Job Finder's Guide 2000

Also by Les Krantz

JOBS RATED ALMANAC

The Best and Worst Jobs –
250 in all – Ranked by More than
a Dozen Vital Factors Including
Salary, Stress, Benefits and More

Job Finder's Guide 2000

THE ONLY BOOK YOU NEED TO GET THE JOB YOU WANT

LES KRANTZ
Foreword by Tony Lee

St. Martin's Griffin
New York

Library of Congress Cataloging-in-Publication Data
available on request.

ISBN 0-312-25503-9

First Published in the United States by World Almanac
Books, on imprint of K-III Reference Corporation.

Second St. Martin's Edition: January 2000

10 9 8 7 6 5 4 3 2 1

STAFF/CONTRIBUTORS
Managing Editor: Sue Sveum
Contributing Editor: Bob Kalish
Production Director: Denise Boynton
Research Associates:
Andy Coan
Robert Hurda
Dan Lin
Yuri Salinas-Martynovski
Contributing Writer: Mark Scheffler
Technical Consultant Adrienne Brown

Special Thanks to Editor Kristen Macnamara, St. Martin's

CONTENTS

CONTENTS

FOREWORD

One of my favorite job-hunting stories involves an accountant living in Northern New Jersey who had lost his position after many years with the same firm. He started answering ads and scheduling interviews, but none of the jobs he targeted worked out, usually because of his high salary level.

After a few months, the accountant's search really started to drag. Answering newspaper ads and contacting recruiters wasn't paying off. He'd often heard that networking was the most effective way to land a new position, but he was uncomfortable with the process. He knew that it meant telling friends, friends of friends and even casual acquaintances that he was out of work.

At first, his pride prevented him from seeking support and leads from others. But he slowly realized that without networking, his search campaign may last forever. So he started sharing his story with others, which lead to a few interviews. Then one Friday afternoon, the accountant struck gold.

On his way home after a frustrating day, he stopped at his local service station for a fill-up. As usual, the station owner pumped his gas, and asked offhandedly how he was doing. But instead of answering the usual way with a "just fine" or "okay," he told the truth. He explained that he wasn't doing well because he was out of work. The owner asked what he did for a living, and expressed surprise when he heard accounting. "My sister is a partner in an accounting practice in the next town, and they're looking for a new partner," he said. By the following Friday, the accountant had a new job. He'd asked the owner for his sister's name, scheduled an appointment for the following Monday and impressed everyone he met with his networking story, as well as the interviewing skills he'd refined during the preceding few months.

Landing a new job can be a horrendous task or a challenging adventure. Your attitude will make a big difference, but so will your level of understanding about the process. That's how this book will help. The *Job Finder's Guide* offers advice on every key aspect of job hunting, including networking, interviewing, writing a great resume and negotiating a healthy compensation package. It even provides strategies for using the Internet effectively to search job listings and applying online.

Once you create a list of target companies, the Guide offers key data on more than 1,000 major employers, including a summary of each company's business outlook. With this book in hand, you'll become more comfortable with the process, and be able to conduct a more knowledgeable search that will bear fruit sooner, not later.

Tony Lee, Editor in Chief & General Manager,
careers.wsj.com, The Wall Street Journal Interactive Edition

INTRODUCTION

TODAY'S JOB MARKET CAN REALLY BE A JUNGLE, especially if you're not prepared for it. Companies are merging, being acquired, and downsizing; technology is rapidly changing; markets are becoming ever more global. The result is that competition for jobs, at virtually all levels, is becoming ever more fierce.

THIS BOOK, THE MOST COMPREHENSIVE JOB SEARCH BOOK AVAILABLE, was written to help you find your way through that jungle—to give you the essential skills, knowledge, and resources you need to find the job you want. More than any other point, it addresses how to *outrun the competition*. It teaches you how to beat others to the job openings and ads, how to put together a stronger resume, how to write better application and follow-up letters, and how to perform better at interviews than anyone else. In addition, this book provides you with key resources you can use in your job search. You will now have valuable information at your fingertips on thousands of employers, agencies, and organizations, all in one handy, easy-to-use volume.

TO COMPETE SUCCESSFULLY in today's job market, you need to know who else is out there; that is, you need an idea of what kinds of job seekers there are. The following table, based on information from the U.S. Census Bureau and the U.S. Department of Labor, estimates the number of Americans who confront different job search situations each year.

EIGHT COMMON GOALS FOR JOB SEEKERS TODAY

Switching careers to a new occupation	12,000,000
Changing jobs within current field	11,000,000
Reentering the work force	10,000,000
Seeking summer employment	3,000,000
Getting an entry-level job	2,000,000
Relocating to another city	2,000,000
Temping	2,000,000
Working abroad	2,000,000
Total	**44,000,000** *job seekers*

IN ALL, THERE ARE MORE THAN 40 MILLION Americans out there each year looking for a job. Almost every one has at least one of the eight employment goals listed in the table above. The content of this book was developed to give you all the essential strategies and information you need to reach your own goal successfully, despite the competition. To get the most from this book, you need to know some essential facts about how it is organized·

SECTION I: REACHING YOUR GOAL

THIS OPENING SECTION IS PERHAPS THE MOST ESSENTIAL to your success. It consists of eight "overview" essays—starting points for job seekers with each of the eight basic employment goals. You can think of each of these overviews as veritable talks with a career counselor trained to help you through specific situations. For example, if your goal is summer employment, you'll receive counsel about landing a summer job in the chapter "Summer Employment." If you wish to return to the work force after a period of unemployment, consult the chapter "Reentering the Work Force."

TO MAKE THE ADVICE OFFERED EVEN MORE EFFECTIVE, each of these chapters contains valuable cross-references that steer you to other relevant portions of the book They will point you to data about sources you might not even know exist—industries and companies to prospect, strategies, literature, and a wealth of other information that can be applied toward reaching your employment goal. Note that valuable cross-references are also found throughout the book, not just in Section I.

SECTION II: TESTING YOUR WATERS

THIS SECTION CONSISTS OF A TEST you may wish to take to help you determine if it is in your best interest to begin looking for a new job. It can help you decide whether you're ready to move on voluntarily, or recognize the clues that your job may be in jeopardy

SECTION III: ESSENTIAL SKILLS

THIS FIVE-CHAPTER SECTION HONES IN ON THE SKILLS YOU NEED to compete with the over 40 million Americans who annually seek new jobs. It lays out how to interview, write letters, network, and write resumes. These are all vital skills that win jobs for those who master them and eliminate others from consideration. You'll also learn how to negotiate salaries—a useful skill not just for a new position but also for the next time you're up for review at your present job

SECTION IV: OCCUPATIONAL FACTS

IF THERE IS ANY CRUCIAL EMPLOYMENT INFORMATION you as a job seeker need to learn, it's likely you'll find it here. And now you have the opportunity to get that information early in the game. There are job descriptions for hundreds of jobs—the key responsibilities and workaday activities of workers in different fields. There is an annual income report that tells you what the average worker in hundreds of occupational fields makes, besides giving you typical salaries for beginners and for top earners in each field. Other chapters in this section help you determine where to get more information on various occupations and industries, such as in professional journals and directories.

SECTION V: JOB OPPORTUNITIES

THIS IS THE LARGEST PORTION of the book, replete with information about thousands of employers. Whether you are looking to work in corporate America, in government service, or elsewhere, you will find indispensable information: employer names, addresses, contacts, phone numbers, and hiring data. In addition, students seeking summer jobs and/or internships will find listings covering hundreds of opportunities available across America.

SECTION VI: JOB HUNTING IN CYBERSPACE

IF YOU'VE BEEN WANTING TO PLUG INTO THE INFORMATION SUPERHIGHWAY to job prospect, this section will tell you everything you need to know. You'll acquire the basics to get started, as well as the locations of specific sites in Cyberspace that advertise jobs. Four chapters provide tips on beating the competition, a guide to using the Internet, and data on company databases, ad banks, and the commercial on-line services.

SECTION VII: SERVICES

THERE ARE MANY SPECIALIZED SERVICES, besides typical employment agencies or career counselors, that target more specific areas that may be relevant. There are, for example, agencies that specialize in placing executives, or workers in the computer industry, or people seeking sales-related careers. In this section, you can find hundreds of agencies of all types, including temp agencies.

SECTION VIII: ORGANIZATIONS

FEW PEOPLE KNOW about the wide range of help available for those seeking employment. Whether you need information on employment prospects overseas or on specific professions, there are many specialized organizations that can and will help you. Hundreds of organizations are listed here, including chambers of commerce and professional associations.

WITH THIS BOOK IN HAND, you have access to the know-how and resources you need to outrun the competition—and reach the goal you set for yourself. Just prepare yourself, and go about your job search in a thorough and methodical way. And good luck!

Les Krantz

REACHING YOUR GOAL

There are eight common goals that job seekers wish to reach. The chapters in this section lay out the essential points job seekers should know about reaching them. Within each chapter, cross-references steer you to portions of the book that are relevant to each specific goal.

REACHING YOUR GOAL

GETTING YOUR FIRST JOB

EACH YEAR, THOUSANDS OF NEW COLLEGE GRADUATES enter the job market looking for their first jobs. According to many observers, the picture for these job seekers is grim. Corporate recruitment is down to record lows on campuses across the country. But there are some positives to consider, too.

Yes, many employers want experience for entry-level jobs, but many don't; they are willing to train new workers, and in fact, some prefer to. These employers know that a four-year college degree can demonstrate ability, willingness to learn, and "stick-toitiveness"— a trio of valuable assets they like. What about employers who do want experience when you have none to offer? You can highlight certain life experiences, such as volunteer work, school or club activities, and hobbies, to gain an edge.

IF YOU DON'T HAVE A COLLEGE DEGREE, don't despair: It is not always a negative. Be up-front about it and let prospective employers know—and actually tell them at the interview—that you have certain definable abilities that are transferable to employment situations—perhaps to the very job they are seeking to fill. Abilities that you already have, coupled with the will to develop them further, can be more important than learned skills. And if you're motivated to develop your abilities, let the hiring authority know. This attitude is basic but powerful. Many people—especially the most educated ones—don't always feel this motivation to develop and grow. If you do, *let it be known!* However, don't be naive enough to think prospective employers will believe you can master a job just because you are determined. Instead, give them real reasons to believe you will be effective in a reasonable period of time. Be prepared to persuade your interviewer that you are a self-starter with transferable skills—those life experiences that are portable and valuable. People skills, the ability to deal with problems, mechanical aptitude, and a host of other talents are examples of transferable skills to call attention to.

CONSIDER STUDENT INTERNSHIPS if you're still a student. ➤**See "Internships for Students," pp. 447-495.** New job seekers can put their last semester or summer in college or high school to good use working at a newspaper, in local government, or in a hospital. Hundreds of opportunities exist. If the internship is not in your chosen occupation, that doesn't always matter. By successfully completing any internship, you demonstrate to a prospective employer that you have experienced and conformed to the rigors of the workaday world.

SUMMER JOBS ALSO PROVIDE OPPORTUNITIES FOR STUDENTS. ➤**See "Summer Jobs for Students," pp. 497-530; and "Summer Employment," pp. 26-29.** A natural increase in the nation's economy happens during those languid days of summer. Some industries, like tourism and food service, are very dependent on student workers. Summer jobs may offer other pleasant surprises, too, in addition to work experience and a paycheck. They may be the beginning of a wonderful web of future contacts.

LOOK TO A TEMPORARY JOB to build experience. ➤**See "Temp Agencies," pp. 616-626; and "Temping," pp. 30-33.** Temporary jobs can last from one day to months; many turn into full-time job offers. In recent years temping has become an accepted and common avenue to a full-time career slot. Microsoft, as just one example, has recruited full-time employees from the ranks of temporary workers who have staffed the company's customer service lines.

Highlighting pertinent experience is only

part of the story. Employers who take a chance on a new job seeker look for a strong showing in three areas: communications skills, people skills, and a zest for the task.

COMMUNICATIONS SKILLS ARE IMPORTANT in all types of jobs. Even manufacturing and technical jobs demand competency in communication. For manufacturing or technical jobs, the ability to read manuals and apply them to the task at hand and to understand objectives and give coworkers and supervisors feedback is important, even if you're never called upon to compose a formal letter. In the white-collar world, being able to compose a clear, concise memo, report, or business letter is a quick way to gain favorable attention. Demonstrate this ability, if you have it. Write a good letter thanking the person for the interview and recapping your skills. And make sure to demonstrate the abilities you have in the interview; there's nothing wrong with doing it verbally, as long as you do it. If you don't do it, no one will know that you have such vital skills.

PEOPLE SKILLS include the ability to work with or motivate others in a group project and to demonstrate leadership and/or empathy, and even the willingness to follow another's good lead. As for a zest for the task, in today's competitive job climate, even entry-level positions demand enthusiasm, and those who look enthusiastically for challenges and experiences that will benefit the company's bottom line are the most desirable employees. All three areas—communication, people skills, and enthusiasm—add up to relationship skills. Most employees are hired on their ability to relate to others, including their ability to form a relationship with the person interviewing them for a particular job.

PUT YOUR RELATIONSHIP SKILLS TO GOOD USE when searching for a job. It's never too early to start networking. ➥**See "Networking the Hidden Job Market," pp. 52-58.** Make a list of everyone you or your family knows, and organize it by keeping a professional address book. Collect business cards, and jot notes on the back of each card to help refresh your memory and determine which contacts will be the most help in seeking a particular position. Consider alumni organizations you've been involved with and even people you meet in chance encounters. According to a national survey done by the American Management Association, 60 percent of all jobs are found through informal contacts.

LOOK TO OTHER JOB-FINDING OPTIONS you may not have considered. For example, large corporations and other agencies offer toll-free numbers that give job seekers job application information. ➥**See "Job Hotlines," pp. 410-446.** For the computer literate, look at job banks on-line. ➥**See "The Internet and the World Wide Web," pp. 536-540; "Commercial On-Line Services," pp. 541-547.**

ANOTHER QUICK REFERENCE to simplify sorting through a cluttered informational field is available from the federal government. ➥**See "Literature Available From the Federal Government," pp. 128-130.** It is called the *Occupational Outlook Handbook*, and along with reports on earnings and literature about careers, it can help narrow your focus down to a particular industry or occupation.

And remember to consult this book for a good overview of the state of American industry as it pertains to more than 1,000 large companies. The essential facts have been gathered that will help you determine which are the best companies and industries for job prospects. ➥**See "U.S. Employers," pp. 158-378; and "Industry Overviews," pp. 395-409.**

CONSIDER SMALL COMPANIES, TOO, in your search. ➥**See "Industry Directories," pp. 148-155.** Many first-time job seekers think only of large corporations because of their visibility both on campus and through major advertising. But small companies are thousands of times more numerous and collectively employ more people than the *Fortune* 500. More importantly for first-time job seekers, small companies can offer cross-training opportunities, more flexibility, and more opportunities for skill acquisition, and they may be willing to give not only an opportunity to new employees but personal mentoring as well.

To locate small companies, get to know employers in your community or in communities that you are targeting for your job search. Many small business owners are active in local chambers of commerce. These chambers generally make listings of their members available upon request. Telephone directory listings can also be a good source, as well as business license lists from local municipalities. Many times, these lists also have owners' names and mailing addresses. Local employers are also well-known supporters of local school teams, yearbooks, and other projects, and they may respond favorably to a local graduate, whether in small towns or big cities.

JOB SEEKERS WILLING TO RELOCATE anywhere in the country, or even just within the state, have more opportunities available, particularly in lesser-known or less-publicized professions. Employees in general are becoming more resistant to transfers, especially those with dependent children and a working spouse. Companies that are expanding are thus having to hire from the local economy more so than in the past. So be open to the possibility of moving, and check out industries in various metropolitan areas. **➤See "Relocating to Another City," pp. 22-25.**

OCCUPATIONAL OPPORTUNITIES CAN BE FOUND IN UNUSUAL PLACES, which is something first-time job seekers may not realize. Journalists, for example, need to realize that large corporations hire writers for in-house organs, and large hospitals need media-relations people as well as writers to produce patient information and employee newsletters. Nurses can be employed by school districts or large companies as part of wellness programs, and printers can work for college in-house print plants.

NEWSPAPER WANT ADS are standard fare for job seekers, but consider looking at want-ad listings in professional journals, particularly if you are willing to relocate. **➤See "Professional Magazines/ Journals," pp. 118-130.** Reading trade journals is also an excellent way to gain "insider" knowledge about a target company. If someone you're acquainted with is listed in an issue as having just received a promotion at which he or she is likely be a prospective hiring authority, add that name to your professional address book, and follow up with a contact.

A GOOD RESUME won't outpace the competition by itself, but having a well-written one can avoid common traps and help you put the best possible spin on yourself. **➤See the section on entry-level resumes in "Resume Writing," p. 41-51.** Don't give out people's names as references unless you call them first to feel out how they might respond to a request for information on you. Sometimes it's a good idea to remind them how pleased you thought they were with the job you did on a particular project. If they truly were pleased, you've planted a seed. They'll know it's something they can positively comment on if someone calls for a reference.

DISCUSS ACCOMPLISHMENTS, NOT DUTIES, in your resume. For example, state that you revised the database for the college yearbook, not that you served on the yearbook committee. Place college degrees in a prominent place on your resume. Since employers look for multifaceted individuals, take special care to list any minors or certificates earned in a particular area. If a career requires a specific credential, emphasize attainment in this area. But if your degree isn't critical to the type of job you are seeking, give your experience more prominence in the resume.

INTERVIEWING SKILLS ARE CRITICAL TO SUCCESS, and to the inexperienced job seeker, they may not come naturally. **➤See "Interviewing to Win," pp. 68-74.** Role-playing with a supportive person may take the edge off your nerves. Dressing for the interview in professional but reasonably subdued clothing is important. Shabby clothes, a know-it-all attitude, a passive posture, poor eye contact, being late for appointments, complaining—all will reflect negatively on you. If the interview goes well and the job seems to your liking, don't be afraid to ask for it. If the answer is no, politely ask why. The knowledge gained will help you in the next job search. And know how to write a good follow-up letter to every interview. **➤See "Letters for Applying and Following Up," pp. 59-67.**

EDUCATE YOURSELF ON A JOB'S SALARY LEVELS before the interview. **➤See "Annual Earnings Survey," pp. 117-127.** Understanding salary levels as well as environmental factors for various industries—that is, the actual physical surroundings in which one must work—are part of developing realistic expectations of what it takes to enter the work force. Entry-level paychecks may seem pathetically low, but take heart. The *Wall Street Journal's Jobs Rated Almanac* showed jobs netted an average increase of 391 percent over time; that's a fourfold increase.

When the time is appropriate for salary

negotiations, don't let having reasonable expectations of what a job will pay stop you from negotiating from the strongest position possible for the most income. ➥See "Salary Negotiations," pp. 75-81.

LOOK AT JOB PROFILES WITH DE-SCRIPTIONS of workaday responsibilities to avoid rude surprises about the demands of a job. ➥See "Job Descriptions," pp. 84-116. Check out descriptions of the economic health of the nation's major industries to avoid parachuting into a battle zone. ➥See "Industry Overviews," pp. 395-409. Be aware, though, that even in the most unhealthy industries there are often companies that are prosperous. Seek them out. ➥See "U.S. Employers," pp. 158-378. That chapter rates the companies with the best prospects with one or two stars. Concentrate on those companies. And remember that even companies that are not rated as highly frequently have many openings as a result of their sheer size.

When reading about different industries, realize that a high employee turnover rate may signal a correspondingly high degree of employee dissatisfaction. On the other hand, it may herald well for first-time job seekers. High turnover may also mean that it is easier to break into a field where more positions are open at any given time.

RESEARCHING WHICH INDUSTRIES are likely to have jobs available is only part of the story. The other half is understanding which occupation best suits your individual temperament. Vocational testing is the scientific way to find out. Organizations that specialize in vocational services can offer tests and counseling to pinpoint the best career for your temperament and life situation. ➥See "Career Counselors and Vocational Services," pp. 552-561.

GETTING THAT FIRST JOB NAILED DOWN is a wonderful feeling. Three months later, the realities of the workaday world may set in, undermining your natural enthusiasm. But keeping enthusiasm strong is the best way to ensure a more rapid progression up the salary ladder.

Don't think getting this first job will be the last job hunting you'll do. The workplace rules have changed dramatically in the last quarter century. Expect to seek out more opportunities with different companies, different industries, and even different occupations during your working career.

REACHING YOUR GOAL

CHANGING JOBS WITHIN YOUR CURRENT FIELD

THE AVERAGE AMERICAN CHANGES JOBS eight times in a lifetime. Since each job hunt typically lasts from two to four months, you could spend up to two years of your life job hunting. If that thought sobers you a bit, take heart: The skills you gain prospecting for a new job are a foundation for your future as well as a stepping-stone for deeper career satisfaction.

IN TODAY'S FICKLE WORK ENVIRONMENT, it often pays to forget about the old notion of moving vertically up the ladder of success within a company. Instead, look to move horizontally. This means developing skills that are portable—that is, learning things that you can apply from job to job or company to company. These types of skills are general ones, like selling, managing, or researching, to name just a few. Having a litany of abilities like these—or even just a few of them—means that many employers can use your talents. These abilities can also bring a deeper sense of fulfillment in your work life, since you aren't saddled to a corporate job or even a specific industry. Instead, you are the one who is dynamically in charge of your career growth, not the corporate personnel department or the health of a given industry. A new position can mean not just an end to a job that has grown boring or stagnant, not just a release from a place where your earning potential has topped out, but a chance to experience a new and invigorating challenge in life.

WHEN AND HOW SHOULD YOU LEAVE your present job? The main reason people stay in jobs they don't like is that they doubt their ability to find another job that's as good or better. But satisfying that urge for security can lead to the loss of your present job—that is, if it's time to change and you don't recognize it. Recognizing the need to change, in fact, should be a basic part of every working person's repertoire. ➤See "Is It Time to Change Jobs?" pp. 38-39. The lifetime job simply is no longer a part of the American way, as much as some of us would like it to be.

SEVERAL DANGER SIGNS can point to a job loss. The most obvious one, general job dissatisfaction, is impossible to hide forever, and eventually your negative attitude becomes obvious to others, your superiors included. Another danger sign is lack of communication with your co-workers. If the people at work stop sharing important job-related news with you, your job performance will suffer, and with that, your job could be in jeopardy. Another warning is that your company is having bad economic times. Pay attention to rumors of impending layoffs. Yet another warning sign is failing to meet objectives. Busywork doesn't substitute for functioning in the specific role you were hired to do.

Try to be objective and ask yourself if your performance is viewed negatively by others. Some people assume that they just won't get fired no matter how bad a performance review they receive. That is dangerous thinking. So is continuing at a job at which you are not highly productive. Sooner or later, even profitable companies will look to pare deadwood.

DON'T GET STUCK IN A BAD SITUATION. And don't let fear stop you from making the next logical step, which is to begin job hunting at the beginning of these danger signs, rather than when your job is terminated or hanging by a thread.

IF YOU THINK IT'S TIME TO PART COMPANY, should you quit first or job hunt while still on the job? Many people are convinced you should never leave a job until you have another to take its place, but it is also true that finding the right job is a full-time occupation. Devoting 40 or 50 hours a week to a job search has its obvious benefits, if you can afford the temporary loss of income. Your emotional health is also a consideration. If job dissatisfaction is so bad that it is ruining your performance in a way that might follow you for life or causing you such unhappiness that personal relationships might suffer, quitting first is at least one option to consider. By all means consider all the risks before you act, one of which is being in a weaker salary negotiating position. Out-of-work applicants are often perceived as being desperate to renew their income strength.

On the other hand, no job is free from problems, and some people hop from one job to the next, when the real issue is a personal one they are reluctant to face. Consider your own idiosyncrasies and the part they may play in your current dissatisfaction. A competent career counselor with experience in psychological testing might help you uncover some personal attributes and actions that are stifling your career growth. **➻See "Career Counselors and Vocational Services," pp. 552-561.**

IF YOU CURRENTLY HAVE JOB PROBLEMS, you may find yourself ambushed again unless you change your work habits or analyze what it is about your current job environment that is creating dissatisfaction. You don't want the problem duplicated somewhere else. It is prudent to make a comparison between your working environment and those of others in the same career field. **➻See "Job Descriptions," pp. 84-116.** Perhaps your employer has created a different environment than the ones your career-peers work in. Is it worse? Maybe. And surprisingly, it could even be better, but it pays to know.

Environmental factors can include how much confinement you experience, physical demands, working conditions such as loud noise, personality issues such as the amount of competitiveness and public contact, and perils or hazards faced on the job. A specific environmental factor, and not your occupational choice, may have you looking for alternatives. If so, consider that some seemingly unlikely industries may utilize people in your occupational field differently or in a different environmental context that is more to your liking. For example, a chef who prefers regular hours and a more institutional setting than offered by most restaurants can find new job opportunities with a hospital that is seeking to recruit more elective surgical and birthing patients by offering a five-star menu. Or a newspaper worker who is no longer willing to cope with daily deadlines may opt to work for a corporate in-house newsletter.

PERSONAL CHEMISTRY PROBLEMS cause a surprisingly large number of people to change jobs. They just don't hit it off with the boss. On your next interview, be prepared to analyze your future boss's personality and even the corporate culture to see if the match will be compatible. **➻See "Interviewing to Win," pp. 68-74.**

IF YOU THINK YOU ARE GOING TO GET FIRED, it's better to confront the issue than to wait for something to happen. Find out if you are going to be fired by asking—that is, if there is sufficient cause for real alarm. If you are told you will be terminated or that there is a chance of it, ask about severance pay. Find out from your state department of unemployment insurance if you qualify for unemployment compensation. It is also prudent to inquire about possible outplacement assistance, continuation of your medical insurance (if you have it), and continuation of other perks that may tide you over during a full-time job search.

It is often possible to negotiate your way out of a job on terms that work for you. Always remember that some bosses feel badly when they have to fire someone. Like you, they are human—and no matter how poorly they may regard your job performance, they may be real softies when it comes to helping you get over the trauma of losing a job.

When it's truly time to go, a lack of confidence in finding a better job can hold you back, if you let it. The solution is to approach job hunting in a systematic way, one that is tried and true.

TAKE THAT SYSTEMATIC APPROACH TO FINDING A BETTER JOB. Your willingness to do so is irrevocably related to the ease or hardship by which you find a new job. The systematic approach treats each job hunt as though it might mean a complete change in occupations (even if you're staying in your current field). You need to analyze your skills to see if they are taking you where you want to go, package yourself as the product for sale to your future employer, prepare your marketing materials and your marketing plan, and look at the best methods and targets for your job search.

SELF-ASSESSMENT SHOULD BE A BASIC AND PERIODIC TASK for all working people. You need to do it even if you are sticking with the same profession—and who knows, maybe in the process you will see the need to change occupations. Your strengths are your portable skills, which should be prominently displayed on your resume and on other self-marketing materials. Actually seeing them in print can build your confidence for selling yourself in interviews.

You may wish to undergo vocational testing, which can be either sobering or reassuring. It is often the latter, however, because it is likely to confirm feelings you have about yourself and how they relate to your occupational choice. ➼See "Career Counselors and Vocational Services," pp. 552-561.

TAKING AN INVENTORY OF YOUR SKILLS is part of the jobsearch process. Listing personal accomplishments is the next step. Come up with several dozen examples; you can cull them later. Use actions words like "achieved," "created," or "negotiated." Quantify accomplishments whenever possible with hard numbers. For example, if you increased efficiency in your department, by how much and over what period of time?

WHEN YOU PUT TOGETHER YOUR RESUME, beware of a tendency to use the exercise as a way to procrastinate on your job search. Some people can spend weeks polishing and revising their resume as an excuse not to move on to the active marketing phase of the job search.

A chronological resume is usually preferred by employment screeners of all kinds, from the personnel department to the line manager who will supervise you. They have so many resumes to rate that a chronological listing of your jobs and accomplishments makes it easier to compare you with other applicants in an efficient manner. Novel approaches may backfire for this reason. It's just too much trouble for employment screeners to assess them. ➼See "Resume Writing," pp. 41-51. Unless you have hard-to-explain gaps in your job history, a chronological listing will probably serve you better in a job change situation.

JOB SEARCH TECHNIQUES encompass making personal contact, sending unsolicited letters to companies, answering ads, and using various services such as recruiters and employment agencies. Many people make the wrong assumptions about the most effective search techniques and consequently spend too much time on the long shots (ads, for example, have a success rate of only 5 percent) and too little time on the more successful methods (networking offers a success rate of some 70 percent). Your job search time should be proportionally allotted to match the expected success rate of each method. So even though answering ads might seem like low odds, one out of 20 job seekers do find jobs that way, so it pays to spend a small amount of time each week doing just that.

EXECUTIVE RECRUITERS, though not at the top of the list for effectiveness, can serve as useful job search tools, particularly for those with a salary history above $50,000 per year. ➼See "Executive Recruiters," pp. 592-609. Working with several firms is important, as each usually carries separate job opportunities. For those making less money, employment agencies can also offer a modest opportunity for success. ➼See "Employment Agencies," pp. 569-591.

NETWORKING IS THE BEST METHOD for finding a new job, but it is also the most intimidating for most people. ➼See "Networking the Hidden Job Market," pp. 52-58. It is less threatening to mail out resumes or answer ads, but you also miss opportunities from the hidden job market. This hidden job market doesn't represent some type of silent conspiracy. It's more simple and yet more complex than that. Companies that are experiencing rapid growth may not have the time to quantify job descriptions for new positions that are needed, so the jobs are not advertised. Instead, by depending upon personal contacts and networking, companies can more informally match applicants to the most current, if somewhat vaguely defined, opportunities. In addition, sometimes companies do not want to alert existing employees to the possibility that they may be replaced. Other times, companies may be experiencing problems that are hard to pin down until networking brings your special talents to the attention of someone who is in a position to hire you away.

MANY LARGE COMPANIES ARE EXPANDING AND HIRING, contrary to popular opinion spurred by news of continuing layoffs among large industries. The ones that are expanding and hiring can be identified by the rating system in this book. ➤See "U.S. Employers," pp. 158-378. However, don't overlook smaller companies, particularly if you are looking to build expertise on your career ladder. Such firms still produce over 60 percent of new job opportunities. In order to locate them, consult various directories. ➤See "Industry Directories," pp. 133-139.

Consider returning to your college job placement office for assistance in your job search, even if you've been out of college for a long time. Professional organizations might help, too, particularly through enabling you to spot economic trends and opportunities in the industry. ➤See "Professional Associations," pp. 644-655. They are also a gold mine for networking.

REACHING YOUR GOAL
SWITCHING CAREERS

THE U.S. CENSUS BUREAU ESTIMATES that over 10 million Americans will switch to a new occupation this year. In fact, more people will switch careers this year than will change jobs within the same field or reenter the work force after a period of unemployment.

Switching careers is a difficult subject to cover in a few pages, and not just because of the magnitude of such a shift. Career switching means a period of soul-searching and measured thinking prior to taking action. Nevertheless, the following overview will help you think through your options.

BEWARE OF ANY PRECONCEIVED NOTIONS you may have about seeking new employment opportunities in midlife, be it changing careers or otherwise. For example, don't be too intimidated by stories of laid-off midlife managers job hunting for a year or more. According to a 1996 report on the NBC *Today Show*, the average time people over 50 spent looking for a job was four months. Or consider this: One avenue of career switching may involve entrepreneurship, but that doesn't necessarily mean raising money to build a factory that makes widgets. Today's career switcher may enter the ranks of a new breed of entrepreneur, one who may be a telecommuter who creates a series of mini-jobs under a contract arrangement, perhaps even working for one or more of the *Fortune* 500 companies.

THE MOST IMPORTANT TASK FACING YOU as you contemplate switching careers involves asking yourself two critical questions: What are your skills? And what are your great desires?

All job-related skills can be sorted into a surprisingly few categories of capabilities and concepts. For example, a group of skills commonly considered part of an artist's repertoire—an eye for color, form, shape, and design—can relate to other professions requiring strength in the visual skills. Examples include architects, pilots, industrial designers, and drafters. Categories of skills like this are transferable to many careers.

AN INVENTORY OF SKILLS is only half of the equation, though. A burning desire is just as important. Someone who excels in oratory skills, for example, has the potential to be an excellent salesperson. But the woman who struggles through public speaking, yet has an overwhelming desire to interact with people, may also find success in sales. Her people skills may be so strong that she fights the butterflies and learns to speak well enough to deliver a credible sales pitch. In other words, when you want something badly enough, you can develop the necessary skills.

When you know what your skills are and have mapped your desires, a simple test may help you decide if this is the right time to make a career move. ➥See "Is It Time to Change Jobs?" pp. 38-39. If it is, it's time to consider your possibilities.

AVENUES TO SWITCH CAREERS ARE AS ABUNDANT and diverse as the people who seek them. Ways for people to apply skills and dreams to new careers include (1) engaging in entrepreneurship, (2) retreating to greener pastures, (3) retraining, (4) dedicating yourself to humanitarianism, (5) "going for the gold," and (6) facing retirement challenges. Let's examine them.

ENTREPRENEURSHIP INVOLVES START-UP BUSINESSES, which have required a lot of financing in the past. However, today's new breed of entrepreneur may not need a lot of start-up cash. This new-breed entrepreneur may run a one-person office, comfortably ensconced at home, doing business by fax machine and modem. He just needs to make sure he has enough money to maintain himself until the first client check comes in. Cash flow is more important than start-up capital. His potential clients may be the same companies he would have previously prospected for full-time employment. Instead, today's new entrepreneur is contracting with major U.S. companies for individual work—

that is, taking on assignments as an independent contractor. In today's business environment of downsizing, many companies are hiring independent contractors more and more. For example, companies that previously had a public relations staffer write speeches for their CEO are now having them written by an outside person. If you have a special skill that a firm could make use of, call it to the attention of a department head at a large company. ➤See "U.S. Employers," pp. 158-378. To target smaller companies for your entrepreneurial success, network with chambers of commerce and otherwise search out smaller firms. ➤See "Industry Directories," pp. 148-155.

CULTIVATE NETWORKING RELATIONSHIPS through professional associations and professional journals. ➤See "Professional Magazines/Journals," pp. 131-147; and "Professional Associations," pp. 644-655. Such sources can also yield leads for assignments when you carefully analyze the content of both ads and articles for companies that may give you business. Industry directories and descriptions of industries can also reveal either potential clients or specific areas to target for your efforts. ➤See "Industry Directories," pp. 148-155; and "Industry Overviews," pp. 395-409.

IF YOU'RE THINKING ABOUT RETREATING TO GREENER PASTURES as part of switching careers, remember to jettison those preconceived notions about a move to the country. Interesting job possibilities exist, even in the hinterlands. Job opportunities in rural areas can be found in unusual places, as telecommuting technology opens up new venues for relocaters. This is related to entrepreneurship. For example, designers who wish to work with large manufacturing companies have found roundabout ways of achieving their goal, even in the most isolated rural areas. They've found that you can design everything from widgets

to window coverings far, far away from the plant in Cleveland.

NETWORKING WITH OTHER SMALL CONTRACTORS over the Information Highway is another way for someone ensconced in a mountain retreat to get work as an independent contractor. You'd be surprised how many independent contractors, similar to those discussed in the section on entrepreneurship above, are seeking subcontractors to help them. Just a few fields where it's happening are computers, sales of high-tech equipment, small manufacturing, and publishing.

AND DON'T FORGET THAT YOUR BIG-CITY SKILLS may be quite salable to an employer in Podunk. Many small communities have even smaller talent pools, so perhaps your talents will be in big demand in Smallsville. Don't be afraid to show your wares or talents. They may dazzle some small-town employer who's getting ready to advertise a senior position at his company in the *New York Times* classified section.

TIPS ON MOVING TO ANOTHER CITY are available from many sources, but first check out general information on moving. ➤See "Relocating to Another City," pp. 22-25. For ideas on unusual businesses in which to find a job, be creative when considering all possibilities. For example, nurses can be employed by paper mills, and photographers by agricultural product manufacturers. Try to come up with options for your own situation.

RETRAINING CAN BE AN IMPORTANT STEP in switching careers. If you wish to enter a new area, you may well need to go back to school. Professional schools today are attracting a new breed of students in finance, medicine, health care, engineering, law, and other high-earning, high-status fields. And even more pressure to retrain may come to bear in blue-collar fields in the nation's manufacturing businesses. New technology can signal the unemployment line for workers unable or unwilling to learn new technical skills.

For both areas, new avenues mean hitting the books. For professionals, the most important choice may begin with deciding where to apply. In certain professions—law, for one—the ability to join a high-profile firm may hinge almost solely on the type of school you attend. Schools are also places to make contacts, especially if such schools cater to the middle-aged.

TO INCREASE YOUR CHANCES OF ACCEPTANCE at the school of your choice, search out manuals and/or courses that prepare you to pass admissions tests. Would-be doctors should consult books on the Medical College Admission Test and *Millers Analogy*. For law school, consider enrolling in one of the courses that prepare people for the Law School Admission Test. There are also books on the Graduate Record Examinations, with sample admissions tests for 20 fields of study. Ask a good bookstore for recommendations. There are study manuals for admissions tests relevant to almost every type of professional and technical school.

DO YOU WANT TO DEDICATE YOURSELF to humanitarianism? Nice guys don't always finish last, even though baseball manager Leo Durocher thought so. Some humanitarians even earn a lot of money. Charitable organizations have many jobs that are not only fulfilling, but financially remunerative. Local, state, and federal governments employ many people at humanitarian jobs—the Peace Corps, for one. Other humanitarian jobs include employment in social work, public health, hospices, child welfare, and the environment. In fact, some organizations dedicated to bettering the quality of life don't get enough highly qualified professionals applying for their job openings. Try one! ➥**See "Jobs in the Federal Government," pp. 379-394.** Other sources of information include directories of nonprofit associations and organizations, which are available at most libraries.

THOSE DESIRING GREATER WEALTH have many avenues to follow. The first places to consider, at least for career switchers, are careers that pay commissions, not salaries. These careers present a smaller risk to employers hiring those new to the field, because they are paid on the basis of success. They are therefore easier for the career switcher to enter. At the same time, they have an open-ended earning potential, meaning that there is virtually no reasonable limit to earnings. Just a few of these high-yielding positions are stockbroker, real estate agent, sales positions involving pharmaceuticals, agricultural and industrial equipment, advertising, and so on. ➥**See "Job Descriptions," pp. 84-116.**

FOR RETIREES OR THOSE NEARING RETIREMENT, changes in anticipated life expectancy have drastically rewritten the rules. For many, a second or third career is mandatory in order to avoid endless days of boredom.

If you are approaching retirement and your employment was terminated involuntarily, looking for another career is also important to your financial security. In order to avoid a serious drop in your earnings, bone up on the finer points of salary negotiations so your job search meets your needs for income. ➥**See "Salary Negotiations," pp. 75-81.**

IF YOU ARE CONSIDERING ENTREPRENEURING—both the type described in this chapter as well as traditional entrepreneuring—some lenders will be more likely to give you a business loan because they know that mature borrowers are better credit risks. You may also be more likely to buy an existing business, because you have the confidence and experience to run it successfully. Other very productive avenues for retirees include the "going for the gold" careers that are outside sales positions, like stockbrokering.

THE BOTTOM LINE ON RETIREMENT CHALLENGES is that you can do most things young people can do, and you are often more likely to be given a chance to do them when you're older. Read each section of this chapter carefully, because all of them apply to retirees, too.

Whatever avenue is destined to bring you to your goal, increase your chances for success by researching the industries in which you are seeking to gain employment. In fact, do it so well that you know more about it than many of the other people who are also going on the interview circuit. ➥**See "Industry Overviews," pp. 395-409; and "Professional Magazines/Journals," pp. 131-147.**

RESUMES TAKE ON A NEW TWIST for career switchers. ➥**See the section on functional resumes in "Resume Writing," pp. 41-51.** That old standby—a resume with jobs held listed in chronological order—does not always do the job for switchers. Consider a format that lists transferable skills instead. Cull and groom noteworthy projects you've accomplished, placing high on the list those that most closely apply to new objectives. Put aside your past identity, and don't let it overshadow your new resume.

If you have a college degree in accounting and are looking for a position as a recreational director, delete the major and list only your degree.

If entrepreneurship is your avenue, you will still need a resume. Consider one that is specific for consultants. ➡**See the section on consultant/freelance resumes in "Resume Writing," p. 41.**

A RESUME WON'T OPEN THE DOOR by itself, and career switchers would be wise to engage in heavy-duty networking. ➡**See "Net-working the Hidden Job Market," pp. 52-58.** Done correctly, it's not manipulative but collaborative. Both sides can gain. Networking also gives career switchers a head start on researching new occupations, as well as practice at forming new identities as they associate with future potential colleagues.

IF YOU ARE GOING TO ANSWER A HELP WANTED AD, make sure you are prepared to explain why you are switching career fields. A person who is switching fields has a harder sell—but so did Ronald Reagan, the former actor, and Harry Truman, the former haberdasher. Your resume may be full of wiggles and jiggles that squirm out of the rigid boxes employers look for in applicants. Search firms don't want to deal with career switchers for the same reason. Direct contact usually works better. Be prepared to sell yourself directly to a prospective company as someone with transferable skills who can turn those career jiggles into a picture of a person who is bent on doing well at whatever he or she does, whether it's a lifelong career in one field or several careers in different fields.

Always remember that when you are interviewing for a job in a new career field, you are usually competing with longtime workers in that field. But most of them weren't good enough at their jobs to be in the front office hiring people as your interviewer is now doing. In other words, experience in the field carries only so much weight, and your interviewer knows this well. The real "heavy" at a job interview is someone with skills that are portable from job to job or industry to industry—and of course, the ability to communicate that he or she has them.

REACHING YOUR GOAL

REENTERING THE WORK FORCE

YOU WANT BACK IN and you're not alone. Ten million other Americans seek to reenter the work force each year, according to an estimate of the U.S. Census Bureau. Some have been unemployed for just a few weeks, some long enough to have serious financial concerns.

WHETHER YOU'VE BEEN OUT OF WORK for two weeks or 20 years, there are many avenues to finding the right job. Even if you don't have the credentials for the job you want, reconsider some assumptions you may be harboring—they may no longer be valid, since things have changed dramatically in the last 10 years. And when you have surveyed current employment conditions, be prepared to look for exceptions to the rules, at least those that may be keeping you out of work. Such exceptions become clearer when you change the way you perceive what shape careers take in the 2000s.

THERE ARE SEVERAL NEW CAREER AVENUES you may not have considered, ones that are replacing the cradle-to-grave, straight-line careers of yesterday. Some are more sophisticated and flexible versions of the move-up-the-ladder careers your parents had. Two that apply especially well to those reentering the work force are "patchwork employment" and a "holding pattern job." These are options you may want to consider if that right career position does not materialize as fast as you'd like.

PATCHWORK EMPLOYMENT INVOLVES WORKING AT SEVERAL OCCUPATIONS rather than only one. This type of employment can involve professional temping, freelancing, consulting, part-time work, entrepreneuring, and interim positions of all kinds. Besides paying your bills, such an approach may open up possibilities for long-term employment. Since most job seekers want only long-term, full-time employment, there aren't enough people willing to work in these short-term or sporadic types of employment. If you are, you may be surprised how easy it is to get work at one of these "untraditional" jobs, though they might not be as untradi-

tional as you think. More and more, these "little jobs" are the livelihood of millions. And they are often jobs that were considered career positions at one time, but are no longer.

THE STRATEGY OF A HOLDING PATTERN JOB differs from that of patchwork employment in that the goal of the former is not to build a career at your present job; rather, the goal is to continue working at that job until you are able to get the job you really want—waiting tables, for example, while auditioning for parts in the theater. The holding pattern job, then, is a strategy that provides you with financial means while you're hoping to get that break. It can also be a good way for you to bide your time—and without too much deprivation—while you're seeking a traditional career position rather than a big break.

AVENUES FOR CAREER CHANGERS are also open to those reentering the work force, particularly after a long absence (the basics are similar). ➤See "Switching Careers" pp. 14-17. Starting a business, going back to professional or technical school, satisfying creative or charitable urges, or relocating to rural areas can open up new vistas as well as enrich your life.

Another effective strategy for anyone seeking employment is to target small companies. Many industry-specific directories (for advertising agencies, medical supply companies, food distributors, and so forth) list smaller companies that may not be found in larger, more general directories. ➤See "Industry Directories," pp. 148-155. Such firms are more likely to be expanding and therefore easier to approach. Moreover, getting a direct line to the manager is far easier in a 10-person firm than it is in a large corporation. Direct communication can allow you to showcase your work experiences in a way that is far easier than trying to fit your lifestyle into a corporate mold.

TO DISCOVER YOUR BEST AVENUE FOR SUCCESS, try using the following tools. It seems basic, but taking an inventory of your skills and your desires is the first step. People who are out of the workplace actually have a unique opportunity to sit back and reflect on who they are and what they want out of a job. Opening your mind to new possibilities may reveal avenues that combine your skills with your desires. One man who lost a job directing a large salesforce for a big company had always wanted to be a professional athlete. Now in his 40s, the dream seemed impossible. However, he realized that professional sports teams need business managers, and he eventually found a management position with a pro hockey team.

THOSE SEEKING TO REENTER THE WORK FORCE usually find networking to be effective—approximately seven in 10 jobs are found in this way. ➤See "Networking the Hidden Job Market," pp. 52-58. Many people are uncomfortable networking because they have a natural reticence to approaching strangers for help. However, networking doesn't mean asking someone for a job or even a favor, but simply for advice and information. You might even think of it as "talking shop," something few people object to if you're not too nosy or too personal. If the person is employed in your target field, ask him or her about current trends in the industry and about which companies may be expanding or undergoing a transition. Ask everyone you talk to for the name of someone else with whom you could speak regarding advice about your job search. Very often that person may be hiring at that moment or will be soon. The possibility also exists that he or she might tell you about a job opening elsewhere.

HOW YOU PREPARE YOUR MOST EF-FECTIVE RESUME depends on your circumstances. ➤See "Resume Writing," pp. 41-51. The functional resume—listing skills and achievements instead of a chronological job history—might be more effective for returning homemakers and others who have spent the past several years doing nonpaid activities, as well as for those looking for patchwork employment or a holding pattern job. A resume listing your chronological job history might be better for someone out of work but seeking the same kind of work. And make sure you have a strong cover letter to accompany your resume. ➤See "Letters for Applying and Following Up," pp. 59-67.

WHEN YOU LAND AN INTERVIEW, and you believe your personal circumstances may raise questions with employers—for example, if you are a displaced homemaker, a disabled person or someone who has recovered from a serious illness, or a senior citizen—confront the issue head on. ➤See "Interviewing to Win," pp. 68-74. Even though these are topics that may have legal restrictions on what employers can ask, you can be certain the employer is thinking about it anyway. Address these concerns, but do it indirectly. For example, one man who walked into an interview on crutches persuaded the interviewer that his "handicap" was not a handicap at all. He walked the interviewer through his morning—how he had risen early (before most people do), arrived at the airport, hitched a ride on a special vehicle (one of those golf carts that operates on airport concourses), and so on. In other words, he let the interviewer know he can go anywhere—and in the same time frame—that anyone else can. He got the job.

However, don't react with hostility if an employer asks an inappropriate question. As one example, if an older person is asked, "How old are you anyway?", he or she might respond, "Based on what you've told me about the job, I don't think my age is a problem." And lay out a few reasons why it isn't. Be prepared for uncomfortable questions, and don't let them elicit emotional responses.

IF YOU WERE FIRED FROM YOUR LAST JOB, be sure to work through any negative emotions you may have about your last employer before you begin the job-hunting process. Even though you may feel panicky, don't approach would-be employers right away about getting a new job. You may scare them off. Losing a job is a powerful jolt to your emotions, and people will read it all over your face.

After you've talked through your feelings with a supportive person and spent several days recovering from the loss, start by reviewing what your former employer can do for you. Even though you may still be smarting, don't forget how critical good references will be to finding a new job. It is very important to control the reference story from the beginning and to make sure it matches what you will present to potential employers. Even if you and your former boss parted on terrible terms, you should expect that he or she will be called as a reference. If you think the reference will be bad, warn the future employer first, but leave out the hostility in your voice. Simply explain that you had some points of disagreement. Then, even a negative reference will confirm your story. Balance out that negativity with carefully chosen references who will give a broader picture of your skills and talents, and make sure they will by reviewing your reference statement with them beforehand.

ONE CARDINAL RULE ABOUT REFERENCES that should always be followed: *Call your references before giving their names to a prospective employer.* Sometimes a "good" reference will turn out to be a bad reference. A call beforehand will prevent such a disaster. Even if you think a former boss will give you a bad reference, a phone call can sometimes turn things around. Many bosses later regret having fired someone, and some will even try to help out a fired employee. Find out if that ex-boss is one of them. Since he or she is likely to be called anyway, there's little harm that can be done in calling beforehand, unless of course you were in such a bloody war that a tip-off will only make him or her prepare to do you more dirt when the call comes in.

During interviews, be extra careful to avoid making any potentially damaging or hostile statements about your previous employers. Stay on neutral ground.

IF YOU'RE AMONG THE LONG-TERM UNEMPLOYED, consider several new avenues to finding a job. If you've been seeking employment for a long time, consider why your strategies haven't worked. Have you approached your job search in a systematic way? Have you undergone self-assessment, prepared a strong resume, and researched and applied job-search strategies? Have you put enough time and work into it? It's perfectly normal to receive only one or two leads for every 100 letters you mail. Are you maintaining frequent contact with several dozen members of your network, do you respond to an average of three or four want ads per week, and have you sent direct mailings to over 100 companies?

CONSIDER NEW AVENUES if these conventional job strategies haven't worked. The holding pattern job, which involves taking a less-desirable job while you continue your search, may be a reasonable choice at this time. Or patchwork employment, which focuses on more flexible work options, may also buy you time or even lead you in a new direction you'll eventually find more fulfilling. For many long-term unemployed workers, starting a business has been the eventual solution for their job-finding needs. However, even more drastic possibilities may sometimes need to be considered. Is it time to think about a geographical change in order to expand your possibilities? Those caught in mill-town layoffs are familiar with this bind, but even white-collar workers may find greener pastures in smaller towns, which can offer unfilled niches begging to be filled. Be aware that research is critical before you consider such a move. ➡ See "Relocating to Another City," pp. 22-25.

QUESTION ALL YOUR ASSUMPTIONS about the type of job you are seeking. If you dropped out of the work force years ago for personal reasons, don't think you are automatically locked out of jobs you want because you scan the want ads and they all require more education or work experience than you have. You may be able to get the training you need by simply taking a few courses. In addition, question all of the assumptions you may have about credentials. Wait until you put all your personal accomplishments on paper. Accomplishments mean you achieved more with the same resources, made something easier, did something important and useful that had not been done in that organization before, or solved a problem with little or no increase in resources. People who have reared children, worked in a volunteer capacity, or even recovered from a tremendous personal injury or crisis may have valuable experience to offer. Norman Cousins, for example, the famous editor and author, was hired as adjunct professor in the school of medicine at UCLA. He held honorary medical degrees for his ability to recover from a crippling illness, and he inspired countless others in their desire to heal themselves. Previous to his entry into the field of medicine, he had spent his entire professional life in publishing. Similar opportunities open up every day for those who value their personal life experiences enough to see that those experiences get the credit they deserve.

FOR HOMEMAKERS REENTERING THE WORK FORCE following a divorce or the death of a spouse, community colleges offer low-cost training. In addition, resource centers for women are located throughout the country. If you are over 35, you may be eligible for services from a government-funded Displaced Homemaker Center. Widows, widowers, and the recently divorced might consider temporary work. The first year following a death or a traumatic divorce is not the ideal time to start a new, demanding career. Instead, consider taking a holding pattern job.

IF YOU'RE A RETIREE SEEKING A RETURN TO WORK, you're not alone: One out of three retired men do so within two years, according to a recent survey by the American Association of Retired Persons.

To avoid age discrimination, seek employers who are small, new, selling to or serving seniors, or using temporary and/or part-time workers. A helpful resource is the National Association of Older Workers Employment Services in Washington, DC, at 202-479-1200.

CAREERS THAT PRESENT A SMALLER RISK TO EMPLOYERS because they are paid on a success basis—stockbrokering or selling real estate, pharmaceuticals, industrial equipment, or advertising, to name a few—usually mean open-ended earning potential as well as an easier way in for the older job seeker. These careers can be quite lucrative for retirees, who may also be able to work at such professions on a flexible or part-time basis.

REACHING YOUR GOAL

RELOCATING TO ANOTHER CITY

IN THE 2000S, AMERICANS STILL REMAIN ON THE MOVE, and changing jobs because you've changed your address puts you in the company of around 2 million other job seekers each year. Some are spousal tagalongs, trooping off with a wife or husband who has been transferred. Others catch that pioneer spirit and strike out for new territory, looking for a better life and better opportunities in one of America's dynamic cities or maybe in a quiet small town removed from urban problems. Some will move in order to be closer to family or to take care of an elderly relative.

NATURALLY, ONE OF THE MOST OBVIOUS PLACES to look for a job is at major employers in the community, the largest of which are listed in this book. ➤See "U.S. Employers," pp. 158-378. Many of these large companies have regional offices or plants throughout the United States. Within the "U.S. Employer" chapter (organized in part by state), look for "Other Locations," which, if applicable, is found within each company listing. Also, if you know the industries in which you wish to prospect, there are industry directories that list companies throughout the country. ➤See "Industry Directories," pp. 148-155.

IF YOU'RE MOVING WITH A SPOUSE, chances are good that you will have some help from your spouse's company. Fifty percent of American corporations surveyed provide some type of spousal employment assistance for company transferees. The typical transferee, according to statistics gathered by the Employee Relocation Council, is a middle manager, not an executive, and 75 percent of the time, he or she is married. Only 15 percent of transferees are female, so spousal employment assistance is more commonly geared toward women.

IF YOU'RE MOVING ON YOUR OWN, you're the kind of person with initiative, which will serve you well in finding a job in a new city or town. You won't have the benefit of being able to network through an extensive list of contacts, since you're new on the scene. But that doesn't mean you don't have some powerful techniques to help you get a jump start on your move.

Even if your spouse's company is providing you with some assistance, you can still do a lot for yourself in the weeks and days before you move to ensure a better job.

BEFORE YOU MOVE, GET AN EARLY START on your job hunt. If you're the spouse of a company transferee, as soon as you get word that you're moving, call the corporate personnel office and find out what employment benefits may be available to you. Even if you're not married, you may still qualify for partner benefits. Almost a quarter of companies recently surveyed provide partner assistance either formally or informally if requested.

IT'S IMPORTANT TO TAKE THE INITIATIVE, since half of the companies that offer spousal employment assistance do so informally or on an as-needed basis. The number one choice among companies in assistance is payment of fees for employment counselors or placement agencies, and either or both could be an important part of your job-seeking strategy. In fact, you can start employment counseling before you pack even one box. ➤See "Career Counselors and Vocational Services," pp. 552-561. Almost one in five companies will actually try to find you a position within your spouse's firm, and an equal number will give you referrals to job contacts outside the company.

NO MATTER THE REASON FOR YOUR MOVE, you need to do a career assessment. Perhaps you have no plans to change your occupation. On the other hand, this move may represent a unique opportunity to redirect your career onto a new track. Regardless, it's important to take the time to figure out exactly what you want to do with your work future.

Vocational testing and career counseling can point out the need for a change in your work environment or give you the knowledge you need to take advantage of the kind of new opportunities available to you following a move to a new city. ►See "Career Counselors and Vocational Services," pp. 552-561. You'll gain confidence in your abilities to tackle the challenge.

MAKE A LIST OF YOUR PERSONAL ACCOMPLISHMENTS, both in paid and in nonpaid capacities. You'll need these for a new resume or for use in an introductory letter (more about that later), but they'll also be important confidence builders. In a new city, you'll have so many new things to process—new navigation routes for commuting, a new neighborhood, even new climatic conditions—that you can feel rattled and disconnected in your first few weeks. Reviewing this list will give you confidence in selling yourself to potential employers.

When you make your list, focus on active verbs and quantifiable data. For example, you raised your department's sales by more than 20 percent in your previous year on the job, or you chaired a community group that raised enough funds to build a new wing on the local hospital.

AS SOON AS YOU GIVE YOUR NOTICE on your current job, start collecting letters of reference. Bosses can move, become ill, or transfer. Two or three months from now, while you're still in the midst of an active job search, the person who knew you best on the job might no longer be readily available. Plus, these letters will again fuel your confidence and quell your nerves as you beat the pavement in a new city. This can also be a good way to uncover potential negative references before you make the mistake of using one when applying for a new job. Anyone who is hesitant about signing a letter endorsing you as a candidate for another job may feel too uncomfortable about you to offer a good phone recommendation once you move.

Even though you may not yet know your future address, start putting together your resume before you move. You can always revise it later, and to be most effec-

tive, you won't use just one resume anyway. You should instead target resumes to each particular opportunity. ►See "Resume Writ-ing," pp. 41-51.

WHEN YOU DRAFT YOUR RESUME, if you don't know what type of job you will be searching for, a chronological format—where previous jobs are listed in a timeline beginning with the last job held—is the safest bet. Unconventional resumes are disliked by many personnel screeners and recruiters. You'll want to avoid anything that smacks of avant-garde, sticking to the conventional route whenever possible, since you don't have as much networking potential as competing job seekers who already live in town. If you're changing careers during the move, however, a functional format—listing skills and accomplishments rather than jobs—can be an important way to communicate that you've broken with the past and are now ready for a new challenge. ►See "Switching Careers," pp. 14-17.

DO AS MUCH RECONNAISSANCE as possible about your new city before you move. Many people spend a lot of time researching neighborhoods with real estate agents, but it's just as important to research your new community's economic profile, and several tools for this purpose are readily available. The first one—a copy of the Yellow Pages for your new town—may be available at your library. If not, you can easily order your own copy by calling the local phone provider for the new city. Particularly in a small town, this reference can yield volumes of information on what kinds of employers are located in your area, including addresses and markets. By analyzing their ads, you'll be able to figure out who their customers are.

Later, you can use such information, in combination with economic development information, to see which companies may be on the upswing. If you know you want to move and haven't settled on a particular community, or if you are trying to narrow the field among several promising communities, this economic data can be critical in choosing a place that has both the career opportunities and the lifestyle that meet your needs.

LOCAL GOVERNMENTS CAN PROVIDE remarkably detailed economic data on the community, usually free. The city hall or the local or state chamber of commerce is likely to know how and where to locate this information. Reports such as these, which the federal government often requires of communities that receive federal economic development dollars, contain a lot of information about economic opportunities. They can also provide you with facts about which industries and which companies are expanding and contracting and about areas of new growth.

Another consideration when analyzing these data is which industries in your new locale will offer the best occupational opportunities for you. For example, in the Silicon Valley a large number of computer workers are employed in the computer or semiconductor industry, but in the eastern United States a large number are employed in the insurance and finance industries.

Before you move, you can also contact employment placement agencies located in the area to which you are moving. Many are especially suited to your career needs. For example, some agencies specialize in placement for certain occupations. ➻See "Employment Agencies," pp. 569-591; "Temp Agencies," pp. 616-582; "Executive Recruiters," pp. 592-609; "Computer-Search Agencies," pp. 562-568; and "Sales Recruiters," pp. 610-615.

AFTER YOU MOVE, YOU'LL NEED TO HIT THE GROUND RUNNING. But your desire for a steady paycheck is only one reason to get a quick start in job hunting. The longer you are without a job, the more suspiciously potential employers are likely to view the employment gap on your resume. Unlike job seekers who don't relocate, you can't usually retain your current job until you've found another, unless you've had time before the move and money to pay for long-distance job-hunting expenses. This means that you should begin your job search as soon as you can.

BE SURE TO BALANCE YOUR NEED FOR SPEED WITH YOUR NEED FOR QUALITY. It takes time to get a well-paying, long-term job. If you think your job search may take longer than your income comfortably allows, consider taking temporary work. According to a recent university survey, taking on temporary work lengthens your job search by only five weeks, yet results in a higher-paying job for the majority of people who do it.

➻See "Temping," pp. 30-33; and "Temp Agencies," pp. 616-626.

TRADITIONAL JOB-SEARCH TECHNIQUES include networking, responding to ads (including those on-line), using the services of placement agencies, and contacting potential employers directly. Networking, the most powerful technique, results in a job for some two-thirds of all job seekers, but it is difficult for someone new in the community to network. However, it's not impossible, and you can spend your first few weeks cultivating some powerful contacts. For those who have a spouse who is transferring, your spouse's company may offer networking assistance. It's a great place to start, and the local personnel office may have some excellent referrals free for the asking.

OTHER CONTACTS THAT CAN PAY OFF are organizations you currently belong to that have a branch in your new community. For example, the American Association of University Women, the Rotary, the Lion's Club, fraternities and sororities, and religious organizations can give you an automatic calling card for beginning your networking. ➻See "Networking the Hidden Job Market," pp. 52-58.

HELP WANTED ADS ARE AN OBVIOUS CHOICE for a newcomer to town, and you can increase your chances for success by submitting a strong introductory letter either in place of or in addition to a resume. A good introductory letter that stands out can help you get past resume screeners by focusing attention on your most pertinent, powerful qualifications. ➻See "Letters for Applying and Following Up," pp. 59-67.

One job-hunting resource that can be used even before you move is job listings on-line through various companies such as CompuServe or America Online. ➻See "The Internet and the World Wide Web," pp. 536-540; and "Commercial On-Line Services," pp. 541-547. If you are responding on-line with your resume, make sure you prepare it so that it avoids the electronic trashcan. ➻See "Resume Writing," pp. 41-51.

CAREER COUNSELORS AND VOCATIONAL SERVICES are potentially useful once you arrive in town. At some companies, such as the one that transferred your spouse, employment consultation for a spouse is reimbursable. ➻See "Career Counselors and Vocational Services," pp. 552-561.

If you plan to contact companies directly, make good use of the economic development data you requested earlier to pick the most promising leads. Chambers of commerce will also have member lists to share, as will tourism bureaus for those in the hospitality industry.

FINALLY, DON'T RULE OUT SELF-EMPLOYMENT as a viable alternative, particularly if you have relocated to a small town, where opportunities for your career may be limited. As one example, in a one-newspaper community where a small weekly fills the niche, there aren't many jobs for news photographers. It may be time to consider opening a photography business.

Or, a corporate communications officer may find a great niche doing newsletters for businesses that previously looked to professional firms from large cities. You may find it easy to compete with overpriced and overextended firms that don't want the local business anyway. The bottom line is that you may bring a rare talent to town, one that is in demand, but you must let it be known.

REACHING YOUR GOAL

SUMMER EMPLOYMENT

ONE OF THE INITIATIONS INTO ADULTHOOD is finding that first job, usually one that takes place during the summer months. Jobs tailored to students seeking income during the summer break are generally plentiful, and many also offer a taste of the workaday world. Many of these two- or three-month stints also offer adventure, camaraderie, and a special type of learning experience that would be difficult to duplicate under any other circumstance.

THE BASICS OF FINDING A SUMMER JOB are the same as finding most types of work. Therefore, much of the information and many of the strategies offered in this book will be useful. Depending on your experience, some sections and chapters will be more useful than others. It is recommended that you familiarize yourself with—or even just brush up on—the basics of breaking into the work force. ➤**See "Getting Your First Job," pp. 6-9.** That chapter offers many useful suggestions, even if you are just seeking summer work. The rudimentary steps that need to be taken are the same as those leading to a permanent job. For example, networking, interviewing, and writing letters to potential employers are basic skills you need to master.

DON'T BE OVERLY ZEALOUS, HOWEVER. As a student seeking a summer job, you aren't expected to be a shining star at an interview, nor do you need a highly polished resume, though a basic one cannot hurt you. Read about all of these things, however, in this book. There are a few dos and don'ts that are likely to give you an edge over other applicants for the job.

Other portions of this book that list employers, job profiles, industry overviews, and industry directories all will be useful. Each of these areas will be touched on in the paragraphs that follow.

THE CLASSIC SUMMER JOB, as the name suggests, is intended to be seasonal and primarily focused on outdoor activities. Unlike internships, such jobs aren't necessarily geared to introducing students to the everyday workings of a professional field. Many summer jobs are positions that employers need to fill regularly because of increased employee requirements during the summer months. Naturally, many are positions at camps or recreational facilities. There are also teaching positions available during the summer months at academic/ leadership-oriented sites, as well as jobs with the government and at national parks. Numerous job opportunities such as these are listed in this book. ➤**See "Summer Jobs for Students," pp. 497-530.**

SINCE THERE ARE SO MANY SUMMER JOB OPPORTUNITIES, many are not listed in this book. However, simply knowing what types of jobs are available will help you determine where to find them in your area. For example, students who are interested in the performing arts have a variety of opportunities with summer stock theater groups and festivals. Most likely, the chamber of commerce in your city has a list of these theater groups and festival sponsors, which are excellent sources to prospect for jobs. Summer stock theaters often have summer-long positions available. And festivals are a wonderful place for budding performers of all stripes to work, even if it's just for a short fair. Artists and craftspeople who are willing to travel around their state are likely to find opportunities selling their creations or teaching techniques at traveling festivals. Guidelines for seizing these opportunities are usually obtainable from the festival's sponsors or organizers.

AMUSEMENT PARKS, which are easy to find around the nation, also employ large amounts of summer help. Workers perform in a variety of capacities, from operating rides to providing kitchen help, informational services, and maintenance. Apply early, however, as these positions fill up quickly.

CAMPS ALSO OFFER JOBS for students during the summer. Among the many positions offered are camp directors, counselors, waterfront supervisors, and instructors of all kinds. There are thousands of camps, the names of which are obtainable in the Yellow Pages in your area. Many camp jobs are also found in this book. ➵See "Summer Jobs for Students," pp. 497-530. Many other camps are run by schools, churches, and religious organizations. If a camp job is what you want, in addition to consulting the sources listed in this book, query various religious organizations and groups, most of which run or know of camp situations. Seek them out in your community or in far-off locales in which you may wish to spend the summer.

OTHER OUTDOOR JOBS ARE OFFERED by government units at the local, state, and federal level. Though America is a nation of private property, the "great outdoors" is primarily owned and operated by the largest landholder of all, the government. Whether it's at a city park or a state or national forest, there are thousands of jobs to be filled during the summer months. At the local level, job prospectors can usually find the source for employment through city governments, some of which have telephone hotline numbers you can call to learn about employment opportunities. Some states also have hotlines that are possible sources of information. ➵See "Job Hotlines," pp. 410-446. Many states also have an Internet site that lists employment opportunities. ➵See "The Internet and the World Wide Web," pp. 536-540.

One of the most fruitful sources for jobs dealing with nature and the environment is the federal government, principally the U.S. Department of the Interior. ➵See "Jobs in the Federal Government," pp. 379-394. Many of the job openings are at national parks, which are some of the most majestic locations in the United States. While the pay is usually on the lower end of the scale, the opportunity to interact with tourists from all over the world at a location with beautiful scenery can often prove to be compensation enough. Be aware that the competition is usually strong at most of the major parks; employees are often people who have been working for the parks for many years in a variety of different capacities.

THE RANGE OF POSITIONS AT NATIONAL PARKS varies tremendously, and the staff ranks swell as high season approaches each year. Preference is given to U.S. armed forces veterans, and the employment conditions and qualifications must be completely met before consideration can be made. Parks are usually looking for food service, retail, grounds-keeping, and visitor information personnel to staff their concession stands and education centers. They also hire rangers, interpreters, fire fighters, biologists, historians, and a host of other titles. The Park Service suggests that the chances of employment increase if candidates apply at smaller, lesser-known parks for off-season positions. Details about them can be obtained from the National Park Service, 18th and C Sts., Washington, DC 20240. ➵See "Jobs in the Federal Government," pp. 379-394.

Since the federal government is the largest landholder in the United States, it needs summer help in places besides the national parks. Other federal agencies hire students over the summer as well, and they too should be fruitful areas to prospect. In particular, the Bureau of Land Management has 270 million acres to maintain. Jobs can be physically demanding, involving hauling timber, for example. The U.S. Fish and Wildlife Service hires majors in environmental sciences and other related fields, as well as others willing to work during summer. ➵See "Jobs in the Federal Government," pp. 379-394.

AN INTERNSHIP IS ANOTHER OPTION for summer work. Internships deal more with the nuts and bolts of the professional working world than most classic summer jobs. Therefore, an intern should be prepared for a less than leisurely summer, but the hard work will be compensated by valuable professional experience. Internships provide hands-on experience in a multitude of different industries. Many times they also serve as recruiting tools for corporations to fill full-time positions. Many intern positions can be found in this book. ➵See "Internships for Students," pp. 447-495. Many of them are for the summer months only, while others are for other seasons.

ONE DRAWBACK TO INTERNSHIPS is that they are unlikely to offer fun-in-the-sun recreational opportunities or high income, though they will provide a valuable addition to your resume. Some internships do pay well. But be prepared, in at least some instances, to have a relatively high cost of going to work. Formal business attire may be required, as well as the need to cover expenses such as lunches and transportation to and from work.

INCOME POTENTIAL AND OTHER RELEVANT FACTS are also offered in the internship chapter of this book. While using these entries, be alert to the fact that in addition to wages, some positions may provide "perks"—that is, stipends to cover transportation and living expenses. And many will provide you with future useful contacts and letters of recommendation.

In addition to the internships listed in this book, there are many more to be found. Some of them are not formally announced. In order to tap into them, contact large corporations. ➤See "U.S. Employers," pp. 158-378. You are almost certain to learn of more internships if you do. Some smaller companies also have internships. You are likely to find some of them by querying firms in an industry in which you are interested in working. Prospect companies in your area as well as those you find in various industry directories. ➤See "Industry Directories," pp. 148-155.

WHAT ABOUT TRADITIONAL CORPORATE JOBS? While it's fun to work in the great outdoors and practical to get professional experience via an internship, there are some traditional jobs available during the summer months that should be considered. Despite some of the gloom and doom you might hear about getting jobs in general, America still needs more workers during the summer months. About 40 percent of all annual economic activity takes place between Labor Day and the end of December. That translates into corporations needing to get ready for it during the summer. Jobs in manufacturing, administration, and the service sector usually pick up a significant portion of the student work force. But how do you tap into these jobs? The first step is becoming aware of some of the jobs and their basic duties. ➤See "Job Descriptions," pp. 84-116.

Then you need to find out about some of the necessary skills for job hunting. A section of this book is devoted to this and is aptly named "Essential Skills." It is divided into five chapters, all of which relate to the basics of finding jobs: resume writing, networking, writing letters to answer ads, interviewing, and salary negotiating. Networking is one of the most useful—and in fact, one of the most accessible—strategies open to students. ➤See "Networking the Hidden Job Market," pp. 52-58.

NETWORKING CAN BE AN ONGOING PROCESS that will be useful as you get your education or your on-the-job experience. While networking consists of tapping many sources for job leads, the most effective source for students seeking summer employment is likely to be your circle of family, friends, and acquaintances. Don't forget to include members of social clubs or any recreational groups you or your family belong to. Other people you know in the community via churches, charitable associations, and schools are likely sources as well. Effective networking involves not only letting it be known that you want a summer job but the career field you prefer. This gets your contacts thinking about companies and situations they may know of.

COLD CALLING, IN ADDITION TO NETWORKING, does work for many. This means contacting companies without prior knowledge of specific leads. There are thousands of corporate employers listed in this book. ➤See "U.S. Employers," pp. 158-378; and "Job Hotlines," pp. 410-446. If you contact enough of them—and do it early—you're likely to find some summer employment opportunities. Also prospect companies in your area as well as those you find listed in useful directories. ➤See "Industry Directories," pp. 148-155.

WHENEVER YOU MAKE CONTACT WITH A COMPANY, in addition to asking about summer employment, also ask about temping and how temp jobs are obtained. ➤See "Temping," pp. 30-33. Most companies are more likely to have temporary positions open than summer jobs. Temp agencies are also an excellent source. ➤See "Temp Agencies," pp. 616-626. Some temp positions require certain skills. For example, some companies seek temporary workers who know how to use specific software programs (such as Microsoft Office, Lotus, Excel, or WordPerfect) and value such skills more than actual on-the-job experience.

If you are particularly adroit at learning computer programs, make some calls to temp agencies to determine what applications are in demand, then learn them on your own time. During summer months when full-time employees take vacations, temps with computer skills are in demand. Temp agencies and companies during the summer also need to fill clerical jobs, sales jobs, and warehouse positions (to process incoming shipments needed for autumn operations).

THE BOTTOM LINE ON SUMMER JOBS is that they are relatively plentiful and that there are jobs of every stripe. Don't necessarily take the first opportunity you hear of. Shop around. Your summer months can be spent in valuable career pursuits as well as at exotic vistas while you earn and learn. Consider your student summers to be rare opportunities to work in situations that may never come your way again. Or you can think of them another way: Once you begin a career or a family, it is unlikely that you will have three months to deal with in such a discretionary fashion. That much time and that many options are something rare.

Treat them as such.

REACHING YOUR GOAL
TEMPING

THE GROWTH OF TEMPORARY WORK virtually exploded in the 1990s, and according to recent surveys, 90 percent of U.S. companies now use temporary workers. The temporary staffing industry hit the $40 billion mark in 1995, and gross revenues have doubled since 1991. This skyrocketing growth spells more opportunities than ever before for temporary work, spanning virtually all trades and professions.

Though half of all temporary employees are clerical workers, and a third work in industry—with such blue-collar jobs as shipping, receiving, hauling, and working assembly lines—the rest are engaged in technical and professional positions. Virtually every occupation is represented today in temporary work: nurses, attorneys, computer programmers, drafters, illustrators, even management personnel.

A MORE COMPETITIVE, INTERNATIONALLY BASED economy means companies now prune their permanent work forces down to the minimum levels. However, work loads continue to fluctuate with the ups and downs typical in a complex economy. Using temporary employees offers companies a way to deal with temporary overloads, without suffering the morale problems that come when an overstaffed work force runs out of work during an inevitable slowdown.

RECRUITMENT AND PERSONNEL COSTS have also risen as a result of increased government regulations and the complexities of employee benefits programs. So using temporary workers also allows companies to try out a full-time position at the beginning of a work load expansion before committing to a permanent full-time post.

At the same time, the employer is evaluating the temporary employee as a potential permanent employee. This is why, for almost four out of 10 temporary employees, temping results in an offer for a permanent job.

THERE ARE MANY BENEFITS OF TEMPORARY WORK for employees, and some may surprise you. Temping offers freedom, flexibility, and paid on-the-job training. But you can also increase your chances for finding a higher-paying permanent job, if that is your goal, simply by taking on a temporary job. Why? Because temping can take the financial pressure off and allow you more time for your job search. According to a recent university survey, temporary work lengthens the job search by just five weeks, yet pays off in a better-paying job. And contrary to what some think, taking a temporary job did not lessen the employee's chance for permanent employment.

Temporary employment is indeed different from permanent employment, but the advantages outweigh the disadvantages for many. In fact, 40 percent of temporary employees recently surveyed said that given their choice, they would continue on as temps indefinitely.

TEMPORARY WORK IS VERY DIFFERENT from regular, permanent employment, and many times the traits that serve permanent employees well can work against you in a temporary setting. For example, people who value routine and faithfully perform repetitive tasks under stress day in and day out may find it difficult to tackle a new job assignment every week or every month, or even every day. That's why the flexibility that draws many people to temporary work is a double-edged sword.

THE FLEXIBILITY OF TEMPORARY EMPLOY-MENT is one of its biggest advantages. It offers you a chance to try out a variety of different positions to gain new skills and to make valuable contacts. Half of all temps confirm that free on-the-job training is one of the major perks of temping. On the other hand, temporary work requires you to be flexible, too. You have to be able to enter a new working environment and hit the ground running, with a minimum of training and set-up time. You'll have unfamiliar procedures and workstyles, and you may not have the chance to form relationships with coworkers or feel like you really belong and are one of the team. Flexibility costs you the personal on-the-job relationships that many people find so rewarding. One way to deal with this is to form a close working relationship with the placement officer at the temporary agency you contract with, if you choose to seek temporary assignments through an agency, as most temps do.

HOURLY RATES ARE LIKELY TO BE LOWER for temporary work than you would receive for comparable work in a full-time permanent setting. Pay rates among temp workers themselves are usually pretty competitive, and many times, a full range of benefits are offered by many temporary employment companies, including medical insurance and vacation pay. However, you may find that the permanent employees you work with side-by-side earn more than you. Consider their seniority, experience, and other factors, when evaluating pay potential. You'll need to balance the lower pay with the freedom you have to turn down new job assignments and take more time off to pursue personal goals, or even to look for a better, full-time permanent job. If you're not sure of the salary level for a prospective temporary assignment in a specific career field, an earnings survey can give you an idea of what you can expect to make. **➤See "Annual Earnings Survey," pp. 117-127.**

UNLIKE A FULL-TIME PERMANENT EMPLOYEE, you may not be able to work all the time as a temporary employee, because you may not be able to secure enough temporary assignments to be fully booked. You thus may have extended gaps without a paycheck. Then again, you may find yourself working steadily for months, if your field is in high demand.

However, if the temporary staffing agency you contract with can't offer you a reasonable outlook for full-time employment and that is what you want, then register with more than one company. Almost 40 percent of temporary employees do just that.

IF A COMPANY HIRES YOU DIRECTLY as a temporary employee without using an agency, you will probably be given a good idea of the length of the assignment at the time you are hired. When the assignment is over, you'll be job hunting again, but for the duration of the assignment you'll probably have steady work.

HOW DO YOU FIND A TEMPORARY JOB? The majority of temporary workers use one or more temporary staffing agencies, which place workers with companies. Both the company and the worker are under contract with the agency, which acts as the legal employer of the temporary worker, handling all personnel matters. In essence, the temporary agency hires the temporary worker, who then fulfills specific duties for client companies of the agency. (In most cases, the employer allows the agency to take a commission, which is based on the fee they pay for temp workers. In other words, the agency is paid by the employer.)

LOCATING TEMPORARY AGENCIES is relatively easy—many are simply listed in the Yellow Pages as well as in this book. **➤See "Temp Agencies," pp. 616-626.** Another way to locate agencies is through the National Association of Temporary and Staffing Services, a trade organization for temporary agencies, located at 119 S. Saint Asaph St., Alexandria, VA 22314; telephone 703-549-6287. This association offers Internet Web access to a fully searchable member database, which includes the local telephone numbers of 1,400 staffing companies with a total of 9,000 offices. This database can be of great help if you're relocating to a new city. The Web site, or URL on the Internet, is www.natss.com/staffing.

Temporary agencies frequently advertise through local classified ads, and those that do probably have a fair number of job assignments available, though assignments in your particular area of expertise may not be available. You may also find temporary agencies listed in the Yellow Pages under specific service listings such as nursing.

YOU CAN ALSO APPROACH COMPANIES DIRECTLY for temporary work assignments through all the same avenues you would use for seeking regular employment. Big corporations do occasionally recruit temporary workers without the use of a temporary agency, as one large software company recently admitted. Such recruitment can be done on a case-by-case basis, and effective networking can uncover such opportunities, which can lead to full-time permanent employment if that is what you desire. ➟See "Networking the Hidden Job Market," pp. 52-58. Information on temporary work assignments is also often provided on the job hotlines operated by different companies. ➟See "Job Hotlines," pp. 410-446.

MANY MUNICIPALITIES AND GOVERNMENT AGENCIES, as well as businesses, occasionally offer temporary work through advertised listings. Government agencies commonly use temps for grant-funded projects that have a particular expiration date, at which time the employment will probably be terminated. Hiring workers as temps allows such municipalities or businesses to avoid union issues and the payment of a full benefits package. Some companies may be awarded contracts for certain projects and do not want to hire full-time staff, only to have to lay them off at a later date. Hiring a temporary work force, where the duration of the job is advertised up-front, avoids such problems. Such opportunities can be good stepping stones for more lucrative permanent jobs.

OBTAINING AN INTERVIEW at a temporary agency is usually much easier than getting one with a permanent employer. However, don't underestimate the importance of appearing just as professional and just as prepared. It is critical that you dress professionally and have a good resume that highlights your abilities as a quick starter and a flexible, independent worker. ➟See "Interviewing to Win," pp. 68-74. Though you may receive assignments without putting out the extra effort, you are competing with a growing pool of temps, and you may lose out on the choicer, better-paying assignments by appearing too casual or not considering a temp agency a "real" employer.

THINK ABOUT YOUR PRIORITIES before the interview. You may not receive all of your wishes, so think about which of the following are the most important to you right now: benefits, salary, training opportunities, the chance for transitioning into permanent employment, or flexibility in your schedule.

When you meet with the temporary agency representative, sell yourself like you do with any other employer, but also pay attention to how you are treated. Can you enjoy the relationship with this person? Your interactions with him or her might be the only "warm fuzzies" you have a chance to develop on shorter temporary assignments.

DO THE PROPOSED ASSIGNMENTS MEET YOUR NEEDS? Make sure you can handle them successfully. A comfortable stretch in your abilities will assist you in gaining new skills, but don't accept assignments that are completely over your head. The resulting failure could demoralize you.

If you're looking for a transition into permanent work via a temporary job, be sure you ask about the temporary agency's policies regarding acceptance of a permanent position. Sometimes employers have to pay a fee if they hire you directly from the agency or during a certain amount of time, even after you are no longer under contract. This can mean that some companies will be hesitant to hire a temp on a permanent basis, simply to avoid paying the agency fee. On the other hand, some temporary agencies are also in the business of filling permanent openings, often with the temporary workers they send out. Obviously, this kind of a situation can be an open door to trying out jobs before you plunge into a permanent position.

YOU MAY ALSO QUALIFY FOR BONUSES for seniority as a temporary employee, as well as bonuses for referring other workers who sign on as temps. After the interview, you will be offered various job assignments. Evaluate each one carefully. Some commitments can be very long-term and may interfere with your desire for flexibility. Other assignments may be jobs that you just don't want to do. To get a better idea of the kind of temporary work you would enjoy the most, look at job profiles. ➟See "Job Descriptions," pp. 84-116.

If the agency is not affiliated with a national group or association, be careful to check its references through the Better Business Bureau or some other organization. By no means do smaller, localized temp agencies have a bad reputation, as a whole. Some, in fact, carry more weight in the local business community than the big national chains.

WHEN APPLYING DIRECTLY TO AN EMPLOYER for a temporary job, use the same techniques as job seekers looking for permanent employment. In some grant-funded assignments, particularly, a year-long temporary job can draw stiff competition from other job seekers with heavy credentials. ➤See "Interviewing to Win," pp. 68-74.

WHAT IF YOUR GOAL IS PERMANENT EMPLOYMENT? If you're hoping to use temporary work as a stepping-stone to a permanent job, temping can give you an excellent opportunity to be offered a full-time position with the company you've been assigned to by the temporary agency or that has hired you directly as a temporary employee. For those with less on-the-job experience, temporary work can give you a chance to prove your abilities to increasingly skittish employers. The way to impress an employer is through stellar job performance, while at the same time seeking opportunities to document your efforts. For example, if you are working in customer service, keep copies or make notes of any customer compliments you receive.

ESTABLISH A POSITIVE RELATIONSHIP with your immediate supervisor, and enlist his or her aid when the time has come to apply for a full-time permanent position. Don't be shy about asking for letters of recommendation or a job review letter. Finally, research company issues, challenges, and opportunities with diligence.

If you are offered a chance to interview for a permanent position, prepare your resume. A functional resume may better highlight your accomplishments while on the job, particularly if you are short on actual work experience prior to taking on temporary work. ➤See "Resume Writing," pp. 41-51. During the interview, discuss your research and observations about the company, detailing ideas you would put into operation if given the opportunity to come aboard as a permanent employee.

IF YOU ARE USING TEMPORARY EMPLOYMENT as a way to keep the cash coming in while you job hunt for better opportunities, consider the timing of scheduling your job-hunting activities with accepting new temporary assignments. You may find that accepting weeklong assignments gives you enough leeway to take alternate weeks off for intensive job-hunting activities, since you undoubtedly do not want to take time off during assignments. Such behavior would probably draw complaints from the company and may dry up your source of future assignments as a result.

If you need to boost your credentials in a particular field, consider seeking assignments that provide training and expertise in that area. Tell your temporary agency representative that training is your top priority in accepting assignments.

REACHING YOUR GOAL

WORKING ABROAD

THOUGH THE NUMBER OF AMERICANS WORKING ABROAD in nonmilitary positions constitutes less than 0.6 percent of the total U.S. labor force, the historic changes in the global arena in the 1990s have given way to increasing employment prospects for civilians outside the United States. The U.S. military, however, is still the traditional choice for Americans who wish to live and work abroad.

FOR CIVILIAN EMPLOYMENT, the trend toward corporate globalization has increased job opportunities abroad in a dramatic fashion. In addition, far-reaching events like the fragmentation of the former Soviet Union, the crumbling of the Berlin Wall, and the emergence of the Southeast Asian business community have brought on increased trading activities and opened up numerous job opportunities overseas.

With many countries now participating in international commerce, there has been a substantial increase in trade in manufactured goods. And sectors besides manufacturing are growing. Forecasts indicate that for the next eight to 10 years, the service sector will experience the greatest overseas job growth. Translators, computer programmers, electricians, equipment operators, and word processors will be in high demand.

JUST WHO IS HIRING ABROAD? The federal government, and its many agencies, is a huge overseas employer—in fact, the largest employer of U.S. civilians abroad. ➥See "Jobs in the Federal Government," pp. 379-394. If you get a government job, you will be able to take advantage of U.S. government employee benefits, and you also may not initially be required to speak a foreign language. Many of the larger government agencies abroad have foreign language courses available when you arrive.

FOREIGN CORPORATIONS are among the largest employers of American civilians abroad. Another option is working abroad for a U.S.-based company. Information on these companies can be found in this book. ➥See "U.S. Employers," pp. 158-378. Though most industries have at least some employment opportunities abroad, the most fruitful U.S. companies are in the following industrial categories: Airlines, Automotive, Chemicals, Computers/Peripherals, Mining and Metals, Personal/Household Products, Petroleum/Gas, and Travel/Hospitality. There are directories you can consult, specifically on the topic of international employment, for more leads. ➥See "Industry Directories," pp. 148-155.

You should browse through the entire chapter on U.S. employers in this book. ➥See "U.S. Employers," pp. 158-378. Pay particular attention to "Other Locations," a subparagraph of the company profiles. Here, you will find hundreds of corporate offices outside the United States. Usually, the U.S.-based human resources department has information on how to apply for positions abroad.

MANY U.S. COMPANIES IN THE PRIVATE SECTOR look to their in-house personnel to fill the relatively small number of vacancies abroad, which means that many foreign positions are filled internally by those familiar with the company's operations. If you are considering a job in the United States with the hope of being transferred abroad, make your desire known before you accept a position.

JOB OPPORTUNITIES EXIST ABROAD in many categories. Jobs in international business run the spectrum from skilled workers, like assemblers in aircraft manufacturing plants, to management and upper management specialists. Among the latter category, finance officers are especially in demand. In the category of skilled workers, pipe fitters, welders, clerks, tradespeople, and heavy equipment operators are being hired.

VARIOUS MANAGEMENT SPECIALISTS—including accountants, marketers, and those in production, personnel, and purchasing—are also finding jobs abroad. They are required to be highly knowledgable about specific nations and often fluent in their languages. Upper management and professional positions routinely filled by multinational corporations include senior managers, lawyers, engineers, geologists, and economists.

Another place to look are the U.S. chambers of commerce around the world, which employ a large number of American citizens in major cities abroad. ➤See "Chambers of Commerce," pp. 628-643.

BUT JUST WHICH NATIONS have jobs? If you are interested in working in the private sector overseas but are more concerned with a particular country than company, take into account the size of a country's economy. Naturally, the jobs are in the most industrialized nations, chiefly in Western Europe, Scandinavia, Japan, Hong Kong, Singapore, Taiwan, and some parts of South America.

A country's economic growth rate can also help you gauge the job climate. In light of the rapidly changing political and technological conditions in today's global marketplace, it is possible that U.S. corporations in countries with smaller gross national products, but with higher economic growth rates, will be expanding more rapidly than U.S. corporations in larger, but more static, economies. Company expansion can translate into more job openings. The Organization for Economic Cooperation and Development, or OECD (located at 2001 L St., NW, Washington, DC 20036; 202-785-6323) collects and disseminates economic information and provides listings of annual growth rates for the world's most developed countries.

MANY OF THE COUNTRIES AND TERRITORIES ON THE PACIFIC RIM—Hong Kong, Indonesia, Thailand, and neighboring countries like Australia and India—are experiencing surges in population and increased economic growth due to technological advancements. These areas are among the decade's most promising in terms of job opportunities. Also, sweeping changes in Eastern Europe are creating economic opportunities.

While a country's economic size and growth rate are reliable factors to consider, population size is another. Many corporations that deal with inexpensive consumer goods have a substantial presence in Mexico, the Philippines, and elsewhere.

LAST, A COUNTRY'S PARTICIPATION IN INTERNATIONAL TRADE plays a part in determining the nature of its job opportunities. Countries in the center of global trade activities depend on the presence of American and other multinational companies. As such, places like Singapore, Hong Kong, and the Netherlands, which are home for many American corporate branches, offer not only manufacturing jobs but also positions in communications, insurance, banking, and transportation.

BEFORE YOU DEPART FOR A FOREIGN NATION to seek employment, contact the chambers of commerce within the nation in which you wish to work. In addition to these, most nations have a chamber on U.S. soil, which can and should be contacted prior to your departure. ➤"Chambers of Commerce," pp. 628-643. Both types of offices are knowledgeable about companies within their nations, and some will provide American job seekers with lists of these companies to prospect. Some will circulate resumes, others will post ads for you, and some will do even more.

INTERNATIONAL AGENCIES LIKE THE UNITED NATIONS, NATO, and the World Bank are also major employers. Other organizations that work to promote world peace and social well-being, like Africare and Catholic Relief Services, serve as additional job sources. Universities and colleges provide international opportunities via fellowships and exchanges for professors. Trade associations and foundations employ people for the purposes of monitoring global developments and coordinating various academic research and education programs. And public policy organizations, like the Brookings Institution, employ people to conduct research into international concerns.

THE WORLD BANK and the International Monetary Fund, two major international financing groups in the business of offering developmental support to countries, have continual needs for bankers, economists, and global businesspersons.

THE FEDERAL GOVERNMENT, as previously stated, is the largest single employer of U.S. civilians abroad. ➤See **"Jobs in the Federal Government," pp. 379-394.** At the head of the hiring line is the Department of Defense. People with technical and scientific experience, high-end computer knowledge, engineering and economic backgrounds, and translating skills will be in high demand in the coming years. Since the Department of Defense is broken up into many different parts—each representing a different facet of defense and each having its own hiring procedures and qualifications—there is no one office to contact for information. Instead, several major agencies can serve as springboards. Among them are the National Security Agency and the U.S. military branches.

THE CENTRAL INTELLIGENCE AGENCY is the next largest overseas employer in the federal government. The CIA draws from a multitude of professions to staff its ranks, including graphic arts, engineering, history, international studies, photography, and political science.

THE STATE DEPARTMENT is the branch of government concerned with overseeing American foreign policies abroad. The Foreign Service, a major component of the State Department, is primarily concerned with diplomatic relations and serves as a good source for job opportunities. There are thousands of Foreign Service Officers (FSOs) at any given time, and they generally rotate from Washington to one of the 140 embassies or 100 other overseas posts administered by the State Department. Applicants must pass the foreign service examination, as well as an intensive oral exam.

THE U.S. AGENCY FOR INTERNATIONAL DEVELOPMENT (AID) deals with issues of economic development overseas. As its tasks abroad are concentrated on environmental welfare, agronomy, economic policy, health, nutrition, rural infrastructure, and energy, many of the positions the AID offers are filled by teachers, economists, and agriculture specialists.

THE U.S. INFORMATION AGENCY (USIA) works to inform the world about various American cultural programs through the radio broadcasts of Voice of America and television shows put forth by WORLDNET. Most USIA staffers come by way of the foreign service examination and include journalists, broadcasters, and radio and television technicians.

THE PEACE CORPS puts approximately 6,000 people to work in over 70 developing countries. Peace Corps volunteers (who receive a modest monthly stipend) assist communities in agriculture education, health care practices, and business organization. Almost any background is considered for admittance to the Peace Corps, but the primary focus centers around those who have experience in agriculture, the trades, life sciences, engineering, and education.

THE U.S. DEPARTMENT OF COMMERCE, though it has fewer jobs, has many choice jobs in major international cities. Among its agencies that employ U.S. citizens overseas is the U.S. Travel and Tourism Administration, which promotes visitation of foreign tourists and business groups to the United States. The U.S. and Foreign Commercial Services division of the Commerce Department acts as a U.S. liaison with foreign companies.

Other federal agencies worth checking into for foreign employment are the Federal Maritime Commission, the Foreign Agricultural Service, the U.S. Geological Survey, the International Criminal Police Organization—U.S. National Central Bureau, and the U.S. Secret Service.

TESTING YOUR WATERS

K nowing if—and above all when—you should seek a new job is one of the most essential career assessments. An easy-to-take test will open your eyes to how satisfactory or unsatisfactory your current job is, and how pressing your need is to move on.

TESTING YOUR WATERS

IS IT TIME TO CHANGE JOBS?

ALMOST EVERYONE CONSIDERS CHANGING JOBS at one time or another, even those who wind up working at one company for life—very rare individuals indeed, at least nowadays. In most cases today, eventually a job and the person working at it are no longer a good match. Even if they are, other factors can come into play that lead you to consider moving on, such as personality conflicts, downsizing, or a natural disaster that causes a plant to close. Whatever the reason, in America of late, there is usually a time when the big decision is begging to be made: Should you leave or should you stay?

Sometimes it's prudent to ride out some bad spots and stay where you are. Other times, the handwriting is on the wall: It's time to change jobs.

BUT WHEN IS THE RIGHT TIME to jump off the ship? Certainly not after you're thrown overboard or when the ship sinks. Though you may not think of working for a living as navigating the seas, in some ways that's precisely what you're doing. Like sailing, there are situations when you should change course, and there are times to keep an even keel.

HERE IS A SELF-TEST that will help you test your waters. It is followed by an evaluation of your responses. The test will help you determine if it's in your best interest to get a new job or to stay where you are. Only check the boxes next to the statements that apply, and skip over those that do not.

❑ You are worried that you may lose your job.

❑ You have heard reports (substantiated or otherwise) that your company is going to be acquired by or merged with another firm.

❑ Your employer does not seem thankful when you do a good job.

❑ You are earning below the market rate for your job.

❑ When you are not at work, you seldom think about your job.

❑ Your company is being outshone by rival firms.

❑ Your company or department is not performing its mission as well as it has in the past.

❑ You have no friends at work or feel alienated from your fellow workers.

❑ You have seriously thought about switching to a new career field in the last year.

❑ You would consider taking a new job for the same salary.

❑ You have fewer important job responsibilities now than you did last year.

❑ You have not been promoted to a higher-paying position or earned a more prestigious job title in the last five years.

❑ You find it necessary to work at an extra job to meet your immediate needs.

❑ You are not getting the recognition you deserve at work.

❑ Your health is being negatively affected by your job.

❑ On your day off, you get depressed when you think about going back to work.

❑ People outside your place of work suggest that you make a career move.

❑ Your pay has not increased even though you have taken on more job responsibilities.

❑ Your leisure time is being compromised because you are taking on more responsibilities at work.

❑ You are not consulted directly or indirectly regarding company decisions that will affect your job environment or job responsibilities.

IS IT TIME TO CHANGE JOBS?

- ❑ Your income level is not satisfactory.
- ❑ You are not able to save money from your present salary.
- ❑ You find getting to and from work an unreasonable hassle.
- ❑ You believe that your career ambitions cannot be fulfilled at your present company.

THE FOREGOING MIGHT SEEM like a form of career psychology. In some ways, that is exactly what it is. Not only does this test require you to examine some facts—it also helps you think about your attitude, which is as important as the details of your present job situation. Together, they dictate the condition of the waters in which you are sailing—that is, the soup you're in, or the smooth sailing you are experiencing but may not be aware of.

Which is it? Let's examine the general situations most workers are in. Determining the one that you fit into will help you reach one of the most important decisions of your life: whether or not to change jobs.

PERHAPS YOU HAVE A GOOD DEAL GOING. If you checked fewer than seven boxes, you are like most people. You moan and groan about work here and there, which is normal. Work can be frustrating, but overall, your complaints are manageable, and it is not likely that a new job would satisfy you any more than your present one.

Of course, you might eliminate some gripes by taking a new job, but it's likely you'd find there would be other points of dissatisfaction at a new position that you don't have at your present position. Be aware, however, that if you checked several boxes that are interrelated (such as ones indicating low pay), and particularly if you've also checked the last box in the test (indicating that your career ambitions cannot be fulfilled), your gripes may be serious enough to justify making a closer examination about a job change.

BE MINDFUL AS WELL THAT CERTAIN NEGATIVES, even one, can be so powerful that they are enough to warrant making a move. For example, if you don't have sizable career ambitions and don't really care about the money, a long and difficult commute may be such a hassle that it ruins your whole day—five days each week! Watch for other examples like this. The rule of thumb is *trust your gut.* If you absolutely hate several aspects of your situation, that may be enough to make you decide to change jobs.

THE TEST MAY SHOW THAT YOU NEED TO MAKE A REAL EVALUATION of your current situation. If you checked seven to 12 boxes, you have many major contentions related to your job. This does not always mean that you should change jobs, since some prob-

lems can be fixed. Determine which ones can and which ones cannot. For example, if salary is an issue, have you asked for a raise? At some companies, particularly small ones, this is the only way workers can increase their income. Many employers assume that if you don't speak up, you're happy with what you make.

HOW SHOULD YOU COPE if you're in this category? You can divide the situations you've checked into two separate lists: (1) the things that you can change or at least can influence, and (2) the things that are unlikely to change, no matter what you do. If too many fall into the second group, you should consider looking around.

REVIEW THESE TWO LISTS in a few months to determine how the situations have changed. Were you able, for example, to get a raise? Is your leisure time still affected by your job? Did your company avoid a hostile takeover? The bottom line is that if you fall into this category of having serious problems at work, don't jump the gun. Things change, especially if you try to change them.

Also be aware that if you fall into this category, it may be because you've peaked at your job. If so, you need either a promotion or a new job. It is possible that you can get a new position at your present company. This is a real possibility that should be investigated before you begin the arduous task of looking for a new job.

IF YOU CHECKED 13 BOXES OR MORE—over half of the 24 situations in the test—you are working in a negatively charged work environment. It is doubtful that most people can change an overall work situation like the one you are in. The possibility also looms large that you will be involuntarily dismissed. In other words, your job may be in grave danger if you fit into this category. The only possible exception is if you can cause a palace coup—that is, take over the company or department operations. This is unlikely, but possible. And even then, the needed changes will happen slowly, and that may not be fast enough or sweeping enough to make it worth your while to stay on. It may be time to begin job prospecting, possibly toward a new field altogether. ➤See "Changing Jobs Within Your Current Field," pp. 10-13; and "Switching Careers," pp. 14-17.

ESSENTIAL SKILLS

No matter how well-honed your skills on the job are, the skills needed to seek new employment opportunities are very different. The chapters in this section define and describe the five most essential job-finding skills and teach you how to polish and perfect them.

ESSENTIAL SKILLS

Resume Writing

WRITING A RESUME DOESN'T HAVE TO BE A TRIAL BY FIRE. Some people obsess about it, spending days—even weeks—attempting to craft the ultimate document. They mistakenly believe that a resume is the single key to getting a job.

A resume is important, but it's only one part of the picture. It's your calling card, your marketing piece, and, hopefully, your invitation to a job interview. However, it's also a relatively simple thing to craft. If you follow a few rules, it won't take you weeks to write one. You can produce powerful resumes, that honestly represent your special talents and experience, without the exercise becoming an obsession. That's right: resumes in the plural.

ONE OF THE MOST BASIC RULES OF RESUME WRITING is that you often need to customize each one you send out to meet each specific job-hunting need. Fortunately, because of word processors, customizing has never been easier, and with the boom in personal computers and high-quality printers, custom-fit resumes have become standard practice. Employers who regularly screen hundreds of resumes select only those that specifically meet their needs. A generic resume accompanied by a generic cover letter is equivalent to trying to hunt in the dark by firing random shots. Sooner or later you'll probably hit something, but it's the targeted approach that nets the biggest game—and the biggest gain.

A COVER LETTER IS ALSO IMPORTANT, and it offers you a further means of customizing your approach. ➤**See "Letters for Applying and Following Up," pp. 59-67.** The time you spend briefly researching a company, when possible, and composing a personalized cover letter is an essential investment. A standard cover letter can be as boring as a steady diet of vanilla pudding to job screeners, who must read hundreds, maybe even thousands of such letters in a given month, particularly for personnel professionals in large corporations. To make yours stand out, don't count on bright paper or other such gimmicks. Instead, consider a cover letter that specifically but briefly describes those qualities and experiences that exactly match the job requirements as you know them.

Once you've sent your letter and resume,

appropriate follow-up steps can also be important. There is a fine line between nagging a potential employer for a response to your resume and appearing enthusiastic and appropriately aggressive in your career aspirations. It's quite all right to send a follow-up letter, and maybe more than one, in a week. Even a reply postcard can help ensure that you're not left in limbo. ➤**See "Letters for Applying and Following Up," pp. 59-67.**

A SUCCESSFUL RESUME INCORPORATES FIVE SIMPLE CONCEPTS, but each one is crucial. Failure to include any one of the following guidelines can sabotage your efforts.

Rule 1: Brag a little. Our culture sends a strong message that people who brag are rude and impolite. However, modesty will not serve you well in applying for a job. This is a situation in which you need to tout your own talents and accomplishments. Don't downplay what you're worth and what you've accomplished.

Rule 2: Adopt a simple, clean approach to your layout. Eliminate clutter, odd paper, crass colors, unusual typefaces, and any other nonstandard elements, which are sometimes used as attention-getting devices but only draw the wrong kind of attention. To be noticed in a positive light, emphasize your accomplishments rather than your responsibilities. Avoid boring lists of "my duties were blah, blah, blah," and instead put down succinct, action-packed descriptions of what you're proud of—for example, raising sales figures by 25 percent in six months, designing innovations that saved the company $50,000 in one year, or decreasing proposal turnaround time by 15 percent.

Rule 3: Create an inventory of your skills. You have two types of skills that need to be included in any resume. The first type, the functional skills, are easy because they are obvious. These refer to your ability to perform specific job functions that can be quantitatively measured: familiarity with a word processing program, knowledge of how to operate specific machinery, understanding the technical requirements of your position, training and credentials in areas specifically related to your chosen career path. However, the second type, your transferable skills, are just as important. In fact, for some employers transferable skills are more important than job-specific skills. They include talents and character traits—for example, meeting deadlines with grace, having a fine eye for detail, or being especially gifted visually—as well as more generic job tasks involving people management and sales performance.

Rule 4: Prioritize your skills and experience to meet the requirements specified in the job description. An individualized resume is more important and much more effective than a single generic resume worked to perfection and sent out to hundreds of companies. You must learn to match your skills to the job opportunity you are targeting. This means customized resumes: target shooting versus a scattershot approach. If one job description emphasizes managerial responsibilities over accounting skills, put your management experience at the forefront.

Rule 5: Don't list references unless you call them first to feel out each person on how he or she might respond to a request for information about you. More people than you would think have shot themselves in the foot by putting down a reference who later turns out to be a "foe" in disguise, sabotaging their efforts to get the job. Even if you've checked out the references ahead of time, in most cases you're better off omitting them from your resume entirely. Save them for when you're asked during the final stages of job application, after you've had an opportunity to interview for the job.

THESE GENERAL GUIDELINES WILL HELP you construct a good resume, but certain types of resumes work better in some situations than in others. A career switcher needs a different type of overall approach from that taken by a first-time job seeker. A parent who is returning to the workplace after a long hiatus to raise a child is not necessarily best served by the old standby—a chronological resume. Choose carefully among the six types of resumes described below for the one that best meets your individual job-seeking needs.

THE CHRONOLOGICAL RESUME is what many people think of first, and its basic concept is simple: You list the jobs you've had in chronological order, beginning with the last one held at the top of the resume and ending with the first job held at the end of the resume. The idea for such an approach was born during a period of corporate dominance in the economy, when the type of job that required a resume represented a logical career progression, beginning with a college degree and then moving through a succession of increasingly more responsible positions, and finally reaching a pinnacle of performance in the most recent or current job held. For some people, it's still the way the work force operates. ►See "Changing Jobs Within Your Current Field," pp. 10-13. For others, however, such a format can be harmful. Take a look at the advantages and disadvantages.

IN ITS FAVOR, THE CHRONOLOGICAL RESUME is an acceptable and conservative course of action. If you don't use it, people may think you've got something to hide: You haven't been on the straight and narrow, you've been goofing off, you've dropped out of the workplace, or you've had a change of heart and career midstream. In other words, you don't fit the corporate profile. Of course, for people who have taken a straight path to success, there is no better vehicle to showcase their talents.

On the other hand, a chronological format can hurt those people whose careers have taken a circuitous or less direct progression. Homemakers, people who've taken time off because of a disabling or major illness, those who've taken sabbaticals or who have gone through long periods of unemployment will have significant gaps in their employment history. These gaps can be negatively highlighted in a chronological format.

ANOTHER GROUP OF PEOPLE WHO SHOULD CONSIDER a different resume style are those who have an uninterrupted employment record but who, because of layoffs or other financial distress, have gone from positions of authority to lower-level jobs. In other words, their work history has not been a steady progression up, but perhaps a series of ups and downs.

FOR CAREER SWITCHERS, a chronological format places the emphasis exactly where you don't want it to be: on your old career rather than on your new goals that have yet to be reached. Your major strength—transferable skills—gets scant attention in a chronological resume.

If you think the chronological format is the one most suited to your needs, take a look at the first of the sample resumes at the end of this chapter for some ideas about how to structure a clean, concise marketing tool that will work for you.

THE FUNCTIONAL RESUME does not emphasize a timeline and corresponding job titles. Rather, it highlights your skills, talents, and accomplishments, grouping them within certain functional areas or according to your overall job goals and objectives. This style, shown in the second sample at the end of this chapter, is a relatively new approach. This may put it at a disadvantage among many personnel professionals. The advantages of this approach for some career switchers, however, can be quite powerful, negating any potential adverse effects.

THIS STYLE IS WONDERFUL for merging paid and unpaid work experience. If you've spent a considerable amount of creative activity in nonpaid work, you can receive important credit for this experience. A chronological format just won't do the same for you. You can also place the most relevant experience at the top even if it's dated. For people who've suffered significant setbacks that have forced them to work at jobs well beneath their abilities, this can be a critical advantage. The same goes for people who have had extended gaps in employment or been forced to change jobs more quickly than they wanted to. ➛See "Reentering the Work Force," pp. 18-21. For others who've been stalemated by slow-growing companies, where advancements were few and far between, a lack of chronological advancement isn't such a detrimental factor when chronological dates aren't emphasized. For career switchers it focuses attention on

what you can do rather than where you did it. ➛See "Switching Careers," pp. 14-17.

A functional resume can have either a chronological job listing at the end or a simple statement such as "Job history available upon request." The decision depends on individual factors. For example, if you were fired from your last job, you might want to explain the situation in person during an interview rather than listing the job on your resume. If there was a scandal at one of your previous companies, there may be a danger that you will be unfairly associated with it. Therefore, you may not want to list that job on your resume; you would probably prefer to explain the situation during an interview, when you have already had a chance to a make a positive impression. On the other hand, if there were no problems at your previous jobs or if your job history is generally impressive, you may want to provide a short list of jobs on your resume. The deciding factor essentially is whether the overall impact of the resume makes you look good—which is the real purpose of any type of resume.

SOME EMPLOYERS JUST DON'T LIKE FUNCTIONAL RESUMES because they make it harder to weed out the specific problems that they are designed to deemphasize. Professional job screeners, in particular, can find them irritating because they make objective and speedy comparisons with other, more traditional resumes difficult. This type of resume can also be more difficult to compose because you may find it hard to arrange your experience in functional categories.

THE CUSTOMIZED RESUME is the third type. This form, shown in the third sample at the end of this chapter, attempts to combine the best of both functional and chronological resumes by dividing the resume into two abbreviated sections. One section features chronological listings, and the other section emphasizes accomplishments. Sometimes this form of resume combines both dates and accomplishments under the more traditional job listing. Usually, the date section comes in an abbreviated form at the bottom.

Since it combines features of both chronological and functional resumes, a customized resume attempts to merge the greater acceptability that comes with a timeline format with the advantages that come from focusing attention on accomplishments rather than job titles. By placing dates at the end, hard-to-explain gaps in job history aren't as noticeable, although they haven't disappeared either. One drawback, however, is that traditional job screeners may still find the format objectionable because it just doesn't fit their idea of purism in form. In essence, it's a hedge.

PERHAPS THE GREATEST ADVANTAGE this format offers is the ability to tailor your specific skills to the prospective employer's specified needs.

ENTRY-LEVEL RESUMES, the fourth type, do not necessarily have to fit a particular style. However, functional and customized formats can be useful since entry-level job seekers (usually new graduates) often have more nonpaid experience than paid. Volunteer experience or scholastically related organizational experience— for example, with sports teams, clubs, or associations—can provide proof to employers that you have the requisite skills for the job you are seeking. ➥See "Getting Your First Job," pp. 6-9.

STUDENTS AND NEW GRADUATES CAN HIGHLIGHT THEIR SKILLS AND AC-COMPLISH-MENTS in the following ways. When listing your nonpaid and paid experience, be careful to discuss accomplishments rather than duties. For example, to say you revised the database for the college yearbook committee emphasizes your accomplishment, which sounds a lot more impressive than saying you worked on the college yearbook committee. Since your degree has required a significant investment of your time, do list it in a prominent place. If you're short on paid work experience, be sure to list any minors or special certificates too. These can demonstrate your well-roundedness as a potential employee. Careers that require specific credentials mean you should emphasize your accomplishments in those areas. Recent graduates should list grade point averages on their resumes only if they are quite high.

An example of an entry-level resume is presented in the fourth sample at the end of this chapter.

THE CONSULTANT/FREELANCE RESUME, shown in the fifth sample at the end of this chapter, is for someone who is self-employed. This is a very different type of resume. In essence, each time a consultant or freelancer bids on a new project, he or she is competing for a "mini-job" against perhaps just as many people as any corporate job seeker. A resume and proposal screening for a big project may be just as rigorous as well, so your resume needs to stand out from the crowd.

TARGETING YOUR RESUME TO EACH BID is critical. You simply cannot use the same generic description of your credentials for every contract opportunity. Highlight those accomplishments that are most specifically related to the particular project you're bidding on. If you have worked with big-name firms or people, including their names can be extremely useful. On the other hand, a chronological listing of your accomplishments is not particularly useful. Try instead to spotlight large clients and successful projects.

THE LAST CATEGORY OF RESUMES consists of those for other purposes. If you have special circumstances, you need to tailor your resume.

PEOPLE LEAVING THE MILITARY represent a large group of career switchers and, like other career switchers, for them using a functional resume is the best bet. These people generally offer more salable skills than they give themselves credit for, but they may be lacking in information about how to sell themselves as civilian employees. Concentrating on specific accomplishments that can be applicable to civilian jobs is the best approach. For example, officer duties can readily be translated into management skills, as in the following excerpt from a fictional military resume:

> Over two decades of experience in managing physical plant facilities, personnel development, program implementation, budgeting, and supervision of maintenance of highly technical and expensive telecommunications and transportation equipment.

PROFESSIONAL EDUCATORS AND ACADEMICIANS should give priority to educational credentials. These job seekers have resumes that differ from others in that items like speeches to professional groups, research papers, studies in progress, and other experiences specifically related to an academic career should be included.

Specific accomplishments that mention some of these items can fit neatly within a chronological format, as in the following excerpt from a fictional elementary teacher's resume. Under the listing of a recent job as a third-grade teacher, this person included the following information about the job:

> Developed innovative program emphasizing hands-on science teaching techniques for third-graders, which resulted in overall test score improvement of 10 percent over previous class year.

Within the same job description, the teacher also includes these certifications:

> Received Associate Master Teacher Certification from State of Texas. Awarded certificate from Gesell Institute as a Developmental Screener—a designation that acknowledges expertise in correct placement of students in developmentally appropriate situations.

IF YOU'RE A RETURNING HOMEMAKER, providing an accurate accounting of your nonpaid work experience is critical. One of the biggest hurdles you face is something you can change: your own underestimate of your worth in the workplace. The best way to circumvent this trap is to do an accurate skill inventory. Then cite specific volunteer-based accomplishments within a functional resume format, as in this example:

> Headed aggressive public relations program for local hospital fundraising drive, which exceeded board-set goal by 25 percent and grossed a total of $225,000 in three months.

> Served on search committee and provided oversight for position of religious education director, who increased church youth attendance by 30 percent in her first year.

PEOPLE WHO ARE AGGRESSIVELY SEEKING NEW OPPORTUNITIES within their company also need resumes, and in these cases, their resumes should concentrate on accomplishments that closely match the new position's requirements. Naturally, giving more weight to the current job description and what you've managed to do with that position is ap-propriate. A creative format may suit this need very well, since the chronological review isn't as important as current job performance.

A NEW CATEGORY OF RESUMES has recently come on the scene, and what sets these resumes apart is not how they are constructed but how they are reviewed. Some employers are now using computers to sort resumes after scanning them in electronically, and with this new technology comes a whole new way for employers to screen out would-be job seekers. Certain large companies are even requesting that you submit your resume electronically. ➤See "Getting the Edge on Rival Job Prospectors in Cyberspace," pp. 508-510. By using electronic search features, they can hone in on keywords, and if your resume doesn't have the magic ones, your submission won't even come before human eyes before it hits the electronic trash can. Electronic screening also makes it easier for employers to compare hundreds of resumes against very tightly defined measurements almost instantly.

THE FIRST TIP FOR MAKING SURE YOUR RESUME SURVIVES electronic scanning is to set it conservatively in an easy-to-scan type with a generous amount of white space. If the computer can't read it, chances are no human will either. Don't waste valuable space on irrelevant information. Focus your resume around a specific concept, citing specific examples that define your experience in terms of the job as offered, and don't submit more than one tailored resume. The computer will realize you've sent multiple submissions. Last, put your most valuable contributions at the beginning because, in some cases, the computers are programmed to scan for critical attributes within a certain word count.

THERE ARE SOME COMMON MISTAKES PEOPLE MAKE when preparing resumes. Whatever style you choose, make sure you avoid these pitfalls when drafting and sending out your resume:

- Not emphasizing a degree that is unrelated to your field. Most employers consider any four-year degree from an accredited college a demonstration of your ability to complete long-term, difficult tasks, regardless of the specific material you studied.
- Using a "canned" resume. Don't use borrowed language from a book.

Make your resume your own personal marketing statement, and use your own voice. Copying language from someone else's resume can trip you up later, perhaps during an interview. You need to be fam-iliar with the statements in your re-sume so that you can believably restate salient points with your potential employer.

- Exceeding one or two pages. Some experts think all resumes should be limited to one page, but certain highly accomplished or older people find it impossible to portray their accomplishments accurately on one page. If you need more than one page, be sure to use two separate pieces of paper rather than a double-sided sheet.

- Including your salary history. Putting it in hurts your negotiating position later on, when you are actually offered the job, because the employer may offer you less when he or she has a better idea of what it will take to hire you. You could even nix your chances of being offered an interview, because many employers use salary history as a way to screen out resumes as they whittle down the pile. ➡See "Salary Negotiations," pp. 75-81.

- Stating your reason for leaving your previous job or jobs. Save such discussions for the interview (or possibly your cover letter). Again, bringing up such an issue in your resume can result in an automatic disqualification. Once you are in an interview, you can bring inter-personal skills to bear by discussing your reasons face to face.

- Listing grade point average. Generally, don't do it unless it's excellent. Anything less than the best draws attention to a mediocre performance.

- Using a boring, laundry-list format detailing responsibilities. Intelligent people know what most job descriptions entail. Instead, focus on your attention-getting accomp-lishments.

- Addressing resumes and cover letters "to whom it may concern." Get the name of the person even if you need to call the company to find out who the recipient of your resume will be. If a name is not obtainable, use a box number (in the case of a blind ad) or a job title such as Accounts Payable Manager or Human Re-sources Manager.

- Including bad jokes or off humor. Use humor sparingly, if at all.

- Having errors or otherwise using a sloppy presentation. This seems so obvious, yet resume experts can cite sad but humorous examples of unbelievable goofs and bad grammatical errors.

- Using poor formatting, with little or no white space. This can be deadly dull. You can give your resume an appealing, graphic look without straying outside the bounds of conservatism by framing your type within generous margins and using double-spacing, when appropriate.

- Using big words or technical terms that many people may be unfamiliar with. You won't impress anyone with your command of arcane language. Technical terms usually do not belong on resumes, but watch for common-sense exceptions such as when you know the resume is going directly to a technical person. Make sure, however, that you are positively certain you are using the term appropriately.

- Including negative information. If it needs to be broached, try to do it during the interview, when face-to-face relationships can assist you in explaining yourself. There is nothing to be gained by saying in your resume that you were fired from your last job or that you were demoted on a previous job because of a serious error on your part. In an interview, you can do more effective damage control if such information must be shared.

- Stating a poorly written objective. Avoid vague wording and generalized goals. The latter category includes statements im-plying that you seek ideal working conditions, such as a boss you can look up to or a job with no overtime. When stating an objective, consider using the job title you're seeking in a specific position.

- Using the pronoun "I." It's obvious you are talking about yourself, and therefore starting every sentence with "I" is awkward and distracting.

- Detailing personal information. Don't do it unless it is considered essential to per-formance of job duties. For example, a model or actress would be expected to list physical measurements and personal features, as well as including a photo.

- Using gimmicky or clever touches. Eliminate cutesy graphics or typography. Stick to a clean, professional look.

EXAMPLE OF A CHRONOLOGICAL RESUME

Ben Wilson
17 Easy Valley Road
Sycamore, New York 12345
555-123-4567

Objective: Management position with dynamic commercial real estate firm

Pertinent Experience:

Leasing Agent, Sulfur Springs Commercial Ventures, Sycamore, NY
1993 - Present

- Handled leasing arrangements for large commercial tenants in 10 regional malls and five office complexes within five-county area.
- Scrutinized financial solvency and viability of prospective commercial tenants.
- Successfully completed leasing arrangements 30 days before projected construction date for 200,000-square-foot shopping complex, with 100 percent occupancy.

Manager, Thompson Properties, Inc., Upsprings, NY
1989-1993

- Marketed properties ranging from a 40,000-square-foot riverside commercial mall to a 200,000-square-foot warehouse space.
- Managed a total portfolio of more than 2 million square feet of preexisting and under-construction properties, exceeding yearly goals by 30 percent in three successive years.

Property Manager, Global Enterprises, Inc., Sarasota, NY
1985-1989

- Executed leases for firm with $4 million in annual sales.
- Developed new database for prospecting and sales.
- Managed advertising budget and developed marketing strategy.

Education: BS/BA, City College of New York, Marketing Major, 1985

License: New York Real Estate Broker's License

Civic and Professional Affiliations:

- Chair, Hospital Construction Fund-Raising Committee, Sycamore, NY
- Chair, Sycamore City Recreation Board
- Member, Mortgage Bankers of America
- President, Sycamore Realtors Association, 1994-1996
- Recipient, Local Citizen of the Year Award, 1994, Sycamore City Commission

EXAMPLE OF A FUNCTIONAL RESUME THAT DOES NOT INCLUDE EMPLOYMENT HISTORY

Note: The same hypothetical job seeker who prepared the previous chronological resume has presented his background in a functional format so you can compare the differences in style.

Ben Wilson

17 Easy Valley Road

Sycamore, New York 12345

555-123-4567

Objective: Management position with dynamic commercial real estate firm

Career Qualifications:

- Twelve years of property management experience with diverse firms
- Board presidencies for community and professional organizations
- Fiscal responsibility for millions of dollars in commercial portfolio property
- Proven track record for exceeding leasing and sales goals

Pertinent Experience:

Business Management

- Managed a total portfolio of more than 2 million square feet of preexisting and under-construction properties, exceeding yearly goals by 30 percent in three successive years.
- Scrutinized financial solvency and viability of prospective commercial tenants.
- Headed team that raised over $2 million in local contributions for new hospital wing construction.
- Created new quality-control feedback mechanism for city recreation department.
- Supervised team of five real estate professionals in leasing department.

Marketing and Sales

- Executed leases for firm with $4 million in annual sales.
- Developed new database for prospecting and sales.
- Managed advertising budget and developed marketing strategy.
- Marketed properties ranging from a 40,000-square-foot riverside commercial mall to a 200,000-square-foot warehouse space.
- Successfully completed leasing arrangements 30 days before projected construction date for 200,000-square-foot shopping complex, with 100 percent occupancy.

Public Relations and Development

- Handled leasing arrangements for large commercial tenants in 10 regional malls and five office complexes within five-county area.
- Created advertising campaign for local Realtors Association, which raised local awareness of the group by measurably significant amounts as assessed by six-month follow-up survey.

Education: BS/BA, City College of New York, Marketing Major, 1985

License: New York Real Estate Broker's License

EXAMPLE OF A CUSTOMIZED RESUME

Note: The same person who prepared the chronological and functional resumes has presented his background in a hybrid format so you can compare the differences in style.

Ben Wilson
17 Easy Valley Road
Sycamore, New York 12345
555-123-4567

Objective: Management position with dynamic commercial real estate firm

Pertinent Experience:

Business Management

- Managed a total portfolio of more than 2 million square feet of preexisting and under-construction properties, exceeding yearly goals by 30 percent in three successive years.
- Scrutinized financial solvency and viability of prospective commercial tenants.
- Headed team that raised over $2 million in local contributions for new hospital wing construction.
- Created new quality-control feedback mechanism for city recreation department.
- Supervised team of five real estate professionals in leasing department.

Marketing and Sales

- Executed leases for firm with $4 million in annual sales.
- Developed new database for prospecting and sales.
- Managed advertising budget and developed marketing strategy.
- Marketed properties ranging from a 40,000-square-foot riverside commercial mall to a 200,000-square-foot warehouse space.
- Successfully completed leasing arrangements 30 days before projected construction date for 200,000-square-foot shopping complex, with 100 percent occupancy.

Public Relations and Development

- Handled leasing arrangements for large commercial tenants in 10 regional malls and five office complexes within five-county area.
- Created advertising campaign for local Realtors Association, which raised local awareness of the group by measurably significant amounts as assessed by six-month follow-up survey.

Employment Overview:

1993-Present Leasing Agent, Sulfur Springs Commercial Ventures, Sycamore, NY

1989-1993 Manager, Thompson Properties, Inc., Upsprings, NY

1985-1989 Property Manager, Global Enterprises, Inc., Sarasota, NY

Education: BS/BA, City College of New York, Marketing Major, 1985

License: New York Real Estate Broker's License

EXAMPLE OF AN ENTRY-LEVEL RESUME

Jacqueline Rogers
34554 Frickson Highway
Hobbleson, Iowa, 67890
555-345-6789

Objective: Reporter for *Des Moines Herald*, education beat

Education:
University of Iowa, Des Moines, GPA 3.9
Bachelor of Arts in Journalism, June 1996

Honors: Dean's List—six semesters
National Merit Finalist
National Honor Society

Accomplishments:
- Headed Students Against Drunk Driving Task Force. Coordinated public affairs campaign to increase community awareness of drunk driving fatalities among those under 21.

- Managed college yearbook committee in 1995. Produced largest volume ever at 10 percent under budget. Introduced new section: "Students in the News."

- Awarded "Most Promising New Journalist" in *Iowa Business News Journal's* writing contest, 1995.

- Produced quarterly community newsletter for Hobbleson Public Schools, 1994-1996.

- Sold five feature articles on student affairs to several news agencies in the state, including the *Des Moines Herald*.

Civic Activities:
- Literacy tutor for adults.

- Summer storytime coordinator for Hobbleson Public Library.

- Volunteer for local public radio station. Hosted weekly half-hour jazz show.

EXAMPLE OF A CONSULTANT/FREELANCE RESUME

Janet Williamson
34 Happy Lane
Serene Valley, California 45678
555-567-8910

Experience:

1992-Present   *Desktop Computer Productivity Consultant*

- Provide in-depth productivity-enhancement knowledge and software troubleshooting assistance for small to medium-size firms, with a focus on desktop publishing.

Clients:

- *Daily Record Herald,* North Bend, California

  Revamped software configuration for 25-employee firm, which boosted newsroom productivity by 25 percent in the first three months of operation. Diagnosed and resolved long-term crashing problem with network server.

- *Big River Business Journal,* North Bend, California

  Designed new database system for automating news tracking, customer sales, and billing, fully integrating system. Company was able to cut staff by one full position for a net savings of over $20,000 per year.

- Little Bear Books, Inc., Big Fork, California

  Revised system procedures and installed training and tracking program for new mail-order operation.

- Credit Union of North Bend, North Bend, California

  Supervised installing of new desktop workstations and training for 10 employees.

- Big Fork Furniture Warehouse, Big Fork, California

  Installed new accounting and inventory system software and conducted training sessions for three employees.

- West End Restaurant, Big Fork, California

  Integrated computer systems for three-store operation, fully combining inventory tracking and buying operations. Estimated productivity increased by 25 percent in first six months.

1989-1992   *Production Department Supervisor*
        Grant City News Corp., Grant City, California

- Supervised newsroom production for 10,000-circulation daily newspaper, fully utilizing Macintosh-based desktop publishing system.
- Installed software and trained crew of five to convert to fully automated graphic production.

1985-1989   *Customer-Service Technician*
        Micro Systems, Inc., San Francisco, California

- Handled incoming calls for desktop software customers, troubleshot technical difficulties, and researched software incompatibilities.

Education: BA, Northern California University, 1985
        Computer Science major

ESSENTIAL SKILLS
NETWORKING THE HIDDEN JOB MARKET

STATISTICALLY, MORE PEOPLE FIND JOBS through an informal, person-to-person contact known as networking than they do through any other method. Approximately seven in 10 jobs are found in this way. What makes this statistic all the more surprising is that most people don't understand the networking process. Though it is misunderstood, sometimes abused, and often maligned, the fact is that understanding networking and applying it in a systematic fashion significantly increases your odds of getting a job.

ONE REASON NETWORKING IS MALIGNED is that many people view it as a high-pressure form of begging. Others believe there is some "standard" way of finding a job and any other way is a form of cheating and subterfuge. They think networking is a backdoor, sneaky method for hitting people up for a job.

Successful networking is not about any of these things. It is about relaxed, low-key interactions that do not involve asking for a job but merely asking for information: developments in your industry, feedback on your approach, and knowledge of others who might know of industry openings or opportunities elsewhere.

MANY PEOPLE WHOM YOU ASK FOR INFORMATION will one day, perhaps very soon, know of a job suitable for you. One person you talk with may even be hiring, if not now, then later. Or he may steer you to a friend or business relation who has information or even a job for you, though he may not know it at the time he suggested the contact. The possibilities are endless. Those who venture out, follow up on leads, and get around bump into all kinds of things.

ALTHOUGH NETWORKING IS AN IN-FORMAL, HUMAN-CONTACT ACTIVITY, it is not a random process. Networking is a systematic method of acquiring names, establishing contact with those people, then seeking out a second and third tier of contacts who refer you to still others, and meanwhile periodically circling back to your initial contacts to check on new developments. It is, in essence, the building of a human tree, each branch leading to another and another until eventually you've discovered the rich node of growth that leads to the perfect job.

Some people look at this tree and see only work: an immense amount of time and energy spent following each lead—or branch—until they are thoroughly exhausted and out on a limb. Effective networking, however, means going beyond the metaphor of a tree. It turns each person in your contact tree into a listening device, a sensitive radar that becomes tuned to your frequency. Each person is now aware of your talents and your search and will think of you when some piece of information comes her way that reminds her of your search for a job. By networking, you don't need to sweat blood to dig up each piece of information yourself. If you've conducted the net working process properly, you have created a benign army that will work for you and let you know of any useful information they receive through their many personal and professional contacts.

NETWORKING CAN HELP YOU TAP INTO THE HIDDEN JOB MARKET, and no other job search method can do that. What is this hidden job market—some type of silent conspiracy? Actually, it's both more simple and more complex than that. Representing one facet of this hidden job market are companies that are experiencing rapid growth and, instead of advertising their job openings, are depending on the tried-and-true grapevine—the network. Via the network, many companies find they can more informally match applicants to their most current, if somewhat vaguely defined, present or future opportunities.

Sometimes companies do not want to alert existing employees to the possibility that they may be replaced. In such cases, they don't advertise for applicants. At other times, companies may experience problems that are hard to pin down until, via the network, someone comes along with a solution, which can be either the person herself or an idea she expressed in an informal networking situation.

THE PROCESS OF EFFECTIVE NETWORKING begins by your making a list of the people who will make up your network. The people on your list generally fall into four categories, depending on their abilities to help you and their degree of commitment and motivation to the process of networking.

IN THE FIRST CATEGORY you list your circle of family, friends, and acquaintances. This includes your dentist, your hairdresser, and other service providers who together form a significant pool of people. This group will have the highest level of motivation because they are emotionally involved with you, either as a person or as a customer. The disadvantage is that they may know only the personal, as opposed to professional, side of you. They don't necessarily have a clear picture of the kind of person you are at work and of the latest update on your professional accomplishments or goals. When thinking about this category, don't forget to include members of any social clubs or recreational groups you belong to—even, for example, your son's little league parents' group.

IN THE SECOND CATEGORY, list all of your industry-related contacts. These people run the gamut from employees of vendors who sell to your former or current employer, to people you know from professional groups who may work in your field, to people you know in your current or former job, to customers of your firm and government regulators. (You should also include here alumni from your college who have indicated to the school placement office that they are willing to speak to students or other graduates about career matters.) This overall group may know your professional side better than your first group of contacts, but they will also expect you to show a higher level of professionalism as you conduct your networking activities. They can also be the most sensitive to feeling hit upon for a job.

IN THE THIRD CATEGORY, list people you know as members of community groups. This includes people you know in the community via organized groups such as clubs, churches, charitable associations, and schools. A word of caution: If you've given only a half-hearted effort to any of these groups—skipping board meetings, gaining a reputation as a critic—you might find networking favors among these participants to be in short supply. Your ability to network here is only as good as your reputation in the community groups to which you belong.

THE FOURTH CATEGORY depends entirely on chance. Here you should list the strangers you meet, whether on plane trips, as you hail the

same cab, or in the waiting room of your doctor's office. They are strictly chance encounters, and you need to be aware of each happenstance meeting so that you can strike up a friendly conversation, perhaps trade business cards, and gain a valuable lead. Most such leads will get you nowhere, but it takes only one with the right contact to help you find the career opportunity of a lifetime.

WHAT YOU SAY TO EACH OF THESE

CONTACTS depends on which category they're in. By now, you've probably begun to realize that you have quite a large number of people to include in your networking tree. Before you begin, however, you need to polish your act and decide how you are going to answer the inevitable questions about your professional goals and your package of credentials. A professional, community, or chance encounter contact will want to size you up and absorb enough of your pitch to be able to pass along a tip or recommendation. Your personal circle of contacts needs to know the "career" you and desires the same information.

THE ART OF NETWORKING INVOLVES designing a compact, powerful message that can be delivered in a minute or two. It's like a short, dynamic resume that describes what you are doing and where you want to go and asks for suggestions about how you can get there.

You'll need to include the following information in your preplanned presentation, and you'll need to practice it enough so that you can deliver it flawlessly when those chance encounters occur in unlikely places:

- *Your level of experience and technical skills.* Most people can recite this part fairly well, even when beset by nerves or in a stressful situation. This is the meat of your job skills.

- *Your abilities and transferable skills.* Portability is the key word in describing this category of talents. Even if you are new to the work force, you have undoubtedly developed certain capabilities that set you apart from your peers. Perhaps you are excellent with people, have perfect pitch, or have the kind of visual acuity that can spot discrepancies in graphic presentations.

- *Your work history.* Your aides in networking will need to have a brief summation, in a sentence or two, of your work history.

- *Your personal traits.* This sums up your career goals and experience through the lens of your personal viewpoint. What drives you? What rewards do you seek?

IF YOU ARE SWITCHING CAREERS, another piece of critical information to add to your self-presentation is a summary of your motivations and goals. "Why do you want to go into the ministry when you've been a stockbroker for 10 years? Why the change of heart? What is it that you seek?" Talk about the reasons for your job or career change. ➤See "Switching Careers," pp. 14-17.

Though this may sound like more than a simple pitch, it shouldn't be. Come up with a conversational tone that packs powerful, descriptive words in a few paragraphs. Make sure you jettison any negative comments. If something happened that you feel badly about—if you were fired, for example—be careful how you phrase it. "We didn't share the same vision" has a much better feel than "I was fired because I argued a lot with the boss."

MAKE AN EFFORT TO UNDERSTAND THE MOTIVATIONS OF YOUR NETWORKING CONTACTS. Each category of potential networking colleagues has its own motivations for agreeing to participate in the networking process. Understanding these motivations will help you to avoid feeling guilty or lacking confidence as you approach your networking colleagues.

YOUR PERSONAL NETWORK OF CONTACTS values you as a human being. You have emotional ties to these people, even if it's just a dentist-patient relationship. For family and friends, the bond is obvious. Even acquaintances feel an important, if less intense, emotional connection to you as a person, perhaps for no other reason than familiarity. For them, participating in your network will usually be an easy choice, and most assume that you would do the same for them if the need arose. However, this group is limited by a lack of specific knowledge about you as an employee. You need to make a special effort to educate them about how valuable a contribution you can make in the right spot at the right company.

FOR THE OTHER THREE CATEGORIES— community ties, professional contacts, and the random person that you meet on street—four motivations are at work in your favor. As long as you don't overstay your welcome in meeting with them, they will gain from the networking contact in the following ways:

- Gathering favors owed is a time-honored form of business currency. It's an exchange that we all keep track of and call upon when necessary. By agreeing to help you, they have made you indebted to them, and they can feel free to call upon you at a later date should they need a similar favor.

- They could gain from the information exchange. You may have some tidbits of information that are of interest to them. It's worth a few minutes of their time to find out what you know.

- It's a boost to their ego to have you seek out their expertise. Everyone loves to be asked for advice, for the simple reason that it allows them to pump up their ego.

- They are repaying past favors of others who helped them. Mentoring you repays the person in their past who mentored them.

NOW IT'S TIME TO PRIORITIZE YOUR CONTACT LIST and decide how to contact them. Since networking involves many individual meetings, you can quickly overload yourself with a huge commitment of time. Effective networking is therefore prioritized networking. You need to make a master list of all your contacts and rate them according to how effective you think each will be.

OF COURSE, BEFORE YOU CAN RATE THEM, you need to list them. A brainstorming session is useful here. Go through each of the first three categories—personal, professional, and community—and try to think of every possible person with whom you have some kind of connection or familiarity. That's enough to justify your initial networking telephone call or note. Review holiday card lists, club rosters, old college roommates: Give your mind free rein for several days to remember as many people as you can. Keep a notebook handy for jotting down names.

WHEN YOU HAVE COMPLETED YOUR LIST, you will probably have at least 100 names on it. Now's the time to refine your list, evaluating each name against three criteria: the people you know the best, the people who are highly knowledgeable or well-connected in your field, and the people who truly have the power to get things done.

It's easiest to start with the people you know best. Practicing your spiel is infinitely easier in a low-pressure situation, as would be offered by a close friend or colleague. Next, branch out to those who are well-connected and knowledgeable in your field. These people help you "reality-test" your career goals and capabilities within the context of current industry conditions. When you have successfully met with these people, you should begin to form a firmer idea of what particular niche you're aiming for. This is when the third category—the real movers and shakers—can be of most help. Don't waste their time with analysis or helping you figure out where you are going. If you have a powerful contact, really use that person to open doors.

WHEN YOU HAVE PRIORITIZED YOUR LIST, it's time to start putting it to work by asking specific people to meet with you. How do you do this? Is the telephone better than sending a personal letter? Each has advantages and disadvantages. Phone calls require more nerve on the part of the caller, whereas a letter or personal note is more low-key. However, requests by phone, since they put people on the spot, can be harder to refuse. Letters, on the other hand, can be ignored, sometimes for quite some time. But letters can also set the stage for a more successful phone call at a later date.

BEFORE YOU DECIDE, CONSIDER THESE FACTORS: How well can you handle yourself over the phone? How well can you compose a letter? How much more power and prestige does the other person have than you? Too great a disparity may call for a letter first, since your phone call may be screened, and you should usually try to avoid letting a secretary or executive assistant translate your message. Ask yourself if the person is more likely to be swamped by phone calls or letters. Pick the one that he or she is likely to receive fewest of in order to avoid getting lost in the shuffle. How much explanation does your situation require? If it's more than a few breathfuls, use written communication rather than leaving a phone message. Once a letter arrives explaining what you want, a very busy person may be more likely to take your phone call.

E-MAIL IS ANOTHER VIABLE OPTION. Messages sent via E-mail are less likely to be ignored, and they are easier to answer. But don't abuse or overuse E-mail, and keep it short and to the point.

If the person eventually takes your phone call, ask for a face-to-face meeting. If the answer is no, start a phone meeting then and there, since you have the person on the line. Sometimes you can acquire important information in what sounds like a casual "thanks anyway." If he begins to talk to you and you sense a rapport, you might try a simple, "I know you don't have time for a meeting in your office, but can we have coffee or a drink some time?" However, don't try this until you've spent some productive time on the phone. Wait until you've established some agenda or common interest. Then the momentum might sway him to have a face-to-face meeting with you.

THE BEST NETWORKING SESSIONS ARE RELAXED and at least appear to be informal. Too much intensity can poison the atmosphere. This appearance can be deceiving, however, since it takes some real orchestration on your part to see that the session flows in the right direction: low-key, informal, friendly. You win good feelings, good information, and powerful feedback when you perform your role as planner and organizer. You reap only resentment and blame, however, if you fail in your role as conductor.

A SUCCESSFUL MEETING FOLLOWS SEVERAL STAGES. Think about each one as well as the best way to move most gracefully from one stage to the next.

THE FIRST STAGE INVOLVES opening the meeting and setting the agenda. Here you explain succinctly why you called the person, where you are in your job search, and what you expect to gain from the meeting.

YOU THEN PROCEED TO GIVE YOUR SPIEL, which represents the second stage, taking care to make it sound as fresh and conversational as possible. Avoid giving a canned effect.

The third phase of the meeting occurs when you have brought the person up to date on what you're looking for and where you are now. At this point it's time for you to ask specific questions concerning your abilities and skills, the current market conditions for job hunting in your particular industry, and suggestions for looking for leads and contacts that could eventually lead to an employment offer.

THE QUESTIONING SESSION OF THE MEETING can drag on, so it's important to keep an eye on the clock and put an end to this stage if the meeting is taking more than the half-hour you promised. Then it's time for the next stage: asking for names of others who might be helpful in your networking. Be careful to phrase your request so that it doesn't sound like begging. Instead, say things like: "Do you know someone who would be receptive . . ." or "Do you think it would it be beneficial if I spoke with . . ."

Ask the person if it's okay before you jot down specific names. Jotting down the right name is only part of the story. When you call the new lead, you will have the most effect if you are able to mention the name of the person who gave you her name. This can be a very touchy situation; one good way to defuse it is to ask whether you may mention that the two of you spoke when you call the contact.

ONCE YOUR QUESTIONS HAVE BEEN ANSWERED, you've used your allotted time, and hopefully, a few names have been shared. You may wish to give the person your resume now. ➤See "Resume Writing," pp. 41-51. (Giving it to the person earlier in your meeting might distract him or her from your conversation.) At this point, it is time for you to close the meeting. Later, after you have taken at least one piece of advice or action offered by your contact, you must follow up with a handwritten thank-you note. It's important to give the person who has taken the time to help you a feeling of satisfaction by specifying how you benefited from the meeting.

THE MECHANICS OF A NETWORKING MEETING actually work on two levels. First, there is the planned meeting agenda as outlined above, in which your logical mind takes the issue and moves it forward in a systematic fashion. Second, there are the mechanics of human interaction, which are based on hunches, feelings, body language, perceptions, and all the human touches that take place when two people are communicating.

Be aware of these mechanics, since it's very important for you to create a likable impression among the people you are asking for favors. Pay attention to your hunches, and if they tell you that the meeting is turning bad, listen and take steps to steer things back on course. Be aware of body language, of appearing too pushy or controlling. If the other person starts to look uncomfortable, try to find out why and address his or her concerns. Your voice is also important. Are you running along at full speed, talking too fast because you're nervous, or allowing your inflection to rise at the end of each sentence? Or maybe you're delivering a monologue—talking so much and so fast that the other person can't get in a single word without interrupting you.

Although you are attempting to steer a meeting that needs to appear to the other person to be relaxed and low-key, you still must pay attention to nonverbal communication clues and respond immediately to subtle hints. For example, if the person stands up, it's time to end the meeting quickly and politely.

WHAT IF, DESPITE YOUR BEST EFFORTS, the meeting turns sour? Your hunches may tell you that the person is irritated, confused, or ready to end the meeting after five minutes. If so, it's not too late to bring the agenda back on track. Remember, he *did* agree to meet with you, so steer the conversation directly to the subject he agreed to talk about. You'll stand a better chance of regaining your momentum if you talk about the thing he obviously found acceptable to converse about in the first place.

If the person with whom you are meeting rambles on, evades your request for information with generic well-wishes, or jumps ahead and is prepared to give you names of other contacts before you have asked for them, be flexible and friendly but try to steer the meeting back to your agenda.

AVOID USING TOO MANY TECHNICAL TERMS, since the person you meet with will probably be too embarrassed to tell you if she doesn't understand your terminology. Be particularly careful in your handling of sensitive information, for example, regarding firings or other bad news from your past. It's safest to be candid about bad news, so the person can rest assured that you aren't hiding any skeletons in your closet.

FOLLOWING UP WITH YOUR NETWORKING CONTACTS is essential to your success. If you've successfully navigated your way through several dozen meetings, you may be wondering why you need to follow up with these same people. You need to keep going forward—looking for new leads and new contacts, continuing to follow the branches of your tree higher and higher until you reach your goal, right? However, there are compelling reasons why you should check back with your contacts.

There may be new developments. A check back by phone helps you jog your contact's memory so he or she will remain alert for new information, but more important, you may be able to repay the favor with information you've learned by contacting his or her referrals. Suppose, for example, that you follow up on a suggested contact and gain a valuable piece of insider industry news. This is an excellent opportunity for a call-back and the perfect icebreaker for doing so.

If you don't have a good opportunity like that, it can help to schedule a day to check back with a lot of your contacts all at once. However, be careful not to stress a relationship that's fragile, which many networking relationships are. Don't be a pest, and don't circle back until at least two to three months have passed.

WHEN YOU DO FOLLOW UP, be prepared to offer some simple statements to refresh the person's memory, offering a quick review of what you discussed in your last meeting and your efforts at following his advice or leads.

Then give a quick review of your progress to date. Finally, gently remind him of his offer to keep an ear out, and ask if he has heard of any new developments since you last met. Successful follow-ups can be your final key to effective networking.

ESSENTIAL SKILLS

LETTERS FOR APPLYING AND FOLLOWING UP

JOB SEEKERS MAKE CONTACT WITH POTENTIAL EMPLOYERS in numerous ways—during personal interviews, on the telephone, and through their resumes. Another key way is through letters, which can be sent as an introduction, in reply to ads, or as a follow-up to some earlier contact. A good cover letter can help determine whether or not you make it to the next step. It can help you get your resume read, be called for an interview, and maybe even get hired.

A good resume is, of course, important, and virtually every job seeker now uses a resume. ➤See "Resume Writing," pp. 41-51. However, you need more than a resume to land the job you want. This chapter offers some tools that may help tilt the odds in your favor.

WHEN ANSWERING AN AD, instead of sending a basic cover letter that looks like everyone else's, why not send a slightly different letter, one that will more likely stand out? This is the perfect match letter. The perfect match letter has a power that rests upon its brevity and specificity. Simply put, it is a short letter that lists your qualifications, matched point for point to the requirements of the job.

This type of introductory letter is the ideal cover letter to go with a resume, but it can also be used without an accompanying resume; the decision on whether to include a resume rests on what the ad asks for. Remember that 95 percent of applicants send resumes, most of them looking and sounding alike. A well-crafted perfect match letter, however, is a rarity, and it may give you the edge you need if a resume is not specifically requested.

THE POWER OF THIS LETTER lies in its succinct ability to summarize the precise match between you and the position that needs to be filled. Because it gets right to the point, it can help you navigate through the gauntlet of professional job screeners in personnel departments. It's the equivalent of a billboard advertisement: attention-getting for the few seconds necessary to let you into the next stage, which is an invitation to talk more, submit more, or meet in person.

This tool must be brief—that is one of its key ingredients. Most letters should be limited to one page, but for higher-level jobs, two pages are acceptable. In this case, the first page is more of a cover letter, with page two noting your qualifications as they directly match the listed job.

THE CUSTOMIZED APPROACH of this letter is the other reason for its attention-grabbing power. You aren't merely sending in a generic resume. Instead, you are targeting this particular job in a bull's-eye. Employers like that. It shows you have a keen interest in what you can do for the company.

CONSTRUCTING THE LETTER IS EASY. Start with a simple, to-the-point introduction. Then list the job's descriptive points, followed by your matching credentials. It's important to back up your assertions with factual accomplishments that can later be verified. End the letter with information on how the decision maker can reach you. (Again, you don't need to include your resume if it is not requested. Only do so if you think it will help direct your application toward the pile reaching the next stage.)

On the next page you will find a fictionalized example of a perfect match letter, used in response to an ad for an administrative position. It is followed by a variation.

EXAMPLE OF A PERFECT MATCH LETTER

123 Herald Lane
Simpsonville, IL 12345
555-123-4567
May 1, 2000

Jane Smith
Simpsonville Herald
456 Lincoln Street
Simpsonville, IL 12345

Re: Administrative Assistant Position

Dear *[Note: Insert the name, department, or company mentioned in the ad, or use the box number if you don't know any of the first three]*:

Your ad in the *Simpsonville Herald* indicated your search for a person who possesses:
- Highly refined office supervisory skills.
- An in-depth understanding of Macintosh computer operations.
- Excellent public relations skills.

My qualifications match your requirements precisely. I have:
- Supervised a staff of 15 clerical workers and shipping personnel.
- Operated Macintosh computers in a variety of settings for six years and familiar with all the major business and medical-office application software.
- Interfaced with the general public face-to-face and via telephone contact, including resolving difficult complaint situations successfully.

My resume is enclosed. I would like to meet with you to discuss how I can help your company. Your reply is eagerly anticipated.

Sincerely,

Bill Monroe

VARIATION OF THE PERFECT MATCH LETTER

123 Herald Lane
Simpsonville, IL 12345
555-123-4567
May 1, 2000

Jane Smith
Simpsonville Herald
456 Lincoln Street
Simpsonville, IL 12345

Re: Administrative Assistant Position

Dear *[Note: Insert the name, department, or company mentioned in the ad, or use the box number if you don't know any of the first three]*:

I am responding to your ad in the *Simpsonville Herald* because my qualifications match your requirements precisely.

YOUR NEEDS	MY QUALIFICATIONS
Highly refined office supervisory skills.	Supervised a staff of 15 clerical workers and shipping personnel.
An in-depth understanding of Macintosh computer operations.	Operated Macintosh computers for six years; have familiarity with all the major business and medical-office application software.
Excellent public relations skills.	Interfaced with the public face-to-face and via telephone contact, and resolved difficult complaint situations successfully.

If you would care to meet with me, I can relate more of my experience, which is extensive. If you would prefer to see my resume first, kindly write or call me at your convenience.

Sincerely,

Bill Monroe

THE SUGGESTED FORM OF ADDRESS is indicated in the sample letters. However, there is another way to address your letter so that it carries more weight, though it will take a little more time. By researching the company, you can direct your letter to the person actually making the hiring decision and not to the personnel department, which screens replies and then forwards the winnowed pile to the person who actually does the hiring. This procedure is particularly followed in larger companies, but even small companies have administrative assistants who screen job applicants.

IF YOU KNOW WHICH COMPANY is advertising for the position, it is possible to call and ask who is doing the actual hiring. Many times, lower-echelon people will be surprisingly candid. If not, go up the ladder a bit. Names of individuals in management or even those in staff positions can often be found in directories. ➡See "Industry Directories," pp. 148-155. A personally addressed letter carries a tremendous amount of weight.

INTRODUCTORY, UNSOLICITED LETTERS — those that are not written in response to specific ads—need to be directed to the appropriate individual, not just to "Personnel Department" or "Human Resources." Again, you can call companies directly to find out who is in charge of specific departments or functions.

WHEN WRITING AN UNSOLICITED LETTER, do your research first. Find out as much as you can about the company you are contacting and the overall industry. ➡See "U.S. Employers," pp. 158-378; and "Industry Overviews," pp. 395-409. Also keep informed of general business news affecting that company and industry through newspapers and magazines and periodicals published by professional groups. ➡See "Professional Magazines/Journals," pp. 131-147; and "Professional Associations," pp. 644-655. Then tailor your letter to that firm's specific situation. Is the company launching a new product line, and you have experience with similar marketing ventures? Has the company recently purchased a division in a completely new field, but one in which you've done an internship? These are the kinds of things you want to highlight in an unsolicited introductory letter.

The next page gives an example of an unsolicited letter.

THERE IS ANOTHER TOOL YOU MIGHT CONSIDER using, especially when contacting a company that has not advertised a job opening or if you are involved in consulting or freelance work. It is called a professional assessment and will often linger in the recipient's mind much longer than a run-of-the-mill resume. The professional assessment doesn't resemble a traditional job-hunting tool at all. This is exactly what makes it and you stand out.

THE PROFESSIONAL ASSESSMENT CONSISTS OF A FEW PAGES that describe some essential how-to information that, ideally, addresses a problem the company or hiring authority you've targeted is trying to solve. (You have, of course, researched the company to determine what problem to focus on.) Here are some examples of problems and the titles that go with them:

- Five tips for instituting quality control among sales teams: Maintaining control without reining in your staff's enthusiasm and profits.
- Six ways to create positive customer feedback: Making those complaints work for your bottom line.
- Seven tips for improving employee morale: You can improve productivity in 30 days with the smile-creating program.

It's often a long shot that you've been involved with a project identical to the one at hand at the company to which you're applying. Your professional assessment, therefore, should be reasonably analogous to a situation at or goal of the company. If you don't have something that fits, send something else. It can still help you if it's a good example of how well you've performed at a past or present job.

ACCOMPANY YOUR PROFESSIONAL ASSESS-MENT with a cover letter, which should point out the relevance of this professional assessment to the job you're applying for. If it's not relevant, the letter should explain that you know that the assessment may not be related to specific job duties the company requires, but it is an example of how you attack and solve problems. Problems and solutions, after all, are relevant to all jobs. Point this out.

EXAMPLE OF AN UNSOLICITED LETTER

12 Thomas Street
Bestville, MD 23456
555-345-6789
May 1, 2000

Todd Brown
Managing Editor
Big Valley News
456 Trigger Road
Bestville, MD 23456

Dear Mr. Brown:

It has been widely reported that *Big Valley News* will soon be launching a new specialty publication focusing on local businesses. Three years ago, as the associate editor for a small newspaper publisher in suburban Baltimore, I played a major role in creating the prototype and later performing numerous editorial duties for just such a targeted publication. The newspaper, which was profitable from its first issue and soon drew a circulation of 5,000 in a town with a population of only 30,000, targeted the local business community. As the associate editor, I conducted market research and assisted the advertising sales department in soliciting ads for the first issue. I also had full responsibility for developing ties with local businesspeople and reporting their achievements and developments in each weekly issue.

My editorial, developmental, organizational, and planning skills were all called upon in this successful venture. I feel these same skills could be of direct benefit to *Big Valley News* as you undertake your new publication.

I am enclosing my resume. I will be calling you within the next five days to discuss how I can help you in your new area. I look forward to speaking with you.

Yours truly,

Michelle Chen

IF YOU HAVE A REASON FOR NOT USING A RESUME, the professional assessment used in its stead has some benefits. There are some successful job applicants who don't circulate resumes, perhaps because their vital statistics don't look very impressive on paper. The professional assessment can look even better to a hiring authority than a resume.

BY TARGETING THE TOPIC CAREFULLY, you can make even a lengthy unsolicited document hard for the recipient to resist. Since you have automatically positioned yourself as an author, a problem solver, and someone who does not always do things in the conventional way, your name will stand out—especially if you follow up with a phone call.

SEVERAL MAIN ELEMENTS GO INTO WRITING a professional assessment. Just as a headline in a print ad grabs your attention, a headline that compels the reader to go further is fundamental. A subtitle is a nice touch. The headline must have a benefit apparent to the recipient. In the profit-oriented world of business, the benefit is either making money or saving it, both of which can improve the bottom line.

A one-paragraph introduction signals to the reader that you are personally experienced with what you are writing about and think the recipient will benefit from the information.

A HALF-DOZEN USEFUL TIPS make up the heart of the professional assessment. Examples are: six ways to eliminate software incompatibility crashes in employee desktop systems, or the six critical elements in putting together a powerful marketing presentation that signs new real estate clients.

YOUR NAME, ADDRESS, AND PHONE NUMBER should have prominent display on all the pages, either at the top or bottom, so that everyone knows just who authored the professional assessment. A short bio, such as you would see in a magazine, should follow at the end.

FINISH THE PROFESSIONAL LOOK with a nice binding of some sort. For a small fee, a quick print shop can do a perfect binding, where the pages are glued, or a spiral binding, either with a nice cover. You can also buy plastic covers and do your own binding.

ANOTHER IMPORTANT TYPE OF CORRESPONDENCE is the follow-up letter, which can be as important as an introductory letter since it helps to build rapport. Generally speaking, there are two types of follow-ups: (1) those sent after the initial contact—that is, the very next contact you make after having sent your perfect match letter, resume, or professional assessment; and (2) those sent after an interview.

FOLLOW-UPS SENT AFTER THE INITIAL CONTACT assume you have not yet met with anyone at the company regarding your first correspondence. It is sometimes effective to make a phone call instead of sending a follow-up letter. In many cases, your cover letter, or introductory letter, can tell the recipient that you intend to call in a few days or a week. When you call, have a note sheet handy and take careful notes. If you get through to the hiring authority, quickly confirm that he or she did receive your materials, and offer to answer any questions. If the person wants to talk, take advantage of the situation to sell yourself and partake in a mini-interview.

Sometimes phone calls are not possible, such as when an ad states, "No phone calls, please," or you are not sure who the employer is, as in a blind ad with just a box number.

THE SIMPLEST WAY TO FOLLOW UP is with a short, polite letter, stating that you are writing to follow up and you are still interested in the job "for these reasons," which you list in a paragraph. You can also put in a brief reminder that you have certain skills and experiences and think the job's requirements are an excellent match for your expertise. Wrap it up with your thoughts of what the next step might be. An interview is your first choice, but since the employer already knows that, offer something else. If you have not sent a resume, offer it now. If your initial contact was not a professional assessment, offer that now. (But remember, if you've never heard the term "professional assessment," they haven't either, so describe it as a report pertaining to some specific.) The overall idea is to restate your qualifications and offer the employer even more proof than what he or she already has.

IT CAN BE APPROPRIATE TO FOLLOW UP in a few days with a second note, and even a third might not be too outlandish. There is a fine line between appearing enthusiastic and looking like a nag, so be careful and use your best judgment.

SOME APPLICANTS FAVOR A RESPONSE CARD, which is a stamped, self-addressed postcard with a few boxes for the recipient to check. It might have the following:

❑ We expect to call you for an interview by.

❑ We will keep your name on file.

❑ We have not made a decision yet, but you are still under consideration.

❑ We do not think you are the right match for us at this time.

Be aware that applicants for executive-level jobs might position themselves as merely one of the pack if they use a method as impersonal as the response card above. A more formal, professional-looking letter asking what the next step might be would be more in order.

THE SECOND TYPE OF FOLLOW-UP is a thank-you note sent after an interview. Above all, it should be sent no later than a day or two after the interview. The time frame says something about you: No grass grows under your feet.

YOUR LETTER SHOULD BE SHORT and should remind your interviewer of what you spoke about, at least the things that reflected well on you. The letter should never be intended to "polish someone's apple" or to sing praises of the company. The intention of the letter is to confirm what the interviewer already knew when you walked in the door: that you had the necessary qualifications. Otherwise, you'd never have been asked to interview.

THE LETTER SHOULD CITE SOMETHING the interviewer liked about you, not what you liked about the company. In addition, the letter should make reference to the next step. If the interviewer has given you a cue as to what that may be, express it again in your letter. For example: "As you suggested, I'd be delighted to meet with Steve Richmond and show him my portfolio. Next Wednesday is especially convenient. Can we set up a time?" If you were not given a cue, you may have to think of the next step yourself. You can set this up as you leave the interview. For example: "Have you seen the report I did on markets in Indochina? Based on what you said, it might be useful when you plan next year's sales estimates." Then in your follow-up letter, you can offer to bring the report to a second interview.

The next two pages show two sample follow-up letters.

THE PERFECT MATCH LETTER can also be an excellent follow-up to an interview, unless of course the hiring authority has seen it before. If you use it as a follow-up, however, make sure to adapt it so that you remind the employer of something he/she liked about you and address the issue of the next step.

HERE ARE FOUR ADDITIONAL TIPS for effective letters:

• Make them as warm, sincere, and personal as you can, avoiding stilted formality and awkward construction. Avoid long words, sticking with short syllables and an easy flow. Certainly your grammar and spelling should be impeccable, and don't saddle your letters with technical jargon. This makes them boring and hard to read and can put people off.

• Don't write the letter by hand, but sometimes an added handwritten note can be appropriate and give a nice personal touch. For example, it can be helpful to handwrite a short P.S., or a note in the top right margin mentioning some pertinent point or expressing enthusiasm for the company or the position.

• Edit mercilessly and keep your letters short and to the point. Busy people resent wading through a rambling letter. Several short paragraphs with generous margins and with doublespacing between paragraphs make for a better presentation.

• Keep copies of all correspondence and notes on phone calls related to a position, as well as a copy of the original ad. This way, at a moment's notice, you can respond accurately in a follow-up call or letter.

EXAMPLE OF A FOLLOW-UP LETTER

12 Breckenridge Lane
Townley, MD 12345
555-123-4567
May 1, 2000

Beverly Johnson
Director of Manufacturing
Trace Brake Manufacturing
345 Trace Lane
Eatonville, MD 67890

Dear Ms. Johnson:

You may know that I recently submitted a resume *[or something else]* last week pertaining to the advertised position for a quality control supervisor. I am sure that it will be obvious to anyone at Trace Brake who reads it that I am one of the most qualified candidates for the job currently available.

Could you kindly let me know what the next step might be? Would you, for example, like to see *[my resume, a professional assessment, or something the addressee has not yet viewed]*?

Sincerely,

John Howard

EXAMPLE OF A LETTER FOLLOWING UP ON AN INTERVIEW

12 Hughes Road
Los Angeles, CA 12345
555-123-4567
May 1, 2000

Bradley Benjamin
News Herald
P.O. Box 3456
Los Angeles, CA 12345

Dear Mr. Benjamin:

Thank you for our pleasant and interesting meeting. I particularly enjoyed discussing *[cite something Mr. Benjamin found interesting]*.

Based on what you told me about your department and what you expect from your employees, I am even more confident that my professional experience and your expectations for a managing editor match almost perfectly.

Is there anyone else at the *Herald* with whom you would like me to meet? Perhaps you might also wish to see the four-part story I did for the *Times* that you were so interested in?

Whatever you deem our next step to be, I'd like to go forward. How may we proceed?

Best regards,

Jackie Winston

ESSENTIAL SKILLS

INTERVIEWING TO WIN

SOMETIMES IT JUST DOESN'T SEEM FAIR. Though hundreds of applicants may apply for a position, only a handful win the privilege of an interview. These chosen few have been carefully screened, their credentials have been closely analyzed, and their qualifications have been held up to stiff competition. Whether there are five or 10 people or some number in between, they are the handpicked, select few. Yet only one will be offered a job. For what reasons is that one person hired and the others not?

Contrary to popular opinion, it isn't necessarily the most qualified person who gets hired. Being the most qualified candidate is not the deciding factor once a person makes it to the interview stage. At that point, new criteria are used. The one who gets the job is often not at all the one with the best skills or experience. However, he or she far exceeds the others in demonstrating the three critical elements of an interview: (1) attitude, (2) communication, and (3) people skills. Let's examine them one at a time.

THE NEED TO CULTIVATE AND DEMONSTRATE AN ENTHUSIASTIC ATTITUDE is at the top of the list of important interviewing skills. Energy, a smile, an upbeat attitude, even love of the job: for a prospective employer, these are signs that you will tackle the job with the same kind of enthusiasm you showed in the interview. How do you demonstrate this attitude? It's not just a matter of expressing your feelings. What is more important is drawing specific examples from your life or career experiences that demonstrate your enthusiasm for this particular career field.

Before the interview, jot down some specific events that demonstrate your enthusiastic attitude. In other words, be prepared to tell a good story or two. There is no better way to demonstrate your positive traits than a well-told anecdote.

A SURE METHOD OF RUINING YOUR INTERVIEW and revealing your lack of enthusiasm is to appear passive, show indifference about the subject matter being discussed, or approach the interview with the attitude of, "I just need a job, okay?" Presumably you've been selective in your job search, and you've chosen to interview for a position that will enhance your long-term career plans. Even if you regard the job as a temporary fill-in while you wait for a better opportunity, you still need to demonstrate a certain amount of respect for the job.

CONFIDENCE IS NEARLY AS IMPORTANT AS ENTHUSIASM in demonstrating a positive attitude. It can be difficult to show in an interview, which is often a high-tension experience for most people. However, knowing what you'll be asked in an interview can assuage your fears and help you maintain a confident attitude. Further on in this chapter, some of the questions that you can expect in a job interview are provided, along with suggestions on how they can be handled.

But there is also another kind of confidence that will shine through even during a tense interview situation: the confidence that comes from having mapped out your career goals long before the interview. Setting career goals is important because without them you can come across in an interview as if you expect your prospective employer to do that work for you. Convey a sense of focus and maturity. Let the interviewer know you have a plan for your career and you're here to find out if this position and this company fit that plan. Your goal is more than earning a paycheck: It's your heart's desire and your own personal plan for making a mark on the world, or at least making it a better place.

CONVEYING THE RIGHT ATTITUDE also involves taking the time to research the company that has offered you the opportunity to apply for a job or to be interviewed. If you're not sold on the company, they won't be sold on you. Know the specifics—the ins and outs of that particular firm and industry—and you'll field questions successfully. ➤See "U.S. Employers," pp. 158-378, and "Industry Overviews," pp. 395-409. Most local libraries have reference material with information on local firms or can tell you where to get it. You might even start with a phone call to the company's receptionist, who often knows what literature the company has available. Your knowledge, which will be revealed during the question-and-answer period of the interview, will demonstrate your enthusiasm for the job. You'll be the candidate with the right attitude.

A common mistake is to be caught ill-prepared when the interviewer assumes you know about the company's recent merger, new product, or new logo. Your prospective employer will not be impressed by your lack of knowledge about obvious and newsworthy developments in the company. Keep informed by reading up on business news. ➤See "Professional Magazines/Journals," pp. 131-147, and Professional Associations," pp. 644-655.

If you have contacts with employees who work for the firm, take advantage of the opportunity to network with them and find out what the company's current issues and pressing concerns are *before* your appointment. ➤See "Networking the Hidden Job Market," pp. 52-58.

PROPER GRAMMAR AND THE ABILITY TO SPEAK INTELLIGENTLY are the foundation for the kind of communications skills necessary to navigate a job interview. But they are only the beginning. Most communication occurs at the nonverbal level, and this is the area to examine most closely as you prepare for your "performance."

You'll be on stage. Naturally, you'll be somewhat nervous. No matter how much you practice for your performance, you won't be nearly as good in the actual interview. That's okay. Your performance doesn't have to be flawless. However, there are some good habits to begin cultivating right now that will serve you well. You can change those bad habits, which seem like minor offenses but be-

come deadly sins when committed during an interview. They include (1) a "fishy" limp handshake, (2) poor eye contact, and (3) poor posture. Let's look at each of them.

A "FISHY" LIMP HANDSHAKE can be a problem because this is usually your first contact with the interviewer. A firm, confident handshake is a form of body language. When accompanied by a smile and good eye contact, it says something positive and sets a tone for all that follows.

REGARDING POOR EYE CONTACT, shifting your eyes frequently, averting your gaze, or looking downward are unmistakable signs that you are ill at ease, lacking confidence, or hiding something. It's no way to build a relationship.

WHAT ABOUT YOUR POSTURE? Do you tend to slouch or fold into the furniture? Check yourself to make sure you are comfortably upright, not stiff, not slouching, but projecting just the right air of quiet confidence. A positive approach means you'll lean forward at appropriate times, expressing your interest in the job as well as the person who's interviewing you. Watch your hands, too, lest your prospective employer finds them fidgeting or, worse yet, wandering toward your mouth to indulge in nervous nail-biting.

THERE ARE BASIC RULES GOVERNING PROFESSIONAL BEHAVIOR that may seem obvious, but a surprising number of people violate them often. For example, be on time. Being late to an interview usually means you've blown your opportunity. However, if you're on the freeway and unavoidably detained because of a traffic accident or other such obstacle, it's better to pull off and make a call even though it will make you even later. At least you can offer the employer a chance to reschedule.

GIVE SPECIAL CARE TO THE WAY YOU DRESS FOR THE INTERVIEW. Make sure you overdress for the position. Casual clothes are deadly to your chances of being hired, even though once on the job they would be perfectly appropriate. Wearing personalized jewelry or symbols, strong perfume or aftershave, earrings for men, exotic hairdos for women—all of these are likely to send off danger signals to the potential employer and should therefore be carefully avoided.

TELEPHONE ETIQUETTE is an area of professional behavior that is often overlooked, particularly by recent graduates who have roommates or who share other group-living situations. Be sure you inform everyone who shares your number that you are involved in a job search, and instruct them to answer the phone in a professional manner. Have a message pad and pencil near the phone. If you have an answering machine, be sure the message is programmed to be as simple and as courteous as possible.

Critical remarks made about other people during the interview usually reflect poorly on *you*, not on the person you're putting down, particularly if that person is your former boss or teacher. Your interviewer may justifiably assume that you would be just as quick to adopt a critical attitude toward your new employer.

LYING ABOUT YOUR CREDENTIALS OR ABILITIES IS THE GRAVEST ERROR you could make and, if discovered, could forever thereafter mark you as an untrustworthy person. Even if you have been employed for years, a discovery that you lied about your credentials during your hiring process may result in your immediate termination.

Other mistakes in human relations are:

- *A lack of courtesy.* Don't be too familiar too quickly. Use a formal address or title. Stand when others enter the room, and offer to shake hands. Thank the interviewer for his or her time in talking with you.

- *A disclosure of prejudice.* Even if you think the person may share your attitudes, keep them to yourself. Better yet, work on ridding yourself of such attitudes, since they will also give you trouble on the job.

- *A tendency to complain.* Don't complain or whine about past events. Management usually gets many complaints from employees or customers each week, and they don't need to hear any during the interview. Also, don't make excuses. You can express your responsibility for unfavorable occurrences while still putting a positive spin on events.

- *An inclination to act like a "know-it-all."* Very few people appreciate an overbearing attitude, particularly during an interview, where a touch of humble pie is more appropriate.

THESE MISTAKES CAN SIGNAL BAD TIDINGS for job interviews, but a positive attitude, good people skills, and good communication, especially nonverbal communication, can help you quickly form a relationship with your prospective employer. To prepare fully for your interview, you also need to be prepared for the kinds of questions you'll be asked. Regardless of the job, all employers' questions can be broken down into four categories: (1) what skills you can bring to the job; (2) why you applied to the company; (3) what your deficiencies are, and how they'd affect your performance; and (4) what kind of salary you're asking for.

WHAT SKILLS CAN YOU BRING TO THE JOB? Dealing with questions pertaining to skills involves defining your talents, leaving as little as possible to the imagination. When doing so, remember to show enthusiasm. One suggested strategy is to offer the employer a menu, a veritable summarized list of your skills. Then ask him what he would be most interested in hearing more about. Posing this question to the interviewer is important. His answer ensures that you will be talking about the personal characteristics he regards as the most valuable. What better topic to spend time talking about?

USE STORIES WHEN DESCRIBING YOUR SKILLS, telling them enthusiastically. What, after all, sounds better, the statement "I am a conscientious worker" or a short narrative about the time you demonstrated meticulousness and it paid off for you and your company? And which is more believable, the statement or the story with the proof of the pudding in evidence?

In addition to industry-specific questions (which obviously can't be addressed here) other generic questions of this type may include: Are you a self-starter? How good are you at motivating other people? What new procedures have you initiated in previous positions?

WHY DID YOU APPLY TO THE COMPANY? That is the second thing an employer will want to know. Most people handle this type of question incorrectly, by attempting to assure the employer that her company is great, huge, full of opportunities, and so forth in an effort to present an enthusiastic attitude. The problem is that this answer is not very believable. A better approach is to be honest. You have researched the company, but you're at this interview to find out if the fit is right for both parties. You might consider telling the interviewer about your own job goals. Then you have an opportunity to turn the tables and ask her, "Can my goals be realized here?" If the answer is yes, this well-timed question makes a powerful statement directly to the interviewer about the match she is trying to make with the applicant. This approach not only opens up a dialogue, it may also give you enough information to decide if you really want the job. Moreover, it's a demonstration for the interviewer of your collaborative and professional negotiating skills.

WHAT ARE YOUR DEFICIENCIES, and how will they affect your performance? This next category of questions is meant to unnerve you and, from the employer's viewpoint, uncover any information about you that the employer would find incompatible with the company's goals or management style. They can be summed up in one simple question: "What's wrong with you?" Everyone has his or her faults, and these questions are meant to uncover yours, particularly those deficiencies which would affect your performance.

IN ORDER TO FIELD THESE QUESTIONS, you need to find out specifically what the employer's concerns are and attempt to address them. For example, if the employer asks you why your current salary is so low in light of your professed accomplishments, his concern is probably obvious: that you are not what you claim to be. Attempt to clarify his concerns by asking, "It sounds like you're concerned that I am overselling my credentials for this particular position. Is that the case?"

THEN GO ON TO ANSWER THE QUESTION using positive phrases. "Up until now, I've been so interested in the kind of work I've done that salary has been of less importance to me, and I was willing to take less than I am truly worth. But now, I'm equally concerned with income." Or, you could say, "My last company has a lower than usual pay scale but compensated me with a very generous benefits package."

Here's another example. If your employment record of moving through four jobs in five years is questioned, you can give it a positive spin with an explanation or, better yet, a story about how quickly

you've mastered new responsibilities at previous jobs and soon outgrew the positions. Then, seize the opportunity and turn the tables, asking the interviewer, "Can this company offer me an opportunity to grow as fast as my job skills do?"

OCCASIONALLY, YOU WILL ENCOUNTER an interviewer who tries to provoke you by purposely making you uncomfortable. The person may be conducting a "stress interview," a specific technique designed to uncover "the real you," or she may simply not be very skilled at interviewing.

In either case, inappropriate questions may surface. Some of these may only be improper; others may be illegal. These include questions about your plans for marriage or children, about your spouse's attitude toward your working, and about your feelings about being supervised by the opposite sex. You may be tempted to defend your legal rights. Don't do it. Instead, rather than answering the questions directly, attempt to address the unstated concern without blatantly pointing out the poor behavior of the interviewer. For example, if she is worried that as a male you won't like your female boss, reassure her that you are a mature person who works well with others. If she's concerned that the company will invest in a lot of training only to see you go on extended maternity leave, reassure her that you are dedicated to your work and your personal concerns are just that: personal. You need say no more.

HOW MUCH MONEY WILL IT TAKE TO HIRE YOU? Questions regarding salary require special handling and, with very few exceptions, need to be diplomatically postponed until you are made an offer for the job. In many cases, employers have a range rather than a salary in mind. Your goal, if offered the job, is to get the highest end of that range. This can be done only if the employer has the highest regard for you. If you disclose salary information too early, you run several risks.

Employers use salary information to screen candidates they believe may be too high priced or not really qualified on the basis of their salary history. If you allow an employer to set the salary and allow yourself little or no room to negotiate, you may end up being underpaid, which only gives you a negative attitude about your job and may possibly even cost you your job over time. Of course, the worst part is actually getting short-changed on what should rightfully be yours: top dollar for your skills and experience.

WHEN INTERVIEWERS ASK ABOUT SALARY before you have adequately demonstrated your worth to the company, redirect the question. For example, ask how important this or that talent is to the job. Then you might assert that if the company places that much weight on those abilities, salary won't be a problem. Move on to the next topic, attempting to show confidence that salary is not a problem. After all, you both agree that matching abilities to the job is the goal at hand. Stick to this strategy, even if pressed. If you have a very pushy interviewer, chances are he will be the first to toss out salary figures. But usually salaries are not seriously discussed before the decision has been made that you are right for the job. If you are pressed, you might say something like, "Your company doesn't have a reputation for paying unfairly, but it does have a reputation for hiring the best people. If you think I'm one of them, we'll be able to agree on a salary." ➤**See Salary Negotiations," pp. 75–81.**

WHEN AND IF YOU ARE OFFERED THE JOB, don't be the first to quote a figure. Wait for the employer. If you feel the need to bargain for more, be prepared to cite figures gathered through your research. Researching a salary range for a job title is essential to getting your worth. ➤**See "Annual Earnings Survey," pp. 117–127.** Networking will also yield information regarding salary expectations. ➤**See Networking the Hidden Job Market," pp. 52–58.** Quote them, and the sources if necessary, but be respectful of the interviewer. Making him or her come off as a cheapskate will kill whatever rapport you've built. If the interviewer quotes you too low, in addition to citing your research, ask if the company pays a bit more for experiences or talents that go beyond the norm. This is the most tactful way to increase the ante, provided the interviewer is sold on your talents and that your demands are not unreasonably high. Your preinterview research will reveal if they are.

TURN THE TABLES DURING THE CLOSE OF THE INTERVIEW. After the interviewer has set forth all of her questions and you've sensed that the session is about to come to a close, pose questions of your own that will help you decide if you and the job are a good match. If you've taken careful note of the description of the four basics that interviewers ask questions about, you have already discovered that answering each one involves turning the tables and questioning the interviewer. It's all right to ask questions here and there during the interview, but a rally of questions is best saved for the end. Always remember, however, that if you've been effective at posing questions *during the interview*, it shouldn't be necessary to interrogate the interviewer at the end.

There may be lots of questions remaining, but your goal at your *first* interview—there is often a second, third, or even more before a job is offered—is to establish rapport with the interviewer, leaving a positive impression as a person who handled the basic elements of the interview well: (1) attitude, (2) communication, and (3) people skills. If you have accomplished this goal, the interviewer is likely to be persuaded to take you to the next level. This usually involves meeting another member of the company, often the interviewer's boss or a department head for whom the interviewer is screening candidates.

ASKING SEVERAL QUESTIONS IN THE CLOSING MINUTES of an interview, however, will never hurt you. For example, you might ask if you've adequately answered various questions, particularly those that you sensed were important. However, if you didn't provide good answers initially, don't underscore them by calling even more attention to them. If you did answer certain questions well and feel a need to reinforce them—for example, if your positive answers overshadowed a weakness the interviewer seemed to be concerned about—ask if she was adequately informed.

IF YOU'RE INTERESTED IN PURSUING THE JOB OPENING, it might be prudent for you to ask what the next step is. Since that almost always involves another meeting, frequently with a higher-level employee of the company, the best impression you can leave is that you are someone the interviewer will want to meet with again and will take pride in being the one who suggested you meet with those in command.

TAKE STEPS IMMEDIATELY AFTER THE INTERVIEW to prepare yourself for the next one. Just because the interview is over, you shouldn't end your efforts to secure the job. There are steps you can take to turn the tide in your favor. Even if you don't get the job, follow-up activities can generate good will and leave the door open for future opportunities or even for networking possibilities. If you've been successful in developing a rapport with the employer even if he or she did not hire you, you can still continue to work the relationship.

YOUR FIRST STEP IS TO TAKE NOTES immediately after the interview. Jot down all the important points covered in the interview, including the ways in which you think you were impressive, any potential deficiencies that were uncovered, and the job tasks deemed most important by the employer. Do this while the experience is still fresh in your mind. If you are called back for a second interview, this information can be critical. You can attempt to address any weaknesses and look for more ways to emphasize the perfect match between the employer's needs and your credentials and experience.

EVEN IF YOU DON'T GET THE JOB, *analyzing the information you've noted will be an invaluable* way to prepare for future interviews. Consider each interview a rehearsal that will eventually lead to a starring role. In doing so, you may discover missed opportunities or better ways to present certain background material about yourself.

AFTER YOU'VE NOTED SPECIFICS ABOUT THE INTERVIEW, send the interviewer a thank-you note. ➥**See Letters for Applying and Following Up," pp. 59-67.** If he or she gave you unmistakable signals that you were not going to get the job or you've decided that you don't want the job, then a simple note thanking the person for his or her time is not only courteous but leaves the door open for future opportunities. The same company may have a new position in the future that is more to your liking or better suited to your qualifications. Such a courtesy will be remembered and regarded favorably.

Such a sample letter might read:

> Thank you for your time in interviewing me for the position of recreation director. I appreciated the opportunity to find out more about Redway Corporation and some of the exciting projects you have on the agenda.
>
> If offered a position with your company, I would seriously consider it.

A SECOND TYPE OF THANK-YOU NOTE applies to situations in which you want the job and think you have a decent chance of getting it. Open with a sentence or two of thanks, then briefly summarize the job's most significant tasks and responsibilities, linking each one to your skills and abilities. Say you're interested in the job, and if you have something significant you'd like to show the company that might clinch the job opportunity for you, make them an offer.

A sample note of this type might read:

> Thank you for your time in interviewing me for the position of recreation director. The job certainly sounds like a challenging one.
>
> As you know, I have been involved in scheduling and supervising 30 athletic programs during my tenure as a recreation director. As we discussed, my previous employer asked that I write a report to management justifying our proposed $1.6 million budget. This report was so well received that the first year we received every dollar. The following year, the board of directors increased our budget to $1.85 million based on my updated report, not to mention providing me with an executive assistant.
>
> I'd like to show you this report, which demonstrates how I can be effective in a similar capacity at your company. If you would like to arrange another meeting, I am available any day but Wednesday during the week of the 20th.

IF YOU HAVEN'T HAD A REPLY TO YOUR LETTER in a week to 10 days, consider a phone call. Sometimes the interviewer will acknowledge your note, but if not, have something to offer as an addendum to it and then wait quietly for a response.

You'll either get the bad news you wish was not in the offing or the good news that you are being strongly considered.

IF YOU DON'T GET THE JOB, ask for feedback and for additional leads to other jobs. If you are being considered with reservations, counter them. You may be successful. If you're not, you should still ask for leads to other jobs.

IF YOU ARE A STRONG CANDIDATE, try to build on the relationship. If you're aware of some new development about the company, that may be a good icebreaker. You can ask what effect it might have on the job you've discussed. If a specific problem was disclosed during the interview and you've had time to think about some solutions, now's a great time to say so and to offer an invitation to get together and discuss your ideas in more detail. If you are juggling more than one offer, say so and you may prod your contact into hurrying the decision along.

IN SUM, BUILDING RELATIONSHIPS IS THE KEY to the interview process. If this is done well, good follow-up skills serve as reminders of the good impression you made at the interview. The follow-up also cements the relationship you've built. When you put your follow-up in writing, it can also serve as a springboard to get you to the next step.

SALARY NEGOTIATIONS

MOST JOB SEEKERS UNDERSTANDABLY EXPEND a greater amount of energy on finding the right job than on negotiating a salary. While the process of job searching can take weeks or even months, the time it takes to negotiate your actual salary after you are offered a job can pass by in literally seconds. If you do not understand the importance of and techniques for negotiating your salary well in advance of those fleeting moments, you may be settling for a salary that is 10 or 20 percent less than what you deserve. Since every future raise or job you have will probably be based on that salary, you are shortchanging yourself for a lifetime. Multiply that 10 or 20 percent over the span of a career, based on the average annual salary, and you could end up with over $100,000 less in lifetime income!

Though the material in this chapter is skewed toward negotiating mid- and upper-level salaries, by no means does that imply that salaries for lower-level or entry-level jobs cannot be negotiated upward. Even the salary for, say, a receptionist has some room for enhancement. Maybe a receptionist can negotiate overtime pay that is not initially offered, or another 50 cents per hour—which could later mean $1,000 a year.

NEVER LOSE SIGHT OF THE FACT that if you are applying for a job for which many candidates qualify, it probably will pay less than jobs for which there are few qualified candidates. This is the chief reason that applicants who have made themselves stand out from the pack can command more money than the company was originally willing to pay. Even if you are applying for the lowest-level job, coming off as a standout will make it that much more possible to negotiate a salary upward. If your interviewer can say something like, "Oh, that's splendid, we didn't anticipate an applicant who can do word processing," or "You're the only candidate for comptroller who speaks Spanish well enough to write directives for our Puerto Rican office," then you've given her a good reason to offer you more than she originally planned.

Try to conform the ideas that follow to your specific situation. If you cannot see how to adopt them, then *adapt* them. They can often apply if you are creative.

TO GRASP THE ESSENCE OF NEGOTIATING SALARIES, you must accept that the relationship between an employer and an employee is, at least in economic terms, an adversarial one. The company seeks to minimize its labor costs, while at the same time shooting for the best possible talent for the price. The employee wants the most in salary, while aiming for the best in working conditions. By arming yourself with key negotiating skills—at the very beginning of your job search—you can come out the winner in the relationship.

YOU MAY ALSO BE ABLE TO AVOID THE EVEN DEADLIER TRAP of "winning" a salary that's really too high for your qualifications. It can be dangerous to negotiate a salary so high that it defeats the company's goal of paying you in a way that is profitable to the firm's bottom line. Inevitably, within six months or a year, the company will realize that you are being paid more than you are really worth, and you may lose your job and big paycheck altogether. So effective negotiating skills can make both you and your employer a winner by creating a perfect match: You get the top dollar that you're actually worth, and the company gets a quality employee who will more than earn every penny he is paid.

WHAT STOPS MOST PEOPLE FROM NEGOTIATING for top dollar is the fear that taking such a stance, particularly too early in the game, will anger the prospective employer and maybe even ruin one's chances of being offered the job. Part of the fear is justified. If you press your stance too early in the interviewing process, more than likely you will send the wrong signals to a prospective employer, who may think you care more about your pay than what you have to offer the company. But you should press for all you're worth—as long as you do so at the right time.

TIMING IS EVERYTHING IN SALARY NEGOTIATIONS. It's amazing to realize that in a matter of a minute or two, you and your prospective employer will probably come to terms on your pay, which is one of the most important financial decisions of your life. That moment can pass by quickly. That's why you must be prepared to get the most out of each second of that critical interaction. So even though you must prepare for salary negotiations from the very first moment of your job search, the actual nitty-gritty of bargaining should occur only in that moment when you are offered the job.

MOST EMPLOYERS WILL PRESS for an earlier discussion of salary. It's an easy way for them to screen out both job seekers they consider too high priced for their budget and potential employees who may not be truly qualified for the job, based on their previous salary history. Thus, many employers will press the salary issue early, perhaps even at the beginning of the interview, and want you to reveal your salary history and goals before they disclose their intended level of pay to you. It will take diplomacy on your part to postpone salary negotiations until the tide has turned to your favor. *That critical moment is when the employer becomes the seller instead of the buyer*—in other words, when she is ready to hire you and wants to sell you on working for her. That's when you have the power to negotiate for the best money, without the fear that doing so will cost you an opportunity for the right job.

YOU WANT TO BE IN CONTROL of deciding whether this job suits you or not (and if it does, of commanding a higher salary than the employer intended to pay when the job was first made available). By postponing salary discussions and avoiding the employer's screening efforts, you can do a more effective sales job on what you have to offer the company. If the employer perceives that not only can you do the job as intended but

actually solve even greater problems for the company, you could end up with a much higher salary. Some people have even managed to double the salary budgeted for a position by convincing the employer to expand their duties and redefine the position before they even start the job. You certainly won't be able to do that if you allow the employer to short-circuit the process with the salary-screening technique.

ALLOWING SALARY DISCUSSIONS TO OCCUR BEFORE that critical moment when you are offered the job can lead to another hazard: when you quote a figure that's too low. It can happen all too easily. You find yourself face-to-face with the interviewer, who casually interrupts the discussion about job duties to ask you something along the following lines: "By the way, what did you have in mind for a salary?" If you name a figure that is below what the employer expected to pay, one possibility is that the employer immediately assumes that you are just not a quality candidate. If you were, you would certainly have expected a higher salary commensurate with your experience. You lose the job offer.

The other possibility is that the employer thinks he's gotten a great deal, because apparently you are willing to accept the job for thousands less than the department's budget had allowed. You get the job, but you lose money that should have been yours. Either way, when you succumb to pressure and quote a figure that is too low, you lose.

And it can get worse. If you take the job for less pay than you know you are worth, it's only human nature that you will become resentful over time. That can ultimately cost you your job or, at the minimum, the kind of raises, advances, and enjoyment that should be your reward for hard work.

WHAT IF YOU QUOTE HIGH, just as you would when you are trying to sell a used car because you figure you must start high and then face attempts to bargain you down? Chances are the employer will be in no mood to bargain. She will likely scratch you off the prospect list altogether. The employer will worry that if the company does hire you for less than you quoted, you'll become resentful and eventually turn into a problem employee. Why bother? She'll look to another candidate who gave a figure more to her liking, or even more wisely, who held out to avoid early salary negotiation and then worked out a figure pleasing to both parties.

UNTIL YOUR POTENTIAL EMPLOYER IS SOLD ON YOUR SPECIAL CONTRIBUTION—how you can help him and his company achieve greater profits—quoting too high can kill a potential job offer. So what you really need to do is *diplomatically stall* for time, which can actually create respect, not rejection. Potential employers will be impressed with your poise and firm convictions, but most of all with your continued emphasis on discussing what you can do for their companies, before you talk about what they can do for you. The specific techniques for effective salary negotiation are not difficult and will generate the kind of respect that will get you the job offers you deserve.

THE FIRST STEP IN EFFECTIVE SALARY NEGOTIATIONS is postponing salary discuss-ions until you are offered the job. Even discussing salary history can be harmful, as this is used as a screening tool. There are a variety of tension-diffusing phrases you can use when an employer puts the ball in your court before making an offer to hire you. Any of the following statements can effectively prevent you from having to reveal your salary expectations first:

- "I doubt we'll disagree about compensation. Before we talk about it, can we look at your department's goals and how I can help you meet them?"
- "I'm sure you'll be able to afford me. Shall we see if we have a good match here first? That seem to be the real issue for now."
- "If this job is what your ad said it is, I'm sure salary won't be an issue. Could you tell me more about the job re-sponsibilities?"

Note that the last response posed a question to the interviewer. Now the ball is in her court. Most likely her response will be to discuss the job duties, and you've successfully moved the conversation away from salary. This ploy is well worth trying because it usually works.

YOU WILL NEED TO PRACTICE and invent your own personal response that feels most comfortable for you. *Be prepared to fend off salary inquiries more than once.* You may find the employer steering you back to the topic several times. The important thing is to exude confidence in your replies. Send the message back that the discussion on salary will take care of itself when you two have a meeting of the minds on what the significance of your contribution will be.

REFUSE TO BE BOXED IN by discussing salary history up front. Be aware that when the hiring authority is making a big issue over your salary history, it is likely because he feels the salary the company had in mind is too low. A statement from you like, "I've heard your company pays fairly, which is how I'm used to being paid" takes some pressure off the interviewer. It might make him feel more at ease, and he'll go on to something else. You might even take the opportunity to pose a new or related topic if the interviewer seems satisfied with what you just said.

YOU ARE READY FOR THE NEXT STEP when the employer accepts your negotiating stance and agrees to postpone further salary discussions until the moment when he is ready to offer you the job. At this point, when he has asked you what it will take for you to join the firm, the employer is once again trying to get you to name your price first. Be confident and ask, "What salary did you have in mind?" Again, you have thrown the ball back to him.

WHEN THE EMPLOYER SETS FORTH A FIGURE or a range, your most powerful tool now comes into play: silence. Again, you're putting the onus upon her to continue with something. She might wonder if she underbid for your talents. If so, you might hear a higher figure. Or you might hear a qualifier, such as: "It may be lower than you deserve, but we can arrange a salary review after a few months." She might even lay out some noncash compensations, such as a company car.

WHENEVER YOU RESPOND WITH SILENCE, always look as if you're contemplating what else may be in the offing. Frequently there's more, or there can be if you've made the employer sweat a little.

At this juncture, you either have the initial offer to respond to or, better yet, the employer has upped the first figure and you have a second one to consider. Your next step is to respond truthfully to the offer. Is it more than you wanted? A lot more? Be cautious here. Perhaps you have oversold your abilities and you will have a difficult time earning such a figure. If so, address that concern with some caution. Allow yourself some time to think about the job so you can do more research to make sure that the position is one in which you can excel, not just barely manage to tread water.

IS THE SALARY EXACTLY WHAT YOU HAD IN MIND? Though this is usually not the case—because most employers will quote a lower figure, at least to start—it may be an amount that fits your research. Then say so, and move on to closing the deal.

IS THE FIGURE DISAPPOINTING? If you have researched the going rate for this position, you can now negotiate a successful resolution. (See the section of this chapter on how to conduct useful research on salary levels.) If you have convincing research at your disposal, the employer is likely to be motivated to try and meet your expectations because she is convinced that you are right for the job. If you can say to her, "according to my research," it will give your negotiations more power.

SPEND A SERIOUS AMOUNT OF TIME arming yourself with salary research. The best negotiating skills will do you little good if you don't understand the economics of salaries.

HOW DO COMPANIES DETERMINE what to pay? There are three rules that almost universally apply to how companies compensate employees.

- *Rule 1:* Companies always try to get the best quality for the least cost. In this competitive age, companies know they must pay for quality. Labor is a critical component of a firm's competitiveness, and smart managers understand it's foolhardy to fudge on labor costs. But at the same time, they might try to get you for less and spend the money they saved on something else.

- *Rule 2:* Salaries are matched to the level of job responsibility. The principle of negotiating more responsibilities, rather than more pay, frequently nets you more pay. Though it is not necessary to wrangle more job responsibilities at your interview, you are likely to get them if you've sold yourself as someone capable of not just handling the job but doing even a bit more. Let the boss decide what you should be doing, but plant a seed by selling your capabilities beyond

just managing the responsibilities in the job description.

There is a reverse of this that is deadly: taking a job for which you are overqualified. One of the things you need to avoid is applying for a job at which the pay will be not be commensurate with your level of experience or will be below your minimum income threshold. If the job challenges you but doesn't overwhelm you, then chances are excellent that the salary offered will be in an acceptable range. Therefore, don't shoot too low, even if income is not your primary reason for working.

- *Rule 3:* You must always earn your salary back in profits for your company, whether directly or indirectly. In a capitalistic society, you must pay your way. This applies to people who may seem far removed from the sales department. Even if you are not actually selling or servicing for the company, your position had better be part of the matrix that makes the company money. If not, in lean times, it will be the first to go.

THESE ARE THE BASICS IN SALARY ECONOMICS, but how do you find out what your particular circumstances warrant in pay? You need to research the right salary for a specific job. ➤See "Annual Earnings Survey," pp. 117-127. You may find you need more definitive information for your particular specialty than provided in this book. One up-to-date source is periodic literature—specifically, trade journals. Many professional journals produce an annual salary survey. ➤See "Professional Magazines/Journals," pp. 131-147. General business magazines may also do salary surveys from time to time. You can research these at your local library.

THE FEDERAL GOVERNMENT also has salary information available. ➤See "Literature Available From the Federal Government," pp. 128-130. One publication in particular, the *Occupational Outlook Handbook,* is an excellent source, as is *Employment and Earnings.* Contact the Government Printing Office, 732 N. Capitol St., NW, Washington, DC 20401, for information on obtaining copies.

These sources will give you generalities. To get more specifics for your area, you may need to do your own local salary survey. The advantage to this method is that it can give you an accurate picture of local salary conditions. It can also be critically important if you are relocating to a distant city where salaries differ greatly from those in your own area.

SALARY IS PROBABLY ONE OF THE MOST TABOO SUBJECTS in conversation. The very fact that it is, however, works in your favor during the survey. Anything that is taboo elicits extensive curiosity. People working in positions similar to the one you're seeking will want to know what everybody else is making, probably just as badly as you want to know what they are making.

TO DO YOUR OWN SURVEY, choose several businesses that employ positions similar to yours, and phone and request to speak to the person occupying that position. When you've been put through, explain that you are discussing salary requirements for a position like the one she currently occupies. Describe the job's responsibilities, and say that you are calling other places to learn about salary ranges. If she wants to be part of your survey, offer her a copy of your results when it is complete. Most people's interest will be piqued at this point. Have a brief list of questions ready including: level of seniority, years on the job, size of business, number of employees the person is responsible for, and title of the person's boss. This will give you the information you need during your negotiations.

COACHING YOURSELF FOR SUCCESS is extremely important for those negotiations. It may seem simple to negotiate for the best possible salary, and you will presumably be armed with the facts, but if the thought of sparring with a potential employer gives you a case of nerves, practice is the best strategy.

A SIMPLE WAY TO INCREASE YOUR COMFORT LEVEL is to role-play with your friends or a tape recorder. Coach your friend on what type of responses a wary employer might give, and practice your responses. By recording the interactions, you can analyze your weak points and work to correct them.

PROFESSIONAL CAREER COUNSELORS can also assist you in acquiring negotiating skills with employers, and particularly in improving your confidence level and presentation. They can coach you on body language and how to project confidence while you discuss uncomfortable subjects. ➤See "Career Counselors and Vocational Services," pp. 552-561.

In the final tally, however, the most important way to dispense with your fears and gain powerful confidence is to practice. Pick particular phrases that you feel the most comfortable with, and work so that you deliver them with poise, diplomacy, and confidence.

ONCE YOU'VE AGREED ON SALARY, you may be thinking that you've won one of the biggest challenges of your career. However, salary is only part of the equation. Once you and your new employer have agreed on a salary, you also need to discuss your total compensation package. The time to talk about your benefits and perquisites is right after you've nailed down the salary agreement.

Once you've agreed on a specific figure for salary, pin down the exact salary structure. For example, what does it involve in the way of commissions, bonuses, or incentives? You don't have to be in sales to earn commissions. Supervisors of departments can sometimes tie in performance pay to their position, if not in the form of a commission, then in the form of a bonus or other incentive.

THE TIME TO TALK ABOUT THIS IS after you've agreed to take the job, but not until you've had a night to think about it. Ideally, you should schedule a meeting with the appropriate company representative a day or two later, at which you hash the package out. It's imperative that you get the agreement down in writing, at least prior to giving notice on your current job.

YOUR FIRST PERFORMANCE REVIEW should also be addressed now. Try to avoid a year's wait for the first one. That just means a longer wait for your first raise. Determine what the company's policy is toward a cost-of-living adjustment, and try to have your performance review merit a possible salary adjustment in addition to the cost-of-living adjustment. Otherwise, it's not really a raise at all, and you are only keeping pace with inflation. Point out to your employer that you intend to offer a star performance, and you'd appreciate the additional incentive of having a chance to discuss that performance in six months (or whenever you think you can prove your worth). Be sure to give yourself enough time to perform, and don't cut yourself short.

JOB BENEFITS ARE THE NEXT THING TO discuss once you have negotiated the complete salary structure and your first performance review. These include insurance, vacation, and sick leave. In some high-level executive jobs, these benefits can add up to 30 or even 40 percent of your total compensation package. At other jobs, particularly those at very low levels, benefits are minimal or even nonexistent, so they are not a topic for negotiation.

INSURANCE COSTS are one area of labor expense that companies are looking seriously to reduce because of escalating health care costs, so it pays to be vigilant here. Things you might consider asking about include the amount of the deductible, reducing or eliminating the waiting period for eligibility if there is one, how long the coverage will last if you leave the job, and the availability of other insurance, such as disability and life. Again, these matters may not be up for negotiation at some jobs.

MORE VACATION TIME is an absolutely wonderful thing to have. By phrasing the request in the right way, you may be able to gain an extra week or some extra days scattered throughout the year. You may even suggest that you be rewarded for perfect attendance with well days off instead of sick leave. Say to your employer that you intend to work so hard that you could use some periods of refreshment.

THE LAST CATEGORY TO DISCUSS IS COMPANY PERKS—things like use of a company car, club memberships, parking spaces, company dining privileges, tuition assistance, and child care assistance. (These often apply only to top-level jobs.) At the start of your job search, take the time to compile an extensive list of all possible job perks, and be prepared to ask about them when you're offered a job.

When all is said and done, get it in writing, sleep on it for at least one night, and then agree to the deal, knowing that you negotiated for the best possible package.

THERE ARE OTHER THINGS TO CONSIDER. You may find yourself in the enviable position of fielding two or more offers at the same time. What a wonderful situation, but how do you handle it? You can either negotiate for more time with company A while you await company B's offer, or you can try to hurry up company B's offer. The second is the better choice. It helps to be honest with company B and to tell your prospective employer, particularly if you have established good rapport, exactly what your situation is and that you need to make a decision within the time frame of company A.

IF YOU HAVE NO WORK EXPERIENCE, does that affect your ability to negotiate for the best possible salary? Recent graduates aren't the only ones to find themselves in this position. People changing careers can also be short on experience in their new field, as can people in highly technical fields where technology is being replaced with new equipment and procedures they are not accustomed to. No matter what your situation, you are being hired mainly for your talent, personality, and transferable skills. The company expects to train employees for specific tasks, but good managers know that quality people make the difference. Remember to stress your quality and your worth (particularly to yourself), and the resulting confidence will enable you to negotiate for the best possible salary.

SOMETIMES IT CAN SEEM IMPOSSIBLE TO AVOID giving away salary information, when the very ad or job application demands it in no uncertain terms. Employers are simply seeking to screen out replies, because in today's job market, an ad can bring in hundreds of replies. You can still avoid giving away salary information as long as you respect the employer's need to handle this problem. One way to deal with this request in an ad or application is to reassure the employer that you are currently paid a market value for your present job, that your are positive salary needs will not be a problem, and that you will be happy to broach the matter in an interview. Of course, once you find yourself in an interview, simply use the techniques discussed earlier to delay being the first one to cite specific salary figures. You can also list your salary as competitive and simply say no more about it, particularly on an application.

THE IMPORTANT THING TO REMEMBER is to maintain a sense of respectfulness while at the same time holding on to your principles and your negotiating position. If you've targeted your application to a job that is appropriate to your experience and professional abilities, and that offers you a challenge, respectfully postponing the citing of specific salary figures should not affect your chances in applying for the job.

THERE IS AN EXCEPTION TO EVERY RULE, and the one place that it is advisable to discuss salary information up front is with recruiters and employment agencies. These people are just as interested as you are in getting you the highest possible salary. After all, most of them are compensated with a commission that is based on a percentage of your earnings. In order to get you the highest-paying job, they need an honest appraisal of the salary you are seeking as well as your salary history. Your credibility to these people is doubly important, because they are putting themselves and their company on the line when they represent you to a potential employer. Never inflate or lie about your salary history. If you misrepresent your salary expectations, you could end up on a futile quest, as employment agents send you to jobs that are inappropriate to your skills levels or needs.

OCCUPATIONAL FACTS

Knowing about the job you seek—from the responsibilities to the income potential—is one of the key ingredients of getting hired. The chapters in this section give you essential data, as well as information about how to gather more facts, such as how to locate both large and small employers and uncover literature that will give you an insider's perspective.

OCCUPATIONAL FACTS

JOB DESCRIPTIONS

THIS CHAPTER CONTAINS PROFILES of 250 jobs. Jobs were chosen to represent common occupational fields and professions in the United States. If you cannot find the job you are looking for below, it may be because the title is different. For example, "Engineer" appears here as "Aerospace Engineer," "Electrical Engineer," and so on. So be flexible in how you look for the title. Information on salaries of many of these jobs appears elsewhere in this book. ➤See "Annual Earnings Survey," pp. 117-127.

ACADEMIC COUNSELOR

Academic counselors provide educational and vocational guidance for individuals or groups. Through tests, interviews, and other procedures, counselors determine a client's aptitudes and abilities as they pertain to educational and career prospects. They also assist students with emotional or social problems and can refer individuals in need of additional assistance.

ACCOUNTANT

While some accountants assist organizations by ordering financial data, others advise clients about investments and compliance with tax laws. A typical worker in this field prepares and analyzes financial reports to assist managers in business, industry, and government. Those with a CPA (certified public accountant) certificate can dramatically increase their earnings.

ACTING COACH

Acting coaches teach dramatic techniques, assess students' talents through script readings, and adapt or create training methods to sharpen performers' abilities. They focus specifically on improving an actor's script analysis abilities, voice projections, and character interpretations.

ACTOR

Actors play parts in movies, radio, television, and on the live stage. A typical worker in this field entertains and/or informs an audience by interpreting dramatic or comedic roles. Facial expressions, gestures, and verbal communication are tools of the actor's trade.

ACTUARY

Insurance companies and some government agencies employ actuaries to predict potential losses, while other organizations employ actuaries to manage their pension and welfare plans. A typical worker in this field interprets statistics to estimate probabilities of accidents, sickness, and death, and the occurrence rate of theft and natural disasters leading to loss of property. Actuaries use information they assemble to calculate anticipated events, primarily related either to health or casualties and sometimes to financial outcomes.

ACUPUNCTURIST

An acupuncturist's primary function is to assist patients, through a process of inserting needles at various bodily pressure points, in alleviating physical pain, stress, or tension. They use a patient's medical history, the supervising physician's diagnosis, and their own physical findings to pinpoint a disorder and determine the best method for applying acupuncture techniques.

ADVERTISING ACCOUNT EXECUTIVE

A typical advertising account executive supervises all aspects of a client's advertising and, to some extent, the marketing of the client's product. They are the "salespersons" for advertising agencies; that is, they pitch new business and coordinate the efforts of the advertising agency personnel who work on their client's advertising program. They also frequently implement marketing and advertising ideas.

ADVERTISING COPYWRITER

Advertising copywriters work in print and broadcast media to sell or promote goods and services. They develop a creative advertising campaign, write advertising copy, and monitor trends in the industry. They usually consult with sales and marketing personnel to ensure that their advertising schemes target specific demographics.

ADVERTISING SALESPERSON

A typical advertising salesperson calls on businesses (clients) and their advertising agencies in order to sell them publication space, radio and television time, billboards, and other advertising media. They may also work with clients to gear advertising strategies toward particular audiences.

AEROSPACE ENGINEER

Aerospace engineers design and supervise the production of new and developing technologies related to aircraft and space flights. In addition to air- and spacecraft, aerospace engineers work with missiles, satellites, and various space systems.

AGENCY DIRECTOR (NONPROFIT)

Directors of nonprofit agencies need excellent people skills, diplomacy, energy, fundraising ability, and a genuine desire to work with volunteers motivated not by career ambitions but by devotion to a charitable cause. A typical professional in the field serves as a public representative and manages the operations of a charitable or nonprofit organization.

AGRICULTURAL SCIENTIST

Agricultural scientists improve the quantity and quality of field crops and livestock and seek practical answers to agricultural production problems. They are employed primarily by local, state, and federal governments and by colleges and universities. In the private sector, they often work for fertilizer companies and horticultural research laboratories.

AGRONOMIST

Agronomists are concerned with finding newer, more efficient ways to grow crops. They usually work at experiment stations or farms, conducting studies to determine ways in which to improve crop adaptations to soil and climate conditions and resistance to pests and diseases. They are interested in developing new methods of planting, cultivation, and harvesting and in finding new ways to combat noxious weeds.

AIR TRAFFIC CONTROLLER

Air traffic controllers route the flow of air traffic in and out of airports and through stations along the way. They usually begin as ground controllers and advance to the positions of local controller, departure controller, and arrivals controller, respectively. Once experienced, an air traffic controller routes several aircraft at any given time and must often make quick decisions based on the activities of each plane.

AIRPLANE NAVIGATOR

Airplane navigators are responsible for locating the position and directing the course of an airplane using charts, maps, sextants (an instrument for measuring angular distances), slide rules, celestial indicators, or dead reckoning. They work to plot alternative courses in cases of wind shifts, atmospheric changes, and other inclement weather and also maintain the flight log.

AIRPLANE PILOT

Airplane pilots operate aircrafts to transport passengers and cargo to appointed destinations. Three-fifths of all pilots work for commercial airlines. Others are employed by air freight companies and air taxi services. During flight, pilots must constantly monitor instruments, fuel consumption, and weather conditions.

ALLERGIST
Allergists treat conditions and diseases associated with allergic or immunologic causes. They generally diagnose patients based on patch and blood tests and prescribe treatments based on test results and patient histories. They treat ailments such as asthma, dermatological disorders, connective tissue syndrome, and complications of transplantation.

ANESTHESIOLOGIST
Anesthesiologists administer anesthetics to render patients insensible to pain during surgical, obstetrical, and other medical procedures. Their primary tasks are to determine the patient's surgical risk, decide on the appropriate anesthetic, and confer with attending physicians about findings and strategy. During the medical procedure, they monitor the patient for signs and symptoms of adverse reactions and complications and adjust dosages accordingly.

ANIMAL BREEDER
Animal breeders are concerned with breeding desirable characteristics—such as strength, maturity rate, disease resistance, and meat quality—into economically valuable animals. They may, for example, breed livestock to increase their market value or breed horses or dogs for people who are looking for an animal with a particular pedigree.

ANTHROPOLOGIST
Anthropologists contribute to our understanding of the world by studying and explaining the customs and values of persons in primitive, nonindustrialized societies, or modern urbanized cultures. A typical worker in this field studies the social customs, language, and physical attributes of people throughout the world. They work with educators, government officials, and world leaders to increase our understanding of our own way of life in relation to the broader global environment.

ANTIQUE DEALER
In addition to selling antiques, antique dealers spend time acquiring pieces for an inventory and maintaining a network of clients and lists of their interests and the specific pieces they want. A typical worker in this field provides a source for clients collecting within particular fields. Antique collectibles dealers seek out and purchase antiques within their specialty and either maintain an in-store inventory of items or deal by appointment or through shows.

ARCHAEOLOGIST
Archaeologists conduct research into ancient, often preliterate cultures. They study artifacts and architectural structures uncovered by excavation to determine cultural identity and the age of their subjects. They frequently specialize in a specific geographical area or time period.

ARCHITECT
Considering aesthetic and utilitarian aspects of buildings, architects apply scientific and mathematical theories to plan and design spaces according to the specifications of their clients. Drafting tools and computers are among the equipment architects use; a thorough knowledge of structural materials is also necessary.

ART THERAPIST
Art therapists work with mentally, emotionally, or physically handicapped individuals on a variety of art and art-related projects designed to encourage creative discovery and self-actualization. They work in conjunction with medical professionals to determine the needs of each particular patient and to design programs to meet their aptitudes.

ARTIST (COMMERCIAL)
Commercial artists design and/or illustrate the materials used to sell a product or concept to a specific audience. Graphic artists—including medical, scientific, and fashion illustrators, cartoonists, and editorial artists—are usually salaried employees who work in studios or offices, often at a drafting table.

ARTIST (FINE ART)
Fine artists create artwork, usually in the form of painting, drawing, sculpture, or related visual-art mediums. Painters use a variety of colorful substances such as acrylic and oil paints; sculptors use steel

or stone and clay to create artistic images. Most fine artists are self-employed and sell their pieces to museums, galleries, and private collectors.

ASTRONOMER

Astronomers spend only a few weeks each year in actual observation; most of their time is spent researching and interpreting data. A typical worker in this field uses principles of physics and mathematics to understand the workings of the universe. Colleges or universities and the federal government are the largest employers of astronomers, who use such tools as telescopes, radio telescopes, and sophisticated photographic equipment.

ATHLETIC DIRECTOR

Athletic directors are the people behind the scenes of professional sports. They develop and implement extramural athletic policies and employ and discharge coaches, either on their own initiative or at the direction of the athletic board. They prepare the annual sports schedules, supervise publicity activities, and also serve on the financial end of athletics, preparing budgets and reviewing reports of income from ticket sales.

ATTORNEY

Contrary to popular opinion, once in their own practice few attorneys spend much time in courtrooms. Instead, a typical attorney counsels clients in legal matters, using interpretation of laws and previous judicial rulings to advise and represent businesses and individuals. Lawyers also act as executors, trustees, or guardians.

AUDIOLOGIST

Audiologists use electro-acoustical instru-mentation and speech audiometers as they plan and conduct rehabilitation programs. A typical worker in this field diagnoses and treats hearing problems by attempting to discover the range, nature, and degree of hearing function. Many audiologists assist in hearing-aid selection and orientation and counsel individuals with varying degrees of hearing loss.

AUDIOVISUAL TECHNICIAN

Audiovisual (AV) technicians are responsible for installing and repairing tape recorders, film and slide projectors, public address systems, videotape players, and other presentation equipment. They often work either with an educational institution or in a repair shop that specializes in repairing AV equipment.

BALLISTICS EXPERT

Ballistics experts work with criminal investigation units in order to collect facts that may contribute to the apprehension and prosecution of suspects. Their duties involve testing firearms and examining both spent bullets and the crime scene for relevant evidence. They determine the caliber of a gun, generally test-fire the weapon allegedly used so as to allow for microscopic comparisons between bullets from the test weapon and those at the crime scene, and attempt to determine the angles and distances from which the crime weapon was fired.

BANK OFFICER

Bank officers assist in the direction of policies and procedures for operating a financial institution. This job entails executing financial planning and loan packages within an existing framework of regulations established by a board of directors and the government.

BIOLOGIST

Biologists conduct research as a means of understanding living organisms. A typical biological scientist studies the relationship of plants and animals to their environment. They use laboratory equipment in testing and computers to help with statistics and in the writing of reports. Ornithology, botany, and zoology are all subfields of biological science.

BOOKKEEPER

Bookkeepers maintain financial records and prepare statements of a company's income and daily operating expenses. Many bookkeepers participate in tax preparation, often working with their companies accounting firm. A bookkeeper may also be responsible for payroll disbursement, billing, and interest computation.

BOTANIST

Botanists are interested in researching the life processes, heredity, anatomy, and economic value of plants for application in fields like forestry, horticulture, pharmacology, and agronomy. They use microscopes and staining techniques to research a plant's chromosome behavior, internal and external structure, and plant-cell chemistry. They are often involved in gauging the effects on plant life of rainfall, temperature, climate, soil, and elevation.

BROADCAST TECHNICIAN

Broadcast technicians run and maintain the equipment used to transmit radio and television messages. They are employed by radio and television studios, where they use hand signals and wear headsets to relay messages to others during broadcast.

BUDGET ANALYST

Budget analysts are primarily concerned with analyzing accounting records to determine the financial resources required to implement programs. They are also responsible for preparing and justifying budget requests, submitting recommendations for budget allocations, and advising on fiscal appropriations.

BUILDING INSPECTOR

Building inspectors examine a building's structure and safety to see if they are in compliance with building, grading, and zoning laws. They consider several factors as they review a site, such as whether or not footings, floor framing, chimneys, and stairways meet regulations and adhere to fire-safety codes.

BUYER

Buyers order merchandise and maintain inventory control for wholesale and retail sales firms. They rely heavily on the use of computers to facilitate inventory control and to assist in the selection of goods. Over 60 percent of buyers work for retail establishments, purchasing merchandise from wholesale firms or from the manufacturer for resale directly to consumers.

CARDIOLOGIST

Cardiologists specialize in the diagnosis and treatment of heart disease. Using medical instruments and equipment, they examine patients for symptoms of heart disorders and study diagnostic images and electrocardiogram (EKG) recordings. They prescribe medications and recommend various remedial programs such as diet and exercise regimens.

CARDIOVASCULAR TECHNICIAN

Cardiovascular technicians (CTs) obtain electrocardiogram (EKG) results from patients by attaching electrodes to their chests, arms, and legs. CTs generally perform this heart-monitoring, stress-testing procedure as part of a general physical exam before a patient undergoes surgery. CTs also perform more advanced variations of the EKG, including Holter monitors, stress tests, and treadmill tests.

CARPENTER

Carpenters assist in the construction, repair, and remodeling of buildings and other structures. Contractors are the largest employers of carpenters; others work for government agencies, utility companies, and manufacturing firms, or are self-employed. Work includes framing out houses; installing doors, flooring, and general woodwork; constructing concrete; and erecting scaffolding.

CATERER

Caterers are involved in coordinating the food-service activities at various social gatherings such as parties, banquets, picnics, concerts, and other special events. They confer with clients and their food-service staffs to plan menus and decide on dining room, bar, and banquet operations. They either make the dishes themselves or are involved as the food suppliers, and they are almost always in charge of serving the courses.

CHEF/COOK

In America, unlike in Europe, the line between a chef and a cook is somewhat blurred except in fine restaurants. In haute cuisine restaurants, meals are prepared by highly paid, highly trained "chefs." In large fine restaurants, a head chef supervises the work of other members of the kitchen staff (including assistant chefs and pastry chefs) and plans menus, determines meal portions, and often purchases food supplies. A "cook," on the other hand, has likely not attended culinary school or received advanced training. Cooks play almost no role in the planning and management of a restaurant and usually follow recipes prepared by the restaurant's owner or manager.

CHEMICAL ENGINEER

Chemical engineers design equipment and develop processes pertaining to the production or use of chemicals and chemical products. Because their field is interdisciplinary and involves many different methods of application, chemical engineers are frequently knowledgeable in the principles of physics, math, and mechanical and electrical engineering. Chemical engineers often specialize, either in a specific operation such as oxidation or polymerization or in a particular area such as pollution control or automotive plastics production.

CHEMIST

Most chemists specialize in a specific area of chemistry such as biochemistry or organic chemistry. A typical professional in this field develops substances through research of properties and composition and assists industry and individuals through the study of chemical structures of products. Private industry, state and federal governments, universities, and high schools employ chemists to study and explain the physical properties of substances.

CHILD-CARE WORKER

Child-care workers tend to the basic needs of young children during their parents' absence. A typical worker in this field cares for infants and toddlers when parents are at work or otherwise unable to do so. Approximately two-thirds of all child-care workers are self-employed; others work for child-care centers, residential institutions, government agencies, and hospitals. They provide nutritious meals, structured play, and educational activities for the children in their care and also watch for any possible physical or developmental problems.

CHIROPRACTOR

Chiropractors use a variety of techniques to diagnose and treat impairments of the nervous system, which they believe to be at the root of most physical problems. A typical worker in this field treats physical problems by manipulating various parts of the body, especially the spinal column. Other treatments include water and heat massage and ultrasound and light therapy. In many states chiropractors are prohibited from prescribing surgery or drugs, but they can and do prescribe exercise, rest, and proper diet for their patients.

CHOREOGRAPHER

Choreographers instruct performers and develop and interpret dance routines for stage and other presentations. They use sound systems and musical instruments to assist them in their work. Most choreographers are employed by dance companies and educational institutions, where they teach ballet, as well as stylized, traditional, and modern dance techniques.

CIVIL ENGINEER

Civil engineers apply scientific and mathematical theories to design and implement plans for structures that make our lives easier and more efficient. A typical worker in this field plans and supervises the building of roads, bridges, tunnels, and structures. Most civil engineers work for manufacturing companies or engineering and architectural firms; others are employed by management consulting companies and by federal, state, and local governments.

COMPOSER

Building on their knowledge of harmonics, of rhythmic, melodic, and tonal structures, and of various dimensions of music theory, composers create musical pieces for instruments and/or vocals. They sometimes write within existing forms such as sonatas, symphonies, or operas. At other times composers seek to create new and original forms of musical expressions.

COMPOSITOR/TYPESETTER

Compositors/typesetters lay out pages, check page proofs for errors, and make corrections as instructed by editors. Over half of all compositors and typesetters work in newspaper or commercial printing plants; others work for graphic design and commercial art firms, publishing companies, and other firms that do their own printing. In printing shops and plants, compositors often prepare preliminary printing mechanicals. Increasingly, typesetting tasks are performed by computers into which typesetters enter the desired specifications.

COMPTROLLER

Comptrollers are responsible for preparing reports that detail and forecast a company's business activities and financial positions in the areas of income, expenses, and earnings based on past, present, and anticipated operations. They also ensure that the firm has met all tax and regulatory requirements.

COMPUTER CONSULTANT

Computer consultants are retained by firms that wish to introduce or expand high-tech automation in their business procedures. Working closely with management, consultants are charged with determining system architecture and then facilitating the installation of hardware and software which best meet the needs of the firm they are servicing. They are also normally responsible for training users on the new software or system.

COMPUTER OPERATOR

The duties of a computer operator include loading computers with tapes, disks, and paper and recording malfunctions in log books. Computer operators must respond to all error messages, locate the source of the problem, and either find a solution or terminate the program. Today's computer operators work not on personal computers but on mainframe or super computers, the sort used by such institutions as banks, insurance companies, hospitals, and government agencies. Operators run consoles and sometimes peripheral equipment.

COMPUTER PROGRAMMER

Computer programmers write detailed instructions for computers to process data and to solve problems in a logical order. Knowledge of computer languages is therefore essential. Programmers often include comments in their instructions that allow other programmers to work with the system. They then test the operation of the program to be sure that it is understandable and working according to the specifications of users.

COMPUTER SERVICE TECHNICIAN

Typical computer service technicians repair malfunctioning computer equipment, maintain service according to manufacturers' sched-ules, and sometimes install computers and peripheral equipment. Technicians are also responsible for keeping all equipment in good running order. Wholesalers and computer manufacturers are the largest employers of computer service technicians. Others work for large companies that own and operate their own computer systems.

COMPUTER SYSTEMS ANALYST

Computer systems analysts design and develop computer systems for businesses and scientific institutions. After assessing the needs of a business, analysts use charts and diagrams to show managers how a particular system has been developed and what it can accomplish. Most computer systems analysts specialize in either business, engineering, or scientific applications because of their varied and complex uses of computers.

CONSERVATIONIST

Conservationists typically conduct research into range problems and manage range lands to make efficient use of livestock and wildlife without destroying their habitats. Range managers study range lands to determine optimal grazing seasons and the number and kind of animals to graze. They also direct improvements such as corralling and building of water reservoirs plan for reseeding and plant growth in relation to environmental suitability, and protect range lands from fire and rodent damage.

CONSTRUCTION FOREMAN

Construction foremen and forewomen, also known as blue-collar supervisors, train and supervise employees, and recommend them for promotion. They ensure proper, safe, and effective use of equipment and materials on production lines in manufacturing plants or at construction sites. In companies with labor unions, foremen consult with union represent-atives about problems and grievances.

CONSTRUCTION MACHINERY OPERATOR

Construction machinery operators usually work for contracting firms that specialize in construction, extractive, and foundation work, or in structural steel building. Workers are classified according to the type of machine they operate, such as trench excavators, tower cranes, or air compressors. But many are expected to know how to operate such various pieces of machinery as bulldozers, cranes, steamrollers, and jackhammers.

CONTRACT ADMINISTRATOR

Contract administrators coordinate the contracting activities for the purchase or sale of equipment, materials, products, or services. They must examine performance requirements and delivery schedules and estimate material, equipment, and production costs. They prepare bids, review bids from other firms, negotiate contracts with customers or bidders, and request or approve amendments to or extensions of the contract.

CORRECTIONS OFFICER

Corrections officers supervise inmates at work and recreation and enforce regulations in jails, prisons, and other correctional facilities. At some penal institutions, they counsel on avoiding the hazards of prison life, such as violence, boredom, and low self-esteem.

COSMETOLOGIST

Also called beauty operators, hair stylists, or beauticians, cosmetologists shampoo, cut, style, color, and curl hair. They create hairstyles and advise clients about caring for their hair between appointments. To succeed in this field, one must keep up with new fashions in hair treatment.

COURT CLERK

Court clerks work in courts of law. They examine legal documents for adherence to various court procedures, administer the court oath to witnesses, and explain procedures to parties in the case. Clerks may also secure information for judges; contact witnesses, attorneys, and litigants to obtain information; and prepare case folders and the calendar of cases to be called.

COURT REPORTER/STENOGRAPHER

Court reporters/stenographers report testimony, judicial opinions, or judgments of the court by transcribing depositions and judicial proceedings of all kinds. They may use typewriters, recording machines, and stenotype machines. Most are employed at federal, state, and local courts and by agencies of the legislative and executive branches of government.

CREATIVE DIRECTOR

Creative directors conceive basic presentational approaches and direct the art, copywriting, and production departments in the development of promotional materials such as television and radio commercials, print ads, and brochures. They work with materials and information provided by the client in designing the best possible presentation concept. Since they coordinate all the creative activities at an agency and present the final concept to the client, creative directors have final approval on art or copy ideas.

CYTOLOGIST

Cytologists study plant and animal cells, specifically those cells concerned with reproduction and the means by which chromosomes divide or unite. They also study the physiology of unicellular organisms and the influence that physical and chemical factors have on malignant and normal cells as well as on growth.

DATA-ENTRY CLERK

Data-entry clerks enter information into a computer or onto a magnetic tape or disk using a keyboard, optical scanner, or other entry device. The information they enter may consist of alphabetic, numeric, or symbolic data, and the clerk must either compare data entered with source documents or else reenter it in a verifications format in order to detect errors, making corrections as needed.

DENTAL HYGIENIST

Dental hygienists are licensed to clean teeth by removing deposits and stains, using rotating brushes, rubber caps, and cleaning compounds. They also take medical and dental histories, operate X-ray equipment and develop films, and instruct patients about proper practice of oral hygiene. Most dental hygienists are employed by private dental offices.

DENTAL LABORATORY TECHNICIAN

Dental laboratory technicians make and repair dentures, crowns, and orthodontic devices. Dental laboratory technicians work for commercial dental laboratories, dentists' offices, hospitals and federal agencies. They use hand tools, molding equipment, bunsen burners, and bench fabricating machines to fabricate and repair dental appliances according to prescriptions written by dentists. Using stone or plaster models of dental impressions, they also work with ceramics, metals, and acrylics to make and repair teeth.

DENTIST

Dentists examine, clean, and repair teeth, and diagnose and treat diseases and abnormalities of the mouth. Caring for and maintaining the overall dental health of his or her patients is the dentist's most important function. In pursuit of this goal, dentists use X rays, and a variety of equipment to fill cavities, repair decayed teeth, and perform surgical procedures. While most dentists are general practitioners, some specialize in orthodontics (correcting irregularies of the teeth), periodontics (treatment of gum disease), or pediatric dentistry.

DERMATOLOGIST

Dermatologists diagnose and treat diseases and problems that are particular to the human skin. They examine skin using blood samples, physical inspection, and smears from the infected area in order to identify disease-causing organisms or pathological conditions. They prescribe and administer medications and treat scars, abscesses, baldness, and skin injuries. They are also qualified to surgically excise cutaneous malignancies, cysts, birthmarks, and other growths.

DIETITIAN

Dietitians instruct patients in proper diet and food selection and provide nutritional therapy for critically or terminally ill individuals. They also consult with a variety of medical professionals to determine patients' dietary habits and needs. Dietitians often use computers to formulate nutritional care plans and to coordinate food intake with institutional menus.

DISK JOCKEY

Disk jockeys select and play recordings and comment on subjects of interest to a particular radio audience. The average disk jockey, or DJ, specializes in a particular type of music: rock, jazz, country, classical, and so forth. Most are employed by radio stations, though some work live shows at parties or dance clubs. In small radio stations, disk jockeys may also announce the news, weather, and sports.

DRESSMAKER

Dressmakers, often referred to as "seamers" or "seamstresses" in the apparel trade, follow design instructions and operate a sewing machine to join, reinforce, and decorate parts of garments or other textiles. Garment seamers assemble parts of an article of clothing such as legs, arms, collars, and pockets. Other seamers work on household articles, such as bedspreads, linens, and curtains. Sometimes these workers may also be responsible for oiling machines, changing needles, and placing modifying attachments on equipment.

DRYWALL APPLICATOR/FINISHER

Drywall applicators/finishers install and prepare surfaces of drywall panels for commercial or residential interiors. Most are employed by construction contractors. Drywall applicators fasten sheetrock to the framework of buildings; finishers ready wall surfaces for painting or papering.

ECONOMIST

Economists study and analyze the effects of resources such as land, labor, and raw materials on costs and their relation to industry and government. Analyzing and reviewing industry data as well as preparing reports are their chief functions. Most economists work in a particular area of expertise such as finance, insurance, labor, or government.

EDITOR (BOOK)

Book editors oversee the process of turning a manuscript into a book. Before accepting a manuscript for publication, editors consider whether it is salable and if it meets the publisher's established aesthetic criteria. Once a manuscript is accepted, book editors confer with the publisher and author to negotiate publication date, royalties, and number of copies to print. Editors then work with the author in the editing and revising of the book for publication.

EDITOR (PUBLICATION)

Nearly all publication editors work for newspapers, magazines, or book publishers. Some are employed by businesses and nonprofit organizations. Publication editors edit, rewrite, and sometimes assign writing projects; they supervise most editorial matters. Senior editors give writing assignments and then organize and edit the resulting material. Editors help determine the content of their publications by frequently discussing stories or editorial objectives with their publishers and staff.

EDITORIAL ASSISTANT

Under the direction of editors, editorial assistants work on a variety of tasks in the production of a publication or book. They proofread, fact-check, edit, write, and rewrite materials scheduled for print, in addition to sometimes performing clerical tasks. They must make sure that copy conforms to a publication's style and editorial policy and often confer with authors regarding editorial decisions. Editorial assistants also may choose and crop illustrations or photographs and prepare page layouts.

ELECTRICAL ENGINEER

Electrical engineers conduct research and plan and direct design, testing, and manufacture of various types of electrical equipment. Electrical equipment manufacturers, engineering and business consulting firms, and government agencies employ electrical engineers to develop and supervise the manufacture of electrical equipment. Many specialize in a particular area such as electrical energy generation, instrumentation, computers, or communications.

ELECTRICAL EQUIPMENT REPAIRER

Electrical equipment repairers install and repair electronic equipment for military installations, manufacturers, and businesses. They follow blueprints and use diagnostic tools such as voltmeters and oscilloscopes to locate and correct malfunctions in electronic control panels, X-ray equipment, and transmitters. In accordance with preventive maintenance procedures, many workers keep logs of servicing dates and schedules for re-servicing.

ELECTRICIAN

Electricians follow blueprints or prepare sketches to indicate location of wiring prior to construction of walls, ceilings, and floors. They use a variety of hand tools to assemble and install wiring and electrical conduits in residential and commercial structures. Electricians also test circuitry to ensure safety and electrical compatibility.

EMERGENCY MEDICAL TECHNICIAN (EMT)

Emergency medical technicians (EMTs) often referred to simply as ambulance attendants, are usually the first medical personnel to reach the scene of an emergency. They attend to situations that demand immediate medical attention such as automobile accidents, heart attacks, and gunshot wounds. Upon arriving at an emergency, they determine the nature of the problem and, if necessary, provide life-saving measures until the patient is out of danger before transporting him or her to the hospital. EMTs are employed by fire departments, private ambulance services, police departments, and hospitals.

ENTOMOLOGIST
Entomologists study insects and their relationships to plant, animal, and human life. Their duties often include classifying species of insects and aiding in the control and elimination of pests that threaten agriculture and forests. They may be able to suggest biological and cultural solutions for pest control. They also study the ecological impact of insect life.

ENVIRONMENTAL ANALYST
Environmental analysts develop and administer state governmental programs to assess the environmental impact of proposed recreational projects. In instances where they conclude that a specified project may be insensitive to the environment, they help draft alternative proposals and plans. They are responsible for gathering environmental information regarding planned projects, and they must prepare budgets for the impact-statement preparation program.

ESTATE PLANNER
Estate planners review the various assets and liabilities of an estate (that is, an individual's property to be left after death) in order to determine if insurance coverage is adequate for financial protection of the property. In assessing values, they peruse wills, trusts, business agreements, life insurance policies, and government benefits. They must also figure in expenses, taxes, and debits to determine adjusted gross values. They then prepare or discuss the most optimal insurance programs with the client.

EXECUTIVE SEARCH CONSULTANT
The chief goal of executive search consultants is to bring together a hiring authority and a job seeker. They assist companies in finding ideal executives for a vacant position, in part by maintaining a large database of candidates and marketing those people to corporate clients. Often called headhunters, they are compensated either on a success (or contingency) basis or a fixed retainer. Contingency professionals search for candidates to fill vacancies and get paid only when someone is hired. Consultants on a retainer are paid in advance or in progress payments whether or not they fill the position.

FACILITIES PLANNER
Facilities planners apply their knowledge of organizational efficiency to figure out how best to utilize space and facilities for a government agency or business establishment. They consider whether or not a building space is suitable for optimal occupancy in terms of air circulation, lighting, location, and size. They compute how much square footage of personal space each employee will be allotted determining if minimum space restriction can be met, and they may be involved in making sure real estate contracts comply with government specifications and guidelines for occupational wellness.

FASHION DESIGNER
Fashion designers design articles or complete lines of clothing for men, women, or children. They study fashion trends, fabrics, and demographics, taking into account their company's market as well as their own tastes. Designers also determine fabrics and color schemes and consult with retail buyers and fashion critics. Designers have various areas of expertise such as lingerie, swimwear, or outerwear.

FIELD SERVICE TECHNICIAN
Field service technicians install, program, and repair equipment such as programmable controllers, robot controllers, end-of-arm tools, conveyers, and part orienters. In order to perform their duties, they must be efficient in handling and knowledgeable about electronics, circuits, me-

chanics, hydraulics, and programming. In performing repairs they use hardware such as power and hand tools as well as blueprints, schematic diagrams, and field manuals.

FINANCIAL PLANNER

Financial planners manage investment portfolios and offer a broad range of services to help individuals manage and plan their financial future. Many have finance backgrounds as accountants, securities brokers, or corporate executives. Financial planners help monitor savings and investment programs and analyze all sorts of financial objectives, dealing with such things as mortgages, insurance, college payment, and retirement plans. They plan strategies for the client to best meet his or her goals through savings and investments, including bank certificates of deposit, mutual funds, or portfolios of stocks and bonds.

FIREFIGHTER

Firefighters protect individuals and save lives and property from the ravages of fire. In addition, firefighters educate students and civic groups about safety procedures and inspect public buildings for hazardous conditions. Heavy reliance on the support of other firefighters in emergencies and dangerous conditions fosters a communal spirit among members of this profession.

FISH AND GAME WARDEN

Fish and game wardens patrol wildlife areas—by car, boat, horse, or on foot—to prevent game-law violations and to compile biological data about wildlife. They are on the lookout for hunters or fishermen who are not properly licensed, are sporting out of season, or have not complied with various sporting regulations. Wardens are authorized to serve warrants and make arrests, as well as seize equipment. They also gather information on the conditions of fish and wildlife in their habitat and suspected pollution areas.

FLIGHT ATTENDANT

Flight attendants tend to the care and comfort of passengers on commercial and corporate aircraft. Before taking off, attendants prepare the plane for boarding and instruct passengers on the use of emergency equipment; during the flight, they answer questions and serve meals and drinks. As a preparation for a flight, attendants learn about current weather conditions and special passenger problems from the flight captain. After the flight has arrived at its destination, attendants—who are typically away from home one-third of the time—assist passengers as they leave the plane and prepare reports on equipment conditions.

FLORIST

Florists cut and arrange flowers according to the wishes of customers. Many florists are also floral designers and are employed by retail flower shops. Retail florists make arrangements for special events such as weddings, birthdays, anniversaries, and funerals. Florists use cutters and wire and work with live or artificial flowers to evoke particular sentiments for customers.

FORESTRY TECHNICIAN

Forestry technicians collect data on species and population sizes of trees, gauge the impact of disease and insect damage on the forest, and determine conditions that lead to forest fires. They often instruct conservation workers in projects such as tree planting, forest-fire fighting, and facility maintenance. Most technicians work for the government.

FUNDRAISER

Fundraisers solicit donations for charities, nonprofit organizations, and other causes. They must demonstrate that the organization they are representing is worthy of a financial donation. They often contact potential contributors either by telephone or in person. Fundraisers often handle sponsorship events and special promotional tie-in campaigns, and they may coordinate social functions or prepare fundraising brochures for solicitation programs.

GEMOLOGIST

Gemologists study stones in order to appraise their quality and monetary value. They use plariscopes, refractometers, microscopes, and other optical instruments in order to distinguish between stones, identify rare specimens, and detect flaws that may diminish value. They also immerse stones in chemical solutions to determine specific gravities and properties and grade stones for color and quality of the cut.

GENETICIST
Geneticists often specialize in a particular branch of genetics such as molecular or population genetics. They are concerned with trait inheritance and variation of characteristics. They are often involved in conducting experiments to determine the laws, mechanisms, and environmental factors as they pertain to the origin, transmission, and development of inherited traits. Geneticists study the scenarios that determine traits such as color, size, and immunity in order to better understand the relationship that heredity plays in biological processes like maturity and fertility.

GEOGRAPHER
Geographers study the uses of the earth's surface and interpret the interactions of physical and cultural phenomena. They often specialize in a single area: Economic geographers examine the distribution of resources and economic activities; political or cultural geographers study various phenomena relating to societal groups; physical geographers study variations in climate, vegetation, soil, and land forms and their implications for human activity; urban geographers study transportation, regional activities, and the various phenomena of metropolitan areas; and medical geographers study health care systems and the effect of the environment on health.

GEOLOGIST
Geologists' main function is to gain knowledge of oil- and gas-exploration sights and to consult in developing techniques to bring resources to the surface. A typical geologist studies and analyzes the physical properties of the earth's surface for oil companies, federal and state agencies, and colleges and universities. Many geologists use sonar devices and X-ray equipment in order to study mineral deposits within the earth's crust. Some seek fossil specimens to further scientific knowledge about the earth.

GUNSMITH
Gunsmiths repair, adjust, or modify firearms according to blueprints or customer specifications. They may also design guns. Some of the tasks they perform include installing metallic or optical sights, pistol grips, recoil pads, or decorative pieces, as well as reboring barrels to enlarge the caliber. They test firearms with proof loads to determine strength characteristics, correct alignment and structural components, and sometimes refinish wooden stocks on rifles and shotguns.

HAZARDOUS WASTE MANAGEMENT SPECIALIST
Hazardous waste management specialists play an important role in providing information about the treatment and containment of hazardous waste. They survey industries to determine the type and magnitude of the disposal problem and suggest treatment alternatives. Often they will be involved in developing spill prevention programs. In cases where a spill has occurred, specialists work to determine the hazardous impact and take corrective measures.

HEAD COACH
Head coaches plan and direct the training activities of their team as well as coordinate field tactics during a game. The objectives for any coach are a winning season and a championship, and in order to meet those goals, coaches must be skilled both in assessing players' skills and in teaching various techniques to improve performance. They also must be shrewd tacticians in terms of playing to the opposing team's weaknesses.

HEATING/REFRIGERATION MECHANIC
Heating/refrigeration mechanics diagnose problems, make repairs, and perform off-season maintenance on heating and cooling systems. A typical worker in this field installs and services air-conditioning and furnace systems in businesses and residences. Most mechanics specialize in the installation and

servicing of certain equipment, for example, furnaces or air-conditioning systems.

HELICOPTER PILOT

Helicopter pilots perform many of the same duties as airline pilots in that they both adhere to safety precautions and are in the business of transporting passengers and cargo. They follow a checklist of preflight inspections that greatly decrease the chances of complications while airborne. Since their crafts are maneuverable and can hover, helicopter pilots often conduct flights for police and medical units, photographers, firefighters, and news and traffic reporters.

HISTORIAN

Historians analyze and record historical information from a specific era or according to a particular area of expertise. Common areas of specialization are sociology, economics, and art. Historians frequently study historic news reports, court documents, and various published documents. Most historians work for universities, museums, and research firms. Some work almost exclusively as independent contractors, writing books and various published material.

HOME ECONOMIST

Home economists study and instruct students about efficiency in homemaking and developing economical household budgets. They are employed by schools, home health care agencies, nursing homes, and other health care establishments and social service agencies. Consulting for hotels, restaurants, and food service organizations is common. Others work at companies involved in the manufacture of household products. Other areas of involvement include the development of nutrition, hygiene, and health programs for companies and institutions.

HOME HEALTH AIDE

Home health aides work with elderly, disabled, or ill individuals who are living in their own homes. Aides help with housekeeping, plan meals, and provide emotional support for their clients. They also provide personal-care services, which include helping patients move around the house, bathe, dress, and groom. Often aides check pulses, take temperatures, and assist with simple exercises and medication routines.

HORTICULTURIST

Horticulturists specialize in growing fruits, nuts, berries, vegetables, flowers, and ornamental plants. They are interested not only in determining the optimal methods of breeding, storing, processing, and transporting their goods, but also in experimenting to improve the variety or yield of goods that have higher nutritional levels, stronger resistance to disease, and greater adaptability traits.

HOSPITAL ADMINISTRATOR

Hospital administrators are responsible for the effective management of programs, staff, and budgets of health care establishments. They oversee department heads to ensure that services and programs are running smoothly. Senior administrators plan budgets and organize training programs. Administrators no longer work exclusively for hospitals; increasingly, they are employed by health maintenance organizations, physicians' offices, and outpatient facilities.

HOTEL MANAGER

Hotel managers at all levels—from national chains to small motels or hotels—supervise staff, organize recreational activities, and manage hotel marketing and accounting services. They also handle customer complaints and, in smaller establishments, the processing of reservations. Knowledge of computers is essential since they are relied on for budget management, housekeeping, and reservations. Day-to-day problem solving is a large part of the job.

HUMAN RESOURCES SPECIALIST

Human resources specialists are an integral part of any business or organization. Their responsibilities include recruiting and interviewing prospective employees, advising on hiring decisions, and working with top management personnel to establish policies, qualifications, and requirements for current and future employees. They also assist firms in creating more conducive working environments and increasing office efficiency.

HYDROLOGIST

Hydrologists study the distribution, development, and cycles of water as it pertains to land areas. They examine degrees of precipitation and the routes by which water returns to the ocean or the atmosphere. They are interested in mapping water flow and disposition of sediment, measuring changes in water volume due to evaporated and melted snow, and determining the rate of ground absorption. Hydrologists may also help develop drainage, irrigation, water power, and flood-control systems.

INDUSTRIAL DESIGNER

Industrial designers design and develop manufactured products of all kinds, although they usually specialize in one field, for example, automobiles or home appliances. Their tools include calipers and drafting equipment and, increasingly, computer-aided design systems. Once they determine customer preferences for color, size, and material, they prepare sketches or models for completed designs.

INDUSTRIAL ENGINEER

Industrial engineers are employed primarily by manufacturing firms to find ways to improve operational efficiency. They make recommendations to management on staff utilization as well as employment of machinery based on their studies of worker motions and space layout.

INSURANCE AGENT

Insurance agents sell insurance and advise clients about coverage based on needs and circumstances. Many agents are self-employed, while others work at large insurance firms or agencies. In addition to selling, agents may need to calculate premiums for the three types of insurance—casualty, health, and life—although some agents are committed to only one type of insurance.

INSURANCE UNDERWRITER

Insurance underwriters assess and analyze the risks inherent in insuring potential policy holders before making recommendations to the insurance companies that employ them. A typical workday involves reviewing applications and loss and medical reports. Knowing actuarial figures, which are used to determine the feasibility of insuring groups and individuals, is also vital. Specialties of underwriters include property and liability, life, or health insurance.

INTERIOR DESIGNER

Interior designers conceive and implement layout schemes for the interior spaces of private homes, public buildings, and commercial establishments. They take into account a client's tastes, needs, and budget in developing a design that will work on practical and aesthetic levels. Their design effects are often achieved through the creative use of mirrors, lighting, furniture, and wall hangings. They consider color coordination, floor coverings, building code specifications, and handicapped accessibility.

INTERPRETER

Interpreters perform many of the same tasks as translators, except that interpreters deal primarily with verbal instead of written language. Depending on the nature of the occasion, they perform either simultaneous or consecutive translation and give either an approximate or verbatim translation. Deaf interpreters work with deaf people, translating between spoken language and sign language. They may, for example, translate television broadcasts for deaf viewers.

JEWELER

Jewelers manufacture and repair pins, rings, bracelets, and necklaces using precious and semiprecious metals and stones. Slightly less than half of all jewelers operate retail or repair shops. Those whose work at retail counters alter rings, reset stones, and replace various jewelry elements. Others work for jewelry manufacturing firms. Some jewelers repair watches and do engraving; a few design jewelry and are qualified to do appraisals.

LABOR RELATIONS SPECIALIST

Labor relations specialists analyze collective bargaining agreements in order to determine the intent and terms of the contract. They advise union officials in the development and application of labor relations practices. They coordinate meetings between business representatives of labor unions and the workers, supervisors, and managers with grievances. They monitor policies regarding wages, hours, and working conditions.

LANDSCAPE ARCHITECT

Landscape architects are responsible for designing functional, aesthetically pleasing, and environmentally harmonious areas, such as parks, residential neighborhoods, college campuses, shopping centers, and industrial parks. Their tasks may run the gamut from planning the locations of a particular building or road to the arrangement of flowers, shrubs, trees, and greenery at a public site.

LIBRARIAN

Librarians select and organize materials to make information available to the public. Most librarians work at public libraries, schools, and academic institutions and are classified in several ways. For example, reference librarians work with the public while acquisitions librarians generally meet with library book wholesalers, publishers, editors, and other librarians in order to develop library contents and acquire new books. Responsibilities of librarians vary according to the size of their library's collections.

LINGUIST

Linguists study the functions of a specific language within a social framework. They prepare descriptions of sounds, forms, or vocabularies and apply linguistic theories to the teaching of foreign languages and the development of language-teaching materials. They may also be involved in translating previously unwritten languages to standardized written form. Much of their work is performed within an educational context, and one of their specialties is to prepare tests that gauge language-learning aptitudes and proficiencies.

LITHOGRAPHER/PHOTOENGRAVER

Lithographers/photoengravers use cameras and metal printing plates to prepare printed materials for presswork. They photograph material to be printed before making a plate from the film, and this plate is then inked and pressed through rollers to print on paper. Most lithographers work for commercial printing plants, newspapers, and printing trade service firms. Some are designated as camera operators; others, called strippers, use strips of adhesive tape to bind printing film together, typically specially developed picture negatives that go with text. Still other lithographers, known as platemakers, use this film to make printing plates.

LOBBYIST

Lobbyists work for specific people or groups, or for the general public, and their job is to persuade legislators and other public office holders to support legislation that is in the best interests of their clients. Lobbyists may contact individuals and groups with similar interests in order to boost support for their efforts. They may prepare news releases and conduct news conferences in order to inform voters of particular legislative activities. They also coordinate meetings with lobby members and elected officials to discuss various issues.

MACHINIST

Machinists operate machinery in a manufacturing plant for fabrication of industrial parts. A machinist's typical day is spent setting up and operating the machinery used to make metal parts. Some work primarily on motor vehicles, others on industrial machinery and aircraft manufacturing. Tools of their trade include micrometers and gauges, which they use to measure the accuracy of their work.

MARINE BIOLOGIST

Marine biologists study aquatic animals and plants and the environmental conditions affecting them. For example, they might study temperature, acidity, light, oxygen content, and other water conditions in order to gauge how plants and animals are adapting. Some marine biologists specialize in breeding or raising aquatic life.

MARKET RESEARCH ANALYST

Market research analysts research and evaluate trends in consumer spending to help businesses develop new products and make sales forecasts. Most are employed by consulting firms that both collect data and assist in management decisions for their clients. They meet with corporate contacts and others to devise marketing strategies, and their work involves conducting research analyses and surveys, preparing reports about new products, and projecting future sales.

MARRIAGE AND FAMILY COUNSELOR

Marriage and family counselors work with individuals, couples, and families to help them identify their intersituational problems and develop effective developmental and communication methods. They use interviewing, observation, and assessment to determine the best treatment course or to refer clients to other specialists or institutions. While their therapeutic programs are usually based on verbal interactions between the parties, they may also incorporate hypnosis or psychotherapy.

MASSEUR/MASSEUSE

Masseurs and masseuses perform full-body or specific area massages and administer other body condition treatments for therapeutic and remedial purposes. They apply alcohol, lubricants, and lotions and employ such techniques as kneading, rubbing, and stroking flesh to stimulate blood circulation and soothe tightened muscles. They may also administer steam or dry heat and ultraviolet, infrared, or water treatments under the direction of the customer or a physician.

MATHEMATICIAN

Mathematicians apply knowledge of mathematical theories and formulas to teach or to solve problems in a business, educational, or industrial climate. Most are employed at corporations, research laboratories, and institutions of higher learning. Many mathematicians are involved in scientific research and engineering projects as well as development of software and other applications.

MECHANICAL ENGINEER

Mechanical engineers develop mechanical products and coordinate the operation and repair of power-using and power-producing machinery. They often develop specialized expertise in one type of machinery, for example, internal combustion engines or refrigeration and air-conditioning equipment. Their job responsibilities often include designing mechanical systems and products, directing the testing and repair of machinery, and coordinating the operation and maintenance of manufacturing machinery.

MEDIA SPECIALIST

Media specialists work in advertising or public relations departments, developing and implementing media programs. In order to create successful media directives, specialists must meet with agency representatives, product managers, and the corporate advertising staff to discuss media goals, objectives, and strategies within the advertising budget. They study demographic data and consumer profiles to identify target audiences and keep up on trends, innovations, and changes that affect media planning.

MEDICAL ILLUSTRATOR

Medical illustrators draw images, pictures, and paintings and construct three-dimensional models that accurately represent medical or biological subjects. They work mainly in the subject areas of anatomy, physiology, histology, pathology, or surgical procedures. Medical illustrators' work is for use in books, exhibits, and research and teaching programs.

MEDICAL LABORATORY TECHNICIAN

Medical labroatory technicians conduct routine laboratory tests and analyses used in the detection, diagnosis, and treatment of disease. They perform tests on body fluids and tissues to detect changes in cell structures as well as the presence of parasites, viruses, or bacteria. Their data help physicians diagnose and treat their patients. Technicians must follow proper sterilization and handling procedures to reduce the possibility of exposure to infectious substances.

MEDICAL RECORDS TECHNICIAN

Medical records technicians keep medical records for use in treatment, billing, and statistical surveys. Their job responsibilities include coding symptoms, diseases, and treatments and recording medical histories. Records are coded and filed using a standardized system, often on computers. Most are employed at health care institutions. Increasingly, however, workers in this field are employed by insurance companies, law firms, and accountants.

MEDICAL TECHNOLOGIST

Medical technologists perform laboratory analyses used in the detection, diagnosis, and treatment of disease. They may also perform research, develop laboratory techniques, or carry out administrative tasks. Unlike medical technicians, medical technologists are required to have a bachelor's degree in science. Job responsibilities often include performing tests of a bacteriological, chemical, or hematological nature in order to detect diseases or to determine blood cholesterol levels. Specialization is common in such categories as biochemistry, cytotechnology, histology, and microbiology.

MEMBERSHIP DIRECTOR

Membership directors work to establish chapters of fraternal societies, lodges, or like organizations. They contact interested parties to present the goals and ideals of the organization for charters or recognition. Since membership directors spend time surveying conditions in established branches in their efforts to organize new chapters, they are in a unique position to advise societies or lodges experiencing either financial or membership problems.

MENTAL RETARDATION AIDE (MRA)

Mental retardation aides (MRAs) provide self-care training and therapeutic treatment to residents of a mental retardation center. They instruct and counsel residents in bathing and dressing practices, positive social interaction, and shopping for personal items. They may work in conjunction with other aides in facilitating various physical exercises, arts and crafts, and recreational games. Part of their job consists of observing the resident's speech, feeding patterns, and toilet training in order to assess treatment and further instruction needs.

MERCHANDISE DISTRIBUTOR

Merchandise distributors compile inventory information pertaining to specific stock on hand and the amount sold for retail chains. They route merchandise from one branch store to another on the basis of sales. They usually specialize in one type of merchandise such as dresses, lingerie, or sportswear.

METALLURGICAL ENGINEER

Metallurgical engineers (MEs), who develop new types of metal alloys, work within one of three branches of metallurgy: (1) extractive or chemical, (2) physical, and (3) mechanical or process. Extractive MEs deal with the removal of metals from ores; physical MEs study various methods of processing metals; and mechanical MEs work to develop and improve metal-working processes.

METEOROLOGIST

Meteorologists study the physical characteristics, motions, and processes of the earth's atmosphere by collecting data on air pressure, temperature, humidity, and wind velocity. They also make long- and short-term weather predictions. Physical meteorologists study the effects of the atmosphere on the transmission of light, sound, and radio waves, and investigate factors affecting formation of clouds, storms, and tornadoes. Those who forecast weather are known as operational or synoptic meteorologists.

JOB DESCRIPTIONS

MICROBIOLOGIST

Microbiologists study bacteria and other microorganisms for the purpose of observing their effects upon the living tissues of plants, animals, humans, and other organisms, and on dead organic matter. They work in laboratories, and their primary instrument is the microscope. In order to study microorganisms fully, they must isolate and make cultures of them, all the while controlling life factors such as moisture, aerations, temperature, and nutrition.

MILITARY (COMMISSIONED OFFICER)

Commissioned military officers are members of one of the branches of the armed forces, including the U.S. Army, Navy, Air Force, Marines, Coast Guard, and National Guard. A typical officer supervises enlisted personnel and performs a variety of military tasks in defense of the nation, ranging from combat leadership to support services. Officers are concentrated in the areas of administration, medical specialties, and combat activities. These personnel may hold positions as ship's officers, aircraft pilots, or as infantry, intelligence, or communications officers. Officer training is provided by the service academies, ROTC, officer candidate schools, and other programs.

MILITARY (ENLISTED PERSON)

Persons enlisted in the military perform any number of military tasks involved in the defense of the nation, from engaging in combat to working as a payroll clerk in an office. Enlistees in the armed forces choose among the U.S. Army, Navy, Air Force, Marines, Coast Guard, and National Guard. Their job responsibilities often include operation, maintenance, and repair of military-related equipment. Approximately 15 percent are required to be combat-ready as foot soldiers, members of gun crews, or seamanship specialists, while most are employed at support roles in such areas as supply, personnel, communications, and administration. All enlistees undergo a rigorous period of basic training.

MILITARY (WARRANT OFFICER)

There are three types of licenses for military service: enlistment contracts, commissions, and warrants. Warrant officers generally hold the ranks between noncommissioned and commissioned officers. A typical warrant officer performs any number of specialized duties in the military, from combat support to military band leader. To qualify for a warrant, individuals normally must fulfill requirements concerning knowledge or experience in a particular field of expertise. Warrant officers can be flight specialists, supply officers, or medical experts; work in food preparation and distribution, or perform any number of other functions. They generally enjoy the rank and privileges accorded other officers in the military.

MINERALOGIST

Mineralogists, similar to geologists and gemologists, analyze and classify minerals, gems, and precious stones after first isolating specimens from ore, rock, or matrices. Using a microscope, a mineralogist examines features such as shape and surface markings, and conducts tests and X rays to determine the specimen's composition and type of crystalline structure. Through these procedures, mineralogists develop theories about the origins, occurrences, and possible uses of minerals.

MINISTER

Ministers traditionally focus on biblical study, preparing sermons, and providing spiritual leadership to the community. A typical Protestant clergy leader directs a congregation's worship services and performs the rites of the church in Protestant congregations. Most are expected to engage in charitable activities or teach in seminaries and schools. In smaller churches, ministers often interact closely with parishioners, but in larger ones they often have fewer opportunities to do so. Ministers also manage church affairs and work with volunteer laity members, who perform nonliturgical functions such as preparing church budgets or office work.

MOTION PICTURE EDITOR

Along with the picture's directors, motion picture editors oversee all aspects of the filming and editing of motion pictures used for entertainment, business, and educational purposes. After becoming familiar with a screenplay, an editor can interpret it in his or her own manner by establishing the locations of cameras and lights, instructing actors on how to move through a scene and deliver lines, and choosing the cuts to be used in the the final version.

MUSEUM CURATOR

Museum curators plan and direct the activities of museum workers and arrange for the exhibition of articles of interest to museum visitors. They frequently direct art restoration and supervise the installation of exhibits. They may also coordinate research and obtain new acquisitions. Most are employed at museums, colleges, universities, and libraries.

MUSICIAN

Musicians usually specialize in either classical or popular styles, although many perform in both genres. Besides playing musical instruments, many musicians compose and/or perform vocal pieces as well. They may perform their work live or for radio or television soundtracks or commercials. They play with orchestras, bands, jazz combos, or solo. Few musicians work full-time; instead, they generally perform at night and on weekends and are often traveling.

NEUROLOGIST

Neurologists diagnose and treat diseases and disorders of the nervous system. Most of their diagnostic information comes from the results of chemical, microscopic, biological, and bacteriological analyses of a patient's blood and cerebrospinal fluid. They identify pathological blood conditions or parasites and prescribe and administer drugs accordingly. They also review the results of electroencephalograms or X rays to detect abnormalities in brain wave patterns or brain structure.

NEWS WRITER

News writers write items for newspapers, magazines, and radio and television news departments. They seek to capture their reader's or listener's attention while relaying facts in an objective, nonbiased manner. Writers at major broadcast outlets work with stories written by reporters and on rewrites of international wire services, whereas writers at wire services and city news bureaus typically research local stories and condense them into more concise articles.

NEWSCASTER

Newscasters help their news team prepare news stories and then deliver them on radio or television. The anchorperson, who holds the most prestigious news job of all, delivers the day's top news stories, while broadcast news analysts and commentators interpret stories or relate greater details about them. At smaller stations, many newscasters prepare their own material, and some also write advertising copy. Most newscasters specialize in such areas as politics, courts, current events, sports, and weather.

NUCLEAR ENGINEER

Nuclear engineers research, design, and oversee the operation and maintenance of nuclear reactors and power-plant equipment. Some conduct research and prepare reports on experiments in radiation and nuclear energy. Others coordinate the service and operation of nuclear power plants, during which time they must employ every precaution to avoid the constant threat of nuclear accidents. Over one-quarter of all nuclear engineers in the United States are federally employed by the Nuclear Regulatory Commission, the Tennessee Valley Authority, or the Department of Energy.

NUCLEAR MEDICINE TECHNICIAN

Nuclear medicine technicians are in charge of preparing, measuring, and administering radioactive pharmaceuticals in diagnosis and treatment of diseases. After treatments are given, technicians use cameras to track the radioactive drug in the patient's body. They then monitor the characteristics of the tissues and organs that the drugs have localized.

NURSE (LICENSED PRACTICAL)

Licensed practical nurses (LPNs) assist registered nurses as well as physicians in the care of physically or mentally ill patients. Most are employed at hospitals, clinics, schools, and other institutions such as nursing homes and prisons. Other LPNs work for state and local governments, HMOs, and home health care agencies. LPNs monitor blood pressure and temperature, administer medicines, chart patients' progress, and perform other bedside functions such as changing dressings and assisting with personal hygiene. Those who work in private homes may prepare meals, provide companionship to boost patients' morale, and teach family members how to provide basic care for patients.

NURSE (REGISTERED)

Registered nurses (RNs) assist physicians in administering medical care and treating patients. Most are employed at clinics, hospitals, public health centers, and HMOs. They provide bedside care and administer treatment prescribed by physicians. Many nurses specialize in such areas as surgery, pediatrics, or obstetrics. Private-duty nurses provide individualized care, most often in private residences, for patients requiring intensive treatment and supervision. Community-health nurses provide group care for patients in public schools, clinics, and retirement homes, while office nurses assist physicians and dental surgeons in private practice.

OBSTETRICIAN/GYNECOLOGIST

Obstetricians/gynecologists (OB/GYNs) specialize in the medical treatment of women. Obstetricians treat women during prenatal, natal, and postnatal periods; deliver infants; and care for the mothers for a prescribed period of time following childbirth. Obstetricians may also perform cesarean sections or other procedures in order to preserve the mother's and infant's safety. Gynecologists perform routine examinations on women and treat conditions involving menstruation, menopause, and so on.

OCCUPATIONAL SAFETY HEALTH INSPECTOR

Occupational safety health inspectors examine places of business for equipment and work conditions that endanger the health and safety of employees. Most are employed by the U.S. Department of Labor or by state governments. Inspectors must have knowledge of federal laws governing safety in the workplace and proper inspection procedures. They visit a wide range of places of employment, from manufacturing and industrial plants to restaurants and hospitals, to detect unsafe work equipment, machinery, and procedures and unhealthy work conditions. They also discuss findings with employers or managers, advise on steps to correct violations, and urge compliance with regulations.

OCCUPATIONAL THERAPIST

Occupational therapists develop individualized programs of activity for mentally, physically, developmentally, and emotionally impaired persons to aid them in achieving self-reliance. They use a variety of routine chores to encourage motor skills, concen-tration, and motivation in patients, as well as to prepare them for the rigors of independent living. Most therapists are employed by hospitals; others work for school systems, nursing homes, and other health care agencies and centers.

OCEANOGRAPHER

Oceanographers study the physical characteristics of marine environments and the organisms that inhabit the seas. More and more oceanographers are self-employed consultants. Many are employed as faculty members of colleges and universities or on the staffs of research institutes. Physical or geological oceanographers study ocean currents, the topography of the ocean floor, and the chemical composition of sea water. Most divide time between laboratory work and research at sea.

OPERATING ROOM TECHNICIAN

Operating room technicians assist the surgical team before, during, and after an operation. Prior to the operation, they set out needed instruments, perform equipment checks, and prepare patients for surgery. During the procedure, they pass instruments, cut sutures, and count sponges, needles, supplies, and instruments. After an operation, they may help transport the patient to the recovery room and restock the operating room.

OPHTHALMIC LAB TECHNICIAN

Ophthalmic lab technicians make prescription eyeglasses through a process of cutting, grinding, edging, and finishing according to the specifications of an eye care specialist. They may also manufacture lenses for instruments such as telescopes, microscopes, and binoculars. Half of all technicians are employed by optical laboratories, while others work in retail stores that sell prescription glasses.

OPHTHALMOLOGIST

Ophthalmologists are medical doctors who diagnose and treat eye afflictions. Like optometrists, they examine patients for ocular disorders like cataracts, glaucoma, and refractive problems and determine the extent of injury or infection. They also prescribe eyeglasses and contact lenses. However, unlike optometrists, ophthalmologists are also qualified to perform eye surgery and laser treatment.

OPTICIAN

Opticians fill optometrists' or ophthalmologists' prescriptions for eyeglasses and contact lenses. They also assist customers in the selection of eyeglass frames and perform measurements of the eyes to determine placement of lenses. Another aspect of their job involves checking glasses and contacts for prescription fidelity and making minor adjustments to ensure proper and comfortable fit. Most opticians are employed at optical shops and in retail stores with optical departments.

OPTOMETRIST

Optometrists diagnose visual disorders and prescribe and administer corrective and rehabilitative treatments. They check eyes for signs of cataracts and other disease and test for depth perception, color differentiation, focus, and coordination.

Most optometrists prescribe glasses, contact lenses, and other optical aids and design exercises to develop and strengthen ocular coordination and muscular control.

ORTHODONTIST

Orthodontists diagnose and correct deviations in dental growth, development, and position. They design, fabricate, and install braces, space maintainers, space retainers, labial and lingual arch wires, head caps, and other intra- and extra-oral appliances to alter the positions and relationships of teeth and jaws and to restore or maintain normal appearance and function.

OSTEOPATH

Osteopaths perform medical examinations, diagnose illnesses, and treat patients with ailments of the muscular and skeletal system. Doctors of Osteopathy (DOs) differ from MDs in that they place special emphasis on the muscular and skeletal systems and attempt to correct ailments and relieve pain by manually manipulating body parts. They also prescribe drugs, perform surgery, and counsel patients on preventive health care.

OTOLARYNGOLOGIST

Otolaryngologists diagnose and treat disorders and infections of ears, noses, and throats. Their primary instruments for assessing affected organs are audiometers, prisms, nasoscopes, microscopes, X-ray machines, and fluoroscopes. They prescribe and administer drugs and perform surgery when necessary. They also conduct tests to gauge hearing and speech loss. Those who specialize in the throat are called laryngologists, ear doctors are called otologists, and nose doctors are called rhinologists.

PALEONTOLOGIST

Paleontologists study fossil evidence found in rock formations in order to trace the evolution of plant and animal life and the geological history of the earth. As scientists, they must carefully record their findings and classify them according to their botanical or zoological family and probable age. They may organize various expeditions and supervise the removal of fossils from rock.

PARALEGAL

Paralegals assist attorneys in preparing legal documents, collecting depositions and affidavits, and investigating, researching and analyzing legal issues. Their specific duties include writing motions, taking depositions, conducting independent legal research, and filing court papers as well as performing less critical clerical tasks. Paralegals work under the supervision of attorneys. While they cannot do all of the work that attorneys do, those with experience perform many functions traditionally performed only by lawyers.

PAROLE OFFICER

Parole officers monitor, counsel, and report on the progress of individuals who have been released from correctional institutions to serve parole. Most are employed by municipal, state, and federal departments of corrections. Their primary responsibility is to monitor parolees to ensure that the terms of their parole are not being violated. Parole officers may also provide counseling on educational and employment opportunities, assist with family and social adjustment, and otherwise help parolees enter the mainstream of society.

PATHOLOGIST

Pathologists study the nature, cause, and development of diseases and the functional changes that result from them. By examining body tissues, fluids, secretions, and other specimens, they are able to diagnose the presence and stages of diseases. They also perform autopsies to determine cause of death and the effects of treatment efforts. They may be classified according to specialties, such as clinical, forensic, or surgical pathologists.

PEDIATRICIAN

Pediatricians provide medical services to children from the time they are born until they reach adolescence. They are interested in making sure that a child goes through the growth and developmental phases in good mental and physical health. Pediatricians conduct periodic exams and tests on patients to detect symptoms and diseases and prescribe medications for various infections and maladies.

PERSONNEL RECRUITER

Personnel recruiters interview prospective employees, administer tests, and provide information about company policies and available jobs. Most are employed by employment agencies and personnel recruitment agencies as well as by consulting and outplacement firms. Recruiters evaluate job candidates and usually pass recommendations on to personnel offices or hiring committees for final determination. They often must spend time traveling to college campuses, job fairs, and conventions to meet with job candidates. Recruiters may conduct screening interviews or discuss in depth the educational background, work experience, and career goals of prospective employees, in relation to what the company is looking for and has to offer.

PETROLEUM ENGINEER

Petroleum engineers plan drilling sites and effective production methods for optimal access to oil and natural gas. They prepare maps of subsurfaces to determine exact locations of natural gas and oil reservoirs and evaluate production costs and drilling rates to establish effective recovery methods. The majority of petroleum engineers are employed by major oil companies; others work for independent oil firms, government agencies, or private consulting firms.

PHARMACIST

Pharmacists prepare and dispense prescriptions. Most are employed at drugstores, hospitals, and pharmaceutical companies. Some pharmacists counsel patients and doctors about the side effects of prescribed medications and drug treatments and about the proper use and storage of medicines. At larger chain stores, pharmacists hire and supervise personnel at drug departments and counters.

JOB DESCRIPTIONS

PHOTOGRAPHER

Photographers use cameras and, increasingly, digital video, to portray events visually. They use a variety of mechanical and optical instruments to achieve graphic effects and adapt lighting conditions. Many photog-raphers specialize in scientific, medical, or engineering photography. Others specialize as advertising and catalog photographers. Photojournalists capture newsworthy events for newspaper and magazine publication, and portrait photographers take pictures of individuals or groups in posed settings.

PHOTOGRAPHIC-PROCESS WORKER

Photographic-process workers develop photo-graphic film, make prints and slides, prepare enlargements, and retouch photographs. To develop prints and slides, they expose film to chemical solutions and use projection printers. Most are employed at photo-finishing labs that work with amateur and professional photographers. Others work for portrait photographers, commercial studios, motion picture producers, and newspapers. At large, sophisticated labs, photographic-process workers specialize as airbrush artists, photographic retouchers, colorists, and color laboratory technicians.

PHOTOJOURNALIST

Photojournalists photograph news events for print media, especially newspapers and magazines. They receive assignments from editors and normally travel with reporters to news sites, where they capture visually striking images that help convey the meaning of a particular story. Photojournalism requires a keen sense for news and a good eye for the visual image. Some photojournalists are salaried employees on the staffs of newspapers, magazines, and other publications; many others work freelance.

PHYSICAL THERAPIST

Physical therapists plan and direct treatment to improve mobility and alleviate pain in persons disabled by injury or disease. Therapists typically work with persons recovering from debilitating accidents and afflictions such as multiple sclerosis, cerebral palsy, and stroke. Treatments include exer-cise, electrical stimulation, heat massage, and ultrasound to relieve pain and promote muscle and skin development. Most are employed at hospitals; others work in rehabilitation cen-ters, nursing homes, and home health agencies.

PHYSICIAN (GENERAL PRACTICE)

Physicians in general practice perform examinations, diagnose medical conditions, and prescribe treatment for individuals suffering from injury, discomfort, or disease. Most are employed in group practice with several physicians. Approximately one-quarter serve on the staffs of hospitals, either as residents or on a full-time basis. They take patients' medical histories, order tests such as X rays, and analyze medical reports before prescribing treatments and medications. They also advise patients in proper diet and other preventive health measures.

PHYSICIAN ASSISTANT

Physician assistants (PAs) perform essential medical procedures, freeing physicians to attend to more specialized duties. They take medical histories, perform physical exams and laboratory tests, and sometimes prescribe treatments. Physicians in private practice employ the largest number of physician assistants; hospitals, clinics, and HMOs also provide opportunities for PAs. Under law, most perform their duties under the supervision of a licensed supervising physician, but increasingly, more states are allowing PAs to work independently of doctors.

PHYSICIST

Physicists research and develop theories concerning the physical forces of nature. Most study one or more branches of physics, including elementary-particle physics, atomic or molecular physics, optics, acoustics, or the physics of fluids. Universities are the largest employers of physicists; others work for the federal government and in private industry. They use specialized instruments such as lasers, particle accelerators, computers, and semiconductors. Much of federal grant money given to physicists is intended for research for military applications.

PHYSIOLOGIST

Physiologists study the life functions of plants and animals, both in their natural habitats, and under experimental or abnormal conditions. Most hold teaching and research positions at universities; others work for commercial research companies and in the food industry. Physiologists are expected to know about all aspects of the life cycles of organisms, such as growth, reproduction, photosynthesis, and metabolism. They also analyze the function of organic systems, such as the circulatory, nervous, and immune systems in animals and the root systems of plants.

PLUMBER

Plumbers build and repair water, waste disposal, drainage, and gas delivery systems for residential, commercial, and industrial structures. Using manual and power tools, they fit pipes, cutting them to exact specifications. Some frequently consult blueprints and drawings indicating the location of these pipes.

PODIATRIST

Podiatrists treat foot ailments, such as corns, bunions, ingrown toenails, and skin and nail diseases. Required training and education normally includes a degree from a college of podiatric medicine, classroom and laboratory study, and clinical experience. Specializations are common and include podiatric surgery similar to that of orthopedics, which involves the treatment of bone, joint, and muscle disorders. The treatment they offer may include prescribing and fitting corrective devices or implants, performing surgery, recommending programs of therapy, or referring patients with arthritis or other diseases to other physicians.

POLICE DETECTIVE

Police detectives perform investigations in an effort to prevent crimes or solve criminal cases. By pursuing leads, gleaning information from key witnesses, or gathering clues from a crime scene, detectives attempt to put together a case that will help either to apprehend or prosecute a suspected criminal. They arrest alleged felons and assist in presenting the police department's case to the courts. Detectives can work in various divisions, including homicide, vice, narcotics, grand theft auto, or juvenile delinquency.

POLICE OFFICER

Police officers provide protection against crime, investigate criminal activity, and work with the public on crime-prevention measures. Increasingly, police officers work with community leaders, educators, and corrections workers. Job responsibilities include monitoring surroundings, reacting to suspicious or dangerous situations, and responding to radio instructions from police headquarters. In large forces, patrol officers are supplemented by mounted and canine corps, firearms and fingerprint experts, mobile rescue and SWAT teams, laboratory experts, and numerous other specialists.

POLITICAL SCIENTIST

Political scientists study the origin, development, and operation of political institutions in order to formulate, develop, and validate political theories. Most are employed at institutions of higher learning, though many political scientists are employed by consulting firms, political organizations, and government intelligence agencies. Many political scientists specialize in a specific geographical, political, or philosophical aspect of people's political behavior.

POLLUTION CONTROL ENGINEER

Pollution control engineers analyze and evaluate pollution problems, methods of pollution control, and methods of testing pollution sources. The engineers determine the physiochemical nature and concentration of contaminants in polluted areas. They also make sure that industrial complexes are in compliance with pollution control regulations. Based on their assessments, they may recommend either issuing or denying construction permits. They are often subcategorized as air-pollution engineers, noise-abatement engineers, or water quality-control engineers.

POSTAL INSPECTOR
Postal inspectors are officially designated U.S. marshals, whose job is to enforce the laws and regulations governing the operation of the postal system. They monitor the function of the postal system, ensuring smooth, safe, and legal postal service operations, and investigate criminal activities, such as theft of mail or use of the postal system for fraudulent purposes. Investi-gations, which take up most of their time, involve digging into mismanagement, performing financial audits, and working with the Internal Revenue Service and other agencies on special projects.

PRIEST
In addition to serving parishioners, Catholic priests may teach in seminaries, perform missionary work, or work with community and charitable organizations. Priests attend to the spiritual, moral, and educational needs of church members. They prepare and deliver sermons, administer the sacraments, preside at weddings and funerals, comfort the sick, and counsel those in need of help or spiritual guidance.

PRINTER
Printers reproduce copy and/or graphic arts materials. They often work in small print shops or printing departments, and they perform their tasks using some of the following procedures: They prepare aluminum plates for reproduction in an offset lithographic process, touch up negatives, assemble film flats, and operate offset-duplicating machines or small printing presses to reproduce materials. They also operate bindery equipment to cut, assemble, staple, or bind materials.

PRIVATE INVESTIGATOR
Private investigators (PIs) specialize in ob-taining missing information, conducting background checks, performing covert observations, and exposing insurance or financial fraud. They often conduct surveillance in order to uncover various types of illegality or illicit behavior. Almost half of all PIs are self-employed or work for detective agencies. PIs often have backgrounds or schooling in insurance, collections, the military, law enforcement, finance, or government.

PRODUCER (MOVIE/TV)
Movie/TV producers handle play or script selection, arrange financing, and determine the size and content of the production and its budget. They participate in casting decisions and choose directors and production professionals. As the financial backers of a project, they are responsible for negotiating various contracts with artistic personnel. And in the course of putting together a project, they may coordinate the activities of writers, directors, and other personnel.

PROFESSOR
Professors instruct college and university students in a highly specialized field of expertise. In addition to teaching responsibilities, they prepare lectures, develop and administer exams, grade papers, and promote class discussion. At some colleges and universities, professors are under intense pressure to conduct research and publish.

PROOFREADER
Proofreaders read written materials to detect errors in spelling, grammar, type, or composition. They use standardized correction marks to indicate clearly the mistakes in the text. Once the text has been scrutinized by the proofreader, the copy is then revised, and the proofreader once again makes sure that the new version is correct. Proofreaders may also measure the dimensions, spacing, and positioning of page elements to ensure that they meet various format specifications.

PROPERTY MANAGER
Property managers take on the duties in cases where owners of apartments, office buildings, or retail and industrial property lack the time or expertise to carry out the day-to-day management responsibilities of their real-estate investments. Managers serve as agents for the property and, as such, they market vacant space,

handle lease agreements, establish rental rates, and take care of financial and building maintenance operations.

PROSTHETIST

Prosthetists work in conjunction with physicians to fit patients with artificial limbs. They assist in determining a patient's prosthetic needs and specifications and are involved in fitting patients. They design limbs by selecting the materials and components as well as make casts and model modifications. They evaluate how well the patient is able to utilize the prosthetic and make adjustments to assure function and comfort.

PSYCHIATRIST

Behavioral abnormalities are the stock and trade of psychiatrists, who are physicians trained in medicine, psychology, and neurology. A typical professional in this field studies, diagnoses, and treats mental, emotional, and behavioral disorders. Psychiatrists treat both the psychological and biological pathology of human thought processes, using, for example, dream interpretation, programs of psychoactive medication, and behavior modification. Most are employed in their own practices, while others may also work for hospitals.

PSYCHOLOGIST

Psychologists study human behavior, emotion, and mental processes and provide counseling and therapy for individuals on the basis of experiments, tests, interviews, surveys, and clinical studies. Most are employed in education, health care, social service organizations, private businesses, and government agencies. About one-quarter own private practices. Experimental psychologists study motivation, learning, perception, and neurological factors in behavior, while clinical psychologists assist the emotionally or mentally disturbed in adjusting to life, often through psychotherapy. Developmental psychologists investigate patterns of change that occur in the maturing and aging processes.

PUBLIC RELATIONS EXECUTIVE

Public relations executives help government bodies, businesses, and individuals maintain a good public image. They assess and communicate reaction to a company's policies from customers, employees, the press, community organizations, and special interest groups to decision makers of all kinds. Because each client's objectives are different, public relations executives must develop custom-tailored programs.

PURCHASING AGENT

Purchasing agents, who buy raw materials, supplies, and equipment of all kinds, must have a thorough knowledge of the specific products and suppliers they work with, as well as the inventory and needs of their own companies. Agents make purchases both spontaneously and based on predetermined schedules, either at departmental requests or by examining computerized inventory reports. Most work in manufacturing, others at construction companies, schools, advertising firms, and government agencies, especially the Department of Defense.

QUALITY ASSURANCE ANALYST

Quality assurance analysts evaluate new or modified software programs to verify that they function according to user requirements and meet establishment guidelines. They review various elements of a program, such as flowcharts, documentation, and diagrams, in order to ensure that they will perform as they should. They also check a program's validity, accuracy, and reliability to see that they meet company standards. They then recommend improvements to or identify errors for computer programmers.

RABBI

Rabbis should have a desire to serve others, good social and rhetorical skills, and knowledge of Jewish laws and tradition. Rabbis are the spiritual leaders of Jewish congregations. They advise and teach their congregations and conduct religious services. They also visit the infirmed, work with community organizations, conduct weddings and funerals, supervise Sunday schools and Hebrew classes, and console grieving families. Unlike some Christian clergy, rabbis have an abundance of autonomy, reporting mainly to their congregations and boards rather than outside authorities.

RADIATION THERAPIST
Radiation therapists administer doses of ionizing radiation to patients' body parts as part of the treatment for cancer. They operate linear accelerators with electron capabilities and other equipment and are also responsible for monitoring patients' reactions to radiation side effects.

RADIO/TELEVISION ANNOUNCER
Radio/television announcers serve as the voice of a network or radio station by introducing or closing shows and announcing such things as station breaks, public service announcements, commercials, and station-identification messages. They coordinate broadcasts with the daily schedule by cuing transmitted programs from network central stations or other pickup points. Announcers disseminate breaking news stories as they arrive at the station, and may rewrite news bulletins from wire services to fit a specific time slot or program.

RADIOGRAPHER
Radiographers produce X rays of various sections of the human body in order to assist in diagnosing medical problems. They position radiographic equipment at the correct angles and heights over the area of the patient's body specified by the attending medical specialist. To prevent unnecessary radiation exposure, they use lead shields or blankets or limit the size of the X-ray beam. Experienced radiographers perform fluoroscopies or operate computerized tomography scanners.

REAL ESTATE AGENT
Real estate agents act as intermediary between buyer and seller in real estate transactions, usually as the prime salesperson of a property. They are usually independent salespersons who work for licensed brokers. Agents usually sell either residential or commercial properties, and those who sell the latter often specialize in industrial or agricultural real estate.

RECREATIONAL THERAPIST
Recreational therapists plan and coordinate medically approved activities for patients in order to help them remediate the effects of illness, build confidence levels, and interact with their surroundings. If they are employed at hospitals and/or rehabilitation centers, therapists often specialize in patients with specific medical problems. In nursing homes and residential facilities, they may also treat medical problems, but their first priority is to improve general health and well-being.

REPORTER
Reporters cover newsworthy events for newspapers, magazines, broadcasters, and wire services. Reporters work closely with editors, photojournalists, and newsmakers. There are several types of reporters. General assignment reporters cover local events; beat reporters cover specific assignments, such as police headquarters or city hall; and investigative reporters go into stories in depth, often filing series reports to cover a particular angle or uncover injustice or corruption.

RESPIRATORY THERAPIST
Respiratory therapists treat and rehabilitate patients suffering from cardiopulmonary (heart and lung) ailments. They administer a variety of routine and emergency treatments. Respiratory therapists configure, operate, and monitor a variety of special medical devices, including oxygen tents, ventilators, and breathing machines. Most are employed at hospitals. Others are employed in private clinics or nursing homes or provide in-home care.

RESTAURANT MANAGER
Restaurant managers make sure that their establishments run efficiently and profitably. They ensure that menu items are well prepared and appropriately priced, provide a clean dining environment with good service, and see that the food and other supplies are used efficiently. They work in a variety of locations, ranging from fast food to fine dining restaurants, from cafeterias to banquet halls.

SALES REPRESENTATIVE (WHOLESALE)

Wholesale sales representatives work for wholesalers and/or distributors, selling their products to stores, manufacturers, and businesses. They are also expected to keep sales records, develop new clients, and advise existing clients about marketing and advertising strategies. The primary employers of wholesale sales representatives are firms that sell machinery, equipment, and other products to business and industrial users. Others work for food product companies, hardware distributors, and companies that sell electrical goods.

SALESPERSON (RETAIL)

Retail salespeople provide sales service to customers in retail stores. They provide information on products, give demonstrations of available models, discuss prices, and otherwise assist potential buyers. They work at various establishments, from drugstores and department stores to specialized shops for home entertainment equipment, clothing, and furniture. Some work on commission, others on a salary plus bonuses based on their sales. For some, however, the job consists primarily of handling transactions and wrapping purchases.

SCREENWRITER

Screenwriters create scripts for motion pictures and television, sometimes on their own, sometimes by assignment. They may research factual materials in order to authenticate their storyline. They may work with directors or producers in developing and revising scripts.

SECRETARY

Secretaries perform various administrative tasks for either an executive or a group of office workers, the nature of which depends on the kind of organization for which they work. In some organizations, secretaries work together in small groups, forming a secretarial pool. In most cases they organize and maintain files, answer questions of callers and schedule appointments, type and perform word-processing functions, and take dictation for employers.

SEISMOLOGIST

Seismologists analyze data from seismographs and geophysical instruments to locate earthquakes and faults. They work to establish the direction, motion, and stress of the earth's movements before, during, and after an earthquake. They may indicate areas of seismic risk to existing or proposed buildings.

SOCIAL WORKER

Social workers assist individuals, families, and groups in need of counseling and special social services. They may provide counseling on specific problems, such as alcoholism, housing, and child care, or refer people to available resources and agencies. This work requires compassion, understanding, and the ability to communicate effectively. State, county, and local government agencies employ a large percentage of social workers. In the private sector, most are employed at charitable and nonprofit agencies.

SOCIOLOGIST

Sociologists study human behavior by examining the interaction of social groups and institutions, using data culled through surveys or direct observation and analyzed by means of statistical and computer techniques. Most work at government agencies, research firms, corporations, and welfare organizations. Their findings are used by educators, policy makers, and other professionals to develop and implement reforms. Sociologists may also direct services in welfare agencies and consult on programs that improve those agencies.

SOFTWARE ENGINEER

Software engineers develop and maintain software systems and programs for medical, scientific, and industrial purposes. They may also analyze computer hardware requirements and determine if a product under design will work efficiently. They also develop and direct software testing procedures, programming, and documentation and consult with customers concerning system maintenance and installation.

SPEECH PATHOLOGIST

Speech pathologists evaluate hearing, speech, and language disabilities and provide therapy. Their job responsibilities often vary from job to job. Those employed at hospitals diagnose and identify speech abnormalities and work closely with physicians and other professionals to develop therapeutic programs. Those employed at educational institutions have a wider range of responsibilities. They may consult with parents and school administrators and instruct classroom teachers on developing the communications skills of students.

SPORTS INSTRUCTOR

Sports instructors teach, coach, and develop athletic skills. Most are employed at elementary and secondary schools, colleges and universities, and recreational facilities. Some work with private individuals and families. They may teach calisthenics and other exercises and supervise sports activities of all kinds. They may also coach varsity or intercollegiate teams. Some work at health clubs, golf courses, and tennis clubs, where they confer with members about physical conditioning.

STATIONARY ENGINEER

Stationary engineers operate and maintain power plants and industrial heating, cooling, and ventilation systems. They maintain generators, pumps, turbines, compressors, condensers, boilers, and diesel engines in order to meet consumer and industrial power, heating, refrigeration, and ventilation needs. They may also monitor meters, gauges, and other mechanical indicators so they can assess the condition and performance of their equipment.

STATISTICIAN

Through data culled from experiments and surveys, statisticians predict the conduct of groups by studying the behavior of representative smaller samples. Their conclusions are applied in almost every area in which large groups of individuals interact with one another. They not only study people but also deal with physical phenomena, from the weather to random mechanical occurrences of all kinds, particularly in the manufacturing and insurance industries.

STOCKBROKER

Stockbrokers trade in securities through representatives on the floors of securities exchanges, or over the counter directly with dealers. They may serve private parties or institutions. Most work at brokerage houses, investment firms, and financial management companies. Stockbrokers may discuss stock options with clients and place orders, advise clients of investment opportunities, and manage their financial portfolios.

STORE MANAGER

Store managers operate retail establishments that sell merchandise, such as groceries, clothes, jewelry, and furniture. Managers either delegate or perform the following tasks: preparing work schedules, determining pricing policies, bookkeeping, coordinating promotional activities, and advertising. They may also hire and fire, handle customer complaints, and order products.

SURGEON

Surgeons both diagnose disorders and correct them. They may specialize in one area of treatment, such as heart surgery, brain surgery, plastic surgery, or orthopedics. Most surgeons are affiliated with hospitals or other large health care establishments, such as research institutions. They use precision instruments and diagnostic equipment, such as scalpels, sutures, and lasers.

SURVEYOR

Surveyors measure construction and mining sites, write technical property descriptions for deeds and leases, and prepare maps and charts. They may also prepare reports, plott charts, perform computations, and plan surveys for offices. Most are employed by surveying firms or governments, though some work for engineering and architectural firms. Most state and municipal surveyors work for highway or urban planning agencies.

TAX EXAMINER/COLLECTOR

Tax examiners and collectors assess tax liability and collect taxes from individuals, estates, and corporations. This profession requires accounting skills and a broad knowledge of state and federal tax codes. Tax examiners and collectors are employed by federal and state internal revenue departments. They examine the financial records—receipts, income statements, and the like—of businesses and individuals, to determine tax liability and compare it with actual taxes paid. They may then impose penalties.

TEACHER

Teachers introduce school-age children to reading, mathematics, language, science, social studies, and other subjects offered at the schools in which they work. Teachers also observe and assist students' social and emotional development and monitor their health. Most are employed at public schools. Teachers may use visual instruction aids, such as films and slides, to help children become interested in learning. They also meet with school officials and parents to discuss students' performance, prepare lessons, and grade papers.

TECHNICAL WRITER

Most technical writers prepare instruction manuals, catalogs, parts lists, and brochures for use by sales representatives, technicians, and owners of high-tech equipment. They transform scientific and technical information into "user friendly" material. Though good writing skills are essential, a background in a particular scientific or technical field is also required in this profession.

THEATER DIRECTOR

Theater directors work to convert their artistic interpretations of written plays into productions for the stage. They audition and select cast members, conduct rehearsals, and direct the activities on stage according to their reading of the script. By advising ensemble members on their acting, voice, and movements, directors attempt to achieve the best possible performance. Many also have the final say on set design, costumes, choreography, and music.

TRANSLATOR

Translators are bilingual or multilingual professionals who translate from one language to another. They may specialize in a particular area, such as the translation of news, legal documents, or scientific reports. They must make sure that nuances are not lost in translation and that their versions are grammatically and mechanically correct.

TRAVEL AGENT

Travel agents use their knowledge of various destinations to arrange flights, make hotel accommodations, and schedule tourist packages. They must also learn the specific needs of individuals and businesses. They gather information on customs regulations, travel documents, and exchange rates for international travelers. To familiarize themselves with the places to which they send their clients, agents must travel to them, and often do so at deeply discounted rates.

TRAVEL GUIDE

Travel guides arrange excursions for tour groups, coordinating itineraries according to the wishes of their groups. They also arrange for both transportation and accommodations. They are responsible for the safety of their groups, and may need to know various first-aid or life-saving procedures. As tour leaders, they must be familiar with the terrain—whether it be city or country—and able to inform tourists about various points of interest.

TYPIST/WORD PROCESSOR

Typists and word processors prepare and edit typed or electronic copies of handwritten, printed, or magnetically recorded documents. They may create custom headings for form letters, transcribe from handwritten drafts, and address envelopes. They may also perform related office chores, such as filing, photocopying, and answering telephones. Senior typists—those who have developed exceptional speed, accuracy, and discretion—often work with technical materials and rough drafts.

ULTRASOUND TECHNICIAN
Also known as sonographers, ultrasound technicians use an ultrasound machine to transmit nonionizing, high-frequency sound waves through a patient's body. These sound waves, which echo back to form an image, are used by physicians as interpretive and diagnostic tools. Ultrasound is often used in obstetrics to view fetuses, but technicians may also specialize in neural, vascular, cardi-ological, abdominal, and ophthalmological areas.

UNDERTAKER
Undertakers, or morticians, prepare bodies for burial and arrange and direct funerals. After bodies are delivered to funeral homes, undertakers treat them with embalming fluid to prevent decomposition. In arranging funerals, they work with families, a job that requires compassion and sensitivity. Many also consult clergy to ensure religious rites are properly performed.

URBAN/REGIONAL PLANNER
Urban/regional planners both collect and analyze data about communities in order to plan land use for citizens and corporations. They conduct interviews and surveys to assist them in evaluating land use. They may work with government officials, corporations, and community members to anticipate changes in the development of land. They must be aware of shifts in the economy and population, and develop programs according to the specific needs of a community.

VETERINARIAN
Veterinarians have various areas of expertise, some with small animals, (dogs, cats, and other small pets), others with livestock such as cattle, horses, sheep, or poultry. Most work at small hospitals, colleges and universities, and health agencies. Many are employed by the federal government to inspect livestock and help prevent the transmission of diseases through food products. Many also work in research and teaching. Veterinarians may also perform autopsies, mainly on farm animals.

VOCATIONAL COUNSELOR
Most vocational counselors are employed at secondary schools and colleges and universities, where they assess educational and career choices based on a student's mental, emotional, social, and educational status. They use academic records, vocational tests, and interviews in their work. They often measure vocational skills to assist in career planning and may also help students find solutions to special problems.

WEB DEVELOPER
Web developers are employed by a very wide range of industries. Usually working closely with Marketing and IT/MIS departments, developers are often called upon to design websites ranging from single-page, text-oriented sites to elaborate multi-page sites replete with real-time interface capabilities and extensive graphics and animation, depending largely on the function of the site. Developers require expertise in various web programming media.

WEB MANAGER
Web managers are charged with facilitating the implementation, upkeep, and upgrade of employers' servers and electronic communication systems. They oversee the testing, installation, and maintenance of communications software and hardware and are in charge of establishing and maintaining network security, expanding browser com-patibility, researching and implementing technological advancements for website programming, and the tracking of website interactivity and utility by target users. Web general managers also often work closely with marketing departments to create and execute website promotion strategies.

WOODWORKER
There are two types of woodworkers. Production woodworkers are employed by sawmills, plywood mills, and wood products manufacturing plants. Precision woodworkers work in small shops that make architectural woodwork and other specialty items. Both kinds of woodworkers usually operate woodworking machines to cut and shape objects from lumber.

ZOOLOGIST

Zoologists study animals and their behavior. Many concentrate on a single animal group. Ornithologists, for example, study birds, mammalogists study mammals, herpetologists study reptiles, and ichthyologists study fish. While some zoologists work with live animals, in natural or simulated-natural habitats, others dissect dead animals in laboratories to study their physiology.

OCCUPATIONAL FACTS

A NNUAL EARNINGS SURVEY

T HE TABLE IN THIS CHAPTER presents estimates of annual salaries nationwide for over 400 occupations. Jobs were chosen to represent the most common occupational fields as well as some of the most visible jobs such as President of the U.S., sports jobs and others.

Income figures are derived from a variety of sources, but principally the U.S. Bureau of Labor Statistics (BLS). In many cases they also come from professional organizations like the Society of Actuaries. Commissions were calculated on annual basis. When reliable data could not be found, estimates were culled from professionals familiar with incomes in the given field. All the annual incomes shown have been systematically updated to reflect estimated incomes for the beginning of the year 2000, using a cost-of-employment index similar to that used by economists at the BLS. While incomes reflect 2000 estimates, be aware that no one knows for sure how coming economic conditions will influence earnings in the future.

Three earnings figures are provided for each job listed here. The "Beginning" figure is that of the lowest-paid workers in the field or, in cases like those of actors, the lowest earnings that those calling themselves "professionals" might make. The "Midlevel" figure reflects what the average worker is paid. In many cases this figure is exactly an average of the income of all workers in the field. When averages were not available, median incomes were often used, meaning that half the workers in this field make less than the figure shown, and half make more. The "Top" figure gives earnings in the 90th percentile in the occupation, which reflects the level that the most talented or experienced individuals might reasonably expect to make. It does not represent the highest or near-highest income in the field. For example, movie stars may earn some 10 million per film. However, they do not represent "top" income among actors; rather, the top is 56,000—what a successful actor in the 90th percentile of his or her profession might earn.

Descriptions of many of the jobs listed here can be found elsewhere in this book. ➤See "Job Descriptions," pp. 84-116.

Job Title	Beginning	Midlevel	Top
Academic Counselor	$ 25,000	$ 45,000	$ 65,000
Accountant	33,000	59,000	74,000
Acting Coach	10,000	12,000	29,000
Actor	3,000	15,000	56,000
Actuary	41,000	90,000	133,000
Acupuncturist	19,000	30,000	49,000
Admissions Evaluator	15,000	23,000	58,000
Advertising Account Executive	30,000	51,000	93,000
Advertising Copywriter	21,000	54,000	116,000
Advertising Salesperson	16,000	31,000	74,000
Aerobics Instructor	16,000	20,000	45,000
Aerospace Engineer	40,000	67,000	114,000
Agency Director (Nonprofit)	46,000	67,000	143,000
Agricultural Scientist	27,000	65,000	66,000
Agronomist	32,000	39,000	44,000
Air Conditioning Mechanic	13,000	32,000	47,000
Air Traffic Controller	32,000	51,000	74,000

ANNUAL EARNINGS SURVEY

Job Title	Beginning	Midlevel	Top
Airbrush Artist	$ 13,000	$ 23,000	$ 41,000
Aircraft Mechanic	27,000	40,000	51,000
Airplane Navigator	52,000	83,000	166,000
Airplane Pilot	11,000	114,000	212,000
Allergist	58,000	292,000	350,000
Anesthesiologist	58,000	309,000	350,000
Animal Breeder	12,000	16,000	19,000
Animal Caretaker	10,000	14,000	22,000
Anthropologist	21,000	40,000	72,000
Antique Dealer	30,000	47,000	85,000
Appliance Repairer	14,000	33,000	49,000
Archeologist	24,000	40,000	74,000
Architect	31,000	52,000	106,000
Architectural Drafter	22,000	36,000	54,000
Art Therapist	16,000	26,000	37,000
Artist (Commercial)	28,000	34,000	54,000
Artist (Fine Art)	18,000	31,000	45,000
Assayer	30,000	35,000	39,000
Astronaut	59,000	78,000	93,000
Astronomer	38,000	71,000	114,000
Athletic Director	12,000	42,000	54,000
Athletic Trainer	25,000	36,000	57,000
Attorney	45,000	68,000	133,000
Auctioneer	13,000	33,000	66,000
Audiologist	25,000	39,000	62,000
Audiovisual Technician	24,000	26,000	30,000
Author (Books)	6,000	30,000	64,000
Auto Wrecker	13,000	18,000	26,000
Automobile Assembler	16,000	31,000	38,000
Automobile Body Repairer	14,000	27,000	45,000
Automobile Mechanic	14,000	27,000	45,000
Automobile Painter	13,000	24,000	40,000
Automobile Salesperson	30,000	42,000	63,000
Baggage Porter	5,000	12,000	14,000
Bailiff	26,000	35,000	37,000
Baker	12,000	15,000	42,000
Ballistics Expert	26,000	44,000	72,000
Bank Officer	25,000	46,000	87,000
Bank Teller	13,000	19,000	27,000
Barber	25,000	32,000	47,000
Bartender	11,000	18,000	28,000
Baseball Player (Major League)	175,000	442,000	4,250,000
Baseball Umpire (Major League)	75,000	144,000	180,000
Basketball Coach (NCAA)	30,000	56,000	135,000
Basketball Player (NBA)	249,000	1,540,000	5,100,000
Beautician	13,000	19,000	23,000
Biologist	25,000	41,000	70,000
Blaster	25,000	26,000	30,000

ANNUAL EARNINGS SURVEY

Job Title	Beginning	Midlevel	Top
Boilermaker	$ 29,000	$ 35,000	$ 56,000
Bookbinder	12,000	24,000	51,000
Bookkeeper	16,000	24,000	35,000
Border Guard	22,000	37,000	58,000
Botanist	36,000	41,000	54,000
Bricklayer	14,000	28,000	49,000
Broadcast Technician	19,000	34,000	106,000
Budget Analyst	35,000	41,000	50,000
Building Inspector	24,000	42,000	72,000
Bus Driver	13,000	27,000	40,000
Butcher	15,000	21,000	39,000
Buyer	21,000	38,000	67,000
Cake Decorator	12,000	18,000	30,000
Camera Operator	20,000	24,000	48,000
Cardiologist	65,000	170,000	655,000
Cardiovascular Technician	20,000	23,000	30,000
Carpenter	15,000	27,000	46,000
Carpet Installer	15,000	27,000	46,000
Cashier	9,000	14,000	26,000
Caterer	15,000	19,000	26,000
Catholic Priest	12,000	15,000	33,000
Chauffeur	38,000	51,000	63,000
Chef/Cook	13,000	18,000	33,000
Chemical Engineer	47,000	58,000	77,000
Chemist	29,000	57,000	89,000
Child Care Worker	8,000	14,000	21,000
Chiropractor	35,000	95,000	180,000
Choreographer	32,000	28,000	54,000
Civil Engineer	37,000	53,000	96,000
Collection Agent	15,000	24,000	39,000
College Professor	35,000	58,000	98,000
Communications Equipment Mechanic	14,000	34,000	52,000
Community Organization Worker	16,000	19,000	26,000
Composer	26,000	45,000	67,000
Compositor/Typesetter	13,000	24,000	39,000
Comptroller	25,000	52,000	99,000
Computer Consultant	30,000	65,000	104,000
Computer Operator	15,000	26,000	44,000
Computer Programmer	22,000	45,000	69,000
Computer Service Technician	19,000	35,000	52,000
Computer Systems Analyst	28,000	53,000	80,000
Concrete Mason	15,000	26,000	47,000
Congressional District Aide	15,000	30,000	55,000
Congressperson/Senator	138,000	153,000	177,000
Conservationist	22,000	53,000	62,000
Construction Foreman	31,000	59,000	106,000
Construction Machinery Operator	15,000	26,000	43,000

ANNUAL EARNINGS SURVEY

Job Title	Beginning	Midlevel	Top
Construction Worker (Laborer)	$ 11,000	$ 19,000	$ 34,000
Consumer Loan Officer	35,000	48,000	58,000
Contract Administrator	33,000	42,000	52,000
Cook/Chef	13,000	16,000	40,000
Corporate Executive (Senior)	59,000	181,000	319,000
Correction Officer	23,000	30,000	48,000
Corrections Officer	22,000	31,000	56,000
Cosmetologist	13,000	21,000	25,000
Cost Estimator	24,000	38,000	95,000
Counter/Rental Clerk	12,000	13,000	16,000
Court Clerk	20,000	23,000	26,000
Court Reporter/Stenographer	18,000	32,000	36,000
Cowboy	16,000	30,000	40,000
Crane Operator	23,000	35,000	48,000
Creative Director	26,000	56,000	125,000
Customer Service Clerk (Retail)	13,000	20,000	37,000
Customs Inspector	25,000	44,000	86,000
Cytologist	37,000	41,000	54,000
Dairy Farmer	11,000	53,000	106,000
Dancer	5,000	19,000	54,000
Data-Entry Clerk	15,000	22,000	42,000
Deli Cutter	12,000	14,000	22,000
Dental Hygienist	20,000	39,000	54,000
Dental Laboratory Technician	16,000	28,000	54,000
Dentist	64,000	144,000	160,000
Dermatologist	110,000	200,000	287,000
Dietitian	31,000	36,000	42,000
Dishwasher	10,000	11,000	11,000
Disk Jockey	8,000	21,000	54,000
Dock Supervisor	18,000	35,000	65,000
Dog Groomer	11,000	12,000	13,000
Dramatist	2,000	8,000	50,000
Dressmaker	13,000	16,000	25,000
Drill-Press Operator	16,000	27,000	41,000
Drywall Applicator/Finisher	11,000	25,000	46,000
Economist	33,000	84,000	96,000
Editor (Book)	19,000	39,000	77,000
Editor (Publication)	32,000	54,000	84,000
Editorial Assistant	13,000	22,000	30,000
Electrical Engineer	39,000	64,000	96,000
Electrical Equipment Repairer	19,000	35,000	52,000
Electrical Technician	16,000	36,000	58,000
Electrician	20,000	35,000	54,000
Elevator Operator	12,000	13,000	14,000
Elevator Technician	19,000	33,000	42,000
Emergency Medical Technician	13,000	29,000	35,000
Engineering Technician	24,000	37,000	54,000

ANNUAL EARNINGS SURVEY

Job Title	Beginning	Midlevel	Top
Entomologist	$ 37,000	$ 43,000	$ 54,000
Environmental Analyst	22,000	41,000	90,000
Escrow Officer	18,000	29,000	44,000
Estate Planner	23,000	47,000	152,000
Etcher	12,000	13,000	14,000
Excavator	13,000	19,000	26,000
Executive Search Consultant	35,000	71,000	247,000
Exhibit Display Representative	31,000	42,000	49,000
Exterminator	15,000	18,000	30,000
Fabric Layout Worker	12,000	18,000	19,000
Facilities Planner	30,000	32,000	35,000
Farmer	11,000	28,000	40,000
Fashion Designer	16,000	34,000	69,000
Fashion Model	11,000	89,000	212,000
Fast Food Worker	12,000	13,000	23,000
Field Service Technician	14,000	37,000	45,000
File Clerk	13,000	20,000	24,000
Financial Planner	21,000	99,000	186,000
Fire Ranger	19,000	22,000	25,000
Firefighter	22,000	37,000	52,000
Fish And Game Warden	12,000	24,000	35,000
Fish Hatchery Worker	12,000	15,000	22,000
Fisherman	19,000	25,000	37,000
Flight Attendant	16,000	38,000	74,000
Florist	15,000	27,000	37,000
Football Player (NFL)	163,000	824,000	5,000,000
Forestry Technician	18,000	35,000	66,000
Forklift Operator	15,000	26,000	43,000
Foundry Worker	13,000	20,000	21,000
Fundraiser	13,000	19,000	33,000
Furniture Finisher	15,000	22,000	25,000
Furniture Upholsterer	14,000	21,000	35,000
Furrier	11,000	13,000	16,000
Gambling Dealer	13,000	15,000	18,000
Garbage Collector	11,000	19,000	34,000
Gardener	12,000	19,000	37,000
Gas And Oil Servicer	12,000	13,000	14,000
Gemologist	16,000	38,000	67,000
Geneticist	37,000	43,000	54,000
Geographer	22,000	49,000	91,000
Geologist	34,000	68,000	114,000
Glazier	16,000	34,000	47,000
Government Caseworker	21,000	30,000	78,000
Grocery Clerk	12,000	15,000	25,000
Guard	11,000	20,000	38,000
Gunsmith	12,000	19,000	23,000
Hazardous Waste Management Specialist	26,000	36,000	44,000

ANNUAL EARNINGS SURVEY

Job Title	Beginning	Midlevel	Top
Head Coach	$ 34,000	$ 42,000	$ 78,000
Hearings Officer	37,000	48,000	54,000
Heating/Refrigeration Mechanic	16,000	31,000	47,000
Helicopter Pilot	52,000	83,000	166,000
Highway Patrol Officer	22,000	39,000	62,000
Home Economist	20,000	26,000	37,000
Home Health Aide	12,000	16,000	26,000
Horticulturist	13,000	15,000	19,000
Hospital Administrator	30,000	64,000	202,000
Hotel Manager	44,000	62,000	86,000
House Painter	14,000	25,000	45,000
Human Resources Specialist	16,000	35,000	63,000
Hydrologist	21,000	32,000	79,000
Industrial Designer	31,000	55,000	148,000
Industrial Engineer	41,000	64,000	108,000
Industrial Machine Repairer	19,000	32,000	49,000
Insulation Specialist	12,000	18,000	42,000
Insurance Agent	18,000	36,000	81,000
Insurance Underwriter	24,000	42,000	74,000
Interior Designer	12,000	18,000	26,000
Interpreter	19,000	25,000	30,000
Inventory Clerk	12,000	15,000	25,000
Ironworker	18,000	34,000	51,000
Irrigator	13,000	18,000	29,000
Jackhammer Operator	12,000	19,000	34,000
Janitor	10,000	18,000	30,000
Jeweler	26,000	37,000	61,000
Jockey	13,000	36,000	70,000
Judge (Federal)	115,000	146,000	146,000
Labor Relations Specialist	36,000	44,000	60,000
Landscape Architect	39,000	45,000	54,000
Librarian	33,000	40,000	62,000
Lifeguard	13,000	15,000	22,000
Line Installer	12,000	24,000	50,000
Linguist	19,000	41,000	66,000
Lithographer/Photoengraver	21,000	36,000	54,000
Lobbyist	30,000	41,000	56,000
Locker-Room Attendant	12,000	14,000	16,000
Locomotive Engineer	26,000	32,000	35,000
Lumberjack	13,000	27,000	38,000
Machine Product Assembler	15,000	20,000	35,000
Machine Tool Operator	14,000	25,000	41,000
Machinist	18,000	31,000	46,000
Maid	10,000	15,000	22,000
Mail Carrier	33,000	39,000	43,000
Mailroom Supervisor	13,000	24,000	32,000
Makeup Artist	16,000	22,000	29,000
Manicurist	13,000	19,000	35,000

ANNUAL EARNINGS SURVEY

Job Title	Beginning	Midlevel	Top
Marine Biologist	$ 36,000	$ 45,000	$ 54,000
Marine Engineer	19,000	39,000	72,000
Market Research Analyst	31,000	71,000	79,000
Marriage And Family Counselor	15,000	20,000	32,000
Masseur/Masseuse	15,000	24,000	32,000
Mathematician	35,000	68,000	96,000
Mayor	13,000	24,000	92,000
Meat Cutter	15,000	20,000	42,000
Mechanical Engineer	37,000	58,000	125,000
Medical Illustrator	13,000	23,000	37,000
Medical Laboratory Technician	16,000	30,000	45,000
Medical Records Technician	19,000	24,000	35,000
Medical Secretary	22,000	34,000	41,000
Medical Technologist	16,000	38,000	45,000
Mental Retardation Aide (MRA)	16,000	20,000	21,000
Merchandise Distributor	15,000	18,000	30,000
Messenger	16,000	20,000	32,000
Metallurgical Engineer	41,000	50,000	54,000
Meteorologist	22,000	63,000	225,000
Meter Reader	13,000	24,000	39,000
Microbiologist	36,000	42,000	54,000
Military (Commissioned Officer)	23,000	38,000	97,000
Military (Enlisted Person)	12,000	21,000	37,000
Military (Warrant Officer)	16,000	28,000	52,000
Millwright	22,000	43,000	59,000
Mineralogist	37,000	45,000	54,000
Mining Engineer	37,000	47,000	55,000
Minister	22,000	35,000	58,000
Motion Picture Editor	24,000	56,000	114,000
Motion Picture Projectionist	12,000	20,000	29,000
Mover	14,000	19,000	29,000
Muffler Installer	12,000	15,000	16,000
Munitions Handler	18,000	31,000	54,000
Museum Curator	27,000	55,000	64,000
Musical Instrument Repairer	18,000	32,000	49,000
Musician	3,000	54,000	128,000
Neurologist	170,000	287,000	655,000
News Writer (Radio/TV)	31,000	38,000	53,000
Newscaster	29,000	74,000	212,000
Newspaper Carrier	8,000	16,000	26,000
Newswriter (Radio/TV)	24,000	34,000	71,000
Nuclear Engineer	41,000	68,000	114,000
Nuclear Medicine Technician	36,000	44,000	54,000
Nuclear Plant Decontamination Technician	19,000	26,000	34,000
Nurse (Licensed Practical)	19,000	27,000	36,000
Nurse (Registered)	24,000	40,000	56,000
Nurse's Aide	13,000	16,000	24,000

Job Title	Beginning	Midlevel	Top
Obstetrician/Gynecologist	$ 65,000	$ 200,000	$ 655,000
Occupational Safety/Health Inspector	22,000	39,000	65,000
Occupational Therapist	37,000	52,000	59,000
Oceanographer	34,000	69,000	90,000
Office Machine Repairer	19,000	33,000	52,000
Oil Pumper	24,000	30,000	33,000
Operating Room Technician	24,000	29,000	36,000
Ophthalmic Lab Technician	18,000	23,000	30,000
Ophthalmologist	49,000	199,000	367,000
Optician	26,000	30,000	35,000
Optometrist	37,000	91,000	133,000
Orthodontist	170,000	245,000	319,000
Osteopath	56,000	95,000	170,000
Painter	12,000	22,000	36,000
Paleontologist	36,000	49,000	53,000
Paper Hanger	14,000	25,000	47,000
Paralegal Assistant	26,000	38,000	49,000
Park Naturalist	25,000	60,000	72,000
Parking Enforcement Officer	16,000	16,000	20,000
Parking Lot Attendant	12,000	14,000	22,000
Parole Officer	31,000	38,000	56,000
Pathologist	65,000	218,000	350,000
Payroll/Timekeeping Clerk	12,000	20,000	49,000
Pediatrician	47,000	211,000	373,000
Personnel Recruiter	16,000	37,000	74,000
Petroleum Engineer	47,000	90,000	114,000
Pharmacist	32,000	57,000	75,000
Philosopher	35,000	74,000	91,000
Photographer	16,000	35,000	79,000
Photographic Process Worker	13,000	25,000	35,000
Photojournalist	13,000	39,000	88,000
Physical Therapist	23,000	43,000	69,000
Physician (General Practice)	36,000	146,000	355,000
Physician Assistant	45,000	69,000	70,000
Physicist	38,000	74,000	114,000
Physiologist	22,000	41,000	78,000
Piano Tuner	18,000	32,000	49,000
Plasterer	14,000	30,000	51,000
Plumber	22,000	39,000	56,000
Podiatrist	51,000	104,000	149,000
Police Captain	29,000	36,000	47,000
Police Detective	23,000	35,000	37,000
Police Officer	26,000	47,000	68,000
Political Scientist	21,000	40,000	72,000
Pollution Control Engineer	49,000	57,000	87,000
Postal Inspector	26,000	63,000	86,000
Precision Assembler	12,000	20,000	33,000

ANNUAL EARNINGS SURVEY

Job Title	Beginning	Midlevel	Top
President (U.S.)	$ 200,000	$ 200,000	$ 200,000
Priest	10,000	14,000	38,000
Printer	20,000	32,000	44,000
Private Investigator	13,000	23,000	39,000
Producer (Movie/TV)	23,000	44,000	116,000
Professor	42,000	68,000	98,000
Proofreader	14,000	23,000	35,000
Property Manager	13,000	29,000	61,000
Prosthetist	60,000	77,000	92,000
Protestant Minister	9,000	34,000	54,000
Psychiatrist	111,000	141,000	234,000
Psychologist	22,000	56,000	90,000
Public Relations Executive	26,000	53,000	103,000
Public Safety Dispatcher	18,000	23,000	32,000
Publication Editor	24,000	53,000	71,000
Purchasing Agent	21,000	38,000	67,000
Rabbi	42,000	79,000	106,000
Race Car Driver (Indy Class)	30,000	472,000	5,550,000
Radiation Therapist	36,000	45,000	52,000
Radio/Television Announcer	13,000	20,000	31,000
Radiographer	26,000	37,000	63,000
Railroad Conductor	39,000	54,000	51,000
Real Estate Agent	14,000	36,000	80,000
Receptionist	12,000	19,000	31,000
Recreation Worker	13,000	22,000	40,000
Recreational Therapist	16,000	26,000	37,000
Reporter (Newspaper)	20,000	26,000	54,000
Respiratory Therapist	21,000	36,000	52,000
Restaurant Host/Hostess	13,000	15,000	18,000
Restaurant Manager	18,000	29,000	73,000
Roofer	12,000	21,000	42,000
Roustabout	20,000	24,000	29,000
Sales Representative (Wholesale)	19,000	41,000	79,000
Salesperson (Retail)	11,000	15,000	27,000
School Principal	37,000	74,000	69,000
Screenwriter	19,000	31,000	41,000
Script Reader	29,000	37,000	47,000
Seaman	16,000	30,000	53,000
Secretary	20,000	31,000	43,000
Security Guard	20,000	24,000	33,000
Seismologist	36,000	54,000	73,000
Set Designer	15,000	34,000	69,000
Sewage Plant Operator	18,000	31,000	43,000
Sewing Machine Operator	12,000	14,000	16,000
Sheet Metal Worker	19,000	29,000	54,000
Ship Captain	29,000	45,000	72,000
Shipping/Receiving Clerk	13,000	24,000	39,000

ANNUAL EARNINGS SURVEY

Job Title	Beginning	Midlevel	Top
Shoemaker/Repairer	$ 13,000	$ 21,000	$ 33,000
Singer	3,000	54,000	106,000
Social Worker	32,000	38,000	54,000
Sociologist	21,000	40,000	72,000
Software Engineer	43,000	53,000	88,000
Speech Pathologist	25,000	39,000	62,000
Sports Instructor	9,000	22,000	40,000
Stationary Engineer	20,000	42,000	55,000
Statistician	34,000	55,000	71,000
Stenographer/Court Reporter	15,000	27,000	44,000
Stevedore	11,000	19,000	34,000
Stock Clerk	12,000	22,000	39,000
Stockbroker	35,000	98,000	176,000
Stonemason	12,000	36,000	44,000
Store Manager	12,000	18,000	52,000
Street Cleaner	12,000	16,000	20,000
Subway Operator	39,000	45,000	50,000
Surgeon	138,000	265,000	303,000
Surveyor	26,000	39,000	54,000
Symphony Conductor	41,000	118,000	743,000
Tailor	13,000	19,000	22,000
Tax Examiner/Collector	22,000	31,000	39,000
Taxi Driver	11,000	22,000	45,000
Teacher	27,000	43,000	44,000
Teacher's Aide	13,000	22,000	24,000
Technical Writer	26,000	51,000	70,000
Telephone Installer/Repairer	20,000	40,000	57,000
Telephone Operator	12,000	21,000	32,000
Theater Director	25,000	57,000	127,000
Ticket Agent	12,000	24,000	38,000
Tool Grinder	22,000	25,000	29,000
Tool-And-Die Maker	28,000	41,000	62,000
Town Clerk	10,000	12,000	14,000
Toxicologist	41,000	70,000	127,000
Traffic Technician	15,000	24,000	32,000
Translator	13,000	20,000	29,000
Travel Agent	19,000	26,000	35,000
Travel Guide	10,000	12,000	15,000
Tree Cutter	11,000	18,000	44,000
Truant Officer	15,000	25,000	44,000
Truck Driver	22,000	36,000	48,000
Typist/Word Processor	16,000	25,000	29,000
Ultrasound Technician	33,000	45,000	49,000
Undertaker	21,000	34,000	57,000
Upholsterer	12,000	29,000	43,000
Urban/Regional Planner	27,000	54,000	74,000
Vending Machine Repairer	14,000	24,000	43,000
Veterinarian	37,000	64,000	96,000

ANNUAL EARNINGS SURVEY

Job Title	Beginning	Midlevel	Top
Vocational Counselor	$ 22,000	$ 41,000	$ 64,000
Waiter/Waitress	14,000	15,000	25,000
Watch Repairer	15,000	35,000	52,000
Web Developer	31,000	51,000	79,000
Website Manager	19,000	77,000	160,000
Welder	15,000	27,000	43,000
Woodworker	18,000	22,000	26,000
Zoologist	25,000	41,000	70,000

OCCUPATIONAL FACTS

LITERATURE AVAILABLE FROM THE FEDERAL GOVERNMENT

THIS CHAPTER CONTAINS A LIST of publications available from the federal government that are particularly relevant to the job seeker. Most of the materials, which are relatively inexpensive, are available from the U.S. Government Printing Office and may be ordered by mail. For ordering information, contact: U.S. Government Printing Office, 945 N. Capital St. Washington, DC 20401; 202-512-1993, 202-783-3238 (for orders). Many of the publications listed below may be found at local libraries as well.

Some materials are also available at regional U.S. Government Printing Offices. However, their inventory is not always complete, so call first to verify what is on hand. Here are the telephone numbers of GPO branches outside of Washington, DC:

Atlanta, GA	404-347-1900	Kansas City, MO	816-767-8225
Birmingham, AL	205-731-1056	Los Angeles, CA	213-239-9844
Boston, MA	617-720-4180	Milwaukee, WI	414-297-1304
Chicago, IL	312-353-5133	New York, NY	212-264-3825
Cleveland, OH	216-522-4922	Philadelphia, PA	215-636-1900
Columbus, OH	614-469-6956	Pittsburgh, PA	412-644-2721
Dallas, TX	214-767-0076	Portland, OR	503-221-6217
Denver, CO	303-844-3964	Pueblo, CO	719-544-3142
Detroit, MI	313-226-7816	San Francisco, CA	415-512-2770
Houston, TX	713-228-1187	Seattle, WA	206-553-4271
Jacksonville, FL	904-353-0569		

AMERICAN WORK FORCE: 1992–2005
Provides Bureau of Labor Statistics employment projections for the year 2005.
Price: $9.50.
Published: 1994.

AMERICANS WITH DISABILITIES ACT TECHNICAL ASSISTANCE MANUAL
Gives a general overview of the Americans With Disabilities Act, which ensures equal employment, accommodation in public places, and access to government services for those with disabilities.
Price: $24.00/$25.00 (Title II/Title III).
Published: 1997.

AREA TRENDS IN EMPLOYMENT AND UNEMPLOYMENT
Lists eligible labor surplus areas in which employers are given preference in bid ding on federal procurement contracts.
Price: $5.00 per issue.
Published: Monthly.

CAREER GUIDE TO INDUSTRIES
Examines the state of American industries.
Price: $12.00.
Published: 199.

COLLEGE LABOR MARKET: OUTLOOK, CURRENT SITUATION, AND EARNINGS
Contains four articles from the Summer 1992 issue of the *Occupational Outlook Quarterly* especially pertinent to the college student or recent graduate.
Price: $1.75.
Published: 1992.

DICTIONARY OF OCCUPATIONAL TITLES
Defines and indexes over 20,000 jobs.
Price: $40.00 for two books.
Published: 1991.

DIRECTORY OF CULTURAL RESOURCE EDUCATION PROGRAMS AT COLLEGES, UNIVERSITIES, CRAFT AND TRADE SCHOOLS IN THE UNITED STATES, 1994–1995

Contains information about training or education programs pertaining to the preservation and management of cultural resources and cultural heritage in the United States.
Price: $6.50.
Published: 1994.

DIRECTORY OF NONTRADITIONAL TRAINING AND EMPLOYMENT PROGRAMS SERVING WOMEN

Contains information on 125 programs and services for women seeking jobs in trades and technology.
Price: $9.00.
Published: 1991.

EMPLOYMENT AND EARNINGS

Contains up-to-date data on employment, hours, and earnings for the United States, individual states, and more than 200 local areas.
Price: $14.00 per issue.
Published: Monthly.

FEDERAL STAFFING DIGEST

Describes current activities and programs in the areas of job recruiting, college recruiting, and affirmative action employment.
Price: $2.50 per issue.
Published: Quarterly.

HOW TO FILE A CLAIM FOR YOUR BENEFITS

Contains information on what to do if your health, disability, or severance benefits are denied. Also discusses the law, waiting periods, and other information.
Price: 50 cents.
Published: 1991.

IS THERE ANOTHER DEGREE IN YOUR FUTURE?

Explores how to choose a graduate school.
Price: $1.50
Published: 1994.

JOB OUTLOOK IN BRIEF, 1990–2005

Contains brief sketches of employment data for each of the occupations listed in the *Occupational Outlook Handbook*.
Price: $2.25.
Published: 1994.

JOB PATTERNS FOR MINORITIES AND WOMEN IN PRIVATE INDUSTRY

Contains statistics and tables.
Price: $30.00.
Published: Annually.

JOB SEARCH GUIDE: STRATEGIES FOR PROFESSIONALS

Contains material on job searching, handling job loss, career self-assessment, researching the job market, networking, and other areas of job prospecting.
Price: $5.50.
Published: 1993.

MILITARY CAREERS

Provides information about career opportunities in the military, from job descriptions to advancement prospects.
Price: $30.00.
Published: 1998.

MONTHLY LABOR REVIEW

Provides information on economic develop-ments, labor-management relations, business conditions, and social trends.
Price: $7.00 per issue.
Published: Monthly.

NEW TEACHERS IN THE JOB MARKET— 1991 UPDATE, CONTRACTOR REPORT

Contains a summary of findings from the Recent College Graduates study and focuses on the makeup of the teaching force.
Price: $6.00.
Published: 1993.

OCCUPATIONAL AND EDUCATIONAL OUTCOMES OF RECENT COLLEGE GRADUATES 1 YEAR AFTER GRADUATION, 1991

A progress report on students with bachelor's degrees.
Price: $6.00.
Published: 1993.

OCCUPATIONAL OUTLOOK HANDBOOK

Describes, in extensive detail, approximately 250 career fields and hundreds of

jobs related to them.
Price: $32.00.
Published: 1996-97.

OCCUPATIONAL OUTLOOK QUARTERLY

This magazinelike publication contains current information on various aspects of the work force and the job market.
Price: $9.50 per annual subscription; $3.00 per issue.
Published: Quarterly.

PIPELINES OF PROGRESS: AN UPDATE ON THE GLASS CEILING INITIATIVE

A report on what is taking place in America to ensure that artificial barriers to career
advancement are broken down.
Price: $3.25.
Published: 1992.

PROFESSIONAL WORKERS AS LEARNERS: THE SCOPE, PROBLEM, AND ACCOUNT-ABILITY OF CONTINUING PROFESSIONAL EDUCATION IN THE 1990'S

Contains seven essays about continuing education for professionals.
Price: $14.00.
Published: 1992.

RESUMES, APPLICATION FORMS, COVER LETTERS, AND INTERVIEWS

Contains information on job search strategies.
Price: $1.00.
Published: 1995.

STAY-IN-SCHOOL PROGRAM: THE FEDERAL GOVERNMENT IN PARTNERSHIP WITH EDUCATION

Provides information about federal employment for high school students who have a financial need or disability.
Price: $10.00.
Published: 1992.

TOMORROW'S JOBS

Provides projections of the labor force, economic growth, industry output and employment, and occupational employment to the year 2005. Also contains information on career training.
Price: $1.25.
Published: 1994.

UNITED STATES GOVERNMENT POLICY AND SUPPORTING POSITIONS

Contains information on 9,000 federal civil service leadership and support positions in the legislative and executive branches.
Price: $14.00.
Published: 1992.

WE'VE GOT THE WHOLE WORLD IN OUR HANDS: ENVIRONMENTAL CAREERS

Contains information on environmental jobs.
Price: $1.25.
Published: 1994.

WORKER TRAINING: COMPETING IN THE NEW INTERNATIONAL ECONOMY

Focuses on the training given in the workplace to employed workers.
Price: $13.00.
Published: 1990.

WORKING FOR AMERICA WORKS FOR YOU: A GUIDE TO FEDERAL CAREERS IN WASHINGTON, DC

Covers the whole spectrum of job hunting on Capitol Hill.
Price: $31.00.
Published: 1992.

WORKING FOR THE UNITED STATES IN THE 1990'S

A great resource for those seeking employment in the federal government. Tells where to find vacancies and how to apply.
Price: $2.00.
Published: 1995.

OCCUPATIONAL FACTS

Professional Magazines/Journals

THIS CHAPTER CONTAINS A LISTING OF MAGAZINES AND JOURNALS that cover or concern specific professions and occupations. Perusing trade or specialty publications is one of the best ways to stay up-to-date on a specific field. These magazines and journals often contain company profiles and industry overviews that are ideal for providing job hunters with information about an industry's primary and secondary players. These publications also examine cutting-edge business developments and make forecasts about the repercussions of mergers, downsizings, and expansions going on within particular sectors of commerce.

Aside from covering current business activities within specific fields, magazines and trade journals also introduce job hunters to the contours of an industry. In other words, they may serve as a reference for contacts or as a valuable tool in determining which companies are hiring or which, by contrast, are experiencing difficult financial times.

Note that many magazines and journals often contain at least a few job listings or potential networking sources in each issue. In the listings here, if a publication has an extensive help wanted section, such information has been noted.

Numerous occupational fields are represented in this chapter and are given in the Industry List below. Cross-references indicate where you may find additional magazines pertaining to your interests. For instance, magazines aimed at engineers will certainly be found in the "Engineering" section, but there also may be magazines of interest to engineers in other fields, such as "Aerospace" or "Technology."

Job seekers looking for jobs in specific fields should also be aware that most industries hire individuals in many occupational fields. For example, most companies in the aviation industry hire accountants. Thus, those looking for jobs in accounting may find valuable information—a help wanted ad, for example—in an aviation magazine. Similarly, job seekers who want advertising jobs may find listings for advertising jobs or other useful information in magazines that serve industries other than advertising. In other words, keep an open mind, and check a few industry magazines that may not be specifically targeted to the career field in which you wish to work.

Other chapters in this book may also help you. ➥**See "Professional Associations," pp. 644-655; "U.S. Employers," pp. 158-378; and "Industry Overviews," pp. 395-409.**

INDUSTRY LIST

ACCOUNTING (*Also see:* Finance)
ADVERTISING (*Also see:* Consumer Products, Marketing, Public Relations, Retail, Sales)
AEROSPACE (*Also see:* Aviation, Engineering)
AGRICULTURE
ARCHITECTURE (*Also see:* Construction)
ARTS (*Also see:* Broadcasting, Design, Entertainment, Fashion)
AUTOMOTIVE

AVIATION (*Also see:* Aerospace, Engineering)
BROADCASTING (*Also see:* Arts, Entertainment)
CONSTRUCTION (*Also see:* Architecture)
CONSUMER PRODUCTS (*Also see:* Advertising, Fashion, Food and Beverages, Hospitality, Retail, Sales)
DESIGN (*Also see:* Arts, Fashion)
EDUCATION (*Also see:* Library Science)

ENGINEERING (*Also see:* Aerospace, Aviation, Science, Technology)
ENTERTAINMENT (*Also see:* Arts, Broadcasting, Fashion)
FASHION (*Also see:* Arts, Consumer Products, Design, Entertainment)
FINANCE (*Also see:* Accounting)
FOOD AND BEVERAGES (*Also see:* Consumer Products, Hospitality)
FOREST/PAPER PRODUCTS
GOVERNMENT (*Also see:* Social Services)
HEALTH SERVICES
HOSPITALITY (*Also see:* Consumer Products, Food and Beverages)
INSURANCE
INTERNATIONAL EMPLOYMENT
LAW
LIBRARY SCIENCE (*Also see:* Education)
MANAGEMENT
MARKETING (*Also see:* Advertising, Public Relations, Sales)
NATURAL RESOURCES (*Also see:* Petroleum, Utilities)

PETROLEUM (*Also see:* Natural Resources, Utilities)
PLASTICS
PUBLIC RELATIONS (*Also see:* Advertising, Marketing, Sales)
PUBLISHING
RETAIL (*Also see:* Advertising, Consumer Products, Sales)
SALES (*Also see:* Advertising, Consumer Products, Marketing, Public Relations, Retail)
SCIENCE (*Also see:* Engineering, Technology)
SECRETARIAL
SOCIAL SERVICES (*Also see:* Government)
TECHNOLOGY (*Also see:* Engineering, Science, Telecommunications)
TELECOMMUNICATIONS (*Also see:* Technology)
TRANSPORTATION
TRAVEL
UTILITIES (*Also see:* Natural Resources, Petroleum)
WASTE MANAGEMENT

❶ A C C O U N T I N G

ACCOUNTING TODAY
425 Park Ave., New York, NY 10022; 212-756-5155
Additional Information: Biweekly.

THE CALIFORNIA CPA QUARTERLY
California Society of CPAs, 275 Shoreline Dr., Redwood City, CA 94065; 415-802-2600
Additional Information: Quarterly.

CPA JOURNAL
530 Fifth Ave., New York, NY 10036; 212-719-8300
Additional Information: Monthly.

FLORIDA CPA TODAY
Florida Institute of CPAs, P.O. Box 5437, 325 W. College Ave., Tallahassee, FL 32314; 904-224-2727
Additional Information: Monthly.

INTERNAL AUDITOR
P.O. Box 140099, Orlando, FL 32889; 407-830-7600
Additional Information: Bimonthly; available to Internal Auditor members.

JOURNAL OF ACCOUNTANCY
Harborside Financial Ctr., 201 Plaza 3, Jersey City, NJ 07311; 201-938-3000
Additional Information: Monthly; contains extensive job listings.

MANAGEMENT ACCOUNTING
Institute of Management Accountants, P.O. Box 433, 10 Paragon Dr., Montvale, NJ 07645; 201-573-9000
Additional Information: Monthly.

NATIONAL PUBLIC ACCOUNTANT
National Society of Pubic Accountants, 1010 N. Fairfax St., Alexandria, VA 22314; 703-549-6400
Additional Information: Monthly.

THE PRACTICAL ACCOUNTANT
11 Penn Plaza, New York, NY 10001; 800-535-8403
Additional Information: Monthly.

❶ A D V E R T I S I N G

ADVERTISING AGE'S CREATIVITY
220 E. 42nd St., New York, NY 10017; 212-210-0280
Additional Information: Weekly; good help wanted section and industry overviews.

ADWEEK
1515 Broadway, New York, NY 10036; 212-764-7300
Additional Information: Weekly; good help wanted section and industry coverage.

COMMUNICATION ARTS
410 Sherman Ave., P.O. Box 10300, Palo Alto, CA 94303; 415-326-6040
Additional Information: Eight issues per year; displays the finest advertising art.

❶ AEROSPACE

AEROSPACE AMERICA
370 L'Enfant Promenade SW, Washington, DC 20024; 202-646-7471
Additional Information: Daily; newsletter sent to government officials and aerospace executives.

AVIATION WEEK AND SPACE TECHNOLOGY
1221 Ave. of the Americas, New York, NY 10020; 212-512-2793
Additional Information: Weekly; covers the entire industry.

DEFENSE NEWS AND SPACE NEWS
6883 Commercial Dr., Springfield, VA 22159; 800-424-9335
Additional Information: Weekly.

❶ AGRICULTURE

AG CONSULTANT
37733 Euclid Ave., Willoughby, OH 44094; 216-942-2000
Additional Information: Nine issues per year; geared toward agriculture professionals.

AGRI FINANCE
6201 W. Howard, Niles, IL 60648; 847-647-1200
Additional Information: Nine issues per year; covers the financial aspects of agriculture.

FEED MANAGEMENT
122 S. Wesley Ave., Mt. Morris, IL 61054; 815-734-4171
Additional Information: Monthly; aimed at feed industry professionals.

CORN FARMER
1716 Locust St., Des Moines, IA 50336; 515-284-3000
Additional Information: Monthly; extensive industry overviews.

❶ ARCHITECTURE

ARCHITECTURAL RECORD
P.O. Box 564, Hightstown, NJ 08520; 800-257-9402
Additional Information: Monthly; contains extensive job listings.

PROGRESSIVE ARCHITECTURE
P.O. Box 1361, 600 Summer St., Stamford, CT 06904; 203-348-7531
Additional Information: Monthly; contains extensive job listings.

❶ ARTS

AMERICAN ARTIST
1515 Broadway, New York, NY 10036; 212-764-7300
Additional Information: Monthly.

ART SEARCH
Theatre Communications Group, 355 Lexington Ave., New York, NY 10017; 212-697-5230
Additional Information: Bimonthly; contains job listings for a variety of arts careers.

ARTFORUM
65 Bleecker St., New York, NY 10012; 212-475-4000
Additional Information: Ten issues per year.

ARTWEEK
2149 Paragon Dr., Suite 100, San Jose, CA 95131; 408-441-7065
Additional Information: Weekly.

PROFESSIONAL PHOTOGRAPHER
57 Forsyth St., Suite 1600, Atlanta, GA 30303; 404-522-8600
Additional Information: Monthly; publication of the Professional Photographers of America.

❶ AUTOMOTIVE

WARD'S AUTO WORLD
3000 Town Center, Suite 2750, Southfield, MI 48075; 810-357-0800

Additional Information: Monthly; aimed at dealership owners, managers, and suppliers.

AUTOMOTIVE EXECUTIVE
National Auto Dealers Association, 8400 Westpark Dr., McLean, VA 22102; 703-821-7150
Additional Information: Monthly; sent to NADA members.

AUTOMOTIVE INDUSTRIES
2600 Fisher Bldg., Detroit, MI 48202; 313-875-2090
Additional Information: Monthly; aimed at design, manufacturing, management, and sales professionals.

AUTOMOTIVE MARKETING
Chilton Way, Radnor, PA 19089; 610-964-4395
Additional Information: Monthly; aimed at parts retailers and manufacturers.

AUTOMOTIVE NEWS
1400 Woodbridge Ave., Detroit, MI 48207; 313-446-6000
Additional Information: Weekly; extensive industry coverage and good help wanted section.

❶AVIATION

AIR CARGO NEWS
P.O. Box 777, Jamaica, NY 11431; 718-476-5250
Additional Information: Monthly.

AIRLINE PILOT
P.O. Box 1169, Herndon, VA 22070; 703-689-4176
Additional Information: Monthly; magazine for Air Line Pilots Association members.

AIRPORT PRESS
P.O. Box 879, Jamaica, NY 11430; 718-244-6788
Additional Information: Monthly.

AVIATION EMPLOYMENT MONTHLY
Box 8286, Saddle Brook, NJ 07662; 800-543-5201
Additional Information: Monthly; contains listings of international positions for aviation personnel.

BUSINESS AND COMMERCIAL AVIATION
4 International Dr., Rye Brook, NY 10573; 914-939-0300
Additional Information: Monthly.

PROFESSIONAL PILOT
3014 Colvin St., Alexandria, VA 22314; 703-370-0606
Additional Information: Monthly.

❶BROADCASTING

BROADCASTING & CABLE
1705 DeSales St., NW, Washington, DC 20036; 202-859-2340
Additional Information: Weekly; geared toward network and station staffs; contains good help wanted section.

ELECTRONIC MEDIA
740 N. Rush St., Chicago, IL 60611; 312-649-5350
Additional Information: Weekly; covers all areas of the broadcast industry.

TELEVISION BROADCAST
460 Park Ave. S, 9th Floor, New York, NY 10016; 212-378-0400
Additional Information: Monthly; aimed at media production, management, and engi-neering personnel.

VIDEO WEEK
Television Digest, Inc., 2115 Ward Ct., NW, Washington, DC 20037; 202-872-9200
Additional Information: Weekly; provides industry coverage.

❶CONSTRUCTION

BUILDING DESIGN AND CONSTRUCTION
P.O. Box 5080, Des Plaines, IL 60017; 847-635-8800
Additional Information: Monthly; aimed at building designers, developers, and contractors.

BUILDINGS
P.O. Box 1888, Cedar Rapids, IA 52406; 319-364-6167
Additional Information: Monthly; aimed at industry professionals.

HIGHWAY AND HEAVY CONSTRUCTION
P.O. Box 5080, Des Plaines, IL 60017; 847-635-8800
Additional Information: Monthly.

PROFESSIONAL BUILDER/REMODELER
1350 E. Touhy, Des Plaines, IL 60017; 847-635-8800
Additional Information: Eighteen issues per year.

---

❶ CONSUMER PRODUCTS

APPLIANCE
1110 Jorie Blvd., Oak Brook, IL 60522; 630-990-3484
Additional Information: Monthly.

APPLIANCE MANUFACTURER
5900 Harper Rd., Suite 105, Solon, OH 44139; 216-349-3060
Additional Information: Monthly.

COSMETIC INSIDERS REPORT
7500 Old Oak Blvd., Cleveland, OH 44130; 216-243-8100
Additional Information: Bimonthly.

DRUG AND COSMETIC INDUSTRY
270 Madison Ave., New York NY 10016; 212-891-2689
Additional Information: Monthly; aimed at manufacturers and merchandisers.

HOUSEHOLD AND PERSONAL PRODUCTS INDUSTRY
Box 555, Ramsey, NJ 07446; 201-825-2552
Additional Information: Monthly; deals with the soap, detergent, cosmetics, toiletries, and fragrance industries; contains many employment opportunities.

PRODUCT DESIGN AND DEVELOPMENT
Chilton Way, Radnor, PA 19089; 610-964-4000
Additional Information: Monthly.

SOAP/COSMETICS/CHEMICAL SPECIALTIES
445 Broad Hollow Rd., Melville, NY 11747; 516-845-2700
Additional Information: Monthly.

---

❶ DESIGN

AMERICAN INSTITUTE OF GRAPHIC ARTS JOURNAL
164 Fifth Ave., New York, NY 10010; 212-807-1990
Additional Information: Quarterly; contains news and calendar events.

COMPUTER GRAPHICS WORLD
10 Tara Blvd., 5th Floor, Nashua, NH 03062; 603-891-0123
Additional Information: Monthly.

DESIGN NEWS
275 Washington St., Newton, MA 02158; 617-964-3030
Additional Information: Semimonthly; covers design engineering.

GRAPHIC ARTS MONTHLY
245 W. 17th St., New York, NY 10011; 212-463-6835
Additional Information: Monthly; focuses on advertising art.

GRAPHIC DESIGN: USA
1556 Third Ave., Suite 405, New York, NY 10128; 212-534-5500
Additional Information: Monthly.

INTERIOR DESIGN
275 Washington St., Newton, MA 02158; 617-964-3030
Additional Information: Monthly.

---

❶ EDUCATION

AMERICAN EDUCATORS
555 New Jersey Ave., NW, Washington, DC 20001; 202-879-4420
Additional Information: Quarterly.

AMERICAN SCHOOL AND UNIVERSITY
9800 Metcalf, Overland Park, KS 66212; 913-341-1300
Additional Information: Monthly; aimed at school administrators.

AMERICAN TEACHER
555 New Jersey Ave., NW, Washington, DC 20001; 202-879-4400
Additional Information: Monthly.

CHANGE: THE MAGAZINE OF HIGHER LEARNING
1319 18th St., NW, Washington, DC 20036; 202-362-6445
Additional Information: Bimonthly.

CHRONICLE OF HIGHER EDUCATION
1255 23rd St., NW, Washington, DC 20037; 202-466-1000
Additional Information: Monthly; aimed at college faculty and administrators; good job listings section.

EDUCATION WEEK
4301 Connecticut Ave., NW, Suite 432, Washington, DC 20008; 202- 606-0800
Additional Information: Weekly; aimed at elementary and secondary educators.

EDUCATIONAL LEADERSHIP
1250 N. Pitt, Alexandria, VA 22314; 703-549-9110
Additional Information: Eight issues per year; aimed at supervisors.

INSTRUCTOR
555 Broadway, New York, NY 10012; 212-505-4900
Additional Information: Monthly; aimed at elementary education teachers.

LEARNING
P.O. Box 9753, Greensboro, NC 27429; 910-854-0309
Additional Information: Bimonthly.

TEACHER
4301 Connecticut Ave., NW, Suite 432, Washington, DC 20008; 202-686-0800
Additional Information: Monthly.

❶ E N G I N E E R I N G

AEROSPACE ENGINEERING
400 Commonwealth Dr., Warrenville, PA 15096; 412-772-7114
Additional Information: Monthly.

CHEMICAL AND ENGINEERING NEWS
1155 16th St. NW, Washington, DC 20036; 202-872-4572
Additional Information: Weekly; contains industry roundups and extensive job listings.

CIVIL ENGINEERING
345 E. 47th St., New York, NY 10017; 212-705-7514
Additional Information: Monthly; contains extensive job listings.

ELECTRIC ENGINEERING TIMES
600 Community Dr., Manhasset, NY 10022; 516-562-5000
Additional Information: Weekly.

ENGINEERING NEWS-RECORD
1221 Ave. of the Americas, New York, NY 10020; 800-512-2793
Additional Information: Weekly; contains good help wanted section.

ENGINEERING TIMES
1420 King St., Alexandria, VA 22314; 703-684-2875
Additional Information: Monthly; contains career resources and general information.

ENVIRONMENT TODAY
1483 Chain Bridge Rd., McLean, VA 22101; 703-448-0336
Additional Information: Eight issues per year; aimed at environmental engineers.

IEEE SPECTRUM
P.O. Box 1331, Piscataway, NJ 08855; 908-981-9334
Additional Information: Monthly; contains extensive job listings; publication of the Institute of Electrical and Electronics Engineers.

MECHANICAL ENGINEERING
345 E. 47th St., New York, NY 10017; 212-705-7782
Additional Information: Monthly; contains extensive job listings.

PLANT ENGINEERING
P.O.Box 5080, Des Plaines, IL 60017; 847-635-8800
Additional Information: Sixteen issues per year.

POLLUTION ENGINEERING
P.O. Box 5080, Des Plaines, IL 60017; 847-635-8800
Additional Information: Monthly.

❶ E N T E R T A I N M E N T

AMERICAN CINEMATOGRAPHER
1782 N. Orange Dr., Los Angeles, CA 90028; 213-876-5080
Additional Information: Monthly.

BACK STAGE/SHOOT
1515 Broadway, New York, NY 10036; 212-764-7300
Additional Information: Weekly; newspaper covering all areas of the entertainment and commercial production fields.

BILLBOARD
1515 Broadway, New York, NY 10036; 800-669-1002
Additional Information: Weekly; covers the music production industry.

BOX OFFICE
6640 Sunset Blvd., Suite 100, Los Angeles, CA 90028; 213-465-1186
Additional Information: Monthly; geared toward theater professionals and film production and distribution personnel.

CASH BOX
6464 Sunset, Suite 605, Hollywood, CA 90028
Additional Information: Weekly; aimed at music industry professionals.

DAILY VARIETY
5700 Wilshire Blvd., Los Angeles, CA 90036; 213-857-6600
Additional Information: Daily; covers the film and television production industry.

DANCE MAGAZINE
33 W. 60th St., New York, NY 10029; 212-245-9050
Additional Information: Monthly.

DRAMA-LOGUE
P.O. Box 38771, Los Angeles, CA 90038; 213-464-5079
Additional Information: Weekly; contains extensive entertainment job listings on the West Coast.

FILM JOURNAL
244 W. 49th St., New York, NY 10019; 212-246-6460
Additional Information: Monthly.

HOLLYWOOD REPORTER
5055 Wilshire Blvd., Los Angeles, CA 50036; 213-525-2000
Additional Information: Daily; provides extensive coverage of the Hollywood production community.

SCREEN
16 W. Erie St., Chicago, IL 60610; 312-664-5236
Additional Information: Weekly; covers all aspects of Chicago's production scene; contains good help wanted section.

VARIETY
249 W. 17th St., New York, NY 10011; ; 212-237-6900
Additional Information: Weekly.

❷ FASHION

BOBBIN
P.O. Box 1986, Columbia, SC 29202; 803-771-7500
Additional Information: Monthly; aimed at industry executives.

CALIFORNIA APPAREL NEWS
110 E. Ninth St., Los Angeles, CA 90079; 213-627-3737
Additional Information: Weekly; covers the California fashion industry.

DAILY NEWS RECORD
7 W. 34th St., New York, NY 10001; 212-630-4000
Additional Information: Daily; newspaper for apparel manufacturers, buyers, retailers, and wholesalers.

FOOTWEAR NEWS
7 W. 34th St., New York, NY 10001; 212-630-4230
Additional Information: Weekly; aimed at footwear designers, marketers, buyers, and suppliers.

WOMEN'S WEAR DAILY
7 W. 34th St., New York, NY 10001; 212-630-4230
Additional Information: Daily; covers all aspects of the women's clothing industry.

❸ FINANCE

ABA BANKING JOURNAL
345 Hudson St., New York, NY 10014; 212-620-7200
Additional Information: Monthly; aimed at upper-level banking professionals; publication of the American Banking Association.

AMERICAN BANKER
1 State St. Plaza, New York, NY 10004; 212-943-6700
Additional Information: Daily; newspaper aimed at senior-level executives; contains good employment section.

BARRON'S NATIONAL BUSINESS AND FINANCIAL WEEKLY
200 Liberty St., New York, NY 10281; 212-416-2700
Additional Information: Weekly; news-

paper aimed at finance executives and investors.

FE/FINANCIAL EXECUTIVE

P.O. Box 1938, Morristown, NJ 07962; 201-898-4621
Additional Information: Bimonthly; aimed at finance executives.

FINANCIAL SERVICES REPORT

7811 Montrose Rd., Potomac, MD 20854; 301-340-2100
Additional Information: Monthly.

FINANCIAL WORLD

1328 Broadway, New York, NY 10001; 212-594-5030
Additional Information: Monthly; geared toward options and commodity traders.

INC.

38 Commercial Wharf, Boston, MA 02110; 617-248-8000
Additional Information: Monthly; contains information on frequently hiring companies.

INSTITUTIONAL INVESTOR

488 Madison Ave., New York, NY 10022; 212-303-3300
Additional Information: Monthly; geared toward investment industry professionals.

JOURNAL OF COMMERCE

2 World Trade Ctr., New York, NY 10048; 212-837-7000
Additional Information: Daily; covers the business world.

PENSIONS & INVESTMENTS AGE

220 E. 42nd St., New York, NY 10007; 212-210-0100
Additional Information: Biweekly; newspaper aimed at pension plan professionals.

❶ FOOD AND BEVERAGES

BEVERAGE WORLD

150 Great Neck Rd., Great Neck, NY 11021; 516-829-9210
Additional Information: Monthly; aimed at industry executives; publishes annual profile of leading companies.

CONVENIENCE STORE NEWS

233 Park Ave. S, New York, NY 10003; 212-979-4100
Additional Information: Sixteen issues per year; aimed at executives, suppliers, and distributors.

FOOD BUSINESS

301 E. Erie St., Chicago, IL 60611; 312-644-2020
Additional Information: Monthly; provides extensive industry coverage.

FOOD ENGINEERING

Chilton Way, Radnor, PA 19089; 610-964-4448
Additional Information: Monthly; aimed at food industry personnel.

FROZEN FOOD DIGEST MAGAZINE

271 Madison Ave., New York, NY 10016; 212-557-8600
Additional Information: Quarterly.

HEALTH FOODS BUSINESS

445 Broad Hollow Rd., Melville, NY 11747; 516-845-2700
Additional Information: Monthly.

MEAT PROCESSING

122 S. Wesley Ave., Mt. Morris, IL 61054; 815-734-4171
Additional Information: Monthly.

NATURAL FOODS AND MERCHANDISER

1301 Spruce St., Boulder, CO 80302; 303-939-8440
Additional Information: Monthly.

SUPERMARKET NEWS

7 W. 34th St., New York, NY 10001; 800-247-2160
Additional Information: Weekly; aimed at food store operators.

❶ FOREST/PAPER PRODUCTS

WOOD TECHNOLOGY

600 Harrison St., San Francisco, CA 94104; 415-905-2200
Additional Information: Monthly.

PULP & PAPER FORECASTER

600 Harrison St., San Francisco, CA 94107; 415-905-2200
Additional Information: Monthly; aimed at industry managers, technicians, and supervisors.

❶ GOVERNMENT

FEDERAL CAREER OPPORTUNITIES
P.O. Box 1059, Vienna, VA 22183; 703-281-0200
Additional Information: Semiweekly; contains extensive job listings.

FEDERAL JOBS DIGEST
325 Pennsylvania Ave., SE, Washington, DC 20003; 800-824-5000
Additional Information: Bimonthly; contains extensive job listings with grade and salary information.

JOBS AVAILABLE
P.O. Box 1040, Modesto, CA 95353; 209-571-2120
Additional Information: Semiweekly; contains listings for public administration and research jobs.

THE NATIONAL JOURNAL
1501 M St., NW, Suite 300, Washington, DC 20005; 800-424-2921
Additional Information: Weekly; provides extensive coverage of government affairs.

PUBLIC EMPLOYEE
1625 L St., NW, Washington, DC 20036; 202-429-1144
Additional Information: Bimonthly; contains information about government employment.

PUBLIC SECTOR JOB BULLETIN
P.O. Box 1222, Newton, IA 50208; 515-791-9019
Additional Information: Biweekly; lists public sector jobs.

❷ HEALTH SERVICES

AMERICAN JOURNAL OF HOSPITAL PHARMACY
7272 Wisconsin Ave., Bethesda, MD 20814; 301-657-3000
Additional Information: Monthly; contains extensive job listings.

AMERICAN JOURNAL OF NURSING
555 W. 57th St., New York, NY 10019; 212-582-8820
Additional Information: Monthly; for American Nursing Association members.

AMERICAN NURSE
600 Maryland Ave. SW, Suite 100W, Washington, DC 20024; 202-651-7026
Additional Information: Monthly; aimed at registered nurses.

AMERICAN PHARMACY
2215 Constitution Ave., NW, Washington, DC 20037; 202-429-7519
Additional Information: Monthly.

BIOMEDICAL PRODUCTS
Box 650, Morris Plains, NJ 07950; 201-292-5100
Additional Information: Monthly; aimed at professionals involved in biopharmaceutical research and development.

BIOTECHNIQUES
154 E. Central St., Natick, MA 01760; 508-655-8282
Additional Information: Monthly; aimed at bioresearchers.

CONTEMPORARY LONG TERM CARE
355 Park Ave. S., New York, NY 10010; 212-592-6200
Additional Information: Monthly.

DENTAL ASSISTANT
919 N. Michigan Ave., Chicago, IL 60611; 312-541-1550
Additional Information: Bimonthly.

DVM: THE NEWSMAGAZINE OF VETERINARY MEDICINE
101 Fieldcrest Ave., Edison, NJ 08837; 908-225-9500
Additional Information: Monthly; contains job listings for doctors of veterinary medicine.

EMERGENCY: THE JOURNAL OF EMERGENCY SERVICES
6300 Yarrow Dr., Carlsbad, CA 92009; 619-438-2511
Additional Information: Monthly; aimed at EMTs (emergency medical technicians) and paramedics.

HEALTH FACILITIES MANAGEMENT
737 N. Michigan Ave., Chicago, IL 60611; 312-440-6800
Additional Information: Monthly; aimed at managers of health facilities.

HEALTHCARE EXECUTIVE
840 N. Lake Shore Dr., Chicago, IL 60611; 312-943-0544
Additional Information: Bimonthly.

JAMA (JOURNAL OF THE AMERICAN MEDICAL ASSOCIATION)
515 N. State St., Chicago, IL 60611; 312-464-5000
Additional Information: Weekly; publication of the American Medical Association.

JOURNAL OF THE AMERICAN DENTAL ASSOCIATION
211 E. Chicago Ave., Chicago, IL 60611; 312-440-2736
Additional Information: Nine issues per year; aimed at ADA professionals; contains extensive job listings.

JOURNAL OF DENTAL HYGIENE
444 N. Michigan Ave., Chicago, IL 60611; 312-440-8900
Additional Information: Nine issues per year.

LONG-TERM CARE NEWS
2 Northfield Plaza, Suite 300, Northfield, IL 60093; 847-441-3700
Additional Information: Monthly; aimed at nursing home professionals.

MODERN HEALTHCARE
740 Rush St., Chicago, IL 60606; 312-649-5341
Additional Information: Biweekly; aimed at health care professionals.

NEW ENGLAND JOURNAL OF MEDICINE
10 Shattuck St., Boston, MA 02115; 617-734-9800
Additional Information: Weekly.

NURSING MANAGEMENT
P.O. Box 908, Spring House, PA 19477; 215-646-8700
Additional Information: Monthly; aimed at nurse supervisors.

NURSINGWORLD JOURNAL
470 Boston Post Rd., Weston, MA 02193; 617-899-2702
Additional Information: Monthly.

PHARMACEUTICAL PROCESSING
Box 650, Morris Plains, NJ 07950; 201-292-5100
Additional Information: Monthly; aimed at the pharmaceutical production industry.

PHARMACEUTICAL TECHNOLOGY
Box 10460, Eugene, OR 97401; 541-343-1200
Additional Information: Monthly.

---

❶ HOSPITALITY

CORNELL HOTEL AND RESTAURANT ADMINISTRATION QUARTERLY
Cornell University School of Hotel Administration, 327 Statler Hall, Ithaca, NY 14853; 607-255-5093
Additional Information: Quarterly.

HOTEL
1350 E. Touhy Ave., Des Plaines, IL 60018; 847-635-8800
Additional Information: Monthly; aimed at executives, management firms, and developers.

HOTEL AND MOTEL MANAGEMENT
7500 Old Oak Blvd., Cleveland, OH 44130; 216-243-8100
Additional Information: Twenty-one issues per year.

LODGING HOSPITALITY
1100 E. Superior Ave., Cleveland, OH 44114; 216-696-7000
Additional Information: Monthly; aimed at lodging and food service management specialists.

RESTAURANT BUSINESS
355 Park Ave. S., New York, NY 10010; 212-592-6500
Additional Information: Eighteen issues per year; aimed at food service executives, manufacturers, and distributors.

RESTAURANT HOSPITALITY
1100 E. Superior Ave., Cleveland, OH 44114; 216-696-7000
Additional Information: Monthly; geared primarily toward table-service restaurant owners and managers.

RESTAURANTS AND INSTITUTIONS
1350 E. Touhy Ave., Des Plaines, IL 60618; 847-635-8800
Additional Information: Biweekly; aimed at industry managers.

VACATION INDUSTRY REVIEW
6262 Sunset Dr., Penthouse I, Miami, FL 33143; 305-667-0202
Additional Information: Quarterly.

❶ I N S U R A N C E

AMERICAN AGENT AND BROKER
330 N. Fourth St., St. Louis, MO 63102; 314-421-5445
Additional Information: Monthly; aimed at insurance agents, brokers, and adjusters.

BEST'S REVIEW
Ambest Rd., Oldwick, NJ 08858; 908-439-2200
Additional Information: Monthly; aimed at insurance executives; contains extensive employment opportunities.

BUSINESS INSURANCE
740 Rush St., Chicago, IL 60611; 312-649-5200
Additional Information: Weekly.

NATIONAL UNDERWRITER
505 Gest St., Cinncinnati, OH 45203; 513-721-2140
Additional Information: Weekly; geared toward management professionals.

❶ I N T E R N A T I O N A L EMPLOYMENT

INTERNATIONAL EMPLOYMENT GAZETTE
1525 Wade Hampton Blvd., Greenville, SC 29609; 800-882-9188
Additional Information: Biweekly; contains extensive job listings.

INTERNATIONAL EMPLOYMENT HOTLINE NEWSLETTER
P.O. Box 3030, Oakton, VA 22124; 800-291-4618
Additional Information: Monthly; contains extensive job listings.

INTERNATIONAL JOBS BULLETIN
University Placement, Woody Hall B-208, Southern Illinois University, Carbondale, IL 62901; 618-453-2391
Additional Information: Bimonthly; contains extensive listing of international jobs.

❶ L A W

ABA JOURNAL
750 N. Lake Shore Dr., Chicago, IL 60611; 312-988-6003
Additional Information: Monthly; available to American Bar Association members.

AMERICAN LAWYER
600 Third Ave., New York, NY 10016; 212-973-2800
Additional Information: Ten issues per year; contains insightful industry overviews.

BUSINESS LAW TODAY
750 N. Lake Shore Dr., Chicago, IL 60611; 312-988-6056
Additional Information: Quarterly.

NATIONAL LAW JOURNAL
345 Park Ave. S., New York, NY 10003; 212-779-9200
Additional Information: Weekly; contains extensive job listings.

❶ L I B R A R Y   S C I E N C E

AMERICAN LIBRARIES
50 E. Huron St., Chicago, IL 60611; 800-545-2433
Additional Information: Monthly; contains job listings that can be made available in advance of publication.

LIBRARY JOURNAL
249 W. 17th St., New York, NY 10011; 212-463-6819
Additional Information: Semimonthly; contains numerous job listings.

SCHOOL LIBRARY JOURNAL
249 W. 17th St., New York, NY 10011; 212-463-6759
Additional Information: Monthly.

❶ M A N A G E M E N T

ACROSS THE BOARD
845 Third Ave., New York, NY 10022; 212-759-0900
Additional Information: Monthly; a prestigious publication of the Conference Board.

CORPORATE MEETINGS/INCENTIVES
63 Great Rd., Maynard, MA 01754; 508-897-5552
Additional Information: Monthly; aimed at planners of business meetings.

FACILITIES DESIGN & MANAGEMENT
1515 Broadway, New York, NY 10036; 212-869-1300
Additional Information: Monthly; aimed at corporate facilities managers.

HARVARD BUSINESS REVIEW
Harvard School of Business Administration, Soldiers Field Rd., Boston, MA 02163; 617-495-6800
Additional Information: Bimonthly; provides excellent business coverage.

HR MAGAZINE
606 N. Washington St., Alexandria, VA 22314; 703-548-3440
Additional Information: Monthly; aimed at human resources professionals.

INDUSTRY WEEK
1100 Superior Ave., Cleveland, OH 44114; 216-696-7000
Additional Information: Semimonthly; aimed at the industrial management field.

MANAGEMENT REVIEW
135 W. 50th St., New York, NY 10020; 212-903-8063
Additional Information: Monthly; publication available to American Management Association members.

NATIONAL BUSINESS EMPLOYMENT WEEKLY
P.O. Box 300, Princeton, NJ 08543; 609-520-4306
Additional Information: Weekly.

PERSONNEL JOURNAL
245 Fischer Ave., B-2, Costa Mesa, CA 92626; 714-751-4106
Additional Information: Monthly; aimed at human resources professionals.

RECREATION RESOURCES
2101 S. Arlington Heights Rd., Arlington Heights, IL 60005; 847-427-9512
Additional Information: Nine issues per year; aimed at recreation managers.

LOGISTICS MANAGEMENT
275 Washington St., Newton, MA 02158; 617-964-3030
Additional Information: Monthly.

TRAINING
50 S. 9th St., Minneapolis, MN 55402; 612-333-0471
Additional Information: Monthly; aimed at staffs of corporate and university training programs.

❶ MARKETING

BUSINESS MARKETING
Crain Communications, 740 N. Rush St., Chicago, IL 60601; 312-649-5200
Additional Information: Monthly.

DIRECT MARKETING
724 Seventh St., Garden City, NY 11530; 516-746-6700
Additional Information: Monthly.

MARKETING NEWS
250 S. Wacker Dr., Suite 200, Chicago, IL 60606; 312-648-0536
Additional Information: Biweekly.

SALES AND MARKETING MANAGEMENT
355 Park Ave. S., New York, NY 10010; 212-592-6300
Additional Information: Fifteen issues per year; major industry magazine.

❶ NATURAL RESOURCES

COAL
745 5th Ave., New York, NY 10151; 212-251-1500
Additional Information: Monthly; aimed at industry executives in all areas.

ENGINEERING AND MINING JOURNAL
745 5th Ave., New York, NY 10151; 212-251-1500
Additional Information: Monthly; covers the mining industry.

NEW STEEL
191 S. Gary Ave., Carol Stream, IL 60188; 630-462-2286
Additional Information: Monthly; covers the iron industry.

NORTH AMERICAN MINING
100 W. Grove St., Suite 240, Reno, NV 89509; 702-827-1115
Additional Information: Monthly; aimed at mining professionals.

❶ PETROLEUM

OIL AND GAS JOURNAL
3050 Post Oak Blvd., Suite 200, Houston, TX 77056; 713-621-9720
Additional Information: Weekly; aimed at oil production, exploration, and marketing professionals.

WORLD OIL
P.O. Box 2608, Houston, TX 77252; 713-529-4301
Additional Information: Monthly; aimed at scientists, corporate executives, production engineers, and a variety of industry professionals.

❶ P L A S T I C S

MODERN PLASTICS
1991 Avenue of the Americas, New York, NY 10020; 212-512-6245
Additional Information: Monthly; aimed at engineers, developers, technicians, and other professionals in the plastics industry.

❶ P U B L I C   R E L A T I O N S

O'DWYER'S PR MARKETPLACE
271 Madison Ave., New York, NY 10016; 212-679-2471
Additional Information: Biweekly; newsletter providing public relations employment prospects.

PR REPORTER
PR Publishing Co., Inc., Box 600, Exeter, NH 03833; 603-778-0514
Additional Information: Weekly; newsletter sent to public relations professionals.

PUBLIC RELATIONS JOURNAL
PR Society of America, 33 Irving Pl., New York, NY 10003; 212-995-2230
Additional Information: Monthly; contains extensive resources for public relations professionals.

❶ P U B L I S H I N G

COLUMBIA JOURNALISM REVIEW
700A Journalism Bldg., Columbia University, New York, NY 10027; 212-854-2716
Additional Information: Bimonthly.

EDITOR AND PUBLISHER
11 W. 19th St., New York, NY 10011; 212-675-4380
Additional Information: Weekly; aimed at newspaper editors.

MAGAZINE & BOOKSELLER
322 Eighth Ave., New York, NY 10001; 212-620-7330
Additional Information: Monthly; aimed at retailers and wholesalers.

PUBLISHERS WEEKLY
249 W. 17th St., New York, NY 10011; 800-842-1669
Additional Information: Weekly.

THE WRITER
120 Boylston St., Boston, MA 02116; 617-423-3157
Additional Information: Monthly; aimed primarily at freelance writers.

WRITER'S DIGEST
1507 Dana Ave., Cincinnati, OH 45207; 513-531-2222
Additional Information: Monthly; aimed at freelance writers; contains market information.

❶ R E T A I L

CHILDREN'S BUSINESS
7 W. 34th St., New York, NY 10001; 212-630-4230
Additional Information: Monthly; provides coverage of the children's apparel and accessories industries.

DISCOUNT MERCHANDISER
233 Park Ave. S., New York, NY 10003; 212-979-4800
Additional Information: Monthly; aimed at discount store buyers, managers, and executives.

DRUG STORE NEWS
425 Park Ave., New York, NY 10022; 212-756-5000
Additional Information: Biweekly; aimed at chain and independent drugstore professionals.

KIDS' SHOW GUIDE
485 Seventh Ave., New York, NY 10018; 212-594-0880
Additional Information: Monthly; aimed at children's clothing retailers.

MASS MARKET RETAILERS
220 Fifth Ave., New York, NY 10001; 212-213-6000
Additional Information: Biweekly; aimed at supermarkets and drug and discount store executives.

❶ SALES

AGENCY SALES MAGAZINE
P.O. Box 3467, Laguna Hills, CA 92654;
714-859-4040
Additional Information: Monthly; aimed
at manufacturing representatives.

INDUSTRIAL DISTRIBUTION
275 Washington St., Newton, MA 02158;
617-558-4432
Additional Information: Monthly; aimed
at sales representatives.

SALES MANAGER'S BULLETIN
Bureau of Business Practice, 24 Rope Ferry
Rd., Waterford, CT 06386; 860-442-4365
Additional Information: Monthly.

SUCCESSFUL MEETINGS
355 Park Ave. S., New York, NY 10010; 212-
592-6200
Additional Information: Monthly; aimed
at managers of sales and marketing
meetings.

❶ SCIENCE

AMERICAN LABORATORY NEWS
P.O. Box 870, Shelton, CT 06484; 203-926-
9300
Additional Information: Monthly; aimed
at research chemists and biologists.

AMERICAN SCIENTIST
P.O. Box 13975, Research Triangle Park, NC
27709; 919-549-0097
Additional Information: Publication of
Sigma Xi, a society for research scientists
and engineers.

BIOSCIENCE
730 11th St., NW, P.O. Box 20001, Washington, DC 20001; 202-628-1500
Additional Information: Monthly.

FEDERAL ARCHEOLOGY REPORT
P.O. Box 37127, Washington, DC 20013;
202-343-4101
Additional Information: Quarterly;
contains information on volunteering and
training programs.

PHYSICS TODAY
1 Physics Ellipse, College Park, MD 20740;
301-209-2440
Additional Information: Monthly; contains numerous job listings and general
industry features.

SCIENCE
1333 H St., NW, Washington, DC 20005;
202-326-6500
Additional Information: Weekly; provides widespread coverage of the science
field.

WEATHERWISE
1319 18th St., NW, Washington, DC 20036;
202-362-6445
Additional Information: Bimonthly.

❶ SECRETARIAL

SECRETARY
2800 Shirlington Rd., Arlington, VA 22206;
703-998-2534
Additional Information: Monthly.

❶ SOCIAL SERVICES

CORRECTIONS TODAY
8025 Laurel Lakes Ct., Laurel, MD 20797;
301-206-5100
Additional Information: Seven issues
per year; aimed at those pursuing a career
in the corrections field.

LAW AND ORDER
1000 Skokie Blvd., Wilmette, IL 60091; 847-
256-8555
Additional Information: Monthly; aimed
at law enforcement professionals.

NASW NEWS
750 First St., NE, Washington, DC 20002;
202-408-8600
Additional Information: Ten issues per
year; publication of the National Association of Social Workers; contains extensive job listings.

NATIONAL EMPLOYMENT LISTING SERVICE
Sam Houston University, Criminal Justice
Ctr., Huntsville, TX 77341; 409-294-1692
Additional Information: Monthly; lists
jobs in law enforcement, corrections, and
social work.

SOCIAL SERVICE JOBS
10 Angelica Dr., Framingham, MA 01701;
508-626-8644
Additional Information: Biweekly;
contains many job listings in the social
services field.

❶ TECHNOLOGY

COMPUTER RESELLER NEWS
600 Community Dr., Manhasset, NY 11030; 516-562-5000
Additional Information: Weekly; aimed at systems professionals, engineers, and manufacturers.

NETWORK WORLD
P.O. Box 9172, Framingham, MA 01701; 508- 875-6400
Additional Information: Weekly; provides extensive coverage of the computer industry.

DATA COMMUNICATIONS
1221 Ave. of the Americas, New York, NY 10020; 212-512-6150
Additional Information: Monthly; aimed at computer network integration professionals.

DATAMATION
275 Washington St., Newton, MA 02158; 617-964-3030
Additional Information: Semimonthly; aimed at information systems professionals; publishes annual directory.

DIGITAL NEWS AND REVIEWS
275 Washington St., Newton, MA 02158; 617-964-3030
Additional Information: Biweekly; aimed at manufacturers of hardware and software as well as dealers and retailers.

ECN ELECTRONIC-COMPONENT NEWS
Chilton Way, Radnor, PA 19089; 610-964-4347
Additional Information: Monthly; aimed at design engineers.

ELECTRONIC BUSINESS
275 Washington St., Newton, MA 02158; 617-964-3030
Additional Information: Semimonthly; covers the computer and electronics industry; publishes annual directory of leading companies.

ELECTRONIC DESIGN
611 Rte. 46 W., Hasbrouck Heights, NJ 07604; 201-393-6060
Additional Information: Biweekly; aimed at design engineers and managers.

ELECTRONIC NEWS
488 Madison Ave., New York, NY 10022; 800-883-6397
Additional Information: Weekly; newspaper aimed at sales, design, and computer professionals.

HIGH TECHNOLOGY CAREERS
4701 Patrick Henry Dr., Suite 1901, Santa Clara, CA 95054; 408-970-8800
Additional Information: Bimonthly; contains extensive listings of high-tech jobs.

INFO WORLD
155 Bovet Rd., San Mateo, CA 94402; 415-572-7341
Additional Information: Weekly; provides extensive coverage of the information systems industry.

INFORMATION TODAY
143 Old Marlton Pike, Medford, NJ 08055; 609-654-4888
Additional Information: Monthly; aimed at users and producers of electronic information services.

❶ TELECOMMUNICATIONS

AMERICA'S NETWORK
233 N. Michigan Ave., 2 Illinois Ctr., Chicago, IL 60601; 312-938-2378
Additional Information: Semimonthly; aimed at phone company managers, technicians, and executives.

TELECOMMUNICATIONS
685 Canton St., Norwood, MA 02062; 617-769-9750
Additional Information: Monthly; aimed at engineers, technicians, and specs professionals.

TELEPHONY
55 E. Jackson Blvd., Chicago, IL 60604; 312-922-2435
Additional Information: Weekly; aimed at engineers, specifiers, and buyers.

❶ TRANSPORTATION

AMERICAN SHIPPER
P.O. Box 4728, Jacksonville, FL 32201; 904-355-2601
Additional Information: Monthly.

COMMERCIAL CARRIER JOURNAL
201 King of Prussia Rd., Radnor, PA 19089; 610-964-4523

Additional Information: Monthly; aimed at trucking executives.

DISTRIBUTION

201 King of Prussia Rd., Radnor, PA 19089; 610-964-4384
Additional Information: Monthly; aimed at traffic and transportation managers, shippers, packers, and other industry professionals.

HEAVY DUTY TRUCKING

P.O. Box W, Newport Beach, CA 92658; 714-261-1636
Additional Information: Monthly; aimed at professionals with fleets of 26,000 pounds and over.

INBOUND LOGISTICS

5 Penn Plaza, New York, NY 10001; 212-629-1560
Additional Information: Monthly; covers the inbound freight business.

OWNER–OPERATOR: THE BUSINESS MAGAZINE OF INDEPENDENT TRUCKING

201 King of Prussia Rd., Radnor, PA 19089; 610-964-4262
Additional Information: Nine issues per year; aimed at small fleets and independents.

PRO TRUCKER

610 Colonial Park Dr., Roswell, GA 30075; 404-587-0311
Additional Information: Monthly.

RAILWAY AGE

345 Hudson St., New York, NY 10014; 212-620-7200
Additional Information: Monthly; covers the rapid transit and railroad professions.

SHIPPING DIGEST

51 Madison Ave., New York, NY 10010; 212-689-4411
Additional Information: Weekly; aimed at executives involved in exporting American goods overseas.

❶ TRAVEL

BUSINESS TRAVEL NEWS

1 Penn Plaza, 10th Floor, New York, NY 10119; 212-869-1300
Additional Information: Thirty-six issues per year.

TRAVEL AGENT

801 Second Ave., New York, NY 10017; 212-370-5050
Additional Information: Weekly.

TRAVEL TRADE

15 W. 44th St., New York, NY 10036; 212-730-6600
Additional Information: Weekly; aimed at travel agents, tour operators, resort managers, and hospitality personnel.

TRAVEL WEEKLY

500 Plaza Dr., Secaucus, NJ 07096; 201-902-2000
Additional Information: Weekly; provides extensive industry coverage.

TRAVELAGE MIDAMERICA

Official Airline Guides, Inc., 2000 Clearwater Dr., Oakbrook, IL 60521; 630-574-6000, ext. 6963
Additional Information: Weekly; aimed at travel agents in middle America, Ontario, and Manitoba.

TRAVELAGE WEST

Official Airline Guides, Inc., 49 Stevenson, #460, San Francisco, CA 94105; 415-905-1155
Additional Information: Weekly; covers the travel industry in the western states.

❶ UTILITIES

ELECTRICAL WORLD

11 W. 19th St., New York, NY 10011; 212-337-4069
Additional Information: Monthly; aimed at executives and engineers.

PUBLIC POWER

2301 M St., NW, Washington, DC 20037; 202-467-2900
Additional Information: Bimonthly; publication of the American Public Powers Association.

PUBLIC UTILITIES FORTNIGHTLY

8229 Boone Blvd., Suite 401, Vienna, VA 22182; 703-847-7720
Additional Information: Semimonthly; aimed at industry professionals.

TRANSMISSION & DISTRIBUTION

P.O. Box 12901, Overland Park, KS 66212; 913-341-1300
Additional Information: Monthly; aimed at electric utilities executives, technicians, and other professionals.

❶WASTE MANAGEMENT

ENVIRONMENTAL PROTECTION NEWS
Box 2573, Waco, TX 76702; 817-776-9000
Additional Information: Nine issues per year; aimed at pollution control specialists.

ENVIRONMENTAL SOLUTIONS
312 W. Randolph St., Suite 600, Chicago, IL 60606; 3112-553-8900
Additional Information: Monthly; aimed at hazardous waste specialists.

OCCUPATIONAL FACTS

Industry
DIRECTORIES

INDUSTRY DIRECTORIES

T HIS CHAPTER LISTS DIRECTORIES OF COMPANIES within specific industries. This is an idealsupplement to the chapter on "U.S. Employers," which is primarily made up of major U.S. companies. Smaller firms, too, are excellent prospects for employment, and a large number of them can be found in these industry directories. The directories can also help you to find the names of specific department heads and many middle managers at companies of all sizes. Some of the directories even specialize in listing such potential contacts and employers.

Since most directories are extremely expensive, it may not be economical to purchase them. However, most libraries have extensive collections of directories. You just have to know which ones to ask for.

Various industries are represented in this chapter. While the fields themselves are broken down fairly specifically, you should also consider consulting directories outside your particular area of interest. For instance, directories aimed at engineers will certainly be found in the "Engineering" section, but there also may be directories of interest to engineers in other fields, such as aerospace and manufacturing.

Other chapters in this book may also be useful. ➤➤**See Industry Overviews," pp. 395-409; "U.S. Employers," pp. 158-378;** and **Professional Associations," pp. 644-655.**

INDUSTRY LIST

ACCOUNTING (*Also see:* FINANCE)
ADVERTISING (*Also see:* Consumer Products, Public Relations, Retail, Sales)
AEROSPACE (*Also see:* Aviation, Engineering)
AGRICULTURE
ARTS (*Also see:* Broadcasting, Design, Entertainment, Fashion, Performing Arts)
AUTOMOTIVE
AVIATION (*Also see:* Aerospace, Engineering)
BROADCASTING (*Also see:* Arts, Entertainment)
CHEMICALS (*Also see:* Science, Technology)
CONSUMER PRODUCTS (*Also see:* Advertising, Food and Beverages, Hospitality, Retail, Sales)
DESIGN (*Also see:* Arts, Fashion)
EDUCATION
ENGINEERING (*Also see:* Aerospace, Aviation, Manufacturing, Science, Technology)
ENTERTAINMENT (*Also see:* Arts, Broadcasting, Fashion, Performing Arts)

ENVIRONMENT
FASHION (*Also see:* Arts, Design, Entertainment)
FINANCE (*Also see:* Accounting)
FOOD AND BEVERAGES (*Also see:* Consumer Products, Hospitality, Natural Resources)
FOREST/PAPER PRODUCTS (*Also see:* Natural Resources)
GOVERNMENT
HEALTH SERVICES
HOSPITALITY (*Also see:* Consumer Products, Food and Beverages)
INSURANCE
INTERNATIONAL EMPLOYMENT
LAW
LIBRARY SCIENCE
MANAGEMENT
MANUFACTURING (*Also see:* Engineering, Technology)
METALS (*Also see:* Natural Resources, Petroleum)
NATURAL RESOURCES (*Also see:* Forest/Paper Products, Metals, Petroleum, Utilities)

INDUSTRY DIRECTORIES

PERFORMING ARTS (*Also see:* Arts, Entertainment)
PETROLEUM (*Also see:* Metals, Natural Resources, Utilities)
PUBLIC RELATIONS (*Also see:* Advertising, Sales)
PUBLISHING
REAL ESTATE
RETAIL (*Also see:* Advertising, Consumer Products, Sales)
SALES (*Also see:* Advertising, Consumer Products, Public Relations, Retail)

SCIENCE (*Also see:* Chemicals, Engineering, Technology)
TECHNOLOGY (*ALSO SEE:* CHEMICALS, ENGINEERING, MANUFACTURING, SCIENCE)
TELECOMMUNICATIONS (*Also see:* Technology)
TRANSPORTATION
UTILITIES (*Also see:* Natural Resources, Petroleum)

❶ ACCOUNTING

ACCOUNTANT'S DIRECTORY
5711 S. 86th Circle, P.O. Box 27347, Omaha, NE 68127; 402-593-4600

FIRM ON FIRM DIRECTORY
American Institute of CPAs, Harborside Financial Ctr., 201 Plaza 3, Jersey City, NJ 07311; 800-862-4272

❶ ADVERTISING

AMERICAN ASSOCIATION OF ADVERTISING AGENCIES ROSTER AND ORGANIZATION
666 Third Ave., New York, NY 10017; 212-682-2500

MACMILLAN DIRECTORY OF INTERNATIONAL ADVERTISERS AND AGENCIES
121 Chanlon Rd., New Providence, NJ 07974; 800-521-8110

STANDARD DICTIONARY OF ADVERTISING AGENCIES
121 Chanlon Rd., New Providence, NJ 07974; 800-521-8110

❶ AEROSPACE

AEROSPACE CONSULTANTS DIRECTORY
Society of Aerospace Engineers, 400 Commonwealth Dr., Warrendale, PA 15096; 412-776-4841

INTERNATIONAL ABC AEROSPACE DIRECTORY
1340 Braddock Pl., Suite 300, P.O. Box 1436, Alexandria, VA 22313; 703-683-3700

❶ AGRICULTURE

DIRECTORY OF INFORMATION RESOURCES IN AGRICULTURE AND BIOLOGY
U.S. Government Printing Office, Washington, DC 20402; 202-783-3238

DIRECTORY OF STATE DEPARTMENTS OF AGRICULTURE
U.S. Government Printing Office, Washington, DC 20402; 202-783-3238

FARMS DIRECTORY
5711 S. 86th Circle, Omaha, NE 68127; 402-593-4600

❶ ARTS

AMERICAN ART DIRECTORY
121 Chanlon Rd., New Providence, NJ 07974; 800-521-8110

FOUNDATION GRANTS TO INDIVIDUALS
Foundation Ctr., 79 Fifth Ave., New York, NY 10003; 212-620-4230

ARTIST'S MARKET
1507 Dana Ave., Cincinnati, OH 45207; 513-531-2222

CREATIVE BLACK BOOK
866 Third Ave., New York, NY 10022; 212-702-9700
Foundation Ctr., 79 Fifth Ave., New York, NY 10003; 212-620-4230

HUMOR AND CARTOON MARKET
1507 Dana Ave., Cincinnati, OH 45207; 513-531-2222

INDUSTRY DIRECTORIES

❶ AUTOMOTIVE

AUTOMOTIVE NEWS MARKET DATA BOOK
1400 Woodbridge Ave., Detroit, MI 48207;
313-446-6000

❶ AVIATION

ANNUAL REPORT OF THE COMMUTER RE-GIONAL AIRLINE INDUSTRY
1101 Connecticut Ave., NW, Washington, DC
20036; 202-857-1170

WORLD AVIATION DIRECTORY
1200 G St., NW, Washington, DC 20005;
202-383-3700

❶ BROADCASTING

BROADCASTING & CABLE MARKETPLACE
P.O. Box 31, New Providence, NJ 07974;
800-323-4345

BROADCASTING YEARBOOK
1705 DeSales St., NW, Washington, DC
20036; 202-659-2340

GALE DIRECTORY OF PUBLICATIONS AND BROADCAST MEDIA
835 Penobscot Bldg., Detroit, MI 48226; 800-877-4253

❶ CHEMICALS

CHEM SOURCES—INTERNATIONAL
Box 1824, Clemson, SC 29633; 864-646-7840

CHEM SOURCES—USA
Box 1824, Clemson, SC 29633; 864-646-7840

CHEMICALS DIRECTORY
275 Washington St., Newton, MA 02158;
617-964-3030

DIRECTORY OF CHEMICAL PRODUCERS U.S.A.
333 Ravenswood Ave., Menlo Park, CA
94025; 415-859-3627

❶ CONSUMER PRODUCTS

APPLIANCE MANUFACTURERS ANNUAL DIRECTORY
5900 Harper Rd., Suite 105, Solon, OH
44139; 216-349-3060

DIRECTORY OF CONSUMER ELECTRONICS, PHOTOGRAPHY, AND MAJOR APPLI-ANCE RETAILERS AND DISTRIBUTORS
425 Park Ave., New York, NY 10022; 212-756-5252

❶ DESIGN

DESIGN FIRM DIRECTORY
Wefler & Associates, P.O. Box 1167,
Evanston, IL 60204; 847-475-1866

GRAPHIC ARTISTS GUILD DIRECTORY
Graphic Arts Guild, 11 W. 20th St., New
York, NY 10011; 212-463-7730

GRAPHIC ARTS BLUE BOOK
79 Madison Ave., New York, NY 10016; 212-679-0770

❶ EDUCATION

OPPORTUNITIES ABROAD FOR EDUCATORS: FULBRIGHT TEACHER EXCHANGE PROGRAM
E/ASX, Room 353, U.S. Information Agency,
Washington, DC; 202-619-4555

PATTERSON'S AMERICAN EDUCATOR
P.O. Box 199, Mt. Prospect, IL 60056; 847-459-0605

❶ ENGINEERING

DIRECTORY OF CHEMICAL ENGINEERING CONSULTANTS
American Institute of Chemical Engineers,
345 E. 47th St., New York, NY 10017; 212-705-7338

DIRECTORY OF ENGINEERING SOCIETIES
1111 19th St., NW, Suite 608, Washington,
DC 20002; 202-296-2237

DIRECTORY OF ENGINEERS IN PRIVATE PRACTICE
National Society of Professional Engineers,
1420 King St., Alexandria, VA 22314; 703-684-2882

❶ ENTERTAINMENT

BILLBOARD INTERNATIONAL RECORDING STUDIO & EQUIPMENT DIRECTORY
1515 Broadway, New York, NY 10036; 212-764-7300

CASH BOX ANNUAL WORLD WIDE DIRECTORY
345 W. 58th St., New York, NY 10019; 212-245-4224

RADIO & RECORDS RATINGS REPORT & DIRECTORY
1930 Century Park W., Los Angeles, CA 90067; 310-553-4330

RECORDING ENGINEER/PRODUCER BLACK BOOK
9800 Metcalf, Overland Park, KS 66212; 913-341-1300

WHO'S WHO IN THE MOTION PICTURE INDUSTRY
P.O. Box 2187, Beverly Hills, CA 90213; 213-854-0276

❶ E N V I R O N M E N T

CONSERVATION DIRECTORY
National Wildlife Foundation, 1400 16th St., NW, Washington, DC 20036; 800-432-6564

❶ F A S H I O N

AMERICAN APPAREL MANUFACTURERS ASSOCIATION DIRECTORY
2500 Wilson Blvd., Arlington, VA 22201; 703-524-1864

APPAREL TRADES BOOK
1 Diamond Hill Rd., Murray Hill, NJ 07974; 908-665-5000

FASHION RESOURCE DIRECTORY
7 W. 34th St., New York, NY 10001; 212-630-4000

❶ F I N A N C E

AMERICAN BANKER YEARBOOK
1 State St. Plaza, New York, NY 10004; 212-943-6700

AMERICAN FINANCIAL DIRECTORY
6195 Crooked Creek Rd., Norcross, GA 30092; 800-247-7376

AMERICAN SAVINGS DIRECTORY
6195 Crooked Creek Rd., Norcross, GA 30092; 800-247-7376

CORPORATE FINANCE SOURCEBOOK
121 Chanlon Rd., New Providence, NJ 07974; 800-323-6772

DIRECTORY OF AMERICAN FINANCIAL INSTITUTIONS
6195 Crooked Creek Rd., Norcross, GA 30092; 800-247-7376

MOODY'S BANK AND FINANCIAL MANUAL
99 Church St., New York, NY 10007; 212-553-0300

POLK'S BANK DIRECTORY—INTERNATIONAL EDITION
P.O. Box 3051000, Nashville, TN 37230; 800-827-2265

POLK'S BANK DIRECTORY—NORTH AMERICAN EDITION
P.O. Box 3051000, Nashville, TN 37230; 800-827-2265

SECURITIES INDUSTRY YEARBOOK
120 Broadway, New York, NY 10271; 212-608-1500

❶ F O O D   A N D   B E V E R - A G E S

AMERICAN FROZEN FOOD INDUSTRY DIRECTORY
1764 Old Meadow Lane, McLean, VA 22102; 703-821-0770

FOOD ENGINEERING'S DIRECTORY OF U.S. FOOD AND BEVERAGE PLANTS
Chilton Way, Radnor, PA 19089; 610-687-8200

HERELD'S 5000: THE DIRECTORY OF LEADING U.S. FOOD, CONFECTIONARY, BEVERAGE AND PET FOOD MANUFACTURERS
200 Leeder Hill Dr., Suite 341, Hamden, CT 06517; 203-281-6766

❶ F O R E S T / P A P E R   P R O D U C T S

DIRECTORY OF THE FOREST PRODUCTS INDUSTRY
6600 Silacci Way, Gilroy, CA 95020; 408-848-5296

INTERNATIONAL PULP AND PAPER DIRECTORY
6600 Silacci Way, Gilroy, CA 95020; 408-848-5296

WALDEN'S ABC GUIDE AND PAPER PRODUCTION YEARBOOK
225 N. Franklin Turnpike, Ramsey, NJ 07446; 201-818-8630

❶ G O V E R N M E N T

CONGRESSIONAL YELLOW BOOK
104 Fifth Ave., New York, NY 10011; 212-627-4140

FEDERAL REGIONAL YELLOW BOOK
104 Fifth Ave., New York, NY 10011; 212-627-4140

STATE AND REGIONAL ASSOCIATIONS OF THE UNITED STATES
1212 New York Ave., NW, Suite 300, Washington, DC 20005; 202-898-0662

U.S. COURT DIRECTORY
U.S. Government Printing Office, Washington, DC 20402; 202-512-1800

❶ H E A L T H   S E R V I C E S

AMERICAN HOSPITAL ASSOCIATION GUIDE TO THE HEALTH CARE FIELD
840 N. Lake Shore Dr., Chicago, IL 60611; 312-280-6000

DUN'S GUIDE TO HEALTH CARE COMPANIES
3 Sylvan Way, Parsippany, NJ 07054; 201-605-6000

HOSPITAL PHONE BOOK
121 Chanlon Rd., New Providence, RI 07974; 800-521-8110

MEDICAL AND HEALTH INFORMATION DIRECTORY
835 Penobscot Bldg., Detroit, MI 48226; 800-877-4253

NATIONAL DIRECTORY OF HEALTH MAINTENANCE ORGANIZATIONS
1129 20th St., NW, Suite 600, Washington, DC 20036; 202-778-3247

NURSING CAREER DIRECTORY
1111 Bethlehem Pike, Springhouse, PA 19477; 215-646-8700

U.S. MEDICAL DIRECTORY
121 Chalon Rd., New Providence, RI 07974; 800-521-8110

❶ H O S P I T A L I T Y

CHAIN RESTAURANT OPERATORS
425 Park Ave., New York, NY 10022; 212-756-5000

DIRECTORY OF HOTEL AND MOTEL SYSTEMS
1201 New York Ave., NW, Washington, DC 20005; 202-289-3162

DIRECTORY OF HOTEL/MOTEL RESTAURANT MANAGEMENT COMPANIES
7500 Old Oak Blvd., Cleveland, OH 44130; 216-243-8100

FOOD SERVICE INDUSTRY DIRECTORY
1200 17th St., NW, Suite 800, Washington, DC 20036; 202-331-5900

HIGH VOLUME INDEPENDENT RESTAURANTS
425 Park Ave., New York, NY 10022; 212-756-5000

WHO'S WHO IN THE LODGING INDUSTRY
1201 New York Ave., NW, Washington, DC 20005; 202-289-3162

❶ I N S U R A N C E

INSURANCE ALMANAC
50 E. Palisade Ave., Englewood, NJ 07631; 201-569-8808

INSURANCE PHONE BOOK AND DIRECTORY
121 Chalon Rd., New Providence, NJ 07974; 800-323-6772

❶ I N T E R N A T I O N A L   E M - P L O Y M E N T

DIRECTORY OF AMERICAN FIRMS OPERATING IN FOREIGN COUNTRIES
50 E. 42nd St., New York, NY 10017; 212-697-4999

FORTUNE WORLD BUSINESS DIRECTORY
Rockefeller Ctr., New York, NY 10020; 212-522-2581

OPPORTUNITIES ABROAD FOR EDUCATORS: FULBRIGHT TEACHER EXCHANGE PROGRAM
E/ASX, Room 353, U.S. Information Agency, Washington, DC 20547; 202-619-4555

WORLD MARKETING DIRECTORY
3 Sylvan Way, Parsippany, NJ 07054; 800-526-0651

INDUSTRY DIRECTORIES

❶ L A W

LAW FIRM YELLOW PAGES
104 Fifth Ave., New York, NY 10011; 212-627-4140

NATIONAL PARALEGAL ASSOCIATION DIRECTORY
P.O. Box 406, Solebury, PA 18963; 215-297-8333

❶ LIBRARY SCIENCE

AMERICAN LIBRARY ASSOCIATION—ORGANIZATION AND MEMBERSHIP DIRECTORY
50 E. Huron St., Chicago, IL 60611; 800-545-2433

AMERICAN LIBRARY DIRECTORY
P.O. Box 31, New Providence, NJ 07974; 800-521-8110

DIRECTORY OF FEDERAL LIBRARIES
4041 N. Central, Suite 700, Phoenix, AZ 85012; 800-279-6799

GUIDE TO LIBRARY PLACEMENT SOURCES
50 E. Huron St., Chicago, IL 60611; 800-545-2433

WORLD GUIDE TO LIBRARIES
P.O. Box 31, New Providence, NJ 07974; 800-521-8110

❶ MANAGEMENT

AMERICAN MANAGEMENT ASSOCIATION'S EXECUTIVE EMPLOYMENT GUIDE
135 W. 50th St., New York, NY 10020; 212-586-8100

DUN & BRADSTREET MILLION-DOLLAR DIRECTORY
3 Sylvan Way, Parsippany, NJ 07054; 800-526-0651

DUN & BRADSTREET REFERENCE BOOK OF CORPORATE MANAGEMENT
3 Sylvan Way, Parsippany, NJ 07054; 800-526-0651

WOMEN DIRECTORS OF THE TOP 1,000 CORPORATIONS
1440 New York Ave., NW, Suite 300, Washington, DC 20005; 202-393-5257

❶ MANUFACTURING

AMERICAN MANUFACTURERS DIRECTORY
5711 S. 86th Circle, Omaha, NE 68127; 402-593-4600

APPLIANCE MANUFACTURERS ANNUAL DIRECTORY
5900 Harper Rd., Suite 105, Solon, OH 44139; 216-349-3060

❶ METALS

DIRECTORY OF IRON AND STEEL PLANTS
3 Gateway Ctr., Suite 2350, Pittsburgh, PA 15222; 412-281-6323

DIRECTORY OF STEEL FOUNDRIES IN THE UNITED STATES, CANADA, AND MEXICO
455 State St., Des Plaines, IL 60016; 847-299-9160

DUN'S INDUSTRIAL GUIDE: THE METAL-WORKING DIRECTORY
3 Sylvan Way, Parsippany, NJ 07054; 201-455-0900

IRON & STEEL WORKS OF THE UNITED STATES AND CANADA
1101 12th St., NW, Washington, DC 20036; 202-452-7100

❶ NATURAL RESOURCES

REFINING, NATURAL GAS PROCESSING, AND ENGINEERING CONTRACTORS
1120 E. 4th St., Tulsa, OK 74102; 918-582-2000

WHOLE WORLD OIL DIRECTORY
121 Chanlon Rd., New Providence, NJ 07974; 800-323-6772

❶ PERFORMING ARTS

AMERICAN DANCE GUILD MEMBERSHIP DIRECTORY
31 W. 21st St., New York, NY 10010; 212-627-3790

REGIONAL THEATER DIRECTORY
P.O. Box 519, Dorset, VT 05251; 802-867-2223

ROSS REPORTS TELEVISION
40-29 27th St., Long Island City, NY 11101;
718-937-3990

SUMMER THEATER DIRECTORY
P.O. Box 519, Dorset, VT 05251; 802-867-2223

❶ PETROLEUM

OIL & GAS DIRECTORY
P.O. Box 130508, Houston, TX 77219; 713-529-8789

WEST COAST PETROLEUM INDUSTRY DIRECTORY
15314 Devonshire, Suite D, Mission Hills, CA 91345; 818-892-1121

❶ PUBLIC RELATIONS

DIRECTORY OF MINORITY PUBLIC RELATIONS PROFESSIONALS
33 Irving Pl., New York, NY 10003; 212-995-2230

O'DWYER'S DIRECTORY OF PUBLIC RELATIONS FIRMS
271 Madison Ave., New York, NY 10016; 212-679-2471

PUBLIC RELATIONS CONSULTANTS DIRECTORY
5707 S. 86th Circle, Omaha, NE 68127; 402-331-7169

❶ PUBLISHING

AMERICAN BOOK TRADE DIRECTORY
121 Chalon Rd., New Providence, NJ 07974; 908-464-6800

EDITOR AND PUBLISHER INTERNATIONAL YEARBOOK
11 W. 19th St., New York, NY 10011; 212-675-4380

EDITOR AND PUBLISHER MARKET GUIDE
11 W. 19th St., New York, NY 10011; 212-675-4380

EDITOR AND PUBLISHER SYNDICATE DIRECTORY
11 W. 19th St., New York, NY 10011; 212-675-4380

GALE DIRECTORY OF PUBLICATIONS AND BROADCAST MEDIA
835 Penobscot Bldg., Detroit, MI 48226; 800-877-4253

INTERNATIONAL LITERARY MARKETPLACE
121 Chanlon Rd., New Providence, NJ 07974; 908-464-6800

JOURNALISM CAREER AND SCHOLARSHIP GUIDE
Box 300, Princeton, NJ 08543; 609-452-2820

LITERARY MARKETPLACE: THE DIRECTORY OF AMERICAN BOOK PUBLISHING
121 Chanlon Rd., New Providence, NJ 07974; 908-464-6800

MAGAZINE INDUSTRY MARKETPLACE
121 Chanlon Rd., New Providence, NJ 07974; 908-464-6800

PUBLISHERS DIRECTORY
835 Penobscot Bldg., Detroit, MI 48226; 800-877-4253

WRITER'S GUILD DIRECTORY
8955 Beverly Blvd., Los Angeles, CA 90048; 310-205-2502

❶ REAL ESTATE

REAL ESTATE SOURCEBOOK
121 Chanlon Rd., New Providence, NJ 07974; 800-323-6772

❶ RETAIL

DIRECTORY OF CONSUMER ELECTRONICS, PHOTOGRAPHY, AND MAJOR APPLIANCE RETAILERS AND DISTRIBUTORS
425 Park Ave., New York, NY 10022; 212-756-5252

DIRECTORY OF DEPARTMENT STORES
425 Park Ave., New York, NY 10022; 212-756-5252

DIRECTORY OF GENERAL MERCHANDISE/VARIETY CHAINS AND SPECIALTY STORES
425 Park Ave., New York, NY 10022; 212-756-5252

INDUSTRY DIRECTORIES

❶ S A L E S

MANUFACTURERS' AGENTS AND REPRESEN-TATIVES
5711 S. 86th Circle, P.O. Box 27347, Omaha, NE 68127; 402-593-4600

SALESMAN'S GUIDE: NATIONAL DIREC-TORY OF CORPORATE MEETING PLAN-NERS
P.O. Box 31, New Providence, NJ 07973; 800-323-6772

❶ S C I E N C E

DIRECTORY OF INFORMATION RESOURCES IN AGRICULTURE AND BIOLOGY
U.S. Government Printing Office, Washington, DC 20402; 202-783-3238

❶ T E C H N O L O G Y

DIRECTORY OF TOP COMPUTER EXECUTIVES
P.O. Box 82266, Phoenix, AZ 85071; 602-995-5929

WHO'S WHO IN ELECTRONICS REGIONAL SOURCE DIRECTORY
2057 Aurora Rd., Twinsburg, OH 44087; 216-425-9000

❶ T E L E C O M M U N I C A T I O N S

MOBIL COMMUNICATIONS DIRECTORY
1201 Seven Locks Rd., Suite 300, Potomac, MD 20854; 800-326-8638

TELECOMMUNICATIONS DIRECTORY
835 Penobscot Bldg., Detroit, MI 48226; 800-877-4253

TELEPHONE ENGINEER & MANAGEMENT DIRECTORY
131 W. First St., Duluth, MN 55802; 800-346-0085

TELEPHONE INDUSTRY DIRECTORY AND SOURCEBOOK
1201 Seven Locks Rd., Suite 300, Potomac, MD 20854; 800-326-8638

❶ T R A N S P O R T A T I O N

AMERICAN MOTOR CARRIER DIRECTORY
424 W. 33rd St., New York, NY 10001; 212-714-3100

DIRECTORY OF TRUCKLOAD CARRIERS
210 Teaberry Lane, Clarks Summit, PA 18411; 717-586-9023

NATIONAL TANK TRUCK CARRIER DI-RECTORY
2200 Mill Rd., Alexandria, VA 22314; 703-838-1960

❶ U T I L I T I E S

AMERICAN PUBLIC GAS ASSOCIATION DIREC-TORY
P.O. Box 11094D, Lee Highway, Suite 102, Fairfax, VA 22030; 703-352-3890

BROWN'S DIRECTORY OF NORTH AMERI-CAN & INTERNATIONAL GAS COMPANIES
131 W. First St., Duluth, MN 55802; 218-723-9200

DIRECTORY OF GAS UTILITY COMPANIES
1120 E. 4th St., Tulsa, OK 74120; 918-582-2000

ELECTRICAL WORLD DIRECTORY OF ELECTRIC UTILITIES
1221 Sixth Ave., New York, NY 10007; 212-553-0300

JOB OPPORTUNITIES

In a nation with millions of public- and private-sector employers, finding a job involves knowing where the right opportunities are and are not. The chapters in this section provide employer names, addresses, contacts, and information on specific opportunities. Also provided is an assessment of the potential to find a job at legions of companies and in the many industries in which they function.

JOB OPPORTUNITIES
U.S. EMPLOYERS

THIS CHAPTER CONTAINS PROFILES OF MORE THAN 1,000 U.S. EMPLOYERS. You will find here the essential information needed to prospect for jobs in mainstream corporate America. In addition, the companies—which cover a broad range of industries—are rated according to how favorable or poor employment prospects are there. The rating system is described in further detail below.

The employers listed here generally represent the largest companies in America—that is, those employing 1,000 or more individuals. Of course, small companies also represent excellent employment prospects for job seekers. Overall in America today, small companies employ approximately twice as many people as do all the companies listed below. Information about small U.S. companies can be found by consulting directories about different industries or keeping current on them by reading professional publications and availing yourself of the resources offered by professional organizations. **➜See "Industry Directories," pp. 148-155; "Professional Magazines/Journals," pp. 131-147; and "Professional Associations," pp. 644-655.** Employment information for other smaller companies can also be found elsewhere in this book. **➜See "Job Hotlines," pp. 410-446; "Internships for Students," pp. 447-495; and "Summer Jobs for Students," pp. 497-530.**

You can also get information on different companies not listed here, and the most current information on all companies, by finding their sites on the Internet. **➜See "The Internet and the World Wide Web," pp. 536-540, and "Getting the Edge on Competition in Cyberspace," pp. 548-550.**

The rating system used for companies in this chapter needs some explanation. When two stars (★★) appear after a company's name, it means that the firm's sales, revenues, or assets and the number of people it employs have increased consistently in the last several years. One star (★) means that there have been similar increases, but to a lesser extent than at a company given two stars. If companies are rated with one or two stars, it generally indicates that employment prospects for job seekers are good to excellent, respectively. When no stars appear following a company's name, it means that employment prospects are not as good—for example, employee cutbacks may be taking place or have recently occurred, sales may have dropped, and so on.

Bear in mind that all companies have hiring priorities—that is, they may be hiring vigorously in one occupational category while remaining flat or even cutting back in another, or vice versa. Therefore, the ratings given here do not always indicate the potential for finding a job, since they do not take into account what occupations are in demand at a particular company. Even companies that have decreasing sales and declining employee bases hire people on a regular basis, at least at very large corporations. This means that a very large corporation, with decreasing sales and a declining employee base, may actually have more job openings than a company given two stars that has lower sales or fewer employees. (To make it easier to spot potential situations such as this, each entry contains the number of employees at the company.)

In total, the 1,000-plus companies listed below employ more than 40 million people. Like all large corporations, each has an attrition rate, which means that many of them, if not most, have job openings at any given time. Those that are rated with one or two stars are likely to have the most openings, at least in proportion to their current employee base.

The entries here are organized by industry, then alphabetically within each industry by state. Finally, the companies themselves are listed alphabetically within each state. (A list of industries covered appears below.) Note that some of the companies listed are the U.S. subsidiaries of multinational corporations whose headquarters are located in other countries. These companies are thus apt to be employers of significant numbers of people both in the United States and in other nations—something to consider if you are interested in working abroad. ➤See "Working Abroad," pp. 34-36.

Each entry contains essential contact information, such as address, phone number, and sometimes Web site. Key personnel are also listed, such as some of the top executives at the company or the heads of important divisions. (Unless otherwise noted, for subsidiaries, these are the key people at the subsidiary, not the parent company.)

Also given are the number of employees and the annual sales, revenues, or assets of each company, depending on what figure the company reports. Banks, for example, often report assets. (Note that all such figures are rounded off, and some are estimated.) These figures can give you a good idea of how large each company actually is. But be aware that for subsidiaries, unless otherwise noted, these figures are totals for the parent companies. In addition, economic figures for multinationals are sometimes reported in the foreign currency of the country where the company is headquartered.

A profile of each company is then presented, giving information on the company's activities, important projects, products, and/or services. Important partnerships are often discussed, as well as how recent industrial and societal trends have affected the company. In addition, if the company is the subsidiary of a larger conglomerate, that relationship is noted as well.

The last section of some profiles is "Other Locations." If the primary company listed is the U.S. subsidiary of a multinational corporation, information on the parent company's worldwide headquarters (address and phone number) is given here. In addition, this section lists where the company has other facilities, branches, offices, and so on, both in the United States and abroad.

Though every effort has been made to reflect current information at the time this list and the ratings were compiled, unforeseen events can affect hiring policies and company operations. Therefore, the information below may have changed. Bear this in mind, and try to keep up-to-date on industry matters by reading the business section of newspapers and/or business publications.

To find a specific company here, first refer to the list of the industries below into which the companies are categorized. Then find that category in the chapter. Note that some companies, particularly large conglomerates, are engaged in many industries, so they may not be listed in the industrial category that represents the activities that you are most familiar with. If you are primarily interested in geographic locations, look for the relevant states in each industry category.

Refer elsewhere in the book for information on how major U.S. industries are faring overall. ➤See "Industry Overviews," pp. 395-409.

INDUSTRY LIST

ACCOUNTING (*Also see:* Finance)
ADVERTISING/PUBLIC RELATIONS
AEROSPACE/DEFENSE
AIRLINES
ALCOHOLIC BEVERAGES (*Also see:* Food and Beverages)
APPAREL/FOOTWEAR
APPLIANCES (*See:* Consumer Electronics and Appliances)
ARCHITECTURE (*See:* Construction/Engineering)
ATHLETICS/RECREATIONAL AND LEISURE ACTIVITIES (*Also see:* Entertainment, Gaming, Toys)
AUTO/TRUCK RENTAL

AUTOMOTIVE (*Also see:* Industrial/Farm Equipment and Tools, Transportation Equipment)
BANKING (*Also see:* Finance)
BEVERAGES (*See:* Alcoholic Beverages, Food and Beverages)
BOOKS (*See:* Publishing/Information)
BROADCASTING (*See:* Entertainment)
BUILDING MATERIALS (*Also see:* Industrial/ Farm Equipment and Tools)
BUSINESS SERVICES (*Also see:* Accounting, Advertising/Public Relations, Construction/ Engineering, Environment/Waste Management)
CHEMICALS

U.S. EMPLOYERS

COMPUTERS/PERIPHERALS (*Also see*: Electronics/ Electrical Equipment, Semiconductors, Software)

CONSTRUCTION/ENGINEERING

CONSUMER ELECTRONICS AND APPLIANCES (*Also see:* Electronics/Electrical Equipment, Photographic Equipment and Film)

COSMETICS (*See:* Personal/Household Products)

DEFENSE (*See:* Aerospace/Defense)

DISTRIBUTORS/WHOLESALERS

DIVERSIFIED

ELECTRONICS/ELECTRICAL EQUIPMENT (*Also see:* Consumer Electronics and Appliances)

EMPLOYMENT SERVICES (*See:* Business Services)

ENTERTAINMENT (*Also see*: Athletics/Recreational and Leisure Activities, Gaming, Toys, Travel/Hospitality)

ENVIRONMENT/WASTE MANAGEMENT

FASHION (*See:* Apparel/Footwear)

FINANCE (DIVERSIFIED) (*Also see:* Accounting, Banking, Insurance)

FOOD (RETAIL)

FOOD AND BEVERAGES (*Also see:* Alcoholic Beverages)

FOREST/PAPER PRODUCTS

FREIGHT/TRANSPORTATION (*Also see*: Railroads)

FURNITURE

GAMING (*Also see:* Athletics/Recreational and Leisure Activities, Entertainment, Travel/Hospitality)

HEALTH CARE (*Also see:* Medical/Biotechnology)

HOUSEHOLD PRODUCTS (*See:* Personal/ Household Products)

HOTELS (*See:* Travel/Hospitality)

INDUSTRIAL/FARM EQUIPMENT AND TOOLS

INFORMATION SERVICES (*See:* Publishing/ Information)

INSURANCE

INTEREST GROUPS AND ORGANIZATIONS

MAGAZINES (*See:* Publishing/Information)

MEDICAL/BIOTECHNOLOGY (*Also see:* Health Care)

METALS (*See:* Mining and Metals)

MINING AND METALS

MISCELLANEOUS GOODS AND SERVICES

NEWSPAPERS (*See:* Publishing/Information)

OFFICE EQUIPMENT

PERSONAL/HOUSEHOLD PRODUCTS

PETROLEUM/GAS

PHARMACEUTICALS

PHOTOGRAPHIC EQUIPMENT AND FILM

PRINTING

PUBLISHING/INFORMATION

RADIO (*See:* Entertainment)

RAILROADS (*Also see*: Freight/Transportation)

RECREATION (*See:* Athletics/Recreational and Leisure Activities)

REAL ESTATE

RESTAURANT CHAINS

RETAILING (GENERAL MERCHANDISE)

SECURITIES (*See:* Finance)

SEMICONDUCTORS

SHOES (*See:* Apparel/Footwear)

SOFTWARE

STEEL (*See:* Mining and Metals)

TELECOMMUNICATIONS SERVICES

TELEVISION (*See:* Entertainment)

TEXTILES

TOBACCO PRODUCTS

TOOLS (*See*: Industrial/Farm Equipment and Tools)

TOYS (*Also see*: Athletic/Recreational and Leisure Activities)

TRANSPORTATION EQUIPMENT (*Also see*: Automotive, Industrial/Farm Equipment and Tools)

TRAVEL/HOSPITALITY

UTILITIES

WASTE MANAGEMENT (*See:* Environment/ Waste Management)

WHOLESALERS (*See:* Distributors/Wholesalers)

FIM—*Finnish markkaa*	**PFO**—*Principal Financial Officer*	**SF**—*Swiss francs*
FL—*Dutch Florins*		**SVC**—*Senior Vice Chairman*
HK$—*Hong Kong dollars*	**PLC**—*Public Limited Corporation*	**SVP**—*Senior Vice President*
HQ—*Headquarters*	**PP**—*Philippine pesos*	**S$**—*Singapore dollars*
IR£—*Irish pounds*	**£**—*British pounds*	**VC**—*Vice Chairman*
Lit—*Italian liras*	**R**—*Indian rupees, South African rand*	**VP**—*Vice President*
M$—*Malaysian ringgits*		**W**—*South Korean won*
NA—*Not available*	**SEK**—*Swedish kronor*	**Y**—*Japanese yen*
NT$—*New Taiwan dollars*	**SEVP**—*Senior Executive Vice President*	
NZ$—*New Zealand dollars*		

❶ ACCOUNTING

ILLINOIS

ANDERSEN WORLDWIDE ★★

33 W. Monroe St., Chicago, IL 60603; 312-580-0033
http://www.arthurandersen.com
Employees: 123,900
Sales: $13,900 million
Key Personnel: Acting CEO and Partner: Robert W. Grafton. Managing Partner: Arthur Andersen, Jim Wadia. Manager, Human Resources: Peter Pesce.
One of the largest accounting and management consulting companies in the world, Andersen Worldwide is made up of two branches. Arthur Andersen & Co. provides auditing, tax services, and management advice. Andersen Consulting provides technology consulting and strategic services. The company is rapidly expanding, and its sales and work force are increasing.
Other Locations: Worldwide HQ: Arthur Andersen & Co., S.C., 18, quai General-Guisan, Geneva 3, Switzerland; phone: +41-22-214444.

NEW YORK

DELOITTE TOUCHE TOHMATSU ★★

1633 Broadway, New York, NY 10019-6754; 212-492-4000
Employees: 82,000
Sales: $9,000 million
Key Personnel: Managing Partner, Deloitte & Touche LLP: James E. Copeland, Jr. Human Resources Contact: Martyn Fisher.
http://www.deloitte.com
One of the largest accounting firms in the world, Deloitte Touche Tohmatsu has primarily existed in the past as an auditor of large corporations. However, the increasing number of lawsuits between clients and auditors is causing the company to seek more business consulting work. Its sales and work force are growing.
Other Locations: The company has 700 branches in more than 130 countries.

ERNST & YOUNG LLP ★★

787 Seventh Ave., New York, NY 10019; 212-773-3000
http://www.eyi.com
Employees: 85,000
Sales: $10,900 million
Key Personnel: Chairman: Philip A. Laskawy. CEO: William L. Kimsey. Human Resources Contact: Lewis A. Ting.
Ernst & Young is the fourth largest accounting practice in the United States. The company—an amalgamation of two other big firms, Ernst & Whinney and Arthur Young—serves an international list of clients with auditing, accounting, and consulting services. Its sales and work force are on the rise.
Other Locations: The company has 701 offices in more than 130 countries.

KPMG INTERNATIONAL ★

345 Park Ave., New York, NY 10154; 212-909-5000
http://www.kpmg.com
Employees: 85,300
Sales: $10,600 million.
Key Personnel: Chairman: Colin Sharman. U.S. Chairman, CEO: Stephen G. Butler. Human Resources Partner, KPMG Peat Marwick LLP: Timothy P. Flynn. Human Resources Contact: Timothy P. Flynn.
KPMG (Klynveld Peat Marwick Goerdeler) is the third largest of the Big Five accounting firms, with operations in 800 cities around the world. It is unique in that it is the only one larger in Europe

than in North America. In the U.S. the firm operates under the name KPMG Peat Marwick. KPMG and Ernst & Young have dropped their merger plans, which would have made them the number 1 firm in the world. Both work force and sales have increased during the past year.
Other Locations: Main European Office, Klynveld Peat Marwick Goerdeler, P.O. Box 74555; 1070 BC Amsterdam, The Netherlands; phone: +31-20-656-7578.

PRICE WATERHOUSE COOPERS ★★
1301 Ave. of the Americas, New York, NY 10019; 212-596-7000
http://www.pwcglobal.com
Employees: 140,000
Sales: $15,000 million
Key Personnel: Chairman: Nicolas G.Moore. CEO: James J. Schiro. Human Resources Contact: Lennert S. Lindegren.
One of the Big Five largest accounting companies in the world, Price Waterhouse Coopers was formed last year from the merger of Coopers & Lybrand and Price Waterhouse. The company has retained its global client base after running into trouble years ago with the scandal at the Bank of Credit & Commerce. As of last year, its sales and work force are growing.
Other Locations: The company has more than 850 offices in 150 countries.

---

❶ ADVERTISING/PUBLIC RELATIONS

ILLINOIS
TRUE NORTH COMMUNICATIONS, INC. ★★
101 E. Erie St., Chicago, IL 60611-2897; 312- 425-6500
Employees: 11,448
Revenues: $ 1,242.3 million.
Key Personnel: Chairman, CEO: David Bell. President, FCB International: Harry Reid. VP, Director of Human Resources: Paul Sollitto.
True North was formerly Foote, Cone & Belding Communications, an old and prominent advertising agency. It is now a global company, having acquired agencies in Asia, Latin America, and the United States. The company has been restructuring for the past several years. It is now creating a virtual agency that will

operate without an actual office through computer networking. The company's sales and work force are rising.
Other Locations: The company has operations in 60 countries.

NEW YORK
DCA ADVERTISING ★★
666 Fifth Ave, New York, NY 10103; 212-397-3333
Employees: 6,000
Revenues: $1,620 million
Key Personnel: President, CEO: Tetsuo Machida. Treasurer: Masaki Yaegashi. EVP, Douglas Fidoten. EVP: Steve Penchina.
DCA Advertising, is a subsidiary of Dentsu, one of the largest advertising agencies in the world. Dentsu is a major force in the Japanese advertising market. With demand slipping, the company is diversifying into multimedia development, film and video production, and many other areas not traditionally visited by ad agencies. Sales and work force are up.
Other Locations: Worldwide HQ: Dentsu, Inc., 1-11-10 Tsukiji, Chuo-ku, Tokyo, 104-8426, Japan; phone: +81-3-5551-5111. The company and its affiliates have offices in 34 countries.

INTERPUBLIC GROUP ★★
1271 Avenue of the Americas, New York, NY 10020; 212-399-8000
http://www.interpublic.com
Employees: 34,000
Revenues: $3,844.3 million.
Key Personnel: Chairman, President, and CEO: Philip H. Geier Jr. EVP, CFO: Sean F. Orr. SVP Human Rresources: C. Kent Kroeber. SVP Planning and Business Development: Barry R. Linsky.
The Interpublic Group is one of the world's largest advertising companies. It is a holding company for a group of advertising agencies, including McCann-Erickson World Group. The agencies serve clients in more than 110 countries. Sales and employee growth has been substantial.

YOUNG & RUBICAM, INC.
285 Madison Ave., New York, NY 10017; 212-210-3000
http://www.yr.com
Employees: 13,000 **Revenues:** $1,522.5

million.

Key Personnel: Chairman, CEO, Young & Rubicam Advertising: Peter A. Georgescu. President, Young & Rubicam Advertising: John P. McGarry Jr. Human Resources contact: Bob Wells.

One of the largest conglomerations of advertising and public relations operations in the world, Young & Rubicam concentrates on five main areas. It serves its clients with advertising, public relations, sales promotion and direct marketing, corporate and product identity consulting, and health care communications. Its sales are declining, but its work force is expanding.

Other Locations: The company has 331 offices in 76 countries. Its public relations subsidiary, Burson-Marsteller, has 63 branches in 32 countries.

OMNICOM GROUP INC. ★★
437 Madison Ave., New York, NY 10022; 212-415-3600
http://www.omnicomny.com
Employees: 35,600
Revenues: $4,092.0 million.
Key Personnel: Chairman: Bruce Crawford. EVP, CFO: Randall J. Weisenburger.

Omnicom is one of world's largest advertising groups. Included in the Omnicom stable is BBDO Worldwide, DDB Needham, GGT Group and TBWA Chiat/Day. The company offers its clients consumer market research, marketing consultation, design and production of merchandising and promotion programs, and corporate image development. Sales growth in 1997 was over 18 percent.

TEXAS
HERITAGE MEDIA CORPORATION ★★
13355 Noel Rd., Suite 1500, Dallas, TX 75240; 214-702-7380
Employees: 16,000*
Revenues: $440 million
Key Personnel: Chairman: James M. Hoak. President, CEO: David N. Walthall. Manager, Human Resources: Amy Kruckemeyer.

Although Heritage Media owns several U.S. television and radio stations, its main enterprise is ACTMEDIA, which puts ads on freezers, carts, and shelves in over 36,000 grocery stores and pharmacies in the United States and Europe. Heritage also owns ACTRADIO, the top

U.S. in-store radio network. The company's sales and work force are growing. (*Employee figures include 12,000 part-time and 4,000 full-time workers.)

❶ AEROSPACE/DEFENSE

CALIFORNIA
BEI TECHNOLOGIES, INC. ★★
One Post St., Suite 2500, San Francisco, CA 94104; 415-956-4477
http://www.bei-tech.com
Employees: 1,100
Sales: $124.3 million
Key Personnel: Chairman, President, and CEO: Charles Crocker. VP, Chief Technology Officer: Lawrence A. Wan. Human Resources: William T. Aber.

Electronic sensors, servo systems, and DC motors are just a portion of BEI Technologies' (formerly BEI Electronics) product line. The company manufactures a wide variety of high-technology gadgets for transportation, medical, and other commercial uses. Its sales and workforce are both up.

HUGHES ELECTRONICS CORPORATION
7200 Hughes Terrace, P.O. Box 80028, Los Angeles, CA 90045-0066; 310-568-7200
http://www.hughes.com
Employees: 15,000
Sales: $5,963.9 million
Key Personnel: Chairman, CEO: Michael T. Smith. VC: Steven D. Dorfman. SVP, CFO: Roxanne S. Austin. Human Resources: Sandra Harrison.

Under the auspices of General Motors, Hughes Electronics derives a large portion of its business from the satellite-based telecommunications industry. It has a fleet of communications satellites in orbit and is responsible for DIRECTV, a satellite broadcasting system with several million subscribers. Its sales are up, but its workforce numbers are stagnant.

LITTON INDUSTRIES, INC. ★★
21240 Burbank Blvd., Woodland Hills, CA 91367-6675; 818-598-5000
http://www.littoncorp.com
Employees: 34,900
Sales: $4,399.9 million
Key Personnel: Chairman, President, and CEO: Michael R. Brown. EVP, COO: Harry Halamandaris. Human Re-

sources: Nancy L. Gaymon.

Litton Industries runs a myriad of operations in aerospace, defense, electronics, and information systems. Litton does most of its work for the U.S. government, making navigational and control systems, electronic warfare systems, and building ships for the Navy. The company has expanded its commercial shipbuilding interests with its recent acquisition of Avondale industries. Sales are up moderately, and workforce growth has been strong.

NORTHROP GRUMMAN CORPORATION

1840 Century Park E., Los Angeles, CA 90067; 310-553-6262

http://www.northgrum.com
Employees: 49,600
Sales: $8,902 million
Key Personnel: Chairman, President, and CEO: Kent Kresa. VP, President and CEO of Logicon: Herbert W. Anderson. Corporate VP, President of Integrated Systems & Aerostructures Sector. Corporate VP, Chief Human Resources Officer: Marvin Elkin.

An amalgamation of two giants, Northrop Grumman sprung from the merger of Northrop Corporation and Grumman Corporation. The company makes electronics for military aircraft and parts for commercial aircraft, as well as a variety of other military technologies. The company is restructuring to adjust to decreases in demand for its products. Sales and workforce growth have been tepid.
Other Locations: The company has facilities in 18 states.

ROCKWELL INTERNATIONAL CORP. ★

600 Anton Blvd., Suite 700, Costa Mesa, CA 92628-5090; 714-424-4200

http://www.rockwell.com
Employees: 41,000
Sales: $6,752 million
Key Personnel: Chairman, President, and CEO: Don H. Davis Jr. SVP Finance and Planning, CFO: W. Michael Barnes. Human Resources: Joel R. Stone.

Rockwell International is shifting its business away from the aerospace/defense industry (having sold those divisions to Boeing), toward industrial automation. The company makes a wide variety of products for both the public and private sector, including the space shuttle orbiter, industrial motors, and worker-machine interface devices. Its

sales and work force are increasing steadily.

CONNECTICUT

UNITED TECHNOLOGIES CORPORATION

One Financial Plaza, Hartford, CT 06101; 860-728-7000

http://www.utc.com
Employees: 178,800
Sales: $25,687 million
Key Personnel: Chairman, CEO: George David. President, COO: Karl J. Krapek. SVP Human Resources and Organization: William L. Bucknall, Jr.

United Technologies Corporation is an amalgamation of several prominent manufacturers, including Carrier, Hamilton, Standard, Otis, Pratt & Whitney, Sikorsky, and UT Automotive. The company has been a major defense contractor, supplying such products as the Army's Black Hawk helicopters. Overall sales and work force growth have been slow and stagnant, respectively.
Other Locations: The company has facilities in Africa, Asia, Australia, Canada, Europe, Latin America, Mexico, the Middle East, and the United States.

KANSAS

LEARJET, INC. ★★

One Learjet Way, Wichita, KS 67277-7707; 316-946-2000

http://www.learjet.com
Employees: 5,000
Sales (overall Bombardier): $7609.9 million
Key Personnel: President: Jim Sigler. VP Finance: Chris Krawshaw. VP Human Resources: Jeff Bahr.

Learjet is an American subsidiary of Bombardier, Canada's largest aerospace interest. In addition to Lear, Bombardier also owns de Havilland and other commercial aerospace companies. Lear makes what many regard to be the leading small jet aircraft. Its sales and work force are rising.
Other Locations: Worldwide HQ: Bombardier, Inc., 800 Rene-Levesque Blvd. W Montreal, Quebec H3B1Y8, Canada; 514-861-9481.

MARYLAND

LOCKHEED MARTIN CORPORATION

6801 Rockledge Dr., Bethesda, MD 20817; 301-897-6000

http://www.lockheedmartin.com/index.htm

Employees: 165,000
Sales: $26,266 million
Key Personnel: Chairman and CEO: Vance D. Coffman. President and COO: Peter B. Teets. Human Resources: Terry Powell.

The largest defense contractor in the United States, Lockheed Martin is an amalgamation of Lockheed and Martin Marietta. The company produces a wide variety of products including the Trident II missile, communications satellites, and night navigation systems, and was recently selected by NASA to build a new experimental rocket, the X-33. Sales and workforce are both up slightly.

MASSACHUSETTS

EG&G, INC. ★
45 William St., Wellesley, MA 02481;
781-237-5100
http://www.egginc.com
Employees: 13,000
Sales: $1,407.9 million
Key Personnel: Chairman, President, and CEO: Gregory L. Summe. SVP: Angelo D. Castellana. SVP, Human Resources: Richard F. Walsh.

EG&G, which had several lucrative contracts with the U.S. government in nuclear weapons testing and research, abandoned the field because of cutbacks. The company now manufactures a wide array of sensors and screening instruments used in medical testing, food decontamination and other applications. Sales growth is slow, but workforce numbers have shown a healthy increase.

RAYTHEON COMPANY ★
141 Spring St., Lexington, MA 02421;
781-862-6600
http://www.raytheon.com
Employees: 108,200
Sales: $19,530 million
Key Personnel: Chairman, President, and CEO: Daniel P. Burnham. EVP, Chairman and CEO Raytheon Engineers and Constructors. EVP, Chairman and CEO Raytheon Systems: William H. Swanson. Human Resources: Dennis M. Donovan.

Following its acquisition of the defense divisions of Texas Instruments and Hughes Electronics, Raytheon has become the #3 U.S. aerospace and defense company (after Boeing and Lockheed Martin). Electronics, aircraft, and engineering/construction are Raytheon's three chief areas of operations. The company makes systems for environmental testing, broadcasting, and defense (Tomahawk and Patriot missiles). Raytheon is also a leading manufacturer of small passenger aircraft. Sales are skyrocketing and jobs have experienced a healthy increase.

MINNESOTA

ALLIANT TECHSYSTEMS, INC. ★
600 Second St., NE, Hopkins, MN 55343; 612-931-6000
http://www.atk.com
Employees: 6,110
Sales: $1,090.4
Key Personnel: Chairman, CEO: Paul David Miller. President, COO: Peter A. Bukowick. Human Resources: Robert E. Gustafson.

Defense and Aerospace manufacturer Alliant Techsystems has three chief areas of operation: defense systems, conventional munitions, and space and strategic systems. Heavily dependent on sales to the U.S. government, these three operations allow the company to cater to a variety of defense and space needs. Gunpowder, rocket propulsion systems, smart bombs, and unmanned military vehicles are only a few of Alliant's products. Sales growth has been meager, but jobs are up measurably.

NEW JERSEY

ALLIEDSIGNAL, INC.
101 Columbia Rd., Morristown, NJ 07962; 973-455-2000
Employees: 70,400
Sales: $15,128 million
Key Personnel: Chairman, CEO: Lawrence A. Bossidy. President and COO: Frederic M. Poses. Human Resources: Donald J. Redlinger.

Growth by acquisition has been the mainstay of AlliedSignal in recent years. Among its purchases are a Polish brake plant from Fiat and Ford's U.K. spark plug plant. The company has three main segments: aerospace, automotive, and engineered materials. It is in the midst of acquiring Honeywell and plans to adopt that name. Sales have increased slightly, but work force numbers are static.
Other Locations: The company has more than 300 operations in 40 countries.

NEW YORK

ITT INDUSTRIES, INC. ★★
4 W. Red Oak Ln., White Plains, NY 10604; 914-641-2000
Key Personnnel: Chairman, President, and CEO: Travis Engen. President, COO: Louis J. Giuliano. Human Resources: James P. Smith, Jr.
ITT Industries, a manufacturing conglomerate, was founded in 1995 when ITT Corporation's operations were split into three companies. The various divisions of ITT manufacture everything from defense and aerospace products to auto parts and fluid-handling valves. ITT Defense Products & Services, a subsidiary of ITT Industries, makes electronic warfare systems, radar instruments, and night-vision gear for the U.S. military. Sales and workforce growth are through the roof.

LORAL SPACE AND COMMUNICATIONS, LTD. ★★
600 3rd Ave., New York, NY 10016; 212-697-1105
http://www.loral.com
Employees: 3,900
Sales: $1,301.7 million
Key Personnel: Chairman, CEO: Bernard L. Schwartz. President, COO: Gregory J. Clark. Human Resources: Stephen L. Jackson.
Loral Space & Communications is what remains after Lockheed Martin's acquisition of most of the former giant, Loral Corp. The new Loral deals primarily in satellite production and transmission services. It manages and/or owns a variety of satellite-based telecommunications providers, including Cyberstar, Skynet, and Orion Network Systems. Sales are flat, but workforce growth is through the roof.

OHIO

THE BF GOODRICH COMPANY
4020 Kinross Lakes Pkwy., Richfield, OH 44286-9368; 330-659-7600
http://www.bfgoodrich.com
Employees: 17,175
Sales: $3,950.8 million
Key Personnel: Chairman, President, and CEO: David L. Burner. EVP, President and COO Aerospace Segment: Marshall O. Larsen. Human Resources: Gary L. Habegger.

BF Goodrich makes aircraft parts and provides aircraft maintenance, repair, and overhaul services to such customers as Boeing and Lockheed Martin. The company also develops specialty chemicals for use in manufacturing, pharmaceuticals, paper, and more. Although BF Goodrich earned its name making tires, it no longer does, having licensed the Goodrich name to Michelin. Sales are way up, but jobs are static.

PENNSYLVANIA

ALLEGHENY TELEDYNE, INC.
1000 Six PPG Place, Pittsburgh, PA 45222-5479; 412-394-2800
http://www.alleghenyteledyne.com
Employees: 21,500
Sales: $3,923.4 million
Key Personnel: Chairman, President, and CEO: Richard P. Simmons. VC: Robert P. Bozzone. SVP Human Resources: Judd R. Cool.
Allegheny Teledyne, the result of a 1996 merger of Diversified Teldyne and Allegheny Ludlum, has its chief operations in specialty metals, aerospace, electronics, and defense. It makes aircraft piston engines, parts for microwaves, and dental lab equipment. Metals operations acount for more than half the company's sales and it is currently making efforts to sell or spin off its non-metals businesses. Sales and workforce growth have both been slow.

RHODE ISLAND

TEXTRON, INC.
40 Westminster St., Providence, RI 02903; 401-421-2800
http://www.textron.com
Employees: 64,000
Sales: $9,683 million
Key Personnel: Chairman, CEO: Lewis B. Campbell. President, COO: John A. Janitz. Human Resources: John D. Butler.
One of the oldest industrial conglomerates in the United States, Textron has four chief areas of operation: aircraft (subsidiaries include Cessna and Bell); plastic automotive parts; industrial manufacturing; and finance. It also owns companies such as Orag Inter AG, the largest distributor of lawn care and golf equipment in Europe. Its sales are up, but its workforce is holding steady.
Other Locations: The company has 138

facilities in the United States and nine in foreign countries.

UTAH

CORDANT TECHNOLOGIES, INC. ★★
15 W. South Temple, Ste. 1600, Salt Lake City, UT 84101-1532; 801-933-4000
http://www.cordanttech.com
Employees: 17,400
Sales: $1,779.3 million
Key Personnel: Chairman, President, and CEO: James R. Wilson. SVP, CFO: Richard L. Corbin. EVP Human Resources and Administration: James E. McNulty.

Formerly Thiokol Corporation, Cordant Technologies is in the midst of a dazzling move away from defense manufacturing toward commercial and other non-military propulsion systems. Although it still depends on government contracts (as NASA's only solid booster supplier and the manufacturer of crucial Trident missile components), Cordant's subsidiaries—which produce specialty fasteners for transportation and construction—have begun to really pull their weight. Sales and workforce numbers have each more than doubled.
Other Locations: The company has operations in France, Germany, the United Kingdom, and the United States.

VIRGINIA

BRITISH AEROSPACE NORTH AMERICA, INC. ★★
15000 Conference Center Dr., Ste. 200; Chantilly, VA 20151; 703-802-0080
http://www.bae.co.uk
Employees (overall BAe): 47,900
Sales (overall BAe): $11,48.7 million
Key Personnel: SVP, General Manager: Paul L. Harris. VP Finance, Treasurer: Steve Massey. VP Human Resources: Maria Gill.

British Aerospace North America is a subsidiary of British Aerospace (Bae), the largest defense contractor in Europe. With the downturn in the defense industry, it has recently been aggressively diversifying. Along with its participation in the Airbus Industrie consortium, it has gotten into such areas as automobiles and civil engineering. Sales are up dramatically, as its workforce
Other Locations: Worldwide HQ: British Aerospace PLC, Warwick House, P.O. Box 87, Farnborough Aerospace Centre, Farnborough, Hampshire, GU146YU, United Kingdom; phone: +44-125-237-3232.

GENERAL DYNAMICS CORPORATION ★
3190 Fairview Park Dr., Falls Church, VA 22042-4523; 703-876-3000
http://www.gendyn.com
Employees: 31,000
Sales: $4,970 million
Key Personnel: Chairman, CEO: Nicholas D. Chabraja. President, COO: James E. Turner, Jr. Human Resources: W. Peter Wylie.

General Dynamics builds nuclear submarines and tanks. Once a much larger company, it has sold off major chunks in order to stay afloat. After this downsizing (in the early 1990's), the company has begun acquiring related businesses to broaden its base. Gulfstream Aerospace, a subsidiary, makes business jets. Sales and workforce numbers are showing marked improvement.
Other Locations: The company builds submarines in Connecticut, New Jersey, and Rhode Island, tanks in Michigan and Ohio.

NEWPORT NEWS SHIPBUILDING, INC.
4101 Washington Ave., Newport News, VA 23607-2770; 757-380-2000
http://www.nns.com
Employees: 18,200
Sales: $1,862 million
Key Personnel: Chairman, CEO: William P. Fricks. SVP, CFO: Thomas C. Schievelbein. Human Resources: Alfred Little, Jr.

Newport News Shipbuilding (NNS) is the #2 shipbuilder in the U.S., behind General Dynamics. Building,, refurbishing, and otherwise servicing nuclear submarines and aircraft carriers for the Navy provides 90 percent of its business. NNS lost the recent bidding war over Avondale Industries to Litton, which was only one setback among many for a company that has suffered from defense cutbacks. Sales are up moderately, but workforce growth has been static.

ORBITAL SCIENCES CORPORATION ★★
21700 Atlantic Blvd., Dulles, VA 20166; 703-406-5000
http://www.orbital.com
Employees: 4,400
Sales: $734.3 million

Key Personnel: Chairman, President, and CEO: David W. Thompson. EVP, CFO: Jeffrey V. Pirone. Human Resources: Mary Ann Welding.

Orbital Sciences' products include launch vehicles, data communications systems, and ground control systems. Orbital focuses on small to medium-sized satellites for low and medium-earth orbit. Working jointly with auto parts manufacturer Magna International, Orbital is designing a navigation system for c ars. Its sales are rising, as is its workforce.

ROLLS–ROYCE, NORTH AMERICA INC.

11911 Freedom Dr., Reston, VA 20190-5602; 703-834-1700
http://www.rolls-royce..com
Employees (overall Rolls-Royce): 42,000
Sales (overall Rolls-Royce): $7,463.1 million
Key Personnel: President, CEO: James M. Guyette. VP Corporate Communications: Robert N. Baugniet. VP Human Resources: Rebecca Blackman.

The third largest manufacturer of jet engines in the world, Rolls-Royce also makes equipment for and constructs power plants and builds marine oil and gas pumps. Its jet engines are used both in military and civilian applications. The company's aerospace component has suffered from cutbacks in military spending. Both its sales and its workforce growth have been slow to non-existent.
Other Locations: Worldwide HQ: Rolls-Royce PLC, 65 Buckingham Gate, London, SW1E6AT, United Kingdom; phone: +44-171-222-9020.

WASHINGTON

THE BOEING COMPANY

7755 E. Marginal Way S., Seattle, WA 98108; 206-655-2121
http://www.boeing.com
Employees: 231,000
Sales: $56,154 million
Key Personnel: Chairman, CEO: Philip M. Condit. President, COO: Harry C. Stonecipher. Human Resources: James B. Dagnon.

Boeing has been the largest commercial aircraft manufacturer in the world for more than 30 years. With the pruchase of McDonnell Douglas, its rival and the number one military aircraft maker, Boeing is now the largest aerospace firm in the world and the only maker of commercial jet airplanes in the U.S. In addition to its extensive line of commercial aircraft, the company also makes the B-2 bomber, V-22 Osprey, and many other defense and space vehicles. Sales have increased substantially, but workforce growth has been slow.
Other Locations: The company has facilities in 11 states and two Canadian provinces.

❶ AIRLINES

ARIZONA

AMERICA WEST AIRLINES, INC.

400 East Sky Harbor Blvd., Phoenix, AZ, 85034; 480-693-0800.
http://www.americawest.com
Employees: 12,204
Sales: $ 2,023.3 million
Key Personnel: Chairman, CEO: William A. Franke. President, CEO: Richard R. Goodmanson. SVP Human Resources: Bruce A. Johnson.

America West controls about 3 percent of the domestic airlines market, with flights mostly to Western states. The company filed for Chapter 11 bankruptcy in 1991, laying off thousands of employees in a restructuring effort. It has regained profitability in the last few years flying to over 60 U.S. destinations.

CALIFORNIA

QANTAS AIRWAYS, LTD.

841 Apollo St., Suite 400, El Segundo, CA 90245; 310-726-1400
http://www.qantas.com.au
Employees: 30,000
Sales: $ 5,047.6 million
Key Personnel: Chairman: Gary M. Pemberton. Managing Director: James A. Strong. HR Contact: George Elsey

Qantas is Australia's largest airline. It primarily serves Asia and the Pacific. The company recently purchased Australia Airlines and agreed to a partnership arrangement with British Airways. The company aggressively cut its work force in 1992. Recently, the decrease in travel has resulted in less sales.
Other Locations: Worldwide HQ: Qantas Airways, Ltd., Qantas Centre, 203 Coward St., Mascot, NSW 2020, Australia; phone: +61-2-691-3636.

SINGAPORE AIRLINES, LTD.
5670 Wilshire Blvd., Suite 1800, Los
Angeles, CA 90036; 323-934-8833
http://www.singaporeair.com
Employees: 27,516
Sales: $4,786.3 million
**Key Personnel: Chairman: Michael Y.
O. Fam.** Deputy Chairman, CEO:
Cheong Choong Kong. HR Contact:
Chris Lee.
Singapore Airlines is considered the best
airline in the world, known for its elegant
cabin furnishings and gourmet meals.
The Singapore government owns 54 per-
cent of the airline, which has the most
modern fleet of all the international carri-
ers. The company has suffered from a re-
cent slump in air travel.
Other Locations: Worldwide HQ: Sin-
gapore Airlines, Ltd., Airline House, 25
Airline Rd., 819829, Singapore; phone:
+65-542-3333.

CONNECTICUT

VIRGIN ATLANTIC ★★
747 Belden Ave., Norwalk, CT 06850;
203-750-2000.
http://www.fly.virgin.com/
Employees: 24,000
Sales: $5,000 million
Key Personnel: Chairman: Richard
Branson. CFO: David Tait. Human Resources contact: DeloraBrathwaite.
Virgin Group is the owner of Virgin Atlantic Airways, Britain's second largest
airline. The London-based company is
expanding. It doubled the size of its fleet
and the aggressive airline also added
routes to San Francisco and Hong Kong
several years ago.. The company continues to increase sales and work force as it
acquires an increasing share of the market.
Other Locations: Worldwide HQ: Virgin Group PLC, 120 Campden Hill Rd.,
London, W8 7AR, United Kingdom;
phone: +44-171-229-1282.

GEORGIA

DELTA AIR LINES, INC. ★★
1030 Delta Blvd., Atlanta, GA 30320-
6001; 404-715-2600
http://www.delta-air.com
Employees: 70,846
Sales: $ 14,711 million
Key Personnel: President, CEO: Leo F.
Mullin. EVP Operations: Malcom B.

Armstrong. Human Resources contact:
Robert L. Colman.
Although Delta Air Lines is one of the
top carriers in the United States, it has
not been profitable since 1989. The company, which has 4,900 daily flights to
U.S. locations and abroad and recently
announced a new budget carrier—Delta
Express—has seen consistently increasing sales.

ILLINOIS

UAL CORPORATION
1200 E. Algonquin Rd., Elk Grove
Township, IL 60007; 847-700-4000
http://www.ual.com
Employees: 95,035
Sales: $ 17,561 million
Key Personnel: Chairman, CEO, UAL
and United Airlines: James E. Goodwin.
President, UAL and United Airlines:
Rono J. Dutta. Human Resources contact:
William P. Hobgood.
UAL operates United Airlines, the top carrier in the world. After three years of losses,
the company gave up 55 percent ownership
to its employees in 1994 in exchange for
wage concessions. Following several years
of losses, its sales and workforce have increased modestly.

MINNESOTA

NORTHWEST AIRLINES CORPORATION
5101 Northwest Drive, St. Paul, MN
55121-3034; 612-726-2111
http://www.nwa.com
Employees: 50,600
Sales: $ 9,044.8 million
Key Personnel: Chairman: Gary L. Wilson. President, CEO: John H. Dasburg.
SVP Communications, Advertising, and
Human Resources: Christopher E.
Clouser.
Northwest Airlines is the fourth largest
airline in the world. It came close to bankruptcy after a leveraged buyout in 1989.
However, its employees agreed to nearly
$1 billion in wage concessions in return
for 26 percent of the company's stock.
KLM Royal Dutch Airlines owns 25 percent of Northwest. Sales and work force
continue to increase, but increased labor
costs due to "wage snapbacks" promised
in 1993 were expected to curtail overall
growth.

MISSOURI

TRANS WORLD AIRLINES, INC.

1 City Ctr., 515 N. 6th St., St. Louis, MO 63101; 314-589-3000
Employees: 21,261
Sales: $ 3,259.1 million
http://www.twa.com
Key Personnel: Chairman: Gerald L. Gitner. President, CEO: William Compton. Human Resources contact: Kathleen A. Soled.

Although Trans World Airlines—which has scheduled service throughout the United States and in Europe and the Middle East—once led the pack in transatlantic flights, its prospects are uncertain today. It went to bankruptcy court in 1995 for the second time in four years and has long been downsizing in an effort to remain in business. However, in the past two years its revenues and workforce have decreased modestly.

NEVADA

MESA AIR GROUP, INC.

3753 Howard Hughes Pkwy, Suite 200, Las Vegas, NE89109; 702-892-3773
http://www.mesa-air.com
Employees: 2,500
Sales: $423.5 million
Key Personnel: President, CEO, Director: Jonathan Ornstein. COO: Michael Lotz. Treasurer, CFO: Blaine M. Jones. VP Human Resources: Rodena Turner Bojorquez.

Mesa Airlines serves about 120 cities in 28 states. The company is coming off a couple years of bad sales and a management shakeup. The company generates 70 percent of its income from sharing agreements with other airlines.

NEW YORK

ALL NIPPON AIRWAYS

630 Fifth Ave., Suite 646, New York, NY 10111; 212-956-8200
http://www.ana.co.jp
Employees: 15,200
Sales: $ 8,119.8 million
Key Personnel:. President, CEO: Kichisaburo Nomura. HR Contact: Yoji Ohashi.

All Nippon Airways is the second largest airline in Japan and one of the largest in the world. Along with its tremendous passenger volume, the company also has significant income from its hotel, travel, and real estate subsidiaries. The Japanese recession caused severe profit reductions in recent years.
Other Locations: Worldwide HQ: All Nippon Airways Co., Ltd., Kasumigaseki Bldg., 3-2-5, Kasumigaseki, Chiyoda-ku, Tokyo 100-6027, Japan; phone: +81-3-3592-3065.

BRITISH AIRWAYS (U.S.)

7520 Astoria Blvd., Flushing, NY 11370; 718-397-4000
http://www.british-airways.com
Employees: 60,770
Sales: $ 14,446.8 million
Key Personnel: Chairman: Sir Colin Marshall. CEO: Robert Aylin. SVP Human Resources, Bulova Corp. Center (U.S.): Irv Rudowitz.

British Airways is the largest international airline in the world. Based in London, the company flies to 165 cities in 75 countries. The company's sales have been fluctuating in recent years after it purchased a 25 percent share of USAir in 1993. British Airways has been shrinking its work force since 1991.
Other Locations: Worldwide HQ: British Airways PLC, Waterside, PO Box 365 Harmondsworth UB70GB, United Kingdom; phone: +44-181-562-4444.

FLIGHTSAFETY INTERNATIONAL, INC. ★★

Marine Air Terminal, La Guardia Airport, Flushing, NY 11371; 718-565-4100
http://www.flightsafety.com
Employees: 3,500
Sales: $ 858 million
Key Personnel: Chairman, President: Albert L. Ueltschi. EVP: Bruce N. Whitman. Human Resources Director: Thomas W. Riffe.

FlightSafety International is the world's largest cockpit-simulation operator. The company, a subsidiary of Berkshire Hathaway,trains aircraft pilots and ship operators and also sells simulation equipment. The company's sales and work force have been increasing nicely.

JAPAN AIRLINES

655 Fifth Ave., New York, NY 10022; 212-310-1318
http://www.japanair.com
Employees: 17,863
Sales: $ 11,981.5 million

Key Personnel: President, CEO: Isao Kaneko. SVP Human Resources: Hidekazu Funayama.

Japan Airlines is the largest airline in Japan and one of the largest in the world. The company carries 23 million passengers a year. It also owns a 25-percent share of the courier service DHL International. The company's sales have remained steady despite the Japanese recession, although its work force has decreased slightly.

Other Locations: Worldwide HQ: Japan Airlines Co., Ltd.,4-11, Higashi-shinagawa 2-chome, Shinagawa-ku, Tokyo 140-8637, Japan; phone: +81-3-5460-3191.

KLM ROYAL DUTCH AIRLINES USA ★

565 Taxter Rd., Elmsford, NY 10523; 914-784-2000

http://www.klm.nl
Employees: 28,374
Sales: $ 5,717.8 million
Key Personnel: Chairman: C. J. Oort. VP and Area Manager: Jan Meurer. Human Resources contact: Cees van Woudenberg.

Based in Amsterdam, Koninklijke Luchtvaart Maatschappij, or KLM Royal Dutch Airlines, is the world's oldest international airline. The Dutch government owns a 38.2-percent stake in the company, which has become increasingly diversified. KLM is now the fifth largest cargo carrier in the world. KLM's work force and sales have remained steady in recent years.

Other Locations: Worldwide HQ: KLM Royal Dutch Airlines, Koninklijke Luchtvaart Maatschappi N.V., Amsterdamseweg 55, Amstelveen, The Netherlands; phone: +31-20-649-91-23.

LUFTHANSA GERMAN AIRLINES

680 Fifth Ave., New York, NY 10019; 212-479-8801

http://www.lufthansa.de
Employees: 54,867
Sales: $13,592.4 million
Key Personnel: Chairman: Jurgen Weber. Chief Executive, Technical Services: Klaus Nittinger. Manager, Human Resources, Lufthansa (U.S.):Thomas Facone.

Lufthansa is the second largest airline in Europe. The German government owns a 51.4-percent share of the company. Along with its cargo transport operation, the company owns interests in several other airlines and travel-related businesses. A downturn in European travel forced the layoff of thousands in the early 1990s, but sales have remained strong.

Other Locations: Worldwide HQ: Deutsche Lufthansa AG, Von-Gablenz-Strasse 2-6, Cologne, 21, Germany; phone: +49-221-8260.

T E X A S

AMR CORPORATION

4333 Amon Carter Blvd., Fort Worth, TX 76155; 817-963-1234

http://www.amrcorp.com
Employees: 92,000
Sales: $ 19,205 million
Key Personnel: Chairman, President, CEO:Donald J. Carty. EVP Operations, American Airlines: Robert W. Baker. Human Resource contact, American Airlines: A. Jaynne Allison.

AMR Corporation owns American Airlines, the number-one carrier in the United States. The company also owns American Eagle, a regional shuttle system operating mainly in the Eastern United States, and the SABRE reservation system. Although sales have increased moderately, the work force continues to decrease.

CONTINENTAL AIRLINES, INC. ★★

1600 Smith St., Dept. HQSEO, Houston, TX 77002; 713-324-5000

http://www.continental.com
Employees: 43,900
Sales: $ 7,951 million
Key Personnel: Chairman, CEO: Gordon M. Bethune. President, COO: Gregory D. Brenneman. SVP Human Resources: Mike Campbell.

Financially troubled Continental Airlines flies to over 100 cities in the United States and over 50 cities in Asia, Australia, Europe, and Latin America. The company's declining sales and decreasing workforce turned around in 1996-97, with a slight increase in both sales and workforceand has continued to rebound nicely.

SOUTHWEST AIRLINES CO. ★

2702 Love Field Dr., Dallas, TX 75235; 214- 792-4000

http://www.southwest.com
Employees: 25,844

Sales: $ 4,164 million
Key Personnel: Chairman, President, CEO: Herbert D. Kelleher. EVP, COO: James C. Wimberly. VP People: Elizabeth P. Sartain.

Southwest Airlines has used a low-cost, no-frills approach to business to become the eighth largest airline in the United States. Although the competition is stiff, the company continues to come up with innovative approaches to keep its market niche. Its sales and work force increased moderately in recent years. Currently, the company is expanding into the eastern U.S

UTAH
SWIRE PACIFIC HOLDINGS, INC. ★
875 S. West Temple St., Salt Lake City, UT 84101; 801-530-5300
http://www.irasia.com/listco/hk/swire
Employees: 60,000
Sales: $ 3,162.8 million
Key Personnel: Chairman: Peter D. A. Sutch. President, CEO, Swire Pacific (U.S.): Jack Pelo. Director of Human Resources, Swire Pacific (U.S.): Kristin Roberts

Swire Pacific has major holdings in Cathy Pacific and Dragonair, a regional Chinese carrier. The company, which is based in Hong Kong, also does extensive business in real estate and property management, as well as apparel, food, and other manufacturing operations. It is also a Coca-Cola bottler in southern China.
Other Locations: Worldwide HQ: Swire Pacific, Ltd., 35/F, Two Pacific Place, 88 Queensway, Hong Kong; phone: +852-840-8888.

VIRGINIA
US AIRWAYS GROUP, INC.
2345 Crystal Dr., Arlington, VA 22227; 703- 872-7000
http://www.usairways.com
Employees: 42,625
Sales: $ 8,688 million
Key Personnel: Chairman: Stephen M. Wolf. President, CEO: Rakesh Gangwal. SVP Human Resources, US Airways, Inc.: Michelle V. Bryan

USAir Group owns USAir, Allegheny Airlines, and other subsidiary companies. USAir is the sixth largest airline in the United States and operates primarily on the East Coast. Invester Warren Buffet's Berkshire Hathaway owns 10% of the US Airways. With sales decreasing for more than six years because of intense competition, the company has been downsizing in an effort to maintain its market share.

WASHINGTON
ALASKA AIR GROUP, INC. ★
19300 Pacific Highway S., Seattle, WA 98188; 206-431-7040
http://www.alaska-air.com
Employees: 9,244
Sales: $ 1,897.7 million
Key Personnel: Chairman, President, CEO; Chairman, Alaska Airlines and Horizon Air: John F. Kelly. President, CEO, Horizon Air: George D. Bagley. VP Employee Services, Alaska Airlines: Timothy R. Metcalf.

Alaska Airlines is a dominant force in the travel market on the West Coast. Although the company suffered losses in 1992 and 1993, things turned around in the mid-1990's after cutting costs and expanding services. Both sales and work force have remained steady during the past two years.

❶ ALCOHOLIC BEVERAGES

CALIFORNIA
E. & J. GALLO WINERY ★★
P.O. Box 1130, 600 Yosemite Blvd., Modesto, CA 95353; 209-341-3111
http://www.gallo.com
Employees: 5,500
Sales: $1,500 million (est.)
Key Personnel: Chairman: Ernest Gallo. Co-President: James E. Coleman. Co-President: Joseph E. Gallo. Human Resources: Mike Chase.

The largest wine producer in the world, E. & J. Gallo has found its market in the low-priced niches in the past. However, as wine consumption has decreased, the company has marketed an increasing quantity of upscale varietals. The company's successful distribution network has aided this transition. Its sales and work force are rising slightly.

KIRIN BREWERY OF AMERICA, LLC
2400 Broadway St., Suite 240, Santa Monica, CA 90404; 310-829-2400
http://www.kirin.com
Employees: 8,400

Sales: $6,648.9 million
Key Personnel: President: Takeshi Shimazu. VP Administration and Management, Human Resources: Jutei Watanabe.
Kirin Brewery of America is a subidiary of the ailing Kirin Brewery Company, once the largest beer maker in Japan. A fiercely competitive Japanese beer market has forced Kirin to branch out internationally, investing in locally-brewed beers and pharmaceutical interests—operations which have brought the company a much-needed resurgence. Kirin also makes teas, canned drinks, coffees, and sports drinks. Sales are up substantially; work force numbers show moderate growth.
Other Locations: Worldwide HQ: Kirin Brewery Co., Ltd., 10-1 Shinkawa 2-chome, Chuo-ku, Tokyo 104-8288, Japan; +81-3-5540-3411. The company has 15 breweries in Japan and affiliated operations in 11 countries.

SAN MIGUEL, INC.

1900 S. Norfolk, Suite 270, San Mateo, CA 94404; 415-345-1330
http://www.sanmiguel.com.ph
Employees (overall San Miguel Corp.): 15,923
Sales (overall San Miguel Corp.): $1,910.5 million
Key Personnel: Chairman, CEO: Eduardo M. Cojuangco, Jr. VC: Renato C. Valencia. President, COO: Francisco C. Eizmendi, Jr.
San Miguel is one of the largest manufacturing company in the Philippines. The company makes beer, soft drinks, packaging material, and various processed foods. It also has livestock, insurance, and real estate interests. Its sales and work force are up markedly.
Other Locations: Worldwide HQ: San Miguel Corp., 40 San Miguel Ave., P.O. Box 271, Mandaluyong City, Metro Manila 1550, Philippines; +63-2-632-3000.

COLORADO

ADOLPH COORS COMPANY

17735 W. 32nd Ave., Golden, CO 80401; 303-279-6565
http://www.coors.com
Employees: 5,800
Sales: $1,899.5 million
Key Personnel: Chairman, President, and Chairman, Coors Brewing: William K. Coors. VC: Joseph Coors. Human Resources: Robert W. Ehret.

One of the largest brewers in the United States, Adolph Coors is expanding to both Europe and Asia. The company has been increasing its product line for several years, although Coors Light, the #4 U.S. beer, still accounts for about two-thirds of sales. The company recently opened breweries in Spain and South Korea. While sales remain steady, workforce numbers have been static.
Other Locations: The company has facilities in Colorado, Tennessee, and Virginia and in South Korea and Spain.

CONNECTICUT

FORTUNE BRANDS, INC.

1700 E. Putnam Ave., P.O. Box 811, Old Greenwich, CT 06870-0811; 203-698-5000
http://www.fortunebrands.com
Employees: 26,040
Sales: $5,240.9 million
Key Personnel: Chairman, CEO: Thomas C. Hays. VC: John T. Ludes. President, COO: Norman H. Wesley. Human Resources: Anne C. Linsdau.
Fortune Brands (formerly American Brands) is comprised of subsidiaries making distilled spirits, hardware and home improvement supplies, and office products. All its companies are at the top of their markets, among them Jim Beam, Master Lock, and ACCO. Sales and work force growth have been moderate.
Other Locations: The company has subsidiaries in Asia, Australia, Europe, and North America.

UNITED DISTILLERS AND GUINNESS IMPORT CO. ★★

6 Landmark Sq., Stamford, CT 06901; 203-359-7100
http://www.guinness.ie
Employees (overall Diageo): 77,029
Sales (overall Diageo): $29,497.3 million
Key Personnel: Chairman: Tony Greener. Group CEO: John McGrath. President, CEO United Distillers & Vinters North America.
United Distillers and Guiness Import Co. are the U.S. divisions of Diageo PLC, the result of Guinness's merger with Grand Metropolitan. The company is the world's top producer of alcoholic drinks and leading food brands, such as Pillsbury and Green Giant. Its product lines include many premium brands, such as Johnnie Walker scotch and Guinness

Stout. The company also has several other businesses, including Guinness Publishing. Its sales and workforce have risen dramatically.

Other Locations: Worldwide HQ: Diageo PLC, 8 Henrietta Place, London W1M 9AG, United Kingdom; phone: +44-171-927-5200. The company's products are made in 46 countries and sold in over 130.

LABATT USA ★★
101 Merrit 7, Norwalk, CT 06856; 203-750-6600
http://www.labattblue.com/home.html
Employees (overall Interbrew): 16,727
Sales (overall Interbrew): $4,216.8 million
Key Personnel: President: Paul Cooke. VP Marketing: Bill Bessette. EVP Human Resources, Interbrew Americas: Luc Luyten.

A subsidiary of the Belgium-based Interbrew, Labatt U.S.A. imports Labatt Blue and Labatt Ice from Canada, along with an assortment of other premium beers from other countries. The company also makes Rolling Rock and the Mexican beers Dos Equis and Tecate. Sales and workforce are up substanially.

Other Locations: Worldwide HQ: Interbrew S.A., Vaarstraat 94, B-3000 Leuven, Belgium.

KENTUCKY

BROWN–FORMAN CORPORATION ★★
850 Dixie Highway, Louisville, KY 40201; 502-585-1100
http://www.brown-forman.com
Employees: 7,600
Revenues: $ 1,776 million
Key Personnel: Chairman, CEO: Owsley Brown II. VC, President, CEO, Brown-Forman Beverages Worldwide: William M. Street. Human Resources: James D. Wilson.

One of the leading U.S. makers of wine and spirits, Brown-Forman also sells durable goods. The company's spirits and wines, including Southern Comfort, Jack Daniel's, Bolla, and Korbel, are at the tops of their markets. Its china and crystal, sold under the brands Dansk, Gorham, and Lenox, are also popular. Sales and work force are up moderately.

Other Locations: The company's wines and spirits operation has 18 facilities in the United States, two in Canada, two in the Virgin Islands, and one in Ireland. Its consumer durables operation has 19 facilities and 86 retail stores in the United States.

MICHIGAN

DIVERSEY CORP.
12025 Technical Ctr. Dr., Livonia, MI 48150; 313-458-5000
Employees: 15,000
Sales: (C$, millions) 2,967
Key Personnel: President: Andrew Engleman. VP, CFO: Peter Kenan. Director of Human Resources: Chris Millsap.

Diversey is a subsidiary of Molson, Inc. Although Molson is Canada's largest brewer, beer is not its largest operation. Institutional cleaning is the company's leading activity. The company also retails home improvement products and owns the successful Montreal Canadiens hockey team. The company is expanding its beer exports to China. Sales and work force are down.

Other Locations: Worldwide HQ: Molson, Inc., Scotia Plaza, 40 King St. W., Ste. 3600, Toronto, Ontario M5H 3Z5, Canada; 416-360-1786.

MISSOURI

ANHEUSER–BUSCH COMPANIES, INC.
One Busch Pl., St. Louis, MO 63118; 314-577-2000
http://www.anheuser-busch.com
Employees: 23,344
Sales: $11,245.8 million
Key Personnel: Chairman, President, Anheuser Busch, Inc.: August A Busch III. VP, Group Executive, President, Anheuser-Busch, Inc.: Patrick T. Stokes. Human Resources: William L. Rammes.

Anheuser-Busch is the world's largest brewer, responsible for such brands as Budweiser, Michelob, and Busch. The company is aggressively expanding its markets overseas, with new facilities in Brazil, China, India, and other countries. The company also has subsidiaries involved in many activities, such as grain processing, communications, and real estate development. Its sales remain steady, but its work force is growing moderately.

NEW YORK

CANANDAIGUA BRANDS, INC. ★★
300 Willowbrook Office Park, Fairport, NY 14450; 716-218-2169
Employees: 4,230
Revenues: $1,497.3 million
Key Personnel: President, CEO: Richard Sands. Chairman: Marvin Sands. Human Resources: George Murray.
Canandaigua Brands, formerly Canandaigua Wine, is the one of the largest wine producers in the United States. The company is also a major beer importer and grape juice producer. Recently, it has been buying other wine brands to sell through its successful distribution network. Product lines include Amaden, Corona, and St. Pauli Girl. Sales and work force have increased dramatically.

HOUSE OF SEAGRAM ★★
375 Park Ave., New York, NY 10152; 212-572-7900
http://www.seagram.com
Employees (overall Seagram): 24,200
Sales (overall Seagram): $12,312 million
Key Personnel: Chairman: Edgar M. Bronfman. President, CEO: Edgar Bronfman, Jr. VC, CFO: Robert W. Matschullat. Human Resources: John D. Borgia.
In the face of declining demand for its core product, Seagram has diversified. The company's sales of alcoholic drinks, especially in the United States, have given way to entertainment industry sales as its biggest money-earners. It holds interests in DuPont, Time Warner, MCA, and owns almost all of Universal Studios. Sales and workforce are up impressively.
Other Locations: Worldwide HQ: The Seagram Co., Ltd., 1430 Peel St., Montreal, Quebec H3A 1S9, Canada; 514-849-5271. The company has facilities in 36 countries.

LVMH MOET HENNESSY LOUIS VUITTON, INC.
2 Park Ave., Suite 1830, New York, NY 10016; 212-340-7480
http://www.lvmh.com
Employees (overall LVMH): 33,000
Sales (overall LVMH): $8,100.3 million
Key Personnel: Chairman, CEO: Bernard Arnault. VC: Antoine Bernheim. Executive Committee, Human Resources: Concetta Lanciaux.
The world's top champagne maker, LVMH Moet Hennessy–Louis Vuitton is also a major manufacturer of luxury goods. Along with Dom Perignon, the company makes successful lines of luggage, perfumes, and beauty products. Among its popular brands are Christian Dior and Christian Lacroix. Its sales and work force have increased only slightly.
Other Locations: Worldwide HQ: LVMH Moet Hennessy Louis Vuitton, SA, 30, avenue Hoche, 75008 Paris, France; +33-1-44-13-22-22.

HEINEKEN USA, INC.
50 Main St., White Plains, NY 10606-1955; 914-681-4100
http://www.heineken.com
Employees (overall Heineken): 33,511
Sales (overall Heineken): $7,360.8 million
Key Personnel: President, CEO: Michael Foley. VP Finance: Dan Walsh. VP, Human Resources: Art Masarky.
Heineken USA is a subsidiary of Heineken, N.V. the second largest brewer in the world. Heineken faces decreased demand in Europe, its top market, but has expanded operations in Asia and Africa to combat the decrease. Its sales and workforce are up moderately.
Other Locations: Worldwide HQ: Heineken N.V., Tweede Weteringplantsoen 21, 1017ZD Amsterdam, The Netherlands; +31-20-523-92-39. The company has more than 90 breweries in over 150 countries.

WISCONSIN

MILLER BREWING COMPANY
3939 W. Highland Blvd., Milwaukee, WI 53208-2688; 414-931-2000
http://www.millerbrewing.com
Employees: 5,900
Sales: $4,105 million
Key Personnel: President, CEO: John D. Bowlin. SVP Marketing: Robert L. Mikulay. VP Human Resources: Gary Booher.
A subsidiary of Phillip Morris and the #2 U.S. beer maker, Miller Brewing Company controls roughly 20 percent of U.S. beer sales. It brews more than 50 brands of beer, including Miller Lite, Miller Genuine Draft, Ice House, and Sharp's. With the purchase of many Pabst and Stroh brewery brands, Miller became the

#1 seller of malt liquor in the U.S. as well. Sales and workforce are up slightly.

❶ APPAREL/FOOTWEAR

CALIFORNIA

LEVI STRAUSS ASSOCIATES, INC. ★★

1155 Battery St., San Francisco, CA 94111-1230; 415-544-6000
http://www.levistrauss.com
Employees: 37,700
Revenues: $6,900 million
Key Personnel: Chairman, CEO: Robert D. Haas. President, COO: Peter A. Jacobi. SVP Human Resources: Donna J. Goya.
The largest clothing manufacturer in the world, Levi Strauss Associates gets nearly three-quarters of its income from the sale of jeans, sold under the Levi's and Britannia brands. It is currently expanding its Dockers line of clothing and pushing its customfit line of jeans. Sales are increasing slightly and work force remains steady.
Other Locations: The company has facilities in 74 countries.

ILLINOIS

FRUIT OF THE LOOM, INC.

5000 Sears Tower, 233 S. Wacker Dr., Chicago, IL 60606; 312-876-1724
http://www.fruit.com
Employees: 32,900
Revenues: $2,139.9 million
Key Personnel: Chairman, CEO: William Farley. SVP, Chief Information Officer: Robert F. Heise. Human Resource contact: Burgess D. Ridge.
Fruit of the Loom, the top U.S. underwear manufacturer, got caught in a squeeze recently. The company had just purchased several additional companies, such as Gitano, to expand its women's apparel line when cotton prices went up. Consequently, the company (which is the largest U.S. buyer of cotton) was forced to move more production abroad to cut costs. Sales and work force are down.
Other Locations: The company has facilities in Canada, El Salvador, Honduras, Ireland, Jamaica, Mexico, the United Kingdom, and the United States.

HARTMARX CORPORATION

101 N. Wacker Dr., Chicago, IL 60606; 312-372-6300
http://www.apparelmart.com
Employees: 8,100
Sales: $718.1 million
Key Personnel: President, COO: Homi B. Patel. EVP, CFO: Glenn R. Morgan. Manager of Employee Relations: Lorraine Dickson.
Changing fashions have changed the fortunes of Hartmarx. The company makes a variety of clothing for men and women under brands such as Pierre Cardin. It has been shutting down its stores, such as Kuppenheimer and Country Miss, and factories for the past several years as more people are opting for casual clothing the company doesn't sell. Both sales and workforce are down..
Other Locations: The company has production plants in nine states and owns 132 stores nationwide.

MASSACHUSETTS

REEBOK INTERNATIONAL, LTD.

100 Technology Ctr. Dr., Stoughton, MA 02072; 617-341-5000
http://www.reebok.com
Employees: 6,948
Revenues: $3,643.5 million
Key Personnel: Chairman, President, CEO: Paul B. Fireman. EVP, President, CEO, Reebok Division: Robert Meers. EVP; President, CEO, The Rockport Co.: Angel R. Martinez.
One of the largest athletic footwear manufacturers in the nation, Reebok International makes a wide variety of footwear and athletic apparel. The company is actively pursuing the top of the market through an intense marketing effort. It expects growth in its Rockport line, which caters to the tastes of baby boomers. Both sales and workforce are up slightly.

NEW YORK

CYGNE DESIGNS, INC.

1372 Broadway, New York, NY 10018; 212-354-6474
Employees: 1,000
Sales: $ 254 million
Key Personnel: Chairman, CEO: Bernard M. Manuel. VP, Secretary, General Counsel: Paul D. Baiocchi.
Cygne Designs is a top producer of private-label women's apparel.. The com-

pany sells primarily to the Limited, which also sells merchandise through its Lerner stores. Recently it divested itself of the Ann Taylor partnership. Although it was plagued with cash-flow problems in the late 1980s, it has recovered and is now expanding through acquisition. The company owns production facilities in several offshore locations, including Brazil, Hong Kong, and South Korea. Although its workforce has been reduced substantially, sales are increasing.

LIZ CLAIBORNE, INC.
1441 Broadway, New York, NY 10018; 212-354-4900
http://www.lizclaiborne.com
Employees: 7,100
Revenues: $2,412.5 million
Key Personnel: President,CEO: Paul R. Charron. President: Denise V. Seegal. SVP Human Resources: Jorge L. Figueredo.

Liz Claiborne is among the largest women's apparel manufacturers in the United States. Sales in its women's sportswear products have been declining, and the company has been closing some stores and shifting the focus of others in response. It has also been opening new outlets overseas in such places as Asia and the Middle East. While the workforce is down, sales are increasing slightly.
Other Locations: The company has production facilities in more than 50 countries.

POLO/RALPH LAUREN CORPORATION
650 Madison Ave., New York, NY 10022; 212-318-7000
http://www.ralphlaurenfragrance.com
Employees: 4,000
Sales: $1,180.4 million
Key Personnel: VC, COO: Michael J. Newman. SVP, Human Resources: Karen Rosenback.

Owned by one of the apparel industry's top designers, Polo/Ralph Lauren has had its ups and downs. The company got off to a shaky start in the 1970s with serious financial problems but hit it big in the 1980s, when upscale yuppies developed a liking for its upscale designs. The company is faltering again as tastes change. Sales ar down, but work force is up.

NIKE, INC. ★★
One Bowerman Dr., Beaverton, OR 97005; 503-671-6453
http://www.info.nike.com
Employees: 21,800
Revenues: $ 9,186.5 million
Key Personnel: President, COO: Thomas E. Clarke. VP, General Manager, Sports and Fitness: Harry C. Carsh. VP, General Manager, Consumer Product Marketing: Mark G. Parker.

Nike is the world's number one shoe company, controlling more than 40 percent of the U.S. athletic shoe market. The company designs and sells shoes for just about every sport, in addition to operating NIKETOWN shoe and sportswear stores in such cities as New York, Boston and Chicago. In 1997 alone, Nike's sales increased over 40 percent and its workforce grew by over 25 percent.

V.F. CORPORATION
1047 N. Park Rd., Wyomissing, PA 19610; 610-378-1151
http://www.vfc.com
Employees: 62,800
Revenues: $5,222.1 million
Key Personnel: Chairman: Lawrence R. Pugh. President, CEO: Mackey J. McDonald. Human Resource contact: Susan Larson Williams.

One of the largest jeans manufacturers in the United States, V.F. sells its jeans under the Wrangler, Rustler, and Lee brands. The company also sells industrial work clothes, lingerie and loungewear, sportswear, and children's clothes, under the Red Kap, Vanity Fair, Jantzen, and Healthtex brands. The company is currently involved in several expansion projects. Sales are up, but work force is down.

HAGGAR CORP.
6311 Lemmon Ave., Dallas, TX 75209; 214-352-8481
Employees: 4,300
Sales: $406 million
Key Personnel: President, COO: Frank D. Bracken. SVP Marketing: Alan Burks. Human Resources contact: Sandra K. Stevens.

The top manufacturer of tailored pants,

Haggar primarily makes boys' and men's apparel. Its products are usually made from wrinkle-resistant natural fibers. More than a quarter of the company's sales are from JCPenney. The company markets clothing to the midpriced market under its Haggar brand, while it appeals to cheaper sales with its Reed St. James label. Sales and work force are both down.

WISCONSIN
OSHKOSH B'GOSH, LTD
112 Otter Ave., Oshkosh, WI 54901; 414-231-8800
http://www.oshkoshbgosh.com
Employees: 4,700
Sales: $395.2 million
Key Personnel: President, CEO: Douglas W. Hyde. EVP, COO: Michael D. Wachtel. Human Resource contact: Donald M. Carlson.

Sales are declining in children's apparel and rising in menswear at OshKosh B'Gosh. The company is one of the top manufacturers of fashionable children's clothes. It blames its problems on quickly changing fashions and intends to cut costs by shifting more of its manufacturing overseas. Sales have managed to turn around, but the work force is still decreasing.
Other Locations: The company owns 20 facilities in the United States.

❶ ATHLETICS/ RECREATIONAL AND LEISURE ACTIVITIES

CALIFORNIA
BELL SPORTS CORP.
6350 San Ignacio Ave., San Jose, CA 95119; 408-574-3400
http://www.bellsports.com
Employees: 1,320
Sales: $207.2 million
Key Personnel: Chairman, President, CEO, COO: Mary J. George. CFO, EVP: Richard S. Willis. President, U.S. Group: William L. Bacy. Human Resources contact: Celine Schafer.

Bell Sports is well-known for its bicycle and motorcycle helmets. The company is a dominant force in the industry, having captured 65-percent market share. One key to its prominence is its sales of auto racing helmets, that are worn by the highly visible stars of the racing world. The company recently merged with American Recreation, a bicycle helmet and bicycle manufacturer and is being bought by investment firms Harvard Private Capital and Brentwood Associates. Sales and work force are down.

CALLAWAY GOLF COMPANY
2285 Rutherford Rd., Carlsbad, CA 92008-8815; 760-931-1771
http://www.callawaygolf.com
Employees: 2,252
Sales: $697.6 million
Key Personnel: SEVP, Chief Merchant: Bruce Parker. SEVP, Chief of Manufacturing: Ronald A. Drapeau. SEVP, Chief of New Products: Richard C. Helmstetter. Human Resources contact: Elizabeth O'Mea.

Maker of the Big Bertha golf club, Callaway Golf is riding a wave of popularity. Demand for the company's metal wood driver is so high that it cannot keep the product in stock. The club is designed for long shots and features a large sweet spot. The company makes a complete line of golf clubs.

ILLINOIS
WMS INDUSTRIES, INC. ★
3401 N. California Ave., Chicago, IL 60618; 773-961-1111
http://www.wms.com
Employees: 1,100
Sales: $187.3 million
Key Personnel: Chairman, President, CEO: Louis J. Nicastro. VP, COO: Kevin L. Verner. Director of Human Resources: Michael Sirchio.

WMS Industries is the top manufacturer of coin-operated pinball machines in the world. The company began in the 1930s and was the first to introduce many of the game's commonly known features, such as the tilt mechanism. It also makes a variety of arcade video games, slot machines, and lottery terminals. The company has also branched into video games, with releases like Mortal Kombat. Lottery terminals and slot machines are also a product of the company and accounts for more than half of the company's sales.

❶ AUTO/TRUCK RENTAL

FLORIDA

RYDER SYSTEM, INC. ★
3600 NW 82nd Ave., Miami, FL 33166;
305-500-3726
http://www.ryder.com
Employees: 45,373
Revenues: $5,188.7 million
Key Personnel: Chairman, CEO: M.
Anthony Burns. President, COO: Gregory T. Swienton. EVP, Chief Human Resources Officer: Carol A. Kiryluk.
The leading commercial truck rental and leasing company in the world, Ryder System has a fleet of over 180,000 vehicles. The company is also the largest transporter of new cars and trucks in North America. Ryder is expanding its foreign facilities, especially in Europe and Mexico. Sales and work force remain steady.
Other Locations: The company provides truck rentals through facilities in Canada, Germany, Mexico, Poland, the United Kingdom, and the United States.

MISSOURI

ENTERPRISE RENT-A-CAR CO. ★
600 Corporate Park Dr., St. Louis, MO
63105; 314-512-5000
http://www.pickenterprise.com
Employees: 37,000
Revenues: $4,180 million
Key Personnel: Chairman: Jack C.
Taylor. President, CEO: Andrew C.
Taylor. SEVP, COO: Donald L. Ross.
VP Human Resources: Jerry Spector.
One of the two largest car rental companies (along with Hertz) in the United States, Enterprise Rent-A-Car targets the replacement-car market. Replacement car renters are customers looking for temporary transportation after their cars have been stolen or damaged. The company also operates several subsidiaries that primarily serve the travel and insurance industries. The company's sales and work force are growing.
Other Locations: The company has more than 1,400 branches in the United States.

NEVADA

U-HAUL INTERNATIONAL, INC. ★
1325 Airmotive Way, Suite 100, Reno,
NV 89502; 775-688-6300
http://www.uhaul.com
Employees: 14,400
Revenues: $1,551.9 million
Key Personnel: Chairman, President,
CEO: Edward J. Joe Shoen. VP: James P.
Shoen. Human Resources contact: Henry
P. Kelly.
Although it was once the top truck and trailer rental company in the United States, family bickering nearly brought U-Haul International to its knees. Disagreements over capital improvements and other issues have allowed the company's rivals to dominate the market. The company's rental fleet includes 190,000 trucks, trailers, and tow dollies. The company's sales and work force are now on the increase.

NEW JERSEY

HERTZ CORPORATION ★★
225 Brae Blvd., Park Ridge, NJ 07656-
0713; 201-307-2000
http://www.hertz.com
Employees: 24,800
Revenues: $4,153.6 million
Key Personnel: Chairman, CEO: Frank
A. Olson. President, COO: Craig R.
Koch. SVP Employee Relations: Donald
F. Steele.
The originator of the car rental business, Hertz is not only the world's largest car rental firm but also the largest industrial equipment rental firm. A large portion of the company is owned by Ford Motors. The company's sales and work force continue to increase.
Other Locations: The company has more than 6,000 car rental locations in the United States and 140 other countries.

NEW YORK

AVIS RENT A CAR, INC. ★
900 Old Country Rd., Garden City, NY
11530; 516-222-3000
http://www.avis.com
Employees: 19,000
Revenues: $2,297.6 million
Key Personnel: Chairman: Martin
Edelman. President, COO: F. Robert
Salerno. SVP Sales: Thomas J. Byrnes.
Human Resources contact: Kevin P.
Carey.
Among the top automobile rental and leasing companies in the United States, Avis is fighting aggressive competition

from newer companies, such as Alamo Rent-A-Car. The company has also had difficulties keeping overhead costs down. It is currently implementing various improvements to its customer service. Sales and workforce are up

Other Locations: The company operates in 140 countries.

❶ AUTOMOTIVE

CALIFORNIA

AMERICAN HONDA MOTOR CO., INC. ★

1919 Torrance Blvd., Torrance, CA 90501; 310-783-2000

http://www.honda.com

Employees: 112,200

Sales: $52,371.9 million

Key Personnel: President: Koichi Amemiya. VP Human Resources: Gary Kessler.

Honda is the top motorcycle manufacturer in the world and among the top makers of automobiles. Although stiff competition and Japanese economic problems hurt its U.S. sales, the company is working aggressively to bounce back. It has recently entered the minivan and sport-utility markets and shifted some manufacturing to North America to cut costs. Sales and work force are both up.

Other Locations: Worldwide HQ: Honda Motor Co., Ltd., Honda Giken Kogyo Kabushiki Kaisha, No. 1-1, 2-chome, Minami-Aoyama, Minato-ku, Tokyo, 107-8556, Japan; phone: +81-3-3423-1111.

AMERICAN ISUZU MOTORS INC.

2300 Pellissier Place, Whittier, CA 90601; 562-699-0500

http://www.isuzu.com/

Employees: 13,520

Sales: $13,523.7 million

Key Personnel: President: Yasuyuki Sudo. SVP,General Manager Light Vehicles: Robert Reilly. Human Resources Manager: Rhonda Parry.

Among the world's largest truck manufacturers, Isuzu makes a wide variety of recreational and commercial vehicles. The company also makes a popular line of diesel engines. It recently began making pickup trucks in its factory in Louisiana. Although the company used to make cars, it discontinued the line to cut costs. General Motors owns 49% of the company.

Other Locations: Worldwide HQ: Isuzu Motors, Ltd., Isuzu Jidosha Kabushiki Kaisha, 26-1, Minami-oi 6-chome Shinagawa-ku, Tokyo, 140-8722, Japan; phone: +81-3-5471-1141.

AMERICAN SUZUKI MOTOR CORPORATION

3251 E. Imperial Highway, Brea, CA 92821; 714-996-7040

http://www.suzuki.com

Employees: 13,820

Sales: $11,188 million

Key Personnel: President: Masao Nagura. Human Resources Manager: Ahmad Tarzi.

As a small manufacturer of small cars and trucks, Suzuki has found its greatest success in developing countries. It is one of the world's largest motorcycle manufacturers. The company keeps costs down by locating its factories outside Japan. It also makes electric wheelchairs and marine engines.

Other Locations: Worldwide HQ: Suzuki Motor Corp., 300 Takatsuka-cho, Hamamatsu, Shizuoka, 432-8611, Japan; phone: +81-53-440-2061. The company has facilities in 28 countries.

FLEETWOOD ENTERPRISES, INC. ★

3125 Myers St., Riverside, CA 92503-5527; 909-351-3500

http://www.fleetwood.com

Employees: 19,000

Sales: $3,490.2 million

Key Personnel: Chairman, CEO: Glenn F. Kummer. President, COO: Nelson W. Potter. Human Resource contact: Dundee Kelbel.

Recreational vehicles and manufactured housing are the twin specialties of Fleetwood Enterprises. The company is the largest recreational vehicle maker and the largest manufactured housing builder in the United States. It is working to expand its market share in Europe. Sales and work force are slightly on the rise.

Other Locations: The company has 22 recreational vehicle factories and 38 manufactured housing factories in 19 states, Canada, and Germany.

HYUNDAI MOTOR AMERICA

10550 Talbert Ave., Fountain Valley, CA 92728-0850; 714-965-3000

http://www.hyundaiusa.com

Employees: 46,300

Sales: $7,384.1 million
Key Personnel: President:Juhn Myung - Huhn. Director of Finance: Jim Hanne-field. VP Administration (Human Resources): Keith Duckworth.

Hyundai Motor America is a subsidiary of Hyundai Group, one of the largest conglomerates in South Korea. The company, which has interests in many heavy industries such as shipbuilding, has capitalized on that country's cheap labor. However, as wages are rising, it is switching to higher-wage industries, such as telecommunications and aerospace. In the United States, the company's primary activity is automobile manufacturing. Sales and work force have been hurt by the weak Asian economy.
Other Locations: Worldwide HQ: Hyundai Group, 140-2, Kye-Dong, Chongro-ku, KPO Box 672, Seoul, South Korea; phone: +82-2-746-1114.

MAZDA MOTOR OF AMERICA, INC. ★★

7755 Irvine Ctr. Dr., Irvine, CA 97218; 949-727-1990
http://www.mazdausa.com
Employees: 31,665
Sales: $15,341 million
Key Personnel: President, CEO Mazda North American Operations: Richard N. Beattie. Human Resources contact: Andrea Kelly.

The smallest of the major Japanese automobile manufacturers, Mazda is suffering from recessions in Europe, Japan, and the United States. Ford controls the company and recently upped its membership on Mazda's board at the request of the Japanese company's creditors. Mazda is currently cutting costs by shifting production to Asian facilities. The company's sales and work force are up.
Other Locations: Worldwide HQ: Mazda Motor Corp., 3-1, Shinchi, Fuchu-cho, Aki-gun, Hiroshima, 730-91, Japan; phone: +81-82-282-1111. The company has facilities in Japan and 20 other countries.

NEW UNITED MOTOR MANUFACTURING INC.

45500 Fremont Blvd., Fremont, CA 94538-6326; 510-498-5500
http://www.nummi.com
Employees: 4,800
Sales: $4,699 million
Key Personnel: President, CEO: Kanji Ishii. EVP: Gary Convis. VP Human Resources: Gregg Vervais.

New United Motor Manufacturing is a joint venture between Toyota and General Motors. The company builds the Toyota half-ton pickup, the Toyota Corolla, and the Geo Prizm in its plant in Fremont, Calif. The operation is an experiment to see if Toyota's techniques for manufacturing cars can be successfully imported to the United States. Sales and work force are rising slightly.

NISSAN NORTH AMERICA INC.

18501 S. Figueroa St., Gardenia, CA 90248; 310-771-5631
http://www.nissan-na.com
Employees: 137,201
Sales: $27,191.7 million
Key Personnel: President: Nobuo Araki. Manager, Human Resources: Kathy Doi.

Among the largest car manufacturers in the world, Nissan has been cutting costs and shifting production facilities around the world in order to fight sagging profits. The company's problems stem from a recession in Japan, where it is the number 3 automaker. Sales and work force are falling.
Other Locations: Worldwide HQ: Nissan Motor Co., Ltd., 17-1, Ginza 6-chome, Chuo-ku, Tokyo, 104-8023, Japan; phone: +81-3-5565-2147.

TOYOTA MOTOR SALES, U.S.A., INC. ★

19001 S. Western Ave., Torrance, CA 90509; 310-618-4000
http://www.toyota.com
Employees: 159,035
Sales: $107,040.7 million
Key Personnel: President, CEO: Yoshio Ishizaka. EVP: Yale Gieszl. SVP, General Manager: Donald Esmond.

Toyota is the largest automobile manufacturer in Japan and the fourth largest in the world. The company makes a wide variety of cars and light trucks and is among the world's top three car makers. Because of the high value of the yen relative to the dollar, the company shifted much of its manufacturing activities out of Japan. Sales and work force are up.
Other Locations: Worldwide HQ: Toyota Motor Corp., 1, Toyota-cho, Toyota City, Aichi Prefecture, 471-8571, Japan; phone: +81-565-28-2121. The company has 50 factories in more than 25 countries.

CONNECTICUT

PIRELLI TIRE NORTH AMERICA

500 Sargent Dr., New Haven, CT 06536;
203-784-2200
http://www.pirelli.com
Employees: 36,226
Sales: $6,580.4 million
Key Personnel: President: Carlo Bianconi. Manager, Human Resources: Debbie Bragdon.

Pirelli Armstrong Tire is a subsidiary of Pirelli S.P.A. Pirelli is best known for tires; it is one of the largest companies of its type in the world. It makes tires for a wide variety of applications. The company also has a large cable manufacturing division. Its cable products include telecommunications, power, and building cables. Sales are up, but work force has shown no substantial increase.
Other Locations: Worldwide HQ: Pirelli S.p.A, Viale Sarca, 222, 20126 Milan, Italy; phone: +39-02-6442-4688.

FLORIDA

BREED TECHNOLOGIES, INC. ★★

5300 Old Tampa Highway, Lakeland, FL 33807-3050; 941-668-6000
http://www.breedtech.com
Employees: 16,300
Sales: $1,385.3 million
Key Personnel: Chairman Emeritus: Allen K. Breed. Chairman, CEO: Johnnie C. Breeed. Human Resources Manager: Susan Rider.

Automotive airbags and airbag components are the specialty of Breed Technologies. The company is one of the top U.S. manufacturers of steering wheels, electromechanical sensors, inflators, and complete airbag systems. The company is developing a line of electronic sensors. Its business is expanding rapidly. Sales and work force are growing.

GEORGIA

SAAB CARS USA INC. ★

4405A International Blvd., Norcross, GA 30093; 404-279-0100
http://www.saabusa.com
Employees: 9,974
Sales: $3,507.4 million
Key Personnel: President, CEO: Joel K. Manloy. VP Finance and Administration: Ken Adams. Director of Human Resources: Thomas Reis.

Saab Cars USA is a subsidiary of Saab-Scania Holdings Group. The company produces trucks and buses through its Scania subsidiary, and aircraft and defense equipment through its Saab subsidiary. It also imports automobiles, such as Audis and Porsches. The company operates Saab Automobile, a joint venture with General Motors, which manufactures a line of luxury automobiles. Sales and work force are increasing.
Other Locations: Worldwide HQ: Saab-Scania Holdings Group, S-581 88, Linkoping, Sweden; phone: +46-13-18-00-00. The company has facilities in 21 countries.

ILLINOIS

BORG–WARNER AUTOMOTIVE, INC.

200 S. Michigan Ave., Chicago, IL 60604; 312-322-8500
http://www.bwauto.com
Employees: 10,100
Sales: $1,836.8 million
Key Personnel: Chairman, CEO: John F. Fiedler. EVP: Ronald M. Ruzic. VP Human Resources: Geraldine Kinsella.

Borg-Warner Automotive makes parts for all the world's major car makers. Among its products are automatic transmissions, timing chain systems, and transfer cases. The company aims to double its revenues by the year 2000 and is expanding its markets overseas. It is entering joint ventures in both Europe and Asia.
Other Locations: The company has more than 50 factories in Asia, Europe, and the United States.

NAVISTAR INTERNATIONAL CORPORATION ★

455 N. Cityfront Plaza Dr., Chicago, IL 60611; 312-836-2000
http://www.navistar.com
Employees: 17,558
Sales: $7,830 million
Key Personnel: Chairman, President, CEO, Navistar and Navistar International Transportation: John R. Horne. EVP, President, Truck Group and Navistar International Transportation: Donald DeFosset Jr. SVP, Human Resources: Pamela J. Hamilton.

Although it is one of the top manufacturer of school buses and medium and heavy trucks, Navistar International has suffered for many years because of sluggish demand. However, demand for its products picked up in the mid-1990s, al-

lowing the company to upgrade its product line. It also builds diesel engines. Sales and work force remain steady.
Other Locations: The company operates factories in the United States, Canada, Mexico, and Brazil.

ROBERT BOSCH CORPORATION

2800 S. 25th Ave., Broadview, IL 60153; 708-865-5200
http://www.uni-stuttgart.de
Employees: 188,017
Sales: $30,200.1 million
Key Personnel: Chairman, President, CEO: Robert S. Oswald. EVP, CFO: Gary M. Saunders. VP, Human Resources: Robert B. Cummins.
Robert Bosch Corporation, a wholly-owned subsidiary of Germany's Robert Bosch GmbH, is the top manufacturer of fuel injection and antilock braking systems in the world. Demand for the company's products has slipped in Japan and Western Europe because of slowing economies. The company also makes automotive audio equipment and many other components. Sales and work force are on the rise.
Other Locations: Worldwide HQ: Robert Bosch GmbH, Robert Bosch Platz 1, Postfach 10 60 50, D-70049 Stuttgart, Germany; phone: +49-711-811-0. The company has facilities in 27 countries.

INDIANA

CUMMINS ENGINE COMPANY, INC. ★

500 Jackson St, Columbus, IN 47201-3005; 812-377-5000
http://www.cummins.com
Employees: 28,300
Sales: $6,266 million
Key Personnel: Chairman, CEO: James A. Henderson. President, COO: Theodore M. Solso. Human Resources contact: Jean S. Blackwell.
The largest independent manufacturer of diesel engines in the world, Cummins sells its products to nearly all major North American truck manufacturers. Approximately one-third of all midsized and heavy trucks sold in the United States have Cummins engines. The company is expanding its facilities overseas. Sales and work force are up.
Other Locations: The company has facilities in 14 countries.

WABASH NATIONAL CORPORATION ★★

1000 Sagamore Pkwy. S., Lafayette, IN 47905; 765-771-5300
http://www.wabashnational.com
Employees: 5,302
Sales: $1,292.3 million
Key Personnel: Chairman, President, CEO: Donald J. Ehrlich. VP Manufacturing: Charles R. Ehrlich. Human Resources contact: Charles E. Fish.
Trailers are the business of Wabash National. The company is the #1 designer and builder of truck trailers. Among its most popular products are its bimodal trailers, which can be towed on roadways or mounted on railroad cars. The company expects to expand in China, Europe, and Southeast Asia. Sales and work force are up.

MICHIGAN

DAIMLERCHRYSLER AG ★★

1000 Chrysler Dr., Auburn Hills, MI 48326; 248-576-5741
http://www.daimlerchrysler.com
Employees: 441,500
Sales: $154,615 million
Key Personnel: Co-Chairman, Co-CEO: Robert J. Eaton. Co-Chairman, Co-CEO: Juergen E. Schrempp. Human Resources contact: Heiner Tropitzsch.
DaimlerChrysler, formed by the merger of Chrysler and Germany's Daimler-Benz, is the world's #3 automobile manufacturer. The company manufactures Chrysler's brands as well as luxury sedans, sport utility vehicles, and aerospace products. The combination of Daimler's international influence and Chrysler's market savvy provides a big boost to the company. Sales and work force are up.
Other Locations: Worldwide HQ: DaimlerChrysler AG, Epplestrasse 225, D-70546 Stuttgart, Germany; phone: +49-711-17-1.

FORD MOTOR COMPANY

The American Rd., Dearborn, MI 48121-1899; 313-322-3000
http://www.ford.com
Employees: 345,175
Sales: $144,416 million
Key Personnel: Chairman: William C. Ford Jr. President, CEO: Jacques A. Nasser. Chairman, President, CEO, Ford Financial Services Group: Philippe Paillart. Human Resource contact: David L. Mur-

phy.

Although Ford Motor Company is the second largest automobile manufacturer in the world, it is revamping its operations in an effort to achieve first place. The company is working to design a "world car" that it can sell worldwide with minimal alterations for local preferences. The company recently aquired the automobile division of Volvo. It is also expanding its rental business, having bought Hertz, the number one rental firm in the U.S.

Other Locations: The company has facilities in 34 countries.

GENERAL MOTORS CORPORATION

100 Renaissance Center, Detroit, MI 48243-7301, 313-556-5000
http://www.gm.com
Employees: 594,000
Sales: $161,315 million
Key Personnel: Chairman, CEO: John F. Smith, Jr. President, COO: G. Richard Wagoner, Jr. VC: Harry J. Pearce. EVP, New Business Strategies: Louis R. Hughes. Human Resources contact: Kathleen S. Barclay.

General Motors is the largest car manufacturer in the world. It builds over 75 types of trucks and cars. Among its brand names are Buick, Chevrolet, Cadillac, Pontiac, and Saturn. The company is cutting costs and streamlining operations. It recently spun off its computer services division, Electronic Data Systems. Sales and work force are down.

Other Locations: The company has facilities in Austria, Belgium, Brazil, Canada, Germany, Mexico, Spain, the United Kingdom, and the United States.

SPARTAN MOTORS, INC. ★★

1000 Reynolds Rd., Charlotte, MI 48813; 517-543-6400
http://www.spartanmotors.com
Employees: 1,025
Sales: $255.3 million
Key Personnel: Chairman, CEO: George W. Sztykiel. President, COO: John E. Sztykiel. EVP: Anthony G. Sommer. Director of Personnel: Janine Nierenberger.

Heavy-duty chassis are the main products of Spartan Motors. The company manufactures chassis from standard parts, which it purchases from outside providers. Its products are used for a variety of vehicles, including motor homes, fire trucks, buses, and tank trucks. Among its customers are Winnebago and Gulfstream Coach. Sales and work force are both up.

VOLKSWAGEN OF AMERICA, INC. ★

3800 Hamlin Rd., Auburn Hills, MI 48326; 248-340-5000
http://www.vw.com
Employees: 297,916
Sales: $80,546.6 million
Key Personnel: President, CEO: Verd Klauss. Executive Director, Human Resources: Thomas Stretlien.

Europe's #1 automobile manufacturer, Volkswagen produces over 4.8 million cars, trucks, and vans per year. The company makes cars and trucks under both its own name and the Audi brand. The company is at work to cut production costs by increasing manufacturing efficiency. Sales and work force are up.

Other Locations: Worldwide HQ: Volkswagen AG, Brieffach 1848-2, D-38436 Wolfsburg, Germany; phone: +49-53-61-90.

NEW JERSEY

BMW (U.S HOLDING CORP. ★

300 Chestnut Ridge Rd., Woodcliff Lake, NJ 07675; 800-956-4269
http://www.bmwusa.com
Employees: 115,927
Sales: $37,880.8 million.
Key Personnel: Chairman, CEO, BMW (U.S.): Heinrich Heitmann. President: Victor Doolan. VP Marketing: Jim McDowell. Human Resource contact: John Brunner.

Among the top automobile manufacturers in Europe, BMW also makes motorcycles and aircraft engines through its subsidiary, BMW Rolls-Royce. The company is known for its commitment to long-term investments in technology. BMW is expanding into new areas, such as computers and telephone equipment. It recently opened a manufacturing plant in the United States. Sales and work force are up.

Other Locations: Worldwide HQ: Bayerische Motoren Werke AG, Petuelring 130, BMW Haus, Postfach 40 20 40, D-80788 Munich, Germany; phone: +49-893 822-4272.

NEW YORK

FIAT U.S.A., INC.
375 Park Ave. Suite 2073, New York, NY 10152; 212-355-2600
http://www.fiatusa.com
Employees: 234,454
Sales: $56,634.5 million
Key Personnel: President and CEO: Danieoe Rulli. President, Fiat Finance North America: Enrico Zecchini. VP Human Resources: John Loffman.
One of the largest car makers in Europe, Fiat is the biggest of Italy's private industrial enterprises. Along with cars, the company also makes industrial and agricultural equipment. The company is updating its line of automobiles and expanding its marketing efforts in Latin America, Eastern Europe, and China. Sales and work force are down.
Other Locations: Worldwide HQ: Fiat S.p.A, 250 Via Nizza, 10135 Turin, Italy; phone: +39-011-6-831-1111. The company has facilities in 66 countries.

RAMERICA INTERNATIONAL, INC.
One Rockefeller Plaza Ste. 2404, New York, NY 10020, 212-218-6990
Employees: 37,178
Sales: $5,793.7 million
Key Personnel: VP Human Resources Management: Tamer Sahinbas. General Manager, Ramerica International (U.S.): Davut Okutcu. CFO, Director of Human Resources, Ramerica International (U.S.): Gunduz Yalcin.
Ramerica International is a subsidiary of Koc Holding, the largest company in Turkey. Its interests fall into three areas: automotive; industrial, commercial, and energy; and finance and foreign trade. More than half of its income comes from its automotive businesses. It is a leading manufacturer of cars, trucks, and buses. Its work force and sales are down.
Other Locations: Worldwide HQ: Koc Holding A.S., Nakkkastepe Azizbey Sok. No. 1, Kuzguncuk, Istanbul, Turkey; phone: +90-216-341-46-50. The company has offices in France, Germany, Italy, the United Kingdom, and the United States.

OHIO

DANA CORPORATION ★★
4500 Dorr St., Toledo, OH 43615; 419-535-4500
http://www.dana.com
Employees: 86,400
Sales: $12,463.6 million
Key Personnel: Chairman: Southwood J. Woody Morcott. President, CEO: Joseph M. Magliochetti. Human Resources Manager: Pat Gehagen.
Dana manufactures a wide variety of components for motor vehicles. Much of its sales are to Ford, DaimlerChrysler, and parts distributors. Among the products the company makes are piston rings, drive shafts, valves, and filters. The company recently opened an office in Vietnam as part of its overall Asian expansion plan. Sales and work force are up.
Other Locations: The company has facilities in more than 30 countries.

EATON CORPORATION
Eaton Center, Cleveland, OH 44114-2584; 216-523-5000
http://www.eaton.com
Employees: 49,500
Sales: $6,625 million
Key Personnel: Chairman, CEO: Stephen R. Hardis. President, COO: Alexander M. Cutler. Human Resources Manager: Susan J. Cook.
Eaton provides precision products to auto makers. It also manufactures electronic components for many applications. The company's products are used in aerospace, appliances, construction, and defense. It recently purchased the Australian company Email, Ltd., in an effort to gain a presence in the Pacific Rim. The company is also focused on expansion into Asia, Latin America, and Eastern Europe.
Other Locations: The company has facilities in 25 countries.

GOODYEAR TIRE & RUBBER COMPANY
1144 E. Market St., Akron, OH 44316-0001; 330-796-2121
http://www.goodyear.com
Employees: 96,950
Sales: $12,626.3 million
Key Personnel: Chairman, President, CEO: Samir F. Gibara. President, North America Tires: William J. Sharp. VP Human Resources and Total Quality Culture: Mike L. Burns.
Known for its tires and its blimp, Goodyear is among the largest of the world's tire manufacturers. It also makes a wide variety of other rubber-based products for commercial and consumer markets.

The company also manages an oil pipeline between Texas and California and rubber plantations in Guatemala and Indonesia. Sales have remained steady, and the workforce has increased slightly.
Other Locations: The company operates over 900 retail stores in the U.S. and over 80 plants worldwide.

THOR INDUSTRIES, INC. ★★
419 W. Pike St., Jackson Center, OH 45334-0629; 937-596-6849
http://www.thorindustries.com
Employees: 3,304
Sales: $715.6 million
Key Personnel: Chairman, President, CEO: Wade F. B. Thompson. SVP: Clare G. Wentworth.
Thor Industries is one of the largest manufacturers of recreational vehicles and small- and medium-sized buses in the U.S. Airstream, Dutchmen, and Four Winds are among its subsidiaries. It also makes suspension systems and axles. The company recently purchased Skamper, which makes a line of folding trailers. Both its sales and work force are on the rise.

TRW, INC
1900 Richmond Rd., Cleveland, OH 44124-3760; 216-291-7000
http://www.trw.com
Employees: 78,000
Sales: $11,886 million
Key Personnel: Chairman, CEO: Joseph T. Gorman. President, COO: Ronald D. Sugar. EVP, Human Resources and Communications: Howard V. Knicely.
Operating in two main areas of business, TRW supplies products and services to the automotive and aerospace markets. The company has long been a major supplier of automotive and aircraft engine valves. It is currently working on a 12-satellite communications network. The company is trying to control debt by selling noncore auto units.
Other Locations: The company has 93 facilities in 25 states and 82 facilities in 19 countries abroad.

PENNSYLVANIA

MACK TRUCKS, INC.
2100 Mack Blvd., Allentown, PA 18105; 610-709-3011
http://www.macktrucks.com
Employees: 138,321
Sales: $43,430.1 million

Key Personnel: President, CEO: Michel Gigou. Human Resources contact: Samuel L. Torrence.
Mack Trucks is a subsidiary of Regie Nationale des Usines Renault. Known for making cars with personality, Renault has had its ups and downs in recent years. The company's majority owner is the French government, which is planning to sell some of its interest. A recent merger with Volvo fell through after four years of negotiations. Sales are up, and work force is steady.
Other Locations: Worldwide HQ: Regie Nationale des Usines Renault S.A., 34, quai du Point-du-Jour, 92109 Boulogne Billancourt Cedex, France; phone: +33-1-41-04-50-50.

SOUTH CAROLINA

MICHELIN NORTH AMERICA, INC
One Parkway South, Greenville, SC 29615; 864-458-5000
http://www.michelin.com
Employees: 127,241
Sales: $15,301.2 million
Key Personnel: Chairman, President: Jim Micali. EVP, Personnel: Jean-Pierre Gervais.
The pioneer of the radial tire design, Michelin is the #2 tire maker in the world. The company manufactures 3,500 different types of tires at a rate of 785,000 tires a day. The company also makes wheels, steel cables, and tubes and publishes a series of travel guides. The company has been reorganizing its management structure for several years. Sales and work force are rising slightly.
Other Locations: Worldwide HQ: Compagnie Generale des Etablissements Michelin, 12, cours Sablon, 63000 Clermont-Ferrand, France; phone: +33-4-73-98-59-00.

TENNESSEE

BRIDGESTONE/FIRESTONE, INC.
50 Century Blvd., Nashville, TN 37214; 615-872-5000
http://www.bridgestone.com
Employees: 97,800
Sales: $19,689.3 million
Key Personnel: Chairman, CEO: Masatoshi Ono. President: Kenji Shibata. Human Resource contact: Frank R. Doman.
Bridgestone/Firestone, Inc. is a subsidiary of Bridgestone, the #1 tire maker in the

world. The company, which purchased Firestone in 1988, supplies tires to many major auto manu-facturers, such as General Motors, Porsche, Lamborghini, and Ford. It also makes tires for heavy equipment and aircraft and makes a variety of building materials and other goods.
Other Locations: Worldwide HQ: Bridgestone Corp., 10-1, Kyobashi 1-chome, Chuo-ku, Tokyo, 104-8340, Japan; phone: +81-3-3567-0111. The company has manufacturing facilities in 16 countries.

WASHINGTON

PACCAR, INC ★★
PACCAR Bldg., 777 106th Ave. NE, Bellevue, WA 98004; 425-468-7400
http://www.paccar.com
Employees: 23,000
Sales: $7,894.8 million
Key Personnel: Chairman, CEO: Mark C. Pigott. President: David J. Hovind. VP Employee Relations (Human Resources): Laurie L. Baker.
One of the largest heavy truck manufacturers in the world, PACCAR makes Peterbilt, Foden, and Kenworth trucks. The company manufactures oil field equipment, winches, and medium-duty trucks. It is exploring the possibility of a joint venture with Russian truck manufacturer ZiL and may build a new U.S. Peterbilt factory. Sales and work force are rising.
Other Locations: The company has 15 facilities in Australia, Belgium, Canada, Mexico, the Netherlands, the United Kingdom, and the United States.

WISCONSIN

HARLEY-DAVIDSON, INC.
3700 W. Juneau Ave., Milwaukee, WI 53208; 414-342-4680
http://www.harley-davidson.com
Employees: 6,200
Sales: $2,064 million
Key Personnel: Chairman, President, CEO: Jeffrey L. Bleustein. VP, Treasurer, Controller: James M. Brostowitz. VP Human Resources: C. William Gray.
Harley-Davidson is the only major motorcycle manufacturer in the U.S. The company's products are so popular that its factories often can't keep up with demand. The company makes lines of delivery trucks, recreational vehicles, office furniture, and other products. Sales and workforce have declined slightly.
Other Locations: The company has six

plants in Indiana, Pennsylvania, and Wisconsin.

OSHKOSH TRUCK CORPORATION ★★
2307 Oregon St., Oshkosh, WI 54903; 920-235-9150
http://www.oshkoshtruck.com
Employees: 3,500
Sales: $902.8 million
Key Personnel: President, CEO: Robert G. Bohn. EVP, President, Defense Business: Paul C. Hollowell. Human Resources contact: James D. Voss.
One of the top military vehicle manufacturers in the world, Oshkosh Truck makes a variety of vehicles for commercial use, too. Among the company's products are snow removers, fire trucks, and concrete carriers. It is expanding its product line to include motor home chassis to compensate for decreased demand for its defense-related products. Sales and work force at Oshkosh are both up.

---

❶ BANKING

ALASKA

NATIONAL BANCORP OF ALASKA, INC.
310 W. Northern Lights Blvd., Anchorage, AK 99503; 907-276-1132
http://www.nationalbankofalaska.com
Employees: 1,098
Sales: $273.1 million
Key Personnel: Chairman: Edward B. Rasmuson. President: Richard Strutz. Human Resources: Cathy Richter.
National Bancorp of Alaska is the largest bank in Alaska. The company provides a comprehensive line of services to both commercial and residential customers, including construction loans and individual retirement accounts. It is currently in the process of streamlining its operations. Sales are up, but workforce has suffered a slight decline.
Other Locations: The bank has over 50 branches.

CALIFORNIA

COUNTRYWIDE CREDIT INDUSTRIES, INC. ★★
4500 Park Granada, Calabasas, CA 91302-1613; 818-225-3000
http://www.countrywide.com

Employees: 11,378
Sales: $2,952.8 million
Key Personnel: President: David S. Loeb. Chairman, CEO: Angelo R. Mozilo. Managing Director of Human Resources: Anne McCallion.
Countrywide Credit Industries is the largest independent mortgage bank in the United States. It buys, sells, originates, and services mortgages through its subsidiary, Countrywide Funding Corporation. Nearly half of the loans it services are in California. The company's sales and work force have been increasing for many years.

WELLS FARGO & COMPANY ★★

420 Montgomery St., San Francisco, CA 94163; 800-411-4932
http://www.wellsfargo.com
Employees: 92,178
Sales: $20,482 million
Key Personnel: Chairman: Paul Hazen. President, CEO: Richard Kovacevich. Human Resources: Patricia R. Callahan.
After merging with Norwest, Wells Fargo is one big bank, boasting 6,000 locations across the country and the #1 mortgage banking operation in the U.S. The company provides full-service consumer and business banking, in addition to a bevy of investment and loan services. Norwest banks will be renamed Wells Fargo by 2000.

GEORGIA

SUNTRUST BANKS, INC. ★★

303 Peachtree St. NE, Atlanta, GA 30308; 404-588-7711
http://www.suntrust.com
Employees: 30,452
Sales: $7,392.1 million
Key Personnel: Chairman, President, and CEO: L. Phillip Humann. Chairman, CEO: Richard G. Tilghman. Human Resources: Carolyn Cartwright.
Although SunTrust is based in Atlanta, its biggest customer base is among the many retirees in Florida. The bank provides a full range of commercial and personal banking services for its customers. Additional services include credit cards, asset management, and mortgage banking. The company's sales and workforce are increasing.
Other Locations: SunTrust has some 1,000 branches in the Southeast.

ILLINOIS

BANK ONE CORPORATION ★★

One First National Plaza, Chicago, IL 60670; 312-732-4000
http://www.bankone.com
Employees: 93,310
Sales: $25,595 million
Key Personnel: Chairman: Verne G. Istock. President, CEO: John B. McCoy. Human Resources: Timothy P. Moen.
When Banc One purchased First Chicago NBD, it changed its name to Bank One. The purchase boosted its operations to include more than 2,000 branches in 14 states across the Midwest and Southwest and made the company one of the top five U.S. banks. Bank One also issues more credit cards than any other bank and provides a wide array of commercial, corporate and institutional banking services. Sales and workforce are up dramatically.

HARRIS BANKCORP INC. ★★

111 W. Monroe St., Chicago, IL 60603; 312-461-2121
http://www.harrisbank.com
Employees: 11,084
Sales: $1,767 million
Key Personnel: Chairman, CEO, Harris Bankcorp: Alan G. McNally. VC: Edward W. Lyman, Jr. Human Resources: Michael B. Lowe.
Harris Bankcorp is a subsidiary of the Bank of Montreal, one of the largest banks in Canada, with more than 1,100 branches. The company is currently expanding its U.S. customer base. It provides a full range of both personal and commercial financial services. Sales and work force are up dramatically.
Other Locations: Worldwide HQ: Bank of Montreal, 119 St. Jacques, Montreal, Quebec H2Y 1L6, Canada; 514-877-7110.

MASSACHUSETTS

BANKBOSTON CORPORATION

100 Federal St., Boston, MA 02110; 617-434-2200
http://www.bankboston.com
Employees: 24,500
Sales: $7,609 million
Key Personnel: Chairman, CEO: Charles K. Gifford. VC: Paul F. Hogan. Executive Director of Human Resources: Helen G. Drinan.
When its planned acquisition by Fleet

Financial is finalized, BankBoston will be the largest bank in New England. For now, it sits atop the Boston market. With branches as far off as Shanghai, the company already has the strongest global presence of any bank in the area. BankBoston was formed by the 1996 merger of Bank of Boston Corporation and BayBanks, Inc. Since that merger, BankBoston's Sales and workforce have been increasing steadily.

Other Locations: Bank of Boston has some 430 branches in the United States and 23 countries around the world.

FLEET FINANCIAL GROUP, INC. ★

1 Federal St., Boston, MA 02110-2010; 617-346-4000

http://www.fleet.com

Employees: 36,000

Sales: $10,002 million

Key Personnel: Chairman, CEO: Terrence Murray. VC: H. Jay Sarles. SVP Human Resources: M. Anne Szostak.

Fleet Financial Group is the largest bank in New England. The company's primary business is in mortgages and consumer finance, though it also provides many other services, including investment and brokerage services. Fleet Financial is acquiring BankBoston. The move has forced Fleet to divest nearly 300 of its 1,200 branches to avoid anti-trust penalties.

MICHIGAN

COMERICA INCORPORATED

Comerica Tower at Detroit Center, 500 Woodward Ave., Detroit, MI 48226; 313-222-4000

http://www.comerica.com

Employees: 10,739

Sales: $3,219.9 million

Key Personnel: Chairman, President, and CEO: Eugene A. Miller. VC: John D. Lewis. Human Resources: Ted Bennett.

Comerica is a holding company, with Business Bank, Individual Bank and Investment Bank operating units. The company specializes in providing consumer loans to average borrowers, but it also works with very substantial business clientele. Comerica also operates more than 350 traditional retail banking branches under its own name. Sales are up modestly, but workforce has dropped slightly.

NEW YORK

BANK OF NEW YORK CO., INC.

One Wall St., New York, NY 10286; 212-495-1784

http://www.bankofny.com

Employees: 17,157

Sales: $5,793 million

Key Personnel: Chairman, CEO: Thomas A. Renyi. VC, Bank of New York Company and Bank of New York: Alan R. Griffith. Human Resources: Thomas Angers.

Founded in 1784 by Alexander Hamilton, the Bank of New York is the city's oldest bank and currently the number #1 retail banking organization in the metropolitan area. The bank also operates in the multinational arena and some specialty niches, such as securities transaction processing and trust services. The Bank of New York's Sales and workforce are increasing.

Other Locations: The Bank of New York has 360 branches in the Northeast. Its subsidiaries operate throughout the United States and in 24 foreign countries.

CHASE MANHATTAN CORPORATION ★

270 Park Ave., New York, NY 10017; 212-270-6000

http://www.chase.com

Employees: 72,683

Sales: $32,590 million

Key Personnel: Chairman: Walter V. Shipley. VC, President and CEO: William B. Harrison Jr. Human Resources: John J. Farrell.

The 1996 merger of Chase Manhattan Corporation and Chemical Banking Corporation created the largest banking enterprise in the United States. But Chase didn't stay on top for long; Bank of America recently bumped it from the top spot down to #2. The company provides business, consumer and investment banking in more than 50 countries across the globe. Sales and workforce are up.

CITIGROUP, INC. ★★

399 Park Ave., New York, NY 10043; 212-559-1000

http://www.citi.com

Employees: 173,700

Sales: $76,431 million

Key Personnel: Co-Chairman, Co-CEO: Sanford I. Weill. Co-Chairman, Co-CEO: John S. Reed. Human Resources: Lawrence R. Phillips.

Travelers Group merged with Citicorp, one of the world's largest credit card companies, to form Citicorp, a truly titanic financial services company. The business, which will continue to use the Travelers' umbrella logo, now offers credit card, insurance, and assorted financial and investment services. Its subsidiaries include brokerage firm Saloman Smith Barney, mutual fund-operator Primerica Financial, and others. As a result of the merger, sales and workforce have more than doubled.

CREDIT SUISSE FIRST BOSTON, INC. ★★

11 Madison Ave., New York, NY 10010-3629; 212-325-2000
http://www.csfb.com
Employees: 14,126
Sales: $6,713 million
Key Personnel: Chairman: Rainer E. Gut. CEO: Allen D. Wheat. Human Resources: David O'Leary.

A subisidiary of Credit Suisse, Switzerland's #2 bank, CS First Boston is a formidable investment banking force in its own right. The company has some 50 offices across the globe, and specializes in business finance and the privatization of government companies. It is now focusing on expanding markets in the former Soviet Union, Latin America, Asia and other newly developing regions. Sales are down, but workforce is up substantially.
Other Locations: Worldwide HQ: Credit Suisse Group, Paradeplatz 8, Postfach 1, 8070 Zurich, Switzerland; +41-1-212-1616.

DAI-ICHI KANGYO BANK

One World Trade Ctr., Ste. 4911, New York, NY 10048; 212-466-5200
http://www.dkb.co.jp
Employees: 17,100
Sales: $17,514 million
Key Personnel: President, CEO: Katsuyuki Sugita. Deputy President: Yoshiro Aoki. Director of Human Resources, New York Branch: Edward Zinser.

The Dai-Ichi Kangyo Bank is the Japan's fourth largest bank. Headquartered in Tokyo, more than 70 percent of the bank's business occurs in Japan. Its sales and workforce have been decreasing in the wake of Japan's recession.
Other Locations: Worldwide HQ: Dai-Ichi Kangyo Bank, Ltd., 1-5, Uchisaiwaicho I-chome, Chiyoda-ku, Tokyo 100, Japan; +81-3-3596-1111. The bank has 400 offices in Japan and more than 75 in the United States and around the world.

HSBC HOLDINGS, INC. ★

140 Broadway, New York, NY 10005; 212-658-5500
http://www.hsbcgroup.com
Employees (overall HSBC): 144,521
Sales (overall HSBC): $43,402.7 million
Key Personnel: Chairman: John R.H. Bond. Group CEO: Keith R. Whitson. Human Resources: Robert A. Tennant.

HSBC Holdings PLC, or the Hong Kong & Shanghai Banking Corporation, is one of the largest banks in the world. It owns Britain's largest bank, Midland Bank, and the #1 bank in Hong Kong, Hong Kong and Shanghai Bank. Its sales and workforce are up.
Other Locations: Worldwide HQ: HSBC Holdings PLC, 10 Lower Thames St., London EC3R 6AE, United Kingdom; +44-171-260-0500. The bank has some 550 offices around the world.

J. P. MORGAN & CO., INC.

60 Wall St., 46th Floor, New York, NY 10260-0060; 212-483-2323
http://www.jpmorgan.com
Employees: 15,674
Sales: $18,425 million
Key Personnel: Chairman, President and CEO: Douglas A. Warner III. VC: Roberto G. Mendoza. Human Resources: Nancy Baird Harwood.

J. P. Morgan is one of the top international banks in the United States. It is primarily involved in trading government securities and types of asset management. The company is currently restructuring with some staff reductions expected, although sales continue to increase.
Other Locations: J. P. Morgan has branches in seven cities in the United States and in 35 foreign countries.

NATIONAL WESTMINSTER BANK PLC

175 Water St., New York, NY 10038; 212-547-7000
http://www.natwestgroup.com
Employees: 74,900
Sales: $22,232.3 million.
Key Personnel: Chairman: Robert Alexander. Group CEO: Derek Wanless. Human Resources: J. Christopher Wathen.

National Westminster is one of the world's leading investment banks and one of the largest banks in the United Kingdom. Some of the company's top management were accused of violations of securities disclosure laws in the early 1990s. Its sales are up modestly, but its work force has been shrinking in recent years.
Other Locations: Worldwide HQ: National Westminster Bank PLC, 41 Lothbury, London EC2P 2BP, United Kingdom; +44-171-726-1000. The bank has more than 1,700 branches in the United Kingdom and several hundred more around the world.

ROYAL BANK OF CANADA ★★
Financial Sq., New York, NY 10005-3531; 212-428-6200
http://www.royalbank.com
Employees (overall RBC): 60,035
Sales (overal RBC): $12,803.2 million.
Key Personnel: Chairman, CEO: John E. Cleghorn. VC: J. Emilien Bolduc. Human Resources: E. Gay Mitchell.
The Royal Bank of Canada is the #2 bank in Canada. It holds a leading percent of the country's personal deposits, residential mortgages and consumer loans. Sales and workforce have increased.
Other Locations: Worldwide HQ: Royal Bank of Canada, One Place Ville Marie, Montreal, Quebec H3B 1Z8, Canada; 514-874-2110. The bank has more than 1,400 branches in Canada and more than 100 subsidiaries in 33 other countries.

NORTH CAROLINA

BANK OF AMERICA CORPORATION ★★
100 N. Tryon St., 18th Fl., Charlotte, NC 28255; 704-386-5000
http://www.bankofamerica.com
Employees: 170,975
Sales: $51,794 million
Key Personnel: Chairman, CEO: Hugh L. McColl, Jr. VC, CFO: James H. Hance, Jr. Human Resources: Charles Cooley.
Former #3, NationBank, and former #4, BankAmerica, got together and the result is #1—Bank of America is the largest bank in the U.S. The company, which offers a full range of consumer, commercial and corporate banking services, operates approximately 11,500 branches

across the country. Bank of America also provides investment and mutual fund services, and brokerage insurance. Sales and workforce are way up.

FIRST UNION CORPORATION ★★
One First Union Center, Charlotte, NC 28288-0570; 704-374-6565
http://www.firstunion.com
Employees: 71,486
Sales: $21,543 million
Key Personnel: Chairman, CEO: Edward E. Crutchfield. VC: B. J. Walker. EVP Human Resources: Don R. Johnson.
First Union Corporation offers a full range of personal and commercial financial services. The bank tries to combine a lean management style with responsive customer service in its branches throughout the Southeast. It also offers services on the Internet. Sales and workforce are increasing dramatically.
Other Locations: First Union Corporation has more than 2,400 branches in the southeastern United States.

NORTH DAKOTA

COMMUNITY FIRST BANKSHARES, INC. ★★
520 Main Ave., Fargo, ND 58124-0001; 701-298-5600
http://www.cfbx.com
Employees: 2,839
Sales: $509.5 million
Key Personnel: Chairman, President and CEO: Donald R. Mengedoth. VC: Ronald K. Strand. Human Resources: Harriette S. McCaul.
Multi-bank holding company, Community First Bankshares operates banks at approximately 150 local sites across the West and Midwest. Its banks provide a full range of consumer and commercial services. In 1998, Community First acquired four banks in Colorado and it is currently acquiring its first California bank. Both sales and workforce are up.
Other Locations: The company operates banks in 11 states.
OHIO

KEYCORP ★
127 Public Sq., Cleveland, OH 44114-1306; 216-689-6300
http://www.keybank.com
Employees: 25,862
Sales: $6,050 million
Key Personnel: Chairman, CEO: Robert W. Gillespie. President, COO: Henry L.

Meyer III. Human Resources: Thomas E. Helfrich.

KeyCorp was formed in 1994 through the merger of Society Corporation of Columbus, Ohio and KeyCorp of Albany, N.Y. Based in Cleveland, the new company provides a full array of banking and financial services for consumer, corporate and institutional clientele. Sales are increasing, as is workforce.
Other Locations: KeyCorp has more than 1,000 branches in 13 states.

PENNSYLVANIA

MELLON BANK CORPORATION
One Mellon Bank Ctr., Pittsburgh, PA 15258-0001; 412-234-5000
http://www.mellon.com
Employees: 28,500
Sales: $5,814 million
Key Personnel: Chairman, CEO: Martin G. McGuinn. VC, President and COO: Christopher M. Condron. Human Resources: Charles Singleton.
Mellon Bank Corporation operates a number of subsidiaries, including The Boston Company, The Dreyfus Corp., and Mellon Bank. The company's services include investment management, credit cards, and real estate loans. Both sales and work force have been increasing in recent years.

PNC BANK CORP.
One PNC Plaza, 249 Fifth Ave., Pittsburgh, PA 15222-2707;412-762-1553
http://www.pncbank.com
Employees: 25,500
Sales: $7,936 million
Key Personnel: Chairman, CEO: Thomas H. O'Brien. President, COO: James E. Rohr. Human Resources: William E. Rosner.
Formed in 1983 by the merger of Pittsburgh National and Provident National of Philadelphia, PNC has since acquired banks throughout the Northeast. It is currently consolidating operations in its more than 740 branches in an effort to streamline operations and cut costs. Its Sales continue to increase, and workforce is up modestly.
Other Locations: PNC has 10 subsidiary banks in seven states and more than 80 nonbanking subsidiaries.

TEXAS

TORONTO–DOMINION BANK (USA), INC.
909 Fannin St, Houston, TX 77010; 713-653-8200
Employees (overall TD): 28,001
Sales (overall TD): $7,439.0 million.
Key Personnel: Chairman, CEO: A. Charles Baillie. SVP USA Division: Michael P. Mueller. SVP Human Resources: Lourie MacDonald.
The Toronto-Dominion Bank is Canada's fifth largest financial institution. Its primary focus is the securities business, and it has the country's largest brokerage. Sales continue to increase, and workforce is up.
Other Locations: Worldwide HQ: Toronto-Dominion Bank, Toronto-Dominion Centre, King St. W. & Bay St., Toronto, Ontario M5K 1A2, Canada; 416-982-8222. The bank has 1,000 branches in Canada and offices in the major financial centers of the world.

❶ BUILDING MATERIALS

ALABAMA

VULCAN MATERIALS COMPANY
1200 Urban Center Dr., Birmingham, AL 35242; 205-298-3000
http://www.vulcanmaterials.com
Employees: 6,971
Sales: $1,776.4 million
Key Personnel: Chairman, CEO: Donald M. James. VC: A. Frederick Gerstell. Human Resources: J. Wayne Houston.
The largest producer of crushed rock, Vulcan Materials is also a top manufacturer of chemicals for industry. The company supplies materials used in road building and industrial chemicals and provides transportation for various industrial applications. Sales are up, but workforce is down slightly.
Other Locations: The company has more than 330 plants in the United States and Mexico, as well as seven chemical plants and other facilities in the U.S. and Canada.

COLORADO

JOHNS MANVILLE CORPORATION ★★
717 17th St., Denver, CO 80202; 303-978-2000
http://www.jm.com
Employees: 9,500

Sales: $1,781.2 million
Key Personnel: Chairman, President, and CEO: Charles L. Henry. SVP, CFO: John P. Murphy. Human Resources: Ron L. Hammons.

Johns Manville Corporation (formerly the Manville Corporation) is the owner of several subsidiaries, including Riverwood, one of the largest manufacturers of linerboard packaging for canned drinks, and Stillwater Mining, a producer of palladium, platinum, and other metals. The company is the #2 U.S. manufacturer of building insulation and was once the world's largest asbestos producer. Sales and workforce are up.

CONNECTICUT

LOCTITE CORPORATION

10 Columbus Blvd., Hartford, CT 06106; 860-520-5000
http://www.loctite.com
Employees: 4,518
Sales: $890.4 million
Key Personnel: Chairman, President and CEO: David Freeman. CFO: Joseph De-Forte. EVP Human Resources: Bruce Vakiener.

The manufacturer of Super Glue, Loctite Corporation has long been one of the largest industrial firms in the world. Along with the famous adhesive, the company manufactures an extensive line of sealants and chemical specialties. It is currently expanding into the lucrative Asian market. In early 1997, Loctite became a wholly owned subsidiary of German chemical manufacturer Henkel. Sales have increased, but workforce is down.

FLORIDA

WATSCO, INC. ★★

2665 S. Bayshore Dr., Ste. 901, Coconut Grove, FL 33133; 305-714-4100
http://www.watsco.com
Employees: 2,900
Sales: $1,008.8 million
Key Personnel: Chairman, President and CEO: Albert H. Nahmad. VP Finance, CFO: Barry S. Logan. Human Resources: Anna Romero.

Watsco is a leader in the manufacture of climate control products and also provides personnel services. The company's climate control division makes residential air conditioners and related equipment. Its personnel division supplies permanent and temporary workers through its subsidiary, Dunhill Personnel System. Both sales and work force are on the rise.

GEORGIA

KUBOTA MANUFACTURING OF AMERICA CORPORATION

Gainesville Industrial Park N., 2715 Ramsey Rd., Gainesville, GA 30501; 770-532-0038
Employees: 15,156
Sales: $8,071.5 million
Key Personnel: Chairman, Representative Director: Osamu Okamoto. President: Yoshikuni Dobashi. Executive Managing Director: Hiroyuki Kisaka.

Farm equipment, water and sewer pipes, roofing equipment—they're all made by Kubota. One of Japan's top manufacturers, it also makes environmental controls, prefab houses, engines, and many other things. The company has suffered during Japan's recent recession and as a result is planning to move more of its manufacturing capacity overseas. Sales and work force are down.
Other Locations: Worldwide HQ: Kubota Corp., 2-47 Shikitsuhigashi 1-chome, Naniwa-ku, Osaka 556-8601, Japan; +81-6-6648-2111.

ILLINOIS

ACE HARDWARE CORPORATION

2200 Kensington Ct., Oak Brook, IL 60523; 630-990-6600
http://www.acehardware.com
Employees: 4,672
Sales: $3,120.4 million
Key Personnel: Chairman: Howard J. Jung. President, CEO: David F. Hodnik. Human Resources: Fred J. Neer.

One of the largest hardware wholesalers in the United States, Ace Hardware is a dealer-owned cooperative. Its 5,300 dealers around the world buy as a group to get the best prices on wholesale goods. The company also manufactures its own line of paint. Sales are up, but workforce is down slightly.

USG CORPORATION ★

125 S. Franklin St., Chicago, IL 60606-4678; 312-606-4000
http://www.usg.com
Employees: 13,700
Sales: $3,130 million
Key Personnel: Chairman, CEO: William C. Foote. President, COO: P. Jack

O'Bryan. Human Resources: Brian J. Cook.

USG is a holding company that operates a number of subsidiary manufacturers of building materials. Its main subsidiary is North American Gypsum, the world's largest producer of gypsum wallboard. USG's subsidiaries are also leading manufacturers of ceiling tiles and other construction products. Demand keeps USG's facilities near maximum capacity. Sales and work force are growing healthily.

MICHIGAN

MASCO CORPORATION ★★
21001 Van Born Rd., Taylor, MI 48180; 313-274-7400
http://www.masco.com
Employees: 31,700
Sales: $4,345 million
Key Personnel: President, COO: Raymond F. Kennedy. Chairman, CEO: Richard A. Manoogian. Human Resources: Daniel R. Foley.

A leader in the home improvement market, Masco Corporation has a major market share in several areas. It is the top U.S. maker of faucets, cabinets, and furniture. The growth in the U.S. home building and home improve-ment markets has created growth for Masco. Sales are healthy, as is workforce.
Other Locations: The company has more than 150 factories in 23 states and 17 countries.

MINNESOTA

HONEYWELL, INC.
Honeywell Plaza, Minneapolis, MN 55408; 612-951-1000
http://www.honeywell.com
Employees: 57,000
Sales: $8,426.7 million
Key Personnel: Chairman, CEO: Michael R. Bonsignore. President, COO: Giannantonio Ferrari. VP Human Resources: James T. Porter.

One of the largest manufacturers of switches and sensors in the world, Honeywell is the company that invented the thermostat. It is a major manufacturer of controllers for homes, communications, aerospace, and many other industries. Honeywell is being purchased by Allied Signal. The company's sales have been rising, but workforce is down.
Other Locations: The company has facilities in 95 countries.

NEW JERSEY

AMERICAN STANDARD COMPANIES, INC. ★★
One Centennial Ave., Piscataway, NJ 08855; 732-980-6000
http://www.americanstandard.com
Employees:57,100
Sales: $6,653.9 million
Key Personnel: Chairman, President, and CEO: Emmanuel A. Kampouris. VC: Horst Hinrichs. Human Resources: Adrian B. Deshotel.

American Standard manufactures plumbing products, air conditioning systems, and braking systems for trucks and buses. With plants all over the world, American Standard customizes its products to fit the local markets. The company's rapid expansion has caused consistent losses since the late 1980s. However, its sales and work force are rising.
Other Locations: The company has 120 factories in 35 countries.

FEDDERS CORPORATION
505 Martinsville Rd., Liberty Corner, NJ 07938-0813; 908-604-8686
http://www.fedders.com.
Employees: 2,700
Sales: $322.1 million
Key Personnel: Chairman: Salvatore Giordano. VC, President, CEO: Salvatore Giordano Jr. Human Resources: Marlene Volte.

As the largest manufacturer of room air conditioners and dehumidifiers in North America, Fedders Corporation holds a 25-percent market share. Sales in North America have always been seasonal, so the company has been expanding into warmer climates to create a steadier cash flow. Sales are up, but workforce is static.

NEW YORK

CORNING, INC.
One Riverfront Plaza, Corning, NY 14831-0001; 607-974-9000
http://www.corning.com
Employees: 15,400
Sales: $3,484 million
Key Personnel: Chairman, CEO: Roger G. Ackerman. Co-COO, Sector President: John W. Loose. Human Resources: Pamela C. Schneider.

Corning is a world leader in specialty glass materials, including fiber-optic cable (which it invented two decades ago).

The company also produces many communications products, such as optical fibers and photnic components. Corning is the parent company of Dow Corning, the much maligned breast implant manufacturer. Both its sales and work force are on the decline.
Other Locations: The company has laboratories in 10 countries and 41 factories in eight countries.

OHIO

OWENS-CORNING FIBERGLAS CORPORATION

One Owens Corning Pkwy., Toledo, OH 43659; 419-248-8000
http://www.owenscorning.com
Employees: 21,000
Sales: $5,009 million
Key Personnel: Chairman, CEO: Glen H. Hiner. SVP: Robert C. SVP, CFO: J. Thurston Roach.
The largest manufacturer of glass fiber insulation material, Owens-Corning also makes many other products sold to the housing market around the world. Along with Fiberglass, it also produces Miraflex fiber, another insulating material, and many other building products. The company's sales are on the increase, especially in Europe, but its work force is shrinking.
Other Locations: The company has factories in the United States and 11 other countries.

OWENS-ILLINOIS, INC. ★★

One SeaGate, Toledo, OH 43666; 419-247-5000
http://www.owens-illinois.com
Employees: 38,800
Sales: $5,306.3 million
Key Personnel: Chairman, CEO: Joseph H. Lemieux. SVP, CFO: David G. Van Hooser. Human Resources: John Frechette.
Owens-Illinois is the largest manufacturer of glass containers in the world. The company is also one of the largest makers of packaging products, including pharmaceutical containers and plastic beverage containers. Demand for glass packaging has peaked in the United States, and the company is restructuring. Sales are increasing, but workforce is down.
Other Locations: The company has manufacturing facilities in more than 170 cities across the globe.

SHERWIN-WILLIAMS COMPANY

101 Prospect Ave. NW, Cleveland, OH 44115-1075; 216-566-2000
http://www.sherwin-williams.com
Employees: 24,822
Sales: $4,934.4 million
Key Personnel: Chairman, CEO: John G. Breen. President, COO: Thomas A. Commes. Human Resources: Thomas E. Hopkins.
The largest manufacturer of paints and varnishes in North America, the Sherwin-Williams Company also produces other types of coatings. The company makes many best-selling brands of paint (such as Dutch Boy), as well as several store brands. It also runs more than 2,000 retail stores. Sales are up modestly, but workforce has suffered modest declines.
Other Locations: The company has some 140 automotive branches and 2,200 specialty paint stores in Canada, Puerto Rico, and the United States, as well as subsidiaries in Brazil, Canada, Curaçao, the Grand Cayman Islands, Jamaica, Mexico, and the Virgin Islands.

PENNSYLVANIA

AMPCO-PITTSBURGH CORP.

600 Grant St., Ste. 4600, Pittsburgh, PA 15219; 412-456-4400
Employees: 1,332
Sales: $187.9 million
Key Personnel: Chairman: Louis Berkman. President, CEO: Robert A. Paul. Human Resources: Robert F. Schultz.
Ampco-Pittsburgh manufactures a variety of air handling systems, pumps, and heat exchange coils for several industries, including marine defense, chemical processing, electric utility, and refrigeration. Its customers are primarily commercial and industrial businesses in the United States. Sales are up healthily; workforce is up slightly.

ARMSTRONG WORLD INDUSTRIES, INC. ★★

2500 Columbia Ave., Lancaster, PA 17604-3001; 717-397-0611
http://www.armstrong.com
Employees:18,900
Sales: $2,746.2 million
Key Personnel: Chairman, President and CEO: George A. Lorch. SVP: Frank A. Riddick III. SVP Human Resources: Douglas L. Boles.
A major manufacturer of floor coverings,

furniture, and industrial specialty items, Armstrong World Industries has been growing along with the housing market. The company also has been expanding into the growing Asian market and building factories there as well. Sales and workforce are up substantially.

Other Locations: The company has 69 factories in the United States and 14 in other countries.

CERTAINTEED CORPORATION ★★

750 E. Swedesford Rd., Valley Forge, PA 19482; 610-341-7000
http://www.certainteed.com
Employees: 7,718
Sales: $1,813 million
Key Personnel: CEO, SVP, Compaigne de Saint-Gobain: Gian-Paolo Caccini. VP, Finance: George B. Amoss. VP Human Resources: Dennis Baker.

CertainTeed is a subsidiary of Saint-Gobain, one of the largest companies in Europe. Saint-Gobain has approximately 300 subsidiaries and has industrial units in 37 countries. CertainTeed manufactures a variety of building materials, such as tiles, windows, pipes, and drainage systems. Sales and workforce are up substantially.

Other Locations: Worldwide HQ: Compagnie de Saint-Gobain, Les Miroirs, 18 Avenue d'Alsace, F-92400 Courbevoie, France; +33-1-47-62-30-00.

PPG INDUSTRIES, INC.

One PPG Pl., Pittsburgh, PA 15272; 412-434-3131
http://www.ppg.com
Employees: 32,500
Sales: $7,510 million
Key Personnel: Chairman, CEO: Raymond W. LeBoeuf. EVP: Frank A. Archinaco. SVP Human Resources and Administration: Russell L. Crane.

One of the largest glass manufacturers in the United States, PPG Industries makes windows for many applications, including cars, airplanes, and buildings. The company also produces coating materials, such as paints and optical resins, and is the second largest maker of fiberglass. Sales and workforce are up modestly.

Other Locations: The company has manufacturing facilities in the United States and 15 other countries.

TEXAS

PITT–DES MOINES, INC. ★★

1450 Lake Robbins Dr., Ste. 400, The Woodlands, TX 77380; 281-765-4600
http://www.pdm.com
Employees: 2,479
Sales: $566.7 million
Key Personnel: CEO, President: William W. McKee. Treasurer, VP Finance and Administration: R. A. Byers. Human Resources: Ken Boesiger.

Pitt-Des Moines has been in operation since 1892. The company provides products and services for the construction of a wide variety of structures, including bridges, skyscrapers, water and oil tanks, and wind tunnels. It also distributes a line of carbon steel products, such as plates, sheets, and tubes. Sales and workforce are up dramatically.

❶ BUSINESS SERVICES

CALIFORNIA

ADECCO, INC.

100 Redwood Shores, Redwood, CA 94065; 650-610-1000
http://www.adecco.com
Employees (overall Adecco): 350,000
Sales (overall Adecco): $11,141.2 million
Key Personnel: CEO: John P. Bowmer. CFO: Felix Weber. VP Human Resources: John Wilson.

Adecco, Inc. is the U.S. division of Adecco S.A., the largest temporary employment agency in the world. The result of a merger between Adia and Ecco, Adecco S.A. is also one of the few temp agencies that operates internationally. The company places both skilled and unskilled workers in temporary and sometimes permanent positions. It also provides job counseling services. Sales are way up, but workforce has dropped sharply.

Other Locations: Worldwide HQ: Rue de Langeallerie 11, Postale 2, 1000 Lausanne 4, Switzerland; phone: +41-2-13-21-66-66.

ANACOMP, INC. ★★

12365 Crosthwaite Circle, Poway, CA 92064, 858-679-9797
http://www.anacomp.com
Employees: 3,400

Sales: $499 million
Key Personnel: Co-Chairmen: Richard D. Jackson, Lewis Solomon. President, CEO: Ralph W. Koehrer. Human Resources: Wally Boehm.

Anacomp is a leading provider of information storage products and services. Its microfilm-transfer products line is one of the largest in the world. The company also offers an extensive line of electronic data and image management products and services, such as optical disk storage systems. Sales and work force are up.

COMPUTER SCIENCES CORPORATION ★★
http://www.csc.com
2100 E. Grand Ave., El Segundo, CA 90245; 310-615-0311
http://www.csc.com
Employees: 50,000
Sales: $7,660 million
Key Personnel: Chairman, President, CEO: Van B. Honeycutt. VP: Harvey N. Bernstein. Human Resources: Frederick E. Vollrath.

Supplying information technology to companies around the world, Computer Sciences Corporation provides a broad range of services. Communications network engineering, information system development, and office automation are among the company's offerings. Sales and work force are increasing.

CONNECTICUT

ADVO, INC.
One Univac Lane, Windsor, CT 06095; 860-285-6100
http://www.advo.com
Employees: 4,600
Sales: $1,046.5 million
Key Personnel: Chairman: Robert Kamerschen. President, CEO: Gary M. Mulloy. Human Resources: Mardelle Pena.

ADVO is the largest full-service direct mail company in the United States. The company is the biggest of the U.S. Postal Service's bulk mail customers. It offers a wide variety of programs to its advertisers and also rents its mailing list of over 100 million residential addresses. The company's sales have increasd modestly, while its workforce has fallen slightly.

EMCOR GROUP, INC. ★
101 Merritt Seven Corporate Park, Seventh Fl., Norwalk, CT 06851; 203-849-7800

http://www.emcorgroup.com
Employees: 15,000
Sales: $2,210.4 million
Key Personnel: Chairman , CEO: Frank T. MacInnis. President, COO: Jeffrey M. Levy. VP Human Resources: Jim Murphy.

When the large conglomerate JWP filed for bankruptcy in 1994, it was reorganized into two separate companies, one of which was EMCOR. EMCOR is one of the biggest electrical and mechanical service organizations in North America. Sales and workforce are increasing.
Other Locations: The company has 45 branches in Europe, North America, and the Middle East.

GEORGIA

EQUIFAX, INC. ★★
1600 Peachtree St. NW, P.O. Box 4081, Atlanta, GA 30309; 404-885-8000
http://www.equifax.com
Employees: 14,000
Sales: $1,621 million
Key Personnel: President, CEO: Thomas F. Chapman. CFO: David A. Post. Human Resources: Karen H. Gaston.

The largest credit reporting agency in the United States, Equifax keeps tabs on more than 300 million people. Although Equifax derives most of its income from the U.S. and Canadian economies, it has been increasing its market share in Europe. The company's sales and work force are up.
Other Locations: The company has branches in Canada, Europe, Latin America, and the United States.

PER-SE TECHNOLOGIES, INC.
2840 Mount Wilkinson Pkwy., Ste. 300, Atlanta, GA 30339; 770-444-4000
http://www.medaphis.com
Employees: 6,600
Sales: $349.8 million
Key Personnel: Chairman: David E. McDowell. President, CEO Allen W. Ritchie. Human Resources: Julie L. Molleston.

Fomerly Medaphis, Per-Se Technologies handles billing, collections, and office management for the health services industry. The company's clients include 20,000 physicians and 2,700 hospitals across the U.S. After rapid growth, Per-Se is reorganizing its operations. Sales and workforce are down sharply.

TOTAL SYSTEM SERVICES, INC. ★★
1200 Sixth Ave., Columbus, GA 31901;
706-649-2310
http://www.totalsystem.com
Employees: 3,935
Sales: $396.2 million
Key Personnel: President: Philip W. Tomlinson. Chairman, CEO: Richard W. Ussery. Human Resources: Brenda Reed.
One of the largest credit-card data processors in the world, Total System Services handles over 35.5 million accounts. The company provides services such as credit authorization and payment processing. Through its subsidiaries, it also sells and leases computer equipment, offers commercial printing, and provides direct mail services. Its sales and work force are increasing.

ILLINOIS

BAKER & MCKENZIE ★
One Prudential Plaza, 130 E. Randolph Dr., Ste. 2500, Chicago, IL 60601; 312-861-880
http://www.bakerinfo.com
Employees: 6,700
Sales: $784.5 million
Key Personnel: Chairman: John C. Klotsche. CFO: Suzanne M. Meyers. Human Resources: Jennifer Pingolt.
Baker & McKenzie is one of the largest law firms in the world. It has more than 2,000 lawyers in more than 50 offices worldwide and can offer its clients expertise in almost any field of law. The company employs local lawyers in its foreign operations to enhance its success abroad. Its sales and work force continue to grow.

COMDISCO, INC. ★★
6111 N. River Rd., Rosemont, IL 60018; 847-698-3000
http://www.comdisco.com
Employees: 2,800
Sales: $3,243 million
Key Personnel: President, CEO: Nicholas K. Pontikes. EVP, CFO: John J. Vosicky. Human Resources: Lucie A. Buford.
Leasing, buying, and selling computer systems is the main business of Comdisco. Although the company was built primarily around mainframe computers, in the 1990s it branched into networked computers and medical products. It has recently entered into an agreement to sell its original mainframe leasing business. About a quarter of Comdisco's business comes from outside the U.S. The company's sales and workforce have increased.

INFORMATION RESOURCES, INC. ★★
150 N. Clinton St., Chicago, IL 60661; 312-726-1221
http://www.infores.com
Employees: 7,500
Sales: $511.3 million
Key Personnel: Chairman, President, and CEO: Joseph Durrett. EVP, CFO: Gary M. Hill. Human Resources: Gary Newman.
Gathering and utilizing marketing data is the specialty of Information Resources Inc. (IRI). The company sells services that allow retailers to track purchases and analyze consumer trends by compiling information gathered at the checkout stand with the store's bar-code scanner. The company's domestic expansion opportunities are slowing, and it is looking overseas for new options. Sales and work force are up.

MASSACHUSETTS

ACQUENT ★★
711 Boylston St., Boston, MA 02116; 617 535-5000
http://www.acquent.com
Employees: 12,500
Sales: $130 million
Key Personnel: CEO: John Chuang. VP: Nikki Granner. VP Human Resources: Charlotte Evans.
Unlike other temporary employment agencies, Acquent (formerly MacTemps) specializes in employing people who are computer literate. The company does not provide training but instead screens to find qualified candidates. The company began by specializing in Macintosh computer, hence its former name. Sales and workforce are healthy.
Other Locations: The company has more than 30 offices in the U.S. and several foreign countries.

PRIMARK CORPORATION
1000 Winter St., Ste. 4300N, Waltham, MA 02154; 781-466-6611
http://www.primark.com
Employees: 2,900
Sales: $434.5 million
Key Personnel: Chairman, President and

CEO: Joseph E. Kasputys. EVP, CFO: Stephen H. Curran. Human Resources: Diane Robesen.

Formerly the manager of a public utility in Michigan, Primark now provides extensive information, financial, health care data management, and weather graphic systems services. Its customers include 1,200 commercial weather clients and 1,500 financial organizations. Sales and work force are increasing rapidly.

MICHIGAN

KELLY SERVICES, INC. ★★

999 W. Big Beaver Rd., Troy, MI 48084; 248-362-4444
http://www.kellyservices.com
Employees: 740,000
Sales: $4,092.3 million
Key Personnel: Chairman, President and CEO: Terence E. Adderley. EVP Field Operations: Carl T. Camden. Human Resources: David Beckstrand.

One of the largest temporary employment services in the world, Kelly Services has benefited from the reduction in the number of permanent workers in the world's labor force. Kelly, which began by placing only secretaries and other clerical assistants, now offers high technology and professional staffing services. The company's sales are up, but workforce is down slightly.
Other Locations: The company has offices in Puerto Rico, the U.S., and 18 foreign countries.

MINNESOTA

CERIDIAN CORPORATION ★★

8100 34th Ave. S., Minneapolis, MN 55425; 612-853-8100
http://www.ceridian.com
Employees: 9,600
Sales: $1,162.1 million
Key Personnel: Chairman, CEO: Lawrence Pearlman. President, COO: Ronald L. Turner. SVP Human Resources: Shirley Hughes.

Ceridian's has multiple operations. The largest of these is its Human Resource Services (HRS) division, which provides payroll and employee assistance programs. Comdata, which accounts for nearly a quarter of the company's business, offers information services to trucking companies. Arbitron, Ceridian's third major unit, is the largest U.S. supplier of audience demographics for radio.

Sales and workforce are increasing.
Other Locations: The company has operations in Canada, the United Kingdom, and the United States.

NEW JERSEY

AUTOMATIC DATA PROCESSING, INC. ★★

One ADP Blvd., Roseland, NJ 07068; 973-994-5000
http://www.adp.com
Employees: 34,000
Sales: $5,540.1 million
Key Personnel: Chairman, CEO: Arthur F. Weinbach. President, COO: Gary C. Butler. VP Human Resources: Richard C. Berke.

The movement in business away from mainframe computers has added to the business of Automatic Data Processing. The largest payroll and tax-filing processor in the United States, ADP offers many other services, such as auto collision estimates for insurance companies. The company also sells the popular Peachtree accounting software. Its sales and work force are growing.
Other Locations: The company has 53 branches in the United States, one in Canada, and two in Europe.

BISYS GROUP, INC. ★★

150 Clove Rd., Little Falls, NJ 07424; 973-812-8600
http://www.bisys.com
Employees: 2,200
Sales: $472.7 million
Key Personnel: Chairman, CEO: Lynn J. Mangum. EVP, CFO: Dennis R. Sheehan. Human Resources: Mark J. Rybarczyk.

Administrative computing and marketing services are the focus of BISYS Group. The company provides its services to more than 9,000 financial institutions. Those services fall into three categories: loan administration, financial computing support, and investment administration. The company continues to sign on new clients as more banks seek to outsource services. Sales and work force are increasing.

NEW YORK

ENTEX INFORMATION SERVICES

Six International Dr., Rye Brook, NY 10573; 914-935-3600
http://www.entex.com
Employees: 5,800

Sales: $483.6 million
Key Personnel: President: John A. McKenna, Jr. EVP Finance, CFO: Kenneth A. Ghazey. Human Resources: Mark G. Mindell.
Individualized computer configurations are the specialty of Entex Information Services. The company is a nationwide information services provider primarily supplying services to large corporations. Its services include network design and installation, equipment acquisition, and emergency technical service. After dumping its resale products division, which provided 80 percent of sales, the company's sales and work force are down sharply.

MCKINSEY & COMPANY, INC.

55 E. 52nd St., New York, NY 10022; 212-446-7000
http://www.mckinsey.com
Employees: 8,500
Sales: $2,500 million
Key Personnel: Managing Director: Rajat Gupta. CFO: Donna Rosenwasser. Director Personnel: Jerome Vascellaro.
The oldest business consulting company in the U.S., McKinsey & Company studies the functions of its clients and then creates strategic analyses that hopefully point the way to greater success. Like its competitors, McKinsey's advice hasn't always been effective, but it still attracts major clients. Sales are up healthily, but workforce is static.
Other Locations: The company has 74 branches in United States and across the globe.

OGDEN CORPORATION

Two Pennsylvania Plaza, New York, NY 10121; 212-868-6000
http://www.ogdencorp.com
Employees: 21,970
Sales: $1,692.4 million
Key Personnel: Chairman: George L. Farr. CEO, President: Scott G. Mackin. Human Resources: Alane G. Baranello.
Ogden Corporation operates in three arenas. It provides management services to major organizations in the public and private sectors. It serves the aviation, entertainment, and sports industries with catering and other services. And it is also the biggest developer of waste-to-energy facilities in the United States. The company plans to sell its aviation and entertainment businesses to focus on its energy unit. Sales and work force are down.

OLSTEN CORPORATION ★★

175 Broad Hollow Rd., Melville, NY 11747-8905; 516-844-7800
http://www.olsten.com
Employees: 700,850
Sales: $4,602.8 million
Key Personnel: Chairman: Stuart Olsten. President and CEO: Edward H. Blechschmidt. Human Resources: Maureen K. McGurl.
In an age when flexibility is sometimes the key to business success, Olsten is thriving. The company is one of the world's largest temporary employment agencies. It places staff in a wide variety of fields, including health services, clerical, and finance. The company also offers its temps training programs and other benefits. It is currently in the process of selling its staffing businesses to Adecco. Sales and work force are growing nicely.

PAYCHEX, INC. ★

911 Panorama Trail S., Rochester, NY 14625; 716-385-6666
Employees: 5,500
Sales: $1,175.4 million
Key Personnel: Chairman, President and CEO: B. Thomas Golisano. VP: Diane Rambo. Human Resources: Augustin Melendez.
The second largest payroll accounting company in the United States, Paychex has more than 300,000 clients. Along with payroll services, the company offers tax and human resources services. Paychex focuses on small to midsized businesses, typically those with 200 or fewer employees. Both its sales and work force are on the increase.

O H I O

BATTELLE MEMORIAL INSTITUTE

505 King Ave., Columbus, OH 43201-2693; 614-424-6424
http://www.battelle.org
Employees: 7,250
Sales: $710.1 million
Key Personnel: Chairman: Willis S. White, Jr. First VC: John J. Hopfield. Human Resources: Bob Lincoln.
The developer of many well-known inventions, Battelle Memorial Institute is the oldest and largest contract research organization in the world. Among its many successes are the copy machine,

the copper-nickel sandwich coin, and cruise control. Battelle is actively seeking contracts from companies too small to do their own research and development. Its sales are decreasing, but its work force is up slightly.

DIEBOLD, INC.

5995 Mayfair Rd., North Canton, OH 44720; 330-490-4000
http://www.diebold.com
Employees: 6,489
Sales: $1,185.7 million
Key Personnel: Chairman, President and CEO: Robert W. Mahoney. EVP, CFO: Gerald F. Morris. Human Resources: Charles B. Scheurer.
Diebold is one of the largest manufacturers of security products and ATM machines in the United States. The company began making safes nearly 140 years ago and now makes a wide variety of electronic and physical security systems. Diebold is expanding its international market, especially in Asia. Its sales and work force are on the decline.

THE REYNOLDS AND REYNOLDS COMPANY

115 S. Ludlow St., Dayton, OH 45402; 937-485-2000
http://www.reyrey.com
Employees: 9,152
Sales: $1,486 million
Key Personnel: Chairman, CEO: David R. Holmes. President, COO: Lloyd G. Waterhouse. Human Resource: Tom Momchilov.
Reynolds and Reynolds has been supplying business forms since the 1860s. The company supplies general forms and sells more specialized forms to the automotive sales and health care markets. Reynolds also sells computer software for the automotive and health markets that helps with administrative details. The company's sales are up, as is workforce.

PENNSYLVANIA

ARAMARK CORPORATION

1101 Market St., Philadelphia, PA 19107; 215-238-3000
http://www.aramark.com
Employees: 150,000
Sales: $6,377.3 million
Key Personnel: President, COO: William Leonard. EVP, CFO: L. Frederick Sutherland. VP Human Resources: Brian G. Mulvaney.
From hot dogs to uniforms, ARAMARK offers it all. The company provides a wide variety of catering and institutional services at national parks, prisons, sports arenas, and many other venues. ARAMARK is now adjusting its image to provide more cross-marketing opportunities among its branches. Its sales are up slightly and workforce is static.

RIGHT MANAGEMENT CONSULTANTS, INC. ★★

1818 Market St., Philadelphia, PA 19103; 215-988-1588
http://www.right.com
Employees: 1,406
Sales: $168.3 million
Key Personnel: Chairman, CEO: Richard J. Pinola. President, COO: John J. Gavin. CFO: G. Lee Bohs.
Right Management Consultants offer a specialized form of career counseling. The company counsels employees who have been terminated, helping them get necessary training and finding jobs for them. The company has approximately 170 offices, some of which it owns and some of which are franchised. Right's sales and work force are increasing.
Other Locations: The company has 170 branches in Canada, Europe, and the United States.

SAFEGUARD SCIENTIFICS, INC. ★★

435 Devon Park Dr., Wayne, PA 19087; 610-293-0600
http://www.safeguard.com
Employees: 5,120
Sales: $2,275.1 million
Key Personnel: Chairman, CEO: Warren V. Musser. President, COO: Harry Wallaesa. Human Resources: Gerald M. Hogan.
Safeguard Scientifics is a high-tech incubator. It provides business and management assistance to high-tech start-ups and then sells all or part of its interest once the company's stock is appealing. Among its current subsidiaries are Cambridge Technology Partners and CompuCom Systems. Its sales and work force are on the rise.

SEI INVESTMENTS COMPANY ★★

One Freedom Valley Dr., Oaks, PA

19456-1100; 610-676-1000
http://www.seic.com
Employees: 1,309
Sales: $366.1 million
Key Personnel: Chairman, CEO: Alfred P. West, Jr. EVP: Richard B. Lieb. EVP Human Resources: Scott Budge.

Formerly SEI Corporation, SEI Investments Company began by providing computerized training for bank executives. The company's primary functions are now benefits administration, pension and investment consulting, data processing, software development, and financial services. The company has recently reorganized its operation. Sales and workforce are up.

TEXAS

ELECTRONIC DATA SYSTEMS CORPORATION ★
5400 Legacy Dr., Plano, TX 75024-3199; 972-604-6000
http://www.eds.com
Employees: 120,000
Sales: $16,891 million
Key Personnel: Chairman, CEO: Richard H. Brown. President, COO: Jeffrey M. Heller.

Founded by Ross Perot, Electronic Data Systems is one of the largest data-processing companies in the U.S. However, the com-pany, which until recently was a subsidiary of General Motors, has been losing market share for several years. In 1995, EDS purchased A. T. Kearney in the hopes of gaining expanding its overseas business. The company's sales continue to increase, as does its workforce.

KANEB SERVICES, INC.
2435 N. Central Expwy., Richardson, TX 75080 ; 972-699-4000
http://www.kaneb.com
Employees: 1,857
Sales: $375.9 million
Key Personnel: Chairman, President and CEO: John R. Barnes. SVP: Edward D. Doherty II. Director Human Resources: William H. Kettler, Jr.

Industrial maintenance and testing are the main business of Kaneb. The company mainly services energy and chemical plants. Kaneb also owns Pipe Line Partners, which operates an oil pipeline running from Kansas to North Dakota. Along with facility servicing, Kaneb also provides testing and emergency repairs. The company's sales and work force are growing.

PEROT SYSTEMS CORPORATION ★
12404 Park Central Dr., Dallas, TX 75251; 972-340-5000
http://www.perotsystems.com
Employees: 6,000
Sales: $993.6 million
Key Personnel: Chairman, President, and CEO: Ross Perot. VP, CFO: Terry Ashwill. Human Resources: Kelly Parsons.

Perot Systems Corporation is a business consulting firm specializing in office automation and networking systems. The company, which was founded by Ross Perot (who also founded the similar Electronic Data Systems), has an international client base. It is owned jointly by Perot and its employees. Sales and work force are increasing.

UTAH

FRANKLIN COVEY CO.
2200 W. Parkway Blvd., Salt Lake City, UT 84119-2331; 801-975-1776
http://www.franklincovey.com
Employees: 4,247
Sales: $546.6 million
Key Personnel: Co-Chairman: Hyrum W. Smith. Co-Chairman: Stephen R. Covey. Human Resources: Daken Tanner.

With the acquisition of Stephen Covey's firm, Franklin Covey now offers a variety of printed products, computer software, videos, audio cassettes and seminars on time management. Many of the country's corporate and government leaders participate in its seminars, including employees of the IRS and Chrysler. Sales are up, especially in the company's retail stores. Work force, however, is shrinking.
Other Locations: The company owns operations or has franchises in more than 30 countries.

VIRGINIA

PRC, INC.
1500 PRC Dr., McLean, VA 22102; 703-556-1000
http://www.prc.com
Employees: 5,800
Sales: $834 million

Key Personnel: President: Leonard Pomata. SVP Civil Division: Richard Braun. SVP Human Resources: Walter Goodlett.

A subsidiary of Litton Industries, PRC's services focus on high-technology. The company provides information, primarily to government agencies. Among its many projects, the company has converted engineering drawings to digital format and created a computer to track drug smugglers. PRC's sales and workforce are up.

WISCONSIN

FISERV, INC. ★★

255 Fiserv Dr., Brookfield, WI 53005; 414-879-5000

http://www.fiserv.com
Employees: 12,500
Sales: $1,233.7 million
Key Personnel: Chairman, CEO: George D. Dalton. VC, President and COO: Leslie M. Muma. SVP Corporate Human Resources: Jack P. Bucalo.

The third largest financial dataprocessing company in the United States, Fiserv works with more than 7,000 banks and credit unions around the world. Along with processing data on retirement accounts, Fiserv also does electronic fund transfers and automated teller services. The company's sales and work force are increasing.

MANPOWER, INC.

5301 N. Ironwood Rd., Milwaukee, WI 53217; 414-961-1000

http://www.manpower.com
Employees: 2,015,000
Sales: $8,814.3 million
Key Personnel: Chairman, President and CEO: Mitchell S. Fromstein. EVP U.S. Temporary Services: Terry A. Hueneke. Human Resources: Marion Aymie.

The second biggest temporary employment agency in the world, Manpower puts more than two million people to work. Along with its temporary employment services, the company also provides its customers with permanent employment, testing, and training services. Sales are up, but workforce is static.

❶ CHEMICALS

CONNECTICUT

UNION CARBIDE CORPORATION

39 Old Ridgebury Rd., Danbury, CT 06817-0001; 203-794-2000

http://www.unioncarbide.com
Employees: 11,627
Sales: $5,659 million
Key Personnel: Chairman, President and CEO: William H. Joyce. VP: Bruce D. Fitzgerald. VP Human Resources: Malcolm A. Kessinger.

The top producer of ethylene oxide, ethylene glycol, and polyethylene in the world, Union Carbide is finally recovering from its 1984 plant disaster in Bhopal, India. Dow Chemical is in the process of buying the company. Sales and workforce are down.

DELAWARE

E. I. DU PONT DE NEMOURS AND COMPANY

1007 Market St., Wilmington, DE 19898; 302-774-1000

http://www.dupont.com
Employees: 101,000
Sales: $24,767 million
Key Personnel: Chairman, CEO: Charles O. Holliday, Jr. EVP: Richard R. Goodmanson. Human Resources: John D. Broyles.

Delaware-based Du Pont is the largest chemical company in the United States. The company has many subsidiaries that manufacture a wide variety of products, including fuels, pesticides, consumer products, and pharmaceuticals. It has been aggressively restructuring for several years, laying off more than 30,000 employees since 1990. Sales have dropped sharply, but workforce has experienced a modest rebound.
Other Locations: The company has operations in more than 45 countries.

HERCULES, INC. ★★

Hercules Plaza, 1313 N. Market St., Wilmington, DE 19894-0001; 302-594-5000

http://www.herc.com
Employees: 12,357
Sales: $2,145 million
Key Personnel: President, COO: Vincent J. Corbo. SVP: Dominick W. DiDonna. Human Resources: June B.

Barry.

Originally a part of Du Pont forced out of the nest by an antitrust suit, Hercules is a major supplier of industrial chemicals. The company produces materials for the paper, paint, and food industries and many others. It is expanding its Mexican operations to supply chemicals to Central and South America. Its sales and work force are rising.

Other Locations: The company has facilities in 18 countries.

ICI AMERICAS, INC.

Concord Plaza, 3411 Silverside Rd., Wilmington, DE 19850; 302-887-3000

http://www.icinorthamerica.com

Employees: 23,443

Sales (overall ICI): $15,093.2 million

Key Personnel: Chairman: John R. Danzeisen. VP, CFO: John Forrest. Human Resources: D.I. Hartnett.

ICI Americas is a subsidiary of Imperial Chemical Industries PLC, Great Britain's largest chemical manufacturer and the sixth largest chemical company in the world. The company recently spun off its agricultural, pharmaceutical, and specialty chemical operations and is now concentrating on explosives, industrial chemicals, paints, and materials. Its overall sales are increasing, but its work force is decreasing.

Other Locations: Worldwide HQ: Imperial Chemical Industries PLC, Imperial Chemical House, 9 Millbank, London SW1P 3JF, United Kingdom; +44-171-834-4444.

FLORIDA

W. R. GRACE & CO.

1750 Clint Moore Rd., Boca Raton, FL 33487; 561-362-2000

http://www.grace.com

Employees: 6,300

Sales: $1,463 million

Key Personnel: Chairman, President and CEO: Paul J. Norris. SVP: James R. Hyde. Human Resources: William L. Monroe.

One of the world's largest manufacturers of specialty chemicals, W. R. Grace also leads in specialty health care products. The company makes a full range of products for kidney dialysis and runs 550 dialysis centers worldwide. Sealants, water treatment chemicals, and petroleum cracking catalysts are among its other products. In recent years Grace has sold off more than two dozen businesses. Sales are down and workforce is static.

Other Locations: The company has facilities around the world.

ILLINOIS

AKZO NOBEL, INC.

300 S. Riverside Plaza, Chicago, IL 60606; 312-906-7500

http://www.akzonobelusa.com

Employees (overall AN): 68,900

Sales (overall AN): $14,556.7 million

Key Personnel: President, CEO and CFO: Piet Provo Kluit. Chief Human Resources Officer: Dan Barker.

When Akzo and Nobel Industries merged in 1994, it created the world's largest paint company. The company also manufactures a wide variety of other chemicals, including salt, polymers, and pharmaceuticals. Akzo Nobel is in the process of expanding its capital investments and world market, especially in Asia. Sales are up, but workforce is static.

Other Locations: Worldwide HQ: Akzo Nobel N.V., Velperweg 76, P.O. Box 9300, 6800 SB Arnhem, The Netherlands; +31-26-366-4433. The company has facilities in more than 65 countries.

FMC CORPORATION

200 E. Randolph Dr., Chicago, IL 60601; 312-861-6000

http://www.fmc.com

Employees: 16,216

Sales: $4,378.4 million

Key Personnel: Chairman, CEO: Robert N. Burt. President: Joseph H. Netherland. Human Resources: Michael W. Murray.

Once known as Food Machinery and Chemicals, FMC changed its name to reflect its diversification. The company still makes food processing machines and chemicals. It also builds Bradley fighting vehicles and mines precious metals. Its employees own more than 20 percent of the company. Sales and work force have dropped slightly.

Other Locations: The company has 100 mines and other facilities in the United States and 24 other countries.

MICHIGAN

THE DOW CHEMICAL COMPANY

2030 Dow Ctr., Midland, MI 48674; 517-636-1000

http://www.dow.com

Employees: 39,000

Sales: $18,441 million
Key Personnel: President, CEO: William S. Stavropoulos. EVP: Anthony J. Carbone. VP Human Resources: Larry Washington.

One of the largest chemical companies in the world, Dow Chemical makes a host of products for the consumer, industrial, and agricultural markets. Its consumer products include Ziploc, Saran Wrap, and Fantastik. Several of the company's subsidiaries have been doing poorly in recent years because of lawsuits and changing economic conditions. Dow is in the process of acquiring Union Carbide. Sales and workforce are down.

MISSOURI

HOECHST MARION ROUSSEL, INC.
10236 Marion Park Dr., Kansas City, MO 64137, 816-966-5000
http://www.hmri.com
Employees: 38,109
Sales: $8,242.3 million
Key Personnel: Chairman, CEO: Richard Markham. CFO: Daniel Camus. VP Human Resources: Tommy White.

Hoechst AG is the largest chemical company in the world. From its plants in more than 120 countries, it produces chemicals—including pharmaceuticals, dyes, and plastics—for a broad array of industries. The company's sales are up, but workforce is shrinking.
Other Locations: Worldwide HQ: Hoechst AG, Brueningstrasse 50, D-65926 Frankfurt, Germany; +49-69-305-0.

MONSANTO COMPANY ★★
800 N. Lindbergh Blvd., St. Louis, MO 63167; 314-694-1000
http://www.monsanto.com
Employees: 31,800
Sales: $8,648 million
Key Personnel: Chairman, CEO: Robert B. Shapiro. VC: Richard U. De Schutter. Human Resources: Madonna A. Kindl.

Long one of the largest chemical companies in the United States, Monsanto makes some well-known products in the consumer market, such as aspartame (marketed as NutraSweet). The company also makes many industrial, agricultural, and pharmaceutical products. Monsanto is expanding its biotechnology operations after selling off its chemicals business in 1997 (as Solutia, Inc.). Sales and workforce are up dramatically.

NEW JERSEY

BASF CORPORATION
3000 Continental Dr. N., Mt. Olive, NJ 07828-1234; 201-426-2600
http://www.basf.com
Employees: 15,365
Sales: $7,519.3 million.
Key Personnel:. Chairman, President, and CEO: Peter Oakley. EVP, CFO: Kurt W. Bock. Human Resources: Norman H. Maas.

The second largest chemical company in the world, BASF is most recognized for its audio and videotapes. The company is divided into five sectors: chemicals, polymers, dyestuffs and finishing products, fibers, and consumer products. The company's sales and workforce are up.
Other Locations: Worldwide HQ: BASF AG, Carl-Bosch St. 38, 67056 Ludwigshafen, Germany; +49-621-60-0.

FORMOSA PLASTICS CORP., U.S.A. ★★
9 Peach Tree Hill Rd., Livingston, NJ 07039; 973-992-2090
http://www.fpcusa.com
Employees (overall FPC): 4,897
Sales (overall FPC): $1,471.8 million
Key Personnel: CEO: Susan Wang.

Formosa Plastics Corporation is the largest manufacturer of polyvinyl chloride in the world. Most of the PVC is used in Taiwan in the making of computer motherboards and other plastic products. The company has many powerful subsidiaries in the computer and chemical industries. Though sales are down, workforce has risen dramatically.
Other Locations: Worldwide HQ: Formosa Plastics Corp., 201 Tun Hwa North Rd., Taipei, Taiwan; +886-22-712-2211.

PENNSYLVANIA

AIRGAS, INC.
259 N. Radnor-Chester Rd., Ste. 100, Radnor, PA 19087-5283; 610-687-5253
http://www.airgas.com
Employees: 8,000
Sales: $1,561.2 million
Key Personnel: Chairman, President and CEO: Peter McCausland. President, COO: William A. Rice, Jr. Human Resources: Caren Hosansky.

The largest U.S. independent distributor of custom medical and industrial gases, Airgas has a network of distribution centers that spans North America. Airgas also sells welding equipment. The com-

pany continues to grow through the acquisition of smaller gas distributors. Its sales are up, though workforce has declined slightly.
Other Locations: The company has 700 branches in 44 states, Mexico and Canada.

HENKEL CORPORATION
2200 Renaissance Blvd., Ste. 200, Gulph Mills, PA 19406; 610-270-8100
http://www.henkelcorp.com
Employees (overall Henkel): 56,291
Sales (overall Henkel): $12,801.7 million.
Key Personnel: President, CEO: Robert Lurcott. CFO: John Knudson. VP Human Resources: Bill Read.
Based in Germany, Henkel is not only one of the largest chemical companies in that country but also the world's largest producer of oleochemicals, which are used to make soaps and cosmetics. Henkel is also a top maker of metal surface treatments. Both sales and work force are rising after a downward trend.
Other Locations: Worldwide HQ: Henkel KGaA, Henkelstrasse 67, D-40191 Dusseldorf, Germany; +49-211-797-3937.

TENNESSEE
EASTMAN CHEMICAL COMPANY
100 N. Eastman Rd., Kingsport, TN 37660; 423-229-2000
http://www.eastman.com
Employees: 16,000
Sales: $4,481 million
Key Personnel: Chairman, CEO: Earnest W. Davenport, Jr. VC, EVP: R. Wiley Bourne, Jr. Human Resources: B. Fielding Rolston.
Originally a subsidiary of Eastman Kodak, Eastman Chemical now stands on its own as a leader in the U.S. chemical industry. The company leads in sales of plastics used in packaging and coatings. It also is one of the largest suppliers of inks and resins. Both sales and workforce are decreasing.
Other Locations: The company has facilities in the United States, Latin America, Europe, and Asia.

TEXAS
LYONDELL CHEMICAL COMPANY ★★
1221 McKinney St., Ste. 1600, Houston, TX 77010; 713-652-7200

http://www.lyondell.com
Employees: 10,400
Sales: $1,447 million
Key Personnel: Chairman: William T. Butler. President, CEO: Dan F. Smith. Human Resources: John A. Hollinshead.
Formerly Lyondell Petrochemical, Lyondell Chemical is still one of the largest petrochemical companies in the United States. The company produces petrochemicals for many industrial uses and refines oil to make fuels and lubricants. It is the #1 U.S. maker of ethylene and propylene. Sales have dropped sharply, but workforce has increased dramtically.

UTAH
HUNTSMAN CHEMICAL CORPORATION
500 Huntsman Way, Salt Lake City, UT 84108; 801-532-5200
http://www.huntsman.com
Employees: 10,000
Sales: $5,200 million
Key Personnel: Chairman, CEO: Jon M. Huntsman, Sr. President, COO: Peter R. Huntsman. VP Human Resources: William Chapman.
Already the largest privately held chemical company in the United States, Huntsman Corporation (formerly Huntsman Chemical) doubled its size when it bought Texaco's petrochemical operations in 1994. The company supplies chemicals to a broad range of fields, including the automotive, construction, electronics, and medical industries. Both sales and work force continue to increase.

❶ COMPUTERS/PERIPHERALS

ALABAMA
INTERGRAPH CORPORATION
Huntsville, AL 35894-0001; 256-730-2000
http://www.intergraph.com
Employees: 6,700
Sales: $1,032.8 million
Key Personnel: Chairman, CEO: James W. Meadlock. President, COO: Manfred Wittler. Human Resources: Milford B. French.
Intergraph supplies workstations, servers, and peripherals for the computer-aided engineering, manufacturing, and design markets. The company has struggled to make the transition from Unix to Microsoft Windows and Intel processors. It has

recently sued Intel, alleging anticompetitive practices, and continues its streamlining efforts. Sales and workforce have been on the decline for several years.

SCI SYSTEMS, INC. ★★
2101 W. Clinton Ave., Huntsville, AL 35805; 256-882-4800
http://www.sci.com
Employees: 25,235
Sales: $6,710.8 million
Key Personnel: Chairman: Olin B. King. President, CEO: A. Eugene Sapp, Jr. Human Resources: Francis X. Henry.
Although unknown to most computer purchasers, the contract manufacturer SCI is one of the largest assemblers of computers in the world. The company builds computers for many original equipment manufacturers, including Hewlett-Packard and Apple. The company runs a variety of other operations, including surface mount circuit board assembly. Despite a recent drop in sales, its workforce has experienced substantial growth.
Other Locations: The company has manufacturing facilities in Canada, France, Hong Kong, Ireland, Mexico, Scotland, Singapore, Thailand, and the United States.

CALIFORNIA

ACER AMERICA CORPORATION ★★
2641 Orchard Pkwy., San Jose, CA 95134; 408-433-4985
http://www.acer.com/aac
Employees: 23,000
Sales: $5,268.9 million
Key Personnel: President, CEO and COO (Acer America): Max Wu. Chairman: Stan Shih. SVP Finance: Philip Peng.
Acer is a leader in the computer manufacturing industry. It has designed an extremely efficient logistical system to become the top producer of computer peripherals and components in the world. The company has facilities in countries around the world. Both its sales and work force are on the increase.
Other Locations: Worldwide HQ: Acer, Inc., 21F, 88, Section 1, Hsin Tai Wu Rd., Hsichih, Taipei County 221, Taiwan; +886-2-696-1234.

ADAPTEC, INC.
691 S. Milpitas Blvd., Milpitas, CA 95035; 408-945-8600
http://www.adaptec.com
Employees: 2,123
Sales: $692.4 million
Key Personnel: Chairman: Larry Boucher. President, CEO: Robert N. Stephens. Human Resources: E.J. Tim Harris.
Many computers are connected to their peripheral devices with Adaptec's invention, the Small Computer System Interface, or SCSI. Adaptec is now the largest manufacturer of SCSI systems and produces many related devices. It is expanding its operations and recently opened a subsidiary in Japan. Its sales and work force have fallen sharply.

AMDAHL CORPORATION ★★
1250 E. Arques Ave., Sunnyvale, CA 94088-3470; 408-746-6000
http://www.amdahl.com
Employees: 13,000
Sales: $2,200 million
Key Personnel: Chairman: John C. Lewis. President, CEO: David B. Wright. Human Resources: Anthony M. Pozos.
Formely a mainframe mainstay, Fujitsu subsidiary Amdahl has lately metamorphosed into a technology services provider and software developer. Its services include outsourcing, systems development, integration and data storage. The company's sales and work force are growing rapidly.
Other Locations: The company has support facilities in California, Texas and the U.K. and offices in more than 30 countries around the world.

APPLE COMPUTER, INC.
One Infinite Loop, Cupertino, CA 95014; 408-996-1010
http://www.apple.com
Employees: 9,663
Sales: $5,941 million
Key Personnel: Interim CEO: Steven P. Jobs. EVP, CFO: Fred D. Anderson. Human Resources: Eileen Schloss.
Apple Computer's primary product is its line of Macintosh computers, recently augmented by its popular new iMac. The company has been in losing competition with the manufacturers of IBM-compatible computers for many years. Still, after years of economic ups and downs, the company maintains a dedicated customer base, in spite of vocal critics With the return of co-founder

Steve Jobs, Apple is trying to recover its previous market share. But sales continue to slip in key markets, and work force is shrinking.

CISCO SYSTEMS, INC. ★★

170 W. Tasman Dr., San Jose, CA 95134; 408-526-4000
http://www.cisco.com
Employees: 15,000
Sales: $12,154 million
Key Personnel: Chairman: John P. Morgridge. President, CEO: John T. Chambers. Human Resources: Barbara Beck.
The world's largest provider of networking systems for the Internet, Cisco Systems was also one of the first in the market. The company now has more than a 50-percent market share. Recent acquisitions have enabled the company to expand its market base. Sales and workforce are growing rapidly.

HEWLETT-PACKARD COMPANY

3000 Hanover St., Palo Alto, CA 94304; 650-857-1501
http://www.hp.com
Employees: 124,600
Sales: $47,061 million
Key Personnel: Chairman: Lewis E. Platt. EVP: CEO, President: Carleton S. Fiorina. Human Resources: Susan D. Bowick.
One of the largest manufacturers of office computers and peripherals, Hewlett-Packard is grabbing a share of the home computer market. Its campaign has come complete with brightly colored, multimedia PCs and especially easy setup procedures designed for the home user. Its sales and work force are on the rise.
Other Locations: The company has sales and support offices in over 120 countries and manufacturing facilities in Puerto Rico, the United States, and 16 other countries.

INTEL CORPORATION

2200 Mission College Blvd., Santa Clara, CA 95052-8119; 408-765-8080
http://www.intel.com
Employees: 64,500
Sales: $26,273 million
Key Personnel: Chairman: Andrew S. Grove. President, CEO: Craig R. Barrett. Human Resources: Patricia Murray.
Intel processors have powered IBM-compatible personal computers since 1981, but—as the world's #1 microchip manufacturer—Intel makes chips for more than just PC's. The company's products are also used in military, industrial, and communications applications. Intel operates facilities in the U.S., Europe, and Asia. Sales and workforce are up moderately.

KOMAG, INC.

1704 Automation Pkwy., San Jose, CA 95131, 408-576-2000
http://www.komag.com
Employees: 4,086
Sales: $328.9 million
Key Personnel: President, CEO: Thien Hoo Tan. SVP, CFO: William L. Potts, Jr. VP Human Resources: Elizabeth A. Lamb.
Komag makes parts for hard disk manufacturers.
The company is one of the world's largest makers of magnetic thin-film disks, which are used in computer hard drives. Komag's customers include IBM and Maxtor. The company's sales and workforce have declined.

LOGITECH, INC. ★★

6505 Kaiser Dr., Fremont, CA 94555; 510-795-8500
http://www.logitech
Employees: 4,170
Sales: $448.1 million
Key Personnel: President, CEO: Guerrino De Luca. Chairman: Daniel V. Borel. Human Resources: Patrick Brubeck.
Logitech makes more mice than any other company in the world—for computers, that is. With 35 percent of the market, Logitech sells most of its products to original equipment manufacturers, such as Apple and IBM. The company also makes other peripherals, such as the FotoMan digital camera and joysticks. Its sales and work force continue to increase.
Other Locations: Worldwide HQ: Logitech International SA, Moulin Du Choc D, CH-1122 Romanel-sur-Morges, Switzerland; +41-21-863-51-11.

MAXTOR CORPORATION ★

510 Cottonwood Dr., Milpitas, CA 95035; 408-432-1700
http://www.maxtor.com
Employees: 6,251
Sales: $2,408.5 million

Key Personnel: Chairman: Chong Sup Park. President, CEO: Michael R. Cannon. Human Resources: Phillip C. Duncan.

Maxtor is one of the largest makers of computer hard drives in the United States. It makes magnetic drives for PCs, notebooks, subnotebook computers, and optical drives. Its primary market is original equipment manufacturers, including IBM, Compaq and Dell. Sales are up impressively, as is workforce.
Other Locations: The company has manufacturing plants in the U.S. and Singapore.

PACKARD BELL NEC, INC.

One Packard Bell Way, Sacramento, CA 95828-0903, 916-288-0101.
http://www.packardbell.com
Employees: 3,000
Sales: $2,300 million
Key Personnel: Chairman, President, and CEO: Alain Couder. EVP: Paul Greenwood. Human Resources: Fred Philpott.

Packard Bell NEC, once a the top makers of personal computers in the retail market, has fallen on hard times. It sells its computers through large retailers, such as Sears and Wal-Mart. Since its merger with NEC, which now owns 88 percent of the company, Packard Bell's sales and workforce have fallen off dramatically.

QUALCOMM, INC. ★★

6455 Lusk Blvd., San Diego, CA 92121-2779; 858-587-1121
http://www.qualcomm.com
Employees: 11,600
Sales: $3,347.9 million
Key Personnel: Chairman, CEO: Irwin Mark Jacobs. VC: Andrew J. Viterbi. Human Resources: Daniel L. Sullivan.

A leading manufacturer of communications systems, QUALCOMM is involved in developing a low-orbiting satellite telecommunications system that will extend coverage to nearly every populated area in the world. QUALCOMM publishes Eudora, a leading e-mail software program. Sales and workforce are growing.

QUANTUM CORPORATION ★

500 McCarthy Blvd., Milpitas, CA 95035; 408-894-4000
http://www.quantum.com
Employees: 6,610

Sales: $4,902.1 million
Key Personnel: Chairman, CEO: Michael A. Brown. EVP, CFO: Richard L. Clemmer. EVP Human Resources: Jerald L. Maurer.

Quantum is one of the largest manufacturers of computer storage products and the world's #2 maker of hard disk drives (behind Seagate). Its customers include IBM, Dell, Hewlett Packard, and Compaq. Its products are distibuted in some 25 countries. Despite a drop in sales, workforce has increased.

READ–RITE CORPORATION

345 Los Coches St., Milpitas, CA 95035; 408-262-6700
http://www.readrite.com
Employees: 18,257
Sales: $808.6 million
Key Personnel: President, COO: Alan S. Lowe. Chairman, CEO: Cyril J. Yansouni. Human Resources: Sherry F. McVicar.

Read-Rite is one of the largest manufacturers of computer-disk read-write heads. The company makes a unique ceramic head that is smaller and more efficient than the ferrite metal ones made by its competitors. The company sells its products to original equipment manufacturers such as Maxtor and Samsung; many of its operations and sales are in Asia. Ovreall sales and work force are on the decline.

SEAGATE TECHNOLOGY, INC.

920 Disc Dr., Scotts Valley, CA 95066; 831-438-6550
http://wwwseagate.com
Employees: 82,000
Sales: $6,802 million
Key Personnel: President, CEO: Stephen J. Luczo. EVP, COO: William D. Watkins. Human Resources: J. Kenneth Davidson.

The largest independent hard drive manufacturer in the computer industry, Seagate has an extensive line of data-storage products. It makes hard drives for all types of computers and sells them mainly to original equipment manufacturers, value-added resellers, and distributors. The company is expanding in many areas, including head manufacturing. Seagate's overall sales and work force have both been in decline for the last few years.
Other Locations: The company has

factories in China, Singapore, Thailand, the United Kingdom, and the United States and sales offices in 17 countries.

SILICON GRAPHICS, INC.

2011 N. Shoreline Blvd., Mountain View, CA 94043-1389; 650-960-1980
http://www.sgi.com
Employees: 10,286
Sales: $2,749 million
Key Personnel: Chairman, CEO: Robert R. Bishop. SVP, CFO: Steven J. Gomo. Human Resources: Kirk Froggatt.

Best known for its special effects in movies such as *Jurassic Park*, Silicon Graphics has made forays into software and hardware markets. After recent difficulties in a competitive workstation market, the company plans to streamline operations to focus its on high-end server machines. Sales and workforce have decreased markedly**Error! Bookmark not defined.**.
Other Locations: The company has 63 branches in North America and 55 more in 29 other countries.

SUN MICROSYSTEMS, INC. ★★

901 San Antonio Rd., Palo Alto, CA 94303, 650-960-1300
http://www.sun.com
Employees: 26,300
Sales: $11,726.3 million
Key Personnel: Chairman, CEO: Scott G. McNealy. President, COO: Edward J. Zander. Human Resources: Kenneth M. Alvares.

Sun Microsystems' server systems have become a raging success. The company has won more than 50 percent of the market and continues to bring out new products. Sun is also the top maker of Unix-based workstations, and the originator of Java, a language designed to produce software that can be run on any kind of computer. Its sales and workforce are up substantially.

3COM CORPORATION

5400 Bayfront Plaza, Santa Clara, CA 95052; 408-326-5000
http://www.3com.com
Employees: 13,027
Sales: $5,772.1 million
Key Personnel: Chairman, CEO: Eric A. Benhamou. VC: Casey Cowell. Human Resources: Eileen Nelson.

Founded by Robert Metcalfe—the inventor of Ethernet, a popular high-speed computer networking system—3Com sells a broad range of networking products. The company recently acquired several other companies, including U.S. Robotics, thus expanding its capabilities in local area networking, wireless communications, and remote accessing. 3Com is in the process of dividing into two companies—one based on its Network Products Division and one based on its Personal Connectivity Division. Its sales and work force are growing moderately.

VERIFONE, INC. ★★

4988 Great America Pkwy., Santa Clara, CA 94054-1561, 408-496-0444.
http://www.verifone.com
Employees: 3,300
Sales (overall HP): $47,061 million
Key Personnel: SVP: Pierre Francois Catte. SVP: Tom Kilcoyne. Human Resources: Gary Baty.

Verifone, a subsidiary of Hewlett-Packard, is one of the largest suppliers of transaction automation products. Its machines allow businesses to electronically authorize a wide variety of transactions, including insurance claims, credit cards, and food stamps. More than 3 million of the company's systems have been installed in over 70 countries. Its sales and work force are on the increase.

WESTERN DIGITAL CORPORATION

8105 Irvine Center Dr., Irvine, CA 92618; 949-932-5000
http://www.westerndigital.com
Employees: 13,045
Sales: $2,767.2 million
Key Personnel: Chairman, President and CEO: Charles A. Haggerty. Co-COO: Matthew H. Massengill. Human Resources: Jack Van Berkel.

One of the largest independent makers of hard disk drives, Western Digital also sells a line of circuit boards for PCs. The company primarily sells its products to original equipment manufacturers, such as Dell and Compaq. However, it is currently working to expand its corporate network sales. Its sales and work force are have dropped markedly.
Other Locations: The company has offices in Asia, Europe, and the United States.

WYSE TECHNOLOGY, INC.
3471 N. First St., San Jose, CA 95134-1803; 408-473-1200
http://www.wyse.com
Employees:1,000
Sales: $161.8 million
Key Personnel: Chairman: Morris Chang. President, CEO: Doug Chance. VP Human Resources and Administration: Frederick M. Chancellor.
Wyse Technology is the largest supplier of advanced display computer terminals in the world. The company makes several other products in its Taiwan manufacturing facilities, including monitors. Its terminals are designed to behave like PCs when connected to a mainframe network. The company's sales have rebounded slightly after a long period of decline; workforce is stagnant.

COLORADO

EXABYTE CORPORATION
1685 38th St., Boulder, CO 80301; 303-442-4333
http://www.exabyte.com
Employees: 1,212
Sales: $286.5 million
Key Personnel: Chairman, President, and CEO: William L. Marriner. SVP Marketing: Bruce Huibregtse. Human Resources: Sam Trenka.
The largest manufacturer of tape backup systems for computers is Exabyte. The company makes a backup system that uses a machine similar to a videocassette recorder to store information on inexpensive audiotape. The company has been cutting costs recently but continues to expand its product line. Its sales and work force have declined

STORAGE TECHNOLOGY CORPORATION
2270 S. 88th St., Louisville, CO 80028-4309; 303-673-5151
http://www.stortek.com
Employees: 8,700
Sales: $2,258.2 million
Key Personnel: Chairman, President and CEO: David E. Weiss. EVP, COO: Victor M. Perez. Human Resources: Cindy Bishop.
A leading provider of disk arrays and other computer storage systems, Storage Technology is increasing its market share with high-end direct access storage devices. It continues to increase its product line with more storage products and a line of networking products as well. Its sales and work force are up.
Other Locations: The company manufactures equipment in California, Colorado, Florida, Puerto Rico, and the United Kingdom.

GEORGIA

FIRST DATA CORPORATION
5660 New Northside Dr., Ste. 1400, Atlanta, GA 30328; 770-857-7001
http://www.firstdatacorp.com
Employees: 32,000
Sales: $5,117.6 million
Key Personnel: Chairman, CEO: Henry C. Duques. President, COO: Charles T. Fote. Human Resources: Janet Harris.
First Data Corporation is the country's largest 3rd-party processor of credit card transactions. Its customers are mainly financial institutions, oil companies and retailers. The company also provides mutual fund processing, cost management, document management and customized phone service. Sales and workforce are both down.

KENTUCKY

LEXMARK INTERNATIONAL GROUP, INC. ★★
One Lexmark Centre Dr., 740 New Circle Rd. NW, Lexington, KY 40550; 606-232-2000
http://www.lexmark.com
Employees: 8,800
Sales: $3,020.6 million
Key Personnel: Chairman, President, and CEO: Paul J. Curlander. EVP: Thomas B. Lamb. Human Resources: Kathleen E. Affeldt.
Lexmark is one of the largest makers of printers and printer accessories. Originally a subsidiary of IBM, it was spun off in a leveraged buyout in 1991. The company's primary market is original equipment manufacturers. Its sales and work force are increasing.
Other Locations: Manufacturing facilities in Colorado and France.

MASSACHUSETTS

BULL HN INFORMATION SYSTEMS, INC.
300 Concord Rd., Billerica, MA 01821; 978-294-6000
http://www.us.bull.com
Employees: 1,300
Sales: $199.3 million

Key Personnel: President, CEO Bull Americas: George McNeil. CFO: Bruno Guerin. VP Human Resources: Cecile Wright.

Bull HN Information Systems is a subsidiary of Compagnie des Machines Bull, which is usually called Groupe Bull. It is the third largest computer manufacturer in Europe. Its primary markets are the sales and leasing of computer equipment and data processing services. Sales are down and workforce is static.

Other Locations: Worldwide HQ: Compagnie des Machines Bull, 68 route de Versailles, 78430 Louveciennes, France; phone: +33-1-39-66-60-60.

DATA GENERAL CORPORATION

4400 Computer Dr., Westborough, MA 01580; 508-898-5000
http://www.dg.com
Employees: 4,700
Sales: $1,462.1 million
Key Personnel: President, CEO: Ronald L. Skates. SVP: Joel Schwartz. Human Resources: Erin Motameni.

From manufacturer to value-added reseller was the path taken by Data General. Once a minicomputer maker, the company has completely restructured its operation. It now supplies high-end network servers complemented by a wide variety of supporting products. EMC has entered into an agreement to purchase Data General. Sales and workforce are down.

EMC CORPORATION ★★

35 Parkwood Dr., Hopkinton, MA 01748-9103; 508-435-1000
Employees: 9,700
Sales: $3,973.7 million
Key Personnel: Chairman: Richard J. Egan. President, CEO: Michael C. Ruettgers. Human Resources: Donald W. Amaya.

EMC Corporation is the largest supplier of RAID technology, for redundant arrays of inexpensive disks. The system is much faster and less expensive than other large storage systems, and it allowed EMC to grab a large share of the mainframe storage market from IBM. EMC's sales and work force are growing rapidly.

MINNESOTA

HUTCHINSON TECHNOLOGY, INC. ★

40 W. Highland Park, Hutchinson, MN 55350; 320-587-3797
http://www.htch.com
Employees: 7,764
Sales: $407.6 million
Key Personnel: Chairman: Jeffery W. Green. President, CEO: Wayne M. Fortun. Human Resources: Rebecca A. Albrecht.

Hutchinson Technology is the world's largest manufacturer of disk-drive suspension assemblies. The assemblies are used to move the read-write heads of hard disks. Hutchinson dominates the industry with 70 percent of market share. The company's biggest challenge is making its assemblies smaller to accommodate the needs of higher-capacity drives. Its sales are down, but workforce is up.

NEBRASKA

INACOM CORP ★★

10810 Farnam Dr., Omaha, NE 68154; 402-392-3900
http://www.inacom.com
Employees: 12,000
Sales: $4,258.4 million
Key Personnel: Chairman, President, and CEO: Bill L. Fairfield. EVP, CFO: David C. Guenthner. Human Resources: Larry Fazzini.

One of the largest U.S. distributors of computer products and services, InaCom serves the needs of companies throughout the country. It uses a network of independent value-added resellers and franchised operations to provide products to major computer manufacturers. The company also provides training and technical support. Sales and work force are on the increase.

Other Locations: The company has facilities in California, Nebraska, and New Jersey.

NEW HAMPSHIRE

CABLETRON SYSTEMS, INC.

35 Industrial Way, Rochester, NH 03867; 603-332-9400
http://www.ctron.com
Employees: 5,951
Sales: $1,411.3 million
Key Personnel: Chairman, President, and CEO: Piyush Patel. COO: Romulus Patel. Human Resources: Linda Pepin.

Cabletron Systems has kept its eye on innovations and its overhead low to become the second largest manufacturer of intelligent computer network hubs, or Multi-Media Access Centers. The company's products, which are designed to control traffic on computer networks, have been installed at thousands of sites. Its sales and work force are declining.

NEW YORK

INTERNATIONAL BUSINESS MACHINES CORPORATION ★

New Orchard Rd., Armonk, NY 10504; 914-765-1900
http://www.ibm.com
Employees: 291,067
Sales: $81,667 million
Key Personnel: Chairman, CEO: Louis V. Gerstner Jr. SVP, CFO: Douglas L. Maine. SVP Human Resources: J. Thomas Bouchard.

Once the dominant name in computers, International Business Machines has been selling off parts of its operation for many years in an effort to hit upon a stable formulation. Things are looking up; IBM is the world's #1 hardware provider, has the largest computer service division in the world and ranks second to Microsoft in software sales. The company is currently focusing on its Internet business. Sales and work force are increasing.

NEC AMERICA, INC. ★★

Eight Corporate Center Dr., Melville, NY 11747-3112; 516-753-7000
http://www.nec.com
Employees (overall NEC): 157,800
Sales (overall NEC): $40,334 million
Key Personnel: President, CEO: Kaoru Yano. CFO: Hitoshi Kawamura. Human Resources: Peter Cristallo.

Among the largest computer companies in Japan, NEC owns most of U.S. computer maker Packard Bell, giving it increased access to the US market. NEC also makes a wide variety of electronic products, including mobile communications systems, space electronics, and DRAM (dynamic random access memory) modules. Sales and work force are on the rise.
Other Locations: Worldwide HQ: NEC Corp., 7-1, Shiba 5-chome, Minato-ku, Tokyo, 108-01, Japan; phone: +81-3-3454-1111. The company has 174 subsidiaries and 63 plants in Japan and 30 other countries.

OREGON

SEQUENT COMPUTER SYSTEMS, INC.

15450 SW Koll Pkwy., Beaverton, OR 97006-6063; 503-626-5700
http://www.sequent.com
Employees: 2,646
Sales: $784.2 million
Key Personnel: President, COO: John McAdam. Chairman, CEO: Karl C. Powell, Jr. Human Resources: Jack W. Brooks.

High-performance symmetric multiprocessing computer systems are the business of Sequent Computer Systems. The company sells consulting and professional services to original equipment manufacturers, such as Compaq, and end users. The company has recently expanded its services to include helping customers transfer from proprietary operating systems to open architectures. Sales and workforce are both down.

PENNSYLVANIA

UNISYS CORPORATION

Unisys Way, Blue Bell, PA 19424; 215-986-4011
http://www.unisys.com
Employees: 33,200
Sales: $7,208.4 million
Key Personnel: Chairman, President and CEO: Lawrence A. Weinbach. EVP, President Computer Systems: George R. Gazerwitz. Human Resources: David O. Aker.

One of the largest computer manufacturers in the world, Unisys has had difficulties adapting to the trend away from mainframes. Unisys now focuses on systems integration and its new ClearPath servers, which bring together mainframe, Windows NT, and Unix operating systems in a single platform. Sales and workforce are up.

RHODE ISLAND

AMERICAN POWER CONVERSION CORPORATION ★★

132 Fairgrounds Rd., West Kingston, RI 02892; 401-789-5735
http://www.apcc.com
Employees: 5,443
Sales: $1,125.8 million
Key Personnel: Chairman, President and CEO: Rodger B. Dowdell Jr. CFO: Donald M. Muir. Human Resources: Bruce Grant.

American Power Conversion (APC)

makes products to keep computers running in the event of power failures. Called uninterruptible power supplies, the devices help prevent data loss during storms. The company makes a number of other related products and is the world's top supplier of UPS devices. Its sales and work force are increasing dramatically.

SOUTH DAKOTA

GATEWAY, INC. ★★
610 Gateway Dr., North Sioux City, SD 57049; 605-232-2000
http://www.gateway.com
Employees: 19,300
Sales: $7,467.9 million
Key Personnel: President, COO: Jeffrey Weitzen. Chairman, CEO: Theodore W. Waitt. Human Resources: Gary Glandon.
One of the largest direct marketers of Pentium-based PCs is Gateway. The company specializes in prompt, direct service. Customers can order over the phone or via the company's Web site. Gateway also ovvers portable PCs and add-on components. Sales and work force are growing rapidly.
Other Locations: The company has facilities in Missouri, South Dakota, and Ireland.

TEXAS

COMPAQ COMPUTER CORPORATION ★★
20555 State Highway 249, Houston, TX 77070; 281-370-0670
http://www.compaq.com
Employees: 71,000
Sales: $31,169 million
Key Personnel: Chairman: Benjamin M. Rosen. President, CEO: Michael D. Capellas. Human Resources: Yvonne R. Jackson.
Compaq is the largest PC manufacturer in the world. It has recently been dueling for market share with rivals IBM and Hewlett-Packard. The company is #3 in the world in computer sales behind IBM and HP. Sales and work force are growing rapidly.
Other Locations: The company has facilities in Brazil, China, Scotland, and Singapore.

DELL COMPUTER CORPORATION ★★
One Dell Way, Round Rock, TX 78682-2244; 512-338-4400
http://www.dell.com
Employees: 24,400

Sales: $18,243 million
Key Personnel: Chairman, CEO: Michael S. Dell. VC: Morton L. Topfer. Human Resources: Thomas B. Green.
One of the world's largest computer manufacturers, Dell is also the #1 direct-sale computer seller. The company has recently refocused its marketing, pulling out of retail stores such as Wal-Mart and introducing a new, more powerful line of notebook PCs. The company also sells its own peripheral and software products, and markets such products for other companies. Dell's sales and work force continue to rise dramatically.

FUJITSU-ICL SYSTEMS, INC.
5429 LBJ Freeway, Dallas, TX 75240; 972-716-8300
htttp://www.iclretail
Employees (overall ICL): 19,000
Sales (overall ICL): $4,075.2 million
Key Personnel: President, CEO Fujitsu-ICL Systems: Rod Powell. CEO ICL: Keith Todd. Human Resources: Fiona Colquhoun.
Fujitsu-ICL is a subsidiary of ICL, the largest computer company in the United Kingdom. ICL is owned by the Japanese company Fujitsu. The firm sells hardware, software, and technology services mainly to financial, retail, travel, and transportation companies. Sales are down and workforce is steady.
Other Locations: Worldwide HQ: ICL PLC, 26 Finsbury Sq., London EC2A 1DS, United Kingdom; +44-171-638-5622.

VIRGINIA

NEWBRIDGE NETWORKS, INC.
593 Herndon Pkwy., Herndon, VA 22070; 703-834-3600
http://www.newbridge.com
Employees (overall NNC): 6,530
Sales (overall NNC): $1,227.5 million
Key Personnel: Chairman, CEO: Terence H. Matthews. VC: Peter D. Charbonneau. Human Resources: Michael Williams.
Newbridge Networks, Inc., the U.S. division of Canada's Newbridge Network Corporation, is a top provider of computer networking products. The company, which markets its line under the brand MainStreet, sells hardware and software for local-area and wide-area networks. It is the world's largest manufacturer of asynchronous transfer mode

switches for high-speed telephone and data network multimedia communications. Sales and work force are on the rise.
Other Locations: Worldwide HQ: Newbridge Networks Corp., 600 March Rd., P.O. Box 13600, Kanata, Ontario K2K 2E6, Canada; 613-591-3600.

---

❶ CONSTRUCTION/ ENGINEERING

CALIFORNIA

BECHTEL GROUP, INC. ★★
50 Beale St., San Francisco, CA 94105-1895; 415-768-1234
http://www.bechtel.com
Employees: 30,000
Sales: $12,645.0 million
Key Personnel: Chairman, CEO: Riley P. Bechtel. President, COO: Adrian Zaccaria. VP, Manager of Human Resources: Bob Baxter.
Bechtel Group is primarily a large construction company, working on power plants, airports, and other projects of similar scope. The company also provides civil engineering, hazardous waste cleanup, and mineral exploration services. Bechtel is actively expanding its work in Asia. Its sales are growing, but its work force has remained steady of late.
Other Locations: The company has offices in the United States and several other countries.

FLUOR CORPORATION
One Enterprise Dr., Aliso Viejo, CA 92656; 949-349-2000
http://www.fluor.com
Employees: 56,886
Revenues: $13,504.8 million
Key Personnel: Acting Chairman: Philip J. Carroll Jr. Chairman, CEO, A. T. Massey Coal Co.: Don L. Blankenship. VP Human Resources and Administration: Frederick J. Grisby Jr.
Fluor Corporation is the parent company to several large subsidiaries. Fluor Daniel is one of the largest engineering and construction companies in the world and brings in over 40 percent of the parent company's income. Another subsidiary, A. T. Massey, is one of the largest coal mining companies in the United States. It has 16 coal mines in the East, and ac-counts for an additional 40 percent of sales. Fluor's sales and work force both decreased slightly last year.
Other Locations: The company has offices in more than 80 countries.

PARSONS CORPORATION
100 W. Walnut St., Pasadena, CA 91124; 626-440-2000
http://www.parsons.com
Employees: 11,000
Sales: $1,263.0 million
Key Personnel: President, CEO: Jim McNulty. CFO: Curtis Bower. Human Resources Director: David R. Goodrich.
The Parsons Corporation is one of the largest firms owned totally by its employees. It is primarily a design and engineering company and has a diverse customer base ranging from municipalities to nations. The company builds airports, power plants, and even cities. It is currently operating in all 50 states and 80 foreign countries. Sales are dropping, but its work force is stable.

CONNECTICUT

ASEA BROWN BOVERI INC.
500 Merritt 7, Norwalk, CT 06851; 203-750-2200
http://www.us.abb.com/usa
Employees: 22,000
Sales: $5,700 million
Key Personnel: President, CEO (US): D. Howard Pierce. CFO (US): Philip Widman. VP Human Resources, (U.S.): Daniel M. Kuzmak.
The largest electrical engineering joint venture in the world, ABB Asea Brown Boveri operates in 140 countries, building rail transportation, power generation, industrial buildings, and similar projects. The company is expanding in Eastern Europe and Asia and cutting back in Western Europe and the United States. Its sales and work force are increasing.
Other Locations: Worldwide HQ: ABB Asea Brown Boveri, Ltd., P.O. Box 8131, Zurich, Switzerland; phone: +41-1-317-71-11. The organization operates through 1,300 companies around the world.

HAWAII

SCHULER HOMES, INC. ★★
848 Fort Street Mall, Honolulu, HI 96813; 808-521-5661
Employees: 269

Sales: $285.3 million
Key Personnel: Chairman, President, CEO: James K. Schuler. EVP Operations: Michael T. Jones. Personnel Director: Joanne Halsey.
Buildable land is scarce in Hawaii, and the population is growing. Schuler Homes targeted those Hawaiian customers by building low and moderately priced housing. Recently, they have expanded eastward to Colorado, Northern California, Oregon and Washington State. Typically, they build single family residences, with 61 percent of sales coming from the Melody Homes Branch in the Colorado market. Sales and work force are growing.

ILLINOIS
SQUARE D COMPANY
1415 S. Roselle Rd., Palatine, IL 60067; 847-397-2600
Employees: 92,000
Sales: $56,000 million
Key Personnel: President, CEO, North American Division: Charles W. Denny. President, CEO, Square D (U.S.): William P. Brink. CFO, VP Human Resources, Square D (U.S.): Charles L. Hite.
Square D is the U.S. subsidiary of Groupe Schneider, a French company with a history that dates back to 1782. The company is among the top electrical engineering enterprises in the world. It provides a wide variety of products and services, including contracting, industrial control, and communications networks. Square D's sales and work force are down.
Other Locations: Worldwide HQ: Groupe Schneider, 40, avenue Andre Morizet, Boulogne-Billancourt Cedex, France; phone: 33-1-46-05-38-20.

LOUISIANA
MCDERMOTT INTERNATIONAL, INC.
1450 Poydras St., New Orleans, LA 70112-6050; 504-587-5400
http://www.mcdermott.com
Employees: 20,350
Sales: $3,150.0 million
Key Personnel: Chairman, CEO: Roger E. Tetrault. SVP, CFO: Daniel R. Gaubert. Human Resources Manager: Kevin A. Blasini.
A large construction conglomerate,

McDermott International brings together J. Ray McDermott, the world's largest marine construction company, and several other subsidiaries involved in the construction of power plants. Its marine services include construction of marine pipelines and offshore platforms, while its power generation services focus on nuclear reactors. McDermott International's sales remain steady, but its work force is decreasing.

MICHIGAN
CHAMPION ENTERPRISES, INC. ★★
2701 University Dr., Ste. 300, Auburn Hills, MI 48326; 248-340-9090
http:// www.champent.com
Employees: 14,000
Sales: $2,254.3 million
Key Personnel: Chairman, President, CEO: Walter R. Young Jr. EVP, CFO: Joseph H. Stegmayer. Human Resources Manager: Hugh Beswick.
Champion has become the #1 U.S. manufactured housing maker, surpassing Fleetwood Enterprises. They sell through more than 280 company-owned sales centers, as well as through 3,500 additional retailers. Increasingly, they are focusing on manufactured housing. Both sales and work force numbers are up significantly.
Other Locations: Champion manufactures homes at 60 plants in the U.S. and in Canada.

NEBRASKA
PETER KIEWIT SONS', INC. ★★
1000 Kiewit Plaza, Omaha, NE 68131; 402-342-2052
http://www.kiewit.com
Employees: 16,200
Revenues: $3,403.0 million
Key Personnel: Chairman Emeritus: Walter Scott, Jr. Chairman, CEO: Kenneth E. Stinson. VP Human Resources: Brad Chapman.
One of the largest construction companies in the United States, Peter Kiewit Sons' builds highways, dams, and waste disposal systems. The company also has numerous mining and communications subsidiaries. Most of its income stems from construction, and about half of its jobs are from government contracts. Employees have owned the company since 1979. Sales have increased while the work force has remained steady.

NEW JERSEY

FOSTER WHEELER CORPORATION ★★
Perryville Corporate Park, Clinton, NJ 08809-4000; 908-730-4000
http://www.fwc.com
Employees: 11,120
Sales: $4,536.8 million
Key Personnel: Chairman, President, CEO: Richard J. Swift. VC, CFO: David J. Roberts. Human Resources Manager: James E. Schessler.
Foster Wheeler specializes in design, engineering, construction and project development to industries ranging from pharmaceuticals to power generation. It has a host of subsidiaries specializing in power systems, energy equipment and construction. Both sales and work force have been increasing modestly.

NEW YORK

THE TURNER CORPORATION ★★
375 Hudson St., New York, NY 10014; 212-229-6000
Employees: 3,200
Sales: $3,699.0 million
Key Personnel: Chairman, CEO: Ellis T. Gravette Jr. President, CEO: Robert E. Fee. Human Resources Manager: David J. Smith.
The Turner Corporation is one of the world's leading commercial construction companies. Among its credits is the UN building and Madison Square Garden. A joint venture with Karl Steiner Holding AG gives it a presence overseas. Both sales and work force have been increasing.

NORTH CAROLINA

OAKWOOD HOMES CORPORATION ★★
7800 McCloud Rd., Greensboro, NC 27409-9634; 336-664-2400
http://www.oakwoodhomes.com
Employees: 11,604
Sales: $1,482.6 million
Key Personnel: Chairman, President, CEO: Nicholas J. St. George. EVP, Housing Operations: William G. Edwards. Human Resources Manager: Paul Macksood.
The largest manufactured-home builder in the United States, Oakwood Homes Corporation also develops and manages manufactured-housing communities. It has established communities in several Southeastern states. A new and growing section of the company's market is the more expensive multi-section manufactured home. Its financial service subsidiary provides financing for 85 percent of company sales. Both its sales and work force are rapidly increasing.
Other Locations: The company has 10 manufacturing facilities in California, North Carolina, Oregon, and Texas and some 360 company owned and 700 independent retail centers in 18 states.

PENNSYLVANIA

MICHAEL BAKER CORPORATION ★★
Airport Office Park, 420 Rouser Rd., Bldg. 3, Coraopolis, PA 15108; 412-269-6300
http://www.mbakercorp.com
Employees: 3,824
Sales: $521.3 million
Key Personnel: President, CEO, Michael Baker, Jr., Inc.: Charles I. Homan. EVP, Michael Baker Corp.: Edward L. Wiley. Human Resources Manager: Kimberly W. Foltz.
One of the top engineering and construction companies in the United States is Michael Baker Corporation. The company has extensive experience building bridges, airports, military bases, and similar projects for both public- and private-sector clients. About 90 percent of revenues are generated by U.S. operations. The company continues to expand its sales and work force both domestically and abroad.

TENNESSEE

CLAYTON HOMES, INC. ★★
5000 Clayton Rd., Maryville, TN 37804; 423-380-3000
http://www.clayton.net
Employees: 6,703
Sales: $1,344.3 million
Key Personnel: Chairman, CEO: James L. Clayton. President, COO: Kevin T. Clayton. Director of Human Resources: David Lopater.
The fourth largest builder of manufactured homes in the United States is Clayton Homes, a company that also finances and insures its products. The company sells homes in 28 states, mostly in the Southeast. They own 270 retail centers and sell thorough an additional 800 independent retailers. Clayton also manages 46 manufactured-home communities in eight states. Demand for the

company's products and services is increasing, as are sales. As a result, its work force is expanding as well.

TEXAS

CENTEX CORPORATION ★★
2728 N. Harwood, Dallas, TX 75201-1516; 214-981-5000
http://www.centex.com
Employees: 13,161
Revenues: $5,154.8 million
Key Personnel: Chairman, CEO: Laurence E. Hirsch. EVP,Chairman, CEO, Centrex Homes: Timothy R. Eller. VC, CFO: David W. Quinn. Human Resources Manager: Sarah Hatfield.
The largest home builder in the United States, Centex Corporation has diversified its operations to help avoid ups and downs in the construction market. It has expanded to the UK and its subsidiaries offer home security, pest control and contracts for hospitals, office buildings, and hotels. Its sales and work force are rapidly increasing,.
Other Locations: The company has operations in 20 states and the District of Columbia.

NCI BUILDING SYSTEMS, INC. ★★
7301 Fairview, Houston, TX 77041; 713-466-7788
http://www.ncilp.com
Employees: 3,700
Sales: $675.3 million
Key Personnel: Chairman: C. A. Rundell, Jr. President, CEO: Johnie Schulte, Jr. Director of Human Resources: Karen Rosales.
NCI Building Systems is the second largest manufacturer of metal buildings in the United States. The company designs, fabricates, and markets its products directly to contractors through a network of dealers. The buildings are used in many settings, including agriculture, education, and industry. The company's sales and work force both doubled by acquiring Metal Building Components, Inc., in 1998.
Other Locations: The company has 38 manufacturing facilities in Mexico and 18 states.

❶ CONSUMER ELECTRONICS & APPLIANCES

CALIFORNIA

PIONEER ELECTRONICS (USA), INC. ★★
2265 E. 220th St., Long Beach, CA 90801; 310-835-6177
http://www.pioneerelectronics.com
Employees: 23,647
Sales: $4,701.3 million
Key Personnel: President (North America): Kazunori Yamamoto. President (International): Kaneo Ito. Human Resources Manager (North America): Kim Boyer
Pioneer North America is a subsidiary of Pioneer Electronic Corporation, one of the largest makers of audio equipment in the world. Economic troubles in Japan have caused the company trouble as domestic demand has slipped. The company has refocused its efforts on promoting inexpensive products in Asia, South America, and Eastern and Central Europe. Sales are down, but work force is up.
Other Locations: Worldwide HQ: Pioneer Electronic Corp., 4-1, Meguro 1-chome, Meguro-ku, Tokyo, 153, Japan; phone: +81-3-3494-1111. The company has manufacturing facilities in the United States and seven other countries.

TATUNG CO. OF AMERICA, INC.
2850 El Presidio St., Long Beach, CA 90810; 310-637-2105
http://www.tatung.com
Employees: 19,570
Sales: $2,160.3 million
Key Personnel: President: Hsin-chu Liu. CFO: Michael Lai. Manager, Personnel: Albert Peres.
Tatung has moved beyond the electric fans with which it first began. The company is the largest maker of consumer electronics in Taiwan. It makes a wide variety of products, from televisions to telecommunications systems. Although its consumer products generate the most income, its industrial products have a large market, too. A recent joint venture with Honeywell will produce semiconductors for the U.S. market. Both its sales and work force have decreased.
Other Locations: Worldwide HQ: Tatung Co., 22 Chungshan North Rd., 3rd Sec., Taipei, 104, Taiwan; phone: +886-2-592-5252.

YAMAHA CORPORATION OF AMERICA

6600 Orangethorpe Ave., Buena Park, CA 90620-1396; 714-522-9011
http://www.ysba.com
Employees: 9,044
Sales: $4,733 million
Key Personnel: Chairman, Yamaha Motor Co.: Seisuke Ueshima. President, Yamaha Corp. of America: Noriyuki Egawa. Division Manager, Corporate Personnel, Yamaha Corp. of America: Gil Honeycutt.
The top musical instrument manufacturer in the world, Yamaha has diversified into a broad array of markets. In addition to musical instruments, the company makes computer peripherals, furniture, and many other products. Yamaha has been cutting back its overseas work force, and its sales have dipped because of decreasing demand.
Other Locations: Worldwide HQ: Yamaha Corp., 10-1, Nakazawa-cho, Hamamatsu, Shizuoka, 430, Japan; phone: +81-53-460-2850.

ILLINOIS

ZENITH ELECTRONICS CORPORATION

1000 Milwaukee Ave., Glenview, IL 60025-2493; 847-391-7000
http://www.zenith.com
Employees: 6,800
Sales: $984.8 million
Key Personnel: President, CEO: Jeffrey P. Gannon. SVP, CFO: Edward J. McNulty. Human Resources Manager: Wendy Weil.
Zenith Electronics is the last company in the United States manufacturing color televisions and picture tubes. Zenith also makes a variety of related products in North America and is seeing increasing demand for what it sells, especially outside the United States. In 1995 a majority of Zenith's shares were bought by LG Electronics of South Korea. Sales and work force have decreased drastically as Zenith closes plants and reorganizes under chapter 11 bankruptcy.
Other Locations: The company has facilities in Canada, Mexico, and the United States.

IOWA

MAYTAG CORPORATION ★★

403 W. Fourth St. N., Newton, IA 50208; 515-792-8000
http://www.maytagcorp.com
Employees: 23,938
Revenues: $4,069.3 million
Key Personnel: Chairman, CEO: Lloyd D. Ward. EVP, CFO: Gerald J. Pribanic. Human Resources Manager: Jon O. Nicholas.
The fourth largest maker of large appliances, Maytag makes a wide variety of products under several brand names. Along with its high-end washing equipment made under the Maytag name, the company also makes Jenn-Air kitchen equipment, Magic Chef refrigerators, Hoover vacuum cleaners, and many more machines.
Other Locations: The company has facilities in seven states and in Canada, Mexico, Portugal, and the United Kingdom.

MICHIGAN

WHIRLPOOL CORPORATION

2000 N. M-63, Benton Harbor, MI 49022-2692; 616-923-5000
http://www.whirlpoolcorp.com
Employees: 59,000
Revenues: $10,323.0 million
Key Personnel: Chairman, CEO: David R. Whitwam. EVP, Chief Technology Officer: Ronald L. Kerber. SEVP CFO: Ralph F. Hake.
Whirlpool is the largest manufacturer of washers and dryers in the United States. Along with its U.S. market, the company sells extensively overseas. It manufactures a broad variety of appliances under many brands. Its sales continue to rise, as it concentrates more on overseas and Latin American markets.
Other Locations: The company has facilities in six states and 13 other countries.

NEW JERSEY

CASIO, INC.

570 Mt. Pleasant Ave., Dover, NJ 07801; 973-361-5400
http://www.casio-usa.com
Employees: 17,783
Sales: $3,787.6
Key Personnel: Senior Managing Director: Shigeki Maeno. Senior Managing Director: Shinichi Onoe. President, Casio (U.S.): John J. McDonald. Human Resources Managaer: Doug Poff.
Casio makes gadgets. The company is known for its calculators, fancy digital watches, musical instruments, and personal digital assistants, or PDAs. Sales of

its various types of PDAs are booming, while its once popular musical instruments aren't doing as well. More than 70 percent of its products are now made outside Japan. Sales and work force are up.
Other Locations: Worldwide HQ: Casio Computer Co., Ltd., Casio Keisanki, Shinjuku-Sumitomo Bldg., 2-6-1, Nishi-Shinjuku, Shinjuku-ku, Tokyo, 163-02, Japan; phone: +81-3-3347-4803. The company has subsidiaries and affiliates in 17 countries.

MATSUSHITA ELECTRIC CORPORATION OF AMERICA

One Panasonic Way, Secaucus, NJ 07094; 201-348-7000
Employees: 282,000
Sales: $59,258.9 million
Key Personnel: Managing Director of Personnel Management and General Affairs: Hisao Tahara. Chairman, CEO, Matsushita Electric Corp. of America: Yoshinori Kobe. CFO, Matsushita Electric Corp. of America: Ted Takahaski.
Matsushita Electric Industrial, of which the Matsushita Electric Corporation is a subsidiary, sells a wide variety of consumer electronics gadgetry and entertainment products. Among its many brands are Panasonic, Quasar, and Technics. The company recently purchased the movie production company MCA and already owns Universal Pictures and the book publisher Putnam Berkely. Its sales and work force continue to increase.
Other Locations: Worldwide HQ: Matsushita Electric Industrial Co., Ltd., 1006 Oaza Kadoma, Kadoma City, Osaka, Japan; phone: +81-6-908-1121. The company has facilities in 38 countries.

SEIKO CORPORATION OF AMERICA

1111 MacArthur Blvd., Mahwah, NJ 07430; 201-529-5730
http://www.seiko-corp.co.jp
Employees: 1,023
Sales: $3,072 million
Key Personnel: President: Chushichi Inoue. EVP Administration: Koichi Murano. Manager, Human Resources: Hajime Morokuma.
One of the world's largest watch manufacturers, Seiko is moving into the paging market with wristwatch-like equipment. The move is seen partly as an attempt to revive sales, as the Japanese company counters declining domestic demand for its products. Seiko also

makes many industrial products, including measuring instruments and robots. Its sales and work force are declining.
Other Locations: Worldwide HQ: Seiko Corp., 6-21, Kyobashi 2-chome, Chuo-ku, Tokyo, 104, Japan; phone: +81-3-3563-2111.

NEW YORK

PHILIPS ELECTRONICS NORTH AMERICA CORP.

1251 Avenue of the Americas, New York, NY 10020; 212-536-0500
http://www.philipsusa.philips.com
Employees: 233,686
Sales: $35,521.0 million
Key Personnel: Chairman, President: Cor Boonstra. President, CEO, North American Philips Corp.: Bill Curran. Manager, Human Relations, North American Philips Corp.: James R. Miller.
North American Philips is a subsidiary of Philips Electronics. Although Philips Electronics is best known for its consumer electronics, the company also produces semiconductors, computer systems, and other products as well. The company puts a strong emphasis on research and development. Among its most recent releases is its digital compact cassettes. Its sales are declining but its work force has been increasing.
Other Locations: Worldwide HQ: Philips Electronics N.V., The Rembrandt Tower, Post Box 77900, 1070 MX Amsterdam, The Netherlands; phone: +31-40-786022. The company has facilities in 60 countries.

SANYO NORTH AMERICA CORPORATION ★★

666 Fifth Ave., New York, NY 10103; 212-315-3232
Employees: 67,887
Sales: $14,580.9 million
Key Personnel: Chairman, CEO: Motoharu Iue. President: Masafumi Matsunaga. Human Resources Manager: Patrick Graupp.
Sanyo North America is a subsidiary of Sanyo Electric, one of the largest manufacturers of electric and electronic devices in Japan. Sanyo Electric Company has facilities in 60 countries. The company makes a wide variety of products, including appliances, semiconductors, and communications equipment. The company is a top manufacturer of solar cells. Its sales and work force are on the

rise.

Other Locations: Worldwide HQ: Sanyo Electric Co., Ltd., 5-5 Keihan-Hondori 2-chome, Moriguchi City, Osaka, 570, Japan; phone: +81-6-991-1181.

SONY CORP. OF AMERICA ★★
550 Madison Ave., New York, NY 10022; 212-833-6849
Employees (US): 28,200
Sales (US): $18,109.8 million
Key Personnel: Executive Deputy President (Finance and Personnel): Tsunao Hashimoto. President, CEO, Sony Corp. of America: Michael P. Schulhof. President, COO, Sony Pictures Entertainment: John Calley.

The electronics giant, Sony, moved into the U.S. entertainment business to stimulate sales of its hardware. However, the company's holdings in entertainment have taken on lives of their own, with music and movie sales accounting for nearly 20 percent of the company's overall sales). Sony also makes a wide variety of electronic gizmos, including Apple's PowerBook, computer displays, disk drives, and related equipment. Its sales and work force are growing.

Other Locations: Worldwide HQ: Sony Corp., 7-35 Kitashinagawa 6-chome, Shinagawa-ku, Tokyo, 141, Japan; phone: +81-3-5448-2111.

OHIO

HMI INDUSTRIES, INC.
3631 Perkins, Cleveland, OH 44114; 216-432-1990
Employees: 143
Sales: $39.1 million
Key Personnel: Chairman, CEO: James R. Malone. President, COO: Carl H. Young III. Human Resources Manager: Ellen Gordon.

HMI Industries manufactures high-end vacuum cleaners under the Filter Queen brand. The company also makes central vacuum cleaner systems and tubing for aerospace and commercial uses. It recently sold off many of its subsidiaries to concentrate on core products. Sales and work force are rapidly declining.

ROYAL APPLIANCE MANUFACTURING CO.
650 Alpha Dr., Cleveland, OH 44143; 216-449-6150
http://www.dirtdevil.com
Employees: 1,380

Sales: $282.7 million
Key Personnel: President, CEO: Michael J. Merriman. SVP Administration: Gary J. Dieterich. Human Resources Manager: Timothy J. Araps.

The largest supplier of handheld vacuum cleaners in the United States, Royal Appliance Manufacturing is attempting to stave off the effects of market saturation by expanding its product line. The company, which makes the Dirt Devil line, continues to introduce new varieties of upright vacuum cleaners. Sales are down slightly while employee numbers are up.

WHITE CONSOLIDATED INDUSTRIES, INC.
11770 Berea Rd., Cleveland, OH 44111-1688; 216-252-3700
Employees: 99,322
Sales: $14,505.0 million
Key Personnel: CEO (US): Michael Treschow. SVP, Finance, Controller (US): Ron Zajaczkowski. SVP Human Resources: Joe Burke.

White is a subsidiary of Electrolux, Europe's largest producer of household appliances. Electrolux is also the top maker of floor-care products in the world, which are distributed in the United States under the Eureka brand. In the United States, the company's subsidiary, Frigidaire, is the third largest appliance manufacturer. The company's sales are increasing, but its work force has been shrinking.

Other Locations: Worldwide HQ: Aktiebolaget Electrolux, Luxbacken 1, Stockholm, Sweden; phone: +46-8-738-6000. The company has 625 subsidiaries in 50 countries.

TEXAS

NOKIA TELECOMMUNICATIONS, INC. ★★
6000 Connection Drive, Irving, TX 75039; 972-894-5000
http://www.nokia.com
Employees: 44,543
Sales: $15,553.0 million
Key Personnel: President, CEO, Nokia Corporation: Jorma Ollila. President, Nokia Mobile Phones: Matti Alahuhta. Director, Human Resources: Hallsteing Moerk.

One of the largest companies in Finland, Nokia has risen from a maker of pulp, paper, and rubber products to one of the world's major mobile phone manufacturers. The company's extensive product line also includes television sets, cables, aluminum products, and tires. Its sales are rising, but its work force is shrinking. **Other Locations**: Worldwide HQ: Nokia Group, Etalaesplanadi 12, P.O. Box 226, Helsinki, Finland; phone: +358-0-180-71.

❶ DISTRIBUTORS/ WHOLESALERS

ARIZONA

AVNET, INC. ★
2211 S. 47th St., Phoenix, AZ 85034; 623-643-2000
http://www.avnet.com
Employees: 8,700
Revenues: $6,350.0 million
Key Personnel: President, CEO: Roy Vallee. SVP, CFO: Raymond Sadowski. VP Human Resources: Robert Zierk.
Avnet is one of the largest computer products and electronic components distributors in the world. It has risen from a small radio parts distributor in the 1920s to its current global reach through a series of skillful acquisitions. With a presence in Africa, Asia and Europe, international sales now account for a quarter of their total sales.

MICROAGE ★★
2400 S. MicroAge Way, Tempe, AZ 85282-1896; 602-366-2000
http://www.mocroage.com
Employees: 4,500
Revenues: 5520.0 million
Key Personnel: Chairman, CEO: Jeffrey D. McKeever. EVP Operations: John H. Andrews. Human Resources Manager: Alan R. Lyons.
Beginning with one Arizona computer store in the 1970s, MicroAge has grown to become one of the top computer wholesalers and resellers in the United States. The company has had its ups and downs over the years but continued to grow in spite of its problems. Its distribution subsidiary, Pinacor, accounts for 75 percent of its sales. Sales and work force are up.
Other Locations: The company has warehouses in Arizona and Ohio.

CALIFORNIA
BERGEN BRUNSWIG CORPORATION ★★
4000 Metropolitan Dr., Orange, CA 92868-3598; 714-385-4000
http://www.bergenbrunswig.com
Employees: 5,400
Revenues: $17,121.7 million
Key Personnel: President, CEO: Donald R. Roden. EVP, Chief Procurement Officer: Charles J. Carpenter. Human Resources Manager: Carol E. Scherman.
Among the largest pharmaceutical distribution companies in the United States, Bergen Brunswig has some large customers. More than half of the company's business comes from sales to managed care facilities and hospitals. Among its customers is Columbia/HCA, the largest U.S. hospital chain. It agreed to be bought by rival Cardinal Health, but the government intervened. Sales and work force are rising.
Other Locations: The company has facilities in 64 locations in 29 states.

MARSHALL INDUSTRIES
9320 Telstar Ave., El Monte, CA 91731-2895; 818-307-6000
http://www.marshall.com
Employees: 1,400
Revenues: $1,184.6 million
Key Personnel: President, CEO: Robert Rodin. VP Quality (Chief Technical Officer): Jacob Kuran. Director of Human Resources: Les Jones.
One of the top electronic component distributors in the United States, Marshall Industries primarily sells semiconductors. Japanese semiconductors account for the largest chunk of the company's sales. It recently brought out a new on-line shopping service for computer engineers. Sales and work force are up.

MCKESSON HBOC, INC. ★★
McKesson Plaza, One Post St., San Francisco, CA 94104; 415-983-8300
http://www.mckesson.com
Employees: 24,600
Revenues: $18,153.4 million
Key Personnel: President,CEO: Mark A Pulido SVP National Accounts: Stephen F. Stuber. SVP Marketing: Aldo Zini.
McKesson traces its beginnings to a New York City pharmacy opened in 1833. Now based in San Francisco, the company has grown to become the biggest drug wholesaler in North America. Recently, it purchased HBO & Company, the world leader in health care information systems. It also sells car care products such as Armor All. McKesson is

also part-owner of Nadro S.A. de C.V., the largest drug wholesaler in Mexico. Its subsidiary, McKesson Water Products, is one of the top bottled water enterprises in the nation. Sales and work force are up due to the purchase of HBO & Company.

MERISEL, INC. ★★
200 Continental Blvd., El Segundo, CA 90245-0948; 310-615-3080
http://www.merisel.com
Employees: 2,700
Revenues: $4,553.0 million
Key Personnel: Chairman, CEO: Dwight Sterffensen. President, COO: James E. Illson. SVP Finance, CFO: Timothy N. Jenson. VP Human Resources: Carol Baker..

Among the top computer hardware wholesalers in the world, Merisel angered some of its customers when it purchased the distribution and franchise operations of Computerland International (now called VanStar), stepping over the fence into the reselling end of the business. The company has tried to cut its losses by paring its once-global operations to two units: Merisel Americas (U.S. only) and Merisel Canada. Investment firm Stonington Partners will acquire a majority stake in the company which will help restructure its debt.
Other Locations: The company has offices in the Americas, Australia, and Europe.

FLORIDA

CHS ELECTRONICS, INC. ★★
2000 NW 84th Ave., Miami, FL 33122; 305-908-7200
http://www.chse.com
Employees: 6,800
Revenues: $8,545.8 million
Key Personnel: Chairman, President, CEO: Claudio E. Osorio. COO: Mark E. Keough. Human Resources Manager: Isabel Viteri.

The third largest distributor of computers, networking products, peripherals, and software does very little business in the U.S. CHS is expanding quickly through acquisitions, and is already the top distributor in Latin America. Sales and work force are growing rapidly.
Other Locations: The company has a solid position in Europe and Latin America, and now has a presence in China, India the Middle East, and Southeast Asia.

TECH DATA CORPORATION ★★
5350 Tech Data Dr., Clearwater, FL 33760; 727-539-7429
http://www.techdata.com
Employees: 8,240
Revenues: $11,529.0 million
Key Personnel: Chairman, CEO: Edward C. Raymund. President, COO: Steven A Raymund. Human Resources Manager: Lawrence W. Hamilton.

Tech Data began as a retailer of computer equipment to Florida hospitals in the 1970s. In the 1980s the company focused solely on wholesaling computers to a national market, and it has since grown to be the second largest such company in the United States. It distributes products from 900 manufacturers to more than 100,000 resellers in North America and Europe. Sales and work force are both on the increase at Tech Data.

MARYLAND

U.S. FOODSERVICE ★★
9830 Patuxent Woods Dr., Columbia, MD 21046; 410-312-7100
http://www.usfoodservice.com
Employees: 11,000
Revenues: $6,198.4 million
Key Personnel: Chairman, President, CEO: James L. Miller. SVP Sales, Marketing, and Procurement: Mark P. Kaiser. SVP, CFO: Gerry Megas.

One of the largest food distributors in the United States, U.S. Foodservice (formerly JP Foodservice) offers 130,000 customers over 40,000 products. Its clients are typically large institutional enterprises, such as schools, hotels, restaurants, and colleges. The company now has nationwide reach, with the acquisition of Rykoff-Sexton. The company plans continued expansion through acquisition of smaller wholesalers. U.S. Foodservice's sales and work force are both on the increase.

MICHIGAN

HANDLEMAN COMPANY
500 Kirts Blvd., Troy, MI 48084-4142; 248-362-4400
Employees: 2,300
Revenues: $1,058.6 million
Key Personnel: President, CEO: Stephen Strome. EVP; President, Distribution: Peter J. Cline. SVP Finance, CFO: Leonard Brams. Human Resources Manager: Rodger Apple.

When it comes to wholesale entertainment, Handleman is the top distributor to mass merchandisers. The company provides music and proprietary music/videos to chains such as K-Mart and Wal-Mart. The company recently lost over 2,000 retailers and many more cut back on inventory because of poor economic conditions. Sales and work force are down.

MINNESOTA

CARGILL, INC.
15407 McGinty Rd., Wayzata, MN 55440-5625; 612-742-7575
Employees: 82,000
Sales: $46,000 million
Key Personnel: Chairman: Ernest S. Micek. President, CEO: Warren R. Staley. SVP, Human Resources: Nancy Siska.
Cargill is the largest privately held corporation in the United States. The company's share of the food business is among the country's largest. Cargill is the #1 exporter of grain in the United States, shipping 25 percent of all grain exports. It is currently expanding its production of corn sweeteners, specialty starches, and corn syrups. Cargill is also the #2 salt company, and the Excel division slaughters one-fifth of U.S. cattle.
Other Locations: The company has facilities in 65 countries, and trades in about 130 others.

SUPERVALU, INC.
11840 Valley View Rd., Minneapolis, MN 55344; 612-828-4000
http://www.supervalu.com
Employees: 50,000
Revenues: $17,420.5 million
Key Personnel: Chairman, CEO, President: Michael W. Wright. EVP; President, COO, Retail Food Companies: William J. Bolton. Human Resources Manager: Ronald C. Tortelli..
SUPERVALU is one of the largest food wholesalers in the United States. After several years of declining profits, SUPERVALU has realigned its operations and opened new distribution centers to increase operating efficiency and profitability. The result has seen sales and work force increase.
Other Locations: The company has 29 distibution centers and 350 food stores in the United States.

MISSOURI

GRAYBAR ELECTRI COMPANY, INC. ★★
34 N. Meramec Ave., St. Louis, MO 63105; 314-512-9200
http://www.graybar.com
Employees: 7,900
Revenues: $3,744.1 million
Key Personnel: President, CEO: Carl L. Hall. SVP Electrical Business: Richard H. Haney. Human Resources Manager: Jack F. Van Pelt.
The top U.S. wholesaler of telecommunications and electrical equipment, Graybar Electric began in 1869 as part of Western Electric Manufacturing. The company has been an employee-owned wholesale distributor since the late 1920s, dealing in a wide variety of products, such as fiber-optic cable, wiring devices, and switches. Sales and work force are up.
Other Locations: The company 260 branches in the U.S. and Canada, with additional offices in Latin America and Asia.

NEW YORK

ARROW ELECTRONICS, INC. ★
25 Hub Dr., Melville, NY 11747; 516-391-1300
http://www.arrow.com
Employees: 9,700
Revenues: $8,344.7 million
Key Personnel: President, CEO: Stephen P. Kaufman. EVP, COO: Francis M. Scricco. SVP, CFO: Sam R. Leno. VP Human Resources: Tom F. Hallam.
Arrow Electronics is the top distributor of computer products and electronic components in the world. Its merchandise includes microcomputer circuit boards, semiconductors, and desktop computer systems. Its suppliers include Texas Instruments and Intel. The company sells to original equipment manufacturers. It has been growing by acquisitions for the past decade. Sales and work force are stable.

CONTIGROUP COMPANIES, INC. ★
277 Park Ave., New York, NY 10172-0002; 212-207-5100
Employees: 17,500
Est. Sales: $15,000 million
Key Personnel: President, COO: Paul J. Fribourg. EVP, CFO: James J. Bigham. Human Resources Manager: Teresa McCaslin.
Formerly Continental Grain, ContiGroup has recently shifted focus from selling grain to meat processing and financial

services. The company has several ventures in China, including a liquid petroleum gas facility in Shanghai. The work force is up but sales are down due to the sale of their grain unit.
Other Locations: The company has facilities and offices in over 50 countries.

HAHN AUTOMOTIVE WAREHOUSE, INC. ★
415 W. Main St., Rochester, NY 14608; 716-235-1595
Employees: 1,216
Sales: $133.5 million
Key Personnel: President: Eli N. Futerman. VP Wholesale Operations: Timothy Vergo. VP Direct Distribution: David M. Appelbaum. Human Resources Manager: Ira D. Jevotovsky.
Old cars mean big business for Hahn Automotive Warehouse. The company serves 1,500 independent parts jobbers mostly in the Midwest and East. It also owns approximately 240 Advantage Auto and AUTOWORKS retail parts outlets. The company purchased the AUTOWORKS chain in 1993 for $12.3 million, and in 1997 they filed for Chapter 11 bankruptcy protection. Work force is recovering, but sales are slow.

NORTH CAROLINA
BAKER & TAYLOR, INC. ★
2709 Water Ridge Pkwy., Charlotte, NC 28217, 704-357-3500
http://www.baker-taylor.com
Employees: 2,500
Sales: $1,021.4 million
Key Personnel: Chariman: Patrick W. Gross. President, CEO: Craig M. Richards. EVP, President, Baker & Taylor Entertainment: Richard S. Czuba. Human Resources Manager: Claudette Hampton.
One of the largest book distributors in the world, Baker & Taylor's operations are divided into three sectors: books, videos, and software. It distributes approximately 50 million books annually to retail outlets and libraries worldwide. Its CD-ROM–based ordering system is renowned in the industry for its comprehensive inclusion of hard-to-find titles. It's retailer division sells to companies like Barnes & Noble, Amazon.com, CDNow.com, and Virgin Entertainment. Sales and work force are steady, despite competition from the Internet.
Other Locations: The company has facilities in Australia, Japan, the United Kingdom, and the United States.

OHIO
CARDINAL HEALTH, INC.
5555 Glendon Ct., Dublin, OH 43016; 614-717-5000
http://www.cardinal-health.com
Employees: 11,200
Revenues: $25,033.6 million
Key Personnel: Chairman, CEO: Robert D. Walter. President, COO: John C. Kane. Human Resources Manager: Carole W. Tomko.
Cardinal Health is the second largest U.S. distributor of pharmaceuticals, surgical and hospital supplies, as well as other specialty pharmaceutical, health, and beauty products. It also owns the top maker of gelatin capsules, R.P. Scherer, and the top U.S. medical products distributor, Allegiance. Sales and work force are steady.

OKLAHOMA
FLEMING COMPANIES, INC.
6301 Waterford Blvd., Oklahoma City, OK 73126; 405-840-7200
http://www.fleming.com
Employees: 38,900
Revenues: $15,069.3 million
Key Personnel: Chairman, CEO: Mark S. Hansen. EVP Food Distribution: E. Stephen Davis. SVP Human Resources: Scott M. Northcutt.
Fleming Companies is the second largest wholesale food distribution company in the United States. The company serves over 3,000 grocery stores and also owns 350 more. The company has had its ups and downs in the last few years. It recently restructured operations, selling some assets and cutting back on employees. The company recently bought Scrivner, a food distribution company based in Oklahoma, for $1.09 billion. Sales and work force are stable.

TENNESSEE
INGRAM INDUSTRIES, INC. ★
One Belle Meade Pl., 4400 Harding Rd., Nashville, TN 37205-2244; 615-298-8200
Employees: 6,500
Est. Sales: $2,000 million
Key Personnel: Chairman, CEO: Martha Ingram. VC; Chairman, Ingram Book Group: John R. Ingram. Human Resources Manager: Dennis Delaney.
Ingram Industries is the largest inde-

pendent wholesaler of general-interest books in the world, shipping over 115 million books, audio tapes and CD-ROM's annually. The company, whose roots date back to the mid-1800s, does business in two sectors: wholesale distribution (books, software, periodicals, computer products, and other goods) and energy (barging, oil-drilling equipment, coal). Sales and work force are up.
Other Locations: The company has warehouses in California, Colorado, Connecticut, Georgia, Illinois, Indiana, Maryland, Texas, and Virginia.

TEXAS

AMERISERVE FOOD DISTRIBUTION, INC. ★★

15305 Dallas Pkwy., Addison, TX 75001; 972-364-2000
http://www.ameriserve.com
Employees: 8000
Revenues: $7,421.0 million
Key Personnel: Chairman, CEO: John V. Holten. VC, EVP: Thomas C. Highland. Human Resources Manager: Kurt Twining.
Ameriserve is the second largest distributor of food in the United States, serving over 30 restaurant chains. Customers include Burger King, KFC, Pizza Hut and Olive Garden restaurants throughout the US, Canada, and Mexico. Sales and work force are growing rapidly.

SYSCO CORPORATION ★★

1390 Enclave Pkwy., Houston, TX 77077-2099; 281-584-1390
http://www.sysco.com
Employees: 33,400
Revenues: $17,422.8 million
Key Personnel: Chairman, CEO: Bill M. Lindig. President, COO: Charles H. Cotros. EVP Foodservice Operations: Richard J. Schnieders.
The largest distributor of food in the United States, SYSCO serves the needs of over 300,000 eating spots in the United States, western Canada, and Mexico. Its customers are primarily hotels, hospitals, schools, and large caterers. The company also manufactures food under its own brands, including a number of ethnic foods. Sales and work force are growing.
Other Locations: The company has close to 100 facilities in Canada and the United States.

❶ DIVERSIFIED

CALIFORNIA

PRINCESS CRUISES, INC. ★

10100 Santa Monica Blvd., Los Angeles, CA 90067-4189; 310-553-1770
http://www.princesscruises.com
Employees: 69,533
Sales: $9,831.3 million
Key Personnel: President: Peter G. Ratcliffe. CFO: Colin Rumble. SVP Fleet Services: David Brown.
Princess Cruises is a subsidiary of the Peninsular and Oriental Steam Navigation Company, one of the largest shipowners in the world. It currently draws the majority of its income from construction and property development. Its sales and work force are steady.
Other Locations: Worldwide HQ: Peninsular and Oriental Steam Navigation Co., 79 Pall Mall, London, SW1Y 5EJ, United Kingdom; phone: +44-(01)71-930-4343.

CONNECTICUT

BTR, INC.

333 Ludlow St., Stamford, CT 06902; 203-352-0060
http://www.btr.com
Employees: 115,805
Sales: $16,336.1 million.
Key Personnel: President: John S. Thompson. VP Finance: William Denninger. VP Human Resources: Robert MacQueen.
One of the largest conglomerates in the United Kingdom, BTR has more than 1,000 subsidiaries throughout the world. It has interests in heavy manufacturing, construction, transportation, and packaging, among other areas. The company recently has been expanding into Asia and buying up more high-tech operations. BTR's overall sales are on the increase, but its work force is shrinking.
Other Locations: Worldwide HQ: Invensys PLC, Carlisle Place, London SW1P 1BX, United Kingdom Phone: +44-171-834-3848

TENNECO, INC. ★★

1275 King St., Greenwich, CT 06831; 203-863-1000
http://www.tenneco.com
Employees: 23,600
Revenues: $7,597.0 million
Key Personnel: COO: Paul T. Stecko.

EVP, CFO: Robert T. Blakely. Human Resources Manager: Barry R. Schuman. Once known primarily for its pipeline businesses, Tenneco recently sold its natural gas operations as well as its subsidiaries in chemicals, shipbuilding, and farm and construction equipment. The company now focuses on its packaging and automotive parts businesses. Its sales and work force are decreasing..
Other Locations: Tenneco has manufacturing facilities in 32 other countries.

FLORIDA

NORSK HYDRO USA, INC. ★
100 N. Tampa St., Ste 3350, Tampa, FL 33602, 813-222-3880
http://www.hydro.com
Employees: 38,000
Sales: $12,826.8 million
Key Personnel: President, CEO: Egil Myklebust. EVP: Thorleif Enger. SVP Human Resources: Hans Jorn Ronningen.
Norway's top public industrial enterprise is Norsk Hydro. The bulk of its income comes from its oil and gas operations in the North Sea. The company also produces light metals, such as aluminum, and industrial chemicals. Norsk is currently exploring for oil in Siberia. Its sales and work force are increasing.
Other Locations: Worldwide HQ: Norsk Hydro A.S, Bygdoy alle 2, Oslo, 2, Norway; phone: +47-22-43-21-00.

SANDESTIN RESORTS, INC. ★★
9300 Highway 98 W., Destin, FL 32541; 904-267-8000
http://www.sandestin.com
Employees: 36,000
Sales: $2,923.9 millions
Key Personnel: President: James Rester. VP, Finance: Alvin Liew. Human Resources Director: Sylvia Bell.
Sandestin Resorts is a subsidiary of the Malaysian conglomerate Sime Darby Berhad, one of Asia's largest multinational companies. Much of the company's income comes from investments. Its business activities include heavy equipment manufacturing and property development. It also has plantations, which grow rubber, cocoa, fruit, and other crops. Sales and work force are growing.
Other Locations: Worldwide HQ: Sime Darby Berhad, 21st Floor, Wisma Sime Darby, Jalan Raja Laut, Kuala Lumpur, Malaysia; phone: +60-3-291-4122.

HAWAII

ALEXANDER & BALDWIN, INC.
822 Bishop St., Honolulu, HI 96801-3440; 808-525-6611
http://www.alexanderbaldwin.com
Employees: 2,331
Revenues: $1,292.7 million
Key Personnel: Chairman: Charles M. Stockholm. President, CEO: W. Allen Doane. Human Resources Manager: John Gasher.
Alexander & Baldwin is a diversified company that traces its roots to 1870. The company has subsidiaries in both Hawaii and California. Its subsidiary, Matson Navigation, is an ocean and shore side transportation company. Another subsidiary, A&B–Hawaii, owns California and Hawaiian Sugar Company. Sales are up, but work force is down.

THEO II. DAVIES & CO., LTD. ★
810 Kapiolani Blvd., Honolulu, HI 96813; 808- 592-3900
Employees: 160,000
Sales: $11,229.5 million
Key Personnel: President, CEO: Martin J. Juskot. CFO: Kevin Kurihara. Human Resources Manager: Carol Graff.
Theo H. Davies is a subsidiary of Jardine Matheson Holdings, one of the largest and oldest of Hong Kong's diversified companies. Jardine Matheson Holdings has interests in banking, finance, real estate, shipping, and many other enterprises. The company is preparing for the coming Chinese takeover of Hong Kong by moving some of its interests off the island. Its sales and its work force is down slightly.
Other Locations: Worldwide HQ: Jardine Matheson Holdings, Ltd., Jardine House, 33-35 Reid St., Hamilton, Hong Kong; phone: +852-843-8388.

ILLINOIS

MARMON GROUP, INC.
225 W. Washington St., Chicago, IL 60606; 312-372-9500
http://www.marmon.com
Employees: 35,000
Sales: $6,031.8 million
Key Personnel: President, CEO: Robert A. Pritzker. EVP, Treasurer: Robert C.

Gluth. Personnel Director: Larry Rist.

The Marmon Group is primarily a manufacturing and services conglomerate. The company owns a great range of manufacturing operations, including automotive, building, and consumer products. Its services include liquefied petroleum gas storage, telecommunications, and rail car leasing. Its sales and work force are stable.

Other Locations: They operate 550 facilites in 40 different countries.

QUIXOTE CORPORATION ★★

One E. Wacker Dr., Chicago, IL 60601; 312-467-6755

http://www.quixotecorp.com

Employees: 409

Sales: $72 million

Key Personnel: Chairman, CEO: Philip E. Rollhaus Jr. President, COO, Energy Absorbtion Systems: Leslie J. Jezuit. Human Resources Manager: Dorothy French..

Quuixote's energy absorption system subsidiary is the world's leading maker of energy-absorbing highway crash cushions and highway safety products. The company has shed its CD manufacturing and legal stenography businesses to focus on road safety products. Sales and work force are both increasing.

INDIANA

HILLENBRAND INDUSTRIES, INC.

700 State Rte. 46 E., Batesville, IN 47006-8835; 812-934-7000

http://www.hillenbrand.com

Employees: 10,400

Revenues: $2,001.0 million

Key Personnel: President, CEO: W. August ("Gus") Hillenbrand. SVP, Finance: Tom E. Brewer. VP Human Resources: David L. Robertson.

Life, death, and security are the mainstays of Hillenbrand Industries. The company owns several subsidiaries that specialize in caskets, hospital furniture, and security systems. Its subsidiary, Batesville Casket Company, is the world's largest casket maker. The company has been buying up companies internationally in an effort to expand its market. Sales and work force are steady at Hillenbrand Industries.

Other Locations: The company has offices in Indiana, Virginia, and South Carolina and in France and Germany.

MASSACHUSETTS

HARCOURT GENERAL, INC.

27 Boylston St., Chestnut Hill, MA 02467; 617-232-8200

Employees: 12,000

Revenues: $4,235.3 million

Key Personnel: Chairman, CEO, Harcourt General and Neiman Marcus Group: Richard A. Smith. SVP, CFO: John R. Cook. Human Resources Manager: Gerald T. Hughes.

Publishing, human resources management, and specialty retailing form the core of Harcourt General's business. The company owns several large companies, including Harcourt Brace & Company, one of the largest textbook publishers in the world, and Neiman Marcus Group, which operates fashion and specialty retailers. The company's sales and work force are steady.

Other Locations: The company has approximately 25 Neiman Marcus stores and 290 Contempo Casual stores nationwide, as well as two Bergdorf Goodman stores in New York City. It also has publishing operations in Australia, Canada, Japan, the United Kingdom, and the United States.

NEBRASKA

BERKSHIRE HATHAWAY, INC. ★★

1440 Kiewit Plaza, Omaha, NE 68131; 402-346-1400

http://www.berkshirehathaway.com

Employees: 45,000

Revenues: $13,832 million

Key Personnel: Chairman, CEO: Warren E. Buffett. VC: Charles T. Munger. VP, CFO: Marc D. Hamburg.

With subsidiaries in a wide variety of businesses, Berkshire Hathaway operates in a disparate field of operations. The company sells insurance, books, razors, candy, and many other items. It is owned by Warren Buffett, the second richest man in the world,. Its sales and work force are up.

NEVADA

PACIFIC DUNLOP HOLDINGS, INC.

61221 Lakeside Dr., Ste 200, Reno, NV 89511, 702-824-4600

Employees: 37,619

Sales: $4,339.4 million

Key Personnel: President: Philip Gay. VP Finance: Michael McGetrick. Human Resources Manager: Steve Geerling.

One of the largest companies in Australia, Pacific Dunlop manufactures and markets a diverse group of products. Its subsidiary, Ansell International, is the world's top latex glove and condom maker. The company is aggressively expanding in China and is that country's top maker of ice cream. Its sales and work force are steady.

Other Locations: Worldwide HQ: Pacific Dunlop, Ltd., Level 41, 101 Collins St., Melbourne, Victoria 3000, Australia; phone: +61-03-270-7270.

NEW JERSEY

DAEWOO INTERNATIONAL (AMERICA) CORP.

85 Challenger Rd., Ridgefield Park, NJ 07660-2114; 201-229-4500
http://www.daewoo.com
Employees: 265,044
Sales: $71,526.0 million
Key Personnel: Chairman: K. H. Lee. CEO Finance Division: W.S. Chang.Human Resources Manager: Lisa Park.

South Korea's fourth largest industrial group is Daewoo. The group has 30 domestic and 400 foreign member companies, which operate in more than 100 countries. Daewoo is involved in a wide variety of enterprises, including shipbuilding, electronics, automobiles, and aerospace. The company is expecting to dramatically increase its automobile output. Its sales and work force are increasing.

Other Locations: Worldwide HQ: Daewoo Group, 541 Namdaemunno 5-ga, Chung-gu, Seoul, South Korea; phone: +82-2-759-2114.

HANSON BUILDING MATERIALS

1350 Campus Pkwy., Neptune, NJ 07753; 732-919-9777
Employees: 13,500
Sales: $3,028.9 million
Key Personnel: Chairman: Alan Murray. VP, CFO: Mike Donahue. Chief Executive, Hanson Brick: Alger Moore III.

Hanson is one of the biggest conglomerates of industrial operations in the world. The company sells everything from lumber to cookware through a broad array of subsidiaries. It is known for its constant buying and selling of companies. Recessions worldwide hurt the company in the early 1990s. Its sales and work force are down.

Other Locations: Worldwide HQ: Hanson PLC, One Grosvenor Pl., London, SW1X 7JH, United Kingdom; phone: +44-(01) 71-245-1245. The company has operations in Australia, South Africa, the United Kingdom, and the United States.

METROMEDIA COMPANY

One Meadowlands Plaza, East Rutherford, NJ 07073; 201-531-8000
http://www.metromediarestaurants.com
Employees: 63,000
Est. Sales: $1,950 million
Key Personnel: Chairman, President, CEO: John W. Kluge. SVP, Finance: Robert A. Maresca. Human Resources Manager: Jamie Smith.

Metromedia operates a disparate group of businesses. It is primarily involved in Bonanza, Ponderosa, Bennigan's, and Steak and Ale restaurants and has more than 14,000 restaurants nationwide. But it owns telecommunications and motion picture interests as well. Performance in all sectors has been slower than expected of late, and the company as a result is restructuring its operations. Sales are up, but work force is down.

SAMSUNG AMERICA, INC. ★★

105 Challenger Rd., P.O. Box 260, Ridgefield Park, NJ 07660; 201-229-4000
http://www.sosimple.com
Employees: 267,000
Sales: $57,199.4 million
Key Personnel: President, CEO: Song Bo-Soon. CFO: J. H. Choy. Director of Human Resources: Kevin Won.

Samsung America is a subsidiary of Samsung Group, South Korea's largest industrial conglomerate. More than half of its income derives from financial and information services, but it is also heavily involved in electronics, engineering, consumer products, and chemical production. Its work force has increased, while sales are down sharply.

Other Locations: Worldwide HQ: Samsung Group, CPO Box 1580, Seoul, South Korea; phone: +82-2-724-0361. The company has 254 subsidiaries and branches in 59 countries outside South Korea.

VICKERS AMERICA HOLDINGS, INC.

140 E. Ridgewood Ave., 5th Fl, Paramus,

NJ 07652; 201-986-0225
Employees: 7,132
Sales: $1,481.5 million.
Key Personnel: President, Vickers America: Andrew John. CEO: Baron Paul Buysse. Human Resources Manager: Bernard LeBargy.

With a reputation for premium quality, Vickers has been in business for more than 165 years. The company's subsidiaries operate in the automotive, defense, propulsion technology, and medical equipment markets. Among its products are Cosworth engines, Air-Shields medical equipment, and Challenger tanks. The company has sold its medical equipment line and its Rolls-Royce operations to focus on propulsion technology, automotive engines and defense systems. Its sales and work force are decreasing.
Other Locations: Worldwide HQ: Vickers PLC, Vickers House, Millbank Tower, Millbank, London, SW1P 4RA, United Kingdom; phone: +44-(01)71-828-7777.

NEW YORK

ITOCHU INTERNATIONAL, INC.

335 Madison Ave., New York, NY 10017; 212-818-8000
Employees: 8,400
Sales: $ 116,814.5 million
Key Personnel: Chairman: Minoru Murofushi. President, CEO: Uichiro Niwa. Chairman; CEO, ITOCHU International (U.S.): Jay W. Chai.

One of the largest Japanese industrial conglomerates, ITOCHU has interests in five main areas: basic industries, textiles, food, general merchandise, and forest products. The company is investing heavily in Chinese and Vietnamese businesses. Because of the Japanese recession, its sales are down, but the work force is rebounding.
Other Locations: Worldwide HQ: ITOCHU Corp., 1-3, Kyutaromachi 4-chome, Chuo-ku, Osaka, 541-77, Japan; phone: +81-6-241-2121. The company has 1000 subsidiaries and associated companies that operate worldwide.

KOOR 2000, INC.★

1270 Ave. of the Americas, Suite 2307, New York, NY 10020; 212-765-5050
Employees: 21,500
Sales: $ 3,034.4 million.
Key Personnel: President, CEO, Telrad Telecommunication & Electronic Industries, Ltd.: Israel Zamir. President, CEO, Merhav Ceramic & Building Material Center, Ltd.: Uzi Merom. President, Koor 2000 (U.S.):Adina Brenner.

Israel's largest diversified enterprise is Koor Industries. The company has subsidiaries in construction, agricultural chemicals, telecommunications, electronics, food, and other areas. Koor has plans to create a chain of hotels, a pharmaceutical company, and a biblical amusement park. Recent acquisition of 25 percent by the Claridge Group, owned by Canadian billionaire Charles Bronfman, has led the company to focus more on civilian business. As a result, its sales and work force are growing.
Other Locations: Worldwide HQ: Koor Industries, Ltd., 4 Koifman St., P.O. Box 1514, Tel Aviv, 61014, Israel; phone: +972-3-519-5201.

LOEWS CORPORATION

667 Madison Ave., New York, NY 10021; 212-521-2000
Employees: 34,300
Revenues: $ 21,208.3 million
Key Personnel: Co-Chairman, Co-CEO: Laurence A. Tisch. Co-Chairman, Co-CEO: Preston R. Tisch. President, COO: James S. Tisch. Human Resources Manager: Alan Momeyer.

Insurance and cigarettes are the main income producers for Loews. The company's subsidiary, CNA Financial, is the seventh largest insurance provider in the United States. Its Lorillard subsidiary sells Kent, Newport, and True cigarettes. The company also owns a number of hotels and the Bulova clock company. Its sales and work force are on the stable.

MACANDREWS & FORBES HOLDINGS, INC.

35 E. 62nd St., New York, NY 10021; 212-688-9000
Employees: 29,854
Sales: $6,071 million
Key Personnel: Chairman, CEO: Ronald O. Perelman. President: Bruce Slovin. EVP, SVP: James T. Conroy.

MacAndrews & Forbes Holdings is one of the largest private companies in the United States. Its operations are varied. It owns portions of the gear manufacturer Coleman, the cosmetics maker Revlon, First Nationwide Bank, Mastercraft Boats, and many others. Its sales and work force are steady.

MARK IV INDUSTRIES, INC. ★★

501 John James Audubon Pkwy,Amherst, NY 14226-0810; 716-689-4972

http://www.mark-iv.com

Employees: 17,000

Revenues: $ 1,948.6 million

Key Personnel: Chairman, CEO: Salvatore H. Alfiero. President, COO: William P. Montague. Human Resources Manager: Christine Werth..

Originally begun as a mobile-home construction company, Mark IV Industries is now involved in three main areas. It is the top U.S. supplier of industrial belts, hoses, and temperature control systems to the automotive market. It makes transportation equipment, such as traffic signals. And it also makes audio equipment for the professional recording market. Although sales are down, its work force has increased.

Other Locations: The company has 39 facilities in North America and 13 in Europe.

MARUBENI AMERICA CORP.

450 Lexington Ave., New York, NY 10017; 212-450-0100

Employees: 7,041

Sales: $ 102,506.4 million

Key Personnel: President, CEO (Marubeni America): Katsuo Koh. CFO: Shinichi Saito. Chief Administration Officer (HR): Joe van Dorn.

Marubeni is one of the largest diversified companies in Japan. The company's affiliates manufacture machinery, chemicals, textiles, forest products, food, and more. It is also involved in civil engineering and construction. Among its U.S. operations are Kubota Tractor, Nissan Diesel America, and MAC Fashion. Marubeni's sales and work force are down.

Other Locations: Worldwide HQ: Marubeni Corp., 5-7, Hommachi 2-chome, Chuo-ku, Osaka 541-88 CPO Box 1000, Osaka, 530-91, Japan; phone: +81-6-266-2111. The company has more than 200 offices and nearly 700 related businesses in 83 countries.

MITSUBISHI INTERNATIONAL CORPORATION

520 Madison Ave., New York, NY 10022-4223; 212-605-2000

http://www.mitsubishiintl.com

Employees: 8,401

Sales: $ 118,927.6 million.

Key Personnel: President, CEO: Hiroaki Yano. EVP: James E. Brumm. Director, Human Resources: Richard Lovell.

One of the largest diversified companies in Japan is the Mitsubishi Group. The company's operations are divided into five basic areas: metals; machinery/information systems and services; foods; fuels; and chemicals, textiles, and others. Among its holdings are Mitsubishi Bank and Mitsubishi Heavy Industries. Both its sales and work force are decreasing.

Other Locations: Worldwide HQ: Mitsubishi Group, 6-3, Marunouchi 2-chome, Chiyoda-ku, Tokyo, 100-86, Japan; phone: +81-3-3210-2121. The company has 200 offices around the world.

MITSUI & CO. (U.S.A.), INC.

200 Park Ave., New York, NY 10166; 212-878-4337

Employees: 10,957

Sales: $117,373.0 million

Key Personnel: President, CEO: Naohiko Kumagai. President, CEO (U.S.): Shinjiro Shimizu. EVP: Kazuya Imai.

Mitsui & Co., is the U.S. subsidiary of Mitsui Group, the largest business enterprise in the world. The company has operations in chemicals, food, construction, transportation, metals, and many other areas. The group consists of a network of 742 companies, with more than 300 subsidiaries based outside Japan. The company is aggressively pursuing commercial ventures with China. Sales and work force are decreasing.

Other Locations: Worldwide HQ: Mitsui Group, 2-1, Ohtemachi 1-chome, Chiyoda-ku, Tokyo, 100, Japan; phone: +81-3-3285-1111.

SUMITOMO CORPORATION OF AMERICA

345 Park Ave., New York, NY 10154-0042; 212-207-0700

http://www.sumitomocorp.co.jp

Employees: 9,000

Sales: $94,456.8 million

Key Personnel: CEO: Keitaro Yokohata. CFO: Takehiko Adachi. VP Human Resources: Thomas Stripay..

One of the largest industrial groups in Japan, the Sumitomo Group distributes a wide variety of consumer products, commodities, and industrial products through its subsidiaries. The subsidiaries are related through a network of cross-

ownership. The group is recovering from the recent Japanese recession. Its sales and work force are down.
Other Locations: Worldwide HQ: Sumitomo Group, 2-2, Hitotsubashi 1-chome, Chiyoda-ku, Tokyo, 100, Japan; phone: +81-3-3217-5082. The company has offices in more than 136 cities in 87 countries.

TATA, INC.
101 Park Ave., New York, NY 10178; 212-557-7979
http://www.tata.com
Employees: 270,000
Sales: $1,846.4 million.
Key Personnel:. President, Tata, Inc. (U.S.): Ashok Mehta. VP: Sanjaya Varma. Chairman, Voltas International: A.H. Tobaccowala
Tata is the largest conglomerate in India. Many of its 90 subsidiaries are themselves the largest in their respective fields, including Tata Iron and Steel, Tata Engineering and Locomotive, and Tata Consultancy Services. The last is India's largest software developer. Sales are decreasing while work force is stable.
Other Locations: Worldwide HQ: Tata Enterprises. Bombay House, 24 Homi Mody St., Fort Mumbai, Bombay 400001, India, +91-22-204-9131.

NORTH CAROLINA
UNITED DOMINION INDUSTRIES, LTD. ★★
2300 One First Union Center, Charlotte, NC 28202-6039; 704-347-6800
http://www.uniteddominion.com
Employees: 12,000
Sales: $ 2,020.4 million
Key Personnel: Chairman, CEO: William R. Holland. EVP, CFO: G.A. Eisenberg. VP Human Resources: Timothy Verhagen.
United Dominion Industries makes a variety of industrial and building products. Its subsidiaries operate in communications, energy, hotels, manufacturing, transportation, real estate, and waste management.. The company has restructured to reduce costs and has sold many assets. Sales and work force are down.
Other Locations: Worldwide HQ: Canadian Pacific, Ltd., 910 Peel St., P.O. Box 6042, Station Centre-ville, Montreal, Quebec H3C 3E4, Canada; phone: 514-395-5151.

TEXAS
CONDEA VISTA COMPANY ★★
900 Threadneedle, Houston, TX 77079; 713-588-3000
http://www.condea.com/vista/index.html
Employees: 145,467
Sales: $40,229.6 million
Key Personnel: Chairman: Dieter Drager. President: W. C. Knodel. Manager, Human Resources: Crystal Wright.
Vista Chemical is a subsidiary of RWE Aktiengesellschaft, Germany's biggest electric company. Its biggest income is not from electricity, however. The company is also a petroleum and chemical producer and does mechanical and plant engineering and a variety of related enterprises, including coal mining in the United States. Both sales and work force are rising.
Other Locations: Worldwide HQ: RWE Aktiengesellschaft, Kruppstrasse 5, 45128 P.O. Box 103061, Essen, Germany; phone: +49-201-18-50.

VIRGINIA
THOMSON–CSF, INC.
99 Canal Center Plaza, Suite 450, Arlington, VA 22314; 703-838-9685
http://www.thomson-csf-us.com
Employees: 48,850
Sales: $7,211.4 million
Key Personnel: Chairman, CEO: Denis Ranque. SEVP: Daniel Rapenne. Chairman, CEO, VP North American Region: Francois Gayet. Director of Human Resources: Paul Calandra.
Rescued from bankruptcy by the French government in 1982, Thomson is one of the country's largest diversified companies. Its main areas of operation are defense and consumer electronics. Thomson Consumer Electronics, which owns the GE and RCA brands, is the top U.S. television maker. Its sales and work force are falling.
Other Locations: Worldwide HQ: Thomson S.A., 173 boulevard Haussmann, Paris Cedex, 08, France; phone: +33-153-77-80-00. The company has over 180 subsidiaries in 40 countries.

WISCONSIN
JOHNSON CONTROLS ★★
5757 N. Green Bay Ave., Milwaukee, WI 53201; 414-228-1200
Employees: 89,000

Revenues: $12,586.8 million
Key Personnel: Chairman, President, CEO: James H. Keyes. President, COO: John M. Barth. VP Human Resources: Susan F. Davis.

Four main areas occupy the interests of Johnson Controls: plastic containers, vehicle seating, batteries, and building control systems. The company manufactures products for a large number of companies, including Ford, Coca-Cola, and John Deere. Customers for its facilities management operations include over 9,000 schools and hospitals. Sales and work force are increasing.
Other Locations: The company has more than 500 facilities around the world.

❶ ELECTRONICS/ ELECTRICAL EQUIPMENT

CALIFORNIA

ADVANCED MICRO DEVICES, INC. ★
One AMD Pl., Sunnyvale, CA 94088-3453; 408-732-2400
http://www.amd.com
Employees: 13,800
Revenues: $2,542.1 million
Key Personnel: Chairman, CEO Interim President, COO: W.J. Sanders III. SVP, CFO: Fran Barton. Human Resources Manager: Stanley Winvick.

Advanced Micro Devices is the fourth largest integrated circuit manufacturer in the United States. Generally focusing on low priced models, it makes chips for many applications, including central processing units, telecommunications, and networking. The company recently helped to develop a new standard for microprocessor manufacture. The company's sales and work force are steady.
Other Locations: The company has facilities in California and Texas and in Japan, Malaysia, Singapore, Thailand, and the United Kingdom.

INTEL CORPORATION
2200 Mission College Blvd., Santa Clara, CA 95052-8119; 408-765-8080
http://www.intel.com
Employees: 64,500
Revenues: $26,273.0 million
Key Personnel: Chainman: Andrew S. Glove. President, CEO: Craig R. Barrett. EVP, General Manager, New Business Group: Gerhard H. Parker. Human Resources Manager: Patricia Murray.

Well-known for its 80x86 and Pentium series of microprocessors, Intel is the largest integrated circuit manufacturer in the world. The company's Pentium processors have far exceeded sales from its previous 80486 generation. The company is aggressively expanding its capacity in the face of increasing competition. Both sales and work force are stable.
Other Locations: The company has plants in Ireland, Israel, Malaysia, the Philippines, Puerto Rico, and the United States.

LITTON INDUSTRIES, INC. ★★
21240 Burbank Blvd., Woodland Hills, CA 91367-6675; 818-598-5000
http://www.littoncorp.com
Employees: 34,900
Revenues: $ 4,827.5 million
Key Personnel: Chairman, President, CEO: Michael R. Brown. EVP, COO: Harry Halamandaris. Human Resources Manager: Nancy L. Gaymon.

A major defense contractor operating primarily in the United States and Canada, Litton Industries' main enterprises are advanced electronics and marine engineering. The company builds warships, including the Aegis guided missile destroyer. The company also develops night vision systems and many other electronic products. Two thirds of its sales are to the U.S. government. Its sales and work force are up.
Other Locations: The company has operations in Canada, Germany, Italy, and the United States.

NATIONAL SEMICONDUCTOR CORPORATION
2900 Semiconductor Dr., P.O. Box 58090, Santa Clara, CA 95052-8090; 408-721-5000
http://www.national.com
Employees: 11,600
Revenues: $1956.8 million
Key Personnel: Chairman, President, CEO: Brian L. Halla. EVP, General Manager, Analog Group: Patrick J. Brockett. Human Resources Manager: Richard A. Wilson.

After several years of restructuring, National Semiconductor has come up with a more streamlined product focus. It has sold its Cyrix chip divisions and moved away from the microprocessor market dominated by Intel. Among the company's products are amplifiers, mass storage products, local area network controllers, and products for small computer systems. Its sales and work force have decreased.

Other Locations: The company has factories in Malaysia, the Philippines, Singapore, the United Kingdom, and the United States.

PACIFIC SCIENTIFIC CO. ★★

620 Newport Ctr. Dr., Suite 700, Newport Beach, CA 92658; 714-720-1714
Employees: 2,000
Sales: $300 million
Key Personnel: VP, President, Fisher Pierce Division: Steven L. Breitzka. VP, President, Energy Dynamics Division: Robert L. Day. VP, President, Automation Technology Group: William T. Fejes, Jr.

In business since 1923, Pacific Scientific manufactures electrical and safety equipment. Among the company's products are electric motors and generators, control devices, fire detection and suppression equipment, and flight-control components. Its products are used in many applications, such as highway lighting and aircraft. The company recently purchased Met One, Inc., a manufacturer of precision instruments. Sales and work force are up.

SOLECTRON CORPORATION ★★

777 Gibraltar Dr., Milpitas, CA 95035; 408-957-8500
http://www.solectron.com
Employees: 24,857
Revenues: $ 5,288.3 million
Key Personnel: Chairman, President, CEO: Koichi Nishimura. SVP; President, Solectron Americas: Saeed Zohouri. Human Resources Manager: Thomas Morelli.

The largest provider of contract manufacturing company in the world, Solectron builds circuitry and systems for personal computers, communications, and other markets. The company is known for its blend of American and Japanese management styles. The company is the only company to win the prestigious Malcolm Baldrige Award twice. Among its customers are Sun Microsystems, Hewlett-Packard and 3COM. Its sales and work force are on the rise.

Other Locations: The company has operations in France, Japan, Malaysia, the United Kingdom, and the United States.

COLORADO

THE DII GROUP, INC.. ★★

6273 Monarch Park Place, Ste. 200, Niwot, CO 80503, 303-652-2221
http://www.diigroup.com
Employees: 7,900
Sales: $925.5 million
Key Personnel: Chairman, CEO: Ronald R. Budacz. SVP, CFO, Treasurer: Thomas J. Smach. Humar Resources Manager: Anna Maria Mastronardi.

In the rapidly expanding field of contract electronics manufacturing, DII (formerly DOVatron International) is finding that many businesses want to use its services. The company manufactures circuit boards for such companies as IBM and Apple Computer. The company is currently expanding by acquiring other contract manufacturing companies. DII's sales and work force are on the rise.

Other Locations: The company operates facilities in California, Colorado, and New York and in China, Ireland, Malaysia, Mexico, and Singapore.

CONNECTICUT

GENERAL ELECTRIC COMPANY ★

3135 Easton Turnpike, Fairfield, CT 06431; 203-373-2211
http://www.ge.com
Employees: 293,000
Revenues: $ 99,820.0 million
Key Personnel: Chairman, CEO: John F. Welch Jr. VC: Eugene F. Murphy. SVP Human Resources: William J. Conaty.

Diversification has been key to General Electric's success. One of the largest manufacturers in the world, GE makes generators, jet engines, plastics, and practically everything in between. Most of its markets generate roughly equal income, thereby protecting it from fluctuations. The company recently introduced a new, more efficient generator. GE also owns NBC. Sales and work force have increased.

Other Locations: The company has more than 150 facilities in the United States, Puerto Rico, and 25 other countries.

FLORIDA

GROUP TECHNOLOGIES ★★

10901 Malcolm McKinley Dr., Tampa,

FL 33612; 813-972-6000
http://www.inforagrtk.com
Employees: 1,800
Sales: $240 million
Key Personnel: VP Engineering: Aviram Margalith. VP Business Development: Jack Calderon. VP Operations: Gerald P. Hurley.
Originally a unit of Honeywell, Group Technologies specializes in designing secure communications systems for the U.S. government and performing contract electronics manufacturing for computer makers. Among its customers are IBM, AT&T, and Compaq. Group Technologies also makes the Badger, a portable outdoor computer. The company's overall sales and work force are growing.

HARRIS CORPORATION
1025 W. NASA Blvd., Melbourne, FL 32919; 407-727-9100
http://www.harris.com
Employees: 28,500
Revenues: $1,743.5 million
Key Personnel: Chairman, President, CEO: Phillip W. Farmer. SVP, CFO: Bryan R. Roub. Human Resources Manager: Nick E. Heldreth.
Harris Corporation manufactures electronics products for defense, business, and industry. The company's Lanier Worldwide subsidiary makes dictation systems, copiers, and other office equipment. Other divisions make secure radios for the military. The government makes up 20% of its sales. The company is currently upgrading its computer chip plant in Malaysia. Harris Corporation's overall sales and work force are down.
Other Locations: The company manufactures its products in 29 plants worldwide.

SENSORMATIC ELECTRONICS CORPORATION ★★
951 Yamato Rd., Boca Raton, FL 33431-0700, 561-989-7000
http://www.sensormatic.com
Employees: 5,800
Revenues: $1,017.5 million
Key Personnel: President, CEO: Robert A. Vanourek. SVP, President, North America Retail Operations: Jerry T. Kendall. SVP, CFO: Garrett E. Pierce.
The world's largest provider of loss-prevention equipment, Sensormatic is in the business of closed-circuit television, electronic article surveillance, and other related systems. The company's systems help to prevent internal theft and shoplifting. Sensormatic provided electronic security to the 1996 Olympics. Its sales are steady but its work force is decreasing.

ILLINOIS

A B DICK COMPANY
5700 W. Touhy Ave., Niles, IL 60714; 847-779-1900
http://www.abdick.com
Employees: 1,200
Sales: $456.6 million
Key Personnel: CEO: Gerald McConnell. CFO: James Bryan. Director Human Resources: Lucy Erikson.
A B Dick is a subsidiary of Nesco's Paragon Holdings. It makes a variety of office products, printing equipment, and related products. The firm's history dates back to the very first mimeograph machine in 1897. Both its sales and work force have decreased in recent years.
Other Locations: The company has offices in 80 countries worldwide.

ANDREW CORPORATION ★★
10500 W. 153rd St., Orland Park, IL 60462; 708-349-3300
http://www.andrew.com
Employees: 4,221
Revenues: $852.9 million
Key Personnel: Group President, Communication Products: Thomas E. Charlton. Chairman, President, CEO: Floyd L. English. Human Resources Manager: Roger Blaylock.
Wireless and cable communications systems are the business of Andrew. It makes microwave antennas, cable systems, computer network equipment, and other products for government and commercial markets. The company manufactures and sells its products worldwide, with about 35% of its sales coming from outside the U.S. Demand for its products has decreased. However, its sales and work force are steady.

MOLEX, INC. ★
2222 Wellington Ct., Lisle, IL 60532; 630-969-4550
http://www.molex.com
Employees: 12,455
Revenues: $1,711.6 million
Key Personnel: SVP, Americas: Ray-

mond C. Wieser. President, COO: J. Joseph King. Human Resources Manager: Kathi M. Regas.

Molex makes electrical connectors, ribbon cable, switches, and application tooling. Most of its customers are manufacturers like Ford, Sony and Xerox. The company is named after its original product, an insulation material made from coal tar, asbestos, and Fiberglas. Molex has a uniquely regional approach to business that keeps its managers in contact with customers. Its sales and work force are on the rise.

MOTOROLA, INC.

1303 E. Algonquin Rd., Schaumburg, IL 60196; 847-576-5000
http://www.mot.com
Employees: 133,000
Revenues: $ 29,398.0 million
Key Personnel: Chairman, CEO: Christopher B. Galvin. President, COO: Robert L. Growney. EVP, CFO: Carl F. Koenemann. Human Resources Manager: Glenn A. Gienko.

Motorola is the number one maker of cellular phones in the world. The giant electronics manufacturer also makes radio systems, components for computers, and provides wireless telecom services to developing countries. Its sales and work force are on the decline.
Other Locations: The company has facilities in the United States and 40 other countries.

MASSACHUSETTS

RAYTHEON COMPANY ★

141 Spring St., Lexington, MA 02421; 781-862-6600
http://www.raytheon.com
Employees: 108,200
Revenues: $ 19,530.0 million
Key Personnel: Chairman, President, CEO: Daniel P. Burnham. EVP, Chairman and CEO, Raytheon Systems: William H. Swanson. Human Resources Manager: Dennis Donovan.

As the Cold War era draws to a close, Raytheon is adapting its operations. The company has expanded production of products such as aircraft and appliances (it owns Beech Aircraft and Amana Refrigeration), while decreasing production of missiles and other military products. The new strategy seems to be paying off, since sales have greatly increased.
Other Locations: The company has fa-

cilities in the Americas, Europe, the Middle East, and the Pacific Rim.

SCITEX AMERICA CORP.

8 Oak Park Dr., Bedford, MA 01730; 781-275-5150
http://www.scitex.com
Employees: 3,200
Sales: $640.3 million
Key Personnel: President, CEO: Shlomo Shamir. VC: Mendy Erad. Human Resources Manager: Jack Whelan.

One of the top makers of electronic prepress systems, Scitex has more than 40 percent of the market. In the past the company has targeted primarily large clients, such as R. R. Donnelly. In recent years, it has focused on small- and midsized printers. Sales and work force have decreased.
Other Locations: Worldwide HQ: Scitex Corporation Ltd., Hamada St., Industrial Park, Herzlia, Israel; phone: 972-9-597-222.

SIEMENS NIXDORF INFORMATION SYSTEMS INC.

200 Wheeler Rd., Burlington, MA 01803; 781-313-3816
http://www.siemensnixdorf-usa.com/
Employees: 21,000
Sales: $4,660 million
Key Personnel: Head of Corporate Human Resources: Werner Maly. President, CEO, Siemens Corp. (U.S.): Albert Hoser. President, CEO, Siemens Nixdorf (U.S.): Richard H. Lussier.

Siemens is the second largest company in Germany, and its subsidiary, Siemens Nixdorf Informations systeme, is one of the largest computer makers in Europe. Siemens makes telecommunications, medical engineering, and transportation products, among other goods. The company's computer sales have been suffering recently, which forced layoffs. Sales are up, but work force is down.
Other Locations: Worldwide HQ: Siemens AG, Wittelsbacherplatz 2, D-80333, Munich, Germany; phone: +49-89-2340.

MICHIGAN

SPX CORPORATION

700 Terrace Point Dr., Muskegon, MI 49443; 231-724-5000
http://www.spx.com
Employees: 14,000

Revenues: $ 1,825.4 million
Key Personnel: Chairman, President, CEO: John B. Blystone. VP, Business Development: Drew T. Ladau. VP, Human Resources: Robert B. Foreman.
SPX recently bought General Signal. SPX mainly deals with industrial and technical products like valves, motors and power systems. It has a worldwide presence with plants in North America, Europe, and Asia. Its sales and work force have rapidly increased due to acquisitions.

MISSOURI

EMERSON ELECTRIC CO. ★★

8000 W. Florissant Ave., P.O. Box 4100, St. Louis, MO 63136; 314-553-2000
http://www.emersonelectric.com
Employees: 111,800
Revenues: $ 13,447.2 million
Key Personnel: Chairman, CEO: C. F. Knight. SVC, COO: A. E. Suter. VC: Robert W. Staley. VP Human Resources: P. A. Hutchison.
With more than 40 subsidiaries around the world, Emerson Electric makes a wide range of electrical products. The company's products are targeted toward the commercial, industrial, appliance, and construction markets. It continues to expand its facilities, especially in China and Eastern Europe. Its sales and work force are increasing.
Other Locations: The company has 350 facilities around the world.

NEW JERSEY

OKI AMERICA, INC.

3 University Plaza, Hackensack, NJ 07601; 201-646-0011
http://www.oki.com/english/Home.html
Employees: 23,968
Sales: $5,745.8 million
Key Personnel: President, CEO: Tetsuju Banno. CFO: John McMahon. Director of Human Resources: Lois Stalp.
Oki America is a subsidiary of Oki Electric Industry, one of the largest communications equipment makers in Japan. Oki Electric has suffered during Japan's recession. The company concentrates primarily on the commercial electronics market, with a product line that includes ATM machines, cellular telephones, and printers. It devotes a large portion of its resources to research and development. Sales are down, but work force is up.
Other Locations: Worldwide HQ: Oki Electric Industry Co., Ltd., 7-12, Toranomon 1-chome, Minato-ku, Tokyo, 105, Japan; phone: +81-3-3501-3111. The company has operations in 19 countries.

SHARP ELECTRONICS CORPORATION ★★

Sharp Plaza, Mahwah, NJ 07430-2135; 201-529-8200
http://www.sharp-usa.com
Employees: 57,521
Sales: $ 14,654.8 million
Key Personnel: President: O. Perry Clay. CFO, Secretary, and Treasurer: Manabu Morita. VP Human Resources: Robert Garbutt.
The largest manufacturer of liquid-crystal displays (LCD's), Sharp controls more than 40 percent of the market. The devices are found in an increasing number of electronic gadgets. The company also makes a variety of other electronic equipment, such as fax machines and computers. It is working to expand its business in electronic parts. Sales and work force are up.
Other Locations: Worldwide HQ: Sharp Corp., 22-22 Nagaike-cho, Abeno-ku, Osaka, 545, Japan; phone: +81-6-621-1221.

NEW YORK

ERICSSON, INC. ★

100 Park Ave., Suite 2705, New York, NY 10017; 212-685-4030
http://www.ericsson.com
Employees: 103,667
Sales: $ 22,759.6 million
Key Personnel: President, CEO: Bo Hedfors. CFO: Joe Hagan. Director of Human Resources: Ron Kirchenbauer.
Although it once drew most of its income from the manufacture of wire-based public telephone network equipment, LM Ericsson Telephone is now the largest maker of analog cellular transmission equipment in the world. The company recently became the top supplier of mobile telephone systems to China as well. Its sales and work force continue to increase.
Other Locations: Worldwide HQ: LM Ericsson Telephone Co., S-126 25, Stockholm, Sweden; phone: +46-8-719-0000. The company has operations in more than 100 countries.

EURO RSCG HOLDINGS

350 Hudson St., New York, NY 10014; 212-886-4100
Employees: 23,170
Sales: $8,631.8 million.
Key Personnel: Chairman, CEO: Eric Licoys. EVP, Corporate Services: Nicolas Duhamel. Director, Public Relations: Anne Brucy.

EURO RSCG is a subsidiary of Havas, one of the largest media conglomerates in France. Havas has a wide variety of operations, including radio, television, multimedia advertising, newspapers, and travel. In the United States, EURO RSCG operates a full-service advertising agency. The company also is involved in a joint venture to create interactive software. Sales and work force are steady.
Other Locations: Worldwide HQ: Havas S.A., 136, avenue Charles-de-Gaulle, Neuilly-sur-Seine Cedex, France; phone: +33-1-47-47-30-00. The company has 220 facilities in 65 countries.

HITACHI AMERICA, LTD.

50 Prospect Ave., Tarrytown, NY 10591-4698; 914-332-5800
http://www.hitachi.com
Employees: 328,351
Sales: $ 63,763.9 million
Key Personnel: President: Tomoharu Shimayama. CFO: Katshumi Sakurai. VP, General Manager (Personnel): Iwao Hara.

The largest maker of electrical machinery in Japan, Hitachi's products include communications systems, computers, power equipment, and industrial machinery. Hitachi is the second largest DRAM (dynamic random access memory) module maker in the world. The company is cooperating with Mitsubishi on a project to develop flash-memory chips. Sagging income from its mainframe computer line have caused restructuring. Sales and work force are down.
Other Locations: Worldwide HQ: Hitachi, Ltd., 6, Kanda-Surugadai 4-chome, Tokyo, 101, Japan; phone: +81-3-3258-1111. The company has 700 subsidiaries worldwide.

IEC ELECTRONICS CORP.

105 Norton St., Newark, NY 14513; 315-331-7742
http://www.iec-electronics.com
Employees: 1,536
Sales: $248.2 million

Key Personnel: Chairman, CEO: Russell E. Stingel. President, COO: David W. Fradin. VP, Business Development: Steve Pudles. Human Resources Manager: Lucy Fitzgerald.

In contract electronics manufacturing, IEC Electronics is known as one of the fastest to implement design changes. The company, which builds circuit boards for original equipment manufacturers such as Compaq and IBM, can integrate design changes into its manufacturing process in as little as 24 hours—far faster than its competitors. Sales and work force are falling.
Other Locations: The company has manufacturing facilities in New York, Texas, Mexico, and Ireland.

SYMBOL TECHNOLOGIES, INC.★★

One Symbol Plaza, Holtsville, NY 11742-1300, 516-738-2400
http://www.symbol.com
Employees: 3,700
Sales: $977.9 million
Key Personnel: Chairman and CEO: Jerome Swartz. President, COO: Tomo Razmilovic. EVP: Frederic P. Heiman. Human Resources Manager: Robert W. Blonk.

Symbol Technologies is one of the leading makers of bar-code scanners and portable data terminals. The equipment is used extensively by retailers, such as Wal-Mart and J. C. Penney. It is looking to expand by increasing its share of the small-business market. The company recently went through extensive restructuring. Sales and work force are up.

TOSHIBA AMERICA, INC. ★★

1251 Ave. of the Americas, New York, NY 10020; 212-596-0600
http://www.toshiba.com
Employees: 186,000
Revenues: $41,019.7 million
Key Personnel: Chairman, CEO (U.S.): Shunichi Yamashita. SVP, Human Resources: Jun Morita.

The third largest electronics firm in Japan, Toshiba makes a broad array of products, many in partnership with other companies. Among its partners in commerce are IBM, Apple, and Samsung. Not only is it a major manufacturer of DRAM (dynamic random access memory) modules and light-emitting diodes, but the company also makes elevators and power generation equipment. Its

sales and work force are stable.
Other Locations: Worldwide HQ: Toshiba Corp., 1-1, Shibaura 1-chome, Minato-ku, Tokyo, 105-8001, Japan; phone: +81-3-3457-2096.

OREGON

TEKTRONIX, INC.
26600 SW Parkway Ave., Wilsonville, OR 97070; 503-627-7111
http://www.tek.com
Employees: 7,571
Revenues: $1,861.5 million
Key Personnel: Chairman, President, CEO: Jerome J. Meyer. SVP, CFO: Carl W. Neun. VP Total Quality and Human Resources: Michele M. Marchesi.
The largest manufacturer of oscilloscopes in the world, Tektronix makes a wide variety of testing and measuring equipment. Among its products are frequency counters, video equipment, and color printers. The company is focusing on test and measurement equipment, terminals and printers, and television measuring and production equipment. Sales and work force are down.
Other Locations: The company has operations in 26 countries.

PENNSYLVANIA

ALLEGHENY TELEDYNE INC.. ★
1000 Six PPG Place, Pittsburgh, PA 15222-5479, 412-394-2800
http://www.aleghenyteledyne.com
Employees: 21,500
Revenues: $ 3,923.4 million
Key Personnel: Chairman, President, CEO: Richard P. Simmons. VC: Robert P. Bozzone. SVP Human Resources: Judd R. Cool.
Allegheny Telledyne is the result of a merger between diversified Teledyne and stainless-steel manufacturers Allegheny. The company currently has subsidiaries in aviation and electronics, specialty metals, industrial products, and consumer products. Among its products are seismometers, forklifts, and dental equipment (such as Water Pik). It is selling off its electronics, defense, and consumer businesses to focus on metals.
Other Locations: The company has facilities in 10 states.

AMP, INC.
441 Friendship Rd., Harrisburg, PA 17111; 717-564-0100

http://www.amp.com
Employees: 48,500
Revenues: $ 5,481.6 million
Key Personnel: VC: William J. Hudson Jr. VP: John E. Gurski. Human Resources Manager: William Ward.
The world's top company in manufacture of electrical/electronic connection devices, AMP makes more than 100,000 types of connection devices. The company's growth comes primarily from development of new products. The company holds more than 3,000 issued or pending patents. It is expanding its products to include more networking equipment. Exports make up more than 50% of annual sales. Its sales and work force are stable.
Other Locations: The company has 93 facilities in the United States and 19 other countries.

VISHAY INTERTECHNOLOGY, INC. ★★
63 Lincoln Highway, Malvern, PA 19355-2120; 610-644-1300
http://www.vishay.com
Employees: 21,522
Revenues: $ 1,572.7 million
Key Personnel: Chairman, CEO: Felix Zandman. VC, EVP: Avi D. Eden. President, COO: Gerald Paul. Human Resources Manager: Jack Hain.
Vishay Intertechnology is the biggest producer of fixed resistors, resistive sensors, and tantalum capacitors in Europe and the United States. The company's products are used in all manner of electrical devices, from radios to automobiles. It is focusing its development resources on surface mounted devices. Its sales and work force are growing quickly.
Other Locations: The company has 70 facilities in 12 countries.

WESTINGHOUSE ELECTRIC CORPORATION SEE CBS
Westinghouse Bldg., 11 Stanwix St., Pittsburgh, PA 15222; 412-244-2000
Employees: 77,810
Revenues: $9,610 million
Key Personnel: Chairman, CEO, Westinghouse Broadcasting: Willard C. Korn. Chairman, Electronic Systems: Richard A. Linder. President, Thermo King: James R. Watson.
Westinghouse operates in eight segments of the marketplace: electronic systems, power generation, energy systems, real estate, environmental services, mobile re-

frigeration, broadcasting, and office furniture and equipment. Its broadcasting subsidiary, Group W, continues to acquire new television stations, and the company purchased CBS in 1995 and Infinity Broadcasting, a radio operator, in 1996 (the latter move requiring regulatory approval). Westinghouse has been aggressively restructuring its operations. Sales and work force are down.

Other Locations: The company has more than 900 facilities in the United States and 32 foreign countries.

TENNESSEE

MAGNETEK, INC.
26 Century Blvd., Nashville, TN 37214; 615-316-5100
http://www.magnetek.com
Employees: 14,900
Revenues: $662.5 million
Key Personnel: President, CEO: Ronald N. Hoge. EVP: James E. Schuster. Human Resources Manager: Cyndy Baran.

One of the top manufacturers of discharge ballasts for electrical equipment is MagneTek. The company's products are used in fluorescent and high-intensity lighting. It also makes parts for heating and cooling systems, pool pumps, and other equipment. MagneTek has sold its generators and electric motors business units. Sales are down due to these losses.

NORTEL NETWORKS CORPORATION ★★
Northern Telecom Plaza, 200 Athens Way, Nashville, TN 37228-7388, 615-734-4000
http://www.nortelnetworks.com
Employees: 75,052
Sales: $ 17,575.0 million
Key Personnel: VC, President, CEO (U.S.): John Roth. CFO (U.S.): Jerry Vaughn. Human Resources Manager: Margaret G. Kerr.

The sixth largest telecommunications manufacturer in the world, Northern Telecom primarily sells telephone switching systems, mobile telecommunications equipment, and private branch exchange systems. Its customers include the governments of Israel, Mexico, and Switzerland. The company recently sold part of its electronics components business. Its sales and work force are increasing.

Other Locations: Worldwide HQ: Northern Telecom, Ltd., 3 Robert Speck Pkwy., Mississauga, Ontario L4Z 3C8,

Canada; phone: 905-566-3000. The company's U.S. operations are in California, Georgia, North Carolina, Virginia, and Texas.

TEXAS

ALCATEL USA, INC.
1000 Coit Rd., Plano, TX 75075; 972-519-3000
http://www.usa.alcatel.com
Employees: 118,000
Sales: $24,905.9 million
Key Personnel: CEO: Krish Prabhu. CFO: Hubert de Pesquidoux. Director of Human Resources: Pat Vogler.

One of the largest conglomerates in France, Alcate operates in a number of markets, including telecommunications, electrical engineering, batteries, and financial services. Its Telecom subsidiary is the largest telecommunications manufacturer in the world. Most of the company's business comes from outside France, with Germany being its largest foreign market. Its sales and work force have increased within the U.S.

Other Locations: Worldwide HQ: Alcatel, 54, rue La Boetie, Paris, France; phone: +33-1-40-76-10-10.

COOPER INDUSTRIES, INC.
600 Travis, Ste. 5800, Houston, TX 77002; 713-209-8400
http://www.cooperindustries.com
Employees: 28,100
Revenues: $3,651.2 million
Key Personnel: Chairman, President, CEO: H. John Riley, Jr. EVP Operations: Ralph E. Jackson Jr. SVP Human Resources: David R. Sheil Jr.

Cooper Industries is a conglomerate of companies that manufacture electrical products, hardware, and tools around the world. Among its products are Buss fuses, and Lufkin measuring tapes. It has sold its auto parts division to concentrate on other areas. Demand for its product suffered from downturns in the construction and energy industries. Its sales and work force have decreased.

Other Locations: The company has manufacturing facilities in more than 19 foreign countries.

KENT ELECTRONICS CORPORATION ★★
1111 Gillingham Ln., Sugar Land, TX 77478; 281-243-4000
http://www.kentelec.com

Employees: 1,830
Sales: $ 637.1 million
Key Personnel: Chairman, CEO: Morrie K. Abramson. President, K*TEC Electronics: Larry D. Olson. EVP, President, Kent Datacomm: Mark A. Zerbe. Human Resources Manager: Pamela P. Huffman.
Kent Electronics works in four primary areas: distribution, networking, specialty components and contract manufacturing. The company's distribution operation supplies electrical connectors and other parts to computer, medical, and other equipment makers. Its subsidiary, K*TEC Electronics, is a contract manufacturer of battery power packs and other assemblies for companies such as Apple Computer. Its sales and work force are steady.

RELIANCE ELECTRIC COMPANY

1501 N. Plano Rd., Richardson, TX 75081; 216-266-5800
Employees: 14,000
Sales: $1,610 million
Key Personnel: VP Technology and Corporate Development: Peter J. Tsivitse. VP Telecommunications, President, Comm/Tec: Dudley P. Sheffler. VP, General Manager, Mechanical Group: Joseph D. Swann.
While it is primarily a manufacturer of industrial electronics, Reliance is finding most of its growth in the information business. The company is divided into two sectors. Reliance Electrical Industrial makes generators, transformers, and related products. Reliance Comm/Tec makes telecommunications products, such as video broadband interface devices. Sales are up, but work force is down.
Other Locations: The company has 29 facilities in the United States and 15 plants in nine foreign countries.

TEXAS INSTRUMENTS, INC. ★★

8505 Forest Ln., Dallas, TX 75243-4136; 972-995-3773
http://www.ti.com
Employees: 35,948
Revenues: $ 8,460.0 million
Key Personnel: President, CEO: Thomas J. Engibous. SVP, CFO, and Treasurer: William A. Aylesworth. SVP, Worldwide Human Resources Manager: Stephen H. Leven.
Texas Instruments is the fifth largest computer chip maker in the world.

Among its products are dynamic random access memory chips and digital signal processors. The company recently developed a digital mirror device, which provides clearer images on some computer monitors and televisions. Texas Instruments' sales and work force are down, due to the sale of the defense electronics and memory chip units.
Other Locations: The company has facilities in 18 countries.

---

❶ ENTERTAINMENT

CALIFORNIA

CANAL + U.S.

301 N. Canon Dr., #228, Beverly Hills, CA 90210; 310-247-0994
http://www.cplus.fr/html/english
Employees: 3,816
Sales: $ 2,887.9 million
Key Personnel: CEO: Pierre Lescure. CFO: Mike Metzer. Manager, Human Resources: Victoria Waks.
The French company CANAL+ is the largest operator of pay television in the world. The company, which is similar to HBO, produces and markets television programs and movies. Its subsidiary, CANAL+, is a film production company that invests in French productions and other foreign films. Sales and work force are growing.
Other Locations: Worldwide HQ: CANAL+, 85/89 Quai Andre Citroen, Paris, France; phone: +33-1-44-25-10-00.

WALT DISNEY COMPANY ★★

500 S. Buena Vista St., Burbank, CA 91521; 818-560-1000
http://www.disney.com
Employees: 117,000
Revenues: $ 22,976.0 million
Key Personnel: Chairman, CEO: Michael Eisner. VC: Roy Disney. Human Resources Manager: William J. Wilkinson.
An entertainment conglomerate, Disney owns production studios, theme parks (like Walt Disney World and Disneyland), retail stores, and Capital Cities/ABC. Disney expects to put out 20 films/year, concentrating on the children and family markets, and is expanding its presence in the music area. Sales and work force are up.

COLORADO

JONES INTERCABLE, INC. ★★

9697 E. Mineral Ave., Englewood, CO
80115-3309; 303-792-3111
http://www.jic.com
Employees: 3,060
Sales: $ 460.7 million
Key Personnel: Chairman, CEO: Glenn R. Jones. President: James B. O'Brien. Group VP Operations: Ruth E. Warren. VP Human Resources: Bob Schulz.

Cable television is the main enterprise of Jones Intercable. The company provides cable television services to over 1.4 million people in 17 states. It also operates the Mind Extension University, an on-air college, and Jones Satellite Networks, which supplies cable radio programming. The company has faced stiff competition in recent years. Sales are up but work force is down.

AT&T BROADBAND & INTERNET SERVICES

5619 DTC Pkwy., Englewood, CO
80111-3000; 303-267-5500
http://www.attbis.com
Employees: 37,000
Revenues: $ 7,351.0 million
Key Personnel: President, CEO: Leo J. Hindery Jr. VC: Amos Hostetter. Human Resources Manager: Grace de Latoure.

AT&T recently acquired Tele-Communications, Inc., the top cable television company in the United States. The new company now serves some 12 million subscribers. It also owns a variety of entertainment enterprises, including portions of Courtroom Television Network and Discovery Communications. It is working to develop new technologies to integrate television and telephone systems. They are also focusing on the growing Internet market by providing high speed Internet access with Excite@Home. Currently, sales and work force are stable.

DELAWARE

EMI GROUP INC.

2751 Centerville Rd., Ste. 205, Wilmington, DE 19808, 302-994-4100
http://www.emigroup.com
Employees: 10,292
Sales: $ 3,811.4 million.
Key Personnel: Chairman, CEO: Eric Nicoli. President: Robert White. Director, Human Resources: Jane Sullivan.

The second largest music company in the world, EMI Group (formerly Thorn EMI) pursues business in four main areas: recording and music publishing, equipment rentals, music retailing, and high-tech developments. Among its U.S. subsidiaries are Capitol Records and Rent-A-Center. EMI Music Publishing is the world's number 1 music publisher. Its sales and work force are decreasing.
Other Locations: Worldwide HQ: Thorn EMI PLC, 4 Tenterten St., Hanover Sq., London, W1A 2AY, United Kingdom; phone: +44-(01)71-355-4848. The company has facilities in 40 countries.

GEORGIA

CARMIKE CINEMAS, INC. ★

1301 First Ave., Columbus, GA 31901;
706-576-3400
http://www.carmike.com
Employees: 10,234
Sales: $ 481.6 million
Key Personnel: President, CEO: Michael W. Patrick. SVP Film: Anthony J. Rhead. VP Informational Systems: Larry M. Adams. Human Resources Manager: Sadie Marshall.

Carmike specializes in the small-town motion picture viewing market. The company targets towns with fewer than 100,000 people for its theaters. In most of the its markets, Carmike multiscreen theaters are the only movie outlets available. The company continues to expand through acquisition and construction. Sales are up and work force is steady.
Other Locations: The company operates more than 450 theaters in 36 states.

RANK AMERICA, INC.

5 Concourse Pkwy., Ste. 2400, Atlanta, GA 30328-5350; 770-392-9029
http://www.rank.com
Employees: 43,698
Sales: $3,323.3 million
Key Personnel: EVP, CFO: John Watson. Commercial Director: Douglas M. Yates. VP Human Resources, Rank America: Richard C. Snodgrass.

Rank America is a subsidiary of The Rank Organization. The company operates a number of recreational enterprises as well as providing products and services to the video and film industry. It develops resorts and runs bingo halls and amusement centers. Among its holdings are several Hard Rock Cafes. It also recently won a contract to supply videos of several popular movies. Sales and work force are stable.

Other Locations: Worldwide HQ: Rank Organisation PLC, 6 Connaught Pl., London, W2 2EZ, United Kingdom; phone: +44-(01)71-706-1111. The company has enterprises in Canada, the United Kingdom, and the United States.

TURNER BROADCASTING SYSTEM, INC. SEE TIME WARNER, INC.

One CNN Ctr., Atlanta, GA 30348; 404-827-1700

Employees: 6,000
Revenues: $3,440 million
Key Personnel: Chairman: Ted Turner. VP News: W. Thomas Johnson. VP Advertising, Sales, and Marketing: Steven J. Heyer.

Entertainment and news are the mainstays of Turner Broadcasting System. Along with its eight cable television stations (including CNN, TBS, and TNT), it owns sports interests (such as the Atlanta Hawks basketball team, Atlanta Braves baseball team, and World Championship Wrestling) and many film distribution and production interests. Turner Broadcasting merged with Time Warner, creating the largest entertainment enterprise in the world. Sales are growing, but work force cuts were expected as a result of the merger.

ILLINOIS

ARGOSY GAMING COMPANY ★★

219 Piasa St., Alton, IL 62002; 618-474-7500

http://www.argosycasinos.com
Employees: 4,731
Sales: $ 506.7 million
Key Personnel: Chairman: William F. Cellini. VC: George L. Bristol. President, CEO James B. Perry. Human Resources Manager: Patricia A. Mathews.

With five riverboat casinos in operation on the Ohio, Mississippi, and Missouri Rivers, Argosy Gaming provides a variety of gaming opportunities, including keno and video poker machines, blackjack, roulette, and craps. It is planning an expansion into Indiana. Sales and work force are on the rise.

MISSISSIPPI

ISLE OF CAPRI CASINOS, INC. ★★

711 Washington Loop, Biloxi, MS 39530; 228-436-7000

Employees: 6,000
Sales: $ 480.4 million
Key Personnel: Chariman, CEO: Bernard Goldstein. President, COO: John M. Gallaway. SVP, CFO: Rexford A. Yeisley. VP Human Resources: Robert Boone.

Riverboat gambling is the main business of Casino America. The company owns three floating casinos that operate in Mississippi and Louisiana. It is actively expanding its markets as increasing areas legalize gambling. The company opened Isle of Capri Casino Crowne Plaza Resort, a new resort hotel in Biloxi, Miss., in 1995. Sales and work force are up.

CASINO MAGIC CORP. ★★

711 Washington Loop, Biloxi, MS 39530; 228-467-9257.

http://www.casinomagic.com
Employees: 2,800
Sales: $ 261.5 million
Key Personnel: Chairman, CEO: Bernard Goldstein. President, CEO: Paul R. Alanis. Director Human Resources: Leslie Patrick.

Casino Magic is among the fastest growing casino operators in the United States. Since it began operations in the early 1990s, it has opened seven casinos in the United States and abroad. The company owns two casinos in Mississippi, one in South Dakota, two in Argentina and two in Greece. It plans to expand to other areas of the country as gambling laws are relaxed. Recently, Casino Magic was bought by Hollywood Park Casinos. Sales and work force are up.

NEW YORK

CAPITAL CITIES/ABC, INC. ★★
SEE WALT DISNEY COMPANY

CBS, CORPORATION

51 W. 52nd St., New York, NY 10019; 212-975-4321

http://www.cbs.com
Employees: 46,189
Sales: $ 6,805.0 million
Key Personnel: Chairman: David McLaughlin. President, CEO: Mel Karmazin. Human Resources Manager: David Zemelman.

CBS (formerly Westinghouse Broadcasting) is the number 1 ranked broadcasting network, helped by its acquiring the stations of Infinity Broadcasting in its merger with Westinghouse. It is currently focusing on its TV and radio as it sells off its industrial operations. The company's cable holdings include TNN, CMT, and Eye on People. Viacom is bidding to take over CBS in the largest media deal ever. Sales and work force have dropped since its merger with Westinghouse.

TIME WARNER, INC. ★★
75 Rockefeller Plaza, New York, NY 10019; 212-484-8000
http://www.timewarner.com
Employees: 67,500
Revenues: $ 14,582.0 million
Key Personnel: Chairman, CEO: Gerald M. Levin. VC: Robert E. "Ted" Turner III. President: Richard D. Parsons. Human Resources Manager: Andrew J. Kaslow.

One of the largest media conglomerates in the world, Time Warner has operations in magazines (*Time*, *Sports Illustrated*, *People*, and so on), books (Warner Books and Little, Brown), music, television, and movies (Warner Bros.). Among its other operations are Warner Music Group, the largest music publisher in the world, and Home Box Office, a top distributor and producer of television programs, videos, and films. On top of all this, Time Warner recently merged with Turner Broadcasting. Assets and work force are rising.

VIACOM, INC. ★★
1515 Broadway, New York, NY 10036; 212-258-6000
http://www.viacom.com
Employees: 111,730
Revenues: $12,096.1 million
Key Personnel: President, CEO: Sumner M. Redstone. SVP, CFO: George S. Smith, Jr. SVP, Corporate Relations: Carl D. Folta. Human Resources Manager: William A. Roskin.

With the purchase of CBS, Viacom will become the second largest of the world's media enterprises, behind only Time Warner. Viacom has interests in entertainment, broadcasting, publishing, video and music retailing, and theme parks. Paramount Pictures, MTV Networks, Nickelodeon, MacMillan Publishing USA, Simon & Schuster, and Blockbuster Video are some of its companies. Sales and work force are stable, but expected to drop with the merger.

TEXAS
BLOCKBUSTER ENTERTAINMENT GROUP
1201 Elm St., Dallas, TX 75720, 214-854-3000
http://www.blockbuster.com
Employees: 82,400
Sales: $ 3,893.4 million
Key Personnel: Chairman, CEO: John Antioco. EVP, COO: Gary J. Peterson. EVP, CFO: Gary J. Peterson.

Already the largest video seller in the United States, Blockbuster was purchased in 1994 by Viacom. It was combined with Paramount Parks, which operates a chain of theme parks, and Showtime Networks, which provides subscription cable television, to form Blockbuster Entertainment Group. The company is actively expanding its presence in Europe and South and Central America. Viacom is expected to sell most of its interest in the company by the end of the year. Sales and work force are increasing.
Other Locations: The company has over 4,000 video outlets and 542 music outlets in the United States and 2,250 video stores in 25 other countries.

VIRGINIA
INTERNATIONAL FAMILY ENTERTAINMENT ★★
1000 Centerville Turnpike, Virginia Beach, VA 23463; 804-523-7301
Employees: 1,000
Sales: $210 million
Key Personnel: SVP Advertising Sales: Stephen D. Lentz. SVP Marketing and Corporate Communications: John B. Damoose. Director of Personnel: Carol Kleiber.

Wholesome entertainment is the key to International Family Entertainment. The company, which is headed by television evangelist Pat Robertson, operates The Family Channel, which is among the biggest cable-television networks supported by advertising. It also owns Cable Health Club and other operations. The company purchased MTM Entertainment in 1993. Sales and work force are growing.

FELD ENTERTAINMENT, INC.
8607 Westwood Ctr. Dr., Vienna, VA 22182; 703-448-4000
Employees: 2,500

Est. Sales: $550 million
Key Personnel: Chairman, CEO: Kenneth Feld. President, COO: Stuart Snyder. VP, Human Resources: Richard Felsenstein.

Circuses are the bread and butter of Irvin Feld & Kenneth Feld Productions. The company owns Ringling Bros. and Barnum & Bailey Circus, Walt Disney's World on Ice, and many other traveling shows. It also produces television, film, and theater programs through its subsidiary, Pachyderm Entertainment. Sales are down, but work force is steady.

❶ ENVIRONMENT/WASTE MANAGEMENT

CALIFORNIA ENVIROTEST SYSTEMS CORPORATION ★★

246 Sobrante Way, Sunnyvale, CA 94086-4807, 408-774-6300
Employees: 2,993
Sales: $140.7 million
Key Personnel: Chairman: Chester C. Davenport. President, CEO: F. Robert Miller. Human Resources Manager: James Burley.

Envirotest Systems Corporation is the largest U.S. provider of centralized vehicle emissions testing programs. The company provides testing programs under exclusive contracts with states and municipalities throughout North America. Envirotest also designs and builds vehicle emissions testing stations. The company's sales and work force continue to increase.

ILLINOIS

WMX TECHNOLOGIES, INC. ★★

SEE WASTE MANAGEMENT INC.

3003 Butterfield Rd., Oak Brook, IL 60521; 630-572-8800
Employees: 73,200
Revenues: $10,980 million
Key Personnel: President, CEO: Phillip B. Rooney. President, Waste Management Technology Services: Michael J. Cole. VP Human Resources: Edward Kalebich.

WMX Technologies is the largest waste collection and disposal company in the world. The company has more than 12 million residential clients as well as municipal and commercial accounts in the United States and 21 other countries. It is currently reorganizing to streamline its operations and in 1995 entered the New York City waste market. Its sales and work force are up.

OHIO

MID-AMERICAN WASTE SYSTEMS, INC.

1006 Walnut St., Canal Winchester, OH 43110; 614-833-9155
Employees: 1,000
Sales: $170 million
Key Personnel: Chairman, President, CEO, COO: Christopher L. White. VP Landfill Operations and Solid Waste Management Services: R. Jay Roberts. Human Resources Director: Alan Howald.

Mid-American Waste is a national trash collection and disposal company. Since 1985 it has grown by acquiring facilities throughout the United States. Unfortunately, there is an excess of capacity in the trash business, and Mid-American has been forced to lower its fees. Although its sales are still rising slowly, its work force has decreased slightly.

SOUTH CAROLINA

SAFETY-KLEEN CORPORATION ★★

1301 Gervais St., Ste. 30, Columbia, SC 29201; 803-933-4200
http://www.safety-kleen.com
Employees: 11,500
Revenues: $ 1,185.5 million
Key Personnel: Chairman: James R. Bullock. President, CEO: Kenneth W. Winger. EVP, COO: Michael J. Bragagnolo. Human Resources Manager: Robert Arquilla.

The largest supplier of parts and tool-cleaning services in the world, Safety-Kleen, a subsidiary of Laidlaw Environmental, primarily aims for small businesses. Its typical clients are auto repair shops, printers, and dry cleaners. The company collects, disposes of, and recycles lubricants, industrial liquids, and solvents. Safety-Kleen recently expanded into the photochemical recovery business as well. Its sales and work force are growing.
Other Locations: The company has more than 300 branches in North America and Europe and licenses additional operations in Israel, Japan, and South Korea.

TEXAS

BROWNING-FERRIS INDUSTRIES, INC.
757 N. Eldridge Rd., Houston, TX
77079; 281-870-8100
http://www.bfi.com
Employees: 26,000
Revenues: $ 4,745.7 million
Key Personnel: Chairman, President,
CEO: Thomas H. Van Weelden. VP,
CFO: Henry L. Hirvela. Director, Human
Resources: Christine Caprice.
Browning-Ferris Industries is the second
largest waste management company in
the world. Along with trash collection,
the company operates waste transfer stations, landfills, medical-waste treatment
facilities, and recycling centers in many
countries. The company has been growing quickly, primarily by acquiring
smaller operations. Both its sales and
work force are increasing.
Other Locations: The company has operations in 650 locations in Asia, Australia, Europe, the Middle East, New Zealand, and North America.

WASTE MANAGEMENT, INC. ★★
1001 Fannin, Suite 4000, Houston, TX
77002, 713-512-6200
http://www.wm.com
Employees: 68,000
Sales: $12,703.5 million
Key Personnel: Chairman: Ralph V.
Whitworth. CEO: Robert S. "Steve"
Miller. EVP, CFO: Donald R. Chappel.
VP Human Resources and Employee
Relations: Susan J. Piller.
Waste Management Inc., formerly USA
Waste Services, has acquired several
other companies to become the largest
U.S. waste disposal firm. Waste Management serves municipal, commercial,
industrial and residential customers in all
48 states, Canada and Mexico. To reduce
debt, it plans the sale of its international
division. The company's sales and work
force continue to expand.

❶ FINANCE (DIVERSIFIED)

CALIFORNIA

CHARLES SCHWAB CORPORATION ★★
101 Montgomery St., San Francisco, CA
94104; 415-627-7000
http://www.schwab.com
Employees: 13,300
Revenues: $3,388.1 million
Key Personnel: President, COO: David
S. Pottruck. VC: Steven L. Scheid. VP
Human Resources: George A. Rich.
Charles Schwab is the largest discount
brokerage in the United States. The company, which has more than 2.5 million
accounts, gives its customers responsibility for their own investments. It also
provides an automated telephone transaction system. The company is currently
broadening its mutual fund operations. It
is also attempting a partnership with Fidelity. Its sales and work force are
growing.
Other Locations: The company has
some 290 branches in 46 states and the
United Kingdom.

TRANSAMERICA CORPORATION ★★
600 Montgomery St., San Francisco, CA
94111; 415-983-4000
http://www.transamerica.com
Employees: 9,200
Revenues: $ 6,428.6 million
Key Personnel: Chairman, President,
CEO: Frank C. Herringer. EVP: Thomas
J. Cusack. EVP, CFO: Edgar H. Grubb.
Human Resources Manager: Rona K.
Pehrson.
An amalgamation of numerous subsidi-
aries and affiliates, Transamerica's focus
is on financial services and insurance.
The company provides consumer and
commercial lending, leasing, and real
estate services. The company's sales have
been rebounding after being hurt by eco-
nomic problems in the California area.
Both its sales and work force increasing.
Other Locations: The company has ap-
proximately 600 agencies operating in
Canada and the United States.

DISTRICT OF COLUM-
BIA

FANNIE MAE ★★
3900 Wisconsin Ave., NW, Washington,
DC 20016-2892; 202-752-7000
http://www.fanniemae.com
Employees: 3,800
Revenues: $ 31,499.0 million
Key Personnel: Chairman, CEO: Frank-
lin D. Raines. President, COO: Law-
rence M. Small. EVP, CFO: J. Timothy
Howard. Human Resources Manager:
Thomas R. Nides.
Created in 1938 by President Franklin D.
Roosevelt, the Federal National Mort-

gage Association, or Fannie Mae, is the largest financial company in the United States. It is a federally mandated for-profit corporation set up to provide credit for home buyers in the low- to moderate-income brackets. Its assets and work force are increasing.
Other Locations: The company has of-fices in California, Georgia, Illinois, Pennsylvania, and Texas.

NATIONAL ASSOCIATION OF SECURITIES DEALERS, INC. ★★
1735 K St., NW, Washington, DC 20006-1500; 202-728-8000
http://www.nasd.com
Employees: 2,900
Sales: $ 739.5 million
Key Personnel: Chairman, CEO: Frank G. Zarb. President, EVP: Richard G. Ketchum. Human Resources Manager: Diane E. Carter.
The National Association of Securities Dealers oversees the second largest stock exchange in the world after the NYSE. The NASD Automated Quotations sys-tem operates electronically without a trading floor. The organization also po-lices the trading of over-the-counter stocks. NASD has acquired the American Stock Exchange (AMEX), the third larg-est exchange. Its sales and work force are increasing.

FLORIDA

RAYMOND JAMES FINANCIAL, INC. ★★
880 Carillon Pkwy., St. Petersburg, FL 33716; 813-573-3800
http://www.rjf.com
Employees: 3,790
Sales: $ 1,082.9 million
Key Personnel: Chairman, CEO: Tho-mas A. James. VC: Robert F. Shuck. President, EVP: Francis S. Godbold. VP Human Resources: Chris Lindaman.
With a substantial presence in both the United States and Europe, Raymond James Financial provides a comprehen-sive inventory of services to its clients. Its services include investment banking and research, asset management, and un-derwriting. The company also owns a chain of nursing homes. Its sales and work force are growing.
Other Locations: The company's sub-sidiaries have more than 1000 offices in the United States and Europe.

GEORGIA

FIRST DATA CORPORATION ★★
5660 New Northside Dr., Ste. 1400, At-lanta, GA 30328; 770-857-7001
http://www.firstdatacorp.com
Employees: 32,000
Sales: $ 5,117.6 million
Key Personnel: Chairman, CEO: Henry C. "Ric" Duques. President, COO: Charles T. Fote. EVP, CFO: Lee Adrean. Human Resources Manager: Janet Harris.
First Financial Management merged with First Data to create the largest third party processor of credit card transactions. The company does business in two main ar-eas: merchant services, such as TeleCheck and billing services; and fi-nancial services like processing mutual funds and database management. The company plans to introduce new on-line services, and sell its investor services branch. Its sales are up, but its work force is down.

ILLINOIS

HOUSEHOLD INTERNATIONAL,INC. ★★
2700 Sanders Rd., Prospect Heights, IL 60070; 847-564-5000
http://www.household.com
Employees: 23,500
Revenues: $ 8,707.6 million
Key Personnel: Chairman, CEO: Wil-liam F. Aldinger. VC: Robert F. Elliott. Human Resources Manager: Colin P. Kelly.
Household International is one of the largest credit-card issuers in the U.S. The company also offers home equity and consumer loans through its Household Finance subsidiary. The company also offers revolving credit administration for retail businesses. Its sales and work force are increasing, due to the purchase of Beneficial in 1998.
Other Locations: The company has more than 750 offices in Canada, the United Kingdom, and the United States.

THE KEMPER INSURANCE COMPANIES
One Kemper Dr., Long Grove, IL 60049-0001; 847-320-2000
http://www.kemperinsurance.com
Employees: 9,500
Sales: $3,380.3 million
Key Personnel: Chairman, CEO: David B. Mathis. President, COO: William D. Smith. EVP, CFO: Walter L. White. VP Human Resources: Frederic C. McCul-

lough.

Restructuring has been at the top of the list for Kemper, who has been streamlining its operations for several years. Kemper sells insurance and asset management services and is licensed in 50 states and operates offices in Australia and the UK. Sales and work force are stable.

MARYLAND

DEUTSCHE BANC ALEX BROWN INCORPORATED ★★

One South St., Baltimore, MD 21202; 410-727-1700

http://www.alexbrown.com

Employees: 2,680

Sales: $1,059 million

Key Personnel: CEO: Mayo A. Shattuck III. President: Ted Virtue. Managing Director: W. Gar Richlin. Human Resources Manager: Sherry Edelstein.

Deutsche Banc Alex Brown (formerly known as Alex Brown), currently is a subsidiary of Deutsche Banc, the worlds largest bank. The company provides a variety of investment services, doing business with both institutional and individual investors. It also offers real estate advice and correspondent services. Sales and work force are increasing.

T. ROWE PRICE ASSOCIATES, INC. ★★

100 E. Pratt St., Baltimore, MD 21202; 410-547-2000

http://www.troweprice.com

Employees: 3,500

Sales: $ 886.1 million

Key Personnel: Chairman , President: George A. Roche. Managing Director: James S. Riepe. Human Resources Manager: Marie Nalywayko.

One of the top mutual fund managers in the United States, T. Rowe Price Associates makes most of its money from management and consultation fees. The company has been on an expansion program for several years. It spends approximately 8 percent of its income on advertising. Sales and work force are growing.

MASSACHUSETTS

FMR CORPORATION ★★

82 Devonshire St., Boston, MA 02109; 617-570-7000

http://www.fidelity.com

Employees: 28,000

Sales: $ 6,770.0 million

Key Personnel: Chairman, CEO: Edward C. Johnson III. President, COO: James C. Curvey. EVP, CFO: Stephen P. Jonas. Human Resources Manager: Ilene B. Jacobs.

FMR Corporation is a holding company for many major businesses, including Fidelity Investments, Fidelity Brokerage Services, and Wentworth Galleries. The company also has operations in publishing, real estate, and transportation. The company is expanding into employee benefits management with its new Fidelity Benefits Center. Its sales and work force are growing.

MINNESOTA

GREEN TREE FINANCIAL CORPORATION ★★

1100 Landmark Towers, 345 St. Peter St., St. Paul, MN 55102-1639; 651-293-3400

http://www.gtfc.com

Employees: 6,500

Sales: $ 1,389.6 million

Key Personnel: President: Bruce A. Crittenden. EVP, Commerical Finance: Jerry W. Britton. Human Resources Manager: Barbara J. Didrikson..

Financing manufactured housing is the business of Green Tree Financial. The company also writes loans for home improvements, motorcycles, recreational vehicles, and boats. Green Tree has recently experienced unprecedented growth and now has nearly 30 percent of the market for manufactured home loans. Its sales and work force are rising.

U.S. BANCORP PIPER JAFFRAY INC. ★

222 S. Ninth St., Minneapolis, MN 55402; 612-342-6000

http://www.piperjaffray.com

Employees: 3,180

Revenues: $601.9 million

Key Personnel: Chairman, CEO: Addison L. Piper. President: Andrew S. Duff. CEO, Piper Capital Management: Paul P. Karos. Human Resources Manager: Rose Koning.

Piper Jaffray Companies was acquired by U.S. Bancorp to extend the bank's position in the brokerage industry. U.S. Bancorp Piper Jaffray Inc., as it is called now, is a financial services company operating in the Midwest, Mountain, Southwest, and Pacific Coast states. It offers a broad range of services, including securities brokerage. It recently settled a

class action suit over the performance of one of its funds. The company's revenues are up, and its work force has increased.
Other Locations: The company has approximately 90 offices in the 17 states.

MISSOURI

H & R BLOCK, INC. ★★
4400 Main St., Kansas City, MO 64111; 816-753-6900
http://www.handrblock.com
Employees: 86,500
Revenues: $ 1,521.5 million
Key Personnel: President, CEO: Frank L. Salizzoni. EVP, COO: Mark A. Ernst. Human Resources Manager: Doug D. Waltman.
Originally begun as a tax-preparation business, H & R Block now offers highly diverse services through its many subsidiaries. The company sold its 80 percent stake in the online service Compuserv, but offers investment and securities trading advice in addition to tax preparation.. Sales and work force continue to rise.
Other Locations: The company has more than 10,500 offices in Australia, Canada, Europe, and the United States.

NEW YORK

AMERICAN EXPRESS COMPANY ★★
World Financial Ctr., American Express Tower, 200 Vesey St., New York, NY 10285; 212-640-2000
http://www.americanexpress.com
Employees: 85,000
Revenues: $19,132.0 million
Key Personnel: Chairman, CEO, American Express Travel Related Services: Harvey Golub. VC, CFO: Richard K. Goeltz. Human Resources Manager: Ursula F. Fairbairn.
The operations of American Express fall into three main areas. Its Travel Related Services provides travelers checks and operates a travel agency. American Express Financial Services sells various types of insurance. And American Express Bank offers retail banking services in 37 countries. Sales and work force are up after much restructuring.
Other Locations: The company has operations in more than 160 countries.

BEAR STEARNS COMPANIES, INC. ★★
245 Park Ave., New York, NY 10167; 212-272-2000

http://www.bearstearns.com
Employees: 9,200
Revenues: $ 7,882.0 million
Key Personnel: President, CEO: James E. Cayne. COO, CFO: William J. Montgoris. Managing Director of Personnel: Stephen A. Lacoff.
One of the most prominent companies in the area of securities trading, brokerage, and investment banking, the Bear Stearns Companies have a major presence both domestically and overseas. The firm is aggressively expanding its investments in Asia, especially in China. Its sales and work force continue to increase.
Other Locations: The company has branches in 10 states and the District of Columbia and 12 offices overseas.

MORGAN STANLEY DEAN WITTER & CO. ★★
1585 Broadway, New York, NY 10036; 212-761-4000
http://www.msdw.com
Employees: 45,712
Revenues: $ 31,131.0 million
Key Personnel: Chairman, CEO: Phillip J. Purcell. President, COO: John J. Mack. SVP Human Resources: Michael Cunningham.
Morgan Stanley Dean Witter & Co. is the result of the 1997 merger between Morgan Stanley, the investment bank, and the retail brokerage firm of Dean Witter, Discover. Dean Witter's retail brokerage is the third largest in the U.S. and its Discover unit has been one of the leading credit card issuers. Its sales are up and work force is steady.
Other Locations: The company has more than 430 offices in the United States and 30 more abroad.

GOLDMAN SACHS GROUP, LP ★★
85 Broad St., New York, NY 10004; 212-902-1000
http://www.gs.com
Employees: 14,170
Sales: $ 22,478.0 million
Key Personnel: Co-Chairman, CEO: Henry M. Paulson Jr. Co-Chairman: Jon S. Corzine. Human Resources Manager: Bruce Larson.
Goldman Sachs is now a public partnership that operates as an investment banker, asset manager, equities and fixed income broker, underwriter, and commodities trader. The company has had difficulties in recent years because of an unexpected downturn in the stock market

coupled with the retirement of several of its partners, but has rebounded well by going public. Its sales and work force are up.

Other Locations: The company has offices in Belgium, France, Germany, Hong Kong, Japan, Singapore, the United Kingdom, and the United States.

LEHMAN BROTHERS HOLDINGS, INC.★

3 World Financial Ctr., New York, NY 10285; 212-526-7000
http://www.lehman.com
Employees: 8,873
Revenues: $19,894.0 million
Key Personnel: Chairman, CEO: Richard S. Fuld Jr. COO: Mark Rufeh. CFO: John L. Cecil. Human Resources Manager: MaryAnne Rasmussen.
Lehman Brothers Holdings is one of the world's top investment banks. The company raises money for both government and corporate clients. It also provides asset management and brokerage services. Recent decreases in the bond market have forced the company to restructure its operations. Its sales and work force are increasing.
Other Locations: The company has some 45 offices worldwide.

MERRILL LYNCH & CO., INC. ★★

World Financial Ctr., North Tower, 250 Vesey St., New York, NY 10281-1332; 212-449-1000
http://www.ml.com
Employees: 63,800
Revenues: $ 35,853.0 million
Key Personnel: Chairman, CEO: David H. Komansky. VC: John L. Steffens. Human Resources Manager: Mary E. Taylor.
Merrill Lynch is the largest brokerage in the United States. The company began an expansion program in 1995 to open 250 new small-town, full-services branches. The company is active in the profitable U.S. merger and acquisitions market and it is one of the largest mutual fund managers in the world. It was one of the last brokerage firms to add on-line trading services. Its sales and work force are increasing.

NEW YORK STOCK EXCHANGE, INC.

11 Wall St., New York, NY 10005; 212-656-3000
http://www.nyse.com

Employees: 1,500
Sales: $ 728.7 million
Key Personnel: Chairman, CEO: Richard A. Grasso. President, COO: William R. Johnston. VC: Deryck C. Maughan. Human Resources Manager: Frank Z. Ashen.
The New York Stock Exchange is the largest and oldest U.S. stock market. For the past several years, it has been fiercely competing with NASDAQ for listings. The organization has recently been upgrading its services and cutting costs. Its sales are increasing, and its work force is stable.

NOMURA SECURITIES INTERNATIONAL, INC. ★

2 World Financial Ctr., Bldg. B, New York, NY 10281-1198; 212-667-9300
http://www.nomurany.com
Employees: 9,888
Sales: $7,581.8 million
Key Personnel: Co-Chairman, CEO: Joseph R. Schmuckler. Cochairman, CEO: Atsushi Yoshikawa. Human Resources Manager: Elizabeth Skrobisch.
The third largest brokerage company in Japan, Nomura Securities is also a top bond underwriter and is heavily involved in equity-related issues in the Euromarket. The company's main focus is stock brokerage. Nomura is investigating increased investments in China and other Asian countries. Difficulties in Russian and Asian markets have made growth difficult. Its and work force are decreasing.
Other Locations: Worldwide HQ: Nomura Securities Co., Ltd., 1-9-1, Nihonbashi, Chuo-ku, Tokyo, 103, Japan; phone: +81-3-3211-1811.

PAINE WEBBER GROUP, INC. ★★

1285 Ave. of the Americas, New York, NY 10019; 212-713-2000
http://www.painewebber.com
Employees: 17,800
Revenues: $ 7,249.6 million
Key Personnel: Chairman, CEO: Donald B. Marron. SVP, CFO: Regina A. Dolan. EVP Administration (Human Resources): Matthew Levitan.
A full-service brokerage, the Paine Webber Group has a significant presence in the United States and abroad. Among its services are asset management, municipal securities underwriting, and real estate services. The company recently pur-

chased a new high-tech system to monitor trading activities. Its sales and work force have increased.
Other Locations: The company has nearly 300 offices in France, Hong Kong, Japan, Puerto Rico, Switzerland, the United Kingdom, and the United States.

SALOMON SMITH BARNEY HOLDINGS, INC. ★★

388 Greenwich St. New York, NY 10013; 212-816-6000
http://www.smithbarney.com
Employees: 36,293
Revenues: $ 20,673.0 million
Key Personnel: Co-CEO: Deryck C. Maughan.Co-CEO: James Dimon. VC Equities: Steven Black. Human Resources Manager: Colleen O'Hora.
Salomon Smith Barney Holdings (formerly Salomon Inc.) , is a subsidiary of Traveler's Group. It was formed from the 1997 merger of investment banking firm Salomon Inc. with Traveler's Smith Barney brokerage. Salomon Smith Barney provides asset management and financial research. Its Philbro Division is a commodities trading company. Salomon is also involved in many investment activities and oil refining, through a Russian joint venture.
Other Locations: The company has some 500 offices in 100 countries worldwide.

STUDENT LOAN CORPORATION

99 Garnsey Rd., Pittsford, NY 14534, 716-248-7187
http://www.studentloan.com
Employees: 464
Revenues: $648.9 million
Key Personnel: Chairman, CEO: Carl E. Levinson. VP, CFO: Yiannis Zographakis. Human Resources Manager: Gerald J. Bystrak.
The Student Loan Corporation Marketing Association, is a publicly mandated private corporation. It lends money to banks for student loans and buys student loans. The company also finances capital purchases and provides loan management services for schools and universities. Its sales are up, but work force has decreased.

TEXAS

ASSOCIATES FIRST CAPITAL CORP. ★★
250 E. Carpenter Fwy., Irving, TX

75062-2729; 972-652-4000
http://www.theassociates.com
Employees: 28,662
Sales: $ 9,376.8 million
Key Personnel: Chairman, CEO: Keith W. Hughes. SEVP, CFO: Roy A. Guthrie. Human Resources Manager: Michael E. McGill.
Associates First Capital is the largest consumer finance company in the U.S. They offer home equity loans (one-third of its portfolio), personal loans; MasterCard, Visa, and a variety of oil, retail and credit cards for companies like Texaco and Shell. It also offers financing and leasing of heavy equipment. Work force and sales continue to grow rapidly. Associates First has 4000 offices in 16 countries.

PENNSYLVANIA

ADVANTA CORP. ★★
Welsh and McKean Rd, Spring House, PA 19477; 215-657-4000
Employees: 2,568
Assets: $ 662.7million
Key Personnel: Chairman, CEO: Dennis Alter. President: Olaf Olafsson. Human Resources Manager: John Walp.
Advanta began in the 1950s as a home business providing unsecured loans to teachers. It has since expanded into a diversified corporation that leases equipment, services and originates home mortgages, and offers various types of insurance to its customers. It has eliminated its consumer credit card business and its auto finance department. Its assets and work force are dropping.

❶ FOOD (RETAIL)

ALABAMA
BRUNO'S, INC. ★★
800 Lakeshore Pkwy., Birmingham, AL 35211; 205-940-9400
http://www.brunos.com
Employees: 12,700
Sales: $1,883.2 million
Key Personnel: Chairman, President, and CEO: James A. Demme. SVP Merchandising, Bruce A. Efird. SVP Human Resources: Laura Hayden.
Long a family business, Bruno's was purchased in 1995 by Kohlberg Kravis Roberts. The company runs several

chains of food stores, including Food-Max, Bruno's Food and Pharmacy, and Food Fair. It has typically followed a policy of refurbishing existing stores rather than opening new ones. Currently operating under Chapter 11 bankruptcy protection, sales and work force are both up after large drops.

Other Locations: The company has more than 100 stores in four states.

CALIFORNIA

SAFEWAY, INC. ★★

5918 Stoneridge Mall Rd., Pleasanton, CA 94588; 925-467-3000

http://www.safeway.com

Employees: 170,000

Sales: $24,484.2 million

Key Personnel: Chairman, President and CEO: Steven A. Burd. EVP Labor Relations, Human Resources, Law, and Public Affairs: Kenneth W. Oder.

One of the largest grocers in the North America, Safeway has made a comeback after years of stagnation. In addition to its Safeway stores, it also owns the Vons Companies and many other interests. Its comeback was achieved primarily by cutting staff, benefits, and wages. Sales and work force are now rising.

Other Locations: The company operates approximately 1,500 stores in the United States and Canada.

CONNECTICUT

TOSCO CORPORATION

72 Cummings Point Rd., Stamford, CT 06902; 203-977-1000

http://www.tosco.com

Employees: 26,300

Sales: $12,021.5 million

Key Personnel: Chairman, CEO: Thomas D. O'Malley. EVP, President, Tosco Marketing: Robert J. Lavinia. Human Resources: Wanda Williams.

Tosco bought out Circle K in 1997, shortly after Circle K emerged from bankruptcy. Circle K is the second largest chain of convenience stores with over 2,500 outlets located primarily in the South. With that purchase, Tosco became the country's leading independent petroleum marketer. Sales are up; work force is steady.

FLORIDA

PUBLIX SUPER MARKETS, INC. ★

1936 George Jenkins Blvd., Lakeland,
FL 33815; 941-688-1188

Employees: 117,000

Sales: $12,067.1 million

Key Personnel: President: W. Edwin Crenshaw. EVP: Hoyt R. Barnett. Human Resources: James H. Rhodes II.

Known for its high customer satisfaction, Publix is one of the largest grocers in the United States. The company is largely employee-owned, nonunion, and promotes its employees from within its workforce. It has been accused of racial discrimination and gender bias in promotion and hiring by the United Food and Commercial Workers Union in an ongoing campaign against the company. Sales and work force are up.

Other Locations: The company has more than 510 grocery stores and other facilities in Florida, Georgia, and South Carolina.

WINN-DIXIE STORES, INC.

5050 Edgewood Ct., Jacksonville, FL 32254-3699; 904-783-5000

http://www.winn-dixie.com

Employees: 139,000

Sales: $14,136.5 million

Key Personnel: President: James Kufeldt. EVP Operations: Charles H. McKellar. Human Resources: L.H. May.

Known for its financial stability, Winn-Dixie Stores has grocery stores mainly in the South and the Bahamas. Its stores operate under several names, including Marketplace and Winn-Dixie. The company has been rapidly building new stores and remodeling old ones to compete with new competitors like Kmart and Wal-mart. Sales and work force have risen slightly.

Other Locations: The company has more than 1,100 stores, mostly in the southern United States.

GEORGIA

AHOLD USA, INC. ★★

950 E. Paces Ferry Rd., Ste. 2575, Atlanta, GA 30326; 404-262-6050

http://www.aholdusa.com

Employees: 116,772

Sales: $16,174 million

Key Personnel: President, CEO Ahold USA Support Services: Allan Noddle. CFO: Ernie Smith. EVP Human Resources: Gary Preston.

Ahold USA is a subsidiary of Royal Ahold, the largest food retailer in the

Netherlands. Royal Ahold is also one of the biggest grocers in the United States. Its primary store name in Europe is Albert Heijn. In the United States, it uses the names BI-LO and Edwards, and Stop and Shop among others. The company's goal is to become the dominant supermarket operator in the East. Sales and work force are both rising dramatically.

Other Locations: Worldwide HQ: Royal Ahold N.V., Albert Heijnweg 1, 1500EH Zaandam, The Netherlands; +31-75-659-9111. The company has over 2,100 specialty stores and supermarkets in Belgium, the Czech Republic, the Netherlands, Portugal, and the United States.

IDAHO

ALBERTSON'S, INC. ★

250 Parkcenter Blvd., Boise, ID 83726; 208-395-6200

http://www.albertsons.com
Employees: 100,000
Sales: $16,005.1 million
Key Personnel: EVP Development: Michael F. Reuling. EVP Marketing: Carl W. Pennington. Human Resources: Steven D. Young.

With its recent acquisition of American Stores, Albertson's became the #2 supermarket chain in the U.S. Reaching out to a diverse group of geographic markets has been the strength of Albertson's. The company has less trouble than others with regional economic downturns because it is spread out. Sales and work force are up.

Other Locations: The company has more than 700 stores in 19 states.

MARYLAND

GIANT FOOD, INC.

6300 Sheriff Rd., Landover, MD 20785-4303; 301-341-4100
Employees: 28,000
Sales: $4,230.6 million
Key Personnel: Chairman, President and CEO: Richard Baird. COO: Michael W. Broomfield. SVP Finance, CFO, and Treasurer: Mark H. Berey. Human Resources: Roger D. Olson.

Vertical integration has been the key to Giant Food's success. The company operates numerous supermarkets in the Washington, D.C., area, most combined with drugstores. Rather than hiring outside contractors, its subsidiaries design and build stores, buy real estate, and manufacture some products, such as ice cream and soft drinks. Sales and work force are increasing.

Other Locations: The company has more than 150 supermarkets in Delaware, the District of Columbia, Maryland, and Virginia and several drugstores and other facilities in Maryland.

MASSACHUSETTS

SHAW'S SUPERMARKETS, INC. ★★

140 Laurel St., East Bridgewater, MA 02333; 508-378-7211
http://www.shaws.com
Employees: 22,673
Sales: $4,874.9 million
Key Personnel: Chairman: David Bremner. President, CEO: Ross McLaren. SVP Human Resources: Ruth Bramson.

Shaw's Supermarkets is a subsidiary of J Sainsbury, one of the largest food retailers in the United Kingdom. The company runs a chain of supermarkets in New England. Approximately two-thirds of the company's sales are products sold under its "Shaw's Own" label. Sales and work force are up markedly.

Other Locations: Worldwide HQ: J Sainsbury PLC, Stamford House, Stamford St., London, SE1 9LL, United Kingdom; +44-171-695-6000.

STOP & SHOP COMPANIES, INC.

1385 Hancock St., Quincy Center Plaza, Quincy, MA 02169-5510; 781-380-8000
http://www.stopandshop.com
Employees: 40,000
Sales: $6,187 million
Key Personnel: President, CEO: William J. Grize. EVP, COO: Marc Smith. EVP Human Resources: William M. Vaughan III.

Among the largest supermarket chains in the New England region, Stop & Shop is a subsidiary of the Dutch retailer Royal Ahold. Super Stop & Shop superstores boast an especially wide variety of grocery and non-grocery merchandise. The stores also feature a number of specialty departments, such as floral shops, banks, pharmacies, and small bookstores. Sales and workforce are up.

Other Locations: The company has approximately 200 supermarkets in southern New England and New York.

MICHIGAN

MEIJER, INC.

2929 Walker Ave. NW, Grand Rapids, MI 49544; 616-453-6711

http://www.meijer.com
Employees: 80,000
Sales (Est.): $7,500 million
Key Personnel: Senior Chairman: Fred Meijer. Co-Chairman: Doug Meijer. SVP Human Resources: Windy Ray.

Meijer sells groceries and general merchandise in large stores of more than 200,000 square feet. Its strategy is to attract customers to its general merchandise by offering competitive food pricing. The company relies heavily on advertising to secure its customers. The company is expanding aggressively in the Midwest. Sales and work force are up.
Other Locations: The company has stores, gas stations, and other facilities in Illinois, Indiana, Kentucky, Michigan, and Ohio.

NEW JERSEY

GREAT ATLANTIC & PACIFIC TEA COMPANY, INC.

2 Paragon Dr., Montvale, NJ 07645; 201-573-9700

http://www.aptea.com
Employees: 83,400
Sales: $10,179.4 million
Key Personnel: Chairman: James Wood. President, CEO: Christian W. E. Haub. Human Resources: Laurane Magliari.

The Great Atlantic & Pacific Tea Company is among the largest grocers in the United States. Known best for its A&P stores, the company also has a number of other store names, including Dominion, Farmer Jack, and Food Mart. It also manufactures ice cream, baked goods, and deli products. Sales and work force are steady.
Other Locations: The company has more than 1,100 supermarkets in the United States and Canada.

PATHMARK STORES, INC.

200 Milik St., Carteret, NJ 07008; 732-499-3000

http://www.pathmark.com
Employees: 26,700
Sales: $3,655.2 million
Key Personnel: Chairman, President, and CEO: James L. Donald. EVP Operations: John Sheehan. Human Resources: Kevin Kane.

Pathmark Stores operates a chain of large grocery stores, featuring a wide selection of foods and general items. Most of its sales come from thousands of private-label items sold such as the No Frills, Pathmark, and Pathmark Preferred brands. Pathmark is in the process of being sold to Royal Ahold, which should provide the debt-ridden company with some desperately needed capital. Sales are virtually static, but workforce is up.
Other Locations: The company has more than 130 supermarkets and other facilities in the Northeast.

NORTH CAROLINA

FOOD LION, INC. ★

2110 Executive Dr., Salisbury, NC 28145-1330; 704-633-8250

http://www.foodlion.com
Employees: 92,125
Sales: $10,219.5 million
Key Personnel: SVP Operations, COO: Joseph C. Hall, Jr. SVP Merchandising: Pamela K. Kohn. VP Human Resources: L. Darrell Johnson.

One of the largest supermarket chains in the United States, Food Lion has made a comeback by remodeling stores and instituting a money-back guarantee. Three-fourths of its stores are in the Carolinas, Florida and Virginia. Sales are steady, but work force is increasing.
Other Locations: The company has more than 1,200 food stores in 14 states.

OHIO

THE KROGER CO.

1014 Vine St., Cincinnati, OH 45202; 513-762-4000

http://www.kroger.com
Employees: 213,000
Sales: $28,203.3 million
Key Personnel: Chairman, CEO: Joseph A. Pichler. President, COO: David B Dillon. Human Resources: Reuben Shaffer.

Kroger is the biggest supermarket chain in the United States. The company operates under several store names, including Kroger and City Market. It also operates convenience stores, among them Mini-Mart and Kwik Shop, and manufactures a variety of food products. The company is building new stores and experimenting with concepts, such as a shop-at-home

service. Sales are down, but its work force is up.
Other Locations: The company has more than 2,000 supermarkets and over 800 convenience stores, mostly in the South and Midwest.

OREGON

FRED MEYER, INC. ★
3800 SE 22nd Ave., Portland, OR 97202; 503-232-8844
http://www.fredmeyerstores.com
Employees: 92,000
Sales: $14,878.8 million
Key Personnel: Chairman: Ronald W. Burkle. President, COO: George Golleher. VC, CEO: Robert G. Miller.
One-stop shopping is the specialty of Fred Meyer, Inc., which has been newly acquired by Kroger. The company's stores sell everything from groceries to jewelry, under the same roof. It continues rapid expansions in Idaho, Oregon, Utah, and Washington. Sales have almost tripled and work force is up.
Other Locations: The company has more than 1,000 stores, most of them in the West.

TEXAS

H. E. BUTT GROCERY COMPANY
646 S. Main Ave., San Antonio, TX 78204; 210-938-8000
http://www.heb.com
Employees: 45,000
Sales: $7,000 million
Key Personnel: Chairman, CEO: Charles C. Butt. President, COO: James F. Clingman. SVP Human Resources: Diane Peck.
One of the largest food retailers in Texas, H. E. Butt Grocery has expanded into Louisiana and Mexico. The company operates under several names, including H. E. Butt Food Stores and Pantry Food Stores. Some of its units also incorporate drugstores. The company is expanding its share of the upscale grocery market. Sales are up but workforce numbers are static.
Other Locations: The company has stores and food processing facilities throughout Texas.

RANDALL'S FOOD MARKETS, INC. ★
3663 Briarpark Dr., Houston, TX 77042; 713-268-3500
http://www.randalls.com
Employees: 18,368
Sales: $2,419 million
Key Personnel: Chairman, CEO: R. Randall Onstead. SVP, Chief Information Officer: J. Russell Robinson. SVP Human Resources: Douglas G. Beckstett.
Randall's Food Markets has supermarkets in several Texas cities, primarily Houston. It uses the store names Randalls, Tom Thumb, and Simon David. The company also manufactures several varieties of food, such as baked goods and snacks. It has survived intense competition in recent years and continues to expand geographically. Sales and work force are up.
Other Locations: The company has more than 160 supermarkets in Texas.

7-ELEVEN, INC. ★
2711 N. Haskell Ave., Dallas, TX 75204-2906; 214-828-7011
http://www.7-eleven.com
Employees: 33,368
Sales: $7,257.8 million
Key Personnel: President, CEO: Clark J. Matthews II. VC: Toshifumi Suzuki. SVP: Masaaki Asakura.
Formerly the Southland Corporation, 7-Eleven is the world's largest convience store chain, operating more than 10,000 stores in the United States and in countries around the world. The company's sales come in large part from such products as Slurpees, cigarettes, and Citgo gas. Stores, many of which are franchised, also offer a wide selection of perishable and other grocery items. Sales and workforce are up.

WHOLE FOODS MARKET, INC. ★★
601 N. Lamar, Ste. 300, Austin, TX 78703; 512-477-4455
http://www.wholefoods.com
Employees: 14,200
Sales: $1,389.8 million
Key Personnel: Chairman, CEO: John Mackey. President: Chris Hitt. Human Resources: Jody Hatch.
The trend toward buying more wholesome food led to the success of Whole Foods Market. The company is the largest U.S. grocer specializing in natural foods. It operates more than 80 stores under the Whole Foods name, as well as Bread and Circus, Bread of Life, and Wellspring. Most natural food stores are small operations, but Whole Foods provides a one-stop shopping format. Sales

and work force are up substantially.
Other Locations: The company has stores in twenty states.

● FOOD AND BEVERAGES

ARKANSAS

TYSON FOODS, INC. ★★
2210 W. Oaklawn Dr., Springdale, AR 72762-6999; 501-290-4000
http://www.tyson.com
Employees: 70,500
Sales: $7,414.1 million
Key Personnel: Chairman: John H. Tyson. CEO: Wayne Britt. Human Resources: William P. Jaycox.
As consumers have turned toward chicken as a healthy alternative to beef, Tyson Foods has reaped the benefits. The company is a leader in the U.S. poultry market, with brands like Holly Farm and Weaver, and dominates poultry exports to Japan. It also sells beef, pork, and Mexican food products in domestic and foreign markets. Sales and workforce are up markedly.
Other Locations: The company has facilities in 20 states and 12 foreign countries.

LIFORNIA

DEL MONTE FOODS COMPANY
One Market St., San Francisco, CA 94105; 415-247-3000
http://www.delmonte.com
Employees: 13,450
Sales: $1,505 million
Key Personnel: Chairman: Richard W. Boyce. COO: Wesley J. Smith. Human Resources: Mark J. Buxton.
Del Monte Foods is the largest fruit and vegetable canner in the United States. The company buys approximately 1.2 million tons of produce each year. Its products are purchased by restaurants and government agencies and sold in retail outlets. The company went public in 1999 to combat years of debt problems. Its sales and work force are up.
Other Locations: The company has operations in the Caribbean, Central America, Mexico, the Philippines, and the United States.

DOLE FOOD COMPANY, INC. ★★
31365 Oak Crest Dr., Westlake Village, CA 91361; 805-879-6600

http://www.dole.com
Employees: 53,500
Sales: $4,424.2 million
Key Personnel: Chairman, CEO: David H. Murdock. President, COO: David A. DeLorenzo. VP Human Resources: George R. Horne.
Dole is the largest producer of fresh fruits and vegetables in the world. The company also produces dried foods and is the world's largest flower grower. Dole has been expanding its product line to include value-added products, such as salad kits and freshcut vegetables. Its sales and work force are growing.
Other Locations: The company has operations in 90-plus countries.

NESTLE USA, INC.
800 N. Brand Blvd., Glendale, CA 91203; 818-549-6000
http://www.nestle.com
Employees (overall Nestle): 231,881
Sales (overall Nestle): $52,168.3 million
Key Personnel:. Chairman, CEO: Joe Weller. President, COO: Robert W. Schult. EVP Human Resources: Cam Starrett.
Nestle USA is the U.S. division of Switzerland's Nestle S.A., the world's largest food products company. Known for its chocolate, milk products, and beverages, the company also sells pharmaceuticals under the Alcon brand and several brands of pet food. It has been criticized for promoting infant formula in Africa. Its sales and work force are rising
Other Locations: Worldwide HQ: Nestle S.A., Avenue Nestle 55, CH-1800 Vevey, Switzerland; +41-21-924-21-11. The company has 489 facilities in 69 countries.

GEORGIA

CAGLE'S, INC. ★★
2000 Hills Ave. NW, Atlanta, GA 30318; 404-355-2820
Employees: 3,500
Sales: $352 million
Key Personnel: Chairman, CEO: J. Douglas Cagle. President, COO: Jerry D. Gattis. VP New Product Development: George D. Cagle.
As consumer demand has shifted more toward chicken, Cagle's has adapted to the increase. The company is one of the largest poultry processors in the United States, butchering over 2 million chickens per week. Its subsidiary, Equity

Foods, supplies McDonald's with processed chicken. Sales have risen slightly, but workforce numbers are steady.

COCA-COLA COMPANY

One Coca-Cola Plaza, Atlanta, GA 30313; 404-676-2121
http://www.cocacola.com
Employees: 28,600
Sales: $18,813 million
Key Personnel: Chairman, CEO: M. Douglas Ivester. SVP, CFO: James E. Chesnut, Michael W. Walters.

Although cola consumption is declining, Coca-Cola Company is maintaining its hold on the market by introducing new drinks that appeal to current tastes, such as Fruitopia, Surge, and Barq's Root Beer. It also produces Sprite, Nestea, Minute Maid, and Hi-C. Its products are sold in more than 200 countries. Sales and workforce both remain steady.

ILLINOIS

ARCHER DANIELS MIDLAND COMPANY ★★

4666 Faries Pkwy., Decatur, IL 62526; 217-424-5200
http://www.admworld.com
Employees: 23,132
Sales: $14,283.3 million
Key Personnel: Chairman, CEO: G. Allen Andreas. EVP: Charles T. Bayless. Human Resources: Sheila Witts-Mannweiler.

Processing grain and seed is the specialty of Archer Daniels Midland. The company has 165 facilities, which process 150,000 tons of seed, grain, and vegetable products per day. It also makes a wide variety of other products, including vitamins, foods, and fuels. The company is expanding in Latin America, Eastern Europe, and Asia. In 1996 it agreed to pay record fines in connection with a price-fixing scandal. Its sales and work force are growing.

KEEBLER FOODS COMPANY

677 Larch Ave., Elmhurst, IL 60126; 630-833-2900
http://www.keebler.com
Employees: 12,200
Sales: $2,226.5 million
Key Personnel: Chairman: Robert P. Crozer. CEO, President: Sam K. Reed. Human Resources: Alan Gambrel.

The #2 cookie and cracker maker in the U.S., Keebler makes the most of its formidable cookie franchise by cashing in on a wide variety of markets. Its successful Keebler line of products includes Droxies, Fudge Shoppe, and Sandies cookies. The company also makes cookies and crackers under the Famous Amos, Cheeze-It, and Hi-Ho brands and bakes goods for the Girl Scouts, McDonald's, and Kellogg's. Sales and workforce are extremely healthy.

KRAFT FOODS, INC.

3 Lakes Dr., Northfield, IL 60093-2753; 847-646-2000
http://www.kraftfoods.com
Employees: 37,500
Sales: $17,312 million
Key Personnel: President, CEO: Robert A. Eckert. EVP, President Kraft Cheese: Mary Kay Haben. Human Resources: Terry M. Faulk.

A subsidiary of Phillip Morris, Kraft is the nation's #1 food company. Its products range from Oscar Mayer wieners and bologna to Kool-Aid, Maxwell House Coffee, and Di Giorno frozen pizzas. The company has around 50 manufacturing plants and well over 200 food distribution centers located around the U.S. Sales and workforce are both on the rise.

QUAKER OATS COMPANY ★★

Quaker Tower, 321 N. Clark St., Chicago, IL 60610-4714; 312-222-7111
http://www.quakeroats.com
Employees: 11,860
Sales: $4,842.5 million
Key Personnel: Chairman, President, and CEO: Robert S. Morrison. SVP, CFO: Terence D. Martin. SVP Human Resources: Pamela Hewitt.

A large food conglomerate selling cereals and beverages, Quaker Oats has a comprehensive product line and an effective distribution network. Famous for its line of cereals (such as Quaker Oat Bran, Life, and Cap'n Crunch), the company also sells rice cakes and sports drinks such as Gatorade. It produces Aunt Jemima, Celeste pizza, Van Camp's pork and beans, Ken-L-Ration, and Gaines. Quaker is consolidating its operations, after selling off its unprofitable Snapple operation. Sales are up and work force is up markedly.
Other Locations: The company has operations in Argentina, the Benelux coun-

tries, Brazil, Colombia, France, Germany, Italy, Mexico, the United Kingdom, the United States, and Venezuela.

SARA LEE CORPORATION

3 First National Plaza, Chicago, IL
60602-4260; 312-726-2600
http://www.saralee.com
Employees: 139,000
Sales: $20,012 million
Key Personnel: Chairman, CEO: John H. Bryan. President, COO: C. Steven McMillan. Human Resources: Gary C. Grom.

While Sara Lee is best known for pound cake and other desserts, the company also manufactures a wide variety of other grocery and consumer goods, including jewelry and underwear. Its brands include Ball Park, Hillshire Farms, Hanes, L'eggs, Playtex, and Isotoner. A rapid shift in women's fashion away from sheer hosiery toward casual styles, caused steep drops in the company's profits recently. Sales and workforce remain steady.
Other Locations: The company has 310 plants in 27 states and 35 foreign countries.

TOOTSIE ROLL INDUSTRIES, INC.

7401 S. Cicero Ave., Chicago, IL 60629;
773-838-3400
http://www.tootsie.com
Employees: 1,750
Sales: $388.7 million
Key Personnel: Chairman, CEO: Melvin J. Gordon. President, COO: Ellen R. Gordon. Human Resources: Michael Hale.

Known for sticking to proven strategies, Tootsie Roll Industries has been making its namesake product since the late 1800s. The company also makes many other sweets, including Mason Dots, Charms, and Pom Poms. It is the top lollipop maker in the world. Sales are up slightly, but workforce numbers remain static.

WHITMAN CORPORATION

3501 Algonquin Rd., Rolling Meadows,
IL 60008; 847-818-5000
http://www.whitmancorp.com
Employees: 6,526
Sales: $1,635 million
Key Personnel: Chairman, CEO: Bruce S. Chelberg. EVP: Frank T. Westover.

Human Resources: Peter M. Perez.
Begun as a Midwestern railroad company in the 1800s, Whitman has gone through many iterations. The latest change occured in 1998 when it divested itself of two of its prime operations: Midas Muffler and Hussman Corp. The company now focuses on its Pepsi-Cola General Bottlers, the largest U.S. independent Pepsi bottler. It also distributes other drinks such as Mug Root Beer and Ocean Spray fruit beverages. Both sales and work force are up moderately.
Other Locations: The company's Pepsi facilities are concentrated in 12 U.S. states, Poland, and several former Soviet republics.

WM. WRIGLEY JR. COMPANY ★★

410 N. Michigan Ave., Chicago, IL
60611; 312-644-2121
http://www.wrigley.com
Employees: 9,200
Sales: $2,004.7 million
Key Personnel: President, CEO: William Wrigley, Jr. EVP: John F. Bard. Human Resources: David E. Boxwell.

The world's largest chewing gum manufacturer, Wm. Wrigley Jr., controls nearly half the U.S. market for its products. Its success is attributed to low overhead, low prices, and effective marketing. The company recently sold its Singapore affiliate but is expanding elsewhere in Asia. Sales and work force are up.
Other Locations: The company operates in 27 countries.

MARYLAND

PERDUE FARMS, INC.

Old Ocean City Rd., Salisbury, MD
21804; 410-543-3000
http://www.perdue.com
Employees: 18,000
Est. **Sales:** $2,200 million
Key Personnel: Chairman, CEO: James A. Perdue. President, COO: Robert A. Turley. Human Resources: Rob Heflin.

Perdue Farms started in the chicken business by supplying eggs to the New York City area in the 1920s. The company is now the fourth largest poultry processor in the United States and the leading Northeastern supplier. The company recently began selling substantial amounts of turkey products as well. Its sales and work force are static.
Other Locations: The company has

processing plants in Delaware, Indiana, Maryland, North Carolina, and Virginia.

MASSACHUSETTS

OCEAN SPRAY CRANBERRIES, INC.

One Ocean Spray Dr., Lakeville-Middleboro, MA 02349-0001; 508-946-1000
http://www.oceanspray.com
Employees: 2,350
Sales: $1,479.6 million
Key Personnel: President, CEO: Thomas E. Bullock. EVP, COO: Kevin B. Murphy. Human Resources: Nancy McDermott.

Agricultural cooperative Ocean Spray Cranberries is the largest force in the cranberry industry. Owned by 750 cranberry growers and 150 citrus growers, the co-op is the one of the biggest privately held food companies in the United States. The company's focus is on controlling prices to keep growers' earnings stable. Its sales and workforce are up slightly.

MICHIGAN

KELLOGG COMPANY

One Kellogg Sq., Battle Creek, MI 49016-3599; 616-961-2000
http://www.kelloggs.com
Employees: 14,498
Sales: $6,762.1 million
Key Personnel: Chairman: Arnold G. Langbo. President, CEO: Carlos M. Gutierrez. Human Resources: James W. Larson.

The largest maker of ready-to-eat cereal in the world, Kellogg produces Frosted Flakes, Rice Krispies, and Froot Loops, as well as Pop Tarts and Eggo products. The company is adjusting its approach as the market has become more health conscious. The company is adding brands, such as Healthy Choice, to fill that need. Sales and workforce are up slightly.
Other Locations: The company has manufacturing facilities in 20 countries.

MINNESOTA

ASSOCIATED MILK PRODUCERS, INC.

315 N. Broadway, New Ulm, MN 56073-0455
Employees: 1,600
Sales: $1,100 million
Key Personnel: President: Wayne Bok. Controller: Ken Spoon. Director Human Resources: Gaylee Bjerke.

Associated Milk Producers (AMPI) is the remainder of what was once the largest dairy cooperative in the United States. In 1997, its Southern region split from the group and joined with three other co-ops to found Dairy Farmers of America, the new #1 U.S. dairy cooperative. Still formidable, AMPI has more than 5,000 members in the Midwest. The company accounts for approximately 75 percent of the nation's instant milk sales. Sales are up healthily, but workforce remains static.

GENERAL MILLS, INC. ★★

One General Mills Blvd., Minneapolis, MN 55426; 612-540-2311
http://www.generalmills.com
Employees: 10,200
Sales: $6,246.1 million
Key Personnel: Chairman, CEO: Stephen W. Sanger. VC: Raymond G. Viault. Human Resources: Michael A. Peel.

General Mills is the second largest cereal maker in the United States, selling Wheaties and Cheerios. It makes many consumer products under numerous brand names, including Betty Crocker, Hamburger Helper, and Yoplait. The company is offloading some units to focus on consumer foods. Recently, it acquired the Chex cereal and snack lines from Ralston Purina. Sales are up moderately, but workforce numbers are static.

HORMEL FOODS CORPORATION

One Hormel Pl., Austin, MN 55912-3680; 507-437-5611
http://www.hormel.com
Employees: 11,200
Sales: $3,261 million
Key Personnel: Chairman, President, and CEO: Joel W. Johnson. EVP: Gary J. Ray. Human Resources: James A. Jorgenson.

One of the biggest pork processors in the world, Hormel Foods has found success through brand recognition and internationalization. Among the company's brands are Spam, Dinty Moore, and Herb-Ox. With pork prices low, the company has been expanding and upgrading its operations in the United States and abroad. It is also the #1 turkey processor in the U.S. Sales are static, but work force is up slightly.
Other Locations: The company has facilities in 12 states and joint ventures in

Australia, China, Mexico, and the Philippines.

LAND O' LAKES, INC. ★★
4001 Lexington Ave. N., Arden Hills, MN 55126; 651-481-2222
http://www.landolakesinc.com
Employees: 6,500
Sales: $5,174.2 million
Key Personnel: President, CEO: John E. Gherty. EVP, COO: Duane Halverson. VP Human Resources: Jack Martin.
Land O' Lakes is the largest butter producer in the United States. An agricultural cooperative, it is the only company that markets branded butter. The company also sells cheese, other dairy products, and agricultural supplies. The company serves more than 300,000 farms in the Midwest and Pacific Northwest. Its sales and work force are increasing markedly.

MISSOURI
FARMLAND INDUSTRIES, INC. ★★
3315 N. Oak Trafficway, Kansas City, MO 64116-0005; 816-459-6000
http://www.farmland.com
Employees: 16,100
Sales: $8,775 million
Key Personnel: Chairman: Albert J. Shively. President, CEO: Harry D. Cleberg. VP Human Resources: Holly D. McCoy.
Farmland Industries is the largest agricultural cooperative in the United States. The cooperative is owned by approximately 8,000 livestock producers and 1,500 small cooperatives in the Midwest. Farmland's planned merger with Cenex (#2 U.S. farm co-op) will push membership even higher. Sales of agricultural commodities account for the bulk of the organization's revenue. Sales and work force have been increasing steadily for the past 10 years.
Other Locations: The company has facilities in Iowa, Kansas, Missouri, Nebraska, and Texas.

INTERSTATE BAKERIES CORPORATION ★
12 E. Armour Blvd., Kansas City, MO 64111; 816-502-4000
Employees: 34,000
Sales: $3,459.4 million
Key Personnel: Chairman, CEO: Charles A. Sullivan. President, COO: Michael D. Kafoure. SVP Human Resources:

Russell Baker.
Known for its line of sweet baked goods, Interstate Bakeries is the largest wholesale baking enterprise in the United States after its purchase of Ralston Continental Baking in July 1995. The company also makes several national and regional bread brands including Wonder, Merita, and Home Pride. The company's large fleet of delivery trucks supplies over 250,000 U.S. retailers. Sales and work force are up.
Other Locations: The company has 66 baking facilities in 32 states.

RALSTON PURINA COMPANY ★★
Checkerboard Sq., St. Louis, MO 63164-0001; 314-982-1000
http://www.ralston.com
Employees: 22,435
Sales: $4,653.3 million
Key Personnel: President, CEO: W. Patrick McGinnis. Chairman, CEO, Eveready Battery: J. Patrick Mulcahy. Human Resources: Charles Sommer.
Ralston Purina is the country's number one producer of dry pet food (under the Purina label), and the second largest producer of alkaline batteries (under the Eveready brand). The company recently sold its dry cereal line (Chex) to General Mills. It is now planning to spin off its battery division to further tighten its focus on pet foods and products. Both sales and work force are up.
Other Locations: The company makes human and pet food at 21 facilities, and batteries at 37 plants worldwide.

NEBRASKA
CONAGRA
One ConAgra Dr., Omaha, NE 68102; 402-595-4000
http://www.conagra.com
Employees: 80,000
Sales: $24,594.3 million
Key Personnel: Chairman, President, and CEO: Bruce C. Rohde. EVP, CFO: James P. O'Donnell. Human Resources: Owen C. Johnson.
ConAgra is the second largest food company in the United States. It sells consumer and agricultural products and trades agricultural commodities. Among its product lines are Healthy Choice, Hunt's, and Slim Jim. The company also owns general stores, such as Peavey Ranch and Home, and fabric stores, including Rainbow Bay Crafts. In 1996 the

company restructured, eliminating thousands of jobs. Sales and work force are up slightly.
Other Locations: The company has offices in 35 countries.

NEW JERSEY

CAMPBELL SOUP COMPANY ★★
Campbell Pl., Camden, NJ 08103-1799; 856-342-4800
http://www.campbellsoups.com
Employees: 24,250
Sales: $6,424 million
Key Personnel: President, CEO: Dale F. Morrison. EVP, CFO: Basil L. Anderson. Human Resources: Edward F. Walsh.
Since its inception in 1869, Campbell Soup has been a well-marketed, conservatively managed food company. The company sells its products under an extensive array of brands, both domestically and abroad. Those brands include Franco-American, V-8, Swanson, Prego, Mrs. Paul's, and Pepperidge Farm. Campbell recently acquired the Pace brand, which it will use for a new line of Mexican-style products. Its sales are up and its workforce is up markedly.

BESTFOODS ★
700 Sylvan Ave., International Plaza, Englewood Cliffs, NJ 07632-9976; 201-894-4000
http://www.bestfoods.com
Employees: 42,000
Sales: $8,374 million
Key Personnel: Chairman, President, and CEO: Charles R. Shoemate. EVP, President Bestfoods Europe: Alain Labergere. SVP Human Resources: Richard P. Bergman.
Bestfoods (formerly CPC International) is a major manufacturer and distributor of food throughout the world. With 1,700 trademarked brands (such as Skippy peanut butter, Hellmann's mayonnaise, Mazola corn oil, Arnold bread, and Thomas' English muffins), the company is banking on the strong demand for American brands in foreign markets. More than 60 percent of its income now comes from abroad. Its sales are steady but its work force is up.
Other Locations: The company has 27 plants in the United States and 116 in foreign countries.

NEW YORK

AGWAY, INC.
333 Butternut Dr., DeWitt, NY 13214; 315-449-6436
http://www.agway.com
Employees: 7,100
Sales: $1,562.9 million
Key Personnel: Chairman: Ralph H. Heffner. VC: Gary K. Van Slyke. VP Human Resources: Betty Goyette.
With more than 80,000 members, Agway is the second largest farm cooperative in the United States and the largest in the Northeast. The organization sells a wide variety of goods and services to both the agricultural and consumer markets. Sales and number of employees have steadily declined over the last 10 years. This decline levelled off last year with sales growing moderately and workforce holding steady.
Other Locations: Agway has offices in 12 states.

CHOCK FULL O'NUTS CORPORATION
370 Lexington Ave., New York, NY 10017; 212-532-0300
http://www.chockfullonuts.com
Employees: 1,430
Sales: $396.4 million
Key Personnel: Chairman: Norman E. Alexander. President, CEO: Marvin I. Haas. Human Resources: Peter Baer.
Chock Full o' Nuts is among the oldest trade names in the food service industry. Famous for its coffee, the company was a pioneer in the franchise industry with its chain of restaurants and is returning to that industry after a 12-year hiatus. After initial resistance, the company has agreed to be bought out by food giant Sara Lee. Its sales and work force are up.
Other Locations: The company has facilities in Florida, Missouri, New York, and Oklahoma.

DANNON CO.
120 White Plains Rd., Tarrytown, NY 10591-5536; 914-366-9700
http://www.dannon.com
Employees (US): 876
Sales (US): $522 million
Key Personnel: President, CEO: Thomas Kunz. CFO: Rick Lees. VP Human Resources: Robert Mozdean.
Dannon is a subsidiary of Groupe Danone, one of the largest food producers in the world. The company is a lead-

ing producer of fresh dairy products, mineral water, and biscuits. It has expanded through investments, joint ventures, and acquisitions in Asia and Eastern Europe for several years. Its sales and work force are steady.

Other Locations: Worldwide HQ: Groupe Danone, 7, Rue de Teheran, Paris, France; +33-1-44-35-20-20.

DOMINO SUGAR CORPORATION

1114 Ave. of the Americas, New York, NY 10036; 212-789-9700
Employees (overall T&L): 21,494
Sales (overall T&L): $7,588.1 million
Key Personnel:. President, CEO: Andrew A. Ferrier. CFO: Inder Mathur.
Domino Sugar is a subsidiary of Tate & Lyle, one of the largest processed sugar makers in the world. The company makes sugar, molasses, starches, and other sweeteners from beets and sugarcane. It also makes rum and animal feeds and is involved in the development of artificial sweeteners. Its sales and work force are steady.

Other Locations: Worldwide HQ: Tate & Lyle PLC, Sugar Quay, Lower Thames St., London, EC3R 6DQ, United Kingdom; +44-171-626-6525.

INTERNATIONAL FLAVORS & FRAGRANCES, INC.

521 W. 57th St., New York, NY 10019; 212-765-5500
Employees: 4,670
Sales: $1,407.3 million
Key Personnel: Chairman, President, and CEO: Eugene P. Grisanti. VP, President Flavor Division: Robert G. Corbett. CFO: Douglas J. Wetmore.
One of the world's largest producers of synthetic tastes and scents, International Flavors & Fragrances is getting larger. Its sales of natural flavorings are growing in the United States, as are its European sales of fragrances. The company is introducing new formulations to produce cool, hot, wet, and creamy sensations. Sales and work force are steady.
Other Locations: The company has offices and facilities in 33 countries.

PEPSICO, INC. ★

700 Anderson Hill Rd., Purchase, NY 10577-1444; 914-253-2000
http://www.pepsico.com
Employees: 150,000
Sales: $22,348 million

Key Personnel: Chairman, CEO: Roger A. Enrico. VC: Karl M. von der Heyden. SVP Personnel (HR): William R. Bensyl.
The second largest soft-drink company in the world, producing Pepsi-Cola, Mountain Dew, and Slice, PepsiCo is also the number one maker of snack chips (Frito-Lay, maker of Fritos). The company has shrunk since spinning off its largest division—fast food restaurants such as Taco Bell, Pizza Hut and KFC—as TRICON Global Restaurants. It is aggressively expanding in India and Asia and has recently acquired Tropicana. Sales and work force are on the rise.

NABISCO GROUP HOLDINGS CORPORATION ★

1301 Ave. of the Americas, New York, NY 10019; 212-258-5600
http://www.rjrnabisco.com
Employees: 74,000
Sales: $17,037 million
Key Personnel: Chairman, President, and CEO: Steven F. Goldstone. SVP, General Auditor: Jeffrey A. Kuchar. Human Resources: Gerald I. Angowitz.
In an increasingly hostile legal environment, RJR Nabisco recently split its operation to protect its Nabisco food division from potential legal damages from suits against R. J. Reynolds, its tobacco division. The company sells such foods as Oreos and Ritz and such cigarettes as Winston, Salem, and Camel. Sales are steady and work force is up.

OHIO

BORDEN, INC. ★★

180 E. Broad St., Columbus, OH 43215; 614-225-4000
Employees: 4,200
Sales: $1,399.7 million
Key Personnel: Chairman, President, and CEO: C. Robert Kidder. EVP, CFO: William H. Carter. Human Resources: Nancy A. Reardon.
Although the name Borden is associated with milk and dairy products, the company sold off its dairy division to Southern Foods Coporation.in 1997. It is still one of the largest producers of pasta, soup mixes, adhesives (Elmer's Glue) and industrial adhesives. Since dumping the dairy business, the company's sales and work force have risen dramatically.
Other Locations: The company has 99 facilities in the United States and Puerto Rico and 103 facilities abroad.

CHIQUITA BRANDS INTERNATIONAL, INC. ★

250 E. Fifth St., Cincinnati, OH 45202; 513-784-8000
http://www.chiquita.com
Employees: 37,000
Sales: $2,720.4 million
Key Personnel: Chairman, CEO: Carl H. Lindner. VC: Keith E. Lindner. Human Resources: Jean B. Lapointe.

A leading worldwide fruit and vegetable producer, Chiquita Brands International derives more than 60 percent of its income from bananas. The company also produces and markets other fruit, including avacados, citrus, and mangoes. It has faced stiff price competition in the United States. Sales and work force are both up healthily.

THE J. M. SMUCKER COMPANY ★

One Strawberry Lane, Orrville, OH 44667-0280; 330-682-3000
http://www.smucker.com
Employees: 2,100
Sales: $602.5 million
Key Personnel: Chairman: Timothy P. Smucker. President: Richard K. Smucker. VP Operations: Robert R. Morrison. Human Resources: Robert E. Ellis.

J. M. Smucker is the largest U.S. manufacturer of jellies, jams, and preserves. The company also makes ketchup, peanut butter, and many organic fruit juices. The company is actively expanding its line of natural products, evidenced by its recent purchase of Laura Scudder's Natural Peanut Butter from BAMA. Sales and workforce are up.

PENNSYLVANIA

H. J. HEINZ COMPANY ★

600 Grant St., Pittsburgh, PA 15219; 412-456-5700
http://www.heinz.com
Employees: 38,600
Sales: $9,299.6 million
Key Personnel: President, CEO: William R. Johnson. EVP, CFO: Paul F. Renne. Human Resources: Gary Matson.

Begun as a market garden business in the 1800s, H. J. Heinz has grown to international proportions. The company has a dominant market position in ketchup, frozen potatoes (Ore-Ida), cat food (9 Lives), and diet food (Weight Watchers). It also makes Star-Kist. Heinz is expanding its presence abroad, with acquisitions in the United Kingdom and India. Sales are steady and work force is down.
Other Locations: The company has 88 facilities in 21 countries.

HERSHEY FOODS CORPORATION

100 Crystal A Dr., Hershey, PA 17033; 717-534-6799
http://www.hersheys.com
Employees: 16,200
Sales: $4,435.6 million
Key Personnel: Chairman, CEO: Kenneth L. Wolfe. VC, President, and COO: Joseph P. Viviano. Human Resources: John R. Canavan.

Hershey Foods is more than chocolate. Besides being the largest confectioner in the world (producing Reese's peanut butter cups, Kit Kat, and Almond Joy), the company is also one of the largest U.S. dry pasta makers, with brands such as Ronzoni and American Beauty. It has numerous businesses around the world, including Mexican candy maker Nacional de Dulces. Its sales are up slightly and its work force is holding steady.
Other Locations: The company makes candy in California, Pennsylvania, Virginia, and Ontario.

SOUTH DAKOTA

IBP, INC. ★

800 Stevens Port Dr., Ste. 836, Dakota Dunes, SD 57049; 605-235-2061
http://www.ibpinc.com
Employees: 40,000
Sales: $12,848.6 million
Key Personnel: Chairman, CEO: Robert L. Peterson. President, COO: Richard L. Bond. Human Resources: Kenneth J. Kimbro.

IBP is the one of the largest beef and pork producers in the world. It is expanding into Japan, Eastern Europe, and Russia. The company recently began testing new steam vacuum equipment for removing contaminants from meat. Both sales and work force are rising.
Other Locations: The company has 53 facilities in 13 states and Canada, Japan, and the United Kingdom.

TEXAS

DR PEPPER/SEVEN UP INC. ★

5301 Legacy Dr., Plano, TX 75024-3109; 972-673-7000

Employees (overall Cadbury): 38,656
Sales (overall Cadbury): $6,813.9 million
Key Personnel: President, CEO: Todd Stitzer. President, COO Dr Pepper: Jack Kilduff. President, COO Cadbury Beverages/Seven Up: Michael S. McGrath.
Dr. Pepper/Seven-Up, a subsidiary of Cadbury Schweppes PLC) is the number three soft drink maker in the world and one of the largest soft drink companies in the United States. The company, which has a plant in Missouri, also operates a restaurant service in which it supplies its customers with syrup for soft drinks made on site. Its customers include Burger King and McDonald's. Sales and work force are decreasing.

PILGRIM'S PRIDE CORPORATION
110 S. Texas St., Pittsburg, TX 75686-0093; 903-855-1000
http://www.pilgrimspride.com
Employees: 13,000
Sales: $1,331.5 million
Key Personnel: President, CEO, and COO: David Van Hoose. EVP, CFO: Richard A. Codgill. Human Resources: Ray Gameson.
One of the largest U.S. poultry producers, Pilgrim's Pride also has the second largest poultry operation in Mexico. The company has a comprehensive operation encompassing breeding, hatching, raising, processing, and marketing. Pilgrim sells fresh and processed chicken in retail and food service markets. Its sales are up but its work force is static.
Other Locations: The company has facilities in Arizona, Arkansas, Oklahoma, Texas, and Mexico.

VIRGINIA
INTERBAKE FOODS ★★
2821 Emerywood Pkwy, Ste. 210, Richmond, VA 23294; 804-755-7107
Employees (overall George Weston: 124,000
Sales (overall George Weston): $9,573.5 million
Key Personnel: President, CEO: Raymond A. Baxter. CFO: Don Niemeyer. Director of Human Resources: Page Stowers.
Interbake Foods is a subsidiary of George Weston, a Canadian conglomerate that focuses in three areas. Weston Foods produces candy and dairy and baked products. Weston Resources is a timber

and fishing processing company. Loblaw Companies is Canada's largest food distributor and also has a chain of stores. Sales are up slightly and work force numbers have skyrocketed.
Other Locations: Worldwide HQ: George Weston, Ltd., 22 St. Clair Ave. E., Toronto, Ontario M4T 2S7 Canada; 416-922-2500.

MARS, INC. ★
6885 Elm St., McLean, VA 22101-3810; 703-821-4900
http://www.mars.com
Employees: 30,000
Sales (est.): $15,000 million
Key Personnel: CEO, Co-president: Forrest E. Mars, Jr. Co-president: John F. Mars. VP: Vito J. Spitaleri.
Once the largest confectioner in the world, Mars is now in second place. It is also the fifth largest privately held company in the United States. Its loss of market share has been blamed on the company's failure to introduce new products. Mars also sells pet food and rice. Its sales have held steady and work force numbers are up.
Other Locations: The company has plants in seven states.

❶ FOREST/PAPER PRODUCTS

ALABAMA
MACMILLAN BLOEDEL PACKAGING, INC.
4001 Carmichael Rd., Ste. 300, Montgomery, AL 36106-3635; 334-213-6100
http://www.mbpi.com
Employees: 2,700
Sales (overall MacMillan Bloedel): $2,702.2 million
Key Personnel: President, SVP Packaging Group MacMillan Bloedel Ltd.: Frederick V. Ernst. VP Converting: Larry Barber. VP Human Resources: Charles F. Perkins.
Canada's largest forest products company is MacMillan Bloedel. It manufactures many varieties of building products, including lumber, panelboard, and engineered wood. The U.S. branch of the company also makes packaging materials, such as containerboard and corrugated containers. It is restructuring operations to cut costs. Sales are up, but work force is static.
Other Locations: Worldwide HQ: MacMillan Bloedel Ltd., 925 W. Georgia

St., Vancouver, British Columbia V6C 3L2, Canada; 604-661-8000.

CONNECTICUT

CHAMPION INTERNATIONAL CORP. ★★
One Champion Plaza, Stamford, CT 06921; 203-358-7000
http://www.championpaper.com
Employees: 21,137
Sales: $5,653 million
Key Personnel: Chairman, CEO: Richard E. Olson. VC, Executive Officer: Kenwood C. Nichols. Human Resources: Mark V. Childers.

Champion International is one of the largest paper and wood products manufacturers in the United States. Worldwide economic problems continue to hamper sales, but workforce is up markedly.
Other Locations: The company has facilities in Brazil, Canada, and the United States.

GEORGIA

GEORGIA-PACIFIC CORPORATION
Georgia-Pacific Center, 133 Peachtree St. NE, Atlanta, GA 30303; 404-652-4000
http://www.gp.com
Employees: 45,000
Sales: $13,223 million
Key Personnel: Chairman, President, and CEO: Alston D. Correll. EVP Finance, CFO: John F. McGovern. Human Resources: Patricia A. Barnard.

One of the largest forest products companies in the United States, Georgia-Pacific owns or leases more than 6 million acres of timberland in North America. The company has spent more than $1 billion upgrading its facilities in the 1990s. It makes building, pulp, and paper products. Its sales and work force are both up slightly.
Other Locations: The company has 221 facilities in the United States, two in Canada, and two in Mexico.

ROCK-TENN COMPANY ★
504 Thrasher St., Norcross, GA 30071; 770-448-2193
http://www.rocktenn.com
Employees: 8,856
Sales: $1,293.6 million
Key Personnel: Chairman, CEO: Bradley Currey, Jr. President, COO: Jay Shuster. Human Resources: Brad Newman.

One of the top North American manufacturers of solid-fiber partitions, 100-percent recycled paperboard, and folding cartons, Rock-Tenn is anticipating increased demand for its products. The company has grown in recent years through acquisition of operations that it could vertically integrate with existing divisions. Both sales and work force are up healthily.

IDAHO

BOISE CASCADE CORPORATION
1111 W. Jefferson St., Boise, ID 83728-0001; 208-384-6161
http://www.bc.com
Employees: 23,039
Sales: $6,162.1 million
Key Personnel: Chairman, CEO: George J. Harad. SVP, CFO: Theodore Crumley. Human Resources: J. Michael Gwartney.

The top U.S. supplier of wood, building supplies, office equipment, paper, and furniture, Boise Cascade is also the ninth largest domestic pulp and paper maker. The company's income has been slipping for several years; however, rising paper prices have reversed the trend. Its sales and work force are up.

ILLINOIS

SMURFIT-STONE CONTAINER CORPORATION ★★
150 N. Michigan Ave., Chicago, IL 60601; 312-346-6600
http://www.smurfit-stone.net
Employees: 38,000
Sales: $3,469 million
Key Personnel: Chairman: Michael W.J. Smurfit. President, CEO: Ray Curran. Human Resources: Michael F. Harrington.

The result of a merger between twin giants Jefferson Smurfit and Stone Container, Smurfit-Stone Container Corporation is the world's largest manufacturer of paper packaging and paperboard. Not only is Smurfit-Stone the top maker of paper bags, sacks, and boxes, but it is also a major manufacturer of newsprint and many other types of wood products. In a debt-shedding maneuver, the company plans to dump more than two billion dollars worth of its peripheral operations to focus on containers and paper products. Sales and workforce are both up markedly.
Other Locations: The company has more than 125 facilities in the United States and 60 in foreign countries.

MINNESOTA

BLANDIN PAPER COMPANY

115 SW First St., Grand Rapids, MN
55744; 218-327-6200
Employees (overall UPM): 32,351
Sales (overall UPM): $9,748.1 million.
Key Personnel: President, CEO: Kevin
Lyden. SVP Operations: Raimo Malkki.
VP Human Resources: Edward Zabinski.
Blandin Paper is a subsidiary of UPM-
Kymmene, the Finnish pulp and paper
manufacturer. Along with paper, the
company is involved in oil and gas ex-
ploration. Its sales and work force are up
for the first time in several years.
Other Locations: Worldwide HQ: UPM-
Kymenne Corporation, Etelaesplanadi 2,
PL 380, FIN-00171 Helsinki, Finland.

NEW YORK

INTERNATIONAL PAPER COMPANY

2 Manhattanville Rd., Purchase, NY
10577; 914-397-1500
http://www.ipaper.com
Employees: 80,000
Sales: $19,541 million
Key Personnel: Chairman, CEO: John T.
Dillon. EVP Operations Group: C.
Wesley Smith. Human Resources:
Marianne M. Parrs.
A top supplier of paper and office supply
products, International Paper is one of
the largest industrial corporations in the
United States. Among the company's
products are coated papers, file folders,
containerboard, and photographic films
and plates. Its sales and work force are
rising.
Other Locations: The company has fa-
cilities in 50 countries.

OHIO

MEAD CORPORATION ★★

Courthouse Plaza NE, Dayton, OH
45463; 937-495-6323
http://www.mead.com
Employees: 14,100
Sales: $3,772.2 million
Key Personnel: Chairman, President,
and CEO: Jerome F. Tatar. EVP: Raymond W. Lane. Human Resources: A.
Robert Rosenberger.
Mead Corporation is the largest maker
and distributor of school supplies in the
United States. The company seems to
have weathered the poor pulp and paper
sales of the early 1990s. Its sales and

workforce are up impressively.
Other Locations: The company has 18
packaging and paper mills in the United
States as well as foreign operations in 12
countries.

PENNSYLVANIA

UNISOURCE WORLDWIDE, INC.★

1100 Cassatt Rd., Berwyn, PA 19312;
610-296-4470
http://www.unisourcelink.com
Employees: 13,400
Sales: $7,417.3 million
Key Personnel: President: Charles C.
Tufano. VP, CFO: Matthew C. Tyser.
Human Resources: Gary E. Mask.
Recently purchased by Georgia-Pacific,
Unisource Worldwide is the result of
Alco Standard's 1997 split into two
companies. It is the largest distributor
and marketer of paper and supply systems in North America. The company
distributes printing and imaging products
for offices. The company has been shedding its Mexican interests to concentrate
on U.S. and Canadian business. Sales and
workforce are both up.

TEXAS

KIMBERLY-CLARK CORPORATION

351 Phelps Dr., Irving, TX 75038; 972-
281-1200
http://www.kimberly-clark.com
Employees: 54,700
Sales: $12,297.8 million
Key Personnel: Chairman, CEO:
Wayne R. Sanders. SVP, CFO: John W.
Donehower. VP Human Resources:
Bruce J. Olson.
One of the top makers of consumer tissue
products (like Kleenex), Kimberly-Clark
makes a wide variety of disposable dia-
pers and sanitary products for both children and adults (Huggies, Kotex), paper
towels and wipes, and many other products. The company, which owns approximately 700,000 acres of forest, purchased its competitor, Scott Paper, in
1997. Sales and work force are both rising.
Other Locations: The company has facilities in the United States and 25 foreign countries.

VIRGINIA

CHESAPEAKE CORPORATION ★

1021 E. Cary St., Richmond, VA 23218-
2350; 804-697-1000

http://www.cskcorp.com
Employees: 5,557
Sales: $950.4 million
Key Personnel: Chairman: J. Carter Fox. President, CEO: Thomas H. Johnson. Human Resources: Thomas A. Smith.
Chesapeake and its subsidiaries produce a variety of paper products, including corrugated shipping containers and point of purchase displays. Its tissue segment—which it plans to sell most of—makes over 2,000 varieties of napkins, towels and tissues. In addition, it makes kraft paper, paperboard, and bleached hardwood pulp it sells to other firms.
Other Locations: Chesapeake has facilities in Canada, France and Mexico in addition to the US.

WASHINGTON

WEYERHAEUSER COMPANY
33663 Weyerhaeuser Way South, Federal Way, WA 98003; 253-924-2345
http://www.weyerhaeuser.com
Employees: 35,000
Sales: $10,766 million
Key Personnel: President, CEO: Steven R. Rogel. EVP Wood Products: William R. Corbin. Human Resources: Steven R. Hill.
The largest private holder of softwood forest land, Weyerhaeuser manufactures a wide variety of building, paper, and packaging products. The company is expanding its overseas operations. It is the top exporter of newsprint and logs to Japan and is working with a South African partner on an international log distribution project. Sales and work force are up.

❶ FREIGHT/ TRANSPORTATION

ARKANSAS

AMERICAN FREIGHTWAYS CORPORATION ★
2200 Forward Dr., Harrison, AR 72601; 870-741-9000
http://www.arfw.com
Employees: 13,200
Sales: $986.3 million
Key Personnel: Chairman, CEO: F. Sheridan Garrison. President, COO: Tom Garrison. EVP Human Resources: Terry Stambaugh.
Relaxed interstate commerce regulations

have enhanced the business of American Freightways. The company offers "less-than-truckload" service to destinations in the Midwest, South, Southeast, and West. The company keeps its expenses low by relying on nonunion staff and high-tech equipment. All of its trucks are equipped with computers that track shipments. Its sales and work force are growing.
Other Locations: The company has more than 140 freight terminals in 22 states.

CALIFORNIA

APL, LTD. ★★
1111 Broadway, Oakland, CA 94607; 510-272-8000
http://www.apl.com
Employees: 3,980
Sales: $2,739.1 million
Key Personnel: President, CEO: Timothy J. Rhein. EVP: Michael Goh. VP Human Resources: Mike Maher.
Boasting a coordinated system of truck, rail, and ocean transportation linking Asia, the Middle East, and North America, APL (formerly American President Lines) has become the #2 U.S. shipping company. A subsidiary of Singapore's Neptune Orient Lines Ltd., APL's shipping line has over 25 containerships that serve more than 60 ports. Sales and work force are up.
Other Locations: The company has offices in 45 countries.

CONSOLIDATED FREIGHTWAYS, INC.
175 Linfield Dr., Menlo Park, CA 94025; 650-326-1700
http://www.cfwy.com
Employees: 21,000
Sales: $2,238.4 million
Key Personnel: CEO: W. Roger Curry. President, COO: Patrick H. Blake. Human Resources: Wayne Bolio.
Consolidated Freightways is both a freight and a package delivery company. Its long-haul trucking division is one of the biggest in the United States. The company also provides regional and second-day delivery services in North America, Mexico, and Puerto Rico. Consolidated also provides logistics, equipment supply, custom brokerage, and other services. Its sales and work force are up slightly.
Other Locations: The company has operations in North America, Puerto Rico, and 89 foreign countries.

DHL WORLDWIDE EXPRESS
333 Twin Dolphin Dr., Redwood City, CA 94065; 650-593-7474
http://www.dhl.com
Employees: 60,486
Sales (est.): $5,000 million
Key Personnel: CEO: Rob Kuijpers. Executive Chairman: Patrick Lupo. Human Respources: Bob Parker.
DHL Worldwide Express does business in two separate divisions. DHL International, which has headquarters in Belgium, provides express service for areas outside the United States. DHL Airways serves the U.S. express delivery market. The company's sales and work force are up slightly.
Other Locations: The company has 14 hubs and 1,630 offices in 221 countries.

FRITZ COMPANIES, INC.
706 Mission St., Ste. 900, San Francisco, CA 94103; 415-904-8360
http://www.fritz.com
Employees: 10,000
Sales: $1,387.7 million
Key Personnel: Chairman, CEO: Lynn C. Fritz. President, COO: Dennis L. Pelino. Human Resources: Seamus M. Owen.
Fritz is a top provider of transportation services for exporters. It also makes logistical arrangements for many of its customers. The company has an efficient information system connecting its worldwide office network. Among its customers are Sears and Wal-Mart. Its sales and work force are growing.
Other Locations: The company has 71 offices in the United States and 50 in foreign countries.

DISTRICT OF COLUMBIA

U.S. POSTAL SERVICE ★★
475 L'Enfant Plaza, SW, Washington, DC 20260-3100; 202-268-2000
http://www.usps.gov
Employees: 792,041
Sales: $60,100 million
Key Personnel: Postmaster General, CEO: William J. Henderson. Deputy Postmaster General: Michael S. Coughlin. Human Resources Manager: Yvonne D. Maguire.
Although the U.S. Postal Service has existed since 1775, it has only been an independent agency since 1970. The service delivers 40 percent of the world's mail—more than 190 billion pieces. It continues to expand its services. Sales and work force have increased.

GEORGIA

UNITED PARCEL SERVICE OF AMERICA, INC.
55 Glenlake Pkwy., NE, Atlanta, GA 30328; 404-828-6000
http://www.ups.com
Employees: 328,000
Sales: $24,788 million
Key Personnel: Chairman, CEO: James P. Kelly. SVP Business Development: John W. Alden. Human Resources: Lea N. Soupata.
United Parcel Service of America is the largest package delivery company in the world. In the face of increased competition, the company continues to add to its array of services. Although sales have increased steadily, its work force has been static.
Other Locations: The company has operations in over 200 countries.

IOWA

HEARTLAND EXPRESS, INC. ★★
2777 Heartland Dr., Coralville, IA 52241; 319-645-2728
http://www.heartlandexpress.com
Employees: 1,353
Sales: $263.5 million
Key Personnel: Chairman, President, Secretary: Russell A. Gerdin. EVP Marketing: Richard L. Meehan. Director of Human Resources: Don McGlaughlin.
One of the top short-haul trucking companies in the United States is Heartland Express. The company, which does business primarily in the East, does not have scheduled service. Heartland has benefited from the deregulation of the trucking industry, and the trend in retail of keeping small inventories. The company's short-haul business keeps drivers close to home. Its sales have held steady and work force is up.

KANSAS

YELLOW CORPORATION ★★
10990 Roe Ave., Overland Park, KS 66207; 913-696-6100
http://www.yellowcorp.com
Employees: 29,700
Sales: $2,900.6 million

Key Personnel: Chairman, President and CEO: A. Maurice Myers. SVP Finance, CFO, and Treasurer: Herbert A. Trucksess III. Human Resources: Harold Marshall.

One of the largest trucking companies in the United States, Yellow Corporation operates a fleet of almost 60,000 tractors, trailers, and trucks. Although its core business is long-haul transportation, it has expanded into regional less-than-truckload shipments. Both its sales and work force have increased.

Other Locations: The company has 671 terminals in Canada, Mexico, Puerto Rico, and the United States.

NEBRASKA

UNION PACIFIC CORPORATION

1416 Dodge St., Omaha, NE 68179; 402-271-5000

http://www.up.com

Employees: 65,000

Sales: $10,553

Key Personnel: Chairman, President, and CEO: Richard K. Davidson. EVP Finance: Gary M. Stuart. SVP Human Resources: L. Merill Bryan, Jr.

One of the oldest railroad companies in the U.S., Union Pacific's Union Pacific Railroad is the #1 carrier in the U.S. The company hauls freight over more than 30,000 miles of track in 23 states, carrying loads ranging from chemicals to coal. Sales and workforce are both down.

OHIO

ROADWAY EXPRESS, INC.

1077 Gorge Blvd., Akron, OH 44310-0471; 330-384-1717

http://www.roadway.com

Employees:26,000

Sales: $2,654.1 million

Key Personnel: Chairman, CEO: Michael W. Wickham. President, COO: James D. Staley. VP Human Resources: Thomas V. Lopienski..

Roadway Express was spun off from Caliber System (itself formerly Roadway Services) when Caliber was purchased by Federal Express in 1996. Roadway Express is the #2 less-than-truckload carrier in the U.S. The company operates about 30,000 trailers through a network of about 425 facilities in the U.S, Canada

and Mexico. Sales and workforce have both been static.

Other Locations: The company has operations in Asia, Australia, Europe, and North and South America.

TENNESSEE

FDX CORPORATION

6075 Poplar Ave., Ste. 300, Memphis, TN 38119; 901-369-3600

http://www.fdxcorp.com

Employees: 141,000

Sales: $16,773.5 million

Key Personnel: Chairman, President, and CEO: Frederick W. Smith. EVP, Chief Information Officer: Dennis H. Jones. Human Resources: James A. Perkins.

FDX Corporation is the holding company formed when Federal Express bought trucking company Caliber System. FedEx delivers more than 2.9 million packages to 212 countries per day. Federal Express has the largest fleet of cargo delivery airplanes in the world. Other subsidiaries include RPS, Viking Freight and Caliber Logistics. Its sales and work force are on the increase.

Other Locations: The company has hubs and sorting facilities in Alaska, California, Illinois, Indiana, New Jersey, and Tennessee.

U.S. XPRESS ENTERPRISES, INC. ★★

4080 Jenkins Rd., Chattanooga, TN 37421; 423-510-3000

http://www.usxpress.com

Employees: 7,165

Sales: $581.4 million

Key Personnel: Chairman, President: Patrick E. Quinn. EVP Marketing: E. William Lusk, Jr. Human Resources: Sherry Bass.

U.S. Xpress operates five subsidiaries in the long-haul freight transportation industry. The company's specialty is service that is cheaper than air freight yet nearly as fast. Known for its efficient computer network, the company is considered one of the most rapidly growing truckers in the United States. Its sales and work force are growing.

Other Locations: The company has terminals in 16 states.

TEXAS

KIRBY CORPORATION ★★

1775 St. James Pl., Ste 200, Houston, TX

77056-3453; 713-435-1000
http://www.krntc.com
Employees: 1,250
Sales: $327.1 million
Key Personnel: Chairman: George A. Peterkin, Jr. President, CEO: J.H. Pyne. Human Resources: Jack M. Sims.
The biggest inland tank barge company in the United States, Kirby primarily focuses on two areas. On the Mississippi River and Gulf area, the company carries chemicals and petroleum products. It also carries agricultural chemicals and petroleum products to coastal and offshore areas. Its sales have held steady, while its workforce has grown markedly.

VIRGINIA

CSX CORPORATION

One James Ctr., 901 E. Cary St., Richmond, VA 23219-4031; 804-782-1400
http://www.csx.com
Employees: 46,147
Sales: $9,898 million
Key Personnel: President, CEO: John W. Snow. SVP: Andrew B. Fogarty. Human Resources: Linda Amato.
CSX is not only the nation's third largest railroad, it also engages in ocean shipping, inland barging, and logistics operations. Its subsidiary, CSX Transportation, is the country's largest coal hauler and its Sea-Land Service has about 100 ships serving 120 ports worldwide. Sales and workforce have both been sluggish.
Other Locations: The company's system has links to 20 states and parts of Canada.

❶ FURNITURE

MICHIGAN

HERMAN MILLER, INC. ★

855 E. Main Ave., Zeeland, MI 49464-0302; 616-654-3300
http://www.hermanmiller.com
Employees: 8,555
Sales: $1,766.2 million
Key Personnel: President, CEO: Michael A. Volkema. EVP Financial Services, CFO: Brian C. Walker. Human Resources: Gene Miyamoto.
Herman Miller is the leading manufacturer of modular office furniture and one of the top U.S. producers of office furniture overall. It has manufacturing facilities in the United States and several other countries. The company, which emphasizes its ergonomic designs, has steadily growing sales and work force.

STEELCASE, INC.

901 44th St. SE, Grand Rapids, MI 49508; 616-247-2710
http://www.steelcase.com
Employees: 16,200
Sales: $2,742.5 million
Key Personnel: Chairman: Earl D. Holton. President, CEO: James P. Hackett. Human Resources: Nancy Hickey.
Steelcase is the world's largest office furniture manufacturer. It makes a complete line of products, from desks to integrated systems. The company has been diversifying because of a decrease in demand. It is expanding into other construction products, consulting services, and furniture for the health and hospitality industries. Sales and work force are holding steady.
Other Locations: The company has factories in the United States and 10 other countries.

MISSISSIPPI

RIVER OAKS FURNITURE, INC.

1014 N. Gloster, Tupelo, MS 38801; 662-862-1500
Employees: 1,600
Sales: $126.3 million
Key Personnel: CEO: Thomas Dieterich. Interim CFO: Len York. Treasurer: Walter R. Billingsley, Jr.
River Oaks Furniture manufactures finely crafted love seats, sofas, and chairs. Its midpriced offerings are sold under the River Oaks, Roaring River, River Crest, and Gaines brands. The company sells its furniture to 3,000 regional and national retailers. Both sales and work force are declining.

❶ GAMING

GEORGIA

POWERHOUSE TECHNOLOGIES, INC. ★★

115 Perimeter Pl., Ste. 911, Atlanta, GA 30346; 770-481-1800
http://www.pwrh.com
Employees: 1,380
Sales: $201.2 million
Key Personnel: VC: James J. Davey.

President, CEO: Richard M. Haddrill. Director of Human Resources: Ed Neuman.

Recently acquired by Anchor Gaming, Powerhouse Technologies (formerly Video Lottery Technologies) manufactures video lottery terminals and on-line computer equip-ment. The company is also a major supplier of pari-mutuel betting systems. Although it has enjoyed rapid growth recently from the increase of state-sponsored lottery systems, the company is now diversifying. Sales are up slightly; work force has risen dramatically.

NEVADA

ANCHOR GAMING ★
815 Pilot Rd., Ste. G, Las Vegas, NV 89119; 702-896-6992
Employees: 920
Sales: $248.9 million
Key Personnel: Chairman: Stanley E. Fulton. President, CEO: Michael D. Rumbolz. Human Resources: Susan Delzer.

A top designer and leaser of slot machines, Anchor Gaming also runs two Colorado casinos and provides installation, operation, and repair services for slot machines throughout Nevada. By leasing rather than selling its slot machines, Anchor retains a share of the machines' profits long after they leave the assembly line. Sales and workforce are both up healthily.

INTERNATIONAL GAME TECHNOLOGY ★★
9295 Prototype Dr., Reno, NV 89511; 775-448-7777
http://www.igtgame.com
Employees: 3,400
Sales: $824.1 million
Key Personnel: President, COO: G. Thomas Baker. EVP: Robert M. McMonigle. Human Resources: Randy Kirner.

One of the top companies in the design and manufacture of gaming machines and related software, International Game Technology is best known for its progressive slot machines. Among its other products are blackjack, poker, and video game machines. It is currently researching expansion opportunities abroad. Sales and work force are on the rise.

RHODE ISLAND

GTECH HOLDINGS CORPORATION
55 Technology Way, West Greenwich,

RI 02817; 401-392-1000
http://www.gtech.com
Employees: 4,800
Sales: $972.9 million
Key Personnel: President, CEO: William Y. O'Connor. SVP Technology: Donald L. Stanford. SVP Human Resources: Stephen A. Davidson.

The top operator and supplier of on-line lottery systems, GTECH Holdings recently began selling governmental benefits services too. The company has long been a dominant force in the gambling industry, providing pari-mutuel wagering systems and video lottery games. It recently won a contract to replace food stamps in Texas with an electronic system. Sales are declining and workforce is static.

---

❶ HEALTH CARE

ARKANSAS

BEVERLY ENTERPRISES, INC.
5111 Rogers Ave., Suite 40-A, Fort Smith, AR 72919-0155; 501-452-6712
http://www.beverlynet.com
Employees: 73,000
Sales: $2,812.2 million
Key Personnel: Chairman, CEO: David R. Banks. President, COO: Boyd W. Hendrickson. Human Resources Manager: Carol C. Johansen.

One of the largest nursing home operators in the United States, Beverly Enterprises has more than 700 of those facilities. It recently sold a pharmacy subsidiary. The company is developing Hospice Preferred Choice, a subsidiary that will focus on terminally ill patients. Sales and work force are shrinking.
Other Locations: The company has 727 nursing homes, 53 pharmacies, 40 retirement projects, six transitional hospitals, and four home health care facilities in the U.S.

CALIFORNIA

CATHOLIC HEALTHCARE WEST, INC. ★★
1700 Montgomery St., Ste. 300, San Francisco, CA 94111; 415-438-5500
http://www.chw.edu
Employees (est.): 20,000
Sales: $3,301.3 million
Key Personnel: President, CEO: Richard J. Kramer. EVP, COO: Larry Wilson.

Human Resources: Gene Tange.
The 10th largest nonprofit health services company in the United States, Catholic Healthcare West is the largest operation of its kind in California. It has a network of hospitals in Arizona, California, and Nevada, as well as clinics and other related facilities. Its sales and work force are growing.

FOUNDATION HEALTH SYSTEMS, INC.
21600 Oxnard St., Woodland Hills, CA 91367; 818-676-6000
http://www.fhs.com
Employees: 14,000
Sales: $8,797 million
Key Personnel: Chairman: Richard W. Hanselman. President, COO: Jay M. Gellert. Human Resources: Karin D. Mayhew.
One of the largest in the business of managed care, Foundation Health Systems provides services to more than six million people. It provides a wide variety of services, including H.M.O. plans, eye care, and workers' compensation. In 1996 it merged with Health Systems International, of which it became a subsidiary. The company's sales are up, but workforce is down.
Other Locations: The company provides health management services in 17 states and the United Kingdom.

KAISER FOUNDATION HEALTH PLAN, INC.
One Kaiser Plaza, Oakland, CA 94612; 510-271-5910
http://www.kaiserpermanente.org
Employees: 100,000
Sales: $15,500 million
Key Personnel: Chairman, CEO: David M. Lawrence. President, COO: Richard G. Barnaby. Human Resources: James B. Williams.
The largest health maintenance organization in the United States, Kaiser Foundation Health Plan has more than 6 million members and employs more than 9,500 doctors. The company, which is a nonprofit organization, also operates 28 medical centers. Although HMOs have grown in recent years, much of the increase has bypassed Kaiser. Its sales are up, but its work force is static.
Other Locations: The company has operations throughout the United States.

PACIFICARE HEALTH SYSTEMS, INC.
3120 Lake Center Dr., Santa Ana, CA 92704-5186; 714-825-5200
http://www.pacificare.com
Employees: 8,700
Sales: $9,521.5 million
Key Personnel: Chairman, CEO: Alan R. Hoops. President, COO: Jeffrey M. Folick. Human Resources: Wanda A. Lee.
PacifiCare Health Systems is a fast-growing health care provider. The California company recently began expanding its reach and announced a merger with FHP International Corporation. It now offers managed care services for employer groups and Medicare and Medicaid beneficiaries in six states. The company also recently contracted with the state of California to provide health maintenance organization services to Medi-Cal beneficiaries. Sales are up modestly, but workforce has declined.
Other Locations: The company has operations in California, Florida, Oklahoma, Oregon, Texas, and Washington.

BIO-CYPHER LABORATORIES LTD.
3301 C St., Suite 100E, Sacramento, CA 95816; 916-444-3500
Employees: 1,100
Sales: $65 million.
Key Personnel: CEO: J. Marvin Feigenbaum. VP Finance: Wayne E. Cottrell. Human Resources Director: Carolyn DiMercurio.
One of California's largest independent clinical laboratories, Bio-Cypher Laboratories (formerly the Physicians Clinical Laboratory) has recently emerged from Chapter 11 bankruptcy. It has a network of 17 immediate-response labs, 160 patient service centers, and three main laboratories. The company serves 15 acute-care hospitals in Sacramento, San Francisco, Los Angeles, and the Central Valley area. Although its sales are up modestly, its work force is down.

SALICK HEALTH CARE, INC. ★★
8201 Beverly Blvd., Los Angeles, CA 90048-4520; 323-966-3400
http://www.salick.com
Employees: 1,400
Sales: $209.2 million
Key Personnel: President, CEO: Lawrence D. Piro. CFO: Peter Rogers. Human Resources: Dan Wilbur.
Salick Health Care provides 24-hour cancer and dialysis treatment and is the nation's largest chain of for-profit cancer

treatment centers. Its services are aimed at creating more convenient options for patients with cancer and kidney failure and freeing patients from the restrictive schedules of most hospitals. Most of the company's facilities are in southern California. Sales are up, but work force is static.

Other Locations: The company has operations in California, Florida, Kansas, New York, and Pennsylvania.

TENET HEALTHCARE CORPORATION ★★

3820 State St., Santa Barbara, CA 93105; 805-563-7000

http://www.tenethealth.com
Employees: 116,800
Sales: $10,880 million
Key Personnel: Chairman, CEO: Jeffrey C. Barbakow. President, COO: Michael H. Focht Sr. Human Resources: Alan R. Ewalt.

The second largest hospital chain in the United States, Tenet Healthcare operates more than 120 hospitals in 18 states. The company also offers supervisory/ administrative services for indpendent physicians and groups. Through its subsidiaries, other Tenet interests include: an HMO, a PPO, home health care facilities, and long term facilities. Sales and work force are up markedly.

Other Locations: The company has 70 facilities in the United States and one in Spain.

UNIHEALTH ★★

3400 Riverside Dr., Burbank, CA 91505; 818-238-6000

http://www.unihealth.org
Employees: 11,000
Sales: $1,600 million
Key Personnel: Chairman, CEO: David R. Carpenter. VC: Donald G. Martyn. Human Resources: Barbara Cook.

One of the largest nonprofit health care companies in the United States, UniHealth has numerous subsidiaries, including CliniShare, which provides home health care, and ElderMed America, which provides medical services to seniors. Sales and work force are up slightly.

Other Locations: The company has 11 hospitals, located primarily in southern California.

COLORADO

AMERICAN MEDICAL RESPONSE, INC.

2821 S. Parker Rd., Aurora, CO 80014; 303-614-8500

http://www.amr-inc.com
Employees: 22,000
Sales: $1,659.1 million
Key Personnel: President, CEO: John Grainger. COO: Gregory Guckes. Human Resources: Marsha Williams.

The largest ambulance operator in the United States is American Medical Response. The company has more than 5,000 emergency vehicles in 39 states. It maintains its efficiency through a computerized dispatch system that uses satellites to pinpoint its vehicles. Its growth has mainly been from acquisition of smaller companies. Sales are up dramatically, but workforce has been static.

Other Locations: The company has facilities in 39 states.

CONNECTICUT

OXFORD HEALTH PLANS, INC.

800 Connecticut Ave., Norwalk, CT 06854; 203-852-1442

http://www.oxhp.com
Employees: 5,000
Sales: $4,719.4 million
Key Personnel: Chairman, CEO: Norman C. Payson. President: William M. Sullivan. Human Resources: Nils Lommern.

A leading managed health care provider in the New York City area, Oxford Health Plans offers a variety of health maintenance organization configurations. Its most popular plan allows participants to choose their own physicians. The company also offers employer-funded plans and dental coverage. Its sales are up, but its workforce has dropped sharply.

GEORGIA

MARINER POST-ACUTE NETWORK, INC. ★★

One Ravinia Dr., Suite 1500, Atlanta, GA 30346; 678-443-7000

http://www.marinerhealth.com
Employees: 45,000
Sales: $1,140 million
Key Personnel: Chairman, President, CEO: Keith B. Pitts. SVP: Robert V. Napier. SVP, Human Resources: Ann

Weiser.

The result of a complicated series of mergers between Paragon Health Network, Mariner Health Group, Living Centers of America, and Grancare, Mariner Post-Acute Network is one of the largest long-term care providers in the U.S. The company runs more than 400 inpatient and assisted living facilities across the country. Subsidiaries' operations include pharmacy, home health and rehabilitation therapy. Sales and workforce have grown impressively.

KENTUCKY

HUMANA, INC.

The Humana Bldg., 500 W. Main St., Louisville, KY 40202; 502-580-1000

http://www.humana.com

Employees: 16,300

Sales: $9,597 million

Key Personnel: Chairman: David A. Jones. SVP, General Counsel: Arthur P. Hipwell. SVP Human Resources: Bonnie C. Hathcock.

Humana is one of the major providers of managed health care services in the United States. The company's market spans 15 states, primarily in the Midwest and South, and Puerto Rico. Much of its income is from Medicare payments. Despite impressive sales growth, workforce is down sharply.

OMNICARE, INC. ★★

50 E. Rivercenter Blvd., Covington, KY 41011; 606-291-6800

Employees: 11,560

Sales: $1,517.4 million

Key Personnel: Chairman: Edward L. Hutton. President: Joel F. Gemunder. Human Resources: Janice M. Rice.

Omnicare is the #1 independent provider of pharmacy and services to nursing home market. It purchases, repackages, and dispenses pharmaceuticals on contract for nursing homes located mostly in the Midwest. It also provides administrative and consultative services, including patient drug therapy evaluations. The company plans to broaden its services and expand its market area. Both sales and work force are increasing dramatically.

Other Locations: The company has facilities in 40 states.

MINNESOTA

IN HOME HEALTH, INC.

Carlson Center, Ste. 500, 601 Carlson Pkwy., Minnetonka, MN 55305-5214; 612-449-7500

Employees: 2,055

Sales: $97 million

Key Personnel: President, CEO: Wolfgang von Maack. Interim CFO, Secretary: Robert J. Hoffman, Jr. Human Resources: Susan Garner.

In Home Health is a leading provider of home health care services. The company, which derives more than 70 percent of its income from Medicare payments, supplies its clients with physical therapy, critical care nursing, and other services. It also operates 10 pharmacies. Sales and workforce have both fallen sharply.

Other Locations: The company has 37 centers in Arizona, California, Illinois, Minnesota, Texas, and other states.

MAYO FOUNDATION ★

Mayo Clinic, 200 First St. SW, Rochester, MN 55905; 507-284-2511

http://www.mayo.edu

Employees: 30,497

Sales: $2,565.6 million

Key Personnel: President, CEO: Robert R. Waller. Chair Finance, Treasury: David R. Ebel. Chair Human Resources: Gregory Warner.

Well known for its coordinated approach to medicine, the Mayo Foundation has a team of more than 1,000 scientists and physicians at its many facilities around the country. The company also operates the Mayo Clinic in Rochester, Minnesota, which is the largest private medical facility in the world. Sales and work force are on the rise.

Other Locations: The company has facilities in Arizona, Florida, Iowa, Minnesota, and Wisconsin.

UNITEDHEALTH GROUP

300 Opus Center, 9900 Bred Rd. E., Minnetonka, MN 55343; 612-936-1300

http://www.unitedhealthgroup.com

Employees: 29,200

Sales: $17,106 million

Key Personnel: Chairman, President, and CEO: William W. McGuire. COO: Stephen J. Hemsley. Human Resources: Robert J. Backes.

Formely United Health Care, United-Health Group is the number 3 managed care company in the United States. It owns 16 health maintenance organizations, and manages an additional nine, plus managing preferred provider organizations (PPO's) through a network that reaches to all 50 states. Despite rapidly growing sales, workforce is down slightly.

MISSOURI

EXPRESS SCRIPTS, INC. ★★

14000 Riverport Dr., Maryland Heights, MO 63043; 314-770-1666
http://www.express-scripts.com
Employees: 1,570
Sales: $1,230.6 million.
Key Personnel: President, CEO: Barrett A. Toan. EVP: Stuart L. Bascomb. Human Resources: Karen Matteuzzi.
Keeping down the cost of pharmacy services is the goal of Express Scripts. One of the largest pharmacy benefits management operations in the United States, the company also supplies home-infusion and vision care services to health plan participants. Express is the only pharmacy benefits management company not owned by a pharmaceutical manufacturer. Its sales and work force have more than doubled.

NEVADA

SIERRA HEALTH SERVICES, INC. ★★

2724 N. Tenaya Way, Las Vegas, NV 89128; 702-242-7000
http://www.sierrahealth.com
Employees: 4,700
Sales: $1,037.2 million.
Key Personnel: President, COO: Erin E. MacDonald. Chairman, CEO: Anthony M. Marlon. Human Resources Manager: Ross Lagatutta.
The largest managed care company in Nevada, Sierra Health Services provides home and hospice care, health care administration, and other services. The company also runs an H.M.O. and is the proprietor of Southwest Medical, a multispecialty medical group. Most of the company's primary care physicians are members of its medical group. Sales and work force are up dramatically.

NEW MEXICO

SUN HEALTHCARE GROUP, INC. ★★

101 Sun Ave. NE, Albuquerque, NM 87109; 505-821-3355
http://www.sunh.com
Employees: 80,720
Sales: $3,088.5 million
Key Personnel: Chairman, CEO: Andrew L. Turner. President, COO: Mark G. Wimer. Human Resources: Mary D'ornellas.
Sun Healthcare Group provides long term and related health services through more than 470 facilities in the U.S., Germany, Australia and Spain. Through its subsidiaries, the company provides physical, occupational and speech therapy. Sun also owns pharmacies and provides outpatient therapy in Canada. In 1997, Sun acquired Regency Health Services which added 110 facilities to its stable. Sales and work force are both rising markedly.
Other Locations: The company has facilities in Boston, Chicago, Dallas, Los Angeles, and Tampa.

NORTH CAROLINA

COASTAL PHYSICIAN GROUP, INC.

2828 Croasdaile Dr., Durham, NC 27705; 919-383-0355
Employees: 1,300
Sales: $294.2 million
Key Personnel: Chairman, President, and CEO: Steven M. Scott. EVP, CFO, and Treasurer: Charles Kuoni III. Human Resources: Martha King.
Coastal Physician Group (formerly Coastal Healthcare Group) began in the late 1970s providing contract physicians to hospital emergency rooms. The company is one of the largest providers of contract health and administrative services in the United States, though debt and tough competition have forced it to unload some assets. Coastal also has 27 primary care clinics. Its sales and work force have dropped sharply.

PENNSYLVANIA

HOME HEALTH CORPORATION OF AMERICA.

2200 Renaissance Blvd., Ste. 300, King of Prussia, PA 19406; 610-272-1717
http://www.hhcainc.com
Employees: 3,069
Sales: $174.3 million
Key Personnel: Chairman, CEO: Bruce J. Feldman. CFO: David S. Geller. Human Resources: Bob Simon.
Home Health Corporation of America provides home health care services and

products such as medical equipment, nursing services, infusion therapy and supplies. The company is actively acquiring smaller firms and currently operates about 40 branches across the east and midwest. Despite healthy growth in sales, workforce is static.
Other Locations: The company has branches in Delaware, Florida, Illinois, Maine, Maryland, Massachusetts and Texas.

GENESIS HEALTH VENTURES, INC.
148 W. State St., Kennett Square, PA 19348; 610-444-6350
http://www.ghv.com
Employees: 45,000
Sales: $1,405.3 million
Key Personnel: Chairman, CEO: Michael R. Walker. VC, COO, and EVP: David C. Barr. Human Resources: James W. Tabak.
The primary business of Genesis Health Ventures is specialty geriatric care. It is one of the largest U.S. companies in the nursing home field. Among its services are home care, rehabilitation services, and retirement communities. The company is expanding its medical programs and outpatient therapy services. Sales and work force are up.

NOVACARE, INC. ★★
1016 W. Ninth Ave., King of Prussia, PA 19406; 610-992-7200
http://www.novacare.com
Employees: 53,000
Sales: $1,479.9 million
Key Personnel: Chairman: Timothy E. Foster. President, COO: James W. McLane. Human Resources: Kathryn P. Kehoe.
Having recently sold its orthotic and prosthetic units to Hanger Orthopedic, NovaCare now focuses on rehabilitation serves, of which it is the #2 U.S. provider. The company treats more than 37,000 patients a day and contracts its services to more than 1,900 hospitals and nursing homes. The company's focus is on selling more fixed-price rehabilitation packages to insurance companies. Its sales are down, but work force has still grown dramatically.

TENNESSEE
COLUMBIA/HCA HEALTHCARE CORP.
One Park Plaza, Nashville, TN 37203; 615-344-9551
http://www.columbia-hca.com
Employees: 260,000
Sales: $18,681 million
Key Personnel: Chairman, CEO: Thomas F. Frist, Jr. President, COO: Jack Bovender Jr. Human Resources: Philip Patton.
Columbia/HCA Healthcare is not only one of the largest health service companies in the United States but for several years one of the fastest growing. In recent years it has halted its aggressive expansion and sold its home care operations. Internal problems have plagued the company, resulting in declining sales and workforce.
Other Locations: The company has 445 hospitals and outpatient centers in Switzerland, the United Kingdom, and the United States.

NATIONAL HEALTHCARE CORPORATION
100 Vine St., Murfreesboro, TN 37130; 615-890-2020
Employees: 16,017
Sales: $441.2 million
Key Personnel: Chairman, President: W. Andrew Adams. SVP: Richard F. LaRoche, Jr.
National HealthCare operates long term health care centers and home health care programs in the southeastern U.S. The company provides skilled and intermediate nursing; speech, physical and occupational therapy; and occupational therapy. Sales are down and workforce is static.

TEXAS
HORIZON HEALTH CORPORATION ★★
1500 Waters Ridge Dr., Lewisville, TX 75057-6011; 972-420-8200
Employees: 1,208
Sales: $123.8 million
Key Personnel: Chairman: James K. Newman. President, CEO and CFO: James W. McAtee. Human Resources: Dan Perkins.
Horizon Health Corporation manages mental health and physical rehabilitation programs in 37 states. With over 200 contracts, it handles licensing, accreditation, and Medicare accreditation. Sales and work force are rising steadily.

WASHINGTON

GROUP HEALTH COOPERATIVE OF PUGET SOUND ★★

521 Wall St., Seattle, WA 98121; 206-448-5439
http://www.ghc.org
Employees: 9,602
Sales: $1,300 million
Key Personnel: Chairperson: Jeanne M. Large. President: Cheryl M. Scott. Human Resources: John Nagelman.

A not-for-profit managed care group, Group Health Cooperative of Puget Sound serves 30-plus counties in Washington and several in Idaho. The member-owned company offers HMO, PPO and point-of-service options. In 1997, Group Health affiliated with Kaiser Permanente, the #1 U.S. health services delivery system, in hopes of boosting its somewhat lagging financial performance. Sales and workforce are up markedly.

WISCONSIN

UNITED WISCONSIN SERVICES, INC.

401 W. Michigan St., Milwaukee, WI 53203-2896; 414-226-6900
http://www.uwz.com
Employees: 1,289
Sales: $638.6 million
Key Personnel: Chairman, President and CEO: Thomas R. Hefty. VP: Devon W. Barrix. Human Resources: Sue Fiegel.

Once a part of the Blue Cross/Blue Shield system, United Wisconsin is now the biggest health maintenance organization and managed health care company in Wisconsin. The company's break with its parent was caused by pressure from increased health care costs. It has three HMOs and also offers a number of ancillary services. Sales and work force are up.

❶ INDUSTRIAL/FARM EQUIPMENT AND TOOLS

CONNECTICUT

GERBER SCIENTIFIC, INC.

83 Gerber Rd. W., South Windsor, CT 06074; 860-644-1551
http://www.gerberscientific.com
Employees: 2,700
Sales: $594.6 million
Key Personnel: Chairman, President, and CEO: Michael J. Cheshire. SVP Finance: Gary K Bennet. Human Resources: Becket Q. McNab.

Gerber Scientific manufactures computer-aided-design and computer-aided-manufacturing equipment for a variety of industries, including apparel, automotive, aerospace, electronics, printing, optical, and graphic arts. The company is one of the largest suppliers of automated design and manufacturing equipment to the apparel, signmaking, and screenprinting industries. The company's sales are up markedly, but workforce has suffered a slight decline.

STANLEY WORKS

1000 Stanley Dr., New Britain, CT 06053; 860-225-5111
http://www.stanleyworks.com
Employees: 18,000
Sales: $2,729.1 million
Key Personnel: Chairman, CEO: John M. Trani. VP Engineering: William D. Hill. VP Human Resources: Mark J. Mathieu.

Stanley Works has been putting out tools since 1852. The company currently operates 11 subsidiaries, including MAC Tools and Stanley Door Systems. It manufactures a dizzying array of products, including electronic controls, fasteners, wrenches, shelving, and automatic parking gates. The company is expanding its presence in China, Latin America, and Eastern Europe. Sales are up slightly and workforce is static.
Other Locations: The company owns more than 100 facilities in the United States and 19 foreign countries.

GEORGIA

AGCO CORPORATION

4205 River Green Pkwy., Duluth, GA 30096; 770-813-9200
http://www.agcocorp.com
Employees: 10,500
Sales: $2,941.4 million
Key Personnel: President, CEO: John M. Shumejda. SVP Marketing: Edward R. Swingle. VP Sales: James M. Seaver.
AGCO rose from being a relatively small player to become a significant force in the agricultural machinery business when it purchased tractor maker Massey Ferguson in 1994. The company also makes combines, hay tools, and other related farm equipment. Sales and work force are both currently on the decline.

ILLINOIS

CATERPILLAR, INC. ★★

100 NE Adams St., Peoria, IL 61629-7310; 309-675-1000

http://www.caterpillar.com
Employees: 65,824
Sales: $20,977 million
Key Personnel: Chairman, CEO: Glen A. Barton. Group President: Gerald S. Flaherty. Human Resources: Alan J. Rassi.

The largest manufacturer of bulldozers and similar equipment in the world, Caterpillar also builds gasoline and diesel engines for locomotives, trucks, and electrical power generators. The company has had protracted problems with its union employees for several years. Nearly half of the company's sales currently come from outside the United States. Sales and work force are both on the rise.
Other Locations: The company has dealerships in 128 countries and manufacturing facilities in 12 countries.

DEERE & COMPANY ★

One John Deere Pl.., Moline, IL 61265-8098; 309-765-8000;

http://www.deere.com
Employees: 37,000
Sales: $13,625.8 million
Key Personnel: Chairman, CEO: Hans W. Becherer. SVP Finance, CFO: Nathan J. Jones. Human Resources: John K. Lawson.

Although Deere & Company is the largest farm equipment maker in the world, the company also provides many other products and services. It is among the top producers of lawn care and industrial equipment and provides insurance and financial services, as well. International sales account for more than 20 percent of the company's income. Sales and work force are both on the increase at Deere & Company.

ILLINOIS TOOL WORKS, INC. ★★

3600 W. Lake Ave., Glenview, IL 60025-5811; 847-724-7500

http://www.itwinc.com
Employees: 29,200
Sales: $5,647.9 million
Key Personnel: Chairman, CEO: W. James Farrell. VC: Frank S. Ptak. Human Resources: John Karpan.

Illinois Tool Works makes a wide variety of tools for many different industries. It serves the needs of the food and beverages, automotive, and construction industries, among others. Its products include gears, nails, switches, fastening tools, packing systems, and fasteners. The construction and automotive industries account for nearly two-thirds of its income. The company recently acquired Hobart Brothers Co., which makes welding equipment. Sales and work force are rising.
Other Locations: The company has facilities in Asia, Europe, and the United States.

MARYLAND

BLACK & DECKER CORPORATION

701 E. Joppa Rd., Towson, MD 21286; 410-716-3900

http://www.blackanddecker.com
Employees: 21,800
Sales: $4,559.9 million
Key Personnel: Chairman, President, and CEO: Nolan D. Archibald. EVP: Dennis G. Heiner. Human Resources: Leonard A. Strom.

The top manufacturer of power tools in the world, Black & Decker makes a wide variety of tools for both the industrial and consumer markets. Especially popular are its glass container-making equipment, fasteners, and security hardware. The company's professional power tool lines, Elu and DeWalt, are increasingly successful. Black & Decker also sells a broad range of consumer appliances. Sales and work force are down sharply.

NEW HAMPSHIRE

TYCO INTERNATIONAL, LTD. ★★

One Tyco Park, Exeter, NH 03833; 603-778-9700

http://www.tyco.com
Employees: 87,000
Sales: $12,311.3 million
Key Personnel: Chairman, CEO: L. Dennis Kozlowski. EVP, CFO: Mark H. Swartz. Human Resources: Wendy Desmond.

Fire protection systems are the primary market for Tyco International. The company is the largest maker of fire protection equipment in the world. It also manufactures a variety of packaging products, electronic components, flow control devices, and fiber-optic cable. Sales and work force are up dramatically.

NEW JERSEY

INGERSOLL-RAND COMPANY

200 Chestnut Ridge Rd., Woodcliff Lake, NJ 07675; 201-573-0123
http://www.ingersoll-rand.com
Employees: 46,500
Sales: $8,291.5 million
Key Personnel: Chairman, CEO: James E. Perrella. President, COO: Herbert L. Henkel. Human Resources: Donald H. Rice.

Among the top manufacturers of nonelectrical industrial equipment, Ingersoll-Rand makes a wide variety of products. The company makes air tools, pumps, antifriction bearings, and many other tools. The company strongly emphasizes research and development in its operations. It recently purchased Clark Equipment for $1.5 billion. Despite a marked increase in sales, workforce dropped slightly.
Other Locations: The company has more than 90 factories in Africa, Asia, Canada, Europe, the Far East, Latin America, and the United States.

NEW YORK

DOVER CORPORATION

280 Park Ave., New York, NY 10017-1292; 212-922-1640
http://www.dovercorporation.com
Employees: 23,350
Sales: $3,977.7 million
Key Personnel: Chairman, President, and CEO: Thomas L. Reece. VP Finance: John F. McNiff. VP: George F. Messerole.

Dover Corporation is best known as a manufacturer of elevators, but it also owns companies that make other products ranging from garbage trucks to printing equipment. Other subsidiaries make fuel-handling equipment, can-making machinery, and heat transfer equipment. Sales and work force have declined recently.

MANNESMANN CORPORATION

450 Park Ave., New York, NY 10022; 212-826-0040
http://www.mannesmann.com
Employees (overall Mannesmann):116,247
Sales (overall Mannesmann): $19,783.8 million
Key Personnel: President (U.S.): Peter Prinz Wittgenstein. EVP Administration: Manfred Becker. Human Resources Director (U.S.): Edward Zadravec.

Mannesmann Corporation is the holding company handling the United States operations of Mannesmann AG, one of the world's top manufacturers of steel tubing. The company is also one of the largest con-glomerates in Ger-many. Its products are used in a wide variety of industries, including the telecommunications, automotive, and construction industries. The company also builds steel factories. Sales and work force are down.
Other Locations: Worldwide HQ: Mannesmann AG, Postfach 10 36 41, D-40027 Dusseldorf, Germany; +49-211-820-0.

OHIO

MILACRON, INC.

4701 Marburg Ave., Cincinnati, OH 45209-1086; 513-841-8100
http://www.milacron.com
Employees:11,855
Sales: $1,514.7 million
Key Personnel: Chairman, President, and CEO: Daniel J. Meyer. SVP Finance, CFO: Ronald D. Brown. Human Resources: Barbara G. Kasting.

Milacron is one of the world's top manufacturers of machine tools, plastics machinery, and industrial products. The company sells its products directly through a large sales force and independent distributors. Sales and work force are up.

PARKER HANNIFIN CORPORATION ★★

6035 Parkland Blvd., Cleveland, OH 44124-4141; 216-896-3000
http://www.parker.com
Employees: 39,873
Sales: $4,958.8 million
Key Personnel: Chairman: Patrick S. Parker. President, CEO: Duane E. Collins. SVP Human Resources: Daniel T. Garey.

Parker Hannifin is a leading maker of motion control products for eight product groups that include aerospace, fluid connectors, hydraulics, automation climate, seals and so forth. Their products use hydraulic or pneumatic systems to move and position materials and equipment. Sales and work force are on the increase.

WISCONSIN

BRIGGS & STRATTON CORPORATION
12301 W. Wirth St., Wauwatosa, WI
53222; 414-259-5333
http://www.briggsandstratton.com
Employees: 7,265
Sales: $1,501.7 million
Key Personnel: Chairman, CEO: Frederick P. Stratton, Jr. President, COO:
John S. Shiely. VP Human Resources:
Gerald E. Zitzer.
The largest manufacturer of air-cooled
engines for outdoor power equipment,
Briggs & Stratton's products are used in
such things as garden tillers, lawn mowers, and go-carts. The company is currently working to meet EPA emission
guidelines for its engines. It has kept
costs low through automated manufacturing processes. Although sales have
risen healthily, work force is down.

CASE CORPORATION
700 State St., Racine, WI 53404; 414-636-6011
http://www.casecorp.com
Employees: 17,700
Sales: $6,149 million
Key Personnel: Chairman, CEO: Jean-Pierre Rosso. President, COO: Steven G.
Lamb. Human Resources: Marc J. Castor.
Case is the world's largest manufacturer
of light to medium-sized construction
equipment and the #2 maker of farm
equipment in North America. The company has expanded to the point that almost half its sales are foreign. New Holland is in the process of acquiring Case.
Sales are up, but workforce is down.

GIDDINGS & LEWIS, INC.
142 Doty St., Fond du Lac, WI 54935;
920-921-9400
http://www.giddings.com
Employees: 3,100
Sales: $763 million
Key Personnel: Chairman, CEO: Marvin
L. Isles. Group VP: Carmine Bosco. Human Resources: Robert N. Kelley.
Giddings & Lewis is into robots. The
company, a subsidiary of Thyssen Krupp
AG in Germany, is the largest North
American manufacturer of industrial
automation tools and products. The tools
are popular in aerospace, automotive,
electronics, and other industries. The
company has reversed a downward trend
of the last several years. While sales are
up, work force is down.

HARNISCHFEGER INDUSTRIES, INC.
3600 S. Lake Dr., St. Francis, WI 53235-3716; 414-486-6400
http://www.harnischfeger.com
Employees: 13,700
Sales: $2,042.1 million
Key Personnel: CEO: John N. Hanson.
SVP: Robert W. Hale. Human Resources:
Joseph A. Podawiltz.
Harnischfeger Industries provides heavy
machinery for a variety of industries. The
company's Beloit Industries subsidiary
makes papermaking machines. The Joy
Mining Equipment subsidiary, which is
the largest company of its type, manufactures underground mining equipment.
Harnischfeger Corp., makes surface
mining machinery. Sales and work force
have dropped sharply.

SNAP-ON, INC.
10801 Corporate Dr., Kenosha, WI
53141-1430; 414-656-5200
http://www.snapon.com
Employees: 12,000
Sales: $1,772.6 million
Key Personnel: Chairman, President,
and CEO: Robert A. Cornog. SVP Operations: Frederick D. Hay. Human Resources: Sharon M. Brady.
In a change that represents the evolution
of its operations, Snap-On Tools changed
its name to Snap-On, Inc., in 1995. The
company, which was among the first to
sell socket wrenches, has branched out to
sell a variety of computerized equipment,
such as automotive diagnostic devices
and medical specialty tools. It also sells a
long list of hand and power tools, tool
cabinets, and other products. Sales and
work force are rising.
Other Locations: The company has facilities in Australia, Brazil, Canada, Ireland, Japan, the Netherlands, the United
Kingdom, and the United States.

---

❶ INSURANCE

CALIFORNIA

ALLIANZ INSURANCE CO.
3400 Riverside Dr., Ste. 300, Burbank,
CA 91505-4691; 818-972-8000
Employees (overall Allianz): 105,676
Sales: $68,479.5 million.
Key Personnel: Chairman, President and
CEO: Wolfgang Schlink. EVP, CFO:
Paul Kaduk. VP Human Resources: Ste-

phen Williams.

Allianz Insurance Co. is the U.S. division of Allianz AG of Germany. The world's second largest insurance company, based on sales from premiums, Allianz AG has stakes in numerous larger companies in Germany. Its holdings are predominantly in banking, insurance, and chemical and pharmaceutical manufacturing. The company's increasing international business is raising sales to new heights and workforce has nearly doubled in the last year alone.

Other Locations: Worldwide HQ: Allianz AG, Koniginstrasse 28, D-80802 Munich, Germany; +49-89-3-80-00.

FIDELITY NATIONAL FINANCIAL, INC.

3916 State St., Ste. 300, Santa Barbara, CA 93105; 805-563-1566
http://www.fnf.com
Employees: 7,400
Sales: $1,288.5 million
Key Personnel: President: Frank P. Willey. COO: Patrick F. Stone. Human Resources: Ann Russell.

One of the biggest U.S. title insurance companies, Fidelity National Financial has operations in many of the largest markets in the real estate industry. The company's business has increased in recent years as the real estate market responded to lower interest rates with increased sales and housing starts. Both sales and work force are up substantially.

PACIFIC MUTUAL HOLDING COMPANY ★★

700 Newport Ctr. Dr., Newport Beach, CA 92660-6397; 949-640-3011
http://www.pacificlife.com
Employees: 3,422
Sales: $2,574.4 million
Key Personnel: Chairman, CEO: Thomas C. Sutton. President: Glenn S. Schafer. SVP Human Resources: Anthony J. Bonno.

Among the largest U.S. life insurance companies, Pacific Mutual Life Insurance is the largest company of its type based in California. Along with life insurance, it provides asset management, pension benefits, and employee benefits services. It is currently working on a program to reduce paperwork and eliminate fraud and abuse. Sales and workforce are up markedly.

CONNECTICUT

AETNA INC.

151 Farmington Ave., Hartford, CT 06156; 860-273-0123
http://www.aetna.com
Employees: 40,300
Sales: $18,540.2 million
Key Personnel: Chairman, President, CEO: Richard L. Huber. EVP Aetna Healthcare: Michael J. Cardillo. Human Resources Manager: Elease E. Wright.

Once a leader in the insurance industry, Aetna (formerly Aetna Life and Casualty) is now a leader in managed health care. In 1998 it sold its individual life insurance business to Lincoln National, but continues to sell group insurance. After selling its property casualty operations to Travelers and buying U.S. Healthcare, the company's position improved. Sales are rising, but workforce has dropped substantially.

GENERAL RE CORPORATION

695 E. Main St., Stamford, CT 06904; 203-328-5000
http://www.genre.com
Employees: 3,869
Sales: $8,251 million
Key Personnel: Chairman, President, and CEO: Ronald E. Ferguson. President, COO, General Reinsurance Corp.: Tom N. Kellogg. Human Resources: James Hamilton.

General Re, itself a subsidiary of Berkshire Hathaway, is the parent company of General Reinsurance, the #1 U.S. property/casualty reinsurer. In addition, General Re owns General Re-New England, an insurance consulting company, and National Re, a leader in direct reinsurance. General Re is one of the largest operations of its type in the world.

Other Locations: The company has operations in the United States and 13 foreign countries.

THE HARTFORD FINANCIAL SERVICES GROUP INC.

Hartford Plaza, 690 Asylum Ave., Hartford, CT 06115; 860-547-5000
http://www.thehartford.com
Employees: 25,000
Sales: $15,022 million
Key Personnel: Chairman, President, and CEO: Ramani Ayer. EVP, CFO: David K. Zwiener. Human Resources: Helen G. Goodman.

The Hartford Financial Services Group (formerly ITT Hartford Group) offers a variety of personal and commercial property/ casualty insurance products through its Hartford Fire Insurance unit. Another unit, Hartford Life, was spun off in 1997, but Hartford Financial owns over 80 percent of the new company. Sales are up, but workforce has remained static.

DISTRICT OF COLUMBIA

GEICO CORPORATION ★★

One GEICO Plaza, Washington, DC 20076; 301-986-3000
http://www.geico.com
Employees: 15,000
Sales: $4,033 million
Key Personnel: President, CEO, Insurance Operations: Olza M. Nicely. President, CEO, Capital Operations: Louis A. Simpson. Group VP Human Resources: David L. Schindler.

One of the largest providers of automobile insurance in the United States, GEICO is a holding company for the Government Employees Insurance Company. GEICO mainly targets military personnel and govern-ment employees and recently phased out its consumer finance and homeowners insurance operations. The company is owned by the Berkshire Hathaway investment firm. Assets and work force are up.
Other Locations: The company has operations throughout the United States and serves U.S. military personnel in Germany, Italy, Turkey, and the United Kingdom.

GEORGIA

AFLAC, INC. ★★

1932 Wynnton Rd., Columbus, GA 31999; 706-323-3431
http://www.aflac.com
Employees: 4,450
Sales: $7,104 million
Key Personnel: President, CEO: Daniel P. Amos. EVP Corporate Finance: Norman P. Foster. Human Resources: Angie Hart.

The top supplier of supplemental medical insurance in the Japanese and U.S. markets, AFLAC aims to carry on where other insurance policies leave off. More than three-quarters of its business is done in Japan. The company also owns several television stations. Despite a slight decline in sales, the company's workforce continued its impressive upward trend.

Other Locations: The company has offices in Canada, Japan, Taiwan, and the United States.

ILLINOIS

THE ALLSTATE CORPORATION

Allstate Plaza, 2775 Sanders Rd., Northbrook, IL 60062-6127; 847-402-5000
http://www.allstate.com
Employees: 53,000
Sales: $25,976 million
Key Personnel: Chairman, President, and CEO: Edward M. Liddy. SVP, CFO: John L. Carl. Human Resources: Joan M. Crockett.

One of the largest auto and home insurance companies in the United States, Allstate is a recent spin-off from Sears. The company also sells property and liability insurance to small businesses, life insurance, and pension products. The company is seeking to expand its market by selling additional products to existing customers. Its sales and work force are up moderately.
Other Locations: The company has operations in Canada, Japan, Puerto Rico, South Korea, and the United States.

BLUE CROSS AND BLUE SHIELD ASSOCIATION

225 N. Michigan Ave, Chicago, IL 60601-7680; 312-440-6000
http://www.blueshield.com
Employees: 150,000
Sales: $94,700 million
Key Personnel: President, CEO: Patrick G Hays. EVP Business Alliances: Harry P. Cain II. Human Resources: Bill Clybourne.

The 69 Blue Cross and Blue Shield health insurance companies are coordinated by the Blue Cross and Blue Shield Association. The organization comprises the largest and oldest health insurance carrier. Historically, the Blues were not for profit but now, to compete with other managed care operations, more and more are going public. Sales and work force have held steady.
Other Locations: The organization has operations in Australia, Canada, Jamaica, the United Kingdom, and the United States.

CNA SURETY CORPORATION.

CNA Plaza, 333 S. Wabash, Chicago, IL 60685; 312-822-2000

http://www.cna.com
Employees: 848
Sales: $283.8 million
Key Personnel: CEO, President: Mark C. Vonnahme. EVP Legislative Affairs: Dan L. Kirby. Human Resources: Melita H. Geoghegan.
CNA Surety Corporation was formed through the merger of Capsure Holdings and CNA Financial's surety business. The company's product includes small and large contract and commercial surety bonds. CNA Surety is the largest US surety company based on premiums. Sales have quadrupled, but workforce is only up slightly.

STATE FARM MUTUAL AUTOMOBILE INSURANCE COMPANY ★

One State Farm Plaza, Bloomington, IL 61710-0001; 309-766-2311
http://www1.statefarm.com
Employees: 76,257
Sales: $27,706 million
Key Personnel: Chairman, CEO: Edward B. Rust Jr. VC, President, and CEO: Vincent J. Trosino. Human Resources: Arlene Hogan.
One of the largest insurers in the United States, State Farm is owned by its policyholders. The company provides a broad range of insurance services through its affiliates, including property/casualty insurance. It is currently restructuring its target market, pulling out of some areas and recruiting customers in others. Despite a slight decline in sales, workforce is up healthily.
Other Locations: The company has operations in Canada and the United States.

INDIANA

CONSECO, INC. ★★

11825 N. Pennsylvania St., Carmel, IN 46032; 317-817-6100
http://www.conseco.com
Employees: 14,000
Sales: $7,716 million
Key Personnel: Chairman, President, and CEO: Stephen C. Hilbert. EVP, CFO: Rollin M. Dick. VP Human Resources: Dennis J. Dunlap.
Conseco is a full-service insurance company. It offers traditional insurance, annuities, and other financial services through its affiliates and subsidiaries. The company is currently one of the fastest growing insurance enterprises in the United States, achieving its expansion through acquisitions. Sales are up dramatically and workforce has more than doubled.

LINCOLN NATIONAL CORPORATION

200 E. Berry St., Fort Wayne, IN 46802-2706; 219-455-2000
http://www.lnc.com
Employees: 8,015
Sales: $6,087.1 million
Key Personnel: President, CEO: Jon A. Boscia. EVP, CFO: Richard C. Vaughan. Human Resources: George E. Davis.
Lincoln National is one of the world's largest life and health reinsurers and writers of individual annuities. The company sells coverage and risk management services to other insurers, HMO's, and self-insurance programs. The company is expanding its financial services business. Despite rapid growth in sales, workforce has declined.

IOWA

THE PRINCIPAL FINANCIAL GROUP

711 High St., Des Moines, IA 50392-0001; 515-247-5111
http://www.principal.com
Employees: 16,837
Sales: $7,697 million
Key Personnel: Chairman, CEO: David J. Drury. President: J. Barry Griswell. Human Resources: Thomas J. Gaard.
The Principal Financial Group does business through its subsidiary, Principal Mutual Life Insurance, among the largest life insurance companies west of New York City. The company sells individual insurance, pension plans, as well as group health and life insurance. It changed its name in 1986 from Bankers Life and is trying to recapture its name recognition. Sales and workforce are down.
Other Locations: The company has operations in Canada, Puerto Rico, and the United States.

MASSACHUSETTS

JOHN HANCOCK MUTUAL LIFE INSURANCE COMPANY ★★

200 Clarendon St., Boston, MA 02117; 617-572-6000
http://www.jhancock.com
Employees: 7,959
Sales: $13,653.4 million
Key Personnel: Chairman, CEO: Stephen L. Brown. President, COO: David F. D'Alessandro. Human Resources: A.

Page Palmer.

Although John Hancock Mutual Life Insurance is primarily involved in selling insurance, the company also provides many other financial services. Besides its comprehensive line of insurance offerings, it provides services such as banking and mortgage loans. The company has been streamlining its operations by consolidating offices and adding automation. Sales and work force are up substantially.
Other Locations: The company has operations throughout Canada and the United States. It also does business in 45 foreign countries through its subsidiaries and affiliates.

LIBERTY MUTUAL INSURANCE GROUP ★★

175 Berkeley St., Boston, MA 02117; 617-357-9500
http://www.libertymutual.com
Employees: 37,000
Sales: $10,964 million
Key Personnel: Chairman: Gary L. Countryman. President, CEO: Edmund F. Kelly. Human Resources: Helen Sayles.

In the workers' compensation insurance market, Liberty Mutual is at the top of the heap. The company is an innovator in the field, with groundbreaking programs in site analysis and worker rehabilitation. It also offers a variety of other services, including group health, life, and property/casualty insurance and financial services. Sales and work force are growing rapidly.
Other Locations: The company has operations in Canada, Mexico, the United Kingdom, and the United States.

MASSACHUSETTS MUTUAL LIFE INSURANCE COMPANY

1295 State St., Springfield, MA 01111; 413-788-8411
http://massmutual.com
Employees: 7,885
Sales: $11,728.4 million
Key Personnel: Chairman: Thomas B. Wheeler. President, CEO: Robert J. O'Connell. Human Resources: Susan A. Alfano.

Massachusetts Mutual Life Insurance has four main areas of operations: insurance and financial management, life and health benefits management, pension management, and investment management. The company is currently focusing on insurance products for small, family-owned businesses. It recently became the founding member of the American Alliance of Family-Owned Businesses. Sales are up and work force is holding steady.

MINNESOTA

THE ST. PAUL COMPANIES, INC. ★★

385 Washington St., St. Paul, MN 55102; 651-310-7911
http://www.stpaul.com
Employees: 14,000
Sales: $9,108.4
Key Personnel: Chairman, President, and CEO: Douglas W. Leatherdale. President, COO James E. Gustafson. Human Resources: David R. Nachbar.

One of the nation's largest insurers through its acquisition of USF&G, St. Paul sells property/casualty insurance, reinsurance, and investment services through such subsidiaries as St. Paul Fire and Marine and St. Paul Re. The John Nuveen Company offers investment advice. Both sales and work force have risen dramatically.

NEBRASKA

MUTUAL OF OMAHA COMPANIES

Mutual of Omaha Plaza, Omaha, NE 68175; 402-342-7600
http://www.mutualofomaha.com
Employees: 7,111
Sales: $3,700 million

Mutual of Omaha Companies is a top seller of individual health and accident insurance and a leading life insurance and annuities provider. Its Mutual of Omaha subsidiary focuses on the former, its United of Omaha on the latter. To adapt to a changing market, the company has been developing managed care alternatives. Sales and work force are down.

NEW JERSEY

CHUBB CORPORATION

15 Mountain View Rd., Warren, NJ 07061-1615; 908-903-2000
http://www.chubb.com
Employees: 10,700
Sales: $6,349.8 million
Key Personnel: Chairman, CEO: Dean R. O'Hare. President: John J. Degan. EVP, CFO: David B. Kelso.

Chubb sells insurance to affluent individuals and businesses. Its services include property/casualty insurance, specialty coverage, and a new reinsurance operation, Chubb Re. The company is expanding its presence overseas and already has a presence in Asia, Europe, and Latin America. It has been consolidating its operations in the United States for several years. Sales and work force are down.

Other Locations: The company has operations in Puerto Rico, the United States, the Virgin Islands, and 25 other countries.

PRUDENTIAL INSURANCE COMPANY OF AMERICA

751 Broad St., Newark, NJ 07102; 973-802-6000
http://www.prudential.com
Employees: 50,000
Sales: $27,087 million
Key Personnel: Chairman, CEO: Arthur F. Ryan. EVP Financial Management: E. Michael Caulfield. EVP Human Resources: Michele S. Darling.

Prudential Insurance offers a broad range of products to its customers, including life, health, and property insurance; asset management; estate and financial planning; and residential real estate services. The company has recently been hit with fines for misrepresenting its products and large claims from natural disasters. Scandal and corporate streamlining have pushed sales and workforce down.

Other Locations: The company has operations in Canada, China, Italy, Japan, South Korea, Spain, Taiwan, the United Kingdom, and the United States.

NEW YORK

AMERICAN INTERNATIONAL GROUP, INC. ★★

70 Pine St., New York, NY 10270; 212-770-7000
http://www.aig.com
Employees: 48,000
Sales: $30,760 million
Key Personnel: Chairman, CEO: Maurice R. Greenberg. VC Life Insurance: Edmund S.W. Tse. Human Resources: Axel I. Freudmann.

Among the world's largest insurance companies, American International Group has a major share of the property/casualty insurance market. Although it has a strong U.S. presence, it derives slightly more than half its income from abroad. It is adding commercial insurance operations in China, Russia, Paki-

stan, and Uzbekistan. Sales and workforce are up substantially.

Other Locations: The company has operations in the United States and 130 foreign countries.

AXA FINANCIAL, INC. ★★

1290 Ave. of the Americas, New York, NY 10104; 212-554-1234
http://www.equitable.com
Employees: 14,700
Assets: $10,919 million
Key Personnel: President, CEO: Edward D. Miller. VC, COO: Michael Hegarty. Human Resources: Carolyn Greene.

Formerly The Equitable Companies, AXA Financial is nearly 60 percent owned by French Insurance titan AXA. With nearly half its income derived from sales of individual insurance and annuities, AXA Financial targets the baby-boomer market. It also provides cash management, investment services, and other financial services. The company also has major interests in the management and development of commercial real estate. Sales are up healthily, as is workforce.

GUARDIAN LIFE INSURANCE COMPANY OF AMERICA

7 Hanover Sq., New York, NY 10004; 212-598-8000
http://www.theguardian.com
Employees: 4,800
Sales: $7,179.8 million
Key Personnel: President, CEO: Joseph D. Sargent. EVP, Chief Investment Officer: Frank J. Jones. VP Human Resources, Administrative Support: Douglas C. Kramer.

Known for its conservative and successful management style, Guardian Life Insurance provides a full range of insurance coverage, including life, health, and disability. The company also offers financial services to its customers, such as its Baillie Gifford International Fund. Its sales are up, but workforce has dropped.

MARSH & MCLENNAN COMPANIES, INC. ★★

1166 Ave. of the Americas, New York, NY 10036-2774; 212-345-5000
http://www.marshmac.com
Employees: 54,300
Sales: $7,190 million
Key Personnel: Chairman, CEO: A. J.

C. Smith. SVP, CFO: Frank J. Borelli. SVP Human Resources and Administration: Francis N. Bonsignore.

Marsh & McLennan Companies group together Marsh & McLennan, the world's biggest insurance brokerage, Frizzell Financial Services, the top U.K. group insurance provider, Seabury & Smith, the top U.S. group insurance provider, and several other subsidiaries (including recent acquisition Johnson & Higgins). Worldwide economic ebbs and flows have caused fluctuations, but the conglomerate's sales and work force are up substantially.

Other Locations: The company has branches in over 80 countries.

METROPOLITAN LIFE INSURANCE COMPANY OF NEW YORK

One Madison Ave., New York, NY 10010; 212-578-2211
http://www.metlife.com
Employees: 45,000
Sales: $27,077 million
Key Personnel: Chairman, CEO: Robert H. Benmosche. VC, CFO: Stewart G. Nagler. Human Resources: Lisa M. Weber.

One of the largest life insurance companies in North America, Metropolitan Life Insurance offers a broad range of services to its clients. Among its services are employee benefits administration and mutual funds. Its health plans and some real estate and trust operations were recently sold. The company's merger with New England Mutual Life Insurance in 1996 broadened its traditionally middle-class client base to include wealthier demographics. Sales are up, but the company's work force has been static.

Other Locations: The company has operations in Canada, Mexico, Portugal, South Korea, Spain, Taiwan, the U.K. and the U.S.

NEW YORK LIFE INSURANCE COMPANY

51 Madison Ave., New York, NY 10010; 212-576-7000
http://www.newyorklife.com
Employees: 13,000
Sales: $18,350 million
Key Personnel: Chairman, President, and CEO: Seymour Sternberg. EVP, CFO: Howard I. Atkins. Human Resources: Richard A. Hansen.

One of the largest life insurance companies in the United States, New York Life Insurance also provides mutual funds, disability insurance, and other services. It recently closed its Canadian operations and sold its health care operations, but is expanding in other areas, such as Asia and Latin America. Sales and work force are up.

Other Locations: The company has operations in Argentina, Bermuda, China, Hong Kong, Indonesia, Mexico, South Korea, Taiwan, the United Kingdom, and the United States.

TEACHERS INSURANCE AND ANNUITY ASSOCIATION–COLLEGE RETIREMENT EQUITIES FUND

730 Third Ave., New York, NY 10017-3206; 212-490-9000
http://www.tiaa-cref.org
Employees: 5,000
Sales: $45,898.5 million
Key Personnel: Chairman, President, and CEO: John H. Biggs. VC, Chief Investment Officer: Martin L. Leibowitz. Human Resources: Matina S. Horner.

Providing retirement and insurance benefits to employees of research and educational organizations is the focus of Teachers Insurance and Annuity Association–College Retirement Equities Fund. TIAA–CREF operates the largest private pension fund in the United States and has considerable influence in the investment community. Sales and work force are up.

Other Locations: The company has operations in Canada and the United States.

TOKIO MARINE MANAGEMENT, INC. ★

101 Park Ave., New York, NY 10178; 212-297-6600
Employees: 15,294
Sales: $10,782.7 million.
Key Personnel: President: Masaharu Nakamura. Controller: William Mullins. Human Resources: Sonya Glatzhofer.

In the Japanese insurance market, Tokio Marine and Fire is the largest nonlife company. Tokio Marine Management is its U.S. subsidiary. It offers fire and casualty, marine, personal accident, automobile, and other services. The company is affiliated with the Mitsubishi Group. It is currently expanding its services in China and Vietnam. Assets and work force are on the rise.

Other Locations: Worldwide HQ: Tokio Marine and Fire, 2-1, Marunouchi 1-chome, Chiyoda-ku, Tokyo, 100, Japan; phone: +81-3-3212-6211.

CITIGROUP, INC. ★★
399 Park Ave., New York, NY 10043;
212-559-1000
http://www.citi.com
Employees: 173,700
Sales: $76,431 million
Key Personnel: Co-Chairman, Co-CEO:
Sanford I. Weill. Co-Chairman, Co-CEO:
John S. Reed. Human Resources: Lawrence R. Phillips.
Travelers Group merged with Citicorp, one of the world's largest credit card companies, to form Citicorp, a truly titanic financial services company. The business, which will continue to use the Travelers' umbrella logo, now offers credit card, insurance, and assorted financial and investment services. Its subsidiaries include brokerage firm Saloman Smith Barney, mutual fund-operator Primerica Financial, and others. As a result of the merger, sales and workforce have more than doubled.

OHIO

AMERICAN FINANCIAL GROUP, INC.
One E. Fourth St., Cincinnati, OH 45202;
513-579-2121
http://www.amfnl.com
Employees: 10,000
Sales: $4,050 million
Key Personnel: Chairman, CEO: Carl H.
Lindner. Co-President: Keith E. Lindner.
Human Resources: Lawrence Otto.
American Financial is primarily a provider of casualty, life, and property insurance through its subsidiary, Great American Insurance. However, the company has many other subsidiaries, which distribute food, publish magazines, and own radio stations. More than half the company's sales come from insurance premiums. Sales and work force are rising.

NATIONWIDE INSURANCE ENTERPRISE ★★
One Nationwide Plaza, Columbus, OH
43215-2220; 614-249-7111
http://www.nationwide.com
Employees: 32,815
Sales: $25,301.1 million
Key Personnel: President: Galen R.
Barnes. EVP, CFO: Robert A. Oakley.
Human Resources: Donna A. James.
Nationwide Insurance Enterprise offers a wide variety of coverage. Its services are divided into four areas: long-term savings, exclusive agency lines, commercial services, and investments. The company also owns real estate. It is currently restructuring its operations to improve efficiency through increased automation. Sales and work force are up.
Other Locations: The company has operations in 10 states, Puerto Rico, and Germany.

PENNSYLVANIA

CIGNA CORPORATION
One Liberty Pl., Philadelphia, PA 19192-1550; 215-761-1000
http://www.cigna.com
Employees: 49,900
Sales: $21,437 million
Key Personnel: Chairman, CEO: Wilson H. Taylor. EVP, CFO: James G. Stewart.
Human Resources: Donald M. Levinson.
Natural disasters have cost CIGNA. The company's property/casualty and reinsurance operations suffered from a number of disasters, both manmade and natural, in the early 1990s. However, it remains one of the top insurance companies in the United States and offers a broad range of services. Sales and work force are up.
Other Locations: The company has operations in Asia, Europe, Latin America, and the United States.

TEXAS

AMERICAN GENERAL FINANCIAL GROUP
2929 Allen Pkwy., Houston, TX 77019-2155; 713-522-1111
http://www.agc.com
Employees: 16,100
Sales: $10,251 million
Key Personnel: Chairman, President, and CEO: Robert M. Devlin. VC: Jon P. Newton. Human Resources: Laura Nichol.
One of the top life insurance companies in the United States, American General offers financial services as well. Among its services are business services, home equity loans, and retirement plans. The company is growing rapidly by acquiring other companies. Its sales are up, but workforce has declined slightly.
Other Locations: The company has operations in Canada, Puerto Rico, the United States, and the Virgin Islands.

UICI. ★★
4001 McEwen Dr., Ste. 200, Dallas, TX
75244; 972-392-6700

Employees: 4,000
Sales: $1,179.9 million
Key Personnel: Chairman: Ronald L. Jensen. EVP, COO: Richard J. Estell. Human Resources: Richard Hooton.
UICI (formerly United Insurance Companies) sells its wares to small, nonstandard markets. It concentrates on the self-employed and students. The company also provides additional services, such as credit cards, telemarketing, and long-distance telephone services. Its sales and its work force are up markedly.

USAA ★★
9800 Fredericksburg Rd., USAA Bldg., San Antonio, TX 78288; 210-498-2211
Employees: 20,120
Sales: $7,687 million
Key Personnel: Chairman, CEO: Robert T. Herres. President, COO: Robert G. Davis. Human Resources: Elizabeth Conklyn.
USAA (United Services Auto Association) specializes in providing insurance to military personnel and their dependents. The company provides automobile and property/casualty insurance and discount buying services. Its full range of services is open only to active or retired military personnel; however, it offers insurance services to some government officials and their families. Sales and work force are up.
Other Locations: The company has offices in California, Colorado, Florida, Virginia, and Washington and in Germany and the United Kingdom.

WISCONSIN
NORTHWESTERN MUTUAL LIFE INSURANCE COMPANY ★
720 E. Wisconsin Ave., Milwaukee, WI 53202-4797; 414-271-1444
http://www.northwesternmutual.com
Employees: 4,117
Sales: $13,479 million
Key Personnel: President, CEO: James D. Ericson. EVP: John M. Bremer. Human Resources: Susan A. Lueger.
Operating through more than 7,000 independent agents, Northwestern Mutual Life Insurance is one of the largest insurance companies in the United States. It is well-known in the industry for its superior agent training programs. The company's investment policies allowed it to profit in recent ups and downs of the financial markets. Sales are up, as is work force.

---

❶ INTEREST GROUPS/ ORGANIZATIONS

DISTRICT OF COLUMBIA
AARP ★
601 E St., NW, Washington, DC 20049; 202-434-2277
http://www.aarp.org
Employees: 2,000
Sales: $471.5 million
Key Personnel: Chairman: Allan W. Tull. President: Joseph S. Perkins. Human Resources: J. Robert Carr.
Among the most influential lobbying groups in the United States, the American Association of Retired Persons has over 33 million members. Its focus is the needs of people over 50. The AARP has often been criticized for its uncompromising opposition to cuts in Social Security and Medicare spending. Sales are down, but workforce has increased.

AMERICAN RED CROSS
430 17th St. NW, Washington, DC 20006-5307; 202-737-8300
http://www.redcross.org
Employees (est.): 30,000
Sales: $2,080.4 million
Key Personnel: President, CEO: Norman R. Augustine. COO: E. Matthew Branam. Human Resources: Nancy Breseke.
The American Red Cross is a nonprofit organization dedicated to relieving human suffering. The group maintains the nation's biggest blood supply and also conducts programs to collect and distribute other human fluids and tissues, among its many duties. It is primarily staffed by volunteers. Sales are up and work force is up slightly.

SMITHSONIAN INSTITUTION
1000 Jefferson Dr., SW, Washington, DC 20560; 202-357-2700
http://www.si.edu
Employees: 6,469
Sales: $728.8 million
Key Personnel: Provost: J. Dennis O'Connor. Inspector General: Thomas D. Blair. Human Resources: Carolyn E.

Jones.

The Smithsonian Institution turned 150 years old in 1996. The organization, which is primarily funded by the U.S. government, operates 16 museums (in the District of Columbia and elsewhere) and publishing enterprises. It also supervises a variety of research programs and runs the National Zoo. It is currently suffering financial difficulties due to budget cutbacks. Sales have rebounded slightly, but workforce has slipped.

VIRGINIA

UNITED WAY OF AMERICA

701 N. Fairfax St., Alexandria, VA 22314; 703-836-7100
http://www.unitedway.org
Employees: 15,000
Sales: $3,250 million
Key Personnel: President: Betty Stanley Beene. Chairman: Paul J. Tagliabue. VC Human Resources: Dorothy Miles.

Recovery is the watchword for the United Way of America. The nonprofit organization conducts fundraising for a wide variety of charitable causes. It was slammed in the early 1990s by a corruption scandal that went straight to the top of its leadership. The group has hired new leaders and reformed its practices. Sales are up and workforce has held steady.

❶ MEDICAL/ BIOTECHNOLOGY

CALIFORNIA

ACUSON CORPORATION

1220 Charleston Rd., Mountain View, CA 94043-7393; 415-969-9112
http://www.acuson.com
Employees: 1,894
Sales: $455.1 million
Key Personnel: Chairman, CEO: Samuel H. Maslak. President: Daniel R. Dugan. Human Resources: Charles H. Dearborn.

Acuson is one of the leading makers of ultrasound diagnostic imaging equipment. The company's products are popular in spite of their relatively high price because of high quality and easy upgrades. After a period of instability, Acuson's sales and work force are up modestly.

ALLERGAN, INC.

2525 Dupont Dr., Irvine, CA 92612; 714-246-4500
http://www.allergan.com
Employees: 5,972
Sales: $1,296.1 million
Key Personnel: President, CEO: David Pyott. Corporate VP Research and Development: Lester J. Kaplan. Human Resources: Tom Burnham.

Allergan is one of the largest makers of therapeutic eye and skin products. The company manufactures a wide range of ophthalmic products, including intraocular lenses. The company was spun off by SmithKline in 1989 and has been restructuring since then. It is actively expanding its foreign sales and operations. Sales and work force are rising slowly.

ALZA CORPORATION ★★

950 Page Mill Rd., Palo Alto, CA 94303; 650-494-5000
http://www.alza.com
Employees: 1,845
Sales: $584.5 million
Key Personnel: Chairman, CEO: Ernest Mario. SVP, CFO: Bruce C. Cozadd. SVP Human Resources: Harold Fethe.

In the design and production of therapeutic rate-controlled drug delivery systems, ALZA is the leader. The company leases this technology to pharmaceutical companies, such as Ciba-Geigy, receiving royalties in return. ALZA is currently developing technology to transport drugs through the skin with electric currents. Its sales and work force are up.

CHIRON CORPORATION

4560 Horton St., Emeryville, CA 94608-2916; 510-655-8730
http://www.chiron.com
Employees: 3,247
Sales: $736.7 million
Key Personnel: Chairman, President, and CEO: Sean P. Lance. VC: Edward E. Penhoet. Human Resources: Linda W. Short.

Chiron is a leader in the biotechnology field, working in diagnostics, therapeutics, and vaccines. The company has recently sold its vision and diagnostics divisions to focus on core operations in biopharmaceuticals, blood testing, and vaccines. As a result of its downsizing sales and work force have been cut almost in half.

GENENTECH, INC.

One DNA Way., S. San Francisco, CA 94080; 650-225-1000
http://www.gene.com
Employees: 3,389
Sales: $1062.1 million
Key Personnel: President, CEO: Arthur D. Levinson. COO: William D. Young. Human Resources: Judith A. Heyboer.

Genentech sells several products developed in its biotechnology laboratories, including the growth hormones Protropin and Nutropin, breast cancer drug Herceptin and the clot-dissolving enzyme Activase. The company has several products under development, in-cluding treatments for asthma, and renal failure. Sales and work force continue to rise.

SUNRISE MEDICAL, INC.

2382 Faraday Ave., Ste. 200, Carlsbad, CA 92008; 760-930-1500
http://www.sunrisemedical.com
Employees: 4,400
Sales: $660.2 million
Key Personnel: Chairman, President, and CEO: Richard H. Chandler. SVP, CFO: Ted N. Tarbet. Human Resources: Roberta C. Baade.

As the world's population ages, the need for wheelchairs rises. Sunrise Medical makes some of the most popular electric and manual wheelchairs on the market. The company also makes products such as walkers, crutches, and nursing home beds. The company is expanding through acquisition of similar companies. Both its sales and work force are up modestly.

CONNECTICUT

PE CORPORATION ★★

761 Main Ave., Norwalk, CT 06859; 203-762-1000
http://www.perkin-elmer.com
Employees: 7,188
Sales: $1,531.2 million
Key Personnel: Chairman, President, and CEO: Tony L. White. SVP, CFO: Dennis L. Winger. Human Resources: Rafael Garofalo.

Formerly Perkin-Elmer, PE Corporation is the largest maker of analytical instruments and life science systems. Scientists wishing to know the molecular structure of chemical substances use the company's spectrophotometers, thermal analyzers, and polarimeters. The company also makes instruments designed to analyze biological molecules such as DNA. Its sales and workforce are up dramatically.

UNITED STATES SURGICAL CORPORATION

150 Glover Ave., Norwalk, CT 06856; 203-845-1000
http://www.ussurg.com
Employees: 5,776
Sales: $1,172.1 million
Key Personnel: President: Larry Heaton. CFO: Steve Amelio. Senior Director Human Resources: Bruce Reardon.

United States Surgical Corporation, a new acquisition of Tyco International, is the largest manufacturer of surgical staplers in the world. It is also a leading maker of endoscopy devices. The company faces stiff competition from rival Johnson & Johnson for both the surgical staple and the endoscope markets. Its sales have increased, but workforce is down.
Other Locations: The company manufactures its products in Connecticut and in Germany, Puerto Rico, and Switzerland. It has offices in the United States and 23 other countries.

FLORIDA

MAXXIM MEDICAL, INC.

10300 49th St. N, Clearwater, FL 33762; 727-561-2100
http://www.maxximmedical.com
Employees: 4,068
Sales: $522.5 million
Key Personnel: Chairman, President, CEO: Kenneth W. Davidson. SEVP, COO: Peter M. Graham. Human Resources: Suzanne R. Garon.

MAXXIM Medical markets lines of physical therapy equipment, surgical and medical procedural supplies, and sterile drapes and clothing. Each of the company's divisions has its own sales force. MAXXIM currently has plans to expand its foreign sales force. The company's sales have dropped, but workforce has increased modestly.

SAFESKIN CORPORATION ★★

12671 High Bluff Dr., San Diego, CA 92130; 858-794-8111
http://www.safeskin.com
Employees: 7,200
Sales: $231.8 million
Key Personnel: Chairman, President, and CEO: Richard Jaffe. EVP, CFO:

David L. Morash. Human Resources: Robert Zabaronick, Sr.

With the threat of AIDS infection a very real possibility in medicine and research, Safeskin has become the top manufacturer of hypoallergenic latex gloves. The company makes several types of specially treated latex gloves that reduce the incidence of skin irritation and allergic reactions with prolonged use. Its sales and work force are up dramatically.

ILLINOIS

BAXTER INTERNATIONAL, INC.

One Baxter Pkwy., Deerfield, IL 60015; 847-948-2000
http://www.baxter.com
Employees: 42,000
Sales: $6,599 million
Key Personnel: Chairman: Vernon R. Loucks, Jr. President, CEO: Harry M. Jansen Kraemer, Jr. Human Resources: Michael J. Tucker.

The top U.S. maker and distributor of medical and laboratory products is Baxter International. The company makes a line of medical specialties, including cardiovascular devices and dialysis systems. Baxter also makes laboratory products, such as anesthetics and intravenous systems. Its sales and workforce are both on the rise.

Other Locations: The company has 71 manufacturing facilities, 25 research facilities, and 149 distribution centers around the world.

INDIANA

BIOMET, INC. ★

Airport Industrial Park, Warsaw, IN 46581-0587; 219-267-6639
http://www.biomet.com
Employees: 2,150
Sales: $757.4 million
Key Personnel: President, CEO: Dane A. Miller. VC: Jerry L. Ferguson. Human Resources: Darlene K. Whaley.

The fourth largest manufacturer of orthopedic appliances in the world, Biomet also sells a line of bone regrowth stimulation devices. Its products are sold in over 100 countries. The company has developed a strong research and development operation and has acquired many related companies in recent years. Both sales and work force are up.

MASSACHUSETTS

GENZYME CORPORATION

One Kendall Sq., Cambridge, MA 02139; 617-252-7500
http://www.genzyme.com
Employees: 3,500
Sales: $688.5 million
Key Personnel: Chairman, President, and CEO: Henri A. Termeer. EVP: Earl M. Collier, Jr. Human Resources: John V. Heffernan.

A top research company in the field of gene therapy treatment for cystic fibrosis (done in partnership with the University of Iowa), Genzyme also makes a number of other health care and diagnostic products, pharmaceuticals, and fine chemicals. Its sales are up and workforce has held steady.

THERMEDICS, INC. ★

470 Wildwood St., P.O. Box 2999, Woburn, MA 01888-1799; 781-938-3786
http://www.thermedicsinc.com
Employees: 2,045
Sales: $313.1 million
Key Personnel: President, CEO: John T. Keiser. SVP: Victor L. Poirier. Human Resources: Anne Pol.

Thermedics makes products that require precise chemistry, biomedical research, and electronics. This combination has produced an unusual product line that includes both an artificial heart pump and an explosive-detection system used in many airports. The company, a subsidiary of Thermo Electron, also makes contaminant detection devices and intestinal nutrition delivery systems. Sales are up modestly and workforce growth has been strong.

MINNESOTA

MEDTRONIC, INC. ★★

7000 Central Ave. NE, Minneapolis, MN 55432-3576; 612-514-4000
http://www.medtronic.com
Employees: 21,794
Sales: $4,134.1 million
Key Personnel: Chairman, CEO: William W. George. President, COO: Arthur D. Collins, Jr. SVP Human Resources: Janet S. Fiola.

Medtronic is the largest manufacturer of therapeutic implantable biomedical devices in the world. Among the company's products are implantable pacemakers that regulate a patient's heartbeat, heart valve replacements, and implantable drug delivery systems. The company is expanding its European and Asian markets. Its sales and work force have skyrocketed.

ST. JUDE MEDICAL, INC. ★
One Lillehei Plaza, St. Paul, MN 55117; 651-483-2000
http://www.sjm.com
Employees:3,984
Sales: $1,016 million
Key Personnel: President, CEO: Terry L. Shepherd. President Daig Division: Daniel J. Starks. Human Resources: Jan M. Webster.
One of the largest manufacturers of mechanical heart valves, St. Jude Medical develops and markets medical devices used for cardiovascular applications. These include pacesetters, angiography catheters, and so forth. The company is entering the implantable cardioverter defibrillator market. Sales and work force are rising.

NEW JERSEY

BECTON, DICKINSON AND COMPANY ★★
One Becton Dr., Franklin Lakes, NJ 07417; 201-847-6800
http://www.bd.com
Employees: 21,700
Sales: $3,116.9 million
Key Personnel: Chairman, President, and CEO: Clateo Castellini. EVP: Edward J. Ludwig. Human Resources: James V. Jerbasi.
Becton, Dickinson makes diagnostic systems and medical supplies. It is the largest supplier of IV catheters in the world. The company has a comprehensive product line that includes products used for tissue culture, cellular analysis, and blood collection. It is expanding its operations in Asia. Sales and work force are up.

C. R. BARD, INC.
730 Central Ave., Murray Hill, NJ 07974; 908-277-8000
http://www.crbard.com
Employees: 7,700
Sales: $1,164.7 million
Key Personnel: President, COO: William H. Longfield. Group President: Guy J. Jordan. Human Resources: Hope Greenfield.
Known for its Foley catheter, the top

bladder drainage device in the United States, C. R. Bard makes a wide variety of medical products. The company is a trailblazer in the development of disposable medical products. Its most popular items are its cardiovascular supplies, such as balloon angioplasty catheters. The company's sales and work force have both decreased.
Other Locations: The company has manufacturing facilities in Ireland, Malaysia, and the United Kingdom.

MERCK & CO., INC. ★
One Merck Dr., Whitehouse Station, NJ 08889-001; 908-423-1000
http://www.merck.com
Employees: 57,300
Sales: $26,898.2 million
Key Personnel: Chairman, President, and CEO: Raymond V. Gilmartin. EVP: Edward M. Scolnick. Human Resources: Wendy Yarno.
A world leader in prescription drugs, Merck makes drugs to treat ailments ranging from high cholesterol to AIDS to male pattern baldness. The company's newest drugs include AIDS treatment Crixivan and a hot-selling drug to relieve arthritis pain called Vioxx. Sales and workforce are both healthy.

NEW YORK

BAUSCH & LOMB, INC. ★★
One Bausch & Lomb Place, Rochester, NY 14604-2701; 716-338-6000
http://www.bausch.com
Employees: 15,000
Sales: $2,362.8 million
Key Personnel: Chairman, CEO: William M. Carpenter. President, COO: Carl E. Sassano. SVP Human Resources: Daryl M. Dickson.
One of the top makers of eye care products, Bausch & Lomb also manufactures many products for medical and dental markets. Among its products are contact lenses and dental implants. The company also has an optics division, which manufactures telescopes, binoculars, and related products. Its sales and work force are both increasing.
Other Locations: The company has facilities in 35 countries.

NOVO NORDISK OF NORTH AMERICA, INC. ★★
405 Lexington Ave., Suite 6400, New

York, NY 10017; 212-867-0123
Employees (overall Novo Nordisk): 14,175
Sales (overall Novo Nordisk): $2,480.5 million
Key Personnel: President: Steve Zelson. CFO: John Riley. Human Resources: Sarah Savage.

Novo Nordisk of North America is the U.S. branch of Novo Nordisk A/S. The top insulin producer in the world, Novo Nordisk also has a major share of the industrial enzyme market. The company, which began as a home business in the 1930s, is aggressively expanding its enzyme product line as competition in the insulin market gets increasingly fierce. Its sales are down slightly, though workforce continues to increase modestly.
Other Locations: Worldwide HQ: Novo Nordisk A/S, Novo Alle, Bagsvaerd, Denmark; phone: +45-44-44-88-88. The company has offices in 51 countries.

---

❶ MINING AND METALS

ARIZONA

PHELPS DODGE CORPORATION

2600 N. Central Ave., Phoenix, AZ 85004-3014; 602-234-8100
http://www.phelpsdodge.com
Employees: 13,924
Sales: $3,063.4 million
Key Personnel: Chairman, CEO: Douglas C. Yearley. President, COO: J. Steven Whisler. SVP Human Resources: David L. Pulatie.

Phelps Dodge was on the brink of bankruptcy when it risked its future on a new copper extraction process, called solvent extraction/ electrowinning. The process, which is much cheaper than traditional methods, made the company the lowest-cost copper producer in the market. It also has a variety of other mining and manufacturing interests. Hurt by record-low copper prices, the company's sales and workforce have decreased.
Other Locations: The company has operations in 25 countries.

CALIFORNIA

BHP MINERALS

550 California St., San Francisco, CA 94104; 415-774-2030
Employees (overall BHP): 55,000

Sales (overall BHP): $15,341.4 million
Key Personnel: Chairman: Jeremy K. Ellis. General Manager, Finance: D. F. Collins. SVP, Group General Manager Human Resources: C.W. Mudge.

BHP Minerals is the U.S. subsidiary of Broken Hill Proprietary, the largest company in Australia. Broken Hill Proprietary has interests in many resource-related industries, including minerals, petroleum, and steel. In addition to producing gold, copper, iron, and manganese, it also mines coal for both thermal and metallurgical markets. Its sales and work force are down.
Other Locations: Worldwide HQ: Broken Hill Proprietary Co., Ltd., BHP Tower, 600 Bourke St., Melbourne 3000, Australia; +61-3-9609-3333.

COLORADO

CYPRUS AMAX MINERALS COMPANY

9100 E. Mineral Circle, Englewood, CO 80112; 303-643-5000
http://www.cyprusamax.com
Employees: 7,200
Sales: $2,566 million
Key Personnel: Chairman, President, and CEO: Milton H. Ward. EVP: Garold R. Spindler. Human Resources: Chris Cowl.

Cyprus AMAX Minerals is a top supplier of many vital materials. The company is not only one of the largest U.S. suppliers of copper and coal but a leading supplier of molybdenum, gold, and other key metals. It continues to expand its operations in many areas of the world. Due to the company's recent downsizing and the poor metals market of late, sales and work force are down sharply.
Other Locations: The company has facilities in Australia, Chile, the Netherlands, Peru, Sweden, the United Kingdom, and the United States.

GEORGIA

POLYSIUS KRUPP USA, INC.

180 Interstate N. Pkwy., Atlanta, GA 30339-2194; 770-955-3660
http://www.krupp-ag.com
Employees (overall Thyssen Krupp): 116,174
Sales (overall Thyssen Krupp): $26,097.4 million
Key Personnel: President: Daniel R. Fritz. VP Finance: Andreas Penninger. Director Human Resources: Mike Dow-

ell.

Krupp USA is a subsidiary of Thyssen Krupp AG, a large German industrial conglomerate. The U.S. branch of the company develops products for cement and raw-materials processing and consults, designs, and does research for the construction of industrial plants. Sales are up, but workforce is down.
Other Locations: Worldwide HQ: Thyssen Krupp AG, August-Thyssen-Strasse 1, D-40221 Dusseldorf, Germany; +49-211-824-1000.

ILLINOIS
RYERSON TULL, INC.
2621 W. 15th Pl., Chicago, IL 60608; 773-762-2121
http://www.ryersontull.com
Employees: 5,100
Sales: $2,782.7 million
Key Personnel: Chairman, President, and CEO: Neil S. Novich. EVP, CFO: Jay M. Gratz. Human Resources: William Korda.
Formerly Inland Steel Industries, Ryerson Tull processes steel and distributes industrial materials both nationally and internationally. The company recently divested itself of its steelmaking business and took on the name of its Ryerson Tull subsidiary for the parent company. It is working with companies from Canada, South Africa, and Hong Kong in export ventures. Sales are up, but work force is down.

NIPPON STEEL U.S.A., INC.
900 N. Michigan Ave., Chicago, IL 60611; 312-751-0800
http://www.nsc.co.jp/english/index.htm
Employees (overall Nippon): 85,500
Sales (overall Nippon): $23,119.6 million
Key Personnel: President, CEO: Mosaki Sato. VP: Tomukatsu Kobayashi. Human Resources Manager: Makoto Haya.
Nippon Steel is the largest steel manufacturer in the world. With demand for steel decreasing, the company has been diversifying, expanding operations in such areas as communications and electronics. It also provides engineering and construction services for large projects, such as harbors and airports. Sales are down and workforce is static.
Other Locations: Worldwide HQ: Nippon Steel Corp., 6-3, Otemachi 2-chome,

Chiyoda-ku, Tokyo 100-8071, Japan; +81-3-3242-4111.

LOUISIANA
FREEPORT-MCMORAN COPPER & GOLD INC.
1615 Poydras St., New Orleans, LA 70112; 504-582-4000
http://www.fcx.com
Employees: 6,349
Sales: $1,757.1 million
Key Personnel: Chairman, CEO: James R. Moffett. VC: Rene L. Latiolais. Human Resources: Allison Lauricella.
Freeport-McMoRan Copper & Gold operates the vast open-pit Grasberg mine in Indonesia's remote Irian Jaya province. The company operates other mines in Southeast Asia and Europe. Sales are decreasing, but work force is up slightly.

MICHIGAN
BUDD COMPANY
3155 W. Big Beaver Rd., Troy, MI 48084; ; 248-643-3500
http://www.buddcompany.com
Employees: 9,794
Sales: $3,648.1 million
Key Personnel: Chairman, CEO: Siegfried Buschman. President, COO: David P. Williams. Human Resources: Nancy L. Hutcheson.
The Budd Company is a subsidiary of Thyssen Krupp, a German conglomerate with three main operations: steel, manufactured goods, and trading and services. Budd makes auto components. The company is restruc-turing its operations in the face of decreased demand for steel. Sales and work force are up.
Other Locations: Worldwide HQ: Thyssen Krupp AG, August-Thyssen-Strasse 1, D-40221 Dusseldorf, Germany; +49-211-824-1000.

NEW YORK
ASARCO, INC.
180 Maiden Lane, New York, NY 10038; 212-510-2000
http://www.asarco.com
Employees: 11,800
Sales: $2,721 million
Key Personnel: Chairman, CEO: Francis R. McAllister. President, COO: Kevin R. Morano. Human Resources: David B. Woodbury.
Once just a custom smelter, ASARCO

now has mining operations in the U.S. and abroad. The company also provides environmental services and does a limited chemical manufacturing business. ASARCO is in the process of merging with Cyprus Amax Mineral; the resulting operation will be the largest publicly held copper company in the world. Sales and workforce are both down.

Other Locations: The company has mines in Arizona, Colorado, Idaho, Missouri, Montana, and Tennessee and in Argentina, Australia, Canada, Mexico, and Peru.

INCO, LTD.

One New York Plaza, New York, NY 10004; 212-612-5500
http://www.incoltd.com
Employees (overall Inco): 11,007
Sales (overall Inco): $1,766 million
Key Personnel: President: Scott M. Hand. EVP: Peter J. Goudie. Director of Human Resources, Inco, Ltd. (U.S.): Lorne M. Ames.

One of the world's top nickel producers, Inco is facing stubborn competition from Eastern European countries. The company—which is the U.S. division of Toronto-based Inco, Ltd.— also produces cobalt, platinum, liquid sulfur, and many other key industrial minerals. It is in the process of opening a mining equipment manufacturing plant in Chile. Sales and work force are down sharply.

Other Locations: Worldwide HQ: Inco, Ltd., 145 King St. W., Ste. 1500, Toronto, Ontario M5H 4B7, Canada; 416-361-7511. The company has facilities in 21 nations.

NORTH CAROLINA

NUCOR CORPORATION

2100 Rexford Rd., Charlotte, NC 28211; 704-366-7000
http://www.nucor.com
Employees: 7,200
Sales: $4,151.2 million
Key Personnel: Chairman, President, and CEO: H. David Aycock. EVP Steel Products: D. Michael Parrish. Human Resources: Jim Coblin.

Low-cost, high-production steel is the forte of Nucor. The company achieves its goal through a combination of high technology and cheap, nonunion labor. It is a trailblazer in the use of mini-mills, which make steel more quickly and cheaply. Nucor is building a new South Carolina

mill that will make flat-rolled steel. Sales are down slightly, but work force has risen moderately.

Other Locations: The company has operations in nine states and in Trinidad and Tobago.

OHIO

ALCAN ALUMINIUM CORPORATION ★

100 Erieview Plaza, Cleveland, OH 44101; 216-523-6800
http://www.alcan.com
Employees (overall Alcan): 36,000
Sales (overall Alcan): $7,789 million
Key Personnel: President, CEO: Jacques Bougie. EVP: Robert L. Ball. Human Resources: Gaston Ouellet.

One of the largest manufacturers of aluminum in the world, Alcan Aluminum has faced stiff competition from Russia since the end of the Cold War. The company did a comprehensive study of the aluminum market and used the results as the basis for its recent restructuring. Alcan Aluminum's sales and workforce have risen with its recent acquisitions of Pechiney and Alusuisse Lonza.

Other Locations: Worldwide HQ: Alcan Aluminum, Ltd., 1188 Sherbrooke St. W., Montreal, Quebec H3A 3G2, Canada; 514-848-8000.

LTV CORPORATION

200 Public Sq., Cleveland, OH 44114-2308; 216-622-5000
http://www.ltvsteel.com
Employees: 14,800
Sales: $4,273 million
Key Personnel: Chairman, President, and CEO: J. Peter Kelly. EVP: James F. Haeck. Human Resources: W. R. Huenefeld.

Among the largest steel companies in the United States, LTV is recovering from bankruptcy. The company runs two steel manufacturing facilities: Indiana Harbor Works (in Chicago) and the Cleveland Works (in Cleveland). LTV's products include sheet and strip steel used in auto bodies, industrial machines, and office products, and tubular products used in a variety of applications. Sales and workforce are down.

Other Locations: The company has facilities in 11 countries around the world.

OKLAHOMA

KERR–MCGEE CORPORATION

Kerr-McGee Ctr., 123 Robert S. Kerr Ave., Oklahoma City, OK 73102; 405-270-1313
http://www.kerr-mcgee.com
Employees: 3,367
Sales: $1,396 million
Key Personnel: CEO: Luke R. Corbett. VC: Tom J. McDaniel. Human Resources: Julius C. Hilburn.

Oil, natural gas, coal, and inorganic chemicals are the focuses of Kerr-McGee. The company has both natural resource exploration and extraction operations. Its chemical production includes titanium dioxide and specialty chemicals. The company also produces nearly half of all railroad ties sold in the United States. Sales and work force are down.
Other Locations: The company has oil and gas extraction operations in Canada, the South China Sea, the Gulf of Mexico, and the North Sea and coal mining operations in Illinois, West Virginia, and Wyoming.

OREGON

OREGON STEEL MILLS, INC.

1000 SW Broadway, Ste. 2200, Portland, OR 97205; 503-223-9228
http://www.osm.com
Employees: 2,426
Sales: $892.6 million
Key Personnel: Chairman, CEO: Thomas B. Boklund. President, COO: Joe E. Corvin. Human Resources: Claudia Adamson.

Oregon Steel Mills is a small, diversified steel manufacturer. The company produces seamless tubes, wire products, carbon and alloy steel plates, rods, and bars. Since its employees purchased the company through an employee stock option plan in 1984, it has expanded internationally and upgraded its manufacturing facilities. Its sales are up substantially and work force has grown modestly.

PENNSYLVANIA

ALCOA, INC. ★★

Alcoa Corporate Center, 201 Isabella St., Pittsburgh, PA 15212-5858; 412-553-4545
http://www.alcoa.com
Employees: 103,500
Sales: $15,339.8 million

Key Personnel: President, CEO: Alain J. P. Belda. EVP, CFO: Richard B. Kelson. Human Resources: Robert F. Slagle.
Considered a pioneer in the aluminum industry, Alcoa (formerly Aluminum Company of America) is the largest aluminum company in the world. Its operations include all phases of aluminum production: bauxite mining, refining and processing of alumina, and smelting. After signing agreements with car manufacturers Chrysler and Mercedes-Benz, it has begun building a new Ohio plant to manufacture auto frames. Sales and work force are up dramatically.
Other Locations: The company has operations in 26 countries.

BETHLEHEM STEEL CORPORATION ★

1170 Eighth Ave., Bethlehem, PA 18016; 610-694-2424
http://www.bethsteel.com
Employees: 17,000
Sales: $4,477.8 million
Key Personnel: Chairman, CEO: Curtis H. Barnette. President, COO: Roger P. Penny. Human Resources: Dorothy L. Stephenson.
Bethlehem Steel is one of the largest steel companies in the United States. Once a major supplier of structural steel, it decided to get out of that market in 1996. The company provides much of the steel used in the automotive and railroad industries. Bethlehem operates some of the most efficient steel mills in the industry. Sales are down, but work force is up.
Other Locations: The company has mills and mines in Indiana, Maryland, Pennsylvania, and West Virginia.

CROWN CORK & SEAL COMPANY, INC.

One Crown Way, Philadelphia, PA 19154; 215-698-5100
http://www.crowncork.com
Employees: 38,459
Sales: $8,300 million
Key Personnel: Chairman, CEO: William J. Avery. President, COO: John W. Conway. Human Resources: Gary L. Burgess.
In this age of prepackaged foods, Crown Cork & Seal is a leading manufacturer of food packaging. The company makes a large variety of cans, bottles, and other containers, as well as equipment to fill and case the packages. More than 80 percent of its sales come from metal packaging. Crown Cork & Seal's sales and

work force are both decreasing.
Other Locations: The company has 80 factories in the United States and 70 overseas.

USX—U.S. STEEL GROUP

600 Grant St., Pittsburgh, PA 15219-4776; 412-433-1121
http://www. ussteel.com
Employees: 19,169
Sales: $6,184 million
Key Personnel: Chairman, CEO: Thomas J. Usher. President, U.S. Steel Group: Paul J. Wilhelm. SVP Human Resources: Dan D. Sandman.

The large industrial conglomerate USX has three parts, of which the U.S. Steel Group is one. The company is the biggest and one of the oldest steel companies in the United States. It produces more than 10 percent of all domestic integrated steel. The company is battling low-cost foreign and domestic competitors. Both its sales and workforce are down.
Other Locations: The company has raw steel plants in Alabama, Indiana, and Pennsylvania.

UTAH

KENNECOTT UTAH COPPER

8315 W. 3595 South, Magna, UT 84044; 801-252-3000
http://www.riotinto.com
Employees: 2,239
Sales: $688 million
Key Personnel: President, CEO: B.D. Farmer. SVP Finance and Control: R.P.Johnson. VP Human Resources: D.M. Scartezina.

Kennecott Utah Copper, formerly Kennecott Corporation, is the subsidiary of Rio Tinto plc, one of the largest metal refining and mining companies in the world. Rio Tinto extracts copper, gold, borax, silica, talc, coal, iron, diamonds, manganese, and uranium. The company is one of the largest producers of copper and coal in the United States. The company's exploration budget totals almost $200 million. Sales and work force are down.
Other Locations: Worldwide HQ: Rio Tinto plc, 6 St. James's Sq., London, SW1Y 4LD, United Kingdom; +44-171-930-2399. The company has operations in Australia, Brazil, South Africa, and the United States.

VIRGINIA

REYNOLDS METALS COMPANY

6601 W. Broad St., Richmond, VA 23261-7003; 804-281-2000
http://www.rmc.com
Employees: 20,000
Sales: $5,859 million
Key Personnel: Chairman, CEO: Jeremiah J. Sheehan. VC, Executive Officer: Randolph N. Reynolds. Human Resources: F. Robert Newman.

One of the biggest manufacturers of aluminum in the world, Reynolds Metals also produces plastics and construction materials and processes gold. Having divested many of its own subsidiaries to reduce debt, the company is in the process of being purchased by Alcoa. Sales and work force are down sharply.
Other Locations: The company has facilities in 22 countries.

❶ MISCELLANEOUS GOODS AND SERVICES

CALIFORNIA

EARL SCHEIB, INC.

8737 Wilshire Blvd., Beverly Hills, CA 90211-2795; 310-652-4880
http://earlscheib.com
Employees: 1,172
Sales: $55 million
Key Personnel: Chairman: Philip W. Colburn. President, CEO: Christian K. Bement. SVP, CFO: John D. Branch.

One of the largest automobile painting companies in the United States, Earl Scheib is facing stiff competition from smaller painting centers. Although the company once dominated the market, it has been closing down centers for several years, The company's sales have rebounded modestly; workforce is also up, slightly.
Other Locations: The company has facilities in 170 U.S. cities.

JENNY CRAIG, INC.

11355 N. Torrey Pines Rd., La Jolla, CA 92037; 858-812-7000
http://www.jennycraig.com
Employees: 4,100
Sales: $321 million
Key Personnel: Chairman, CEO: Sidney Craig. President, COO: Philip Voluck. Human Resources: Roberta C. Baade.

Jenny Craig is one of the largest operators of weight-loss clinics in the United States. In addition to North America, it has weight-loss centers in Australia and New Zealand, most of which are owned by the company. Bad press and a variety of mishaps have depressed demand for the company's services. Sales and workforce are down.

Other Locations: The company has over 600 company-owned stores and nearly 200 franchised operations in the United States and abroad.

CONNECTICUT

STURM, RUGER, & COMPANY, INC. ★

Lacey Pl., Southport, CT 06490; 203-259-7843

http://www.ruger-firearms.com
Employees: 2,171
Sales: $211.6 million
Key Personnel: Chairman, CEO, and Treasurer: William B. Ruger. VC, President, and COO: William B. Ruger, Jr. Human Resources: Carol Markland.

Sturm, Ruger is the largest firearms manufacturer in the United States. The company manufacturers all varieties of firearms, as well as metal castings for the automotive, sporting goods, and aerospace industries. It is working to increase its overseas sales. The company's sales and work force are on the rise.

ILLINOIS

THE SERVICEMASTER COMPANY ★★

One ServiceMaster Way, Downers Grove, IL 60515-1700; 630-271-1300

http://www.servicemaster.com
Employees: 51,740
Sales: $4,724.1 million
Key Personnel: President, CEO: Carlos H. Cantu. VC, COO: Phillip B. Rooney. Human Resources: Patricia Asp.

ServiceMaster is a leading provider of health care plant operations and maintenance, housekeeping, laundry and linen services through its Management Service Division. The Consumer Services division provides lawn care, domestic housecleaning, and termite and pest control to more than 10 million customers. Sales and work force are rising.

KENTUCKY

RES-CARE, INC. ★★

10140 Linn Station Rd., Louisville, KY 40223; 502-394-2100

http://www.rescare.com
Employees: 18,500
Sales: $522.7 million
Key Personnel: Chairman, President, and CEO: Ronald G. Geary. SEVP: E. Halsey Sandford. VP Human Resources: Steve Kraus.

Res-Care provides provides training, support, and residential services for more than 17,000 developmentally disabled and mentally retarded people. It also operates several vocational training centers (as part of the federal Job Corps program) and is a part-owner of Home Care Affiliates, which provides home nursing care in the Southeast. Sales and work force are growing rapidly.

Other Locations: The company has facilities in nine states.

MINNESOTA

REGIS CORPORATION. ★★

7201 Metro Blvd., Edina, MN 55439; 612-947-7777

http://www.regiscorp.com
Employees: 25,000
Sales: $713.2 million
Key Personnel: President, CEO: Paul D. Finkelstein. COO: Marvin Goldstein. EVP: Christopher A. Fox.

Regis Corporation is the world's largest owner and franchiser of hair salons and retail product salons. The company operates Regis Hairstylists, Supercuts, MasterCuts and Trade Secret salons, among others. It sells its own line of hair products in addition to other lines such as Paul Mitchell, Nexxus and Redken. Sales and workforce are both up substantially.

Other Locations: The company owns or franchises more than 5,000 salons in Canada, Mexico, Puerto Rico and the United States.

NEW YORK

MONRO MUFFLER BRAKE, INC. ★★

200 Holleder Pkwy., Rochester, NY 14615; 716-647-6400

http://www.monro.com
Employees: 2,811
Sales: $193.5 million
Key Personnel: President, CEO: Robert

Gross. EVP Store Operations: G. Michael Cox. Human Resources: Brad Schramek.

With more people keeping their cars longer and with cars becoming more complex, Monro Muffler Brake has found a growing market niche. The company supplies a complete range of automobile repair services for brake, exhaust, steering, and suspension systems. Located primarily in the Northeast, it plans continued expansion. Sales and work force are on the rise.

Other Locations: The company operates more than 550 facilities in Connecticut, Massachusetts, New York, Ohio, Pennsylvania, Virginia, and other states.

TEXAS

CASH AMERICA INTERNATIONAL, INC. ★
1600 W. 7th St., Fort Worth, TX 76102-2599; 817-335-1100
Employees: 3,035
Sales: $342.9 million
Key Personnel: Chairman, CEO: Jack R. Daugherty. President, COO: Daniel R. Feehan. VP Human Resources: Robert D. Brockman.

Cash America is the world's largest pawnbroking company. The company has done much to clean up the traditionally low-brow image of the industry by maintaining a more pleasant ambiance in its stores. Cash America continues to expand both its sales and its work force.

Other Locations: Cash America has more than 350 stores throughout the Midwest and South.

EZCORP, INC. ★★
1901 Capital Pkwy., Austin, TX 78746; 512-314-3400
http://www.ezpawn.com
Employees: 2,200
Sales: $197.4 million
Key Personnel: Chairman: Sterling B. Brinkley. President, CEO: Vincent A. Lambiase. VP Human Resources: Filbert A DiNardo.

The second largest chain of pawnshops in the United States is also the fastest growing. EZCORP, which began in 1991, already has around 300 stores. The company uses computer systems to track inventory and has a central facility to refurbish forfeited jewelry for resale. Its sales and work force are growing.

❶ OFFICE EQUIPMENT

CONNECTICUT
PITNEY BOWES, INC.
1 Elmcroft Rd., Stamford, CT 06926-0700; 203-356-5000
http://www.pitneybowes.com
Employees: 26,792
Revenues: $4,220 million
Key Personnel: President, COO: Marc C. Breslawsky. President, U.S. Mailing Systems: John N. D. Moody. VP Personnel: Johnna G. Torsone.

The leading manufacturer of postage meters and mailing equipment, Pitney Bowes is readjusting the focus of its business. The company is shedding non-core operations such as Dictaphone, which sells voice processing equipment, and Monarch Marking Systems, which sells bar code systems, to upgrade its mailing equipment to current market requirements. Sales and work force are up.
Other Locations: The company has facilities in Connecticut and the United Kingdom.

XEROX CORPORATION ★★
800 Long Ridge Rd., Stamford, CT 06904; 203-968-3000
http://www.xerox.com
Employees: 92,700
Revenues: $19,449 million
Key Personnel: Chairman: Paul A. Allaire. President, COO: G. Richard Thoman. Human Resources Manager: Patricia M. Nazemetz.

The first company to sell copy machines, Xerox is an innovator in the office equipment industry. The company makes a wide variety of office products, including laser printers, scanners, and document-processing software. It is expanding its market in Europe and China through joint ventures. Sales and work force are up.

NEW JERSEY
MINOLTA CORPORATION (U.S.A.)
101 Williams Dr., Ramsey, NJ 07446-1293; 201-825-4000
http://www.minolta.com
Employees: 4,600
Sales: $3,684 million.
Key Personnel: President, CEO: Osamu Kanaya. EVP, Treasurer: Ko Ikeuchi. Director of Human Resources: Tadashi

Arai.

Although Minolta was once primarily a manufacturer of single-lens-reflex cameras, stiff competition drove the company to diversify. It is now a leader in many areas of the office equipment market, which accounts for nearly 70 percent of its sales. Among its products are laser printers, color copiers, and lenses. Sales and work force are down.

Other Locations: Worldwide HQ: Minolta Co., Ltd., 3-13, Azuchi-machi 2-chome, Chuo-ku, Osaka, 541, Japan; phone: +81-6-271-2251.

OLIVETTI USA, INC.

765 Highway 202 S., Bridgewater, 08807; 908-526-8200
http://www.olivetti.it
Employees: 17,000
Sales: $4,344.6 million
Key Personnel: Chairman: Antonio Tesone. CEO: Roberto Colaninno.

The second largest computer maker in Europe, Olivetti has not earned a profit since 1990. The company, which has a broad product line including office products, has suffered in the competition for the lowest prices on the market and in 1996 announced plans to sell its personal computer division. Olivetti is moving into the telecommunications arena in the hopes of offsetting its losses in other areas. Its sales and work force are shrinking.

Other Locations: Worldwide HQ: Olivetti Group, Via Jervis 77 Ivrea, Torino, Italy; phone: +39-0125-52-2500. The company has sales and support branches in 48 countries.

RICOH CORPORATION

5 Dedrick Pl., West Caldwell, NJ 07006; 201-882-2000
http://www.ricoh.jp
Employees: 63,600
Sales: 10,545.9 million
Key Personnel: Chairman: Hiroshi Hamada. President: Masamitsu Sakurai. HR Contact: Ted Graske.

One of the largest manufacturers of office equipment in the world, Ricoh also makes photographic equipment. The company is also one of the top sellers of facsimile machines. It recently expanded its U.S. market with the purchase of Savin, a copy machine maker. Sales and work force are up.

Other Locations: Worldwide HQ: Ricoh Co., Ltd., 15-5, Minami-Aoyama 1-chome, Minato-ku, Tokyo, 107, Japan; phone: +81-3-3479-3111.

NEW YORK

CANON U.S.A., INC. ★★

One Canon Plaza, Lake Success, NY 11042-1113; 516-488-6700
http://www.usa.canon.com
Employees: 79,800
Sales: $24,364.4 million
Key Personnel: President and CEO: Kinya Uchida. SVP, General Manager: James Rosetta. VP Human Resources: Marylou Ponzi.

A major manufacturer of a wide variety of office equipment, Canon has conquered approximately one-quarter of the photocopier market in the United States. Although cameras were once its top product, they now account for only 10 percent of sales. The company is developing a new ferroelectric liquid display methodology. Sales and work force are up.

Other Locations: Worldwide HQ: Canon, Inc., 30-2, Shimomaruko 3-chome, Ohta-ku, Tokyo, 146, Japan; phone: +81-3-3758-2111.

❶ PERSONAL/HOUSEHOLD PRODUCTS

ARIZONA

DIAL CORP ★★

15501 N.Dial Blvd., Scottsdale, AZ 85260-1619; 623-754-3425
http://www.dialcorp.com
Employees: 3,759
Revenues: $1,524.5 million
Key Personnel: Chairman, CEO: Malcolm Jozoff. SVP ,Sales: Arthur E. Hanke. Head of Human Resources: Bernhard J. Welle.

Primarily focused on consumer products and services, Dial is in a highly competitive market and recently went through an aggressive restructuring period. In 1996 it separated into two companies: The Dial Corporation (focusing on consumer products) and Viad Corp. (concentrating on services). Among Dial's many brands are Armour Star, Liquid Dial, Breck, and Purex. Its sales and work force are rising.

CALIFORNIA

CLOROX COMPANY ★★

1221 Broadway, Oakland, CA 94612-1888; 510-271-7000
http://www.clorox.com
Employees: 6,600
Revenues: $4,003 million
Key Personnel: Chairman, President, CEO: Craig G. Sullivan. President and COO: Gerald E. Johnston. Group VP: Peter N. Louras Jr. Human Resources Manager: Janet M. Brady.

Known for its bleach, Clorox manufactures many other consumer products too. The company has a strong focus on cleaning products, such as Formula 409, Pine-Sol, and Soft Scrub, but also makes many other products, including Match Light charcoal briquettes, Hidden Valley Ranch salad dressings, Combat insecticides, and Control cat litter. Its sales and work force are up.

Other Locations: The company has more than 38 manufacturing facilities in Argentina, Canada, Chile, Mexico, Puerto Rico, South Korea, and the United States.

CONNECTICUT

FIRST BRANDS CORPORATION

83 Wooster Heights Rd., Bldg. 301, Danbury, CT 06813-1911; 203-731-2300
http://www.firstbrands.com
Employees: 4,800
Revenues: $1,203.7 million
Key Personnel: President, CEO: William V. Stephenson. President: Thomas H. Rowland. Human Resources Manager: Ronald F. Dainton.

First Brands' products are well-known in the consumer, pet, and industrial markets. Its best-selling products are in the consumer market. They include Glad and Surtec plastic bags, which make up more than half its sales. In the pet industry, the company's products includes Jonny Cat and Scoop-Away. The company also makes STP auto products. Company was acquired by Clorox in 1999. Sales and work force are up.

Other Locations: The company has manufacturing facilities in 10 states, Canada, Hong Kong, and the Philippines and distributes its products to more than 100 countries.

ILLINOIS

ALBERTO-CULVER COMPANY

2525 Armitage Ave., Melrose Park, IL 60160-1163; 708-450-3000
http://www.alberto.com
Employees: 12,700
Sales: $1,834.7 million
Key Personnel: Chairman: Leonard H. Lavin. President, CEO: Howard B. Bernick. Human Resources Manager: Douglas E. Meneely.

Alberto-Culver makes hair care and personal care products, plus other products such as Molly McButter and Sugar Twin seasonings, and Static Guard household items. Through its Sally Beauty subsidiary, the company sells products direct to professional beauty supply distributors. Sales and work force are rising.

HELENE CURTIS INDUSTRIES, INC.

325 N. Wells St., Chicago, IL 60610; 312-661-0222
http://www.yoursalon.com
Employees: 1,850
Sales: $1,068 million
Key Personnel: Chairman: Gerald S. Gidwitz. VC: Joseph L. Gidwitz. President, CEO: Ronald J. Gidwitz. Human Resources Manager: Barbara Gardner.

Helene Curtis Industries, a subsidiary of Unilever, is a producer of brand-name personal care products. The company manufactures hair care products under the Finesse, Vibrance and Suave brand names. It makes deodorants, hair products and cosmetics for salons. Sales and work force are down.

PREMARK INTERNATIONAL, INC. ★

1717 Deerfield Rd., Deerfield, IL 60015; 847-405-6000
http://www.premarkintl.com
Employees: 19,300
Revenues: $2,739.1 million
Key Personnel: Group VP, President, Food Equipment Group: Joseph W. Deering. SVP: Lawrence B. Skatoff. SVP Human Resources: Kirk H. Mueller.

Premark International was best known for Tupperware, which it sold off in 1996. Now Premark concentrates on manufacturing major commercial products including food service equipment, building products and small appliances under such brand names as Hobart, Florida Tile, and West Bend. Its sales and work force are growing.

Other Locations: The company has manufacturing facilities in 15 countries.

MASSACHUSETTS

GILLETTE COMPANY

Prudential Tower Bldg., Boston, MA 02199; 617-421-7000
http://www.gillette.com
Employees: 43,100
Revenues: $10,056 million
Key Personnel: President, CEO: Michael C. Hawley. EVP North Atlantic Group: Robert G.King. EVP Diversified Group: Archibald Livis.

Best known for its razors and blades, Gillette also makes a wide variety of other consumer products. Its Oral-B subsidiary is one of the largest manufacturers of dental care products in the world. The company also makes toiletries (Right Guard deodorant, Foamy shaving cream), appliances (Braun), and many leading brands of writing instruments (including Parker, Paper Mate, and Waterman). It recently purchased Duracell International, the battery maker. Sales and work force are up.

Other Locations: The company has 57 manufacturing facilities in 28 countries.

MICHIGAN

AMWAY CORPORATION ★★

7575 Fulton St. E., Ada, MI 49355; 616-787-6000
http://www.amway.com
Employees: 13,000
Est.Sales: $5,700 million
Key Personnel: President, Chairman: Richard M. DeVos Jr. SVP: Lawrence Call. SVP Human Resources: Pamela Linton.

One of the largest direct sales businesses in the world, Amway sells more than 5,000 products through a network of over 2 million independent dealers in nearly 60 countries. The company sells products in many categories, including health and beauty, home care, business, and education. Its sales and work force are growing.

Other Locations: The company has operations in nearly 60 countries.

MINNESOTA

MINNESOTA MINING AND MANUFACTURING COMPANY (3M)

3M Ctr., St. Paul, MN 55144; 651-733-1110
http://www.mmm.com
Employees: 73,564
Revenues: $15,021 million
Key Personnel: Chairman ,CEO: Livio D. DeSimone. EVP Industrial and Consumer Sector: Ronald A. Mitsch. EVP Life Science Sector: W. G. Meredith. EVP Human Resources: M. Kay Grenz.

Minnesota Mining and Manufacturing operates in three markets: industrial and consumer; information, imaging and electronics; and life sciences. The company, which is best known as 3M, sells Scotch Tape and Post-It notes. It has long been devoted to research and development. Among its products are computer storage devices and communications systems. Sales are down, but work force is up.

Other Locations: The company has facilities in the United States and 60 other nations.

NEW JERSEY

GUEST SUPPLY, INC.

4301 U.S. Hwy. One, Monmouth Junction, NJ 08852-0902; 609-514-9696
Employees: 864
Sales: $236.7 million
Key Personnel: President, CEO: Clifford W. Stanley. VP Operations: Eugene R. Biber. Human Resources Manager: Joan Constanza.

Guest Supply is the top provider of consumable products to the hospitality industry. The company's shampoo, soap, housekeeping supplies, and other products are used by hotels around the world. It recently began selling textile products and is expanding its production plants. Although sales are growing, work force is down.

RECKITT & COLMAN, INC. ★

1655 Valley Rd., Wayne, NJ 07470; 201-633-3600
Employees: Sales: $3,655.9 million
Key Personnel: President, CEO: Joseph Healy. CFO: Craig Steeneck. VP Human Resources: Craig Saline.

Reckitt & Colman manufactures a wide variety of household products, including such products as Saniflush, Woolite, Mr. Bubble, and Black Flag. Sales and work force are down.

Other Locations: Worldwide HQ: Reckitt & Colman PLC, One Burlington Lane, London, W4 2RW, United Kingdom; phone: +44-81-994-6464.

WATERFORD WEDGWOOD USA, INC.
1330 Campus Pkwy., Wall, NJ 07719;
732-938-5800
Employees: 9,271
Sales: $856.3 million.
Key Personnel: CEO, Waterford Wedgwood USA, Inc.: Christopher J. McGillivary. CFO: Tony Cappiello. VP Human Res.: John Soi.

Waterford Wedgwood is an amalgamation of two venerable companies: Waterford Crystal, a glassware manufacturer, and Josiah Wedgwood & Sons, a manufacturer of fine china. The company has suffered from decreasing demand for its premium products. It recently introduced a cheaper line of glassware that has been selling well and has not cannibalized existing product sales. Sales and work force are steady.
Other Locations: Worldwide HQ: Waterford Wedgwood PLC, Killbarry, Waterford, United Kingdom; phone: +353-517-3311.

NEW YORK

AVON PRODUCTS, INC. ★★
1345 Ave. of the Americas, New York, NY 10105; 212-282-5000
http://www.avon.com
Employees: 33,900
Revenues: $5,212.7 million
Key Personnel: Chairman, CEO: Charles R. Perrin. President: Andrea Jung. Human Resources Manager: Jill Kanin-Lovers.

Direct sales of such products as cosmetics and toiletries have been the calling card for Avon Products. The company has successfully exported its sales approach to countries such as Brazil, where it has more than 400,000 representatives. But the company has faced stiff competition in the United States and Western Europe, where retail distribution channels are more established. Sales and work force are growing.
Other Locations: The company has 18 manufacturing facilities in the United States and abroad.

COLGATE–PALMOLIVE COMPANY ★★
300 Park Ave., New York, NY 10022; 212-310-2000
http://www.colgate.com
Employees: 38,300
Revenues: $8,971.6 million
Key Personnel: President, COO: William S. Shanahan. SVP: Andrew D. Hendry. Human Resources Manager: Robert J. Joy.

The largest U.S. toothpaste manufacturer, Colgate-Palmolive is among the leaders in many other products. It makes Palmolive soap, Ajax detergent, and Colgate toothpaste, among other things. Although the company is facing stiff competition in the United States, its Third World markets are growing rapidly. The company is restructuring its pricing from promotion-induced purchasing to everyday low prices based on changes in consumer demand. Sales and work force are increasing.
Other Locations: The company has 66 plants in the United States and 235 facilities in 60 foreign countries.

COSMAIR, INC. ★★
575 Fifth Ave., New York, NY 10017; 212-818-1500
http://www.cosmair.com
Employees: 6,000
Sales: $2,649.2 million
Key Personnel: President, CEO: Guy Peyrelongue. CFO: Roger Dolden. SVP Human Resources:Bob Niles.

Cosmair is the U.S. subsidiary of L'Oreal. The world's largest cosmetics company, L'Oreal sells a wide variety of products at all levels of the market. The company sells consumer lines of personal products for men and women, as well as professional products, such as the Redken line, sold to hairdressers. Sales and work force are up.
Other Locations: Worldwide HQ: L'Oreal SA, 41, rue Martre, Clichy, France; phone: +33-1-47-56-70-00.

ESTEE LAUDER COMPANIES, INC. ★
767 Fifth Ave., New York, NY 10153; 212-572-4200
http://www.elcompanies.com
Employees: 15,300
Revenues: $3,961.3 million
Key Personnel: Chairman: Leonard A. Lauder. President, COO: Fred H. Langhammer. SVP: Robert J. Bigler. SVP Human Resources: Andrew J. Cavanaugh.

Comprised of a large group of similar manufacturers, Estee Lauder has been described as the world's largest privately held cosmetics and fragrances company. Among the group members are Clinique Laboratories, Aramis, and Origins Natural Resources. The company appeals primarily to the high end of the market. Sales and work force are up.

SHISEIDO COSMETICS (AMERICA), INC.

900 Third Ave., 15th Fl., New York, NY 10022; 212-805-2300
http://www.shiseido.co.jp/e
Employees:23,688
Sales: $5,073.4 million
Key Personnel:. President, CEO, Shiseido Cosmetics (America), Ltd.: Takashi Yamaguchi. CFO: Brian Liston. Human Resources Manager: Barbara Aubin.

The biggest cosmetics manufacturer in Japan, Shiseido has been fighting slow growth in recent years. To prevent a slide, the company is diversifying into pharmaceuticals and other areas. Shiseido also owns restaurants and health clubs. It is researching joint disease treatments and expanding its U.S. sales of skin-care products. Sales and work force are down.
Other Locations: Worldwide HQ: Shiseido Co., Ltd., 7-5-5, Ginza, Chuo-ku, Tokyo, 104-10, Japan; phone: +81-3-3572-5111.

UNILEVER UNITED STATES, INC. ★★

390 Park Ave., New York, NY 10022-4698; 212-888-1260
Employees: 267,000
Sales: $48,969.5 million
Key Personnel:. President, CEO, Unilever U.S.: Richard A. Goldstein. SVP, Finance: J.W. Allgrove. VP Human Resources, Unilever U.S.: Jan Peelen.

Unilever is a consumer goods conglomerate. The company sells an abundance of foods, soap, personal products, clothing, and cosmetics. Unilever's brand names include Birds Eye, Calvin Klein, Pepsodent, and Sunlight. The company is expanding its presence in Asia, Central Europe, and Latin America.Though its sales are increasing, its work force is down.
Other Locations: Worldwide HQ: Unilever, P.O. Box 62, Unilever House, Blackfriars, London, EC4P 4BQ, United Kingdom; phone: +44-(01) 71-822-5252.

O H I O

PROCTER & GAMBLE COMPANY

One P & G Plaza, Cincinnati, OH 45202; 513-983-1100
http://www.pg.com
Employees:110,000

Revenues: $38,125 million
Key Personnel: President, COO: Durk I. Jager. EVP North America: Wolfgang C. Berndt. SVP Human Resources: Richard Antoine.

One of the largest household products manufacturers in the world, Procter & Gamble receives more than half its income from foreign sales. Among its brands are Ivory, Cheer, Tide, Zest, Crest, Prell, Head and Shoulders, Noxzema, Pepto-Bismol, Pampers, Folgers, Charmin, Crisco, and Duncan Hines. The company has been reorganizing and restructuring to create a more international and lower-cost operation. Sales and work force are increasing.

RUBBERMAID, INC. ★

1147 Akron Rd., Wooster, OH 44691-6000; 216-264-6464
http://www.rubbermaid.com
Employees: 12,759
Revenues: $2,470 million
Key Personnel: Chairman, CEO: William P. Sovey. President,COO: Thomas A.Ferguson. Human Resources Manager: David L. Robertson.

Manufacturing a comprehensive array of plastic products, Rubbermaid is restructuring in the face of shrinking demand. The company makes housewares, gardening accessories, furniture, toys, and many other products. Its has been expanding its product lines and its geographic range with purchases in France, Japan, and Mexico. Company merged with Newell Co. in 1999. Its sales and work force are steady.
Other Locations: The company has facilities in 14 states and nine foreign countries.

T E X A S

MARY KAY COSMETICS, INC. ★★

16251 Dallas Pkwy., Dallas, TX 75248; 972-687-6300
http://www.marykay.com
Employees: 3,600
Sales: $1,046 million
Key Personnel: CEO: John P. Rochon. CFO: David Holl. Human Resources Manager: Darell Overcash.

Mary Kay Cosmetics sells cosmetics directly to its customers, skipping traditional retail distribution channels. It is the second largest company of this type in the United States. Mary Kay has more women employees making greater than $50,000 per year than any other U.S.

company. Its sales and work force are rising.

Other Locations: The company has more than 325,000 sales consultants in 21 countries.

UTAH

NATURE'S SUNSHINE PRODUCTS, INC. ★★
75 E. 1700 S., Provo, UT 84606; 801-342-4300

http://www.nsponline.com
Employees: 971
Sales: $296.1 million
Key Personnel: President, CEO: Daniel P. Howells. EVP, COO: Douglas Faggioli. SVP Customer Relations: Eugene L. Hughes.

In the alternative medicine market, Nature's Sunshine is one of the largest companies in the United States. The company makes a wide variety of vitamins, homeopathic treatments, health food, and other similar products. Its sells its products through a network of distributors similar to those of Mary Kay and Amway. Sales and work force are up.

WISCONSIN

S. C. JOHNSON & SON, INC. ★★
1525 Howe St., Racine, WI 53403; 414-260-2000

http://www.scjohnsonwax.com
Employees: 13,200
Est. Sales: $5,000 million
Key Personnel: President, COO: William D. Perez. EVP: Fisk H. Johnson. Human Resources Manager: Gayle P. Kosterman.

Best known for its popular Johnson Wax, S. C. Johnson & Son is among the world's largest manufacturers of consumer specialty products. Its products include Raid insecticides, OFF! insect repellents, Windex cleaners, and Glade air fresheners. The company leads the industry in its recycling and toxic waste emission reduction programs. Sales and work force are growing at S. C. Johnson & Son.

❶ PETROLEUM/GAS

CALIFORNIA

ATLANTIC RICHFIELD COMPANY
515 S. Flower St., Los Angeles, CA 90071-2256; 213-486-3511

http://www.arco.com
Employees: 18,400
Revenues: $10,303 million
Key Personnel: Chairman, CEO: Mike R. Bowlin. President: William E. Wade Jr. Human Resources Manager: John H. Kelly.

Atlantic Richfield is among the largest oil companies in the United States, producing a wide variety of refined products. Although most of its oil reserves are in the U.S., including the Alaskan oil fields, the company has been focusing on international exploration and production. Sales and work force are up.

Other Locations: The company has oil and gas wells in China, Dubai, Indonesia, the United Kingdom, and the United States and coal mines in Australia and the United States.

CHEVRON CORPORATION
575 Market St., San Francisco, CA 94105; 415-894-7700

http://www.chevron.com
Employees: 39,191
Revenues: $26,187 million
Key Personnel: Chairman, CEO: Kenneth T. Derr. VC: James N. Sullivan. Human Resources Manager: Gregory Matiuk.

Among the largest oil companies in the United States, Chevron conducts a broad range of activities, including exploration, refining, and chemical manufacturing. The company has the largest oil refining operation in the United States. Decreased demand in the 1990s has forced the company to cut costs. Sales and work force are down.

Other Locations: The company has operations in approximately 100 countries.

OCCIDENTAL PETROLEUM CORPORATION
10889 Wilshire Blvd., Los Angeles, CA 90024; 310-208-8800

http://www.oxy.com
Employees: 9.,190
Revenues: $9,6,596 million
Key Personnel: EVP, Senior Operating Officer: Dale R. Laurance. EVP; President, CEO, Occidental Oil and Gas Corp.: David R. Martin. EVP, Corporate Development: Donakd P. de Brier. Occidental Petroleum's operations include exploration, production, and marketing of natural gas and crude oil. The company also manufactures plastics, fertilizers, and industrial chemicals. The US

accounts for about 78 percent of the company's sales. The company recently bought a majority stake in a California oil field. Sales and work force are down.

UNOCAL CORPORATION ★★
2141 Rosecrans Ave., Suite 4000, El Segundo, CA 90245; 310-726-7600
http://www.unocal.com
Employees: 7,880
Revenues: $5,003 million
Key Personnel: President: John F. Imle Jr. CFO: Timothy H. Ling. Human Resources Manager: Carl D. McAulay.
Unocal is among the largest U.S. oil companies. It is also the biggest geothermal energy producer in the world. The company's main activities are marketing and retailing of natural gas and petroleum products, and it is also a maker of agricultural and industrial chemicals. It is expanding its operations in Southeast Asia. Sales and work force are down.
Other Locations: The company has production activities in the United States and six foreign countries.

COLORADO

TOTAL FINA, S.A..
900 19th St., Denver, CO 80202; 303-291-2000
Employees: 57,166
Sales: $28,417.8 million
Key Personnel: President, CEO: Thierry M. Desmarest. VP Human Resources: J.J. Guibaud.
One of the largest gas and oil producers in Europe, TOTAL FINA is formed in merger of french TOTAL and Belgian PetroFina. It has weathered recent economic storms in the oil industry by virtue of its chemical manufacturing division, which produces inks, adhesives, and other specialty petrochemicals. The company, whose business spans the full spectrum of the petrochemical industry, has gas stations in Africa, Europe, and the United States. Sales and work force are down.
Other Locations: Worldwide HQ: TOTAL, 24 Cours Michelet, Paris, France; phone: +33-1-41-35-40-00.

ILLINOIS

AMOCO CORPORATION★★
200 E. Randolph Dr., Chicago, IL 60601-7125; 312-856-6111
http://www.amoco.com

Employees: 96,650
Revenues: $68,304 million
http://www.amoco.com
Key Personnel: President: William G. Lowrie. EVP Chemical Sector: Enrique J. Sosa. EVP Human Resources: John F. Campbell.
One of the largest producers of natural gas in North America, Amoco is also among the largest integrated chemical and oil companies in the world. It has refining and marketing operations, gas and oil exploration and production operations, and chemical manufacturing operations. The company is increasing its Asian capacity for polyester production. Sales and work force are up.
Other Locations: The company has facilities in 40 countries.

KANSAS

KOCH INDUSTRIES, INC. ★
4111 E. 37th St. N., Wichita, KS 67220-3203; 316-832-5500
http://www.kochind.com
Employees: 16,000
Est. Sales: $35,300 million
Key Personnel: President, COO: William W. Hanna. EVP Operations: Bill R. Caffey. EVP Human Resources: Paul Wheeler.
Koch Industries is the one of the largest privately held, family-operated U.S. companies. The company's operations span many sectors, including refining and chemicals, agriculture, and transportation. Its refineries, which manufacture a variety of products, boast a combined output of 440,000 barrels per day. Sales are up, and work force is steady.
Other Locations: The company has operations in Canada, Europe, and the United States.

KENTUCKY

ASHLAND OIL, INC.
50 E. RiverCenter Blvd., Covighton, KY 41012; 606-815-3333
http://www.ashland.com
Employees: 21,200
Revenues: $6,534 million
Key Personnel: Chairman, CEO: Paul W. Chellgren. EVP: John A. Brothers. Human Resources Manager: Philip W. Block.
Ashland is among the largest U.S. producers of plastics and industrial chemicals and independent oil refiners. The

company manufactures motor oils under the Valvoline brand. It also owns APAC, one of the biggest highway contractors in the United States. The company is currently upgrading its refining capacity. Sales and work force are up.

Other Locations: The company has natural gas and oil exploration activities in Australia, Morocco, Nigeria, and the United States and refineries in Kentucky, Minnesota, and Ohio.

MISSOURI

FERRELLGAS PARTNERS, L.P.

One Liberty Plaza, Liberty, MO 64068; 816-792-1600
http://www.ferrellgas.com
Employees: 4,325
Sales: $667.4 million
Key Personnel: Chairman, CEO: James E. Ferrell. President, CFO: Danley K. Sheldon. Human Resources Manager: Caroline Newberry.

One of the largest suppliers of propane in the United States, Ferrellgas has more than 600,000 commercial and residential customers. Its operations are concentrated in the Great Lakes, Southeast, and Midwest regions. The company continues to grow by acquiring other existing operations. Sales and work force are up.

NEW YORK

AMERADA HESS CORPORATION

1185 Ave. of the Americas, New York, NY 10036; 212-997-8500
http://www.hess.com
Employees: 9,777
Revenues: $6,590.0 million
Key Personnel: Chairman, CEO: John B. Hess. President, COO: W. Sam H. Laidlaw. EVP Refining and Marketing: Michael W. Press.

Amerada Hess operates in several phases of the energy business. The company explores for natural gas and oil, produces and refines them, and runs a chain of gas stations and convenience stores in the Northeast. Its refinery in the Virgin Islands is one of the largest in the world. Sales are up, but work force is down.
Other Locations: The company has oil and natural gas exploration activities in Canada, Denmark, Egypt, Gabon, Namibia, the North Sea, Thailand, and the United States and refineries in New Jersey and the Virgin Islands.

ELF AQUITAINE, INC. ★★

280 Park Ave., New York, NY 10017; 212-922-3000
Employees: 84,350
Sales: $37,865.0 million
Key Personnel: Chairperson, CEO: Dominique Paret. Comptroller: George Mihalik. Director, Human Resources: Jean-Luc Vergne.

Elf Aquitaine is the largest industrial enterprise in France, partly owned by the French government. The company's main business is in chemicals, health, hygiene products, and hydrocarbons. Hydrocarbons are the company's main operation, with activities divided between exploration, refining, and production of petroleum products. Elf Aquitaine's overall sales and work force are both growing.
Other Locations: Worldwide HQ: Elf Aquitaine, Tour Elf Cedex 45, Paris, La defense, France; phone: +33-1-47-44-45-46.

ENI USA

666 Fifth Ave., New York, NY 10103; 212-887-0330
Employees: 78,906
Sales: $35,143.2 million
Key Personnel: Managing Director: Franco Bernabe. EVP: Roberto Jaquinto. Human Resources Manager: Francesco Furci.

ENI is a subsidiary of Ente Nazionale Idrocarburi, one of the largest companies in Italy. Ente Nazionale Idrocarburi is a government-owned oil company. It was recently hit with a bribery scandal that went to the top of its management. The current management is reorganizing the company in preparation for its transition to private ownership. Many noncore assets are consequently being divested. Sales are rising, but work force is currently falling.
Other Locations: Worldwide HQ: Ente Nazionale Idrocarburi S.p.A., Piazzale Enrico Mattei 1, Rome, Italy; phone: +39-6-59-002-141.

PDV AMERICA CORP.

750 Lexington Ave., New York, NY 10022; 212-339-7944
Employees: 56,592
Sales: $34,801.0 million
Key Personnel: President: Hector Ciavaldini. Coordinator, Exploration and Production: Francisco Pradas. Coordi-

nator, Human Resources: Nelson E. Ol-medillo. Chairman, President, CEO, PDV America Corp.: Fernando Sanchez.

PDV America is a subsidiary of Petroleos de Venezuela, one of the world's biggest oil companies. Owned by the Venezuelan government, it is known to most as PDVSA. Its U.S. subsidiary, PDV America, operates a chain of CITGO service stations. Most of the company's reserves are outside Venezuela. It is seeking foreign investors to help increase its production capacity. Sales and work force are rising.

Other Locations: Worldwide HQ: Petroleos de Venezuela, S.A., Torre Este, Av. Libertador, La Campina, Apartado Postal 169, Caracas, 1010-A, Venezuela; phone: +58-2-708-4111.

TEXACO, INC. ★

2000 Westchester Ave., White Plains, NY 10650; 914-253-4000

http://www.texaco.com
Employees: 24,628
Revenues: $ 30,910.0 million
Key Personnel: Chairman, CEO: Peter I. Bijur. SVP: Robert C. Black. VP Human Resources: Janet L. Stoner.

Among the largest U.S. oil companies, Texaco has been reorganizing and selling noncore assets in order to put more emphasis on its gas and oil business. The company is expanding its production capacity by upgrading old oil fields and developing new ones. It is looking to China, Colombia, and Russia for expansion opportunities. Sales are up, but work force is steady.

Other Locations: The company has operations in western Africa, Europe, the Far East, Latin America, the Middle East, and the United States.

OHIO

BP AMERICA, INC.

200 Public Sq., Cleveland, OH 44114-2375; 216-586-4141
Employees: 96,650
Sales: $ 68,304.0 million
Key Personnel: Chairman: Peter D. Sutherland. Group Chief Executive: Sir John P. Browne. Human Resources Manager: Nick Starritt.

BP America is a subsidiary of British Petroleum, one of the largest oil companies in the world. British Petroleum is the largest corporation in the United Kingdom. The company's holdings are pri-marily in Alaska and the North Sea. It is currently exploring in Alaska, Colombia, the North Sea, and Vietnam. Its sales are rising, but its work force is shrinking.

Other Locations: Worldwide HQ: British Petroleum Co., PLC, Britannic House, One Finsbury Circus, London, EC2M 7BA, United Kingdom; phone: +44-171-496-4000.

OKLAHOMA

MATRIX SERVICE COMPANY

10701 E. Ute St., Tulsa, OK 74116; 918-838-8822
Employees: 2,473
Sales: $ 211.0 million
Key Personnel: Chairman: Doyl D. West. President, CEO: Bradley S. Vetal. Human Resources Manager: C. William Lee.

Above-ground storage tanks are the business of Matrix Service. The company builds, maintains, and provides support services for tanks designed to hold oil, petrochemicals, water, and other liquids. In addition, it aids companies in meeting safety and environmental guidelines. The company plans to expand its market in Mexico, the United Kingdom, and Western Europe. Sales and work force are up.

Other Locations: The company provides services in Canada, Saudi Arabia, the United Kingdom, and the United States.

PHILLIPS PETROLEUM COMPANY

Phillips Bldg., Bartlesville, OK 74004;918-661-6600

http://www.phillips66.com
Employees: 17,300
Revenues: $ 11,845.0 million
Key Personnel: President, COO: James J. Mulva. EVP: K.L. Hedrick. Human Resources Manager: Charles L. Bowerman.

Among the largest integrated oil companies in the world, Phillips has done well recently in spite of sluggish demand for oil because of its strong presence in the natural gas and chemical markets. It expects to increase its refining and manufacturing operations in Puerto Rico soon. The company's employees own more than 20 percent of its stock. Though sales are up, work force is down.

Other Locations: The company has operations in Nigeria, Norway, the United Kingdom, and the United States.

PENNSYLVANIA

CASTLE ENERGY CORPORATION
100 Matsonford Rd., Suite 250, Radnor, PA 19087; 610-995-9400
Employees: 21
Sales: $72.6 million
Key Personnel: Chairman, CEO: Joseph L. Castle. CFO: Richard E. Staedtler. Director of Human Resources: David Williamson.
Refining, production, and exploration were the businesses of Castle Energy. Now the company has downsized its employees and is focusing on becoming an exploration and production company with properties in Oklahoma, Louisiana and six other states. Its revenues fluctuate and it has been having difficulty lately. Sales and work force are down.

SUN COMPANY, INC. ★★
1801 Market St., Philadelphia, PA 19103; 215-977-3000
Employees: 11,100
Revenues: $6,854.0 million
Key Personnel: Chairman, CEO: Robert H. Campbell. President, COO: John G. Drosdick. Human Resources Manager: David C. Shanks.
Sun Company is surviving difficult times in the oil industry with relatively good performance. The company conducts a full range of activities, from exploration to crude oil production to gasoline retailing. Its SUNOCO gasoline stations are in 17 states. The company also produces natural gas and operates pipelines and related services. Sales are up, but work force is down.
Other Locations: The company has operations in Canada, the United Kingdom, and the United States.

TEXAS

BAKER HUGHES, INC.
3900 Essex Lane, Houston, TX 77027-5177; 713-439-8600
http://www.bakerhughes.com
Employees: 32,300
Revenues: $6,311.9 million
Key Personnel: Chairman, CEO: Max L. Lukens. SVP: Thomas R. Bates. SVP: Andrew J. Szescila.
Baker Hughes is among the top companies in the field of oil drilling and mining equipment and services. The company supplies drilling fluids, drill bits, and other products and services. Demand for

the company's products and services is linked to the overall oil, gas, and mining markets, which are currently down. Sales and work force are up.
Other Locations: The company has 43 facilities in the United States and 29 abroad.

CALTEX PETROLEUM CORPORATION
125 E. John Carpenter Freeway, Irving, TX 75062; 214-830-1000
http://www.caltex.com
Employees: 7,900
Sales: $17,174.0 million
Key Personnel: Chairman, CEO: David Law-Smith. SVP: John McPhail. VP Human Resources: Stephen H. Nichols.
Caltex Petroleum is a joint venture between Chevron and Texaco. It is actively expanding its capacity in Asia, upgrading a refinery in China. It has recently opened offices and service stations in Southeast Asia. Sales are up, but work force is down.
Other Locations: The company operates in 61 countries.

COASTAL CORPORATION ★★
Coastal Tower, 9 Greenway Plaza, Houston, TX 77046; 713-877-1400
http://www.coastalcorp.com
Employees: 13,300
Revenues: $7,368.2 million
Key Personnel: Chairman, President, CEO: David A. Arledge. EVP: Coby C. Hesse. SVP: James A. King.
Coastal is predominantly involved in two areas of the energy business: production and sales of refined petroleum products, and transmission and storage of natural gas. The company also explores for new sources of gas and oil, manufactures chemicals, and performs other related activities. It is preparing to expand its Asian operations. Sales and work force are down.

ENRON CORP.
1400 Smith St., Houston, TX 77002; 713-853-6161
http://www.enron.com
Employees: 17,800
Revenues: $31,260.0 million
Key Personnel: President, COO: Jeffrey K. Skilling. VC: Joseph W. Sutton. Human Resources Manager: Doy G. Jones .
Among the largest suppliers of natural

gas in the United States, Enron has operations around the world. Among its many activities, the company manages gas pipelines and supplies natural gas for electricity generation. It recently agreed to market a Russian company's gas in Europe. About 14 percent of the company is owned by its employees. Sales and work force are up.

Other Locations: The company has natural gas pipelines in North and South America.

EXXON CORPORATION

5959 Las Colinas Blvd., Irving, TX 75039-2298; 214-444-1000

http://www.exxon.com
Employees: 79,000
Revenues: $ 100,697 million
Key Personnel: Chairman, CEO: Lee R. Raymond. SVP: Robert E. Willhelm. Human Resources Manager: T. J. Hearn.

Among the largest publicly owned integrated oil companies in the world, Exxon has exploration activities around the world. The company, which was rocked by scandals in the 1990s, is restructuring to increase efficiency and cut costs to help pay for a $5 billion fine levied by an Alaskan court over the Valdez oil spill. While sales remain steady, work force is down.

Other Locations: The company has operations in over 100 countries.

HALLIBURTON COMPANY

3600 Lincoln Plaza, 500 N. Akard St., Dallas, TX 75201-2611; 214-978-2600

http://www.halliburton.com
Employees: 107,800
Revenues: $ 17,353.1 million
Key Personnel: Chairman: William E. Bradford. CEO: Richard B. Cheney. VC: Dale P. Jones. Human Resources Manager: Paul M. Bryant.

Halliburton is one of the largest energy, engineering, and construction services companies in the world. It supplies oil exploration companies with equipment, products, and services; does engineering and construction for industrial and government clients; and issues property/casualty insurance. The company recently built an offshore drilling platform near the coast of Vietnam. Sales and work force are up.

Other Locations: The company has operations in over 100 countries.

RELIANT ENERGY INC.

1111 Louisiana St., Houston, TX 77002; 713-207-3000

http://www.houind.com
Employees: 12,916
Revenues: $ 11,488.5 million
Key Personnel: President, COO: Don D. Jordan. EVP: Lee W. Hogan. Human Resources Manager: Susan D. Fabre.

Reliant Energy, Inc. (formerly known as Houston Industries) bought out NorAm in 1997 and thus expanded from the electricity to natural gas markets. The company has electric utilities and natural gas customers in the U.S., Argentina, Brazil and India. Sales and work force are up.

Other Locations: The company's principal operations are in Arkansas, Louisiana, Minnesota, Mississippi, Missouri, Oklahoma, and Texas.

NABORS INDUSTRIES, INC.

515 W. Greens Rd., Suite 1200, Houston, TX 77067; 713-874-0035

Employees: 6,835
Sales: $ 968.2 million
Key Personnel: Chairman, CEO: Eugene M. Isenberg. President, COO: Anthony G. Petrello. VP, Corporate Secretary (Human Resources): Daniel McLachlin.

The biggest land-based oil and gas drilling contractor in the world, Nabors Industries has operations in nearly all major geothermal, oil, and gas markets. The company has found success in moving drilling equipment to areas of high activity, such as Venezuela and Yemen. It continues to grow by acquiring smaller drilling companies. Sales and work force are up.

PENNZOIL–QUAKER STATE COMPANY

700 Milam St., Houston, TX 77002; 713-546-4000

http://www.pzl.com
Employees: 13,200
Revenues: $1,801.7 million
Key Personnel: Chairman, CEO: James L. Pate. President, COO: Stephen D. Chesebro. Human Resources Manager: Darlene Cox.

Formed by the 1998 merger of Pennzoil and Quaker State, the company makes the U.S.'s #1 brand of motor oil (Pennzoil) and venerable brand Quaker State; it controls about 35 percent of the U.S. motor oil market. Pennzoil-Quaker State targets three areas of the petroleum market: franchised oil change centers, oil and gas exploration and production, and motor oil sales. Sales of oil products are the company's top business, and its Pennzoil-Quaker State brand holds the largest market share. Its Jiffy Lube chain is the largest of its kind in the world. Sales are steady, but work force is up.

Other Locations: The company has operations in California, Louisiana, Pennsylvania, Texas, and Utah, and in Canada, Indonesia, and Qatar.

PETROBRAS AMERICA, INC. ★★

10777 Westheimer, Suite 1200, Houston, TX 77042; 713-781-9799
Employees: 38,225
Sales: $14,908.7 million
Key Personnel: President: Luiz Antonio Nascimento Reis. Planning and Financial Manager (CFO): Jorge Nahas Neto. Administrative Assistant (Personnel): Regis Ferreira.

Petrobras America is a subsidiary of Petroleo Brasiliero, or Petrobras, Brazil's biggest industrial company. It is owned primarily by the government and has a monopoly on production and exploration in the country. It is considered a world leader in offshore drilling technology. The company is currently building a gas pipeline from Brazil to Bolivia. Gross operating revenue and work force are down.

Other Locations: Worldwide HQ: Petroleo Brasiliero S.A., Av. Republica do Chile, Rio de Janeiro, CEP 20035-900, Brazil; phone: +55-21-534-1200.

SHELL OIL COMPANY

One Shell Plaza, P.O. Box 2463, Houston, TX 77002; 713-241-6161
http://www.shellus.com
Employees: 19,800
Sales: $15,451 million
Key Personnel: President, CEO: Jack E. Little. VP Finance, CFO: P. G. Turberville. VP Human Resources: B. W. Levan.

Royal Dutch/Shell Group is a long-standing alliance between Royal Dutch Petroleum and British "Shell" Transport and Trading. In the United States, Shell Petroleum, Inc., is one of the largest industrial enterprises in the country. The company is well-known in the industry for its expertise in deep-sea drilling. Sales and work force are down.

Other Locations: Worldwide HQ: Royal Dutch/Shell Group, 30 Carel van Bylandtlaan, HR The Hague, Holland; phone: +44-(01)71-934-1234.

STAR ENTERPRISE

12700 Northborough Dr., Houston, TX 77067; 713-874-7000
Employees:7,658
Sales: $7,080 million
Key Personnel: President, CEO: Seth L. Sharr. COO: John F. Boles. Director of Human Resources: James M. Trickett.

Star Enterprise is a joint venture between Saudi Aramco and Texaco that markets Texaco petroleum products and operates StarMart convenience stores in the United States. Owned by the Saudi Arabian government, Saudi Aramco is the largest producer of crude oil in the world. Texaco is one of the largest U.S. retailers of branded gasoline. Sales are down, but work force is steady.

USX–MARATHON GROUP

5555 San Felipe Rd., Houston, TX 77253-3128; 713-629-6600
http://www.marathon.com
Employees: 24,344
Revenues: $21,726 million
Key Personnel: VC, President: Victor G. Beghini. EVP: Carl P. Giardini. Human Resources Manager: Daniel J. Sullenbarger.

Marathon Group is a subsidiary of the industrial conglomerate USX. The group is a holding company for Marathon Oil, Carnegie Natural Gas, Emro Marketing, and others. The company's operations include exploration, refining, and marketing through its chain of Marathon gas stations. Sales and work force are down.

Other Locations: The company has exploration and development operations in 17 countries.

ZAPATA CORPORATION ★★

100 Meridian Center, Ste. 350, Houston, TX 77056; 713-242-2000
http://www.zapatacorp.com
Employees:1,322
Sales: $133.6 million
Key Personnel: President, CEO: Avram A. Glazer. SVP: Eric T. Furey. Human Resources Manager: Vivian Schott.

Although Zapata was once both an oil and a gas company, it rearranged its operations in the past few years to emphasize natural gas to increase sales. The company offers a variety of services, including construction and servicing of natural gas compression packages, and is now attempting to get into the food business. Sales and work force are down.

VIRGINIA
MOBIL CORPORATION
3225 Gallows Rd., Fairfax, VA 22037; 703-846-3000
http://www.mobil.com
Employees: 41,500
Revenues: $46,287 million
Key Personnel: Chairman, CEO: Lucio A. Noto. President, COO: Eugene A. Renna. Human Resources Manager: Robert F. Amrhein.

One of the world's largest oil companies, Mobil owns or operates 21 refineries in 12 countries. Besides its extensive petroleum exploration and production operations, the company also manufactures many products, including storage bags and packaging films. Sales and work force are down.
Other Locations: The company has facilities in over 120 countries.

❶ PHARMACEUTICALS

CALIFORNIA
AMGEN, INC. ★★
1840 Dehavilland Dr., Thousand Oaks, CA 91320-1789; 805-447-1000
http://wwwext.Amgen.com
Employees: 5,500
Revenues: $2,642.3 million
Key Personnel: SVP Development: N. Kirby Alton. President, COO: Kevin W. Sharer. Human Resources Manager: Edward F. Garnett.

Amgen is one of the largest biotechnology companies in the world. The company uses recombinant genetic technology to create new drugs. Currently the company's most popular products are EPOGEN, used in treating certain types of anemia, and NEUPOGEN, used to stimulate the immune system in chemotherapy patients. Both sales and work force are on the rise.
Other Locations: The company has facilities in Asia, Europe, and North America.

ICN PHARMACEUTICALS, INC.
3300 Hyland Ave., Costa Mesa, CA 92626; 714-545-0100
http://www.icnpharm.com
Employees: 13,266
Sales: $838.1 million
Key Personnel: Chairman, President, CEO: Milan Panic. President, COO: Adam Jerney. Director of Human Resources: Jack L. Sholl.

Headed by the prominent Yugoslavian Milan Panic, ICN Pharmaceuticals is the parent of three subsidiaries: SPI Pharmaceuticals, ICN Biomedicals, and Viratek. Its pharmaceutical branch is actively expanding in Eastern Europe. Viratek is performing research on antiviral drugs such as ribavirin, which it claims is effective against AIDS. Its sales and work force are down.

ILLINOIS
ABBOTT LABORATORIES
100 Abbott Park Rd., Abbott Park, IL 60064; 847-937-6100
http://www.abbott.com
Employees: 56,236
Revenues: $2,477.8 million
Key Personnel: President, COO: Miles D. White. EVP: Paul N. Clark. Human Resources Manager: Thomas M. Wascoe.

One of the leading health care companies in the United States, Abbott Laboratories divides its resources between its pharmaceutical and nutritional division and its hospital and laboratory products division. Abbott is the world's top producer of erythromycin. Its sales and work force continue to increase.

INDIANA
ELI LILLY AND COMPANY
Lilly Corporate Ctr., Indianapolis, IN 46285; 317-276-2000
http://www.lilly.com
Employees: 29,800
Revenues: $9,236.8 million
Key Personnel: President, Coo: Sidney Taurel. EVP: Charles E. Golden. Human Resources Manager: Pedro P. Granadillo.

With a broad product line that includes the antibiotic Ceclor and the antidepressant Prozac, Eli Lilly is one of the top drug producers in the United States. The company supplies medicines for both human and animal disorders. It has recently sold or reorganized several of its divisions. Its sales and work force are up.

Other Locations: The company has facilities in 27 countries.

MICHIGAN

PHARMACIA & UPJOHN

100 Rte. 206 North Peapack, Kalamazoo, MI 49001; 908-901-8000
Employees: 30,000
Revenues: $6,893.0 million
Key Personnel: SVP U.S. and Canadian Pharmaceutical Operations: Ley S. Smith. EVP: Goran A. Ando. Human Resources Manager: Paul Matson.

When Upjohn merged with Pharmacia in 1995, they became one of the world's largest pharmaceutical companies. Pharmacia is a major Swedish drug maker. In the last several years, patents expired on the tranquilizers Xanax and Halcion, the diabetes treatment Micronase, and the contraceptive Depo-Provera. The company is moving into generic drugs to counteract the income loss. Revenues and work force are falling.

MISSOURI

HOECHST MARION ROUSSEL.

10236 Marion Park Dr.; Kansas City, MO 64137-1405 816-966-5000
Employees: 38,109
Sales: $8,242.3 million
Key Personnel: President, COO: Richard J. Markham. EVP Research and Development: Frank L. Douglas. VP Human Resources: Tommy White.

Hoechst Marion Roussel (formerly Marion Merrell Dow) is part of the German pharmaceutical company Hoechst, which is the third largest drug company in the world. Although it sells over 140 different compounds, the bulk of its sales come from two lines: its Cardizem cardiovascular drugs and Seldane antihistamines. Sales are down, but work force is up.
Other Locations: Worldwide HQ: Hoechst AG, Frankfurt am Main, Germany; phone: +49-69-3050. The company has manufacturing facilities in Canada, France, Italy, Japan, Spain, and the United States.

NEW JERSEY

AMERICAN HOME PRODUCTS CORP. ★★

5 Giralda Farms, Madison, NJ 07940-0874; 973-660-5000
http://www.ahp.com
Employees: 52,984
Revenues: $13,462.7 million

Key Personnel: Chairman, President, CEO: John R. Stafford. EVP: Robert Essner. VP Human Resources: Rene R. Lewin.

American Home Products merged with American Cyanamid in 1994 and is now the fourth largest pharmaceutical company in the United States. The company's diverse activities include the manufacture of drugs (Advil, Anacin, Robitussin), consumer products, animal and agricultural supplies, and medical supplies. It sold its food division in 1996. Sales are up but work force is down.

HOFFMANN-LA ROCHE, INC.

340 Kingsland St., Nutley, NJ 07110; 973-235-5000
Employees: 66,707
Sales: $17,932.1 million
Key Personnel: President, CEO: Patrick Zenner. SVP: Matthias Wahren. Director, Human Resources: Bradley Smith.

Hoffmann-La Roche is a subsidiary of Roche Group, one of the world's top drug makers. Roche Group also makes many other chemical products as well. The company, which owns 66 percent of the California biotechnology firm Genentech, also produces fragrances, vitamins, and fine chemicals. Its sales have increased, but its work force is down.
Other Locations: Worldwide HQ: Roche Group, Grenzacherstrasse 124 Postfach CH-4070, Basel, Switzerland; phone: +41-61-688-1111. The company has facilities in 54 countries.

JOHNSON & JOHNSON

One Johnson & Johnson Plaza, New Brunswick, NJ 08933; 732-524-0400
http://www.jnj.com
Employees: 93,100
Revenues: $23,657.0 million
Key Personnel: Chairman, CEO: Ralph S. Larsen. VC: Robert N. Wilson. Human Resources Manager: Russell C. Deyo.

One of the largest and most diversified pharmaceutical companies in the world, Johnson & Johnson makes consumer products (Band-Aids), pharmaceuticals (Tylenol), and professional products for the medical market, such as surgical instruments and joint replacement systems. The company frequently buys and sells subsidiaries. Its sales and work force are rising.
Other Locations: The company has facilities in 50 countries.

MERCK & CO., INC. ★★
One Merck Dr., Whitehouse Station, NJ
08889; 908-423-1000
http://www.merck.com
Employees: 57,300
Revenues: $ 26,898.2 million
Key Personnel: Chairman, President,
CEO: Raymond V. Gilmartin. EVP: Edward M. Scolnick. Human Resources
Manager: Wendy Yarno.
The world's second largest pharmaceutical company is Merck & Co. Vasotec, the
world's most popular cardiovascular
medication, is Merck's biggest income
producer. The company also makes many
other drugs and chemicals, including
animal health products and pesticides. It
is currently developing treatments for
asthma, osteoporosis, and schizophrenia.
Its sales and work force are growing.

SCHERING-PLOUGH CORPORATION ★★
One Giralda Farms, Madison, NJ 07940;
973-822-7000
http://www.sch-plough.com
Employees: 25,100
Revenues: $8,077.0 million
Key Personnel: President, CEO: Richard
Jay Kogan. EVP: Jack L. Wyszomierski.
SVP Human Resources: John Ryan.
Schering-Plough manufactures many
pharmaceuticals and animal health and
consumer products. Among its most
popular are Claritin, the top-selling antihistamine in the United States, and
Eulexin, a treatment for prostate cancer.
The company's consumer brands include
Dr. Scholl's and Coppertone. It is expanding its sales and manufacturing
abroad. Sales and work force are rising.

WARNER-LAMBERT COMPANY ★★
201 Tabor Rd., Morris Plains, NJ 07950-
2693; 973-540-2000
http://www.warner-lambert.com
Employees: 41,000
Revenues: $10,213.7 million
Key Personnel: President, COO:
Lodewijk J.R. de Vink. EVP: John F.
Walsh. Human Resources Manager:
Raymond M. Fino.
One of the top makers of consumer
health care and other products (such as
Benadryl, Efferdent, Listerine, and
Schick razors), Warner-Lambert also
makes pharmaceuticals and confectionery
products, such as Certs, Trident, and
Bubblicious. Among the drugs it makes

are Dilantin and Accupril. The company
is currently establishing consumer health
care and confectionery manufacturing facilities in China. Its sales and work force
are on the rise.
Other Locations: The company manufactures its products at 72 facilities in 34
countries.

NEW YORK

BRISTOL-MYERS SQUIBB COMPANY
345 Park Ave., New York, NY 10154-
0037; 212-546-4000
http://www.bms.com
Employees: 54,700
Revenues: $18,284.0 million
Key Personnel: EVP, President, Pharmaceutical Group: Hamed M. Abdou.
SVP, CFO: Michael F. Mee. Human Resources Manager: Charles G. Tharp.
With a focus on anticancer, antiinfective,
and cardiovascular drugs, Bristol-Myers
Squibb is one of the largest pharmaceutical makers in the United States. The
company has additional operations in
medical devices, toiletries, and consumer
health. Among its products are Ban antiperspirant, Clairol hair items, Bufferin,
and Enfamil infant formula. Its sales and
work force continue to increase.

CARTER-WALLACE, INC.
1345 Ave. of the Americas, New York,
NY 10105; 212-339-5000
Employees: 3,310
Sales: $ 668.9 million
Key Personnel: Chairman, CEO: Henry
H. Hoyt Jr. President, COO: Ralph Levine. Human Resources Manager: Thomas B. Moorhead.
One of the largest health care and consumer products companies in the United
States, Carter-Wallace makes many topselling products, such as Arrid deodorant,
Rise shaving cream, Trojan condoms,
and Nair depilatory. The company's
pharmaceutical line has been hit hard by
FDA regulators recently for various
complaints. Its sales and work force are
down.
Other Locations: The company has 16
facilities in eight countries.

PFIZER, INC. ★★
235 E. 42nd St., New York, NY 10017;
212-573-2323
http://www.pfizer.com
Employees: 46,400

Revenues: $13,544.0 million
Key Personnel: EVP, President, Hospital Products Group: Henry A. McKinnell. EVP: John F. Niblack. Human Resources Manager: William J. Robison.

More than 70 percent of Pfizer's sales come from sales of its pharmaceutical products. Among its most popular products are its families of cardiovascular, antiinflammatory, and diabetes treatments.The best selling Viagra is a Pfizer product. It also sells medical and consumer products (Visine, Ben-Gay). Its sales and work force are on the rise.
Other Locations: The company has manufacturing facilities in 33 countries.

SANDOZ CORP.

608 Fifth Ave., New York, NY 10020; 212-307-1122
Employees: 57,300
Sales: (SF, millions) 14,780
Key Personnel: CEO: Heinz Imhof. SVP Finance: Roland Losser. VP Human Resources: Richard Bilotti.

The 10th largest drug manufacturer in the world, Sandoz is also a leader in chemical production. With its purchase of baby food maker Gerber Products, it now has a leading position in the nutrition market too. The company also has subsidiaries involved in construction, environmental products, and seeds. Its sales are up, but its work force has decreased.
Other Locations: Worldwide HQ: Sandoz, Ltd., Lichtstrasse 35, Basel, Switzerland; phone: +41-61-324-11-11.

NORTH CAROLINA

GLAXO, INC. ★★

5 Moore Dr., Research Triangle Park, NC 27709; 919-483-2100
Employees: 54,350
Sales: $ 13,247.8 million
Key Personnel: President, CEO: George J. Morrow. CFO: Thomas Haber. VP Human Resources: Donald Cashion.

Glaxo Wellcome is the largest drug company in the world. It is the result of a 1995 merger of two British pharmaceutical giants, Glaxo and Wellcome. The company's biggest money maker is the antiulcer medication rantidine, which is sold as Zantac. Its sales and work force are on the rise.
Other Locations: Worldwide HQ: Glaxo Wellcome PLC, Landsdowne House, Berkeley Sq., London, W1X 6BQ, United Kingdom; phone: +44-(01) 71-

493-4060. The company has facilities in 31 countries.

PENNSYLVANIA

AMERISOURCE HEALTH ★★

300 Chester Field Pkwy., Malvern, PA 19355; 610-296-4480
http://www.amerisrc.com
Employees: 3,298
Revenues: $8,668.8 million
Key Personnel: Chairman: Lawrence C. Karlson. President, CEO: David R. Yost. VP: John A. Aberant.

AmeriSource Health is one of the biggest U.S. pharmaceutical distribution companies. It supplies companies, such as hospitals and nursing homes, with lower-cost drugs and other merchandise and services. The company has an aggressive sales program. It distributes its products primarily in the East. Sales and work force continue to increase.
Other Locations: The company has facilities in 13 states.

SMITHKLINE BEECHAM CORPORATION

One Franklin Plaza, 200 N. 16th St., Philadelphia, PA 19101; 215-751-4000
http://www.sb.com
Employees: 58,300
Sales: $ 13,416.0 million
Key Personnel: CEO: Jan Leschly. COO: Jean-Pierre Garnier. Human Resources Manager: Daniel Phelan.

Once the leading seller of the ulcer medication Tagamet, SmithKline Beecham is moving on to other challenges now that its patent on the popular drug has expired. The company, which makes many popular over-the-counter preparations, is the fifth largest drug company in the world. Its sales and work force are up.
Other Locations: Worldwide HQ: SmithKline Beecham PLC, New Horizons Ct., Brentford, Middlesex, TW8 9EP, United Kingdom; phone: +44-(01) 81-975-2000.

VIRGINIA

APPLIED BIOSCIENCE INTERNATIONAL

4350 N. Fairfax Dr., Arlington, VA 22203; 703-516-2490
Employees: 1,630
Sales: $150 million
Key Personnel: President, CEO, Pharmaco LSR International, Inc.: Charles L. Defesche. President, APBI Environmental Sciences Group: Swep T. Davis.

CEO, ENVIRON: Joseph H. Highland. Applied Bioscience International does business in two basic areas. Most of its business comes from biological safety testing and clinical research on the effects of drugs on humans. The company also provides environmental risk management and assessment services. Applied Bioscience International's sales and work force have both decreased of late.

❶ PHOTOGRAPHIC EQUIPMENT AND FILM

MASSACHUSETTS

POLAROID CORPORATION ★★
784 Memorial Dr., Cambridge, MA 02139; 781-386-2000
http://polaroid.com
Employees: 9,274
Revenues: $ 1,845.9 million
Key Personnel: EVP, CFO: Judith G. Boynton. EVP Business Development: William J. O'Neill Jr. Human Resources Manager: Joseph G. Parham Jr.
Known for its line of instant photography, Polaroid also develops and sells such new imaging products using holographic and polaroization technologies. For the graphic arts market, the company is introducing a new image-setting system and a color-proofing system. Sales and work force are both down.
Other Locations: The company has facilities in Massachusetts, Mexico, the Netherlands, and Scotland.

NEW YORK

EASTMAN KODAK COMPANY
343 State St., Rochester, NY 14650; 716-724-4000
http://www.kodak.com
Employees: 86,200
Revenues: $ 13,406.0 million
Key Personnel: President, COO: Daniel A. Carp. EVP: Carl F. Kohrt. Human Resources Manager: Michael P. Morley.
One of the dominant forces in the photography business, Eastman Kodak has approximately 70 percent of the U.S. market for 35mm film. The company is expanding its digital imaging capabilities, as well as its market for photographic film and supplies to the youth, elderly, and childless couples. While sales are down, work force continues to rise at Eastman Kodak.

FUJI PHOTO FILM U.S.A., INC. ★★
555 Taxter Rd., Elmsford, NY 10523; 914-789-8100
Employees: 36,580
Sales: $ 10,439.9 million
Key Personnel: President: Yasuo "George" Tanaka. Treasurer: Noboru Tanaka. Director of Human Resources: Joe Convery.
Fuji Photo Film is Japan's biggest maker of photosensitive materials. The company also makes a comprehensive array of other products, including cameras, tape recorders, computer disks, and photofinishing systems. It is working on new digital imaging products, a market the company expects will grow in the near future. Sales and work force are up.
Other Locations: Worldwide HQ: Fuji Photo Film Co., Ltd., 26-30, Nishiazabu 2-chome, Minato-ku, Tokyo, 106, Japan; phone: +81-3-3406-2844. The company has facilities in Brazil, Canada, Europe, Japan, the Pacific Basin, and the United States.

❶ PRINTING

ILLINOIS

GENERAL BINDING CORPORATION
One GBC Plaza, Northbrook, IL 60062; 847-272-3700
http://www.gbc.com
Employees: 5,332
Revenues: $ 922.4 million
Key Personnel: President, CEO: Govi C. Reddy. SVP Corporate Development: Walter M. Hebb. Human Resources Manager: Perry S. Zukowski.
General Binding is either holding things together or tearing them apart. The company is a top maker of binding and laminating machines and also manufactures a line of paper shredders. Its products are used in many areas, including government, education, and business. Sales and work force are on the increase at General.

R. R. DONNELLEY & SONS COMPANY
77 W. Wacker Dr., Chicago, IL 60601-1696; 312-326-8000
http://www.rrdonnelley.com
Employees: 36,300
Revenues: $ 5,018.4 million
Key Personnel: President, COO: Jonathan P. Ward. VC: James R. Donnelley. EVP: Cheryl A. Francis.

The largest commercial printer in the United States, R. R. Donnelley & Sons also markets mailing lists and distributes software. The company's printing operations account for the majority of its income. It replicates and distributes CD-ROMs and diskettes for companies such as Microsoft. It recently expanded its software operations. Sales and work force are up.

MASSACHUSETTS

QUEBECOR PRINTING (USA) CORP. ★★
125 High St., Boston, MA 02110; 617-346-7300
http://www.quebecorprinting.com
Employees: 27,535
Sales: $3,808.2 million
Key Personnel: President, CEO: Charles G. Cavell. EVP, COO: Pierre K. Peladeau. VP Human Resources: Serge Reynaud.
One of the largest printers in North America, Quebecor is both a publisher and a commercial printer. The company publishes many books, magazines, and newspapers in Canada and also in the United States, under its Quebecor Printing subsidiary. The company also has a pulp and paper operation. Its sales and work force are increasing.
Other Locations: Worldwide HQ: Quebecor, Inc., 612 Saint-Jacques St., Montreal, Quebec H3C 4M8, Canada; phone: 514-877-9777.

MINNESOTA

DELUXE CORPORATION ★
3680 Victoria St., N. Shoreview, MN 55126-2966; 612-483-7111
http://www.deluxe.com
Employees: 15,100
Revenues: $1,931.8 million
Key Personnel: EVP, COO: Lawrence J. Mosner. SVP, CFO: Thomas W. Van Himbergen. VP Human Resources: Sonia St. Charles.
Deluxe is one of the largest printers of checks and other similar documents. In addition, the company provides banks with a variety of services, including new-account verification help, electronic funds transfer, and marketing services. It is increasingly expanding into computer-related services. Sales and work force are down.
Other Locations: The company has production facilities in Canada, Puerto Rico, the United Kingdom, and the U.S.

MERRILL CORPORATION ★★
One Merrill Circle, St. Paul, MN 55108; 651-646-4501
http://www.merrillcorp.com
Employees: 3,933
Sales: $509.5 million
Key Personnel: President, CEO: John W. Castro. VP Operations: Rick R. Atterbury. VP Human Resources: Kathleen A. Larkin.
The third largest financial printer in the United States, Merrill provides full-service printing, distribution, and communications services to legal, financial, and corporate clients. Merrill has kept its costs down by centralizing its printing facilities, while allowing a distributed sales network. Its sales and work force are increasing.

NEW YORK

DNP (AMERICA), INC.
2 Park Ave., Suite 1405, New York, NY 10016; 212-686-1919
http://www.dnp.co.jp
Employees: 32,682
Sales: $10,044.4 million
Key Personnel: Managing Director: Ryozo Kitami. President, COO, DNP (America): Hideki Fuchigami. Personnel Assistant, DNP (America): Naomi Reis.
DNP is a subsidiary of Dai Nippon Printing, the largest printing company in the world. Dai Nippon Printing does a wide variety of commercial and specialty printing. The company has print plants in Hong Kong, Japan, and Singapore. It also puts out electronic books and multimedia software on CD-ROMs. It recently began expanding into photomask production, which is used in semiconductor manufacturing. Sales and work force are up.
Other Locations: Worldwide HQ: Dai Nippon Printing Co., Ltd., 1-1, Ichigaya Kagacho 1-chome, Shinjuku-ku, Tokyo 162-01, Japan; phone: +81-(0)-3-3266-2111.

AMERICAN BANKNOTE CORP.
200 Park Ave., 49th Fl., New York, NY 10166-4999; 212-557-9100
Employees: 3,380
Sales: $336.6 million
Key Personnel: Chairman, CEO: Morris Weissman. EVP, CFO: John T. Gorman. Head of Personnel: Serge Droujinsky.
One of the world's largest private-sector security printers, American Banknote

prints travelers checks, food coupons, visas, and a host of other related products. The company is an amalgamation of American Banknote Company, ABN-Brazil, and American Banknote Holographics. The latter is the top producer of holograms used for security. Sales and work force are down.

❶ PUBLISHING/ INFORMATION

CALIFORNIA
TIMES MIRROR PUBLISHING COMPANY
Times Mirror Sq., Los Angeles, CA 90053; 213-237-3700
http://www.tm.com
Employees: 20,619
Revenues: $3,009.1 million
Key Personnel: President, CEO: Mark H. Willes. President, CEO, Los Angeles Times: Kathryn M. Downing. Human Resources Manager: James R. Simpson.
The publisher of the *Los Angeles Times*, Times Mirror is one of the largest newspaper publishers in the United States. The company owns a number of newspapers, book publishers, and magazines (*Field & Stream, Popular Science*) and is currently restructuring its operations. Sales and work force remain steady.

CONNECTICUT
GROLIER, INC.
Sherman Turnpike, Danbury, CT 06816; 203-797-3500
http://www.grolier.com
Employees: 2,060
Est. Sales: $467 million
Key Personnel: COO: Brian Beckwith. EVP Marketing: Dante Cirilli. VP Human Resources: Anne Graves.
Among the top publishers of multimedia reference materials and reference books, Grolier is a subsidiary of the French company Lagardere, a media conglomerate. Among its products are the *Encyclopedia Americana*, the *Grolier Multimedia Encyclopedia*, and the *Guinness Multimedia Disc of Records*. The company continues to expand its electronic publishing operations. Sales and work force are growing.
Other Locations: Worldwide HQ: Lagardere Groupe, 4, Rue de Presbourg, Paris, France; phone: +33-1-40-69-16-00.

THE THOMSON CORPORATION
The Metro Ctr., One Station Pl., Stamford, CT 06902; 203-969-8700
http://www.thomcorp.com
Employees: 48,000
Sales: $6,269.0 million
Key Personnel: Chairman: Kenneth R. Thomson. President, CEO: Richard J. Harrington. Human Resources Manager: Theron S. Hoffman.
The Thomson Corporation is involved in specialty publishing and information, travel, and newspaper publishing. The company supplies reference, banking, and law information in a variety of formats. The Thomson Corporation owns several travel businesses, including Britannia Airways, and a number of newspapers, such as the *Toronto Globe and Mail*. Sales and work force are down.
Other Locations: Worldwide HQ: Thomson Corp., Toronto Dominion Bank Tower, Suite 2706, P.O. Box 24, Toronto Dominion Centre, Toronto, Ontario M5K 1A1, Canada; phone: 416-360-8700.

DISTRICT OF COLUMBIA
NATIONAL GEOGRAPHIC SOCIETY
1145 17th St., NW, Washington, DC 20036; 202-857-7000
http://www.nationalgeographic.com
Employees: 1,214
Revenues: $488.9 million
Key Personnel: President, CEO: John M. Fahey. SVP: Terry Adamson . SVP Human Resources: John Blodger.
Renowned for its studies of cultural and environmental issues, the National Geographic Society is a nonprofit educational organization. Its main activity is publishing *National Geographic* magazine. The society also publishes several other magazines and produces television documentaries. It recently introduced a Japanese-language version of *National Geographic*. Revenues and work force are down.

WASHINGTON POST COMPANY ★★
1150 15th St., NW, Washington, DC 20071; 202-334-6000
http://www.washpostco.com
Employees: 7,445
Revenues: $2,110.4 million
Key Personnel: President, COO: Alan G. Spoon. VP, President, COO, *Newsweek*: Richard M. Smith. VP Human Resources: Beverly R. Keil.

The Washington Post Company divides its efforts among magazines, newspapers, and television. The company, which puts out the venerable *Washington Post*, also publishes *Newsweek*, the second most popular weekly newsmagazine in the world (it is actually published in New York City). The company recently helped to create the New Century Network, an on-line provider of entertainment, news, sports, and tickets. Sales and work force are rising.

FLORIDA

AMERICAN MEDIA, INC.

600 S. East Coast Ave., Lantana, FL 33462; 561-540-1000
http://www.nationalenquirer.com
Employees: 2,050
Sales: $293.5 million
Key Personnel: VC Publishing Operations: Michael J. Boylan. EVP Publishing Operations, President, National Enquirer, Inc., and Country Weekly, Inc., Editor-in-Chief, *Enquirer*: Iain Calder. President, Star Editorial, Inc., Publication Director, *Star*: Roger Wood.

With a reputation for sensational stories about celebrities, American Media's Enquirer/Star Group boasts one of the largest single-copy sales rates in the United States. The company, which publishes the *National Enquirer*, *Star*, *Soap Opera Magazine*, and other publications, has a weekly circulation exceeding 7 million. Sales and work force are down.

KNIGHT-RIDDER, INC. ★★

50 W. San Fernando St., Miami, FL 33132; 408-938-7700
http://www.kri.com
Employees: 22,010
Revenues: $3,091.9 million
Key Personnel: VP Operations: Frank McComas. SVP: Ross Jones. SVP Human Resources: Mary J. Connors.

One of the largest newspaper publishers in the United States, Knight-Ridder has won more than 60 Pulitzer Prizes for its editorial and reporting quality. The company publishes the *Philadelphia Inquirer*, the *Detroit Free Press*, and the *San Jose Mercury News*, among others. It has been increasing its electronic offerings, among them SourceOne and DIALOG Direct. Sales and work force are up.
Other Locations: The company puts out newspapers in 16 states and has offices around the world.

GEORGIA

COX ENTERPRISES, INC. ★★

1400 Lake Hearn Dr., Atlanta, GA 30319; 404-843-5000
http://www.CoxEnterprises.com/icorpatlcei
Employees: 55,500
Sales: $5,355.4 million
Key Personnel: President, COO: David E. Easterly. SVP: Robet C. O'Leary. VP Human Resources: Marybeth H. Leamer.

Among the biggest U.S. media conglomerates, Cox Enterprises' holdings are many and varied. They include companies in the radio, television, and newspaper industries, including the *Atlanta Constitution* and Discovery Communications. Its owns radio and television stations in many major markets. The company is looking to expand onto the Information Superhighway. Sales and work force are increasing.

ILLINOIS

ENCYCLOPAEDIA BRITANNICA, INC.

310 S. Michigan Ave., Chicago, IL 60604; 312-347-7000
http://www.eb.com
Employees: 2,000
Est. Sales: $ 300.0 million
Key Personnel: CEO: Don Yannias. COO: Paul Hoffman. VP Human Resources: Karl Steinberg.

Encyclopaedia Britannica is in a pitched battle for survival. The company, which sells one of the most highly regarded print encyclopedias, is facing stiff competition from rivals such as Microsoft and Grolier, which sell cheaper electronic encyclopedias. Sales and work force are down.

JOHNSON PUBLISHING COMPANY

820 S. Michigan Ave., Chicago, IL 60605; 312-322-9200
http://www.ebony.com
Employees: 2,647
Sales: $371.9 million
Key Personnel: Chairman, CEO: John H. Johnson. President, COO: Linda Johnson Rice. Personnel Director: La Doris Foster.

The largest publisher of magazines targeting black audiences, Johnson Publishing is also one of the largest businesses under black ownership. Among its publications are *Jet* and *Ebony*. The company also sells cosmetics and owns two radio stations. It sponsors the American Black Achievement Awards on television each year. Sales are rising, but work force is shrinking.

PLAYBOY ENTERPRISES, INC.

680 N. Lake Shore Dr., Chicago, IL 60611; 312-751-8000
http://www.playboy.com
Employees: 773
Sales: $317.6 million
Key Personnel: Chairman, CEO: Christie Hefner. EVP, President, Entertainment Group: Anthony J. Lynn. Human Resources Manager: Denise M. Bindelglass.

With its U.S. market shrinking, Playboy Enterprises is declining as cultural values change. The company—whose flagship, *Playboy* magazine, has been on the decline since the early 1970s—is looking to overseas markets to increase sales. It also markets a wide variety of videos, clothing, and accessories in the United States and abroad. Sales and work force are up.

RAND MCNALLY & COMPANY

8255 Central Park Ave., Skokie, IL 60076-2970; 847-329-8100
http://www.randmcnally.com
Employees: 1,010
Sales: $175.0 million
Key Personnel: President,CEO: Henry J. Feinberg. VP Sales: Bob Amico. Human Resources Manager: Mary Lynn Smedinghoff.

A top cartography enterprise since the late 1800s, Rand McNally actually gets the most income from its DocuSystems division, which produces baggage tags and tickets for the travel industry. The company is best known, though, for its line of atlases, including the recently released TripMaker, a vacation-planning computer program on CD-ROM. Sales and work force are stable.

TRIBUNE COMPANY ★★

435 N. Michigan Ave., Chicago, IL 60611; 312-222-9100
Employees: 12,700
Revenues: $2,980.9 million
Key Personnel: Chairman, President, CEO: John W. Madigan. SVP: David D. Hiller. Human Resources Manager: Luis E. Lewin.

Among the largest media enterprises in the United States, Tribune owns four daily newspapers, 16 television stations, and five radio stations. It also owns several book publishers, including Contemporary Books. One of its divisions, Tribune New Media/Education, focuses on publishing reference and educational materials. The company also owns the Chicago Cubs baseball team. Tribune continues to expand its holdings in publishing and electronic media. Although sales are down, work force is rising.
Other Locations: The company has operations in 11 states.

MASSACHUSETTS

COURIER CORPORATION

15 Wellman Ave. N. Chelmsford, MA 01863; 978-251-6000
http://www.courier.com
Employees: 1,254
Sales: $151.6 million
Key Personnel: SVP, Chief Marketing Officer: Thomas G. Osenton. VP Religious Books, President, National Publishing Co.: George Q. Nichols. Human Resources Manager: Diana L. Sawyer.

One of the largest book manufacturers in the United States, Courier publishes in traditional paper formats and in newer electronic formats too. Many of the company's products are on CD-ROMs and computer diskettes. Among its products are Bibles, dictionaries, trade books, and medical journals. Sales and work force are up.
Other Locations: The company has facilities in Indiana, Massachusetts, and Pennsylvania.

HOUGHTON MIFFLIN COMPANY ★★

222 Berkeley St., Boston, MA 02116-3764; 617-351-5000
http://www.hmco.com
Employees: 2,830
Sales: $861.7 million
Key Personnel: Chairman, President, CEO: Nader F. Darehshori. EVP: Gail Deegan. Human Resources Manager: Arthur S. Battle Jr.

Houghton Mifflin is a top publisher of textbooks for university, high school, and elementary students. It has two primary subsidiaries, Riverside Publishing Company and McDougall Littell, Inc. It also puts out a variety of other titles, including reference books, fiction, and trade books. Sales and work force are up.

INTERNATIONAL DATA GROUP ★★

One Exeter Plaza, 15th Floor, Boston,
MA 02116-2851; 617-534-1200
http://www.idg.com
Employees: 11,500
Sales: $2,050.0 million
Key Personnel: President: Kelly P.
Conlin. COO: James Casella. Human Resources Manager: Tom Mathews.
Computers, information technology, and electronics are the business of International Data Group. The company puts out over 235 newspapers and magazines in 67 countries. It also puts on more than 60 trade shows in 22 countries each year and provides market data to nearly 4,000 customers. Sales and work force are up.

MINNESOTA

WEST GROUP★★

610 Opperman Dr., Eagan, MN 55123;
612-687-7000
http://www.westgroup.com
Employees: 8,000
Sales: $1,452.3 million
Key Personnel: EVP, COO: Howard M.
Zack. EVP, CFO: Dennis J. Beckingham.
VP Human Resources: Jim Greenwalt.
Among the top legal book publishers in the United States, West Group— a subsidiary of The Thomson Corporation— puts out a comprehensive array of printed materials and software for the legal community. Its publications include indexes, encyclopedias, and court opinions. It also provides many of its works in digital format and operates a legal research division on-line. Sales are up but work force has declined.

MISSOURI

HALLMARK CARDS, INC. ★★

2501 McGee St., Kansas City, MO
64108; 816-274-5111
http://www.hallmark.com
Employees: 20,945
Sales: $3,900.0 million
Key Personnel: President, CEO: Irvine
O. Hockaday, Jr. President, CEO, Hallmark Entertainment: Robert Halmi, Jr.
VP Human Resources: Ralph N. Christensen.
Known for its conservative approach to the greeting card business, Hallmark Cards is gradually losing market share to its competitors. The company, which sells more than 20,000 card designs, is the largest greeting card maker in the world. To keep up with the times, it is expanding its television production activities. Sales and work force are up.
Other Locations: The company has production plants in Kansas and Missouri and distribution operations in Connecticut and Missouri.

NEW JERSEY

DUN & BRADSTREET CORPORATION

One Diamond Hill Rd., Murray Hill, NJ
07974; 908-665-5000
http://www.dnbcorp.com
Employees: 12,500
Revenues: $1,934.5 million
Key Personnel: Chairman, CEO: Volney
Taylor. SVP: Frank S. Sowinski. SVP
Human Resources: Peter J. Ross
One of the top providers of business information, Dun & Bradstreet serves five market niches. The company provides marketing information, software, directory information, risk management and business marketing information, and business support. Its subsidiary, Dun & Bradstreet Information Services, is the top credit reporting agency in the world. Sales and work force are decreasing.

NEW YORK

ADVANCE PUBLICATIONS, INC. ★

950 Fingerboard Rd., Staten Island, NY
10305; 718-981-1234
http://www.advance.net
Employees: 24,050
Est. Sales: $3,859.1 million
Key Personnel: President: Donald E.
Newhouse. CFO: Arthur Silverstein.
President, CEO, Random House: Alberto
Vitale.
One of the biggest U.S. media groups is owned by the holding company Advance Publications. Among the company's holdings are Random House, the top publisher of consumer books in the United States. (Divisions of Random House include Knopf, Ballantine, and Crown.) Advance also owns Condé Nast, a top U.S. magazine publisher, and Newhouse Newspapers and Newhouse Broadcasting. Although sales are down, work force is rising.
Other Locations: The company has cable television and newspaper operations in the United States. It has magazine and book operations in New York as well as in Europe.

BANTAM DOUBLEDAY DELL PUBLISHING GROUP, INC. ★★

1540 Broadway, New York, NY 10036; 212-354-6500
http://www.bdd.com
Employees: 57,807
Sales: $12,701.5 million
Key Personnel: President, CEO: Jack Hoeft. EVP, COO: Erik Engstrom. SVP, Director of Human Resources: Robert Sherwood.

Bantam Doubleday Dell Publishing Group is owned by German media conglomerate Bertelsmann, one of the world's biggest book publishers. Bantam Doubleday Dell publishes a broad range of magazines, books, and audiocassettes. It also has several book clubs. The company is currently trying to reduce costs and increase efficiency. Sales and work force are up.
Other Locations: Worldwide HQ: Bertelsmann AG, Bertelsmann Aletiengesellschaft, Gutersloh, Germany; phone: +49-52-41-80-0.

BLOOMBERG L.P. ★★

499 Park Ave., New York, NY 10022; 212-318-2000
http://www.bloomberg.com
Employees: 4,900
Est. Sales: $1,500.0 million
Key Personnel: President, CEO: Michael R. Bloomberg. COO: Susan Friedlander. VP Marketing: Elisabeth DeMarse. VP Human Resources: Linda Norris.

Combining computer technology with information was the key to success for Bloomberg. The company provides financial information through several sources. Bloomberg Direct is the company's satellite television station. *Bloomberg* magazine provides monthly business features, analysis, and news. And Bloomberg News Radio, which owns WBBR-AM in New York City, broadcasts business news. Sales and work force are on the rise.

CMPMEDIA, INC. ★★

600 Community Dr., Manhasset, NY 11030; 516-562-5000
http://www.cmp.com
Employees: 1,822
Sales: $477.6 million
Key Personnel: President, CEO: Michael S. Leeds. EVP: Kenneth D. Cron.

Human Resources Manager: Mary Jones-Herbert.

CMP Publications puts out 16 trade newspapers and magazines targeting those with an interest in computers and electronics. Among its publications are *NetGuide* and *CommunicationsWeek*. It also supplies information and marketing services to business and consumer clients. The company makes all of its publications available on the Internet. Sales and work force are up.

DOW JONES & COMPANY, INC. ★★

200 Liberty St., New York, NY 10281; 212-416-2000
http://www.dowjones.com
Employees: 8,300
Revenues: $2,758.1 million
Key Personnel: Chairman, CEO; Publisher, *Wall Street Journal*: Peter R. Kann. President, COO: Kenneth L. Burenga. VP Employee Relations: James A. Scaduto.

Dow Jones supplies a many-faceted array of news and information about business. The company's operation provides data to its customers through radio, television, print, and on-line sources. It is best known for the *Wall Street Journal*, its daily newspaper, and *Barron's*, its weekly financial publication. However, the company's on-line offerings are expanding. Sales are up but work force is down.

HACHETTE FILIPACCHI MAGAZINES, INC.

1633 Broadway, New York, NY 10019; 212-767-6227
Employees: 8,768
Sales: $ 2,413.0 million
Key Personnel: President, CEO: Jack Kliger. CFO: John O'Connor. VP Human Resources: Joan Fila.

Hachette Filipacchi Magazines is a subsidiary of Lagardere Groupe, which deals in a wide variety of markets, including defense, automobiles, publishing, banking, and aerospace. Although its defense contracts are decreasing, the company is increasing efforts in the communications and multimedia arenas. Its primary activity in the United States is magazine publishing. Its sales and work force are shrinking.
Other Locations: Worldwide HQ: 149-151, rue Anatole France 92300 Levallois-Perret, France; phone: +33-1-41-34-60-00.

HARPERCOLLINS PUBLISHERS, INC.
10 E. 53rd St., New York, NY 10022;
212-207-7000
http://www.harpercollins.com
Employees: 2,900
Revenues: $737.0 million
Key Personnel: President, CEO: Jane Friedman. SVP Human Resources: Eileen Cross.
HarperCollins is the result of a 1989 merger of Harper & Row and William Collins, both publishing companies owned by Rupert Murdoch's News Corp. The company publishes a comprehensive list of consumer, business, reference, and other books under many imprints, including HarperBusiness, HarperPaperbacks, and HarperEdge. Sales and work force are decreasing.

HEARST CORPORATION ★★
959 Eighth Ave., New York, NY 10019;
212-649-2000
http://www.hearstcorp.com
Employees: 13,555
Sales: $2,375.0 million
Key Personnel: President, CEO: Frank A. Bennack Jr. EVP, COO: Victor F. Ganzi. Human Resources Manager: Ruth Diem.
Among the largest diversified media enterprises in the world, Hearst Corporation has operations in newspapers, books, magazines, and broadcasting. The company's publications include 12 daily newspapers and 20 consumer magazines. The Hearst Book Group is comprised of several publishing companies, including Avon and William Morrow & Co. The corporation owns stakes in Web browser Netscape; has part of education software distributor KidSoft; and Books That Work, a multimedia developer. Sales and work force are up.

JOHN WILEY & SONS, INC. ★
605 Third Ave., New York, NY 10158-0012; 212-850-6000
http://www.wiley.com
Employees: 2,100
Sales: $508.4 million
Key Personnel: President, CEO: William J. Pesce. EVP: Robert D. Wilder. SVP Human Resources: William J. Arlington.
John Wiley & Sons has been renowned in the field of scientific publishing since the 1800s. The company now publishes instructional materials, professional, trade, and reference books. It is aggressively expanding into electronic publishing, with the release of many scientific titles in digital form and on-line releases as well. Sales and work force are stable.

PRIMEDIA, INC.★★
745 Fifth Ave., New York, NY 10151;
212-745-0100
http://www.primediainc.com
Employees: 7,600
Revenues: $1,573.6 million
Key Personnel: Chairman, CEO: William F. Reilly. President: Charles G. McCurdy. Vice Chairman: Beverly C. Chell. Human Resources Manager: Michaelanne C. Discepolo.
With its array of media interests, PRIMEDIA (formerly K-III Communications) is a major force in the industry. Among its many holdings is *Weekly Reader* (a top publisher of newspapers for students), *The World Almanac, Funk & Wagnalls New Encyclopedia, Seventeen* and *New York* magazines, and Channel One, which broadcasts news programs to schools. The company is continuing to expand by acquisitions and internal growth. Sales and work force are rising.

MARVEL ENTERTAINMENT GROUP, INC.
387 Park Ave. S., New York, NY 10016;
212-696-0808
http://www.marvel.com
Employees: 1,100
Sales: $335.5 million
Key Personnel: President, CEO: Joseph Calamari. EVP, CFO: August J. Liguori. VP Administration, Human Resources: Ann Yarmark.
The largest publisher of comic books in North America, Marvel Entertainment Group has been rapidly diversifying. Although comics were its mainstay in the 1980s, trading cards have now climbed to the top. Marvel is also involved in a variety of joint ventures, licensing characters such as X-Men and Spider-Man, to promote restaurants and theme parks. Sales and work force are down.

MCGRAW-HILL, INC.
1221 Ave. of the Americas, New York, NY 10020; 212-512-2000
http://www.mcgraw-hill.com

Employees: 15,897
Revenues: $3,729.1million
Key Personnel: President, COO: Harold W. McGraw III. EVP New Ventures: Michael K. Hehir. VP Human Resources: Michael McGlynn.

One of the largest textbook publishers in the United States, McGraw-Hill serves a wide array of markets including government, professional, and business. Its offerings are increasingly in digital formats, such as CD-ROMs, software, and placements on electronic networks. The company also publishes several magazines, including *Business Week*, and owns four television stations. Sales and work force are up.

NEW YORK TIMES COMPANY

229 W. 43rd St., New York, NY 10036; 212-556-1234
http://www.nytco.com
Employees: 13,200
Revenues: $2,936.7 million
Key Personnel: Publisher, *New York Times*: Arthur Ochs Sulzberger, Jr. President, CEO: Russell T. Lewis. SVP Human Resources: Cynthia H. Augustine.

Publisher of the *New York Times*, the top metropolitan daily newspaper in the United States, the New York Times Company is a diversified communications business. It owns nearly 30 newspapers, including the *Boston Globe*, 10 leisure and sports magazines, and many other news and information services, including TV and radio stations. Sales and work force are up.

NEWS AMERICA HOLDINGS, INC. ★★

1211 Ave. of the Americas, New York, NY 10036-8703; 212-852-7000
http://www.newscorp.com
Employees: 28,220
Sales: $13,585.0 million
Key Personnel: Chairman, Managing Director, CEO, News America: Keith Rupert Murdoch. CFO, Finance Director, CFO, News America: David F. DeVoe. EVP Human Resource, EVP Human Resources, News America: William A. O'Neill.

News America Holdings is a subsidiary of The News Corporation, the largest newspaper publisher in the world. The biggest chunk of its income is derived from film producer Twentieth Century Fox Film Corporation. News America has numerous holdings in the newspaper, magazine, and television industries, including the *New York Post*, *TV Guide*, and Fox Broadcasting. Sales and work force are on the rise.

Other Locations: Worldwide HQ: News Corp., Ltd., 2 Holt St., Sydney, NSW 2010, Australia; phone: +61-2-288-3000. The company has operations in Australia, the Pacific Rim, the United Kingdom, and the United States.

PEARSON, INC.

One Rockefeller Plaza, New York, NY 10020; 212-713-1919
Employees: 18,400
Sales: $3,975.6 million
Key Personnel: Chief Executive: Marjorie M. Scardino. Executive Director, Finance: John Makinson. Director of Human Resources: Randall Keller.

Books and newspapers are the main enterprises of Pearson. The company owns the book publishers Addison-Wesley Longman/Penguin, as well as several newspapers and magazines, including the *Financial Times* and *The Economist*. Among its other holdings are Thames Television and the Lazard Brothers investment bank. Sales and work force are up.

Other Locations: Worldwide HQ: Pearson PLC, 3 Burlington Gardens, London W1X 1LE, United Kingdom; phone: +44-(01) 71-411-2000.

PRODIGY INC.

44 S. Broadway, White Plains, NY 10601; 914-448-8000
http://www.prodigy.com
Employees: 394
Est. Sales: $136.1 million
Key Personnel: President, CEO: David C. Trachtenberg. SVP Marketing: Jim L'Heureux. Human Resources Manager: Pat Anderson .

Prodigy, Inc. (formerly Prodigy Services) is one of the four largest commercial on-line services. Even though it was the first to offer its subscribers access to the World Wide Web, it has fallen to last place behind America Online and Microsoft. It has shifted its focus to becoming an Internet service provider (ISP). Although it has regained sales, its work force has decreased..

RANDOM HOUSE, INC. ★★

201 E. 50th St., New York, NY 10022;

212-751-2600
http://www.randomhouse.com
Employees: 19,500(est.)
Est. Sales: $1,350 million
Key Personnel: Chairman, President, CEO: Alberto Vitale. President, COO: Erik Engstrom. VP Human Resources: Christine Names.

Random House is part of Advance Publications, one of the biggest media conglomerates in the United States. With its various imprints, Random House is the leading U.S. trade publisher. Those imprints include the Knopf Publishing Group, Ballantine, Crown, Fodor's, and Modern Library. The media giant Bertelsmann AG (which owns Bantam Doubleday Dell) is planning to acquire Random House. Sales and work force are growing.

READER'S DIGEST ASSOCIATION, INC.
Reader's Digest Rd., Pleasantville, NY 10570-7000; 914-238-1000
http://www.readersdigest.com
Employees: 5,500
Revenues: $2,532.2 million
Key Personnel: Chairman, CEO: Thomas O. Ryder. SVP: Gregory G. Coleman. SVP Human Resources: Gary S. Rich.

Although *Reader's Digest* magazine is put out in 18 languages and has a readership of 100 million, books and home entertainment products are the biggest income producers of the Reader's Digest Association. The company sells a broad range of videos, CDs, and reference materials, among other things. Nearly two-thirds of its sales come from outside the United States. Sales and work force are down.

REUTERS AMERICA HOLDINGS, INC. ★★
1700 Broadway, New York, NY 10019; 212-603-3300
http://www.reuters.com
Employees: 16,938
Sales: $ 5,031.6 million
Key Personnel: Chairman, CEO: Sir Christopher A. Hogg. President: Andre Villeneuve. EVP: Patrick Burns.

Reuters has been supplying news and financial information since the late 1800s. The company, which rose to prominence at about the same time as the telegraph, is now one of the most respected sources of financial news in the world. It has an international computer network spanning some 150 countries and also provides financial transaction and media services. Sales and work force are up.
Other Locations: Worldwide HQ: Reuters Holdings PLC, 85 Fleet St., London, EC4P 4AJ, United Kingdom; phone: +44-(01) 71-250-1122. The company has operations in 150 countries.

SCHOLASTIC CORPORATION ★★
555 Broadway, New York, NY 10012; 212-343-6100
http://Scholastic.com
Employees: 7,540
Sales: $1,154.7 million
Key Personnel: Chairman, President, CEO: Richard Robinson. EVP: Kevin J. McEnery. VP Human Resources: Larry V. Holland.

Among the top publishers of educational materials, Scholastic targets many markets, including textbooks, children's fiction, educational software, and professional magazines. Among its titles are the extremely successful Goosebumps and Babysitters Club series, the *Charles in Charge* television show, and *Home Office Computing* magazine. It recently introduced a line of interactive books designed to entice children to turn off the television. Sales and work force are growing.
Other Locations: The company has subsidiaries in Australia, Canada, New Zealand, the United Kingdom, and the United States.

SIMON & SCHUSTER
1230 Ave. of the Americas, New York, NY 10020; 212-698-7000
http://www.simonandschuster.com
Employees: 2,300
Sales: $564.6 million
Key Personnel: President, CEO: Jonathon Newcomb. EVP, CFO: Sam Judd. Human Resources Manager: James Young.

The largest book publisher in the world, Simon & Schuster has been on an expansion program for 20 years, buying up many other publishing enterprises. The company, which is a subsidiary of Viacom, has recently been expanding its electronic offerings, both on-line and on CD-ROM. Sales and work force are down.

TIME WARNER, INC. ★
75 Rockefeller Plaza, New York, NY

10019; 212-484-8000
http://www.timewarner.com
Employees: 67,500
Sales: $14,582.0 million
Key Personnel: Chairman, CEO: Gerald M. Levin. VC: Ted Turner. President: Richard D. Parsons.

Time Warner is the biggest media and entertainment conglomerate in the world. The magazines it publishes include *Time*, *Sports Illustrated*, *Fortune*, and *People*. Time also operates a variety of other publishing enterprises, such as the book publisher Little, Brown, and Co., Book-of-the-Month Club, Time Warner AudioBooks, Sunset Publishing, and Time Warner Electronic Publishing. The company is continuing to expand by acquiring existing publishing companies. Sales are and work force are up.

VNU, USA, INC. ★★

1515 Broadway, New York, NY 10036-8986; 212-764-7300
Employees: 12,059
Sales: $2,847.7 million
Key Personnel: President, CEO: G.S. Hobbs. CFO: Rosalee Lovett. VP Human Resources: Debbie Kahlstrom.

A top European publisher, VNU concentrates on women's magazines and regional newspapers. It puts out over 100 magazines in Europe. The company also publishes professional journals and educational materials and is part owner of several Dutch television stations. Sales and work force are up.
Other Locations: Worldwide HQ: nv Verenigd Bezit VNU, Ceylonpoort 5-25, Haarlem, The Netherlands; phone: +31-23-546-3463. The company has facilities in Belgium, the Czech Republic, France, Hungary, Italy, the Netherlands, Spain, the United Kingdom, and the United States.

GOLDEN BOOKS FAMILY ENTERTAINMENT, INC.

888 Seventh Ave. New York, NY 10106; 212-547-6700
http://www.goldenbooks.com
Employees: 950
Sales: $193.6 million
Key Personnel: Chairman, CEO: Richard E. Snyder. President: Eric Ellenbogen. SVP Human Resources: Christian Fritz.

Children's books are the business of Golden Books Family Entertainment (formerly Western Publishing Group). The company is the largest U.S. publisher and manufacturer of children's books. Among its products are picture, pop-up, story, and paper doll books. Its Golden Books imprint is well-known in the United States. Many of its products are generated from licensing agreements with Walt Disney. The compnay's sales and work force are up.

OHIO

AMERICAN GREETINGS CORPORATION ★★

1 American Rd., Cleveland, OH 44144; 216-252-7300
http://www.amgreetings.com
Employees: 35,475
Revenues: $2,205.7 million
Key Personnel: President, COO: Edward Fruchtenbaum. SVP Consumer Products: Erwin Weiss. SVP Human Resources: Patricia A. Papesh.

One of the largest greeting card publishers in the world, American Greetings puts out its products in 69 countries and in 16 languages. The company sells its lines of cards, gifts, and accessories under many brands, including Carlton and Forget Me Not. Sales and work force are growing.
Other Locations: The company has facilities and offices in Canada, France, Ireland, Mexico, the United Kingdom, and the United States.

COMPUSERVE INTERACTIVE SERVICES, INC.

5000 Arlington Ctr. Blvd., Columbus, OH 43220; 614-457-8600
http://www.compuserve.com
Employees: 3,100
Sales: $970 million
Key Personnel:. President, CEO: Mayo Stuntz Jr. VP Human Resources: Anita Marcus.

Among the oldest and largest of the commercial computer network services, CompuServe now operates as a brand of American Online. The company offers a wide variety of services, including electronic mail, reference services, and opportunities to socialize with other subscribers. Work force and sales are rising.

E. W. SCRIPPS COMPANY

312 Walnut St., Cincinnati, OH 45201; 513-977-3000
http://www.scripps.com
Employees: 7,900

Revenues: $1,454.6 million
Key Personnel: SVP Television: Paul Gardner. SVP Corporate Development: Craig G. Standen. SVP Cable: F. Steven Crawford.

Although primarily a newspaper publisher, E. W. Scripps is increasing its operations in the entertainment industry. The company publishes several top daily newspapers, including the *Knoxville News-Sentinel* and the *Rocky Mountain News*. It owns nine television stations and several medium-sized cable operations. It also produces television shows. Sales are up, but work force is down.

❶ RAILROADS

DISTRICT OF COLUMBIA
NATIONAL RAILROAD PASSENGER CORPORATION
60 Massachusetts Ave., NE, Washington, DC 20002; 202-906-3000
http://www.amtrak.com
Employees: 24,000
Sales: $2,285.2 million
Key Personnel: Chairman: Gov. Tommy G. Thompson. President, CEO: George D. Warrington. Human Resources: Lorraine A. Green.

Known to most people as Amtrak, the National Railroad Passenger Corporation gets almost $1 billion annually in federal subsidies. The company is a private, for-profit organization set up by Congress in 1970. It carries over 20 million passengers per year but has never turned a profit. Sales are up dramatically, and work force is growing.
Other Locations: The company has operations in 45 states.

NEBRASKA

UNION PACIFIC CORPORATION
1416 Dodge St., Omaha, NE 68179; 402-271-5000
http://www.up.com
Employees: 65,000
Sales: $10,553 million
Key Personnel: President; Chairman, CEO: Richard K. Davidson. SVP Information Technologies: L. Merill Bryan Jr. SVP Human Resources: Barbara Schaefer.

With its acquisition of Southern Pacific in 1996, Union Pacific became the largest railroad enterprise in North America. With the newest fleet of locomotives in the United States, Union Pacific connects the Gulf of Mexico to the Midwest and the West with more than 36,000 miles of track. Sales and work force are down.
Other Locations: The company has rail service in the western two-thirds of the United States, trucking service in the United States and southeastern Canada, and gas, mining, and oil operations in the United States, the Gulf of Mexico, and Canada.

PENNSYLVANIA
CONRAIL, INC.
2001 Market St., 2 Commerce Sq., Philadelphia, PA 19101; 215-209-4000
http://www.conrail.com
Employees: 22,000
Sales: $3,863 million
Key Personnel: Chairman, CEO: David M. Levan. President: Timothy T. O'Toole. SVP Operations: Ronald J. Conway.

The dominant freight railroad in the Northeast is Conrail, a holding company for six bankrupt rail companies. It has over 11,000 miles of track running from Illinois to Massachusetts and through the Northeast, Quebec, and the Midwest. In 1996 a bidding war developed when both the CSX Corporation and the Norfolk Southern Corporation proposed a takeover of Conrail. They have now divided most of Conrail's operations between them, though the company still oversees interests in Detroit, Philadelphia and New Jersey. While sales are up slightly, the work force is static.

TEXAS
BURLINGTON NORTHERN SANTA FE CORPORATION
2650 Lou Menk Dr., 2nd Floor, Fort Worth, TX 76131-2830; 817-333-2000
http://www.bnsf.com
Employees: 42,900
Sales: $8,941 million
Key Personnel: Chairman, CEO: Robert D. Krebs. President, COO: Matthew K. Rose. Human Resources: Ricki Gardner.

Operating over 34,000 miles of main and secondary track, Burlington Northern Santa Fe has one of North America's longest freight rail systems. The company is the result of the merger between

Burlington Northern, Inc., and the Santa Fe Pacific Corporation. The company's rails stretch from Florida to British Columbia. Transport of coal and agricultural commodities are the company's top income producers. Its sales are up, but its work force is down.

RAILTEX, INC. ★

4040 Broadway, Ste. 200, San Antonio, TX 78209; 210-841-7600
http://www.railtex.com
Employees: 950
Sales: $161 million
Key Personnel: Chairman, President, and CEO: Ronald A. Rittenmeyer. VP, CFO: Joseph P. Jahnke. Human Resources: Felita Rodriguez.

The top short-haul railroad in the United States is RailTex. The company purchases short feeder lines that larger rail companies can't run profitably. Its employees tend to be less specialized and receive less pay than their counterparts in the major rail companies. Sales and work force are up.

VIRGINIA

CSX CORPORATION

1 James Center, 901 E. Cary St., Richmond, VA 23219-4031; 804-782-1400
http://www.csx.com
Employees: 46,147
Sales: $9,898 million
Key Personnel: Chairman, President, and CEO: John W. Snow. EVP, CFO: Paul R. Goodwin. Human Resources: Linda Amato.

CSX's primary subsidiary (CSX Transportation) operates rail lines in 23 U.S. states and Canada, making it the #3 U.S. rail system. CSX also owns nearly half of Conrail and Sea-Land Service, one of the top container shippers in the world. Sales and workforce are down.

NORFOLK SOUTHERN CORPORATION

3 Commercial Pl., Norfolk, VA 23510-2191; 804-629-2600
http://www.nscorp.com
Employees: 24,300
Sales: $4,221 million
Key Personnel: Chairman, President, CEO: David R. Goode. VC, CFO: Henry C. Wolf. Human Resources: Paul N. Astin.

Norfolk Southern is more than just a freight rail system. The company also has coal, natural gas, and timber holdings in the Appalachians. The company is often cited as an example of efficiency and service in the rail industry. In late 1996, the firm joined with CSX to acquire Conrail, and later sold off its North American Van Lines to better focus on its rail service.. Sales are holding steady and work force is shrinking.
Other Locations: The company's rail system operates in 20 eastern states and one eastern Canadian province.

❶ REAL ESTATE

FLORIDA

LENNAR CORPORATION ★★

700 NW 107th Ave., Miami, FL 33172; 305-559-4000
http://www.lennar.com
Employees: 2,173
Sales: $1,303 million
Key Personnel: President, CEO: Stuart A. Miller. SVP: Irving Bolotin. Human Resources Manager: Carl Garraffo.

Lennar is the fifth largest homebuilder in the United States. The company builds homes mainly in the sunbelt states of Arizona, California, Florida, Neveda and Texas. The company also provides mortgage, title and escrow services. In 1997 the company spun off its LNR division, which owned and managed apartments, hotels and office buildings. Sales and work force are up dramatically.

MARYLAND

THE ROUSE COMPANY

10275 Little Patuxent Pkwy., Columbia, MD 21044-3456; 410-992-6000
http://www.therousecompany.com
Employees: 4,126
Sales: $768.3 million
Key Personnel: Chairman, President, and CEO: Anthony W. Deering. EVP, CFO: Jeffrey H. Donahue. Human Resources: Janice Allan Fuchs.

The Rouse Company develops, owns and manages commerical real estate, focusing on retail shopping centers. Its holdings include Faneuil Hall Marketplace in Boston and Baltimore's The Gallery at Harborplace. Having started on the east coast, the company has diversified with holdings in California and Nevada. Sales are down, but workforce is up slightly.

NEW YORK

HELMSLEY ENTERPRISES, INC.
230 Park Ave., New York, NY 10169; 212- 679-3600
http://www.helmsleyhotels.com
Employees: 7,800
Sales (est.): $1,000 million
Key Personnel: Owner: Leona Helmsley. CFO: Abe Wolf. Director Human Resources: Josephine Keenan.
Helmsley Enterprises is the remains of the real estate empire amassed by the late Harry Helmsley and is currently run by his widow Leona. The company owns and manages approximately 100 million square feet of real estate, including apartments, commercial space, and hotels. Among its most notable holdings is a lease on the Empire State Building in New York City. Sales and work force are down sharply.

OHIO

EDWARD J. DEBARTOLO CORPORATION ★★
7620 Market St., Youngstown, OH 44512; 330-965-2000
Employees: 4,000
Sales (est.): $250 million
Key Personnel: Chairman, CEO: Marie Denise DeBartolo York. EVP: John C. York II. SVP, CFO: Lynn E. Davenport.
At one time one of the top U.S. developers of covered shopping malls, Edward J. DeBartolo Corporation is now known more for its ownership of the perennial NFL champions San Francisco 49ers. The company, which is a pioneering force for mall development outside of California, recently raised money by taking portions of its operation public. In 1996 it merged with Simon Property, making it North America's largest publicly traded real estate company. Sales are steady, but workforce is up dramatically.
Other Locations: The company has more than 85 million square feet of retail space in California, Florida, Indiana, New Jersey, Ohio, Pennsylvania, and Texas.

❶ RESTAURANT CHAINS

CALIFORNIA

FRESH CHOICE, INC.
2901 Tasman Dr., Ste. 109, Santa Clara, CA 95054-1169; 408-986-8661
http://www.freshchoiceinc.com
Employees: 2,060
Sales: $73.9 million
Key Personnel: Chairman: Charles A. Lynch. President, CEO: Everett F. Jefferson. Human Resources: Joan M. Miller.
Healthy food for health-conscious people is the strategy of Fresh Choice. The company owns a chain of more than 50 restaurants, mainly in California, that feature a buffet selection of pastas, salads, and soups. The company is looking for expansion opportunities in the East. Sales are up slightly, but workforce is down.

SIZZLER INTERNATIONAL, INC.
6101 W. Centinela Ave., Culver City, CA 90230; 310-568-0135
Employees: 7,300
Sales: $226.3 million
Key Personnel: President, CEO: Charles L. Boppell. CEO International Division: Kevin W. Perkins. Human Resources: Diane M. Hardesty.
Dogged by many difficulties, Sizzler International is persevering. The company, which owns numerous Sizzler and Kentucky Fried Chicken restaurants, has been closing some locations and restructuring, after filing for bankruptcy in 1996. Sales are down, but work force has rebounded slightly.
Other Locations: The company has operations mainly in Australia and the United States.

COLORADO

BOSTON CHICKEN, INC. ★★
14123 Denver West Pkwy., Golden, CO 80401; 303-278-9500
http://www.bostonchicken.com
Employees: 12,470
Sales: $261.1 million
Key Personnel: Chairman, President, and CEO: J. Michael Jenkins. SVP, CFO: Greg Uhing. VP Human Resource Administration: Chris B. Dodge.
After filing for Chapter 11 Bankruptcy in 1998, Boston Chicken shut down more

than 200 stores. Boston Chicken still runs and franchises nearly 900 Boston Market restaurants, in addition to its interests in Einstein/Noah Bagels. Although the company began with its specialty rotisserie chicken, Boston Market has expanded its menu, adding ham, meat loaf, and turkey. Sales and work force are growing.

ROCK BOTTOM RESTAURANTS, INC. ★★

248 Centennial Pkwy., Ste. 100, Louisville, CO 80027; 303-664-4000
http://www.rockbottom.com
Employees: 4,766
Sales: $160.1 million
Key Personnel: Chairman, President, and CEO: Frank B. Day. EVP, COO: Ned R. Lidvall. VP Finance: Theresa D. Shelton..

Rock Bottom Restaurants offers two types of eating experiences, both of which revolve around beer. Old Chicago has a menu emphasizing pizza and over 100 selections of beer from breweries worldwide. Rock Bottom Brewery provides five to seven varieties of beer brewed on the premises. Sales are up, but workforce is down.
Other Locations: The company has operations in Colorado, Minnesota, Oregon, and Texas.

VICORP RESTAURANTS, INC.

400 W. 48th Ave., Denver, CO 80216; 303-296-2121
http://www.vicorpinc.com
Employees: 11,800
Sales: $346.2 million
Key Personnel: Chairman, President, and CEO: Charles R. Frederickson. EVP, CFO: Richard E. Sabourin. Human Resources: Sheila Marko.

VICORP is known mainly for its two restaurant chains: Bakers Square, which serves fresh-baked pies, lunch, and dinner, and Village Inn, which is a popular breakfast eatery. The company has been trying to recover from buying the bankrupt Sambo's Restaurant chain in the mid-1980s, just as the economy took a downturn. Sales are up, but work force has declined.
Other Locations: The company franchises or operates three chains of restaurants in 26 states.

FLORIDA

CHECKERS DRIVE-IN RESTAURANTS, INC.

4255 49th St. North, Bldg. #1, Clearwater, FL 33762; 727-519-2000
Employees: 4,600
Sales: $145.7 million
Key Personnel: President, CEO: James J. Gillespie. EVP, COO: Harvey Fattig. Human Resources: Steve Cohen.

Checkers Drive-In Restaurants operates more than 400 fast food restaurants, about two-thirds of which are company-owned. The company has been battling for market share with larger chains like McDonald's. In 1999, the company acquired its rival Rally's, doubling its size. Sales are up slightly, while workforce is falling.

ELXSI CORPORATION

3600 Rio Vista Ave., Ste. A, Orlando, FL 32805; 407-849-1090
Employees: 2,752
Sales: $98.6 million
Key Personnel: Chairman, President, and CEO: Alexander M. Milley. VP, President Bickford's: Daniel E. Bloodwell. Human Resources: Kenneth Allen.

Originally begun as Trilogy in the 1980s, ELXSI started as a mainframe computer company. However, development difficulties forced the company to change its tune. It now operates more than 60 Bickford's Family Restaurants as well as four Abdow's Family Restaurants. The company also owns Cues, a manufacturer of repair and inspection equipment for sewer systems. Sales are increasing, but work force has declined.

OUTBACK STEAKHOUSE, INC. ★

550 N. Reo St., Ste. 200, Tampa, FL 33609; 813-282-1225
http://www.outback.com
Employees: 36,500
Sales: $1,358.9 million
Key Personnel: President, COO: Robert D. Basham. SVP: J. Timothy Gannon. Human Resources: Trudy I. Cooper.

Outback Steakhouse combines Australian ambiance and recipes with a skillful building plan. The company, which limits its menu offerings to dinner, locates its restaurants in residential areas in order to keep real estate costs down. It currently has over 400 Outback Steakhouse restaurants and numerous Carrabba's Italian Grills. The company plans to open many additional restaurants. Both sales and work force are growing.

ILLINOIS

MCDONALD'S CORPORATION ★
McDonald's Plaza, Oak Brook, IL 60523; 630-623-3000
http://www.mcdonalds.com
Employees: 284,000
Sales: $12,421.4 million
Key Personnel: Chairman, CEO: Jack M. Greenberg. EVP, CFO: Michael L. Conley. Human Resources: Stanley R. Stein.

One of the most successful retail enterprises in the United States, McDonald's is the largest food service retailer in the world. The fast food company has recently been adjusting its menus to follow an evolving market. Approximately 80 percent of its restaurants are franchised, with the rest company-owned. Sales and work force are both on the increase.
Other Locations: The company has over 18,000 restaurants in 89 countries.

KANSAS

APPLEBEE'S INTERNATIONAL, INC. ★★
4551 W. 107th St., Ste. 100, Overland Park, KS 66207; 913-967-4000
http://www.applebees.com
Employees: 20,300
Sales: $647.6 million
Key Personnel: President, CEO, and COO: Lloyd L. Hill. EVP, CFO: George D. Shadid. Human Resources: Louis A. Kaucic.

Among the top casual-dining restaurant chain owners, Applebee's mainly targets the midpriced market. The company is best known for its Applebee's Neighborhood Grill and Bar establishments, which emphasize chicken, burgers, and salads. Most of its restaurants are franchised, but about 25 percent are company-owned. The company is building more restaurants and broadening its menu offerings. Sales and work force are growing.
Other Locations: The company has more than 1,100 restaurants in the United States and abroad.

LONE STAR STEAKHOUSE & SALOON, INC.
224 E. Douglas, Ste. 700, Wichita, KS 67202; 316-264-8899
Employees: 19,400
Sales: $616.7 million
Key Personnel: Chairman, CEO: Jamie B. Coulter. EVP, CFO: John D. White. Director Personnel: Reeve Zimmerman.

Offering a casual atmosphere and generous portions of mesquite-grilled steak, chicken, and other Texas-style foods, Lone Star Steakhouse & Saloon is popular in the Midwest. The company is expanding its reach internationally, having opened restaurants in Australia and planning more in Asia. It has also added the upscale Del Frisco's Double Eagle Steak House Sullivan's Steakhouses to its stable of restaurants. Sales are up, but workforce is on the decline.
Other Locations: The company has more than 300 restaurants in Australia and the United States.

KENTUCKY

PAPA JOHN'S INTERNATIONAL, INC.
11492 Bluegrass Pkwy., Ste. 175, Louisville, KY 40299; 502-266-5200
http://www.papajohns.com
Employees: 14,321
Sales: $669.8 million
Key Personnel: Chairman, CEO: John H. Schnatter. VC, President: Blaine E. Hurst. Human Resources: Mary A. Palmer.

Quality ingredients and narrow focus are the keys to success for Papa John's International. The company has kept its focus on pizza, rather than adding other foods to its menus. It also requires that its franchisees purchase ingredients from company-owned suppliers to maintain quality control. Sales are growing, and workforce is up slightly.

MASSACHUSETTS

BERTUCCI'S, INC.
14 Audubon Rd., Wakefield, MA 01880; 781-246-6700
Employees: 4,685
Sales: $136.7 million
Key Personnel: Chairman, President: Joseph Crugnale. SVP, COO: Theodore R. Barber. Human Resources: Kim Erickson.

Pizza is on the menu at Bertucci's. The

company runs a chain of approximately 85 gourmet pizzerias in the East. The restaurants feature prominently displayed kitchens with brick ovens, which apparently provide the ideal environment for baking pizza. The company targets the adult and family markets. The company was recently purchased by NE Restaurant Company (Chili's, On the Border). Sales are increasing, but workforce is down slightly.

UNO RESTAURANT CORPORATION ★★

100 Charles Park Rd., West Roxbury, MA 02132; 617-323-9200
http://www.pizzeriauno.com
Employees: 5,590
Sales: $191.3 million
Key Personnel: President, COO: Craig S. Miller. EVP, COO: Paul W. MacPhail. Human Resources: Rita McCormick.

Uno Restaurant Corporation owns and franchises a chain of pizzerias that sell popular varieties of deep-dish pizza. Many of its more than 170 restaurants are located in New York and Massachusetts. The company also sells a line of fresh refrigerated pizzas to consumers with increasing success. It has won praise for its financial management. Despite a healthy rise in sales, workforce has declined.

MICHIGAN

DOMINO'S PIZZA, INC.

30 Frank Lloyd Wright Dr., Ann Arbor, MI 48106-0997; 734-930-3030
http://www.dominos.com
Employees: 14,200
Sales: $1,176.8 million
Key Personnel: VP Corporate Operations: Patrick Kelly. VP, Managing Director, Domino's Pizza International: Gary McCausland. VP Marketing and Product Development: Cheryl A. Bachelder.

The world's leading pizza delivery company, Domino's Pizza has had many ups and downs. Stiff competition for price and other market elements have cut into the company's share of customers. The company has more than 6,000 stores worldwide. Its sales are rising, and workforce is holding steady.

LITTLE CAESAR ENTERPRISES, INC.

2211 Woodward Ave., Detroit, MI 48201-3400; 313-983-6000
http://www.littlecaesars.com
Employees: 9,000
Sales: $619 million
Key Personnel: Chairman, CEO: Michael Ilitch. COO: Harsha V. Agadi. Human Resources: Darrel Snygg.

Owned by Ilitch Ventures (created by Michael and Marian Ilitch to control their assorted Detroit businesses), Little Caesar Enterprises is a family concern. With more than 4,600 stores, the company is the #3 chain of pizza stores in the United States. Ilitch Ventures owns many other businesses, including the Detroit Tigers baseball team. Little Caesar is facing increasing pressure from its formidable new competitor Papa John's. Sales are holding steady, and workforce is decreasing.
Other Locations: The company has stores in Canada, Puerto Rico, the United Kingdom, and the United States.

MINNESOTA

BUFFETS, INC. ★★

10260 Viking Dr., Ste. 100, Eden Prairie, MN 55344-7229; 612-942-9760
http://www.buffet.com
Employees: 24,350
Sales: $868.9 million
Key Personnel: Chairman, CEO: Roe H. Hatlen. VC: C. Dennis Scott. Human Resources: K. Michael Shrader.

Buffets specializes in providing lots of food for cost-conscious diners. With over 380 restaurants, mainly in the Midwest, the company has successfully targeted families with children and senior citizens. Its restaurants are called HomeTown Buffet and Old Country Buffet. Recently the company introduced two new concepts: PizzaPlay, which offers entertainment; and Country Roadhouse Buffet & Grill, which offers display cooking in addition to a buffet. Sales are up, but workforce has declined.

INTERNATIONAL DAIRY QUEEN, INC. ★

7505 Metro Blvd., Minneapolis, MN 55439; 612-830-0200
http://www.dairyqueen.com
Employees (est.): 700

Sales: $420 million
Key Personnel: President, CEO: Michael P. Sullivan. EVP, COO: Edward A. Watson. Human Resources: Signe M. Pagel.

International Dairy Queen services more than 5,900 fast food restaurant franchises. The company's primary operation is Dairy Queen restaurant, but it also services Karmelkorn, Orange Julius, and Golden Skillet restaurants. The company has been aggressively cutting costs to increase sales in a competitive market. Sales and workforce are up.
Other Locations: The company has operations in 26 countries.

NEW YORK

ARK RESTAURANTS CORPORATION
85 Fifth Ave, New York, NY 10003;
212-206-8800
http://www.arkrestaurants.com
Employees: 2,616
Sales: $104.3 million
Key Personnel: President: Michael Weinstein. VP, COO: Robert Towers. Human Resources: Marilyn Guy.

Unique, high-profile restaurants are the focus of Ark Restaurants. Rather than using the cookie-cutter approach of franchising, Ark has purchased or developed a chain of more than 25 individualized restaurants, such as El Rio Grande, Louisiana Community Bar & Grill, and Lutece, mostly in New York City and Washington, D.C. The company continues to expand by building and acquisition. Sales are up healthily, but workforce is down.

OHIO

BOB EVANS FARMS, INC. ★★
3776 S. High St., Columbus, OH 43207;
614-491-2225
Employees: 32,363
Sales: $968.5 million
Key Personnel: Chairman, CEO: Daniel E. Evans. President, COO: Stewart K. Owens. Human Resources: James B. Radebaugh.

Bob Evans Farms owns a chain of more than 400 restaurants in the South and Midwest. Most of them are Bob Evans Restaurants, although the company also owns several Owens Family Restaurants, Small-Town Restaurants, and Cantina del Rio restaurants. It also sells a variety of sausage and salad products in grocery stores. Sales and work force are growing.

MAX & ERMA'S RESTAURANTS, INC.
4849 Evanswood Dr., Columbus, OH 43229; 614-431-5800
http://www.max-ermas.com
Employees: 3,899
Sales: $100.5 million
Key Personnel: Chairman, President, and CEO: Todd B. Barnum. COO: Mark F. Emerson. EVP, CFO: William C. Niegsch, Jr.

Gourmet hamburgers are the specialty of Max & Erma's restaurants. The company has more than 40 locations, mostly in the Midwest. It has found its customer base shrinking and is taking steps to expand by building new restaurants in high-traffic areas. Several new locations are planned for Georgia and the Carolinas. Sales and work force are up.

WENDY'S INTERNATIONAL, INC.
4288 W. Dublin Granville Rd., Dublin, OH 43017-0256; 614-764-3100
http://www.wendysintl.com
Employees: 39,000
Sales: $1,948.2 million
Key Personnel: Chairman, President, and CEO: Gordon F. Teter. CFO: Frederick R. Reed. Human Resources: Kathleen A. McGinnis.

Although the company is only the third largest hamburger chain in the world, Wendy's gets top ratings from industry experts for food quality. The company recently began an innovative stock options program for its employees to cut turnover. It is planning expansions both in the United States and overseas. Sales have dropped, and workforce has dropped sharply.
Other Locations: The company has more than 5,000 restaurants in the United States and abroad.

OKLAHOMA

SONIC CORP.
101 Park Ave., Oklahoma City, OK 73102; 405-280-7654
http://www.sonicdrivein.com

Employees: 8,307
Sales: $219.1 million
Key Personnel: President, CEO: J. Clifford Hudson. EVP, COO: Kenneth L. Keymer. Human Resources: Jill M. Hudson.

One of the largest drive-in fast food restaurant chains in the United States, Sonic features carhops on rollerskates and rapid service. The company's strategy has been to keep costs down by locating restaurants in small towns where overhead is low and competition is less. Sales and work force are rising.
Other Locations: The company has more than 1,800 franchised and company-owned restaurants, primarily in the south central United States.

SOUTH CAROLINA

ADVANTICA RESTAURANT GROUP, INC.
203 E. Main St., Spartanburg, SC 29319-9966; 864-597-8000
http://www.advantica-dine.com
Employees: 54,000
Sales: $1,720.5 million
Key Personnel: Chairman, President, and CEO: James B. Adamson. EVP, CFO: Ronald B. Hutchinson. Human Resources: Stephen W. Wood.

Advantica Restaurant Group (formerly Flagstar) owns or franchises over 2,000 restaurants, including Denny's, Coco's, El Pollo Loco and Carrows. After selling its Hardee's and Quincy's restaurant chains, the company emerged from Chapter 11 bankruptcy protection in 1998. Now it is slimming down to concentrate on its central focus of restaurants. Sales and work force are down dramatically.
Other Locations: The company has more than 2,000 restaurants in Canada, the United States, and other countries.

TENNESSEE

CBRL GROUP, INC. ★
Hartmann Dr., Lebanon, TN 37088-0787; 615-444-5533
http://www.crackerbarrelocs.com
Employees: 38,815
Sales: $1,531.6 million
Key Personnel: Chairman, CEO: Dan W. Evins. EVP, COO: Michael A. Woodhouse. SVP Human Resources:

Norman J. Hill.

CBRL Group (formerly Cracker Barrel Old Country Store) has a formula: home-style cooking in a spot near an interstate. The company successfully implements this strategy in over 300 locations throughout the Midwest and Southeast. It recently started to experiment with stores that offer only take-out food. Sales and work force are up.
Other Locations: The company has nearly 400 restaurants in 19 states.

RUBY TUESDAY, INC.
150 W. Church Ave., Maryville, TN 37801; 423-379-5700
http://www.rubyweb.com
Employees: 27,200
Sales: $722.3 million
Key Personnel: Chairman, CEO: Samuel E. Beall III. SVP, CFO: J. Russell Mothershed. SVP Human Resources: Sherry Turner.

Spun off from Morrison Restaurants when the latter was acquired by Piccadilly, Ruby Tuesday has nearly 400 casual-dining units that it either runs or franchises. The Ruby Tuesday chain, which offers entrees ranging from ribs to fajitas, accounts for more than 80 percent of these. The company also owns Mozzarella's American Cafes, which serves Italian Food, and Tia's, a Tex-Mex chain. Most of its restaurants are housed in shopping malls in the Southeastern U.S., though it is hoping to build more free-standing units. Sales are up modestly, and workforce has grown substantially.

SHONEY'S, INC.
1727 Elm Hill Pike, Nashville, TN 37210; 615-391-5201
Employees: 26,000
Sales: $1,130.1 million
Key Personnel: Chairman: Raymond D. Schoenbaum. President, CEO: J. Michael Bodnar. Human Resources: Jodie Wait.

Shoney's owns or franchises around 1,200 restaurants in 28 states, mostly in the south. The company's primary chain, Shoney's, offers full-service family dining. Other outlets include Captain D's (seafood), Pargo's (casual dining) and Fifth Quarter (steakhouse). Shoney's had to sell off its BarbWire chain to offset static sales in the mid 1990s. Sales and workforce are down sharply.

TEXAS

BRINKER INTERNATIONAL, INC. ★★
6820 LBJ Freeway, Dallas, TX 75240;
972-980-9917
http://www.brinker.com
Employees: 53,000
Sales: $1,870.6 million
Key Personnel: VC, CEO: Ronald A. McDougall. President, COO: Douglas H. Brooks. EVP Human Resources: Carol Kirkman.
Among the biggest U.S. companies in the casual dining business, Brinker International has five chains of restaurants. The company operates Chili's Grill & Bar, Romano's Macaroni Grill, Grady's American Grill, On the Border, and Spageddies. It has over 850 restaurants. Sales and work force are up healthily.

LANDRY'S SEAFOOD RESTAURANTS, INC. ★★
1400 Post Oak Blvd., Ste. 1010, Houston, TX 77056; 713-850-1010
http://www.landrysseafood.com
Employees: 14,355
Sales: $399.5 million
Key Personnel: President, CEO: Tilman J. Fertitta. VP Finance, CFO: Paul S. West. Human Resources: Lisa Moore.
Landry's Seafood Restaurants serve four market niches. It operates Landry's Seafood Houses, the Crab House, Willie G's, and Joe's Crab Shack. The company is rapidly expanding. Sales and work force are on the rise.
Other Locations: The company has restaurants in 26 states.

LUBY'S, INC.
2211 NE Loop 410, P.O., San Antonio, TX 78265-3069; 210-654-9000
http://www.lubys.com
Employees: 12,800
Sales: $508.9 million
Key Personnel: President, CEO: Barry J. C. Parker. SVP, CFO: Laura M. Bishop. Human Resources: Sue Elliott.
Luby's (formerly Luby's Cafeterias) runs a chain of restaurants in southern and midwestern states, mostly located in regional shopping malls. The restaurants, which typically seat 300 people, serve a variety of lunch and dinner items in a cafeteria-style environment. The company is increasing its take-out food menu and building more restaurants. Sales and

work force are up.
Other Locations: The company has more than 220 cafeteria-style restaurants, the majority of them in Texas.

WASHINGTON

STARBUCKS CORPORATION
2401 Utah Ave. S., Seattle, WA 98134; 206-447-1575
http://www.starbucks.com
Employees: 26,000
Sales: $1,308.7 million
Key Personnel: President, COO: Orin C. Smith. President, Starbucks Coffee International: Peter Maslen. Human Resources: Sharon E. Elliott.
Gourmet coffee by the cup and a variety of coffee-related merchandise are the basis of Starbucks, whose establishments are patterned after Italian espresso shops. The company, which draws its name from a character in the novel *Moby Dick*, has been expanding nationwide since the mid-1980s. Sales and workforce are up.
Other Locations: The company has more than 2,100 coffee shops in numerous cities.

❶ RETAILING (GENERAL MERCHANDISE)

ALABAMA

BOOKS-A-MILLION, INC.
402 Industrial Lane, Birmingham, AL 35211; 205-942-3737
http://www.booksamillion.com
Employees: 4,500
Sales: $347.9 million
Key Personnel: CEO: Clyde B. Anderson. President: Sandra B. Cochran. Human Resources: Tom Sherk.
Books-A-Million is one of the largest and most profitable bookstore operators in the United States. The company has a reputation for understanding its customers' needs and for keeping costs low. It operates about 180 bookstores in 17 states, mostly in the south. It also operates Joe Muggs coffee bar/newstands. Sales and work force are up.
Other Locations: The company has stores in Alabama, Florida, Georgia, Mississippi, Tennessee, and several other states.

ARIZONA

PETSMART INC. ★★

19601 N. 27th Ave., Phoenix, AZ 85027;
623-580-6100

http://www.petsmart.com
Employees: 21,600
Sales: $2,109.3 million
Key Personnel: President and CEO:
Phillip L. Francis. EVP, CFO: Neil T.
Watanabe. Human Resources: Carol M.
Cox.

PETsMART caters exclusively to people
with pets. The company operates large,
warehouse-style stores and offers discount prices on pet supplies. It also has
veterinary clinics in some of its stores
and operates pet adoption centers. The
company plans to continue its rapid expansion. Sales and work force are up.
Other Locations: The company owns
approximately 530 stores in the U.S.,
Canada, and the U.K.

ARKANSAS

DILLARD'S, INC. ★★

1600 Cantrell Rd., Little Rock, AR
72201; 501-376-5200

http://www.dillards.com
Employees: 54,921
Sales: $7,796.7 million
Key Personnel: CEO: William Dillard
II. President: Alex Dillard. Human Re-
sources: Joyce Wisner.

One of the biggest upscale department
store chains in the U.S., Dillard Department Stores focuses on home furnishings
and fashion clothing for middle-income
and upper-middle-income customers.
Suffering sales led to a decision to focus
more on private-label merchandise. The
decision has paid off, since both sales
and work force have risen in recent years.
Other Locations: The company has approximately 430 stores in 30 states.

WAL-MART STORES, INC. ★★

702 SW Eighth St., Bentonville, AR
72716-8611; 501-273-4000

http://www.wal-mart.com
Employees: 910,000
Sales: $137,634 million
Key Personnel: VC, COO: H. Lee Scott,
Jr. President, CEO: David D. Glass. Human Resources: Coleman Petersen.
International growth is the name of the
game for Wal-Mart Stores, the biggest
retail operator in the world. In addition to
its U.S. facilities, the company owns
more than 320 stores abroad and is rapidly opening more. Its discount stores
remain the company's most successful
component, and it is continuing to open
more Supercenters and Sam's Club
warehouses. Sales and work force are
growing.
Other Locations: The company has approximately 3,600 stores in Argentina,
Brazil, Canada, China, Mexico, the
United States, and other countries.

CALIFORNIA

FREDERICK'S OF HOLLYWOOD, INC.

6608 Hollywood Blvd., Los Angeles, CA
90028; 323-466-5151

http://www.fredericks.com
Employees: 1,500
Sales: $160 million
Key Personnel: President, CEO: Linda
LoRe. VP, Chief Information Officer:
Henry Torres. VP Personnel: Al Simon.
Long known for its risque approach to
lingerie sales, Frederick's of Hollywood
has toned down a bit as cultural values
have changed. The company still sells its
own line of intimate apparel in retail
stores and by mail order, but gone are the
sex aids, X-rated videos, and other merchandise. Sales are up, but work force is
static.
Other Locations: The company has
more than 200 stores in 39 states.

FRY'S ELECTRONICS, INC. ★★

600 Brokaw Rd., San Jose, CA 95112;
408-487-4700

Employees: 4,000
Sales (est.): $1,250 million
Key Personnel: President, CEO: John
Fry. EVP: Randy Fry. VP Human Resources: Kathryn Kolder.
For the most avid computer users in California, Fry's Electronics stores represent
the ultimate shopping experience. Each
store is decorated with a unique theme—
for example, one store looks like an old
mine inside. Unlike most electronics
stores, Fry's stores also sell items such as
beer, snacks, and over-the-counter drugs.
Sales are up, but work force is static.
Other Locations: The company has sixteen stores in California.

THE GAP, INC. ★★

One Harrison St., San Francisco, CA 94105; 415-427-2000
http://www.gap.com
Employees: 111,000
Sales: $9,054.5 million
Key Personnel: President, CEO: Millard S. Drexler. COO: John B. Wilson. Human Resources: Anne B. Gust.

Private-label casual clothing is the specialty of The Gap. In addition to its Gap stores, the company operates stores under the names GapKids, Old Navy Clothing Co., and Banana Republic. The company continues to build new stores, while its sales and work force are growing.
Other Locations: The company has about 2,600 stores in Canada, France, Puerto Rico, the United Kingdom, and the United States.

THE GOOD GUYS, INC. ★★

7000 Marina Blvd., Brisbane, CA 94005-1840; 650-615-5000
http://www.thegoodguys.com
Employees: 5,000
Sales: $928.5 million
Key Personnel: Chairman, CEO: Ronald Unkefer. SVP Finance, CFO: Dennis Carroll. Human Resources: Geradette M. Vaz.

The Good Guys sell consumer electronics. The company, which operates a chain of stores predominantly in California and Washington, sells high-end equipment at discount prices. Salespeople are paid incentives for making sales to repeat customers. The company is aggressively expanding in a highly competitive market. Sales and work force are up.
Other Locations: The company has more than 80 stores in the West.

THE GYMBOREE CORPORATION

700 Airport Blvd., Ste. 200, Burlingame, CA 94010; 650-579-0600
http://www.gymboree.com
Employees: 6,500
Sales: $457.2 million
Key Personnel: VC, CEO: Gary White. President: Melanie Bordeaux Cox. SVP Human Resources: Kenneth F. Meyers.

Gymboree began as a system of play and exercise classes for parents and infants in the mid-1970s. The company has since branched into designing, manufacturing, and retailing play clothes for children age six and under, which is now its dominant business. The company is one of the few with a female majority on its executive board. It is rapidly expanding in a number of markets. Sales are growing, but workforce is static.
Other Locations: The company has 162 stores in the United States and franchised classes at 400 play centers in Australia, Canada, France, Israel, Mexico, South Korea, Taiwan, and the United States.

LONGS DRUG STORES CORPORATION ★

141 N. Civic Dr., Walnut Creek, CA 94596; 510-937-1170
http://www.longs.com
Employees: 18,500
Sales: $3,266.9 million
Key Personnel: Chairman, CEO: Robert M. Long. President: Stephen D. Roath. SVP Marketing: Terry Burnside.

The Longs Drug Stores company is known for its entrepreneurial management style and its service. The company, which is one of the largest U.S. pharmacy chains, allows its local store managers substantial autonomy and pays them more for bringing in greater profits. It has stayed out of price competition promoted by companies such as Wal-Mart, instead emphasizing customer service. Sales and work force are up.
Other Locations: The company operates approximately 380 pharmacies in Alaska, California, Colorado, Hawaii, and Nevada.

NATURAL WONDERS, INC.

4209 Technology Dr., Fremont, CA 94538; 510-252-9600
Employees: 2,600
Sales: $149.8 million
Key Personnel: President, CEO: Kathleen M. Chatfield. COO: Peter G. Hanelt. Human Resources Manager: Karen A. Daley.

Natural Wonders seeks to capitalize on the theme of environmental awareness through the merchandise it sells. The company, whose stores are typically located in shopping malls, sells binoculars, mineral specimens, science kits, and other items that help its customers get in touch with nature. Sales and work force are up modestly.

Other Locations: The company has more than 200 stores in California, Florida, Illinois, Michigan, New Jersey, Ohio, Texas, Washington, and other states.

SHARPER IMAGE CORPORATION

650 Davis St., San Francisco, CA 94111; 415-445-6000

http://www.sharperimage.com

Employees: 1,300

Sales: $243.1 million

Key Personnel: Chairman, CEO: Richard Thalheimer. VC, COO: Barry Gilbert. Human Resources: Mary Tanner.

Unusual gadgets are the specialty of Sharper Image. The company sells its line of upscale merchandise through its catalog, its retail stores, and via television shopping programs. Sales are up and workforce is holding steady.

Other Locations: The company owns or licenses more than 100 stores in Australia, Japan, Mexico, Switzerland, and the United States.

VIKING OFFICE PRODUCTS, INC. ★★

950 W. 190th St., Torrance, CA 90502; 310-225-4500

http://www.vikingop.com

Employees: 3,226

Sales: $1,492.1 million

Key Personnel: Chairman: Irwin Helford. President, CEO: Bruce Nelson. Human Resources: Geri River.

Sales of office products and equipment are the basis of Viking's business. However, the company adds a twist to its approach by selling through direct marketing programs and catalogs. Approximately half of its business comes from European sales, and it plans continued expansion into the European market. Sales and work force are growing.

Other Locations: The company has regional distribution centers in Australia, France, the United Kingdom, and the United States.

COLORADO

CORPORATE EXPRESS, INC.

1 Environmental Way, Broomfield, CO 80021; 303-664-2000

http://www.corporate-express.com

Employees: 25,700

Sales: $752.6 million

Key Personnel: President, CEO: Robert L. King. EVP, CFO: Gary M. Jacobs. Director Human Resources: John O'Loughlin.

Corporate Express specializes in selling office supplies and furniture to corporations with more than 100 employees. The company is one of the largest of its type in the United States. It operates 28 strategically located warehouses to fill orders rapidly. It has been growing rapidly in recent years by acquiring other companies. Corporate Express is being purchased by Buhrmann, a Dutch office products company. Sales are increasing, but workforce has declined.

Other Locations: The company has stores in Australia, Canada, and the U.S.

CONNECTICUT

AMES DEPARTMENT STORES, INC. ★★

2418 Main St., Rocky Hill, CT 06067; 860-257-2000

http://www.AmesStores.com

Employees: 36,500

Sales: $2,507.2 million

Key Personnel: President, CEO: Joseph R. Ettore. EVP: Rolando de Aguiar. EVP, COO: Denis T. Lemire.

After emerging from bankruptcy in 1994, Ames Department Stores faces stiff competition from discount retail chains. The company is concentrating on selling fashion apparel to lower-middle- and middle-income shoppers. The company is also expanding its specialty departments, such as crafts and jewelry. Sales and workforce are up dramatically.

Other Locations: The company has more than 450 stores in the East and Midwest.

WORLD DUTY FREE AMERICAS, INC. ★

63 Copps Hill Rd., Ridgefield, CT 06877; 203-431-6057

http://www.dutyfreeint.com

Employees: 2,000

Sales: $563.6 million

Key Personnel: Executive Committee Chairman: David H. Bernstein. COO: Ramon Bosquez. VP Human Resources: Lisa Goettel.

World Duty Free Americas (Formerly Duty Free International) is a subsidiary of BAA and the largest duty-free store operator on the U.S. borders with Canada and Mexico. Its primary emphasis has been on perfumes, cosmetics, and liquors, although it recently began expanding into wines and gourmet foods as well. The company has grown mainly by acquisition, having just acquired Inflight Services Group, and is looking for expansion opportunities. Sales are up modestly and workforce is static.
Other Locations: The company has around 200 stores at northern and southern U.S. border crossings and in airports.

MICRO WAREHOUSE, INC.
535 Connecticut Ave., Norwalk, CT 06854; 203-899-4000
http://www.warehouse.com
Employees: 3,595
Sales: $2,220 million
Key Personnel: Chairman, President, and CEO: Peter Godfrey. EVP Marketing: Adam Shaffer. Human Resources: Michelle Visosky.
Leading the pack in mail-order retailers of computer equipment and software is Micro Warehouse. The company sells over 20,000 software and hardware products to customers worldwide through its MacWAREHOUSE and MicroWAREHOUSE catalogs. It recently began publishing several specialty catalogs, such as Data Comm WAREHOUSE, to expand its business. Sales are up, but workforce is on the decline.

FLORIDA

ECKERD CORPORATION
8333 Bryan Dairy Rd., Largo, FL33777; 727-395-6000
http://www.eckerd.com
Employees: 55,000
Sales: $10,325 million
Key Personnel: Chairman, President, and CEO: Francis A. Newman. EVP Store Operations: Kenneth L. Flynn. Human Resources: Dennis Cuff.
One of the first U.S. drugstore chains, Eckerd is also one of the largest. The company has spent the last several years upgrading its strategy and technology and selling noncore assets. It is currently closing poorly performing stores and opening new ones. Since 1996 Eckerd's has been a subsidiary of JC Penney. Sales and work force are up.
Other Locations: The company has more than 1,800 drugstores in 13 states.

JM FAMILY ENTERPRISES, INC.
100 NW 12th Ave., Deerfield Beach, FL 33442-1702; 954-429-2000
Employees: 3,000
Sales: $6,200 million
Key Personnel: President, CEO: Patricia Moran. EVP, CFO: Jim Foster. EVP Human Resources: Gary L. Thomas.
JM Family Enterprises runs a variety of subsidiary businesses having to do with automobile leasing, distribution, and financing. Among its subsidiaries are Courtesy Insurance, JM Pontiac & GMC Truck (the largest Pontiac dealer in the United States), and Petro Chemical Products. Sales and work force are rising.

OFFICE DEPOT, INC. ★★
2200 Old Germantown Rd., Delray Beach, FL 33445; 561-438-4800
http://www.officedepot.com
Employees: 44,000
Sales: $8,997.7 million
Key Personnel: President, COO: John C. Macatee. EVP, CFO: Barry J. Goldstein. EVP Human Resources: Thomas Kroeger.
Selling brand-name office equipment and supplies at discount prices has made Office Depot the largest company of its type in the United States. The company sells in a warehouse-style format primarily to small- and medium-sized businesses. The company has recently acquired catalog retailer Viking Office Products, which has expanded Office Depot's market overseas. Sales and work force are up dramatically.
Other Locations: The company has more than 800 stores in the U.S. and Canada.

CHS ELECTRONICS, INC. ★★
2000 NW 84th Ave., Miami, FL 33122; 305-908-7200
http://www.chse.com
Employees: 6,800
Sales: $8,545.8 million
Key Personnel: Chairman, President, and CEO: Claudio Osorio. Chief Tech-

nology Officer: Clifford Dyer. Human Resources: Isabel Viteri.

CHS Electronics is the world's third largest distributor of microcomputer-related products. It distributes networking products, peripheral hardware, software, and computers to more than 150,000 resellers in 45 countries. Most of its sales are in Europe and Latin America. Sales and work force are rising rapidly.

GEORGIA

THE HOME DEPOT, INC. ★★
2455 Paces Ferry Rd., Atlanta, GA 30339; 770-433-8211
http://www.homedepot.com
Employees: 157,000
Sales: $30,219 million
Key Personnel: President, CEO, and COO: Arthur M. Blank. EVP: Ronald M. Brill. Human Resources: Stephen R. Messana.

Home Depot sits at the top of the do-it-yourself home improvement retailing market. The company operates a chain of almost 800 superstores in the United States and Canada and is expanding south to Mexico and South and Central America. Sales and work force are growing.
Other Locations: The company has stores in across the U.S. and in Canada.

HAWAII

DAIEI USA, INC. ★
801 Kaheka St., Honolulu, HI 96814; 808-973-6600
http://www.daiei.co.jp
Employees: 16,600
Sales: $25,085.3 million
Key Personnel: Chairman: Isao Nakauchi. President: Tadasu Toba. Human Resources: Kiyoshi Oyamada.

Known throughout Japan for its chain of supermarkets, Daiei is that country's largest retailer. It runs more than 400 superstores and approximately 6,700 convenience stores. Approximately 90 percent of its income is derived from sales within Japan; however, it is aggressively expanding into other Asian consumer markets. Sales and workforce have followed the Japanese economy downward.
Other Locations: Worldwide HQ: The

Daiei, Inc., 4-1-1, Minatojima, Naka-machi, Chuo-ku, Kobe, 650-0046, Japan; +81-78-302-5001.

ILLINOIS

FOLLETT CORPORATION ★
2233 West St., River Grove, IL 60171; 708-583-2000
http://www.follett.com
Employees: 8,000
Sales: $1,200 million
Key Personnel: Chairman, President, and CEO: Kenneth Hull. VP: Kathryn Stanton. Director Human Resources: Richard Ellspermann.

Follett operates college bookstores. The company, which is owned and operated by the Follett family, also publishes textbooks and wholesales books to elementary and secondary school libraries. It currently has over 500 outlets and serves more than 45,000 schools. Sales and work force are up.
Other Locations: The company runs more than 500 stores at universities and colleges in 48 states.

MONTGOMERY WARD HOLDING CORP.
Montgomery Ward Plaza, Chicago, IL 60671; 312-467-2000
http://www.mward.com
Employees: 49,000
Sales: $3,634 million
Key Personnel: Chairman, CEO: Roger V. Goddu. EVP: Tom Austin. Human Resources: Sherry Harris.

Montgomery Ward Holding is one of the biggest U.S. department store businesses. The company owns the Montgomery Ward chain, the mail-order retailer Montgomery Ward Direct, and many other enterprises. The company filed for Chapter 11 protection several years ago and, since closing more than 100 stores, has emerged from bankruptcy. Sales and work force are declining rapidly.
Other Locations: The company operates approximately 250 stores in some 30 states.

SEARS, ROEBUCK AND CO.
3333 Beverly Rd., Hoffman Estates, IL 60179; 847-286-2500
http://www.sears.com

Employees: 324,000
Sales: $41,322 million
Key Personnel: Chairman, CEO, Sears Merchandise Group: Arthur C. Martinez. EVP, COO: Julian Day. Human Resources: John T. Sloan.

Sears, Roebuck and Co. has been selling assets and streamlining operations for several years to focus on its core merchandising operations. Along with discontinuing its well-known "Great American Wish Book" catalog, the company has sold Allstate Insurance; Dean Witter, Discover; and other operations. It even left the Sears Tower in downtown Chicago. It is remodeling some stores to focus more on a narrower product line and upgrading inventories. Sales are holding steady and workforce has declined.
Other Locations: The company operates around 3,000 stores in Canada, Mexico, and the United States.

SPIEGEL, INC.

3500 Lacey Rd., Downers Grove, IL 60515; 630-986-8800
http://www.spiegel.com
Employees: 11,200
Sales: $2,893.2 million
Key Personnel: Chairman: Michael R. Moran. Office of the President, CFO: James W. Sievers. VP, Treasurer: John R. Steele.

Among the largest U.S. specialty retailers, Spiegel primarily sells apparel and household furnishings through its catalogs. Besides its Spiegel catalog, the company publishes several other catalogs, including a line of Eddie Bauer catalogs. It is planning to continue opening new outlet stores in the United States and abroad. Sales and work force are down.
Other Locations: The company owns more than 300 Eddie Bauer stores and Spiegel stores in Canada, Japan, and the United States.

WALGREEN CO. ★

200 Wilmot Rd., Deerfield, IL 60015; 847-940-2500
http://www.walgreens.com
Employees: 90,000
Sales: $15,307 million
Key Personnel: Chairman, CEO: L. Daniel Jorndt. President, COO: David W. Bernauer. Human Resources Director: John A. Rubino.

Walgreen operates more than 2,700 stores, making it the biggest chain of retail drugstores in the United States. Some 1300 locations offer drive-thru pharmacies. Walgreen is currently expanding rapidly and plans to have 3,000 stores open by the year 2000. Sales and work force are up healthily.

MAINE

L. L. BEAN, INC. ★★

Casco St., Freeport, ME 04033; 207-865-4761
http://www.llbean.com
Employees: 4,000
Sales: $1,070 million
Key Personnel: President, CEO: Leon A. Gorman. SVP Marketing: Chris McCormick. VP Human Resources: Bob Peixotto.

Beginning with the Maine Hunting Shoe in 1912, L. L. Bean has been a pioneer in the mail-order outdoor clothing market. The company also sells household goods and furnishings, active wear, and sporting goods. It manufactures 190 of its own products and is expanding by opening retail stores in the United States and abroad. Sales are holding steady, but workforce has risen in the past year.
Other Locations: The company has retail locations in the United States and 11 stores in Japan.

MARYLAND

CROWN BOOKS CORPORATION

3300 75th Ave., Landover, MD 20785; 301-226-1200
http://www.crownbooks.com
Employees (est.): 3,000
Sales: $225 million
Key Personnel: President, COO: Anna Currence. VP Operations, Acting CFO: Stephen Pate.

Crown Books operates a chain of bookstores in several major U.S. cities. The company grew quickly in the 1980s but has recently run into problems. It was recently driven into bankruptcy as a result of lawsuit-related payments heavy debt. Competition from Borders and Barnes & Noble has hurt sales, which have suffered sharp declines. Workforce is also down dramatically.

Other Locations: The company has approximately 90 stores in California, the District of Columbia, Illinois, and Washington.

MASSACHUSETTS

DESIGNS, INC.

66 B St., Needham, MA 02194; 781-444-7222

Employees: 1,800
Sales: $201.6 million
Key Personnel: President, CEO: Joel H. Reichman. EVP: Scott N. Semel. Human Resources: Mary Ann Ryan.

Designs is one of several retailers that specializes in the products of Levi Strauss. The company has approximately 110 stores, which are all located east of the Mississippi River. Most of its stores are called Levi's Outlet by Designs, but some operate as Boston Trading Co. and Buffalo Jeans. A recent and unsuccessful attempt at launching its own label cost the company dearly. Sales and workforce are down.

LAURIAT'S, INC.

333 Bolivar St., Canton, MA 02021; 781-821-0071

http://www.lauriats-books.com
Employees: 1,000
Sales (est.): $110 million
Key Personnel: President, CEO: Matthew Harrison. CFO: Todd Miller. Director Human Resources: Richard Markiewicz.

One of the largest chains of bookstores in the United States, Lauriat's takes a different tack from its competition. The company favors the small, personal approach instead of the discount superstore approach. Due to over-expansion, the company filed for Chapter 11 bankruptcy protection in 1998. Sales are down and workforce is static.

Other Locations: The company has approximately 100 stores in 11 states and the District of Columbia.

STAPLES, INC.

One Research Dr., Westborough, MA 01581; 508-370-8500

http://www.staples.com
Employees: 21,580
Sales: $7,123.2 million
Key Personnel: Chairman, CEO: Thomas G. Sternberg. EVP Merchandising: Richard R. Gentry. EVP Human Resources: Susan S. Hoyt.

Among the largest discount office supply retailers in the United States, Staples was also one of the first to try selling office supplies in a warehouse-superstore format. The company sells a comprehensive array of products, including computers and furniture. It is continuing to expand even after the FTC blocked its attempt to buy its main competitor, Office Depot, on anti-trust grounds. Sales have jumped by more than a third, but workforce is down by nearly the same amount.

Other Locations: Staples owns or operates through joint venture more than 1,000 stores in 10 foreign countries and the United States.

THE TJX COMPANIES, INC. ★

770 Cochituate Rd., Framingham, MA 01701; 508-390-1000

http://www.tjx.com
Employees: 62,000
Sales: $7,949.1 million
Key Personnel: President, CEO: Bernard Cammarata. EVP, COO: Richard Lesser. VP Human Services: Mark O. Jacobson.

Among the largest retailers selling discount apparel, TJX has been struggling in the past few years because of decreased demand. The company operates several chains, including T. J. Maxx, Hit or Miss, Marshalls, Winners Apparel, and T. K. Maxx. The company is also expanding its HomeGoods chain, which sells home furnishings. Sales and workforce are up.

Other Locations: The company operates about 1,100 stores in Canada, the U.K. and the U.S.

MICHIGAN

BORDERS GROUP, INC. ★★

100 Phoneix Dr., Ann Arbor, MI 48108; 734-477-1100

http://www.bordersgroupinc.com
Employees: 27,200
Sales: $2,595 million
Key Personnel: Chairman, President,

and CEO: Robert F. DiRomualdo. VC: Bruce A. Quinnell. CFO: Kenneth E. Scheve.

Owner of several chains of retail specialty shops, Borders Group is the owner of Waldenbooks, one of the largest U.S. mall-based bookstore chains; Planet Music, a music superstore chain; and Borders, a book superstore chain. Sales and work force are growing.

Other Locations: The company has bookstores across the U.S. and Planet Music stores in Maryland, North Carolina, Tennessee, Texas, and Virginia.

KMART CORPORATION ★

3100 W. Big Beaver Rd., Troy, MI 48084; 248-643-1000
http://www.kmart.com
Employees: 278,525
Sales: $33,674 million
Key Personnel: Chairman, President, and CEO: Floyd Hall. VC: Michael Bozic. EVP Human Resources: Warren F. Cooper.

For years Kmart diversified its operations by acquiring companies such as Office-Max, Borders, and Waldenbooks, while neglecting its core retail business. As a result, Wal-Mart began to seriously cut into the company's sales. Kmart has recently begun to repair the damage by selling off noncore assets (like Borders) to gather the cash needed to refurbish its aging stores. Sales and workforce are up.

Other Locations: The company has retail operations in the Czech Republic, Mexico, Puerto Rico, Singapore, Slovakia, and the U.S.

MINNESOTA

BEST BUY CO., INC. ★★

7075 Flying Cloud Dr., Eden Prarie, MN 55344; 612-947-2000
http://www.bestbuy.com
Employees: 45,000
Sales: $10,077.9 million
Key Personnel: President, COO: Bradbury H. Anderson. Chairman, CEO: Richard Schulze. Human Resources: Nancy C. Bologna.

Best Buy is the largest consumer electronics retailer in the United States. The company uses a superstore format and keeps costs low by maintaining a small staff. It has recently begun installing automated kiosks that supply answers to customers' questions. The company continues to add new stores to its chain. Sales and work force are growing.

Other Locations: The company has over 310 stores in more than 40 states.

DAMARK INTERNATIONAL, INC.

7101 Winnetka Ave. N., Minneapolis, MN 55428; 612-531-0066
http://www1.damark.com
Employees: 1,945
Sales: $484.4 million
Key Personnel: Chairman, President, CEO: Mark A. Cohn. President, COO: George S. Richards. Human Resources: Nancy Reller.

Among the top retailers in the direct marketing arena, DAMARK focuses on well-to-do men. It puts out more than 70 different catalogs selling consumer electronics, computers, sporting goods, and other items. Consumer electronics and computers together account for more than half the company's sales. Sales and work force are down.

DAYTON HUDSON CORPORATION ★

777 Nicollet Mall, Minneapolis, MN 55402-2055; 612-370-6948
http://www.dhc.com
Employees: 244,000
Sales: $30,951 million
Key Personnel: Chairman, CEO: Robert J. Ulrich. SVP, CFO: Douglas A. Scovanner.

Dayton Hudson operates a number of department store chains, including Target, Mervyn's, Dayton's, Hudson's, and Marshall Field's. Its top chain is Target, which focuses on discounted merchandise for an upscale market. Mervyn's has been less successful than expected lately, and the company is testing new approaches to increase sales. Sales and work force are up.

MISSOURI

BROWN SHOE COMPANY, INC.

8300 Maryland Ave., St. Louis, MO 63105; 314-854-4000
http://www.brownshoecompany.com
Employees: 11,000
Sales: $1,538.5million
Key Personnel: Chairman, President,

and CEO: Ronald A. Fromm, Jr. EVP, CFO: Harry E. Rich. Human Resources: James Preuss.

Best known for its line of Buster Brown shoes, Brown Shoe Company (formerly Brown Group) also sells a variety of other footwear, including Naturalizer and Life Stride. The company owns Famous Footwear, one of the largest U.S. shoe store chains. Sales and work force are down.

Other Locations: The company manufactures shoes in 10 U.S. and two Canadian locations.

EDISON BROTHERS STORES, INC.

501 N. Broadway, St. Louis, MO 63102; 314-331-6000

Employees: 14,639
Sales: $949.9 million
Key Personnel: Chairman: Karl W. Michner. EVP,CFO, and CAO: John Burtelow. Human Resources: Marion K. Doyle.

Edison Brothers sells a variety of goods in mall-based specialty stores. The company operates several chains, such as Bakers (footwear), Jeans West (men's apparel), and 5-7-9 (women's apparel). The company emerged from bankruptcy in 1997 after it closed some 1,000 stores and sold its entertainment centers. It refiled in 1999. Sales and work force are down.

Other Locations: The company has stores in Mexico, Puerto Rico, the United States, and the Virgin Islands.

MAY DEPARTMENT STORES COMPANY ★

611 Olive St., St. Louis, MO 63101; 314-342-6300

http://www.maycompany.com
Employees: 127,000
Sales: $13,413 million
Key Personnel: Chairman: Jerome T. Loeb. President, CEO: Eugene S. Kahn. Human Resources: Douglas J. Giles.

May Department Stores is among the top retailers in the nation's upscale department store market. The company operates several chains, including Foley's, Lord & Taylor, Hecht's, and Kaufmann's. The company also owns the Payless ShoeSource chain, the top self-service chain of family shoe stores in the United States. Sales and workforce are up.

Other Locations: The company owns more than 400 department stores in the United States and over 4,400 shoe stores in Puerto Rico, the United States, and the Virgin Islands.

NEW JERSEY

BED BATH & BEYOND, INC. ★★

650 Liberty Ave., Union, NJ 07083; 908-688-0888

http://www.bedbath.com
Employees: 9,400
Sales: $1,397.2 million
Key Personnel: Co-Chairman, Co-CEO: Warren Eisenberg. Co-Chairman, Co-CEO: Leonard Feinstein. Director of Human Resources: Connie Van Dyke.

Bed Bath & Beyond uses a finely tailored approach to sell domestic items in a superstore format. The company keeps its costs down in a variety of ways. For example, it locates its stores in strip malls to minimize real estate costs and advertises with inexpensive direct mail pieces. The company is facing aggressive competition by expanding geographically. Sales and work force are up.

Other Locations: The company has approximately 200 stores in over 35 states.

BURLINGTON COAT FACTORY WAREHOUSE CORPORATION

1830 Rte. 130, Burlington, NJ 08016; 609-387-7800

http://www.coat.com
Employees: 20,000
Sales: $2,005.7 million
Key Personnel: Chairman, President, and CEO: Monroe G. Milstein. EVP, COO: Mark A. Nesci. Human Resources: Chris Pilla.

Burlington Coat Factory Warehouse runs several chains of discount retail stores, featuring apparel, and assorted other products ranging from bath accessories to children's furniture. The company is responsible for Burlington Coat Factory, Luxury Linens, Cohoes Fashions, and others. Sales are up, but workforce is static.

LECHTERS, INC.

One Cape May St., Harrison, NJ 07029; 973-481-1100

http://www.lechters.com
Employees: 6,246
Sales: $428.2 million
Key Personnel: Chairman, CEO: Donald Jonas. President: James A. Shea. SVP Human Resources: Robert J. Harloe.
One of the largest companies selling housewares in the United States, Lechters operates stores under several names. Besides Lechters, the company also owns Lechters Housewares, The Kitchen Place, and Famous Brand Housewares. The company has plans to close some poorly performing store locations and open new stores. Sales and work force are up.
Other Locations: The company operates nearly 600 stores in the United States.

TOYS "R" US, INC.

461 From Rd., Paramus, NJ 07652; 201-262-7800
http://www.toysrus.com
Employees: 70,000
Sales: $11,170 million
Key Personnel: Chairman, Interim CEO: Michael Goldstein. EVP, CFO: Louis Lipschitz. SVP Human Resources: Roger C. Gaston.
Toys "R" Us, once the the largest toy retailer in the world, has recently lost this distinction to Wal-Mart's vanguard of discount superstores. The company operates almost 1,500 worldwide, and sells toys, sporting equipment, and other merchandise in its catalog and on its website. Many of its stores also sell children's clothing. Toys "R" US is currently restructuring to improve its fiscal efficiency. Sales and workforce have dropped sharply.
Other Locations: The company owns nearly 1,500 stores in Canada, France, Germany, Japan, Spain, the United Kingdom, the United States, and other countries.

NEW YORK

BARNES & NOBLE, INC. ★★

122 Fifth Ave., New York, NY 10011; 212-633-3300
http://www.shareholder.com/bks
Employees: 29,000
Sales: $3,005.6 million
Key Personnel: Chairman, CEO: Leonard Riggio. COO: J. Alan Kahn. Human Resources: Michelle Smith.
Barnes & Noble is the nation's top book-store operator. The company operates several chains of stores under such names as B. Dalton Bookseller, Scribner's Bookstore, Bookstop, and others. It also publishes books and sells books by direct mail. The company has aggressively gone online—with its own website, and through America Online—to fend off Internet rival Amazon.com. Sales are up, but workforce has declined.
Other Locations: The company has approximately 1,000 stores across the U.S.

BENETTON USA CORP.

597 Fifth Ave., 11th Floor, New York, NY 10017; 212-593-0290
http://www.benneton.com
Employees (overall Benetton): 7,235
Sales (overall Benetton): $2,318 million
Key Personnel: Chairman: Luciano Benetton. Joint Managing Director: Carlo Gilardi. Human Resources: Gianmario Tondato.
Known for its politically charged advertising, the Italian company Benetton Group sells a variety of products in 120 countries, primarily from its United Colors of Benetton stores. It sells mainly clothing, but also eyewear, cosmetics, and other items. Its controversial ads have drawn fines, bans, and criticism. Sales are up, but work force is down.
Other Locations: Worldwide HQ: Benetton Group S.p.A, Via Villa Minelli 1, 31050 Ponzano Veneto, Italy; +39-0422-4491.

CENDANT CORPORATION

9 W. 57th St., New York, NY 10019; 212-213-1800
http://www.cendant.com
Employees: 35,000
Sales: $5,283.8 million
Key Personnel: Chairman, President, and CEO: Henry R. Silverman. VC, General Counsel: James E. Buckman. Human Resources: Thomas D. Christopoul.
Cendant was formed by the merger of CUC International, a leading provider of membership-based discount services, and HFS, the hospitality franchiser. Through HFS, which owns Century 21 and Coldwell Banker real estate, Cendant can cross market to CUC's clientele providing home improvement referrals. Sales and work force are rising.

J. CREW GROUP, INC. ★★
770 Broadway, New York, NY 10003; 212-209-2500
http://www.jcrew.com
Employees: 8,900
Sales: $824.2 million
Key Personnel: Chair, Chief Designer: Emily C. Woods. CEO: Mark Sarvary. SVP Women's Design: Scott Formby.
J. Crew Group targets 30-year-olds seeking goods to complement a casual but elegant lifestyle. The company mainly sells through mail order catalogs, but it has been expanding its web-based sales and its retail stores operations. Sales are down slightly, but workforce has grown dramatically.
Other Locations: The company has nearly 180 retail stores in the United States and Japan.

LILLIAN VERNON CORPORATION★★
1 Theall Rd., Rye, NY 10580; 914-925-1200
http://www.lillianvernon.com
Employees: 1,500
Sales: $255.2 million
Key Personnel: Chairwoman, CEO: Lillian Vernon. Acting President: Jonah Gitlitz. EVP: Laura L. Zambano. Human Resources: William L. Sharkey, Jr.
Among the biggest of the mail-order specialty retailers in the United States, Lillian Vernon sells a wide variety of household and personal goods through its catalogs. The catalogs, of which there are eight different editions, are sent to 175 million people. The company has recently begun to diversify into specialty markets, such as children's products and garden accessories. Sales are down and work force is static.

MARKS AND SPENCER U.S. HOLDINGS, INC.
346 Madison Ave., New York, NY 10017; 212-697-3886
http://www.marks-and-spencer.co
Employees (overall M & S):71,297
Sales (over all M & S): $13,786.5 million
Key Personnel: Chairman: Brian Baldock. Managing Director Overseas Retail: Guy McCracken. Human Resources: Clara Freeman.
Marks and Spencer sells food, clothing, and household items worldwide. The company, which has been in business since the late 1800s, pioneered many current retailing concepts, such as buying directly from suppliers instead of wholesalers. In the United States, the company operates several chains, including Brooks Brothers. Sales and work force are up.
Other Locations: Worldwide HQ: Marks and Spencer PLC, Michael House, 37-67 Baker St., London W1A 1DN, United Kingdom; +44-171-935-4422.

SOTHEBY'S HOLDINGS, INC.
1334 York Ave., New York, NY 10021; 212-606-7000
http://www.sothebys.com
Employees: 1,921
Sales: $447.1 million
Key Personnel: President, CEO: Diana D. Brooks. Chairman: A. Alfred Taubman. Human Resources: Susan Alexander.
Although it is best known for its high-profile auctions, Sotheby's Holdings is primarily involved in many smaller transactions. The company is the world's largest auction house. Besides its auction business, the company loans money using art as collateral and provides luxury real estate services. Sales are growing rapidly, but workforce has experienced more modest growth.
Other Locations: The company has operations in the United Kingdom, the United States, and 34 other countries.

VENATOR GROUP, INC.
233 Broadway, New York, NY 10279-0003; 212-553-2000
http://www.venatorgroup.com
Employees: 75,118
Sales: $4,555 million
Key Personnel: President, COO: Dale W. Hilpert. SVP, CFO: Bruce L. Hartman. Human Resources: John F. Gillespie.
Venator Group (formerly Woolworth Corporation) operates over 7,000 specialty stores, including Foot Locker, Northern Reflections, and Kinney Shoes. Although Woolworth was known for its five-and-dime stores, Venator has closed all of them and is now concentrating on the specialty market. Sales are down and workforce is static.
Other Locations: The company owns more than 6,000 retail outlets in 12 countries.

NORTH CAROLINA

THE BODY SHOP, INC. ★

5036 One World Way, Wake Forest, NC 27587; 919-554-4900
http://www.the-body-shop.com
Employees: 5,217
Sales: $485.9 million
Key Personnel: President, CEO: Peter Saunders. CFO: Alan Minker. VP Human Resources: Kathi Schwartz.

Using a variety of social causes as a springboard to promote its line of natural cosmetics and toiletries, The Body Shop is finding success all over the world. The company owns and franchises stores in 47 countries, selling products such as massage oils, body lotions, perfumes, and shampoos. It is encountering stiff competition and has brought out a Tupperware-style marketing campaign. Management of its U.S. operation is being turned over to a joint venture with Bellamy Retail. Sales and work force are up.
Other Locations: Worldwide HQ: The Body Shop International PLC, Watersmead, Littlehampton, West Sussex BN17 6LS, United Kingdom; +44-1903-731-500. The company has more than 1,500 stores in 47 countries.

FAMILY DOLLAR STORES, INC. ★★

PO Box 1017, Charlotte, NC 28201-1017; 704-847-6961
http://www.familydollar.com
Employees: 26,100
Sales: $2,361.9 million
Key Personnel: Chairman: Leon Levine. President, CEO, and COO: Howard R. Levine. Human Resources: Dennis C. Merriam.

Family Dollar Stores has been steadily expanding, in spite of the competition it has faced from Wal-Mart. The company has opened more than 3,000 stores during the past 10 years and expects its expansion to continue. Although it still sells a wide variety of goods, competition has driven it to focus more tightly on high-margin merchandise. Sales and workforce are both on the increase.
Other Locations: The company has more than 3,300 stores in 38 states.

LOWE'S COMPANIES, INC. ★★

State Highway 268 E., North Wilkesboro, NC 28659; 336-658-4000
http://www.lowes.com
Employees: 66,000
Sales: $12,244.9 million
Key Personnel: Chairman, President, and CEO: Robert L. Tillman. EVP, COO: Larry D. Stone. VP Human Resources: Perry G. Jennings.

Among the largest U.S. retailers in the home improvement market, Lowe's sells a comprehensive array of building supplies, appliances, hardware, and other merchandise. The company typically locates its stores in small towns where it faces little competition for market share. It plans to increase its chain to 600 stores by the year 2000. Sales and work force are both growing.
Other Locations: The company has approximately 530 stores in 37 states.

TANGER FACTORY OUTLET CENTERS, INC. ★★

1400 W. Northwood St., Greensboro, NC 27408; 336-274-1666
http://www.tangeroutlet.com
Employees: 125
Sales: $98.8 million
Key Personnel: President, COO: Steven B. Tanger. EVP: Rochelle G. Simpson. Personnel Manager: Mary Anne Williams.

Tanger Factory Outlet Centers develops and operates factory outlet malls. The malls, a relatively new concept in retailing, are located near tourist destinations. Tenants sell merchandise from only one manufacturer, such as Timberland shoes or Lenox china. The company is continuing to expand. Sales and work force are growing.
Other Locations: The company has approximately 30 factory outlet malls in 23 states.

OHIO

ABERCROMBIE & FITCH CO. ★★

Four Limited Pkwy. East, Reynoldsburg, OH 43068; 614-577-6500
http://www.abercrombie.com
Employees: 9,500
Sales: $815.8 million
Key Personnel: Chairman, CEO: Michael S. Jeffries. VP: Diane Chang. VP Human Resources: Raymond Attanasio.

Abercrombie & Fitch operates almost 200 stores specializing in high-end casual merchandise for men and women. The company is more than 100 years old and began by selling outdoor equipment. Now, its catchy marketing campaign, which relies partly on the store's catalog/magazine *A&F Quarterly*, appeals to fashion-conscious college students. Sales and workforce are up dramatically.

FEDERATED DEPARTMENT STORES, INC.

Seven W. Seventh St., Cincinnati, OH 45202; 513-579-7000
http://www.federated-fds.com
Employees: 118,800
Sales: $15,833 million
Key Personnel: Chairman, CEO: James M. Zimmerman. VC: Ronald W. Tysoe. EVP Legal and Human Resources: Thomas G. Cody.

After its purchase of the bankrupt R. H. Macy department store chain, Federated Department Stores became the biggest department store retailer in the country. The company also runs Bon Marche, Bloomingdale's, Goldsmith's, Stern's, and many other chains. The company is consolidating and streamlining while selling some of its specialty stores. Sales and work force are up.
Other Locations: The company has more than 400 stores in 33 states.

THE LIMITED, INC. ★★

Three Limited Pkwy., Columbus, OH 43216; 614-415-7000
http://www.limited.com
Employees: 126,800
Sales: $9,346.9 million
Key Personnel: Chairman, President, CEO: Leslie H. Wexner. EVP, CFO: V. Ann Hailey. Director Human Resources: Arnold F. Kanarick.

The Limited operates approximately 3,700 stores across the U.S., focusing primarily on women's apparel. The company's stores operate under the Express, Lerner and Lane Bryant names, in addition to The Limited. In 1998 it divested itself of its 84 percent stake in Abercrombie & Fitch. Sales are up slightly, but workforce is down.
Other Locations: The company has approximately 3,700 stores in the United States.

SUN TELEVISION & APPLIANCES, INC.

6600 Port Rd., Groveport, OH 43125; 614-492-5600
Employees: 2,900
Sales: $508.1 million
Key Personnel: Chairman, CEO, President: R. Carter Pate. EVP, COO: Dennis L. May. Director Human Resources: Kimberly Oeberst.

Sun Television and Appliances is the biggest consumer electronics retailer in the state of Ohio. Since filing Chapter 11 bankruptcy in 1998, the company has begun selling off its stores. It has an aggressive style and pays its salespeople commissions. Sales and work force are both decreasing.
Other Locations: The company has stores in Kentucky, New York, Ohio, Pennsylvania, and West Virginia.

PENNSYLVANIA

AMERICAN EAGLE OUTFITTERS, INC. ★★

150 Thorn Hill Dr., Warrendale, PA 15086-7528; 724-776-4857
http://www.ae-outfitters.com
Employees: 7,576
Sales: $587.6 million
Key Personnel: President, Chief Merchandising Officer: Roger S. Markfield. VC, COO: George Kolber. VP Human Resources: Michael E. Bergdahl.

Quality, private-label men's and women's clothing is the business of American Eagle Outfitters. The company sells its wares primarily from stores located in enclosed shopping malls. The company's goal is to increase to 1,000 stores within a few years. Sales and work force are growing.
Other Locations: The company has close to 400 stores, mainly in the East and Midwest.

GENERAL NUTRITION COMPANIES, INC. ★★

300 6th Ave., Pittsburgh, PA 15222; 412-288-4600
http://www.gnc.com
Employees: 16,888
Sales: $1,417.7 million
Key Personnel: President, CEO: William E. Watts. Chairman: Jerry D. Horn. Human Resources: Eilene D. Scott.

Riding the wave of increasing concern with health, General Nutrition Companies is the largest seller of nutritional supplements in the United States. The company's stores are mainly in shopping malls. Its customers are mostly over 35 years old. It recently purchased its competitor, Nature Food Centres. Sales and work force are rising.

Other Locations: The company has more than 4,200 company-owned and franchised stores in the United States.

RITE AID CORPORATION ★

30 Hunter Lane, Camp Hill, PA 17011-2404; 717-761-2633
http://www.riteaid.com
Employees: 89,900
Sales: $12,731.9 million
Key Personnel: Chairman, CEO: Martin L. Grass. President, COO: Timothy J. Noonan. Human Resources: Robert R. Sounder.

Rite Aid has been restructuring. The company bought the Thrifty PayLess chain and other smaller regional chains to make it one of the top three drugstore chains in the country. In addition, it is expanding many of its stores to 10,500 square feet. The company also operates Eagle Managed Care, a company that markets prescription benefit programs. Sales and work force are up.

Other Locations: The company owns nearly than 4,000 drugstores in the U. S.

RHODE ISLAND

CVS CORPORATION ★★

One CVS Dr., Woonsocket, RI 02895; 401-765-1500
http://www.cvs.com
Employees: 90,000
Sales: $12,738.2 million
Key Personnel: Chairman, CEO: Thomas M. Ryan. President, COO: Charles C. Conway. SVP Human Resources: Rosemary Mede.

CVS (formerly Melville) operates about 4,200 drugstores under the names of Arbor, CVS, and Revco in more than 25 states, making it the #2 drugstore operator in the US. As the Melville Corporation the company had diversified into other retail operations. It has divested itself of those and now concentrates on the drug business. Sales and work force are rising.

Other Locations: The company owns over 4,000 stores in Canada and the U.S.

SOUTH CAROLINA

ONE PRICE CLOTHING STORES, INC.

1875 E. Main St., Hwy. 290, Commerce Park, Duncan, SC 29334; 864-433-8888
Employees: 3,900
Sales: $328.1 million
Key Personnel: President, CEO: Larry I. Kelley. SVP: Ronald C. Swedin. VP Human Resources: James S. Overstreet.

One Price Clothing Stores primarily sells apparel for women and children. Due to falling sales, the company has had to abandon its signature one price format, though most items are still priced between $7 and $15. Unlike similar stores, it does not sell flawed merchandise. Sales and work force are decreasing.

Other Locations: The company has more than 620 stores in Florida, Georgia, North Carolina, South Carolina, Texas, and other states.

TENNESSEE

AUTOZONE, INC. ★★

123 S. Front St., Memphis, TN 38103; 901-495-6500
http://www.autozone.com
Employees: 38,500
Sales: $3,242.9 million
Key Personnel: President, COO: Timothy D. Vargo. EVP: Robert J. Hunt. SVP: Gene Auerbach.

Among the largest retailers of auto parts in the United States, AutoZone primarily targets the do-it-yourself market. It sells a comprehensive line of products under a variety of brand names, including Deutsch and Valucraft. It is expanding rapidly, adding about 100 stores per year. Sales and work force are growing.

Other Locations: The company has more than 2,700 stores in 39 states.

SERVICE MERCHANDISE COMPANY, INC.

7100 Service Merchandise Dr., Brentwood, TN 37027; 615-660-6000
http://www.servicemerchandise.com
Employees: 23,409

Sales: $3,169.5 million
Key Personnel: Chairman: Raymond Zimmerman. CEO: Sam Cusano. Human Resources: C. Stephen Moore.

Among the biggest catalog showroom retail businesses in the United States, Service Merchandise sells a variety of appliances, cameras, housewares, toys, and other merchandise. The company puts out 16 million catalogs each year. Since filing for bankruptcy, it has begun revamping its customer service operations and repositioning itself as a home and jewelry specialty retailer, in an effort to regain its slipping customer base. Sales and work force are both currently decreasing.
Other Locations: The company owns more than 220 stores in 32 states.

TEXAS

ARMY & AIR FORCE EXCHANGE SERVICE
3911 S. Walton Walker Blvd., Dallas, TX 75236; 214-312-2011
http://www.aafes.com
Employees: 44,697
Sales: $7,200 million
Key Personnel: Commander, CEO: Major General Barry D. Bates. COO: W. Michael Beverly. Human Resources: James K. Winter.

The Army & Air Force Exchange Service is among the nation's largest retailers, selling a wide variety of consumer goods. It is an agency of the U.S. Department of Defense, but it does not receive money from the department. It does not pay rent or income taxes for its approximately 10,000 facilities at Army posts and Air Force bases worldwide. Half of its employees are related to military personnel or retirees. Sales are up slightly, while workforce remains static.
Other Locations: The agency has facilities in all states and 26 areas overseas.

THE BOMBAY COMPANY, INC.
550 Bailey Ave., Ste. 700, Fort Worth, TX 76107; 817-347-8200
http://www.bombayco.com
Employees: 5,000
Sales: $356.7 million
Key Personnel: CEO: Robert S. Jackson. President, COO: Carmie Mehrlander. Human Resources: James D. Johnson.

Specializing in a narrowly focused niche, The Bombay Company has become one of the most rapidly expanding U.S. home furnishings retailers. The company sells reasonably priced, fashionable wood furniture and accessories in prominent mall locations. It sells only pieces that can be carried out or assembled at home. Sales and work force are growing.
Other Locations: The company has more than 445 stores in Canada and the U.S.

COMPUCOM SYSTEMS, INC. ★★
7171 Forest Ln., Dallas, TX 75230; 972-856-3600
http://www.compucom.com
Employees: 4,800
Sales: $2,254.5 million
Key Personnel: Chairman, Interim CEO: Harry Wallaesa. President, COO: Tom Lynch. Human Resources: David A. Loeser.

CompuCom Systems sells desktop computers and network systems to large corporate clients. The company sells a wide variety of brand-name products without using a storefront. Instead, customers call a central sales office to begin a transaction. The company also delivers and services its merchandise. Sales and work force are up.
Other Locations: The company has more than 40 locations in the United States.

COMPUSA, INC. ★
14951 N. Dallas Pkwy., Dallas, TX 75240; 972-982-4000
http://www.compusa.com
Employees: 19,700
Sales: $6,321.4 million
Key Personnel: President, CEO: James F. Halpin. EVP, COO: Harold F. Compton. Human Resources: Melvin D. McCall.

One of the largest computer retailers in the United States, CompUSA's acquisition of Tandy Corporation's Computer City chain added 100 stores to its assets. The company recently began restructuring its approach to favor novice computer users rather than experienced clients. Sales and work force are on the rise.
Other Locations: The company has more than 200 stores in over 40 states.

J.C. PENNEY COMPANY, INC.

6501 Legacy Dr., Plano, TX 75024-3698; 972-431-1000
http://www.jcpenney.com
Employees: 262,000
Sales: $30,678 million
Key Personnel: Chairman, CEO: James E. Oesterreicher. EVP: Charles R. Lotter. EVP, Chief Human Resources Officer: Gary L. Davis.

JCPenney is hoping to increase its momentum by looking for sales overseas and by expanding its drugstore business. The company is among the largest department store operators in the United States. However, its management feels that the U.S. market is saturated, so the company is preparing to open stores abroad. With the acquisition of Eckerd, Penney is one of the largest U.S. drugstore retailers. Sales and work force are growing.
Other Locations: The company owns nearly 1,200 retail stores and about 2,900 drugstores.

THE MEN'S WEARHOUSE, INC. ★★

5803 Glenmont Dr., Houston, TX 77081; 713-295-7200
http://www.menswearhouse.com
Employees: 6,800
Sales: $767.9 million
Key Personnel: Chairman, CEO: George Zimmer. President: David Edwab. SVP Human Resources: Charles Bresler.

Tailored clothing for men is the business of The Men's Wearhouse. Best known for its television advertising featuring George Zimmer—the company's CEO—it provides specially trained staff and other customer service perks, along with discount prices. The company has grown quickly in the last five years as department stores have eliminated tailored business clothes from their inventories. Sales and work force are up.
Other Locations: The company has approximately 600 stores.

BABBAGE'S ETC. ★

2250 William D. Tate, Grapevine, TX 76051; 817-424-2000
http://www.gamelord.com
Employees (est.): 3,500
Sales (est.): $375 million
Key Personnel: CEO: R. Richard Fontaine. President, COO: Daniel A. DeMatteo. Director Human Resources: David Shuart.

Babbage's Etc. (formerly NeoStar Retail Group) sells video games, eductional software, PC accessories and computer books. It operates about 475 Babbage's and Software Etc. stores and supplies Barnes &Noble bookstore chain with software. In 1996, as NeoStar, the company filed for bankruptcy. Barnes & Noble head Leonard Riggio bought 450 of NeoStar's 650 stores and renamed the company Babbage's Etc. Since then sales and work force have risen.

PIER 1 IMPORTS, INC. ★

301 Commerce St., Ste. 600, Fort Worth, TX 76102; 817-252-8000
http://www.pier1.com
Employees: 12,600
Sales: $1,138.6 million
Key Personnel: Chairman, President, and CEO: Marvin J. Girouard. SVP: Jay R. Jacobs. Human Resources: E. Mitchell Weatherly.

Distinctive imported items are the foundation of Pier 1 Imports' business. The company sells a wide variety of products including home furnishings, kitchen accessories, and furniture. Its stores are typically located in highly populated areas. The company has been upgrading its inventory to follow its market's changing tastes. Sales and work force are up modestly.
Other Locations: The company operates more than 750 stores in California, Florida, Illinois, New York, Texas, and other states.

TANDY CORPORATION

100 Throckmorton St., Ste. 1800, Fort Worth, TX 76102; 817-415-3700
http://www.tandy.com
Employees: 38,200
Sales: $4,787.9 million
Key Personnel: Chairman, President, and CEO: Leonard H. Roberts. SVP: Richard J. Borinstein. Human Resources: George J. Berger.

Tandy is cutting back its operations to focus on retailing. The company sold many of its computer manufacturing interests and shut down some of its stores, and is selling its Computer City chain to

CompUSA. The bulk of its sales come from its Radio Shack chain. Sales and work force are down.
Other Locations: The company owns or franchises approximately 7,000 retail outlets in Canada, Europe, and the United States.

TUESDAY MORNING CORPORATION
14621 Inwood Rd., Dallas, TX 75001; 972-387-3562
http://www.tuesdaymorning.com
Employees: 4,209
Sales: $396.1 million
Key Personnel: Chairman, President, and CEO: Jerry M. Smith. SVP: G. Michael Anderson. Director Human Resources: Cynthia Allison.
Specialized planning goes into offering deep discounts for customers at Tuesday Morning. The company is the largest retailer of discount upscale merchandise in the United States. To be able to offer 50- to 80-percent discounts on housewares, gifts, and other goods, the company uses strategies such as hiring part-time workers and renting space in inexpensive strip malls. Sales and work force are growing.
Other Locations: The company owns more than 350 stores in the United States.

V I R G I N I A
CIRCUIT CITY STORES, INC. ★★
9950 Mayland Dr., Richmond, VA 23233; 804-527-4000
http://www.circuitcity.com
Employees: 54,430
Sales: $810,804.5 million
Key Personnel: President, COO: W. Alan McCollough. Chairman, CEO: Richard L. Sharp. SVP Human Resources: Jeffrey S. Wells.
A pioneer in the retailing of consumer electronics, Circuit City Stores is known in the industry for the strategy of overwhelming its competition by establishing many stores in a single market. The company has successfully dominated many Southern and Western markets and is turning its attention to the Northeast. Sales and work force are growing.

HEILIG-MEYERS COMPANY
12560 W. Creek Pkwy, Richmond, VA 23238; 804-784-7300
http://www.hmyco.com
Employees: 23,500
Sales: $2,431.2 million
Key Personnel: Chairman, CEO: William C. DeRusha. President, COO: Donald S. Shaffer. Human Resources: Brent Langford.
For Heilig-Meyers, success has meant concentrating on smaller markets. The company sells furniture, consumer electronics, jewelry, and other items, primarily in areas with a population of 50,000 or less. As a big fish in a small pond, the company is able to dominate these markets. It recently purchased a chain of 92 furniture stores. Sales and work force are up.
Other Locations: The company has approximately 900 stores in over 11 states.

W A S H I N G T O N

EGGHEAD.COM INC.
521 SE Chkalov Dr., Vancouver, WA 98683; 360-883-3447
http://www.egghead.com
Employees: 295
Sales: $148.7 million
Key Personnel: Chairman, CEO: George P. Orban. VP Merchandising: James F. Kalasky. Human Resources Director: Machelle Johnson.
Among the largest retailers of computer software, Egghead.com (formerly Egghead) is facing stiff competition. Not only are computer superstores cutting into its sales, but so are hardware manufacturers who bundle lots of software with new computers to entice customers. In response, the company has shut its 200 stores and now conducts business solely on the Internet and a 1-800 number. Sales and work force are down.

NORDSTROM, INC.
1617 Sixth Ave., Seattle, WA 98101; 206-628-2111
http://www.nordstrom.com
Employees: 42,000
Sales: $5,027.9 million
Key Personnel: Co-President: Blake W. Nordstrom. Co-President: Erik B. Nordstrom. VP Human Resources: Joseph V.

Demarte.

Customer service is the foundation of Nordstrom's success. One of the top retailers in the upscale shoe and apparel market, the company has a reputation for encouraging its employees to go to exceptional lengths to please customers. The company continues to expand geographically and through a mail-order catalog it recently introduced. Nordstrom's sales and work force are both on the increase.

Other Locations: The company has approximately 90 stores in California, the District of Columbia area, Hawaii, Oregon, Utah, and Washington and in Guam.

COSTCO COMPANIES, INC. ★★
999 Lake Dr., Issaquah, WA 98207; 206-313-8100
http://www.costco.com
Employees: 36,000
Sales: $24,269.9 million
Key Personnel: President, CEO: James D. Sinegal. EVP, CFO: Richard A. Galanti. SVP Human Resources: John Matthews.

Costco Companies (formerly Price/Costco) is the result of a 1993 merger between Price Club and Costco Wholesale. The resulting company is the largest U.S. operator in the wholesale club market. It sells merchandise to its 27 million members in a warehouse format at discount prices. The company is expanding in the United States and overseas. Sales and work force are up.
Other Locations: The company has more than 300 stores in Canada, the United Kingdom, and the United States.

WISCONSIN
LANDS' END, INC.
Lands' End Lane, Dodgeville, WI 53595; 608-935-9341
http://www.landsend.com
Employees: 8,450
Sales: $1,2371.4 million
Key Personnel: President, CEO: David F. Dyer. EVP: Lee Eisenberg. Human Resources: Kelly A. Ritchie.

Lands' End is primarily a mail-order retailer, selling apparel, soft goods, and home furnishings. The company markets through a number of catalogs and also owns approximately 20 outlet stores. It is currently conducting a rapid expansion of its catalog business to Japan and other foreign countries. Sales are up, but workforce is down.
Other Locations: The company's stores are located in California, Illinois, Iowa, and Wisconsin and in the United Kingdom.

❶ SEMICONDUCTORS

CALIFORNIA
APPLIED MATERIALS, INC.
3050 Bowers Ave., Santa Clara, CA 95054; 408-727-5555
http://www.appliedmaterials.com
Employees: 12,060
Revenues: $ 4,041.7 million
Key Personnel: Chairman, CEO: James C. Morgan. President: Dan Maydan. SVP Worldwide Product Operations: Sasson Somekh. SVP Worldwide Business Operations: David N. K. Wang. Human Resources Manager: Seitaro Ishii.

One of the top manufacturers of semiconductor fabrication equipment, Applied Materials spends heavily on research and development. The company recently developed a process to apply extremely small circuits to silicon wafers using chemical vapors. Its Japanese joint venture, Applied Komatsu, makes flat-panel display fabrication machines. Sales and work force are stable.

ATMEL CORPORATION ★★
2325 Orchard Pkwy., San Jose, CA 95131; 408-441-0311
http://www.atmel.com
Employees: 6,138
Sales: $1,111.1 million
Key Personnel: Chairman, President, CEO: George Perlegos. EVP, General Manager: Gust Perlegos. VP Technology: Tsung-Ching Wu. Human Resources Manager: Joann Morano.

Atmel's products are used in everything from aerospace systems to television remote controls. The company manufactures and designs many types of nonvolatile logic and memory integrated circuits. It is known for its use of complementary metal-oxide semiconductor, or CMOS, technology. Its products are popular in portable systems because they use less power Motorola accounts for 14 percent of sales. Sales and work force are up.

CIRRUS LOGIC, INC.
3100 W. Warren Ave., Fremont, CA
94538; 510-623-8300
http://www.cirrus.com
Employees: 1,331
Sales: $628.1 million
Key Personnel:. President, CEO: David
D. French. President, Cirrus Logic: Ki-
mio Fujii. SVP Human Resources: Patrick V. Boudreau.
Cirrus Logic is one of the largest developers and manufacturers of integrated
circuits for markets such as multimedia,
mass storage, and graphics. The company
has enjoyed great success recently as the
popularity of multimedia computers has
surged. It is currently working on products to be used in personal digital assistants, such as the Apple Newton. Sales
and work force are down.

CYPRESS SEMICONDUCTOR CORPORA-
TION
3901 N. First St., San Jose, CA 95134;
408-943-2600
http://www.cypress.com
Employees: 2,901
Sales: $486.8 million
Key Personnel: President, CEO: T.J.
Rodgers. EVP: James D. Kupec. Human
Resources Manager: Julie Pestka-
Schardt.
Cypress Semiconductor makes a wide variety of products for telecommunications,
personal computers, military, and other
applications. The company has been a
fierce proponent of U.S. technology and
has long resisted moving its operations
overseas. They sell to product makers
such as 3Com, Cisco, Motorola, and
Nortel Networks. It recently purchased
several other semiconductor companies,
including Contaq Microsystems. Sales
and work force are steady.

LAM RESEARCH CORPORATION ★★
4650 Cushing Pkwy., Fremont, CA
94538; 510-659-0200
http://www.lamrc.com
Employees: 3,300
Sales: $648.0 million
Key Personnel: Chairman, CEO: James
W. Bagley. President, COO: Stephen G.
Newberry. Human Resources Director:
Bill Minor.
One of the top makers of semiconductor

fabrication equipment, Lam Research is a
leader in the deposition and etch processes. The deposition process puts a film
on silicon wafers, while etching uses
chemicals to cut grooves in them. Both
processes create circuits on the wafers.
Lam's equipment is being used in the
manufacture of flat-panel displays. Sales
and work force are up.

LSI LOGIC CORPORATION ★★
1551 McCarthy Blvd., Milpitas, CA
95035; 408-433-8000
http://www.lsilogic.com
Employees: 6,420
Revenues: $1,490.7 million
Key Personnel: Chairman, CEO: Wil-
fred J. Corrigan. EVP, CFO: R. Douglas
Norby. VP Human Resources: Lewis C.
Wallbridge.
Semiconductors for the Information Superhighway are the specialty of LSI
Logic. The company creates a variety of
high-density microchips for telecommunications, computer networking, digital
video, and other applications. Sun Microsystems and Sony are some of the company's largest clients, and the company
has numerous joint ventures with companies such as Zenith and Kawasaki Steel.
Sales and work force are rising rapidly.

SILICON VALLEY GROUP, INC.
101 Metro Dr., Suite 400., San Jose, CA
95110; 408-411-6700
http://www.svg.com
Employees: 2,660
Sales: $608.6 million
Key Personnel: President, COO: William Hightower. President, SVG-
Tinsley: Robert J. Aronno. Human Resources Manager: Randy Watkins.
Silicon Valley Group manufactures
semiconductor fabrication equipment.
The company's products are used to etch
patterns in silicon wafers during the process of producing computer chips. Three
main customers, chip makers Intel, IBM,
and Motorola, together account for about
70 percent of SVG's sales. It recently
formed a partnership with the Japanese
company Canon. Sales and work force
are up.

VLSI TECHNOLOGY, INC.
1109 McKay Dr., San Jose, CA 95131;

408-434-3100
Employees: 2,500
Sales: $547.8 million
Key Personnel: President, CEO, COO: Alfred J. Stein. SVP Operations: Ted Malanczuk. Human Resources Director: Art Gemmell.

Microprocessors for personal computers have been the primary business of VLSI Technology. The company was the manufacturer of Apple Computer's 68000 series central processing unit. It is currently focusing on telecommunications and consumer technology OEMs, who use Integrated Circuits for cellular phones, video games and so forth. It is now a subsidiary of Philips Electronics. Sales and work force are decreasing.

ZILOG, INC.

910 E. Hamilton Ave., Campbell, CA 95008; 408-558-8500
http://www.zilog.com
Employees: 1,611
Sales: $ 204.7 million
Key Personnel: President, CEO: Curtis J. Crawford. SVP, CFO: James Thorburn. Human Resources Manager: Steven C. Mizell.

Application-specific microprocessors are the specialty of Zilog. The company provides microprocessors primarily for consumer product controllers, data communications, and other niche markets. Among its products are digital phase lock loops, closed caption controllers, and V-Chips for use in new televisions. Much of the company's business takes place overseas, especially in Asia. Sales and work force are down.

IDAHO

MICRON TECHNOLOGY, INC.

8000 S. Federal Way, Boise, ID 83707-0006; 208-368-4000
http://www.micron.com
Employees: 11,400
Sales: $ 3,011.9 million
Key Personnel: Chairman, President, CEO: Steven R. Appleton. VP Operations: Jay L. Hawkins. VP Human Resources: Nancy M. Self.

Micron Technology is the second largest producer of random access memory chips in the United States. It is also the largest employer in Idaho's private sector. The company is currently working on a broader range of products, including embedded memory for digital video and dynamic random-access memories (DRAMs). Sales and work force are falling.

MASSACHUSETTS

ANALOG DEVICES, INC.

One Technology Way, Norwood, MA 02062-9106; 781-329-4700
http://www.analog.com
Employees: 7,200
Revenues: $ 1,230.6 million
Key Personnel: President, CEO: Jerald G. Fishman. VP Finance, CFO: Joseph E. McDonough. VP Human Resources: Ross Brown.

After establishing a reputation with its digital signal processing integrated circuits, Analog Devices is branching out. Currently, it makes analog and digital curcuits and multi-chip modules. The company is among the largest suppliers of semiconductors in the European cellular telecommunications marketplace. It is currently working to gain a foothold in the U.S. market. Sales and work force are steady.

PENNSYLVANIA

AMKOR TECHNOLOGY, INC. ★★

1345 Enterprise Dr., West Chester, PA 19380; 610-431-9600
http://www.amkor.com
Employees: 10,000
Sales: $1,568.0 million
Key Personnel: Chairman, CEO: James J. Kim. President, COO: John N. Boruch. Human Resources Manager: Cathy Loucks.

Amkor Technology (formerly Amkor Electronics) is a subsidiary of Anam Group. Anam Group also owns Anam Industrial, which is now the largest assembler of semiconductors in the world. The company's other subsidiaries make electronic equipment, such as televisions, and sell software. Amkor Electronics distributes Anam computer chips in the United States. Both its sales and work force are increasing.
Other Locations: Worldwide HQ: Anam Group, 151-22 Hayana-dong, Songdong-gu, Seoul, South Korea; phone: +82-2-460-5171.

➊ SOFTWARE

CALIFORNIA

ADOBE SYSTEMS, INC. ★★
345 Park Ave., San Jose, CA 95110-2704; 408-536-6000
http://www.adobe.com
Employees: 2,680
Sales: $894.8 million
Key Personnel: President, Co-Chairman: Charles M. Geschke. EVP, CFO: Harold Covert. Human Resources Manager: Rebecca M. Guerra.

Best known for its PostScript page description language and typeface software, Adobe Systems is a top enterprise in the desktop publishing market. The company's purchase of Aldus, the publisher of the popular PageMaker typesetting program, in 1994 gave Adobe still greater market share. Currently, its Acrobat Reader is popular on the Internet for reading PDF documents. Sales and work force are steady.

AUTODESK, INC. ★★
111 McInnis Pkwy., San Rafael, CA 94903; 415-507-5000
http://www.autodesk.com
Employees: 2,712
Sales: $740.2 million
Key Personnel: Chairman, President, CEO: Carol A. Bartz. VP, CFO: Steve Cakebread. Human Resources Manager: Stephen McMahon.

Autodesk is one of the largest suppliers of computer-aided-design (CAD) automation software, which is widely used in various engineering applications. The company recently introduced additional products designed for use in multimedia and other development enterprises. Its products are distributed worldwide in a variety of languages. Sales and work force are growing.

INPRISE CORPORATION. ★★
100 Borland Way, Scotts Valley, CA 95066; 831-431-1000
http://www.inprise.com
Employees: 900
Sales: $189.1 million
Key Personnel: President, CEO Dale Fuller. VP Corporate Communications: Marilee Adams. Human Resources Manager: Nancy Hauge.

The publisher of such programs as dBASE, Paradox, C++, and Delphi, Inprise Corporation (formerly Borland International) is facing stiff competition in the software publishing market. The company is among the top publishers of software for desktop computers, but it has been criticized for long delays in getting new software to market. Currently it is focusing on the fast growing Internet market. Overall sales and work force are up.
Other Locations: The company has subsidiaries in the United States and 18 foreign countries.

CADENCE DESIGN SYSTEMS, INC.★★
2655 Sealy Ave., Bldg 5., San Jose, CA 95134; 408-943-1234
http://www.cadence.com
Employees: 4,200
Sales: $1,216.1 million
Key Personnel: President, CEO: H.Raymond Bingham. SVP: M. Robert Leach. Human Resources Director: Ron Kirchenbaur.

Cadence Design Systems is in the business of providing software tools for designing integrated circuits. Demand for its products has been slipping recently as a result of market saturation. The company has grown during recent years by purchasing its competitors, but since 1995 it has been embroiled in a code-theft suit against EDA firm Avant!. Sales and work force are up.

ELECTRONIC ARTS, INC. ★★
209 Redwood Shores Pkwy., Redwood City, CA 94065; 650-628-1500
http://www.ea.com
Employees: 2,500
Sales: $1,221.9 million
Key Personnel: Chairman, CEO: Lawrence F. Probst III. President, COO: John S. Riccitiello. Human Resources Manager: J. Russell Rueff.

The number one computer game publisher in the U.S., Electronic Arts sells most of its products on Sega and Nintendo game cartridges. It distributes almost 1,000 titles internationally. It is also sells a larger number of floppy-disk and CD-ROM products. Sales and work force are rising.

INFORMIX CORPORATION ★★

4100 Bohannon Dr., Menlo Park, CA
94025; 650-926-6300
http://www.informix.com
Employees: 3,984
Sales: $735.0 million
Key Personnel: Chairman: Robert J. Finocchio Jr. President, CEO: Jean-Yves Dexmier. Human Resources Director: Susan Daniel.

Database management is the key to Informix. The company sells a line of software designed for management of Unix-based databases. The company's products include servers and application development utilities. Along with software, the company also offers its clients support services. Its NewEra software is designed to work with client/server networks. Sales and work force are growing.

INTUIT, INC. ★

2535 Garcia Ave., Mountain View CA
94043; 650-944-6000
http://www.intuit.com
Employees: 2,860
Sales: $847.6 million
Key Personnel:: Chairman: William V. Campbell. President, CEO: William H. Harris Jr. Human Resources Manager: Mari J. Baker.

A leading provider of financial software for desktop computers, Intuit sells the popular Quicken application. Among its other software titles are MacInTax, TurboTax, and QuickBooks. Intuit has moved into electronic information by producing several web sites, including a financial news site in conjunction with CNN. Sales are up and work force is steady.

ORACLE CORPORATION ★★

500 Oracle Pkwy., Redwood City, CA
94065; 415-506-7000
http://www.oracle.com
Employees: 43,800
Revenues: $8,827.3 million
Key Personnel: Chairman, CEO: Lawrence J. Ellison. President, COO: Raymond J. Lane. EVP: Gary Bloom. Human Resources Manager: Carole Goldberg.

Among the largest software merchants in the world, Oracle's leading product is its relational database management software. The company, whose sales were once heavily based on mainframe users, has successfully made the transition to users of smaller networked computers. Oracle 8, released in 1997, provides support for network computer systems. It also sells a variety of other products and services, including database integration and accounting applications products. Sales and work force are increasing.

SYBASE, INC.

6475 Christie Ave., Emeryville, CA
94608; 510-922-3500
http://www.sybase.com
Employees: 4,196
Revenues: $867.5 million
Key Personnel: Chairman, President, CEO: John S. Chen. EVP, CIO: Robert S. Epstein. VP Human Resources: Nita C. White-Ivy.

Sybase is one of the largest suppliers of client/server software. Its software is used predominantly for creating relational database management systems (RDBMS). The systems allow large numbers of networked users to access the databases at the same time. Subsidiary Powersoft develops object-oriented application development software. Sales and work force are down.

SYMANTEC CORPORATION ★

10201 Torre Ave., Cupertino, CA 95014-2132; 408-253-9600
http://www.symantec.com
Employees: 2,400
Sales: $633.9 million
Key Personnel: Chairman, President, CEO: John W. Thompson. VP Alliances: John Bruce. Human Resources Manager: Rebecca Ranninger.

Expansion by acquisition has been the strategy of Symantec. The company, which is the top seller of utility programs for MS-DOS-compatible computers, has earned a reputation for buying up cutting edge companies to expand its capabilities in a race to keep from being overwhelmed by competitor Microsoft. Among its offerings are Norton Utilities, THINK C, and ACT! Sales and work force are down.

SYNOPSYS, INC. ★★

700 E. Middlefield Rd., Mountain View,

CA 94043; 650-962-5000
http://www.synopsys.com
Employees: 2,592
Sales: $717.9 million
Key Personnel: Chairman, CEO: Art J. de Geus. President, COO: Chi-Foon Chan. EVP: William W. Lattin. Human Resources Director: Ernst W. Hirt.
Synopsys is one of the largest providers of electronic design automation software for integrated circuit engineers. The company is best known for its reliance on designing circuits through function instead of structure. Among its titles are ModelSource 3000, DesignWare, and VHDL System Simulator. Sales and work force are rising.

ILLINOIS

PLATINUM TECHNOLOGY, INC. ★★
1815 S. Meyers Rd., Oakbrook Terrace, IL 60181-5241; 708-620-5000
http://www.platinum.com
Employees: 4,330
Revenues: $623.5 million
Key Personnel: President, CEO: Andrew Filipowski. EVP Product Development, COO: Paul L. Humenansky. EVP Sales: Thomas A. Slowey. Human Resources Director: Marc L. Ugol.
PLATINUM technology Inc. is one of the largest providers of software for mainframe computers. The company's main products are designed to enhance the performance of networked computing environment and of databases such as Oracle, Sybase and Microsoft SQL. Sales and work force are growing.

SPYGLASS, INC.
Naperville Corporate Ctr., 1230 E. Diehl Rd., 4th Floor, Naperville, IL 60563; 630-505-1010
http://www.spyglass.com
Employees: 127
Sales: $20.5 million
Key Personnel: President, CEO: Douglas P. Colbeth. EVP Business Development: Michael F. Tyrrell. Human Resources Director: Susan L. Kizman.
Spyglass markets software that puts a friendly face on the Internet. The company's Mosaic application runs on most popular desktop computers and allows users to navigate the Internet and the World Wide Web with a point-and-click interface. The software was originally developed by the University of Illinois National Center for Supercomputing Applications and subsequently commercialized by Spyglass. The company's sales and work force are down.

SYSTEM SOFTWARE ASSOCIATES, INC. ★★
500 W. Madison St., 32nd Floor, Chicago, IL 60661; 312-258-6000
http://www.ssax.com
Employees: 2,200
Revenues: $420.8 million
Key Personnel: Chairman, CEO: Robert R. Carpenter. EVP, CFO: F.H. "Terry" Cloudman. Human Resources Manager: Bob Corbett.
Business information systems are the mainstay of System Software Associates. The company provides a variety of products that facilitate supply chain management, global financial solutions, and other business processes. The company's software supports open architecture networks and runs on many different platforms, including several Unix-based systems. Revenues and work force are down.

MASSACHUSETTS

LOTUS DEVELOPMENT CORPORATION
55 Cambridge Pkwy., Cambridge, MA 02142; 617-577-8500
http://www.lotus.com
Employees: 6,000
Sales: $1,400 million
Key Personnel: President, CEO: Jeff Papows. EVP: Michael D. Zisman. Human Resources Director: Jeffrey Yanagi.
Lotus Development, owned by IBM, is one of the top software developers in the world. The company is best known for its 1-2-3 spreadsheet program and Notes network communications product. These products are used by 34 million people worldwide, mostly in business intranets. Sales and work force have remained steady.

PARAMETRIC TECHNOLOGIES
128 Technology Dr., Waltham, MA 02154; 781-398-5000
http://www.ptc.com
Employees: 4,911

Sales: $ 1,018.0 million
Key Personnel: Chairman, CEO: Steven C. Walske. President, COO: C. Richard Harrison. Human Resources Manager: Carl Ockerbloom.
Parametric Technology makes a unique and popular line of engineering software that cuts manufacturing costs through design automation. Its core product is Pro/ENGINEER. Parametric is an industry leader in facilitating solid modeling technology at a competitive price. Among the company's clients are Motorola, Ford, and Hughes Aircraft. Sales and work force are up, due to the acquisition of Computervision.

PROGRESS SOFTWARE CORPORATION ★★

14 Oak Park, Bedford, MA 01730; 781-280-4000
http://www.progress.com
Employees: 1,201
Sales: $239.9 million
Key Personnel: President: Joseph W. Alsop. VP Sales: David P. Vesty. VP Human Resources: Joseph A. Andrews.
Concentrating its marketing efforts on value-added resellers has been a successful strategy for Progress Software. The company sells a set of tools designed to aid in the development of relational database management systems. The tools are used by resellers who develop databases for their clients. The company continues to market its products through its direct sales force. Sales and work force are up.

THE LEARNING COMPANY, INC.

One Athenaeum Street, Cambridge, MA 02142; 617-494-1200
http://www.learningco.com
Employees: 1,525
Revenues: $839.3 million
Key Personnel: Chairman, CEO: Michael J. Perik. President: Kevin O'Leary. EVP, CFO: R. Scott Murray. Human Resources Director: Bill Shupert.
Undercutting the competition has been a successful strategy for The Learning Company (formerly Softkey International). The company became one of the world's top software publishers by selling inexpensive game, productivity, and leisure software. Among its titles are Calendar Creator, Key Fonts, and Where in the World is Carmen Sandiego. The company is now one of the two top players in the field, the other being Cendant, after acquiring Minnesota Educational Computing and Compton's Multimedia Publishing Group. Sales and work force are rising.

ARDENT SOFTWARE, INC. ★★

50 Washington St, Westborough, MA 01581-1021; 508-366-3888
http://www.ardentsoftware.com
Employees: 623
Sales: $119.3 million
Key Personnel: President, CEO: Peter Gyenes. EVP Sales: Jason E. Silvia. Human Resources Manager: Mary Murphy.
Ardent Software (formerly VMARK Software) is one of the largest companies selling Unix operating systems. The company sells a variety of applications to go with Unix and Windows NT platforms, including JET, a word processor; CompuSheet+, a spreadsheet; and HyperSTAR, a graphical user interface. Services account for about half of all revenue. Sales and work force are climbing.

GENTRONICS NV. ★★

600 Technology Park, Billerica, MA 08121; 508-459-5000
http://www.gentronics.com
Employees: 12,458
Revenues: $1,842.1 million
Key Personnel: VC: Ken Bajaj. EVP: Franklyn A. Caine. Human Resources Manager: Albert A. Notini.
Gentronics NV bought U.S. IT firm Wang Laboratories in 1999 to secure a foothold in the growing North American market. The Netherlands based company offers systems integration and networking (60 percent of sales), human resources services, outsourcing, and IT consulting. Sales and work force are up.

NEW JERSEY

VIZACOM, INC. ★

3 Oak Rd., Fairfield, NJ 07004; 973-808-1992
http://www.spco.com
Employees: 151
Sales: $18.3 million

Key Personnel: President, CEO, COO: Mark E. Leininger. VP Sales: Joseph Drop. VP Human Resources: Egie Rambarose.

Vizacom Inc. (formerly Software Publishing Corporation) puts out a variety of business software, including Harvard Graphics, PFS:Write, OfficeWriter, and DrawPlus 4. They also make e-mail software (ActiveMail), how-to CD-ROMs, and interactive multimedia.. Sales and work force are up.

NEW YORK
COMPUTER ASSOCIATES INTERNATIONAL ★★

One Computer Associates Plaza, Islandia, NY 11749; 516-342-5224
http://www.cai.com
Employees: 14,650
Revenues: $5,253.2 million
Key Personnel: Chairman, CEO: Charles B. Wang. EVP Research and Development: Russell M. Artzt. SVP Human Resources: Deborah J. Coughlin.

The third largest independent software vendor in the world, Computer Associates primarily serves the mainframe market. Among the company's more than 300 products are CASE technologies, DB2 tools, and enterprise information solutions. In the last few years the company has been acquiring various other software firms, including the Legent Corp. and the ASK Group, Inc. They are looking to acquire more computer services providers. Sales and work force are up.

NORTH CAROLINA
SAS INSTITUTE, INC. ★

SAS Campus Dr., Cary, NC 27513; 919-677-8000
http://www.sas.com
Employees: 5,400
Sales: $871.4 million
Key Personnel: President: James H. Goodnight. VP, Information Systems: Charlie Dunham. Director Human Resources: David Russo.

The largest independent providers of software in the world, SAS Institute sells a variety of products that facilitate data management. It uses a modular approach, selling a core program called Base SAS and allowing users to purchase additional parts to add capabilities. The programs run on a broad range of computer systems, including Macintosh, Windows, OS/2, and Unix. Sales and work force are up.

OREGON
MENTOR GRAPHICS CORPORATION

8005 SW Boeckman Rd., Wilsonville, OR 97070-7777; 503-685-7000
http://www.mentorg.com
Employees: 2,600
Sales: $490.4 million
Key Personnel: President, CEO: Walden C. Rhines. EVP, CFO, COO: Gregory K. Hinckley. VP Human Resources: Gary Rebello.

Mentor Graphics is one of the top companies in the automation of circuit design. Among its product is Falcon Framework, an electrical design automation package. The company's customers are mainly electronics, aerospace, and computer manufacturers. Sales and work force are stable.

SOUTH CAROLINA
POLICY MANAGEMENT SYSTEMS CORP.

One PMS Ctr., Blythewood, SC 29016; 803-333-4000
http://www.pmsc.com
Employees: 5,839
Sales: $607.5 million
Key Personnel: Chairman, President, CEO: G. Larry Wilson. EVP: David T. Bailey. Human Resources Manager: Gilbert D. Johnson.

Among the top suppliers of software to insurance companies, Policy Management Systems sells a broad range of products. Its software serves all phases of the insurance industry, including billing, group administration, and demographics. Sales and work force are up.

TEXAS
BMC SOFTWARE, INC. ★★

2101 CityWest Blvd., Houston, TX 77042-2827; 713-918-8800
http://www.bmc.com
Employees: 4,914
Sales: $1,303.9 million

Key Personnel: Chairman, President, CEO: Max P. Watson, Jr. SVP, CFO: William M. Austin. Director of Human Resources: Roy J. Wilson.

BMC Software is among the top producers of database utilities for IBM mainframes, selling over 200 products. It principally supplies software to support the IMS and DB2 database platforms. The company's 1994 purchase of Patrol Software, a company that sells to the client/server market, signaled BMC's entry into the nonmainframe market sector. In 1999 it purchased rival management software maker Boole & Babbage. Sales and work force are growing.

STERLING SOFTWARE, INC. ★★

300 Crescent Ct., Suite 1200, Dallas, TX 75201; 214-981-1000
http://www.sterling.com
Employees: 3,500
Revenues: $719.9 million
Key Personnel: President, CEO: Sterling L. Williams. EVP, COO: Geno P. Tolari. Human Resources Director: Steve Fallon.

One of the world's top suppliers of software products and services, Sterling Software targets the electronic commerce, systems management, and applications management markets. They have over 20,000 customers worldwide, including 90 of the top 100 U.S. industrial and service firms. The company also provides technical services to the U.S. government. Sales and work force are rising at Sterling Software.

UTAH

NOVELL, INC. ★

122 E. 1700 South, Provo UT 84606; 801-861-7000
Employees: 4,510
Revenues: $1,083.9 million
Key Personnel: Chairman, CEO: Eric E. Schmidt. VC: John A. Young. SVP: Dennis R. Raney. Human Resources Director: Jennifer A. Konecny-Costa..

Networking is one of the top priorities at Novell. The company sells NetWare, a popular computer networking software package, and Novell Embedded Systems, or NEST, which facilitates network connections to a wide variety of devices. Sales are up and work force is down.

VIRGINIA

SOFTWARE AG OF NORTH AMERICA, INC. ★★

11190 Sunrise Valley Dr., Reston, VA 22091; 703-860-5050
http://www.sagus.com
Employees: 2,096
Sales: $349.2 million
Key Personnel: President, CEO: Erwin W. Konigs. VP Technical: Marius Abel. VP Human Resources: William McGowan.

Software AG of North America is a subsidiary of Germany's Software AG, one of the largest software distributors in the world. Although the company once focused mainly on mainframe software, it now sells a wide variety of products for the client/server market, such as NATURAL, an application development environment, and NETMAP, a data searching tool. Sales and work force are down.
Other Locations: Worldwide HQ: Software AG, Uhlandstrasse 12, D-64297 Darmstadt, Germany; phone: +49-6151-92-0.

WASHINGTON

ATTACHMATE CORPORATION ★★

3617 131st Ave. SE, Bellevue, WA 98006; 425-644-4010
http://www.attachmatecom
Employees: 1,900
Est. Sales: $300.0 million
Key Personnel: Chairman, CEO: Frank W. Pritt. President: William Boisvert. VP Technical Support: Robert Flynn. Human Resources Manager: Daniele Costello.

Attachmate sells software that connects mainframes to desktop computers. The company's products work with a wide variety of configurations, including Windows, OS/2, and Macintosh operating systems, and IBM, Unix and other mainframe computers. Most of the company's customers are government agencies and larger businesses. Sales and work force are up.
Other Locations: Along with field offices in the United States, the company has sales offices around the world.

MICROSOFT CORPORATION ★★

One Microsoft Way, Bldg 8, Redmond, WA 98052; 425-882-8080
http://www.microsoft.com
Employees: 27,055
Revenues: $19,747.0 million
Key Personnel: Chairman, CEO: William H. Gates III. EVP, COO: Robert J. Herbold. EVP Human Resources: Chris Williams.

Software giant Microsoft sells more than 70 different software products to the consumer and business market. It is the largest independent software company in the world, and its leader, Bill Gates, is regularly in the news. The company is involved in numerous joint ventures has taken steps to position itself as the number 2 Internet service company, behind AOL. Sales and work force are up.
Other Locations: The company does marketing and support in 47 countries.

---

❶ TELECOMMUNICATIONS SERVICES

COLORADO

QWEST COMMUNICATIONS INTERNATIONAL INC.

700 Qwest Tower, 555 17th St. Denver, CO 80202; 303-992-1400
http://www.qwest.net
Employees: 8,700
Sales: $2,242.7 million
Key Personnel: President, COO: Afshin Mohebbi. EVP: Scott A. Baxter. Human Resources Manager: Thomas J. Matthews.

Concentrating on small- to midsized markets has been the foundation of Qwest (formerly USLD)'s success. The company operates over 14,000 miles of fiber-optic network in the US and Mexico. Qwest offers local, long distance, Internet and multimedia services. It agreed to merge with Baby Bell US WEST. Sales and work force are both currently on the increase.

U S WEST, INC.

1801 California St., Ste. 5200, Denver, CO 80202; 800-879-4357
http://www.uswest.com
Employees: 54,483

Revenues: $12,378.0 million
Key Personnel:. President, CEO, U S WEST: Solomon D. Trujillo. EVP, Retail Markets: Betsy J. Bernard. Human Resources Director: Mark D. Roellig.

U S WEST provides local phone service to more than 25 million customers in 14 western and midwestern states. The company is upgrading its telephone network and pursuing new businesses, such as wireless personal communication and long distance telephone systems. The compnay was one of two separately traded units of the parent company, US West Inc. which in 1998 split off the cable TV provider US West Media Group. Assets are up, but work force is down.
Other Locations: The company has operations in Europe, Japan, and the United States.

GEORGIA

BELLSOUTH CORPORATION

1155 Peachtree St. NE, Atlanta, GA 30309-3610; 404-249-2000
http://www.bellsouth.com
Employees: 88,400
Revenues: $23,123.0 million
Key Personnel: Chairman, President, CEO: F. Duane Ackerman. EVP, CFO: Ronald M. Dykes. Human Resources Director: Richard D. Sibbernsen.

Wireless communications is a top priority for BellSouth. The company is among the largest U.S. providers of cellular and paging services. It also offers an array of personal communications services, such as database products and electronic mail. It has developed partnerships with companies such as Microsoft and Lotus. It is looking to expand sales to Central and South America. Sales and work force are increasing.
Other Locations: The company has operations in nine southern states.

PREMIERE TECHNOLOGIES, INC ★★

3399 Peachtree Rd., NE, Suite 600, Atlanta, GA 30326; 404-262-8400
http://www.premierecomm.com
Employees: 2,301
Sales: $444.8 million
Key Personnel:: Chairman, CEO: Boland T. Jones. President, COO: Jeffrey A. Allred. Human Resources Manager:

James B. Cichanski.

Premier Technologies offers integrated suites of information and telecommunications services, including long-distance, voice mail, news, weather, conference calling and so forth It delivers its services through its network management system (NMS). Its 1998 acquisition of Xpedite Systems increased its size tenfold. Sales and work force are on the rise.

ILLINOIS

AMERITECH CORPORATION

30 S. Wacker Dr., Chicago, IL 60606; 312-750-5000

http://www.ameritech.com
Employees: 70,525
Revenues: $17,154.0 million
Key Personnel: Chairman, President, CEO: Richard C. Notebaert. EVP Corporate Strategy and Business Development: W. Patrick Campbell. SVP Human Resources: W. M. Oliver.

Ameritech, which Baby Bell SBC is buying, provides local telephone and cellular telecommunications services to the Great Lakes region and several foreign countries, including New Zealand and Norway. It has expanded into interactive services through several joint ventures with companies such as BellSouth and Disney. Sales and work force are steady.

TELEPHONE AND DATA SYSTEMS, INC. ★★

30 N. LaSalle St., Suite 4000, Chicago, IL 60602; 312-630-1900

http://www.teldta.com
Employees: 9,907
Revenues: $1,805.7 million
Key Personnel: President, CEO: Leroy T. ("Ted") Carlson, Jr. President, TDS Telecommunications Corp.: James Barr III Human Resources Manager: C. Theodore Herbert.

One of the nation's largest cellular phone companies, Telephone and Data Systems is a holding company that has prospered by purchasing many smaller telecommunications companies. Among its subsidiaries is TDS Telecommunications, which owns more than 90 phone companies, and United States Cellular, which has more than 290,000 subscribers. Other

subsidiaries provide computing services and custom printing. Sales and work force are rising.

KANSAS

SPRINT CORPORATION ★★

2330 Shawnee Mission Pkwy., Westwood, KS 66205; 913-624-3000

http://www.sprint.com
Employees: 64,900
Revenues: $16,016.9 million
Key Personnel: Chairman, CEO: William T. Esrey. President, COO: Ronald T. LeMay. Human Resources Director: I. Benjamin Watson.

Long distance services is now just one of several markets for Sprint. The company is rapidly expanding into cable television, through partnerships with companies such as Cox Communications and Comcast, and wireless personal communications. It is also in the process of creating an international telecommunications system in a joint venture with Deutsche Telekom and France Telecom. Sales and work force are growing.

Other Locations: The company has facilities in 19 states.

LOUISIANA

CENTURYTEL, INC.

100 Century Park Dr., Monroe, LA 71203; 318-388-9000

http://www.centurytel.com
Employees: 5,800
Sales: $1,499.3 million
Key Personnel: VC, President, CEO: Glen F. Post III. President, Telecommunications Services: W. Bruce Hanks. Human Resources Manager: Ivan Hughes.

One of the largest local telephone companies in the United States, Century Telephone Enterprises has over 2 million subscribers. The company, which serves customers in 21 states, offers voice mail, paging, and video conferencing, in addition to land-based and cellular telephone services. It is currently upgrading its network to fiber-optic cables and digital switches. Sales and work force are growing.

Other Locations: The company has operations in 21 states.

MASSACHUSETTS

ISI SYSTEMS, INC. ★★

2 Tech Dr., Andover, MA 01810; 508-682-5500
Employees: 5,351
Sales: $3,388.9 million
Key Personnel: President, CEO: Paul Lamontagne. VP Finance and Operations: Claude Seguin. Director of Human Resources: Brigitte Bourque.

ISI Systems is a U.S. subsidiary of the Canadian company Teleglobe, one of the largest telecommunications companies in the world. In the United States, ISI sells insurance services. Teleglobe, which hed a monopoly on Canadian international telecommunications until 1997, recently began working together with TRW to construct an international wireless telephone network. Sales and work force are growing.
Other Locations: Worldwide HQ: Teleglobe, Inc., 1000 de la Gauchetiere St. W., Montreal, Quebec H3B 4X5, Canada; phone: 514-868-8124.

MISSISSIPPI

MCI WORLDCOM, INC. ★★

515 E. Amite St., Jackson, MS 39201-2702; 601-360-8600
http://www.wcom.com
Employees: 77,000
Revenues: $17,678.0 million
Key Personnel: President, CEO: Bernard J. Ebbers. CFO: Scott Sullivan. VP Human Resources and Administration: Dennis Sickle.

Originally known as Long Distance Discount Services, or LDDS, WorldCom has been rapidly buying up competing long-distance providers. In 1998 it acquired the number two long-distance carrier in the US, MCI. The company is now the second largest long-distance provider in the United States behind AT&T. It supplies service nationwide and to more than 200 foreign countries. Sales and work force are up.

NEW YORK

AT&T CORPORATION

32 Ave. of the Americas, New York, NY 10013-2412; 212-387-5400
http://www.att.com
Employees: 107,800
Revenues: $53,223.0 million
Key Personnel: President: John D. Zeglis. EVP: James W. Cicconi. Human Resources Manager: Harold W. Burlingame.

Although it no longer holds a virtual monopoly on U.S. telephone service, AT&T is still the number one long-distance carrier. It faces increased competition and as a response has restructured, focusing on its communications services. These include wireless phone service, Internet access, cable TV service and international telephone service. After cutting about 40,000 jobs in 1996, their work force has stabilized, and sales are stable.

BT NORTH AMERICA, INC.

40 E. 52nd St., New York, NY 10022; 212-418-7800
http://www.bt.com
Employees: 124,700
Sales: $27,321.5 million
Key Personnel: Chief of Service Operations: Nick Williams. CFO: Martin Traill. Director of Human Resources: Dave Brown.

BT North America is a U.S. subsidiary of British Telecommunications, the largest company in the United Kingdom. BT's activities in the United States have represented the company's move toward providing worldwide service, inspired by increased competition in the British telecommunications market. Sales are up, but work force is down.
Other Locations: Worldwide HQ: British Telecommunications PLC, BT Centre, 81 Newgate St., London, EC1A 7AJ, United Kingdom; phone: +44-71-356-4008.

BELL ATLANTIC CORPORATION

1095 Ave. of the Americas, New York, NY 10036; 212-395-2121
http://www.bellatlantic.com
Employees: 140,000
Revenues: $31,565.9 million
Key Personnel: Chairman, CEO: Ivan G. Seidenberg. President, COO: James G. Cullen. EVP Human Resources: Donald J. Sacco.

When Bell Atlantic purchased NYNEX

in 1997 it created the second largest telecommunications in the country. The company provides local telephone service to customers in 13 eastern states. It also offers cellular, wireless, Internet access, and other services. Sales and work force are rising.

Other Locations: The company has facilities in the Northeast and abroad in Asia and Europe.

OHIO

CINCINNATI BELL, INC.

201 E. Fourth St., Cincinnati, OH 45202; 513-397-9900
http://www.cinbellinc.com
Employees: 3,500
Revenues: $885.1 million
Key Personnel: President, CEO: Richard G. Ellenberger. EVP: Mary E. McCann. SVP, Human Resources: Thomas J. Hattersley.

Cincinnati Bell is a holding company for a variety of telecommunications, data processing, and marketing operations. Its largest subsidiary is Cincinnati Bell Telephone, which provides telecommunications services in Ohio and Kentucky. It has separated from its other subsidiaries creating Convergys, a combination of Cincinnati Bell Information Systems and MATRIXX Marketing. Sales and work force are down.

TENNESSEE

NORTHERN TELECOM INC.

200 Athens Way, Nashville, TN 37228-7388; 615-734-4000
http://www.nortel.com
Employees: 22,500
Sales: $15,449 million
Key Personnel: President, COO: John Roth. CFO: Jerry Vaughn.

Northern Telecom Inc. is a U.S. subsidiary of Northern Telecom Limited, which is the largest telecommunications company in Canada. Northern is among the world's largest manufacturers of telecommunications equipment in the world, involved in a wide range of activities including cable television and multimedia in both the United States and Canada. The company's sales and work force are both on the decrease.

Other Locations: Worldwide HQ: BCE, Inc., 1000, rue de La Gauchetiere Quest, Bureau 3700, Montreal, H3B 4Y7 Quebec, Canada; phone: 514-397-7000.

TEXAS

GTE CORPORATION ★

1255 Corporate Dr., Irving, TX 75038; 972-507-5000
http://www.gte.com
Employees: 120,000
Revenues: $25,473.0 million
Key Personnel: VC, President, International: Michael T. Masin. President: Kent B. Foster. Human Resources Manager: J. Randall MacDonald.

Among the largest telecommunications companies in the world, GTE provides telephone services to about 23 million customers in 28 states in the domestic market. The company also has extensive holdings overseas, such as in China, where it is developing a new network for telecommunications. It has numerous projects in the works in the United States aimed at marketing personal communications services. Sales and work force are rising.

Other Locations: The company has operations in Argentina, Canada, China, the Dominican Republic, the United States, and Venezuela.

SBC COMMUNICATIONS, INC. ★★

175 E. Houston, San Antonio, TX 78205-2233; 210-821-4105
http://www.sbc.com
Employees: 129,850
Revenues: $28,777.0 million
Key Personnel: Chairman, CEO: Edward E. Whitacre Jr. SEVP: James D. Ellis. VP Human Resources: Karen E. Jennings.

Expansion into nontraditional markets is the focus of SBC Communications' strategy. The company, formerly known as Southwestern Bell, has been enlarging its market geographically and through the introduction of new services. It now serves 5.5 million people in 78 markets, including seven of the top 10 metropolitan areas. Sales and work force are up.

Other Locations: The company has facilities in Arkansas, Kansas, Missouri, Oklahoma, and Texas.

❶ TEXTILES

GEORGIA

MOHAWK INDUSTRIES, INC. ★★

160 S. Industrial Blvd., Calhoun, GA
30701; 706-629-7721
http://www.mohawkind.com
Employees: 18,200
Revenues: $ 2,639.2 million
Key Personnel: Chairman, CEO: David
L. Kolb. President, COO: Jeffrey S. Lor-
berbaum. Director of Human Resources:
Jerry Melton.

Among the largest rug manufacturers in
the world, Mohawk Industries finds its
success in a broad approach in a variety
of markets. The company makes many
types of carpets and rugs under brands
such as Karastan, Aladdin, and Alexander Smith. It is currently emphasizing
area rugs, a small but expanding sector of
its business. Sales and work force are
both currently on the increase at Mohawk
Industries.
Other Locations: The company has facilities in Georgia, North Carolina, and
South Carolina.

SHAW INDUSTRIES, INC.

616 E. Walnut Ave., Dalton, GA 30720;
706-278-3812
http://www.shawinds.com
Employees: 30,300
Sales: $3,542.2 million
Key Personnel: Chairman, CEO: Robert
E. Shaw. EVP, CFO: Kenneth G. Jack-
son. Human Resources Manager: Mike
Roberts.

Shaw Industries is the world's number
one carpet manufacturer and the number
one carpet retailer in the United States,
contolling 34% of the market. The company sells about 2,500 styles of woven
and tufted carpet to nearly 45,000 distributors, and operates about 350 stores
under the Shaw, CarpetSmart and Car-
petland USA names. Sales and employees are steady.

NORTH CAROLINA

BURLINGTON INDUSTRIES, INC. ★★

3330 W. Friendly Ave., Greensboro, NC
27410; 336-379-2000
http://www.burlington-ind.com
Employees: 18,900
Sales: $2,010.4 million
Key Personnel: Chairman, CEO: George
W. Henderson III. VC: Abraham B.
Stenberg. VP Human Resources and
Public Relations: James M. Guin.

Apparel products are the mainstay of
Burlington Industries. The company is
the largest manufacturer of specialty
denim in the United States. It also makes
a variety of other products, including
synthetic yarns, carpeting, blinds, and
upholstery. The company recently went
through extensive restructuring to improve production and product development durations. Sales and work force are
down slightly.
Other Locations: The company has operations in Mexico and the United States.

SOUTH CAROLINA

MILLIKEN & COMPANY, INC

920 Milliken Rd., Spartanburg, SC
29303-9301; 864-573-2020
http://www.milliken.com
Employees: 16,000
Est. Sales: $3,200 million
Key Personnel: President, COO: Tho-
mas J. Malone. Director of Marketing:
Kay Shannon. VP Human Resources:
Tommy Hodge.

Milliken makes use of the latest in textile
technology. The company is the biggest
privately held U.S. textile manufacturer.
Its products are used for numerous applications, including uniforms, swimsuits,
tires, and tablecloths. The company is
owned by the Milliken family, which is
strongly antiunion and supportive of
trade practices that hinder imports. Sales
and work force are stable.
Other Locations: The company has facilities in Georgia, North Carolina, and
South Carolina and in Europe.

SPRINGS INDUSTRIES, INC.

205 N. White St., P.O. Box 70, Fort Mill,
SC 29715; 803-547-1500
http://www.springs.com
Employees: 17,500
Revenues: $ 2,180.5 million
Key Personnel: Chairman, President,
CEO: Crandall C. Bowles. EVP, CFO:
Jeffrey A. Atkins. SVP Human Re-
sources: Gracie P. Coleman.

Springs Industries is among the biggest specialty fabric and home furnishings makers in the United States. Along with unusual fabrics, such as Ultrasuade, the company also makes sheets, pillowcases, and many other products. Sales and work force are decreasing.
Other Locations: The company has manufacturing facilities in eight states and in Asia, Canada, and Mexico.

❶ TOBACCO PRODUCTS

KENTUCKY

BROWN & WILLIAMSON TOBACCO CORP.
401 S. Fourth Ave., Suite 200, Louisville, KY 40202; 502-568-7000
http://www.bw.com
Employees: NA
Sales: $ 4,543.0 million
Key Personnel: Chairman, CEO: Nick G. Brookes. EVP, CFO: Carl Schoenbachler. VP Human Resources: Henry Frick.
Brown & Williamson is a subsidiary of B.A.T. Industries, one of the largest tobacco conglomerates in the world. It sells the brands Carlton, Barclay, Benson & Hedges, and Lucky Strike. The company owns subsidiaries in insurance and financial services and restaurants. Its 1994 purchase of American Tobacco was quickly followed by drastic staffing cuts. Sales and work force are steady.
Other Locations: Worldwide HQ: B.A.T Industries PLC, Windsor House, 50 Victoria St., London, SW1H 0NL, United Kingdom; phone: +44-(01)71-222-7979.

NEW YORK

PHILIP MORRIS COMPANIES, INC.
120 Park Ave., New York, NY 10017; 917-663-5000
http://www.irin.com
Employees: 144,000
Revenues: $74,391.0million
Key Personnel: Chairman, CEO: Geoffrey C. Bible. COO: William H. Webb. SVP Human Resources and Administration: Timothy A. Sompolski.
Long known for its tobacco interests, Philip Morris Companies is big in food and beer as well. The company owns food maker Kraft Foods, one of the largest food companies in the U.S., and Miller Brewing, the second largest beer maker. Some of its brands are Marlboro and Virginia Slims cigarettes; Miller and Lowenbrau beer; and Jell-O, Entenmann, Maxwell House, and Oscar Mayer foods. The company is streamlining its operations to speed growth. Its sales are rising, but its work force is shrinking.

VIRGINIA

UNIVERSAL CORPORATION
1501 N. Hamilton St., Richmond, VA 23230; 804-359-9311
Employees: 25,000
Revenues: $4,004.9 million
Key Personnel: President, COO: Allen B. King. VP, CFO: Hartwell H. Roper. Human Resources Director: Mike Oberschmidt Jr.
The largest tobacco buyer in the world, Universal has had some ups and downs recently because of decreases in demand and excesses in supply. The company's primary customers are cigarette retailers, such as Philip Morris. The company also has operations in lumber and various agricultural products. It expects rising overseas demand for tobacco to translate into future sales increases. Sales and work force are down.

❶ TOYS

CALIFORNIA

MATTEL, INC. ★★
333 Continental Blvd., El Segundo, CA 90245-5012; 310-252-2000
http://www.mattel.com
Employees: 29,000
Revenues: $4,781.9 million
Key Personnel: Chairman, CEO: Jill E. Barad. President: Ned Mansour. SVP Human Resources and Administration: Alan Kaye.
From its beginning as a garage-based toy business, Mattel has grown to be one of the largest toy manufacturers in the world. Its famous Barbie dolls account for approximately a third of the company's sales. Its other primary brands are

Hot Wheels, Disney, and Fisher-Price. It recently purchased The Pleasant Company, which manufactures American Girl dolls. Sales and work force are up.
Other Locations: The company conducts manufacturing operations in China, Indonesia, Italy, Malaysia, and Mexico.

RHODE ISLAND

HASBRO, INC.
1027 Newport Ave., Pawtucket, RI 02861; 401-431-8697
http://www.hasbro.com
Employees: 10,000
Revenues: $3,304.5 million
Key Personnel: Chairman, President, CEO: Alan G. Hassenfeld. VC: Harold P. Gordon. Human Resources Manager: Bob Carniaux.
Among the top toy makers in the world, Hasbro has been fighting to retain its market share. It now has exclusive rights to the Star Wars trilogy action figures. The company has entered the elelectronic media with CD-ROM versions of such board games as Monopoly and Frogger. It has also sought to reduce toy development time from a year to six months. Among its toy brands are Playskool, Kid Dimension, and Parker Brothers. Among its products are Play-Doh and G. I. Joe. Sales are up, but work force is down.
Other Locations: The company has manufacturing facilities in the United States and 25 other countries.

❶ TRANSPORTATION EQUIPMENT

ILLINOIS

BRUNSWICK CORPORATION ★
One N. Field Ct., Lake Forest, IL 60045-4811; 847-735-4700
http://www.brunswickcorp.com
Employees: 25,500
Revenues: $3,945.2 million
Key Personnel: Chairman, CEO: Peter N. Larson. EVP, CFO: Peter B. Hamilton. Human Resources Director: B. Russell Lockridge.
The world's largest manufacturer of pleasure boats and equipment, Brunswick also makes a wide variety of other equipment destined for the leisure market. Approximately 75 percent of its in-

come stems from boating equipment. The company is also well-known for many other products, including its bowling equipment, treadmills, coolers and bicycles. Sales are up and work force is steady.
Other Locations: The company has 35 factories in the United States and five in other countries.

OUTBOARD MARINE CORPORATION ★★
100 Sea Horse Dr., Waukegan, IL 60085; 847-689-6200
http://www.omc-online.com
Employees: 6,400
Revenues: $1,025.7 million
Key Personnel: President, CEO: David D. Jones Jr. VC: Richard Katz. Human Resources Manager: Kimberly K. Bors.
The pioneer of outboard boat motors, Outboard Marine is also the largest manufacturer of the popular boat propulsion machine. The company is among the largest boat makers as well. It introduced a new technology that uses less fuel. During a tug of war between Detroit Diesel and Greenmarine Holding, the latter won control of OMC. Its major brands include Evinrude, Johnson, Grumman, and Chris-Craft. Sales and work force are down.
Other Locations: The company has 16 plants in the United States and 10 abroad.

MINNESOTA

ARCTIC CAT, INC. ★★
600 Brooks Ave. S., Thief River Falls, MN 56701; 218-681-8558
http://www.arctic-cat.com
Employees: 1,685
Sales: $480.3 million
Key Personnel: President, CEO: Christophere A. Twomey. VP Manufacturing: Ronald G. Ray. Human Resources Manager: Terry Blount.
Arctic Cat (formerly known as Arctco) manufactures and sells snowmobiles, all-terain vehicles and personal watercraft. The company's Arctic Cat snowmobiles account for approximately two-thirds of its income. However, Tigershark, its recently introduced personal watercraft, is rapidly catching up. The company also sells replacement parts and accessories for its vehicles. Sales and work force are down.

TEXAS

TRINITY INDUSTRIES, INC. ★

2525 Stemmons Fwy., Dallas, TX
75207-2401; 214-631-4420
Employees: 17,450
Sales: $2,926.9 million
Key Personnel: President, COO: Timothy R. Wallace. EVP: John L. Adams. Human Resources Director: Judy Arrington.

Trinity Industries is a leading manufacturer of metal products, with operations in transportation, construction products and industrial products. The company makes railroad tanks, gondola cars, airport conveyor belts, and even gas storage tanks. The company is expanding its market. Sales and work force are up.

❶ TRAVEL/HOSPITALITY

CALIFORNIA

HILTON HOTELS CORPORATION

9336 Civic Ctr. Dr., Beverly Hills, CA
90210; 310-278-4321
http://www.hilton.com
Employees: 38,000
Revenues: $1,769.0 million
Key Personnel: President, CEO: Stephen F. Bollenback. EVP: Matthew J. Hart. Human Resources Manager: Bethany Ellis.

Among the biggest innkeepers in the world, Hilton Hotels also operates a large gambling operation. It operates five hotel casinos in Nevada, among other interests. Hilton Hotels merged with Bally Entertainment Corporation in late 1996, becoming the largest hotel and gambling company in America. However, it plans to split into two companies; one handling hotel operations, the other operating gaming facilities. Sales and work force are down significantly.
Other Locations: The company owns, manages, or franchises over 220 hotels in Australia, Belgium, Hong Kong, Ireland, Turkey, the United Kingdom, and the United States.

FLORIDA

CARNIVAL CORPORATION ★★

3655 NW 87th Ave., Miami, FL 33178-2428; 305-599-2600
http://www.carnivalcorp.com
Employees: 22,000
Sales: $3,009.3 million
Key Personnel: Chairman, CEO: Micky Arison. VC, COO: Howard S. Frank. SVP, CFO: Gerald R. Cahill. Human Resources Director: Susan Herrmann.

Carnival is the largest operator of overnight cruises in the world. The company appeals to two markets: Carnival Cruise Lines for the cost-conscious, and Windstar Cruises for the well-to-do. The company also provides tours of Alaska and Canada via buses, boats, and trains, among its other operations. Sales and work force are growing.

HILTON INTERNATIONAL CO. ★

901 Ponce de Leon Blvd., Suite 700,
Coral Gables, FL 33134; 305-444-3444
Employees: 46,702
Sales: $7,769.4 million
Key Personnel: CEO: David Michels. VP Finance: Brian G. Wallace. VP Human Resources: Brian Taker.

Hilton International is a subsidiary of Ladbroke Group, which is primarily a betting and gaming concern. Ladbroke Group also operates hotels and does retailing and property management. The company's subsidiary, Ladbroke Racing, is the world's biggest commercial off-track-betting business. Ladbroke Group runs 159 hotels outside the United States through Hilton International. Sales and work force are down.
Other Locations: Worldwide HQ: Ladbroke Group PLC, 10 Cavendish Pl., London, W1M 9DJ, United Kingdom; phone: +44-(01)71-323-5000.

GEORGIA

BASS HOTELS & RESORTS ★

3 Ravinia Dr., Suite 2900, Atlanta, GA
30346-2149; 770-604-2000
http://www.holiday-inn.com
Employees: 19,100
Sales: $1,026.7 million
Key Personnel: Chairman, CEO: Thomas R. Oliver. EVP: Andrew MacFarlane. SVP Human Resources: Cindy Durning.

Bass Hotels & Resorts owns Holiday Inn Worldwide, and is itself a subsidiary of Bass, the largest brewer in the U.K. Bass initiated a massive hotel expansion project that resulted in a total of 2,700 hotels with about 450,000 rooms worldwide. Its sales are down, but work force is growing.

Other Locations: Worldwide HQ: Bass PLC, 20 N. Audley St., London, W1Y 1WE, United Kingdom; phone: +44-(01)71-409-1919. The company has 1,925 hotels in over 90 countries and nearly 3,000 pubs in the United Kingdom.

ILLINOIS

HYATT CORPORATION ★
200 W. Madison St., Chicago, IL 60606; 312-750-1234
http://www.hyatt.com
Employees: 80,000
Est. Sales: $3,400 million
Key Personnel: President: Thomas V. Pritzker. SVP: Frank Borg. SVP Human Resources: Linda Olson.

Long recognized for its luxurious amenities, Hyatt Corporation is one of the nation's largest hotel operators with more than 110 full-service luxury hotels and resorts in North America and the Caribbean, plus 80 hotels overseas in 35 countries. It also manages casinos and a vacation ownership resort. Sales and work force are stable.

Other Locations: The company operates 110 hotels in North America and the Caribbean and 80 hotels abroad.

MARYLAND

HOST MARRIOTT CORPORATION ★
10400 Fernwood Rd., Bethesda, MD 20817; 301-380-9000
http://www.hostmarriott.com
Employees: 191
Revenues: $3,442.0 million
Key Personnel: President, CEO: Terence C. Golden. EVP, COO: Christopher J. Nassetta. Human Resources Director: Arezu Ingle.

Among the biggest hotel owners in the United States, Host Marriott was created when Marriott Corporation split in two in 1993. The other half of the split was Marriott International. Along with hotels, Host Marriott operates numerous airport and turnpike concessions in the United States and abroad. The company is spinning off its retirement properties and restructuring as a real estate investment trust (REIT). Sales are up and work force is down.

Other Locations: The company has operations in Australia, Barbados, Bermuda, Canada, New Zealand, and the United States.

MARRIOTT INTERNATIONAL, INC.
10400 Fernwood Rd., Bethesda, MD 20817; 301-380-3000
http://www.marriott.com
Employees: 133,000
Revenues: $7,968.0 million
Key Personnel: President, COO: William J. Shaw. EVP, CFO: Arne Sorenson. SVP Human Resources: Brendan M. Keegan.

Marriott International was formed in 1998 when Marriott International split its lodging opoerations from its food and facilities management services. The latter is run by Sodexho Marriott Services. Marriott International has extensive operations in hotel franchising and management worldwide, including 49 percent of Ritz-Carlton Hotel Company. Work force is up, but sales are down.

Other Locations: The company has operations in the United States and 22 other countries.

MINNESOTA

CARLSON COMPANIES, INC. ★★
Carlson Pkwy., Minneapolis, MN 55441; 612-540-5000
http://www.carlson.com
Employees: 147,000
Est. Sales: $7,800 million
Key Personnel: VC, President, CEO: Marilyn Carlson Nelson. EVP: Martyn R. Redgrave. Human Resources Manager: Terry M. Butorac.

One of the largest travel services companies in the United States, Carlson Companies also provides hospitality and marketing services. Operating jointly with Accor, Carlson Wagonlit Travel has over 4,000 offices worldwide. The company also owns Radisson Hotel, Country Inn, and T.G.I. Friday's restaurant, as well as provides motivational training. Sales and

work force are up.
Other Locations: The company has operations in 125 countries.

LAKES GAMING, INC.
130 Cheshire Ln., Minnetonka, MN 55305; 612-449-9092
http://www.lakesgaming.com
Employees: 30
Sales: $ 92.3 million
Key Personnel: President: Thomas J. Brosig. CFO: Timothy J. Cope. EVP, COO: Joseph Galvin.

Grand Casinos operates a number of gambling operations in Mississippi and Minnesota. Four of its operations are on Native American land. It recently opened Stratosphere, a Las Vegas casino that features the highest observation tower in the country. The company is being bought by Hilton Hotels. Sales and work force are down.

NEVADA
CIRCUS CIRCUS ENTERPRISES, INC.
2880 Las Vegas Blvd. S., Las Vegas, NV 89109; 702-734-0410
http://www.circuscircus.com
Employees: 20,200
Revenues: $1,354.3 million
Key Personnel: VC, EVP: William A. Richardson. President, Treasurer: Glenn W. Schaeffer. SVP Human Resources: Kit Turner.

Circus Circus Enterprises owns or operates casinos and hotels in three states -- Nevada, Illinois, and Mississippi -- making it one of the largest casino operators in the United States. The company is developing a mile-long site at the south end of the Las Vegas Strip with hotels, casinos and retail and entertainment facilities. Sales and work force remain steady.
Other Locations: The company has operations in Illinois and Nevada.

MIRAGE RESORTS, INC.
3400 Las Vegas Blvd. S., Las Vegas, NV 89109; 702-791-7111
http://www.mirageresorts.com
Employees: 29,850

Revenues: $1,523.7 million.
Key Personnel: Chairman, President, CEO: Stephen A. Wynn. SVP External Affairs: Thomas L. Sheer. Human Resources Manager: Arte Nathan.

Mirage Resorts operates casinos primarily in Las Vegas. Their properties include the tropically-themed Mirage, with its erupting volcano, pirate-themed Treasure Island casino and the Golden Nugget, an older, simpler casino located in downtown Las Vegas. The company is spending more than $1 billion on its Bellagio property, which promises to be the most luxurious casino property in Las Vegas.

NEW JERSEY
PRIME HOSPITALITY CORPORATION ★★
700 Rte. 46 E, Fairfield, NJ 07004; 973-882-1010
Employees: 6,800
Sales: $469.4 million
Key Personnel: Chairman, President, CEO: A. F. Petrocelli. EVP: Paul H. Hower. SVP Human Resources: David Johnson.

Prime Hospitality (formerly Hospitality Franchise Systems) owns and operates or manages about 145 hotels in the U.S., under the names of Marriott, Radisson, Sheraton, Holiday Inn and Ramada. The company locates its properties in secondary markets, mostly in the southern and central United States. Sales are up significantly and work force is growing.

NEW YORK
ACCOR NORTH AMERICA CORP. ★★
245 Park Ave. South, New York, NY 10167; 212-949-5700
Employees: 126,908
Sales: $6,566.3 million
Key Personnel: President, CEO, Accor North America: John Lehodey. VP Finance (CFO), Accor North America: Dan Berry. Director of Human Resources, Novotel (U.S.): Dale Weilgus.

Accor is a French travel and hospitality conglomerate with a worldwide reach. The company owns hotels, travel agencies, and catering services in Europe, North America, and Asia. In the United States, the company owns Motel 6, Regal Inns, and Carlson Companies, among others. It is aggressively expanding in Asia. Sales and work force are up.

Other Locations: Worldwide HQ: Accor SA, 2, rue de la Mare-Neuve, Evry Cedex, France; phone: +33-1-60-87-43-20.

STARWOOD HOTELS & RESORTS WORLDWIDE, INC. ★★

777 Westchester Ave., White Plains, NY 10604; 914-640-8100

http://www.starwoodlodging.com

Employees: 130,000

Revenues: $4,700.0 million

Key Personnel: Chairman, CEO: Barry S. Sternlicht. EVP Acquisition and Development: Steven R. Goldman. Human Resources Director: Susan R. Bolger.

Starwood Hotels and Resorts is the world's largest lodging company, with more than 650 hotels, resorts, and casinos in over 70 countries. One of the reasons it's so big is that in 1998 it bought the Westin Hotel chain and ITT Corp., which owns the Sheraton hotels and Caesar's Palace. Sales and work force are on the rise.

CANADIAN PACIFIC LIMITED

805 Third Ave., New York, NY 10022; 212-715-7000

http://www.princesshotels.com

Employees: 39,804

Sales: $6,557.5 million

Key Personnel: Chairman, President, CEO: David P. O'Brien. EVP: William R. Fatt. VP Personnel: Roseann Mac-Donald.

Canadian Pacific is a highly diversified holding company. It has 640 subsidiaries in 48 countries. The majority of its profits come from its African operations, which include commercial food production and motor-vehicle distribution. It plans to sell off many of its assets to concentrate on hotels, agriculture, and mining. Sales and work force have decreased.

Other Locations: Worldwide HQ: 1800 Bankers Hall East, 855 2nd St. SW, Calgary, Alberta T2P 4Z5, Canada.

TRUMP ORGANIZATION

725 Fifth Ave., New York, NY 10022-2519; 212-832-2000

Employees: 22,000

Sales: $6,900 million

Key Personnel: Chairman: Donald J. Trump. VP Finance: John Burke. VP Human Resources: Norma Foerderer.

Operating primarily in the hospitality industry, the Trump Organization is the owner of four Atlantic City casinos and real estate in New York City. The company has overcome its financial difficulties suffered in the early 1990s. Its sales and work force are on the rise.

T E N N E S S E E

PROMUS HOTEL CORPORATION. ★★

755 Crossover Ln., Memphis, TN 38117; 901-374-5000

http://www.promus.com

Employees: 40,000

Sales: $1,061.8 million

Key Personnel: Chairman, CEO: Norman P. Blake Jr. EVP, CFO: Dan L. Hale. EVP Human Resources: Peter Leddy.

Promus Hotel is a leading lodging company with its more than 1,300 hotels managed or owned in North America. Among them are Embassy Suites, Hampton Inns, Doubletree Hotels and Guest Suites, and Homewood Suites. The company also operates time-share vacation resorts in California, Florida, and Hawaii. Sales and work force are steady.

❶ UTILITIES

A R I Z O N A

PINNACLE WEST CAPITAL CORPORATION

400 E. Van Buren St., Suite 700, Phoenix, AZ 85004; 602-379-2500

http://www.pinnaclewest.com

Employees: 7,333

Revenues: $2,130.6 million

Key Personnel: Chairman, President, and CEO: Richard Snell. President, CEO, Arizona Public Service: William J. Post. Human Resources Manager: Pat Jones.

Pinnacle West Capital is a holding company whose primary asset is Arizona Public Service, an electric utility serving approximately 767,000 people in 11 Arizona counties. The power company generates electricity with coal, gas, oil, and nuclear fuel. Pinnacle also owns SunCor, a real estate development enterprise. The company hopes to develop ties with Mexico, a promising market for electricity. While sales are up, work force is stable.

CALIFORNIA

PACIFIC GAS AND ELECTRIC COMPANY
One Market, Spear Tower, Suite 2400, San Francisco, CA 94105; 415-973-7000
http://www.pgecorp.com
Employees: 23,300
Revenues: $19,942.0 million
Key Personnel: President, COO: Robert D. Glynn, Jr. SVP, Corporate Development: Tony F. DiStefano. SVP Corporate Services (Human Resources): G. Brent Stanley.
With a history dating back to the 1850s, Pacific Gas and Electric is the oldest gas and electric utility in the West, and the number two public utility in the country, behind Duke Power. It has approximately 3.7 million gas subscribers and 4.5 million electric subscribers, making it the biggest U.S. public gas and electric utility. The company is involved in several generation facility development projects in partnership with Bechtel. Sales are up while work force is stable.

EDISON INTERNATIONAL★
2244 Walnut Grove Ave., Rosemead, CA 91770; 626-302-1212
http://www.edison.com
Employees: 13,177
Sales: $10,208.0 million
Key Personnel: Chairman, CEO: John E. Bryson. EVP: Alan J. Fohrer. SVP Public Affairs: Robert G. Foster.
Edison International (formerly SCECorp) is involved in a variety of real estate and construction projects, but its main income is from Southern California Edison, one of the top U.S. electric utilities. The company has over 11 million electric subscribers in southern and central California. Among the company's other operations is Mission Energy, a developer of independent energy projects. Sales and work force are increasing.

FLORIDA

FPL GROUP, INC.
700 Universe Blvd., Juno Beach, FL 33408; 561-694-4000
http://www.fplgroup.com
Employees: 10,375
Revenues: $6,661.0 million
Key Personnel: Chairman, President, CEO: James L. Broadhead. President, FP&L: Paul J. Evanson. Human Resources Director: Lawrence J. Kelleher.
Although FPL Group (for Florida Power & Light) is one of the biggest publicly owned power utilities in the United States, power is not the company's only business. The company supplies power to over 3.7 million customers in Florida—about half the state. But it is also involved in citrus farming, management consulting, and independent energy projects. Sales and work force are increasing.

GEORGIA

AGL RESOURCES INC
303 Peachtree St. NE, One Peachtree Ctr., Atlanta, GA 30308; 404-584-9470
http://www.aglr.com
Employees: 2,791
Revenues: $1,338.6 million
Key Personnel: Chairman, President, CEO: Walter M. Higgins. SVP: J. Michael Riley. Human Resources Director: James W. Connally.
AGL Resources is a holding company for Atlanta Gas Light. Atlanta Gas Light supplies natural gas to customers in the metropolitan Atlanta and Chattanooga, Tenn. areas. Nearly half of the company's business comes from its Atlanta customers. The company also supplies liquefied petroleum gas to customers in Georgia and Alabama. It is currently restructuring its operations and is decreasing staff through retirement and attrition. Sales is up while work force is down.

SOUTHERN COMPANY ★★
270 Peachtree St. NW, Atlanta, GA 30303; 404-506-5000
http://www.southernco.com
Employees: 31,848
Revenues: $11,403.0 million
Key Personnel: President, CEO: S.

Marce Fuller. EVP; President, CEO, Southern Co. Services: Paul J. DeNicola. Human Resources Manager: Christopher C. Womack

Southern Company owns five utilities serving the needs of over 3.8 million people in the Southeast: Alabama Power, Georgia Power, Gulf Power, Mississippi Power, and Savannah Electric and Power Companies, all owned by Southern. The company is expanding its services to include wireless communications and is expanding the number of power plants abroad. It recently acquired 80 percent of Consolidated Electric Power Asia Ltd., a major power producer in Asia. While sales are up, work force is down.

Other Locations: The company has facilities in Alabama, Florida, Georgia, and Mississippi and in the Caribbean, South America, and the United Kingdom.

HAWAII

HAWAIIAN ELECTRIC INDUSTRIES, INC.
900 Richards St., Honolulu, HI 96813; 808-543-5662
http://www.hei.com
Employees: 3,722
Revenues: $1,485.2 million
Key Personnel: President: Robert F. Clarke. CFO: Robert F. Mougeot. Human Resources Director: Faye Maeda.

Hawaiian Electric Industries is a holding company for a variety of subsidiaries. Its largest operation is Hawaiian Electric Corporation, which provides electric service for most of the Hawaiian Islands. The company also owns numerous other subsidiaries involved in a wide variety of enterprises, including real estate development, banking, and shipping. Sales and work force are steady.

IDAHO

IDACORP, INC.
1221 W. Idaho St., Boise, ID 83702-5627; 208-388-2200
http://www.idahopower.com
Employees: 1,669
Revenues: $1,122.0 million
Key Personnel: Chairman, CEO: Joseph W. Marshall. President, COO: Jan B. Packwood. VP, CFO: J. LaMont Keen.

One of the few investor-owned public utilities in the United States that is primarily based in hydroelectric power sources, Idaho Power provides electricity to an area of approximately 20,000 square miles in southern Idaho, eastern Oregon, and northern Nevada. The company operates 17 hydroelectric plants and is part-owner of three coal-fired generating plants. Sales are up, but the work force is steady.

ILLINOIS

ILLINOVA CORPORATION
500 S. 27th St., Decatur, IL 62525; 217-424-6600
http://www.illinova.com
Employees: 3,965
Revenues: $2,430.6 million
Key Personnel: Chairman, President, CEO: Charles E. Bayless. SVP: George W. Miraben. SVP: Alec G. Dreyer.

Illinova Corporation is a holding company whose principal subsidiary is Illinois Power Company, which supplies electricity and natural gas for the state of Illinois. The company has two other subsidiaries. Illinova Generating Company invests in energy-related projects worldwide, and Illinova Power Marketing markets energy and energy-related services. Revenues are down and work force is up.

UNICOM CORPORATION
10 S. Dearborn St., 37th Floor, Chicago, IL 60690-3005; 312-394-7399
http://www.ceco.com
Employees: 15,962
Revenues: $7,151.3 million
Key Personnel: Chairman, President, CEO: John W. Rowe. SVP: John C. Bukovski. Director of Human Resources: Frank Wturrigao.

One of the largest public utilities in the country, Unicom, a holding company created in 1994, owns Commonwealth Edison. The holding company was created to enhance business opportunities for ComEd in the more competitive deregulated power industry. The company supplies approximately 70 percent of Illinois's population. Sales are up, but work force is down.

I O W A

MIDAMERICAN ENERGY HOLDINGS COMPANY

666 Grand Ave., Des Moines, IA 50303; 515-252-6400
http://www.midamerican.com
Employees: 3,703
Revenues: $2,555.2 million
Key Personnel: Chairman, CEO: David L. Sokol. SVP, CFO: Alan L. Wells. Human Resources Manager: Keith D. Hartje.
MidAmerican Energy was created through the 1995 merger of Iowa-Illinois Gas and Electric, and Midwest Resources. The new company provides service to 635,000 electricity and 600,000 gas customers in Illinois, Iowa, Nebraska, and South Dakota. The company is reducing its work force, mostly through retirement and attrition. Revenues are up.

L O U I S I A N A

CLECO CORPORATION ★

2030 Donahue Ferry Rd., Pineville, LA 71360-5226; 318-484-7400
http://www.cleco.com
Employees: 1,210
Assets: $515.2 million
Key Personnel: President, CEO: Gregory L. Nesbitt. VP: David M. Eppler. VP Employee and Support Services: Catherine C. Powell.
Cleco (formerly Central Louisiana Electric Company) supplies electricity to more than 240,000 customers in a 14,000-square-mile area of Louisiana. The company is full- or part-owner of four steam electric generators and a gas turbine with a total generating capacity of 1,693,000 kilowatts. The company uses coal and oil to fuel its steam generators. Sales are up, and work force is steady.

ENTERGY CORPORATION

639 Loyola Ave., New Orleans, LA 70113; 504-529-5262
http://www.entergy.com
Employees: 12,816
Revenues: $11,494.8 million
Key Personnel: President, COO: Wayne Leonard. VC: Jerry L. Maulden. Human Resources Director: Gary Clary.

With approximately 2.5 million customers, Entergy is among the top publicly owned utilities in the United States. It supplies power mainly to mid-southern states. About 30 percent of the company's energy comes from nuclear power. It is involved in a number of projects overseas in countries such as Australia, Brazil, and China. Sales is up while work force is down.
Other Locations: The company has facilities in Arkansas, Louisiana, Mississippi, and Texas.

M A I N E

CMP GROUP, INC. ★

83 Edison Dr., Augusta, ME 04336; 207-623-3521
http://www.cmpco.com
Employees: 1,607
Revenues: $950.3 million
Key Personnel: President, CEO: David T. Flanagan. EVP: Arthur W. Adelberg. VP Human Resources: Kathleen Case.
Central Maine Power is an investor-owned public utility operating throughout the state of Maine. The company's 880-megawatt nuclear generating plant was shut down for good in 1998 for safety reasons. The company has joined forces with New York State Electric & Gas to bring natural gas to the area. Recent changes in state law require the company to divest itself of its generating plants by the year 2000. Sales and work force are stable.

M I C H I G A N

DTE ENERGY COMPANY

2000 Second Ave., Detroit, MI 48226; 313-235-4000
http://www.dteenergy.com
Employees: 8,482
Sales: $4,221.0 million
Key Personnel: President, COO: Anthony F. Earley Jr. VP Business Ventures: Gerard M. Anderson. VP Human Resources: Sandra J. Miller.
DTE Energy is the holding compnay for Detroit Edison, a public utility supplying electricity to a 7,600-square-mile area in southeastern Michigan, about 13 percent of the state's land area. The company

produces electricity through fossil fuels, nuclear power, and purchased electricity. It intends to pursue alternative markets to offset income losses caused by rate decreases. Revenues and work force are up slightly.

MONTANA

THE MONTANA POWER CO. ★
40 E. Broadway, Butte, MT 59701-9989; 406-723-5421
http://www.mtpower.com
Employees: 2,906
Revenues: $1,253.7 million
Key Personnel: Chairman, CEO: Robert P. Gannon. CFO: Jerrold P. Pederson. Human Resources Manager: Pamela K. Merrell.
Montana Power is a diversified energy company. Its primary operations are conducted through its subsidiary, Entech, which operates coal, oil, and gas exploration and extraction. The company also provides electric service to 191 communities in Montana and natural gas to 109 of the state's communities. The company's Touch America unit has a fiber-optic network in the Northwest. Sales are up while the work force is stable.

NEW JERSEY

PUBLIC SERVICE ENTERPRISE GROUP, INC.
80 Park Plaza, P.O. Box 1171, Newark, NJ 07101; 973-430-7000
http://www.pseg.com
Employees: 10,126
Revenues: $5,931.0 million
Key Personnel: President, COO, PSE&G: E. James Ferland. VP, CFO: Robert C. Murray. VP Human Resources, PSE&G: Martin P. Mellet.
The controlling organization for a variety of operations, Public Service Enterprise Group derives most of its income from Public Service Electric & Gas, or PSE&G, the biggest gas and electric utility in New Jersey. The company also owns Enterprise Diversified Holdings, Inc. (EDHI), which is involved in several businesses, including commercial real estate. Sales and work force are down.

NEW YORK

CONSOLIDATED EDISON, INC.
4 Irving Pl., New York, NY 10003; 212-460-4600
http://www.conedison.com
Employees: 14,322
Revenues: $7,093.0 million
Key Personnel: Chairman, CEO: Eugene R. McGrath. President, COO: J. Michael Evans. SVP Human Resources: Richard P. Cowie.
Consolidated Edison is the holding company for Consolidated Edison of New York, which supplies gas and electricity for most of New York City. The company is among the largest publicly owned utilities of its type in the United States and serves over 8 million customers. Deregulation has increased competition and forced the company to cut costs. Sales are steady. Con Ed has been decreasing its work force for two decades.

NORTH CAROLINA

DUKE ENERGY CORPORATION ★
422 S. Church St., Charlotte, NC 28202-1904; 704-594-6200
http://www.duke-energy.com
Employees: 22,000
Revenues: $17,610.0 million
Key Personnel: President, COO: Paul M. Anderson. EVP: Ricahrd J. Osborne. VP Organization Effectiveness (Human Resources): Christopher C. Rolfe.
Duke Energy was formed by the merger of electric utility Duke Power Co. and gas pipeline operator PanEnergy Corp. Among the biggest U.S. publicly owned utilities, Duke Power supplies electricity to over 1.7 million people. The company generates power through fossil fuels, hydroelectric generation, and nuclear power. However, more than 60 percent of its electricity comes from nuclear power. Its territory includes a 20,000-square-mile section of North and South Carolina. Sales and work force are steady.

NORTH DAKOTA

MDU RESOURCES GROUP, INC. ★★
918 E. Divide Ave., Bismarck, ND 58506; 701-222-7900

http://www.mdures.com
Employees: 2,882
Assets: $896.6 million
Key Personnel: President, CEO: Martin A. White. EVP, COO: Douglas C. Kane. VP, Treasurer, CFO: Warren L. Robinson.

MDU Resources Group is a diversified natural resource company. The company's largest segment is Montana-Dakota Utilities, which provides electricity, natural gas, and propane to communities in North and South Dakota, Montana, and Wyoming. They serve 113,000 electricity consumers and 200,000 gas customers. The company is also involved in a variety of other activities, including coal mining and oil and gas exploration. Assets and work force are up.

OHIO

AMERICAN ELECTRIC POWER COMPANY

1 Riverside Plaza, Columbus, OH 43215; 614-223-1000
http://www.aep.com
Employees: 17,943
Revenues: $6,345.9 million
Key Personnel: Chairman, President, CEO: E. Linn Draper, Jr. Treasurer, EVP Administration, Chief Accounting Officer, AEP Service Corp.: Paul D. Addis. EVP Power Generation, AEP Service Corp.: James J. Markowsky.

With over 7 million subscribers, American Electric Power is among the biggest utilities in the United States owned by investors. Through its subsidiaries, the company runs nearly 40 generating units, which are gas-fired, hydroelectric, or nuclear. It recently provided home automation systems and interactive communications for 25,000 residential customers. Sales are up, and work force is steady.
Other Locations: The company provides power to regions of Indiana, Kentucky, Michigan, Ohio, Tennessee, Virginia, and West Virginia.

TENNESSEE

TENNESSEE VALLEY AUTHORITY ★★

400 W. Summit Hill Dr., Knoxville, TN 37902; 423-632-2101
http://www.tva.gov
Employees: 13,818
Sales: $6,729.0 million

Key Personnel: President, COO: O.J. Zeringue. EVP Financial Services: David N. Smith. EVP Human Resources: Wally Tanksley.

Originally set up by Congress, the Tennessee Valley Authority is owned by the U.S. government but supports itself through its operations. The company supplies electricity to 7 million subscribers in the South. It also conducts a variety of nonpower programs, such as flood control and agricultural development. Sales are up but work force is decreasing.
Other Locations: The company has facilities in all of Tennessee and in parts of six other states.

TEXAS

RELIANT ENERGY, INC.

1111 Louisiana, Houston, TX 77002; 713-207-3000
http://www.houind.com
Employees: 12,916
Revenues: $11,488.5 million
Key Personnel: Chairman: Don D. Jordan. EVP, CFO: Stephen W. Naeve. VP Human Resources: Susan D. Fabre.

Reliant Energy, Inc. (formerly Houston Industries) provides electricity to over 2.8 million subscribers in six states The company also has power projects in Latin America and India. Its subsidiary NorAm Energy, a natural gas utility, supplies natural gas to customers in Arkansas, Louisiana, Minnesota and Texas Sales are up and work force is steady.

TEXAS UTILITIES COMPANY ★★

1601 Bryan St., Dallas, TX 75201-3411; 214-812-4600
http://www.txu.com
Employees: 22,055
Revenues: $14,736.0 million
Key Personnel: President, COO: David W. Biegler. EVP: Michael J. McNally. Human Resources Director: Pitt Pittman.

Among the biggest electric utilities in the nation, Texas Utilities conducts business through several subsidiaries. It supplies electricity to approximately 5.7 million subscribers in the Dallas-Fort Worth metropolitan area through Texas Utilities Electric Company. Its other operations include coal mining, oil and gas extraction, and wireless communications. Sales and work force are up.

JOB OPPORTUNITIES
JOBS IN THE FEDERAL GOVERNMENT

THE AGENCIES AND BRANCHES of the federal government listed in this chapter represent those that offer the greatest number of government jobs in that field. Be sure to ask if a field for which you wish to apply is not shown.

Each agency listed not only has different employment criteria but also different hiring procedures. It is essential that you contact each department to get the precise guidelines for how to proceed in prospecting for a job. Also note that most of the offices presented here are in the Washington, DC. area. However, many of the units have employees located throughout the United States. Again, ask about possible other locations when you contact the agency.

Useful information may also be found elsewhere in this book. ➥**See "Job Hotlines," pp. 410-446.**

ADMINISTRATION FOR CHILDREN AND FAMILIES (ACF)

370 L'Enfant Promenade, SW, Washington, DC 20447
MANAGEMENT, PUBLIC AFFAIRS, SOCIAL SCIENCES
ACF is involved in administering programs for the welfare and betterment of families, various ethnic and special groups, and community service and public affairs agencies.

ADMINISTRATIVE OFFICE OF THE UNITED STATES COURTS (AOUSC)

Thurgood Marshall Federal Judiciary Bldg., 1 Columbus Circle, NE, Washington, DC 20544; 202-273-2777
BUSINESS, CRIMINAL JUSTICE, LAW, MATHEMATICS, SOCIAL SCIENCES, TECHNOLOGY
AOUSC oversees the administrative business of the U.S. court system.

ADVANCED RESEARCH PROJECTS AGENCY (ARPA)

3701 N. Fairfax Dr., Arlington, VA 22203
ELECTRONICS, ENGINEERING, SCIENCE, TECHNOLOGY
ARPA engages in research and development projects and creates prototype projects, all of which are essential to the Department of Defense.

AGENCY FOR INTERNATIONAL DEVELOPMENT (USAID)

Recruitment Division, 320 21st St., NW, Washington, DC 20523; 703-302-4101
ACCOUNTING, AGRICULTURE, BUSINESS, ECONOMICS, EDUCATION, HEALTH SERVICES, INTERNATIONAL AFFAIRS, NUTRITION, SOCIAL SCIENCES
USAID administers economic and humanitarian programs to people in developing and Third World countries.

AGRICULTURAL MARKETING SERVICE (AMS)

Dept. of Agriculture Div, Rm 1716 South Bldg., 14th St. and Independence Ave. SW, Washington, DC 20250; 202-720-6190
AGRICULTURE, BUSINESS, MARKETING, SCIENCE
AMS deals with the marketing of agricultural products. The agency handles market news, grading and inspection services for products, and commodity standards.

AGRICULTURAL RESEARCH SERVICE (ARS)

Personnel Division, Bldg. 003, BARC-W, Beltsville, MD 20705; 301-344-4456
Internet Listing:
http://www.arsgrin.gov:80/ars/afmvacancy.html
AGRICULTURE, AGRONOMY, ENGINEERING, SCIENCE

ARS researches the country's food and fiber supply and develops various technologies aimed at solving national agricultural problems.

ANIMAL AND PLANT HEALTH INSPECTION SERVICE (APHIS)

Field Servicing Office, Human Resources, Bulter Sq. W., 100 N. 6th St., Minneapolis, MN 55403; 800-762-2738
ENVIRONMENTAL SCIENCE, SCIENCE, VETERINARY MEDICINE
APHIS administers programs that protect and improve animal and plant health for the betterment of the environment and the nation's population.

BALLISTIC MISSILE DEFENSE ORGANIZATION (BMDO)

The Pentagon, Washington, DC 20301
ELECTRONICS, ENGINEERING, SCIENCE, TECHNOLOGY
BMDO oversees the Defense Department's missile acquisition programs and researches new missile technologies.

BUREAU OF ALCOHOL, TOBACCO, AND FIREARMS (ATF)

Personnel Staffing Specialist, Employment Branch, Bureau of Alcohol, Tobacco, and Firearms, 650 Mass. Ave. NW, Washington, DC 20226; 202-927-8423 (job hotline)
ACCOUNTING, BUSINESS, CRIMINAL JUSTICE, LAW
BATF enforces and administers laws pertaining to firearms, explosives, and the production and distribution of alcohol and tobacco products.

BUREAU OF THE CENSUS

Public Information Office, Rm 3227-3, Washington, DC 20233; 301-457-3371
DATA ENTRY, ECONOMICS, MATHEMATICS, STATISTICS, TECHNOLOGY
The Census Bureau collects data every ten years about the size and characteristics of the U.S. population.

BUREAU OF ECONOMIC ANALYSIS (BEA)

Public Information Office, 1441 L St. NW, Rm. 3009 Washington, DC 20230; 202-606-9900
ACCOUNTING, ECONOMICS, FINANCE, STATISTICS, TECHNOLOGY
BEA handles the nation's accounting activities. The bureau is concerned with charting economic growth, regional development, and the nation's position in the world economy.

BUREAU OF ENGRAVING AND PRINTING (BEP)

Public Affairs Office, Rm. 202-A, 14th and C Sts., SW, Washington, DC 20228; 202-874-0972
ENGINEERING, GRAPHIC DESIGN, PRINTING, SCIENCE, STATISTICS
BEP designs and prints currency, postage and revenue stamps, Treasury securities, and identification cards.

BUREAU OF INDIAN AFFAIRS (BIA)

Personnel Services, 1951 Constitution Ave., NW, MS331, SIB, Washington, DC 20245; 202-208-2682 (Job Hotline)
EDUCATION, ENGINEERING, ENVIRONMENTAL SCIENCE, FORESTRY, PUBLIC AFFAIRS, SOCIAL SCIENCES
BIA is involved in helping Native American communities manage their affairs under a trust relationship with the federal government.

BUREAU OF LABOR STATISTICS (BLS)

Special Programs, 2 Massachusetts Ave., NW, Washington, DC 20212; 202-606-6600
DATA ENTRY, ECONOMICS, MATHEMATICS, STATISTICS, TECHNOLOGY
BLS collects, analyzes, and disseminates data pertaining to everything that falls under the heading of labor economics, from unemployment to industrial relations.

BUREAU OF LAND MANAGEMENT (BLM)

Public Affairs, Dept. of the Interior, Washington, DC 20240; 202-501-6724
ARCHAEOLOGY, CARTOGRAPHY, ENGINEERING, FORESTRY, GEOLOGY, LAW, PUBLIC AFFAIRS, SCIENCE
BLM oversee the more than 270 million acres of U.S. public land. The bureau manages timber, solid minerals, oil, gas, energy, wildlife habitats, wilderness areas, and other resources.

BUREAU OF MINES

Office of Public Information, 810 7th St., NW, Washington, DC 20241
ENGINEERING, GEOLOGY, METALLURGY, SCIENCE

The Bureau of Mines collects data pertaining to the availability of nonfuel minerals for security and other needs. It also researches processing and recycling technologies.

BUREAU OF PRISONS

320 1st St., NW, Washington, DC 20534; 202-307-3204
BUSINESS, CRIMINAL JUSTICE, HEALTH SERVICES, LAW, SOCIAL SCIENCES
The Bureau of Prisons oversees the country's prison systems and community treatment centers.

BUREAU OF PUBLIC DEBT

999 E St., NW Rm 206-1 PKBJ, Washington, DC 20239; 202-480-7799
ACCOUNTING, BUSINESS, FINANCE, TECHNOLOGY
The Bureau of Public Debt borrows the money necessary to run the federal government, accounts for the public debt, and issues Treasury securities.

BUREAU OF RECLAMATION (BR)

Human Resources, P.O. Box 25007, Denver, CO 80225-0007; 303-236-3819
AGRICULTURE, AGRONOMY, ECONOMICS, ENGINEERING, ENVIRONMENTAL SCIENCE, GEOLOGY, HYDROLOGY, METEOROLOGY, SCIENCE
BR oversees the nation's water resources and ensures that they are being managed under the considerations of health, the environment, and economics.

BUREAU OF TRANSPORTATION STATISTICS (BTS)

400 7th St., SW, Room 9113, Washington, DC 20590
ENGINEERING, MATHEMATICS, STATISTICS, TECHNOLOGY
BTS compiles, analyzes, and publishes informational data pertaining to the Department of Transportation.

CENTERS FOR DISEASE CONTROL AND PREVENTION AND AGENCY FOR TOXIC SUBSTANCES AND DISEASE REGISTRY (CDC AND ATSDR)

Human Resources Management Office, 4770 Buford Highway, Atlanta, GA; 404-332-4577 (Job Hotline)
EDUCATION, ENVIRONMENTAL SCIENCE, HEALTH SERVICES, MANAGEMENT, PSYCHOLOGY, PUBLIC AFFAIRS, SCIENCE, SOCIAL SCIENCES, TECHNOLOGY
CDC components are involved in international health, epidemiology, immunization, public and environmental health, injury prevention, occupational health, and health statistics analysis.

CENTRAL IMAGERY OFFICE (CIO)

Suite 300, 8401 Old Courthouse Rd., Vienna, VA 22182
CARTOGRAPHY, ENGINEERING, GEOGRAPHY, GEOLOGY, TECHNOLOGY
CIO handles the Defense Department's imagery needs, whether they be mapping, charting, or geodesy, in order to support national security.

CENTRAL INTELLIGENCE AGENCY (CIA)

Office of Personnel, P.O.Box 12727, Arlington, VA 22209-8727; 703-492-7303
ACCOUNTING, BUSINESS, ECONOMICS, ENGINEERING, SCIENCE, TECHNOLOGY
CIA is responsible for gathering, evaluating, and disseminating information on political, military, economic, and scientific developments abroad for national security purposes.

CIVIL SERVICE

US Dept. of State, 22nd and D Streets, NW, Rm 2819, Washington, DC 20502; 202-647-7284
LAW, PUBLIC AFFAIRS, TECHNOLOGY
Civil Service representatives handle the internal operations of the State Department.

COMMODITY FUTURES TRADING COMMISSION (CFTC)

3 Lafayette Center, 4th Fl., 1155 21st St., NW, Washington, DC 20581; 202-418-5009/5003
ACCOUNTING, BUSINESS, ECONOMICS, LAW, TECHNOLOGY, TRADING
CFTC regulates futures trading and analyzes economic impacts on trading.

CONGRESSIONAL BUDGET OFFICE (CBO)

Congressional Budget Office, 410 Ford House Office Bldg., Washington, DC 20515; 202-226-2628
ECONOMICS, PUBLIC AFFAIRS
CBO assesses the federal budget's impact on the economy.

CONSOLIDATED FARM SERVICES ADMINISTRATION (CFSA)

Public Affairs Staff, P.O. Box 2415, Washington, DC 20013
ACCOUNTING, AGRICULTURE, AGRONOMY, BUSINESS, FINANCE
CFSA administers farm commodity and conservation programs, handles crop insurance, and grants loans for agriculture and rural development.

CONSUMER PRODUCT SAFETY COMMISSION (CPSC)

East-West Towers, 4330 East-West Highway, Bethesda, MD 20814
ENGINEERING, LAW, PUBLIC AFFAIRS, SCIENCE, TECHNOLOGY
CPSC protects the public against defective consumer products by evaluating products, developing safety standards, and researching accident causes and prevention measures.

COOPERATIVE STATE RESEARCH, EDUCATION, AND EXTENSION SERVICE (CSREES)

Coopertive Management Staff, USDA, Rm 3547, South Bldg., 14th St. and Independence Ave. SW, Washington, DC 20250; 202-690-48088
AGRICULTURE, AGRONOMY, BIOLOGY, CUSTOMER SERVICE, EDUCATION, HOME ECONOMICS, HORTICULTURE
CSREES connects the research and education resources and activities of the U.S. Department of Agriculture.

DEFENSE COMMISSARY AGENCY (DCA)

Director of Corporate Communications, Ft. Lee, VA 23801
BUSINESS, FINANCE, MANAGEMENT
DCA manages a worldwide system of commissaries for military servicepeople, their families, and other authorized patrons.

DEFENSE CONTRACT AUDIT AGENCY (DCAA)

Executive Officer,Bldg. 4, Cameron Station, Alexandria, VA 22304-6178; 703-767-2200
ACCOUNTING, FINANCE, TECHNOLOGY
DCAA handles all auditing functions for the Department of Defense.

DEFENSE INFORMATION SYSTEMS AGENCY (DISA)

Chief, Corporate Public Affairs, 701 S. Courthouse Rd., Arlington, VA 22202
ELECTRONICS, ENGINEERING, INFORMATION SYSTEMS, MATHEMATICS, SCIENCE, TECHNOLOGY
DISA handles communications facets and information systems for the military, White House, and State Department pertaining specifically to defense readiness.

DEFENSE INTELLIGENCE AGENCY (DIA)

7400 Defense Pentagon, Washington, DC 20301-7400; 202-695-0071
ECONOMICS, ENGINEERING, GEOGRAPHY, INTERNATIONAL AFFAIRS, LAW, MATHEMATICS, POLITICAL SCIENCE, SCIENCE, TECHNOLOGY
DIA collects and disseminates intelligence information in order to provide military support during peacetime, crisis, contingency, and combat scenarios.

DEFENSE INVESTIGATIVE SERVICES (DIS)

Chief, Office ofof Information and Public Affairs, 1340 Braddock Pl., Alexandria, VA 22314-1651; 703-325-6177
CRIMINAL JUSTICE, LAW ENFORCEMENT, POLITICAL SCIENCE, SPECIAL INVESTIGATIONS
DIS conducts background checks on employees requiring security clearance and investigates allegations of subversive affiliations or other matters affecting security concerns.

DEFENSE LOGISTICS AGENCY (DLA)

Civilian Personnel Support Office, DCPSO-HS, 380 Morrison Rd., Columbus, OH 43213; 614-692-5975
ACCOUNTING, BUSINESS, ENGINEERING, ENVIRONMENTAL SCIENCE, FINANCE, TECHNOLOGY
DLA provides worldwide logistics support to the U.S. military and other Department of Defense agencies and authorities. The agency specifically deals with procuring supplies and services.

DEFENSE MAPPING AGENCY (DMA)

Human Resources Directorate, Office of Personnel, 8613 Lee Highway, Fairfax, VA 22031-2137; 703-285-9148
CARTOGRAPHY, GEOGRAPHY, GEOLOGY
DMA produces and distributes maps, charts, and geodetic products and serv-

ices for purposes of national security and Defense Department support.

DEPARTMENT OF EDUCATION

600 Independence Ave., SW, Washington, DC 20202; 202-401-0559
ACCOUNTING, BUSINESS, ECONOMICS, EDUCATION, LAW, MANAGEMENT, PUBLIC AFFAIRS
The Education Department develops and administers policies for most federal assistance to education. It works to promote educational access and excellence.

DEPARTMENT OF ENERGY

Personnel Services Division, Rm 4H-08, 1000 Independence Ave., SW, Washington, DC 20585; 202-586-8591
ACCOUNTING, ARCHITECTURE, BUSINESS, ECONOMICS, ENGINEERING, ENVIRONMENTAL SCIENCE, FINANCE, SCIENCE, SOCIOLOGY, TECHNOLOGY
The Energy Department coordinates the energy functions of the federal government and engages in the research and development of energy technologies.

DEPARTMENT OF HOUSING AND URBAN DEVELOPMENT (HUD)

451 7th St., SW, Washington, DC 20410; 202-708-0416
ACCOUNTING, ARCHITECTURE, BUSINESS, CONSTRUCTION, ECONOMICS, FINANCE, PUBLIC AFFAIRS, TECHNOLOGY
HUD is concerned with implementing programs designed to address the nation's housing needs and opportunities, as well as the improvement and development of its communities.

DEPARTMENT OF THE INTERIOR

1849 C St., NW, Washington, DC 20240
ENGINEERING, ENVIRONMENTAL SCIENCE, PUBLIC AFFAIRS, SOCIAL SCIENCES
The Interior Department is responsible for managing the nation's public lands and natural resources, as well as maintaining ties with Native American reservations and U.S. island locations.

DEPARTMENT OF JUSTICE

10th St. and Pennsylvania Ave., NW, Washington, DC 20530; 202-514-3396
CRIMINAL JUSTICE, LAW, LAW ENFORCEMENT, PUBLIC AFFAIRS
The Justice Department handles the legal counseling for the nation's citizens.

DEPARTMENT OF LABOR

200 Constitution Ave., NW, Washington, DC 20210; 202-219-6666
ACCOUNTING, ECONOMICS, LAW, PUBLIC AFFAIRS, SOCIAL SCIENCES
The Labor Department is concerned with developing the welfare of wage earners, improving their working conditions, and increasing their employment opportunities.

DEPARTMENT OF STATE

2201 C St., NW, Washington, DC 20520
DIPLOMACY, ECONOMICS, HISTORY, INTERNATIONAL AFFAIRS, LANGUAGES, LAW, POLITICAL SCIENCE, TECHNOLOGY
The State Department has three main objectives: It advises the president on foreign policy, is concerned with ensuring national security, and represents the United States overseas.

DEPARTMENT OF TRANSPORTATION

400 7th St., SW, Washington, DC 20590
BUSINESS, ENGINEERING, MATHEMATICS, SCIENCE, STATISTICS, TECHNOLOGY, TRANSPORTATION
The Department of Transportation sets safety standards for the whole spectrum of transportation vehicles. It also researches fuel efficiency and implements highway safety measures.

DEPARTMENT OF THE TREASURY

1500 Pennsylvania Ave., NW, Washington, DC 20220
ACCOUNTING, BUSINESS, CRIMINAL JUSTICE, ECONOMICS, LAW, POLITICAL SCIENCE, SCIENCE, TECHNOLOGY
The Treasury Department formulates economic, financial, tax, and fiscal policies; enforces laws; manufactures coins and currency; and serves as the financial office for the government.

DEPARTMENT OF VETERANS AFFAIRS (DVA)

Human Resources Division, Rm 1260, 810 Vermont Ave., NW, Washington, DC 20420; 202-273-5400
EDUCATION, HEALTH SERVICES, PHARMACOLOGY, PSYCHOLOGY, RECREATIONAL THERAPY, RELIGIOUS ACTIVITIES, SOCIAL SCIENCES

The Department of Veterans Affairs is concerned with developing and administering benefits programs for veterans and their families.

DRUG ENFORCEMENT ADMINISTRATION (DEA)

Personnel Office, Washington, DC 20537; 202-633-1000
CRIMINAL JUSTICE, LAW, LAW ENFORCEMENT, SCIENCE
DEA regulates and enforces narcotics and controlled substance laws and policies.

ECONOMIC DEVELOPMENT ADMINISTRATION (EDA)

14th St. and Constitution Ave., Washington, DC 20230; 202-482-5113
ACCOUNTING, BUSINESS, ECONOMICS, ENGINEERING, FINANCE
EDA works—through loans, grants, and technical assistance—to direct federal resources to economically distressed areas and to assist in the development of local economies.

ECONOMIC RESEARCH SERVICE (ERS)

Examining Unit, Rm 1447 South Bldg., 14th St. and Independence Ave., SW, Washington, DC 20250; 202-219-0309
AGRICULTURE, ECONOMICS, LAW, MATHEMATICS, POLITICAL SCIENCE, SOCIAL SERVICES, STATISTICS
ERS provides economic and social information for policy and decision makers on issues pertaining to agricultural performance and the state of rural America.

EMPLOYMENT AND TRAINING ADMINISTRATION (ETA)

Office of Public Affairs, 200 Constitution Ave., NW, Rm S5214, Washington, DC 20210; 202-535-8744
ECONOMICS, PERSONNEL RELATIONS, SOCIAL SCIENCES
ETA manages programs that aim to give work experience or training to groups having difficulty entering or reentering the work force.

EMPLOYMENT STANDARDS ADMINISTRATION (ESA)

Office of Public Affairs, 200 Constitution Ave., NW, Rm. S3316, Washington, DC 20210; 202-219-7545
ECONOMICS, LAW, POLITICAL SCIENCE, PUBLIC AFFAIRS, SOCIAL SCIENCES
ESA administers programs that pertain to minimum wage, overtime standards, wage rates on government contracts, workers' compensation issues, and non-discrimination matters.

ENVIRONMENTAL PROTECTION AGENCY (EPA)

Client Services Division, 401 M St., SW, Washington, DC 20460; 202-260-2090
CRIMINAL JUSTICE, ENGINEERING, ENVIRONMENTAL SCIENCE, GEOLOGY, LAW, PUBLIC AFFAIRS, SCIENCE, VETERINARY MEDICINE
EPA regulates environmental laws enacted by Congress, with a particular focus on pollution and toxic cleanups.

EQUAL EMPLOYMENT OPPORTUNITY COMMISSION (EEOC)

Personnel Office, 1801 L St., NW, Washington, DC 20507; 202-663-4900
LAW, PUBLIC AFFAIRS, SOCIAL SCIENCES
EEOC works to eliminate discrimination in the workplace by investigating cases of alleged discrimination, enforcing EEOC regulations, filing lawsuits, and conducting assistance programs.

EXPORT–IMPORT BANK OF THE UNITED STATES (EXIMBANK)

Office of Human Resources, 811 Vermont Ave., NW, Washington, DC 20571: 202-565-3300
ACCOUNTING, BUSINESS, ECONOMICS, FINANCE, INTERNATIONAL AFFAIRS, LAW
EXIMBANK offers loans, guaranties, and insurance programs to help finance U.S. export activities.

FEDERAL AVIATION ADMINISTRATION (FAA)

800 Independence Ave., SW, Washington, DC 20591; 202-267-8007 (Job Hotline)
ENGINEERING, TECHNOLOGY
FAA regulates air commerce and safety standards, controls the use of air space for both civil and military purposes, and promotes civil aeronautics.

FEDERAL BUREAU OF INVESTIGATION (FBI)

9th St. and Pennsylvania Ave., NW, Washington, DC 20535; 202-324-3000
ACCOUNTING, CRIMINAL JUSTICE, ECONOMICS, ENGINEERING, LAN-

GUAGES, LAW, SCIENCE, TECH-
NOLOGY

FBI investigates federal law violations. The bureau gathers and reports evidence, locates witnesses, and compiles information in an attempt to apprehend and prosecute suspected felons.

FEDERAL COMMUNICATIONS COMMISSION (FCC)

Personnel Resources Branch, 1919 M St., NW, Rm 216, Washington, DC 20554; 202-418-0130
ELECTRONICS, ENGINEERING, LAW, PUBLIC AFFAIRS

FCC regulates interstate and foreign radio, television, wire, satellite, and cable communications.

FEDERAL CROP INSURANCE CORPORATION (FCIC)

USDA Bldg., Independence Ave., Washington, DC 20250
ACCOUNTING, AGRICULTURE, BUSINESS, MARKETING, STATISTICS

FCIC works to improve the economic stability of agriculture by administering crop insurance programs.

FEDERAL DEPOSIT INSURANCE CORPORATION (FDIC)

550 17th St., NW, Washington, DC 20429; 202-393-8400
ACCOUNTING, BUSINESS, ECONOMICS, FINANCE

FDIC insures banks and thrift deposits and examines state-chartered, non-Federal Reserve banks for safety and soundness.

FEDERAL ELECTION COMMISSION (FEC)

Office of Personnel, Rm. 812, 999 E St., NW, Washington, DC 20463; 202-219-4290
ACCOUNTING, LAW, POLITICAL SCIENCE, PUBLIC AFFAIRS

FEC ensures that political campaigns make full disclosures of their financial activities, regulates political contributions, and enforces public funding of elections.

FEDERAL EMERGENCY MANAGEMENT AGENCY (FEMA)

Office of Personnel, Rm 816, 500 C St., SW, Washington, DC 20472; 202-646-4040
BUSINESS, ENGINEERING, PUBLIC AFFAIRS, TECHNOLOGY

FEMA works with local, state, and federal governments on matters of emergency planning, preparedness, mitigations, response, and recovery.

FEDERAL ENERGY REGULATORY COMMISSION (FERC)

810 1st St., NE, Rm. 418, Washington, DC 20426; 202-219-2800
ACCOUNTING, AGRICULTURE, BUSINESS, ECONOMICS, ENGINEERING, ENVIRONMENTAL SCIENCE, SCIENCE, TECHNOLOGY

FERC determines rates and charges for the sale and transportation/transmission of natural gas and electricity.

FEDERAL HIGHWAY ADMINISTRATION (FHWA)

400 7th St., SW, Rm 4334, Washington, DC 20590; 202-366-0541
BUSINESS, ECONOMICS, ENGINEERING, MARKETING, MATHEMATICS, SCIENCE, TRANSPORTATION

FHA seeks to coordinate highways with other modes of transportation to achieve the most effective balance of transportation systems under federal transportation polices.

FEDERAL JUDICIAL CENTER (FJC)

Thurgood Marshall Federal Judiciary Bldg., 1 Columbus Circle, NE, Washington, DC 20544
EDUCATION, LAW, MANAGEMENT, STATISTICS

FJC handles the judicial branch's continuing education programs, policy research, and systems development.

FEDERAL LABOR RELATIONS AUTHORITY (FLRA)

Director of Personnel, 607 14th St., NW, Washington, DC 20424; 202-482-6660
LABOR RELATIONS, LAW, POLITICAL SCIENCE, PSYCHOLOGY, PUBLIC AFFAIRS

FLRA protects the rights of employees of the federal government.

FEDERAL LAW ENFORCEMENT TRAINING CENTER (FLETC)

Public Affairs, Glynco, GA 31524
BUSINESS, CRIMINAL JUSTICE, INTERNATIONAL AFFAIRS, LAW ENFORCEMENT, TECHNOLOGY

FLETC provides training for federal law enforcement organizations.

FEDERAL MARITIME COMMISSION (FMC)

Office of Personnel, 800 N. Capitol St., NW, Rm 924, Washington, DC 20573; 202-523-5773
ECONOMICS, INTERNATIONAL AFFAIRS, LAW
FMC regulates foreign and domestic offshore commerce of the United States.

FEDERAL MEDIATION AND CONCILIATION SERVICE (FMCS)

Office of Public Affairs, 2100 K St., NW, Washington, DC 20427; 202-606-5460
BUSINESS, LABOR RELATIONS
FMCS works to promote and ensure stable labor-management relations by mediating collective bargaining disputes.

FEDERAL RAILROAD ADMINISTRATION (FRA)

Office of Human Resources, 400 7th St., SW, Washington, DC 20590; 202-366-4194
ACCOUNTING, BUSINESS, ECONOMICS, ENGINEERING, SCIENCE, TRANSPORTATION
FRA's role is threefold: to enforce rail safety regulations, administer railroad financial assistance programs, and develop improved rail safety measures and rail transport policy.

FEDERAL RESERVE SYSTEM (FRS)

Director, Division of Personnel, Board of Governors of the FRS, 20th and Constitution Aves., NW, Washington, DC 20551; 202-452-3880
ACCOUNTING, BUSINESS, ECONOMICS, FINANCE, LAW
FRS administers and implements policy for the country's credit and monetary affairs in the interests of maintaining a stable banking industry.

FEDERAL TRADE COMMISSION (FTC)

Director of Personnel, Pennsylvania Ave. at 6th St., Rm. 122, Washington, DC 20580; 202-326-2020
ACCOUNTING, CLERICAL, ECONOMICS, LAW, LAW ENFORCEMENT, MARKETING
FTC prevents unfair competition in commerce exchange and presides over consumer protection laws.

FINANCIAL MANAGEMENT SERVICE (FMS)

Public Affairs, Room 555, 401 14th St., NW, Washington, DC 20227; 202-874-7090
ACCOUNTING, BUSINESS, ECONOMICS, FINANCE, MANAGEMENT, TECHNOLOGY
FMS is responsible for maintaining or improving the quality of government financial management as it pertains to Social Security, public monies, and accounting and finance systems.

FOOD AND CONSUMER SERVICES (FCS)

Department of Agriculture, 3101 Park Center Dr., Rm. 614, Alexandria, VA 22302; 703-305-2326
BUSINESS, HEALTH SERVICES, HOME ECONOMICS, NUTRITION, PUBLIC AFFAIRS
FCS develops and implements programs that work to provide food assistance and information to various segments of the population.

FOOD AND DRUG ADMINISTRATION (FDA)

5600 Fishers Lane, Rm 7-59, Rockville, MD 20857; 301-443-4473
HEALTH SERVICES, NUTRITION, PHARMACOLOGY, SCIENCE, STATISTICS, VETERINARY MEDICINE
FDA is responsible for ensuring that drugs, foods, cosmetics, and other potentially hazardous products meet standards of safety, purity, and effectiveness.

FOOD SAFETY AND INSPECTION SERVICE (FSIS)

Personnel Division, Room 3161, South Bldg., 14th St. and Independence Ave., SW, Washington, DC 20250; 202-720-6617
FOOD SCIENCE, VETERINARY MEDICINE
FSIS ensures that meat, poultry, and egg products meet federal standards in terms of safety, wholesomeness, and labeling.

FOREIGN AGRICULTURAL SERVICE (FAS)

Rm. 5627, South Bldg., 14th St. and Independence Ave., Washington, DC 20250; 202-720-5267
AGRICULTURE, BUSINESS, ECONOMICS, INTERNATIONAL AFFAIRS, MARKETING
FAS provides information about agricultural markets abroad. The agency also administers the Agriculture Department's export and foreign food assistance programs.

FOREIGN SERVICE

P.O. Box 9317, Arlington, VA 22210; 703-875-7490
BUSINESS, DIPLOMACY, ECONOMICS, INTERNATIONAL AFFAIRS, LANGUAGES, LAW, POLITICAL SCIENCE
The Foreign Service is engaged in diplomatic missions and embassy administration in an effort to implement U.S. foreign policy.

GENERAL ACCOUNTING OFFICE (GAO)

Office of Public Affairs, 441 G St., NW, Washington, DC 20548; 202-512-4900
ACCOUNTING, BUSINESS, ECONOMICS, LAW, PUBLIC AFFAIRS, TECHNOLOGY
GAO handles investigations on all matters involving the receipt and disbursement of public funds.

GENERAL SERVICES ADMINISTRATION (GSA)

Office of Personnel, Rm. 6242, 18th and F Streets, NW, Washington, DC 20405; 202-501-0370
ACCOUNTING, BUSINESS, ELECTRONICS, ENGINEERING, MANAGEMENT
GSA manages the government's properties, supplies, records, transportation, traffic, communications, and data processing.

GOVERNMENT PRINTING OFFICE (GPO)

Office of Congressional, Legislative, and Public Affairs, N. Capitol and H Streets, NW, Washington, DC 20401; 202-512-1137
DESIGN, PRINTING, TECHNOLOGY
GPO handles all congressional and executive departmental printing needs.

GRAIN INSPECTION, PACKERS, AND STOCKYARD ADMINISTRATION (GIPSA)

South Bldg., 14th St. and Independence Ave., SW, Washington, DC 20250
AGRICULTURE, BUSINESS, ECONOMICS
GIPSA establishes grading standards for grain and administers a nationwide inspection and weighing system.

HEALTH CARE FINANCING ADMINISTRATION (HCFA)

7500 Security Blvd., C2-08-13, Baltimore, MD 21244-1850; 410-786-5505
ACCOUNTING, BUSINESS, ECONOMICS, HEALTH SERVICES, PUBLIC AFFAIRS, SOCIAL SCIENCES
HCFA oversees the operations and policy developments for the Medicare and Medicaid programs and implements quality assurance standards.

HEALTH RESOURCES AND SERVICES ADMINISTRATION (HRSA)

Office of Personnel, 5600 Fishers Lane, Rm. 14A-46, Rockville, MD 20857; 301-443-5460
HEALTH SERVICES, PUBLIC AFFAIRS, SCIENCE, SOCIAL SCIENCES
HRSA is concerned with matters pertaining to health care access, equity, quality, and cost.

IMMIGRATION AND NATURALIZATION SERVICE (INS)

Office of Information, 425 I St., NW, Washington, DC 20536; 202-514-2530
CRIMINAL JUSTICE, LAW ENFORCEMENT
INS controls the entry of foreign persons into the United States. INS agents may take part in inspections and investigations, as well as deportation and detention of illegal aliens.

INDIAN HEALTH SERVICE (IHS)

12300 Twinbrook Pkwy, Suite 100, Rockville, MD 20857; 301-443-4242
ENGINEERING, HEALTH SERVICES, PSYCHOLOGY, SCIENCE, SOCIAL SCIENCES
IHS's main objective—through the development of health programs and coordination of health planning—is to raise the health levels of Native Americans and Alaska Natives.

INTER-AMERICAN FOUNDATION

901 N. Stuart St., Arlington, VA 22203
ECONOMICS, PUBLIC AFFAIRS, SOCIAL SERVICES
The Inter-American Foundation supports, through grants and social programs, the social and economic development of Latin American and Caribbean areas.

INTERNAL REVENUE SERVICE (IRS)

IRS Bldg., 1111 Constitution Ave., Rm. 1034, NW, Washington, DC 20224; 202-622-6340
ACCOUNTING, BUSINESS, CRIMINAL JUSTICE, ECONOMICS, FINANCE, LAW, POLITICAL SCIENCE, TECHNOLOGY

IRS is responsible for both collecting taxes that finance the federal government and enforcing revenue laws.

INTERNATIONAL TRADE ADMINISTRATION (ITA)

14th St. and Constitution Ave., Rm.4809, Washington, DC 20230; 202-482-1533
BUSINESS, ECONOMICS, FINANCE, INTERNATIONAL AFFAIRS, LAW
ITA works to stimulate world trade activities and strengthen the nation's position in the international trade arena.

INTERSTATE COMMERCE COMMISSION (ICC)

Personnel Services, Room 3130, 12th St. and Constitution Ave., NW, Washington, DC 20423
BUSINESS, ECONOMICS, MATHEMATICS, PUBLIC AFFAIRS, SOCIAL SCIENCES, TRANSPORTATION
ICC regulates interstate surface transportation, including trains, trucks, buses, water carriers, household goods transporters, and pipelines.

LIBRARY OF CONGRESS

Human Resources,101 Independence Ave., SE, Washington, DC 20559; 202-707-5620
LANGUAGES, LAW, LIBRARY SCIENCE, TECHNOLOGY
The Library of Congress oversees the national library and has some of the world's largest collections in areas such as American history, music, and law.

MARITIME ADMINISTRATION (MA)

400 7th St., SW, Washington, DC 20590
ACCOUNTING, ECONOMICS, ENGINEERING, TRANSPORTATION
MA implements programs designed to promote and assist with the operations of the U.S. merchant marine. It also directs emergency ship operations.

MERIT SYSTEMS PROTECTION BOARD (MSPB)

1120 Vermont Ave., NW, Rm. 850, Washington, DC 20419; 202-653-5916
LAW, PUBLIC AFFAIRS
MSPB works to protect the rights of federal employees working in the federal merit systems.

MINE SAFETY AND HEALTH ADMINISTRATION (MSHA)

Office of Public Affairs, 4015 Wilson Blvd., Room500, Arlington, VA 22203;703-235-1352
ENGINEERING, HEALTH SERVICES
MSHA implements programs and standards designed to prevent and reduce mining accidents and foster occupational health in the mining industry.

MINERALS MANAGEMENT SERVICE (MMS)

Staffing and Classification Branch, MS 2400, 381 Eden St., Herndon, VA 22070-4817; 703-787-1414
ACCOUNTING, ENGINEERING, ENVIRONMENTAL SCIENCE, GEOLOGY, MATHEMATICS, METEOROLOGY, OCEANOGRAPHY, SCIENCE
MMS evaluates the extent and recoverability, as well as the value, of leasable minerals on the outer continental shelf.

MINORITY BUSINESS DEVELOPMENT AGENCY (MBDA)

14th and Constitution Aves. NW, Washington, DC 20230; 202-482-1936
BUSINESS, ECONOMICS, FINANCE, MANAGEMENT, MARKETING, PUBLIC AFFAIRS
MBDA provides technical and managerial expertise to minority businesses entering or operating in the American free enterprise system.

NATIONAL AERONAUTICS AND SPACE ADMINISTRATION (NASA)

Personnel Director, NASA Headquarters, 2 Independence Square, 300 E St., SW, Rm. 3j11, Washington, DC 20546; 202-358-0100
ENGINEERING, MATHEMATICS, PUBLIC AFFAIRS, SCIENCE, TECHNOLOGY
NASA researches, develops, and implements equipment used in satellite communications and the peaceful exploration of space.

NATIONAL AGRICULTURAL LIBRARY (NAL)

Agricultural Research Service, 6303 Ivy Lane, Room 360, Greenbelt, MD 20770; 301-344-3953
AGRICULTURE, LIBRARY SCIENCE
NAL contains an extensive collection of agricultural resource materials that are available to everyone, from scientists to the general public.

NATIONAL AGRICULTURAL STATISTICS SERVICE (NASS)

Information Division, Economics Management Staff, Department of Agriculture, Washington, DC20250; 202-447-7657
AGRONOMY, BUSINESS, MATHEMATICS, SCIENCE, STATISTICS
NASS conducts surveys and prepares informational material such as reports and estimates for the orderly operation of the U.S. agricultural economy.

NATIONAL ARCHIVES AND RECORDS ADMINISTRATION (NARA)

Personnel Operations Branch, Room 2002, 9700 Page Blvd., St. Louis, MO 63123; 800-827-4898
BUSINESS, DATA ENTRY, EDITORIAL SERVICES, HISTORY, LIBRARY SCIENCE
NARA establishes policies and procedures for managing the U.S. government's records.

NATIONAL CREDIT UNION ADMINISTRATION (NCUA)

Office of Human Resources, 1775 Duke St., Rm. 3041, Alexandria, VA 22314; 703-518-6510
ACCOUNTING, FINANCE
NCUA charters, insures, supervises, and examines federal credit unions.

NATIONAL FOUNDATIONS FOR THE ARTS AND THE HUMANITIES (NFAH)

1100 Pennsylvania Ave., NW, Rm. 208, Washington, DC 20506; 202-682-5405
ADMINISTRATION, ARTS, BUSINESS, PUBLIC AFFAIRS
NFAH provides endowments to and promotes support of the arts and the humanities.

NATIONAL HIGHWAY TRAFFIC SAFETY ADMINISTRATION (NHTSA)

400 7th St., SW, Rm. 5306, Washington, DC 20590; 202-366-1784
ENGINEERING, MATHEMATICS, PSYCHOLOGY, PUBLIC AFFAIRS, SCIENCE, TECHNOLOGY
NHTSA is concerned with administering programs pertaining to the safety performance of motor vehicles, drivers, occupants, and pedestrians. It also researches speed limits and their effects.

NATIONAL INSTITUTE OF STANDARDS AND TECHNOLOGY (NIST)

Room A123, Administration Bldg., Gaithersburg, MD 20899; 301-975-3008
ENGINEERING, MATHEMATICS, SCIENCE, TECHNOLOGY
NIST advances U.S. economic growth by helping industries develop and apply new technologies, measurements, and standards.

NATIONAL INSTITUTES OF HEALTH (NIH)

9000 Rockville Pike, Bldg. 31, Bethesda, MD 20205; 301-496-5979
HEALTH SERVICES, LIBRARY SCIENCE, PSYCHOLOGY, SCIENCE, TECHNOLOGY
NIH is the primary biomedical research agency within the federal government.

NATIONAL LABOR RELATIONS BOARD (NLRB)

1099 14th St., NW, Washington, DC 20570; 202-273-3900
LABOR RELATIONS, LAW
NLRB is concerned with preventing unfair labor practices and safeguarding employees' rights to have unions as bargaining representatives.

NATIONAL OCEANIC AND ATMOSPHERIC ADMINISTRATION (NOAA)

Human Resources Management Office, OA22,1315 East-West Highway, Silver Spring, MD 21910; 301-713-0534
CARTOGRAPHY, MATHEMATICS, METEOROLOGY, OCEANOGRAPHY, SCIENCE, TECHNOLOGY
NOAA collects and disseminates scientific information about the earth's environment, oceans, and atmosphere. The agency reports the weather for the United States and issues severe weather warnings.

NATIONAL PARK SERVICE (NPS)

Public Affairs, P.O. Box 37127, Washington, DC 20013
ANTHROPOLOGY, ARCHAEOLOGY, ENGINEERING, ENVIRONMENTAL SCIENCE, GEOGRAPHY, HISTORY, HOSPITALITY, JOURNALISM, LANDSCAPE ARCHITECTURE
NPS is concerned with preserving and protecting the country's natural and cultural resources. NPS also manages programs aimed at promoting the National Park System's significant allures.

NATIONAL RAILROAD PASSENGER CORPORATION (AMTRAK)

60 Massachusetts Ave., NE, Washington, DC 20002

ENGINEERING, SCIENCE, TECH-
NOLOGY, TRANSPORTATION
AMTRAK develops modern rail services
to meet the nation's intercity passenger
transportation needs.

NATIONAL SCIENCE FOUNDATION (NSF)

*Human Resource Management, 4201
Wilson Blvd., Arlington, VA 22230; 703-
306-1182*
ACCOUNTING, BUSINESS, ECO-
NOMICS, ENGINEERING, MATHE-
MATICS, SCIENCE, SOCIAL SCI-
ENCES
NSF, through grants and programs, pro-
motes the progress of science, engineer-
ing, and education.

NATIONAL SECURITY AGENCY (NSA)

*Recruitment Branch, Attn: M322, Ft.
Meade, MD 20755; 301-859-6444*
BUSINESS, ENGINEERING, LAN-
GUAGES, MATHEMATICS, SCI-
ENCE, TECHNOLOGY
NSA is in charge of securing information
systems and producing foreign intelli-
gence information.

NATIONAL TECHNICAL INFORMATION SERVICE (NTIS)

*5285 Port Royal Rd., Springfield, VA
22161; 703-487-4680*
DATA ENTRY, FINANCE, INFOR-
MATION SYSTEMS, MARKETING,
TECHNOLOGY
NTIS serves as a resource for govern-
ment-sponsored scientific, technical, engineering, and other business-related information.

NATIONAL TELECOMMUNICATIONS AND INFORMATION ADMINISTRATION (NTIA)

*14th St. and Constitution Ave., Wash-
ington, DC 20230*
COMMUNICATIONS, ENGINEER-
ING, PUBLIC AFFAIRS, TECHNOL-
OGY
NTIA researches and develops telecommunications policies and prescribes policies for and manages the federal use of
the radio frequency spectrum.

NATIONAL TRANSPORTATION SAFETY BOARD (NTSB)

*Human Resources Division, 490
L'Enfant Plaza East, SW, Rm. 6103,
Washington, DC 20594; 202-382-6717*
ENGINEERING, SCIENCE, TECH-
NOLOGY, TRANSPORTATION

NTSB investigates accidents, conducts
studies, and makes recommendations to
government agencies, the transportation
industry, and others on safety measures
and practices.

NUCLEAR REGULATORY COMMISSION (NRC)

*Office of Personnel, Mail Stop T3A2,
Washington, DC 20555; 301-415-7047*
ENGINEERING, ENVIRONMENTAL
SCIENCE, SCIENCE
NRC regulates the use of nuclear energy
in order to protect the nation's public
health and environment.

OCCUPATIONAL SAFETY AND HEALTH ADMINISTRATION (OSHA)

*200 Constitution Ave., Rm. N3308, NW,
Washington, DC 20210; 202-219-8006*
ENGINEERING, HEALTH SERVICES,
PSYCHOLOGY, PUBLIC AFFAIRS,
SOCIAL SCIENCES
OSHA develops and implements safety
and health standards and regulations and
conducts inspections and investigations
to ensure that employers are in compli-
ance with policies.

OFFICE OF THE AMERICAN WORKPLACE (OAW)

*Public Affairs Team, RoomC5516, 200
Constitution Ave., NW, Washington, DC
20210; 202-219-6656*
BUSINESS, LAW, MANAGEMENT,
PERSONNEL RELATIONS, SOCIAL
SCIENCES
OAW administers programs pertaining
to human resources practices, skills en-
hancement, worker morale, labor union
relations, and training regimens.

OFFICE OF THE COMPTROLLER OF THE CURRENCY (OCC)

*Director for Human Resources, 250 E
St., SW, Washington, DC 20219; 202-
874-4500*
ACCOUNTING, BUSINESS, ECO-
NOMICS, FINANCE
OCC regulates banks by reviewing applications for charters, enforcing regulations, and implementing rules for banking
practices.

OFFICE OF JUSTICE PROGRAMS (OJP)

*Office of Congressional and Public Af-
fairs, 633 Indiana Ave., NW, Washington, DC 20531*
CRIMINAL JUSTICE, LAW, LAW

ENFORCEMENT
OJP is involved in making sure that the nation's justice system is working efficiently and effectively in preventing and controlling crime.

OFFICE OF PERSONNEL MANAGEMENT (OPM)
Human Resources, 1900 E St.,Rm. 1447, NW, Washington, DC 20415; 202-606-2440
BUSINESS, EDUCATION, LABOR RELATIONS, PERSONNEL RELATIONS, PUBLIC AFFAIRS, SOCIAL SERVICES
OPM ensures that the federal government provides an array of personnel services to applicants and employees.

OFFICE OF SURFACE MINING (OSM)
Personnel Division, 1951 Constitution Ave NW, Rm. 44, Washington, DC 20240; 202-20802773
ACCOUNTING, ENGINEERING, ENVIRONMENTAL SCIENCE, MINING, SCIENCE
OSM works to implement programs designed to protect society and the environment from negative effects of mining, while ensuring that steps are taken to replenish resources.

OFFICE OF TECHNOLOGY ASSESSMENT (OTA)
600 Pennsylvania Ave., SE, Washington, DC 20510
HEALTH SERVICES, RESEARCH, SCIENCE, TECHNOLOGY
OTA gauges the scientific and technical impact of government policies and legislative initiatives.

OFFICE OF THRIFT SUPERVISION (OTS)
1700 G St., NW, Washington, DC 20552; 202-906-6060
ACCOUNTING, BUSINESS, ECONOMICS, FINANCE, LAW, TECHNOLOGY
OTS charters and regulates thrift institutions.

PATENT AND TRADEMARK OFFICE (PTO)
Office ofPersonnel 2011 Crystal Dr., Washington, DC 20231; 703-305-8231
ENGINEERING, LAW, SCIENCE, TECHNOLOGY
PTO reviews applications for and issues three kinds of patents: design, plant, and utility. The office also issues trademarks and publishes various kinds of patent and trademark information.

PEACE CORPS
1990 K St., NW, Rm 4100, Washington, DC 20526; 202-606-3336
AGRICULTURE, EDUCATION, ENGINEERING, HEALTH SERVICES, LANGUAGES, SCIENCE
The Peace Corps promotes world peace by conducting various training programs in developing countries.

PENSION AND WELFARE BENEFITS ADMINISTRATION (PWBA)
PWBA, 200 Constitution Ave., NW, Rm. C5516, Washington, DC 20210; 202-219-6677
ACCOUNTING, BUSINESS, ECONOMICS, FINANCE, INSURANCE, LAW
PWBA is responsible for managing pension plans and other benefits.

PENSION BENEFIT GUARANTY CORPORATION (PBGC)
1200 K St., NW, Suite 120, Washington, DC 20005; 202-326-4110
ACCOUNTING, BUSINESS, FINANCE
PBGC guarantees payment of nonforfeitable pension benefits in covered, private sector-defined benefit pension plans.

POSTAL RATE COMMISSION (PRC)
Personnel Office, 1333 H St., NW, Rm. 300, Washington, DC 20268; 202-789-6840
ACCOUNTING, ECONOMICS, ENGINEERING, LAW, MARKETING, STATISTICS
PRC participates in regulating postage rates, fees, and mail classifications.

RESEARCH AND SPECIAL PROGRAMS ADMINISTRATION (RSPA)
Office of Program and Policy Support, 400 7th St., SW, Rm 8401, Washington, DC 20590; 202-366-5608
ENGINEERING, SCIENCE, TECHNOLOGY, TRANSPORTATION
RSPA is concerned with the safe transport of hazardous materials, pipeline safety, and other matters dealing with safety regulations, emergency preparedness, and transmodal development.

RURAL UTILITIES SERVICE (RUS)
Personnel Management Division, 14th St. and Independence Ave., SW, Wash-

ington, DC 20250; 202-720-2930
ACCOUNTING, BUSINESS, ELEC-
TRONICS, ENGINEERING, FINANCE,
TECHNOLOGY, TELECOMMUNICA-
TIONS
RUS is involved in providing access to
various telecommunications and electric
technologies for populations in rural ar-
eas. The agency often makes or guaran-
tees loans for such purposes.

SECURITIES AND EXCHANGES COMMISSION (SEC)

*Personnel Management, 450 5th St., NW,
Washington, DC 20549; 202-942-4070*
BUSINESS, ECONOMICS, FINANCE,
LAW, TRADING
SEC regulates federal securities laws to
protect investors.

SMALL BUSINESS ADMINISTRATION (SBA)

*409 3rd St., SW, Washington, DC 20416;
202-205-6793*
ACCOUNTING, BUSINESS, ECO-
NOMICS, FINANCE, MARKETING,
PUBLIC AFFAIRS
SBA aids, counsels, assists, and protects
the interests of small businesses and
small business owners.

SMITHSONIAN INSTITUTION

*Human Resources, Suite 2100, 955
L'Enfant Plaza, SW, Washington, DC
20560; 202-287-3100*
BIOLOGY, BOTANY, HISTORY, LIFE
SCIENCES, PHYSICAL SCIENCES
The Smithsonian Institution represents
the arts, history, technology, and science
through exhibits, as well as conducting
research, publishing studies, and participating in educational programs.

SOCIAL SECURITY ADMINISTRATION (SSA)

*Office of Personnel, 6401 Security Blvd.,
Rm. G-120, Baltimore, MD 21235; 410-
965-4506*
BUSINESS, ECONOMICS, INSUR-
ANCE, PUBLIC AFFAIRS, SOCIAL
SCIENCES
SSA administers the federal retirement,
survivors, disability, and health insurance
programs for U.S. citizens. It also studies
problems related to the above areas.

SUBSTANCE ABUSE AND MENTAL HEALTH SERVICES ADMINISTRATION (SAMHSA)

*Division of Personnel Management, 5600
Fishers Lane, Rm. 14C-14, Rockville,*

MD 20857; 301-443-5407
HEALTH SERVICES, PHARMACOL-
OGY, PSYCHOLOGY, SOCIAL SCI-
ENCES
SAMHSA is interested in making sure
that scientific knowledge and state-of-
the-art practices are incorporated into the
prevention and treatment of mental disorders.

SUPREME COURT, LOWER COURTS, AND SPECIAL COURTS

*Public Information Office, Supreme
Court Bldg., 1 First St., NE, Washington,
DC 20543; 202-479-3404*
CRIMINAL JUSTICE, LAW, LIBRARY
SCIENCE
The Supreme Court is the country's
highest court. The lower courts handle
appeals and foreign trade matters, among
other cases. Special courts handle federal
claims and other cases.

TRADE AND DEVELOPMENT AGENCY (TDA)

*Room 309, State Annex 16, Washington,
DC 20523*
BUSINESS, ECONOMICS, FINANCE,
INTERNATIONAL AFFAIRS, LAN-
GUAGES
TDA is involved in economic develop-
ment and U.S. export traffic in various
developing and middle-income nations.

U.S. ARMS CONTROL AND DISARMAMENT AGENCY (ACDA)

320 21st St., NW, Washington, DC 20451
INTERNATIONAL AFFAIRS, PO-
LITICAL SCIENCE
ACDA formulates and implements arms
control policies to promote national secu-
rity and international relations.

U.S. COAST GUARD (USCG)

*Information Office, 2100 2nd St., SW,
Washington, DC 20593; 202-267-2331*
COMMUNICATIONS, ENGINEER-
ING, ENVIRONMENTAL SCIENCE,
HEALTH SERVICES
The Coast Guard, which is part of the
Transportation Department, enforces
maritime laws, performs search and res-
cue missions, and manages waterways.

U.S. CUSTOMS SERVICE (USCS)

*1301 Constitution Ave., NW, Washing-
ton, DC 20229; 202-634-5005*
BUSINESS, CRIMINAL JUSTICE, IN-
TERNATIONAL AFFAIRS, LAW,

LAW ENFORCEMENT
USCS oversees and enforces all import/export regulations.

U.S. FISH AND WILDLIFE SERVICE (FWS)

18th and C Sts.,NW, Rm. 3458, Washington, DC 20240; 202-208-6104
ENVIRONMENTAL SCIENCE, SCIENCE, ZOOLOGY
FWS is concerned with managing natural resources in order to protect the habitats of birds, endangered species, certain marine mammals, and inland sport fisheries.

U.S. AND FOREIGN COMMERCIAL SERVICE (US&FCS)

Human Resources Office, 14th and Constitution Avenues, NW, Washington, DC 20230; 202-482-3505
BUSINESS, INTERNATIONAL AFFAIRS, MARKETING
US&FCS works to develop, produce, market, and manage products and services as they pertain to the marketing needs of the U.S. exporting and international business community.

U.S. FOREST SERVICE (USFS)

P.O. Box 96090, Washington, DC 20090; 703-235-8102
ARCHAEOLOGY, ANTHROPOLOGY, BIOLOGY, BOTANY, EDUCATION, ENGINEERING, FORESTRY, HORTICULTURE, WILDLIFE MANAGEMENT, ZOOLOGY
USFS manages the country's national parks.

U.S. GEOLOGICAL SURVEY (USGS)

12201 Sunrise Valley Dr.MS 601, Reston, VA 22092; 703-648-6131
CARTOGRAPHY, ENVIRONMENTAL SCIENCE, GEOGRAPHY, GEOLOGY, GEOPHYSICS, HYDROLOGY, SCIENCE
USGS studies the country's land, water, mineral, and energy resources; researches global changes; and investigates the impact and occurrence of natural disasters.

U.S. INFORMATION AGENCY (USIA)

Office of Personnel, 301 4th St., SW, Rm 518, Washington, DC 20547;202-619-4656
BROADCASTING, COMMUNICATIONS, EDITORIAL SERVICES, INTERNATIONAL AFFAIRS, LANGUAGES, POLITICAL SCIENCE

USIA works to inform foreign communities of U.S. national interests through the means of radio and television broadcasts, lectures, and exchange programs, among others.

U.S. INTERNATIONAL TRADE COMMISSION (ITC)

500 E St., SW, Rm.314-B,Washington, DC 20436; 202-205-2651
ACCOUNTING, BUSINESS, ECONOMICS, FINANCE, INTERNATIONAL AFFAIRS, LAW
ITC issues studies, reports, and recommendations pertaining to international trade and tariffs to various areas of the government.

U.S. MARSHALS SERVICE (USMS)

Office of Congressional and Public Affairs, Suite 890, 600 Army Navy Dr., Arlington, VA 22202; 202-307-9600
CRIMINAL JUSTICE, LAW ENFORCEMENT
USMS duties include protecting the federal courts, judges, and jurors; apprehending federal fugitives; operating the Witness Protection Program; and managing forfeited property.

U.S. MINT (USM)

Judiciary Sq. Bldg., 633 3rd St., NW,Suite 655, Washington, DC 20220; 202-874-9300
BUSINESS, ECONOMICS, ENGINEERING, FINANCE, MARKETING, METALLURGY
USM produces coin for the nation's trade and commerce exchanges and sells and mints commemorative and specialty coins.

U.S. NATIONAL CENTRAL BUREAU—INTERNATIONAL CRIMINAL POLICE ORGANIZATION (USNCB)

600 E St., NW, Washington, DC 20530
CRIMINAL JUSTICE, INTERNATIONAL AFFAIRS, LANGUAGES, LAW
USNCB serves as a link between the U.S. law enforcement community and its counterparts in foreign countries.

U.S. POSTAL SERVICE

U.S. Postal Service, 475 L'Enfant Plaza, SW, Rm 9671, Washington, DC 20260; 202-268-3643
BUSINESS, ENGINEERING, LABOR RELATIONS, LAW, PUBLIC AFFAIRS

The Postal Service is the major mail-processing and delivering service in the country.

U.S. SECRET SERVICE

Office of Government Liaison and Public Affairs, 1800 G St., NW, Washington, DC 20223; 202-435-5800
ACCOUNTING, BUSINESS, CRIMINAL JUSTICE, LAW, LAW ENFORCEMENT, SOCIAL SCIENCES
The Secret Service is responsible for protecting governmental leaders and premises as well as investigating cases involving fraud, forgery, and counterfeiting.

U.S. SENTENCING COMMISSION (USSC)

Office of Communications, Suite 2-500, S. Lobby, 1 Columbus Circle, NE, Washington, DC 20002
CRIMINAL JUSTICE, LAW, PSYCHOLOGY, SOCIAL SCIENCES
USSC develops sentencing policies for the federal criminal justice system.

U.S. TRAVEL AND TOURISM ADMINISTRATION (USTTA)

14th St. and Constitution Ave., Washington, DC 20230
BUSINESS, INTERNATIONAL AFFAIRS, MARKETING, STATISTICS, TRAVEL
USTTA formulates and executes American tourism policies as they pertain to the nation's economic development and international trade mission.

VETERANS EMPLOYMENT AND TRAINING SERVICE (VETS)

810 Vermont Ave., Rm. 1260, NW, Washington, DC 20210; 202-565-8687
BUSINESS, PSYCHOLOGY, PUBLIC AFFAIRS, SOCIAL SCIENCES
VETS is responsible for administering veterans' employment and training programs and activities to ensure that legislative and regulatory mandates are accomplished.

JOB OPPORTUNITIES

INDUSTRY OVERVIEWS

As the 20th century draws to a close, American industries can reflect the sometimes disruptive and rapid changes that are occurring in society at large. What one day seems like a rock-steady, always-been-here industry can dwindle from being a giant of the economy to playing a relatively minor role in a matter of a few years. (We saw this in the last century with the rising and declining fortunes of the railroads.) In contrast, other industries, such as aerospace or computers, can mushroom from a tiny seed into a large-scale industry employing millions of workers, all within a decade or two.

Changes can also affect industries that have been with us almost since the dawn of time, like agriculture. Various technological developments, trade negotiations, and consumer trends can affect job prospects dramatically in the coming years.

Because of this fluid environment, it has never been more important for job seekers to understand the overlying, general "macro" effects of a particular industry upon the individual companies you might tie your employment prospects to for years or even decades. As you consider your own prospects within the 30 major industry categories discussed in the industry overviews that make up this chapter, certain tips will help you get the most from the information presented. First, each industry is rated and given from zero to two stars for job prospects. (This is the same scale used in the "U.S. Employers" chapter.) Two stars (★★) means that the industry is generally very healthy. The number of people employed in it has increased in the last several years, and a large number of companies that drive it are enjoying increased sales or revenues. One star (★) means basically the same, but to a lesser extent. If there are no stars, the industry is either growing only modestly, is flat, or is in trouble. (The last will be obvious when you read the full text.)

Second, the 30 major industry categories are listed below, along with cross-references to specific sectors that are described in the industry overviews. For example, the apparel sector can be found in the industry of consumer nondurables, and the tools sector can be found in the industry of production machinery.

However, since each industry category includes a wide variety of businesses, as you read each overview, be aware of the following points. The rating system is for the overall industry, but particular sectors of an industry may be doing much better or worse than the industry overall. Thus, pay particular attention to these sector descriptions. Although the entire economy is a vast construction of interdependent webs, certain industries in particular depend very heavily upon other industries for their overall performance. For example, the steel industry is highly dependent upon automobile sales, and the sale of forest products is directly related to interest rates and the health of the real estate sector. Where a direct connection is apparent to you, it might be helpful to look at descriptions in this chapter of these "connected" industries.

A downturn in overall economic conditions, which cannot be entirely predicted in advance, can alter the long-range predictions for some of these industries. An example is the effect that the abrupt ending of the Cold War had on the aerospace industry. Therefore, always temper the forecasts given here in the light of unpredictable and potentially disruptive changes, and do additional research at that time.

For further information on specific industries that are of particular importance in your career plans, consult industry associations and publications. ➤See "Professional Associations," pp. 644-655, and "Professional Magazines/Journals," pp. 131-147.

INDUSTRY OVERVIEWS

INDUSTRY LIST

AEROSPACE AND SPACE COMMERCE

AGRICULTURE/FOOD PRODUCTS

APPAREL (*See:* Consumer Nondurables)

AUTOMOTIVE (*See:* Motor Vehicles/Parts)

AVIATION (*See:* Aerospace and Space Commerce, Freight and Transportation)

BANKING (*See:* Financial Services/Investments)

BUILDING MATERIALS (*See:* Construction/ Real Estate)

BUSINESS SERVICES

CHEMICALS/PLASTICS/RUBBER/ COSMETICS

COMPUTERS/PERIPHERALS

CONSTRUCTION/REAL ESTATE

CONSUMER DURABLES

CONSUMER NONDURABLES

DEFENSE (*See:* Aerospace and Space Commerce)

DRUGS/MEDICAL EQUIPMENT

EDUCATION AND TRAINING

ELECTRICAL AND RENEWABLE ENERGY EQUIPMENT

ELECTRONICS AND APPLIANCES (*See:* Consumer Durables)

ENTERTAINMENT

ENVIRONMENTAL/TECHNICAL SERVICES

FINANCIAL SERVICES/INVESTMENTS

FOOD AND BEVERAGES (*See:* Agriculture/ Food Products)

FOREST/PAPER PRODUCTS

FREIGHT AND TRANSPORTATION

HEALTH SERVICES

HOSPITALITY (*See:* Travel and Lodging)

HOUSEHOLD/PERSONAL PRODUCTS (*See:* Chemicals/Plastics/Rubber/ Cosmetics, Consumer Nondurables)

INDUSTRIAL/ANALYTICAL INSTRUMENTS

INFORMATION SERVICES

INSURANCE

METALS (*Also see:* Natural Resources and Energy)

MINING (*See:* Metals, Natural Resources and Energy)

MISCELLANEOUS EQUIPMENT (*See:* Office/Photographic Equipment, Production Machinery)

MOTOR VEHICLES/PARTS

NATURAL RESOURCES AND ENERGY (*Also See:* Metals)

OFFICE/PHOTOGRAPHIC EQUIPMENT

PRINTING AND PUBLISHING

PRODUCTION MACHINERY

REAL ESTATE (*See:* Construction/Real Estate)

RESTAURANTS (*See:* Retailing)

RETAILING

SEMICONDUCTORS (*See:* Computers/ Peripherals)

SHIPBUILDING AND REPAIR (*See:* Freight and Transportation)

SOFTWARE (*See:* Information Services)

TELECOMMUNICATIONS EQUIPMENT AND SERVICES

TEXTILES (*See:* Consumer Nondurables)

TIRES (*See:* Chemicals/Plastics/Rubber/ Cosmetics)

TOOLS/INDUSTRIAL EQUIPMENT (*See:* Production Machinery)

TOYS (*See:* Consumer Nondurables)

TRAVEL AND LODGING

UTILITIES (*See:* Electrical and Renewable Energy Equipment)

WHOLESALING

AEROSPACE AND SPACE COMMERCE ★

Defense spending is on the upswing, pushing revenues to an all-time high in the aerospace field. Industry sales increased by 5 percent last year and are expected to grow another 3 per-cent this year. Merger madness continues throughout the industry, however, causing a greater competition between companies with fewer left to share in the wealth.

So although this industry is among the health-iest in terms of earnings, mergers will likely mean layoffs for some aero-space and defense workers. Following a 42 percent cut in total employment in the mid 1990s in the aero-space industry, employment in the U.S. grew from 792,000 in the summer of 1996 to over 900,000 by the end of the decade before leveling off.

The commercial aircraft business has a shrinking market overseas, but airline traffic is expected to grow into the year 2000. In 1999, sales figures showed an increase of 8 percent, but operating margins were at only 3 percent or less.

One bright spot is the space commerce industry. This young field includes satellite manufacturing and launching, as well as research partnerships between the government and the private sector. Commercial satellite interests tripled since 1991 and conntinue to look up. Satellite manufacturing continued its high levels of production for the remainder of the 1990s, with demand strengthened by the need to replace satellites at the end of their useful life. The industry is expected to maintain its 60 to 70 percent share of the world market.

The picture in the military aerospace sector is one of change. The Pentagon has moved from development to procurement in its key weapons, such as fighter planes. That will push revenues up slightly from last year. European countries, also, will have more flexibility in their defense budgets in coming years.

AGRICULTURE/FOOD PRODUCTS ★

After a boost in agriculture revenues in the late 90s, farmers are experiencing the downside of market-pricing. Unfortunately, just as the country is producing a record crop, the demand is weakening. The three major U.S. cash crops were all down at the end of this year: corn, down 27 percent; soybeans, down 13 percent; and wheat, down 29 percent. Almost every agricultural product, except dairy, has been hurt by the financial crisis in Asia. Exports dropped by 6% last year and are expected to fall again this year. Other countries are also getting better at producing their own food, a development that could hurt the agriculture industry in future years as well. For livestock producers, the picture is even more dismal. Cattle prices have dropped 20 percent since 1998 and hog prices have plunged to a 50-year low.

Employment in the food manufacturing business was expected to grow. The trend was to more and more ready-made meals, with consumers ever more pressed for time. Food processors are working to explore more overseas markets as well as meet the growing demand for supercenters. Companies like H. J. Heinz and Campbell Soup are looking to form new relationships with food-service operators, which are expanding into supermarkets and even service stations.

Supermarkets are facing stiff competition from restaurants, as fewer meals are eaten at home. Restaurants and food service outlets have seen their share of the food marekt jump to 48%. Large chains are seeing potential in supermarket delis. Food processors like Sara Lee—which is now selling premium meats via a new chain of sandwich shops inside Kroger supermarkets—are lining up to take advantage of this market movement.

Food processors overall can expect 5 percent growth in the near term, but the industry is facing internal competition, and the biggest concerns will win. Companies will be under increasing pressure to jettison low-producing areas to competitors. There will be intense competition to acquire smaller firms that may improve a company's current strong area.

BUSINESS SERVICES ★★

By now it is a familiar story: as companies downsize, much of the work formerly done by staff is out-sourced to outside agencies. This work includes most services -- legal, adver-tising, management services and accounting. Several factors bode well for the business services industry: the growth of Internet web sites, the year 2000 problem, and a continuing tendency to outsource services formerly done on premises.

Business services represent one of the nation's largest industries, with conservative estimates placing total employment at close to 3 million and revenues at over a quarter-trillion dollars. The long-term prospects for the industry are good, with a five-year sales growth rate of 14.9 percent.

Temporary employment services were also expected to see strong growth in the next several years, with annual revenues around $40 billion a year. The largest gains will be by agencies specializing in information technology. Advertising revenues were ex-pected to be up a healthy 8 percent, but long-term prospects may be squeezed by market competition from generic brands. Industrial services companies that supply uniforms or provide cleaning or security should also benefit from the downsizing trend. The average five year sales growth figure of 10.3 percent for this segment of the industry bodes well.

Accounting services were projected to increase in the 5-percent range over the past few years, with total employment running close to a half-million.

Legal services are encountering increased demand due to the growth of legal action in areas such as health care, elder law and environmental issues. The increasing use of computers and a more efficient use of the work force in the legal sector would likely still put the damper on employment prospects. However, some law grads are turning to "temporary" legal work for experience until they are able to find a full-time position.

CHEMICALS/PLASTICS/RUBBER/COSMETICS ★

The chemical industry's fortunes are entwined closely with the health of the overall economy, both in the United States and worldwide, because of the wide variety of products that use chemicals. If key industries—like the housing market, auto sales, and consumer and business electronics—are thriving, then the chemical industry will thrive as well. The industry, which manufactures over 50,000 different substances, is a huge exporter, but almost one-third of import/export business is estimated to be intracompany because of extensive globalization of production facil-ities. The industry, which employs almost a million U.S. workers across virtually every state, has maintained a positive trade balance for over 10 years, but in recent years it has lagged behind the general economy because of lack of pricing power. Industry experts predict that prices for commodity chemicals will continue to fall. It's no surprise that slow markets in Europe are offsetting gains in sales in South America. And the Asian financial crisis did little to help the situation. In fact, the crisis in Asia managed to stop or slow down billions of dollars worth of construction projects that directly impact the chemical industry. Exports to Asian countries have fallen as much as 40 percent.

The industry also suffers from a heavy regulatory burden as many companies try to meet new EPA requirements. This has helped some companies, hindered others. Those that actively participate in the "greening" trend can expect better performance in the coming years.

The changing nature of world competition will be a heavy determining factor on the growth rate of this industry over the rest of the decade. Plastics manufacturing is expected to benefit from increased market demand in the United States and an inevitable restructuring of the European plastics industry, expected within five years. Those gains are balanced by expected increased competition in the petrochemical industry from Middle Eastern countries.

Overall, the industry was expected to grow at a steady pace. The job outlook for the industry in general looks positive. The industry currenlty employs more than 850,000 people, accounting for five percent of the total manufacturing work force. Heavy sales are projected in the growth areas of high performance truck and light truck tires, mirroring these marketing trends in the auto industry. Sales of sports utility vehicles and minivans continue to rise, but for passenger cars, growth is not expected to be spectacular.

COMPUTERS/PERIPHERALS ★

The computer industry will be marked by continuing vitality, intense competition, and continued growth during the next few years. With only about 40 percent of U.S. house-holds owning a personal computer last year, as compared to over 90 percent who own television and videocassette recorders, in-dustry experts predict marked growth in the number of PC-owning households. This year, 70 percent of American households are expected to own a PC.

So after personal computers have saturated the marketplace, the next round of sparring within the computer industry will be over network servers—larger computers that can serve many people at once. The growth of Internet use is driving up demand for these machines. Gross margins for these products are higher—up to 50 percent, compared to a measly 15 percent for personal computers. However, new technological developments in the industry, resulting in cheaper building blocks for the server market, will bring on the kind of competitive environment that will cause these higher margins to diminish, resulting in a predicted job loss in the industry.

There are other bleak spots. Sales of mainframes were expected to give way to cheaper microprocessor machines. And even though global consumption of personal computers was expected to increase, price wars will mean less profit, squeezing job prospects. For the computer manufacturing industry overall, employment should continue its upward trend, but the emphasis will be on comprehensive service providers -- those that can offer training, setup, and support to smaller companies involved in computerizing their companies.

After three years of tough times, the computer industry may be on the upswing. Between the Asian crisis and a U.S. computer inventory glut, the makers of computers and chips took quite a beating. Industry revenue dropped 11 percent worldwide and profits plunged 26 percent. The slump seems to be over, however, with a growth of nearly 10 percent predicted in the coming years for chips and a 14 percent increase in the sale of PCs. One other trend in computer sales bodes well for continued growth in the area of home computers – 45 percent of the PCs sold in retail stores last year were priced at $1,000 or below.

CONSTRUCTION/REAL ESTATE ★

Retail and apartment construction may be in for a fall, but with a housing market come-back and office occupancy up, overall construction and real estate looks good for the future, following some rough years in the mid 1990s. Lower interest rates probably sparked the increase, as homebuilding started its upward trend in 1995. Mortgage rates dropped so much that housing affordability hit a 20-year high last year. Single family housing is expected to increase by 10 percent. Manufactured-housing is also seeing a tremendous growth.

Inventory levels for commercial buildings are surprsingly low, triggering a modest increase in construction over the next few years. While many of the Sun Belt markets continue to see a glut in office space, San Francisco, New York and Boston, along with other major tech and financial centers will see a rise in construction and sales.

A slowdown in demographics for new housing as the baby boomers age and fewer 20-somethings replace them, and a federal budget squeezed to the point of limiting public construction may cause a slowdown in some areas, but a rise in home-ownership among immigrants has caused a boost in real estate markets in U.S. border states, especially California.

Here are some areas to watch: Utility construction will be strong because more plants will reach generating capacity as the demand for electricity soars. Construction of medical buildings, including hospitals, are projected to increase with the aging population. Last, upgrades of an aging stock of buildings are anticipated, particularly if interest rates remain low. In fact, spending on nonresidential repairs may exceed new construction in that sector in the next few years.

Overall, construction is expected to hit a labor squeeze in the next five years, as the availability of new workers falls due to demo-graphic factors. So prospects for employment could benefit. A shortage of labor skills is predicted.

CONSUMER DURABLES ★★

"Durable goods" refers to nonindustrial manufactured products, or so-called hard goods. Household durable goods have shown a solid performance throughout the last decade. Since this industry is highly sensitive to levels of consumer confidence, however, growth could be held back to 2 or 3 percent annually, depending upon levels of consumer debt and taxation.

Demographics appear to be favorable over the next few years, as more Americans enter the age bracket of 35 to 55, which spends the majority of dollars on consumer durables. The top spenders are in the age group of 45 to 55, and record numbers of baby boomers entered that age bracket in the late 1990s. In automobiles, expect stronger growth at the two extremes of the market -- small sport utility vehicles (SUVs) and the high end luxury SUVs such as the Lincoln Navigator and Mercedes ML320. But the sale of passenger cars continues to lag despite rebate incentives offered by the manufacturers.

The household appliance industry is mature, and most sales are targeted to new housing, remodeling, or replacement. Annual growth remained in the 2 percent range throughout the 1990s. One positive development for the industry: The number of women entering the work force is once again increasing, after leveling off in the early 1990s. More women in the work force means a higher demand for labor-saving devices.

In consumer electronics, although sales of televisions, VCRs, and camcorders are expected to stabilize as a result of domestic market saturation, the growth of multimedia devices could zoom as new technologies become available. Overall, expect annual growth rates of 3 percent in this sector.

In household furnishings, overall growth

is expected to be between 3 and 5 percent, but because of expansion in the middle-age higher-income groups, sales of higher-ticket items are expected to increase above that. Also, newer homes are growing in square footage, and larger homes require more furnishings. The average size of a new home rose above 2,000 square feet by the late 1990s.

In lawn and garden equipment, demographics also favor the sale of riding mowers over walk-behinds, while environmental trends favor mulching machines.

Jewelry sales will benefit from a larger higher-income group (age 45 to 55), as well as the growing numbers of working women, who are large purchasers of jewelry. Annual growth in this sector will run between 2 and 3 percent annually for the next several years.

Sales of bicycles will continue to benefit from the popularity of the sport, which is the third most popular participant sport in the country.

CONSUMER NONDURABLES

Employment in the apparel field is on a downward trend in the United States, with imports continuing to swamp any export percentage gained. As a result, though consumer demand is up, imports are benefiting from those sales gains. Employment in the industry has declined in all product lines. The trend is expected to continue as more overseas companies compete with the United States for global market share, and more U.S. firms move plants overseas.

Textile shipments have seen growth rates of only 1 or 2 percent, and employment is continuing to fall, although the declines appear to be leveling off to the rate of 1 percent annually. Over a half-million workers are employed in this segment, half of them in South Carolina, North Carolina, and Georgia.

An overbuilt commercial stock of buildings has hurt floor-covering sales, but increased strength in the housing market should herald some moderate gains in coming years. Carpet purchases are discretionary, so heavy consumer debt or a fall in disposable income will slow growth in this sector.

The nation does remain competitive in the exports of manmade fibers, which include acrylic, nylon, spandex, and polyester, as well as wood-based fibers like rayon. Over the last 15 years, the manmade fiber industry has consolidated and invested in expanded capacity for higher value-added products. Future market opportunities look promising for better performance in these fibers, which increasingly sophisticated consumers are demanding.

Leather products face import pressures, and long-term sales are expected to be in the lower single digits, but the overall outlook appears good, as total hide supplies are expected to increase. This will drop prices and encourage more capital investment in the industry. Luggage and shoes are major end uses for leather. Luggage sales will benefit from demographic factors such as more working women buying briefcases, more well-heeled retirees buying luggage for travel, and growth in the higher-income age bracket of 45 to 55.

As for shoes, in the past 30 years, domestic production of leather footwear has dropped from 640 million pairs a year to less than 200 million pairs. Per capita consumption is up, but imports have swamped the market.

DRUGS/MEDICAL EQUIPMENT ★★

The pharmaceutical industry gets only a small amount of total sales from Asia. As a result, they have barely been touched by that area's economic crisis. New products coupled with price hikes are good forecasters of a record year or two coming up. The industry layoffs that took place earlier in the decade, as well as pressure to cut prices, have given way to higher sales and rising prices

This performance, however, is out of sync with the amount spent by the industry on research and development, which could mean fewer big-selling new miracle products in the short term. One other glitch is the threat of upcoming patent expirations. Industry experts predict that between 1999 and 2002, drugs that generated $14 billion in sales in the U.S. will go off patent. That could lead to a boost in generic versions of those drugs taking over market share.

The medical equipment industry benefits greatly from foreign trade, with its annual trade surplus approaching the $1 billion mark. New technology continues to spur high sales, and growth rates should exceed 6 percent. An aging population in the industrial nations is a major factor in sales growth.

Devices used in less invasive medical procedures will fare better, as the health industry is under increasing cost-containment pressure. Radiological devices will see a contraction in the U.S. market, and product manufacturers will probably turn to marketing efforts focused on emerging markets in Latin America and Asia.

EDUCATION AND TRAINING ★★

Elementary and secondary school enrollment is booming, with high school and college enrollments to follow within the next few years. However, there are advocates who hope to foster more private competition with public schools, and they may put pressure on a system where labor costs are increasing, but outdated labor rules and sinking morale put real limits on hiring and firing decisions in the traditional public school. If extensive privatization does occur, the private firms' more efficient operations could mean a stable or even decreasing work force for kindergarten through high school positions. This could occur, even though enrollments for both public and private schools are expected to grow from 51 million in 1995 to 54.5 million in the year 2005—an increase of almost 7 percent.

Still, even with trends moving toward a demand for higher efficiency and more productivity in the public schools, jobs in elementary education were expected to increase significantly into the next decade. Overall, industry experts expect more than 2 million jobs opening for elementary and secondary teachers through the midway point of the next decade. Though immigration has had a small but noticeable effect on public education, birthrates are the real cause of the increase. After being very low in the 1970s, the birthrate hit a high of over 4 million in 1990. This trend continued throughout the 1990s.

College enrollment should create a booming business in the coming years, as it increases from 14.2 million in the year 1995 to 16.2 million in 2005. High school graduates seeking highly focused career training should keep this increase steady.

The education and training industry is a huge employer, with an estimated work force in excess of 10 million, and as a

percent of the gross domestic product, it is second in size only to the medical industry. Even small increases percentage-wise in job growth could herald significant job openings.

Growth in corporate training expenditures will probably rebound from a recent slump because of the increased training needed overseas from joint ventures, as well as a need to provide remedial education to public school graduates and to upgrade employees' skills to match upgrades in physical plant technology. The biggst boost will come in the area of computer training and technical training and support. Experts predict that technology training will grow from $2.7 in 1999 to $7.8 billion in 2002.

ELECTRICAL AND RENEWABLE ENERGY EQUIPMENT

Deregulation has come to electric utility companies, and legislative change is causing companies to regear and discard their old top-heavy management style for a leaner look. Already many states have passed legislation enabling consumers in those states to shop around for electricity the same way they do for phone service. As a result, power companies are pruning the ranks of middle management and looking for other opportunities to cut costs.

These developments, combined with demands by some heavy users for lower rates, will continue to eat away at utility company profits, continuing a five-year trend. Some companies are cutting rates as much as 10 to 40 percent in an attempt to hold on to big-spending customers.

Another symptom of the prederegulatory fallout: Mergers among electric utility companies. Employment in the industry is expected to continue its falling trend into the next decade.

Costs for electric utility system maintenance will continue to grow because of the aging stock of power plants in the nation.

Electrical equipment shipments will increase, particularly in the niche field of renewable energy equipment. Shipments of wind-energy turbines increased at double-digit rates in the mid 1990s, as did shipments of solar photo-voltaic components.

Industry shipments of switching mechanisms, which stop and start electric motors, increased between 3 and 5 percent per year through the end of the last decade. Motors and generators have recovered from the slump of the early 1990s, as consumers returned to greater purchasing of household appliances. In general, long term growth looks good as the industry restructures for deregulation.

ENTERTAINMENT ★★

Surging demand overseas for American-made movies and music—plus deregulation of telecommunications, ensuring significant investment by phone companies in cable television—will herald strong growth in the years ahead for the entertainment business.

Some of the reasons for such optimism may be summed up with one word: Cable. Cable television has added a million new subscribers a year since 1996. Such growth fuels the Hollywood movie business. This demand, in addition to the increasing demand from overseas for American movies, bodes well for the film industry in general. Recent federal legislation will allow phone companies to compete with cable, forcing cable companies to upgrade services in the quest for future growth. That, plus the new interactive media technology, may herald such far-sweeping changes as to make long-term predictions in the cable industry difficult. While widespread use of the Internet on a television screen is not expected to take off for a year or two, cable subscribers are already signing up for high-speed cable modems that will thrust them into cyberspace.

The networks' share of the viewing audience should stabilize at around 60 to 65 percent, as the major networks halt the slide that has occurred since the popularity of cable television in the last decade began eating away at their dominance. Although motion picture ticket sales were up 10 percent last year, consumers continued to show a strong preference to view videocassettes and movies at home. In videocassette sales, purchases will outstrip rentals in expected growth. Long-term growth in video sales is expected to average 7 percent over the coming years.

As for the music business, it hit a low note with only $12.5 billion in sales last year. Compact disc sales now outnumber cassette sales by two to one. Videogame sales have also leveled off considerably since their peak in 1997.

ENVIRONMENTAL/ TECHNICAL SERVICES ★★

Sales of environmental equipment will increase in future years as the developed countries become more aggressive in their enforcement of antipollution regulations. Globally, this industry could reach sales of $300 billion, exceeding the aerospace industry in worldwide trade importance. Some defense contractors have not missed the implications of this and have established environmental cleanup divisions.

U.S. industries have spent billions of dollars on air cleanup costs in the past few years and will continue the trend in the foreseeable future. The fastest growing sector of air pollution equipment sales is the control of nitrous oxide and volatile organic compounds, with a projected annual growth rate of almost 50 percent. This compares with just under 10 percent for control of airborne particulates.

Projected growth in the amount of coal-generated electricity will also require a large investment in air-cleaning equipment. The number of coal-fired plants is expected to increase from 60 or so to over 150 within 15 years.

Landfill regulations, requiring greater central-ization of landfills and liners, is resulting in a diminishing number of municipal landfills. This will increase technological investment in waste treatment and recycling, as well as the exploration of new markets for disposal.

FINANCIAL SERVICES/ INVESTMENTS ★

Heavy consumer debt may be the drunk that crashed the party for the banking industry's five-year profit-breaking spree. Installment credit increased throughout the 1990s, and more loan delinquencies may be on the horizon. This, coupled with an increase in late payments on bank card account and a rise in delinquency rates will mean that banks will continue to look for ways to cut costs and mergers should continue at a full pace. Analysts predict that by the end of the decade, four-fifths of the industry's assets will lie in the hands of just 50 banks.

One way to cut bank costs is by using technology to encourage consumer banking via phone and on-line, thus reducing the need for expensive branches and electronic banking machines. Sales of this technological equipment should boom. More personnel reductions will undoubtedly follow such trends.

Interest rates are the telling factor for the securities industry, which has been on a roll since 1995. If rates stay low, the stock market will be the bigger draw for investors.

Mergers are expected to continue at their rapid pace. Mergers, however, shouldn't af-fect employment, which the federal government expects to continue in its above average growth rate through the year 2005.

FOREST/PAPER PRODUCTS ★

Though demand for wood products has remained very consistent during the 1990s, supply problems have resulted in an increase of imported wood, as much as 35 percent of market share. The vast majority is from Canadian imports. Employment in lumber and wood products fell from 259,000 jobs in the West to 187,960 jobs in the mid 1990s. The industry in the Southeast has been more stable. However, the lumber industry faces stiff competition from competing materials in the future, as more builders opt for steel instead of wood. Such housing has grown from 500 units to 80,000 in four years.

Hardwood veneer and plywood industries, as well as other domestic wood products in-dustries, should maintain stable employ-ment. Exports will grow because of concerns about tropical hardwood availability. The future of this industry is tied closely to the residential housing market, which uses 70 percent of wood products harvested and imported in the U.S.

The outlook for paper looks relatively flat, due to the same challenges of weak prices, oversupply, and foreign competition. Paper-making capacity is expected to grow only at a snail's pace of 1.5 percent as compared to the 2.6 percent growth rate in the mid-90s.

Corrugated products and folding boxes grew an average of 2 percent a year until the end of the 1990s. The United States was expected to sell over a third of the boxes made worldwide until then. Little market share is expected to be lost to plastic packaging products.

Though the pulp industry is expected to grow at around 2 percent a year, strong growth is an-ticipated in the recycling sector. Production of re-cycled pulp materials has flattened out in recent years, but is expected to increase by the end of the decade.

FREIGHT AND TRANS-PORTATION ★

The outlook for transportation depends upon which form of transportation you're looking at. Airlines and railroads are both undergoing consolidation and this should encourage growth as the transportation systems smooth out the bumps. By the end of the decade the U.S. will have two major eastern railroads and two major western railroads. This should mean im-proved transit times, since transfers from one railroad to another will be obsolete.

Airlines, also, are expected to continue their growth, with mergers still on the horizon.

The Federal Aviation Administration expects U.S. air travel to increase at an annual rate of around 4 percent over the next 15 to 20 years.

More mergers could be in store for the airlines, however. Analysts say such deals could pull companies away from improving service, at least in the short term.

Concerns over commuting congestion in the nation's largest cities could be good news for passenger rail over the long term. Passenger rail is expected to grow between 2 and 3 percent between now and the end of the decade.

Trucking businesses continue to dominate the domestic freight market, with almost 80 percent of the total market. This includes companies that provide their own freight service for their own goods. Too much capacity in the trucking industry, as well as Mexican economic woes (which resulted in fewer exports to that country), gave trucking freight haulers a bad time in the middle of the 1990's, but business seems to be on the upswing. This robustness should continue as trucking edges out rail usage for domestic transport.

U.S. Navy contracts for shipbuilding and repair will comprise the majority of work for America's shipyards, and employment will drop over the next several years as a result of federal spending cutbacks.

HEALTH SERVICES ★★

Cost containment pressures, in the wake

of the failure of health care reform, and the demographics of an aging society have shifted the emphasis in health care away from intensive, long-term hospital stays to outpatient treatment and preventive care. Total hospital admissions are up, but the average length of stay has fallen in the past several years to just 6.7 days. There has been pressure to limit the length of maternity stays, and shorter stays for geriatric patients are possible because of an increase in the network of supportive outpatient resources. Industry experts predict that the unoccupancy rate for hospitals nationwide will continue its upward trend, increasing to 55 percent in the year 2000.

The trend towards managed care continues with the growth of health maintenance organizations (HMOs). Along with the growth has come increased competition, which has led to mergers and consolidation as the new industry sorts itself out. To counteract the competition from HMOs, many hospitals are merging and consolidating into chains that offere HMO-like service.

Another trend is the physician practice-management companies (PPM), which manage doctors and their back-office chores and enable them to negotiate contracts with insurers and health care compnanies. Industry experts predict that by the year 2001, PPMs may capture as much as 50 percent of the physician services market.

Hospitals, HMOs and nursing homes were all targeted by significant changes in Medicare funding and reimbursement systems. After a brief downtown, HMOs and hospitals are seeing healthier returns – mostly because they have dropped out of ailing markets with high price caps and strict regulations.

How all these changes will impact employment is not known. Overall, more than 10 million people are employed in the industry. Annual growth is slowing to just over 10 percent as a result of cost-containment pressures. The unknown factor of future health care reform could change this projection over the next five years.

INDUSTRIAL/ANALYTI-CAL INSTRUMENTS ★★

The manufacture and sale of industrial and analytical instruments is another industry that boasts a positive trade balance. It is anticipated to increase, as the worldwide demand for U.S. technology equipment increases. One research group predicts a 20 percent annual sales growth for this industry between 1998-2001.

Industry/Analytical Instruments includes laboratory equipment, optical instruments, measuring and controlling instruments, and instruments that control fluid flow and measure electricity. Huge sectors that affect this industry include water monitoring, wastewater treatment, the medical industry (for optics), and semiconductor manu-facturing, which uses test equipment included in this industry.

The only area in the overall industry not predicted to have long-term annual growth above 4 or 5 percent is the nuclear controls sector. It is experiencing a slump because of worldwide decline. The only growth areas in this sector for exports are Japan, South Korea, and Taiwan, which have plans for more nuclear power plants.

Double-digit growth was the case in semiconductor manufacturing, until the bottom fell out in 1996. Since then, sales have increased and the long term prospects for semiconductors still looks good. Sales growth rates should be between 15 and 25 percent from now through the begining of the 21st Century.

The same holds true for communications testing equipment, which benefits from a huge U.S. global trade surplus. Canada and Japan are the big buyers of telecommunications testing equipment.

Consumer demand for more processed foods with enhanced flavors and textures, along with growth in life sciences worldwide, is spurring growth for laboratory equipment used in biotechnology. Though domestic demand will not be spectacular, exports to Asian countries and Mexico are expected to experience a healthy increase.

Annual growth of 5 percent is expected over the next few years in optical testing equipment, even though military use is expected to decrease. That will be more than offset by growth in the medical industry.

INFORMATION SERVICES ★★

American software sales continue a meteoric rise, although future volatility make concrete predictions difficult. What is for certain is that the industry as a whole is upwardly mobile. Sales between 1998 and 2001 should rise 10 percent, exceeding $100 billion. Employment in software and data processing should follow suit as several factors point to increased sales and increased demand.

The release of Microsoft's Windows 98 went without a hitch, and although initial sales were not of the catagory of Windows 95, prospects look good for the software giant. The big factor in the industry is the Web-related software, sales of which are expected to exceed $4 billion by the end of the decade. The battle between Microsoft and Netscape should be resolved by then, and most industry analysts see that segment as ripe to explode.

Another area of big growth is that of network-serving computer programs. These programs enable one computer to serve many people, without the expensive costs of mainframe computers. Companies are expected to spend billions on software in the coming years for these expanded PCs or Unix workstation computers. Windows 2000, for office servers, will be one of the powerful operating systems to reap benefits from this trend.

Last, corporate downsizing as a general phenomenon is a blessing to the software industry, as companies need to use more savvy computers to goad ever more efficiency out of an already lean system. By automating certain key functions—customer support, for example—and replacing discordant computer systems with integrated systems (called integrated enterprise software by the industry), companies can further reduce costs. Given the general environment, the only software area that is expected to stagnate is mainframe applications. Mainframe computers are simply being replaced by client server networks using smaller computers, so a stagnation in mainframes is being replaced by gargantuan leaps of profits in these networks.

INSURANCE ★

The key words for the insurance industry continue to be consolidation. With Aetna's acquisition of NYLCare and other recent mergers, the next two years should see a period marked by more consolidation and hot competition both domestically and foreign. Gains in the property-casualty segment of the industry should be modest, with industry analysts predicting growth rates below five percent.

Employment in the life and health insurance industry has been dropping since the mid 1990s and will continue to encounter problems as consumers look to mutual funds instead of life insurance; funds are sold through direct marketing as opposed to a costly agent network. In order to cut distribution costs, which can eat up to two-thirds of product costs, some companies are looking to banks as selling outlets for life insurance.

With all the mergers and acquisitions, downsizing has become a reality in the industry. But with cost cutting, jobs as a whole were expected to increase slightly for the entire industry during the next five years.

Over the next decade, life insurance products have demographics in their favor, since sales are expected to rise as baby boomers become middle-aged and become concerned with retirement issues. This will also increase the demand for health insurance.

For casualty insurance, the long-term prospects are uncertain, depending upon how fast rates rise, the potential failure of a large-scale insurer, and how much streamlining can be done by weaker companies. There is some concern that the industry may be undercapitalized for a major disaster, and this will create some pressure to raise rates.

METALS

Asia accounts for about 45 percent of the world's steel output. In 1998 Asian, Russian and Brazilian imports jumped by 100 percent or more. Steel prices plummeted almost 30 percent under the weight of imports in the spring of that year. Trade lawsuits have caused a slowup of the imported steel, but exporters are looking for ways around this problem. In the meantime, many big steel companies were forced to cut costs and employment has dropped drastically in the industry. Lean times should continue for the next five years, according to industry analysts. Another serious concern is overcapacity. New mills coming on-line will add to the oversupply and put more pressure on larger mills to cut costs. One hope -- China, which could become a large buyer of U.S. steel. China's need for steel rose by 20 million tons in the first three years of the decade. Long-term, China may need as much as 100 million tons by the decade's end.

Aluminum should be headed for long-term growth as aluminum producers continue inroads into new areas, such as automobiles. Another factor is the demand from aircraft manufacturers and the aerospace industry. If demand for new planes inceases, then the industry will be in good shape. The only snag may be periodic price drops.

Over the long term, aluminum could also receive a boost from car makers looking to increase fuel efficiency. Steel could receive a boost from the domestic housing market, where steel framing is becoming a small niche field in the construction industry. Copper consumption around the world and in the United States is expected to increase slightly over the next four years, with China leading expected increases.

Demand for lead will remain consistent, with car batteries the primary use. Provided the automobile market stays stable, lead should see slight growth.

MOTOR VEHICLES/PARTS
★

Price-conscious consumers are looking to a burgeoning used-car market, and this trend had Detroit concerned about prospects for the future. The flood of used vehicles from expiring auto and truck leases will add to pressures that are squeezing manufacturers' profit margins. Actions by automobile manufacturers such as cutting costs, increasing productivity and improving quality have kept automobiles rolling off the lots. Rebates have played a major role and increases in sales of sports utility vehicles (SUVs) and small pick-up trucks have provided a large boost in sales. Industry experts expect a slowdown in sales to continue for the next ten years to reflect the demographics of the baby-boomer population. Therefore, the general employment picture should remain flat, but susceptible to ups and downs of the general economy.

Though new car sales appear to have topped out at just under 16 million units annually, some industry experts see good news in that. Such plateauing of sales means consistency in the industry, with plant managers able to run factory operations at maximum efficiency. Over the long term, all auto makers are looking to the Pacific region for new market growth.

Auto suppliers are seeing their ranks pruned by the big car manufacturers, which are demanding an ever higher level of service from these companies.

Car manufacturers are turning over more and more of the content manufacture of new cars to supply companies—for example, having a company manufacture an entire dashboard instead of just a radio or ashtray. Car makers are also expecting such companies to supply a worldwide array of manufacturing facilities, as U.S. auto makers expand plants overseas. Over the long term, auto manufacturers will shift more research and development costs to the supplier industry. As a result, only the largest suppliers will be able to meet these requirements, and smaller companies will go under.

NATURAL RESOURCES AND ENERGY

Employment in the energy industry looks varied but mostly positive. The last decade saw much consolidation, restructuring and cutting back on costs and labor. The result is an industry that is leaner and more competitive. These factors could mean a positive employment outlook. The Bureau of Labor Statistics predicts the industry is in for a period of slow growth, due to the vagaries of supply and demand in the oil industry. But the good news is that because of all the labor cuts the past ten years, there is a good chance jobs will be there in the coming years.

The coal industry is expected to lose more jobs as labor-saving machinery continues to make inroads into the mines. Number of workers in coal is expected to drop from a current level of 148,000 to 113,000 by the year 2005, continuing a trend started in the 1980s.

A bright spot for the energy industry is the retail sector, where gasoline outlets have become dependable profit generators.

For the long term, energy demand will grow more quickly in developing countries. In the more developed nations such as the United States, demand will grow at a projected anemic rate of 1 percent annually, due to stronger demands for energy conservation.

More than 75 percent of coal mined in the United States goes to electric utilities. Natural gas prices, which held up in the past, are expected to drop this year by as much as 11 percent as U.S. demand weakens.

Nonfuels mining, linked strongly to motor vehicle sales, should increase in the coming years. Aluminum mining will also be aided by a resolution of a long-term worldwide glut.

OFFICE/PHOTOGRAPHIC EQUIPMENT ★★

This industry includes office machines, photo-copiers, and photographic equipment. The photocopier industry is being driven not by new technology in the copying process itself but by machines that combine printing and copying capabilities. Sales of these digital photocopier products, which combine photo-copying capabilities with fax and printing, are expected to continue their upward trend begun with their introduction in the mid 1990s.

Although the use of E-mail continues to climb, the fax machine market remains strong. E-mail is not universally used, so businesses must continue to offer fax capabilities to customers and suppliers who may not have E-mail capabilities. However, since the E-mail arrives at a person's desktop computer, employees are becoming used to having access to E-mail and fax transmissions at their workstations. Therefore, more fax machines are being ordered to meet these expectations.

Printer sales were expected to grow. Color printers could see tremendous growth during the next five years, as sales tripled in the mid 1990s.

Overall, the industry is expected to have modest growth of 2 percent a year, with the photocopier sector compensating for any potential consumer slowdown in the purchase of personal photographic equipment.

PRINTING AND PUBLISHING ★★

Despite living in an increasingly electronic universe, Americans are showing a surprising appetite for the printed word. A growing over-35 population means more newspaper, book, and magazine readers. However, even the under-35 group will see the book market targeting them.

The newspaper industry suffered in the late 1990s when competition from other media cut into circulation and advertising. Ad rates were sluggish, paper prices high, and readership continued its decline. As a result, the industry continued to see labor cutbacks and weaker newspapers closed up shop. The stronger newspapers expanded by buying up other media outlets such as radio and television stations. The bright spot was electronic -- many newspapers have opened up Web sites featuring electronic versions of their product.

In the magazine industry the situation was even worse, exemplified by the closing of Family Media which left more than 250 people without jobs. Even giant Time Warner laid off more than 600 employees. The bright spot continues to be niche marketing, with those magazines aimed at specialized audiences doing well.

With advertising revenues expected to rise, a host of new speciality magazines are expected to hit the newsstands.

Another factor contributing to growth in the industry is demographics, something the book industry in particular, highly depends upon. The increase in the number of school-age children—whose population was projected to grow by 7 percent through the year 2000—will raise demand for elementary and high-school textbooks. The U.S. population as a whole will also increase, and more than 1 million new book buyers in the age group between early adolescence and middle age should enter the market. Last, an ever-increasing educational attainment, as employment pressures demand more educated workers, will contribute positively to the book-buying market. It will also help news-paper and magazine sales. As a result, publishing over the long term should post modest annual gains of around 3 percent over the next few years.

PRODUCTION MACHINERY ★★

As recently as 1995, production machinery sales were up 12 percent, but by 1996 the days of strong growth had tapered off. The late 1990s saw only modest growth. The problem was that despite the growing economy, businesses weren't adding new capacity. Also, companies that depended on a strong foreign market were hurt by the Asian financial crisis and a lag in the European economy. The outlook for the next five years, according to industry analysts, is more of the same -- modest growth with no great gains.

Even such modest growth reflects the overall strength of industrial manufacturing in the United States, where most of the country's major producers realize that continued investment in new machinery will keep manufacturing strong.

Total employment in production machinery was expected to increase, especially among Information Systems (IS) staffers needed to develop software and hardware now used in the manufacturing process.

For the long term, expect growth of around 3 percent annually between now and 2002. Worldwide urban growth, an aging infra-structure, and the pressing need for cash from natural resources harvesting by Third World countries will all contribute to a steady, though modest, demand for industrial equipment.

RETAILING ★★

Job growth in retailing is anticipated to be moderately strong, with the total number of U.S. retail workers more than doubling those employed in manufacturing—a complete reversal of the situation in the early 1980s. Internet sales continue to grow, with major department stores such as Macy's offering their products on-line.

It is a diverse industry, with almost half of all companies employing fewer than five people, and less than 10 percent employing more than 20. One in five nonagricultural employees in the United States works in the retail sector. In fact, sales help is getting harder to find and retain. Stores will be forced to offer more in pay and benefits.

The retail industry's growth and success is tied into the general state of the economy, with sales tending to mirror the rate of increase in the gross national product.

Look for more consolidation, with larger companies buying out smaller ones. One anticipated trend in the industry will be increasing numbers of single-person households, which will lead to a higher demand for single-serving products in the retail food industry—a sector that employs one-third of retail workers.

Convenience stores may see negative growth. Their mainstay customers are men age 18-34, a section of the population that continued its decline during the 1990s. However, a surge in the number of teenagers could lead to an increase in consumer acceptance of alternative retail outlets, such as electronic shopping channels and interactive television.

TELECOMMUNICATIONS EQUIPMENT AND SERVICES ★

With sweeping legislation recently passed allowing cable companies and long-distance and local telephone carriers to compete in each other's markets, the only thing for certain in the future of the telecom-munications industry is a new round of investment and creativity. Demand will be up because consumer use of phone lines and phone time is going up. But companies may enter a vicious round of competition, as they spend billions of dollars to intrude in each other's markets. Mergers, acquisitions, and alliances between companies could shift the employment picture.

Long-distance traffic is expected to increase over the next five years. Several trends are accelerating this demand: telecommuting's in-creasing popularity, the growth of the Internet, an incredible increase in data transmission, and the consumer love affair with cellular phones. Cellular subscribers were expected to hit the 35 million mark by the end of the decade. Revenues for cellular companies are expected to increase in the range of 20 percent over that time.

The long-term prospects for telecommunications equipment manufacturing is good, with annual growth rates forecasted to be between 2 and 4 percent. Fiber-optic cable, cellular station equipment, antennas, and satellite systems are all expected to grow in the coming years.

TRAVEL AND LODGING ★★

Various firms from transportation, service, and retail make up the travel industry, which is a diverse, large, and growing sector of the U.S. economy.

Foreign travel in the United States is growing at a much faster rate than domestic travel. In the 1990s, foreigners traveling within the United States increased their spending by 55 percent. But U.S. citizens traveling within the nation increased spending by only 18 percent. International travel is expected to continue healthy growth throughout the rest of the decade. Travel agents are facing competition from electronic ticketing in air travel and rail traffic. They are promoting new services such as a small fee to find the cheapest rates or complete tours in areas such as golf or culinary interests.

Domestic travelers average three-and-a-half nights lodging while taking domestic trips. Several trends are to be noted. There is a definite shift toward shorter vacations, or mini-vacations. Weekend travel accounts for 55 percent of total domestic trips. Ecotourism, which is tourism that focuses on appreciating the environment, is rapidly growing in popularity. More than 35 million people in the United took an ecotourist trip in the late 1990s. This trend is also leading the travel industry to become more sensitive to travelers' concerns about the environment, and the industry is instituting recycling and other environmentally friendly measures in record numbers. In business, convention travel remains steady, but entertainment travel has declined.

Cruise travel is becoming ever more popular. This sector's policy of all-inclusive pricing gives it a competitive advantage, and other resort-type businesses are noting that and instituting their own pricing changes.

Occupancy rates are up in the lodging business. Hotel chains built and acquired properties as a result of low interest rates. Room rates have increased in the nation's 3 million rooms but are expected to drop by 2001 when the building boom peaks and hotels must fight to attract travelers.

WHOLESALING ★

The wholesale industry is a very stable one in terms of employment and is not subject to large swings because of its fragmentation. This sector is composed of tens of thousands of small firms. Although those numbers have been dwindling due to mergers, acquisitions, and some industry streamlining, the number of firms involved in the industry still total more than a quarter-million. The number of merchant wholesalers, which account for almost two-thirds of industry sales overall, fell by 25 percent in the early 1990s and is expected to fall another 15 percent by the end of the decade.

Wages in this sector tend to be higher than in manufacturing, and over 5 million people are employed in branch, warehouse, and transportation. Analysts portray wholesaling as a steady industry with a solid outlook through the year 2000.

One area of competition in the industry is the growth of direct sales outlets, which bypass wholesale channels and use alternative distribution channels. Wholesalers are becoming more dependent on consumer goods as a product line. However, this same category of goods is also the most vulnerable to usurpation by other alternative channels of distribution, such as discount stores and warehouse clubs. Sales in these areas of alternative distribution are beginning to show some weakening, however.

The product line with the strongest record of growth is capital goods, but these comprise only 20 percent of all wholesale revenues. Bulk goods, comprising a quarter of wholesale revenues and including items such as raw farm goods, have remained flat.

JOB OPPORTUNITIES
JOB HOTLINES

JOB HOTLINES PROVIDE THE JOB SEEKER WITH INSTANT ACCESS to employment opportunities that may not be available anywhere else. Many give up-to-date listings of jobs within an organization, whether it be citywide, statewide, or nationwide. They can offer the caller brief descriptions, an outline of qualifications, and/or information on how to go about applying for the openings. Hotline numbers listed here may also just give you information on how to subscribe, for a fee, to a job hotline service.

An important aspect to consider when conducting your job search is that many companies are listed in this chapter as having a specific function—Coca-Cola, for instance, is classified as in the food and beverages industry. However, most larger companies have in-house public relations, marketing, human resources, and sales departments, among others. In other words, don't limit your search to only the specific industries that match your interests; part of exploring the hidden job market is to search out opportunities in unexpected places.

Unless otherwise indicated, job hotlines in this chapter pertain to general jobs in the relevant organization. If a hotline pertains only to a specific type of job in an organization, the category is noted.

Be aware that some of the hotlines are merely recordings that tell callers where to send their resumes or to leave their names and telephone numbers. Companies in some fields, like entertainment, don't actively pursue applicants quite simply because they don't need to; there are far more candidates than positions. All in all, though, job hotlines are key to tapping resources for a comprehensive job search.

ALABAMA

AMERICAN CAST IRON PIPE COMPANY
❶ MANUFACTURING
Birmingham, AL; 205-325-8010

AUBURN UNIVERSITY
❶ EDUCATION
Birmingham, AL; 205-844-4336

BIRMINGHAM NEWS
❶ JOURNALISM
Birmingham, AL; 205-325-2188

EYE FOUNDATION HOSPITAL
❶ HEALTH SERVICES
Birmingham, AL; 205-325-8589

JEFFERSON COUNTY BOARD OF EDUCATION
❶ EDUCATION
Birmingham, AL; 205-930-3859

MONTGOMERY, CITY OF
❶ CITY GOVERNMENT
Montgomery, AL; 334-241-2217

PROTECTIVE LIFE INSURANCE COMPANY
❶ INSURANCE
Birmingham, AL; 205-868-3125

UNIVERSITY OF ALABAMA
❶ EDUCATION
Birmingham, AL; 205-934-2611

U.S. JOB TRAINING PARTNERSHIP
❶ GOVERNMENT
Huntsville, AL; 205-895-5400

U.S. POSTAL SERVICE
❶ FEDERAL GOVERNMENT
Montgomery, AL; 205-721-7163

ALASKA

ALASKA, STATE OF
❶ STATE GOVERNMENT
Anchorage, AK; 907-563-0200

ALASKA EMPLOYMENT AGENCY
❶ STATE GOVERNMENT
Fairbanks, AK; 907-451-2875

ALASKA EMPLOYMENT SERVICE
❶ STATE GOVERNMENT
Anchorage, AK; 907-269-4740

ALASKA REGIONAL HOSPITAL
❶ HEALTH SERVICES
Anchorage, AK; 907-264-1539

ANCHORAGE, CITY OF
❶ CITY GOVERNMENT
Anchorage, AK; 907-343-4451

ANCHORAGE DAILY NEWS
❶ JOURNALISM
Anchorage, AK; 907-257-4402

ANCHORAGE TELEPHONE
❶ TELECOMMUNICATIONS
Anchorage, AK; 907-564-1515

BLUE CROSS/BLUE SHIELD
❶ HEALTH SERVICES/INSURANCE
Statewide; 206-670-4773

FEDERAL JOB INFORMATION LINE
❶ FEDERAL GOVERNMENT
Anchorage, AK; 907-271-5821

NATIONAL BANK OF ALASKA
❶ BANKING
Anchorage, AK; 907-265-2197

UNIVERSITY OF ALASKA
❶ EDUCATION
Anchorage, AK; 907-786-4887

A R I Z O N A

AMERICA WEST AIRLINES
❶ TRANSPORTATION
Phoenix, AZ; 602-693-8650

ARIZONA LIBRARY ASSOCIATION
❶ LIBRARY SCIENCE
Statewide; 602-275-2325

ARIZONA STATE HOSPITAL
❶ HEALTH SERVICES
Phoenix, AZ; 602-542-4966

ARIZONA STATE JOBLINE
❶ STATE GOVERNMENT
Phoenix, AZ; 602-542-4966

ARIZONA STATE JOBLINE
❶ STATE GOVERNMENT
Tucson, AZ; 520-792-2853

ARIZONA STATE UNIVERSITY
❶ EDUCATION
Tempe, AZ; 602-965-5627

AVIS
❶ TRANSPORTATION
Phoenix, AZ; 602-273-3209

BANK OF AMERICA
❶ BANKING
Phoenix, AZ; 602-594-2500

DISCOVER CARD
❶ FINANCE
Phoenix, AZ; 602-481-2460

INTEL CORPORATION
❶ COMPUTERS/ELECTRONICS
Phoenix, AZ; 602-554-5726

MCDONNELL DOUGLAS HELICOPTER COMPANY
❶ AVIATION
Phoenix, AZ; 602-891-3100

MOTOROLA—GOVERNMENT ELECTRONICS GROUP
❶ ELECTRONICS
Phoenix, AZ; 602-441-3425

PHOENIX, CITY OF
❶ CITY GOVERNMENT
Phoenix, AZ; 602-252-5627
Pertains to: General

PHOENIX, CITY OF
❶ CITY GOVERNMENT
Phoenix, AZ; 602-262-7356
Pertains to: Police, Fire

SCOTTSDALE PUBLIC SCHOOLS
❶ EDUCATION
Scottsdale, AZ; 602-952-6296

TEMPE, CITY OF
❶ CITY GOVERNMENT
Tempe, AZ; 602-350-8217

TUCSON, CITY OF
❶ CITY GOVERNMENT
Tucson, AZ; 520-791-5068

UNIVERSITY OF PHOENIX
❶ EDUCATION
Phoenix, AZ; 602-929-7359

U.S. DEPARTMENT OF AGRICULTURE
❶ FEDERAL GOVERN-

MENT/AGRICULTURE
Phoenix, AZ; 602-225-5382

U.S. FOREST SERVICE
❶ FEDERAL GOVERN-
MENT/ENVIRONMENT
Phoenix, AZ; 602-225-5382

U.S. POSTAL SERVICE
❶ FEDERAL GOVERNMENT
Statewide; 602-223-3624

ARKANSAS

AMERICAN TELEPHONE & TELEGRAPH
❶ TELECOMMUNICATIONS
Statewide; 404-810-7001

COMPUTER SERVICES, DEPARTMENT OF
❶ STATE GOVERN-
MENT/COMPUTERS
Little Rock, AR; 501-682-9500

**FINANCE AND ADMINISTRATION, DE-
PARTMENT OF**
❶ STATE GOVERNMENT/FINANCE
Little Rock, AR; 501-682-5627

FIRST COMMERCIAL CORPORATION
❶ FINANCE
Little Rock, AR; 501-371-3310

GAME AND FISH COMMISSION
❶ STATE GOVERNMENT/WILDLIFE
Little Rock, AR; 501-377-6600

HCA DOCTOR'S HOSPITAL
❶ HEALTH SERVICES
Little Rock, AR; 501-661-4467

LITTLE ROCK, CITY OF
❶ CITY GOVERNMENT
Little Rock, AR; 501-371-4505
Pertains to: General

LITTLE ROCK, CITY OF
❶ CITY GOVERNMENT
Little Rock, AR; 501-377-7919
Pertains to: Waterworks

UNIVERSITY OF ARKANSAS
❶ EDUCATION
Little Rock, AR; 501-569-3038

**U.S. FEDERAL AVIATION ADMINISTRA-
TION**
❶ FEDERAL GOVERN-
MENT/AVIATION
Statewide; 817-222-5855

CALIFORNIA

AC TRANSIT
❶ TRANSPORTATION
Oakland, CA; 510-891-4782

AMERICAN RED CROSS
❶ HEALTH SERVICES
Los Angeles, CA; 213-739-4596

BANK OF CALIFORNIA
❶ BANKING
San Francisco, CA; 415-765-3535

BAXTER HEALTH CARE CORPORATION
❶ HEALTH SERVICES
Glendale, CA; 818-507-8394

BECHTEL CORPORATION
❶ CONSTRUCTION
San Francisco, CA; 415-768-4448

CALIFORNIA, STATE OF
❶ STATE GOVERNMENT
Los Angeles, CA; 213-897-3653
Pertains to: Department of Transportation

CALIFORNIA, STATE OF
❶ STATE GOVERNMENT
Oakland, CA; 510-286-6354
Pertains to: Department of Transportation

CALIFORNIA, STATE OF
❶ STATE GOVERNMENT
Sacramento, CA; 916-445-0538

CALIFORNIA, STATE OF
❶ STATE GOVERNMENT
San Diego, CA; 619-237-6163

CALIFORNIA, STATE OF
❶ STATE GOVERNMENT
Statewide; 916-653-9903
Pertains to: Department of Parks and
Recreation

CALIFORNIA FEDERAL, INC.
❶ FINANCE
Los Angeles, CA; 213-930-6712

**CALIFORNIA INTEGRATED WASTE MAN-
AGEMENT**
❶ WASTE MANAGEMENT
Sacramento, CA; 916-255-2591

CALIFORNIA STATE UNIVERSITY
❶ EDUCATION
Long Beach, CA; 310-985-5491

CHILDREN'S HOSPITAL
❶ HEALTH SERVICES
Oakland, CA; 510-428-3080

CHILDREN'S HOSPITAL OF ORANGE COUNTY
❶ HEALTH SERVICES
Orange, CA; 714-532-8500

COCA-COLA BOTTLING COMPANY
❶ FOOD AND BEVERAGES
Los Angeles, CA; 213-746-5555, ext. 2

COMMUNITY HOSPITALS OF CENTRAL CALIFORNIA
❶ HEALTH SERVICES
Central CA; 800-442-3944

DOUGLAS CORPORATION
❶ AEROSPACE
Long Beach, CA; 310-593-9303

FEDERAL JOB INFORMATION CENTER
❶ FEDERAL GOVERNMENT
Sacramento, CA; 916-551-1464, ext. 2

HEWLETT-PACKARD COMPANY
❶ ELECTRONICS
San Diego, CA; 619-592-8444

HILTON HOTEL
❶ HOSPITALITY
Long Beach, CA; 310-983-3445

HILTON HOTEL—AIRPORT
❶ HOSPITALITY
Los Angeles, CA; 310-410-6111

HYATT REGENCY HOTEL
❶ HOSPITALITY
San Diego, CA; 619-687-6000

KABC-TV
❶ BROADCASTING
Los Angeles, CA; 310-557-4282

LEVI STRAUSS AND ASSOCIATES
❶ APPAREL
San Francisco, CA; 415-544-7828

LONG BEACH, CITY OF
❶ CITY GOVERNMENT
Long Beach, CA; 310-570-6308
Pertains to: Civil Service

LONG BEACH, CITY OF
❶ CITY GOVERNMENT
Long Beach, CA; 310-570-6201
Pertains to: General

LONG BEACH TRANSIT
❶ TRANSPORTATION
Long Beach, CA; 310-591-8234

LOS ANGELES, CITY OF
❶ CITY GOVERNMENT
Los Angeles, CA; 213-847-9424

LOS ANGELES COMMUNITY COLLEGE DISTRICT
❶ EDUCATION
Los Angeles, CA; 213-891-2099
Pertains to: Nonteaching

LOS ANGELES COUNTY
❶ COUNTY GOVERNMENT
Alhambra, CA; 818-458-3926
Pertains to: Public Works

LOS ANGELES COUNTY
❶ COUNTY GOVERNMENT
Los Angeles, CA; 213-972-6217
Pertains to: Transportation Authority

LOS ANGELES TIMES
❶ JOURNALISM
Los Angeles, CA; 213-237-5406
Pertains to: Clerical, Sales

OAKLAND, CITY OF
❶ CITY GOVERNMENT
Oakland, CA; 510-238-3111

ORANGE, CITY OF
❶ CITY GOVERNMENT
Orange, CA; 714-744-7262

ORANGE COUNTY
❶ COUNTY GOVERNMENT
Costa Mesa, CA; 714-966-4025

ORANGE COUNTY
❶ COUNTY GOVERNMENT
Santa Ana, CA; 714-834-5627

PACIFIC BELL
❶ TELECOMMUNICATIONS
San Francisco, CA; 800-924-JOBS
Pertains to: Jobs Within California

RIVERSIDE, CITY OF
❶ CITY GOVERNMENT
Riverside, CA; 909-782-5492

RIVERSIDE COUNTY
❶ COUNTY GOVERNMENT
Indio, CA; 619-863-8970

RIVERSIDE COUNTY
❶ COUNTY GOVERNMENT
Riverside, CA; 909-275-3550

SACRAMENTO, CITY OF
❶ CITY GOVERNMENT
Sacramento, CA; 916-443-9990
Pertains to: General

SACRAMENTO, CITY OF
❶ CITY GOVERNMENT
Sacramento, CA; 916-440-1336
Pertains to: Housing and Redevelopment

SACRAMENTO CITY UNIFIED SCHOOL DISTRICT
❶ EDUCATION
Sacramento, CA; 916-264-4224
Pertains to: Classified Ads

SACRAMENTO COUNTY
❶ COUNTY GOVERNMENT
Sacramento, CA; 916-440-6771

SAN BERNARDINO, CITY OF
❶ CITY GOVERNMENT
San Bernardino, CA; 909-384-5376

SAN BERNARDINO CITY SCHOOL DISTRICT
❶ EDUCATION
San Bernardino, CA; 909-888-9955
Pertains to: Classified Ads

SAN BERNARDINO COMMUNITY COLLEGE DISTRICT
❶ EDUCATION
San Bernardino, CA; 909-384-0853

SAN BERNARDINO COUNTY
❶ COUNTY GOVERNMENT
San Bernardino, CA; 909-387-5611

SAN DIEGO, CITY OF
❶ CITY GOVERNMENT
San Diego, CA; 619-291-0110
Pertains to: Port of San Diego

SAN DIEGO COUNTY
❶ COUNTY GOVERNMENT
San Diego, CA; 619-531-5764

SAN DIEGO SCHOOL DISTRICT
❶ EDUCATION
San Diego, CA; 619-293-8002

SAN FRANCISCO, CITY OF
❶ CITY GOVERNMENT
San Francisco, CA; 415-206-5317
Pertains to: City and County

SAN JOSE, CITY OF
❶ CITY GOVERNMENT
San Jose, CA; 408-277-5627

SANTA CLARA COUNTY
❶ COUNTY GOVERNMENT
San Jose, CA; 408-299-2856

UNIVERSITY OF CALIFORNIA
❶ EDUCATION
Oakland, CA; 510-987-0824

U.S. DEPARTMENT OF HEALTH AND HUMAN SERVICES
❶ FEDERAL GOVERNMENT/HEALTH SERVICES
San Francisco, CA; 415-556-1088

U.S. POSTAL SERVICE
❶ FEDERAL GOVERNMENT
Long Beach, CA; 310-435-4529

U.S. POSTAL SERVICE
❶ FEDERAL GOVERNMENT
San Bernardino, CA; 909-335-4339

U.S. POSTAL SERVICE
❶ FEDERAL GOVERNMENT
San Diego, CA; 619-221-3351

WALT DISNEY PICTURES AND TELEVISION
❶ ENTERTAINMENT/FILM/BROADCASTING
Burbank, CA; 818-567-5800
Pertains to: Mass Marketing/Consumer Products

YOUTH FAIR CHANCE
❶ GOVERNMENT
Fresno, CA; 209-266-3742

COLORADO

AIRPORT SERVICES
❶ HOSPITALITY
Denver, CO; 303-368-4206

ANHEUSER–BUSCH
❶ FOOD AND BEVERAGES

Fort Collins, CO; 970-490-4500, ask for jobline

ARAPAHOE COUNTY
❶ COUNTY GOVERNMENT
Aurora, CO; 303-795-4480

BANK ONE
❶ BANKING
Denver, CO; 303-297-4200

BOULDER, CITY OF
❶ CITY GOVERNMENT
Boulder, CO; 303-441-3434

BOULDER COMMUNITY HOSPITAL
❶ HEALTH SERVICES
Boulder, CO; 303-440-2323

BOULDER COUNTY
❶ COUNTY GOVERNMENT
Boulder, CO; 303-441-4555

BURLINGTON NORTHERN RAILROAD
❶ TRANSPORTATION
Denver, CO; 303-220-3830

CITICORP/DINER'S CLUB
❶ FINANCE
Englewood, CO; 303-649-2800

COLORADO CONVENTION CENTER
❶ HOSPITALITY
Denver, CO; 303-640-8119

COLORADO DIVISION OF WILDLIFE
❶ WILDLIFE
Statewide; 303-291-7527

COLORADO STATE LIBRARY
❶ STATE GOVERNMENT/LIBRARY SCIENCE
Statewide; 303-866-6741

COMPUTER JOB SEARCH
❶ COMPUTERS
Denver, CO; 303-444-5543

DENVER, CITY OF
❶ CITY GOVERNMENT
Denver, CO; 303-640-1234
Pertains to: General

DENVER, CITY OF
❶ CITY GOVERNMENT
Denver, CO; 303-628-6339
Pertains to: Water Department

DENVER GENERAL HOSPITAL
❶ HEALTH SERVICES
Denver, CO; 303-640-3057

DENVER PUBLIC SCHOOLS
❶ EDUCATION

Denver, CO; 303-764-3263

EL PASO COUNTY
❶ COUNTY GOVERNMENT
Colorado Springs, CO; 719-575-8679

JOB SERVICES
❶ STATE GOVERNMENT
Colorado Springs, CO; 719-630-1111, category 5627

KING SOOPERS
❶ RETAIL
Denver, CO; 303-778-3270

MCI SYSTEMS ENGINEERING
❶ TELECOMMUNICATIONS
Colorado Springs, CO; 800-766-2848

NATURAL RESOURCES, DEPARTMENT OF
❶ STATE GOVERNMENT/NATURAL RESOURCES
Statewide; 303-291-7527

TRANSPORTATION, DEPARTMENT OF
❶ STATE GOVERN-MENT/TRANSPORTATION
Statewide; 303-757-9623

UNITED PARCEL SERVICE
❶ TRANSPORTATION
Denver, CO; 303-337-5847, ext. 193
Pertains to: Electronic Job Filing System

UNIVERSITY OF COLORADO
❶ EDUCATION
Boulder, CO; 303-492-5442

U.S. AIR FORCE ACADEMY
❶ FEDERAL GOVERN-MENT/EDUCATION
Colorado Springs, CO; 719-472-2222

U.S. DEPARTMENT OF COMMERCE
❶ FEDERAL GOVERNMENT
Boulder, CO; 303-497-6332

U.S. DEPARTMENT OF HOUSING AND UR-BAN DEVELOPMENT
❶ FEDERAL GOVERNMENT
Denver, CO; 303-672-5042

U.S. INTERNAL REVENUE SERVICE
❶ FEDERAL GOVERNMENT
Denver, CO; 303-446-1087

U.S. NATIONAL PARK SERVICE
❶ FEDERAL GOVERNMENT/PARKS
Denver, CO; 303-969-2010

U.S. POSTAL SERVICE
❶ FEDERAL GOVERNMENT
Denver, CO; 303-853-6030

CONNECTICUT

AMERICAN FROZEN FOODS
❶ FOOD AND BEVERAGES
Stratford, CT; 203-241-7187

AMERICAN TELEPHONE & TELEGRAPH
❶ TELECOMMUNICATIONS
Statewide; 800-858-5417
Pertains to: Management

CONNECTICUT COLLEGE
❶ EDUCATION
New London, CT; 860-439-2466

CONNECTICUT LIBRARY ASSOCIATION
❶ LIBRARY SCIENCE
Statewide; 203-889-1200

DURACELL INTERNATIONAL, INC.
❶ MANUFACTURING
Bethel, CT; 203-796-4650

FLEET BANK
❶ BANKING
Statewide; 800-358-5627, ext. 3

HARTFORD, CITY OF
❶ CITY GOVERNMENT
Hartford, CT; 860-566-1326

HYATT REGENCY
❶ HOSPITALITY
Greenwich, CT; 203-637-1234, ask for jobline

JOB SERVICE
❶ GOVERNMENT
Bridgeport, CT; 203-579-6262

MANCHESTER MEMORIAL HOSPITAL
❶ HEALTH SERVICES
Manchester, CT; 860-647-6424

NEW HAVEN, CITY OF
❶ CITY GOVERNMENT
New Haven, CT; 203-946-8265

SHERATON HOTEL
❶ HOSPITALITY
Hartford, CT; 860-240-7255

UNIVERSITY OF CONNECTICUT
❶ EDUCATION
Storrs, CT; 860-486-2466, ext. 1

DELAWARE

AMERICAN TELEPHONE & TELEGRAPH
❶ TELECOMMUNICATIONS
Statewide; 404-810-7001

DELAWARE DEPARTMENT OF LABOR
❶ STATE GOVERNMENT
Wilmington, DE; 302-577-2750

DELAWARE EMPLOYMENT AND TRAINING DEPARTMENT
❶ STATE GOVERNMENT
Georgetown, DE; 302-856-5625

DELAWARE JOB SERVICE HOTLINE
❶ STATE GOVERNMENT
Dover, DE; 302-739-4434

DELAWARE LIBRARY ASSOCIATION
❶ LIBRARY SCIENCE
Statewide; 302-739-4748, ext. 69

DELMARVA POWER AND LIGHT COMPANY
❶ UTILITIES
Wilmington, DE; 302-429-2450

E. I. DUPONT DE NEMOURS AND COMPANY
❶ CHEMICALS
Wilmington, DE; 302-992-6349

MEDICAL CENTER OF DELAWARE
❶ HEALTH SERVICES
Wilmington, DE; 800-626-5627

MILFORD MEMORIAL HOSPITAL
❶ HEALTH SERVICES
Milford, DE; 302-424-5519

UNIVERSITY OF DELAWARE
❶ EDUCATION
Newark, DE; 302-831-2100
Pertains to: Professional

UNIVERSITY OF DELAWARE
❶ EDUCATION
Newark, DE; 302-831-6612
Pertains to: Salaried

WILMINGTON TRUST COMPANY
❶ FINANCE
Wilmington, DE; 302-427-4555

DISTRICT OF COLUMBIA

AMERICAN UNIVERSITY
❶ EDUCATION
Districtwide; 202-885-2639

BLUE CROSS/BLUE SHIELD OF THE NATIONAL CAPITAL AREA

❶ HEALTH SERVICES/INSURANCE
Districtwide; 202-479-7470

BROOKINGS INSTITUTE
❶ EDUCATION
Districtwide; 202-797-6096

CHILDREN'S NATIONAL MEDICAL CENTER
❶ HEALTH SERVICES
Districtwide; 202-884-2060

CITIBANK
❶ BANKING
Districtwide; 202-429-7760

GEORGETOWN UNIVERSITY HOSPITAL
❶ HEALTH SERVICES
Districtwide; 202-784-2800

GEORGETOWN UNIVERSITY MEDICAL CENTER
❶ HEALTH SERVICES
Districtwide; 202-687-2900

HOWARD UNIVERSITY HOSPITAL
❶ HEALTH SERVICES
Districtwide; 202-364-2080

HUMANA
❶ HEALTH SERVICES/INSURANCE
Districtwide; 202-364-2080

METROPOLITAN WASHINGTON COUNCIL OF GOVERNMENTS LIBRARY COUNCIL
❶ CITY GOVERNMENT/LIBRARY SCIENCE
Districtwide; 202-962-3712

NATIONAL BROADCASTING COMPANY/WRC–TV CHANNEL 4
❶ BROADCASTING
Districtwide; 202-885-4058

SMITHSONIAN INSTITUTE
❶ FEDERAL GOVERNMENT/CULTURAL ORGANIZATIONS
Districtwide; 202-287-3102

U.S. BUREAU OF BROADCASTING
❶ FEDERAL GOVERNMENT/BROADCASTING
Districtwide; 202-619-0909

U.S. BUREAU OF NATIONAL AFFAIRS
❶ FEDERAL GOVERNMENT
Districtwide; 202-452-4335

U.S. BUREAU OF PUBLIC DEBT
❶ FEDERAL GOVERN-MENT/FINANCE
Districtwide; 202-874-4000

U.S. COMMODITY FUTURES TRADING COMMISSION
❶ FEDERAL GOVERNMENT/FINANCE
Districtwide; 202-254-3346

U.S. CORPORATION FOR PUBLIC BROAD-CASTING
❶ FEDERAL GOVERNMENT/BROADCASTING
Districtwide; 202-393-1045

U.S. DEPARTMENT OF COMMERCE
❶ FEDERAL GOVERNMENT
Districtwide; 202-482-5138

U.S. DEPARTMENT OF EDUCATION
❶ FEDERAL GOVERNMENT/EDUCATION
Districtwide; 202-401-0559

U.S. DEPARTMENT OF HEALTH AND HUMAN SERVICES
❶ FEDERAL GOVERNMENT/HEALTH SERVICES
Districtwide; 202-443-1230

U.S. DEPARTMENT OF HOUSING AND URBAN DEVELOPMENT
❶ FEDERAL GOVERNMENT
Districtwide; 202-708-3203

U.S. DEPARTMENT OF TRANSPORTATION
❶ FEDERAL GOVERNMENT/TRANSPORTATION
Districtwide; 202-366-9397

U.S. ENVIRONMENTAL PROTECTION AGENCY
❶ FEDERAL GOVERNMENT/ENVIRONMENT
Districtwide; 202-260-5055

U.S. FEDERAL RESERVE BOARD
❶ FEDERAL GOVERNMENT/FINANCE
Districtwide; 202-452-3038

U.S. FEDERAL TRADE COMMISSION
❶ FEDERAL GOVERNMENT
Districtwide; 202-326-2020

U.S. IMMIGRATION AND NATURALIZATION SERVICE
❶ FEDERAL GOVERNMENT
Districtwide; 202-514-4301

U.S. LIBRARY OF CONGRESS
❶ FEDERAL GOVERN-
MENT/LIBRARY SCIENCE
Districtwide; 202-707-4315

U.S. NATIONAL ENDOWMENT FOR THE ARTS
❶ FEDERAL GOVERNMENT/ARTS
Districtwide; 202-682-5799

U.S. NATIONAL ENDOWMENT FOR THE HUMANITIES
❶ FEDERAL GOVERNMENT
Districtwide; 202-606-8281

U.S. NATIONAL PARK SERVICE
❶ FEDERAL GOVERNMENT/PARKS
Districtwide; 202-619-7256

U.S. NEWS AND WORLD REPORT
❶ PUBLISHING
Districtwide; 202-955-2104

U.S. SENATE
❶ FEDERAL GOVERNMENT
Districtwide; 202-228-5627

WASHINGTON CONVENTION CENTER
❶ CITY GOVERN-
MENT/HOSPITALITY
Districtwide; 202-371-4498

THE WASHINGTON POST
❶ JOURNALISM
Districtwide; 202-334-5350

THE WORLD BANK GROUP
❶ BANKING/FINANCE
Districtwide; 202-473-8151

WUSA–TV CHANNEL 9
❶ BROADCASTING
Districtwide; 202-895-5895

F L O R I D A

AGENCY FOR HEALTH CARE ADMINISTRATION
❶ STATE GOVERNMENT/HEALTH
SERVICES
Tallahassee, FL; 904-488-8356

ALL CHILDREN'S HOSPITAL
❶ HEALTH SERVICES
St. Petersburg, FL; 813-892-4480

AMERICAN SAVINGS OF FLORIDA
❶ BANKING
Miami, FL; 305-770-2019

BARNETT BANK, INC.
❶ BANKING
Tampa, FL; 813-225-8761

BARNETT BANK OF PINELLAS COUNTY
❶ BANKING
Clearwater, FL; 813-539-9300

BAYFRONT MEDICAL CENTER
❶ HEALTH SERVICES
St. Petersburg, FL; 813-893-6080

BROWARD COMMUNITY COLLEGE
❶ EDUCATION
Fort Lauderdale, FL; 954-761-7503

BROWARD COUNTY
❶ COUNTY GOVERNMENT
Fort Lauderdale, FL; 954-357-6450

CAPITOL BANK
❶ BANKING
Miami, FL; 305-270-3930, ext. 1

CARNIVAL CRUISE LINES, INC.
❶ HOSPITALITY
Miami, FL; 305-599-2600, ext. 2793
Pertains to: Shipboard Positions

CITY NATIONAL BANK
❶ BANKING
Miami, FL; 305-868-2929

COMMERCE, DEPARTMENT OF
❶ STATE GOVERNMENT
Tallahassee, FL; 904-488-0869

COMMUNITY AFFAIRS, DEPARTMENT OF
❶ STATE GOVERNMENT
Tallahassee, FL; 904-488-0869

CORRECTIONS, DEPARTMENT OF
❶ STATE GOVERNMENT/LAW AND
CRIMINAL JUSTICE
Orlando, FL; 407-423-6600

CORRECTIONS, DEPARTMENT OF
❶ STATE GOVERNMENT/LAW AND
CRIMINAL JUSTICE
Tampa, FL; 813-871-7142

DADE COUNTY
❶ COUNTY GOVERNMENT
Miami, FL; 305-375-1871

FLORIDA INTERNATIONAL UNIVERSITY
❶ EDUCATION
Miami, FL; 305-348-2500

FLORIDA POWER CORPORATION
❶ UTILITIES
St. Petersburg, FL; 813-866-5627

FLORIDA STATE UNIVERSITY
❶ EDUCATION
Tallahassee, FL; 904-644-6066

FORT LAUDERDALE, CITY OF
❶ CITY GOVERNMENT
Fort Lauderdale, FL; 954-761-5317

GTE FLORIDA
❶ TELECOMMUNICATIONS
Tampa, FL; 813-224-4211

HEALTH AND REHABILITATION SERV-ICES, DEPARTMENT OF
❶ STATE GOVERNMENT/HEALTH SERVICES
Tampa, FL; 813-877-8349

HEALTH AND REHABILITATIVE SERV-ICES, DEPARTMENT OF
❶ STATE GOVERNMENT/HEALTH SERVICES
Miami, FL; 305-377-5747

HEALTH AND REHABILITATIVE SERV-ICES, DEPARTMENT OF
❶ STATE GOVERNMENT/HEALTH SERVICES
Orlando, FL; 407-423-6207

HIALEAH, CITY OF
❶ CITY GOVERNMENT
Hialeah, FL; 305-883-8057

HIALEAH HOSPITAL
❶ HEALTH SERVICES
Hialeah, FL; 305-835-4106

HOLLYWOOD, CITY OF
❶ CITY GOVERNMENT
Hollywood, FL; 954-921-3292

HOME SHOPPING NETWORK
❶ BROADCASTING
Clearwater, FL; 813-573-0500

HUMANA HEALTH CARE PLANS
❶ HEALTH SERVICES/INSURANCE
Tampa, FL; 813-281-6077

HYATT REGENCY
❶ HOSPITALITY
Miami, FL; 305-373-5627

HYATT REGENCY
❶ HOSPITALITY
Orlando, FL; 407-396-5001

HYATT REGENCY
❶ HOSPITALITY
Tampa, FL; 813-287-0666

JACKSONVILLE, CITY OF
❶ CITY GOVERNMENT
Jacksonville, FL; 904-630-1144

LEON COUNTY
❶ COUNTY GOVERNMENT
Tallahassee, FL; 904-922-4944

MAJESTIC TOWERS
❶ HOSPITALITY
St. Petersburg, FL; 813-381-5411, ext. 7103

MARRIOTT HOTEL—WORLD CENTER
❶ HOSPITALITY
Orlando, FL; 407-238-8822

MIAMI, CITY OF
❶ CITY GOVERNMENT
Miami, FL; 305-579-2400

MIAMI OPERATIONS CENTER/SOUTH FLORIDA RECRUITING MAIL BOXES
❶ CITY GOVERNMENT
Miami, FL; 800-826-2217, ext. 9

MIAMI-DADE COMMUNITY COLLEGE
❶ EDUCATION
Miami, FL; 305-237-2050

NORTH MIAMI, CITY OF
❶ CITY GOVERNMENT
North Miami, FL; 305-895-8095

ORANGE COUNTY
❶ COUNTY GOVERNMENT
Orlando, FL; 407-836-4071

ORLANDO, CITY OF
❶ CITY GOVERNMENT
Orlando, FL; 407-246-2178
Pertains to: General

ORLANDO, CITY OF
❶ CITY GOVERNMENT
Orlando, FL; 407-246-2473
Pertains to: Police

ORLANDO UTILITIES COMMISSION
❶ UTILITIES
Orlando, FL; 407-423-9191

PINELLAS COUNTY
❶ COUNTY GOVERNMENT
Clearwater, FL; 813-464-3745

SARASOTA COUNTY
❶ COUNTY GOVERNMENT
Sarasota, FL; 941-951-5495

ST. PETERSBURG, CITY OF
❶ CITY GOVERNMENT
St. Petersburg, FL; 813-893-7033

STATE ATTORNEY
ℹ STATE GOVERNMENT/LAW
Miami, FL; 305-547-0533

SUNBANK
ℹ BANKING
Miami, FL; 305-579-7001

SUNBANK
ℹ BANKING
Orlando, FL; 407-237-6878

SUNBANK
ℹ BANKING
Tampa, FL; 813-224-2001

TAMPA, CITY OF
ℹ CITY GOVERNMENT
Tampa, FL; 813-223-8115

TAMPA GENERAL HEALTHCARE
ℹ HEALTH SERVICES
Tampa, FL; 813-253-4100

TRANSPORTATION, DEPARTMENT OF
ℹ STATE GOVERN-MENT/TRANSPORTATION
Miami, FL; 305-470-5128

UNIVERSAL STUDIOS FLORIDA
ℹ HOSPITALITY
Orlando, FL; 407-363-8080

UNIVERSITY OF FLORIDA
ℹ EDUCATION
Gainesville, FL; 904-392-4631

UNIVERSITY OF MIAMI
ℹ EDUCATION
Coral Gables, FL; 305-284-6918

UNIVERSITY OF TAMPA
ℹ EDUCATION
Tampa, FL; 813-253-6254

U.S. DISTRICT COURTS
ℹ FEDERAL GOVERNMENT/LAW
Miami, FL; 305-530-7834

U.S. FEDERAL RESERVE BANK OF MIAMI
ℹ FEDERAL GOVERN-MENT/FINANCE
Miami, FL; 305-471-6480

U.S. VETERANS ADMINISTRATION MEDI-CAL CENTER
ℹ FEDERAL GOVERN-MENT/HEALTH SERVICES
Miami, FL; 305-324-3154, ext. 3154

WALT DISNEY WORLD
ℹ HOSPITALITY
Lake Buena Vista, FL; 407-345-5701
Pertains to: Auditions

WALT DISNEY WORLD
ℹ HOSPITALITY
Lake Buena Vista, FL; 407-828-3088
Pertains to: Casting, Employment

WESTINGHOUSE ELECTRIC CORPORATION
ℹ ELECTRONICS
Orlando, FL; 407-281-2500

G E O R G I A

AIRPORT HILTON HOTEL
ℹ HOSPITALITY
Atlanta, GA; 404-559-6781

AMERICAN FAMILY LIFE INSURANCE COMPANY
ℹ INSURANCE
Augusta, GA; 706-596-5959

AMERICAN RED CROSS
ℹ HEALTH SERVICES
Atlanta, GA; 404-892-1078

AMERICAN TELEPHONE & TELEGRAPH
ℹ TELECOMMUNICATIONS
Statewide; 404-810-7001

ATHENS—CLARKE COUNTY, CITY OF
ℹ CITY GOVERNMENT
Athens-Clarke County, GA; 706-613-3100

ATLANTA, CITY OF
ℹ CITY GOVERNMENT
Atlanta, GA; 404-330-6456

ATLANTA GASLIGHT COMPANY
ℹ UTILITIES
Atlanta, GA; 404-584-4705

ATLANTA JOURNAL AND CONSTITUTION
ℹ JOURNALISM
Atlanta, GA; 404-526-5092

ATLANTA MEDICAL ASSOCIATION
ℹ HEALTH SERVICES
Atlanta, GA; 404-872-3708

CHATHAM COUNTY
ℹ COUNTY GOVERNMENT
Savannah, GA; 912-652-7931

COLUMBUS, CITY OF
❶ CITY GOVERNMENT
Columbus, GA; 706-571-4738

CREDITOR RESOURCES, INC.
❶ FINANCE
Atlanta, GA; 404-257-8301

DEKALB COUNTY
❶ COUNTY GOVERNMENT
Atlanta, GA; 404-371-2331, ext. 2

EMORY UNIVERSITY
❶ EDUCATION
Atlanta, GA; 404-727-7611

EQUIFAX INFORMATION SERVICES
❶ FINANCE
Atlanta, GA; 404-612-2558

FULTON COUNTY
❶ COUNTY GOVERNMENT
Atlanta, GA; 404-822-7930

GEORGIA, STATE OF
❶ STATE GOVERNMENT
Atlanta, GA; 404-656-2724

GEORGIA INSTITUTE OF TECHNOLOGY
❶ EDUCATION
Atlanta, GA; 404-894-4592

GEORGIA PORTS AUTHORITY
❶ STATE GOVERN-
MENT/TRANSPORTATION
Savannah, GA; 912-964-3970

GEORGIA STATE UNIVERSITY
❶ EDUCATION
Atlanta, GA; 404-651-4270

GTE PERSONAL COMMUNICATIONS SERVICES
❶ COMMUNICATIONS
Atlanta, GA; 404-395-8500

HEWLETT–PACKARD COMPANY
❶ ELECTRONICS
Atlanta, GA; 404-916-8899

HYATT REGENCY
❶ HOSPITALITY
Atlanta, GA; 404-588-3746

LOCKHEED
❶ AEROSPACE
Atlanta, GA; 404-494-5000

MACON, CITY OF
❶ CITY GOVERNMENT
Macon, GA; 912-751-2733

MARIETTA, CITY OF
❶ CITY GOVERNMENT
Marietta, GA; 404-528-0593

MARRIOTT HOTEL–MARQUIS
❶ HOSPITALITY
Atlanta, GA; 404-586-6240

NATIONSBANK OF GEORGIA
❶ BANKING
Atlanta, GA; 404-491-4530

PEPSI—COLA
❶ FOOD AND BEVERAGES
Atlanta, GA; 404-352-7622

UNIVERSITY HOSPITAL
❶ HEALTH SERVICES
Athens, GA; 706-826-8933

UNIVERSITY OF GEORGIA
❶ EDUCATION
Athens, GA; 706-542-5720
Pertains to: Clerical

UNIVERSITY OF GEORGIA
❶ EDUCATION
Athens, GA; 706-542-8722
Pertains to: Lab, Research

UNIVERSITY OF GEORGIA
❶ EDUCATION
Athens, GA; 706-542-5769
Pertains to: Service, Maintenance

UNIVERSITY OF GEORGIA
❶ EDUCATION
Athens, GA; 706-542-5781
Pertains to: Technical, Professional

U.S. ARMY CORPS OF ENGINEERS
❶ FEDERAL GOVERNMENT
Savannah, GA; 912-652-5763

U.S. FEDERAL LAW ENFORCEMENT TRAINING CENTER
❶ FEDERAL GOVERNMENT/LAW
AND CRIMINAL JUSTICE
Glynco, GA; 912-267-8767

U.S. FEDERAL RESERVE BANK
❶ FEDERAL GOVERN-
MENT/FINANCE
Atlanta, GA; 404-521-8767

U.S. INTERNAL REVENUE SERVICE
❶ FEDERAL GOVERNMENT
Atlanta, GA; 404-455-2455

U.S. POSTAL SERVICE
❶ FEDERAL GOVERNMENT
Savannah, GA; 912-235-4629

VETERANS AFFAIRS MEDICAL CENTER
❶ FEDERAL GOVERN-
MENT/HEALTH SERVICES
Augusta, GA; 706-823-2204

HAWAII

FEDERAL JOB INFORMATION CENTER
❶ FEDERAL GOVERNMENT
Statewide; 808-541-2791

FIRST HAWAIIAN BANK
❶ BANKING
Oahu, HI; 808-525-5627

HAWAII, STATE OF
❶ STATE GOVERNMENT
Oahu, HI; 808-587-0977

HAWAII, STATE OF
❶ STATE GOVERNMENT
Statewide; 808-587-1148

HONOLULU, CITY OF
❶ CITY GOVERNMENT
Honolulu, HI; 808-523-4303

HTH CORPORATION
❶ HOSPITALITY
Honolulu, HI; 808-921-6110

ITT SHERATON HOTELS
❶ HOSPITALITY
Oahu, HI; 808-931-8294

KAISER PERMANENTE MEDICAL CENTER
❶ HEALTH SERVICES
Oahu, HI; 808-539-5569

**KAMEHAMEHA SCHOOLS/BISHOP ES-
TATES**
❶ EDUCATION
Oahu, HI; 808-842-8686

OUTRIGGER HOTELS
❶ HOSPITALITY
Oahu, HI; 808-921-6777

ROBERTS HAWAII
❶ TRANSPORTATION
Oahu, HI; 808-539-9406

SAFEWAY
❶ RETAIL
Statewide; 800-255-0812

ST. FRANCIS MEDICAL CENTER
❶ HEALTH SERVICES
Oahu, HI; 808-547-6592

U.S. POSTAL SERVICE
❶ FEDERAL GOVERNMENT
Statewide; 808-423-3690

IDAHO

ADA COUNTY
❶ COUNTY GOVERNMENT
Boise, ID; 208-364-2562
Pertains to: General

ADA COUNTY
❶ COUNTY GOVERNMENT
Boise, ID; 208-377-6707
Pertains to: Sheriff

ALBERTSON'S, INC.
❶ RETAIL
Boise, ID; 208-385-6422

BOISE, CITY OF
❶ CITY GOVERNMENT
Boise, ID; 208-384-3855

BOISE CASCADE CORPORATION
❶ FOREST/PAPER PRODUCTS
Boise, ID; 208-384-4900

ERNST CORPORATION
❶ ENGINEERING
Statewide; 208-621-6880

FIRST INTERSTATE BANK
❶ BANKING
Boise, ID; 208-389-4136

GROUP HEALTH NORTHWEST
❶ HEALTH SERVICES/INSURANCE
Northern ID; 208-838-3390

HEWLETT–PACKARD COMPANY
❶ ELECTRONICS
Boise, ID; 208-396-5200

IDAHO DEPARTMENT OF EMPLOYMENT
❶ STATE GOVERNMENT
Boise, ID; 208-334-6457, ext. 1

IDAHO PERSONNEL COMMISSION
❶ STATE GOVERNMENT
Statewide; 208-334-2568

IDAHO POWER COMPANY
❶ UTILITIES
Boise, ID; 208-383-2950

MCI
❶ TELECOMMUNICATIONS
Statewide; 800-288-9378

SIMPLOT COMPANY
❶ FOOD AND BEVERAGES
Boise, ID; 208-384-8002

ST. LUKE'S REGIONAL MEDICAL CENTER
❶ HEALTH SERVICES
Boise, ID; 208-386-2465

UNIVERSITY OF IDAHO
❶ EDUCATION
Moscow, ID; 208-885-3595

U.S. BUREAU OF RECLAMATION
❶ FEDERAL GOVERNMENT
Boise, ID; 208-378-5144

WASHINGTON MUTUAL SAVINGS BANK
❶ BANKING
Statewide; 800-922-3599

ILLINOIS

ABBOTT LABORATORIES
❶ PHARMACEUTICALS
Lake Bluff, IL; 847-937-6100

AMERICAN AIRLINES
❶ TRANSPORTATION
Chicago, IL; 773-686-4212

AMERITECH CORPORATION
❶ TELECOMMUNICATIONS
Chicago, IL; 800-808-5627

AMOCO OIL
❶ PETROLEUM
Chicago, IL; 312-856-5551

CELLULAR ONE
❶ TELECOMMUNICATIONS
Peoria, IL; 309-303-3444

CHICAGO, CITY OF
❶ CITY GOVERNMENT
Chicago, IL; 312-744-1369

CHICAGO PARK DISTRICT
❶ PARKS
Chicago, IL; 312-747-0946

COMMONWEALTH EDISON
❶ UTILITIES
Chicago, IL; 312-394-4650

COOK COUNTY
❶ COUNTY GOVERNMENT
Chicago, IL; 312-443-6598

DEPAUL UNIVERSITY
❶ EDUCATION
Chicago, IL; 312-362-6803

DRAKE CITY CENTER
❶ HOSPITALITY
Chicago, IL; 312-787-2200, ext. 4236

HARRIS BANK
❶ BANKING
Chicago, IL; 312-461-6900

HEWLETT–PACKARD COMPANY
❶ ELECTRONICS
Bloomington/Chicago/Naperville, IL; 708-245-3909

HILTON HOTEL
❶ HOSPITALITY
Chicago, IL; 312-922-4400

HOTEL INTER–CONTINENTAL
❶ HOSPITALITY
Chicago, IL; 312-321-8819

HYATT REGENCY HOTEL
❶ HOSPITALITY
Chicago, IL; 312-565-1234, ext. 6252

ILLINOIS, STATE OF
❶ STATE GOVERNMENT
Chicago, IL; 312-793-3565

LOYOLA UNIVERSITY
❶ EDUCATION
Chicago, IL; 773-508-3400

MARRIOTT HOTEL
❶ HOSPITALITY
Chicago, IL; 312-245-6909

NATIONAL BROADCASTING COMPANY
❶ BROADCASTING
Chicago, IL; 312-836-5588

NORTHERN ILLINOIS UNIVERSITY
❶ EDUCATION
DeKalb, IL; 815-753-1051

PEORIA COUNTY
❶ COUNTY GOVERNMENT
Peoria, IL; 309-672-6943

QUAKER OATS
❶ FOOD AND BEVERAGES
Chicago, IL; 312-222-7744

RITZ-CARLTON HOTEL
❶ HOSPITALITY
Chicago, IL; 312-266-1000, ask for jobline

SOUTHERN ILLINOIS UNIVERSITY
❶ EDUCATION
Carbondale, IL; 618-536-2116

SPRINGFIELD, CITY OF
❶ CITY GOVERNMENT
Springfield, IL; 217-789-2440

ST. JOHN'S HOSPITAL
❶ HEALTH SERVICES
Springfield, IL; 217-525-5600

SUNSTRAND CORPORATION
❶ AEROSPACE
Rockford, IL; 815-226-6269

UNITED AIRLINES
❶ TRANSPORTATION
Chicago, IL; 847-700-4094

UNITED AIRLINES
❶ TRANSPORTATION
Chicago, IL; 708-952-7200
Pertains to: Flight Attendants

I N D I A N A

ALLEN COUNTY
❶ COUNTY GOVERNMENT
Fort Wayne, IN; 219-428-7510

AMERICAN TELEPHONE & TELEGRAPH
❶ TELECOMMUNICATIONS
Statewide; 404-810-7001

BALL STATE UNIVERSITY
❶ EDUCATION
Muncie, IN; 317-285-8565

BANK ONE
❶ BANKING
Indianapolis, IN; 317-321-7987

BUTLER UNIVERSITY
❶ EDUCATION
Indianapolis, IN; 317-283-9984

COMMUNITY HOSPITAL NORTH
❶ HEALTH SERVICES
Indianapolis, IN; 317-841-5366

COMMUNITY HOSPITALS EAST AND SOUTH
❶ HEALTH SERVICES
Indianapolis, IN; 317-355-5599

EDUCATION FINANCE SERVICES
❶ FINANCE
Indianapolis, IN; 317-469-2184

FIRST OF AMERICA BANK—INDIANA
❶ BANKING
Indianapolis, IN; 317-241-1000

FORT WAYNE, CITY OF
❶ CITY GOVERNMENT
Fort Wayne, IN; 219-427-1186

INDIANA MICHIGAN POWER COMPANY
❶ UTILITIES
Fort Wayne, IN; 219-425-2345

INDIANA STATE EMPLOYMENT DEPARTMENT
❶ STATE GOVERNMENT
Gary, IN; 219-981-4100

INDIANA STATE UNIVERSITY
❶ EDUCATION
Terre Haute, IN; 812-237-4122

INDIANA UNIVERSITY
❶ EDUCATION
Bloomington, IN; 812-855-9102

INDIANA UNIVERSITY MEDICAL CENTER
❶ HEALTH SERVICES
Indianapolis, IN; 317-274-2255

INDIANA UNIVERSITY/PURDUE UNIVERSITY—INDIANAPOLIS
❶ EDUCATION
Indianapolis, IN; 317-274-2255

INDIANAPOLIS POWER AND LIGHT COMPANY
❶ UTILITIES
Indianapolis, IN; 800-735-8515

MACMILLAN PUBLISHING CORPORATION
❶ PUBLISHING
Indianapolis, IN; 317-581-4544

MARSH SUPER MARKETS
❶ RETAIL
Indianapolis, IN; 317-594-2737

PURDUE UNIVERSITY
❶ EDUCATION
West Lafayette, IN; 317-494-7417

RESORT CONDOMINIUMS INTERNATIONAL
❶ HOSPITALITY
Indianapolis, IN; 317-871-9724

SOCIETY NATIONAL BANK
❶ BANKING
Statewide; 219-239-4865

UNIVERSITY OF NOTRE DAME
❶ EDUCATION
South Bend, IN; 219-631-4663

I O W A

ALCOA
❶ MANUFACTURING
Davenport, IA; 319-359-2832

DES MOINES, CITY OF
❶ CITY GOVERNMENT
Des Moines, IA; 515-283-4115

DRAKE UNIVERSITY
❶ EDUCATION
Des Moines, IA; 515-271-4144

HEWLETT–PACKARD COMPANY
❶ ELECTRONICS
Cedar Rapids/Des Moines, IA; 847-245-3909

IOWA DEPARTMENT OF PERSONNEL
❶ STATE GOVERNMENT
Des Moines, IA; 515-281-5820

IOWA STATE UNIVERSITY
❶ EDUCATION
Ames, IA; 515-294-0146

MARRIOTT HOTEL
❶ HOSPITALITY
Des Moines, IA; 515-245-5544

MERCY HOSPITAL MEDICAL CENTER
❶ HEALTH SERVICES
Des Moines, IA; 515-247-3105

PIONEER HI-BRED INTERNATIONAL
❶ AGRICULTURE
Des Moines, IA; 515-270-4000

PRINCIPAL FINANCIAL GROUP
❶ FINANCE
Des Moines, IA; 800-525-2593

QUIK TRIP
❶ RETAIL
Statewide; 800-324-0935

UNIVERSITY OF IOWA
❶ EDUCATION
Iowa City, IA; 319-335-2682

WORK FORCE CENTER, STATE OF IOWA
❶ STATE GOVERNMENT
Cedar Rapids, IA; 319-281-5820

K A N S A S

CESSNA AIRCRAFT COMPANY
❶ AVIATION
Wichita, KS; 316-941-6155

COCA–COLA BOTTLING COMPANY OF MID-AMERICA
❶ FOOD AND BEVERAGES
Kansas City, KS; 913-599-9360

KAISER PERMANENTE
❶ HEALTH SERVICES
Kansas City, KS; 913-967-4701

KANSAS CITY, CITY OF
❶ CITY GOVERNMENT
Kansas City, KS; 913-573-5688

KANSAS DIVISION OF PERSONNEL
❶ STATE GOVERNMENT
Topeka, KS; 913-296-2208

KANSAS STATE UNIVERSITY
❶ EDUCATION
Manhattan, KS; 913-532-6271

LEARJET
❶ AEROSPACE
Wichita, KS; 316-946-2562

PROVIDENCE MEDICAL CENTER
❶ HEALTH SERVICES
Kansas City, KS; 913-596-4990

RAYTHEON AIRCRAFT CORPORATION
❶ AVIATION
Wichita, KS; 316-676-8435

SEDGWICK COUNTY
❶ COUNTY GOVERNMENT
Wichita, KS; 316-383-7633

SHAWNEE COUNTY
❶ COUNTY GOVERNMENT
Topeka, KS; 913-233-8200

ST. FRANCIS REGIONAL MEDICAL CENTER
❶ HEALTH SERVICES
Wichita, KS; 316-268-5191

UNION NATIONAL BANK
❶ BANKING
Wichita, KS; 316-261-4924

UNIVERSITY OF KANSAS

❶ EDUCATION
Lawrence, KS; 913-864-4623

UNIVERSITY OF KANSAS MEDICAL CENTER
❶ HEALTH SERVICES
Kansas City, KS; 913-588-5122

U.S. CENTRAL CREDIT UNION
❶ FINANCE
Kansas City, KS; 913-661-5321

U.S. ENVIRONMENTAL PROTECTION AGENCY
❶ FEDERAL GOVERNMENT/ENVIRONMENT
Kansas City, KS; 913-551-7068

U.S. POSTAL SERVICE
❶ FEDERAL GOVERNMENT
Topeka, KS; 913-295-9164

WICHITA, CITY OF
❶ CITY GOVERNMENT
Wichita, KS; 316-268-4537

KENTUCKY

ACCESS COMPUTER CAREER JOBLINE
❶ COMPUTERS
Louisville, KY; 502-329-0222

ALLIANT MEDICAL PAVILION/KOSAIR CHILDREN'S HOSPITAL/NORTON MEMORIAL
❶ HEALTH SERVICES
Louisville, KY; 502-629-8498

BANK ONE
❶ BANKING
Lexington, KY; 606-231-2760

BROWN-FORMAN CORPORATION
❶ FOOD AND BEVERAGES/CONSUMER PRODUCTS
Louisville, KY; 502-774-6770

COURIER JOURNAL/LOUISVILLE TIMES
❶ JOURNALISM
Louisville, KY; 502-582-7000

GENERAL ELECTRIC
❶ ELECTRONICS/MANUFACTURING
Louisville, KY; 502-452-0006

HUMANA
❶ HEALTH SERVICES/INSURANCE
Louisville, KY; 502-580-3450
Pertains to: Corporate

JEFFERSON COUNTY
❶ COUNTY GOVERNMENT
Louisville, KY; 502-574-6182

JEFFERSON COUNTY PUBLIC SCHOOLS
❶ EDUCATION
Louisville, KY; 502-485-3185

KENTUCKY JOB HOTLINE
❶ LIBRARY SCIENCE
Statewide; 502-564-3008

LIBERTY NATIONAL BANK
❶ BANKING
Louisville, KY; 502-566-1629

LOUISVILLE, CITY OF
❶ CITY GOVERNMENT
Louisville, KY; 502-574-3355

NATIONAL CITY BANK
❶ BANKING
Louisville, KY; 502-581-6453

PHILIP MORRIS USA
❶ CONSUMER PRODUCTS/FOOD AND BEVERAGES
Louisville, KY; 502-566-1234

UNIVERSITY OF KENTUCKY
❶ EDUCATION
Lexington, KY; 606-257-3841

UNIVERSITY OF LOUISVILLE
❶ EDUCATION
Louisville, KY; 502-852-5627

U.S. POSTAL SERVICE
❶ FEDERAL GOVERNMENT
Louisville, KY; 502-454-1625

U.S. VETERANS ADMINISTRATION MEDICAL CENTER
❶ FEDERAL GOVERNMENT/HEALTH SERVICES
Louisville, KY; 502-894-6176

LOUISIANA

AMERICAN TELEPHONE & TELEGRAPH
❶ TELECOMMUNICATIONS
Statewide; 404-810-7001

BATON ROUGE, CITY OF
❶ CITY GOVERNMENT
Baton Rouge, LA; 504-389-4980

CIBA-GEIGY CORPORATION
❶ PHARMACEUTICALS
Baton Rouge, LA; 504-642-1750

COMMERCIAL NATIONAL BANK
❶ BANKING
Shreveport, LA; 318-429-1803

FIRST NATIONAL BANK OF COMMERCE
❶ BANKING
New Orleans, LA; 504-582-7500

HYATT REGENCY
❶ HOSPITALITY
New Orleans, LA; 504-561-1234, ask for job-line

LOUISIANA STATE UNIVERSITY
❶ EDUCATION
Baton Rouge, LA; 504-388-1201
Pertains to: Academic

LOUISIANA STATE UNIVERSITY
❶ EDUCATION
Baton Rouge, LA; 504-388-1101
Pertains to: Classified Ads

LOYOLA UNIVERSITY
❶ EDUCATION
New Orleans, LA; 504-865-3400

MARTIN MARIETTA CORPORATION
❶ AEROSPACE
New Orleans, LA; 504-257-4940

PREMIER BANK
❶ BANKING
Baton Rouge, LA; 504-332-3512

RADISSON HOTEL
❶ HOSPITALITY
New Orleans, LA; 504-522-4500

SCHUMPERT MEDICAL CENTER
❶ HEALTH SERVICES
Shreveport, LA; 318-227-6841

SHERATON HOTEL
❶ HOSPITALITY
New Orleans, LA; 504-525-2500

SHREVEPORT, CITY OF
❶ CITY GOVERNMENT
Shreveport, LA; 318-673-5170

U.S. FEDERAL AVIATION ADMINISTRATION
❶ FEDERAL GOVERN-MENT/AVIATION
Statewide; 800-222-5855

U.S. POSTAL SERVICE
❶ FEDERAL GOVERNMENT
Shreveport, LA; 318-677-2320

M A I N E

AMERICAN TELEPHONE & TELEGRAPH
❶ TELECOMMUNICATIONS
Statewide; 800-858-5417

FEDERAL JOB INFORMATION CENTER
❶ FEDERAL GOVERNMENT
Statewide; 617-565-5900

FLEET BANK OF MAINE
❶ BANKING
Statewide; 800-358-5627, ext. 1

KEY BANK OF MAINE
❶ BANKING
Portland, ME; 207-623-7000, ask for jobline

NEW ENGLAND LIBRARY ASSOCIATION
❶ LIBRARY SCIENCE
Statewide; 617-521-2815

M A R Y L A N D

ALCOHOL, DRUG ABUSE/MENTAL HEALTH
❶ STATE GOVERNMENT/HEALTH SERVICES
Rockville, MD; 301-443-2282

BALTIMORE, CITY OF
❶ CITY GOVERNMENT
Baltimore, MD; 410-576-9675

BALTIMORE COUNTY
❶ COUNTY GOVERNMENT
Baltimore, MD; 410-887-5627

BALTIMORE COUNTY PUBLIC SCHOOLS
❶ EDUCATION
Baltimore, MD; 410-887-4080

BALTIMORE GAS AND ELECTRIC COMPANY
❶ UTILITIES
Baltimore, MD; 410-234-7778

BELL ATLANTIC CORPORATION
❶ TELECOMMUNICATIONS
Statewide; 800-492-9375

BETHLEHEM STEEL CORPORATION
❶ MANUFACTURING
Baltimore, MD; 410-388-7258

CHESAPEAKE HUMAN RESOURCES GROUP
❶ BUSINESS SERVICES
Baltimore, MD; 410-825-5478

DISCOVERY NETWORK
❶ BROADCASTING
Bethesda, MD; 301-986-0444, ext. 2

FEDERAL JOB INFORMATION CENTER
❶ FEDERAL GOVERNMENT

Baltimore, MD; 410-962-3822

FIRST NATIONAL BANK OF MARYLAND
❶ BANKING
Baltimore, MD; 410-347-6562

GIANT FOOD
❶ RETAIL
Baltimore, MD; 410-521-5004

GREATER BALTIMORE MEDICAL CENTER
❶ HEALTH SERVICES
Baltimore, MD; 410-828-3222

HYATT REGENCY
❶ HOSPITALITY
Baltimore, MD; 410-528-1234, ask for
jobline

JOHNS HOPKINS UNIVERSITY
❶ EDUCATION
Baltimore, MD; 410-955-3025

LOYOLA COLLEGE
❶ EDUCATION
Baltimore, MD; 410-617-5037

MARRIOTT HOTEL—INNER HARBOR
❶ HOSPITALITY
Baltimore, MD; 410-962-0202

MARYLAND STATE GOVERNMENT
❶ STATE GOVERNMENT
Baltimore, MD; 410-333-5044

MERCY MEDICAL CENTER
❶ HEALTH SERVICES
Baltimore, MD; 410-332-9414

MONTGOMERY COUNTY PUBLIC SCHOOLS
❶ EDUCATION
Rockville, MD; 301-279-3973

NATIONSBANK OF MARYLAND
❶ BANKING
Bethesda, MD; 301-897-0547

PROCTER & GAMBLE
❶ CONSUMER PRODUCTS
Hunt Valley, MD; 410-785-4600

ROCKVILLE, CITY OF
❶ CITY GOVERNMENT
Rockville, MD; 301-309-3273

SHERATON INNER HARBOR HOTEL
❶ HOSPITALITY
Baltimore, MD; 410-347-1808

UNIVERSITY OF MARYLAND
❶ EDUCATION
Baltimore, MD; 410-706-5562

UNIVERSITY OF MARYLAND
❶ EDUCATION
Baltimore, MD; 410-455-1100

UNIVERSITY OF MARYLAND MEDICAL SYSTEM
❶ HEALTH SERVICES
Baltimore, MD; 410-328-5627

U.S. FOOD AND DRUG ADMINISTRATION
❶ FEDERAL GOVERNMENT/
PHARMACEUTICALS
Rockville, MD; 301-443-1969

U.S. NATIONAL INSTITUTES OF HEALTH
❶ FEDERAL GOVERN-
MENT/HEALTH SERVICES/SCIENCE
Bethesda, MD; 301-496-2403

U.S. NAVAL ACADEMY
❶ FEDERAL GOVERN-
MENT/EDUCATION
Annapolis, MD; 410-293-3821

MASSACHUSETTS

AU BON PAIN
❶ FOOD AND BEVERAGES
Boston, MA; 617-423-2100, ext. 5

BANK OF BOSTON CORPORATION
❶ BANKING
Boston, MA; 617-434-0165

BOSTON EDISON COMPANY
❶ UTILITIES
Boston, MA; 617-424-2000, ext. 4

EMERSON COLLEGE
❶ EDUCATION
Boston, MA; 617-578-8578

FEDERAL JOB INFORMATION CENTER
❶ FEDERAL GOVERNMENT
Boston, MA; 617-565-5900

FLEET BANK
❶ BANKING
Statewide; 800-358-5627

GILLETTE COMPANY
❶ CONSUMER PRODUCTS
Boston, MA; 617-421-7567

HARVARD UNIVERSITY
❶ EDUCATION
Cambridge, MA; 617-495-2771

HYATT REGENCY
❶ HOSPITALITY
Cambridge, MA; 617-492-1234, ask for jobline

MARRIOTT HOTEL
❶ HOSPITALITY
Boston, MA; 617-578-0686

MASSACHUSETTS, STATE OF
❶ STATE GOVERNMENT
Boston, MA; 617-727-3777, ext. 6

**MASSACHUSETTS INSTITUTE OF TECH-
NOLOGY**
❶ EDUCATION
Cambridge, MA; 617-253-4251, ext. 2

NEW ENGLAND MEDICAL CENTER
❶ HEALTH SERVICES
Boston, MA; 617-636-5666

PORT AUTHORITY
❶ STATE GOVERN-
MENT/TRANSPORTATION
Boston, MA; 617-727-3777

RITZ–CARLTON HOTEL
❶ HOSPITALITY
Boston, MA; 617-536-5700

ST. ELIZABETH HOSPITAL
❶ HEALTH SERVICES
Boston, MA; 617-789-2233, ext. 3

U.S. NATIONAL PARK SERVICE
❶ FEDERAL GOVERNMENT/PARKS
Boston, MA; 617-242-6000

WATER AUTHORITY
❶ STATE GOVERNMENT/UTILITIES
Boston, MA; 617-241-6400

MICHIGAN

AMERITECH
❶ TELECOMMUNICATIONS
Detroit, MI; 313-223-8150

COMERICA
❶ FINANCE
Detroit, MI; 313-222-4610

CORRECTIONS, DEPARTMENT OF
❶ STATE GOVERNMENT/LAW AND
CRIMINAL JUSTICE
Lansing, MI; 517-373-4246

DETROIT, CITY OF
❶ CITY GOVERNMENT
Detroit, MI; 313-224-6928

DETROIT PUBLIC SCHOOLS
❶ EDUCATION
Detroit, MI; 313-833-2097

DOW CHEMICAL COMPANY
❶ CHEMICALS
Midland, MI; 517-636-6100

FEDERAL JOB INFORMATION CENTER
❶ FEDERAL GOVERNMENT
Detroit, MI; 313-226-6950

GRAND RAPIDS COMMUNITY COLLEGE
❶ EDUCATION
Grand Rapids, MI; 616-771-3800

HOLIDAY INN
❶ HOSPITALITY
Detroit, MI; 313-965-0200, ask for jobline

INGHAM COUNTY
❶ COUNTY GOVERNMENT
Lansing, MI; 517-887-4329

JOB SERVICE, STATE OF MICHIGAN
❶ STATE GOVERNMENT
Detroit, MI; 313-876-5627
Pertains to: Clerical

MICHIGAN LIBRARY ASSOCIATION
❶ LIBRARY SCIENCE
Statewide; 517-694-7440

MICHIGAN STATE UNIVERSITY
❶ EDUCATION
East Lansing, MI; 517-355-9518

PUBLIC HEALTH DEPARTMENT
❶ STATE GOVERNMENT/HEALTH
SERVICES
Lansing, MI; 517-335-8797

SINAI HOSPITAL
❶ HEALTH SERVICES
Detroit, MI; 313-493-6161

UNIVERSITY OF MICHIGAN
❶ EDUCATION
Ann Arbor, MI; 313-747-2375
Pertains to: General

UNIVERSITY OF MICHIGAN
❶ EDUCATION
Ann Arbor, MI; 313-764-7292
Pertains to: Professional

**UNIVERSITY OF MICHIGAN MEDICAL CEN-
TER**
❶ HEALTH SERVICES
Ann Arbor, MI; 313-329-5550

WAYNE COUNTY
❶ COUNTY GOVERNMENT
Detroit, MI; 313-224-5900

MINNESOTA

AMERICAN EXPRESS ADVISORS
❶ FINANCE
Minneapolis, MN; 612-671-5059

DAYTON'S
❶ RETAIL
Minneapolis, MN; 612-375-2200, ask for jobline

FEDERAL JOB INFORMATION CENTER
❶ FEDERAL GOVERNMENT
Minneapolis/St. Paul, MN; 612-725-3430

GENERAL MILLS
❶ FOOD AND BEVERAGES
Minneapolis, MN; 612-540-2334

HENNEPIN COUNTY
❶ COUNTY GOVERNMENT
Minneapolis, MN; 612-348-4698

HEWLETT–PACKARD COMPANY
❶ ELECTRONICS
Bloomington/St. Paul, MN; 708-245-3909

HONEYWELL
❶ ELECTRONICS
Minneapolis, MN; 612-951-2914

HYATT REGENCY
❶ HOSPITALITY
Minneapolis, MN; 612-370-1202

LAND O' LAKES
❶ FOOD AND BEVERAGES
St. Paul, MN; 651-481-2250

MARRIOTT HOTEL—CITY CENTER
❶ HOSPITALITY
Minneapolis, MN; 612-349-4077

MINNEAPOLIS, CITY OF
❶ CITY GOVERNMENT
Minneapolis, MN; 612-673-2489, ext. 11

MINNEAPOLIS, CITY OF
❶ CITY GOVERNMENT
Minneapolis, MN; 612-673-2666
Pertains to: Open Jobs

MINNEAPOLIS, CITY OF
❶ CITY GOVERNMENT
Minneapolis, MN; 612-673-2999
Pertains to: Promotional Jobs

MINNESOTA DEPARTMENT OF EMPLOYEE RELATIONS
❶ STATE GOVERNMENT
St. Paul, MN; 651-296-2616

MINNESOTA MUTUAL LIFE INSURANCE
❶ INSURANCE
St. Paul, MN; 651-298-7934

NORTH EAST MINNESORTA OFFICE OF JOB TRAINING
❶ STATE GOVERNMENT
Duluth, MN; 218-733-7600

NORTHWESTERN NATIONAL LIFE INSUR–ANCE
❶ INSURANCE
Minneapolis, MN; 612-342-3594

RAMSEY COUNTY
❶ COUNTY GOVERNMENT
St. Paul, MN; 651-266-2666

ST. PAUL, CITY OF
❶ CITY GOVERNMENT
St. Paul, MN; 651-266-6502

UNIVERSITY OF MINNESOTA
❶ EDUCATION
Minneapolis, MN; 612-645-6060

MISSISSIPPI

AMERICAN TELEPHONE & TELEGRAPH
❶ TELECOMMUNICATIONS
Statewide; 404-810-7001

DEPOSIT GUARANTY NATIONAL BANK
❶ BANKING
Jackson, MS; 601-354-8183

JACKSON, CITY OF
❶ CITY GOVERNMENT
Jackson, MS; 601-960-1003

JACKSON/HINDS LIBRARY
❶ LIBRARY SCIENCE
Jackson, MS; 601-968-5829

MISSISSIPPI STATE UNIVERSITY
❶ EDUCATION
Starkville, MS; 601-325-4132

RIVER OAKS HOSPITAL
❶ HEALTH SERVICES
Jackson, MS; 601-936-2200

TRUSTMARK NATIONAL BANK
❶ BANKING
Jackson, MS; 601-949-2337

UNIVERSITY OF MISSISSIPPI
❶ EDUCATION
Oxford, MS; 601-232-7666, ext. 2
Pertains to: Professional

UNIVERSITY OF MISSISSIPPI
❶ EDUCATION
Oxford, MS; 601-232-7666, ext. 1
Pertains to: Support

MISSOURI

ANHEUSER-BUSCH
❶ FOOD AND BEVERAGES
St. Louis, MO; 314-577-2392
Pertains to: General

ANHEUSER-BUSCH
❶ FOOD AND BEVERAGES
St. Louis, MO; 314-577-3871
Pertains to: Plant

BARNES HOSPITAL
❶ HEALTH SERVICES
St. Louis, MO; 314-362-0700

BLUE CROSS/BLUE SHIELD
❶ HEALTH SERVICES/INSURANCE
Kansas City, MO; 816-395-2725

BOATMEN'S NATIONAL BANK
❶ BANKING
Kansas City, MO; 816-691-7000

COMMERCE BANK
❶ BANKING
St. Louis, MO; 314-746-7382

FEDERAL JOB INFORMATION CENTER
❶ FEDERAL GOVERNMENT
St. Louis, MO; 314-539-2285

HYATT REGENCY
❶ HOSPITALITY
Kansas City, MO; 816-283-4473

INDEPENDENCE, CITY OF
❶ CITY GOVERNMENT
Independence, MO; 816-325-7394

JOB SERVICE
❶ STATE GOVERNMENT
Springfield, MO; 417-895-6899

KANSAS CITY, CITY OF
❶ CITY GOVERNMENT
Kansas City, MO; 816-274-1127

KANSAS CITY PUBLIC SCHOOLS
❶ EDUCATION
Kansas City, MO; 816-871-7703

LACLEDE GAS
❶ UTILITIES
St. Louis, MO; 314-342-0762

MARRIOTT HOTEL
❶ HOSPITALITY
St. Louis, MO; 314-259-3381

MCDONNELL DOUGLAS CORPORATION
❶ AVIATION
Hazelwood, MO; 314-232-4222

MISSOURI LIBRARY ASSOCIATION
❶ LIBRARY SCIENCE

Statewide; 314-442-6590

RALSTON PURINA
❶ FOOD AND BEVER-AGES/CONSUMER PRODUCTS
St. Louis, MO; 314-982-2962
Pertains to: Corporate

RALSTON PURINA
❶ FOOD AND BEVER-AGES/CONSUMER PRODUCTS
St. Louis, MO; 314-982-2020
Pertains to: Grocery Products

ST. JOSEPH'S HOSPITAL
❶ HEALTH SERVICES
St. Louis, MO; 314-966-1551, ext. 4

ST. LOUIS COMMUNITY COLLEGE
❶ EDUCATION
St. Louis, MO; 314-539-5200

ST. LOUIS COUNTY
❶ COUNTY GOVERNMENT
Clayton, MO; 314-889-3665

ST. LOUIS UNIVERSITY
❶ EDUCATION
St. Louis, MO; 314-658-2265

ST. MARY'S HEALTH CENTER
❶ HEALTH SERVICES
St. Louis, MO; 314-768-8030

UNIVERSITY HOSPITAL AND CLINICS
❶ HEALTH SERVICES
Columbia, MO; 573-882-8500

UNIVERSITY OF MISSOURI
❶ EDUCATION
Columbia, MO; 573-882-8800

UNIVERSITY OF MISSOURI
❶ EDUCATION
St. Louis, MO; 314-516-5926

U.S. CENTRAL ADMINISTRATION CENTER
❶ FEDERAL GOVERNMENT
Kansas City, MO; 816-426-7463

U.S. INTERNAL REVENUE SERVICE
❶ FEDERAL GOVERNMENT
Kansas City, MO; 816-926-5498

U.S. POSTAL SERVICE
❶ FEDERAL GOVERNMENT
St. Louis, MO; 314-436-3855

MONTANA

BILLINGS, CITY OF
❶ CITY GOVERNMENT
Billings, MT; 406-657-8441

BLUE CROSS/BLUE SHIELD
❶ HEALTH SERVICES/INSURANCE
Helena, MT; 800-821-0264

FRED MEYER
❶ RETAIL
Statewide; 800-401-5627, ext. 4

HELENA, CITY OF
❶ CITY GOVERNMENT
Helena, MT; 406-447-8444

INTERNATIONAL BUSINESS MACHINES
❶ COMPUTERS
Statewide; 415-545-3756, ext. 1

JOB SERVICE
❶ STATE GOVERNMENT
Bozeman, MT; 406-585-9019

JOB SERVICE
❶ STATE GOVERNMENT
Butte, MT; 406-782-1662

JOB SERVICE
❶ STATE GOVERNMENT
Missoula, MT; 406-721-7092

MONTANA STATE UNIVERSITY
❶ EDUCATION
Billings, MT; 406-657-2116

MONTANA STATE UNIVERSITY
❶ EDUCATION
Bozeman, MT; 406-994-3343

MOUNTAIN PLAINS LIBRARY ASSOCIATION
❶ LIBRARY SCIENCE
Statewide; 605-677-5757

ST. VINCENT HOSPITAL
❶ HEALTH SERVICES
Billings, MT; 406-657-8766

UNIVERSITY OF MONTANA
❶ EDUCATION
Missoula, MT; 406-243-6760

U.S. FOREST SERVICE
❶ FEDERAL GOVERN-
MENT/ENVIRONMENT
Bozeman, MT; 406-587-6963

U.S. FOREST SERVICE
❶ FEDERAL GOVERN-
MENT/ENVIRONMENT
Helena, MT; 406-449-5419

U.S. POSTAL SERVICE
❶ FEDERAL GOVERNMENT
Billings, MT; 406-657-5763

YELLOWSTONE COUNTY
❶ COUNTY GOVERNMENT
Billings, MT; 406-248-8880, ext. 1399

N E B R A S K A

AMERICAN LIFE INSURANCE CORPORATION
❶ INSURANCE
Lincoln, NE; 402-467-7199

BLUE CROSS/BLUE SHIELD
❶ HEALTH SERVICES/INSURANCE
Omaha, NE; 402-398-3707

CLARKSON REGIONAL HEALTH SERVICES
❶ HEALTH SERVICES
Omaha, NE; 402-552-3110

JOB SERVICE
❶ STATE GOVERNMENT
Lincoln, NE; 402-471-3607

LINCOLN, CITY OF/LANCASTER COUNTY
❶ CITY GOVERNMENT
Lincoln/Lancaster County, NE; 402-441-7736

LINCOLN GENERAL HOSPITAL
❶ HEALTH SERVICES
Lincoln, NE; 402-435-0092

MUTUAL OF OMAHA INSURANCE COMPANY
❶ INSURANCE
Omaha, NE; 402-978-2040

NATIONAL BANK OF COMMERCE TRUSTS AND SAVINGS
❶ BANKING
Lincoln, NE; 402-434-4700

NEBRASKA, STATE OF
❶ STATE GOVERNMENT
Lincoln, NE; 402-471-2200

NEBRASKA FURNITURE MART
❶ RETAIL
Omaha, NE; 402-392-3231

OMAHA, CITY OF
❶ CITY GOVERNMENT
Omaha, NE; 402-444-5302

OMAHA PUBLIC POWER DISTRICT
❶ UTILITIES
Omaha, NE; 402-636-3046

UNIVERSITY OF NEBRASKA
❶ EDUCATION
Lincoln, NE; 402-472-2303

UNIVERSITY OF NEBRASKA
❶ EDUCATION
Omaha, NE; 402-554-2959

U.S. NATIONAL PARK SERVICE
❶ FEDERAL GOVERNMENT/PARKS
Omaha, NE; 402-221-3434

U.S. POSTAL SERVICE
❶ FEDERAL GOVERNMENT
Lincoln, NE; 402-473-1669

U.S. POSTAL SERVICE
❶ FEDERAL GOVERNMENT
Omaha, NE; 402-348-2523

NEVADA

BANK OF AMERICA
❶ BANKING
Statewide; 702-654-1241

BOULDER CITY, CITY OF
❶ CITY GOVERNMENT
Boulder City, NV; 702-293-9430

CAESAR'S PALACE
❶ HOSPITALITY
Las Vegas, NV; 702-731-7386

CARSON CITY, CITY OF
❶ CITY GOVERNMENT
Carson City, NV; 702-887-2240

CIRCUS CIRCUS ENTERPRISES
❶ HOSPITALITY
Las Vegas, NV; 702-794-3732

CLARK COUNTY
❶ COUNTY GOVERNMENT
Las Vegas, NV; 702-455-3174

FIRST INTERSTATE BANK OF NEVADA
❶ BANKING
Las Vegas, NV; 702-791-6251

HCA MONTEVISTA HOSPITAL
❶ HEALTH SERVICES
Las Vegas, NV; 702-251-1226

HENDERSON, CITY OF
❶ CITY GOVERNMENT
Henderson, NV; 702-565-2318

INTERNATIONAL BUSINESS MACHINES
❶ COMPUTERS
Statewide; 415-545-3756

LAS VEGAS, CITY OF
❶ CITY GOVERNMENT
Las Vegas, NV; 702-229-6346

MIRAGE HOTEL AND CASINO
❶ HOSPITALITY
Las Vegas, NV; 702-792-5627

NEVADA POWER COMPANY
❶ UTILITIES
Las Vegas, NV; 702-367-5200

NEVADA STATE JOBLINE
❶ STATE GOVERNMENT
Carson City, NV; 702-687-4160

NEVADA STATE JOBLINE
❶ STATE GOVERNMENT
Las Vegas, NV; 702-486-2920

NORTHERN NEVADA MEDICAL CENTER
❶ HEALTH SERVICES
Reno, NV; 702-356-4044

RENO, CITY OF
❶ CITY GOVERNMENT
Reno, NV; 702-334-2287

SPRINT CENTRAL TELEPHONE OF NEVADA
❶ TELECOMMUNICATIONS
Las Vegas, NV; 702-877-7566

UNIVERSITIES AND COMMUNITY COLLEGES OF NEVADA
❶ EDUCATION
Statewide; 702-784-1464

U.S. BANK
❶ BANKING
Reno, NV; 800-366-6698

WASHOE COMMUNITY SCHOOL DISTRICT
❶ EDUCATION
Reno, NV; 702-348-0386

WASHOE COUNTY
❶ COUNTY GOVERNMENT
Reno, NV; 702-328-2091

NEW HAMPSHIRE

AMERICAN TELEPHONE & TELEGRAPH
❶ TELECOMMUNICATIONS
Statewide; 800-858-5417
Pertains to: Management

DARTMOUTH COLLEGE
❶ EDUCATION
Hanover, NH; 603-646-3328

EMPLOYMENT SECURITY DEPT.
❶ STATE GOVERNMENT
Manchester, NH; 603-627-7841

FEDERAL JOB INFORMATION LINE
❶ FEDERAL GOVERNMENT
Statewide; 617-565-5900

FLEET BANK
❶ BANKING
Statewide; 800-358-5627, ext. 1

ST. JOSEPH'S HOSPITAL AND TRAUMA CENTER
❶ HEALTH SERVICES
Nashua, NH; 603-598-3309

UNIVERSITY OF NEW HAMPSHIRE
❶ EDUCATION
Durham, NH; 603-862-4473

U.S. POSTAL SERVICE
❶ FEDERAL GOVERNMENT
Statewide; 603-644-4065

NEW JERSEY

ATLANTIC CITY ELECTRICAL COMPANY
❶ UTILITIES
Pleasantville, NJ; 609-625-5848

ATLANTIC CITY SHOWBOAT
❶ HOSPITALITY
Atlantic City, NJ; 609-343-4305

CAESAR'S ATLANTIC CITY HOTEL AND CASINO
❶ HOSPITALITY
Atlantic City, NJ; 609-343-2660

CONTINENTAL AIRLINES
❶ TRANSPORTATION
Newark, NJ; 800-523-3273

CORRECTIONS, DEPARTMENT OF
❶ STATE GOVERNMENT/LAW AND CRIMINAL JUSTICE
Trenton, NJ; 609-633-0496

MID ATLANTIC NATIONAL BANK
❶ BANKING
Edison, NJ; 908-321-2562

MONMOUTH MEDICAL CENTER
❶ HEALTH SERVICES
Monmouth, NJ; 908-870-5214

PERSONNEL, DEPARTMENT OF
❶ STATE GOVERNMENT
Trenton, NJ; 609-292-8668

PRINCETON UNIVERSITY
❶ EDUCATION
Princeton, NJ; 609-258-6130

PRUDENTIAL INSURANCE COMPANY
❶ INSURANCE
Parsippany, NJ; 201-802-8494

RUTGERS UNIVERSITY
❶ EDUCATION
New Brunswick, NJ; 908-445-3045
Pertains to: Clerical, Laboratory, Technical

RUTGERS UNIVERSITY
❶ EDUCATION
New Brunswick, NJ; 908-445-2720
Pertains to: Professional, Administrative, Supervisory

RUTGERS UNIVERSITY
❶ EDUCATION
New Brunswick, NJ; 908-445-3031
Pertains to: Service, Management

STATE COUNTY WORK FORCE
❶ STATE GOVERNMENT
Paterson, NJ; 973-742-9226

TRUMP'S TAJ MAHAL
❶ HOSPITALITY
Atlantic City, NJ; 609-449-5627

NEW MEXICO

ALBUQUERQUE, CITY OF
❶ CITY GOVERNMENT
Albuquerque, NM; 505-768-4636

BERNALILLO COUNTY
❶ COUNTY GOVERNMENT
Albuquerque, NM; 505-768-4887

ETHICON CORPORATION
❶ HEALTH SERVICES
Albuquerque, NM; 505-768-5239

FEDERAL JOB INFORMATION CENTER
❶ FEDERAL GOVERNMENT
Albuquerque, NM; 505-766-5583

HYATT REGENCY
❶ HOSPITALITY
Albuquerque, NM; 505-766-6730

INTEL CORPORATION
❶ COMPUTERS/ELECTRONICS
Rio Rancho, NM; 505-893-3998

MARRIOTT HOTEL
❶ HOSPITALITY
Albuquerque, NM; 505-881-6800

NEW MEXICO STATE UNIVERSITY
❶ EDUCATION
Las Cruces, NM; 505-646-2006

SANTA FE, CITY OF
❶ CITY GOVERNMENT

Santa Fe, NM; 505-984-6742

UNIVERSITY OF NEW MEXICO
❶ EDUCATION
Albuquerque, NM; 505-272-5627

U.S. DEPARTMENT OF ENERGY
❶ FEDERAL GOVERNMENT
Albuquerque, NM; 505-845-4154, ext. 1

U.S. FEDERAL AVIATION ADMINISTRATION
❶ FEDERAL GOVERN-
MENT/AVIATION
Statewide; 817-222-5855

NEW YORK

AVIS
❶ TRANSPORTATION
Garden City, NY; 516-222-3399

BAUSCH & LOMB
❶ CONSUMER PRODUCTS
Rochester, NY; 716-338-8265

BLUE CROSS/BLUE SHIELD OF CENTRAL NEW YORK
❶ HEALTH SERVICES/INSURANCE
Syracuse, NY; 315-448-6735

CHASE BANK
❶ BANKING
New York, NY; 718-242-7573

CITIBANK
❶ BANKING
New York, NY; 718-248-7072

EASTMAN KODAK COMPANY
❶ MANUFACTURING
Rochester, NY; 716-724-4609

FEDERAL JOB INFORMATION CENTER
❶ FEDERAL GOVERNMENT
New York, NY; 212-264-0422

FLEET BANK
❶ BANKING
Statewide; 800-358-5627

GAY MEN'S HEALTH CRISIS
❶ HEALTH SERVICES
New York, NY; 212-337-1910

HILTON HOTEL
❶ HOSPITALITY
New York, NY; 212-261-5719

HYATT GRAND
❶ HOSPITALITY
New York, NY; 212-850-5942

ITT CORPORATION
❶ COMMUNICATIONS

New York, NY; 212-258-1768

MARRIOTT HOTEL MARQUIS
❶ HOSPITALITY
New York, NY; 212-704-8959

MCCAW CELLULAR
❶ TELECOMMUNICATIONS
Statewide; 800-438-3151

METROPOLITAN LIFE INSURANCE
❶ INSURANCE
New York, NY; 212-578-4111

NATIONAL FUEL GAS DISTRIBUTION CORPORATION
❶ TRANSPORTATION
Buffalo, NY; 716-857-7821

NEW YORK DAILY NEWS
❶ JOURNALISM
New York, NY; 212-210-6300

NEW YORK TIMES
❶ JOURNALISM
New York, NY; 212-556-1383

NEWSDAY
❶ JOURNALISM
Long Island, NY; 516-843-2076

PEPSI–COLA
❶ FOOD AND BEVERAGES
Somers, NY; 914-767-6300

PFIZER
❶ PHARMACEUTICALS/CONSUMER PRODUCTS
New York, NY; 212-573-3000

STATE UNIVERSITY OF NEW YORK
❶ EDUCATION
Albany, NY; 518-442-3151

STATE UNIVERSITY OF NEW YORK
❶ EDUCATION
Stony Brook, NY; 516-632-9222

STATEN ISLAND UNIVERSITY HOSPITAL
❶ HEALTH SERVICES
Staten Island, NY; 718-226-9270

U.S. POSTAL SERVICE
❶ FEDERAL GOVERNMENT
Syracuse, NY; 315-452-3438

NORTH CAROLINA

CHARLOTTE, CITY OF
❶ CITY GOVERNMENT
Charlotte, NC; 704-336-3968

DUKE POWER COMPANY
❶ UTILITIES
Charlotte, NC; 800-726-6736

DUKE UNIVERSITY
❶ EDUCATION
Durham, NC; 919-684-8895
Pertains to: Administrative

DUKE UNIVERSITY
❶ EDUCATION
Durham, NC; 919-684-8896
Pertains to: Clerical

DUKE UNIVERSITY
❶ EDUCATION
Durham, NC; 919-684-8899
Pertains to: Daily Listings

DUKE UNIVERSITY
❶ EDUCATION
Durham, NC; 919-684-8898
Pertains to: Skilled Crafts, Service

DUKE UNIVERSITY
❶ EDUCATION
Durham, NC; 919-684-8897
Pertains to: Technical

DURHAM, CITY OF
❶ CITY GOVERNMENT
Durham, NC; 919-560-4636, ext. 332-112

DURHAM PUBLIC SCHOOLS
❶ EDUCATION
Durham, NC; 919-560-3626

FORSYTH COUNTY
❶ COUNTY GOVERNMENT
Winston-Salem, NC; 910-631-6336

GREENSBORO, CITY OF
❶ CITY GOVERNMENT
Greensboro, NC; 919-373-2080

GTE SOUTH
❶ TELECOMMUNICATIONS
Durham, NC; 919-471-6996

GUILFORD COUNTY
❶ COUNTY GOVERNMENT
Greensboro, NC; 919-373-3600

INTERNATIONAL BUSINESS MACHINES
❶ COMPUTERS
Cary/Raleigh/Research Triangle Park, NC;
919-543-5565

KAISER PERMANENTE
❶ HEALTH SERVICES
Statewide; 919-981-6008

RALEIGH, CITY OF
❶ CITY GOVERNMENT
Raleigh, NC; 919-890-3305

UNIVERSITY OF NORTH CAROLINA
❶ EDUCATION
Chapel Hill, NC; 919-990-3000

UNIVERSITY OF NORTH CAROLINA
❶ EDUCATION
Greensboro, NC; 919-334-5023

**UNIVERSITY OF NORTH CAROLINA HOS-
PITALS**
❶ HEALTH SERVICES
Chapel Hill, NC; 919-966-1263

**U.S. ENVIRONMENTAL PROTECTION
AGENCY**
❶ FEDERAL GOVERN-
MENT/ENVIRONMENT
Research Triangle Park, NC; 919-541-3014

U.S. FEDERAL RESERVE BANK
❶ FEDERAL GOVERN-
MENT/FINANCE
Charlotte, NC; 704-358-2484

WACHOVIA BANK OF NORTH CAROLINA
❶ BANKING
Winston-Salem, NC; 910-770-5520

WAKE FOREST UNIVERSITY
❶ EDUCATION
Winston-Salem, NC; 910-759-4448

WINSTON–SALEM, CITY OF
❶ CITY GOVERNMENT
Winston-Salem, NC; 910-631-6496

NORTH DAKOTA

FARGO CLINIC—MERITCARE
❶ HEALTH SERVICES
Fargo, ND; 701-234-2341

FEDERAL JOB OPPORTUNITIES CENTER
❶ FEDERAL GOVERNMENT
Statewide; 800-342-4781

NORTH DAKOTA JOB SERVICE JOBLINE
❶ STATE GOVERNMENT
Bismarck, ND; 701-328-5049

NORTH DAKOTA JOB SERVICE JOBLINE
❶ STATE GOVERNMENT
Williston, ND; 701-857-7658

NORTH DAKOTA STATE UNIVERSITY
❶ EDUCATION
Fargo, ND; 701-231-8273, tape 3008

TACO JOHN'S
❶ FOOD AND BEVERAGES
Fargo, ND; 701-232-5662

UNITED HOSPITAL
❶ HEALTH SERVICES
Grand Forks, ND; 701-780-5123

UNIVERSITY OF NORTH DAKOTA SCHOOL OF MEDICINE
❶ HEALTH SERVICES
Grand Forks, ND; 701-777-3400

U.S. WEST
❶ TELECOMMUNICATIONS
Fargo, ND; 800-822-5853

OHIO

AKRON–SUMMIT COUNTRY PUBLIC LIBRARY – – JOB LISTING SERVICE
❶ COUNTY GOVERNMENT
Akron, OH; 330-643-9000

AMERICAN RED CROSS
❶ HEALTH SERVICES
Columbus, OH; 614-251-1455

AMERITECH
❶ TELECOMMUNICATIONS
Cleveland, OH; 216-822-2711

BANK ONE
❶ BANKING
Columbus, OH; 614-248-0779

CASE WESTERN RESERVE UNIVERSITY
❶ EDUCATION
Cleveland, OH; 216-368-4500, ext. 100

CHILDREN'S HOSPITAL
❶ HEALTH SERVICES
Columbus, OH; 614-722-2270

CHILDREN'S HOSPITAL MEDICAL CENTER
❶ HEALTH SERVICES
Cincinnati, OH; 513-559-4244

CINCINNATI, CITY OF
❶ CITY GOVERNMENT
Cincinnati, OH; 513-352-2489

CLEVELAND, CITY OF
❶ CITY GOVERNMENT
Cleveland, OH; 216-664-2420

CLEVELAND STATE UNIVERSITY
❶ EDUCATION
Cleveland, OH; 216-687-9300

COLUMBUS, CITY OF
❶ CITY GOVERNMENT
Columbus, OH; 614-645-7667

COMP–U–CARD INTERNATIONAL
❶ FINANCE
Columbus, OH; 614-890-9032

CUYAHOGA COUNTY
❶ COUNTY GOVERNMENT
Cleveland, OH; 216-443-2039

DAYTON, CITY OF
❶ CITY GOVERNMENT
Dayton, OH; 513-443-3719

HAMILTON COUNTY
❶ COUNTY GOVERNMENT
Cincinnati, OH; 513-763-4900

HILLSHIRE FARMS
❶ FOOD AND BEVERAGES
Cincinnati, OH; 513-853-1389

MONTGOMERY COUNTY
❶ COUNTY GOVERNMENT
Dayton, OH; 513-225-6128

NATIONAL CITY BANK
❶ BANKING
Columbus, OH; 614-463-6736

NATIONWIDE INSURANCE
❶ INSURANCE
Columbus, OH; 614-249-5725

OHIO STATE UNIVERSITY
❶ EDUCATION
Athens, OH; 740-292-1212
Pertains to: Professional, Administrative

OHIO STATE UNIVERSITY
❶ EDUCATION
Athens, OH; 740-593-4080
Pertains to: Trades, Services

PIZZA HUT
❶ HOSPITALITY
Cleveland, OH; 216-642-3276

PROCTER & GAMBLE
❶ CONSUMER PRODUCTS
Cincinnati, OH; 513-983-7494

PUBLIC UTILITIES COMMISSION
❶ STATE GOVERNMENT/UTILITIES
Columbus, OH; 614-644-5656

SHERWIN WILLIAMS
❶ CONSUMER PRODUCTS
Cleveland, OH; 216-566-2120

U.S. ENVIRONMENTAL PROTECTION AGENCY
❶ FEDERAL GOVERN-MENT/ENVIRONMENT
Columbus, OH; 614-644-2102

U.S. INTERNAL REVENUE SERVICE
❶ FEDERAL GOVERNMENT
Cincinnati, OH; 513-357-5559

U.S. POSTAL SERVICE
❶ FEDERAL GOVERNMENT
Cincinnati, OH; 513-684-5449

OKLAHOMA

AMERICAN FIDELITY
❶ FINANCE
Oklahoma City, OK; 405-523-5627

AMERICAN RED CROSS
❶ HEALTH SERVICES
Tulsa, OK; 918-831-1233

BANK OF OKLAHOMA
❶ BANKING
Tulsa, OK; 918-588-6828

FORD MOTOR COMPANY
❶ AUTOMOTIVE
Tulsa, OK; 918-254-5249

MERCY MEDICAL CENTER
❶ HEALTH SERVICES
Oklahoma City, OK; 405-752-3721

NORMAN, CITY OF
❶ CITY GOVERNMENT
Norman, OK; 405-366-5321

OKLAHOMA CITY, CITY OF
❶ CITY GOVERNMENT
Oklahoma City, OK; 405-297-2419

OKLAHOMA CITY CLINIC
❶ HEALTH SERVICES
Oklahoma City, OK; 405-280-5562

OKLAHOMA DEPARTMENT OF LIBRARIES
❶ STATE GOVERNMENT/LIBRARY SCIENCE
Statewide; 405-521-4202

OKLAHOMA STATE UNIVERSITY
❶ EDUCATION
Stillwater, OK; 405-744-7692

PHILLIPS PETROLEUM COMPANY
❶ PETROLEUM
Bartlesville, OK; 918-661-5547

QUIK TRIP
❶ RETAIL
Tulsa, OK; 800-324-0935

TULSA, CITY OF
❶ CITY GOVERNMENT
Tulsa, OK; 918-596-7444

UNIVERSITY OF OKLAHOMA
❶ EDUCATION
Norman, OK; 405-325-4343

UNIVERSITY OF TULSA
❶ EDUCATION
Tulsa, OK; 918-631-4000

U.S. BUREAU OF PRISONS—SOUTH CENTRAL REGION
❶ FEDERAL GOVERNMENT/LAW AND CRIMINAL JUSTICE
Statewide; 800-726-4473, ext. 2

U.S. POSTAL SERVICE
❶ FEDERAL GOVERNMENT
Oklahoma City, OK; 405-231-1967

U.S. POSTAL SERVICE
❶ FEDERAL GOVERNMENT
Tulsa, OK; 918-599-6861

OREGON

AVIA FOOTWEAR
❶ APPAREL
Portland, OR; 503-520-5322

BANK OF AMERICA
❶ BANKING
Portland, OR; 503-275-2244

BOEING PORTLAND
❶ AVIATION
Portland, OR; 503-661-8318

EUGENE, CITY OF
❶ CITY GOVERNMENT
Eugene, OR; 541-687-5060
Pertains to: General

EUGENE, CITY OF
❶ CITY GOVERNMENT
Eugene, OR; 541-484-3769
Pertains to: Water and Electric Board

GOOD SAMARITAN MEDICAL CENTER
❶ HEALTH SERVICES
Portland, OR; 503-833-3236

INTEL CORPORATION SYSTEMS MANU-FACTURING
❶ COMPUTERS/ELECTRONICS

Hillsboro, OR; 503-696-2580

KGW TV CHANNEL 8
❶ BROADCASTING
Portland, OR; 503-226-4590

LANE COUNTY
❶ COUNTY GOVERNMENT
Eugene, OR; 541-687-4473

MULTNOMAH COUNTY
❶ COUNTY GOVERNMENT
Portland, OR; 503-248-5035

NIKE
❶ APPAREL
Beaverton, OR; 503-644-4224

OREGON STATE JOBLINE
❶ STATE GOVERNMENT
Eugene, OR; 541-686-7652

OREGON STATE JOBLINE
❶ STATE GOVERNMENT
Salem, OR; 503-373-1199

PORTLAND, CITY OF
❶ CITY GOVERNMENT
Portland, OR; 503-823-4352

PORTLAND GENERAL ELECTRIC
❶ ELECTRONICS
Portland, OR; 503-464-7441

SALEM, CITY OF
❶ CITY GOVERNMENT
Salem, OR; 503-588-6162

UNIVERSITY OF PORTLAND
❶ EDUCATION
Portland, OR; 503-283-7536

U.S. POSTAL SERVICE
❶ FEDERAL GOVERNMENT
Eugene, OR; 541-341-3688

U.S. POSTAL SERVICE
❶ FEDERAL GOVERNMENT
Portland, OR; 503-294-2270

U.S. WEST
❶ TELECOMMUNICATIONS
Statewide; 503-242-8593

WASHINGTON MUTUAL SAVINGS BANK
❶ BANKING
Statewide; 800-952-0787

WEYERHAUSER PAPER COMPANY
❶ FOREST/PAPER PRODUCTS
Springfield, OR; 541-741-5910

PENNSYLVANIA

ALLEGHENY GENERAL HOSPITAL
❶ HEALTH SERVICES
Pittsburgh, PA; 412-359-3201

BELL ATLANTIC CORPORATION
❶ TELECOMMUNICATIONS
Philadelphia, PA; 800-967-5422

CORE STATE BANK
❶ BANKING
Philadelphia, PA; 215-973-4556

EMPLOYMENT OPPORTUNITY & TRAINING
❶ STATE GOVERNMENT
Taylor, PA; 717-348-6484

EQUITABLE RESOURCES
❶ FINANCE
Pittsburgh, PA; 412-553-5733

HOSPITAL OF THE UNIVERSITY OF PENNSYLVANIA
❶ HEALTH SERVICES
Philadelphia, PA; 215-662-2999

LEHIGH COUNTY
❶ COUNTY GOVERNMENT
Allentown, PA; 610-820-3386

PENN STATE UNIVERSITY
❶ EDUCATION
University Park, PA; 814-865-5627

PHILADELPHIA ELECTRICAL COMPANY
❶ UTILITIES
Philadelphia, PA; 215-841-4340

PITTSBURGH, CITY OF
❶ CITY GOVERNMENT
Pittsburgh, PA; 412-255-2388

PPG INDUSTRIES
❶ MANUFACTURING
Pittsburgh, PA; 412-434-2002

PROVIDENT NATIONAL BANK
❶ BANKING
Philadelphia, PA; 800-762-5627

UNIVERSITY OF PENNSYLVANIA
❶ EDUCATION
Philadelphia, PA; 215-898-5627

UNIVERSITY OF PITTSBURGH
❶ EDUCATION
Pittsburgh, PA; 412-624-8040

US AIR
❶ TRANSPORTATION
Pittsburgh, PA; 412-472-7693

U.S. FEDERAL RESERVE BANK
❶ FEDERAL GOVERN-
MENT/FINANCE
Philadelphia, PA; 215-574-6100

RHODE ISLAND

AMERICAN TELEPHONE & TELEGRAPH
❶ TELECOMMUNICATIONS
Statewide; 800-858-5417
Pertains to: Management

BROWN UNIVERSITY
❶ EDUCATION
Providence, RI; 401-863-9675

FLEET BANK
❶ BANKING
Statewide; 800-358-5627, ext. 4

LANDMARK MEDICAL CENTER
❶ HEALTH SERVICES
Woonsocket, RI; 401-769-4100, ext. 2379

NEW ENGLAND LIBRARY ASSOCIATION
❶ LIBRARY SCIENCE
Statewide; 617-521-2815

SOUTH CAROLINA

BAPTIST MEDICAL CENTER
❶ HEALTH SERVICES
Columbia, SC; 803-771-5771

CHARLESTON, CITY OF
❶ CITY GOVERNMENT
Charleston, SC; 803-720-3907

CHARLESTON COUNTY
❶ COUNTY GOVERNMENT
Charleston, SC; 803-724-0694

**COLONIAL LIFE AND ACCIDENT INSUR-
ANCE COMPANY**
❶ INSURANCE
Columbia, SC; 803-750-0088

COLUMBIA, CITY OF
❶ CITY GOVERNMENT
Columbia, SC; 803-733-8478

RICHLAND COUNTY
❶ COUNTY GOVERNMENT
Columbia, SC; 803-748-7832

ROPER HOSPITAL
❶ HEALTH SERVICES
Charleston, SC; 803-724-2472

SOUTH CAROLINA, STATE OF
❶ STATE GOVERNMENT
Columbia, SC; 803-734-9334
Pertains to: Clerical, Technical, Skilled

SOUTH CAROLINA, STATE OF
❶ STATE GOVERNMENT
Columbia, SC; 803-734-9333
Pertains to: Professional

**SOUTH CAROLINA DEPARTMENT OF COR-
RECTIONS**
❶ STATE GOVERNMENT/LAW AND
CRIMINAL JUSTICE
Statewide; 803-898-8524

**SOUTH CAROLINA ELECTRIC AND GAS
COMPANY**
❶ UTILITIES
Columbia, SC; 803-748-3001

UNIVERSITY OF SOUTH CAROLINA
❶ EDUCATION
Columbia, SC; 803-777-2100

SOUTH DAKOTA

GATEWAY 2000
❶ COMPUTERS
North Sioux City, SD; 800-846-2000

JOB SERVICE
❶ STATE GOVERNMENT
Sioux Falls, SD; 605-367-5300

PENNINGTON COUNTY
❶ COUNTY GOVERNMENT
Rapid City, SD; 605-394-8090

RAPID CITY, CITY OF
❶ CITY GOVERNMENT
Rapid City, SD; 605-394-5329

RAPID CITY REGIONAL HOSPITAL
❶ HEALTH SERVICES
Rapid City, SD; 605-341-8375

SOUTH DAKOTA, STATE OF
❶ STATE GOVERNMENT
Pierre, SD; 605-773-3326

TENNESSEE

FEDERAL EXPRESS CORPORATION
❶ TRANSPORTATION
Memphis, TN; 901-535-9555

FIRST AMERICAN NATIONAL BANK
❶ BANKING

Statewide; 901-684-3264

HOLIDAY INN
❶ HOSPITALITY
Nashville, TN; 615-885-4491

INTERNATIONAL PAPER COMPANY
❶ FOREST/PAPER PRODUCTS
Memphis, TN; 901-763-7235

KNOXVILLE, CITY OF
❶ CITY GOVERNMENT
Knoxville, TN; 423-521-2562

MARRIOTT HOTEL
❶ HOSPITALITY
Nashville, TN; 615-872-2952

MEMPHIS, CITY OF
❶ CITY GOVERNMENT
Memphis, TN; 901-576-6548

MEMPHIS CITY SCHOOLS
❶ EDUCATION
Memphis, TN; 901-325-5349

NASHVILLE, CITY OF
❶ CITY GOVERNMENT
Nashville, TN; 615-862-6660

NATIONAL BANK OF COMMERCE
❶ BANKING
Memphis, TN; 901-523-3154

**NISSAN MOTOR MANUFACTURING CORPO-
RATION**
❶ AUTOMOTIVE
Smyrna, TN; 615-355-2243

PROMUS COMPANIES
❶ HOSPITALITY
Memphis, TN; 901-748-7626

REGIONAL MEDICAL CENTER
❶ HEALTH SERVICES
Memphis, TN; 901-545-8432

SHARP MANUFACTURING OF AMERICA
❶ ELECTRONICS
Memphis, TN; 901-362-8772

SOUTHERN HILLS MEDICAL CENTER
❶ HEALTH SERVICES
Nashville, TN; 615-781-4132

UNIVERSITY OF TENNESSEE
❶ EDUCATION
Knoxville, TN; 423-974-1911

U.S. INTERNAL REVENUE SERVICE
❶ FEDERAL GOVERNMENT

Memphis, TN; 901-365-5656

U.S. POSTAL SERVICE
❶ FEDERAL GOVERNMENT
Memphis, TN; 901-521-2336, ext. 801

VANDERBILT UNIVERSITY
❶ EDUCATION
Nashville, TN; 615-322-8300

TEXAS

AMERICAN AIRLINES
❶ TRANSPORTATION
Dallas, TX; 214-425-5141

AMERICAN AIRLINES
❶ TRANSPORTATION
Fort Worth, TX; 817-963-1110

ANHEUSER–BUSCH
❶ FOOD AND BEVERAGES
Houston, TX; 713-670-1629

APPLE COMPUTER
❶ COMPUTERS
Austin, TX; 512-919-2011

ARLINGTON, CITY OF
❶ CITY GOVERNMENT
Arlington, TX; 817-265-7938

AUSTIN, CITY OF
❶ CITY GOVERNMENT
Austin, TX; 512-499-3301

BANK OF AMERICA
❶ BANKING
San Antonio, TX; 210-525-5530

BANK ONE OF TEXAS
❶ BANKING
Dallas, TX; 214-290-3637

BANK ONE OF TEXAS
❶ BANKING
Houston, TX; 713-751-2200

BEXAR COUNTY
❶ COUNTY GOVERNMENT
San Antonio, TX; 210-270-6333

BUDGET RENT–A–CAR
❶ TRANSPORTATION
Dallas, TX; 214-716-7954

**COCA–COLA BOTTLING COMPANY OF
NORTH TEXAS**
❶ FOOD AND BEVERAGES

Dallas, TX; 214-902-2634

COCA-COLA BOTTLING COMPANY OF NORTH TEXAS
❶ FOOD AND BEVERAGES
Fort Worth, TX; 817-847-3036

CONTINENTAL AIRLINES
❶ TRANSPORTATION
Houston, TX; 713-834-5300

DALLAS, CITY OF
❶ CITY GOVERNMENT
Dallas, TX; 214-670-5908

DALLAS COMMUNITY COLLEGE DISTRICT
❶ EDUCATION
Dallas, TX; 214-746-2438

DALLAS COUNTY
❶ COUNTY GOVERNMENT
Dallas, TX; 214-653-7637, ext. 6

DALLAS MORNING NEWS
❶ JOURNALISM
Dallas, TX; 214-977-8338, ext. 1

DALLAS/FORT WORTH INTERNATIONAL AIRPORT
❶ TRANSPORTATION
Dallas/Fort Worth, TX; 214-574-8024

DOCTOR'S HOSPITAL
❶ HEALTH SERVICES
Dallas, TX; 214-324-6655

DOCTOR'S HOSPITAL
❶ HEALTH SERVICES
Houston, TX; 713-696-4488

DOW CHEMICAL
❶ CHEMICALS
Houston, TX; 713-978-3300

EXXON CORPORATION
❶ PETROLEUM
Houston, TX; 713-639-2233

FEDERAL JOB INFORMATION CENTER
❶ FEDERAL GOVERNMENT
Houston, TX; 713-759-0455

FEDERAL JOB INFORMATION CENTER
❶ FEDERAL GOVERNMENT
San Antonio, TX; 210-805-2403

FIRST INTERSTATE BANK
❶ BANKING
Dallas, TX; 214-740-1555

FIRST INTERSTATE BANK
❶ BANKING
Houston, TX; 713-250-7356

FORT WORTH, CITY OF
❶ CITY GOVERNMENT
Fort Worth, TX; 817-871-7760

FORT WORTH INDEPENDENT SCHOOL DISTRICT
❶ EDUCATION
Fort Worth, TX; 817-871-2213

HARRIS COUNTY
❶ COUNTY GOVERNMENT
Houston, TX; 713-755-5044

HILTON HOTEL
❶ HOSPITALITY
Dallas, TX; 214-606-3575

HILTON HOTEL
❶ HOSPITALITY
Houston, TX; 713-523-7045

HILTON HOTEL
❶ HOSPITALITY
San Antonio, TX; 210-222-1400, ext. 377

HOUSTON, CITY OF
❶ CITY GOVERNMENT
Houston, TX; 713-658-3798

HOUSTON COMMUNITY COLLEGE SYSTEM
❶ EDUCATION
Houston, TX; 713-866-8369
Pertains to: Clerical, Classified Ads

HOUSTON COMMUNITY COLLEGE SYSTEM
❶ EDUCATION
Houston, TX; 713-868-0711
Pertains to: Professional, Technical

HOUSTON LIGHT AND POWER COMPANY
❶ UTILITIES
Houston, TX; 713-238-5854

HOUSTON NORTH WEST MEDICAL CENTER
❶ HEALTH SERVICES
Houston, TX; 713-440-2233

HUMANA
❶ HEALTH SERVICES/INSURANCE
San Antonio, TX; 210-617-1700

KAISER PERMANENTE
❶ HEALTH SERVICES
Dallas, TX; 214-458-5138

LOCKHEED CORPORATION
❶ AEROSPACE
Fort Worth, TX; 817-777-1000

MILLER BREWING COMPANY
❶ FOOD AND BEVERAGES
Fort Worth, TX; 817-551-3350, ext. 1

NEIMAN–MARCUS
❶ RETAIL
Dallas, TX; 214-401-6975

SAN ANTONIO, CITY OF
❶ CITY GOVERNMENT
San Antonio, TX; 210-207-7280

TEXAS A&M UNIVERSITY
❶ EDUCATION
College Station, TX; 409-845-4444

TEXAS CHRISTIAN UNIVERSITY
❶ EDUCATION
Fort Worth, TX; 817-921-7791

TEXAS COMMERCE BANK
❶ BANKING
Dallas, TX; 214-922-2224

TEXAS COMMERCE BANK
❶ BANKING
Fort Worth, TX; 817-856-5249

TEXAS INSTRUMENTS
❶ ELECTRONICS
Dallas, TX; 214-368-7116

TEXAS WORKFORCE COMMISSION
❶ STATE GOVERNMENT
El Paso, TX; 915-564-6066

UNIVERSITY OF HOUSTON
❶ EDUCATION
Houston, TX; 713-743-5788

UNIVERSITY OF TEXAS
❶ EDUCATION
Austin, TX; 512-471-4295

U.S. INTERNAL REVENUE SERVICE
❶ FEDERAL GOVERNMENT
Austin, TX; 512-477-5627 or 8115

U.S. NASA
❶ FEDERAL GOVERN-
MENT/AEROSPACE
Houston, TX; 713-483-2135

WORKFORCE DEVELOPMENT CORP.
❶ STATE GOVERNMENT
Corpus Christi, TX; 800-735-2989

U T A H

**AMERICAN EXPRESS TRAVELER'S CHECK OP-
ERATIONS CENTER**
❶ FINANCE
Salt Lake City, UT; 801-965-5211

AMERICAN FORKS HOSPITAL
❶ HEALTH SERVICES
Salt Lake City, UT; 801-371-7036

AMERICAN STORES COMPANY
❶ FOOD AND BEVERAGES
Salt Lake City, UT; 800-284-5560

DISCOVER CARD
❶ FINANCE
Sandy, UT; 801-565-5525

GENEVA STEEL
❶ MANUFACTURING
Provo, UT; 801-227-9449

NOVELL
❶ COMPUTERS
Provo, UT; 801-429-5390

NU–SKIN INTERNATIONAL
❶ CONSUMER PRODUCTS
Salt Lake City, UT; 801-345-2525

PROVO, CITY OF
❶ CITY GOVERNMENT
Provo, UT; 801-379-6187

SALT LAKE CITY, CITY OF
❶ CITY GOVERNMENT
Salt Lake City, UT; 801-535-6625

UNIVERSITY OF UTAH
❶ EDUCATION
Salt Lake City, UT; 801-581-5627

UNIVERSITY OF UTAH MEDICAL CENTER
❶ HEALTH SERVICES
Salt Lake City, UT; 801-581-5627

UTAH, STATE OF
❶ STATE GOVERNMENT
Salt Lake City, UT; 801-538-3118

UTAH STATE VETERANS JOB HOTLINE
❶ STATE GOVERNMENT
Statewide; 801-536-7192

WASHINGTON MUTUAL SAVINGS BANK
❶ BANKING
Statewide; 801-537-6994

V E R M O N T

BEN AND JERRY'S
❶ FOOD AND BEVERAGES
Waterbury, VT; 802-882-1240

BURLINGTON, CITY OF
❶ CITY GOVERNMENT
Burlington, VT; 802-865-7147

GREEN MOUNTAIN POWER
❶ UTILITIES
Burlington, VT; 802-660-5698

MEDICAL CENTER HOSPITAL OF VERMONT/FLETCHER HEALTH CARE
❶ HEALTH SERVICES
Burlington, VT; 802-656-2722

MERCHANT'S BANK
❶ BANKING
Burlington, VT; 802-865-1881

UNIVERSITY OF VERMONT
❶ EDUCATION
Burlington, VT; 802-656-2248

VERMONT EMPLOYMENT AND TRAINING DEPARTMENT
❶ STATE GOVERNMENT
Montpelier, VT; 802-828-3939

VERMONT STATE JOBLINE
❶ STATE GOVERNMENT
Montpelier, VT; 802-828-3483

VIRGINIA

FAIRFAX, CITY OF
❶ CITY GOVERNMENT
Fairfax, VA; 703-385-7861

FAIRFAX COUNTY SCHOOLS
❶ EDUCATION
Fairfax, VA; 703-750-8569
Pertains to: Education, Management

FAIRFAX COUNTY SCHOOLS
❶ EDUCATION
Fairfax, VA; 703-993-8799
Pertains to: General

FAIRFAX COUNTY SCHOOLS
❶ EDUCATION
Fairfax, VA; 703-750-8533
Pertains to: Support

KAISER PERMANENTE
❶ HEALTH SERVICES
Norfolk, VA; 800-326-4005

LIFE OF VIRGINIA
❶ INSURANCE
Richmond, VA; 804-281-6127

MARRIOTT CORPORATION
❶ HOSPITALITY
Alexandria, VA; 703-461-6100

MARRIOTT HOTEL
❶ HOSPITALITY
Norfolk, VA; 804-628-6491

MOBIL OIL CORPORATION
❶ PETROLEUM
Fairfax, VA; 703-849-6005
Pertains to: Marketing

MOBIL OIL CORPORATION
❶ PETROLEUM
Fairfax, VA; 703-846-2777
Pertains to: Office, Support

NATIONSBANK
❶ BANKING
Norfolk, VA; 804-441-4451

NEWPORT NEWS, CITY OF
❶ CITY GOVERNMENT
Newport News, VA; 804-928-9281

NORFOLK, CITY OF
❶ CITY GOVERNMENT
Norfolk, VA; 804-627-8768, ext. 353

NORFOLK SHIPBUILDING AND DRYDOCK
❶ MANUFACTURING
Norfolk, VA; 804-494-2964

NORFOLK STATE UNIVERSITY
❶ EDUCATION
Norfolk, VA; 804-683-8184

OLD DOMINION UNIVERSITY
❶ EDUCATION
Norfolk, VA; 804-683-3463

Q ALLIANCE
❶ STATE GOVERNMENT
Arlington, VA; 703-892-6465

RICHMOND, CITY OF
❶ CITY GOVERNMENT
Richmond, VA; 804-780-5888

SENTARA BAYSIDE HOSPITAL
❶ HEALTH SERVICES
Virginia Beach, VA; 804-363-6608

TIDEWATER HEALTH CARE—VIRGINIA BEACH GENERAL HOSPITAL
❶ HEALTH SERVICES
Virginia Beach, VA; 804-481-8668

UNIVERSITY OF RICHMOND
❶ EDUCATION
Richmond, VA; 804-287-6001

U.S. NATIONAL WEATHER SERVICE
❶ FEDERAL GOVERNMENT
Norfolk, VA; 804-441-3720

U.S. POSTAL SERVICE
❶ FEDERAL GOVERNMENT
Norfolk, VA; 804-629-2225

VIRGINIA BEACH, CITY OF
❶ CITY GOVERNMENT
Virginia Beach, VA; 804-427-3580, ext. 815

WASHINGTON GAS AND LIGHT
❶ UTILITIES
Fairfax, VA; 703-750-5814

WASHINGTON

AIRBORNE EXPRESS CORPORATION
❶ TRANSPORTATION
Seattle, WA; 206-281-4815

BOEING COMPANY
❶ AVIATION
Seattle, WA; 206-965-3111

EDDIE BAUER
❶ RETAIL/APPAREL
Seattle, WA; 425-861-4851

FOOD SERVICES OF AMERICA
❶ HOSPITALITY
Seattle, WA; 206-251-1413

GTE
❶ TELECOMMUNICATIONS
Seattle, WA; 206-261-5777

HEALTH TECNA
❶ HEALTH SERVICES
Seattle, WA; 206-395-4473

KING BROADCASTING COMPANY
❶ BROADCASTING
Seattle, WA; 206-448-3915

KING COUNTY
❶ COUNTY GOVERNMENT
Seattle, WA; 206-296-5209

KING COUNTY MEDICAL BLUE SHIELD
❶ HEALTH SERVICES/INSURANCE
Seattle, WA; 206-464-5588

MICROSOFT CORPORATION
❶ COMPUTERS
Seattle, WA; 800-892-3181

NORTH KITSAP SCHOOL DISTRICT
❶ EDUCATION
Seattle, WA; 206-779-8914

OLYMPIA, CITY OF
❶ CITY GOVERNMENT
Olympia, WA; 206-753-8383

RESTAURANTS UNLIMITED
❶ HOSPITALITY
Seattle, WA; 206-634-3082, ext. 777

SEATTLE, CITY OF
❶ CITY GOVERNMENT
Seattle, WA; 206-684-7999
Pertains to: General

SEATTLE, CITY OF
❶ CITY GOVERNMENT
Seattle, WA; 206-443-4376
Pertains to: Housing Authority

SEATTLE, CITY OF
❶ CITY GOVERNMENT
Seattle, WA; 206-233-2181
Pertains to: Lights

SEATTLE, CITY OF
❶ CITY GOVERNMENT
Seattle, WA; 206-728-3444
Pertains to: Port of Seattle

SEATTLE COMMUNITY COLLEGE DIS-TRICT
❶ EDUCATION
Seattle, WA; 206-587-5454

SEATTLE TIMES
❶ JOURNALISM
Seattle, WA; 206-464-2118

UNIVERSITY OF WASHINGTON
❶ EDUCATION
Seattle, WA; 206-543-6969

U.S. BANK OF WASHINGTON
❶ BANKING
Statewide; 206-344-5656

U.S. ENVIRONMENTAL PROTECTION AGENCY
❶ FEDERAL GOVERN-MENT/ENVIRONMENT
Seattle, WA; 206-553-1240

U.S. FEDERAL RESERVE BANK
❶ FEDERAL GOVERN-MENT/FINANCE
Seattle, WA; 206-343-3634

U.S. NATIONAL PARK SERVICE
❶ FEDERAL GOVERNMENT/PARKS
Seattle, WA; 206-220-4053

U.S. POSTAL SERVICE
❶ FEDERAL GOVERNMENT
Seattle, WA; 206-442-6240

WASHINGTON MUTUAL SAVINGS BANK
❶ BANKING
Statewide; 206-585-2714

WASHINGTON STATE FILM AND VIDEO OFFICE
❶ STATE GOVERNMENT
Seattle, WA; 206-464-6074

WASHINGTON STATE JOBLINE
❶ STATE GOVERNMENT
Seattle, WA; 206-464-7378

WEST VIRGINIA

KANAWHA COUNTY BOARD OF EDUCATION
❶ EDUCATION
Charleston, WV; 304-348-6193

WEIRTON STEEL CORPORATION
❶ MANUFACTURING
Weirton, WV; 304-797-4668

WEST VIRGINIA UNIVERSITY
❶ EDUCATION
Morgantown, WV; 304-293-7234

WISCONSIN

AMAZING JOBLYNX
❶ STATE GOVERNMENT
Green Bay, WI; 920-496-2266

DANE COUNTY
❶ COUNTY GOVERNMENT
Madison, WI; 608-266-4123

FLEET MORTGAGE GROUP
❶ FINANCE
Milwaukee, WI; 800-358-5627

GOODWILL INDUSTRIES
❶ PUBLIC SERVICE
Milwaukee, WI; 414-273-9463

MADISON, CITY OF
❶ CITY GOVERNMENT
Madison, WI; 608-266-6500

MARQUETTE UNIVERSITY
❶ EDUCATION
Milwaukee, WI; 414-288-7000

MILWAUKEE, CITY OF
❶ CITY GOVERNMENT
Milwaukee, WI; 414-286-5555

MILWAUKEE COUNTY
❶ COUNTY GOVERNMENT
Milwaukee, WI; 414-278-5321

UNITED HEALTH
❶ HEALTH SERVICES
Milwaukee, WI; 414-347-4343

UNIVERSITY OF WISCONSIN
❶ EDUCATION
Milwaukee, WI; 414-229-6629

WISCONSIN ELECTRIC AND POWER COMPANY
❶ UTILITIES
Milwaukee, WI; 414-221-3091

WISCONSIN GAS COMPANY
❶ UTILITIES
Milwaukee, WI; 414-291-6756

WYOMING

ERNST CORPORATION
❶ ENGINEERING
Statewide; 206-621-6880

INTERNATIONAL BUSINESS MACHINES—WORK FORCE SOLUTIONS
❶ COMPUTERS
Statewide; 415-545-3756

LARAMIE COUNTY SCHOOL DISTRICT
❶ EDUCATION
Laramie, WY; 307-771-2448

SAFECARD SERVICE
❶ FINANCE
Cheyenne, WY; 307-771-2761

UNIVERSITY OF WYOMING
❶ EDUCATION
Laramie, WY; 307-766-5602

WYOMING MEDICAL CENTER
❶ HEALTH SERVICES
Casper, WY; 800-526-5190

JOB OPPORTUNITIES

INTERNSHIPS FOR STUDENTS

ONE OF THE BEST STEPPING-STONES toward eventually landing a job that will match your interests and talents is performing an internship. In the competitive job market, it is essential that along with your educational and vocational history, you actually have some practical professional experience to draw upon—experience that you can also use to demonstrate to employers that you are career-minded, ambitious, and already equipped to hit the floor running.

Internships provide you with an opportunity to get in on the ground floor of the occupational field of your choice. Many internships offer the same responsibilities you would have as an actual employee. Others serve as training grounds or introductory sessions designed to showcase the professional aspects of a particular vocation. Some last only weeks. Others can run as long as a year.

While using the entries listed in this chapter, remember that along with the various levels of compensation, companies and organizations offering internships may provide benefits that run the gamut from food and housing stipends to transportation and living expenses (all of which may not appear in the entries below). This is not to mention that almost all will provide you with valuable future contacts and letters of recommendation.

While many internships are offered year-round, many students prefer to work only during the summer months. There are good reasons for doing so: (1) The student doesn't need to worry about studies during the summer and can therefore focus on the tasks at hand. (2) If the internship doesn't pay, the student has time to schedule an evening or part-time job that offers a wage if necessary. But many internships in today's market do offer pay.

Bear in mind that during the summer, there is greater competition among students looking for internships. However, on the other hand, companies may also increase the number of interns they take on. This can make the learning environment that much more crowded with people trying to get the same caliber of experiences.

When you find an internship that appeals to you, make sure you get in touch with the contact person listed, either through correspondence or via a phone call. Job titles and descriptions of responsibilities can change rapidly, as can wage levels, durations, requirements, available opportunities, and application deadlines. Therefore, it is important that you verify all information before sending in your final application materials. And of course, it's always a good idea to establish personal contact with the internship coordinator.

In some entries listed in this chapter, requirements and job descriptions are not indicated. In the case of requirements, some may be obvious, or companies may be looking for a general level of experience or interest in the field. If job descriptions are not indicated, it is often because the position is self-explanatory or the employer chooses not to define specific job responsibilities. Note that the job descriptions listed here are by no means complete. However, companies will often provide a complete "position profile" along with the application information you request.

Regarding application deadlines, be aware that some employers accept applications at times other than those indicated here. In addition, some might fill a position before the application deadline. As a rule of thumb, always verify the information presented here, as it is subject to change.

The entries in this chapter were chosen because they are representative of the wide sweep of American industries and characteristic of the kinds of positions available all over the country. There are many more internships available than those listed here, and some are not formally announced. In order to tap into them, consult your school placement office. In addition, contact the many other employers listed in this book. You are almost certain to learn of more internships if you do. ➤See "U.S. Employers," 158-378.

These entries, while they may help you find an internship, will also give you a good perspective on the kinds of opportunities available in your specific occupational field. For other seasonal opportunities, ➤see "Summer Jobs for Students," 497-531. That chapter contains positions that are generally more recreational than professional in scope.

ABBREVIATIONS USED IN THIS CHAPTER

CPR—*Cardiopulmonary Resuscitation*
GPA—*Grade Point Average*
LAN—*Local Area Network*

MBA—*Master Of Business Administration*
MFA—*Master Of Fine Arts*

SASE—*Self-Addressed Stamped Envelope*
WPM—*Words per Minute*

A L A B A M A

ALABAMA SHAKESPEARE FESTIVAL
1 Festival Dr., Montgomery, AL 36117-4605
❶ THEATER ARTS
Compensation: No pay.
Duration: One quarter, one semester, or one summer.
Requirements: Marketing, developmental, and administrative positions require command of Lotus 1-2-3, WordPerfect, and PageMaker.
Eligibility: College juniors and seniors, college graduates, graduate students.
Contact: Assistant Managing Director.
*Phone:*334-271-5300.

- MARKETING: Will plan various projects, including ad campaigns.

- DEVELOPMENTAL: Will plan events and help write grant proposals.

- ADMINISTRATIVE: Will work in close contact with business and general managers.

- PRODUCTION: Will work with set design, costume, or electronics department.
Requirements: Technical theater skills.

THE BIRMINGHAM NEWS
2200 4th Ave. N., Birmingham, AL 35203
❶ JOURNALISM
Eligibility: College juniors and seniors, graduate students.
Phone: 205-325-2111.
Apply by: December 15 for summer, April 1 for fall editorial, April 30 for fall advertising.

- NEWS REPORTING
Compensation: $ 325 per week.
Duration: 10-12 weeks.
Requirements: Journalism coursework and experience with campus publication.
Contact: Managing Editor.

- SPORTS REPORTING
Compensation: $ 325 per week.
Duration: 16 weeks.
Requirements: Journalism coursework and experience with campus publication.
Contact: Managing Editor.

- ADVERTISING
Compensation: $6 per hour.
Duration: 10-12 weeks.
Requirements: Advertising coursework and some sales experience.
Contact: Retail Advertising Manager.

ST. VINCENT'S HOSPITAL
P.O. Box 12407, Birmingham, AL 35202
❶ HEALTH SERVICES
Eligibility: College students, college graduates, graduate students.
Contact: Letter and resume to Recruitment Coordinator.
Phone: 205-939-7295.

- ADMINISTRATIVE
Compensation: Paid.
Duration: One year.
Requirements: Master's degree in health or business administration.

- GENERAL: Will work with the personnel, marketing, public affairs, and medical records departments.
Compensation: No pay.
Duration: One quarter or one semester.

WOPP-AM
1101 Cameron Rd., Opp, AL 36467
❶ BROADCASTING
Compensation: No pay.
Duration: Three months.
Eligibility: High school graduates, college students, college graduates, graduate students, career changers, reentrants to the work force.

Contact: General Manager.
Phone: 334-493-4545.
- NEWS GATHERING
- PRODUCTION: Will produce promotional materials and commercials.
- SALES: Will write and sell ads.

ALASKA

ALASKA STATE PARKS VOLUNTEER PROGRAM
3601 C St., Suite 1200, Anchorage, AK 99503
❶ PARKS
Compensation: No pay.
Duration: May 15 to September 15.
Contact: Alaska State Parks, Volunteer Coordinator, Alaska State Parks Volunteer Program.
Phone: 907-269-8708.
Apply by: April 1.
- RANGER ASSISTANCE
Requirements: Some coursework in natural science, knowledge of the outdoors.
  TRAIL CREW
Requirements: Knowledge of the outdoors, experience with hand and power tools.

BUREAU OF LAND MANAGEMENT—ARCTIC DISTRICT
1150 University Ave., Fairbanks, AK 99709
❶ ENVIRONMENT
- RECREATION TECHNICIAN: Will serve the public, collect data, and work to maintain trails, campsites, and waysides.
Compensation: $20 per day.
Duration: One summer.
Requirements: Familiarity with recreational management and natural resource processes.
Eligibility: College juniors and seniors, college graduates, graduate students.
Contact: Natural Resource Specialist.
Phone: 907-474-2300.
Apply by: February 28.

DENALI NATIONAL PARK AND PRESERVE
P.O. Box 9, Denali Park, AK 99755
❶ PARKS
Compensation: No pay.
Duration: One summer.
Eligibility: Minimum age 18.
Contact: Chief of Interpretation or VIP Coordinator.
Phone: 907-683-2294.
Apply by: March 15.
- INTERPRETIVE NATURALISTS: Will research and present various informational programs as well as provide support for the Visitor Center.
Requirements: Good speaker, background in natural history, driver's license.

- BACKCOUNTRY VOLUNTEERS: Will provide informational services and conduct patrols.
- RESOURCE MANAGEMENT VOLUNTEERS: Will assist resource managers and researchers.
Requirements: Background in biology, experience backpacking, driver's license.
- CAMPGROUND HOSTS

KENAI FJORDS NATIONAL PARK
P.O. Box 1727, Seward, AK 99664
❶ PARKS
- GENERAL: Will research and present various visitor information programs, with the potential for working on cruise ships or tour boats.
Compensation: No pay.
Duration: Four months.
Requirements: Good communications and interpretive skills, knowledge of natural history.
Eligibility: College sophomores, juniors, and seniors, college graduates, graduate students, career changers.
Contact: Park Ranger/Volunteer Coordinator.
Phone: 907-224-3175.

KJNP AM–FM RADIO/TELEVISION
P.O. Box 56359, North Pole, AK 99705
❶ BROADCASTING
Compensation: No pay.
Duration: Three months.
Eligibility: High school graduates, college students, college graduates, graduate students, career changers, reentrants to the work force.
Contact: Secretary to the President, P.O. Box 56359.
Phone: 907-488- 2216.

- TV TECHNICIAN
- CAMERA OPERATIONS
- RADIO TECHNICIAN
- ENGINEERING

ARIZONA

ARIZONA FOOD MARKETING ALLIANCE
120 E. Pierce St., Phoenix, AZ 85004
❶ MARKETING
- PUBLICATIONS: Will help write, edit, and design newsletters, brochures, and a monthly full-color magazine.
Compensation: $.50-$6 per hour.
Duration: One semester.
Requirements: Coursework in communications, journalism, or public relations.
Eligibility: College juniors and seniors.
Contact: Resume and writing samples to Publications Director.
Phone: 602-252-9761.
Apply by: August 15 for fall, December 15 for spring, May 15 for summer.

BOYS AND GIRLS CLUB
7502 E. Osborn Rd., Scottsdale, AZ 85251
❶ SOCIAL SERVICES
Compensation: $6-$8 per hour.
Duration: Flexible.
Eligibility: High school students and graduates, college students, college graduates, graduate students.
Contact: Resume and references to Program Development Manager.
Phone: 602-947-6331.

- CULTURAL ENRICHMENT: Will develop programs in the creative, visual, and performing arts.

- SOCIAL RECREATION

- ATHLETIC DIRECTOR ASSISTANT

- COMPUTER SPECIALIST

BUDGET AND RESEARCH DEPARTMENT—CITY OF PHOENIX
200 W. Washington St., 14th Floor, Phoenix, AZ 85003-1611
❶ GOVERNMENT

- MANAGEMENT: Will conduct research and analysis of various administrative or organizational problems, policies, or practices.
Compensation: $2,195 per month.
Duration: One year.
Requirements: Master's degree in public or business administration or related field.
Eligibility: Graduate students, career changers, reentrants to the work force.
Contact: Deputy Budget and Research Director.
Phone: 602-262-4800.
Apply by: January 26.

CH2M HILL
1620 W. Fountainhead Pkwy., Suite 550, Tempe, AZ 85282
❶ ENGINEERING
Compensation: $175 per week for high school students, $250-$450 per week for college students.
Duration: 12-14 weeks during the summer.
Requirements: Chemical engineering or computer science major.
Eligibility: High school students, college juniors and seniors.
Phone: 602-966-8188.

- PROPOSAL DEVELOPMENT

- CALCULATIONS

- DRAFTING

- ADMINISTRATION

THE DIAL CORPORATION CONSUMER PRODUCTS GROUP
1850 N. Central Ave., M/S 1945, Phoenix, AZ 85077

❶ CONSUMER PRODUCTS
Compensation: $450 per week for college students, $650 per week for graduate students.
Duration: 12 weeks during the summer.
Requirements: 3.0 GPA.
Eligibility: College juniors and seniors, graduate students.
Contact: For an application write to Internship Committee.
Phone: 480-754-3425.
Apply by: March 15.

- MARKETING

- HUMAN RESOURCES

- SALES

- ACCOUNTING

PERA CLUB
PER 200, P.O. Box 52025, Phoenix, AZ 85072
❶ RECREATION
Compensation: $75 per week.
Duration: 10-12 weeks during the summer, fall, or spring.
Eligibility: High school seniors, college students, graduate students.
Contact: Internship Coordinator.
Phone: 602-236- 2092.

- RECREATION

- SPECIAL EVENTS COORDINATOR

- AQUATICS PERSONNEL

- SALES

TUCSON CHILDREN'S MUSEUM
P.O. Box 2609, Tucson, AZ 85702
❶ CULTURAL ORGANIZATIONS
Compensation: No pay.
Duration: One semester.
Eligibility: High school students and graduates, college students, college graduates, graduate students, career changers, reentrants to the work force.
Contact: Education Director.
Phone: 520-792-9985, Ext. 103.

- PUBLIC RELATIONS

- EDUCATION

- SPANISH TRANSLATOR

- MARKETING

ARKANSAS

ARKANSAS BEST CORPORATION
3801 Old Greenwood Rd., P.O. Box 10048, Fort Smith, AR 72917
❶ GENERAL BUSINESS

- SYSTEMS PROGRAMMING: Will work in every phase of the development of computer applications systems.
Compensation: $$2,00-2,200 per month.

Duration: Flexible.
Requirements: Coursework in computer information systems, outstanding academic record.
Eligibility: College juniors and seniors, college graduates, graduate students, career changers, reentrants to the work force.
Contact: Consulting Systems Analyst/Programmer.
Phone: 501-784- 8573
Apply by: February 1.

BESS CHISUM STEPHENS YWCA
1200 S. Cleveland, Little Rock, AR 72204
❶ SOCIAL SERVICES
Compensation: No pay.
Eligibility: College students, college graduates.
Contact: Executive Director.
Phone: 501-664-4268.
• YOUTH ACTIVITIES
Duration: Nine months.
• CHILD CARE
Duration: One year.

CALIFORNIA

ACADEMY OF TELEVISION ARTS AND SCIENCES
5220 Lankershim Blvd., North Hollywood, CA 91601-3109
❶ BROADCASTING
Compensation: $2,000.
Duration: Eight weeks.
Eligibility: College sophomores, juniors, and seniors, college graduates, graduate students, individuals who have not been out of school more than one year or who are enrolled in a U.S. university.
Contact: Educational Programs and Services Department.
Phone: 818-754-2830.
Apply by: March 31.
• ENTERTAINMENT NEWS
Requirements: Experience in television production or journalism.
• TELEVISION DIRECTING
• TELEVISION SCRIPTWRITING
Requirements: Writing experience, a prewritten two-page scene.
• FILM EDITING
Requirements: Coursework in film editing.

APPLE COMPUTER, INC.
1 Infinite Loop, MS 75-HR, Cupertino, CA 95014
❶ COMPUTERS
Compensation: Paid.
Duration: Three months.

Eligibility: College sophomores, juniors, and seniors going on to graduate school, graduate students.
Contact: Resume and letter to College Program Coordinator.
Phone: 408-974-0772.
• HARDWARE ENGINEER
• SYSTEMS SOFTWARE ENGINEER
• INFORMATION SYSTEMS AND TECHNOLOGY

BAY AREA DISCOVERY MUSEUM
557 McReynolds Rd., Fort Baker, Sausalito, CA 94965
❶ CULTURAL ORGANIZATIONS
Compensation: No pay.
Duration: 3-6 months.
Eligibility: College sophomores, juniors, and seniors, college graduates, graduate students, career changers, reentrants to the work force.
Contact: Letter and resume to Director of Intern Services.
Phone: 415-289-7282.
• EXHIBITIONS
• EDUCATION
• DEVELOPMENT
• MULTIMEDIA

CALIFORNIA SENATE ASSOCIATES PROGRAM
State Capitol, Room 500A, Sacramento, CA 95814
❶ GOVERNMENT
• GENERAL: Will work on a variety of different legislative activities, including research, bill analysis, and constituent casework.
Compensation: $1,638 per month.
Duration: 11 months.
Requirements: Initiative, analytical and writing skills, assertiveness.
Eligibility: College graduates, graduate students.
Contact: Director, Senate Associates Program Center for California Studies, CSUS, 6000 J St., Sacramento, CA 95819.
Phone: 916-322-7563.
Apply by: February 15.

GLOBAL EXCHANGE
2017 Mission St., Rm 303, San Francisco, CA 94110
❶ INTERNATIONAL RELATIONS
Compensation: Both paid and unpaid positions available.
Duration: 1-6 months.
Requirements: Self-motivated, willing to make a time commitment, creative.

Eligibility: College students, college graduates, graduate students, career changers, reentrants to the work force.

Contact: Letter, resume, two reference letters, and application to Intern Coordinator.

Phone: 415-255-7296.

Apply by: At least one month prior to proposed starting date.

- ALTERNATIVE TRADE: Will attend area festivals as well as write educational materials about country conditions and alternative trade practices.
- CAMPAIGN PROGRAMS: Will work on promotional materials to end the Cold War with Cuba and promote peace in Mexico.
- PUBLICITY
- FUNDRAISING

THE J. PAUL GETTY TRUST—DEPARTMENT OF EDUCATION AND ACADEMIC AFFAIRS

1200 Getty Center Dr., Suite 100, Los Angeles, CA 90049-1687

❶ CULTURAL ORGANIZATIONS

- GENERAL: Undergraduate interns will perform various museum-related and/or artistic projects in Los Angeles museums; graduate interns work in one of the Getty programs.

Compensation: $300 per week for undergraduate interns; $340 for graduate interns.

Duration: 10 weeks during the summer.

Eligibility: College sophomores, juniors, and seniors, graduate students.

Contact: For an application, write Department of Education.

Phone: 310-440-7156.

Apply by: January 8 for graduate interns; March 1 for undergraduates.

KELLY BROADCASTING COMPANY

3 Television Circle, Sacramento, CA 95814

❶ BROADCASTING

Compensation: No pay.

Duration: One semester, 20 hours per week.

Eligibility: College students, college graduates, graduate students.

Contact: News Operations. Manager/Internship Director.

Phone: 916-446-3333.

- NEWS PRODUCTION: Will record news feeds, gather and write news, and perform other duties.

Requirements: Coursework geared toward communications or related fields.

- CONSUMER REPORTING: Will work with reporters on story research, locations, and news coverage.

Requirements: Good research, basic TV production, and communications skills.

- PROMOTIONS: Will work on all aspects of promo production, including field research, studio coordination, and postproduction work.

Requirements: Coursework in communications, journalism, or related major.

- SALES/MARKETING

Requirements: Business, marketing, or communications major, good clerical skills.

KOREAN AMERICAN COALITION

3421 W. Eighth St., Los Angeles, CA 90005

❶ INTERNATIONAL RELATIONS

- GENERAL: Will research issues, coordinate activities, and/or work on publicity materials.

Compensation: $100 per week.

Duration: 10 weeks during the summer, fall, or spring.

Eligibility: College sophomores, juniors, and seniors.

Contact: Internship Coordinator.

Phone: 213-380-6175.

Apply by: February 15 for summer.

KTEH–TV

1585 Shallenberger Rd., San Jose, CA 95131

❶ BROADCASTING

Compensation: No pay.

Duration: Flexible.

Eligibility: High school students and graduates, college students, college graduates, graduate students, career changers, reentrants to the work force.

Contact: Letter and resume to Personnel Manager.

Phone: 408- 795-5400.

- PRODUCTION: Will perform various activities including camera running, floor directing, and set building.

Requirements: Good communications skills, ability to work with others.

- ENGINEERING: Will work as a repair technician both at the studio and in the field.

Requirements: Experience with electronics and TV systems.

- GRAPHIC DESIGN: Will work on desktop publishing tasks.

Requirements: Experience with Macintosh desktop publishing techniques.

LUCAS DIGITAL, LTD./LUCASFILM, LTD./LUCASARTS ENTERTAINMENT COMPANY

Box 2009, San Rafael, CA 94912

❶ FILM/AUDIO/VISUAL

Compensation: $5.25 per hour.

Duration: Nine weeks.

Eligibility: College juniors and seniors, graduate students.

Contact: Human Resources Department–Intern Department.

Phone: 415-662-1800.
Apply by: March 30 for summer, July 25 for fall, October 25 for spring.

- POSTPRODUCTION: Will work as a production assistant for visual effects postproduction.

Requirements: Familiarity with film/video and computers.

- ART: Will work on visual effects production for the art department.

Requirements: Fine arts, illustration, graphic design, or photography major.

- COMPUTER GRAPHICS

Requirements: Ability with high-end 3-D computer graphics, Alias, and Softimage on SGI.

- FINANCE/ACCOUNTING

Requirements: Business, finance, or accounting major, skilled in Lotus or Excel.

SAN FRANCISCO NEIGHBORHOOD LEGAL ASSISTANCE FOUNDATION

225 Bush St., 7th fl., San Francisco, CA 94104

❶ LAW AND CRIMINAL JUSTICE

Contact: Resume and legal writing sample to Director of Litigation.
Phone: No calls.
Apply by: February 15.

- CLERKING: Will work with clients and assist attorneys.

Compensation: $ 10 per hour.
Duration: 3-12 months.
Requirements: Ability to speak Spanish, Cantonese, or Vietnamese.
Eligibility: Eligible for federal work study program, completed one year of law school.

- VOLUNTEER CLERKING: Will provide assistance to attorneys and clients.

Compensation: No pay.
Duration: 3-12 months.
Requirements: Bilingual applicants preferred.
Eligibility: Completed one year of law school, able to commit 10-20 hours per week.

THEATREWORKS

1100 Hamilton Ct., Menlo Park, CA 94025

❶ THEATER ARTS

- TECHNICAL SUPPORT: Will assist in the areas of scene design, costumes, or props. (Note: Part-time positions and apprenticeships also available.)

Compensation: $100 per week.
Duration: 6-10 weeks.
Requirements: Enthusiasm, experience in technical theater preferred.

Eligibility: High school students and graduates, college students, college graduates, graduate students, career changers.
Contact: Associate Artist.
Phone: 415-463-1950, Ext. 107.
Apply by: February 1, April 1, June 1, October 1.

VOLUNTEER CENTER OF SAN FRANCISCO

1160 Battery St., Suite 70, San Francisco, CA 94111

❶ PUBLIC ADMINISTRATION

Compensation: No pay.
Duration: One summer.
Eligibility: Unless otherwise indicated, high school students and graduates, college students, college graduates, graduate students, career changers, reentrants to the work force.
Contact: Executive Director.
Phone: 415-982-8999.

WELLS FARGO BANK

420 Montgomery St., San Francisco, CA 94163

❶ BANKING

Compensation: $216 per week for college students, $391 per week for graduate students.
Duration: 12 weeks during the summer.
Eligibility: College seniors, graduate students.
Contact: Letter and resume to Summer Internship Program, Position #3115.
Phone: 800-541-8980.
Apply by: March 1.

- MARKETING: Will help develop and implement promotion campaigns.

- LENDING: Will handle credit analysis and participate in all areas of credit and loan evaluations.

- FINANCE: Will deal with loan loss factors, data and budget analysis, and financial planning.

- HUMAN RESOURCES: Will analyze data and prepare reports.

Y.E.S. TO JOBS

1416 N. La Brea Ave., Hollywood, CA 90028

❶ ENTERTAINMENT

Compensation: $200 per week.
Duration: 10 weeks during the summer.
Requirements: Minority applicants, 2.5 GPA, minimum age 16.
Eligibility: High school students.
Contact: Executive Director.
Phone: 213-469-2411, EXT 3598.
Apply by: May 1.

- PUBLICITY
- DEVELOPMENT
- CREATIVE
- SALES

YOSEMITE NATIONAL PARK
P.O. Box 577, Yosemite Valley, CA 95389
❶ PARKS
Compensation: No pay.
Duration: Minimum 12 weeks during the summer.
Eligibility: College students, college graduates, graduate students.
Contact: Student Intern Coordinator, P.O. Box 2027.
Phone: 209- 375-9505.
Apply by: February 15.

- INFORMATION RESOURCES: Will conduct tours of the park and provide educational interpretation in the park's visitors' center.

- WILDERNESS MANAGEMENT: Will patrol backcountry areas and provide wilderness education services.

COLORADO

COLORADO WILDLIFE FEDERATION
445 Union Blvd., Suite 302, Lakewood, CO 80228-1243
❶ WILDLIFE/ENVIRONMENT
Compensation: No pay.
Eligibility: College juniors and seniors, college graduates, graduate students, career changers, reentrants to the work force.
Contact: Volunteer Coordinator.
Phone: 303-987-0400.

- SCHOOL PROGRAMS: Will visit elementary and high school students in Denver to address issues pertaining to conservation of the environment.
Duration: One school year.
Requirements: Available for training in late summer so can begin in the fall, available to visit at least one class per week for up to two hours, good with children of all ages.

- ISSUES: Will be involved in all CWF issues decisions, from drafting positions to following resolutions through to legislative hearings.
Duration: Year-round.
Requirements: Proficient research and writing skills.

- ADMINISTRATION/MEMBER RELATIONS: Will serve as the in-house communications assistant.
Duration: Year-round.
Requirements: Good data entry/word-processing skills.

DENVER CENTER THEATRE COMPANY
1050 13th St., Denver, CO 80204
❶ THEATER ARTS
Duration: 30 weeks (12-show season).

Eligibility: College students, college graduates, graduate students.
Contact: Assistant to the Producing Director.
Phone: No calls.
Apply by: August 1.

- SCENIC DESIGN: Will assist in scenery painting for a 12-show season.
Compensation: No pay.

- COSTUME DESIGN: Will work as costume designer and wardrobe upkeeper.
Compensation: $150 per week.

- LIGHTING: Will work on all aspects of lighting design and technique.
Compensation: $150 per week.

- LITERARY: Will help coordinate the screening of new plays.
Compensation: No pay.

DENVER POST
1560 Broadway, Denver, CO 80202
❶ JOURNALISM
Compensation: $440 per week.
Duration: 10 weeks.
Requirements: Background and strong interest in print journalism.
Eligibility: College seniors, graduate students.
Contact: Letter and resume to Associate Editor.
Phone: 303-820-1800.
Apply by: December 1.

- REPORTING

- PHOTOGRAPHY

- COPY EDITOR/GRAPHIC ARTIST

U.S. OLYMPIC COMMITTEE
One Olympic Plaza, Colorado Springs, CO 80909
❶ ATHLETICS/INTERNATIONAL RELATIONS

- GENERAL: Positions available in the broadcasting, accounting, journalism, public relations, computer science, and marketing departments.
Compensation: Paid.
Duration: Spring, fall, or summer semester.
Eligibility: College juniors and seniors, graduate students.
Contact:, Coordinator of Educational Programs.
Phone: 719-632-5551, Ext. 2597.
Apply by: June 1 for fall, October 1 for winter/spring, February 15 for summer.

CONNECTICUT

AETNA LIFE & CASUALTY
151 Farmington Ave., RSAA, Hartford, CT 06156
❶ INSURANCE

- AGENCY ACTIVITIES: Will work in various capacities specific to each assignment.
Compensation: $9-$12 per hour.
Duration: One summer.
Eligibility: College juniors and seniors, graduate students.
Contact: Intern Coordinator, RSAA.
Phone: No calls.
Apply by: February 1.

AUTOMOTIVE RESTORATION, INC.
1785 Barnum Ave., Stratford, CT 06497
❶ AUTOMOTIVE/MANUFACTURING
Duration: Year-round.
Eligibility: High school students and graduates, college students, college graduates, graduate students, career changers, reentrants to the work force.
Contact: President.
Phone: 203-377-6745.

- GENERAL APPRENTICESHIP: Will help tradespeople with specific functions such as panel fabrication, upholstery, car mechanics, body and wood work, and assembly/detail.
Compensation: Minimum $6 per hour.
Requirements: Driver's license, minimum age 18 to work with power tools.

- RACE MANAGEMENT: Will time events, locate parts, and perform general vehicle upkeep.
Compensation: No pay.
Requirements: Ability to travel.

- MARKETING: Will develop marketing strategies, including writing copy, market research, and product development.
Compensation: No pay.

NATURE CONSERVANCY—CONNECTICUT
55 High St., Middletown, CT 06457
❶ ENVIRONMENT
Compensation: Varies.
Duration: Flexible, but usually one semester.
Eligibility: College sophomores, juniors and seniors, college graduates.
Contact: Letter and resume to Stewardship Ecologist.
Phone: 860-344-0716.

- SCIENCE: Will research various species and habitats, develop site conservation strategies, and implement on-site biological management programs.
Requirements: Experience in environmental studies, familiarity with fieldwork.

- LAND PROTECTION: Will conduct inquiries into land ownership and assist with land protection issues.
Requirements: Ability to work independently, demonstrated interest in land issues.

DELAWARE

DELAWARE NATURE SOCIETY
P.O. Box 700, Hockessin, DE 19707
❶ ENVIRONMENT
Eligibility: College sophomores, juniors, and seniors, college graduates.
Contact: Manager of Education.
Phone: No calls.

- EDUCATION: Will teach in a multidimensional education program designed to address ecological and wildlife concerns.
Compensation: $8,500.
Duration: 10 months.
Requirements: Bachelor's degree in science, education, or related field.

- LAND PROTECTION: Will cover a multitude of environmental as well as logistical issues as they pertain to matters of ownership, preservation, and protection.
Compensation: $14,000.
Duration: One year.
Requirements: Bachelor's degree in environment-related area, career-oriented.

DU PONT
Nemours Bldg., Room 12419, Wilmington, DE 19898
❶ CHEMICALS/CONSUMER PRODUCTS
Compensation: $450-$550 per week.
Duration: 8-16 weeks during the summer.
Requirements: Engineering, science, or business major.
Eligibility: College seniors, college graduates entering graduate school.
Contact: Summer Professional Program.
Phone: 302-774-1000.
Apply by: December 31.

- CHEMICALS
- RESEARCH AND DEVELOPMENT
- PIGMENTS AND MINERALS
- PACKAGING AND INDUSTRIAL POLYMERS

HISTORICAL SOCIETY OF DELAWARE
505 Market St., Wilmington, DE 19801
❶ CULTURAL ORGANIZATIONS
Compensation: $5-$6 per hour.
Duration: 13 weeks.
Requirements: Familiarity with and interest in American history.
Eligibility: High school graduates, college students, college graduates, graduate students.
Contact: Resume to Executive Director.
Phone: 302-655-7161.

- CURATORIAL: Will work with various artifacts.

- LIBRARY: Will work as a researcher and processor.

- PROGRAMMING: Will work on educational activities.

QUIET RESORTS PUBLIC RELATIONS
P.O. Box 505, Bethany Beach, DE 19930
❶ PUBLIC RELATIONS
Compensation: No pay.
Duration: One semester.
Eligibility: College sophomores, juniors, and seniors, college graduates, graduate students, career changers, reentrants to the work force.
Contact: Resume and work samples to Publisher.
Phone: 302-537-1585.

- EDITORIAL: Will cultivate, report, and write feature stories, as well as assist with production tasks.
Requirements: Appropriate college coursework, productive work ethic.

- PRODUCTION: Will design, typeset, and paste up stories and advertisements for various newsletters.
Requirements: Computer literacy, coursework in art or graphic design.

- ADVERTISING/SALES: Will cultivate sales leads, work with clients, and create ad campaigns.
Requirements: Coursework in marketing or business.

- PHOTOGRAPHY: Will work as a beginning staff photographer.
Requirements: Art, photography, or graphic design major.

WILM NEWS RADIO
P.O. Box 1990, Wilmington, DE 19899
❶ BROADCASTING

- WRITING: Will collect, write, and rewrite news for broadcast.
Compensation: No pay.
Duration: Three months.
Requirements: Broadcast journalism, communications, or journalism major.
Eligibility: High school students, college students, graduate students.
Contact: Program Director.
Phone: 302-656-9800.
Apply by: Four weeks prior to desired start date.

DISTRICT OF COLUMBIA

THE ACADEMY FOR ADVANCED AND STRATEGIC STUDIES
1647 Lamont St., NW, Washington, DC 20010
❶ RESEARCH

- RESEARCHERS: Will research and address policies surrounding cultural issues.

Compensation: $500-$1,000, room and board.
Duration: 15 weeks to one year during the summer, fall, and/or spring.
Eligibility: High school students and graduates, college students, college graduates, graduate students.
Contact: Internship Coordinator.
Phone: No calls..

ACCURACY IN MEDIA
4455 Connecticut Ave., NW, Suite 330, Washington, DC 20008
❶ JOURNALISM/BROADCASTING
Compensation: $125 per week.
Eligibility: High school graduates, college students, college graduates, graduate students, career changers, international students with proper visa.
Contact: Letter and two writing samples of a political nature to Internship Director
Phone: 202-364-4401.World Wide Web: http://www.aim.org/aim/html

- REPORTING: Will collect and write stories that pertain to foreign affairs.
Duration: 6-18 weeks.
Requirements: Writing samples.

- RESEARCH: Will research topical issues and produce studies or reports on findings.
Duration: 6-18 weeks.

- WRITING: Will research and write stories for *The Campus Report*.
Duration: 6-18 weeks.
Requirements: Writing samples.

- TELEVISION: Will assist in researching material for a weekly commentary show.
Duration: 18 weeks.

AMERICAN FOREIGN SERVICE ASSOCIATION
2101 E St., NW, Washington, DC 20037
❶ PUBLIC ADMINISTRATION/ INTERNATIONAL RELATIONS
Eligibility: College students.
Contact: Executive Director.
Phone: 202-944-5519.
World Wide Web: http://www.afsa.org
Apply by: April 1 for summer, August 1 for fall, December 15 for spring.

- CONGRESSIONAL/OUTREACH: Will monitor legislation on Capitol Hill, help coordinate activities of visiting foreign service speakers, and assist with Diplomats On-Line.
Compensation: No pay.
Duration: One semester, two days per week.
Requirements: Interest in public affairs and international relations.

- SCHOLARSHIP ADMINISTRATION: Will create a database for U.S. dependents and foreign students and provide assistance for the foreign service scholarship program.
Compensation: No pay.
Duration: One semester, two days per week.
Requirements: Background in a college or university financial aid office.

- LABOR MANAGEMENT: Will help field member inquiries and correspondence and assist in periodic reviews of regulations.
Compensation: No pay.
Duration: One semester, two days per week.
Requirements: Interest in labor relations.

- MARKETING: Will market subscriptions and work on advertising for the *Foreign Service Journal*.
Compensation: Paid and unpaid positions available.
Duration: One semester.
Requirements: Business, marketing, or advertising major, basic computer skills.

AMNESTY INTERNATIONAL USA—WASHINGTON OFFICE

304 Pennsylvania Ave., SE, Washington, DC 20003

❶ PUBLIC AFFAIRS/INTERNATIONAL RELATIONS
Compensation: No pay.
Duration: Minimum 10 weeks.
Eligibility: High school graduates.
Contact: Office Manager.
Phone: 202-544-0200.

- AFRICAN AFFAIRS: Will monitor developments in various African regions.

- EUROPEAN/MIDDLE EASTERN AFFAIRS: Will monitor developments in various overseas regions.

- LATIN AMERICAN AFFAIRS: Will monitor developments in Latin American regions.

- CAMPAIGNING: Will prepare materials, coordinate events, and provide evaluations for various campaigns and crisis response activities.

C-SPAN

400 N. Capitol St., NW, Suite 650, Washington, DC 20001 World Wide Web: http://www.c-span.org

❶ BROADCASTING
Compensation: No pay.
Duration: One semester.
Eligibility: College juniors and seniors.
Contact: Letter and resume to Internship Program Coordinator.

Phone: 202-626-7968.

- PROGRAMMING: Positions include field producer, control room producer, and assignment desk editor.

- MARKETING: Will work with departmental planners, create various promotional materials, and conduct market research.

- EDUCATIONAL SERVICES: Will work on procedures for dispersing information.

- PRESS INFORMATION: Will work on news releases, update press lists, conduct media mailings, and transcribe video.

ECONOMIC RESEARCH SERVICE—U.S. DEPARTMENT OF AGRICULTURE

1301 New York Ave., NW, Room 1226, Washington, DC 20005-4788. World Wide Web: http://www.econ.ag.gov

❶ AGRICULTURE/RESEARCH
Compensation: $290-$370 per week for college students, $370-$560 per week for graduate students.
Duration: 8-10 weeks during the summer.
Requirements: 3.0 GPA, academic focus on economics.
Eligibility: College juniors and seniors, graduate students.
Contact: Summer Intern Program.
Phone: 202-219-0307.
Apply by: March 1.

- ECONOMICS
- NATURAL RESOURCES
- AGRICULTURE

FENTON COMMUNICATIONS

1606 20th St., NW, Washington, DC 20009. World Wide Web: http://www.fenton.com

❶ PUBLIC RELATIONS
Eligibility: College sophomores, juniors, and seniors.
Phone: 202- 745-0707.
Apply by: Two months prior to desired start date.

- FULL-TIME PUBLIC RELATIONS: Will perform all facets of public relations, including researching, writing, administrative assistance, database, and phone work.
Compensation: $120 per week.
Duration: One semester or one summer.

HOSTELLING INTERNATIONAL—AMERICAN YOUTH HOSTELS

733 15th St., NW, Suite 840, Washington, DC 20005. World Wide Web: http://www.hiayh.org

❶ HOSPITALITY/TRAVEL
Compensation: $100-$150 per week.
Duration: 10-16 weeks.
Eligibility: College sophomores, juniors, and seniors, college graduates, graduate students, reentrants to the work force.

Contact: Letter, resume, three letters of recommendation, and college transcript to Human Resources Manager.
Phone: 202-783-6161.
Apply by: August 1 for fall, November 1 for winter, February 1 for spring, April 1 for summer.

- MARKETING: Will write and place articles in newspapers and magazines and assist with the nationwide market research program.

Requirements: Experience with advertising and market research.

- PROGRAMS AND EDUCATION: Will work on the Discovery Tours program as well as develop material for nationwide programming.

Requirements: Customer service and word-processing experience, industry experience a plus.

- MANAGEMENT: Will provide informational support to the national network of hostels as well as work on various publicity and developmental materials.

INSTITUTE FOR POLICY STUDIES
5733 15th St.., NW, Washington, DC 20009

❶ RESEARCH/PUBLIC AFFAIRS
Compensation: No pay.
Duration: One semester or one summer.
Eligibility: College juniors and seniors, college graduates, graduate students.
Contact: For application materials, contact Intern Coordinator.
Phone: 202-234-9382.

- BIOGRAPHICAL: Will research issues of cultural concern, such as the Hiroshima Project, Vietnam War, and arms race.

- SOCIAL ISSUES: Will conduct research on child rearing and development as they pertain to the Crisis of Childhood in America Project.

- POLICY: Will monitor the effects of the North American Free Trade Agreement and will research the worldwide labor situation.

- INTERNATIONAL RELATIONS: Will research antiapartheid ordinances, nuclear-free zones, and sister cities.

THE JOHN F. KENNEDY CENTER FOR THE PERFORMING ARTS
2700 F St., NW, Washington, DC 20566.
World Wide Web: http://www.kennedy-center.org

❶ THEATER ARTS
Compensation: $650 per month.
Duration: 3-4 months.

Eligibility: College graduates, graduate students, students who have graduated but have been out of school no more than two years.
Contact: Letter, resume, transcript, writing sample, and three letters of recommendation to Internship Program Manager, Education Department.
Phone: 202-416-8800.

- GENERAL THEATER: Will help coordinate the technical and logistical aspects of the American College Theater Festival.

- ORGANIZATION: Will assist in concert coordination, program development, training, and competition organization.

- PROGRAMS: Will potentially work on a variety of theater training programs, including stage management, drama coaching, and theater production.

- PUBLIC MANAGEMENT: Will assist in organizing special events, volunteer and retail staffs, and materials for community relations.

NATIONAL COUNCIL OF WORLD AFFAIRS ORGANIZATIONS
1726 M St., NW, Suite 800, Washington, DC 20036

❶ INTERNATIONAL RELATIONS

- GENERAL: Will maintain records on World Affairs Councils and help coordinate logistics for visiting global affairs speakers.

Compensation: No pay.
Duration: One semester.
Requirements: Interest in international relations, experience with WordPerfect.
Eligibility: College graduates, career changers, reentrants to the work force.
Contact: Internship Coordinator.
Phone: 202-785-4703.
Apply by: September 15 for fall, November 15 for spring, April 1 for summer.

NATIONAL GEOGRAPHIC SOCIETY
1145 17th St., NW, Washington, DC 20036

❶ GEOGRAPHY
Eligibility: College juniors and seniors and graduate students attending a U.S. university.

- GENERAL: Will conduct editorial research and assist in cartographic design and production.

Compensation: Paid.
Duration: One spring, summer, or fall.
Requirements: Geography or cartography major, excellent research skills.
Phone: 202-857-7161.

- TELEVISION: Will develop and research stories, conduct research, and work in public relations, marketing, and production.

Compensation: No pay.
Duration: One summer.
Contact: NGS Television.
Phone: 202-775-6760.

NATIONAL WILDLIFE FEDERATION
1400 16th St., NW, Washington, DC 20036.
World Wide Web: http://www.nwf.org

❶ ENVIRONMENT

Compensation: $275 per week.
Duration: 24 weeks.
Eligibility: College graduates, graduate students, career changers.
Contact: For application instructions, write to Resources Conservation Internship Program Coordinator.
Phone: 202-797-6800.
Apply by: October 1 for January, March 15 for July.

- FISHERIES/WILDLIFE: Will be involved primarily with researching policy issues, covering government panels, and drafting material for NWF publications.
Requirements: Wildlife, biology, fisheries, or science degree, strong academic record.

- PUBLIC LAND/ENERGY: Will research policy topics, cover congressional proceedings, and work on NWF testimony.
Requirements: Academic experience in forestry, land management, mining, or energy issues.

- GRASS ROOTS: Will serve as an educational source on lobbying issues.
Requirements: Experience in grass-roots activities.

THE NEW REPUBLIC
1220 19th St., NW, Suite 600, Washington, DC 20036

❶ JOURNALISM

- EDITORIAL: Will write short articles and editorials, fact-check, proofread, and examine unsolicited material.
Compensation: $200 per week.
Duration: Three or nine months.
Requirements: Deadline-driven, excellent writing and editing abilities.
Eligibility: College seniors, college graduates.
Contact: Letter, resume, two recommendations, and three to five writing samples to Internship Coordinator.
Phone: No calls.
Apply by: March 1.

RENEW AMERICA
1400 16th St., NW, Suite 710, Washington, DC 20036. World Wide Web: http://www.crest.org

❶ ENVIRONMENT

- LEGISLATION: Will work at the grassroots level with various environmental organizations.
Compensation: Paid and unpaid positions..
Duration: Three to six months.
Eligibility: High school graduates, college students, college graduates, graduate students.
Contact: Letter and resume to Internship Coordinator.
Phone: No phone calls.
Apply by: April 1.

SCIENCE NEWS
1719 N St., NW, Washington, DC 20036

❶ PUBLISHING

- EDITORIAL
Compensation: $1,650 per month.
Duration: Three months during the summer, fall, or spring.
Requirements: Journalism graduate students preferred.
Eligibility: College graduates, graduate students.
Contact: Letter, resume, and at least three writing samples to Managing Editor.
Phone: 202-785-2255.
Apply by: February 1 for summer.

SMITHSONIAN INSTITUTION CONSERVATION ANALYTICAL LABORATORY
MRC 534, Washington, DC 20560

❶ CULTURAL ORGANIZATIONS

Compensation: $3,000
Duration: 10 weeks in summer.
Eligibility:, College seniors, college graduates, graduate students. International applications accepted.
Contact: Send cover letter, resume, two references, to Intern Coordinator.
Phone: 301-238-3700.
Apply by: February 1.

- DESIGN: Will create sketches and scale drawings, using computer.

- EDITORIAL: Will create concepts, formulate designs, and finalize working drawings.

- GRAPHICS: Will interpret and carry out design drawings and layouts, mount exhibits, and work with silk-screening and ink mixing.

W*USA–TV
4100 Wisconsin Ave., NW, Washington, DC 20016

❶ BROADCASTING

Compensation: No pay.
Duration: One semester.
Eligibility: College juniors and seniors, graduate students.
Contact: Resume and enrollment/credit confirmation from school to Internship Coordinator.

Phone: 202-895-5810.

- COMMUNITY AFFAIRS: Will be schooled in copywriting, postproduction, and research techniques and assist in the production of public service spots.
- DOCUMENTARY: Will research investigative topics and gain experience as a documentary producer and scriptwriter.
- SPORTS: Will participate in organizing video footage and storyboarding for the "Eyewitness Sports" news-gathering team.
- PUBLICITY: Will draft press releases, write for the electronic and print media, and participate in postproduction activities in the field and studio.

FLORIDA

FLORIDA STUDIO THEATRE
1241 N. Palm Ave., Sarasota, FL 34236
❶ THEATER ARTS
Compensation: $40 per week.
Duration: 3-12 months.
Eligibility: College students needing an internship for college credit, college graduates.
Contact: Assistant to Artistic Director Intern Coordinator.
Phone: 941-366-9017.

- PRODUCTION: Will coordinate all aspects of the production, from props and sets to costumes.
- MUSIC DIRECTION: Will work on accompaniment and music direction for a variety of in-house and touring productions.
- DRAMATURGY: Will work as a script analyst and evaluator as well as provide input and assistance to the new play program.
- ACTING: Will act in staged readings, workshop exercises, and mainstage productions.

GEORGIA

ATLANTA BRAVES
P.O. Box 4064, Atlanta, GA 30302 World Wide Web: http://www.atlantabraves.com
❶ ATHLETICS
Duration: 10 weeks during the summer.
Requirements: 3.0 GPA.
Eligibility: College juniors and seniors
Contact: Letter, resume, transcript, and recommendations to Career Initiative Program.
Phone: 404-614-1506.
Apply by: February.

- PUBLIC RELATIONS
- STADIUM MANAGEMENT
- MARKETING
- PROMOTIONS

DOWNTOWN ATLANTA YMCA
260 Peachtree St., Atlanta, GA 30303
❶ HEALTH SERVICES
Compensation: No pay.
Duration: Flexible.
Eligibility: High school students and graduates, college students, college graduates, graduate students, reentrants to the work force, elderly, handicapped.
Contact: Resume and application to Fitness Coordinator.
Phone: 404-527-7676.

- HEALTH ENHANCEMENT: Will design and implement weight management and nutritional programs and conduct research for various eating programs.
Requirements: Coursework in sales, nutrition, and physiology.
- EXERCISE PHYSIOLOGY: Will work in all phases of personal training, including design and implementation of fitness programs.
Requirements: Certified personal trainers, knowledge of CPR, Cybex experience.
- AEROBICS: Will implement incentive programs and record-keeping methods, evaluate staff, and coordinate training-program schedules.
Requirements: Certified in aerobics and CPR, exceptional leadership skills.

FLYING DOCTORS OF AMERICA
1951 Airport Rd., PDK, Atlanta, GA 30341
❶ HEALTH SERVICES
Compensation: No pay.
Duration: 3-4 months.
Eligibility: High school graduates, college students, college graduates, graduate students, career changers, reentrants to the work force.
Contact: Assistant to the President.
Phone: 770-452-6670.

- MARKETING: Will help to coordinate fundraising strategies and programs.
Requirements: Knowledge of WordPerfect, excellent communications skills.
- PUBLIC RELATIONS: Will write press releases, communicate with the media, schedule public appearances.
Requirements: Excellent communications skills, knowledge of WordPerfect.
- ADMINISTRATIVE: Will conduct research and correspond with mission participants.
Requirements: Good interpersonal skills, knowledge of WordPerfect.
- DEVELOPMENT: Will write grant proposals, research potential fundraising plans and ideas, and coordinate organizational events.
Requirements: Independence, strong writing and interpersonal skills.

GEORGIA GOVERNOR'S INTERN PROGRAM
115 State Capitol, Atlanta, GA 30334
❶ GOVERNMENT
- GENERAL: Will work on the legislative process in varying capacities.

Compensation: Varies.
Duration: 10-13 weeks.
Requirements: 2.5 GPA, Georgia residents.
Eligibility: College juniors or seniors, graduate students, first- or second-year law students with a minimum GPA.
Contact: Director.
Phone: 404-656-3804.
Apply by: July 15 for fall, October 15 for winter, January 15 for spring, April 15 for summer.

HUMANICS PUBLISHING GROUP,
P.O. Box 7400, Atlanta, GA 30357
❶ PUBLISHING
Compensation: Both paid and unpaid positions available.
Duration: One semester.
Eligibility: College juniors and seniors, college graduates.
Contact: Intern Coordinator, P.O. Box 77766.
Phone: No calls.
- BOOK DESIGN: Will provide input on book and promotion design, illustration, and paste-up.

Requirements: Exceptional communications skills, computer literate, typing ability.
- EDITORIAL: Will write copy for various projects as well as deal with author relations.

Requirements: English or literature coursework, office experience.
- ACQUISITIONS: Will participate in the manuscript selection process, deal with contracts, and assist in author relations.

Requirements: Knowledge of literary trends, good language and negotiation skills.
- BUSINESS ADMINISTRATION: Will deal with all operating aspects of a small business.

Requirements: Relevant background.

THE MATERNAL & CHILD HEALTH INSTITUTE
1252 W. Peachtree St., NW, Suite 551, Atlanta, GA 30309 World Wide Web:
http://www.maternalandchild.org
❶ HEALTH SERVICES
- RESEARCH: Will work on improving welfare of mothers and children.

Compensation: Unpaid.
Duration: 12 weeks during the summer or fall.
Requirements: Coursework in health or public affairs issues.

Eligibility: College juniors and seniors, college graduates, graduate students.
Contact: Community Health Programs Coordinator.
Phone: 404-875-5051.
Apply by: April 1.

NEWS RADIO WGST
1819 Peachtree Rd., Suite 700, Atlanta, GA 30363 World Wide Web:
http://www.wgst.com
❶ BROADCASTING
Compensation: No pay.
Duration: One quarter or one semester.
Eligibility: College students, college graduates, graduate students.
Contact: Resume, dates of proposed internship, and indication of whether academic credit is expected to Operations and Special Events Director.
Phone: No calls.
- NEWS: Will write news copy, take in network and reporter feeds, and make police and fire checks.
- PROGRAMMING: Will provide assistance for remote broadcasts, work on dubbing public service spots, serve as in-house communications source, and screen callers.
- PROMOTIONS: Will assist special-event remote broadcasts and write public service and promotional announcements.

UNIVERSITY OF GEORGIA–MARINE EXTENSION SERVICE
30 Ocean Science Circle, Savannah, GA 31411
❶ EDUCATION/SCIENCE
- GENERAL: Will conduct lectures, labs, and field studies in marine and aquarium topics.

Compensation: $200 per week.
Duration: 50 weeks.
Requirements: Degree in biology, environmental studies, or related field.
Eligibility: College graduates.
Contact: Acting Associate Director, Marine Extension Service.
Phone: 912-598-2496.
Apply by: April 20.

HAWAII

FAMILY PEACE CENTER
938 Austin Lane, Honolulu, Hawaii 96817
❶ SOCIAL SERVICES
- COUNSELING: Will work on domestic violence issues, with responsibilities including counseling, charting, and assessing individuals or groups.

Compensation: No pay.
Duration: Three to six months.

Requirements: Knowledge of abuse issues and group dynamics, maturity, independence.
Eligibility: High school seniors and graduates, college students, college graduates, graduate students, career changers.
Contact: Resume and statement of goals and plans to Program Director.
Phone: 808- 845-1445.

HONOLULU ADVERTISER
Box 3110, Honolulu, HI 96802
❶ JOURNALISM

• GENERAL: Will work in the newsroom on various aspects of the reporting and editing process.
Compensation: $7.50 per hour.
Duration: 12 weeks.
Requirements: Journalism major, knowledge of Hawaiian issues.
Eligibility: Native Hawaiians or Hawaii residents, college undergraduates.
Contact: Letter of application and resume to City Editor.
Phone: 808-525-8090.

PACIFIC/REMOTE ISLANDS NATIONAL WILDLIFE REFUGE
P.O. Box 50167, Honolulu, HI 96850
❶ WILDLIFE/ENVIRONMENT

• MONITORING: Will monitor seabird activities and assist in bird banding, sea turtle counts, and field station maintenance.
Compensation: No pay.
Duration: Minimum 10 weeks.
Requirements: Coursework in wildlife biology, experience with field research.
Eligibility: High school graduates, college students, college graduates.
Contact: Wildlife Biologist.
Phone: 808-541-1201.

I D A H O

BOISE NATIONAL FOREST—MOUNTAIN HOME RANGER DISTRICT
2180 American Legion Blvd., Mountain Home, ID 83647
❶ ENVIRONMENT
Compensation: Both paid and unpaid positions available.
Duration: Flexible.
Eligibility: Minimum age 18.
Contact: Wildlife Biologist.
Phone: 208-587-7961.

• LAND MANAGEMENT: Will catalog range improvements, conduct inspections, and potentially work on construction or maintenance projects.
Requirements: Horseback riding ability, experience driving a four-wheel-drive vehicle.

• WILDLIFE: Will conduct wildlife and habitat surveys and inventories, manipulate vegetation, and maintain and install water-development systems.

I L L I N O I S

ARGONNE NATIONAL LABORATORY—DIVISION OF EDUCATIONAL PROGRAMS
9700 S. Cass Ave., Argonne, IL 60439
❶ RESEARCH/SCIENCE

• GENERAL: Will work with scientists on research in such areas as biology, computer science, mathematics, reactor technology, chemistry, or physics.
Compensation: $225 per week.
Duration: 15-19 weeks during the summer.
Requirements: 3.0 GPA.
Eligibility: College juniors and seniors, college graduates.
Contact: Administrative Assistant.
Phone: 708-252-3366.
Apply by: February 1.

ART INSTITUTE OF CHICAGO
111 S. Michigan Ave., Chicago, IL 60603
❶ CULTURAL ORGANIZATIONS

• GENERAL: Will work on special projects and provide clerical and technical support, public affairs services, and assistance to various art departments.
Compensation: Both paid and unpaid positions available.
Duration: Flexible.
Eligibility: College juniors and seniors, graduate students.
Contact: Letter and resume to Internship Coordinator.
Phone: 312-443-3555.

EDELMAN WORLDWIDE PUBLIC RELATIONS
211 E. Ontario, Chicago, IL 60611
❶ PUBLIC RELATIONS
Compensation: $250 per week.
Duration: 12 weeks (flexible) during the summer, fall, or spring.
Eligibility: College students, college graduates, graduate students.
Contact: Letter, resume, and optional writing samples to Internship Coordinator.
Phone: 312-280-7000.

• MEDIA PRODUCTION

• FINANCE

• EVENT COORDINATION

• MARKETING

FEDERAL RESERVE BANK OF CHICAGO
230 S. LaSalle St., Chicago, IL 60604
❶ BANKING

- GENERAL: Will work individually and with the intern group on economic research, monetary policy, banking issues, and human resources projects.
Compensation: $8.75-$11.25 per hour.
Duration: One summer.
Requirements: Strong computer skills, outstanding academic record, leadership ability.
Eligibility: College sophomores and juniors, graduate students.
Contact: One-page writing sample to Intern Coordinator.
Phone: 312-322- 5490.
Apply by: February 1.

PEORIA JOURNAL STAR
1 News Plaza, Peoria, IL 61643 World Wide Web: http://www.pjstar.com
❶ JOURNALISM
Compensation: $275 per week.
Duration: 3 months.
Requirements: B average or better in journalism coursework, completed junior year of college.
Eligibility: College seniors, graduate students.
Contact: Asst. City Editor.
Phone: 309-686-3255.
Apply by: November 30 for spring, March 15 for summer, July 30 for winter.

- NEWS: Will work as a reporter on assigned stories.
- PHOTOGRAPHY: Will work as a photographer on assigned photo shoots.
- COPY EDITOR
Requirements: Computer scanning experience.

SECOND CITY, INC.
1616 N. Wells, Chicago, IL 60614
❶ THEATER ARTS
- PRODUCTION: Will work on special projects in marketing and promotion.
Compensation: No pay.
Duration: Three months.
Requirements: Ambitious, interest in theater and improvisation.
Eligibility: High school seniors and graduates, college sophomores, juniors, and seniors, college graduates.
Contact: Administrative Director.
Phone: 312-664-4032.

STATE FARM INSURANCE COMPANIES
Three State Farm Plaza, K-1, Bloomington, IL 61791. World Wide Web: http://www.statefarm.com
❶ INSURANCE
- GENERAL: Will work as a programmer and analyst.
Compensation: $12.63 per hour.
Duration: One summer.

Requirements: 3.0 GPA, excellent analysis skills, computer science or information science major.
Eligibility: College sophomores, juniors, and seniors.
Contact: Resume to Human Resources.
Phone: 309-763-2815.
Apply by: March 31.

STEPPENWOLF THEATER COMPANY
1650 N. Halsted St., Chicago, IL 60614.
World Wide Web: http://www.steppenwolf.com
❶ THEATER ARTS
Compensation: No pay.
Duration: 3-12 months.
Eligibility: High school graduates, college students, college graduates, graduate students, career changers, reentrants to the work force.
Contact: Director of Internships.
Phone: 312-335-1888.

- STAGE MANAGEMENT
- FRONT-OF-HOUSE
- PUBLIC RELATIONS
- PRODUCTION

WGN–RADIO 720
435 N. Michigan, Chicago, IL 60611
❶ BROADCASTING
Compensation: $75 per week travel stipend.
Duration: 14 weeks during the summer, fall, spring, or winter.
Requirements: Creativity, ability to meet deadlines, excellent writing and audio production skills.
Eligibility: College juniors and seniors, college graduates, graduate students, career changers, reentrants to the work force.
Contact: Letter, resume, and application to Assistant Program Director.
Phone: 312-222-4973.

- PROGRAMMING: Will book guests, conceive of program ideas, work on promotional materials, and screen calls.
- NEWS: Will provide assistance on major breaking news stories, research and write stories, take feeds, and answer phones.
- AGRIBUSINESS: Will prepare reports or news updates, assist with TV and newsletter production, and answer phones.
- NETWORK: Will organize and prepare programs for distribution to station affiliates.
- PROMOTIONS: Will prepare press releases, edit newsletter, and organize special events.
- SPORTS: Will do interviews, edit copy, cover events, and book guests.

INDIANA

INDIANAPOLIS STAR AND NEWS

307 N. Pennsylvania, Indianapolis, IN
46204.World Wide Web:
http://www.starnews.com

❶ JOURNALISM

Compensation: $472 per week.
Duration: 10 weeks during the summer.
Eligibility: College graduates within one year
of graduation.
Contact: Fellowship Director at P.O. Box
145.
Phone: 317-633-9121

- REPORTERS
- EDITORS
- EDITORIAL WRITERS

DEMOCRATIC CAUCUS OF THE HOUSE OF REPRESENTATIVES

Room 4-1, State House, 200 W. Washington
St., Indianapolis, IN 46204-2786

❶ GOVERNMENT

Compensation: $200 per week.
Duration: 2½ months.
Eligibility: College juniors and seniors, grad
students, Indiana residents/nonresi-dents at-
tending an Indiana college or university.
Contact: Coordinator.
Phone: 317-232-9623.
Apply by: October 1.

- CONSTITUENT SERVICES: Will help
  four representatives on legislative issues,
  conduct constituent problem research, and
  organize material for newsletters.
- MEDIA SERVICES: Will work as an assistant in the caucus media department, researching and writing news reports and organizing press conferences.
  Requirements: Major in a media-related field.
- WAYS AND MEANS: Will assist in fiscal
  analysis for the chief Democratic member of
  the Ways and Means Committee.
  Requirements: Business, economics, or finance major.

INDIANA REPERTORY THEATRE

140 W. Washington St., Indianapolis, IN
46204

❶ THEATER ARTS

Compensation: Paid.
Duration: 8-9 months.
Eligibility: College seniors, college graduates,
graduate students, applicants with profes-
sional experience.
Contact: General Manager.
Phone: 317-635-5277.
Apply by: June 15.

- SCENE DESIGN: Will work on painting
  scenes with the chief designer.

Requirements: Basic knowledge of scenic design techniques.

- ELECTRICS: Will work on all aspects of
  theatrical lighting.
  Requirements: Knowledge of basic board operations and cable techniques.
- SCENE SHOP: Will help construct sets.
  Requirements: Ability to read blueprints, tool
  and woodworking knowledge.
- SOUND: Will work with all aspects of
  sound production.

NATIONAL ASSOCIATION FOR COMMUNITY LEADERSHIP

200 S. Meridian St., Suite 340, Indianapolis,
IN 46225

❶ PUBLIC AFFAIRS

Compensation: Paid.
Duration: One semester.
Eligibility: College students, college gradu-
ates, graduate students.
Contact: President and Chief Executive Offi-
cer.
Phone: No calls.

- MEMBER SERVICES: Will disseminate information to members, coordinate educational seminars, prepare databases, and perform clerical duties.
  Requirements: Excellent communications and
  computer skills, good attitude.
- COMMUNICATIONS: Will write, edit,
  proof, and research for development programs.
  Requirements: Strong communications and
  computer skills.
- LEADERSHIP: Will arrange training sessions, collect data, and assume various management responsibilities.
  Requirements: Good analytic and research
  skills.

IOWA

CRESWELL, MUNSELL, FULTZ, & ZIRBEL

600 E. Court Ave., Des Moines, IA 50309

❶ PUBLIC RELATIONS

Compensation: $300 per week.
Duration: 8-12 weeks.
Eligibility: College sophomores, juniors, and
seniors.
Contact: Letter, resume, transcript, and writ-
ing samples to Vice President/Human Re-
sources Manager.
Phone: 515-246-3500, Ext 589.
Apply by: March 15.

- PUBLIC RELATIONS
- ADVERTISING

DES MOINES REGISTER

715 Locust St., Des Moines, IA 50309

❶ JOURNALISM
Compensation: $410 per week.
Duration: 12 weeks during the summer.
Requirements: College newspaper experience.
Eligibility: College juniors and seniors, college graduates, graduate students, career changers.
Contact: Managing Editor.
Phone: 515-284- 8561.
Apply by: December 15 for summer. March 1 for fall.
- REPORTING
- ART
- PHOTOGRAPHY
- COPY EDITING

KANSAS

KANSAS STATE HISTORICAL SOCIETY
6425 SW Sixth Ave., Topeka, KS 66615.
World Wide Web:
http://www.history.cc.ukans.edu
❶ CULTURAL ORGANIZATIONS
Eligibility: Unless otherwise indicated, high school students and graduates, college students, college graduates, graduate students, career changers, reentrants to the work force.
Contact: Assistant Director.
Phone: 913-272-8681.
Apply by: June 15 for fall, November 15 for spring, April 15 for summer.
- FIELD: Will excavate archaic and historic sites.
Compensation: $8-$10 per hour.
Duration: 6-10 weeks.
Requirements: Physically fit.
- ARCHIVE MANAGEMENT: Will maintain and oversee manuscript records and archival materials from Kansas history.
Compensation: $1,800.
Duration: 10 weeks.
Requirements: College juniors and seniors, coursework in history.
- GENERAL: Will work with archaeologists, archivists, or education specialists.
Compensation: No pay.
Duration: 6-10 weeks.
THE LAND INSTITUTE
2440 E. Water Well Rd., Salina, KS67401
❶ RESEARCH
- GENERAL: Will work on research experiments and a curriculum pertaining to sustainable agriculture.
Compensation: $137 per week.
Duration: 10 months from February to December.
Requirements: Good health, ability to work with groups.

Eligibility: College graduates, graduate students, career changers.
Contact: Director of Education.
Phone: 913-823-5376.
Apply by: October 1.
SPRINT CORPORATION
2330 Shawnee-Mission Pkwy., Westwood, KS 66205. World Wide Web:
http://www.sprint.com
❶ TELECOMMUNICATIONS
Compensation:$4500 per month.
Duration: 2-3 months.
Eligibility: Graduate students.
Contact: Staffing Manager, PO Box 8417, Kansas City, MO 64114-0417.
Phone: No calls.
Apply by: December 1.
- INTERNATIONAL: Will develop and manage projects in key strategic areas.
Requirements: Skilled in leadership, customer service, and team dynamics.
- TREASURY: Will develop projects in key demographic areas.
- STRATEGIC PLANNING: Will pinpoint specific target areas and implement strategies.
- CELLULAR INTERNS: Will assist in project management and assignment development.
WOLF CREEK NUCLEAR OPERATION CORPORATION
P.O. Box 411, Burlington, KS 66839-0411
❶ ENGINEERING
- TRAINEES: Will be concerned with design, maintenance, operations, and analysis of plant systems.
Compensation: $10.50 per hour.
Duration: One semester.
Eligibility: College juniors and seniors.
Contact: Letter, resume, and transcript to Human Resources Specialist.
Phone: 316-364-8831, ext. 8673.

KENTUCKY

CABBAGE PATCH SETTLEMENT HOUSE
1413 S. Sixth St., Louisville, KY 40208
❶ SOCIAL SERVICES
Eligibility: College juniors and seniors, college graduates, graduate students.
Contact: Resume to Assistant Director.
Phone: No calls.
- ASSISTANT: Will assist program leaders.
Compensation: No pay.
Duration: Flexible.

- RECREATION: Will work in day care in various leadership roles and program development positions.
Compensation: $2,300.
Duration: 10 weeks.
Requirements: Experience with youth, CPR and first aid certification, minimum age 21.

STAGE ONE:PROFESSIONAL THEATRE FOR YOUNG AUDIENCES
425 W. Market St., Louisville, KY 40202

❶ THEATER ARTS

- GENERAL: Will work as an actor, administrator, project developer, or marketing specialist.
Compensation: $150 per week.
Duration: 4-9 months.
Requirements: Committed to nonprofit groups, acting interns must audition.
Eligibility: College sophomores, juniors, and seniors, college graduates, graduate students.
Contact: Letter, resume, and at least three references to Education Director.
Phone: 502-589-5946.
Apply by: 2-3 months prior to start date.

WHAS–TV
520 W. Chestnut, Louisville, KY 40202

❶ BROADCASTING
Compensation: No pay.
Duration: One fall, spring, or summer.
Eligibility: College juniors and seniors, graduate students.
Contact: Human Resources Administrator, P.O. Box 1100, Louisville, KY 40201.
Phone: 502-582-7701.
Apply by: 2-3 months prior to start date.

- MARKETING: Will work in the creative services department, preparing materials for promotions and special events.
Requirements: Art major, background in commercial art.

- NEWS: Will participate in all aspects of the news-gathering and writing process.
Requirements: Journalism background, campus or internship news experience.

- SALES: Will work with account executives as they go out on calls, learn the rating structures, and attend sales meetings.
Requirements: Career-oriented, marketing or advertising major.

- SPORTS: Will work with news staff in gathering, writing, and producing sports segments.
Requirements: Extensive sports knowledge, some camera and editing experience.

LOUISIANA

THE ADVOCATE
P.O. Box 588, Baton Rouge, LA 70821.

World Wide Web:
http://www.theadvocate.com

❶ JOURNALISM

- REPORTING: Will work as a full-fledged reporter.
Compensation: $10.88 - $13.26 per hour.
Duration: Two years.
Requirements: Journalism degree, excellent grammar, spelling, and typing skills.
Eligibility: College seniors, college graduates, graduate students in Journalism.
Contact: Human Resources Director.
Phone: 225-388-0171.

KDBS, INC. (KRRV/KRRV–FM)
1515 Jackson St., Alexandria, LA 71301

❶ BROADCASTING
Compensation: Paid and unpaid positions available.
Duration: Flexible.
Eligibility: College sophomores, juniors, and seniors, college graduates, graduate students.
Contact: Letter and resume (including Milam tape for news and promotions applicants) to Vice President/General Manager.
Phone: No calls.

- NEWS: Will work as a reporter.

- SALES: Will assist the sales force.

- PROMOTIONS: Will work on promotional campaigns.

LAKE CHARLES AMERICAN PRESS
P.O. Box 2893, Lake Charles, LA 70602.
World Wide Web:
http://www.americanpress.com

❶ JOURNALISM

- EDITORIAL
Compensation: Paid..
Duration: Two-three months in summer.
Eligibility: College students.
Contact: Letter, resume, and writing samples to Managing Editor.
Phone: 318-494-4081.
Apply by: March 30.

PELICAN COUNCIL OF GIRL SCOUTS
P.O. Box 17950, Shreveport, LA 71138

❶ SOCIAL SERVICES

- MEMBERSHIP: Will be involved in training, recruitment, and program development.
Compensation: $4.35 per hour.
Duration: Six months.
Requirements: Excellent communications and organizational skills.
Eligibility: College sophomores, juniors, and seniors, college graduates, graduate students, career changers, reentrants to the work force.
Contact: Executive Director.
Phone: No calls.

MAINE

ARCADY MUSIC SOCIETY
P.O. Box 780, Bar Harbor, ME 04609
❶ MUSIC

- GENERAL: Will promote shows, sell advertisements, distribute publicity materials, and arrange housing for in-town artists and performers.
Compensation: $800-$1,000.
Duration: 3-4 months during the summer.
Requirements: Good computer and social skills, resourcefulness.
Eligibility: High school students and graduates, college students.
Contact: Executive Director.
Phone: 207-288-3151.
Apply by: March 1.

H.O.M.E., INC.
P.O. Box 10, Orland, ME 04472
❶ SOCIAL SERVICES
Compensation: No pay.
Eligibility: High school graduates.
Contact: Coordinator.
Phone: 207-469-7961.

- CONSTRUCTION: Will learn carpentry and labor techniques while building homes.
Duration: Three months to two years.
Requirements: Basic math skills, interest in construction business.

- WOOD HARVESTER: Will work with saws and shingle mills as well as harvest and process wood.
Duration: Six months to two years.
Requirements: Respect for power tools, math skills, love of the environment.

- ORGANIC GARDENING: Will be involved in managing land resources so as to ensure the future success of cleared forest areas.
Duration: Six months to two years.

- PROGRAMS: Will work with low-income families in all aspects of home building, including land clearing, fence building, and painting.
Duration: Six months to two years.

NORLANDS LIVING HISTORY CENTER
RR 2, Box 1740, Livermore Falls, ME 04254
❶ CULTURAL ORGANIZATIONS
Compensation: $100 per month.
Duration: Minimum three months.
Eligibility: College juniors and seniors, college graduates, graduate students, career changers, reentrants to the work force.
Contact: Director.
Phone: 207-897-4366.

- EDUCATION: Will educate visitors in 19th-century New England customs, attend to livestock, and maintain site.

- AGRICULTURAL: Will work with visitors on 19th-century farming customs.

- ARCHIVAL: Will research and organize archival materials and maintain existing archives.
Requirements: Good research and cataloging skills, archival experience preferred.

- INTERPRETATIONS: Will lead tour groups on visits through the center.

PENOBSCOT BAY PRESS
P.O. Box 36, Stonington, ME 04681
❶ JOURNALISM
Compensation: Paid.
Duration: One summer.
Eligibility: High school seniors and graduates, college students, reentrants to the work force.
Contact: Publisher.
Phone: 207-367-2200.

- EDITORIAL: Will work as a writer, researcher, photographer, production assistant, and office clerk.
Requirements: Interest in journalism, sense of humor, flexibility.

- ADVERTISING: Will work in sales, research, and design as well as assist with various office duties.
Requirements: Sense of humor, adaptability, good sales skills.

- PRODUCTION: Will be involved in computer operations, word processing, and general production activities.
Requirements: Experience with Macintosh software.

THEATRE AT MONMOUTH
P.O. Box 385, Monmouth, ME 04259
❶ THEATER ARTS
Duration: Three months.
Eligibility: High school graduates, college students, college graduates, graduate students, career changers, reentrants to the work force.
Contact: Resume to Managing Director.
Phone: No calls.
Apply by: March 15.

- ACTING: Will work on-stage as a performer, backstage as an assistant, and in the costume and prop shops.
Compensation: $40-$60 per week.
Requirements: Experience in theater.

- TECHNICAL: Will work with all aspects of production.
Compensation: $50-$100 per week.
Requirements: Experience or coursework in carpentry or electronics.

- COSTUME: Will participate in every aspect of costume design.

Compensation: $50-$150 per week.

Requirements: Experience working with costumes.

- OFFICE: Will perform clerical duties and front-of-house functions.

Compensation: $50-$100 per week.

WGME–TV

P.O. Box 1731, Portland, ME 04104, World Wide Web: http://www.wgme-tv.com

❶ BROADCASTING

- REPORTING: Will be involved in the daily operations of the newsroom as a writer and script editor.

Compensation: No pay.

Duration: Flexible.

Requirements: Coursework in journalism or communications.

Eligibility: High school graduates, college students, college graduates, graduate students.

Contact: Business Manager.

Phone: No calls.

MARYLAND

THE AMERICAN PHYSICAL SOCIETY

One Physics Ellipse, College Park, MD 20740-3844. World Wide Web: http://www.aps.org

❶ SCIENCE/RESEARCH

- LAB SUPPORT: Will assist physicists nationwide on a variety of projects.

Compensation: $2,000 per month.

Duration: 12 weeks during the summer.

Requirements: Academic focus on physics.

Eligibility: College graduates within one year of graduation, graduate students.

Contact: ISIP Administrator/APS.

Phone: 301-209-3100.

Apply by: October 20.

CHESAPEAKE WILDLIFE SANCTUARY

17308 Queen Anne Bridge Rd., Bowie, MD 20716-9053. World Wide Web: http://www.pattersonvideo.com

❶ WILDLIFE/ENVIRONMENT

Compensation: No pay.

Duration: Minimum 12 weeks, 40 hours per week.

Eligibility: High school students and graduates, college students, college graduates, graduate students, career changers, reentrants to the work force.

Contact: Send SASE to Internship Coordinator.

Phone: 301-390-7010.

- EDUCATION: Will work with students in grades K-12 in hands-on activities oriented toward the care of sick or injured animals.

- SMALL MAMMALS: Will be responsible for the care of on-site squirrels, rabbits, groundhogs, and bats.

- VETERINARY: Will be involved in administering veterinary care to sick, injured, or orphaned wildlife.

Eligibility: Postgraduate veterinary school students.

- PUBLIC RELATIONS: Will serve as an informational source for the public.

DISCOVERY COMMUNICATIONS, INC.

7700 Wisconsin Ave., Bethesda, MD 20814

❶ BROADCASTING

Compensation: $7 per hour.

Duration: One semester or one summer.

Eligibility: College juniors and seniors, graduate students.

Contact: Letter, resume, writing or production sample, transcript, and two letters of recommendation to Intern Coordinator.

Phone: 301-986-0444.

Apply by: December 1 for spring, April 1 for summer, August 1 for fall.

- EDITORIAL: Will research, proofread, write, and fact-check a variety of stories.

Requirements: Journalism, English, or broadcasting major.

- EDUCATIONAL RELATIONS: Will work on special projects with networks carrying Discovery programming.

Requirements: Firm grasp of Internet operations.

- INTERNATIONAL: Will research international television markets and trends.

Requirements: Middle East studies major, knowledge of Arabic.

- PRODUCTION: Will work with The Learning Channel as a program reviewer, production summary writer, and respondent to viewer inquiries.

GREATER BALTIMORE MEDICAL CENTER

6701 N. Charles St., Baltimore, MD 21204

❶ HEALTH SERVICES

- PUBLIC RELATIONS: Will work on special events and various program publications.

Compensation: No pay.

Duration: 3-4 months.

Requirements: Good writing, phone, and organizational skills.

Eligibility: College students, college graduates, graduate students, career changers, reentrants to the work force.

Contact: Resume and writing sample to Director, Community and Media Relations.

Phone: No calls.

Apply by: 3-4 weeks prior to start date.

OCEAN CITY ADVERTISING AGENCY

108 W. 75th St., Office #18, Ocean City, MD
21842. World Wide Web:
http://www.ecusa.com

❶ ADVERTISING

Compensation: No pay.
Duration: One semester.
Eligibility: College students, college gradu-
ates, graduate students, career changers, reen-
trants to the work force.
Contact: President, P.O. Box 1759, Ocean
City, MD 21842.
Phone: 410-524-5351.
Apply by: Two months prior to start date.

• GRAPHIC DESIGN
Requirements: Advertising, computer graphics, design, or art major.

• COPYWRITING
Requirements: English or advertising major.

• PHOTOGRAPHY
Requirements: Experience, art or photography major.

• HUMAN RESOURCES
Requirements: Business, communications, or
marketing major.

SMITHSONIAN ENVIRONMENTAL RE-SEARCH CENTER

P.O. Box 28, Edgewater, MD 21037. World
Wide Web: http://www.serc.si.edu

❶ ENVIRONMENT

Compensation: $190 per week.
Eligibility: College students, graduate stu-
dents up to one year following graduation.
Contact: For applications materials, contact
Director of Education.
Phone: 301-261-4190.
Apply by: November 1 for January through
May projects, March 1 for May through
August projects.

• FOREST STUDIES: Will examine the relationship between the forest and the lower
atmosphere by monitoring air quality, field
sampling, and data analysis.
Duration: 1-3 semesters.

• NUTRIENT STUDIES: Will provide support services for field and laboratory research as it pertains to the transportation of
nutrients.
Duration: 1-4 semesters.
Requirements: Basic knowledge of ecology,
mathematics, and computers.

• GEOCHEMISTRY: Will examine the impact of acid deposition on forest geochemistry.
Duration: Spring and summer.

Requirements: Knowledge of analytic chemistry.

• GLOBAL CHANGES: Will work on various studies to examine the effects of carbon
dioxide on wetlands wildlife species.
Duration: 1-2 semesters.
Requirements: Coursework in plant physiology and photosynthesis.

UNIVERSITY OF MARYLAND—CENTER FOR INTERNATIONAL DEVELOPMENT AND CONFLICT MANAGEMENT

Room 0145, Tydings Hall, College Park, MD
20742-7231. World Wide Web:
http://www.bsos.umd.edu

❶ INTERNATIONAL RELATIONS

• RESEARCH: Will work on special projects
using on-line sources to monitor and analyze international and international events.
Compensation: No pay.
Duration: 2-12 months.
Requirements: Background in statistics, policy, and/or global affairs, Microsoft Access
experience.
Eligibility: College juniors and seniors, college graduates, graduate students, career
changers, reentrants to the work force.
Contact: Research Coordinator.
Phone: 301-314-7709.

USF&G

5801 Smith Ave., MC0105, Baltimore, MD
21209

❶ INSURANCE

Duration: 10 weeks.
Eligibility: College juniors, graduate students.
Contact: Write to College Relations
Phone: No calls.

• CORPORATE: Will work on various proj-
ects in Baltimore and nationwide branch of-
fices.
Compensation: $8-$15 per hour.
Requirements: Eligible to work in the United
States, 3.0 GPA.

• INFORMATION SCIENCE: Will help with
the corporate transition from mainframe to
client/server environment.
Compensation: $10 per hour.
Requirements: Schooled in applications and
life-cycle development, LAN and C++ experience, 3.0 GPA.

MASSACHUSETTS

A. E. SCHWARTZ & ASSOCIATES

P.O. Box 228, Waverly, MA 02179-9998.
World Wide Web:
http://www.aeschwartz.com

❶ GENERAL BUSINESS

Compensation: Paid.

Duration: Flexible.
Eligibility: High school graduates, college juniors and seniors, college graduates, graduate students, career changers.
Contact: President.
Phone: 617-926-9111.

- SALES/MARKETING: Will cultivate contacts, telemarket to potential clients, organize programs with sponsors, maintain computer systems, and handle inquiries.
- PUBLIC RELATIONS: Will arrange and organize media coverage, write press releases, and place advertisements.
- SOFTWARE SPECIALISTS: Will be involved with Windows software programs instruction, database construction, and desktop publishing.
- PUBLISHING: Will be involved in writing, editing, and text development and evaluation.

AMERICAN CANCER SOCIETY—MASSACHUSETTS DIVISION

30 Speen St., Framingham, MA 01701.
World Wide Web: http://www.ma.cancer.org.

❶ RESEARCH/HEALTH SERVICES

- RESEARCH: Will work with senior researchers on projects oriented around the control of and cure for cancer.

Compensation: $2,500.
Duration: 10 weeks during the summer.
Requirements: Massachusetts resident.
Eligibility: College juniors and seniors, graduate students.
Contact: Fuller Committee.
Phone: 800-952-7664, Ext. 4651.
Apply by: February 1.

AMERICAN REPERTORY THEATRE

64 Brattle St., Cambridge, MA 02138

❶ THEATER ARTS

Compensation: No pay.
Eligibility: High school students and graduates, college students, college graduates, graduate students, career changers, reentrants to the work force.
Contact: Coordinator of Internship Programs, Loeb Drama Center.
Phone: 617-495-2668.

- FUNDRAISING: Will explore potential sponsorship prospects, work with volunteer committees, help organize special events, and maintain records.

Duration: Flexible.
Requirements: Excellent communications skills.

- LITERARY MANAGEMENT: Will provide script evaluation, dramaturgical research, and assistance for special events.

Duration: Flexible.
Requirements: Familiarity with major dramatists and theater production, good typing.

- MARKETING: Will work with audience-demographic studies and ticket sales initiatives.

Duration: Minimum 12 weeks.

- RUNNING CREW: Will handle lighting, wardrobe, sound, and other stage management elements.

Duration: Minimum 12 weeks.

BOSTON MAGAZINE

300 Massachusetts Ave., Boston, MA 02115.
World Wide Web:
http://www.bostonmagazine.com

❶ PUBLISHING

Compensation: No pay.
Duration: One semester.
Eligibility: College sophomores, juniors, and seniors, college graduates, graduate students.
Contact: Letter and resume to Internship Coordinator.
Phone: No calls.
Apply by: April 1 for summer, August 1 for fall, December 1 for spring.

- ACCOUNTING: Will be involved in accounts receivable, billing, collection calling, and credit check activities.

Requirements: Coursework in business and accounting.

- ART: Will be involved in monthly production in conjunction with the art director.

Requirements: Must have a portfolio.

- PROMOTIONS

Requirements: Marketing or advertising background, good computer and writing skills.

- EDITORIAL

Requirements: Coursework in journalism, English, or communications, basic computer skills.

HOUGHTON MIFFLIN COMPANY

222 Berkeley St., Boston, MA 02116-3764.
World Wide Web: http://www.hmco.com

❶ PUBLISHING

Compensation: $8 per hour.
Duration: 12 weeks during the summer.
Eligibility: College students, college graduates, graduate students.
Contact: Letter and resume to Administrative Assistant.
Phone: No calls.
Apply by: April1.

- EDITORIAL
- ART DESIGN
- PERMISSIONS
- PRODUCTION

WORLDTEACH—HARVARD INSTITUTE FOR INTERNATIONAL DEVELOPMENT

One Elliot St., Cambridge, MA 02138. World Wide Web: http://www.igc.org

❶ EDUCATION/INTERNATIONAL RELATIONS

Eligibility: All qualified U.S. applicants.
Contact: Recruiting Director.
Phone: 617-495-5527.
Apply by: Five months prior to departure.

• TEACHING: Will teach English, math, or science to students in developing countries.
Compensation: Paid.
Duration: One year.
Requirements: Bachelor's degree.

• SUMMER TEACHING: Will work as an English teacher in a large-scale cultural exchange with Chinese students.
Compensation: No pay.
Duration: One summer.
Requirements: Enrolled in a college or university.

• SPORTS: Will teach sports activities in black South African townships.
Compensation: No pay.
Duration: Six months.
Requirements: Coaching and athletics experience.

MICHIGAN

AMWAY

7575 Fulton St. E., Ada, MI 49355-0001

❶ MANUFACTURING

Duration: 12 weeks during the summer.
Eligibility: College juniors, graduate students.
Contact: Letter, resume, and college transcript to College Relations, 78-1 C, Senior Adviser, College Relations and EEO.
Phone: No calls.
Apply by: January 31.

• MARKETING
Compensation: $10-$13 per hour.
Requirements: Major in business, marketing, or related fields.

• PURCHASING
Compensation: $10 per hour.
Requirements: Major in business, finance, management, or related fields.

• INFORMATION SERVICES
Compensation: $10-$12 per hour.
Requirements: Computer science major.

• RESEARCH AND DEVELOPMENT
Compensation: $11.90 per hour.
Requirements: Chemistry major.

CHRYSLER FINANCIAL CORPORATION

27777 Franklin Rd., Southfield, MI 48034-8266

❶ FINANCE

• GENERAL: Will work in either the computer science or finance department.
Compensation: Paid.
Duration: 3-4 months.
Requirements: Computer science, finance, or accounting major.
Eligibility: College students.
Contact: Personnel Programs Administrator.
Phone: No calls.
Apply by: April 30.

THE DETROIT FREE PRESS

600 W. Fort St., Detroit, MI 48226. World Wide Web: http://www.freep.com

❶ JOURNALISM

Compensation: $495 per week.
Duration: 12 weeks during the summer.
Eligibility: College juniors and seniors, college graduates, graduate students, career changers.
Contact: Letter explaining what you hope to learn from an internship at *The Free Press.*
Phone: 313-222-6490.

• CITY DESK
• BUSINESS WRITING
• LIFESTYLES WRITER
• EDITORIAL WRITER

DETROIT INSTITUTE OF ARTS

5200 Woodward Ave., Detroit, MI 48202-4094. World Wide Web: http://www.dia.org

❶ CULTURAL ORGANIZATIONS

Eligibility: High school seniors, college sophomores, juniors, and seniors, college graduates, graduate students.
Contact: Student Placement/Department of Education.
Phone: 313-833-1858.

• GRADUATE: Will perform curatorial and other museum departmental work.
Compensation: No pay.
Duration: 3-12 months.
Requirements: Bachelor's degree, enrolled in master's program in art history, museum studies.

• UNDERGRADUATE: Will work in field studies performing clerical and research duties.
Compensation: No pay.
Duration: Minimum one month.
Requirements: Coursework in museum-related studies.

• HIGH SCHOOL PLACEMENT: Will participate in short-term field work in accordance with authorized school programs.
Compensation: No pay.
Duration: Three months.
Requirements: Interest in museum career.

- PROFESSIONAL PROGRAM FOR MINORITIES: Will work with museum employees and curators and participate in various seminars.
Compensation: Paid.
Duration: 3-12 months.
Requirements: Minority, pursuing graduate work in art history, museum studies, or related fields.

HUMAN RESOURCES AND EMPLOYEE DEVELOPMENT SERVICES—CITY OF DETROIT
8220 Second Ave., Detroit, MI 48202
❶ PUBLIC ADMINISTRATION
Eligibility: College students, graduate students.
Contact: Resume to Internship Coordinator.
Phone: No calls.

- DEPARTMENTAL: Tasks will vary according to specific department.
Compensation: No pay.
Duration: Varies.

- GENERAL: Will work in a clerical or technical capacity depending on departmental needs.
Compensation: $5-$6 per hour.
Duration: Nine months.
Requirements: Eligible for work study.

MINNESOTA

HYATT REGENCY MINNEAPOLIS
1300 Nicollet Mall, Minneapolis, MN 55403
❶ HOSPITALITY
Compensation: Paid.
Duration: 3-6 months.
Eligibility: College juniors and seniors.
Contact: Resume and letter outlining career goals to Employment Manager.
Phone: 612-370-1234.
Apply by: February.

- FOOD AND BEVERAGES
- ROOM

MINNESOTA INTERNATIONAL CENTER
711 E. River Rd., Minneapolis, MN 55455
❶ INTERNATIONAL RELATIONS
Compensation: No pay.
Duration: Minimum 12 weeks.
Requirements: Background in intercultural communications, initiative, good computer, organizational, and communications skills.
Eligibility: College sophomores, juniors, and seniors, college graduates.
Contact: Letter and resume to Administrative Manager.
Phone: 612-625-4421.

- DEVELOPMENTAL: Will create press kits, organize special events, assist in research, correspond with potential members, and perform general clerical work.

- WORLD AFFAIRS: Will help coordinate publicity promotions and events, provide general clerical assistance, and handle correspondence.

- INTERNATIONAL VISITOR PROGRAM: Will coordinate the logistics for international visitors, maintain file records, and provide general clerical assistance.

- INTERNATIONAL STUDENT PROGRAM: Will handle phone inquiries, assist with general communications among various parties, and assist with clerical tasks.

MINNESOTA MULTIPLE SCLEROSIS SOCIETY
2344 Nicollet Ave., #280, Minneapolis, MN 55404
❶ SOCIAL SERVICES
Compensation: No pay.
Eligibility: High school graduates, college students, college graduates, graduate students, career changers, reentrants to the work force.
Contact: Manager of Volunteer Services.
Phone: 612-870-1500.

- PUBLIC RELATIONS: Will work on four-page newsletter as well as press kits for the media.
Duration: 8-14 weeks.
Requirements: English, advertising, or mass communications major, writing skills.

- GRAPHIC DESIGN: Will conceptualize, execute, and work on small- and large-scale design projects.
Duration: 8-14 weeks.
Requirements: Coursework in design.

- VOLUNTEER ASSISTANT: Will work in all facets of volunteer management, from recruiting and interviewing to training and coordinating.
Duration: 10 to 14 weeks.
Requirements: Coursework in social sciences or personnel management.

- ASSISTANT TO THE DIRECTOR: Will work in every logistical phase of planning weeklong camp sessions for 60 people, including budget planning, supervision, and development.
Duration: Three months.
Requirements: Coursework in social services, public health, or therapeutic recreation.

THE MINNESOTA ZOO
13000 Zoo Blvd., Apple Valley, MN 55124
❶ ZOOLOGY
Compensation: No pay.
Duration: 10-12 weeks.

Eligibility: College juniors, seniors, college graduates, graduate students.
Contact: Intern Program Coordinator.
Phone: 612-431-9219.
Apply by: August 1 for fall, December 1 for spring, March 1 for summer, October 1 for winter.

- MARKETING: Will write and edit articles, organize special events, and work with the sales department as part of the promotions staff.
- EDUCATION: Will conduct interactive exercises with visitors.
- ANIMAL MANAGEMENT

PROGRAM FOR AID TO VICTIMS OF SEXUAL ASSAULT
32 E. First St., Suite 200, Duluth, MN 55802
❶ SOCIAL SERVICES
Compensation: No pay.
Eligibility: College juniors and seniors, graduate students, career changers.
Contact: Advocacy Coordinator.
Phone: 218-726-1442.

- ADVOCATE: Will work in crisis prevention as well as assist with one-to-one support.
Duration: 3-12 months.
- RESEARCHER: Will work on a research project under supervisor's guidance before presenting it to the PAVSA staff.
Duration: 3-12 months.

ST. PAUL AREA COUNCIL OF CHURCHES
1671 Summit Ave., St. Paul, MN 55105
❶ SOCIAL SERVICES
Compensation: No pay.
Eligibility: College students, college graduates, career changers.
Contact: Executive Director.
Phone: 651-646-8805.

- CHAPLAINCY: Will work with people in a correctional institution setting.
Duration: Flexible.
Requirements: Background in criminal justice.
- POLICE CHAPLAINCY: Will work with the police department in matters of criminal justice and the community.
Duration: Flexible.
Requirements: Background in counseling or human resources.
- NATIVE AMERICAN EDUCATION: Will work as an informational and counseling source for parenting issues.
Duration: Flexible.
- TEACHING: Will work as a tutor and monitor in programs for African-American children age 6-12.
Duration: 3-9 months.

TWIN CITIES PUBLIC TELEVISION
172 E. 4th St., St. Paul, MN 55101
❶ BROADCASTING
Compensation: No pay.
Duration: Three months.
Eligibility: College juniors and seniors, college graduates, graduate students.
Contact: Letter and resume to Compensation and Employee Relations Manager.
Phone: 651-222-1717.

- PRODUCTION: Will write press releases and deal with aspects of promotion and publicity.
- LEGAL: Will research legal issues and work as a human resources assistant.

MISSISSIPPI

BIG BROTHERS/BIG SISTERS OF THE TRI-COUNTY AREA
931 Highway 80 W., Suite 50, Jackson, MS 39204
❶ SOCIAL SERVICES

- GENERAL: Will handle the documenting of casework and interview clients.
Compensation: No pay.
Duration: Flexible.
Eligibility: College students.
Contact: Executive Director.
Phone: 601-355- 3009.

GULF PUBLISHING COMPANY, INC.
P.O. Box 4567, Biloxi, MS 39555-4567.
World Wide Web: http://www.sunherald.com
❶ JOURNALISM
Eligibility: College juniors and seniors, college graduates, graduate students.
Contact: Clips or portfolio to Managing Editor.
Phone: 601-896-2345.
Apply by: March 15.

- REPORTING: Will cultivate, report, and write stories.
Compensation: $8-$12 per hour.
Duration: Three months.
Requirements: Journalism experience, computer skills.
- PHOTOGRAPHER: Will shoot pictures and develop and process film using electronic darkroom.
Compensation: $8 per hour.
Duration: One year.
Requirements: Coursework in photography.
- GRAPHIC ARTS: Will design maps, graphs, and illustrations on a Macintosh.
Compensation: $8 per hour.
Duration: Three months.
Requirements: Knowledge of Quark, Adobe, FreeHand, and Illustrator.

NEW STAGE THEATRE
1100 Carlisle St., Jackson, MS 39202
❶ THEATER ARTS
Compensation: $140 per week.
Duration: 4-9 months.
Requirements: Experience, theater major.
Eligibility: College graduates, career changers, professionals.
Contact: Education Director.
Phone: 601-948-0142.
Apply by: March 24.

* ACTING: Will act in mainstage performances as well as work in an arts-in-education program that tours high schools.
* TECHNICAL

WLOX–TV13
208 De Buys Rd., P.O. Box 4596, Biloxi, MS 39535. World Wide Web: http://www.wlox.com
❶ BROADCASTING
Compensation: No pay.
Eligibility: College students, college graduates, graduate students, career changers, reentrants to the work force.
Contact: Promotions Manager.
Phone: 228-896-1313.

* ART: Will learn computer software programs and assist the graphic design department in producing promotion print articles.
Duration: 18-20 weeks.
Requirements: Coursework in design, computer knowledge.
* SPECIAL PROJECTS: Will be involved with all aspects of public relations.
Duration: One semester.
Requirements: Basic coursework in public relations.
* STUDIO ASSISTANCE: Will work on the development of news shows and various other productions.
Duration: Varies.
* CREATIVE SERVICES: Will work on readying the technical aspects of the set in preparation for going on air.
Duration: Varies.

MISSOURI

BERNSTEIN–REIN
4600 Madison, Suite 1500, Kansas City, MO 64112
❶ ADVERTISING/PUBLIC RELATIONS
Compensation: $188 per week.
Duration: 6 weeks during the summer.
Eligibility: College juniors.
Contact: Vice President/Human Resources.

Phone: 816-756-0640.
Apply by: March 1.

* ACCOUNT MANAGEMENT
* CREATIVE DEVELOPMENT
* PUBLIC/MEDIA RELATIONS

BOYS HOPE/GIRLS HOPE NATIONAL OFFICE
12120 Bridgeton Sq. Dr., Bridgeton, MO 63044-2607
❶ SOCIAL SERVICES
Eligibility: College seniors, college graduates, graduate students, career changers, reentrants to the work force.
Contact: Resume to Director of Personnel and Training.
Phone: 800-545-2697.

* COUNSELING: Will live with at-risk youngsters, providing a stable environment, helping with schoolwork, and assuming a mentoring role.
Compensation: $200 per month.
Duration: One year.
Requirements: Minimum age 21, college-educated, mature, physically fit.
* VOLUNTEER COORDINATOR: Will serve as the communications link between national and local programs, represent the organization at fairs, and recruit new volunteers.
Compensation: $200 per month.
Duration: One year.
Requirements: Minimum age 21, college-educated, mature, physically fit.
* ADMINISTRATIVE: Will assist with fund-raising and public relations tasks as well as provide general administrative support.
Compensation: $200 per month.
Duration: Flexible.
Requirements: Good people skills, office experience.
* CAMP COUNSELING: Will teach outdoor education classes as well as serve as a live-in leader at residence camp.
Compensation: $300.
Duration: Eight weeks during the summer.
Requirements: Minimum age 18, child-care and teaching experience.

ENTERPRISE RENT–A–CAR
600 Corporate Park Dr., St. Louis, MO 63105. World Wide Web: http://www.erac.com
❶ TRANSPORTATION

* GENERAL: Will work in a customer service capacity as well as providing administrative and office support.
Compensation: Paid.
Duration: Three months.

Requirements: Good communications skills, flexibility.
Eligibility: College sophomores, juniors, and seniors, graduate students.
Contact: Human Resources.
Phone: 888-999-3722.

HALLMARK CARDS, INC.
2501 McGee, Kansas City, MO 64141-6580
❶ MANUFACTURING/CONSUMER PRODUCTS
Compensation: Paid.
Duration: Three months.
Requirements: 3.0 GPA, strong leadership skills.
Eligibility: College seniors, graduate students.
Contact: Corporate Staffing Manager.
Phone: No calls.
Apply by: February 1.

- MARKETING: Will collect and evaluate information as it pertains to various product development strategies.
- FINANCIAL ANALYSIS: Will work on plans, forecasts, internal auditing, and other financial projects.
- BUSINESS SERVICES: Will monitor and control inventory as well as production levels.

KSDK NEWS CHANNEL 5
1000 Market St., St. Louis, MO 63101
❶ BROADCASTING
Compensation: No pay.
Duration: One semester.
Eligibility: College juniors and seniors, college graduates, graduate students.
Contact: News Operations Manager.
Phone: 314-444-5164.
Apply by: March 1 for fall and summer, November 1 for winter.

- SPORTS: Will collect statistics, log games, and coordinate satellite feeds.
Requirements: Knowledge of sports and athletes.
- SPECIAL PROJECTS: Will be involved in various programming tasks as well as assisting reporters.
- ASSIGNMENT DESK: Will coordinate incoming and outgoing phone calls.
- ARCHIVES: Will catalog and retrieve all tapes for the news department.

MCDONNELL DOUGLAS AEROSPACE
P.O. Box 516, Mailcode 2761740, St. Louis, MO 63166-0516
❶ AEROSPACE
Compensation: $280-$475 per week.
Duration: 10-17 weeks during the summer, fall, or spring.

Requirements: 3.0 GPA.
Eligibility: College seniors.
Contact: Student Development Programs Administrator.
Phone: 314-234-1297.
Apply by: February 1.

- DEFENSE TECHNOLOGIES
- BUSINESS OPERATIONS
- LOGISTICS
- PHYSICAL/COMPUTER SCIENCES

MISSOURI LEGISLATIVE INTERN PROGRAM
State Capitol, Jefferson City, MO 65101
❶ GOVERNMENT

- GENERAL: Will work on legislation and participate in the workings of government.
Compensation: Paid.
Duration: One semester.
Eligibility: College juniors and seniors.

ST. LOUIS POST-DISPATCH
900 N. Tucker Blvd., St. Louis, MO 63101
❶ JOURNALISM
Compensation: $375 per week.
Duration: 13 weeks.
Eligibility: College juniors and seniors, college graduates, graduate students.
Contact: Resume and samples to Assistant Managing Editor/ News.
Phone: No calls.

- REPORTING
- COPY EDITING
Requirements: Knowledge of Atex pagination.
- PHOTOGRAPHY
Requirements: Knowledge of Scitex, Harris, and PhotoLeaf systems.
- GRAPHIC ART
Requirements: Knowledge of Atex and Macintosh design programs.

MONTANA

MONTANA LEGISLATIVE COUNCIL
Room 138, State Capitol, Helena, MT 59620
❶ GOVERNMENT

- GENERAL: Will assist in the legislative process.
Compensation: No pay.
Duration: Four months.
Requirements: Recommendation by school president, at least one course in government.
Eligibility: College juniors and seniors attending school in Montana.
Contact: Apply through intern coordinator or president of school, and contact the Internship Coordinator.
Phone: No calls.

Apply by: November 7.

MONTANA WILDLIFE FEDERATION

P.O. Box 1175, Helena, MT 59624

❶ WILDLIFE

- ORGANIZATIONAL DEVELOPMENT: Will serve as communications liaison between state board and local affiliates in an effort to increase membership and focus on primary MWF goals.
Compensation: $500-$1,000.
Duration: One summer.
Requirements: Excellent people skills, experience as an organizer/motivator.
Eligibility: College graduates, graduate students.
Contact: Executive Director.
Phone: 406-449-7604.

WILDERNESS WATCH

P.O. Box 9175, Missoula, MT 59807. World Wide Web: http://www.ism.net

❶ ENVIRONMENT

- GENERAL: Could be involved in fundraising, membership drives, and public relations and wilderness projects.
Compensation: No pay.
Duration: Flexible.
Requirements: Public relations and outreach. Commitment to wilderness.
Eligibility: College students, college graduates, graduate students.
Contact: Executive Director.
Phone: 406-542-2048.

NEBRASKA

AGATE FOSSIL BEDS NATIONAL MONUMENT

301 River Rd., Harrison, NE 69346. World Wide Web: http://www.mps.gov

❶ CULTURAL ORGANIZATIONS

- GENERAL: Will work with the public as an information source and/or work as a curator.
Compensation: No pay.
Duration: Flexible.
Requirements: Driver's license.
Eligibility: Minimum age 18.
Contact: Park Ranger.
Phone: 308-668-2211.

BOZELL WORLDWIDE ADVERTISING AND PUBLIC RELATIONS

800 Blackstone Ctr., 302 S. 36th St., Omaha, NE 68131

❶ PUBLIC RELATIONS

- MEDIA LIAISON
Compensation: $240 per week.
Duration: 10-12 weeks during the summer.
Eligibility: College students, college graduates, graduate students.

Contact: Letter, resume, and writing samples to Account Supervisor.
Phone: No calls.

OMAHA MAGIC THEATRE

325 S. 16th St., Omaha, NE 68102

❶ THEATER ARTS

- GENERAL: Will work with all the technical dimensions of theater as well as in box office management.
Compensation: No pay.
Duration: 6-12 months.
Requirements: Passion for all varieties and aspects of theater.
Eligibility: High school students and graduates, college students, college graduates, graduate students, career changers.
Contact: Artistic Director.
Phone: No calls.

OMAHA WORLD–HERALD COMPANY

World Herald Sq., 14th and Dodge, Omaha, NE 68102

❶ JOURNALISM

- NEWS: Will write and edit news and feature stories.
Compensation: $350 per week.
Duration: 12 weeks.
Requirements: Core coursework in journalism and/or experience on campus newspaper.
Eligibility: College seniors.
Phone: 402-444-1000.
Apply by: November 1.

NEVADA

BIG BROTHERS/BIG SISTERS OF SOUTHERN NEVADA

1785 E. Sahara Ave., Suite A-100, Las Vegas, NV 89104

❶ SOCIAL SERVICES

Compensation: No pay.
Duration: Three months.
Requirements: Good communications skills.
Eligibility: High school students and graduates, college students, college graduates, graduate students, career changers, reentrants to the work force.
Contact: Program Director.
Phone: 702-731-2227.

- CASE AIDE: Will work to set up and implement objectives and case plans.

- ASSISTANT COORDINATOR: Will recruit volunteers and establish and maintain case files.

HUMBOLDT NATIONAL FOREST—ELY RANGER DISTRICT

P.O. Box 539, Ely, NV 89301

❶ ENVIRONMENT

Compensation: No pay.
Duration: 4-5 months.
Eligibility: College juniors and seniors, college graduates, graduate students, career changers, reentrants to the work force.
Contact: Volunteer Coordinator.
Phone: 702-289-3031.
CAMPGROUND HOSTING: Will serve as a greeter and informational source to visitors.
Requirements: Should have a camping trailer.

- MAINTENANCE VOLUNTEERS: Will perform general campground upkeep as well as provide maps and information to visitors.

LAS VEGAS REVIEW–JOURNAL
P.O. Box 70, Las Vegas, NV 89125
❶ JOURNALISM
Compensation: $10 per hour.
Duration: Three months during the summer.
Eligibility: College juniors.
Contact: Letter, resume, and writing/photo samples to City Editor.
Phone: 702-383-0264.
Apply by: March 15.

- REPORTERS
Requirements: Journalism major, excellent writing skills.

- PHOTOGRAPHY
Requirements: Journalism major, good photography skills.

ST. JUDE'S RANCH FOR CHILDREN
P.O. Box 61659, Boulder City, NV 89005
❶ SOCIAL SERVICES
Eligibility: College juniors and seniors, college graduates, graduate students, career changers, reentrants to the work force.
Contact: Program Director, P.O. Box 61659, Boulder City, NV 89006.
Phone: 702-294-7105.
Apply by: April 30.

- PROGRAMMING: Will facilitate swimming and recreation activities and assist as a tutor, coach, and counselor.
Compensation: $200 per month.
Duration: Three months.
Requirements: Lifeguard certification, experience with youths with behavior disorders.
- SOCIAL WORK: Will assist social workers by doing intake calling, file updating, and child transportation while cultivating social work skills.
Compensation: Both paid and unpaid positions available.
Duration: 1-2 semesters.
Requirements: Completing a bachelor's or master's degree in social work.
- ART THERAPY: Will work with individuals and groups under the guidance of certi-

fied art therapists in an effort to meet degree requirements.
Compensation: Both paid and unpaid positions available.
Duration: 1-2 semesters.
Requirements: Completing art therapy coursework.

NEW HAMPSHIRE
AMERICAN STAGE FESTIVAL (THE YOUNG COMPANY)
14 Court St., Nashua, New Hampshire 03060
❶ THEATER ARTS
Compensation: No pay.
Duration: Three months.
Eligibility: High school graduates, college students, college graduates, graduate students, career changers, reentrants to the work force.
Contact: Production Manager.
Phone: 603-8889-2330.
Apply by: April 15.

- ACTING: Will perform in children's shows and work as an understudy and assistant for mainstage performances.
- TECHNICAL: Will work on all design elements, including set and prop construction.
- LIGHTING: Will provide technical assistance for mainstage shows.
- DIRECTING: Will assist the mainstage director.

CONCORD COMMUNITY MUSIC SCHOOL
23 Wall St., Concord, NH 03301
❶ MUSIC
- DEVELOPMENT: Will work on publicity and promotion materials as well as advertisements and program development.
Compensation: No pay.
Duration: One semester or one summer.
Requirements: Good communications skills, interest in music and nonprofit work.
Eligibility: High school graduates, college students, college graduates, graduate students.
Contact: Director of Communications and Development.
Phone: 603-228-1196.
STUDENT CONSERVATION ASSOCIATION
P.O. Box 550, Charlestown, NH 03603
❶ ENVIRONMENT
- RESOURCES: Will be involved as an educator and participant in various conservation projects dealing with ecology, forestry, and environmental awareness.
Compensation: No pay.
Duration: 12-16 weeks.
Requirements: Minimum age 18, related education background.

Eligibility: High school graduates, college students, college graduates, graduate students, career changers.
Contact: Recruitment Director.
Phone: 603-543-1700.

WKXL–AM/FM RADIO
37 Redington Rd., P.O. Box 875, Concord, NH 03302
❶ BROADCASTING
Compensation: No pay.
Duration: Three months.
Eligibility: College sophomores, juniors, and seniors, college graduates.
Contact: President and General Manager
Phone: 603-225-5521.

- NEWS
- SALES

NEW JERSEY

BIG BROTHERS/BIG SISTERS ASSOCIATION, INC.
340 Haddon Ave., Westmont, NJ 08108
❶ SOCIAL SERVICES

- CASE MANAGEMENT: Will assist in co-ordinating group activities, client assessment, and case documentation.

Compensation: No pay.
Duration: One year.
Requirements: Access to a car, driver's license, good personality, communications skills.
Eligibility: College students, college graduates, graduate students.
Contact: Executive Director.
Phone: 609-858-3133.

BMW OF NORTH AMERICA
300 Chestnut Ridge Rd., Woodcliff Lake, NJ 07675
❶ AUTOMOTIVE

- GENERAL: Will work in various areas of the company, including sales, distribution, engineering, and service.

Compensation: Paid.
Duration: Three months.
Requirements: Computer literate.
Eligibility: College juniors and seniors, graduate students.
Contact: Resume to Human Resources INT-PET, P.O. BoX 8271, Haledon, NJ 07538.
Phone: No calls.
Apply by: April 1.

NATIONAL POETRY SERIES
100 W. Broad St., Hopewell, NJ 08525
❶ PUBLISHING

- EDITORIAL: Assist in office operations and project work related to a major competition.

Compensation: No pay.
Duration: Flexible.

Requirements: Literature major, typing skills, some computer experience, flexibility.
Eligibility: College students, college graduates, graduate students.
Contact: Coordinator.
Phone: 609-466-4748.
Apply by: August 1 for fall, December 1 for spring, April 1 for summer.

NEW JERSEY SHAKESPEARE FESTIVAL
36 Madison Ave., Madison, NJ 07940. World Wide Web: http://www.njshakespeare.org
❶ THEATER ARTS
Compensation: No pay.
Duration: Minimum 10 weeks.
Eligibility: High school seniors and graduates, college students, college graduates, graduate students, career changers, reentrants to the work force.
Contact: Letter, resume, recent photo, and portfolio for design applicants to Assistant to the Artistic Director.
Phone: 201-408-3278.
Apply by: March 31.

- DIRECTING: Will direct non-Equity members, coach juniors in scenes and monologues, and assist in mainstage productions.

Requirements: Self-motivated.

- BOX OFFICE
- COSTUME DESIGN
- SOUND DESIGN

PRO–FOUND SOFTWARE, INC.
500 Frank W. Burr Blvd., Teaneck, NJ 07666
❶ COMPUTERS

- ENGINEERS: Will be involved in system connectivity, software development, design sessions, and client meetings.

Compensation: $400-$600 per week.
Duration: 3-12 months.
Requirements: Major in computer science, electrical engineering, or related field.
Eligibility: College juniors and seniors.
Contact: Principal.
Phone: 201-928-0400.

NEW MEXICO

BIG BROTHERS/BIG SISTERS OF OTERO COUNTY
821 Alaska Ave., Alamogordo, NM 88310
❶ SOCIAL SERVICES
Compensation: No pay.
Duration: Three months.
Eligibility: High school students and graduates, college students, college graduates, graduate students, career changers, reentrants to the work force.
Contact: Executive Director.
Phone: 505-434-3652.

- **ASSISTANT CASE MANAGEMENT:** Will help set up case plans and objectives for clients.
Requirements: Good writing and verbal skills.

- **ASSISTANT MENTOR:** Will establish and maintain case files and recruit and coordinate volunteers.
Requirements: Good communications skills.

CARLSBAD CAVERNS NATIONAL PARK
3225 National Parks Highway, Carlsbad, NM 88220.World Wide Web: http://www.nps.gov
❶ ENVIRONMENT
Compensation: No pay.
Duration: Flexible.
Eligibility: College students, college graduates, graduate students, career changers, reentrants to the work force.
Contact: Volunteer Coordinator.
Phone: 505-785-2232.

- **CAVE WORKER:** Will monitor cave biology and work to restore and catalog caves.
Requirements: Interest in caves, driver's license.

- **WILDLIFE TECHNICIAN:** Will work to protect and conserve mating grounds and wildlife water areas.

- **CULTURAL RESOURCES:** Will handle office activities, including filing and processing.

- **ARCHAEOLOGY:** Will assist in maintenance and coordination of dig sites.
Requirements: Coursework or background in archaeology.

INTER-HEMISPHERIC RESOURCE CENTER
P.O. Box2178, Silver City, NM 88062
❶ INTERNATIONAL RELATIONS

- **RESEARCH:** Will research and write about issues pertaining to U.S. relations with Mexico, Central America, and the Caribbean.
Compensation: No pay.
Duration: One semester in the fall, spring, or summer.
Requirements: Bilingual in Spanish and English, typing skills.
Eligibility: College seniors, college graduates, graduate students.
Contact: Resume, references, and writing sample to Director.
Phone: 505-388-0208.
Apply by: Three months prior to start date.

ST. ELIZABETH SHELTER
804 Alarid St., Santa Fe, NM 87501
❶ SOCIAL SERVICES

- **GENERAL:** Will work at the homeless shelter coordinating meals, working on case management, writing newsletters, and maintaining the facilities.
Compensation: $55-$85 per week.
Requirements: Strong work ethic, interest in working with the homeless, minimum age 20.
Eligibility: Anyone over age 20.
Contact:: Executive Director.
Phone: 505-982-6611.

WHITE SANDS NATIONAL MONUMENT
P.O. Box 1086, Holloman AFB, NM 88330
❶ ENVIRONMENT
Compensation: $10 per day.
Eligibility: College juniors and seniors, college graduates, graduate students, career changers, reentrants to the work force.
Contact: Volunteer Coordinator.
Phone: 505-479-6124.
Apply by: April 1 for summer, July 15 for fall, December 15 for spring.

- **INTERPRETATION:** Will provide roving tours on bike and foot, present educational talks on nature, and participate in ranger activities.
Duration: 12-16 weeks.
Requirements: Biology, geology, education, or recreation major.

- **RESOURCE MANAGEMENT:** Will work in all areas of environmental monitoring, including bird surveys, water data collecting, report writing, and research assistance.
Duration: Flexible.
Requirements: Good monitoring, research, and computer skills.

NEW YORK

AMERICAN ASSOCIATION OF ADVERTISING
405 Lexington Ave., 18th Fl., New York, NY 10174-1801
❶ ADVERTISING

- **MINORITY ADVERTISING:** Will work in research, media, copywriting, design, or account management in New York, Chicago, Detroit, Los Angeles, or San Francisco.
Compensation: $300 per week.
Duration: 10 weeks during the summer.
Requirements: Good communications and writing skills.
Eligibility: College seniors, graduate students.
Contact: College career placement office.
Phone: 800-676-9333.
Apply by: January3.

AMERICAN MANAGEMENT ASSOCIATION
1601 Broadway, New York, NY 10019.
World Wide Web: http://www.amanet.org
❶ MANAGEMENT
Compensation: $4.25 per hour.

Duration: Flexible.
Eligibility: High school students, college students, college graduates, graduate students, career changers, reentrants to the work force.
Contact: Letter, resume, and two letters of reference (one academic, one business) to Senior Employment Representative.
Phone: 212-903-8021.

- BOOKS: Will help proofread, edit, and lay out books pertaining to business and management training.
Requirements: English/journalism major, WordPerfect and Lotus 1-2-3 skills.

- MARKETING: Will research and analyze markets and assist in new product development.
Requirements: Marketing, economics, or statistics major, WordPerfect and Lotus skills.

- HUMAN RESOURCES: Will assist in audits, conduct research for human resources reports, and analyze personnel reports.
Requirements: Psychology or human resources major, WordPerfect and Lotus 1-2-3 skills.

- PRODUCTION: Will organize preproduction schedule, contact and assist speakers, proofread presentation scripts, and research new production topics.
Requirements: Communications or journalism major, skilled in all editorial areas.

AMERICAN SOCIETY OF MAGAZINE EDITORS
919 3rd Ave., 22nd Fl., New York, NY 10022

❶ PUBLISHING

- EDITORIAL SERVICES: Will work with leading consumer magazines.
Compensation: $300 per week.
Duration: 10 weeks during the summer.
Requirements: Journalism coursework and experience, recommendations.
Eligibility: College seniors.
Contact: For an application, write to Executive Director, ASME.
Phone: No calls.
Apply by: December 15.

ARCHIVE FILMS, INC.
530 W. 25th St., New York, NY 10001.
World Wide Web:
http://www.archivefilms.com

❶ FILM
Compensation: No pay.
Duration: 2-3 months.
Eligibility: College sophomores, juniors, and seniors, college graduates.
Contact: Letter and resume to Intern Coordinator.

Phone: No calls.

- LIBRARY: Will be involved in acquiring, maintaining, and film-to-tape procedures, tape preparation, and voice dubbing.
Requirements: Technical skills, interest in film preservation.

- RESEARCHERS: Will help in areas of tape cuing, fact-checking, collection accessing, and screening.
Requirements: Background in cinema history.

- SALES: Will provide support for client services, screenings, and clerical departments.

- PHOTO SUPPORT: Will handle upkeep, organization, and preservation of the photo files.

THE BUFFALO NEWS
One News Plaza, P.O. Box 100, Buffalo, NY 14240

❶ JOURNALISM

- GENERAL: Will report, write, and edit news stories, take photographs, or work on art and graphics projects depending upon area of interest.
Compensation: $300 per week.
Duration: 3 months.
Eligibility: College juniors, graduate students.
Contact: Letter, resume, and samples of published work to Managing Editor.
Phone: No calls.

CENTER FOR WAR, PEACE, AND THE NEWS MEDIA AT NEW YORK UNIVERSITY
10 Washington Pl., 4th Fl., New York, NY 10003

❶ PUBLIC AFFAIRS

- GENERAL: Will contribute to a variety of public policy projects by analyzing academic articles, creating files, and implementing outreach programs.
Compensation: No pay.
Duration: One semester.
Requirements: Background in politics, economics, and media studies.
Eligibility: College juniors and seniors, college graduates, graduate students.
Contact: Letter, resume, and writing sample to Assistant Director for Administration.
Phone: 212-998-7960.

CHRISTIE'S
502 Park Ave., New York, NY 10022. World Wide Web: http://www.christie's.com

❶ AUCTION HOUSE
Compensation: Unpaid.
Duration: 3 months.
Eligibility: College sophomores, juniors, and seniors, college graduates.

Contact: Human Resources.
Phone: 212-636-2000.

- DECORATIVE ARTS
- HUMAN RESOURCES
- PUBLIC RELATIONS
- PUBLICITY

ENTERTAINMENT WEEKLY
1675 Broadway, New York, NY 10019
❶ PUBLISHING
Compensation: $320 per week.
Duration: One semester.
Eligibility: College students, college graduates, graduate students.
Contact: Letter, resume, and writing samples to Director of Research Services.
Phone: 212-522-2856.
Apply by: March 1 for summer, July 1 for fall, November 1 for spring.

- PHOTOGRAPHY
- EDITORIAL
- MEDIA RELATIONS
- GRAPHIC DESIGN

HARPER'S MAGAZINE FOUNDATION
666 Broadway, New York, NY 10012. World Wide Web: http://www.harpers.org
❶ PUBLISHING
Compensation: No pay.
Duration: 3-5 months.
Eligibility: College students, college graduates, graduate students, career changers.
Contact: Resume, at least two references, and a 500-word personal statement explaining yourself and your interest in the Harper's internship.
Phone: 212-614-6500.
Apply by: June 15 for fall, October 1 for winter, February 15 for summer.

- EDITORIAL: Will assist section editors, work on the Harper's Index, and perform general publishing tasks.
Requirements: Initiative, self-motivation.
Contact: Assistant Editor.
- PROMOTIONS: Will work on corporate and public affairs projects, publicity, and special events.
Requirements: Excellent communications skills, deadline-driven.

HOME BOX OFFICE
1100 Ave. of the Americas, New York, NY 10036
❶ BROADCASTING
- COMMUNICATIONS: Will work in production, programming, advertising, marketing, finance, and many other communications-oriented areas.
Compensation: $500.

Duration: 9-12 weeks.
Eligibility: College students, graduate students.
Contact: Human Resources Officer.
Phone: No calls.

KETCHUM PUBLIC RELATIONS
292 Madison Ave., New York, NY 10017.
World Wide Web: http://www.ketchum.com
❶ PUBLIC RELATIONS
- GENERAL: Will help to develop and implement promotions and publicity campaigns.
Compensation: $250-$350 per week.
Duration: 8-10 weeks.
Requirements: 3.0 GPA, strong writing skills.
Eligibility: College juniors.
Contact: Manager, Communications and Training.
Phone: 212-448-4200.
Apply by: March 31.

THE KITCHEN: CENTER FOR VIDEO, MUSIC, DANCE, PERFORMANCE, FILM, AND LITERATURE
512 W. 19th St., New York, NY 10011.
World Wide Web: http://www.panix.com
❶ ARTS
Compensation: No pay.
Duration: Flexible.
Eligibility: High school graduates, college students, college graduates, graduate students, career changers, reentrants to the work force.
Contact: Specific letter of interest and resume to Production Coordinator.
Phone: 212-255-5793.

- CURATORIAL: Will work with artists' contracts and review and evaluate submissions.
Requirements: Background in the arts, motivated, good organizational skills.
- TECHNICAL: Will work on theater and equipment maintenance.
Requirements: Background in technical theater.
- PUBLICITY: Will work on publicity and public relations projects.
Requirements: Excellent communications and Macintosh skills, journalism background.
- MEDIA SERVICES: Will help coordinate rotating video installations, organize video archives, perform office tasks, and assist with video distribution.
Requirements: Good organizational skills, motivated, video and/or marketing knowledge.

MAGAZINE PUBLISHERS OF AMERICA, INC.
919 Third Ave., New York, NY 10022. World Wide Web: http://www.magazine.org

❶ PUBLISHING

- GENERAL: Will work on business-related tasks as they pertain to magazine publishing.
Compensation: $275-$600 per week.
Duration: 10 weeks.
Requirements: Spreadsheet and word-processing skills.
Eligibility: College juniors, MBA students entering second year.
Contact: School Career Office or Internship Coordinator.
Phone: 212-872-3700.
Apply by: December 30.

THE METROPOLITAN MUSEUM OF ART

1000 Fifth Ave., New York, NY 10028-0198.
World Wide Web:
http://www.metmuseum.org

❶ CULTURAL ORGANIZATIONS

Contact: Letter, resume, two recommendations, transcript, and list of art history coursework to Internship Coordinator.
Phone: 212-570-3710.
Apply by: Call for current deadlines.

- RESEARCH: Will work on research and writing projects as they pertain to the museum's collection or special exhibits.
Compensation: $2,750.
Duration: 10 weeks.
Requirements: Completed one year of graduate school in art history or related field.
Eligibility: Graduate students.

- GENERAL INTERNS: Will work on projects pertaining to the applicant's special area of interest or expertise.
Compensation: $8,000.
Duration: Six months.
Requirements: Art history major.
Eligibility: Disadvantaged minority New York residents, college seniors, recent college graduates, graduate students.

- UNDERGRADUATE INTERNS: Will provide information services, gallery talks, and assistance on departmental projects.
Compensation: $2,500.
Duration: 10 weeks.
Requirements: Art history background.
Eligibility: College juniors and seniors, college graduates.

- VOLUNTEERS: Will work on various projects in the museum.
Compensation: No pay.
Duration: 2-9 months.
Requirements: Art history coursework.
Eligibility: College students, college graduates.

NEW YORK FOUNDATION FOR THE ARTS

155 Ave. of the Americas, 14th Fl., New York, NY 10013. World Wide Web:
http://www.artswire.org

❶ ARTS

Compensation: No pay.
Duration: Flexible.
Eligibility: College sophomores, juniors, and seniors, college graduates, graduate students.
Contact: Education and Information Internship Program.
Phone: 212-366-6900.
Apply by: Two months prior to start date.

- COORDINATOR: Will work to organize the Artist's New Works film series and the annual international film festival.
Requirements: Computer skills, interest in film.

- INFORMATION SERVICES: Will work in an editorial capacity for *FYI*, a quarterly newsletter distributed to the arts, education, and administration communities.
Requirements: Computer and graphic design skills, exceptional communications skills.

- DEVELOPMENTAL: Will work on writing projects, fundraising, special events, and data management.
Requirements: Computer literate, good research and communications skills.

- PROGRAMMING: Will help plan and organize the annual arts conference and seminar series for the arts community.
Requirements: Interest in the arts, computer and communications skills.

SEVENTEEN MAGAZINE

850 Third Ave., 9th Fl., New York, NY 10022

❶ PUBLISHING

Compensation: Paid and Unpaid available.
Duration: Six weeks during the summer, fall, or spring.
Eligibility: High school students, college students, college graduates, graduate students.
Contact: Internship Coordinator.
Phone: 212-407-9700.

- EDITORIAL

- MARKETING

- ADVERTISING SALES

THEATRE FOR THE NEW CITY FOUNDATION, INC.

155 First Ave., New York, NY 10003

❶ THEATER ARTS

Compensation: No pay.
Duration: Flexible.
Eligibility: High school students and graduates, college students, college graduates, graduate students, career changers, reentrants to the work force.
Contact: Administrator.
Phone: 212-254-1109.

- ADMINISTRATIVE: Will work with the theater director on various logistical and office-related tasks.
- TECHNICAL: Will work with the technical director.
- FUNDRAISING: Will work in financial development, writing grants, performing clerical duties, and conducting foundation research.

THE VILLAGE VOICE
36 Cooper Sq., New York, NY 10003
❶ JOURNALISM
- GENERAL: Will perform researching and editing tasks.

Compensation: No pay.
Duration: Three months during the spring, summer, or fall.
Requirements: Journalism experience.
Eligibility: High school students and graduates, college students, college graduates, graduate students, career changers.
Contact: Resume, writing samples, and recommendations to Intern Coordinator.
Phone: 212-475-3300, ext. 2300.

NORTH CAROLINA

AMERICAN DANCE FESTIVAL
Box 90772, Durham, NC 27708
❶ DANCE
- GENERAL: Internships available in administration, press, box office, finance, development, performance, international programs, and facilities.

Compensation: $950.
Duration: 8-9 weeks.
Eligibility: College sophomores, juniors, and seniors, college graduates, graduate students, career changers.
Contact: Director, American Dance Festival on Tour.
Phone: 919-684-6402.
Apply by: February 9.

CONTEMPORARY ART MUSEUM
P.O. Box 66, Raleigh, NC 27602-0066
❶ ART
Compensation: No pay.
Duration: One semester.
Eligibility: College juniors and seniors, college graduates, graduate students, career changers, reentrants to the work force.
Contact: Communications/Curator of Education.
Phone: 919-836-0088
- MARKETING: Will work on membership programs, public relations tasks, and program development.

- EDUCATION: Will help develop special educational outreach programs.

FIELDCREST CANNON, INC.
326 E. Stadium Dr., Eden, NC 27288
❶ MANUFACTURING
Compensation: $2,100 per month.
Eligibility: College juniors.
Contact: Letter, resume, transcript, coursework descriptions, and program of study to Director, Human Resources Department, 204 W. Stadium Dr., Eden, NC 27288.
Phone: No calls.
Apply by: January 15.
- YARN: Will work on hands-on, home textile projects.

Duration: 13-14 weeks.
- FABRIC: Will work with fabrics in the manufacturing of home textile products.

Duration: Three months.
- CUT AND SEW: Will work on fabric and textile design projects.

Duration: Three months.
- INFORMATION SYSTEMS: Will work on computer science-based projects.

Duration: Three months.
Requirements: Coursework in computer science or information systems.

THE NEWS AND OBSERVER PUBLISHING COMPANY
215 S. McDowell St., P.O. Box 191, Raleigh, NC 27602. World Wide Web: http://www.nando.net
❶ JOURNALISM
Compensation: $500 per week.
Duration: 10-12 weeks.
Eligibility: College sophomores, juniors, and seniors, recent college graduates, graduate students.
Contact: Assistant Managing Editor.
Phone: 919-829- 4530.
Apply by: November 15.
- REPORTING
- GRAPHICS
- PHOTOGRAPHY
- COPY EDITING

NORTH CAROLINA AMATEUR SPORTS
P.O. Box 12727, Research Triangle Park, NC 27709
❶ ATHLETICS
Compensation: No pay.
Duration: Flexible.
Eligibility: High school students and graduates, college students, college graduates, graduate students, career changers, reentrants to the work force.
Contact: Director of Support Services.
Phone: No calls.

- OPERATIONS: Will be involved in coordinating facility searches, communications operations, equipment procurement, medical care, and concession plans.
- MEDIA/PROMOTIONS: Will promote events through media outlets and collect scores and statistics for distribution to news agencies and wire services.
- SPECIAL EVENTS: Will work to coordinate in-house media and operations departments for special events.
- VOLUNTEER MANAGEMENT: Will recruit, train, and assign over 1,000 volunteers for the North Carolina State Games.

NORTH CAROLINA GOVERNOR'S OFFICE OF CITIZEN AFFAIRS
116 W. Jones St., Raleigh, NC 27603
❶ PUBLIC ADMINISTRATION
Compensation: Both paid and unpaid positions available.
Duration: One semester or one summer.
Eligibility: High school students and graduates, college students, college graduates, graduate students, career changers, reentrants to the work force.
Contact: Executive Director.
Phone: 919-733-2391.

- ADVOCACY: Will work with the ombudsperson to provide informational, referral, and casework services to constituents.
- COMMUNICATIONS: Will work on special integrated marketing projects via newsletters, public service announcements, and outreach programs.
- NATIONAL AND COMMUNITY SERVICE: Will help support organizations and programs that promote citizen involvement and volunteerism.

NORTH DAKOTA

FARGO–MOORHEAD COMMUNITY THEATRE
P.O. Box 644, Fargo, ND 58107. World Wide Web: http://www.fargoweb.com
❶ THEATER ARTS
Compensation: No pay.
Duration: Flexible, up to one year.
Eligibility: High school students and graduates, college students, college graduates, graduate students, career changers, reentrants to the work force.
Contact: Managing Artistic Director.
Phone: No calls.
Apply by: At least 4-6 weeks prior to start date.

- SCENERY AND LIGHTING

- CHILDREN'S THEATER: Will coordinate and oversee child- or youth-related productions and organize youth theater classes.
- MARKETING
- BOX OFFICE

THEODORE ROOSEVELT NATIONAL PARK
315 Second Ave., Medora, ND 58645
❶ PARKS
Compensation: No pay.
Eligibility: College students, college graduates, graduate students, career changers, reentrants to the work force.
Contact: Chief of Interpretation.
Phone: 701-623-4466.
Apply by: February 15.

- INTERPRETIVE: Will give interactive talks, conduct tours, work at the information desk, lead hikes, and work in volunteer management.
Duration: 2-3 months.
Requirements: Experience as a public speaker.

- BIOLOGICAL SCIENCE: Will work as a technician on resource management projects like exotic pest control and wildlife surveys.
Duration: 3-4 months.

TURTLE MOUNTAIN ENVIRONMENTAL LEARNING CENTER
#2 Lake Metigoshe State Park, Bottineau, ND 58318

❶ ENVIRONMENT

- NATURALIST: Will lead group activities and discussions designed to increase environmental awareness.
Compensation: $400-$450 per month.
Duration: Two months.
Requirements: Teaching ability, environmental knowledge.
Eligibility: College sophomores, juniors, and seniors, college graduates, graduate students, career changers, reentrants to the work force.
Contact: Park Manager, #2 Lake Metigoshe State Park, Bottineau, ND 58318.
Phone: 701-263-4651.
Apply by: March 1.

OHIO

BELLEFAIRE–JCB
22001 Fairmount Blvd., Shaker Heights, OH 44118
❶ SOCIAL SERVICES
Eligibility: Graduate and doctoral students.
Contact: Director of Community and Clinical Services.
Phone: 216-932-2800.
Apply by: December 1.

- CHILD PSYCHOLOGY: Will conduct psychological assessments and supervise individual, family, and group therapy with children and adolescents.
Compensation: $1,000 per month.
Duration: One year.
Requirements: Experience, near completion of an approved doctoral program.
- SOCIAL WORK: Will supervise therapy with children and adolescents.
Compensation: No pay.
Duration: Nine months.
Requirements: Enrolled in a master's program.

CINCINNATI PLAYHOUSE IN THE PARK
Box 6537, Cincinnati, OH 45206. World Wide Web: http://www.cincyplay.com
❶ THEATER ARTS
Compensation: Paid.
Eligibility: College juniors and seniors, college graduates, graduate students.
Phone: 513-345-2242.
Apply by: May 1.

- DIRECTING: Will assist mainstage productions.
Duration: Flexible.
- PRODUCTION: Will be involved all aspects of putting on a play.
Duration: Flexible.
- STAGE MANAGEMENT: Will assist backstage on technical matters.
Duration: Flexible.
Contact: Production Stage Manager.
- ADMINISTRATIVE: Will be involved in front-of-house affairs.
Duration: 2-6 months.
Contact: Buzz Ward.

INTERNATIONAL FIELD STUDIES
709 College Ave., Columbus, OH 43209
❶ SCIENCE
Compensation: Paid.
Duration: 1-2 years.
Requirements: Minimum age 21.
Eligibility: College graduates.
Contact: Executive Director.
Phone: 800-962-3805.

- GENERAL: Will support field staff on marine biology projects in the Bahamas.
Requirements: Mechanical, scuba, snorkeling, and swimming experience.
- FIRST MATES: Will assist the marine biology crew in the sailing program in the Bahamas.
Requirements: Sailing experience.

OHIO DEPARTMENT OF NATURAL RESOURCES—DIVISION OF PARKS AND RECREATION
1952 Belcher, Bldg. C-3, Columbus, OH 43224
❶ PARKS
Compensation: No pay.
Requirements: Minimum age 16.
Contact: Volunteer Coordinator.
Phone: 614-265-6549.

- HOSTS: Will work at one of Ohio's 72 state parks in visitor information services and public relations.
Duration: Six months.
Requirements: Camping experience, familiarity with state parks.
- GROUP VOLUNTEERS: Will work with various clubs, groups, and organizations in park maintenance and beautification.
Duration: One year.
- ADOPT-A-TRAIL VOLUNTEERS: Will adopt and then maintain a trail on a regular basis.
Duration: One year.

PROCTER & GAMBLE COMPANY
Miami Valley Laboratories, Box 538707, Cincinnati, OH 45253-8707
❶ CONSUMER PRODUCTS
- GENERAL: Will work as a full-time researcher at one of the Procter & Gamble corporate technical centers in Cincinnati.
Compensation: $650 per week.
Duration: 10-12 weeks.
Requirements: Aiming for Ph.D. in chemistry, life science, or chemical engineering.
Eligibility: College seniors planning on enrolling in graduate school in the fall, graduate students.
Contact: Manager, Doctoral Recruiting,
Phone: 513-627-1035.
Apply by: March 1.

WEWS-TV 5
3001 Euclid Ave., Cleveland, OH 44115
❶ BROADCASTING
Compensation: No pay.
Duration: One quarter or one semester.
Eligibility: College juniors and seniors, graduate students.
Contact: Letter and resume to Community Affairs Director.
Phone: 216-431-5555.
Apply by: March 1 for spring quarter and summer semester, August 1 for fall, November 1 for winter quarter and spring semester.

- NEWS & EDITORIAL: Will work at the assignment desk, making calls to story contacts and police departments and serving as the liaison for field news crews.
Requirements: Confident, good communications skills.

- SPORTS: Will monitor the sports wires, assist sports director with breaking news, shot-sheet and time interviews, and work with field producers.

Requirements: Exceptional sports knowledge.

- PROMOTIONS

Requirements: Excellent communications skills.

- PRODUCTION
- INVESTIGATIVE AND "TEAM 5" INTERNS

OKLAHOMA

KOTV
P.O. Box 6, Tulsa, OK 74101

❶ BROADCASTING

Compensation: No pay.
Duration: Three months.
Eligibility: College juniors and seniors, graduate students.
Contact: Letter outlining career goals and resume to Producer/Intern Supervisor.
Phone: 918-599-1410.
Apply by: November 30 for spring, March 30 for summer, July 30 for fall.

- NEWSROOM: Will work as an assistant to reporters, photographers, and associate producers as well as perform editing and TelePrompTer operations.

Requirements: Basic knowledge of television operations.

- SPORTS: Will work with sports production team in shooting and editing stories for broadcast.

- PRODUCTION: Will participate in pre- and postproduction activities, run studio cameras, and assist with TelePrompTer operations.

NATIONAL ASSOCIATION OF INTERCOLLEGIATE ATHLETICS—SPORTS INFORMATION
6120 S. Yale Ave., Suite 1450, Tulsa, OK 74136

❶ ATHLETICS

Compensation: $400 per month.
Eligibility: College seniors, college graduates, graduate students, career changers.
Contact: Letter, resume, and publicatons produced to Internship Coordinator.
Phone: 918-494-8828.
Apply by: May 1.

- SPORTS INFORMATION: Will compile ratings and statistics and help publicize and coordinate championship events.

Duration: Nine months.
Requirements: Statistical background, computer literacy, journalism skills.

- INFORMATION SPECIALIST: Will handle scheduling, media guide development, editing, researching, and writing of press releases.

Duration: Two months during the summer.
Requirements: Strong journalism and layout skills, computer literacy.

OREGON

KOIN-TV
222 SW Columbia St., Portland, OR 97201

❶ BROADCASTING

Compensation: No pay.
Duration: One quarter or one semester.
Eligibility: College juniors and seniors.
Contact: Human Resources Manager.
Phone: 503-464-0600.
Apply by: August 1 for fall, November 1 for winter, February 1 for spring, April 1 for summer.

- MARKETING: Will perform research and writing tasks in the development of marketing projects.

Requirements: Motivated, creative, coursework in advertising/marketing.

- PRODUCTION: Will work in the studio and field and on pre- and postproduction tasks.

Requirements: Career-oriented, coursework in broadcast production or communications.

- PROMOTIONS: Will write press releases, staff biographies, video promotional spots, and voiceovers as well as conduct station tours.

- PROGRAMMING: Will help to organize and produce news, talk, and entertainment programming.

NORTHWEST FILM CENTER
1219 SW Park Ave., Portland, OR 97205

❶ FILM

EQUIPMENT AND EDUCATION PR/EXHIBITION

Compensation: No pay.
Duration: One trimester.
Requirements: Strong desire to pursue professional development in arts administration.
Eligibility: High school students and graduates, college students, college graduates, graduate students, career changers.
Contact: Internship Coordinator.
Phone: 503-221-1156.
Apply by: August 10 for fall, December 10 for winter, May 10 for summer.

OREGON ARTS COMMISSION
775 Summer St., NE, Salem, OR 97310.
World Wide Web: http://www.das.state.or.us

❶ ARTS

- GENERAL: Will work on grants administration and special projects.
Compensation: No pay.
Duration: 3-6 months during the spring, summer, or fall.
Requirements: Computer literacy.
Eligibility: College juniors and seniors, college graduates, graduate students, career changers, arts professionals.
Contact: Assistant Director.
Phone: 503-986-0086.

OREGON MUSEUM OF SCIENCE AND INDUSTRY
7171 Southwest Quarry Ave., Redmond, OR 97756
❶ CULTURAL ORGANIZATIONS
Compensation: $10-$15 per day.
Duration: Three months.
Eligibility: College students, college graduates, graduate students.
Contact: Resume and letters of recommendation to Director OMSI Science Camps.
Phone: 541-548-5473.

- NATURALIST: Will research environmental science and natural history so as to develop and teach programs.
Requirements: Strong interest in environmental education.

- DEVELOPMENT: Will build on existing programs to ensure continual curriculum enhancement.
Requirements: Strong interest in environmental education.

U.S. FOREST SERVICE—PACIFIC NORTHWEST REGION AND RESEARCH STATION
P.O. Box 3623, Portland, OR 97208
❶ ENVIRONMENT

- VOLUNTEERS: Will deal with environmental research, timber management, fish and wildlife, geology, or recreation, depending on applicant's objectives.
Compensation: No pay.
Duration: Minimum 6-8 weeks.
Eligibility: High school graduates, college students, college graduates, graduate students, career changers.
Contact: Volunteer Coordinator.
Phone: 503-326-3816.

PENNSYLVANIA

AIR PRODUCTS AND CHEMICALS, INC.
7201 Hamilton Blvd., Allentown, PA 18195-1501. World Wide Web: http://www.airproducts.com
❶ MANUFACTURING
Compensation: Paid.
Duration: 3-9 months.

Requirements: Maturity, good communications skills, excellent academic record, experience in field helpful.
Eligibility: College students, graduate students.
Contact: Two letters of recommendation to University Relations.
Phone: 610-481-7695.
Apply by: February 1.

- RESEARCH ENGINEERING: Will research cryogenic and noncryogenic separation technologies, polymers, plastics, performance chemicals, catalysts, and fertilizers.

- PROCESS ENGINEERING: Will work with design, air separation systems, liquefactions, and cryogenic and noncryogenic processes.

- SAFETY ENGINEERS: Will ensure that optimal safety techniques are being applied in both the lab and field.

- DESIGN ENGINEERS: Will develop heat exchangers, process piping, and other facility components.

THE ANDY WARHOL MUSEUM
117 Sandusky St., Pittsburgh, PA 15212. World Wide Web: http://www.warhol.org
❶ CULTURAL ORGANIZATIONS
Compensation: Unpaid.
Duration: One semester minimum.
Eligibility: High school students and graduates, college students, college graduates, graduate students.
Contact: For an application, write to Internship Coordinator.
Phone: 412-237-8300.

- CURATORIAL

- EDUCATION

- MEDIA RELATIONS

- MUSEUM SHOP

CHILDREN, YOUTH, AND FAMILY COUNCIL
3200 S. Broad St., Philadelphia, PA 19145
❶ SOCIAL SERVICES
Compensation: No pay.
Duration: Flexible.
Eligibility: College juniors and seniors, college graduates, graduate students, career changers.
Contact: Resume and writing sample to Executive Director.
Phone: 215-334-0600.

- RESEARCH

- POLICY ANALYST: Will evaluate policies and assist in determining group positions.

PHILADELPHIA INQUIRER
P.O. Box 8263, Philadelphia, PA 19101
❶ JOURNALISM

Compensation: $573 per week.
Duration: One summer.
Eligibility: Minority applicants, college students, college graduates, graduate students.
Contact: Letter, portfolio of 10-12 samples, and letters of recommendation to Internship Coordinator, Suite 100, 100 E. Hector St., Conshocken, PA 19428.
Phone: 215-854-2000.

- COPY EDITORS: Will train for and work at the copy desk.

- MEDICAL WRITING: Will work on assignments from the medical/science desk.

- PHOTOGRAPHY: Will work as a staff photographer.
Requirements: Experience in photojournalism.

PHILADELPHIA MUSEUM OF ART
Box 7646, Philadelphia, PA 19101-7646
❶ CULTURAL ORGANIZATIONS
Eligibility: College students, college graduates, graduate students, career changers, reentrants to the work force.
Contact: Deputy Manager of Volunteer Services.
Phone: 215-684-7925.
Apply by: April 8 for summer.

- MUSEUM STUDIES: Will work as a curator and administrator in specific departments while also exploring the function and operations of other departments.
Compensation: No pay.
Duration: Two months.

- GENERAL VOLUNTEERS: Will assist departments in clerical, administrative, curatorial, and research capacities.
Compensation: No pay.
Duration: Flexible.

- EDUCATION: Will plan and implement summer programs for school-age children.
Compensation: No pay.
Duration: Flexible.

PITTSBURGH POST-GAZETTE
34 Blvd. of the Allies, Pittsburgh, PA 15222
❶ JOURNALISM

- NEWS DESK: Will participate in the entire news-gathering, writing, and editing process for various departments.
Compensation: $460-$490 per week, daily travel expenses.
Duration: 13 weeks (flexible).
Requirements: Journalism experience.
Eligibility: College seniors, college graduates, graduate students.
Contact: Assistant to the Editor..
Phone: 412-263-1297.
Apply by: December 31.

RUNNING PRESS

125 S. 22nd St., Philadelphia, PA 19103
❶ PUBLISHING
Compensation: No pay.
Duration: Minimum 12 weeks.
Eligibility: College juniors and seniors, graduate students.
Contact: Editor, Internship Coordinator.
Phone: 215-567-5080.

- EDITORIAL
- PUBLICITY

WORLD GAME INSTITUTE
3215 Race St., Philadelphia, PA 19104.
World Wide Web: http://www.worldgame.org
❶ PUBLIC AFFAIRS
Compensation: No pay.
Duration: Flexible.
Eligibility: College juniors and seniors, college graduates, graduate students, career changers, reentrants to the work force.
Contact: Office Manager.
Phone: No calls.
Apply by: Two months prior to preferred start date.

- RESEARCH: Will research global statistics and update materials for workshops designed to help people become responsible global citizens.
Requirements: Good computer skills.

- MARKETING: Will be involved in various market research projects as well as programming a client database.
Requirements: Some background in marketing strategy.

- PUBLIC RELATIONS: Will help research and write grant proposals, press releases, and other developmental materials.
Requirements: Good writing skills.

- EDUCATION: Will research issues for program enhancement and participate in curriculum development.
Requirements: Background in K-12 education.

R H O D E   I S L A N D

MIXED MEDIA
P.O. Box 20568, Cranston, RI 02920
❶ PUBLIC RELATIONS
Compensation: No pay.
Duration: 1-2 semesters.
Eligibility: High school graduates, college students, college graduates.
Contact: President.
Phone: 401-942-8025.

- PUBLICITY: Will write press releases, develop various marketing strategies, and conduct follow-up calls with clients.
Requirements: Excellent communications and writing skills.

- PROMOTIONS: Will monitor airplay statistics and organize promotions.
Requirements: Sales experience, good personality.

- RETAIL: Will work to organize and implement promotional materials for retail aspects of the firm.
Requirements: Ambition, excellent communications skills.

RHODE ISLAND HISTORICAL SOCIETY
110 Benevolent St., Providence, RI 02906
❶ CULTURAL ORGANIZATIONS

- COLLECTIONS: Will work on preservation, cataloging, exhibit installations, data processing, and registration tasks.
Compensation: No pay.
Duration: One semester.
Requirements: Database experience, history coursework.
Eligibility: College juniors and seniors, graduate students.
Contact: Chief Curator.
Phone: 401-331-8575.

TRINITY REPERTORY COMPANY
201 Washington St., Providence, RI 02903
❶ THEATER ARTS
Compensation: No pay.
Duration: One semester, one summer, or one year.
Eligibility: High school seniors, college students, college graduates.
Contact: Letter, resume, and recommendations to Educational Outreach Coordinator.
Phone: 401-521-1100.
Apply by: At least one semester, if not one year, in advance.

- PRODUCTION: Will be involved with stage preparation and management, prop and set construction, and costumes.
- ADMINISTRATIVE: Will work in developing various fundraising and publicity materials as well as educational outreach programs and program development.
Requirements: Liberal arts or business coursework.

UNIVERSITY OF RHODE ISLAND ENVIRONMENTAL EDUCATION CENTER
W. Alton Jones Campus, 401 Victory Highway, West Greenwich, RI 02817. World Wide Web: http://www.uri.edu
❶ ENVIRONMENT
Eligibility: College sophomores, juniors, and seniors, college graduates, graduate students, career changers, reentrants to the work force.
Phone: 401-397-3304, ext. 3304.

- FIELD INSTRUCTION: Will teach educational courses in forestry, team building, farming, Native American history, and ecology issues.
Compensation: $50 per week.
Duration: 4-5 months.
Requirements: Interest in environmental education, great personality.
Contact: Letter and resume to Education Director.

WPRI–TV
25 Catamore Blvd., East Providence, RI 02914. World Wide Web: http://www.wpri.com
❶ BROADCASTING
Compensation: No pay.
Duration: One semester.
Eligibility: High school seniors, college sophomores, juniors, and seniors.
Contact: Resume and school authorization to Assistant Production Manager.
Phone: 401-438-7200.
Apply by: Four weeks prior to start of each semester.

- PRODUCTION: Will help with studio and production operations, including light setup and camera work.
Requirements: Coursework in communications.
- NEWS: Will work in the newsroom on various production tasks.
Requirements: Coursework in journalism.
- ENGINEERING: Will learn and work with videotape processes.
Requirements: Coursework in electronics or electrical engineering.
- PRODUCTION: Will work on early script drafts for commercials.
Requirements: Theater experience, computer literacy, excellent imagination.

SOUTH CAROLINA

BARRIER ISLAND ENVIRONMENTAL EDUCATION CENTER
2810 Seabrook Island Rd., John's Island, SC 29455
❶ ENVIRONMENT

- EDUCATION: Will teach recreation classes and help develop new curriculum.
Compensation: $75 per week.
Duration: Flexible.
Requirements: Interest in children, biological science major, good verbal skills.
Eligibility: College juniors and seniors, college graduates, graduate students.
Phone: 843-768-1337.
Apply by: At least two months prior to start date.

NATIONAL AUDUBON SOCIETY

Francis Beidler Forest, 336 Sanctuary Rd.,
Harleyville, SC 29448

❶ ENVIRONMENT

Compensation: $125 per week.
Duration: 12-14 weeks.
Eligibility: College seniors, college graduates,
graduate students, career changers, reentrants
to the work force.
Contact: Assistant Manager.
Phone: 803-462-2150.
Apply by: January 15 for spring, April 1 for
summer.

- NATURALIST: Will give environmental
education information and guide canoe trips.
Requirements: Canoeing skills, natural history background.
- WARDEN: Will work as a naturalist as well
as in range maintenance.
Requirements: Tool and communications
skills, canoeing ability.

SPOLETO FESTIVAL USA

P.O. Box 157, Charleston, SC 29402-0157

❶ ARTS

Compensation: $200 per week.
Duration: 3-5 weeks.
Eligibility: College students, college gradu-
ates, graduate students, career changers, those
interested in arts careers.
Contact: Letter, resume, and two reference
letters to Apprentice Program Coordinator.
Phone: 843-722-2764.
Apply by: February 13.

- PUBLIC RELATIONS: Will work as a
press contact and assist in coordinating
publicity.
Requirements: Coursework in public rela-
tions/journalism, detail-oriented.
- BUSINESS OFFICE: Will handle financial
matters and personnel and payroll operations.
Requirements: Related academic background,
good organizational skills.
- MERCHANDISING: Will assist in retailing
souvenir merchandise.
Requirements: Customer service-oriented,
some sales experience.
- ORCHESTRA MANAGEMENT: Will help
coordinate the setup and transportation of
instruments.
Requirements: Lifting and van-driving ability.

SOUTH DAKOTA

BADLANDS NATIONAL PARK

Interior, SD 57750. World Wide Web:
http://www.nps.gov/badl

❶ PARKS

- PALEONTOLOGY AND INTERPRETA-
TION: Will work on self-initiated research
projects and present paleontological materi-
als to park visitors.
Compensation: $2,000.
Duration: 10 weeks.
Requirements: Career-oriented geol-
ogy/paleontology students or strong interest in
these areas.
Eligibility: All interested.
Contact: Chief of Interpretation or Park Pale-
ontologist, P.O. Box 6, Interior, SD 57750.
Phone: 605-433-5361.
Apply by: March 15.

D. C. BOOTH HISTORIC NATIONAL FISH HATCHERY

423 Hatchery Circle, Spearfish, SD 57783.
World Wide Web: http://www.fws.gov

❶ CULTURAL ORGANIZATIONS

Compensation: No pay.
Duration: 2-6 months.
Requirements: Museum studies, education,
and/or archival experience.
Eligibility: College students, graduate stu-
dents, career changers, reentrants to the work
force.
Contact: Curator.
Phone: 605-642-7730.

- MUSEUM: Will assist with maintenance
and monitoring of fish culture archives as
well as perform curatorial and informational
duties.
- ARCHIVES: Will maintain and process archives.

BLACK HILLS POSSE BASKETBALL

444 Mt. Rushmore Rd., Rapid City, SD 57701

❶ ATHLETICS

Compensation: No pay.
Duration: Four months.
Eligibility: College juniors and seniors, col-
lege graduates, graduate students.
Contact: Resumes to General Manager.
Phone: No calls.

- SPORTS MANAGEMENT
- PUBLIC RELATIONS

TENNESSEE

INTERNATIONAL PAPER

6400 Poplar Ave., Memphis, TN 38197.
World Wide Web: http://www.ipaper.com

❶ MANUFACTURING

- ENGINEERING: Will work on various
projects in paper manufacturing.
Compensation: Paid.
Duration: Three months.
Eligibility: College sophomores, juniors, and
seniors.

Contact: Recruiting Analyst.
Phone: No calls.

NASHVILLE BANNER
1100 Broadway, Nashville, TN 37203
❶ JOURNALISM

- NEWSROOM: Will work on general assignments as a reporter and writer.
Compensation: $300-320 per week.
Duration: 10-12 weeks.
Requirements: Journalism experience.
Eligibility: College sophomores, juniors, and seniors.
Contact: Resume and clips to Managing Editor.
Phone: 615-726-8982.
Apply by: February 28.

OAK RIDGE NATIONAL LABORATORY
P.O. Box 20008, Oak Ridge, TN 37831
❶ RESEARCH/SCIENCE
Contact: Program Director.
Phone: 615-576-1089.
Apply by: December 1 for spring, February 1 for summer, June 1 for fall, October 1 for winter.

- LAW: Will conduct inquiries into energy-related problems as they pertain to environmental and patent law.
Compensation: $465 per week.
Duration: Three months during the summer.
Eligibility: Completed one year of law school.

- PROFESSIONAL: Will deal with matters of waste management through the scope of chemistry, geology, hydrology, and computer science.
Compensation: $210-$325 per week.
Duration: 3-12 months.
Eligibility: College students, graduate students.

- TECHNOLOGY: Will work in a technical and administrative capacity on a variety of multidisciplinary research projects.
Compensation: $235 per week.
Duration: 1-12 months.
Eligibility: Associate degree students.

TENNESSEE REPERTORY THEATRE
427 Chestnut St., Nashville, TN 37203
❶ THEATER ARTS
Compensation: $5 per hour.
Duration: 11 months.
Eligibility: High school graduates, college graduates.
Contact: Company Manager.
Phone: No calls.
Apply by: May 31.

- SCENE SHOP: Will construct scenery for five mainstage shows as well as work on shop maintenance and stage coordination.
Requirements: Carpentry and scene painting experience.

- COSTUME: Will help design and create costumes for five mainstage shows.
Requirements: Strong sewing and tailoring skills.

- PROPERTIES: Will search for and/or build production props.
Requirements: Access to a car, craftsmanship skills.

TEXAS

THE DALLAS MORNING NEWS
Communications Ctr., P.O. Box 655237, Dallas, TX 75265. World Wide Web: http://www.dallasnews.com
❶ JOURNALISM

- GENERAL: Will work in newsroom environment as a professional journalist.
Compensation: $400 per week.
Duration: 10-12 weeks.
Requirements: Experience or previous internship, strong work ethic.
Eligibility: College juniors and seniors, graduate students.
Contact: Letter, resume, and 8-10 clips to Assistant Managing Editor.
Phone: 214-977-8031.
Apply by: December 1.

DALLAS THEATER CENTER
3636 Turtle Creek Blvd., Dallas, TX75219
❶ THEATER ARTS
Compensation: $500 per month.
Duration: 9-10 months.
Eligibility: College graduates, graduate students, career changers, reentrants to the work force.
Contact: Artistic Director.
Phone: 214-526-8210, ext 281.

- DIRECTOR/LITERARY: Will conduct workshop productions, evaluate new scripts, research and assist mainstage productions, and communicate with playwrights.

- STAGE MANAGERS: Will help usher the productions from their rehearsal phase through mainstage run.

- ARTS ADMINISTRATION: Will work on budgets, board relations, daily operations, and staff and building management.

- EDUCATION: Will assist in developing and coordinating community outreach programs.

DYKEMAN ASSOCIATES, INC.

4115 Rawlins, Dallas, TX 75219. World Wide Web: http://www.dykemanassoc.com

❶ PUBLIC RELATIONS

- GENERAL: Will work on video production, ad development, media contacts, program coordination, and proposal writing.

Compensation: No pay.
Duration: One semester or one summer.
Requirements: Professionalism.
Eligibility: All qualified applicants.
Contact: President/CEO.
Phone: 214-528-2991.
Apply by: One month prior to start date.

HOUSTON INTERNATIONAL PROTOCOL ALLIANCE

801 Congress, Suite 270, Houston, TX 77002

❶ INTERNATIONAL RELATIONS

Compensation: No pay.
Duration: Flexible.
Eligibility: College students, college graduates, graduate students, career changers, reentrants to the work force.
Contact: Letter, resume, and writing sample to Director of Protocol Affairs.
Phone: 713-227-3395.

- PROTOCOL: Will work in event organization, administration, correspondence, and special project coordination.

Requirements: Computer literacy, experience abroad, interest in international affairs.

- PUBLISHING: Will help lay out and write newsletter, design various communications materials, and oversee the printing process.

Requirements: Layout experience, good writing skills, Macintosh desktop publishing skills.

LUNAR AND PLANETARY INSTITUTE

3600 Bay Area Blvd., Houston, TX 77058-1113. World Wide Web: http://www.cass.jsc.nasa.gov

❶ SCIENCE

- GENERAL: Will work with scientists on a variety of planetary and astronomical projects and disseminate new research.

Compensation: $350 per week.
Duration: 10 weeks during the summer.
Requirements: Physical science major, 50-plus semester hours of coursework.
Eligibility: College juniors and seniors, new college graduates.
Contact: Intern Program.
Phone: 281-486-2100.
Apply by: February 7.

SAM HOUSTON NATIONAL FOREST

PO Drawer 1000, New Waverly, TX 77358

❶ ENVIRONMENT

Compensation: No pay.
Duration: Flexible.
Eligibility: High school students and graduates, college students, college graduates, graduate students, career changers, reentrants to the work force.
Phone: 409-344-6205.

- RECREATION: Will perform trail upkeep, construction tasks, and planning and design duties.

Requirements: Carpentry skills, good health.
Contact: Resources Forester

- FIRE MANAGEMENT: Will work with fire safety and burning procedures.

Requirements: Good physical condition.
Contact: Outdoor Recreation Planner.

- BIOLOGY: Will work on wildlife habitat-improvement projects.

Requirements: Background in zoology, biology, or related field.
Contact: Wildlife Biologist.

- BOTANY: Will perform botanical cataloging and plant population maintenance.

Requirements: Coursework in botany or related field.
Contact: Wildlife Biologist.

SOUTHWEST RESEARCH INSTITUTE

6220 Culebra, San Antonio, TX 78238

❶ RESEARCH

Compensation: Paid.
Duration: Three months during the summer.
Eligibility: College juniors and seniors, graduate students.
Contact: Must submit transcript before application will be issued to Student Employment Coordinator, P.O. Drawer 28510, San Antonio, TX 78228.
Phone: 210-522-2223.
Apply by: May 1.

- ENGINEERS: Will work directly with scientists on technology development.

Requirements: 3.0 GPA in chemical, industrial, or mechanical engineering.

- ANALYSTS: Will provide support for senior analysts on a variety of projects.

Requirements: Computer science major, 3.5 GPA.

- SCIENTISTS: Will assist on major projects.

Requirements: 3.0 GPA, physics, chemistry, geology, or hydrology major.

TEXAS ALLIANCE FOR HUMAN NEEDS

2520 Longview, Suite 311, Austin, TX 78705

❶ SOCIAL SERVICES

Eligibility: High school students and graduates, college students, college graduates, graduate students, career changers, reentrants to the work force.

Contact: Executive Director.
Phone: 512-474-5019.

• RESEARCH: Will research and attend hearings on poverty issues.
Compensation: No pay.
Duration: 3-6 months.
Requirements: Excellent report writing skills.

• NEWSLETTER: Will research, write, and help edit articles for the coalition newsletter.
Compensation: No pay.
Duration: 3-6 months.

• FIELD: Will participate in and help coordinate field activities and develop literature on minority issues.
Compensation: No pay.
Duration: 6-12 months.

• MINORITY HEALTH: Will work in minority communities investigating pertinent issues.
Compensation: $300 per month.
Duration: 6-9 months.
Requirements: Excellent communications skills.
Eligibility: Minority individuals.

UTAH

DESERET NEWS
30 E. First South St., Salt Lake City, UT 84111
❶ JOURNALISM

• GENERAL: Will work in all editorial facets.
Compensation: $8 per hour.
Duration: Three months during the summer.
Requirements: Communications or journalism major, Utah residents.
Eligibility: College juniors.
Contact: Personnel Director.
Phone: No calls.

OFFICE OF LEGISLATIVE RESEARCH AND GENERAL COUNSEL
436 State Capitol Bldg., Salt Lake City, UT 84114
❶ GOVERNMENT

• LEGISLATION: Will assist legislators.
Compensation: $300.
Duration: 45 days.
Requirements: Upperclass students from Utah universities, chosen by campus coordinator.
Eligibility: College juniors and seniors, graduate students.
Contact: Internship director at universities in Utah.
Phone: No calls.

VERMONT

DORSET THEATER FESTIVAL

Box 519, Dorset, VT 05251.World Wide Web: http://www.genghis.com
❶ THEATER ARTS
Compensation: $85-$100 per week.
Duration: Three months.
Eligibility: College juniors and seniors, college graduates, graduate students, career changers, reentrants to the work force.
Contact: Artistic Director.
Phone: 802-867-2223.

• TECHNICAL: Will work on sets, costumes, props, and lighting.
Requirements: Experience in appropriate area.

• ARTS MANAGEMENT: Will handle front-of-house tasks, including fundraising, publicity, and box office operations.
Requirements: Theater experience.

WASHINGTON COUNTY YOUTH SERVICES BUREAU
38 Elm St., P.O. Box 627, Montpelier, VT 05602
❶ SOCIAL SERVICES
Compensation: No pay.
Duration: One year.
Requirements: Pursuing a master's degree in counseling or family counseling.
Eligibility: College graduates, graduate students.
Contact: Letter and resume to Associate Director of Treatment.
Phone: 802-229-9151.

• FAMILY COUNSELING
• DRUG COUNSELING
• INDIVIDUAL COUNSELOR

VIRGINIA

AMERICAN ASSOCIATION OF SCHOOL ADMINISTRATORS
1801 N. Moore St., Arlington, VA 22209
❶ EDUCATION
Compensation: A stipend.
Duration: 3-6 months.
Eligibility: College students, graduate students.
Contact: Senior Associate Executive Directors.
Phone: 703-875-0753.

• COMMUNICATIONS: Will handle all editorial tasks and various organizational functions as they pertain to communications.
Requirements: Interest in communications career.

• GOVERNMENT RELATIONS: Will assist in researching and gathering information for dissemination to various levels of government.

ASHOKA: INNOVATORS FOR THE PUBLIC

1700 N. Moore St., Suite 1920, Arlington, VA 22209. World Wide Web: http://www.ashoka.org

❶ INTERNATIONAL RELATIONS
Compensation: No pay.
Duration: Flexible.
Eligibility: College students, graduate students.
Contact: Intern Coordinator.
Phone: 703-527-8300.

- PRODUCTIONS: Will conduct major research, writing, editing, and translating projects as well as participate in crisis management and program support.

- COMPUTER NETWORKING: Will be involved in budgetary planning and analysis of international telecommunications methods.
Requirements: Knowledge of computer networking.

- PRESS/PUBLICATIONS: Will work on in-house publications.
Requirements: PageMaker experience.

- CENTRAL AND EASTERN EUROPE PROGRAM: Will help implement developmental plans for fellowship programs in various regions.

COUNTERPART INTERNATIONAL BUSINESS PARTNERS

2200 Clarendon Blvd., Suite 1410, Arlington, VA 22201

❶ GENERAL BUSINESS

- ASSISTANTS: Will work with an international publishing company collecting data.
Compensation: No pay.
Duration: 3-12 months.
Requirements: Business coursework, foreign language and computer skills.
Eligibility: College juniors and seniors, college graduates, graduate students.
Contact: Executive Vice President.
Phone: No calls.

INNER QUEST, INC.

34752 Charles Town Pike, Purcellville, VA 22132

❶ EDUCATION

- APPRENTICES: Will teach outdoor education and ropes courses to encourage personal growth and skill development.
Compensation: $850.
Duration: 12 weeks.
Requirements: Teaching or counseling background.
Eligibility: High school graduates, college students, college graduates, graduate students, career changers, reentrants to the work force.

Contact: Assistant Director.
Phone: 703-668-6699.

THEATRE VIRGINIA

2800 Grove Ave., Richmond, VA 23221

❶ THEATER ARTS
Compensation: Both paid and unpaid positions available.
Duration: One semester or one season.
Eligibility: College graduates, career changers, reentrants to the work force.
Contact: Letter stating interest, resume, and references with phone numbers to Associate Director of Education and Research.
Phone: 804-353-6100.

- ADMINISTRATIVE: Will assist in development, administration, box office operations, public relations, or management.

- PRODUCTION: Will assist with sets, costumes, props, lights, sound, or production.

WASHINGTON

BOEING COMPANY

P.O. Box 3707, MS 6H-PR, Seattle, WA 98124. World Wide Web: http://www.boeing.com

❶ AVIATION

- GENERAL: Will work in design, engineering, or manufacturing areas.
Compensation: $10.50-$11.50 per hour.
Duration: One summer or one six-month co-op.
Requirements: Pursuing a bachelor's degree in engineering.
Eligibility: College juniors and seniors.
Contact: Boeing Intern/Co-op Program Manager.
Phone: No calls.
Apply by: April 30.

KBRC RADIO

PO Box 250, Mt. Vernon, WA 98273

❶ BROADCASTING

- NEWS: Will perform news and sports reporting, act as weekend disk jockey, produce, and write.
Compensation: No pay (hourly wage for weekend disk jockeys).
Duration: Minimum one quarter or one semester.
Requirements: Excellent communicator.
Eligibility: High school graduates, college students, college graduates, graduate students, career changers.
Contact: General Manager.
Phone: No calls.

OLYMPIC NATIONAL PARK

600 E. Park Ave., Port Angeles, WA 98362

❶ PARKS
Duration: 2-3 months.
Eligibility: All qualified applicants.
Contact: Volunteer Coordinator.
Phone: 360-452-4501.

- INTERPRETATION: Will work in the visitor's information center as well as conduct educational talks on nature.
Compensation: $100 per month.
Requirements: Creativity, photographic skills.

- RANGERS: Will work in backcountry areas on revegetation projects and resource management.
Compensation: $50 per month.

- NATURAL SCIENCE: Will work with biologists and technicians on wildlife management projects.
Compensation: $50 per month.

- HOST: Will provide visitor greetings, informational services, and range maintenance.
Compensation: $50 per month.
Requirements: Background in natural science.

WEST VIRGINIA

CRISS CROSS INC.
PO Box 1831, 115 S. Fourth St., Clarksburg, WV 25302
❶ SOCIAL SERVICES
Compensation: No pay.
Duration: Flexible.
Requirements: Good communications and problem-solving skills.
Eligibility: High school students and graduates, college students, college graduates, graduate students, career changers, reentrants to the work force.
Contact: Resume to Director.
Phone: 304-623-6681.

- GENERAL: Will develop and implement programs and work with clients as both a referral service and consumer credit counselor.

- PUBLIC RELATIONS: Will cultivate media relationships and coordinate public events.

- BUSINESS: Will assist clients with debt management plans.

- COMPUTER: Will work as a programmer.

WCHS-TV
1301 Piedmont Rd., Charleston, WV 25301
❶ BROADCASTING

- NEWS: Will contribute to the news programming by conducting background reporting and fact gathering and also assist in technical areas.

Compensation: No pay.
Duration: 200 hours.
Requirements: Strong interest in broadcast journalism.
Eligibility: College juniors and seniors, career changers, reentrants to the work force.
Contact: Administrative Assistant.
Phone: 304-346-5358.

WEST VIRGINIA KIDS COUNT FUND
1031 Quarrier St., Suite 313, Charleston, WV 25301, World Wide Web:
http://www.westvirginiakidscountfund.
❶ SOCIAL SERVICES
Compensation: No pay.
Duration: Flexible.
Eligibility: College sophomores, juniors, and seniors, college graduates, graduate students.
Contact: Communications Coordinator.
Phone: 304-345-2101.

- COMMUNICATIONS: Will write press releases, cultivate and organize media contacts, and compile information and media results.
Requirements: Experience in media-related areas, good writing skills.

- SOCIAL WORK: Will conduct research and write reports pertaining to the well-being and caretaking of community at-risk children.
Requirements: Social work major.

WISCONSIN

APOSTLE ISLANDS NATIONAL LAKE-SHORE
Rte. 1, Box 4, Bayfield, WI 54814
❶ ENVIRONMENT
Compensation: No pay.
Duration: Three months during the summer.
Eligibility: High school graduates, college students, college graduates, graduate students.
Contact: Volunteer Coordinator.
Phone: 715-779-3397.
Apply by: April 1.

- NATURAL OR CULTURAL: Will explore plant and animal life and compile data for research personnel.

CONSOLIDATED PAPERS, INC.
231 First Ave. N., Wisconsin Rapids, WI 54495-8050
❶ MANUFACTURING
Duration: 3-6 months.
Eligibility: College juniors.
Contact: Professional Employment Manager, P.O. Box 8050, Wisconsin Rapids, WI, 54495.
Phone: No calls.

Apply by: November 30.

- PAPER SCIENCE ENGINEERS: Will be involved in the research, development, and/or manufacturing of coated paper products.

Compensation: $13-$14 per hour.

- PACKAGING ENGINEERS: Will be involved with various projects pertaining to packaging.

Compensation: $12.25 per hour.

- FORESTRY: Will be involved in resource management.

Compensation: $10.25 per hour.

- RISK MANAGEMENT: Will deal with risk control matters.

Compensation: $13 per hour.

MILWAUKEE REPERTORY THEATRE

108 E. Wells, Milwaukee, WI 53202

❶ THEATER ARTS

Compensation: No pay.

Eligibility: College graduates, graduate students.

Contact: Resident Director of Intern Programs.

Phone: 414-224-1761.

Apply by: April 1.

- DIRECTING: Will direct readings of new material, conduct understudy rehearsals, and assist with mainstage directing tasks.

Duration: One year.

Requirements: Experience, training, MFA preferred but not essential.

- ACTING: Will act and be understudy.

Duration: One year.

Requirements: Experience, training, MFA preferred but not essential.

DRAMATURGY: Will read new scripts and research various developmental projects.

Duration: One year.

Requirements: Master's Degree in English literature, dramatic literature, or dramaturgy.

- TECHNICAL: Will work with various aspects of technical theater production.

Duration: Nine months.

Requirements: Background in tech. theater.

PATHFINDERS FOR RUNAWAYS

1614 E. Kane Pl.., Milwaukee, WI 53202

❶ SOCIAL SERVICES

- ASSISTANT ADVOCATES: Will work on the crisis hotline, perform intake assessments, and lead group activities.

Compensation: No pay.

Duration: One semester.

Requirements: Interest in working with teens and families.

Eligibility: High school graduates, college students, college graduates, graduate students, career changers.

Contact: Program Assistant.

Phone: 414-271-1560.

Eligibility: High school graduates, college students, college graduates, graduate students, career changers, reentrants to the work force.

Apply by: April 1 for summer, July 1 for fall, December 1 for spring.

W Y O M I N G

BRIDGER–TETON NATIONAL FOREST, KEMMERER RANGER DISTRICT

PO Box 31, Kemmerer, WY 83101

❶ WILDLIFE

Compensation: $16 per day.

Eligibility: College juniors, seniors, graduates, graduate students, retirees, teachers.

Contact: Natural Resources Specialist.

Phone: 307-877-4415

JOB OPPORTUNITIES

Summer Jobs for Students

SUMMER JOBS ARE A FACT OF LIFE for many students, both as a way to earn money and a way to gain valuable work experience. This chapter includes summer jobs that are generally available—that is, positions that employers need to fill regularly because of increased employee requirements during the summer months. Naturally, many are positions at camps or recreational facilities. There are also teaching positions available during the summer months at academic or leadership-oriented sites, as well as jobs with the government and national parks. Many of these types of jobs are also found in this chapter.

Corporations also hire for the summer. However, most are not listed below because they rarely make formal announcements about summer hiring. This is because companies hire students for the summer based on economic conditions, which are often not known until shortly before summer break. Therefore, in addition to the possibilities listed below, job seekers should prospect companies listed elsewhere in the "Job Opportunities" section of this book. ➔See "U.S. Employers," pp. 158-378; "Jobs in the Federal Government," pp. 379-394; and "Job Hotlines," pp. 410-446. There are also many internships for students available at prestigious corporations, government agencies, and so on. While these may not pay as much as certain summer jobs, they do offer valuable experience and can look extremely impressive on a resume. ➔See "Internships for Students," pp. 447-496.

And don't forget temporary work. Temp agencies often hire qualified students during the summer. ➔See "Temp Agencies," pp. 616-626. There are also job opportunities if you have access to the Internet or the commercial on-line services via a personal computer. ➔See "The Internet and the World Wide Web," pp. 536-540, and "Commercial On-Line Services," pp. 541-547.

Camps are perennial summer employers. Keep in mind that just because a particular camp position may not be listed here doesn't necessarily mean it doesn't exist. Camp jobs can run well into the dozens, so make sure you phone particular camps to get the full range of positions offered. Also, plan on getting full details about a camp. Some camps cater to Girl Scouts, some to the developmentally disabled, others to specific sports, and so on. Get the specifics at the outset, before you apply.

Job descriptions are not always provided in this chapter, either because the positions are self-explanatory or the employers prefer not to define them until an applicant contacts them. In addition, those entries for which there is no information about requirements usually have varying requirements depending on the specifics of the hiring situation. Ask when you call. As for room and board, many camps and resorts provide it free as part of compensation, while others arrange to offer it to their employees at reasonable rates. Again, ask when you call.

Be aware that the application deadlines for many positions listed below are not always enforced. While employers do set deadlines on paper, some actually accept applications only until all the positions are filled. For some jobs, that could be months before summer even begins. Other slots may be open well into the summer, and still other employers accept applications on an ongoing basis. As a result, for some employers, no "apply by" information is given. As a general rule, job seekers should always check with employers regarding application dates.

Students whose primary aim is to make money over the summer for school or other expenses should consider restaurant work. Many restaurants—too numerous and small to list here—hire during the summer. Other employers that do so and are not necessarily listed below are painting companies, city parks and works departments, retail stores, and entertainment facilities.

ABBREVIATIONS USED IN THIS CHAPTER

ACA—*American Camping Association, American Canoe Association*

AYH—*American Youth Hostels*

BCU—*British Canoe Union*

CHA—*Camp Horsemanship Association*

CIT—*Counselor-In-Training*

CPR—*Cardiopulmonary Resuscitation*

EMT—*Emergency Medical Technician*

GPA—*Grade Point Average*

LIT—*Leader-In-Training*

LPN—*Licensed Practical Nurse*

MFA—*Master Of Fine Arts*

MFC—*Marriage And Family Counselor*

NAA—*National Archery Association*

NRA—*National Rifle Association*

PPS—*Pupil Personnel Services*

RA—*Resident Assistant*

RN—*Registered Nurse*

USCG—*U.S. Coast Guard*

USGA—*U.S. Golf Association*

WPM—*Words Per Minute*

WSI—*Water Safety Instructor*

ALABAMA

CAMP SKYLINE
Mentone, AL 35984

❶ CAMPING (GIRLS)
Compensation: $900-$1,200 per season, room and board.
Duration: June 1 to August 10.
Contact: Personnel Director, Camp Skyline, Department SJ, P.O. Box 287, Mentone, AL 35984.

Phone: 256-634-4001.

- SPORTS INSTRUCTION: Will facilitate activities in archery, tennis, swimming, diving, gymnastics, and horseback riding.
- LIFEGUARDING
Requirements: WSI certification.
- ARTS INSTRUCTION: Will work with campers in music, dance, arts and crafts, or drama activities.
- COMPUTER INSTRUCTORS

ALASKA

BRISTOL BAY LODGE
P.O. Box 1509, Dillingham, AK 99576

❶ LODGING
Compensation: Room and board, travel reimbursements.
Duration: June 5 to September 20.
Contact: President/General Manager, Bristol Bay Lodge, 2422 Hunter Rd., Ellensburg, WA 98926.

Phone: 509-964-2094.

Apply by: February 1.

- CHEF
Compensation: $2,000-$2,400 per month.

Requirements: Experience.
- HOUSEHOLD WORK
Compensation: $900 per month.

- PILOTS
Compensation: Varies with experience.
Requirements: Communications, instrumentation, and seaplane ratings (over 1,500 hours).

- FISHING GUIDES
Compensation: $800-$1,200 per month.
Requirements: CPR and first aid certification.

CAMP TOGOWOODS
HC 30, Box 5400, Wasilla, AK 99654

❶ CAMPING (GIRLS)
Compensation: Room and board, health insurance.

Duration: May 31 to August 6.

Contact: Camp Director, Girl Scouts Susitna Council, Camp Togowoods, 3911 Turnagain St., Anchorage, AK 99517.

Phone: 907-248-2250.

Apply by: April 15.

- COUNSELORS: Will work with girls age 7-15 in a variety of activities.
Compensation: $1,700 - $1,850 per season.
- WATERFRONT DIRECTOR
Compensation: $2,500 - $2,700 per season.
Requirements: WSI certification.
- LIFEGUARDS
Compensation: $1,900 - $2,025 per season.
Requirements: Proper certification.
- FOOD SERVICE
Compensation: $2,400 - $2,800 per season.

RAINBOW KING LODGE
P.O. Box 106, Iliamna, AK 99606

❶ LODGING
Compensation: Room and board.
Duration: June 1 to October 1.
Contact: Manager, Rainbow King Lodge, 333 S. State St., Suite 126, Lake Oswego, OR 97034.
Phone: 800-458-6539.
Apply by: April 1.

• FISHING GUIDES
Compensation: $1,050-$1,850 per month.
Requirements: CPR and first aid certification, fly fishing and boating background.

• LODGE WORKERS
Compensation: $1,050-$1,700 per month.
Requirements: Experience preferred.

• MAINTENANCE PERSONNEL
Compensation: $1,050-$1,850 per month.
Requirements: Experience preferred.

ARIZONA

GRAND CANYON NATIONAL PARK LODGES
P.O. Box 699, Grand Canyon, AZ 86023.
World Wide Web:
http://www.coolworks.com
❶ PARKS
Compensation: $5.15 - $7 per hour.
Duration: Flexible, year-round.
Contact: Personnel Department, Department SJ.
Phone: 520-638-2812.

• RETAIL

• TOUR BUS DRIVERS

• ACCOUNTING/CASHIER

• COOKS

• HOUSEKEEPING

ORME SUMMER CAMP
HC 63, Box 3040, Mayer, AZ 86333-9799

CAMPING
Compensation: Room and board.
Duration: June 10 to August 14.
Contact: Director, Orme Summer Camp, Department SJ.
Phone: 602-632-7601.
Apply by: February 1.

• OUTDOOR ADVENTURE INSTRUCTOR
Compensation: $1,000-$1,300 per season.
Requirements: Outward Bound completion or equivalent.

• SENIOR COUNSELORS

Compensation: $750-$1,100 per season.

ARKANSAS

NOARK GIRL SCOUT CAMP
Rte. 3, Box 22, Huntsville, AR 72740
❶ CAMPING (GIRLS)
Compensation: Room and board.
Duration: May 31 to August 8.
Contact: Camp Director, Noark Girl Scout Camp, Department SJ, P.O. Box 1004, Harrison, AR 72602.
Phone: 501-750-2442.
Apply by: April 15.

• UNIT LEADERS
Compensation: $160 per week.
Requirements: Recreation/physical education degree preferred, minimum age 21.

• UNIT COUNSELORS
Compensation: $140 per week.
Requirements: Minimum age 18.

• HEALTH WORKERS
Compensation: $150 per week.
Requirements: RN, LPN, or paramedic license, minimum age 21.

• BUSINESS MANAGEMENT
Compensation: $160 per week.
Requirements: Background in business methods and record keeping.

CALIFORNIA

AMERICAN ADVENTURES
6762A Centinela Ave., Culver City, CA 90230

❶ CAMPING (ADVENTURE)
• LEADERS: Will drive and lead bus tours for international passengers.
Compensation: $210-$330 per week.
Duration: May 1 to October 31.
Requirements: Knowledge of history/culture, bilingual ability, first aid preferred, minimum age 21.
Contact: Operations Manager.
Phone: 310-390-7495.
Apply by: February or March.

CAMP HARMON
Boulder Creek, CA 95006
❶ CAMPING (PHYSICAL AND DE- VELOPMENTAL DISABILITIES)
Compensation: Room and board.
Duration: June 4 to August 24.
Contact: Camp Director, Camp Harmon, Department SJ, 430 West Grant St., Healdsburg, CA 95448.

Phone: 707-433-3530.

Apply by: April 1.

- CABIN COUNSELORS
Compensation: $175 per week.
- PROGRAM SPECIALISTS
Compensation: $200 per week.

CAMP JCA SHALOM
34342 Mulholland Highway, Malibu, CA 90265

❶ CAMPING (RELIGIOUS)

Compensation: $1,000-$3,000 per season, room and board.

Duration: June 24 to August 22.

Contact: Assistant Director.

Phone: 818-889-5500.

Apply by: March 31.

- COUNSELORS
Requirements: High school student.
- SONG LEADER: Will lead campers in a variety of traditional American and Hebrew folk songs.
Requirements: Guitar skills, great spirit.
- NURSE: Will run the infirmary.
Requirements: Interact well with patients, good supervisory skills.
- UNIT HEADS
Requirements: College degree, three years of camping experience, Jewish programs skills.

CAMP WASEWAGAN
42121 Seven Oaks Rd., Angelus Oaks, CA 92305

❶ CAMPING

Compensation: Room and board.

Duration: June 20 to August14.

Contact: Director of Marketing, Camp Fire Council of the Foothills, Camp Wasewagan, 136 W. Lime Ave., Monrovia, CA 91016.

Phone: 818- 305-1200.

Apply by: May 31.

- WATERFRONT ASSISTANCE
Compensation: $975 per season.
Requirements: Lifesaving, CPR, and first aid certification.
- HANDCRAFTS
Compensation: $900 per season.
Requirements: Artistic training and skills.
- OUTDOOR SPECIALIST
Compensation: $900 per season.
Requirements: Knowledge of outdoor activities, athletic.
- ASSISTANT COOK
Compensation: $1,050 per season.

DOUGLAS RANCH CAMPS
33200 E. Carmel Valley Rd., Carmel Valley, CA 93924. World Wide Web: http://www.douglascamp.com

❶ CAMPING

Compensation: Room and board.

Duration: June 12 to August 14.

Contact: Assistant Director, Douglas Ranch Camps, 8 Pala Ave., Piedmont, CA 94611.

Phone: 510-547-3925.

Apply by: May 1.

- SWIMMING INSTRUCTION
Compensation: $2,000 - $2,200 per season.
Requirements: WSI and lifeguard certification.
- HORSEBACK RIDING INSTRUCTION
Compensation: $2,000 - $2,300 per season.
Requirements: Experience teaching riding, background in saddling and general horse care.
- TENNIS INSTRUCTION
Compensation: $2,000 - $2,200 per season.
Requirements: Teaching or team tennis experience.
- ARCHERY INSTRUCTION
Compensation: $2,000 - $2,200 per season.
Requirements: Prior experience.

EMANDAL—A FARM ON A RIVER
16500 Hearst Rd., Willits, CA 95490. World Wide Web: http://www.pacific.net

❶ CAMPING

Compensation: Room and board.

Duration: February 1 to November 30. Year-round positions also available.

Contact: Director.

Phone: 707-459-5439.

Apply by: April 15.

- COUNSELORS
Compensation: $975 per season.
Duration: Six weeks.
- FAMILY CAMP WORKERS
Compensation: $180 per week.
Duration: Six weeks.
- GARDENERS
Compensation: $180 per week.
Duration: Entire summer.
- FARM WORKERS
Compensation: $180 per week.
Duration: Until Thanksgiving.

JAMESON RANCH CAMP
P.O. Box 459, Glennville, CA 93226

❶ CAMPING

Compensation: $2,000 per season, room and board.

Duration: June 21 to September 6.

Contact: Owner/Director.

Phone: 805-536-8888.

Apply by: May 30.

- LIFEGUARDS
Requirements: ALS certification.
- CRAFTS INSTRUCTION
- DRAMA INSTRUCTION
- PHOTOGRAPHY INSTRUCTION

LOS ANGELES DESIGNERS' THEATER
P.O. Box 1883, Studio City, CA 91614

❶ THEATER ARTS

Compensation: Negotiable on a per-show basis.

Duration: Year-round positions available.

Contact: Send nonreturnable items that best demonstrate applicant's artistry to Artistic Director, Department P.

Phone: 323-650-9600.

- DIRECTING
- ACTING
- TECHNICAL
- CREW

SUPERCAMP
Pitzer College, Claremont, CA 91711.
World Wide Web:
http://www.supercamp.com

❶ CAMPING

Compensation: Room and board.

Duration: June 20 to August 20.

Contact: Human Resources Coordinator, SuperCamp, 1725 S. Coast Highway, Oceanside, CA 92054.

Phone: 800-527-5321.

Apply by: May 1.

- TEAM LEADERS: Will work on programs designed to teach teens self-confidence and lifelong self-improvement techniques.
Compensation: $500-$1,000 per season.
Requirements: High school diploma.
- FACILITATORS
Compensation: $1,500-$6,000 per season.
Requirements: Good communications skills, college degree, teaching certificate preferred.
- COUNSELORS
Compensation: $1,000-$4,000 per season.
Requirements: PPS credentials, master's degree in counseling, or MFC license.
- NURSES

Compensation: $1,000-$3,000 per season.
Requirements: RN license.

YMCA CAMP OAKES
P.O. Box 452, Big Bear City, CA 92314

❶ CAMPING

Compensation: Room and board.

Duration: June 18 to September 5.

Contact: Program Director, YMCA Camp Oakes, P.O. Box 90995, Long Beach, CA 90809-0995.

Phone: 310-496-2756.

Apply by: May 31.

- PROGRAM DIRECTORS
Compensation: $190-$250 per week.
Requirements: Three years of experience, minimum age 21.
- AQUATICS
Compensation: $190-$250 per week.
Requirements: WSI, CPR, and first aid certification, minimum age 21.
- CABIN COUNSELORS
Compensation: $150-$170 per week.
Requirements: Completed one year of college, minimum age 18.
- JUNIOR COUNSELORS
Compensation: $110-$130 per week.
Requirements: Minimum age 18.

YOSEMITE CONCESSION SERVICES CORPORATION
P.O. Box 578, Yosemite National Park, CA 95389

❶ PARKS

Compensation: $5.49 per hour and up.

Duration: April 1 to September 5. Spring, winter, Christmas break, and year-round positions also available.

Contact: Manager of Employee Relations and Placement, Department SJ.

Phone: 209-372-1236.

- FRONT DESK
Requirements: Computer experience.
- AUDITORS
Requirements: Accounting experience.
- STABLE HANDS
Requirements: Background in horse care.
- TOUR GUIDES
Requirements: Familiarity with Yosemite, good presentation skills.

COLORADO

ANDERSON WESTERN COLORADO CAMPS, LTD.
7177 Colorado River Rd., Gypsum, CO 81637

❶ CAMPING

Compensation: Room and board.

Duration: May 15 to August 29.

Contact: Director.

Phone: 970-524-7766.

Apply by: April 15.

- WRANGLERS
Compensation: $975-$1,200 per season.
- RIDING INSTRUCTOR
Compensation: $975-$1,125 per season.
- COOKS
Compensation: $150-$400 per week.
- LODGE AND GROUNDSKEEPERS
Compensation y by: $800-$1,000 per season.
ASPEN LODGE AT ESTES PARK
6120 Highway 7, Estes Park, CO 80517

❶ RESORTS

Duration: May 1 to October 31. Year-round positions also available.

Contact: Personnel Manager.

Phone: 970-586-8133.

Apply by: April 15 for summer.

- SPORTS CENTER ATTENDANTS
Compensation: $5.25 per hour.
- CHILDREN'S COUNSELORS
Compensation: $5.25 per hour.
- WAITSTAFF
Compensation: $5.25 per hour.
- GROUNDSKEEPERS
Compensation: $5.25 per hour.
CENTRAL CITY OPERA
621 17th St., Suite 1601, Denver, CO 80206

❶ MUSIC

Compensation: Room and board.

Duration: June 1 to August 15.

Contact: Festival Administrator, Department SJ.

Phone: 303-292-6500.

Apply by: April 1.

- HOUSE MANAGER
Compensation: $ $250-$300 per week.
- MUSIC LIBRARIANS
Compensation: $170-$180 per week.
- PUBLIC RELATIONS
Compensation: $170-$180 per week.
- PRODUCTION
Compensation: $170-$180 per week.
COLORADO MOUNTAIN RANCH
P.O. Box 97, Boulder, CO 80306

❶ CAMPING

Compensation: $900-$975 per season, room and board.

Duration: June 6 to August 19.

Contact: Directors, Colorado Mountain Ranch, 10063 Gold Hill Rd., Boulder, Co 80302.

Phone: 303-442-4557.

Apply by: May 1.

- SWIMMING INSTRUCTORS
Requirements: WSI and/or lifeguard certification.
- WRANGLERS
- KITCHEN WORKERS
- DAY CAMP WORKERS
DON K RANCH
2677 S. Siloam Rd., Pueblo, CO 81005

❶ CAMPING

Compensation: $350-$800 per month, room and board.

Duration: May 15 to September 30.

Phone: 719-784-6600.

Apply by: April 1.

- WRANGLERS
Requirements: Strong background in horseback riding and caretaking.
- CHILDREN'S COUNSELORS
Requirements: Lifesaving certification, ability to plan activities for and work with children.
- CABIN HOUSEKEEPERS
- OUTDOOR MAINTENANCE
FLYING G RANCH, TOMOHAWK RANCH
400 S. Broadway, Denver, CO 80209

❶ CAMPING (GIRLS)

Compensation: Room and board.

Duration: June 8 to August 12.

Contact: Camp Administrator.

Phone: 303-778-8774.

Apply by: May 1.

- TROOP LEADERS
Compensation: $135-$175 per week.
Requirements: Good supervisory skills, experience working with children.
- HORSEBACK RIDING COUNSELORS
Compensation: $115-$130 per week.
Requirements: Experience with Western riding style.
- NATURE SPECIALISTS
Compensation: $115-$155 per week.
- FINE/THEATRICAL ARTS

Compensation: $115-$155 per week.
Requirements: Ability to teach the arts to children.

POULTER COLORADO CAMPS
P.O. Box 772947-P, Steamboat Springs, CO 80477

❶ CAMPING
Compensation: Room and board.
Duration: June 6 to August 20.
Contact: Director.
Phone: 970-879-4816.
Apply by: April 1.

• WRANGLERS
Compensation: $1,000-$1,500 per season.
Requirements: Excellent teaching and horsemanship skills.

• WILDERNESS INSTRUCTORS
Compensation: $1,100-$2,000 per season.
Requirements: Wilderness experience, good teaching and technical skills, minimum age 21.

• SENIOR COUNSELORS
Compensation: $900-$1,000 per season.
Requirements: Lifeguard and first aid certification preferred, experience with youths.

• ASSISTANT COUNSELORS
Compensation: $700 per season.

ROCKY MOUNTAIN VILLAGE—HOME OF THE EASTER SEAL HANDICAMP
2644 Alvarado Rd., Empire, CO 80438

❶ CAMPING (PHYSICAL AND DE-VELOPMENTAL DISABILITIES)
Compensation: Room and board.
Duration: May 15 to August 20.
Contact: Program Director, P.O. Box 115.
Phone: 303-892-6063.
Apply by: April 1.

• ACTIVITY DIRECTOR
Compensation: $1,600 per season.

• COUNSELORS
Compensation: $1,000-$1,200 per season.
Requirements: Minimum age 18.

• MAINTENANCE
Compensation: $1,000-$1,200 per season.
Requirements: Minimum age 16.

VAIL ASSOCIATES, INC.
P.O. Box 7, Vail, CO 81658. World Wide Web: http://www.vail.net

❶ RESORTS
Duration: May 31 to September 1. Spring break, winter break, Christmas break, and year-round positions also available.
Contact: Personnel Office.

Phone: 970-845-2460.

• HOSPITALITY
Compensation: $8 per hour.
• MAINTENANCE
Compensation: $6 per hour.
• LIFT OPERATIONS
Compensation: $ 7.50 - $8 per hour.
• WRANGLERS
Compensation: $7.50 - $8 per hour.

YMCA OF THE ROCKIES—SNOW MOUNTAIN RANCH
P.O. Box 169, Winter Park, CO 80482

❶ RESORTS
Compensation: $100-$110 per week, room and board.
Duration: Summer break, spring break, winter break, Christmas break, and year-round positions available.
Contact: Human Resources Director.
Phone: 303-887-2152.

• LIFEGUARDS
Requirements: Lifeguard certification.
• DAY CAMP COUNSELORS
Requirements: CPR and first aid certification.
• MAINTENANCE PERSONNEL
• FRONT DESK

CONNECTICUT

CAMP WASHINGTON
190 Kenyon Rd., Lakeside, CT 06758

❶ CAMPING
Compensation: Room and board.
Duration: June 25 to August 19.
Contact: Camp Director.
Phone: 860-567-9623.
Apply by: June 1.

• WATERFRONT STAFF
Compensation: $1,300-$1,500 per season.
Requirements: WSI certification, lifeguard training.

• PROGRAMS SPECIALIST
Compensation: $1, 300-$1,500 per season.
Requirements: Teaching ability.

• NURSE
Compensation: $1,500-$3,000 per season.
Requirements: RN license.

• HEAD COUNSELORS
Compensation: $1,800-$2,500 per season.
Requirements: Wilderness challenge and outdoor experience.

CHANNEL 3 COUNTRY CAMP
73 Times Farm Rd., Andover, CT 06232

❶ CAMPING

Compensation: Room and board.
Duration: June 23 to August 23.
Contact: Director.
Phone: 203-742-CAMP.
Apply by: May 15.

• COUNSELORS
Compensation: $1,000-$2,000 per season.
Requirements: Two years of camp experience, college junior or senior.
• CRAFTS
Compensation: $1,100-$2,100 per season.
Requirements: Background in children's crafts, college junior or senior.
• SWIMMING INSTRUCTORS
Compensation: $1,100-$2,100 per season.
Requirements: WSI and ALS certification preferred.
• ATHLETIC INSTRUCTORS
Compensation: $1,100-$2,100 per season.

LAUREL RESIDENT CAMP
175 Clubhouse Rd., Lebanon, CT 06247
❶ CAMPING (GIRLS)
Compensation: Room and board.
Duration: June 21 to August 20. Year-round positions also available.
Contact: Outdoor Program/Property Director, Camping Department, Laurel Resident Camp, 20 Washington Ave., North Haven, CT 06473.
Phone: 203-239-2922.
Apply by: June 10 for summer.

• WATERFRONT
Compensation: $1,500 - $1,900 per season.
Requirements: CPR, first aid, or WSI certification.
• UNIT ASSISTANTS
Compensation: $1,000-$1,200 per season.
Requirements: Camping and child supervision experience.
• HORSEBACK RIDING INSTRUCTORS
Compensation: $750-$1,600 per season.
Requirements: Horsemanship skills.
• BOATING INSTRUCTORS
Compensation: $1,000-$1,300 per season.

UNITED CEREBRAL PALSY ASSOCIATION OF GREATER HARTFORD
301 Great Neck Rd., Waterford, CT 06385
❶ CAMPING (PHYSICAL DISABILITIES)
Compensation: Room and board.

Duration: June 20 to August 20.
Contact: Camp Coordinator, United Cerebral Palsy Assn of Greater Hartford, 80 Whitney St., Hartford, CT 06105.
Phone: 203-236-6201.
Apply by: May 15.

• PROGRAM DIRECTOR
Compensation: $3,000-$5,000 per season.
Requirements: Ability to work with disabled children, directorial experience.
• HEAD COUNSELORS
Compensation: $2,300-$2,700 per season.
Requirements: Experience in caretaking and camp life.
• ACTIVITIES LEADER
Compensation: $2,000-$2,300 per season.
Requirements: Excellent interactional skills.
• GENERAL COUNSELORS
Compensation: $1,825-$2,000.
Requirements: Experience working with disabled children preferred, maturity, eagerness.

DELAWARE

CHESAPEAKE BAY GIRL SCOUT COUNCIL
501 S. College Ave., Newark, DE 19713
❶ CAMPING (GIRLS)
Compensation: Room and board.
Duration: June 20 to August 17.
Contact: Environmental Education Specialist.
Phone: 302-456-7150.
Apply by: May 15.

• LEADERSHIP DEVELOPMENT DIRECTOR
Compensation: $900-$1,400 per season.
Requirements: Bachelor's degree, driver's license, CPR and first aid certification.
• BUSINESS MANAGER
Compensation: $1,300-$1,600 per season.
Requirements: Bachelor's degree, driver's license.
• UNIT LEADERS
Compensation: $1,200-$1,400 per season.
Requirements: Minimum age 21, background in Girl Scouts or camping activities.
• ASSISTANT UNIT LEADERS
Compensation: $900-$1,100 per season.
Requirements: Minimum age 18, CIT or LIT background, group leader course.

DISTRICT OF COLUMBIA

ST. ALBAN'S SUMMER PROGRAMS
Mt. St. Alban, Washington, DC 20016

❶ CAMPING
Duration: June 19 to July 28.
Phone: 202-537-6450.
Apply by: March 15.

• SPORTS COUNSELORS
Compensation: $5.25-$10 per hour.
Requirements: Excellent athletic skills.
• DAY CAMP COUNSELORS
Compensation: $1,000-$2,000 per season.

FLORIDA

ACTIONQUEST PROGRAMS
P.O. Box 5507, Sarasota, FL 34277.
World Wide Web:
http://www.actionguest.com.
❶ CAMPING (ADVENTURE)
Compensation: Room and board.
Duration: June 15 to August 25.
Contact: Director.
Phone: 941-924-2115.

• USCG SAILING TEACHERS OR BRIT-
ISH YACHTMASTERS
Compensation: $3,000 per season.
Requirements: Appropriate certification.
• DIVING INSTRUCTORS
Requirements: Appropriate license and certi-
fication.
Compensation: $2,200 per season.
• WINDSURFING INSTRUCTORS
Requirements: Appropriate certification.
Compensation: $1,000 per season.

CAMP BLUE RIDGE
P.O. Box 2888, Miami, FL 33104
❶ CAMPING
Compensation: Room and board.
Duration: June 22 to August16 .
Contact: Personnel.
Phone: 305-538-3434.

• ARTS AND CRAFTS INSTRUCTOR
Compensation: $1,000-$1,200 per season.
• ATHLETICS INSTRUCTORS
Compensation: $1,000-$1,200 per season.
• DANCE AND DRAMA INSTRUCTORS
Compensation: $1,000-$1,200 per season.
• WATERFRONT SPECIALISTS: Will work
as a swimming, boating and/or water-skiing
instructor.
Compensation: $1,000-$1,500 per season.

CAMP UNIVERSE
Lake Miona, Wildwood, FL 34785
❶ CAMPING
Compensation: $600-$1,800 per season,
room and board.

Duration: June 11 to August 23.
Contact: Director, Camp Universe, 5875
SW 129 Terrace, Miami, FL 33156.
Phone: 305-666-4500.
Apply by: March 15 .

• COUNSELORS: Will work in specialized
areas including soccer, canoeing, arts and
crafts, archery, and riflery.
Requirements: Experience in skill area.
• GUITARISTS/SINGERS
Requirements: Ability to lead groups in a va-
riety of songs.
• DRAMA STAFF
• CIRCUS STAFF

CORKSCREW SWAMP SANCTUARY
375 Sanctuary Rd., Naples, FL 34120
❶ PARKS

• NATURALISTS: Will work on projects
pertaining to resource management and en-
vironmental education.
Compensation: $100 per week.
Duration: May 15 toSeptember 1. Year-round
positions also available.
Requirements: Background in specified areas.
Contact:: Assistant Manager.
Phone: 813-657-3771.
Apply by: March 15 for summer.

SEA WORLD OF FLORIDA
7007 Sea World Dr., Orlando, FL 32821
❶ THEME PARKS
Compensation: $5 per hour.
Duration: May 1 to September 1.
Contact: Human Resources Department,
Department SJ.
Phone: 407-351-3600.

• FOOD SERVICES
• OPERATIONS/CROWD MANAGEMENT
• LANDSCAPE PERSONNEL
Requirements: Background in planting,
draining, and irrigation helpful.
• TOUR GUIDES
Requirements: Good presentation skills.

GEORGIA

CAMP WOODMONT FOR BOYS AND GIRLS ON LOOKOUT MOUNTAIN
1339 Yankee Rd., Cloudland, GA 30731
❶ CAMPING
• COUNSELORS
Compensation: $400-$700 per season, room
and board.
Duration: June 15 to August 15.

Requirements: CPR and first aid certification.

Contact: Camp Directors, Department SJ, 2339 Welton Pl., Dunwoody, GA 30338.

Phone: 404-457-0862.

Apply by: May 1.

HAWAII
CAMP MOKULEIA
68-729 Farrington Highway, Waialua, HI 96791

❶ CAMPING

Compensation: $700-$1,000 per season, room and board.

Duration: June 29 to August17 .

Contact: S.C. Programs Department.

Phone: 808-637-6241.

Apply by: March 1.

• WATERFRONT DIRECTOR
Requirements: WSI, lifeguard, CPR, and first aid certification.

• SPORTS DIRECTOR
Requirements: CPR and first aid certification, outdoors experience, coursework in recreation.

• COUNSELORS
Requirements: CPR and first aid certification.

IDAHO
HIDDEN CREEK RANCH
7600 E. Blue Lake Rd., Harrison, ID 83833

❶ CAMPING

Compensation: Room and board.

Duration: April 1 to October 31.

Requirements: CPR and first aid certification.

Contact: Owner.

Phone: 208-689-3209.

Apply by: April30.

• WRANGLERS
Compensation: $500-$700 per month.
Requirements: Good horsemanship skills.

• HOUSEKEEPING/WAITSTAFF
Compensation: $400-$500 per month.

• GUIDE/MAINTENANCE STAFF
Compensation: $500-$700 per month.
Requirements: Background in outdoor boating and/or recreation.

• CHILDREN'S COUNSELORS

Compensation: $500-$700 per month.
Requirements: Camping experience.
MYSTIC SADDLE RANCH
State Highway 75, Stanley, ID 83278

❶ CAMPING

Compensation: $1,200-$1,800 per month.

Duration: June 1 to November 15. Year-round positions also available.

Requirements: Minimum age 18, no fish and game violations.

Contact: Owner.

Phone: 208-774-3591.

• TRAIL RIDE GUIDES
• HORSE PACKERS
• CORRAL MANAGER
REDFISH LAKE LODGE
Box 9, Stanley, ID 83278

❶ LODGING

Compensation: $682 - $900 per month, room and board.

Duration: May 1 to October 5.

Contact: Manager.

Phone: 208-774-3536.

Apply by: May 15.

• WAITSTAFF
• MARINA STAFF
• STORE STAFF
• MAINTENANCE

ILLINOIS
CAMP CEDAR POINT
1327 Camp Cedar Point Ln., Makanda, IL 62958

❶ CAMPING (GIRLS)

Compensation: Room and board.

Duration: June 3 to August 6.

Contact: Shagbark Girl Scout Council, Camp Cedar Point, Department SJ, P.O. Box 549, Herrin, IL 62984.

Phone: 618-942-3164.

Apply by: May 1.

• WATERFRONT DIRECTOR
Compensation: $195-$230 per week.
Requirements: Minimum age 21, WSI and lifeguard certification.

• UNIT LEADERS
Compensation: $170-$185 per week.
Requirements: Camping experience preferred.

• ENVIRONMENTALIST
Compensation: $155-$180 per week.

Requirements: Minimum age 18, some background in nature studies preferred.

• ARTS AND CRAFTS
Compensation: $155-$180 per week.
Requirements: Some background in arts and crafts preferred.

PEACOCK CAMP
38685 N. Deep Lake Rd., Lake Villa, IL 60046

❶ CAMPING (PHYSICAL DISABILITIES)
Compensation: $1,425 per season, room and board.
Duration: June 10 to August 15.
Contact: Camp Directors.
Phone: 847-356-5201.

• COUNSELORS/WATERFRONT STAFF
Requirements: Lifeguard experience preferred.

• COUNSELORS/ARTS AND CRAFTS
• COUNSELORS/RECREATION

THE ROAD LESS TRAVELED
2053 N. Magnolia Ave., Chicago, IL 60614

❶ CAMPING
Compensation: Pay varies, room and board.
Duration: June 15 to August 30.
Requirements: Lifeguard certification and wilderness experience. First Responder certification. Must be 21 or older.
Contact: Director.
Phone: 773-348-4100.
Apply by: April 1.

• TRIP LEADERS

I N D I A N A

HAPPY HOLLOW children's camp, inc.
3049 Happy Hollow Rd., Nashville, IN 47448

❶ CAMPING (DIABETES AND ASTHMA)
Compensation: Room and board.
Duration: June 1 to August 9.
Contact: Director.
Phone: 812-988-4900.
Apply by: April 1.

• GENERAL COUNSELORS
Compensation: $130-$175 per week.
• PROGRAM INSTRUCTORS

Compensation: $130-$175 per week.
Requirements: Certification in related area.

CULVER SUMMER CAMPS
Box 138 CEF, Culver, IN 46511

❶ CAMPING
Compensation: $1,200-$1,500 per season, room and board.
Duration: June 20 to August 15.
Contact: Director.
Phone: 800-221-2020.
Apply by: December 15.

• AQUATICS INSTRUCTORS
Requirements: WSI and lifeguard certification.

• COUNSELORS
Requirements: Completed at least one year of college, experience with children.

• TENNIS INSTRUCTORS
• MUSIC INSTRUCTORS

HOWE MILITARY SCHOOL SUMMER CAMP
P.O. Box 240, Howe, IN 46746

❶ CAMPING (MILITARY)
Compensation: $1,400-$2,600 per season, room and board.
Duration: June 22 to August 7.
Contact: Camp Director.
Phone: 219-562-2131.
Apply by: May 15.

• WATERFRONT STAFF
Requirements: WSI and lifeguard certification.

• MATH INSTRUCTORS
• ENGLISH INSTRUCTORS
• HIGH ROPES COURSE INSTRUCTORS

I O W A

CAMP COURAGEOUS OF IOWA
12007 190th St., P.O. Box 418, Monticello, IA 52310-0418

❶ CAMPING (DISABILITIES)
Compensation: $550-$900 per month, room and board.
Duration: May 18 to August 15.
Contact: Camp Director.
Phone: 319-465-5916.
Apply by: May 15.

• COUNSELORS
Requirements: Strong interest in working with people with disabilities.
• CANOEING SPECIALIST
Requirements: Lifeguard certification.
• NATURE SPECIALISTS

Requirements: Good presentation skills, experience working with small animals.

• RECREATION SPECIALIST
Requirements: Experience working with people with disabilities.

CAMP HANTESA
1450 Oriole Rd., Boone, IA 50036

❶ CAMPING
Compensation: $1,200 per season, room and board.

Duration: June 1 to August 20.

Contact: Director.

Phone: 515-432-1417.

• COUNSELORS
Requirements: Interest in working with children.

• SWIMMING INSTRUCTOR
Requirements: WSI certification.

• UNIT DIRECTORS
Requirements: Good management skills.

• RIDING INSTRUCTORS
Requirements: Good horsemanship skills, English or Western riding experience.

CAMP HITAGA
5551 Hitaga Rd., Walker, IA 52352

❶ CAMPING
Compensation: Room and board.

Duration: June 10 to August 15.

Contact: Camp Director, Camp Hitaga, Department SJ, 226 29th St. Dr., SE, Suite E-2, Cedar Rapids, IA 52403.

Phone: 319-362-8268.

Apply by: April 15.

• RIDING STAFF HEADS
Compensation: $1,000-$1,250.
Requirements: Background in horsemanship.

• AQUATIC STAFF HEADS
Compensation: $1,000-$1,250.
Requirements: Appropriate certification.

• HEALTH AIDE
Compensation: $1,000-$1,200.

• ASSISTANT DIRECTOR
Compensation: $1,200-$1,500 per season.

KANSAS
FORT LARNED NATIONAL HISTORIC SITE
Rte. 3, Lawrence, KS 67550

❶ PARKS
Compensation: Paid.

Duration: Summer break.

Phone: 402-221-3456

• HISTORIAN: Will work as a researcher and reporter.
Requirements: U.S. citizenship, bachelor's degree, graduate degree preferred. Must submit personal qualification statement, letter of recommendation, and paper demonstrating primary research abilities.
Contact: Summer Program Administrator, HABS/HAER Division, National Park Service, P.O. Box 37127, Washington, DC 20013.

• RANGERS: Will provide visitor services and perform park upkeep.
Contact: National Park Service, 1709 Jackson St., Omaha, NE 68102.

KENTUCKY
CAMP WOODMEN OF THE WORLD
93 Schwartz Rd., Murray, KY 42071

❶ CAMPING
Compensation: $700-$1,100 per season, room and board.

Duration: June 1 to August 8.

Contact: Camp Director, Camp Woodmen of the World, 401 A Maple St., Murray, KY 42071.

Phone: 502-753-4382.

Apply by: May 1.

• ARCHERY INSTRUCTOR
Requirements: Appropriate experience or certification.

• ARTS AND CRAFTS INSTRUCTOR
Requirements: Experience.

• RIFLE INSTRUCTOR
Requirements: NRA certification or experience.

• AQUATICS MANAGER
Requirements: WSI certification.

LIFE ADVENTURE CAMP
Estill County, KY 40336

❶ CAMPING (BEHAVIORAL DISABILITIES)
Compensation: Room and board.

Duration: May 9 to August 20.

Contact: Program Director, Life Adventure Camp, Department SJ, 1122 Oak Hill Dr., Lexington, KY 40505.

Phone: 606-252-4733.

Apply by: May 1.

• COUNSELORS: Will work with emotionally or behaviorally challenged youth in need of enhanced self-esteem and cooperation skills.
Compensation: $1,000-$1,300 per season.

Requirements: CPR and first aid certification, college and leadership camping experience.

• FOOD DIRECTOR
Compensation: $900-$1,000 per season.
Requirements: Driver's license, background in food management.

• HEALTH SUPERVISOR
Compensation: $1,200-$1,400 per season.
Requirements: CPR and first aid experience.

LOUISIANA

CAMP FIRE CAMP WI-TA-WENTIN
2126 Oak Park Blvd., Lake Charles, LA 70601

❶ CAMPING
Compensation: Room and board.
Duration: June 1 to July 15.
Contact: Executive Director.
Phone: 318-478-6550.
Apply by: May 1.

• LIFEGUARDS
Compensation: $600-$675 per season.

• GENERAL COUNSELORS
Compensation: $700-$800 per season.

• CANOE INSTRUCTOR
Compensation: $700-$800 per season.

• WATER SAFETY INSTRUCTOR
Compensation: $900 per season.

MARYDALE RESIDENT CAMP
10317 Marydale Rd., St. Francisville, LA 70775

❶ CAMPING (GIRLS)
Compensation: Room and board.
Duration: May 31 to July 27.
Contact: Program Director, Marydale Resident Camp, Department SJ,545 Colonial Dr., Baton Rouge, LA 70806.
Phone: 800-852-8421.
Apply by: May 1.

• UNIT LEADERS
Compensation: $115-$125 per week.
Requirements: Minimum age 21, camp and leadership experience.

• COUNSELORS
Compensation: $100-$112 per week.
Requirements: Minimum age 18.

• AQUATICS STAFF
Compensation: $100-$125 per week.
Requirements: Red Cross and WSI certification.

• RIDING STAFF

Compensation: $100-$125 per week.
Requirements: CHA certification or experience.

MAINE

ACADIA CORPORATION
85 Main St., Box 24, Bar Harbor, ME 04609

❶ PARKS
Compensation: Starts at $7.00 per hour except waitstaff which starts at $2.58 per hour plus tips.
Duration: May 15 to October 31.
Contact: Personnel.
Phone: 207-288-5592.

• KITCHEN WORKERS
• HOSTS
• GUEST RELATIONS
• MAINTENANCE
• RETAIL
• RESTAURANT
• BARTENDER
• WAITSTAFF
• LEAD COOK
• CASHIER

CAMP ENCORE-CODA FOR A GREAT SUMMER OF MUSIC, SPORTS, AND FRIENDS
Stearns Pond, Sweden, ME 04040

❶ CAMPING (MUSIC)
Compensation: Room and board.
Duration: June 20 to August 17.
Contact: Director, Camp Encore-Coda for a Great Summer of Music, Sports, and Friends, 32 Grassmere Rd., Brookline, MA 02167.
Phone: 617-325-1541.

• WATERFRONT DIRECTOR
Compensation: $2,000-$2,500 per season.
Requirements: WSI or lifeguard certification.

• ARTS AND CRAFTS LEADER
Compensation: $500-$1,000 per season.

• HEAD COUNSELOR
Compensation: $2,000-$3,000 per season.
Requirements: Leadership, camp, and organizational experience.

• TENNIS COUNSELOR
Compensation: $600-$1,200 per season.

CAMP NASHOBA NORTH
Raymond Hill Rd., Raymond, ME 04071.World Wide Web:
http://www.campnashoba.com

❶ CAMPING
Compensation: $1,000-$1,700 per season, room and board.
Duration: June 15 to August16.
Contact: Director, Camp Nashoba North, 140 Nashoba Rd., Littleton, MA 01460.
*Phone:*508-486-8236.
Apply by: June 1.

• WINDSURFING INSTRUCTORS
Requirements: Appropriate certification.
• RIDING INSTRUCTORS
Requirements: Pony club, show, or event experience.
• THEATER INSTRUCTORS
• TRIP INSTRUCTORS

CAMP TAPAWINGO
Rte. 93, Sweden, ME 04040
❶ CAMPING (GIRLS)
Compensation: $900-$1,100 per season, room and board.
Duration: June 21 to August21.
Contact: Assistant Director, Camp Tapawingo, Department SJ, P.O. Box 1353, Scarborough, ME 04070.
Phone: 207-885-0799.

• WATERSKIING INSTRUCTORS
Requirements: Lifeguard certification, instructor rating.
• SWIMMING INSTRUCTORS
Requirements: WSI and lifeguard certification.
• TRIP LEADERS
Requirements: Minimum age 21, CPR, first aid, and lifeguard certification.
• GYMNASTICS INSTRUCTORS

CAMP WINNEBAGO
Rte. 17, RR2, Box 1400, Kents Hill, ME 04349
❶ CAMPING (BOYS)
Compensation: $1,100-$2,000 per season, room and board.
Duration: June 21 to August 20.
Contact: Director, Camp Winnebago, 1606 Washington Plaza, Reston, VA 20190.
Phone: 703-437-0808.

• ATHLETICS INSTRUCTORS
• ARTS AND CRAFTS INSTRUCTORS
• NEWSPAPER INSTRUCTOR
• VIDEOGRAPHY INSTRUCTOR

NEW ENGLAND CAMPING ADVENTURES
Panther Pond, P.O. Box 160, Raymond, ME 04071
❶ CAMPING (ADVENTURE)
Compensation: $1,100-$1,400 per season, room and board.
Duration: June 25 to August 18.
Contact: Owner, New England Camping Adventures, 10 Scotland Bridge Rd., York, ME 03909.
Phone: 207-363-1773.
Apply by: May 1.

• CANOE EXPEDITION LEADERS
• BACKPACKING LEADERS
• ROCK CLIMBING LEADERS
• SAILING INSTRUCTORS

MARYLAND

CAMPS AIRY AND LOUISE
5750 Park Heights Ave., Baltimore, MD 21215. World Wide Web: http://www.airylouise.org
❶ CAMPING
Compensation: Room and board.
Duration: June 13 to August 14.
Contact: Executive Director.
Phone: 410-466-9010.

• COUNSELORS
Compensation: $850-$1,300 per season.
• OUTDOOR LIVING INSTRUCTORS
Compensation: $1,000-$1,600 per season.
• SPECIALISTS
• ADMINISTRATIVE POSITIONS

THE INSTITUTE FOR THE ACADEMIC ADVANCEMENT OF YOUTH—THE JOHNS HOPKINS UNIVERSITY
34th and Charles Sts., Baltimore, MD 21218
❶ CAMPING (ACADEMIC)
Compensation: Room and board.
Duration: June 20 to August 7.
Contact: Assistant Coordinator, CTY/JHU, 3400 N. Charles St., Johns Hopkins University, Baltimore, MD 21218.
Phone: 410-516-0053.
Apply by: January 31.

• SITE DIRECTORS
Compensation: $6,600 per season.
Requirements: Teaching experience, master's degree preferred, administrative background.

- INSTRUCTORS
Compensation: $1,500-$2,000 per season.
Requirements: Bachelor's degree, master's degree preferred, leadership and teaching skills.
- TEACHING/LAB ASSISTANTS
Compensation: $775 per season.
Requirements: 3.2 GPA, experience with youth.
- RESIDENT ADVISERS
Compensation: $875 per season.
Requirements: Experience as a counselor or RA, 3.2 GPA, good planning skills.

YMCA CAMP LETTS
4003 Camp Letts Rd., P.O. Box 208, Edgewater, MD 21037

O CAMPING
Compensation: Room and board.
Duration: June 17 to August 17.
Contact: Executive Director.
Phone: 301-261-4286.

- CREW SKIPPERS
Compensation: $1,800-$2,100 per season.
Requirements: Minimum age 21.
- COUNSELORS
Compensation: $1,400-$1,800 per season.
Requirements: Minimum age 19, completed one year of college.
- PHOTOGRAPHER/EDITOR
Compensation: $1,400-$1,800 per season.
Requirements: Background in editing.
- LAND ACTIVITIES DIRECTOR
Compensation: $1,800-$2,300 per season.
Requirements: Upperclass or graduate status, CPR and first aid certification.

MASSACHUSETTS

CAMP EMERSON
212 Longview Ave., Hinsdale, MA 01235

O CAMPING
Compensation: $1,300 per season, room and board.
Duration: June 15 to August 22.
Contact: Camp Director, Camp Emerson, 78 Deerfield Rd., Sharon, MA 02067.
Phone: 800-782-3395.
Apply by: June 1.

- CREATIVE ARTS INSTRUCTORS
Requirements: Experience in the applied arts, crafts, media, computers, and/or woodworking.
- PERFORMING ARTS INSTRUCTORS
Requirements: Background in theater or musical arts.
- LAND SPORTS INSTRUCTORS
Requirements: Background in recreational and sports activities.
- WILDERNESS INSTRUCTORS
Requirements: Background in outdoor living and recreational activities.

CAPE COD SEA CAMPS
P.O. Box 1880, Brewster, MA 02631.
World Wide Web:
http://www.kidscamps.com

O CAMPING
Compensation: Room and board.
Duration: June 20 to August 16.
Contact: Associate Director.
Phone: 508-896-3451.
Apply by: April 15.

- ACTIVITIES DEPARTMENT
Compensation: $1,900-$2,500 per season.
Requirements: Teaching certification.
- GENERAL COUNSELORS
Compensation: $1,000-$1,500 per season.
Requirements: Camp experience.
- SAILING STAFF
Compensation: $1,100-$ 2,000 per season.
Requirements: Instruction and racing experience.
- SWIMMING INSTRUCTORS
Compensation: $1,000-$1,600 per season.
Requirements: WSI certification.

COLLEGE LIGHT OPERA COMPANY
Highfield Theatre, P.O. Drawer F, Falmouth, MA 02541

O THEATER ARTS (SUMMER STOCK)
Compensation: Room and board.
Duration: June 9 to August 29.
Contact: Producer, College Light Opera Company, 162 S. Cedar St., Oberlin, OH 44074.
Phone: 216-774-8485.
Apply by: March 15.

- VOCALISTS
Compensation: No pay.
- ORCHESTRA STAFF
Compensation: $500 per season.
- COSTUME CREW
Compensation: $500 per season.
- CHORUS MASTERS
Compensation: $900 per season.
Requirements: Experience.

SUMMER THEATER AT MOUNT HOLYOKE COLLEGE
South Hadley, MA 01075

❶ THEATER ARTS (SUMMER STOCK)

Compensation: Room and board.

Duration: May 30 to August 25.

Contact: Producing Director.

Phone: 413-538-2632.

Apply by: March 1.

• ACTORS (NON-EQUITY)
Compensation: $200 per season.

• CARPENTERS
Compensation: $750-$1,000 per season.

• PROP ARTISANS
Compensation: $750-$1,000 per season.

• TECHNICAL DIRECTOR
Compensation: $1,200-$1,800 per season.

WILLIAMSTOWN THEATER FESTIVAL
P.O. Box 517, Williamstown, MA 01267

❶ THEATER ARTS (SUMMER STOCK)

Compensation: Varies.

Duration: June 2 to August 31.

Contact: Company Manager, Williamstown Theater Festival, 100 E. 17th St., 3rd Fl., New York, NY 10003.

Phone: 212-228-2286.

• STAFF
• APPRENTICES
• EQUITY ACTORS
• NON-EQUITY ACTORS
• INTERNS

MICHIGAN

AMERICAN YOUTH FOUNDATION—CAMP MINIWANCA
8845 W. Garfield, Rd., Shelby, MI 49455. World Wide Web: http://www.ayf.com

❶ CAMPING

Compensation: Room and board.

Duration: June 1 to August 31.

Contact: Site Director.

Phone: 616-861-2262.

Apply by: April 1.

• TEAM LEADERS
Compensation: $125-$220 per week.
Requirements: College student or teacher.

• KITCHEN STAFF
Compensation: $125-$175 per week.
Requirements: High school student or retiree.

• CAMP UPKEEP
Compensation: $125-$175 per week.
Requirements: High school student or retiree.

• FACILITY MAINTENANCE
Compensation: $125-$175 per week.
Requirements: High school student or retiree.

BAY CLIFF HEALTH CAMP
Big Bay, MI 49808

❶ CAMPING (SPECIAL NEEDS)

Compensation: Room and board.

Duration: June 14 to August 9.

Contact: Camp Director, Bay Cliff Health Camp, 310 W. Washington St., Suite 300, Marquette, MI 49855.

Phone: 906-228-5770.

Apply by: May 15.

• UNIT LEADERS
Compensation: $2,000 per season.
Requirements: Teaching experience, special education degree preferred.

• COUNSELORS
Compensation: $1,300 per season.
Requirements: Minimum age 18, completed one year of college.

• ROVING COUNSELORS
Compensation: $1,300 per season.
Requirements: Minimum age 18, completed one year of college.

• PHYSICAL THERAPISTS
Compensation: $2,500 per season.
Requirements: Appropriate certification.

BLUE LAKE FINE ARTS CAMP
300 E. Crystal Lake Blvd., Twin Lake, MI 49457

❶ CAMPING (ARTS)

Compensation: Room and board.

Duration: June 1 to August 30.

Contact: Staff Director.

Phone: 616-894-1966.

Apply by: June 15.

• COUNSELORS
Compensation: $850-$1,300 per season.
Requirements: Minimum age 18, completed one year of college, interest in the fine arts.

• HEALTH STAFF
Compensation: $1,000-$2,000 per season.
Requirements: Response to Emergencies certification.

• WATERFRONT DIRECTOR
Compensation: $2,000-$3,000 per season.
Requirements: WSI or lifeguard certification.

- MUSIC LIBRARY STAFF
Compensation: $5 per hour.
Requirements: Clerical skills, knowledge of music.

CIRCLE PINES CENTER SUMMER CAMP
8650 Mullen Rd., Delton, MI 49046.
World Wide Web:
http://www.circlepinescenter.org

❶ CAMPING
Compensation: $600-$1,000 per season, room and board.

Duration: June 16 to August 18.

Contact: Camp Director.

Phone: 616-623-5555.

Apply by: April 15.

- WATERFRONT DIRECTOR
Requirements: WSI, CPR, and lifeguard certification, minimum age 21.

- COUNSELORS
Requirements: Leadership and child supervision skills.

- COOKS
Requirements: Whole foods and large servings experience.

- DRAMA LEADER
Requirements: Children's theater experience.

LAKE OF THE WOODS AND GREENWOODS CAMPS
Decatur, MI 49045

❶ CAMPING
Compensation: $1,200 per season, room and board.

Duration: June 16 to August 19.

Contact: Owner/Director, Lake of the Woods and Greenwoods Camps, 1765 Maple St., Northfield, IL 60093.

Phone: 847-446-2444.

Apply by: June 15.

- SWIMMING INSTRUCTORS
Requirements: WSI and lifeguard certification.

- MODEL ROCKETRY INSTRUCTOR
Requirements: Minimum age 19.

- ARTS AND CRAFTS INSTRUCTORS

- SPORTS COACHES

MINNESOTA

CAMP BUCKSKIN
Box 389, Ely, MN 55731

❶ CAMPING (LEARNING DISABILITIES)

Compensation: Room and board.

Duration: June 3 to August 22.

Contact: Director, Camp Buckskin, 8700 W. 36th St., Suite 6W, St. Louis Park, MN 55426.

Phone: 612-930-3544.

Apply by: May 30.

- COUNSELORS/CANOEING INSTRUCTORS
Compensation: $1,200-$1,700 per season.
Requirements: CPR, first aid, and lifeguard certification.

- COUNSELORS/NATURE EDUCATORS
Compensation: $1,200-$1,700 per season.
Requirements: Nature course certification preferred.

- COUNSELORS/ARTS AND CRAFTS INSTRUCTORS
Compensation: $1,200-$1,700 per season.
Requirements: Creativity, enthusiasm.

- READING TEACHERS
Compensation: $1,500-$2,000 per season.
Requirements: Teaching experience, special education certification preferred.

DEEP PORTAGE CONSERVATION RESERVE
Rte. 1, Box 129, Hackensack, MN 56452

❶ CAMPING (ENVIRONMENTAL)

- INSTRUCTORS/NATURALISTS
Compensation: $125-$150 per week.
Duration: June 5 to August 25.
Requirements: College coursework in nature studies or Camp Director.
Phone: 218-682-2325.

FRIENDSHIP VENTURES/CAMP FRIENDSHIP
10509 108th St., NW, Annandale, MN 55302

❶ CAMPING (DEVELOPMENTAL DISABILITIES)
Compensation: $120-$155 per week, room and board.

Duration: June 1 to August 31.

Contact: Human Resources Director.

Phone: 612-274-8736.

Apply by: May 1.

- COUNSELORS

- WATERFRONT SPECIALISTS
Requirements: WSI and lifeguard certification.

- TRAVEL LEADERS
Requirements: Driver's license, excellent leadership skills.

- MUSIC SPECIALISTS
Requirements: Music, music therapy, or special education major.

STRAW HAT PLAYERS—CENTER FOR THE PERFORMING ARTS
Moorhead State University, Moorhead, MN 56563

❶ THEATER ARTS (SUMMER STOCK)
Compensation: Room and board.
Duration: May 27 to July 26.
Contact: Director of Theater
Phone: 218-236-4613.
Apply by: January 2.

- ACTING
Compensation: $75-$200 per week.
- THEATER TECHNICIANS
Compensation: $100-$300 per week.
- CHOREOGRAPHER
Compensation: $150-$200 per week.
Requirements: MFA or professional background.
- PROP MASTER
Compensation: $150-$200 per week.

VALLEYFAIR FAMILY AMUSEMENT PARK
1 Valleyfair Dr., Shakopee, MN 55379

❶ AMUSEMENT PARKS
Compensation: $2,500-$3,500 per season.
Duration: May 1 to September 30.
Contact: Human Resources Manager.
Phone: 612-445-7600.

- RIDE ATTENDANTS
- FOOD HOSTS/HOSTESSES
- RETAIL CLERKS
- GAME ATTENDANTS

M O N T A N A

BIG SKY RESORT
P.O. Box 160001, Big Sky, MT 59716

❶ RESORTS
Compensation: $6-7 per hour.
Duration: June 2 to October 15.
Contact: Human Resources.
Phone: 406-995-5820.
Apply by: May 1.

- HOUSEKEEPERS
- FOOD AND BEVERAGE POSITIONS
- ACCOUNTANTS
- GOLF COURSE MAINTENANCE

- LIFT OPERATERS
HAMILTON STORES, INC.
P.O. Box 250, West Yellowstone, MT 59758

❶ RETAIL
Compensation: $4. 75-$6.75 per hour, room and board.
Duration: March 15 to October 15.
Contact: Human Resources Department, Hamilton Stores, Inc., 1709 W. College, Bozeman, MT 59715.
Phone: 406-587-2208.
Apply by: August 1.

- SALES CLERKS
- GROCERY CLERKS
- KITCHEN CLERKS
- DORMITORY MANAGERS

N E B R A S K A

CALVIN CREST CAMP, RETREAT, AND CONFERENCE CENTER
RR 2, Box 226, Fremont, NE 68025

❶ CAMPING (RELIGIOUS)
Compensation: $130-$150 per week, room and board.
Duration: May 15 to August 15.
Contact: Administrator.
Phone: 402-628-6455.
Apply by: April 15.

- SWIMMING INSTRUCTORS
Requirements: WSI certification.
- FOOD SERVICE
- HOUSEKEEPING

N E V A D A

LAKE MEAD NATIONAL RECREATION AREA
601 Nevada Highway, Boulder City, NV 89005

❶ PARKS
Compensation: Paid.
Duration: Summer break.
Requirements: U.S. citizen.
Phone: 702-298-8713.
Apply by: April 1.

- RECREATION ASSISTANT: Will work at waterfront areas.
Requirements: Minimum age 18, aquatics supervisory experience.
- LABORER: Will work on trail maintenance and general area upkeep.

- SKILLED TRADES AND CRAFTS: Will work as a carpenter, mechanic, axman, or in other positions.
- PARK RANGER: Will provide visitor services and perform park upkeep tasks.

NEW HAMPSHIRE

BROOKWOODS FOR BOYS/DEER RUN FOR GIRLS

Chestnut Grove Rd., Alton, NH 03809.
World Wide Web:
http://www.brookwoods.org

❶ CAMPING (RELIGIOUS)
Compensation: $1,000-$1,200 per season, room and board.
Duration: June 15 to August 22. Spring break and winter break positions also available.
Contact: Executive Director.
Phone: 603-875-3600.
Apply by: May 1 for summer.

- TRIP STAFF
Requirements: CPR and first aid certification.
- RIDING INSTRUCTORS
Requirements: Minimum age 21, CHA certification.
- RIFLE INSTRUCTOR
Requirements: NRA certification.
- WATER-SKIING INSTRUCTOR
Requirements: Lifeguard certification.

CAMP MERROWVISTA

147 Canaan Rd., Ossipee, NH 03864

❶ CAMPING
Compensation: Room and board.
Duration: June 15 to August 24.
Contact: Program Director.
Phone: 603-539-6607.
Apply by: May 15.

- VILLAGE LEADERS
Compensation: $125-$190 per week.
Requirements: WSI and lifeguard certification, CPR and first aid preferred.
- TRIP LEADERS
Compensation: $160-$215 per week.
Requirements: WSI and lifeguard certification, tour leading experience, CPR preferred.
- WATERFRONT STAFF
Compensation: $800-$2,000 per season.
Requirements: WSI and lifeguard certification.
- SAILING INSTRUCTOR
Compensation: $800-$1,000 per season.
Requirements: Laser I and Laser II experience, lifeguard certification.

CAMP ROBIN HOOD FOR BOYS AND GIRLS

Freedom, NH 03836

❶ CAMPING
Compensation: Room and board.
Duration: June 20 to August 20.
Contact: Director, Camp Robin Hood for Boys and Girls, 344 Thistle Trail, Mayfield Heights, OH 44124.
Phone: 216-646-1911.
Apply by: May 1.

- GENERAL COUNSELORS
Compensation: $600-$800 per season.
- SPORTS COACHES
Compensation: $800-$1,500 per season.
- RIDING INSTRUCTORS
Compensation: $800-$1,500 per season.
Requirements: English riding and teaching experience.
- SAILING AND CANOEING INSTRUCTORS
Compensation: $700-$1,200 per season.
Requirements: Teaching experience.

INTERLOCKEN INTERNATIONAL SUMMER CAMP

RR 2, Box 165, Hillsboro, NH 03244.
World Wide Web:
http://www.interlocken.org

❶ CAMPING
Compensation: $1,100-$1,600 per season, room and board.
Duration: June 15 to August 20.
Contact: Staffing Coordinator.
Phone: 603-478-3166.
Apply by: March 1.

- SPORTS LEADERS
- WILDERNESS LEADERS
- PERFORMING ARTS INSTRUCTORS
- MUSIC INSTRUCTORS

STUDENT CONSERVATION ASSOCIATION

P.O. Box 550, Charlestown, NH 03603

❶ ENVIRONMENT
Compensation: $50 per week, room and board.
Duration: May 1 to September 1. Year-round positions also available.
Contact: Recruitment Director.
Phone: 603-543-1700.

- RESOURCE ASSISTANTS
Requirements: Minimum age 18, high school graduate.
- TRAIL CREW MEMBERS
Requirements: Age 16-18.

NEW JERSEY

APPEL FARM ARTS AND MUSIC CENTER
P.O. Box 888, Elmer, NJ 08318

❶ CAMPING (ARTS/MUSIC)

Compensation: $1,100-$1,500 per season, room and board.

Duration: June 15 to August 18.

Requirements: Minimum age 22.

Contact: Camp Director.

Phone: 609-358-2472.

• MUSIC INSTRUCTORS
Requirements: Proficient in rock, woodwinds, piano, strings, percussion, or voice.

• PHOTOGRAPHY INTERNS
Requirements: Good photography and darkroom skills.

• THEATER INSTRUCTORS
Requirements: Production and directing experience.

• ART INSTRUCTORS
Requirements: Experience in painting, sculpting, weaving, film animating, or ceramics.

COLLEGE GIFTED PROGRAMS
120 Littleton Rd., Suite 201, Parsippany, NJ 07054

❶ CAMPING

Compensation: Pay varies, room and board.

Duration: June 25 to August 22.

Contact: Executive Director.

Phone: 201-334-6991.

Apply by: April 30.

• COUNSELORS

• HOUSEMASTERS/INSTRUCTORS

• INSTRUCTORS

FAIRVIEW LAKE ENVIRONMENTAL TRIP
1035 Fairview Lake Rd., Newton, NJ 07860

❶ CAMPING

Duration: June 15 to August 20.

Requirements: CPR, first aid, and lifeguard certification.

Phone: 973-383-9282.

Apply by: March 1.

• TRIP LEADERS
Compensation: $200-$250 per week.

• TRIP COUNSELORS
Compensation: $180-$200 per week.

NEW JERSEY 4-H CAMPS
50 Nielson Rd., Sussex, NJ 07461

❶ CAMPING

Compensation: $180-$230 per week, room and board.

Duration: June 27 to August 20.

Requirements: Minimum age 18.

Contact: Director.

Phone: 201-875-4715.

Apply by: June 15.

• LIFEGUARDS
Requirements: Appropriate certification.

• BOATING/CANOEING INSTRUCTORS
Requirements: Appropriate certification.

• NATURE INSTRUCTORS

• FISHING INSTRUCTORS

NEW JERSEY SUMMER ARTS INSTITUTE
Ewing, NJ 08648

❶ CAMPING (ARTS)

Compensation: Room and board.

Duration: June 27 to August 6.

Contact: Executive Director, NJSA, 100 Jersey Ave., Suite B-104, New Brunswick, NJ 08901.

Phone: 908-220-1600.

• RESIDENCE SUPERVISORS
Compensation: $1,500-$1,800 per season.
Requirements: Master's degree, preferably in the arts.

• RESIDENCE ADVISERS
Compensation: $900-$1,200 per season.
Requirements: Completed sophomore year of college.

• TEACHING ASSISTANTS
Compensation: $1,000-$1,200 per season.
Requirements: Completed sophomore year of college.

• SOCIAL WORKER
Compensation: $2,500-$3,500 per season.
Requirements: Master's degree in social work, interest in the arts.

NEW MEXICO

BRUSH RANCH CAMPS FOR GIRLS AND BOYS
HC 73, Box 32, Tererro, NM 87573

❶ CAMPING

Compensation: Varies, room and board.

Duration: June 9 to August 10.

Contact: Owner/Director, Brush Ranch Camps for Girls and Boys, P.O. Box 5759, Santa Fe, NM 87502.

Phone: 800-722-2843.

Apply by: May 10.

- ART INSTRUCTORS
Requirements: Experience with ceramics.
- ROPES COURSE INSTRUCTORS
Requirements: 40 hours of training or 100 hours of course leadership in last 12 months.
- DANCE INSTRUCTORS
- DRAMA INSTRUCTORS

GLORIETA CONFERENCE CENTER
P.O. Box 8, Glorieta, NM 87535
❶ CONFERENCE CENTERS
Compensation: Minimum wage.
Duration: May 20 to September 5.
Contact: Administrative Services Coordinator.
Phone: 505-757-6161.
Apply by: March 1.

- DAY CAMP WORKERS
- HOUSEKEEPERS
- CONFERENCE SERVICE WORKERS
- SOUND AND LIGHTING TECHNICIANS

PHILMONT SCOUT RANCH
Cimarron, NM 87714
❶ CAMPING/CONFERENCE CENTERS
Compensation: $520 per month, room and board.
Duration: May 25 to August 25.
Contact: Season Personnel.
Phone: 505-376-2281.
Apply by: May 30.

- FOOD SERVICE STAFF MEMBERS
- CONSERVATION STAFF MEMBERS
- RANGERS
- PROGRAM COUNSELORS

NEW YORK

CAMP HILLCROFT
Box 5, Billings, NY 12510
❶ CAMPING
Compensation: Room and board.
Duration: June 29 to August21.
Contact: Director.
Phone: 914-223-5826.

- GROUP LEADERS
Compensation: $1,200-$1,500 per season.
Requirements: Completed senior year of college, experience working with children.
- OUTDOOR ADVENTURE INSTRUCTORS
Compensation: $1,000-$1,400 per season.
Requirements: Ropes course, climbing, and cooperative games experience.
- CERAMICS AND WOOD INSTRUCTORS
Compensation: $1,000-$1,400 per season.
Requirements: Teaching experience.
- TENNIS AND ARCHERY INSTRUCTORS
Compensation: $1,000-$1,400 per season.
Requirements: Experience and/or proper certification.

CAROUSEL DAY SCHOOL
9 West Ave., Hicksville, NY 11801
❶ CAMPING
Duration: June 29 to August 21.
Phone: 516-938-1137.
Apply by: May 31.

- CRAFTS DIRECTOR: Will develop a crafts program.
Compensation: $2,500 per season.
- SWIMMING INSTRUCTORS AND LIFEGUARDS
Compensation: $1,500-$1,900 per season.
Requirements: WSI and CPR experience.
- SPORTS INSTRUCTORS/COUNSELORS
Compensation: $825-$1,100 per season.
Requirements: Experience coaching basketball, soccer, and baseball.
- GENERAL COUNSELORS
Compensation: $850-$1,200 per season.
Requirements: Enthusiasm.

CHAUTAUQUA INSTITUTION SUMMER SCHOOLS
P.O. Box 1098, Chautauqua, NY 14722
❶ EDUCATION (ARTS)
Duration: June 23 to August 25.
Contact: Vice President.
Phone: 716-357-6232.
Apply by: March 1.

- TECHNICAL DIRECTORS
Compensation: $2,000 per season.
- SCENIC DESIGNERS
Compensation: $2,000 per season.
- STAGE MANAGERS
Compensation: $1,220 per season.
- CARPENTER INTERN
Compensation: $1,220 per season.

FIVE RIVERS CENTER
Game Farm Rd., Delmar, NY 12054
❶ ENVIRONMENT
- NATURALIST INTERNS
Compensation: $100 per week, room and board.
Duration: June 21 to August 30.
Phone: 518-475-0291.
Apply by: February 1.

THE FRESH AIR FUND
Sharpe Reservation, Van Wyck Lake Rd., Fishkill, NY 12524. World Wide Web: http://www.freshair.org
❶ CAMPING
Compensation: Room and board.
Duration: June 20 to August 21.
Contact: Associate Executive Director, The Fresh Air Fund, 1040 Ave. of the Americas, New York, NY 10018.
Phone: 800-367-0003.
Apply by: June 1.

- PROGRAM SPECIALISTS: Will lead photography, arts and crafts, video, music, sewing, hiking, or nature programs.
Compensation: $1,600-$2,000 per season.
Requirements: Appropriate experience.
- GENERAL COUNSELORS
Compensation: $1,450-$1,850 per season.
Requirements: Minimum age 19, experience with children, some college.
- VILLAGE LEADERS
Compensation: $1,800-$2,200 per season.
Requirements: Leadership experience.
- WATERFRONT STAFF
Compensation: $1,600-$2,000 per season.
Requirements: Lifeguard certification.

INTRODUCTION TO INDEPENDENCE
New York Institute of Technology, Central Islip, NY 11722
❶ CAMPING (LEARNING DISABILITIES)

- RESIDENT ADVISERS
Compensation: $1,000 per season.
Duration: July 5 to August 22.
Requirements: Special education, psychology, or social work background, graduate status.
Contact: Introduction to Independence, P.O. Box 465, Islip Terrace, NY 11752.
Phone: 516-348-3354.
Apply by: May 1.

SAIL CARIBBEAN
79 Church St., Northport, NY 11768. World Wide Web: http://www.sailcaribbean.com
❶ ATHLETICS
Compensation: Pay varies, room and board.
Duration: June 18 to August 24.
Contact: Owner/ Operator.
Phone: 800-321-0994.
Apply by: March 1.

- SKIPPERS

- FOOD SUPERVISORS
- ARC LIFEGUARD INSTRUCTORS
- SCUBA INSTRUCTORS

STAGEDOOR MANOR THEATRE AND DANCE CAMP
Karmel Rd., Loch Sheldrake, NY 12759
❶ CAMPING (ARTS)
Compensation: Room and board.
Duration: June 20 to August 26.
Contact: Production Director, SMTDC269 Moneymaker Circle, Gatlinburg, TN 37738.
Phone: 423-436-3030.
Apply by: May 1.

- THEATER DIRECTORS
Compensation: $2,000-$2,500 per season.
Requirements: Bachelor's degree.
- PIANISTS
Compensation: $1,800-$2,500 per season.
Requirements: Ability to read music, musical theater background.
- CHOREOGRAPHERS
Compensation: $1,800-$2,500 per season.
Requirements: Musical theater background.
- TECHNICAL STAFF
Compensation: $1,800-$2,500 per season.
Requirements: Theater background.

TIMBERLOCK CAMP
Indian Lake, NY 12864
❶ CAMPING (ADVENTURE)

- GROUP LEADERS
Compensation: $300-$400 per week, room and board.
Duration: June 25 to August 20.
Contact: Timberlock Camp & Voyageurs, P.O. Box 1052, Sabael, NY 12864.
Phone: 518-648-5494.
Apply by: March 31.

TRAILMARK OUTDOOR ADVENTURES
16 Schuyler Rd., Nyack, NY 10960
❶ CAMPING (ADVENTURE)

- TRIP LEADERS
Compensation: $100-$300 per week, room and board.
Duration: June 15 to August 30.
Requirements: CPR and first aid certification.
Contact: Director.
Phone: 914-358-0262.
Apply by: June 15.

NORTH CAROLINA

CAMP HIGH ROCKS
P.O. Box 127, Cedar Mountain, NC

28718. World Wide Web:
http://www.highrocks.com

❶ CAMPING (BOYS)
Compensation: $170-$230 per week,
room and board.
Duration: June 8 to August 16.
Contact: Camp Director.
Phone: 704-885-2153.
Apply by: April 1.

• ROCK CLIMBING INSTRUCTORS
• HORSEBACK RIDING INSTRUCTORS
• MOUNTAIN BIKING INSTRUCTORS
• ROPES COURSE LEADERS

CAMP SKY RANCH
634 Sky Ranch Rd., Blowing Rock, NC
28605

❶ CAMPING (DEVELOPMENTAL
DISABILITIES)
Compensation: $120-$150 per week,
room and board.
Duration: June 5 to August 10.
Contact: Director.
Phone: 704-264-8600.
Apply by: May 1.

• WATERFRONT DIRECTOR
Requirements: WSI certification.
• LIFEGUARDS
Requirements: Lifeguard certification.
• COUNSELORS/ACTIVITY LEADERS

**DUKE YOUTH PROGRAMS—DUKE UNI-
VERSITY CONTINUING EDUCATION**
203 Bishop's House, Box 90702, Durham, NC 27708

❶ CAMPING (ACADEMIC)
Compensation: Room and board.
Duration: May 1 to August 15.
Contact: Program Coordinator.
Phone: 919-684-2827.
Apply by: February 1.

• RESIDENTIAL COUNSELORS
Compensation: $1,200-$2,000 per season.
• TEACHING ASSISTANTS
Compensation: $500-$1,300 per season.
• OFFICE STAFF
Compensation: $6-$10 per hour.

KEYSTONE CAMP
P.O. Box 829, Brevard, NC 28712

❶ CAMPING (GIRLS)
Compensation: $1,100-$1,800 per sea-
son, room and board.
Duration: June 3 to August 15.

Contact: Associate Director.
Phone: 828-884-9125.
Apply by: April 15.

• AEROBICS INSTRUCTOR
• ART INSTRUCTORS
• HIKING AND OUTDOOR LIVING IN-
STRUCTORS
• SPORTS INSTRUCTORS

**NORTH BEACH SAILING/BARRIER IS-
LAND SAILING CENTER**
Box 8279, Duck, NC 27949

❶ ATHLETICS
Duration: May 1 to October 15.
Contact: President.
Phone: 919-261-6262.
Apply by: May 1.

• WINDSURFING INSTRUCTORS
Compensation: $250-$350 per week.
Requirements: Windsurfing experience, good
teaching skills.
• SAILING INSTRUCTORS
Compensation: $250-$350 per week.
Requirements: Excellent teaching skills.
• RENTAL/DESK STAFF
Compensation: $150-$200 per week.
• RETAIL SALES STAFF
Compensation: $200-$300 per week.
Requirements: Knowledge of sailing and
windsurfing.

YMCA CAMP HANES
Rte. 5, Box 99, King, NC 27021. World
Wide Web: http://www.camphanes.org

❶ CAMPING (SPECIAL NEEDS)
Compensation: $100-$200 per week,
room and board.
Duration: June 1 to August 15.
Contact: Executive Director.
Phone: 910-983-3131.
Apply by: April 15.

• RIDING DIRECTOR
Requirements: Equestrian experience.
• WATERFRONT DIRECTOR
Requirements: WSI certification.
• PROGRAM DIRECTOR
• CABIN COUNSELORS

NORTH DAKOTA

INTERNATIONAL MUSIC CAMP
International Peace Garden, Dunseith,
ND 58329

❶ CAMPING (MUSIC)
Compensation: $175-$250 per week,

room and board.

Duration: June 1 to July 31.

Contact: Camp Director, International Music Camp, 1725 11th St., SW, Minot, ND 58701.

Phone: 701-838-8472.

Apply by: February 28.

• COUNSELORS
Requirements: College senior or college graduate.

• SECRETARIES
Requirements: Type 50 wpm, good computer skills.

• MUSIC LIBRARIANS
Requirements: Knowledge of instruments.

• GROUNDS/HOUSEKEEPER

• CONCESSIONS STAFF

O H I O

CAMP BUTTERWORTH
8551 Butterworth Rd., Maineville, OH 45039

❶ CAMPING (GIRLS)
Compensation: Room and board.

Duration: June 9 to August 14.

Contact: Program Services Manager, Great Rivers Girl Scout Council, Inc., Camp Butterworth, 4930 Cornell Rd., Cincinnati, OH 45242.

Phone: 513-489-1417.

Apply by: May 21.

• WATERFRONT STAFF
Compensation: $1,450-$1,800 per season.
Requirements: Minimum age 18, lifeguard certification.

• NATURALISTS/CRAFTS INSTRUCTORS
Compensation: $1,380-$1,900 per season.

• UNIT LEADERS
Compensation: $1,600-$1,900 per season.
Requirements: Minimum age 21.

• UNIT COUNSELORS
Compensation: $1,380-$1,600 per season.
Requirements: Minimum age 18.

CAMP O'BANNON
9688 Butler Rd., NE, Newark, OH 43055

❶ CAMPING
Compensation: $900-$1,800 per season, room and board.

Duration: June 7 to August 15.

Contact: Camp Director, Camp O'Bannon, 62 W. Locust St., Newark, OH 43055.

Phone: 614-349-9646.

Apply by: March 30.

• COUNSELORS
Requirements: Minimum age 19, completed one year of college.

• OUTPOST COUNSELORS
Requirements: Minimum age 19, completed one year of college.

• LIFEGUARD
Requirements: Minimum age 19, WSI certification preferred.

• NATURE COUNSELOR
Requirements: Minimum age 19, completed one year of college.

FRIENDS MUSIC CAMP
Barnesville, OH 43713

❶ CAMPING (MUSIC)
Compensation: $900 per season, room and board.

Duration: July 8 to August 4.

Contact: Director, Friends Music Camp, P.O. Box 427, Yellow Springs, OH 45387.

Phone: 937-767-1311.

Apply by: March 31.

• MUSIC INSTRUCTORS
Requirements: Appropriate training and/or experience.

• COUNSELORS

GEAUGA LAKE
1060 N. Aurora Rd., Aurora, OH 44202

❶ AMUSEMENT PARKS
Compensation: $180-$220 per week.

Duration: May 10 to November 2

Contact: Employment Coordinator.

Phone: 216-562-8303.

Apply by: March 15.

• EVENT COORDINATOR
Requirements: Excellent organizational and communications skills.

• GIFT SHOP EMPLOYEE
Requirements: Store management ability.

• VOLLEYBALL COORDINATOR
Requirements: Background in volleyball, good communications skills.

• LIFEGUARD
Requirements: Appropriate certification or desire to train for certification.

HIDDEN HOLLOW CAMP
5127 Oppossum Run Rd., Rte. 3, Bellville, OH 44813

❶ CAMPING

- CAMP COUNSELORS
Compensation: $150-$200 per week, room and board.
Duration: July 4 to August 20.
Contact: Director, Hidden Hollow Camp, 380 N. Mulberry St., Mansfield, OH 44902.
Phone: 419-522-0521.
Apply by: January 15.

OKLAHOMA

CAMP RED ROCK
Rte. 1, Box 110B, Binger, OK 73009
❶ CAMPING (GIRLS)
Compensation: Room and board.
Duration: June 1 to August 10.
Contact: Program Specialist.
Phone: 405-528-3535.

- UNIT COUNSELORS
Compensation: $900-$1,100 per season.
Requirements: Minimum age 18, CPR and first aid certification.

- UNIT LEADERS
Compensation: $1,000-$1,200 per season.
Requirements: Minimum age 21, CPR and first aid certification.

- RIDING STAFF
Compensation: $1,000-$1,200 per season.
Requirements: CPR and first aid certification.

- ARCHERY/ROPES/ARTS AND CRAFTS INSTRUCTORS
Compensation: $1,000-$1,200 per season.
Requirements: Minimum age 18, experience.

OREGON

CRATER LAKE COMPANY
Crater Lake National Park, P.O. Box 128, Crater Lake, OR 97604
❶ PARKS
Compensation: $4.75 $6.50 per hour.
Duration: April 10 to October 20. Year-round positions also available.
Contact: Personnel Manager.
Phone: 541-830-4053.
Apply by: April 15 for summer.

- OFFICE WORKERS
Requirements: Good accounting skills.

- FOOD SERVICES

- GIFT SHOP STAFF

- FRONT DESK STAFF

YWCA CAMP WESTWIND
2353 N. Three Rocks Rd., Otis, OR 97368
❶ CAMPING

Compensation: Room and board.
Duration: June 12 to August 31.
Contact: Camp Administrator, YWCA Camp Westwind, 1111 SW 10th Ave., Portland, OR 97205.
Phone: 503-294-7472.
Apply by: June 5.

- COUNSELORS
Compensation: $95-$100 per week.
Requirements: CPR and first aid certification.

- NATURE/MARINE SCIENCE INSTRUCTORS
Compensation: $100-$110 per week.
Requirements: Minimum age 21, CPR and first aid certification.

- WATERFRONT DIRECTOR
Compensation: $100-$110 per week.
Requirements: CPR, first aid, and lifeguard certification, small craft instructor experience.

- KITCHEN STAFF
Compensation: $1,200-$1,300 per season.

PENNSYLVANIA

CAMP AKIBA
Reeders, PA 18352
❶ CAMPING
Compensation: Room and board.
Duration: June 21 to August 15.
Contact: Executive Director, Camp Akiba, Box 840, Bala Cynwyd, PA 19004.
Phone: 610-660-9556.
Apply by: May 1.

- COUNSELORS
Compensation: $950-$1,700 per season.
Requirements: Interest in working with children.

- ARCHERY INSTRUCTORS
Compensation: $950-$1,300 per season.
Requirements: Experience.

- SPORTS INSTRUCTORS
Compensation: $950-$1,500 per season.
Requirements: Background in team sports.

- WATERSKIING INSTRUCTORS
Compensation: $950-$1,800 per season.
Requirements: Experience.

CAMP BALLIBAY FOR THE FINE AND PERFORMING ARTS
Box 1, Camptown, PA 18815
❶ CAMPING (ARTS)
Compensation: $750-$2,000 per season, room and board.
Duration: June 22 to August 27.

Phone: 717-746-3223.

- THEATER DIRECTORS
Requirements: Background in theater directing.
- MUSIC INSTRUCTORS
Requirements: Vocal and/or instrumental proficiency.
- DANCE INSTRUCTORS
- ART INSTRUCTORS

CAMP CAYUGA
Pocono Mountains, Honesdale, PA 18431

❶ CAMPING
Compensation: Room and board.
Duration: June 19 to August 20.
Contact: Camp Director, Camp Cayuga, P.O. Box 452, Department PSJ, Washington, NJ 07882.
Phone: 908-689-3339.
Apply by: June 10.

- SAILING INSTRUCTORS
Compensation: $1,400-$1,700 per season.
Requirements: Lifeguard and arc small craft certification.
- DRAMA INSTRUCTORS
Compensation: $1,250-$1,500 per season.
Requirements: Completed one year of college.
- RADIO BROADCASTING INSTRUCTORS
Compensation: $1,250-$1,500 per season.
Requirements: Completed one year of college, disk jockey experience preferred.
- RIDING INSTRUCTORS
Compensation: $1,300-$1,500 per season.
Requirements: Completed one year of college, stable maintenance and horsemanship skills.

CAMP NOCK-A-MIXON
249 Traugers Crossing Rd., Kintnersville, PA 18930

❶ CAMPING
Compensation: Room and board.
Duration: June 19 to August 14.
Contact: Director, Camp Nock-A-Mixon, 16 Gum Tree Lane, Lafayette Hill, PA 19444.
Phone: 610-941-0128.
Apply by: June 1.

- COUNSELORS
Compensation: $900-$1,300per season.
- SPECIALISTS
Compensation: $900-$1,400per season.
- SWIMMING INSTRUCTORS

Compensation: $1,000-$2,000 per season.
Requirements: WSI and/or lifeguard certification.
- DRAMA SPECIALISTS
Compensation: $900-$1,300 per season.

COLLEGE SETTLEMENT OF PHILADELPHIA
600 Witmer Rd., Horsham, PA 19044

❶ CAMPING
Compensation: $1,600-$2,000 per season, room and board.
Duration: June 10 to August 25.
Contact: Director of Resident Programs.
Phone: 215-542-7974.
Apply by: May 1.

- CABIN COUNSELORS
- UNIT LEADERS
- TRIP LEADERS
Requirements: CPR and first aid certification.
- NATURE SPECIALISTS

HERSHEY PARK
100 W. Hershey Park Dr., Hershey, PA 17033

❶ RESORTS
Compensation: $285-$350 per week.
Duration: May 1 to September 3.
Contact: Entertainment Coordinator.
Phone: 717-534-3349.
Apply by: February 15.

- SINGERS/DANCERS
Requirements: Experience.
- STAGE MANAGERS
Requirements: Experience.
- SOUND TECHNICIANS
Requirements: Experience.
- COSTUME SHOPKEEPERS

PENNSYLVANIA DEPARTMENT OF TRANSPORTATION—BUREAU OF PERSONNEL
555 Walnut St. 9th Fl., Forum Place, Harrisburg, PA 17101-1900

❶ GOVERNMENT
Compensation: $6.25-$7.83 per hour.
Duration: March 1 to October 1.
Contact College Relations Coordinator.
Phone: 717-783-2680.

- ENGINEERING/SCIENTIFIC/TECHNICAL
Requirements: Engineering, math, science, or architecture major.

- GOVERNMENT SERVICE
Requirements: College student.
- TRANSPORTATION/CONSTRUCTION INSPECTORS
Requirements: Two years of construction inspection experience.
- HIGHWAY MAINTENANCE

SPORTS AND ARTS CENTER AT ISLAND LAKE
Island Lake Rd., Starrucca, PA 18462
❶ CAMPING
Compensation: Room and board.
Duration: June 18 to August19.
Contact: Directors, SACIL, P.O. Box 800, Pomona, NY 10970.
Phone: 914-354-5517.
Apply by: May 15.

- SPECIALISTS
Compensation: $1,000-$1,500 per season.
Requirements: Experience in sports and/or performing and visual arts.
- NURSES
Compensation: $200-$500 per week.
Requirements: Experience, appropriate licenses.
- DEPARTMENT HEADS
Compensation: $1,500-$3,000 per season.
Requirements: Experience.
- HEAD COUNSELORS
Compensation: $2,500-$6,000 per season.
Requirements: Experience.

RHODE ISLAND
UNIVERSITY OF RHODE ISLAND SUMMER PROGRAMS—W. ALTON JONES CAMPUS
401 Victory Highway, West Greenwich, RI 02817
❶ CAMPING
Compensation: $160-$180 per week, room and board.
Duration: June 15 to August 21.
Contact: Camp Manager.
Phone: 401-397-3304, ext. 6043.

- LIFEGUARDS
Requirements: Appropriate certification.
- EXPEDITION LEADERS
- COUNSELORS

YMCA CAMP FULLER
PO Box 432, Wakefield, RI 02880
❶ CAMPING
Compensation: Room and board.
Duration: June 15 to August 28.
Contact: Executive Director, YMCA

Camp Fuller, 166 Broad St., Providence, RI 02903.
Phone: 401-521-1470.
Apply by: April 30.

- COUNSELORS
Compensation: $100-$140 per week.
Requirements: Minimum age 19.
- NURSE
Compensation: $300-$350 per week.
Requirements: RN license.
- DIVISION LEADERS
Compensation: $150-$200 per week.
Requirements: Minimum age 21.

SOUTH CAROLINA
CAMP CHATUGA
291 Camp Chatuga Rd., Mountain Rest, SC 29664
❶ CAMPING
Compensation: Room and board.
Duration: June 6 to August 4.
Contact: Director of Personnel.
Phone: 864-638-3728.
Apply by: May 15.

- COUNSELORS
Compensation: $800-$1,100 per season.
- WATERFRONT DIRECTOR
Compensation: $875-$1,200 per season.
Requirements: WSI certification.
- RIDING INSTRUCTOR
Compensation: $875-$1,200 per season.
Requirements: Western-style riding experience.
- PROGRAM DIRECTOR
Compensation: $1,000-$1,500 per season.

CAMP THUNDERBIRD
1 Thunderbird Lane, Lake Wylie, SC 29710
❶ CAMPING
Compensation:$120-$160 per week, room and board.
Duration: June 4 to August 20.
Contact: Assistant Camp Director.
Phone: 803-831-2121.
Apply by: February 28.

- WATERSKIING INSTRUCTORS
Requirements: CPR or first aid certification.
- CHALLENGE COURSE LEADERS
Requirements: CPR or first aid certification.
- RIDING INSTRUCTORS
Requirements: Experience with English-style riding.
- OUTDOOR LIVING LEADERS

SOUTH DAKOTA

AMERICAN PRESIDENTS RESORT
Highway 16A, P.O. Box 446, Custer, SD
57730
❶ RESORTS
Compensation: $5-$6 per hour.
Duration: May 1 to September 8.
Contact: Manager.
Phone: 605-673-3373.
Apply by: April 1.

• DESK CLERKS

• MAIDS

• LAUNDRY WORKERS

CUSTER STATE PARK RESORT COMPANY
HC 83, Box 74-A, Custer, SD 57730
❶ RESORTS
Compensation: Room and board.
Duration: April 15 to October 30.
Contact: President.
Phone: 605-255-4541.
Apply by: June 1.

• SALES PERSONNEL
Compensation: $750-$800 per month.

• WAITSTAFF
Compensation: $600-$750 per month.

• COOKS/CHEFS
Compensation: $800-$1,400 per month.

• KITCHEN STAFF/FOOD PREPARATION
Compensation: $550-$750 per month.

**PALMER GULCH RESORT/MT. RUSH–
MORE KOA**
Box 295, Hill City, SD 57745
❶ RESORTS
Compensation: $210-$240 per week.
Duration: April 1 to October 1.
Contact: General Manager.
Phone: 605-574-2525.

• WATERSLIDE STAFF
Requirements: CPR, first aid, or lifeguard
certification.

• REGISTRATION OFFICE/STORE CLERK

• MAINTENANCE STAFF

• RESERVATIONS STAFF

TENNESSEE

**CHEROKEE ADVENTURES WHITEWATER
RAFTING**
Jonesborough Rd., Erwin, TN 37650
❶ CAMPING (ADVENTURE)
Duration: May 15 to September 16.

Contact: President.
Phone: 423-743-7733.
Apply by: April 30.

• RAFT GUIDES
Compensation: $400-$600 per month.
Requirements: CPR and first aid certification,
excellent personality.

• COOKS/CLEANUP STAFF
Compensation: $4.25-$5 per hour.

• RESERVATIONIST/OFFICE CLERK
Compensation: $4.25-$5 per hour.
Requirements: Good clerical skills, type 50
wpm.

• GROUNDSKEEPER
Compensation: $4.25-$5 per hour.

GIRL SCOUT CAMP SYCAMORE HILLS
Box 40466, Nashville, TN 37204
❶ CAMPING (GIRLS)
Compensation: Room and board.
Duration: June 1 to July 31.
Contact: Outdoor Program Manager.
Phone: 800-395-5318.
Apply by: May 27.

• CAMP DIRECTOR
Compensation: $180-$375 per week.
Requirements: Girl Scout camp experience.

• HIGH ADVENTURE LEADERS
Compensation: $120-$275 per week.
Requirements: Lifeguard certification.

• EQUESTRIAN INSTRUCTORS
Compensation: $110-$140 per week.
Requirements: Experience.

• RAPPELING STAFF
Compensation: $110-$200 per week.
Requirements: Two years of experience.

TEXAS

CAMP BALCONES SPRINGS
HC04, Box 349, Marble Falls, TX 78654
❶ CAMPING (RELIGIOUS)
Compensation: $1,450-$1,500 per sea-
son, room and board.
Duration: May 20 to August 15.
Contact: Personnel/Head Counselor.
Phone: 800-775-9785.
Apply by: April 1.

• AQUATICS STAFF
Requirements: WSI and lifeguard certification.

• RIDING INSTRUCTORS
Requirements: English-style riding experi-

ence.

- SAILING/WINDSURFING INSTRUCTORS

Requirements: Demonstrated experience.

- ARCHERY/RIFLERY INSTRUCTORS

Requirements: NRA and NAA certification.

CAMP EL TESORO

2700 Meacham Blvd., Fort Worth, TX 76137

❶ CAMPING

Compensation: $80-$150 per week, room and board.

Duration: May 28 to August 15.

Contact: Camp Director.

Phone: 817-831-2111.

Apply by: May 1.

- CABIN COUNSELORS

Requirements: Completed one year of college.

- RIDING INSTRUCTOR

Requirements: CHA certification preferred.

- WATERFRONT STAFF

Requirements: CPR, first aid, and lifeguard certification.

- KITCHEN PERSONNEL

CAMP STEWART FOR BOYS

Rte. 1, Box 110, Hunt, TX 78024. World Wide Web: http://www.campstewart.com

❶ CAMPING (BOYS)

Compensation: $1,000-$2,000 per season, room and board.

Duration: May 25 to August 15.

Contact: Codirector.

Phone: 830-238-4670.

Apply by: April 1.

- RIDING INSTRUCTORS

Requirements: Must take CHA certification at Camp Stewart.

- ROCK CLIMBING INSTRUCTORS

Requirements: Appropriate certification.

- CHALLENGE COURSE INSTRUCTORS

Requirements: Appropriate certification.

- ARTS AND CRAFTS INSTRUCTORS

CAMP WALDEMAR

Rte. 1, Box 120, Hunt, TX 78024

❶ CAMPING (GIRLS)

Compensation: $450-$700 per season, room and board.

Duration: May 31 to July 15.

Contact: Owner/Director.

Phone: 830-238-4821.

- RIDING INSTRUCTORS

Requirements: English- or Western-style riding experience.

- TENNIS STAFF

Requirements: Varsity high school or college team experience.

- RIFLE STAFF

Requirements: NRA certification.

- GYMNASTICS/TRAMPOLINE STAFF

Y. O. ADVENTURE CAMP

HC 01, Box 555, Mountain Home, TX 78058. World Wide Web: http://www.kidscamp.com

❶ CAMPING

Compensation: Room and board.

Duration: May 19 to August 18.

Requirements: CPR, first aid, and lifeguard certification.

Contact: Director.

Phone: 210-640-3220.

Apply by: May 1.

- COUNSELORS

Compensation: $425 per month.

- SEASONAL INSTRUCTORS

Compensation: $500 per month.

UTAH

FOUR CORNERS SCHOOL OF OUTDOOR EDUCATION

P.O. Box 1029, Monticello, UT 84535

❶ CAMPING

- OUTDOOR EDUCATION

Compensation: $75 per week, room and board.

Duration: March 15 to October 30.

Requirements: Career-oriented, First Responder and CPR certification.

Contact: Director.

Phone: 435-587-2859.

Apply by: January 15.

WORLD HOST BRYCE VALLEY INN

P.O. Box A, Tropic, UT 84776

❶ RESORTS

Duration: March 15 to October 14.

Contact: Operations Manager.

Phone: 801-679-8811.

Apply by: March 10.

- MAIDS

Compensation: $5-$7 per hour.

- HOSTS/HOSTESSES

Compensation: $5 per hour.

- WAITSTAFF

Compensation: $4.25 per hour.
- SHOP CLERKS
Compensation: $5 per hour.

VERMONT

CAMP THOREAU-IN-VERMONT
RR 1, Box 88, Miller Pond Rd., Thetford Center, VT 05075-9601

❶ CAMPING

Compensation: $1,400-$2,200 per season, room and board.

Duration: June 15 to August 22.

Contact: Director, Camp Thoreau-in-Vermont, 157 Tillson Lake Rd., Wallkill, NY 12589.

Phone: 914-895-2974.

Apply by: February 15.

- COUNSELORS/BOATING INSTRUCTORS
Requirements: Canoeing/sailing/kayaking and other appropriate certification.
- COUNSELORS/WOODSHOP INSTRUCTORS
Requirements: CPR and first aid certification.
- HIKING/OUTDOOR LIVING INSTRUCTORS
Requirements: Outdoors experience, CPR and first aid certification.
- DRAMA INSTRUCTORS

CHALLENGE WILDERNESS CAMP
Bradford, VT 05033

❶ CAMPING (BOYS)

Compensation: $1,200-$2,000 per season, room and board.

Duration: June 18 to August 24.

Contact: Directors, Challenge Wilderness Camp, 300 N. Grove St., #4, Rutland, VT 05701.

Phone: 800-832-HAWK.

- KAYAK INSTRUCTOR
Requirements: ACA or BCU certification.
- ROCK CLIMBING INSTRUCTORS
Requirements: Certified climbing experience.
- MARKSMANSHIP INSTRUCTOR
Requirements: 22 caliber and military experience.
- FOOD SERVICES DIRECTOR
Requirements: Outdoors and cooking experience.

KILLOOLEET
Rte. 100, Hancock, VT 05748

❶ CAMPING

Compensation: $1,000-$1,500 per season, room and board.

Duration: June 10 to August 16.

Contact: Director, Killooleet, 70 Trull St., Somerville, MA 02145.

Phone: 617-666-1484.

Apply by: May 10.

- NATURE INSTRUCTOR
Requirements: Teaching knowledge of ponds, streams, woods, and fields.
- MUSIC INSTRUCTOR
Requirements: Knowledge of folk, rhythm and blues, and funk.
- VIDEO INSTRUCTOR
Requirements: Knowledge of control room and editing practices.
- ELECTRONICS INSTRUCTOR

POINT COUNTER POINT CHAMBER MUSIC CAMP
Lake Dunmore, VT 05733

❶ CAMPING (MUSIC)

Compensation: Starting at $1,500, room and board.

Duration: June 18 to August 12.

Contact: Director, PCPCMC, P.O. Box 3181, Terre Haute, IN 47803.

Phone: 812-877-3745.

Apply by: March 15.

- ACTIVITIES COUNSELORS
Compensation: Starting at $1,500 per season.
Requirements: WSI, CPR, and first aid certification.
- MUSIC FACULTY
Compensation: Starting at $2,500 per season.
Requirements: Violinist, cellist, violist, and/or pianist, performing and teaching background.
- COOKS
Compensation: Negotiable.
Requirements: Experience.

VIRGINIA

CAMP FRIENDSHIP
P.O. Box 145, Palmyra, VA 22963

❶ CAMPING

Compensation: Room and board.

Duration: June 5 to August 20.

Contact: Director.

Phone: 804-589-8950.

Apply by: April 1.

- COUNSELORS/TRIP LEADERS

Compensation: $1, 050-$1,350 per season.
Requirements: Teaching skills.

- RIDING INSTRUCTORS
Compensation: $1,100-$1,500 per season.
Requirements: Riding experience.

- VILLAGE DIRECTORS
Compensation: $1,600-$2,000 per season.
Requirements: College degree, supervisory experience.

- MAINTENANCE
Compensation: $1,200-$1,400 per season.
Requirements: Minimum age 21, driver's license.

CAMP HORIZONS
Rte. 3, Box 374, Harrisonburg, VA 22801

❶ CAMPING
Compensation: $1,050-$2,000 per season, room and board.
Duration: April 1 to November 30.
Contact: Director.
Phone: 540-896-7600.
Apply by: March 1.

- WATERFRONT LEADERS
Requirements: CPR, first aid, and lifeguard certification.

- ACTIVITIES COUNSELORS
Requirements: CPR and first aid certification, swimming, languages, drama, or caving experience.

- RIDING INSTRUCTORS
Requirements: CPR and first aid certification, Western-style riding experience.

- ADVENTURE LEADERS
Requirements: Bachelor's degree, climbing, ropes, hiking, or canoeing background.

CAT'S CAP & ST. CATHERINE'S CREATIVE ARTS PROGRAM
6001 Grove Ave., Richmond, VA 23226

❶ CAMPING (ARTS)
Duration: June 20 to July 30.
Contact: Director.
Phone: 804-288-2804, ext. 45.

- INSTRUCTORS
Compensation: $11-$13 per hour.
Requirements: Background in dance, music, art, theater, or physical education.

- ASSISTANTS
Compensation: $6-$8 per hour.
Requirements: Training or degree in education.

- CANOEING INSTRUCTORS
Compensation: $11 per hour.
Requirements: Appropriate experience.

- RAPPELING INSTRUCTORS
Compensation: $11 per hour.
Requirements: Appropriate experience.

4 STAR TENNIS ACADEMY AT THE UNIVERSITY OF VIRGINIA
Charlottesville, VA 22901

❶ CAMPING (ATHLETIC)
Compensation: Room and board.
Duration: June 15 to August 10.
Contact: Assistant Director, 4 Star Tennis Academy at the University of Virginia, P.O. Box 3387, Falls Church, VA 22014.
Phone: 703-573-0890.
Apply by: May 1.

- TENNIS INSTRUCTORS/COUNSELORS
Compensation: $900-$1,400 per season.
Requirements: College status or older, advanced tennis skills, competition experience.

- EVENING ACTIVITIES/RECREATION DIRECTOR
Compensation: $1,800-$2,250 per season.
Requirements: Excellent organizational skills.

- DORM SUPERVISOR
Compensation: $1,575-$2,025 per season.
Requirements: Good leadership and organizational skills.

- ACADEMIC COUNSELORS
Compensation: Varies.
Requirements: Teaching background.

LEGACY INTERNATIONAL'S GLOBAL YOUTH VILLAGE
Rte. 4, Box 265-D, Bedford, VA 24523

❶ CAMPING (LEADERSHIP TRAINING)
Compensation: Pay is negotiable, room and board.
Duration: June 16 to August 20.
Contact: Codirector.
Phone: 540-297-5982.
Apply by: May 15.

- LEADERSHIP INSTRUCTORS
Requirements: Excellent organizational and teaching skills.

- PERFORMING ARTS INSTRUCTORS
Requirements: Improvisational skills.

- ROPES COURSE LEADERS
Requirements: Certification or documented training in high or low ropes.

- KITCHEN STAFF

WASHINGTON

CAMP BERACHAH
19830 SE 328th Pl., Auburn, WA 98002

❶ CAMPING

Compensation: Room and board.

Duration: June 1 toAugust 30

Contact: Program Director.

Phone: 253-939-0488.

Apply by: May 15.

- COUNSELORS
Compensation: $100-$135 per week.
- RECREATION DIRECTOR
Compensation: $125-$135 per week.
- CRAFTS DIRECTOR
Compensation: $125-$135 per week.
- WRANGLERS/RIDING INSTRUCTORS
Compensation: $900-$1,500 per season.

LONGACRE EXPEDITIONS
Glacier, Washington

❶ CAMPING (ADVENTURE)

Compensation: Room and board.

Duration: June 14 to August 4.

Requirements: Minimum age 21.

Contact: Longacre Expeditions, RD 3, Box 106, Newport, PA 17074.

Phone: 717-567-6790.

- MOUNTAINEERING LEADERS
Compensation: $300-$400 per week.
- ROCK CLIMBING INSTRUCTORS
Compensation: $300-$400 per week.
- SUPPORT STAFF
Compensation: $150-$175 per week.
- ASSISTANT TRIP LEADERS
Compensation: $150-$175 per week.

MT. RAINIER GUEST SERVICES
P.O. Box 108, Ashford, WA 98304.
World Wide Web:
http://www.coolworks.com

❶ RESORTS

Compensation: $216-$240 per week.

Duration: May 1 to October 10.

Contact: Personnel Department.

Phone: 360-569-2400, ext. 119.

- DESK CLERKS
Requirements: Cash handling and communications skills.
- HOUSEKEEPING
- FAST FOOD ATTENDANTS
- RETAIL CLERK

YMCA CAMP SEYMOUR
9725 Carmer Rd. KPN, Gig Harbor, WA 98329

❶ CAMPING

Compensation: Room and board.

Duration: June 11 to August 15.

Contact: Assistant Director of Camping, YMCA Camp Seymour, 1002 S. Pearl St., Tacoma, WA 98465.

Phone: 206-564-9622.

Apply by: May 15.

- CABIN LEADERS
Compensation: $100-$130 per week.
- PROGRAM SPECIALISTS
Compensation: $130-$170 per week.
Requirements: Experience with arts and crafts or outdoor education.
- TRIP LEADERS
Compensation: $130-$180 per week.
Requirements: Background in bike, backpack, canoe, and kayak trips.
- UNIT LEADER
Compensation: $150-$190 per week.

WEST VIRGINIA

CAMP RIM ROCK
Box 69, Yellow Springs, WV 26865

❶ CAMPING (GIRLS)

Compensation: $1,600-$2,400 per season, room and board.

Duration: June 7 to September 2.

Contact: Director.

Phone:800-662-4650.

Apply by: May 1.

- SWIMMING LEADERS
Requirements: WSI certification, teaching ability.
- TENNIS COUNSELORS
Requirements: Experience.
- RIDING INSTRUCTORS
Requirements: Teaching certification.
- SPORTS AND GENERAL COUNSELORS
Requirements: Skilled in sports, ability to work with children.

GREENBRIER RIVER OUTDOOR ADVENTURES
P.O. Box 160, Bartow, WV 24920

❶ CAMPING (ADVENTURE)

Compensation: Room and board.

Duration: June 20 to August 16.

Contact: Directors/ Owners.

Phone: 304-456-5191.

Apply by: May 30.

- GROUP LEADERS
Compensation: $200-$250 per week.
Requirements: CPR and first aid certification, clean driving record.

- SUPPORT STAFF
Compensation: $130 per week.

- CLIMBING SPECIALIST
Compensation: $200-$250 per week.

- SWIMMING INSTRUCTORS
Compensation: $600 per month.
Requirements: WSI certification.

TIMBER RIDGE CAMPS
High View, WV 26808

❶ CAMPING

Compensation: $1,000-$1,500 per season, room and board.

Duration: June 16 to August 18.

Contact: Personnel Director, Timber Ridge Camps, 10 Old Court Rd., Baltimore, MD 21208.

Phone: 410-484-2233.

Apply by: April 1.

- SWIMMING INSTRUCTORS
Requirements: WSI certification.
- TENNIS INSTRUCTORS
- WOODWORKING INSTRUCTORS
- COMPUTER INSTRUCTORS

WISCONSIN

CAMP EDWARDS
P.O. Box 16, East Troy, WI 53120

❶ CAMPING

Compensation: Room and board.

Duration: June 7 to August 14.

Contact: Executive Director.

Phone: 414-642-7466.

- CABIN COUNSELORS
Compensation: $125-$135 per week.
- SUPPORT PERSONNEL
Compensation: $165-$250 per week.
- WATERFRONT DIRECTORS
Compensation: $165-$250 per week.
- UNIT LEADERS
Compensation: $165-$250 per week.

CAMP MANITO–WISH YMCA
Boulder Junction, WI 54512

❶ CAMPING

Compensation: Room and board.

Duration: June 3 to August 10.

Contact: Assistant Director, Camp Manito-Wish YMCA, N14 W24200 Tower Place 205, Waukesha, WI 53188.

Phone: 414-523-1623.

Apply by: May 1.

- WILDERNESS INSTRUCTORS
Compensation: $500-$550 per month.
Requirements: CPR, wilderness First Responder (available at camp), and other appropriate certification.

- ROPES COURSE LEADER
Compensation: $170 per week.

- CABIN COUNSELORS
Compensation: $118-$124 per week.
Requirements: CPR, first aid, and other appropriate certification.

- TRIP ASSISTANTS
Compensation: $106-$111 per week.
Requirements: CPR, first aid, and other appropriate certification.

CAMPS WOODLAND AND TOWERING PINES
Eagle River, WI 54521

❶ CAMPING

Compensation: $150-$200 per week, room and board.

Duration: June 23 to August 14.

Contact: Camps Woodland and Towering Pines, 242 Bristol St., Northfield, IL 60093.

Phone: 847-446-7311.

- BOATING STAFF
Requirements: WSI certification, experience with small crafts.

- RIFLERY/ARCHERY INSTRUCTORS
Requirements: NRA training.

- CRAFTS/INDIAN LORE STAFF

- TENNIS AND GYMNASTICS STAFF

CENTRAL WISCONSIN ENVIRONMENTAL STATION
7290 County MM, Amherst Junction, WI 54407

❶ CAMPING (ENVIRONMENTAL)

Compensation: Room and board.

Duration: May 23 to August 24.

Contact: Summer Camp Director.

Phone: 715-824-2428.

Apply by: May 1.

- SUMMER PROGRAM DIRECTOR
Compensation: $200-$225 per week.
- AQUATICS DIRECTOR
Compensation: $150-$170 per week.
Requirements: WSI and lifeguard certification.
- NATURALISTS/COUNSELORS
Compensation: $120-$140 per week.
- HEALTH LODGE SUPERVISOR
Compensation: $150-$170 per week.
Requirements: EMT or RN, advanced first

aid certification.

GEORGE WILLIAMS COLLEGE EDUCATION CENTERS—LAKE GENEVA CAMPUS

P.O. Box 210, Williams Bay, WI 53191

❶ CONFERENCE CENTERS

Duration: May 15 to September 15.

Contact: Director of Personnel.

Phone: 414-245-5531.

• LIFEGUARDS
Compensation: $6.75-7.50 per hour.
Requirements: Minimum age 18, WSI, CPR, and advanced first aid certification.
• FOOD SERVICES PERSONNEL
Compensation: $5.75 per hour.
• ARTS AND CRAFTS INSTRUCTORS
Compensation: $6-7 per hour.
Requirements: Minimum age 18.

SILVER SANDS GOLF ACADEMY

563 Upper Gardens, Fontana, WI 53125

❶ ATHLETICS

• COUNSELORS/GOLF INSTRUCTORS
Compensation: $150-$200 per week, room and board.
Duration: June 10 to August 10.
Phone: 800-232-1834.
Apply by: May1

W Y O M I N G

ABSAROKA MOUNTAIN LODGE

1231 E. Yellowstone Highway, Wapiti, WY 82450

❶ LODGING

Compensation: $350-$500 per month, room and board.

Duration: May 1 to November 1.

Contact: Owner.

Phone: 307-587-3963.

Apply by: April 1.

• COOKS
Requirements: Experience preferred.
• WRANGLERS
Requirements: Experience.
• MAINTENANCE
Requirements: Experience preferred.
• WAITSTAFF

ALPENHOF LODGE

Box 288, 3255 W. McCollister Ave., Teton Village, WY 83025

❶ RESORTS

Duration: May 20 to October 8.

Contact: Personnel Manager.

Phone: 307-733-3242.

• HOUSEKEEPING
Compensation: $960 per month.
• BELLMEN
Compensation: $840 per month.
• WAITSTAFF

Compensation: $370 per month.
• DISHWASHERS
Compensation: $960-$1,040 per month.

CODY'S RANCH RESORT

2604 Yellowstone Highway, Cody, WY 82414

❶ RESORTS

Compensation: $400-$800 per month, room and board.

Duration: April 15 to November 15.

Contact: Owners.

Phone: 307-587-6271.

• WRANGLERS
Requirements: Horsemanship experience.
• COOKS
Requirements: Culinary experience.
• WAGON DRIVERS
Requirements: Draft horse driving experience, CPR and first aid certification.
• HOUSEKEEPERS

SIGNAL MOUNTAIN LODGE

Grand Teton National Park, P.O. Box 50, Moran, WY 83013

❶ LODGING

Compensation: $4.35-$6 per hour.

Duration: May 1 to October 20.

Contact: Personnel Manager.

Phone: 800-672-6012.

Apply by: April 1.

• FRONT DESK PERSONNEL
Requirements: Typing and communications skills.
• LODGING STAFF
Requirements: Good housekeeping skills.
• PANTRY PERSONNEL
Requirements: Salad and dessert preparation skills.
• ACCOUNTING STAFF

TETON VALLEY RANCH CAMP

Jackson Hole, P.O. Box 8, Kelly, WY 83011

❶ CAMPING

Compensation: Room and board.

Duration: June 5 to August 23.

Contact: Director of Personnel.

Phone: 307-733-2958.

Apply by: April 1.

• COUNSELORS
Compensation: $500-$800 per season.
Requirements: CPR and first aid certification.
• KITCHEN STAFF
Compensation: Starts at $1,600 per season.
• LAUNDRY WORKERS
Compensation: Starts at $1,200 per season.
• MAINTENANCE STAFF
Compensation: $1,400 per season.

JOB HUNTING IN CYBERSPACE

Your computer may be the most useful job-prospecting tool you possess. Whether you're an on-line novice or a seasoned traveler in Cyberspace, the chapters in this section provide valuable information that cuts through the maze of Cyber-clutter that could impede your search. Also provided are numerous hints and tips that will help you beat your competition in Cyberspace.

JOB HUNTING IN CYBERSPACE

YOUR FIRST-TIME CYBER TOUR

EVERYONE HAS HEARD ABOUT IT, and almost 100 million Americans have tapped into it at least once. It goes by several names, all of which refer to the same "place"—the Internet, the Information Superhighway, or Cyberspace. It's not really a place, though; rather, it is a network that links thousands upon thousands of computers worldwide. Users log on to it through a service installed on their personal computer. Once you're logged on, your local telephone or cable line provides access to data in computers around the world.

THE CYBERSPACE REVOLUTION is changing the way we conduct business, and no job search today would be complete without tapping into the vast resources that are available on-line. Thousands of job listings, company profiles, and professional networking opportunities are waiting on-line 24 hours a day. With a computer, modem, phone line, and special software, you can access a virtual library of information on three basic components of Cyberspace: (1) the Internet, which includes one of its most popular facets, the World Wide Web; (2) the commercial on-line services; and (3) electronic bulletin board systems (BBSs).

CYBERSPACE CAN BE A ROUGH ROAD TO TRAVEL if you don't know the territory. Searching through the vast amounts of information can be tedious and time-consuming, and if you do not plan your time well, it can get expensive. However, don't let this scare you away from going on-line. You simply need to follow a few basic guidelines when conducting your on-line job search.

BEFORE YOU LEARN MORE, let's compare navigating Cyberspace with getting from the city you live in to another community miles away. There are some similarities to traveling the Information Superhighway.

Remember the last out-of-town trip you took? Most likely, it wasn't too complicated, but it could have been if you think about it. What vehicles, for example, could have gotten you there? Planes, trains, buses, automobiles? What road did you take? A major interstate, an old highway, maybe some back roads? There are lots of alternatives. There are even alternatives about which town you could have visited. And then there's the question of what part of town to go to, not to mention the streets to take once there. In other words, that last trip you took could have boggled someone else's mind if he or she hadn't traveled much.

THE SAME CAN BE TRUE for traveling in Cyberspace. Once you know the ropes, you don't have to think about it. Yes, you have a few vehicles to pick from, but just a few. We'll call these vehicles the "components" of Cyberspace. We'll call the towns "sites," though some call them "databases," "forums," or various other names, depending on format. It's the same principle as calling Akron a "town," a "city," or a "municipality." There are technical differences in the terms, but they all refer to a place you want to visit to encounter something or somebody firsthand.

Cyberspace is no different from that last out-of-town trip you took. The Information Superhighway is divided into various "regions" or areas: (1) the Internet and the World Wide Web; (2) newsgroups and electronic mail; (3) commercial on-line services; and (4) electronic bulletin board systems. Here is a brief summary of these areas and the sites ("towns") you'll find while traveling there.

THE INTERNET is a collective network of computers, comprised of thousands of interconnected computer networks, with the capability of exchanging data between them in a matter of seconds. It links government, corporate, university, individual, and research networks worldwide. Millions of people use the Internet to send and receive electronic messages, search databases, publish information, exchange data files, use remote computers, and "chat" with other people around the world.

Most people today access the multimedia part of the Internet, the World Wide Web, which contains easy-to-use features that help users link a wide variety of Internet resources. To use the "Web," as it's called for short, you need a "web browser." Once this software is loaded on your computer and you have signed-up with an Internet service provider, you can easily navigate, or "surf," through large amounts of information by pointing and clicking on icons, graphics, and "hypertext links." Hypertext links are cross-references to other documents. Clicking on the link with your mouse pointer takes you to the cross-referenced material, which can sometimes be on a completely different Web site.

THE WAY THAT YOU CONNECT WITH THE INTERNET is by logging on through an Internet service provider (ISP) by dialing into their server with your modem. Most Internet users use small local providers, national direct providers, or an Internet option that is standard fare with the major commercial on-line services (discussed further on in this chapter). If you wish to use a local Internet service provider to connect to the Internet, they can be found by scanning the ads in local and national computer publications, looking in the Yellow Pages, or asking a nearby computer dealer for reliable local sources.

Here are a few major national Internet service providers.

AMERICA ONLINE PRIMEHOST
888–AOL–1111
AT&T WORLDNET SERVICE
800–400–1447
GTE INTERNETWORKING (BBN)
800–472–4565
MCI PRIMIER PLAN
888-213-8379 (residential) **888-212-3089** (business)

Subscribers to Internet providers usually pay a monthly fee for using the service. Internet pricing is competitive. You may be able to subscribe for as little as $19 per month with unlimited connect time available. *Connect time* is the time that your computer is connected via modem to the service. Please note that not all ISP's support all of the types of communication hardware available on the market, so be sure to ask about compatibility in advance to avoid surprises later on.

TO FIND SPECIFIC INFORMATION ON THE INTERNET, you have to enter an Internet address or a Uniform Resource Locator, known as a "URL." These addresses are usually entered on the location line that is provided on your Web browser. These URL addresses are unique and take you directly to the Web site or home page where the information is stored. A Web site is a collection of various Web pages maintained by a company, organization, or person, and the home page is the main page of a Web site, usually the first page you see when you connect to that site. If you do not know the exact URL for the information you want, you can do a Web search for a company name or keywords to obtain a list of possible matches.

NEWSGROUPS ARE ANOTHER RESOURCE ON THE INTERNET for sharing information. A newsgroup is a discussion forum and is part of the Internet service *Usenet*. There are over an estimated 20,000 Usenet groups (newsgroups) around the world. A newsgroup is similar to a bulletin board. You can post messages to a certain group of people who share your interest, and other newsgroup participants who are interested in your messages can respond and offer their comments. This is a good way to network with people from around the world who have similar interests to your own. There are even newsgroups dedicated to recruiting and job searching.

TO PARTICIPATE IN A NEWSGROUP, you can use your Web browser. Also, check with your Internet service provider to see if it offers the Usenet service. Once connected to the Internet, to access a newsgroup, you type in the newsgroup address as follows:

news:<name of newsgroup>

A newsgroup address is formatted like this: "comp.job.offered." The first part of the address is the category the newsgroup is in. Below is a list of the most common categories:

alt	alternative
bio	biosciences
biz	business
clari	premium news
comp	computer-related
misc	miscellaneous
news	information
rec	recreational
sci	science
soc	social issues
talk	debate-oriented

One word of caution: The people who participate in newsgroups usually have been doing so for a long time. When first accessing a newsgroup, make sure you check out the rules of etiquette. Read the FAQ (frequently asked questions) and go to the new member section before participating.

To get started, here are a few newsgroups for you to visit:

alt.building.jobs—construction jobs

bionet.jobs.offered—science positions

biz.jobs.offered—business-related

misc.jobs.contract—contract jobs

misc.jobs.misc—jobs throughout the United States

misc.jobs.offered.entry—entry-level jobs

misc.jobs.resumes—lets you post your resume for employers to view

news.announce.newusers—provides new users with information on newsgroup etiquette and procedures

You can also obtain a list of Usenet groups to suit your needs simply by doing an Internet search.

THE COMMERCIAL ON-LINE SERVICES are another component of Cyberspace. The four major ones are America Online (AOL), CompuServe, Prodigy, and The Microsoft Network. All four of these services have extensive career and job information. ►See "Commercial On-Line Services," pp. 541-548.

Commercial on-line services offer an abundance of information in an easily navigated, organized format. As a member of an on-line service, you have access to reference material, magazines, news-papers, periodicals, specialized forums, games and entertainment, weather forecasts, sports information, business and financial reports, and electronic mail, as well as databases of employment opportunities and career guidance materials not available to non-members. All the major commercial on-line services also offer complete Internet access through either their own Internet browser or a browser provided by another company, such as Netscape Navigator or Microsoft Internet Explorer.

TO SIGN UP FOR A COMMERCIAL SERVICE, you can call the customer service number to receive free software to install on your computer that will allow you to access the service. ►See "Commercial On-Line Services," pp. 541-548. You can also obtain free software in many computer magazines, which will set up your computer to connect to the service. There are various pricing plans available. Often, once you have signed up for a service, you are charged a flat monthly fee that includes a number of free hours. An additional hourly rate is charged after your free hours have expired. Be aware that free hours are used up quickly, and charges can add up to quite a hefty amount as you wander around browsing. To keep costs down, plan your on-line time carefully. Take the time to familiarize yourself with the service's basic commands. Print out these commands as a reference for later. Also, be sure to visit the members' assistance section of the service. This is usually a free section designed to give newcomers a tour around the service, along with instructions on how to get around easily. If you anticipate lengthy online sessions, paying a little more for unlimited usage may end up being your best bet.

THE ELECTRONIC BULLETIN BOARD SYSTEMS, or BBSs, are computer systems that allow users to retrieve and send information by modem. BBSs generally have a narrower focus than the Internet or the commercial on-line services. One of their best features is that the job seeker can target job-related information relevant to his or her career goals. However, the quality of information found on a bulletin board varies. Make sure to check when the information was last updated to see how current it is. Don't waste your time chasing down leads that are out of date.

**WHAT DO YOU NEED TO GET CON-
NECTED?** You can use a wide variety of
computers. To run the most popular on-
line access software, you need either a
PC with a Pentium processor, or a Macintosh with a Power PC or G3 processor.
In either case, your computer should
have at least 32 megabytes of random access memory (RAM) installed. You'll
also need a modem with a speed of at
least 14.4 bits per second (although you
may find it difficult to download large
sites with modems slower than 28.8 bps)
a phone line, and software for whatever
on-line service you want to access. Once
you have your computer system set up,
you can connect to the on-line service
through a local access number. This is
just like making a phone call. Be aware
that you may incur additional phone
charges depending on the access number
you are using. Any additional phone
charges will appear on your phone bill
and are not included in your membership
fee.

WANT TO TRY BEFORE YOU BUY? To get
a feel for which service best fits your
needs, you can sign up and limit your use
to the free hours; similarly, some ISP's
have free introductory periods for this
purpose. If you are not satisfied, then
you can always cancel. Better yet, find a
friend who already is on-line who will
give you a tour and let you browse
through the career section. You can also
visit the library. Many larger libraries
have Internet connections and allow the
public to use their computers on a limited
basis.

THE FIRST TIME YOU GO ON-LINE, take
the time to learn your way around. Putting in a little effort up-front will save
you from headaches later. After you have
signed on to a commercial on-line service
or bulletin board system, your first stop
should be the Help section that lists basic
navigational commands (although the
quality of these Help sections varies from
service to service). Print out these commands so you can read them later. Read
all introductory information and go
through any on-line training tutorials you
find. Tutorials are a great help in explaining how to use the service effectively. Assistance in learning to navigate
the Internet is another matter. There is no
Help feature on the Internet. Although
your Internet service provider can sometimes help you find what you want, there
are search engines and directory services
that can help you locate what you are
looking for in the vastness of Cyberspace. **►See The Internet and the
World Wide Web," pp. 536-540.** Also,
don't be afraid to use the hypertext links
that hook one Web site to another. That's
what the World Wide Web is all about.

JOB HUNTING IN CYBERSPACE

THE INTERNET & THE WORLD WIDE WEB

THIS CHAPTER IS COMPRISED PRIMARILY of listings of Internet sites that are likely to be useful in your job search. In addition to the general listing of sites, there are lists called "State Web Sites" and "Web Search Engines and Directories." Together, these provide all the essentials you need to find almost any job-related site on the Internet.

If you have not read the first chapter in this section, you may wish to do so now to learn the basic concepts of using the Internet and the World Wide Web. **See "Your First-Time Cyber Tour," pp. 532-536.**

EACH **I**NTERNET SITE HAS A LOCATION ADDRESS, or "URL." If you know the exact URL, simply type it into your Web browser in order to contact the site and retrieve information. You must type the address exactly as you see it. Pay careful attention to capitalizations, which more often than not are left in lowercase. IF YOU ARE UNABLE TO CONNECT TO A SITE, the difficulty is probably caused by one of the following situations: (1) You typed the address incorrectly, possibly by entering capital letters; (2) the site was busy; (3) the site has moved; (4) the site no longer exists; or (5) Internet access in general is moving slowly. The last situation comes and goes, particularly during late afternoon and evening hours. In time, this problem may be solved, but for now, Internet users will have to live with it. If you do encounter the second or fifth scenarios, try entering the URL again—sometimes that is all it takes.

GENERAL WEB SITES

AMERICAN FEDERAL JOBS DIGEST LISTINGS
http://www.jobsfed.com
Database of over 10,000 current federal employment opportunities. Updated daily.

AMERICA'S JOB BANK
http://www.ajb.dni.us
Connects over 1,800 State Employment Services offices. Primarily for those seeking entry-level work in the government or military.

BUSINESS JOB FINDER
http://www.cob.ohio-state.edu/dept/fin/osujobs.htm
Maintained by Ohio State University's Fisher College of Business. Allows job seekers to explore business careers, visit major corporations' home pages, and check out employment opportunities. This site also contains dozens of links to other job search sites.

CAREERMOSAIC
http://www.careermosaic.com
Comprehensive guide to job listings on Usenet, company profiles, job fairs, and entry-level job opportunities. Service is also available on Prodigy.

CAREERPATH.COM
http://www.careerpath.com
Provides access to newspaper employment listings from over 65 newspapers broken down by geographic region along with other job search vehicles.

CAREERS.WSJ.COM
See "Wall Street Journal Interactive Edition" on page 509.

CAREERWEB
http://www.cweb.com
CareerWeb's JobMATCH lets you track down the perfect job and participate in virtual career fairs with recruiting managers from top companies. You must register for JobMATCH, but there are

other non-registered postings to search through.

CONTRACTORS EXCHANGE
http://www.contractorsexchange.com
Contractor and construction job listings.

E-SPAN'S JOB OPTIONS
http://www.joboptions.com/esp/plsq/es pan_enter.espan_home
A searchable database of employment openings in a variety of career fields. Lets job seekers create on-line resumes and receive E-mail notices of job listings that fit their qualifications. Service is also available on America Online, CompuServe, and Prodigy.

EMPLOYERS NETWORK

Provides career links to jobs and career-related websites. Also lists government career sites, salary information and offers links to online classified ads.

EXEC-PC
http://www.execpc.com

Job opportunities in the Midwest.

FEDWORLD
http://www.fedworld.gov
Provides information on employment opportunities with the National Technical Information Service, both in the United States and overseas.

FINANCENET
http://www.financenet.gov
Government jobs page lists jobs in government, finance, and accounting and links to general employment resources.

1ST STEPS TO THE HUNT
http://www.interbiznet.com/hunt/companies/
Gives you access to 4,000 companies' job pages. Go to the home page to subscribe to a recruiting newsletter.

FORTUNE CONSULTANTS OF ORLANDO
http://www.fortuneconsultants.com
Job listings for various occupations. Also provides personal consultants and resume advice.

4WORK
http://4work.com

Lists volunteer opportunities, internships, and job openings across the United States.

HELP WANTED—USA
http://iccweb.com
Includes listings of some 10,000 job openings, many in computer-related fields. Job seekers can post their resumes for 6 months for a $25 fee.

HOOVER'S BUSINESS RESOURCES
http://www.hoovers.com
Contains in-depth profiles of more than 2,000 companies, sketches of over 10,000 others, and a vast array of business information. Service is also available on America Online and CompuServe.
HRCOMM
Jobnet page provides a forum for job postings and job inquiries for those in the human resources field.

INTERNET JOB LOCATOR
http://www.joblocator.com/jobs
Database primarily of technical and manage-ment positions. Provides links to hundreds of recruiters and thousands of hiring companies.

JOBBANK USA
http://www.jobbankusa.com
Includes Job MetaSearch, a utility that can search through the Internet's largest job databases for jobs in specific fields.

JOBCENTER
http://www.jobcenter.com
Matches applicants with employers. Lets you post your resume in the database and be notified by E-mail when an appropriate job match is made. Fee for posting a resume is $20 for six months.

JOBHUNT
http://www.job-hunt.org
A guide to the newest and best employment resources on the Internet. Good place for beginners.

JOBSMART
http://www.jobsmart.org
Although this site is targeted primarily toward those searching for career opportunities in California, there are links to several national employers as well as other career counseling and job search sites.

MONSTER BOARD
http://www.monster.com

Contains over 50,000 job listings worldwide, including openings posted by the nation's top companies. Service is also available on Prodigy.

NET TEMPS
http://www.net-temps.com

Contains temporary or permanent job listings from employment agencies.

ONLINE CAREER CENTER
http://www.occ.com/occ

Provides career fairs, career guidance assistance, and links to recruiting sites. Free to browse, and no charge to applicants who enter their own resume on-line, although registration is required. Service is also available on Prodigy.

PURSUITNET JOBS
http://www.tiac.net/users/jobs

Matches employers with applicants who are seeking positions in the $30,000 to $200,000 range. A fee is charged once an offer of employment is accepted.

RECRUITERS ONLINE NETWORK
http://www.ipa.com

Provides employment professionals and human resources personnel with career opportunities and career advice. Free to post a resume and browse extensive listings, but membership is required to browse resumes.

SMALL BUSINESS ADMINISTRATION
http://sba.gov/jobs

Provides a list of jobs posted with the Small Business Administration.

SEARCH 123
http://search123.com

More than 50,000 job listings from around the world.

WALL STREET JOURNAL INTERACTIVE EDITION
http://careers.wsj.com

This site is absolutely one of the best available for those searching for positions in business, advertising, engineering, hi-tech, banking and finance, consulting, and many other industries. Replete with thousands of company listings and job postings, job search advice, e-mail updates, salary info, and career indicators, this comprehensive site offers the job seeker a multitude of resources for successful hunting both in the U.S. and abroad. It also features directories of executive recruiters and venture-capital firms worldwide along with a career counseling service in which candidates can schedule tele-counseling sessions online.

VIRTUAL JOB FAIR
http://www.careerexpo.com/jobsearch.html

Allows the user to search hundreds of companies' high tech job listings.

YAHOO'S EMPLOYMENT HIERARCHY PAGE
http://www.yahoo.com/Business/Employment

Offers hypertext access to Web sites and Usenet newsgroups that have specialized or regional job listings, resume postings, and career resources.

Besides checking the sites just listed, keep in mind that many professional associations now have sites on the World Wide Web, and a number of these sites include listings of current job openings. The sites can be located through Web search engines (discussed later in this chapter); also, many of the site addresses follow this format:

http://www.organization acronym.org

To give just two examples, the Web sites of the American Library Association (http://www.ala.org) and of the Institute of Electrical and Electronics Engineers (http://www.ieee.org) list hundreds of job openings for professionals in those fields.

STATE WEB SITES

Listed below are state Web sites that offer on-line job listings. Both official and unofficial state government sites are included. As of this writing, not all states had job listings on-line. Be aware that new Web sites are starting up everyday, and it is likely that many states that are not listed below will soon be on the World Wide Web. You can find them by using any of several Web search engines (discussed later in this chapter). Note as well that there are many city Web sites that list municipal openings. These can also be found using Web search engines.

ALASKA
http://www.state.ak.us

ARKANSAS
http://www.state.ar.us

COLORADO
http://www.state.co.us

GEORGIA
http://www.state.ga.us/gopher/merit.htm

HAWAII
http://www.aloha.net/~edpso
http://www.hcc.hawaii.edu/hspls/hjobs.html

INDIANA
http://www.ai.org/jobs/index.html

LOUISIANA
http://www.dnr.state.la.us/~cs/csjobopp.htm

MAINE
http://www.state.me.us/labor/jsd/jobserv.htm

MARYLAND
http://dop.state.md.us

MASSACHUSETTS
http://www.state.ma.us/govserv.htm#employ

MISSISSIPPI
http://www.webcom.com/whipcomm/mscareer

MONTANA
http://www.mt.gov

NEBRASKA
http://www.state.ne.us/personnel/per.html

NEVADA
http://www.state.nv.us

NEW HAMPSHIRE
http://www.state.nh.us

NEW JERSEY
http://www.state.nj.us/personnel

NEW MEXICO
http://www.state.nm.us/dol

NEW YORK
http://www.labor.state.ny.us

NORTH DAKOTA
http://www.state.nd.us/www/general.html

OHIO
http://www.state.oh.us

OREGON
http://www.das.state.or.us/jobs

SOUTH CAROLINA
http://www.state.sc.us

TEXAS
http://www.state.tx.us

VERMONT
http://www.state.vt.us/det/dethp.htm

VIRGINIA
http://www.state.va.us

WASHINGTON
http://www.wa.gov/wahome.html

WEST VIRGINIA
http://www.state.wv.us

WISCONSIN
http://www.state.wi.us

WEB SEARCH ENGINES AND DIRECTORIES

Web search engines and directories are on-line utilities located on the World Wide Web. They can assist you in finding a particular piece of information. For instance, if you enter the keyword "jobs," the search engine will search the Internet and compile a list of sites that match the keyword. In the list it brings up, each citation is called a "hit."

All of the search engines and directories listed below have instructions on their Web pages. Since each one is slightly different, you have to learn how to use them individually. They are designed to be user-friendly.

Below are some of the most popular search engines on the World Wide Web.

ALTAVISTA
http://altavista.com

EXCITE
http://www.excite.com

INFOSEEK NET SEARCH
http://www.infoseek.com

LYCOS
http://www.lycos.com

WEBCRAWLER
http://www.webcrawler.com

To the casual user, Web directories appear very similar to Web search engines. However, with a directory, a user's search extends only to the Internet sites that have already been indexed in the directory. Although some directories may have a limited number of indexed sites, others, such as Yahoo!, are quite comprehensive, and a search can access a wide variety of what the Web has to offer. Moreover, some directories also have links to search engines.

Below are some of the most popular directories on the World Wide Web.

HOTBOT
http://www.hotbot.com

MAGELLAN
http://www.mckinley.com

YAHOO!
http://www.yahoo.com

ALL THE SEARCH ENGINES AND DIRECTORIES listed above can help you locate companies, providing they have some Internet presence. Today, most of the very large companies have a Web page. The easiest way to get to them is to bypass the search engine option and simply type in the following Internet address on the location line of your Web browser:

http://www.companyname.com

where "companyname" is the name of the company. For example, http://www.ibm.com is IBM's Internet address. ►See "Getting the Edge on Rival Job Prospectors in Cyberspace," pp. 508-510.

IF YOU CANNOT FIND A COMPANY'S WEB PAGE, it might be because it does not exist. Some companies have been surprisingly slow to get on the Information Superhighway. But if the foregoing method did not work, it does not necessarily mean that the company is not on the Internet. Try simply typing the company's name on the search line provided on any of the search engines. If the firm has a site, all of the engines are likely to find it using this method.

Simply typing the word "jobs" will generate some useful hits. However, you are likely to get more than you bargained for. As a general principle, the more generic the word you type in, the more hits you will get. Hence, a word like "jobs" might net too many hits. One saving grace of most search engines is that they have a hierarchy in the presentation of the hits they find. That is, the hits they deem to be the most useful will come up first. As you go down the list, you will begin to reach a point of diminishing returns. Other general words like "employment" or "career" may give you similar problems.

TRY TO USE PHRASES instead. Phrase or word combinations allow you more specificity. Examples are "jobs, finance" or "jobs in finance." Each search engine has a preferred syntax, so you have to adapt the phases to the search engine you select. Read the instructions provided with the search engine.

Try to be creative and open-minded when it comes to words or phrases on which to base your search. For example, a word like "editor" or "coach," or a specific career field like "real estate," might generate hits that cite various groups or associations that will be useful in your job search. It might also lead you to bulletin boards, newsgroups, or industry overviews, not to mention listings of job openings you want to know about. The most useful piece of advice about using search engines and directories is to try lots of things—some of them are bound to work.

JOB HUNTING IN CYBERSPACE

COMMERCIAL ON-LINE SERVICES

THIS CHAPTER IS COMPRISED PRIMARILY of information on the four major commercial online services: (1) America Online (AOL), (2) CompuServe, (3) Prodigy, and (4) The Microsoft Network. It includes a list of their most valuable sites, instructions on how to get to them, and highlights of their content.

If you have not read the first chapter in this section, you may wish to do so at this time to learn the basics of the commercial online services. ►See "Your First-Time Cyber Tour," pp. 532-535.

ALL FOUR SERVICES, as previously stated, will allow you a free trial—some for as many as 15 hours, some for longer, depending on the specific offer when you start your subscription. In the parts of this chapter that follow on each individual service, telephone numbers and addresses are provided to obtain your trial software. In order to run the software, you need either a PC with a Pentium processor, or a Macintosh with a Power PC or G3 processor. Your computer should also have at least 32 megabytes of random access memory (RAM) and a modem capable of operating at 14.4 or 28.8 bits per second or higher.

Immediately following is information about the four major online services. Be aware that membership fees, usage costs, and free privileges often change. Be sure to call the service to get the most up-to-date information on all possible options.

AMERICA ONLINE (AOL)

P.O. Box 10810
Herdon, VA 22070
Telephone: 800-827-6364
Membership Fee: $9.95 per month (includes five free hours); other options available
Additional Usage: $2.95 per hour

AOL is the most popular of the major services and is considered the most family-oriented of the services. It is also thought by many to have the most prolific "chat rooms"—that is, groups of users who communicate via text in multi-user assemblies. Celebrities also often chat with users online.

For job prospectors, AOL offers its members The AOL Career Center, which includes access to major job databases, resume banks, occupational profiles, resume help, drop-in chat sessions with counselors and AOL members, and private and confidential online career counseling sessions (by appointment). The center is staffed by professional career counselors and experts with decades of experience in career guidance. Use of the center is included in the basic membership fee, but there are additional fees for some of the career guidance material available.

Following is a brief description of some of the most valuable job databases and career resources on AOL. When it is applicable, the "keyword" is given in parentheses. A keyword is the word to type on the line provided after clicking your mouse on the "Go To" button. In most cases, however, keywords are not needed, because the site is accessible from the on-screen menu.

THE CAREER CENTER (KEYWORD: CA-REERS)
This is the apex of the pyramid at which AOL users access all other sites listed below, all of which are options shown on the on-screen menu.

ACCESS.POINT
Forum contains a nonprofit career center for those seeking employment in the nonprofit sector.

AOL CLASSIFIEDS: EMPLOYMENT
Job listings of professional office jobs.

EMPLOYER CONTACTS DATABASE
Contains profiles of over 6,000 American employers.

EMPLOYMENT AGENCY DATABASE
Contains information on search firms throughout the United States.

E-SPAN'S JOB OPTIONS
A pioneer in online employment recruiting, E-Span's Job Options provides electronic advertising through several online services around the world and around the clock. E-Span began its service in 1991 and now has more than 1,000 clients representing a broad spectrum of industries. It features a searchable database of employment openings in a variety of career fields, such as engineering, human resources, manufacturing, and medicine. Updates are made every week, usually on Monday. E-Span's Job Options can be accessed through AOL Internet and is also available on CompuServe and Prodigy, as well as on the Internet via the World Wide Web.

FEDERAL JOB LIBRARY
Information on positions available with the federal government. This service is also available on the World Wide Web.

GONYEA ONLINE CAREER CENTER (KEY-WORD: CAREER CENTER)
Provides access to Help Wanted USA along with other helpful areas such as government jobs, occupational profiles which provide descriptions, earnings, and outlook information for various careers, links to employment agencies, job hunting tips and strategies, and an extensive resume bank.

HELP WANTED—USA
A service of Gonyea and Associates, Inc., the developers of The AOL Career Center. Publishes over 10,000 help wanted ads each week.

HOOVER'S BUSINESS RESOURCES (KEY-WORD: HOOVERS)
Profiles more than 2,000 companies in depth and offers brief sketches of over 10,000 more businesses. It also provides links to over 2,000 corporate Web sites, U.S. and international business resources, investor resources, and other career resources. Its profiles list names, addresses, phone numbers, and key personnel. This service is available in numerous other areas, including CompuServe and the World Wide Web.

TALENT BANK
A searchable resume bank designed to help AOL members market themselves to the entire AOL membership or locate other members with certain credentials.

COMPUSERVE

5000 Arlington Ctr. Blvd.
Columbus, OH 43220
Telephone: 800-848-8990
Membership Fee: $9.95 per month (includes five free hours—other options available)
Additional Usage: $2.95 per hour

CompuServe is the second most popular online service. It is considered by many to be the most business-oriented of the major services, since it has the most databases and business forums. Whereas AOL has a wide reputation for its chat rooms, CompuServe is known for its forums that pertain to special areas of business. A special listing of them is provided below after the listing of databases.

CompuServe provides a wealth of resources for the job seeker and a variety of databases and forums. The forums are special interest groups through which one can find not only potential jobs but also background information about potential employers. Many have at least one section where job opportunities are listed or job seekers have posted notices of their desire to work.

Following is a list of some of the most valuable databases and forums that are available on CompuServe. In order to access the sites listed below: (1) Click the "Go" icon; (2) type in the forum/database name (3) click "OK" or hit enter.

Databases:

Access to some of the databases requires payment of a surcharge above CompuServe's regular charges.

BIZ*FILE (GO BIZFILE)
Provides access to names, addresses, and phone numbers of more than 10 million U.S. and Canadian businesses. The database is searchable by geographic location, company name, phone number, or type of business.

BUSINESS DATABASE PLUS (GO BUSDB)
Makes over 500 regional, national, and

international business periodicals available for search. The service also offers articles from more than 550 specialized business newsletters. Still more articles are provided through sister services: Magazine Database Plus (GO MAGDB), Computer Database Plus (GO COMPDB), and Health Database Plus (GO HLTDB).

THE BUSINESS WIRE (GO TBW)
Provides news articles, press releases, and other information relating to business issues. The service provides information on hundreds of businesses and is updated continuously throughout the day.

D&B DUN'S ELECTRONIC BUSINESS DIRECTORY (GO DUNSEBD)
Provides access to a database of more than 8.5 million businesses and professionals. The database, which can be searched by a variety of methods, contains listings of names, addresses, phone numbers, and other information.

E-SPAN (GO ESPAN)
This service has long been a part of CompuServe Classifieds (GO CLASSIFIEDS), a section of the service designed to emulate newspaper classified advertising. For basic information on E-Span, refer to its listing in this chapter under America Online.

On CompuServe, E-Span users can choose from several activities in addition to searching the job database. You can read job postings, submit a resume to E-Span's resume database, or place your own help wanted advertisement.

E-Span also offers CompuServe members a Career Management Forum. Users can network with other job seekers, share success stories, and access information on the job market.

HOOVER'S COMPANY DATABASE (GO HOOVERS)
Profiles more than 2,000 companies in depth and offers brief sketches of over 10,000 more businesses. It is also available from AOL and via the World Wide Web. For more detailed information, refer to its listing in this chapter under America Online.

INFORMATION PLEASE BUSINESS ALMANAC (GO BIZALMANAC)
Makes available interesting facts, rankings, and advice designed to interest the business community. The service draws from approximately 500 sources to provide information on 700 different topics, and makes available thousands of addresses and phone and fax numbers of businesses. Articles are searchable by category or keyword.

IQUEST (GO IQUEST)
Provides a huge variety of information from 400 databases. The service provides inexpensive access to many of the world's top information resources. Among IQuest's contributors are Dialog Information Services, Inc., NewsNet, Inc., and VU/TEXT Information Services, Inc. Full-featured searching capabilities are available.

MARKETING/MANAGEMENT RESEARCH CENTER (GO MGMTRC)
Makes available nine databases containing indexes and full-text articles from major U.S. and international management, business, and technical magazines; indexes of industry and market research studies and reports; and news releases from both international and U.S. companies. Among the databases available are ABI/INFORM, Findex, and McGraw-Hill Publications Online.

Forums:

Each forum has many separate discussion areas and related libraries of downloadable files. All of the forums listed below have at least one section devoted to employment opportunities.

ALL PROFESSIONS CENTRAL FORUM (GO PROCENTRAL)
Provides links to forums and information in 20 different industries.

AMIA MEDICAL FORUM (GO MEDSIG)
Sponsored by the American Medical Informatics Association, with members from all facets of the medical community.

BROADCAST PROFESSIONAL FORUM (GO BPFORU)
Serves the interests of those involved in radio, television, professional audio and video communications, and several related fields. The forum is also a meeting place for members of AESNET, the online membership of the Audio Engineering Society, and SBENET, the online membership of the Society of Broadcast Engineers.

COMPUTER CONSULTANT'S FORUM (GO CONSULT)

Provides numerous opportunities for com-puter consultants interested in networking with others in their field. The forum provides discussions on marketing and business development and includes help wanted postings from companies looking for consultants.

COURT REPORTERS FORUM (GO CRFORUM)

Participants include representatives from the National Court Reporters Association and the *Journal of Court Reporters*. The forum includes a classified ads section where participants can find help wanted postings, as well as listings of equipment for sale.

DESKTOP PUBLISHING FORUM (GO DTPFORUM)

Provides opportunities for both independent professionals and employees to interact. The forum sponsors a variety of seminars and conferences as well as the usual opportunities for discussion. There is also a classified ads section where participants can post notices for jobs wanted or available.

EDUCATION FORUM (GO EDFORUM)

Discusses all facets of the learning and teaching process, including finding jobs for educational professionals. The forum is the gathering place for a wide variety of individuals, from parents and students to university faculty and textbook publishers.

ENTREPRENEUR'S SMALL BUSINESS SQUARE (GO BIZSQUARE)

Makes available products, services, and franchising and job opportunities. The section is a jumping-off spot for Entrepreneur's Small Business Forum (GO SMALLBIZ), an online version of *Entrepreneur Magazine* (GO ENTMAGAZINE).

E—SPAN CAREER MANAGEMENT FORUM (GO CAREERS)

Sponsored by the E-Span employment service, it provides a place for job seekers and human resources professionals to gather and discuss issues. The forum has its own classified ads section and resume library, as well as a wealth of other information and opportunities for discussion.

INTERNATIONAL TRADE FORUM (GO TRADE)

Allows discussions of customs, trade practices, and international relationships. The forum is a place for professionals from around the world to make contacts and trade information on exciting opportunities.

JOURNALISM FORUM (GO JFORUM)

Has allowed writers interested in print, radio, television, and other areas of the media to gather since 1985. In addition to being a popular place to find job postings and freelance opportunities, the forum is the meeting place for a number of professional writers' organizations.

LEAP FORUM (GO LEAP)

Lets design professionals who use computers to improve productivity gather. Sponsored by the League for Engineering Automation Productivity, it provides discussion of the basic topics of CAD and CAM software and equipment and lets forum participants exchange information about job openings and educational opportunities.

LEGAL FORUM (GO LAWSIG)

Devoted to serving the needs of the legal community. Attorneys, paralegals, corrections officers, and many others get together to discuss a variety of topics, such as copyrights and bankruptcies. The forum has a classified ads section in which members can advertise job openings.

OFFICE AUTOMATION FORUM (GO OAFORUM)

For people who share an interest in business machines. They discuss trends in software and hardware, as well as share information on employment options. The forum is also a home base for vendors such as Dayo Software, FranklinQUEST, and MicroBiz.

PHOTO PROFESSIONALS FORUM (GO PHOTOPRO)

A popular meeting spot for photographers to share tips, trade equipment, and find out about job opportunities.

PR AND MARKETING FORUM (GO PRSIG)

A gathering of professionals in communications, public relations, sales, and marketing. The forum offers discussions on a wide variety of topics, including consumer affairs and government. Its Jobs Online section is one of its most popular areas.

PROJECT AND COST MANAGEMENT FORUM (GO TCMFORUM)

For professionals involved in planning, sched-uling, estimating, and many other facets of project management. Created in 1995 by the Association for Total Cost Management, the forum's many sections include a help wanted section and special interest groups on manufacturing, architecture, and construction.

SOHO FORUM (GO SOHO)

Serves the needs of people working in a small office or home office environment. Sponsored by *PC World*, the forum has extensive libraries, and its message sections feature lively discussions on a wide range of topics.

TELECOMMUNICATIONS PROFESSIONALS FORUM (GO TELEPRO)

Allows the user to participate in discussions about the telecommunications industry as well as research career opportunities in the field.

TRAINERS' AND TRAINING FORUM (GO TRAINERS)

Provides interesting discussions for those involved in training of any type. Among its discussion group sections are presentations, freelancing, and public speaking. There is also a classified ads section.

WOMEN'S WIRE ONLINE (GO WOMEN)

Designed to help women find resources in a variety of areas. There are four departments: (1) Career & $$$, (2) Health & Fitness, (3) News, and (4) Styles & Trends & Women's Wire Picks. The Career & $$$ area features seminars, advice, and other aids for job seekers.

PRODIGY

445 Hamilton Ave.
White Plains, NY 10601
Telephone: 800-PRODIGY
Membership Fee: $9.95 per month (includes five free hours); other options available
Additional Usage: $2.95 per hour

Prodigy was started by Sears, Roebuck and IBM, which sold it off in 1996. Prodigy was originally marketed primarily as a family-oriented online service. Its original emphasis on graphics, color, and

fun provided the impetus a few years ago for Cyberspace operators to dress up their sites. Today, the service is still long on fun, though short on business services. Nonetheless, there are some valuable sites for job prospectors as well as a unique feature that integrates the Internet with Prodigy's own sites. (In addition to its regular online service, Prodigy has launched an internet service—Prodigy Internet (Prodigy Classic is the commercial service). Accessed directly through the World Wide Web at http://www.prodigy.com, this new service allows unlimited Internet access for a fixed price per month and also access to Prodigy proprietary content.

Prodigy simplifies your online job hunt by integrating Prodigy sites and the Internet onto one screen. Job hunters may take advantage of this convenience by accessing Prodigy's Career Connections!, which is a page on the World Wide Web that is accessible only to Prodigy subscribers. Once on this page, users may access both Prodigy sites as well as Web pages of all genres since the software they are using is actually Prodigy's Web browser.

In order to steer you to career sites on the Web, rather than its entire spectrum, icons are provided. When clicked on, they give you other menu options. The icons have titles such as Getting Started, Resume Connections, and The Career Travel Guide.

To arrive at Career Connections!: (1) select the "Go To" menu, and then select "Jump To"; (2) type "Career Connections!"; (3) press Enter. This will get you to the Career Connections! page, from which all Prodigy career-related sites on and off the Internet are accessed.

Following are some of the most valuable sites you can access, some of which are on the World Wide Web and others on Prodigy's own computers. The job databases are free, but many of the resume banks and recruiting services charge a fee.

ADAMS JOBBANK ONLINE

Contains current listings of employment opportunities nationwide.

CAREERMOSAIC

Large database of job listings, resumes, and company profiles. Offers good in-

COMMERICAL ON-LINE SERVICES

formation on entry-level opportunities for new graduates and corporate college recruiting programs. This service is also available on the World Wide Web.

CATAPULT
Provides links to college career services around the world.

CONTRACT EMPLOYMENT WEEKLY
Contract employment opportunities from the current issue of *Contract Weekly*, the largest publication dedicated to contract technical employment. This service is also available on The Microsoft Network.

E–SPAN JOB DATABASE SEARCH
Allows free resume posting, and lets you access the salary calculator to determine the salary you need if you plan to relocate to a new city. This service is also available on AOL, CompuServe, and the World Wide Web. For more details, refer to its listing in this chapter under America Online.

INSURANCE CAREER CENTER
A job database and talent bank for the insurance industry. There is a $25 annual membership fee for posting your resume/profile in the talent bank, but graduating students can get this service free.

JOBTRAK
Job listings for college students and college graduates. At least 500 new jobs are posted each day. This service is also available on the World Wide Web.

MONSTER BOARD DRIVEWAY
Applicants can post and update their resume, search through a database of over 55,000 job listings, and conduct research on prospective employers. This service is also available on the World Wide Web.

NATIONAL BUSINESS EMPLOYMENT WEEKLY
Job openings and employment briefings from Dow Jones's weekly newspaper, *National Business Employment Weekly*, which contains a week's worth of help wanted ads from *The Wall Street Journal*.

NCS CAREER MAGAZINE
Provides job database, resume bank, employer profiles, relocation assistance, and online corporate college recruiting. There is a fee to post a resume online.

ONLINE CAREER CENTER
One of the first online employment services. No charge to post your resume if you enter it online yourself. This service is also available on the World Wide Web.

ONLINE RESUME SERVICES
Listing of several companies that can create an electronic resume for you and assist you in getting your resume in front of potential employers.

REGIONAL EMPLOYMENT OPPORTUNITIES
Listings of job opportunities throughout the United States.

SKILLSEARCH
Online placement service that matches your profile with an employer's request. There is a fee for this service.

THE MICROSOFT NETWORK
One Microsoft Way
Redmond, WA 98052
Telephone: 800-386-5550
Membership Fee: $69.50 per year (includes five free hours/month)
Additional Usage: $2.50 per hour ($19.95/mo. unlimited also available)

The Microsoft Network, or MSN, is the newest of the four commercial online services and has grown to be the third most popular service. This service is available only for PCs running the Windows 95 or 98 operating systems. In addition to providing access to msn.com and the Web, this service features a program viewer that incorporates sound and animation. Members are able to receive news from MSNBC—Microsoft and NBC's cable TV network—and view original entertainment programming. Although much of what can be found on MSN can be accessed through most ISP's, there is a high degree of user-friendliness on the new MSN, and there are still some forums that can be accessed by members only.

Most of the job listings available through MSN can be reached easily through links on the "onstage" page (www.onstage .msn.com--consider setting this as the default home page for easy access). By clicking on the "Business" option under the "Web Directory" list, users are given 3 job-related options: "Careers and work," "Careers and work—other," and "Employment and job search." Each of the aforementioned options immediately provide users with links to several sites with job postings and career information in a wide variety of fields. In addition, MSN has rated each of the sites using a 1-4 star system to aid users in finding the sites MSN deems the most comprehensive and helpful—some of these are profiled below.

As mentioned, the new version of MSN is just that: new. Therefore, the forum choices for job hunting are thus far slim, but more forums may be added in the near future. Choose the "Communicate" option under "Microsoft Network Sites," then choose "MSN Forums" then "Business & Investing" to check for possibly helpful forums.

AMERICA'S EMPLOYERS
Location: Business/Careers and work (3 stars)

This site provides users with over 50,000 job postings and profiles of over 40,000 companies. There are also links to contact forums where one can network and receive job hunting and resume tips.

CAREER MAGAZINE
Location: Business/Careers and work (3 stars)

This online publication provides job seekers with tips and tools for executing successful job searches on the Internet. Job postings, forums, a resume bank, company profiles, and links to other job search sites are provided.

ESCOFFIER ON LINE
Location: Business/Careers and work—other (4 stars)

This site is a gold mine for those searching for careers in the restaurant industry. Job postings for food preparation and restaurant management, information on restaurant career services, and a "positions sought" section aid the culinary professional's job search.

IRS FEDERAL JOB SEARCH
Location: Business/Employment and job search (4 stars)

This is a "how to" and "where to" site for those interested in securing government positions. Upon accessing, users can receive e-mail messages regarding openings, browse current listings, and use the pay scale and calculation tables to find the best government employment opportunities.

QUINTESSENTIAL CAREER AND JOB HUNTING RESOURCES GUIDE
Location: Business/Employment and job search (4 stars)

Practical tutorials on writing resumes and cover letters are helpful features of this site. In addition, there are links to several job sites broken down by industry along with links to and suggestions for other career development resources.

VILLAGE CAREER
Location: Business/Careers and work—other (4 stars)

This site is chock full of helpful information on establishing a new career or developing a current career track. It includes links to job sites, personal career questionnaires, information on working at home, and tips on improving your work habits. Women will find this site especially helpful, as there are several articles and links to sites designed for the working woman.

JOB HUNTING IN CYBERSPACE

Getting the Edge on Competition in Cyberspace

THIS CHAPTER IS INTENDED TO PROVIDE you with an edge on all the other job prospectors who are also logging on to Cyberspace. And there are many competitors out there! Using the World Wide Web as a primary source for job searches is not unusual anymore, so being knowledgeable and prepared may be the key to securing that perfect position.

EVEN THOUGH THERE IS COMPETITION ON-LINE, that does not mean that going on-line exposes you to more rival job prospectors for any given job. Millions of job seekers are out in Cyberspace anyway, regardless of what you do. Most hiring authorities don't necessarily give any preference to those pounding the pavement of the Information Superhighway (unless, for instance, they're hiring for a job like Web Developer or for positions at one of the commercial on-line services), but by going on-line, you avail yourself of job opportunities that you would be unlikely to know about otherwise. This is simply because there is no other medium that allows you so much access to so many job opportunities. That in itself gives you an edge over people who choose not to prospect in Cyberspace.

Among the many who do go on-line, those who follow the seven tips described below will have a better chance of getting their desired job.

TIP #1: **D**EVELOP AN ELECTRONIC RESUME. An on-line job search is immensely more efficient if you have an electronic resume. Generally, there are two options: (1) You can do a fill-in-the-blank resume on a form provided by many posting services, or (2) you can write your own resume, which obviously gives you the option to be more creative and to tailor it to fit your specific needs.

Your electronic resume should be saved as a plain text file in ASCII characters—that is, a DOS text or Windows text format. In these types of text files, only the actual characters, tabs, and carriage returns are saved, so don't worry about

typeface, margins, and other formatting options. Refer to the software manual of the program you used to create your resume for instructions on converting the resume to a text file.

RESUMES THAT YOU SUBMIT TO RESUME BANKS or send by electronic mail to employers are put into databases. Recruiters and employers can search the database by keywords and compile a list of qualified candidates in minutes. Keywords describe your skills and experiences and come from the terminology used in your job field. Presumably, these words are included in your resume.

TIP #2: **S**ET UP AN ELECTRONIC MAIL ADDRESS. People in business today are using electronic mail, or E-mail, more than ever before. It is becoming as vital and basic as the telephone. E-mail messages are sent electronically from one computer to another. The system has many advantages. It's fast, inexpensive, and you can send one message to many people at once. Even long documents and computer files can be sent through E-mail.

E-mail can be sent to people regardless of whether they are using the Internet, a bulletin board system, or a commercial on-line service. As long as someone has an E-mail address, you can send him or her messages—no matter where he or she is in the world. On-line ads and even many classified ads are now asking that responses be sent via E-mail. To conduct a viable on-line job search, you really need an E-mail address.

YOU GET AN E-MAIL ADDRESS when you subscribe to any commercial on-line service or Internet service provider. ➛**See**

The Internet and the World Wide Web," **pp. 536-540,** and **Commercial On-Line Services," pp. 541-547.** E-mail service is included in your membership fee. When you first sign on with a service, you are given an E-mail address that you can change if you like. Like your postal address, your E-mail address tells people where to send messages to you on-line.

AN E-MAIL ADDRESS USUALLY LOOKS like this:

joejones@aol.com

It is made up of two parts: (1) the user name (Joejones), which identifies who the recipient is, and (2) the domain name or post office, (@aol.com), which tells where the mail is being received. In this example, "aol.com" means that the person receives E-mail through America Online.

E-MAIL YOUR RESUME to perspective em-ployers by attaching it to a message. Most e-mail software allows you to attach whole files which can then be opened on the receiving end. If you are not certain that the receiver uses the same or compatible software, it is a good idea to save a version of your resume in "text only" format or, in the case of different versions of MS Word, saving in "rich text format" keeps special characters and formatting intact.

A FEW WORDS OF CAUTION: Keep your user name businesslike. Some services allow you to create any name you want for your E-mail address. But if you are going to use E-mail in your job search, user names like "Pbrain" or "SweetOne" are inappropriate. Also, when you establish an E-mail address with an on-line service, plan to stay a member of that service during your entire job search. If you cancel your service, you are canceling your E-mail address and you won't be able to receive or send messages at that address any longer. Unlike the U.S. Postal Service, there is no general mail forwarding service on the Information Superhighway (although it is not entirely impossible).

TIP #3: PLAN A COURSE OF ACTION. Having a specific plan in mind when you go on-line can save you time and money. Keep in mind what you want to accomplish, and stick to your plan. You can easily get off course in the sea of information that is out there in Cyberspace.

To keep costs down, limit the amount of time you are on-line (unless of course you have paid for unlimited access). Don't read information while you are on-line. Instead, download or print out the information to read when you are off-line and not being charged. To keep track of your downloads, it's a good idea to create a separate directory for them.

MARK THE SITES YOU HAVE VISITED AND FOUND USEFUL so you can return to them without searching. The commercial services and World Wide Web browsers have mechanisms built into the software that let you set a "bookmark" that will allow for easy return visits. There is nothing more frustrating than finding the perfect forum or Web site and then having to search for hours trying to find it again.

KEEP TRACK OF WHICH ADS YOU RESPONDED TO and all of the resume databases where you have posted your resume. Check these sites at least once a week to see if there are any updates. If you are using E-mail to respond to ads, remember to check your E-mail frequently (at least twice a day) for any responses. If your on-line service has a way of quickly logging onto a service to retrieve and send E-mail and then immediately signing out to read and write E-mail responses while not logged onto your service, you should take advantage of this time-saving, cost-cutting method.

TIP #4: CHOOSE DATABASES CAREFULLY. All job databases are not created equal. Look at the job listings carefully and note their dates. You won't want to waste time searching through old job leads. A good database provider updates its listings at least once a week. Also, use job database services that allow you to update your resume at any time and offer you the option of submitting a blind resume or profile. If you do not want your current employer to know you are looking for a job, the blind resume option is your best bet. It allows prospective employers to check out your credentials but not your identity. Also, under most conditions, avoid paying to post your resume. There are many free services available. Be on the lookout, however, for possible exceptions. There may be a database that is so targeted to your job goal that a small fee may be acceptable.

TIP #5: NETWORK. As the saying goes, it's not what you know, it's whom you know. It has been said that most jobs are found through networking, and networking is easy on-line. There are plenty of professional forums and chat groups where you can meet people who share your interests and could help you in your job search.

CHECK OUT SOME OF THE FORUMS OR CHAT GROUPS available on-line. You can read through some of the messages or even drop in on a live on-line chat. (In Cyberspace lingo, hanging around without participating in discussions is called lurking.) When you feel comfortable enough, start participating by asking questions and sharing information. Remember to be discrete when participating in chat groups. Be selective about how much personal information you share. You don't always know whom you're chatting with.

TIP #6: VISIT COMPANY WEB SITES. If you are focusing your job search on specific companies, you can research them directly by visiting their sites on the World Wide Web. Many major corporations list employment opportunities on their Web sites. If you don't know the company's Web address, try typing in the following Internet address:

http://www.companyname.com

where "companyname" is the name of the company. For example, www.ibm.com is IBM's Internet address; Arthur Andersen's address is www.arthurandersen.com; and Ford's address is www.ford.com. You can also find a company's Web site with one of the popular Web search engines. ➤See **The Internet and the World Wide Web," pp. 536-540.**

There are also many company Web addresses in this book. ➤See **U.S. Employers," pp. 158-378.** In that chapter, the Web sites are found under the address and telephone number. The major job databases and some commercial on-line services also offer direct links to many corporate Web sites.

TIP #7: CHECK YOUR STATE'S WEB SITE. Most of the U.S. states and the District of Columbia have a presence on the Internet. Besides general information about the state's government officials and services, many states list available employment opportunities. A list of the states that have on-line job listings can be found in this book. ➤See "The Internet and the World Wide Web," pp. 536-540.

SO WHERE ARE ALL THE JOB POSTINGS in Cyberspace? Some of the best job databases and career resources are located on the major commercial on-line services and bulletin board systems. ➤See Commercial On-Line Services," pp. 541-547. There are also many useful Internet sites where you will want to prospect. ➤See **The Internet and the World Wide Web," pp. 536-540.**

SERVICES

The job hunter need not be the lonely hunter. There are thousands of agencies and experts that can help you get hired in the field of your choice.

SERVICES

CAREER COUNSELORS AND VOCATIONAL SERVICES

CAREER COUNSELORS AND VOCATIONAL SERVICES specialize in helping career switchers and job seekers get oriented in the employment market. They often work either with individuals or groups to determine aptitudes and skill levels as they pertain to the job hunt, as well as their clients' objectives in their job searches. There are many types of career counselors, in terms of both education and area of specialization. Some have master's degrees and advanced training, while others rely on their personal work experiences to assist job hunters.

Career counselors may incorporate some of the following into their services: teaching exercises to build self-confidence, offering resume advice, doing personality testing and/or skills evaluation, and providing access to jobbanks. Counselors give comprehensive interviews and/or tests to job hunters in order to gauge their interests and aptitudes. They also sometimes administer tests to determine personality type, which may indicate the type of career path the person might follow. (An extrovert, for example, might be better at a sales position than an introvert.) In addition, counselors often can provide information on trends in the job market and steer the job seeker toward an area that not only best suits his or her overall personality and skill level but is also a growing field. If job seekers face some kind of internal barrier toward finding a job (low self-esteem, shyness, etc.), some counselors are equipped to work with them in resolving these obstacles. They may be able to provide job leads as well.

There are several things to keep in mind when obtaining the services of a career counselor or vocational service. First, make sure you are informed of the kinds of services provided. Second, make sure you understand the degree to which you are involved in the process. And last, make sure you understand your financial commitment. Some of the career counselors who specialize in executive-level jobs charge fees of several thousand dollars, whereas vocational services pertaining to other types of jobs may be free or cost only a nominal amount.

Some counselors and services specialize in helping particular groups. This is sometimes evident by the name—for instance, "Forty Plus" specializes in middle-aged and older individuals. You might ask if a counselor or service has a specialty when you make the initial contact. Note as well that while some of the centers listed below are located at universities, they do provide at least some services to the general public.

Some career counselors are certified as NCC, for National Certified Counselor. Others are NCCC, for National Certified Career Counselor. An NCCC certification means the counselor has: (1) obtained a graduate degree in counseling or a related field from an accredited higher education institution, (2) completed a minimum of three years of full-time career development work experience, (3) gotten supervised counseling experience, and (4) completed a knowledge-based certification examination.

ABBREVIATIONS USED IN THIS CHAPTER	
NCC—*National Certified Counselor*	NCCC—*National Certified Career Counselor*

ALABAMA

DALE MARTIN, NCC, NCCC
3325 Allendale Pl., Montgomery, AL 36111; 334-241-9577

INTERCHANGE
2 Perimeter Park S., Suite 200W, Birmingham, AL 35243; 205-324-5030

ALASKA

CAREER TRANSITIONS
2221 E. Northern Lights Blvd., Suite 207, Anchorage, AK 99508; 907-278-7350

JAMES RONANA, JR., NCC, NCCC
P.O. Box 220230, Anchorage, AK 99522; 907-271-4514

ARIZONA

BRAD HARPER, NCC, NCCC/TRIGON EXECUTIVE ASSESSMENT CENTER
6991 E. Camelback Rd., Suite B-365, Scottsdale, AZ 85251; 602-423-1776

COLLEGE PLUS CAREER CONNECTIONS
4540 S. Rural Rd., #P-8, Tempe, AZ 85282; 480-730-5246

DARLENE FRITSCHE, NCC, NCCC
2228 E. Vista Ave., Phoenix, AZ 85020; 602-866-6125

MARILYN GILLA BECHTOLD, NCC, NCCC
8686 E. Dahlia Dr., Scottsdale, AZ 85260; 602-224-5000

PEGGY HOLDEN, NCC, NCCC
1414 E. Amberwood Dr., Phoenix, AZ 85048; 602-543-6600

TUCSON/PIMA COUNTY JOB CLUB
110 E. Pennington, Lower Level, Tucson, AZ 85701; 602-884-8280

ARKANSAS

LEE GARNER, NCC, NCCC/ HUMANAGEMENT, INC.
P.O. Drawer 1056, Fordyce, AR 71742; 501-352-5268

CALIFORNIA

ALUMNAE RESOURCES
120 Mongomery St., Suite 1080, San Francisco, CA 94104; 415-274-4700

KATHRYN ANDERSON NCC, NCCC
P.O Box 23641, San Diego, CA 92193; 619-287-0823

CAREER AND PERSONAL DEVELOPMENT INSTITUTE
690 Market St., Suite 402, San Francisco, CA 94104; 415-982-2636

CAREER DEVELOPMENT AND LIFE PLANNING
3585 Maple St., Suite 237, Ventura, CA 93003; 805-656-6220

CAREER DIRECTIONS
215 Witham Rd., Encinitas, CA 92024; 619-436-3994

CAREER PLANNING AND ADULT DEVELOPMENT NETWORK
4965 Sierra Rd., San Jose, CA 95132; 408-559-8211

CAREER STRATEGY ASSOCIATES
1100 Quail St., Suite 201, Newport Beach, CA 92660; 714-252-0515

CENTER FOR CREATIVE CHANGE
2222 F St., San Diego, CA 92102; 619-231-3716

CONSTRUCTIVE LEISURE
511 N. La Cienega Blvd., Los Angeles, CA 90048; 310-652-7389

CONSULTANTS IN CAREER DEVELOPMENT
2017 Palo Verde Ave., Suite 201B, Long Beach, CA 90815; 310-598-6412

FORTY PLUS OF NORTHERN CALIFORNIA
7440 Lockheed St., Oakland, CA 94603; 510-430-2400

FORTY PLUS OF SOUTHERN CALIFORNIA
3450 Wilshire Blvd., Suite 510, Los Angeles, CA 90010; 213-388-2301

LINDA R. GONZALES, NCC, NCCC
64 N. 9th St., Suite 3, San Jose, CA 95112; 408-274-7900, ext. 6689

JOHN F. KENNEDY UNIVERSITY CAREER DEVELOPMENT CENTER
1250 Arroyo Way, Walnut Creek, CA 94596; 510-295-0610

MARY BETH ROGERS, NCC, NCCC
244 Burning Tree Dr., San Jose, CA 95119; 408-578-7446

SACRAMENTO WOMEN'S CENTER
1924 T St., Sacramento, CA 95814; 916-736-6942

BONNIE S. SINCLAIR, NCC, NCCC
7801 Mission Center Court, Suite 200, San Diego, CA 92108; 619-296-7065

TRANSITIONS COUNSELING CENTER
171 N. Van Ness, Fresno, CA 93701; 209-233-7250

TURNING POINT CAREER CENTER
University YMCA, 2600 Bancroft Way, Berkeley, CA 94704; 510-848-6370

COLORADO

ACCELERATED JOB SEARCH
4490 Squires Circle, Boulder, CO 80303; 303-494-2467

AFFILIATED PROFESSIONALS
10767 W. Leyton Pl., Littleton, CO 80127; 303-979-4583

CRS CONSULTING
425 W. Mulberry, Suite 108, Ft. Collins, CO 80521; 970-484-9810

CAREER MANAGER
UNIVERSITY OF COLORADO–DENVER
Campus Box 106, Denver, CO 80217; 303-556-2563

FORTY PLUS OF COLORADO
565800 W. Almeda, Lakewood, CO 80226; 303-937-49

SANDRA TYNES HAGEVIK, NCC, NCCC
1460 Elm St., Denver, CO 80220; 303-388-1374

WILLA SMITH DAVIS, NCC, NCCC
3139 Oak Creek Dr. E., Colorado Springs, CO 80906; 719-573-5071

YWCA OF BOULDER COUNTY
Career Ctr., 2222 14th St., Boulder, CO 80302; 303-443-0419

CONNECTICUT

ACCORD CAREER SERVICES
The Exchange, Suite 305, 270 Farmington Ave., Farmington, CT 06032; 860-674-9654

ROBERT E. PANNONE, NCC, NCCC
177 Patterson Ave., Stratford, CT 06614; 203-377-8104

CAROLE JEAN PRESCOTT, NCC, NCCC
2 Palmieri Rd., Westport, CT 06880; 203-255-4246

BONNIE K. PUMERANTZ, NCC, NCCC
415 Silas Deane, Weathersfield, CT 06109; 203-529-2955

MELVIN S. SILVERSTEIN, NCC, NCCC
12 Newtown Terr., Norwalk, CT 06851; 303-847-6400

DELAWARE

KAMAKAOKALANI SCOTT, NCC, NCCC
P.O. Box 90, Oceanview, DE 19970; 302-537-4956

WILMINGTON SENIOR CENTER—EMPLOYMENT SERVICES
1909 N. Market St., Wilmington, DE 19802; 302-651-3440

DISTRICT OF COLUMBIA

BLACKWELL AND ASSOCIATES
Capitol Hill, 626 A St., SE, Washington, DC 20003; 202-546-6835

COMMUNITY VOCATIONAL COUNSELING SERVICE
George Washington University Counseling Ctr., 718 21st St., NW, Washington, DC 20052; 202-994-4860

GEORGE WASHINGTON UNIVERSITY CENTER FOR CAREER EDUCATION
2020 K St., NW, Washington, DC 20052; 202-994-5299

HORIZONS UNLIMITED, INC.
1133 15th St., NW, Suite 1200, Washington, DC 20005; 202-296-7224

FLORIDA

CAREER CONSULTANTS OF AMERICA, INC.
2701 W. Busch Blvd., Suite 111, Tampa, FL 33618; 813- 265-9262

CAREER MOVES, INC.
5300 N. Federal Highway, Ft. Lauderdale, FL 33308; 954-772-6857

CENTER FOR CAREER DECISIONS
980 N. Federal Highway, Suite 203, Boca Raton, FL 33432; 407-394-3399

ECKERD COLLEGE CAREER AND PERSONAL COUNSELING CENTER
4200 54th Ave., S., St. Petersburg, FL 33711; 813-864-8356

LARRY HARMON, NCC, NCCC
2000 S. Dixie Highway, #103, Miami, FL 33133; 305-285-8900

PEN (PROFESSIONAL EMPLOYMENT NETWORK, INC.)
3421 Lawton Rd., Orlando, FL 32803; 407-897-2886

JOYCE C. PUCKETT, NCC, NCCC
167 Salem Ct., Tallahassee, FL 32301; 904-656-4561

MICHAEL SHAHNASARIAN, NCC, NCCC
10708 Carroll Lake Dr., Tampa, FL 33618; 813-265-9262

GEORGIA

ATLANTA OUTPLACEMENT AND CAREER COUNSELING
1150 Lake Hearn Dr., NE, Suite 200, Atlanta, GA 30342; 404-250-3232

D & B CONSULTING
1175 Peachtree St., 100 Colony Sq., Suite 840, Atlanta, GA 30361; 404-874-9379

JEWISH VOCATIONAL SERVICE
1100 Spring St., Suite 700, Atlanta, GA 30309; 404-876-5872

HAWAII

CAREER DISCOVERY
1441 Kapiolani Blvd., Suite 2003, Honolulu, HI 96814; 808-739-9494

NANCY L. MARTINO, NCC, NCCC
1159 Lauloa St., Kailua, HI 96734; 808-235-7471

RONALD G. SCRONCE, NCC, NCCC
716A Olokele Ave., Suite D, Honolulu, HI 96816; 808-737-5439

IDAHO

JIM S. BAXTER, NCC, NCCC
1751 Ridgecrest Dr., Boise, ID 83712; 208-336-0848

TRANSITIONS
1970 Parkside Dr., Boise, ID 83712; 208-638-0499

ILLINOIS

CAREER CONNECTION
817 Huntleigh Dr., Naperville, IL 60540; 708-369-8778

CAREER WORKSHOPS
5431 W. Roscoe St., Chicago, IL 60641; 773-282-6859

FORTY PLUS OF CHICAGO
28 E. Jackson Blvd., Chicago, IL 60604; 312-922-0285

GRIMARD WILSON CONSULTING
111 N. Wabash Ave., Suite 1006, Chicago, IL 60602; 312-201-1142

HARPER COLLEGE CAREER TRANSITION CENTER
Bldg. A, Room 124, Palatine, IL 60067; 847-459-8233

LUCRATIVE CAREERS, INC.
511 Maple Ave., Wilmette, IL 60091; 847-251-4727

LANSKY CAREER CONSULTANTS
500 N. Michigan Ave., Suite 430, Chicago, IL 60611; 312-494-0022

MIDWEST WOMEN'S CENTER
828 S. Wabash, Suite 200, Chicago, IL 60605; 312-922-8530

UNIVERSITY OF ILLINOIS ALUMNI CAREER CENTER
4400 Alumni Hall, 412 S. Peoria St., Chicago, IL 60607; 312-996-6350

INDIANA

CAREER CONSULTANTS
107 N. Pennsylvania St., Suite 400, Indianapolis, IN 46204; 317-639-5601

INDIANA UNIVERSITY SCHOOL OF CONTINUING STUDIES
Owen Hall, Room 202, Bloomington, IN 47405; 812-855-4991

KCDM ASSOCIATES
10401 N. Meridian St., Suite 300, Indianapolis, IN 46290; 317-581-6230

MICHAEL D. ZLATOS, NCC, NCCC
931 N. 5th St., Suite 3, Terre Haute, IN 47807; 812-238-1723

IOWA

BEERS CONSULTING
5505 Boulder Dr., West Des Moines, IA 50266; 515-225-1245

LINDA PHILIPS, NCC, NCCC/CAREER AND LIFE TRANSITION COUNSELING
3209 Ingersoll Ave., Des Moines, IA 50312; 515-277-4052

UNIVERSITY OF IOWA CENTER FOR CAREER DEVELOPMENT AND COOPERATIVE EDUCATION
315 Calvin Hall, Iowa City, IA 52242; 319-335-3201

KANSAS

VENDA RAYE JOHNSON, NCC, NCCC
1406 N St., Atchison, KS 66002; 913-367-5340

RIGHT ASSOCIATES
6201 College Blvd., Suite 360, Overland Park, KS 66211; 913-451-1100

KENTUCKY

BARBARA S. DEHART, NCC, NCCC
2931 Riedling Dr., Louisville, KY 40206; 502-895-2258

CAROLINE FRANCIS, NCC, NCCC
180 Idle Hour Dr., Lexington, KY 40502; 606-266-1693

SUCCESSFUL TRANSITIONS
P.O. Box 20806, Louisville, KY 40250; 502-495-6292

LOUISIANA

DIVISION OF EDUCATION
Xavier University, 7325 Palmetto St., New Orleans, LA 70125; 504-483-7487

METROPOLITAN COLLEGE CAREER PLANNING AND ASSESSMENT CENTER
University of New Orleans, New Orleans, LA 70148; 504-286-7100

STEWART R. SCHELVER, NCC, NCCC
42219 Deborah Dr., Hammond, LA 70403; 504-345-4968

MAINE

CAREER PERSPECTIVES
75 Pearl St., Suite 204, Portland, ME 04101; 207-775-4487

JOHNSON CAREER SERVICES
34 Congress St., Portland, ME 04101; 207-773-3921

WILLIAM S. WEBB, NCC, NCCC
526 Western Ave., Augusta, ME 04915; 201-623-2600

MARYLAND

CAREER TRANSITION SERVICES
3126 Berkshire Rd., Baltimore, MD 21214; 410-444-5857

CAREERSCOPE, INC.
One Mall N., Suite 216, 1025 Governor Warfield Pkwy., Columbia, MD 21044; 410-992-5042

MARYLAND NEW DIRECTIONS, INC.
2220 N. Charles St., Baltimore, MD 21218; 410-235-8800

CARL MICHAEL SWEENY, NCC, NCCC
16210 Fairview Rd., Hagerstown, MD 21740; 301-791-4170

MASSACHUSETTS

CAREER MANAGEMENT CONSULTANTS
30 Park Ave., Worcester, MA 01605; 508-853-8669

CAREER PLANNING AND MANAGEMENT, INC.
12 Marshall St., Boston, MA 02108; 617-723-7696

CAREERPRO
581 Boylston St., Suite 403, Boston, MA 02116; 617-437-8888

CITY OF BOSTON/COMMISSION OF AFFAIRS OF THE ELDERLY
Boston City Hall, Room 806, Boston, MA 02201; 617-635-4366

COMPETITIVE EDGE
335 Washington St., Suite 22, Woburn, MA 01801; 617-932-3232

ALAN R. GREEN, NCC, NCCC
62 Williston Ave., Easthampton, MA 01027; 413-527-4089

JOYCE K. PICARD, NCC, NCCC
14 Halcyon Rd., Newton, MA 02159; 617-332-7600

RADCLIFFE CAREER SERVICES
77 Brattle St., Cambridge, MA 02138; 617-495-8631

MICHIGAN

CAREER DEVELOPMENT ASSOCIATES
16776 Southfield, Detroit, MI 48235; 313-534-1117

CAREER DIRECTIONS
300 N. 5th Ave., Suite 120, Ann Arbor, MI 48104; 734-663-0677

LANSING COMMUNITY COLLEGE
2020 Career and Employment Development Services, P.O. Box 40010, Lansing, MI 48901; 517-483-1221

NEW OPTIONS: COUNSELING FOR WOMEN IN TRANSITION
2311 E. Stadium, Suite B-2, Ann Arbor, MI 48104; 734-973-0003

DANIEL W. STETZ, NCC, NCCC
2493 Valley Oaks, Flint, MI 48532; 810-762-0357

GWENDOLYN WATTS–PRINGLE, NCC, NCCC
8200 E. Jefferson, Suite 911, Detroit, MI 48214; 313-845-9612

MINNESOTA

CAREER DYNAMICS, INC.
8400 Normandale Lake Blvd., Suite 1220, Bloomington, MN 55437; 612-921-2378

CAREER SENSE
370 Selby Ave., #327, St. Paul, MN 55702; 612-331-6609

EMPLOYMENT ADVISORS
526 Nicollet Mall, Minneapolis, MN 55402; 612-339-0521

FORTY PLUS OF MINNESOTA
14870 Grenada Ave., Suite 315, St. Paul, MN 55124; 615-683-9898

INVENTURE GROUP
8500 Normandale Lake Blvd., #1750, Minneapolis, MN 55437; 612-921-8686

MISSISSIPPI

ACADEMIC & CAREER RESEARCH
2633 Ridgewood Rd., Suite 202, Jackson, MS 39216; 601-982-1900

MISSISSIPPI GULF COAST COMMUNITY COLLEGE CAREER DEVELOPMENT CENTER
Jackson County Campus, P.O. Box 100, Gautier, MS 39553; 601-497-9602

MISSISSIPPI STATE UNIVERSITY CAREER SERVICES CENTER
P.O. Box P, Colvard Union, Suite 316, Mississippi State, MS 39762; 601-325-3344

MISSOURI

ANDREA RIGGS–HEAVRIN, NCC, NCCC/CAREER POTENTIAL
7750 Clayton Rd., Suite 201, St. Louis, MO 63117; 314-644-0104

ARTHUR SMITH, NCC, NCCC
10 Hanely Downs, St. Louis, MO 63141; 314-997-3811

CAREER MANAGEMENT CENTER
8301 State Line Rd., Suite 202, Kansas City, MO 64114; 816-363-1500

MARK L. POPE, NCC, NCCC
4579 Laclede Ave., Suite 436, St. Louis, MO 63108; 314-454-9300

UNIVERSITY OF MISSOURI CAREER CENTER
Community Career Services, 110 Noyes Hall, Columbia, MO 65211; 573-882-6803

MONTANA

BOYER & DIMICH
1236 N. 28th St., Billings, MT 59101; 406-256-9386

ROBIN PUTNAM, NCC, NCCC
127 Fairway Dr., Missoula, MT 59803; 406-549-3865

NEBRASKA

CAREER MANAGEMENT SERVICES
5000 Central Park Dr., Suite 204, Lincoln, NE 68504; 402-466-8427

OLSON COUNSELING SERVICES
8720 Frederick, Suite 105, Omaha, NE 68128; 402-390-2342

NEVADA

CAREER LIFESTYLES
4550 W. Oakey Blvd., Suite 111, Las Vegas, NV 89102; 702-258-3353

MEG PRICE, NCC, NCCC
3785 Baker Lane, Reno, NV 89509; 702-828-9600

NEW HAMPSHIRE

KATHLEEN M. FLORA, NCC, NCCC
95 Hitching Post Ln, Bedford, NH 03110; 603-472-2401

INDIVIDUAL EMPLOYMENT SERVICES
90-A Sixth St., P.O. Box 917, Dover, NH 03820; 603-742-5616

NEW JERSEY

ADULT RESOURCE CENTER
100 Horseneck Rd., Montville, NJ 07045; 201-335-6910

ARISTA CONCEPTS CAREER DEVELOP- MENT SERVICE
P.O. Box 2463, Princeton, NJ 08540; 609-921-0308

CAROLE T. BEER, NCC NCCC
702 Chesterwood Ct., Marlton, NJ 08053; 609-810-0812

FRANK S. KARPATI, NCC, NCCC
28 Summit Ave., Hackensack, NJ 07601; 201-487-0808

KEAN COLLEGE OF NEW JERSEY ADULT ADVISORY SERVICE
Administration Bldg., Union, NJ 07083; 908-527-2210

PROFESSIONAL ROSTER
1000 Herrontown Rd., Princeton, NJ 08540; 609-921-9561

NEW MEXICO

CAREER CENTER
6301 Topke Pl., NE, Albuquerque, NM 87109; 505-883-4513

YWCA CAREER SERVICES CENTER
7201 Paseo del Norte NE, Albuquerque, NM 87113; 505-822-9922

NEW YORK

SHARON B. ALLEN, NCC, NCCC
24 Cambridge Rd., Albany, NY 12203; 518-454-5141

CAREER DEVELOPMENT SERVICE
14 Franklin St., Temple Bldg., Suite 1200, Rochester, NY 14604; 716-325-2274

CRYSTAL/BARKLEY CORP. JOHN C. CRYSTAL CENTER
152 Madison Ave., New York, NY 10016; 212-889-8500

BARBARA K. HERNE, NCC, NCCC
1025 Fifth Ave., New York, NY 10028; 212-249-0410

LIVELIHOOD JOB SEARCH CENTER
301 Madison Ave., New York, NY 10017; 212-687-2411

LONG ISLAND UNIVERSITY CAREER DE- VELOPMENT CENTER
C. W. Post Campus, Brookville, NY 11548; 516-299-2251

PERSONNEL SCIENCES CENTER, INC.
276 Fifth Ave., Suite 704, New York, NY 10001; 212-683-3008

RLS CAREER CENTER
3049 E. Genesee St., Suite 211, Syracuse, NY 13224; 315-446-0500

SANDRA C. SILVERSTEIN, NCC, NCCC
332 Dan Troy Dr., Buffalo, NY 14221

ELINOR DEAN WILDER, NCC , NCCC
19 Grace Court, Brooklyn, NY 11202; 212-998-7060

WIN (WOMEN IN NETWORKING) WORK- SHOPS
1120 Ave. of the Americas, New York, NY 10036; 212-333-8788

NORTH CAROLINA

CAREER SERVICES/UNC–WILMINGTON

Wilmington, NC 28403; 314-882-0697

CAREER, EDUCATIONAL, PSYCHOLOGICAL EVALUATIONS
2915 Providence Rd., Suite 300, Charlotte, NC 28211; 704-362-1942

LIFE MANAGEMENT SERVICES
301 Gregson Dr., Cary, NC 27511; 919-481-9832

JUNE M. MERLINO, NCC, NCCC
5415 Lake Vista Dr., Durham, NC 27712;
919-383-8490

TRAUX CAREER/LIFE PLANNING AND RELOCATION SERVICES
2711 Bears Creek Rd., Greensboro, NC
27406; 919-271-2050

NORTH DAKOTA

BISMARCK STATE COLLEGE
1581 Atlanta Dr., Bismarck, ND 58504; 701-224-5638

CAREER CONNECTIONS
1621 S. University, #215, Fargo, ND 58103;
701-232-4614

OHIO

HENRY W. BRUNER, NCC, NCCC
222 Colgate Ave., Elyria, OH 44035; 216-322-9749

CAREER INITIATIVES CENTER
1557 E. 27th St., Cleveland, OH 44114; 216-574-8998

J & K ASSOCIATES, INC.
607 Otterbein Ave., Dayton, OH 45406; 513-274-3630

PRISCILLA MUTTER, NCC, NCCC
8141 N. Main St., Suite 4, Dayton, OH 45415

PYRAMID CAREER SERVICES, INC.
2400 Cleveland Ave., NW, Canton, OH
44709; 330-453-3767

STUDENT CAREER DEVELOPMENT CENTER
John Carroll University, University Heights,
OH 44118; 216-725-2872

UNIVERSITY OF AKRON ADULT RESOURCE CENTER
Buckingham for Continuing Education, Room
55, Akron, OH 44325; 330-972-7448

OKLAHOMA

CAREER DEVELOPMENT SERVICES
5314 S. Yale, Suite 600, Tulsa, OK 74135;
918-495-1788

SUSAN H. LOCASCIO, NCC, NCCC
235 Mt. Scott Circle, Lawton, OK 73501;
405-529-2149

BRUCE M. STAPP, NCC, NCCC
1623 Glenn Dr., Norman, OK 73071; 405-631-4503

OREGON

CAREER DEVELOPMENT
P.O. Box 850, Forest Grove, OR 97116; 503-357-9233

PERKINS-REED & ASSOCIATES
11830 SW Kerr Pkwy., Suite 304, Lake
Oswego, OR 97035; 503-245-2283

SUZANNE STEGMILLER, NCC, NCCC
8555 NE Duddleson, Portland, OR 97220;
503-256-0126

VERK CONSULTANTS, INC.
1441 Oak St., #7, P.O. Box 11277, Eugene,
OR 97440; 541-687-9170

PENNSYLVANIA

CAREER DEVELOPMENT CENTER
Jewish Family & Children's Ctr., 5737 Darlington Rd., Pittsburgh, PA 15217; 412-422-5627

CAREER MANAGEMENT CONSULTANTS, INC.
3207 N. Front St., Harrisburg, PA 17110;
717-233-2272

CENTER FOR CAREER SERVICES
1845 Walnut St., Philadelphia, PA 19103;
215-854-1800

CREATIVE LIVING CENTER
1388 Freeport Rd., Pittsburgh, PA 15238;
412-963-8765

EDWIN L. HERR, NCC, NCCC
860 Saxton Dr., State College, PA 16801;
814-863-1489

ANN B. MOFFATT, NCC, NCCC
732 W. 7th St., Erie, PA 16502; 814-459-2245

OPTIONS, INC.
225 S. 15th St., Philadelphia, PA 19102; 215-735-2202

MARILYN WOODS, NCC, NCCC
5928 Devon Pl., Philadelphia, PA 19138;
215-848-2914

RHODE ISLAND

CAREER DESIGNS
104 Rankin Ave., Providence, RI 02908; 401-521-2323

ELLEN WEAVER-PAQUETTE, NCC, NCCC
440 Schooner Ave., Jamestown, RI 02835; 401-423-0171

SOUTH CAROLINA

ANDREA R. CAMPBELL, NCC, NCCC
1722 E. Heyward St., Columbia, SC 29205; 803-799-9245

CAREER COUNSELOR SERVICES, INC.
25 Woods Lake Rd., Suite 324, Greenville, SC 29607; 864-370-9453

HARRIET G. FIELDS, NCC, NCCC
412 Juniper St., Columbia, SC 29203; 843-661-8027

GREENVILLE TECHNICAL COLLEGE CAREER ADVANCEMENT CENTER
P.O. Box 5616, Greenville, SC 29606; 864-250-8281

SOUTH DAKOTA

CAREER CONCEPTS PLANNING CENTER, INC.
1602 Mountain View Rd., Suite 102, Rapid City, SD 57702; 605-342-5177

CAREER COUNSELOR
School of Education, University of South Dakota, Vermillion, SD 57069; 605-677-5840

TENNESSEE

MARY E. MCWILLIE, NCC, NCCC
3661 Charleswood, Memphis, TN 38122; 901-722-0331

MID-SOUTH CAREER DEVELOPMENT CENTER
2315 Fisher Pl., Knoxville, TN 37920; 423-573-1340

POINDEXTER & ASSOCIATES, INC.
230 4th Ave. N., 5th Floor, Nashville, TN 37219; 615-256-8077

RANDALL HOWARD & ASSOCIATES, INC.
5353 Flowering Peach Dr., Memphis, TN 38115; 901-365-2700

TEXAS

AUSTIN CAREER ASSOCIATES
4501 Spicewood Springs Rd., Suite 1007, Austin, TX 78759; 512-343-0526

BART BARHAM, NCC, NCCC
1346 Maureen Dr., Dallas, TX 75232; 214-827-2870

CAREER ACTION ASSOCIATES
12655 N. Central Expressway, Suite 821, Dallas, TX 75243; 214-392-7337

CAREER ACTION ASSOCIATES
1325 8th Ave., Ft. Worth, TX 76112; 817-926-9941

CAREER COUNSELOR
University of Houston, 4800 Calhoun, Houston, TX 77004; 713-743-5448

CAREER MANAGEMENT RESOURCES
222 W. Las Colinas, Suite #2114, Irving, TX 75039; 214-556-0786

COUNSELING SERVICES OF HOUSTON
1964 W. Gray, Suite 204, Houston, TX 77019; 713-521-9391

MICHELLE DEATLEY, NCC, NCCC
16650 Huebner Rd., Suite 1121, San Antonio, TX 78248; 210-370-5222

EMPLOYMENT/CAREER INFORMATION RESOURCE CENTER
Corpus Christi Public Library, 805 Comanche, Corpus Christi, TX 78401; 512-880-7004

FRANK M. GAULT, NCC, NCCC
2731 Whispering Trail, Arlington, TX 76013; 817-261-3463

DONNA J. MOORE, NCC, NCCC
6122 Belpree Rd., Amarillo, TX 79106; 806-355-7194

NEW DIRECTIONS COUNSELING CENTER
8140 N. Mopac, Bldg. II, Suite 230, Austin, TX 78701; 512-343-9496

CAREER COUNSELOR
University of Houston, 4800 Calhoun, Houston, TX 77004; 713-743-5448

VOCATIONAL GUIDANCE SERVICE
2600 SW Freeway, Suite 800, Houston, TX 77098; 713-535-7104

UTAH

SUSAN M. LINDER, NCC, NCCC
378N 400W, Suite A, Cedar City, UT 84720; 801-867-1003

UNIVERSITY OF UTAH CENTER FOR ADULT DEVELOPMENT
1195 Annex Bldg., Salt Lake City, UT 84112; 801-581-3228

VERMONT

CAREER NETWORKS
7 Kilburn St., Burlington, VT 05401; 800-918-WORK

VIRGINIA

BERNADETTE M. BLACK, NCC, NCCC
370 N. Granada St., Arlington, VA 22203; 804-225-2290

CHANGE & GROWTH CONSULTING
1334 G St., Woodbridge, VA 22191; 540-494-8271

EDUCATIONAL OPPORTUNITY CENTER
7010-M Auburn Ave., Norfolk, VA 23513; 804-855-7468

OFFICE FOR WOMEN
The Government Ctr., 12000 Government Ctr. Pkwy., Suite 318, Fairfax, VA 22035; 703-324-5730

VIRGINIA COMMONWEATLH UNIVERSITY CAREER CENTER
907 Floyd Ave., Room 2007, Richmond, VA 23284; 804-367-1645

CARYLE H. ZORUMSKI, NCC, NCCC
1215 Warwick Blvd., Suite 300, Newport News, VA 23606

WASHINGTON

CENTERPOINT INSTITUTE FOR LIFE AND CAREER RENEWAL
Career Consultants, 624 Skinner Bldg., 1326 5th Ave., Seattle, WA 98101; 206-622-8070

INDIVIDUAL DEVELOPMENT CENTER, INC. (I.D. CENTER)
1020 E. John, Seattle, WA 98102; 206-329-0600

KEVIN PRATT, NCC, NCCC
N. 2910 E. Oval, Spokane, WA 99205; 509-326-4473

UNIVERSITY OF WASHINGTON EXTENSION CAREER DEVELOPMENT SERVICES
GH-21, 5025 25th Ave. NE, Suite 205, Seattle, WA 98195; 206-543-3900

WEST VIRGINIA

CAREER WORKS ASSOCIATES
1033 Quarrier St., Charleston, WV 25301; 304-344-2273

WISCONSIN

CAREER COUNSELOR
NORTH CENTRAL TECHNICAL COLLEGE
602 N. 72nd Ave., Wausau, WI 54401; 715-675-3331

MARGO W. FREY, NCC, NCCC
1567 E. Blackthorne Pl., Milwaukee, WI 53211; 414-964-6006

MAKING ALTERNATIVE PLANS
Career Development Ctr., Alverno College, 2401 S. 39th St., Box 343922, Milwaukee, WI 53234; 414-382-6010

WYOMING

NATIONAL EDUCATION SERVICE CENTER
P.O. Box 1279, Riverton, WY 82501; 307-766-2398

UNIVERSITY OF WYOMING CAREER PLANNING AND PLACEMENT CENTER
P.O. Box 3195, Knight Hall 228, Laramie, WY 82071; 307-766-2398

SERVICES

COMPUTER-SEARCH AGENCIES

THE TECHNOLOGY BOOM has not only greatly influenced the job market, but it has also spawned specialized employment agencies that focus on finding positions for the influx of computer professionals. These computer-search agencies seek individuals to fill highly specialized positions such as software development professionals, systems analysts, Web developers, LAN (local area network) specialists, and computer operators. Note that at computer-search agencies, "computer operators" means individuals who can operate mainframes, Unisys systems and on-line servers.

Sometimes, computer-search agencies have positions available for data processors as well as those with personal computer skills. These lesser-skilled computer jobs, however, are usually available through employment agencies and temporary agencies. ➛See "Employment Agencies," pp. 569-591, and "Temp Agencies," pp. 616-626.

Most of the computer-search agencies listed in this chapter are compensated by employers looking to fill positions rather than by job seekers. However, be sure to ask at particular agencies to make sure this is the case before going in for the initial interview.

ALABAMA

COMPUSEARCH OF BIRMINGHAM
P.O. Box 381626, Birmingham, AL 35238; 205-408-0848

EMPLOYMENT CONSULTANTS
649 S. McDonough St., Montgomery, AL 36104; 334-264-0649

MANAGEMENT RECRUITERS
3263 Demetropolis Rd., Suite 6C, Mobile, AL 36693; 334-602-0104

SNELLING PERSONNEL SERVICES
1813 University Dr., Huntsville, AL 35801; 256-382-3000

ALASKA

ALASKA EXECUTIVE SEARCH
821 North St., Suite 204, Anchorage, AK 99501; 907-276-5707

ARIZONA

AUSTIN MICHAELS, LTD.
8687 E. Via de Ventura, Suite 303, Scottsdale, AZ 85258; 602-483-5000

COMPUTER STRATEGIES, INC.
7454 E. Broadway, Suite 205, Tucson, AZ 85710; 520-721-9544

ROMAC INTERNATIONAL
5343 N. 16th St., Suite 270, Phoenix, AZ 85016; 602-230-0220

ARKANSAS

MANAGEMENT RECRUITERS/ COMPUSEARCH
1701 Centerview Dr., Suite 314, Little Rock, AR 72211; 501-224-0801

CALIFORNIA

BRODY & ASSOCIATES
P.O. Box 522, Alamo, CA 94507; 510-838-8898

COMPUSEARCH
9455 Ridgehaven Ct., Suite 205, San Diego, CA 92123; 858-565-6600

CRA SYSTEMS
301 E. Ocean Blvd., Long Beach, CA 90802; 310-495-2577

EAGLE SEARCH ASSOCIATES
410 Pacific Ave., San Francisco, CA 94133; 415-398-6066

LOCKHART GROUP
5757 W. Century Blvd., Los Angeles, CA 90045; 310-645-2500

PEGASUS GROUP
5757 W. Century Blvd., Los Angeles, CA 90045; 310-215-1841

ROMAC INTERNATIONAL
4510 Executive Dr., Suite 211, San Diego, CA 92121; 858-550-1600

ROMAC INTERNATIONAL
425 California St., Suite 1200, San Francisco, CA 94104; 415-591-1700

TECH KNOWLEDGE X-CHANGE
6 Venture, Irvine, CA 92718; 714-453-1533

WALTER AND COMPANY
8950 Villa La Jolla Dr., La Jolla, CA 92037; 619-693-4100

C O L O R A D O

ABACUS CONSULTANTS
1777 S. Harrison, Suite 404, Denver, CO 80210; 303-759-5064

SLITZ PROFESSIONAL SEARCH
1526 Spruce St., Boulder, CO 80302; 303-440-0164

ROMAC INTERNATIONAL
7730 E. Belleview Ave., Englewood, CO 80111; 303-773-3700

C O N N E C T I C U T

HIGH-TECH RECRUITERS
30 High St., Suite 104A, Hartford, CT 06103; 860-527-4262

ROMAC INTERNATIONAL
1177 High Ridge Rd., Stamford, CT 06905; 203-324-1265

STEWART ASSOCIATES
410 Asylum St., Hartford, CT 06103; 860-548-1388

D E L A W A R E

J. B. GRONER EXECUTIVE SEARCH, INC.
1502 Society Dr., Claymont, DE 19703; 302-792-9228

D I S T R I C T   O F   C O L U M B I A

BRUCE W. HAUPT ASSOCIATES
P.O. Box 21599, Kalorama Station, Washington, DC 20009; 202-462-1524

GRANT/MURPHY ASSOCIATES
2001 L St., NW, Suite 710, Washington, DC 20036; 202-955-5520

ROMAC INTERNATIONAL
1111 19th St., NW, Suite 620, Washington, DC 20036; 202-223-6000

F L O R I D A

COMPUTER CAREER CONNECTIONS
4300 N. University Dr., Suite C101, Ft. Lauderdale, FL 33351; 954-741-5400

MANAGEMENT RECRUITERS OF TALLAHASSEE
1406 Hays St., Suite 7, Tallahassee, FL 32301; 850-942-2793

ROMAC INTERNATIONAL
15600 NW 67th Ave., Miami Lakes, FL 33014; 305-477-0500

ROMAC INTERNATIONAL
120 W. Hyde Park, Tampa, FL 33607; 813-258-8855

SOUTHPORT INTERNATIONAL ASSOCIATION
562011 Arbor Club Way, Boca Raton, FL 33433; 407-393-6320

G E O R G I A

COMPUTER NETWORK RESOURCES
6000 Lake Forest Dr., Suite 265, Atlanta, GA 30328; 404-843-1331

COMPUTER SEARCH ASSOCIATES
3343 Peachtree Rd., NE, Suite 200, Atlanta, GA 30326; 404-231-0965

ROMAC INTERNATIONAL
4170 NE Ashford Dunwoody Rd., Suite 285, Atlanta, GA 30319; 770-357-1050

H A W A I I

HUMAN RESOURCES MANAGEMENT HAWAII, INC.
210 Ward Ave., Suite 126, Honolulu, HI 96814; 808-536-3438

IDAHO

MANAGEMENT RECRUITERS/COMPUSEARCH
290 Bobwhite Ct., Suite 215, Boise, ID
83706; 208-336-6770

ILLINOIS

COMPUPRO
162 N. Franklin St., Chicago, IL 60606; 312-
236-5507

DALTON–SMITH & ASSOCIATES, INC.
475 River Bend Rd., Suite 105, Naperville, IL
60540; 630-955-0790

DATA CAREER CENTER
1 Prudential Plaza, Suite 2008, Chicago, IL
60601; 312-565-1060

DATA INTERACTION
1815 W. Roscoe St., Chicago, IL 60657; 312-
733-2005

EXECUTIVE SEARCH INTERNATIONAL
4300 N. Brandywine Dr., #104, Peoria, IL
61614; 309-685-6273

M. W. MCDONALD AND ASSOCIATES
455 E. Illinois St., Suite 565, Chicago, IL
60611; 312-304-0795

ROMAC INTERNATIONAL
150 S. Wacker Dr., Suite 400, Chicago, IL
60606; 312-346-7000

INDIANA

DATA FORCE
715 N. Park Ave., Indianapolis, IN 46202;
317-636-9900

ROMAC INTERNATIONAL
135 N. Pennsylvania Ave., Suite 1770, Indianapolis, IN 46204; 317-631-2900

IOWA

EVERGREEN INFORMATION
P.O. Box 704, Fairfield, IA 52556; 515-472-
9626

EXECUTIVE RESOURCES
3716 Ingersoll Ave., Des Moines, IA 50312;
515-287-6880

KANSAS

CONTINENTAL BUSINESS SYSTEMS
5845 Horton St., Shawnee Mission, KS
66202; 913-677-0200

ROMAC INTERNATIONAL
10300 W. 103rd St., Suite 101, Overland
Park, KS 66214; 913-888-8885

KENTUCKY

MANAGEMENT REGISTRY
1256 S. 3rd St., Louisville, KY 40203; 502-
636-5551

ROMAC INTERNATIONAL
2850 National City Tower, Louisville, KY
40202; 502-581-9900

LOUISIANA

A. D. BOUDREAUX AND ASSOCIATES
7701 Sandpiper Dr., New Orleans, LA 70128;
504-245-1930

AMMON'S CAREER CENTER
9622 Airline Highway, Suite C17, Baton
Rouge, LA 70815; 504-926-8378

COMPUTER PERSONNEL SERVICE
2 Canal St., New Orleans, LA 70130; 504-
581-2433

**DUNHILL PERSONNEL SYSTEM OF
SHREVEPORT**
2920 Knight St., Suite 140, Shreveport, LA
71105; 318-861-3576

MAINE

COMPUSOURCE, INC.
P.O. Box 6822, Scarborough, ME 04070;
207-883-1188

EXECUTIVE SEARCH OF NEW ENGLAND
39 Darling Ave., South Portland, ME 04106;
207-772-4677

PROFESSIONAL SEARCH
30 Overlook Dr., Sanford, ME 04073; 207-
929-6885

MARYLAND

A. G. FISHKIN & ASSOCIATES, INC.
P.O. Box 34413, Bethesda, MD 20827; 301-
983-0303

CRAIG WILLIAMSON, INC.
6701 Rockledge Dr., Suite 250, Bethesda,
MD 20817; 301-897-9566

ROMAC INTERNATIONAL
120 E. Baltimore St., Suite 1950, Baltimore,
MD 21202; 410-727-4050

MASSACHUSETTS

ALLEN DAVIS & ASSOCIATES
P.O. Box 2007, Amherst, MA 01004; 413-549-7440

PRATT PARTNERS
303 Congress St., Boston, MA 02210; 617-439-3090

ROMAC INTERNATIONAL
155 Federal St., 10th Floor, Boston, MA 02110; 617-482-8211

SCOTT-WAYNE ASSOCIATES, INC.
100 Charles River Plaza, Boston, MA 02114; 617-723-7007

MICHIGAN

COLLINS AND ASSOCIATES
10188 W. H Ave., Kalamazoo, MI 49009; 616-372-3275

COMPUPRO
1000 S. Woodward Ave., Suite 105-19, Birmingham, MI 48009; 810-549-2552

ROMAC INTERNATIONAL
161 Ottawa Ave., NW, Suite 409, Grand Rapids, MI 49503; 616-459-3600

MINNESOTA

EHS AND ASSOCIATES
3033 Excelsior Blvd., Minneapolis, MN 55146; 612-924-2366

JACKLEY SEARCH CONSULTANTS
7400 Metro Blvd., Suite 112, Minneapolis, MN 55439; 612-831-2344

ROMAC INTERNATIONAL
220 S. 6th St., Suite 810, Minneapolis, MN 55402; 612-630-5000

MISSISSIPPI

DUNHILL PROFESSIONAL SEARCH
13 Northtown Dr., Suite 200, Jackson, MS 39211; 601-956-1060

MISSOURI

AUSTIN NICHOLS TECHNICAL SEARCH
1100 Main St., Suite 1670, Kansas City, MO 64105; 816-471-5575

P & I C ASSOCIATES
107 W. Pine Pl., St. Louis, MO 63108; 314-367-9577

ROMAC INTERNATIONAL
2 City Place, St. Louis, MO 63141; 314-212-8700

SOFTWARE SYNERGY
1200 E. 104th St., Kansas City, MO 64131; 816-941-7444

MONTANA

FORTUNE PERSONNEL
104 E. Main St., Bozeman, MT 59715; 406-585-1332

NEBRASKA

THE REGENCY GROUP, LTD.
256 N. 115th St., Suite 1, Omaha, NE 68154; 402-334-7255

TELE ELECTRONICS COMPANY
206 S. 19th St., Suite 204, Omaha, NE 68102; 402-346-3421

NEVADA

MANAGEMENT RECRUITERS
6875 W. Charleston Blvd., Suite B, Las Vegas, NV 89117; 702-254-4558

NEW HAMPSHIRE

ACCESS DATA PERSONNEL, INC.
503 Beech St., Manchester, NH 03104; 603-641-6300

EXETER 2100
Computers Park, P.O. Box 2120, Hampton, NH 03842; 603-926-6712

NEW JERSEY

BERMAN & LARSON ASSOCIATES, LTD.
140 Route 17 N., Suite 204, Paramus, NJ 07652; 201-262-9200

CAREER PATH, INC.
502 Marion Lane, Paramus, NJ 07652; 201-265-6665

MIS NETWORK ASSOCIATES
1 Passaic St., Ridgewood, NJ 07450; 201-444-3235

QUESTAR CORPORATION
247 Montgomery St., Jersey City, NJ 07302; 201-451-8376

NEW MEXICO

RADIN ASSOCIATES
2373 Brother Abdon Way, Santa Fe, NM 87505; 505-983-2243

NEW YORK

ACCOUNTING AND COMPUTER PERSONNEL
200 Salina Meadows Pkwy., #180, Syracuse, NY 13212; 315-457-8000

THE AYERS GROUP, INC.
370 Lexington Ave., New York, NY 10023; 212-889-7788

DINA WEHN ASSOCIATES
321 W. 13th St., New York, NY 10014; 212-675-3224

EXEK RECRUITERS
35 Flatt Rd., Rochester, NY 14623; 716-292-0550

NATIONWIDE PERSONNEL GROUP
474 Elmwood Ave., Buffalo, NY 14222; 716-881-2144

PATHWAY EXECUTIVE SEARCH, INC.
60 E. 42nd St., Suite 858, New York, NY 10165; 212-557-2650

QUANTEX ASSOCIATION, INC.
219 E. 44th St., New York, NY 10017; 212-661-5450

RITECH MANAGEMENT, INC.
2 Penn Plaza, Suite 1500, New York, NY 10121; 212-268-7778

ROMAC INTERNATIONAL
60 E. 42nd St., New York, NY 10165; 212-883-7300

TECHNO–TRAC SYSTEMS, INC.
251 Central Park W., New York, NY 10024; 212-769-8722

NORTH CAROLINA

DATA MASTERS
338 N. Elm St., Suite H, Greensboro, NC 27401; 919-373-1461

INFORMATION SYSTEMS PROFESSIONALS
5004 Castlerock Dr., Raleigh, NC 27604; 919-954-9100

MANAGEMENT RECRUITERS
2101 Sardis Rd., N, Charlotte, NC 28227; 704-849-9200

SANFORD ROSE ASSOCIATES
2915 Providence Rd., Suite 300, Charlotte, NC 28211; 704-366-0730

NORTH DAKOTA

PROFESSIONALS UNLIMITED, INC.
2620 25th St., Suite 8, Fargo, ND 58103; 701-232-3465

OHIO

INNOVATIVE RESOURCES
1340 Depot St., Suite 210, Cleveland, OH 44116; 216-331-1757

ROMAC INTERNATIONAL
525 Vine St., Suite 2250, Cincinnati, OH 45202; 513-651-4044

ROMAC INTERNATIONAL
3 Summit Park Dr., Suite 550, Cleveland, OH 44131; 216-328-5900

ROMAC INTERNATIONAL
1105 Schrock Rd., Suite 510, Columbus, OH 43229; 614-825-6700

OKLAHOMA

DP SELECT PERSONNEL, INC.
9717 E. 42nd St., Tulsa, OK 74146; 918-663-3847

EDDIE ROBERTSON AND ASSOCIATES
2525 NW Expressway St., Suite 102, Oklahoma City, OK 73112; 405-840-1991

OREGON

ADVANCED PERSONNEL
441 Union St., NE, Salem, OR 97301; 503-581-8906

D. BROWN & ASSOCIATES, INC.
610 SW Alder St., Suite 1111, Portland, OR 97205; 503-224-6860

SANFORD ROSE ASSOCIATES
10200 SW Eastridge St., Suite 200, Portland, OR 97223; 503-768-4546

ROMAC INTERNATIONAL
10220 SW Greenburg., Suite 1140, Portland, OR 97201; 503-223-6160

PENNSYLVANIA

NATIONAL COMPUTERIZED EMPLOYMENT
2014 W. 8th St., Erie, PA 16505; 814-454-3874

ROMAC INTERNATIONAL
1760 Market St., Suite 2702, Philadelphia, PA 19103; 215-665-1717

ROMAC INTERNATIONAL
Foster Plaza Bldg. VI, 681 Andersen Dr., Pittsburgh, PA 15220; 412-928-8300

RHODE ISLAND

COMPUSEARCH OF PROVIDENCE
101 Dyer St., Providence, RI 02903; 401-274-2810

SCHATTLE PERSONNEL CONSULTANTS, INC.
1130 Ten Rod Rd., B-207, North Kingston, RI 02852; 401-739-0500

SOUTH CAROLINA

CONTEMPORARY MANAGEMENT SERVICES
60 Pointe Circle, Box A, Suite 226, Greenville, SC 29606; 864-233-1947

SOUTH DAKOTA

MANAGEMENT RECRUITERS
2600 S. Minnesota Ave., Suite 202, Sioux Falls, SD 57105; 605-334-9291

TENNESSEE

J & D RESOURCES, INC.
6555 Quince Rd., Suite 425, Memphis, TN 38119; 901-753-0500

THE MORGAN GROUP
P.O. Box 121153, Nashville, TN 37212; 615-297-5272

PHOENIX CONSULTING GROUP, INC.
118 Lee Pkwy. Dr., Chattanooga, TN 37421; 423-892-3897

TEXAS

COMPUTER PROFESSIONALS UNLIMITED
13612 Midway Rd., Suite 333, Dallas, TX 75244; 214-233-1773

COX DODSON AND STORY
16051 Addison Rd., Dallas, TX 75248; 214-750-1067

EDP COMPUTERS SERVICE
4600 Post Oak Pl. Dr., Suite 204, Houston, TX 77027; 713-960-1717

ELSWORTH GROUP
10127 Morocco St., Suite 116, San Antonio, TX 78216; 210-341-9197

FRANKEL AND HOWARD RECRUITING
8834 Prichett Dr., Houston, TX 77096; 713-666-1001

KAHN, RICHARDS, AND ASSOCIATES
1 Riverway, Houston, TX 77056; 713-622-7011

MURPHY SEARCH MANAGEMENT
18484 Preston Rd., Suite 102, Dallas, TX 75252; 214-960-7200

O'KEEFE AND ASSOCIATES
3420 Executive Ctr. Dr., #114, Austin, TX 78731; 512-343-1134

ROMAC INTERNATIONAL
5429 LBJ Freeway, Suite 275, Dallas, TX 75240; 214-387-1600

ROMAC INTERNATIONAL
520 Post Oak Ave., Houston, TX 77027; 713-439-1077

UTAH

EXECUSOURCE
4746 S. 900 E., Suite 250, Salt Lake City, UT 84117; 801-261-3179

VERMONT

ECKLER PERSONNEL NETWORK
14 Lincoln St., Woodstock, VT 05091; 802-457-1605

VIRGINIA

HIGH TECHNOLOGY CONSULTANTS
9691 Main St., Suite D, Fairfax, VA 22031; 703-764-0123

PROFESSIONAL EXECUTIVE SEARCH, INC.
6861 Elm St., Suite 400, McLean, VA 22101; 703-506-1868

TECHNICAL SEARCH GROUP
7400 Beaufont Springs Dr., Suite 425, Richmond, VA 23225; 804-323-3000

WASHINGTON

BERKANAN INTERNATIONAL, INC.
18907 Forest Park Dr., NE, Seattle, WA 98155; 206-361-1633

COMPUTER PERSONNEL, INC.
1601 5th Ave., Suite 1730, Seattle, WA 98101; 206-340-2722

MANAGEMENT RECRUITERS OF TACOMA
2114 Pacific Ave., Suite 155, Tacoma, WA 98402 ; 253-572-7542

MCHALE & ASSOCIATES
1001 4th Ave., Suite 3200, Seattle, WA
98154; 206-684-9778

WEST VIRGINIA

AZIMUTH, INC.
1401 Country Club Rd., Fairmont, WV
26554; 304-363-1162

WISCONSIN

EDP CONSULTANTS, INC.
P.O. Box 26066, Milwaukee, WI 53226; 414-
255-9363

ROMAC INTERNATIONAL
1233 N. Mayfair Rd., Suite 300, Milwaukee,
WI 53226; 414-475-7200

WYOMING

SAL ENTERPRISES, INC.
1905 Cy Ave., Casper, WY 82604; 307-472-
1144

S E R V I C E S

Employment Agencies

EMPLOYMENT AGENCIES CAN BE A VALUABLE RESOURCE for job seekers. Such agencies, which typically list available jobs at various companies, arrange interviews for job seekers who meet the respective requirements. If you are fortunate enough to arrive at an agency when an appropriate job is being listed, you may find yourself succeeding quickly in your job search. The employment agencies included in this chapter specialize in permanently staffing all income levels and all ranges of the professional spectrum. Accordingly, some place executives. However, for agencies that specialize in executive-level jobs, ►►see **Executive Recruiters," pp. 592-609.** Likewise, jobs in sales and computers and temporary positions are often available at the employment agencies listed in this chapter. However, for these particular areas of specialization, ►►see **"Sales Recruiters," pp. 610-615; Computer-Search Agencies," pp. 562-568; and Temp Agencies," pp. 616-626.**

Many agencies deal specifically with certain industries or types of jobs. These classifications are found at the end of each agency listing here and are called "Areas of Specialization." Those agencies that do not specialize—referred to here as "General"—can help all types of job hunters match their qualifications with available job situations.

In the following listings, those agencies that specialize in "Technology" are geared toward searches in the computer or electronics fields. "Finance" specialists operate in the banking as well as the financial industry. "Trades" refers to plumbing, carpentry, and so on. The other areas of specialization are self-explanatory. Note that the areas of specialization cited within an agency's listing are only generalizations. Many agencies have positions available that are not in their areas of specializations. You should therefore ask for a more complete list of the types of positions agencies seek to fill.

Many of the entries in this chapter are branches of major nationwide employment agencies. Larger, more established local agencies are also listed. Some newer agencies are included because they specialize in employment areas that the others do not cover. There is also a representative listing in terms of agency areas of specialization and geography.

Most of the agencies listed are compensated by employers looking to fill positions rather than by job seekers. However, be sure to ask at particular agencies to make sure this is the case.

ALABAMA

A-1 EMPLOYMENT SERVICES
1015 Monlimar Dr., Suite 130, Mobile, AL 36609; 334-343-9702
Areas of Specialization: General

CMS
2002 Poole Dr. NW, Suite B, Huntsville, AL 35801; 205-852-7777
Areas of Specialization: General

DUNHILL PERSONNEL
2738 S. 18th St., Birmingham, AL 35209;
205-877-4580
Areas of Specialization: General

LABOR FINDERS
947 Madison Ave., Mongomery, AL 36104; 334-264-4506
Areas of Specialization: General

ALASKA

ALASKA STATE EMPLOYMENT SERVICE
675 7th Ave., Fairbanks, AK 99701; 907-451-2871
Areas of Specialization: General

PERSONNEL PLUS EMPLOYMENT AGENCY
701 E. Tudor Rd., Suite 160, Anchorage, AK
99503; 907-563-7587
Areas of Specialization: General

ARIZONA

ADECCO
333 E. Osborn, Phoenix, AZ 85012; 602-246-1143
Areas of Specialization: Clerical, Human Resources, Law, Manufacturing, Publishing

AMERICAN CAREER GROUP
2400 E. Arizona Biltmore Circle, Phoenix, AZ 85016; 602-381-1667
Areas of Specialization: General

ARIZONA MEDICAL EXCHANGE
777 E. Missouri Ave., Phoenix, AZ 85014;
602-246-4906
Areas of Specialization: Health Services

AIRMATE PERSONNEL
1255 E. Aero Pk. Blvd., Tucson, AZ 85706;
520-573-9699
Areas of Specialization: Administration,
Data Processing, Technology

AUTOMOTIVE CAREERS CENTER, INC.
630-1 E. Thomas Rd., Suite222, Scottsdale,
AZ 85251; 602-970-3952
Areas of Specialization: Automotive

GENERAL EMPLOYMENT
100 Clarendon Ave., Suite 1700, Phoenix, AZ
85013; 602-265-7800
Areas of Specialization: Administration,
Engineering, Manufacturing, Science,
Technology

LCC COMPANY
7975 N. Hayden Rd., Scottsdale, AZ 85258;
602-483-5660
Areas of Specialization: Health Services

VOLT SERVICES GROUP
7102 W. Thomas Rd., Phoenix, AZ85033;
602-849-6780
Areas of Specialization: Accounting,
Design, Engineering, Science, Technology

ARKANSAS

MANAGEMENT RECRUITERS
10816 Executive Ctr. Dr., Suite 110, Little
Rock, AR 72211; 501-224-0801

Areas of Specialization: General

MOORE & ASSOCIATES
5111 Rogers Ave., Ft. Smith, AR72903; 501-478-7052
Areas of Specialization: General

PERSONNEL RESOURCES
14000 Cantrill Rd., Suite 174, Little Rock,
AR 72212; 501-332-4000
Areas of Specialization: General

CALIFORNIA

ACTION PLUS EMPLOYER SERVICES
1211 W. Imperial Highway, Suite 100, Brea,
CA 92621; 714-773-1506
Areas of Specialization: Automotive,
Health Services, Management, Marketing, Sales

ADDISON PERSONNEL
3540 Wilshire Blvd., #515, Los Angeles, CA
90010; 213-386-6238
Areas of Specialization: Accounting, Finance, Law, Management, Manufacturing, Marketing, Sales, Secretarial

APPLE EMPLOYMENT AGENCY
18538 Hawthorne Blvd., Torrance, CA
90505; 310-542-8534
Areas of Specialization: Accounting,
Clerical, Finance, Health Services

APPLE ONE EMPLOYMENT SERVICE
1295 N. Euclid, Anaheim, CA 92801; 714-956-5180
Areas of Specialization: Accounting,
Clerical, Finance, Human Resources,
Marketing, Sales

APPLE ONE SERVICES
1970 Broadway, Suite 110, Oakland, CA
94612; 510-835-0217
Areas of Specialization: Accounting,
Clerical, Finance

ASSURED PERSONNEL SERVICES, INC.
1301 M., S. Beach Blvd., La Habra, CA
90631; 310-723-5020
Areas of Specialization: Accounting,
Clerical, Health Services, Secretarial

BEVERLY HILLS BAR ASSOCIATION PERSONNEL SERVICES
300 S. Beverly Dr., Suite 214, Beverly Hills,
CA 90212; 310-553-4575
Areas of Specialization: Law

BOOKKEEPERS/ACCOUNTANTS PLUS
9442 Garfield Ave., Suite 216, Huntington,

CA 92646; 714-963-7858
Areas of Specialization: Accounting

BRIDECREEK PERSONNEL
12792 Valley View St., #202, Garden Grove, CA 92645; 714-891-1771
Areas of Specialization: Engineering, Management, Manufacturing, Marketing, Sales

BUSINESS SYSTEMS STAFFING & ASSOCIATES, INC.
10680 W. Pico Blvd., Suite 210, Los Angeles, CA 90064; 310-204-6711
Areas of Specialization: Business Services

CAREER VISIONS
3737 Camino Del Rio S., Suite 108, San Diego, CA 92108; 619-280-3554
Areas of Specialization: General

CHOSEN FEW PERSONNEL SERVICES
911 Wilshire Blvd., Suite 1880, Los Angeles, CA 90017; 213-689-9400
Areas of Specialization: Law

COLT SYSTEMS PROFESSIONAL SERVICES
1880 Century Park E., Suite 208, Los Angeles, CA 90067; 310-277-4741
Areas of Specialization: Accounting, Administration, Clerical, Data Processing, Finance, Science, Technology

THE COMPUTER RESOURCES GROUP, INC.
275 Battery St., #800, San Francisco, CA 94111; 415-398-3535
Areas of Specialization: Technology

CT ENGINEERING
2221 Rosecrans Ave., Suite 131, El Segundo, CA 90245; 310-643-8333
Areas of Specialization: Accounting, Clerical, Engineering, Science, Secretarial, Technology

DATA CAREERS PERSONNEL SERVICES, INC.
3320 4th Ave., San Diego, CA 92103; 619-291-9994
Areas of Specialization: Accounting, Engineering, Finance, Technology

DEC & ASSOCIATES HEALTHCARE PERSONNEL
2555 E. Chapman Ave., Suite 300, Fullerton, CA 92631; 714-447-0826
Areas of Specialization: Health Services

DENT-ASSIST PERSONNEL SERVICE
725 30th St., Suite 206, Sacramento, CA 95816; 916-443-1113
Areas of Specialization: Health Services (Dental)

DIAL PERSONNEL ASSOCIATES
1033 E. Imperial Highway, Suite E-10, Brea, CA 92621; 714-671-1726
Areas of Specialization: Accounting, Clerical, Finance

DUNHILL OF OAKLAND, INC.
3732 Mt. Diablo Blvd., Suite 375, Lafayette, CA 94549; 925-283-5300
Areas of Specialization: Accounting, Engineering, Finance, Health Services, Manufacturing, Marketing, Sales, Technology

EMPLOYMENT SERVICE AGENCY
84243 Florence Ave., Downey, CA 90240; 310-869-8811
Areas of Specialization: Accounting, Food and Beverages, Health Services, Manufacturing, Marketing, Sales, Secretarial

EMPLOYMENT SOLUTIONS—AN IBM DIVISION
355 S. Grand Ave., 7th Floor, Los Angeles, CA 90071; 213-621-5895
Areas of Specialization: Accounting, Engineering, Finance, Human Resources, Manufacturing, Marketing, Sales, Science, Secretarial, Technology

GOULD PERSONNEL SERVICES
850 Colorado Blvd., Suite 104, Los Angeles, CA 90041; 213-256-5800
Areas of Specialization: General

HEALTHCARE RECRUITERS
15300 Ventura Blvd., Suite 207, Sherman Oaks, CA 91403; 818-981-9510
Areas of Specialization: Engineering, Health Services, Manufacturing, Marketing, Sales, Science

HUGHES PERSONNEL SERVICES
1535 E. Shaw Ave., Suite 102, Fresno, CA 93710; 209-227-1300
Areas of Specialization: General

IDI PERSONNEL SERVICES
6922 Hollywood Blvd., Suite 211, Hollywood, CA 90028; 213-466-4388
Areas of Specialization: Advertising, Entertainment, Health Services, Law, Management

JAA EMPLOYMENT AGENCY
6404 Wilshire Blvd., Suite 1230, Los Angeles, CA 90048; 213-655-0285
Areas of Specialization: Management, Marketing, Sales

JAMES HOLDER PLACEMENT
160 Pine St., Suite 300, San Francisco, CA 94111; 415-391-5965
Areas of Specialization: Accounting, Clerical, Marketing, Sales, Technology

JOSEPH MICHAELS
1440 Broadway, Suite 506, Oakland, CA 94612; 510-832-1090
Areas of Specialization: Accounting, Finance

JOBS PLUS
1590 Oakland Rd., B104, San Jose, CA 95131; 408-383-0426
Areas of Specialization: General

JUSTUS PERSONNEL SERVICES
10680 W. Pico Blvd., #210, Los Angeles, CA 90064; 310-204-6711
Areas of Specialization: Entertainment, Finance, Health Services, Manufacturing, Nonprofit, Real Estate

MAINSTREAM
1520 Nutmeg Pl., Suite 210, Costa Mesa, CA 92626; 714-641-9190
Areas of Specialization: Engineering

MARK ASSOCIATES
300 Montgomery St., Suite 860, San Francisco, CA 94104; 415-392-1835
Areas of Specialization: Law

MBC EMPLOYMENT AGENCY
3699 Wilshire Blvd., Los Angeles, CA 90010; 213-388-0333
Areas of Specialization: Domestic Services, Food and Beverages

MCCALL PERSONNEL SERVICES
351 California St., Suite 1200, San Francisco, CA 94104; 415-981-3400
Areas of Specialization: Clerical, Secretarial

MICRO TEMPS SYSTEMS AND PROGRAMMING
17320 Red Hill Ave., Suite 320, Irvine, CA 92714; 714-259-1850
Areas of Specialization: Aerospace, Engineering, Science, Technology

MULTAX SYSTEMS, INC.
505 N. Sepulveda Blvd., Suite 7, Manhattan Beach, CA 90266; 310-379-8398
Areas of Specialization: Engineering, Technology

NESCO SERVICE COMPANY
19558 Ventura Blvd., Tarzana, CA 91356; 818-881-8813
Areas of Specialization: Administration, Engineering, Nonprofit, Technology

NURSES EXCHANGE OF AMERICA
3534 Larga Ave., Suite A, Los Angeles, CA 90039; 213-662-1916
Areas of Specialization: Health Services (Nursing)

OLSTEN SERVICES
70 S. Lake Ave., Suite 770, Pasadena, CA 91101; 818-449-1342
Areas of Specialization: Accounting, Advertising, Clerical, Finance, Health Services, Insurance, Law, Manufacturing, Real Estate

INTERIM PERSONNEL
750 W. Gonzales Rd., Suite 140, Oxnard, CA 93030; 805-983-2000
Areas of Specialization: Architecture, Clerical, Construction, Food and Beverages, Health Services, Manufacturing, Marketing, Real Estate, Sales

PIPS PERSONNEL SERVICES
40 Atlantic Ave., Suite D, Long Beach, CA 90802; 310-435-3030
Areas of Specialization: Accounting, Clerical, Finance, Marketing, Sales

PREMIER PERSONNEL SERVICES
2463 208th St., #200, Torrance, CA 90501; 310-320-1023
Areas of Specialization: Accounting, Administration, Finance, Management, Marketing, Sales, Secretarial

REMEDY STAFFING SERVICES
11740 San Vincente Blvd., #202, Los Angeles, CA 90049; 310-826-5065
Areas of Specialization: Data Processing, Human Resources, Marketing, Retail, Sales, Secretarial

ROBERT HALF INTERNATIONAL
1901 Ave. of the Stars, Suite 490, Los Angeles, CA 90067; 310-286-6800
Areas of Specialization: Accounting, Finance, Technology

SAN PABLO PERSONNEL AGENCY
629 El Protal Ctr., San Pablo, CA 94806; 510-233-7363
Areas of Specialization: General

SEARCH WEST OF ENCINO
1888 Century Park E., Suite 2050, Los Angeles, CA 90067; 310-284-8888
Areas of Specialization: General

SNELLING PERSONNEL SERVICES
26229 Eden Landing Rd., Suite 3, Hayward, CA 94545; 510-887-8210
Areas of Specialization: General

STERLING SERVICES
1482 E. Valley Rd., #47, Santa Barbara, CA 93108; 805-565-4444
Areas of Specialization: Domestic Services

SUNDAY & ASSOCIATES, INC.
P.O. Box 21122, Piedmont, CA 94620; 510-644-0440
Areas of Specialization: Science, Technology

SYSTEM ONE
3021 Citrus Circle, Suite 230, Walnut Creek, CA 94598; 510-932-8801
Areas of Specialization: Clerical, Engineering

SYSTEMS CAREERS
211 Sutter St., Suite 607, San Francisco, CA 94108; 415-434-4770
Areas of Specialization: Finance, Food and Beverages, Manufacturing, Marketing, Sales, Technology, Transportation

T. R. EMPLOYMENT AGENCY
406 Wilshire Blvd., Santa Monica, CA 90401; 310-393-4107
Areas of Specialization: Accounting, Engineering, Fashion, Health Services, Manufacturing

YOLAND'S EMPLOYMENT AGENCY
16218 Ventura Blvd., Suite 1, Encino, CA 91436; 213-872-0083
Areas of Specialization: Domestic Services

COLORADO

ADECCO
44 Cook St., Suite 110, Denver, CO 80206; 303-399-7706
Areas of Specialization: Accounting, Clerical, Data Processing, Finance, Insurance, Law, Secretarial, Science, Technology

DUNHILL OF FT. COLLINS, INC.
2120 S. College Ave., Suite 3, Ft. Collins, CO 80525; 970-221-5630
Areas of Specialization: Accounting, Engineering, Health Services, Marketing, Sales

40 PLUS OF COLORADO, INC.
3842 S. Mason St., Ft. Collins, CO 80525; 970-223-2470, ext. 261
Areas of Specialization: General

40 PLUS OF COLORADO, INC.
5800 W. Alameda Ave., Lakewood, CO 80226; 303-937-4956
Areas of Specialization: General

INTERIM PERSONNEL SERVICES OF BOULDER
3000 Pearl St., Suite 200, Boulder, CO 80301; 303-442-8677
Areas of Specialization: Clerical, Customer Service, Data Processing, Law, Manual Labor, Secretarial

INTERIM PERSONNEL SERVICES OF DENVER
1775 Sherman St., Denver, CO 80218; 303-777-7734
Areas of Specialization: Clerical, Customer Service, Data Processing, Law, Manual Labor, Secretarial

JFI/JOBS FOR INDUSTRY
1888 Sherman St., Suite 500, Denver, CO 80207; 303-831-0048
Areas of Specialization: Distribution, Manufacturing

JULIE WEST AND ASSOCIATES
4155 E. Jewell Ave., Suite 210, Denver, CO 80222; 303-759-1622
Areas of Specialization: Accounting, Clerical, Finance, Law, Real Estate, Secretarial

VOLT SERVICES GROUP
102 N. Cascade Ave., Suite 200, Colorado Springs, CO 80903; 719-471-0858
Areas of Specialization: Accounting

CONNECTICUT

A-1 PERSONNEL SERVICES
80 Shield St., W. Hartford, CT 06110; 860-549-5262
Areas of Specialization: Accounting,

Engineering, Finance, Insurance, Manufacturing, Marketing, Sales, Science, Technology

BAILEY ASSOCIATES
1208 Main St., Branford, CT 06405; 203-488-2504
Areas of Specialization: Accounting, Clerical, Engineering, Insurance, Law, Manufacturing, Marketing, Sales, Secretarial, Technology

EMPLOYMENT OPPORTUNITIES
57 North St., Suite 320, Danbury, CT 06810; 203-797-2653
Areas of Specialization: Accounting, Clerical, Engineering, Finance, Food and Beverages, Health Services, Manufacturing, Sales, Science, Technology

LABOR FORCE OF AMERICA
102 New Haven Ave., Milford, CT 06460; 203-878-6821
Areas of Specialization: Accounting, Construction, Data Processing, Engineering, Law, Management, Manual Labor, Marketing, Sales, Science, Secretarial

UNI/SEARCH OF WATERBURY, INC.
195 Grove St., Waterbury, CT 06710; 203-753-2329
Areas of Specialization: General

DELAWARE

CAREERS USA.
3205 Concord Pike, Wilmington, DE 19803; 302-658-6461
Areas of Specialization: Accounting, Engineering, Design, Marketing, Sales, Science, Secretarial, Technology

FIDELITY PERSONNEL
4010 Concord Pike, Wilmington, DE 19803; 302-478-6996
Areas of Specialization: Accounting, Clerical, Engineering, Finance, Insurance, Law, Sales, Science, Technology

DISTRICT OF COLUMBIA

ADMIN ASSISTANCE
1511 K St., NW, Suite 320, Washington, DC 20005; 202-638-6380
Areas of Specialization: Administration, Data Processing, Secretarial

ATLAS PERSONNEL AGENCY
1129 20th St., NW, Suite 400, Washington, DC 20036; 202-293-7210
Areas of Specialization: General

C ASSOCIATES
1619 G St., SE, Washington, DC 20003; 202-544-0821
Areas of Specialization: Technology

DON RICHARD ASSOCIATES OF WASHINGTON, DC
1020 19th St.NW, Suite 650, Washington, DC 20036; 202-463-7210
Areas of Specialization: Accounting, Finance, Technology

MEDICAL PERSONNEL SERVICES
7007 L St., Suite 250, Washington, DC 20036; 202-466-2955
Areas of Specialization: Health Services

NANCY ALLEN AND ASSOCIATES, INC.
1000 16th St., NW, Suite 501, Washington, DC 20036; 202-467-4100
Areas of Specialization: Law

POSITIONS, INC.
1730 K St., NW, Suite 907, Washington, DC 20006; 202-659-9270
Areas of Specialization: Clerical, Data Processing, Secretarial

SIGMAN & SUMMERFIELD ASSOCIATES, INC.
1120 Connecticut Ave., NW, Suite 270, Washington, DC 20036; 202-785-9044
Areas of Specialization: Administration, Law, Nonprofit, Secretarial

TRIFAX CORPORATION
4121 Minnesota Ave., NE, Washington, DC 20019; 202-388-6000
Areas of Specialization: Health Services, Human Resources

FLORIDA

AAA EMPLOYMENT
4035 S. Florida Ave., Lakeland, FL 33813; 941-646-9681
Areas of Specialization: General

AAA EMPLOYMENT
101 Century Dr., Jacksonville, FL 32216; 904-725-9551
Areas of Specialization: General

ALL CARE PROFESSIONAL SERVICES
1065 NE 125th St., N. Miami, FL 33161; 305-895-2080
Areas Of Specialization: General

AVAILABILITY, INC.
P.O. Box 25434, Tampa, FL 33622; 813-286-8800
Areas of Specialization: Clerical, Engineering, Law, Science, Secretarial, Technology

EXECUTIVE DIRECTIONS, INC.
450 N. Park Rd., #302, Hollywood, FL 33021; 954-926-9444
Areas of Specialization: Technology

FIRST EMPLOYMENT CONSULTANTS, INC.
6175 NW 153rd St., Suite 230, Miami Lakes, FL 33014; 305-825-8900
Areas of Specialization: Architecture, Construction, Engineering, Real Estate

JANUS CAREER SERVICE
157 E. New England Ave., Suite 240, Winter Park, FL 32789; 407-628-1090
Areas of Specialization: General

JOB SERVICE OF FLORIDA
5729 Manatee Ave. W., Bradenton, FL 34205; 941-741-3036
Areas of Specialization: General

PERSONNEL ONE, INC.
1650 Sand Lake Rd., Orlando, FL 32809; 407-850-2250
Areas of Specialization: Administration, Law, Marketing, Sales, Secretarial

GEORGIA

ACCOUNTANTS ON CALL
3355 Lenox Rd., Suite 630, Atlanta, GA 30326; 404-233-2040
Areas of Specialization: Accounting, Finance, Technology

BUSINESS PROFESSIONAL GROUP, INC.
3490 Piedmont Rd., Suite 212, Atlanta, GA 30305; 404-262-2577
Areas of Specialization: Accounting, Administration, Advertising, Engineering, Finance, Insurance, Management, Manu-facturing, Sales, Science, Technology

COASTAL EMPLOYMENT
409 E. Montgomery, Savannah, GA 31406; 912-781-0082
Areas of Specialization: General

EMPLOYMENT SOLUTIONS—AN IBM DIVISION
3200 Windy Hill Rd., Marietta, GA 30067;
770-835-7654
Areas of Specialization: Accounting, Engineering, Finance, Manufacturing, Marketing, Sales, Secretarial, Science, Technology

EXECUTIVE RESOURCE GROUP
315 W. Ponce de Leon Ave., #549, Decatur, GA 30030; 404-377-0888
Areas of Specialization: Finance, Gaming, Health Services, Insurance

HINES RECRUITING ASSOCIATES
3880 Habersham Rd., NW, Atlanta, GA 30305; 404-262-7171
Areas of Specialization: Engineering, Human Resources, Manufacturing

INTERNATIONAL INSURANCE PERSONNEL, INC.
P.O. Box 20408, Atlanta, GA 30358; 404-257-9685
Areas of Specialization: Insurance

IPR GROUP, INC.
88097-B Roswell Rd., Atlanta, GA 30350; 404-369-7500
Areas of Specialization: Human Resources

OFFICE SPECIALISTS
6623 Roswell Rd., Atlanta, GA 30328; 404-843-3717
Areas of Specialization: Administration, Clerical, Customer Service, Data Processing, Law, Secretarial

OFFICEMATES OF ATLANTA
400 Colony Sq., Suite 1001, 1201 Peachtree St., Atlanta, GA 30361; 404-892-1900
Areas of Specialization: Accounting, Clerical, Secretarial

PREMIER STAFFING
2 Concourse Pkwy., NE, Atlanta, GA 30328; 404-396-9224
Areas of Specialization: Accounting, Administration, Architecture, Construction, Finance, Insurance, Marketing, Retail, Sales, Secretarial

RANDSTAD STAFFING SERVICE
1002 Broadway, Columbus, GA 31901; 706-596-8344
Areas of Specialization: General

SNELLING PERSONNEL SERVICES
1337 Canton Rd., D-3, Marietta, GA 30066; 770-952-0909
Areas of Specialization: Health Services, Marketing, Sales, Secretarial

HAWAII

ASSOCIATE EMPLOYMENT SERVICE
1141 Union Mall, Suite 41, Honolulu, HI 96812; 808-537-3381
Areas of Specialization: General

BENEFICIAL EMPLOYMENT SERVICE
841 Bishop St., Suite 904, Honolulu, HI 96813; 808-526-4121
Areas of Specialization: General

IDAHO

APPLE ONE
8724 Fairview Ave., Boise ID 83704; 208-377-4844
Areas of Specialization: General

CAREER DEVELOPMENT CENTER
ISU Museum, 3rd Floor, Pocatello, ID 83201; 208-236-2380
Areas of Specialization: General

ILLINOIS

ABA PLACEMENTS
1526 Miner St., Des Plaines, IL 60016; 847-297-3535
Areas of Specialization: Accounting, Food and Beverages, Manufacturing, Marketing, Publishing, Sales

AMERICAN MEDICAL PERSONNEL, INC.
612 N. Michigan Ave., #714, Chicago, IL 60611; 312-337-4221
Areas of Specialization: Health Services, Insurance

AMERICAN TECHNICAL SEARCH, INC.
2215 York Rd., Oak Brook, IL 60521; 630-990-1001
Areas of Specialization: Architecture, Construction, Engineering, Management, Real Estate

BANNER PERSONNEL SERVICE, INC.
122 S. Michigan Ave., Suite 1510, Chicago, IL 60603; 312-704-6000
Areas of Specialization: Accounting, Engineering, Management, Sales, Science, Secretarial, Technology

BANNER PERSONNEL SERVICE, INC.
1701 E. Woodfield Rd., Suite 611, Schaumburg, IL 60173; 847-706-9180
Areas of Specialization: Accounting, Engineering, Management, Marketing, Sales, Science, Secretarial, Technology

BRITT ASSOCIATES, INC.
2709 Black Rd., Joliet, IL 60435; 815-744-7200

Areas of Specialization: Distribution, Transportation

BUSCH EMPLOYMENT AGENCY
185 N. Wabash Ave., Suite 1106, Chicago, IL 60602; 312-372-7260
Areas of Specialization: Food and Beverages, Hospitality

CAREER MANAGEMENT ASSOCIATES
262 N. Phelps Ave., Box 5863, Rockford, IL 61125; 815-229-7815
Areas of Specialization: Accounting, Clerical, Engineering, Finance, Health Services, Insurance, Manufacturing, Secretarial, Technology

DUNHILL OF CHICAGO
68 E. Wacker Pl., Chicago, IL 60601; 312-346-0933
Areas of Specialization: Accounting, Finance, Marketing, Sales, Technology

EMPLOYMENT SOLUTIONS—AN IBM DIVISION
1 IBM Plaza, Chicago, IL 60611; 312-245-7935
Areas of Specialization: Accounting, Engineering, Finance, Manufacturing, Marketing, Sales, Science, Secretarial, Technology

ESQUIRE PERSONNEL SERVICE, INC.
222 S. Riverside Plaza, Suite 320, Chicago, IL 60606; 312-648-4600
Areas of Specialization: Administration, Clerical, Finance, Insurance, Law, Marketing, Retail, Sales, Secretarial

GANS, GANS, AND ASSOCIATES
175 N. Franklin, Suite 401, Chicago, IL 60606; 312-357-9600
Areas of Specialization: Insurance, Law

GROVE PERSONNEL SERVICES
1411 Opus Pl., Executive Towers W. II, Suite 118, Downers Grove, IL 60515; 630-968-2771
Areas of Specialization: Clerical, Finance, Insurance, Management, Marketing, Sales, Secretarial

HUMAN RESOURCES CONNECTION
1900 E. Golf Rd., Suite M100, Schaumburg, IL 60173; 847-995-8090
Areas of Specialization: General

INTERIM PERSONNEL
5411 E. State St., Suite 4, Rockford, IL 61108; 815-227-1030
Areas of Specialization: General

KINGSLEY EMPLOYMENT
208 S. LaSalle St., Suite 1877, Chicago, IL 60604; 312-726-8190
Areas of Specialization: Advertising, Finance

MICHAEL DAVID ASSOCIATES, INC.
133 E. Ogden Ave., Room 202, Hinsdale, IL
60521; 630-654-4460
Areas of Specialization: General

THE MURPHY GROUP
6 S. 235 Steeple Run Dr., Naperville, IL
60540; 630-355-7030
Areas of Specialization: Administration,
Clerical, Data Processing, Management,
Secretarial

THE MURPHY GROUP
1211 W. 22nd St., Suite 221, Oak Brook, IL
60521; 630-653-3660
Areas of Specialization: Accounting, Finance, Insurance, Manufacturing, Marketing, Sales

ROBERT HALF INTERNATIONAL
205 N. Michigan Ave., #3301, Chicago, IL
60601; 312-616-8200
Areas of Specialization: Administration, Secretarial

ON STAFF, INC.
640 Pearson St., Des Plaines, IL 60016; 847-827-1650
Areas of Specialization: Administration, Finance, Data Processing, Marketing, Secretarial

THE OPPORTUNITIES GROUP
53 W. Jackson, Suite 215, Chicago, IL 60604;
312-922-8898
Areas of Specialization: Clerical, Data
Processing, Law, Secretarial

OPPORTUNITY PERSONNEL SERVICE
200 W. Adams, Suite 1702, Chicago, IL
60606; 312-704-9898
Areas of Specialization: Accounting,
Clerical, Finance, Insurance, Law, Manufacturing, Marketing, Sales, Technology

PERSONNEL CONNECTIONS, INC.
960 Clock Tower Dr. E., Springfield, IL
62704; 217-787-9022
Areas of Specialization: General

POL–AM EMPLOYMENT AGENCY
3907 W. Belmont, Chicago, IL 60618; 773-685-6602
Areas of Specialization: Construction,
Domestic Services, Engineering, Health
Services

PROGRESSIVE EMPLOYMENT SERVICES
18525 S. Torrence, Lansing, IL 60438; 708-895-3300
Areas of Specialization: Accounting,
Administration, Engineering, Manufacturing, Secretarial, Technology

PROMISED LAND EMPLOYMENT SERVICE
P.O. Box 4212, Rockford, IL 61110; 815-964-3473
Areas of Specialization: General

ROBERT HALF INTERNATIONAL
205 N. Michigan Ave., Suite 3301, Chicago,
IL 60601; 312-616-8200
Areas of Specialization: Administration,
Technology

RUSH PERSONNEL SERVICES
331 Fulton St., Suite 825, Peoria, IL 61602;
309-637-8303
Areas of Specialization: General

SEARCH DYNAMICS
9420 W. Foster Ave., Suite 200, Chicago, IL
60656; 773-992-3900
Areas of Specialization: Engineering,
Manufacturing, Science, Technology

INDIANA

ADECCO EMPLOYMENT SERVICES
1417 W. Coliseum Blvd., Ft. Wayne, IN
46808; 219-482-2390

DUNHILL PROFESSIONAL SEARCH
950 W. Meridian., Suite I, Indianapolis, IN
46204; 317-237-7878
Areas of Specialization: General

EDGE PERSONNEL CONSULTING
915 Main St., Evansville,IN 47708; 812-424-8814
Areas of Specialization: General

SNELLING PERSONNEL
1000 E. 80th Pl., Merrillville, IN 46410; 219-769-2922
Areas of Specialization: General

IOWA

PERSONNEL, INC.
604 Locust St., Suite 516, Des Moines, IA
50309; 515-243-7687
Areas of Specialization: General

KANSAS

ABLE EMPLOYMENT
10 E. Cambridge Circle Dr., Suite 120, Kansas City, KS 47708; 812-424-8814
Areas of Specialization: General

ABLE STAFFING
615 E. 47th St. S, Wichita, KS 67216; 316-522-1713
Areas of Specialization: General

DUNHILL OF WICHITA
1210 E. 15th St., Wichita, KS 67211; 316-264-4065
Areas of Specialization: General

SERVICE FOR EMPLOYMENT
601 SW Topeka Blvd., Topeka, KS 66603; 785-234-9675
Areas of Specialization: General

KENTUCKY

MANAGEMENT RECRUITERS
1930 Bishop Lane, Suite 426, Louisville, KY 40218; 502-456-4330
Areas of Specialization: General

LOUISIANA

ATS SERVICES
1515 Poydras St., Suite 1060, New Orleans, LA 70112; 504-522-4000
Areas of Specialization: General

SNELLING PERSONNEL
942 Office Park Blvd., Baton Rouge, LA 70809; 225-927-0550
Areas of Specialization: General

MAINE

AMES PERSONNEL CONSULTANTS
34 Hennessey Ave., Brunswick, ME 04011; 207-729-5158
Areas of Specialization: General

BEST EMPLOYMENT SERVICES
58 York St., Portland, ME 04101; 207-874-0055
Areas of Specialization: General

MARYLAND

A. G. FISHKIN AND ASSOCIATES, INC.
P.O. Box 34413, Bethesda, MD 20827; 301-770-4944
Areas of Specialization: Science, Technology, Telecommunications

ADMAN PERSONNEL
1112 Wayne Ave., Silver Spring, MD 20910; 301-565-3900
Areas of Specialization: Accounting, Clerical, Finance, Marketing, Sales, Technology

ATLAS PERSONNEL AGENCY
11820 Parklane Dr., Suite 330, Rockville, MD 20852; 301-984-8075
Areas of Specialization: General

CAPLAN ASSOCIATES
28 Allegheny Ave., Suite 600, Towson, MD 21204; 410-821-9351
Areas of Specialization: Accounting, Finance, Manufacturing, Real Estate, Science, Technology

CAREERS III, INC.
1039 Shady Grove Ct., Gaithersburg, MD 20877; 301-251-1255
Areas of Specialization: Clerical, Customer Service, Data Processing, Secretarial

CONTEMPORARY FAMILY CARE SERVICES, INC./CHEVY CHASE BABYSITTERS
9222 Woodland Dr., Silver Spring, MD 20910; 301-654-4858
Areas of Specialization: Domestic Services

CONTINENTAL ASSISTANCE & SEARCH AGENCY, INC./CASA
914 Silver Spring Ave., Suite 205, Silver Spring, MD 20910; 301-587-0135
Areas of Specialization: Fashion, Finance, Health Services, Law, Real Estate

DUNHILL OF ROCKVILLE
414 Hungerford Dr., Suite 252, Rockville, MD 20850; 301-654-2115
Areas of Specialization: Accounting, Clerical, Finance

J. R. ASSOCIATES
152 Rollins Ave., Suite 200, Rockville, MD 20852; 301-424-0450
Areas of Specialization: Engineering, Marketing, Sales, Science, Technology

SNELLING PERSONNEL
20 S. Charles St., Sun Life Bldg., Baltimore, MD 21201; 410-528-9400
Areas of Specialization: General

TOM MCCALL & ASSOCIATES
506 Equitable Bldg., Baltimore, MD 21202; 410-539-0700
Areas of Specialization: Management, Marketing, Sales

MASSACHUSETTS

ABBOTT PERSONNEL CONSULTING SERVICES, INC.
Faneuil Hall #4, 4th Floor, Boston, MA
02108; 617-423-0202
Areas of Specialization: General

ADVANCE PERSONNEL ASSOCIATES, INC.
50 Mall Rd., Burlington, MA 01803; 617-
273-4250
Areas of Specialization: Advertising,
Engineering, Marketing, Publishing,
Sales, Science, Technology

B & M ASSOCIATES, INC.
199 Cambridge Rd., Woburn, MA 01801;
617-938-9120
Areas of Specialization: Aerospace, Engineering, Manufacturing, Science,
Technology

CAMPBELL ASSOCIATES
18 Tremont St., Boston, MA 02108; 617-227-
2028
Areas of Specialization: Accounting,
Advertising, Finance, Law

HALYS ASSOCIATES
24 Ray Ave., Burlington, MA 01803; 617-
890-1500
Areas of Specialization: Hospitality,
Sales

HILTON ASSOCIATES
252 Elliott St., Beverly, MA 01915; 508-921-
0840
Areas of Specialization: Health Services,
Marketing, Sales

HRI SERVICE, INC.
150 Wood Rd., Suite 3303, Braintree, MA
02184; 617-848-9110
Areas of Specialization: Hospitality

INSURANCE PERSONNEL RECRUITERS, INC.
303 Congress St., Suite 600, Boston, MA
02210; 617-439-0580
Areas of Specialization: Insurance

KINGSTON-DWIGHT ASSOCIATES
100 Franklin St., Suite 300, Boston, MA
02110; 617-350-8811
Areas of Specialization: Accounting, Finance

LANE EMPLOYMENT SERVICE, INC.
370 Main St., Suite 820, Worcester, MA
01608; 508-757-5678

Areas of Specialization: Accounting,
Clerical, Engineering, Finance, Insurance, Manufacturing, Secretarial, Technology

MARTIN GRANT ASSOCIATES, INC.
65 Franklin St., Boston, MA 02110; 617-357-
5380
Areas of Specialization: Insurance

NETWORK PERSONNEL, INC.
P.O. Box 88, Billerica, MA 01866; 508-663-
5378
Areas of Specialization: Accounting,
Advertising, Health Services, Management, Publishing, Sales

NETWORK PERSONNEL, INC.
1661 Worcester Rd., #101, Framingham, MA
01701; 508-879-9251
Areas of Specialization: Accounting,
Clerical, Manufacturing, Secretarial

NEW BOSTONSELECT STAFFING
146 Bowdoin St., Boston, MA 02108; 617-
720-0990
Areas of Specialization: Accounting,
Clerical, Data Processing, Secretarial

NEW BOSTON ASSOCIATES
16 Wheeling Ave., Woburn, MA 01801; 617-
938-1910
Areas of Specialization: Accounting,
Engineering, Finance, Technology

RANDOLPH ASSOCIATES, INC.
P.O. Box 1586, Boston, MA 02104; 617-227-
2554
Areas of Specialization: Engineering,
Manufacturing, Publishing, Science,
Technology

REARDON ASSOCIATES, INC.
990 Washington St., Suite 1500, Dedham,
MA 02026; 617-329-2660
Areas of Specialization: Accounting,
Engineering, Manufacturing, Marketing,
Sales, Science, Technology

THE RESOURCE PARTNERSHIP
20 Park Plaza, Room 605, Boston, MA
02116; 617-350-8921
Areas of Specialization: General

ROMAC AND ASSOCIATES
125 Summer St., Boston, MA 02110; 617-
350-0945
Areas of Specialization: Accounting, Finance

ROUTHIER LEGAL PERSONNEL
100 State St., Boston, MA 02109; 617-742-
2747

Areas of Specialization: Finance, Health Services, Law, Science, Secretarial, Technology

MICHIGAN

ACCENT ON ACHIEVEMENT
189 E. Big Beaver, Suite 202, Troy, MI 48083; 810-528-1390
Areas of Specialization: Accounting, Finance, Human Resources

ACCOUNTANTS ONE, INC.
24133 Northwestern Highway, Suite 202, Southfield, MI 48075; 810-354-2410
Areas of Specialization: Accounting, Finance

BPA ENTERPRISES, INC.
19971 James Couzens Highway, Detroit, MI 48235; 313-345-5700
Areas of Specialization: General

CALVERT ASSOCIATES, INC.
202 E. Washington St., Suite 304, Ann Arbor, MI 48329; 313-673-3800
Areas of Specialization: Marketing, Publishing, Sales

CORPORATE BUSINESS SERVICES, LTD.
913 W. Holmes Rd., Suite 100, Lansing, MI 48910; 517-394-1800
Areas of Specialization: Engineering, Food and Beverages, Insurance, Manufacturing, Marketing, Sales, Technology

DAVIS–SMITH MEDICAL EMPLOYMENT, INC.
24725 W. Twelve Mile Rd., Suite 302, Southfield, MI 48034; 810-354-4100
Areas of Specialization: Clerical, Health Services

DUNHILL OF ANN ARBOR
315 N. Main, Suite 400, Ann Arbor, MI 48104; 313-996-3100
Areas of Specialization: Technology

DUNHILL OF DETROIT
29350 Southfield Rd., Suite 115, Southfield, MI 48076; 810-557-1100
Areas of Specialization: Engineering, Marketing, Sales

GROSSE POINT EMPLOYMENT
18514 Mack Ave., Grosse Point Farms, MI 48236; 313-885-4576
Areas of Specialization: Domestic Services

HARPER ASSOCIATES
29870 Middlebelt Rd., Farmington Hills, MI 48334; 810-932-1170
Areas of Specialization: Architecture, Food and Beverages, Health Services

HUMAN RESOURCES UNLIMITED, INC.
535 N. Capital, Suite 2, P.O. Box 14306, Lansing, MI 48901; 517-371-5220
Areas of Specialization: Engineering, Technology

JOE L. GILES & ASSOCIATES, INC.
18105 Parkside St., Suite 14, Detroit, MI 48221; 313-864-0022
Areas of Specialization: Engineering, Technology

LUDOT & ASSOCIATES
P.O. Box 208, Southfield, MI 48037; 810-353-9720
Areas of Specialization: Automotive, Engineering, Manufacturing

MICHIGAN EMPLOYMENT SECURITY COMMISSION
2827 N. Lincoln Rd., P.O. Box 356, Escanaba, MI 49829; 906-786-6841
Areas of Specialization: General

ROTH YOUNG PERSONNEL SERVICE OF DETROIT, INC.
25505 W. Twelve Mile Rd., Suite 4040, Southfield, MI 48034; 810-948-8800
Areas of Specialization: Accounting, Advertising, Broadcasting, Engineering, Finance, Food and Beverages, Health Services, Manufacturing, Sales, Science, Technology

SOFTWARE SERVICES CORPORATION
2850 S. Industrial, Suite 300, Ann Arbor, MI 48104; 313-971-2300
Areas of Specialization: Engineering, Science, Technology

WILLIAM HOWARD AGENCY
38701 Seven Mile Rd., Suite 4456, Livonia, MI 48152; 313-464-6777
Areas of Specialization: General

WORKFORCE SOLUTIONS—AN IBM DIVISION
200 Galleria Officentre, Southfield, MI 48086; 810-262-3110
Areas of Specialization: Accounting, Data Processing, Engineering, Finance, Manufacturing, Marketing, Sales, Science, Secretarial, Technology

MINNESOTA

PEOPLE MANAGEMENT
701 4th Ave. S., Suite 400, Minneapolis, MN
55415; 612-337-7214
Areas of Specialization: General

MISSISSIPPI

MANAGEMENT RECRUITERS
1755 Lelia Dr., Suite 102, Jackson, MS
39216; 601-936-7900
Areas of Specialization: General

MISSOURI

ABC EMPLOYMENT SERVICE
25 S. Bemiston, Suite 214, Clayton, MO
63105; 314-725-3140
Areas of Specialization: Accounting,
Architecture, Construction, Engineering,
Design, Manufacturing, Marketing,
Sales, Science, Technology

BEST PERSONNEL SERVICE
8901 State Line, Suite 242, Kansas City, MO
64114; 816-361-3100
Areas of Specialization: Accounting,
Clerical, Insurance, Marketing, Sales,
Secretarial

CAREER CONSULTANTS, INC.
8550 Holmes, Suite 120, Kansas City, MO
64131; 816-941-8666
Areas of Specialization: Accounting,
Clerical, Finance, Insurance, Law, Secretarial

THE CHRISTIANSEN BROWN GROUP
2021 S. Waverly, Suite 700, Springfield, MO
65804; 417-883-9444
Areas of Specialization: Advertising,
Engineering, Food and Beverages, Science, Technology

**DECK AND DECKER EMPLOYMENT
SERVICES**
319 Kelly Plaza, Columbia, MO 65202; 573-
449-0876
Areas of Specialization: General

L. P. BANNING, INC.
212 S. Central Ave., Suite 302, Clayton, MO
63105; 314-863-1770
Areas of Specialization: General

NICHOLS PERSONNEL
9201 Wark Pkwy., Kansas City, MO 64114;
816-444-5910
Areas of Specialization: General

STATUSPRO
406 W. 34th St., Kansas City, MO 64111;
816-931-8236
Areas of Specialization: Accounting,
Administration, Advertising, Arts, Manual Labor, Marketing, Public Relations,
Publishing, Sales, Secretarial

TOBERSON GROUP
120 S. Central Ave., Suite 212, Clayton, MO
63105; 314-726-0500
Areas of Specialization: Food and Beverages, Health Services, Hospitality,
Marketing, Sales

MONTANA

BILLINGS EMPLOYMENT CENTER
2310 Broadwater Ave., Suite 9, Billings, MT
59102; 406-652-4990
Areas of Specialization: General

EXPRESS PERSONNEL SERVICES
3709 Brooks St., Missoula, MT 59801; 406-
542-0323
Areas of Specialization: General

FORTUNE PERSONNEL
104 E. Main St., Bozeman, MT 59715; 406-
585-1332
Areas of Specialization: General

NEBRASKA

PROFESSIONAL PERSONNEL SERVICE
3201 Pioneers Blvd., Suite 222, Lincoln, NE
68502; 402-483-7821
Areas of Specialization: General

NEVADA

SNELLING AND SNELLING
6490 S. McCarran Blvd., Reno, NV 89502;
702-825-4404
Areas of Specialization: General

SNELLING PERSONNEL SERVICES
1050 E. Flamingo Rd., #142, Las Vegas, NV
89119; 702-369-0087
Areas of Specialization: General

NEW HAMPSHIRE

ABLE 1 PERSONNEL
126 Daniel St., Portsmouth, NH 03801; 603-
436-1151
Areas of Specialization: Accounting,
Clerical, Engineering, Finance, Health
Services, Insurance, Law, Publishing,
Sales, Secretarial, Technology

ACCESS DATA PERSONNEL
649 2nd St., Manchester, NH 03102; 603-641-6300
Areas of Specialization: General

CAREER CONNECTIONS, INC.
74 Northeastern Blvd., Unit 17, Nashua, NH 03062; 603-880-7184
Areas of Specialization: Accounting, Administration, Clerical, Finance, Secretarial

CAREER/ADVANCE
67 Water St., Suite 210, Laconia, NH 03246; 603-528-2828
Areas of Specialization: Accounting, Finance

EXETER 2100
P.O. Box 2120, Hampton, NH 03842; 603-926-6712
Areas of Specialization: Engineering, Science, Technology

NEW JERSEY

A+ PERSONNEL
1017 Broadway, Bayonne, NJ 07002; 201-437-5594
Areas of Specialization: Accounting, Administration, Finance, Law, Manufacturing, Secretarial, Technology

ABC NATIONWIDE EMPLOYMENT
241 Main St., Hackensack, NJ 07601; 201-487-5515
Areas of Specialization: Engineering, Finance, Law, Manufacturing, Secretarial

ADEL–LAWRENCE ASSOCIATION, INC.
142 Highway 34, Aberdeen, NJ 07747; 908-566-4914
Areas of Specialization: Engineering, Health Services, Science, Technology

ADVANCED PERSONNEL SERVICE
1341 Hamburg Turnpike, P.O. Box 2244, Wayne, NJ 07474; 201-694-0303
Areas of Specialization: General

ALLEN ASSOCIATES OF NEW JERSEY
120 Wood Ave. S., Suite 300, Iselin, NJ 08830; 908-549-7555
Areas of Specialization: Accounting, Human Resources, Secretarial

ARLINE SIMPSON ASSOCIATES, INC.
114 Essex St., Rochelle Park, NJ 07662; 201-343-5885
Areas of Specialization: Accounting, Administration, Fashion, Law, Manufacturing, Marketing, Retail, Sales, Secretarial

BLAKE & ASSOCIATES
P.O. Box 1425, Pleasantville, NJ 08232; 609-645-3330
Areas of Specialization: General

CAREER CENTER, INC.
194 Passaic St., P.O. Box 1036, Hackensack, NJ 07601; 201-342-1777
Areas of Specialization: Accounting, Administration, Advertising, Clerical, Engineering, Fashion, Finance, Insurance, Manufacturing, Sales, Science, Technology

CAREERS FIRST, INC.
305 U.S. Route 130, Cinnaminson, NJ 08077; 609-786-0004
Areas of Specialization: Science, Technology

CITIZENS EMPLOYMENT SERVICES
106 Parsippany Rd., Parsippany, NJ 07054; 201-887-4600
Areas of Specialization: Clerical, Finance, Insurance, Manufacturing, Marketing, Sales

COMMERCE EMPLOYMENT
50 Journal Sq., Jersey City, NJ 07306; 201-798-8000
Areas of Specialization: General

DUNHILL OF CHERRY HILL
1040 Kings Highway N., Suite 400, Cherry Hill, NJ 08034; 609-667-9180
Areas of Specialization: General

FORTUNE PERSONNEL CONSULTANTS OF MENLO PARK
100 Menlo Park, Suite 206, Edison, NJ 08837; 908-494-6266
Areas of Specialization: Engineering, Food and Beverages, Human Resources, Science, Technology

IMPACT PERSONNEL, INC.
3371 Route 1, Lawrenceville, NJ 08648; 609-987-8888
Areas of Specialization: General

JUBILEE EMPLOYMENT SERVICES
494 Madison Ave., Paterson, NJ 07914; 973-

278-5627
Areas of Specialization: General

MADEMOISELLE PERSONNEL
1 Gateway Center, Newark, NJ 07102; 973-624-1200
Areas of Specialization: General

PERSONNEL ONE
20 Nassau St., Princeton, NJ 08542; 609-799-4636
Areas of Specialization: Clerical, Secretarial

PHILADELPHIA SEARCH GROUP, INC.
1 Cherry Hill, Suite 510, Cherry Hill, NJ 08002; 609-667-2300
Areas of Specialization: General

PRINCETON EXECUTIVE SEARCH
2667 Nottingham Way, Trenton, NJ 08619; 609-584-1100
Areas of Specialization: General

RSVP
P.O. Box 8369, Cherry Hill, NJ 08002; 609-667-4488
Areas of Specialization: Engineering, Technology

SELECTIVE PERSONNEL
214 Highway 18, East Brunswick, NJ 08816; 908-497-2900
Areas of Specialization: Accounting, Clerical, Engineering, Health Services, Insurance, Law, Manufacturing, Marketing, Sales, Science, Technology

SNELLING PERSONNEL SERVICES
5425 Route 70, Pennsauken, NJ 08109; 609-662-5424
Areas of Specialization: Accounting, Clerical, Food and Beverages, Human Resources, Marketing, Sales

NEW MEXICO

MARCIA OWEN ASSOCIATES
660 Granada St., Santa Fe, NM 87501; 505-983-7775
Areas of Specialization: General

SNELLING PERSONNEL SERVICE
2601 Wyoming St., NE, Albuquerque, NM 87112; 505-293-7800
Areas of Specialization: General

NEW YORK

ABLE PERSONNEL, INC.
280 Madison Ave., New York, NY 10016;

212-689-5500
Areas of Specialization: Advertising, Architecture, Construction, Engineering, Fashion, Marketing, Publishing, Real Estate, Sales, Transportation

ADAM PERSONNEL
11 E. 44th St., New York, NY 10017; 212-557-9150
Areas of Specialization: Accounting, Advertising, Fashion, Finance, Human Resources, Law, Secretarial

ADECCO EMPLOYMENT SERVICES
551 5th Ave., New York, NY 10017; 212-682-3438
Areas of Specialization: General

ADVICE PERSONNEL
230 Park Ave., Suite 903, New York, NY 10169; 212-682-4400
Areas of Specialization: Accounting, Administration, Finance, Management, Secretarial

ALL HOME SERVICES AGENCY, LTD.
2121 Broadway, New York, NY 10023; 212-799-9360
Areas of Specialization: Domestic Services, Health Services

AMES GROUP
928 Broadway, Suite 1101B-N, New York, NY 10010; 212-475-5900
Areas of Specialization: Accounting, Administration, Finance, Health Services, Insurance, Marketing, Publishing, Sales, Science, Secretarial, Technology

ANALYTIC RECRUITING, INC.
21 E. 49th St., New York, NY 10016; 212-545-8511
Areas of Specialization: Administration, Finance, Marketing, Sales, Technology

ARROW EMPLOYMENT AGENCY
150 Broadhollow Rd., Melville, NY 11747; 516-271-3700
Areas of Specialization: Engineering, Manufacturing, Secretarial, Science, Technology

BEST DOMESTIC SERVICES AGENCY, INC.
10 E. 39th St., #1112, New York, NY 10016; 212-685-0351
Areas of Specialization: Domestic Services

BONFIELD EMPLOYMENT AGENCY
16 E. 79th St., #4G, New York, NY 10021;
212-288-1010
Areas of Specialization: Domestic Services, Secretarial

BREMAR ASSOCIATES
420 Lexington Ave., New York, NY 10170;
212-661-0909
Areas of Specialization: Accounting, Administration, Advertising, Fashion, Finance, Secretarial

BRYANT & STRYATTON
1225 Jefferson Rd., Rochester, NY 14623;
716-292-5627
Areas of Specialization: General

CAREER BLAZERS
590 Fifth Ave., New York, NY 10036; 212-719-3232
Areas of Specialization: General

CAREER CONCEPTS, INC.
25 W. 43rd St., Suite 708, New York, NY
10036; 212-764-1370
Areas of Specialization: Accounting, Fin-ance, Human Resources

COHEN PERSONNEL SERVICES, INC.
475 Fifth Ave., New York, NY 10017; 212-725-1666
Areas of Specialization: Accounting, Ad-ministration, Advertising, Clerical, Data Processing, Health Services, Law, Marketing, Public Relations, Sales, Secretarial

CORPORATE PARTNERS, INC.
6800 Jericho Turnpike, Suite 203W, Syosset, NY 11791; 516-364-7676
Areas of Specialization: Accounting, Fin-ance, Marketing, Sales

CROSS PERSONNEL AGENCY
150 Broadway, New York, NY 10038; 212-227-6705
Areas of Specialization: Clerical, Finance

ECHO STAFFING SERVICES
902 Broadway, New York, NY 10010; 212-995-2400
Areas of Specialization: Accounting, Ad-vertising, Broadcasting, Clerical, Fashion, Finance, Food and Beverages, Insurance, Public Relations, Publishing, Retail, Textiles

EDEN PERSONNEL, INC.
280 Madison Ave., New York, NY 10016;
212-685-8600
Areas of Specialization: Advertising,

Health Services, Law, Publishing, Real Estate, Secretarial

EMPLOYMENT RECRUITERS AGENCY
11821 Queens Blvd., Suite 609, Forest Hills, NY 11375; 718-263-2300
Areas of Specialization: Accounting, Advertising, Architecture, Construction, Fashion, Finance, Health Services, Retail, Sales, Secretarial

FAIRFIELD RESOURCES, LTD.
350 Fifth Ave., Room 7605, New York, NY
10118; 212-268-0220
Areas of Specialization: Administration, Fashion, Manual Labor

FUSCO PERSONNEL, INC.
401 New Karnes Rd., Albany, NY 12205;
518-869-6100
Areas of Specialization: General

HILLARY TAYLOR PERSONNEL
2 John St., New York, NY 10038; 212-619-8200
Areas of Specialization: Accounting, Advertising, Finance, Human Resources, Insurance, Law, Secretarial

MRS. E. E. BROOKE, INC.
420 Lexington Ave., New York, NY 10170;
212-687-8400
Areas of Specialization: Accounting, Administration, Finance, Insurance, Management, Publishing, Secretarial, Transportation, Travel

PARK AVENUE AGENCY, INC.
16 E. 79th St., New York, NY 10021; 212-737-7733
Areas of Specialization: Domestic Services, Health Services

PERSONNEL ASSOCIATES
731 James St., Syracuse, NY 13203; 315-422-0070
Areas of Specialization: General

PHILLIP THOMAS PERSONNEL, INC.
535 Fifth Ave., Suite 606, New York, NY
10017; 212-867-0860
Areas of Specialization: Fashion, Finance, Marketing, Sales, Secretarial

SETH DIAMOND ASSOCIATES, INC.
45 W. 45th St., Suite 801, New York, NY
10036; 212-944-6190
Areas of Specialization: General

SLOAN STAFFING.
317 Madison Ave., New York, NY 10017;
212-949-7200
Areas of Specialization: Clerical, Secretarial

STANTON STAFFING, INC.
189 Broadway, New York, NY 10007; 212-843-6600
Areas of Specialization: Accounting, Ad-ministration, Advertising, Architecture, Construction, Fashion, Marketing, Publishing, Real Estate, Sales, Secretarial

UNITED PERSONNEL AGENCY, INC.
51 E. 42nd St., Suite 417, New York, NY 10017; 212-490-2197
Areas of Specialization: Accounting, Ad-vertising, Broadcasting, Law, Publishing, Secretarial, Technology

VINTAGE RESOURCES, INC.
11 E. 44th St., Suite 708, New York, NY 10017; 212-867-1001
Areas of Specialization: Accounting, Ad-vertising, Clerical, Law, Publishing, Secretarial

WINSTON PERSONNEL, INC.
535 Fifth Ave., Suite 701, New York, NY 10017; 212-557-5000
Areas of Specialization: General

YOURS IN TRAVEL PERSONNEL AGENCY
12 W. 37th St., New York, NY 10018; 212-697-7855
Areas of Specialization: Accounting, Ad-ministration, Hospitality, Marketing, Publishing, Sales, Secretarial, Technology, Travel

NORTH CAROLINA

A-1 PERSONNEL
25 Heritage Plaza, Asheville, NC 28806; 704-252-0708
Areas of Specialization: Accounting, Ad-vertising, Architecture, Finance, Publishing, Retail, Sales

AMOS & ASSOCIATES
633-B Chapel Hill Rd., Burlington, NC 27215; 910-222-0231
Areas of Specialization: Technology

AYERS & ASSOCIATES
157 Blue Bell Rd., Greensboro, NC 27406; 919-378-1761
Areas of Specialization: Apparel, Man-ufacturing, Textiles

CAREER STAFFING
5605 77 Center Dr., Suite 250, Charlotte, NC 28274; 704-525-8400
Areas of Specialization: Clerical, Finance, Technology

CAREERS UNLIMITED, INC.
1911 Hillandale Rd., Suite 1210, Durham, NC

27705; 919-383-7431
Areas of Specialization: Accounting, Clerical, Finance, Sales, Technology

CORPORATE PERSONNEL CONSULTANTS, INC.
P.O. Box 221739, Charlotte, NC 28222; 704-366-1800
Areas of Specialization: Engineering, Environment, Technology

DATA MASTERS
P.O. Box 14548, Greensboro, NC 27415; 919-373-1461
Areas of Specialization: Technology

ELITE PERSONNEL SERVICES, INC.
P.O. Box 52029, Durham, NC 27717; 919-493-1449
Areas of Specialization: Clerical, Secretarial

ELLIS ASSOCIATES
P.O. Box 98925, Raleigh, NC 27624; 919-676-1061
Areas of Specialization: Biotechnology, Pharmaceuticals

EMPLOYMENT SECURITY COMMISSION
1105 S. Briggs Ave., Durham, NC 27624; 919-560-6880
Areas of Specialization: General

A FIRST RESOURCE PERSONNEL SERV-ICE/KLS ENTERPRISES, INC.
8025 N. Point Blvd., Winston-Salem, NC 27106; 910-759-0877
Areas of Specialization: Accounting, Administration, Finance, Management, Pub-lishing, Retail, Sales

FORTUNE PERSONNEL CONSULTANTS OF RALEIGH, INC.
P.O. Box 98388, Raleigh, NC 27624; 919-848-9929
Areas of Specialization: Accounting, Engineering, Finance, Food and Bever-ages, Manufacturing, Technology

GRAHAM & ASSOCIATES
2110-J W. Cornwallis Dr., Greensboro, NC 27408; 919-288-9330
Areas of Specialization: General

GREER PERSONNEL SERVICE
5500 McNelly Dr., Suite 102, Raleigh, NC 27612; 919-571-0051
Areas of Specialization: Accounting, Clerical, Finance, Law

KELLY SERVICES
2701 Coltsgate Rd., Suite 102, Charlotte, NC 28211; 704-364-4790

Areas of Specialization: Accounting, Ad-ministration, Clerical, Insurance, Law, Manufacturing, Publishing, Sales, Technology

KELLY SERVICES
620 Green Valley Rd., Suite 206, Greensboro, NC 27408; 919-292-4371
Areas of Specialization: General

MEDICAL PROFESSIONALS
110 Seaside Lane, Wrightsville Beach, NC 28480; 910-256-8115
Areas of Specialization: Health Services

PERSONNEL SERVICES OF EASTERN NORTH CAROLINA
105 Oakmont Dr., Suite A, Greenville, NC 27858; 919-522-7587
Areas of Specialization: General

ROBERT HALF INTERNATIONAL
300 N. Greene St., Suite 275, Greensboro, NC 27401; 919-274-4523
Areas of Specialization: Accounting, Ad-ministration, Finance, Technology

SNELLING PERSONNEL
5970 Fairview Rd., Charlotte, NC 28217; 704-553-0050
Areas of Specialization: Accounting, Clerical, Manufacturing, Science, Technology

NORTH DAKOTA

SNELLING PERSONNEL SERVICES
609½ 1st Ave. N., #200, Fargo, ND 58102; 701-237-0600
Areas of Specialization: General

OHIO

ACCOUNTANTS ON CALL
250 E. Fifth St., Suite 1630, Cincinnati, OH 45202; 513-381-4545
Areas of Specialization: Accounting

BALDWIN & ASSOCIATES
3975 Erie Ave., Cincinnati, OH 45208; 513-272-2400
Areas of Specialization: Engineering, Man-ufacturing, Science, Technology

CAREER CONNECTIONS
14 W. Union St., Athens, OH 45701; 614-594-4941
Areas of Specialization: Education, Law, Manufacturing, Nonprofit, Secretarial, Technology

CBS PERSONNEL SERVICES
435 Elm St., Suite 700, Cincinnati, OH 45202; 513-651-1111
Areas of Specialization: Clerical, Finance, Technology

CHAMPION PERSONNEL SYSTEM, INC.
668 Euclid St., 300A, Cleveland, OH 44114; 216-781-5900
Areas of Specialization: Accounting, Ad-ministration, Clerical, Finance, Secretarial

N. L. BENKE & ASSOCIATES, INC.
1422 Euclid Ave., Suite 956, Cleveland, OH 44115; 216-771-6822
Areas of Specialization: Accounting, Fin-ance, Insurance, Technology

SELECTIVE SEARCH ASSOCIATES
1206 N. Main St., Suite 112, North Canton, OH 44720; 330-494-5584
Areas of Specialization: Technology

VECTOR TECHNICAL
7911 Enterprise Dr., Mentor, OH 44060; 216-946-8808
Areas of Specialization: Engineering, Man-ufacturing, Science, Technology

WORLD SEARCH
4130 Linden Ave., Suite 105, Dayton, OH 45432; 513-254-9071
Areas of Specialization: Engineering

OKLAHOMA

DUNHILL PERSONNEL
5500 N. Western Ave., Suite 278, Oklahoma City, OK 73118; 405-848-8981
Areas of Specialization: General

OREGON

ACCOUNTEMPS
450 Country Club Rd., Eugene, OR 97401; 541-345-9930
Areas of Specialization: Accounting

MANAGEMENT RECRUITERS
2020 Lloyd Ctr., Portland, OR 97232; 503-287-8701
Areas of Specialization: General

NORTH VALLEY MEDICAL STAFFING
4776 Whitman Circle NE, Salem, OR 97305; 503-463-5730
Areas of Specialization: General

PERSONNEL SOURCE INC.
703 Medford Center, Medford, OR 97504; 541-776-7466
Areas of Specialization: General

PENNSYLVANIA

ADECCO PERSONNEL SERVICES
1760 Market St., 6th Floor, Philadelphia, PA 19103; 215-567-2390

Areas of Specialization: General

ADVANCE PERSONNEL
P.O. Box 8383, Reading, PA 19603; 610-374-4089
Areas of Specialization: Administration, Clerical, Customer Service, Data Processing, Law, Secretarial

ALEXANDER PERSONNEL ASSOCIATES
1 Oxford Valley, Suite 702, Longhorne, PA 19047; 215-757-4935
Areas of Specialization: Accounting, Engineering, Insurance, Management, Manufacturing, Science, Secretarial, Technology

BRENTWOOD SEARCH CONSULTANTS
401 S. 2nd St., Suite 203, Philadelphia, PA 19147; 215-487-7199
Areas of Specialization: General

CAREERS U.S.A.
1825 JFK Blvd., Philadelphia, PA 19103; 215-561-3800
Areas of Specialization: General

DENTAL POWER OF DELAWARE VALLEY, INC.
1528 Walnut St., Suite 1802, Philadelphia, PA 19102; 215-825-2131
Areas of Specialization: Health Services (Dental)

DUNHILL PERSONNEL SYSTEMS OF PHILADELPHIA
801 W. Street Rd., Feasterville, PA 19035; 215-357-6591
Areas of Specialization: Accounting, Clerical, Marketing, Sales

EDEN AND ASSOCIATES, INC.
794 N. Valley Rd., Paoli, PA 19301; 610-889-9993
Areas of Specialization: Consumer Products, Food and Beverages, Wholesale

EXPRESS PERSONNEL SERVICE
260 S. Broad St., Suite 1810, Philadelphia, PA 19102; 215-893-1200
Areas of Specialization: General

FORTUNE PERSONNEL AND ASSOCIATES, INC.
1528 Walnut St., Suite 1625, Philadelphia, PA 19102; 215-546-9490
Areas of Specialization: General

INTERIM PERSONNEL
1617 JFK Blvd., Suite 240, Philadelphia, PA 19103; 215-561-3322
Areas of Specialization: Clerical, Secretarial

KEY PERSONNEL SERVICE
845 Wyoming St., Allentown, PA 18103; 610-435-6355
Areas of Specialization: General

MINORITY PERSONNEL SERVICES
5424 N. 5th St., Philadelphia, PA 19010; 215-457-2672
Areas of Specialization: General

PAL
1239 Vine St., Philadelphia, PA 19107; 215-569-2277
Areas of Specialization: Manual Labor, Trades

PERSONNEL RESOURCES ORGANIZATION
121 S. Broad St., Suite 1030, Philadelphia, PA 19107; 215-735-7500
Areas of Specialization: General

POWERS PERSONNEL
1530 Chestnut St., Suite 310, Philadelphia, PA 19102; 215-563-5520
Areas of Specialization: Clerical, Secretarial

PRATT PERSONNEL
1547 Pratt St., Suite 300, Philadelphia, PA 19124; 215-537-1212
Areas of Specialization: Clerical, Engineering, Manufacturing

THE RICHARDS GROUP
2 Penn Ctr. Plaza, Suite 710, Philadelphia, PA 19102; 215-751-0805
Areas of Specialization: General

ROBERT HALF OF PHILADELPHIA, INC.
2000 Market St., Philadelphia, PA 19103; 215-568-4580
Areas of Specialization: General

SELECT PERSONNEL, INC.
Neshaminy Plaza 2, 3070 Bristol Pike, Salem, PA 19020; 215-741-4700
Areas of Specialization: Engineering, Finance, Human Resources, Manufacturing, Marketing, Sales, Science, Technology

SNELLING PERSONNEL SERVICES
1617 JFK Blvd., Philadelphia, PA 19103; 215-568-1414
Areas of Specialization: General

TODAY'S STAFFING SERVICES, INC.
5601 Chestnut St., Philadelphia, PA 19139; 215-748-8844
Areas of Specialization: General

VOGUE PERSONNEL, INC.
1 Penn Ctr., 1617 JFK Blvd., Philadelphia,

PA 19103; 215-564-0720
Areas of Specialization: Administration, Clerical, Law, Sales, Secretarial

RHODE ISLAND

MANAGEMENT RECRUITERS
101 Dyer St., Suite 5-A, Providence, RI 02903; 401-274-2810
Areas of Specialization: General

SOUTH CAROLINA

DUNHILL PERSONNEL SERVICES
16 Berryhill Rd., #120, Columbia, SC 29210; 803-772-6751
Areas of Specialization: Engineering, Manufacturing, Marketing, Sales, Textiles

THE HAMPTON GROUP
27 Gamecock Ave., Suite 200, Charleston, SC 29407; 803-763-0532
Areas of Specialization: Engineering, Science, Technology

PHELPS PERSONNEL
P.O. Box 4177, Greenville, SC 29608; 864-232-8139
Areas of Specialization: Engineering

ROPER SERVICES
220 Executive Ctr. Dr., Columbia, SC 29210; 803-798-8500
Areas of Specialization: Clerical, Construction, Manufacturing, Marketing, Sales

SEARCH AND RECRUIT EAST
2501 Northforest Dr., North Charleston, SC 29420; 803-572-4040
Areas of Specialization: Accounting, Admin-istration, Engineering, Finance, Food and Beverages, Health Services, Manufacturing, Sales, Technology

STAFFING RESOURCES
1755 St. Julian Pl., Columbia, SC 29204; 803-765-0820
Areas of Specialization: Clerical, Finance, Health Services, Insurance, Manufacturing, Technology

SOUTH DAKOTA

MANAGEMENT RECRUITERS
2600 S. Minnesota Ave., Suite 202, Sioux Falls, SD 57105; 605-334-9291
Areas of Specialization: General

TENNESSEE

BAIVIL MODEL AND TALENT AGENCY

7075 Poplar Pike, Germantown, TN 38138; 901-754-4747
Areas of Specialization: Advertising, Broadcasting, Education, Finance, Human Resources, Marketing, Sales

COBBLE PERSONNEL
8560 Kingston Pike, Bldg. B, Knoxville, TN 37919; 423-690-2311
Areas of Specialization: Accounting, Clerical, Finance, Science, Technology

DUNHILL OF MEMPHIS, INC.
5120 Stage Rd., Suite 2, Memphis, TN 38134; 901-386-0400
Areas of Specialization: Administration, Clerical, Science, Technology

ENGINEER ONE, INC.
P.O. Box 23037, Knoxville, TN 37933; 423-690-2611
Areas of Specialization: Construction, Design, Engineering, Food and Beverages, Manufacturing, Science, Technology

FORTUNE PERSONNEL CONSULTANTS OF NASHVILLE, INC.
102 Hazel Path, P.O. Box 2213, Hendersonville, TN 37077; 615-662-9110
Areas of Specialization: Engineering, Human Resources, Management

MADISON PERSONNEL
1864 Poplar Crest Cove, Memphis, TN 38119; 901-761-2660
Areas of Specialization: Accounting, Clerical, Engineering, Food and Beverages, Manufacturing, Marketing, Sales, Secretarial

OFFICE MANAGEMENT CONSULTANTS, INC.
1000 Morningside Circle, Savannah, TN 38372; 901-925-7874
Areas of Specialization: Administration, Clerical, Finance, Health Services, Insurance, Law, Manufacturing, Marketing, Sales, Technology

RANDALL HOWARD & ASSOCIATES, INC.
5353 Flowering Peach Dr., Memphis, TN 38115; 901-365-2700
Areas of Specialization: Accounting, Finance, Health Services, Law

TEXAS

ACCOUNTANTS EXECUTIVE SEARCH
1990 Post Oak Blvd., Suite 720, Houston, TX 77056; 713-961-5603
Areas of Specialization: Accounting, Finance

ATTORNEY RESOURCE, INC.
2301 Cedar Springs Rd., Suite 350, Dallas, TX 75201; 214-922-8050
Areas of Specialization: Law

BABICH & ASSOCIATES, INC.
6060 N. Central Expressway, Suite 544, Dallas, TX 75206; 214-361-5735
Areas of Specialization: Accounting, Administration, Clerical, Engineering, Finance, Manufacturing, Marketing, Sales, Science, Technology

BABICH & ASSOCIATES, INC.
One Summit Ave., Suite 602, Ft. Worth, TX 76102; 817-336-7261
Areas of Specialization: Accounting, Administration, Clerical, Engineering, Finance, Manufacturing, Marketing, Sales, Science, Technology

BURNETT PERSONNEL CONSULTANTS
9800 Richman, Suite 800, Houston, TX 77042; 713-977-4777
Areas of Specialization: Accounting, Clerical, Construction, Finance, Real Estate

CHAMPION PERSONNEL SERVICE
8326 Wind Willow Dr., Houston, TX 77040; 713-937-6160
Areas of Specialization: Engineering, Environment, Health Services, Manufacturing, Technology

CONTINENTAL PERSONNEL SERVICE
6671 SW Freeway, Suite 101, Houston, TX 77074; 713-771-7181
Areas of Specialization: Engineering, Health Services, Manufacturing, Marketing

THE DANBROOK GROUP
14180 Dallas Pkwy., Suite 400, Dallas, TX 75240; 214-392-0057
Areas of Specialization: Accounting, Construction, Design, Engineering, Finance, Insurance

DOUGAN MCKINLEY STRAIN
The Phoenix Tower, Suite 3300, Houston, TX 77027; 713-960-0747
Areas of Specialization: General

DUNHILL STAFFING OF NORTHEAST DALLAS
14881 Quorum Dr., Dallas, TX 75240; 972-503-2400
Areas of Specialization: Clerical, Engineering

EMPLOYMENT SOLUTIONS
1507 LBJ Freeway, Suite 100, Dallas, TX 75234; 214-280-6680
Areas of Specialization: Engineering, Manufacturing, Publishing, Sales, Technology

EXPRESS PERSONNEL SERVICES
P.O. Box 8136, Waco, TX 76714; 817-776-3300
Areas of Specialization: Accounting, Construction, Finance, Health Services, Insurance, Law, Manufacturing, Marketing, Sales

GULCO INTERNATIONAL RECRUITING SERVICES
15710 JFK Blvd., Houston, TX 77032; 713-590-9001
Areas of Specialization: Accounting, Administration, Engineering, Finance, Health Services, Human Resources, Management, Manufacturing

HEALTHCARE RECRUITERS OF HOUSTON, INC.
9301 SW Freeway, #650, Houston, TX 77074; 713-771-7344
Areas of Specialization: Health Services

HOUSTON AREA URBAN LEAGUE
3215 Fannin St., Houston, TX 77004; 713-526-5127
Areas of Specialization: Clerical, Fashion, Food and Beverages, Insurance, Marketing, Nonprofit, Sales

IMPRIMIS GROUP/FREEMAN AND ASSOCIATES
5550 LBJ Freeway, Suite 150, Lock Box 52, Dallas, TX 75240; 214-419-1700
Areas of Specialization: Clerical, Secretarial

JOB SERVICES
6404 Callaghan Rd., San Antonio, TX 78229; 210-344-3444
Areas of Specialization: General

LEE MANAGEMENT GROUP
12200 Ford Rd., Suite 170, Dallas, TX 75240; 214-484-6044
Areas of Specialization: Apparel, Finance, Textiles

ODELL & ASSOCIATES, INC.
12700 Park Central Pl., Suite 1800, Dallas, TX 75251; 214-458-7900
Areas of Specialization: General

THE PERSONNEL CONNECTION
16479 N. Dallas Pkwy., Suite 110, Dallas, TX 75248; 214-770-7878
Areas of Specialization: Administration,

Clerical, Secretarial

PERSONNEL CONSULTANTS, INC.
4620 Fairmont Pkwy., #106, Pasadena, TX 77504; 713-998-8060
Areas of Specialization: General

PRESTIGE RECRUITERS, INC.
1212 Stonehollow, Humble, TX 77339; 713-359-2525
Areas of Specialization: Administration, Technology

SALINAS & ASSOCIATES PERSONNEL SERVICE
15851 N. Dallas Pkwy., Suite 600, Dallas, TX 75248; 214-770-7878
Areas of Specialization: Accounting, Clerical, Engineering, Law, Manufacturing, Marketing, Sales, Secretarial

SNELLING PERSONNEL SERVICES OF LONGVIEW
1800 NW Loop 281, Suite 205, Longview, TX 75604; 903-297-2223
Areas of Specialization: General

STONE & STONE EMPLOYMENT SERVICE
3000 S. 31st St., Suite 501, Temple, TX 76502; 817-778-3565
Areas of Specialization: General

SUMMIT SEARCH SPECIALISTS
14825 St. Mary's Lane, #275, Houston, TX 77079; 713-497-5840
Areas of Specialization: Insurance

TAD TECHNICAL SERVICES
4300 Alpha Rd., Suite 100, Dallas, TX 75244; 214-980-0510
Areas of Specialization: Aerospace, Clerical, Engineering, Manufacturing, Science, Technology

THOMAS OFFICER PERSONNEL SERVICE, INC.
3909 Flintridge Dr., Irving, TX 75038; 214-934-0472
Areas of Specialization: Accounting, Administration, Clerical, Secretarial

THE URBAN PLACEMENT SERVICE
602 Sawyer St., Suite 460, Houston, TX 77007; 713-880-2211
Areas of Specialization: Accounting, Administration, Engineering, Finance, Food and Beverages, Manufacturing, Marketing, Sales, Science, Technology

VALPERS, INC.
8303 SW Freeway, #750, Houston, TX 77074; 713-771-9420
Areas of Specialization: Engineering, Management, Manufacturing, Marketing, Sales, Secretarial, Technology

VINSON AND ASSOCIATES
4100 McEwen, Suite 180, Dallas, TX 75244; 214-980-8800
Areas of Specialization: Accounting, Clerical, Finance, Insurance, Law, Manufacturing, Marketing, Sales

UTAH

INTERMOUNTAIN STAFFING
2196 S. 700 E., Salt Lake City, UT 84107; 801-467-6500
Areas of Specialization: General

MANAGEMENT RECRUITERS
6600 S. 1100 E., Suite 420, Salt Lake City, UT 84121; 801-264-9800
Areas of Specialization: General

PROFESSIONAL RECRUITERS
220 E. 3900 S. #9, Salt Lake City, UT 84107; 801-268-9940
Areas of Specialization: Clerical, Medical, Technical

VERMONT

MANAGEMENT RECRUITERS
187 St. Paul St., Burlington, VT 05401; 802-865-0541
Areas of Specialization: General

MASIELLO EMPLOYMENT SERVICES
219 Western Ave., Brattleboro, VT 05301; 802-254-5401
Areas of Specialization: General

PERSONNEL CONNECTION
272 S. Main St., Rutland, VT 05701; 802-773-3737
Areas of Specialization: General

VIRGINIA

ACCUSTAFF
550 Oyster Point Rd., #D, Newport News, VA 23602; 757-249-0059

ADECCO EMPLOYMENT SERVICES
7231 Forest Ave;, Suite 101, Richmond, VA 23226; 804-288-4497
Areas of Specialization: General

AFFILIATES
1100 Wilson Blvd., Arlington, VA 22209; 757-474-2752
Areas of Specialization: General

AMERICAN TECHNICAL RESOURCES
1651 Old Meadow Rd., McLean, VA 22102; 703-917-7800
Areas of Specialization: Engineering, Science, Technology

CORE PERSONNEL
8201 Greensborough Rd., Suite 1219,
McLean, VA 22102; 703-556-9610
Areas of Specialization: Technology

MANAGEMENT RECRUITING
2 E. Church St., Virginia Beach, VA 23462;
757-474-2752
Areas of Specialization: General

WASHINGTON
ABLE PERSONNEL SERVICE
NT Office Bldg., N. 4407 Division, Suite 625,
Spokane, WA 99207; 509-487-2734
Areas of Specialization: Accounting,
Clerical, Engineering, Finance, Marketing, Sales

A.S.A.P. EMPLOYMENT SERVICES
4171 Wheaton Way, Suite 7, Bremerton, WA
98310; 206-479-4310
Areas of Specialization: General

EXPRESS PERSONNEL SERVICES
4301 S. Pine St., Suite 110, Tacoma, WA
98409; 253-475-6859
Areas of Specialization: General

HALLMARK SERVICES
520 Pike St., Suite 1450, Seattle, WA 98101;
206-587-5360
Areas of Specialization: Clerical, Law

HOUSER, MARTIN, MORRIS, & ASSOCIATES
P.O. Box 90015, Bellevue, WA 98009; 206-453-2700
Areas of Specialization: Accounting,
Engineering, Finance, Insurance, Manufacturing, Marketing, Sales, Technology

JOBS CO.
E. 8900 Sprague Ave., Spokane, WA 99212;
509-928-3151
Areas of Specialization: Accounting,
Clerical, Engineering, Finance, Health
Services, Manufacturing, Marketing, Science, Secretarial, Technology

PERSONNEL UNLIMITED, INC.
W. 25 Nora, Spokane, WA 99205; 509-326-8880
Areas of Specialization: Accounting,
Clerical, Engineering, Finance, Food and
Beverages, Health Services, Insurance, Law,
Marketing, Sales

SNELLING PERSONNEL
2101 4TH Ave., Seattle, WA 98121; 206-441-8895
Areas of Specialization: Clerical, Finance, Insurance, Marketing, Retail,
Sales

WEST VIRGINIA
CAREER SEARCH
714 Lee St. E., Charleston, WV 25301;
304-343-0682
Areas of Specialization: General

KENT MANAGEMENT GROUP, INC.
836 6th Ave., Huntington, WV 25701; 304-523-8566
Areas of Specialization: General

KEY PERSONNEL, INC.
1124 4th Ave., Suite 300, Huntington, WV
25701; 304-529-3377
Areas of Specialization: General

WISCONSIN
FOODPRO RECRUITERS
913 Ernst Dr., Green Bay, WI 54304; 920-499-6080
Areas of Specialization: Food Service

HS GROUP, INC.
2611 Libal St., Green Bay, WI 54301; 920-432-7444
Areas of Specialization: General

MANAGEMENT RECRUITERS, INC.
1711 Woolsey St., Suite D, Delavan, WI
53115; 414-728-8886
Areas of Specialization: General, Human
Resources
Minimum Salary: Varies

SKILL SEARCH INC.
1140 W. Bluemound Rd., Milwaukee, WI
53226; 414-456-0800
Areas of Specialization: General

SNELLING PERSONNEL SERVICES
10909 W. Greenfield Ave., #208, Milwaukee,
WI 53214; 414-771-3456
Areas of Specialization: General

SNELLING PERSONNEL
9700 W. Bluemound Rd., Milwaukee, WI
53226; 414-771-3456
Areas of Specialization: General

WYOMING
MANAGEMENT RECRUITERS
1008 E. 21st St., Cheyenne, WY 82001; 307-635-8731
Areas of Specialization: General

TRADEMARK PERSONNEL
350 West A St., Suite 200, Casper, WY
82601; 307-234-8181
Areas of Specialization: General

SERVICES

EXECUTIVE RECRUITERS

EXECUTIVE RECRUITERS GENERALLY SEEK to fill jobs at the executive or professional level, usually in the higher-income brackets. Many recruiters specialize in one or several industries, while others provide recruitment services for a wide sweep of industries. These classifications are found at the end of each listing here and are called "Areas of Specialization." Those recruiters that do not specialize in any one area are referred to here as "General."

Salaries for jobs offered by each recruitment agency often vary widely, ranging from beginning and midlevel to the highest echelons of the pay scale. Minimum salaries are listed in each entry below. Whatever the case, executive recruiters can provide the job hunter with access to hidden job opportunities that are rarely available to the general public.

Recruiting agencies generally operate on either a "contingency" or "retainer" basis. Contingency firms are paid only when someone is hired, and their fee is generally based on a percentage of the salary paid during the first year of employment. Retainer agencies, on the other hand, are paid either in advance or in so-called progress payments, whether a placement occurs or not. In most cases, the employer looking to fill a position pays the fee, and therefore it is not important that a job seeker find out whether the agency works on contingency or retainer. However, you should be sure to ask whether the employer or the job applicant is expected to pay the fee. In the few cases in which the applicant pays, you need to know if it is based on contingency or retainer.

The major metropolitan branches of the country's larger executive recruitment firms have been included in this chapter. Other listings were chosen because of the specializations or geographic areas they represent.

ALABAMA

CLARK PERSONNEL SERVICE, INC.
4315 Downtowner Loop N., Mobile, AL 36609
Areas of Specialization: General
Minimum Salary: Varies

FORTUNE PERSONNEL CONSULTANTS OF HUNTSVILLE, INC.
3311 Bob Wallace Ave., Suite 204, Huntsville, AL 35805; 205-534-7282
Areas of Specialization: General
Minimum Salary: $30,000

THE LANGFORD SEARCH, INC.
2025 3rd Ave. N., Suite 301, Birmingham, AL 35203; 205-328-5483
Areas of Specialization: General
Minimum Salary: Varies

RHS ASSOCIATES, INC.
1 Perimeter Park S., Suite 130-N, Birming-

ham, AL 35243; 205-969-1099
Areas of Specialization: General
Minimum Salary: $40,000

LOCKE & ASSOC.
4144 Carmichael Rd., Suite 20, Montgomery, AL 36106; 334-272-7400
Areas of Specialization: Engineering
Minimum Salary: $50,000

ALASKA EXECUTIVE SEARCH
821 North St., Suite 204, Anchorage, AK 99501; 907-276-5707
Areas of Specialization: General
Minimum Salary: $30,000

ARIZONA

ACCOUNTING & BOOKKEEPING PERSONNEL, INC.
1702 E. Highland Ave., Suite 200, Phoenix, AZ 85016; 602-277-8212
Web: www.aafa.com

Areas of Specialization: Accounting
Minimum Salary: $40,000

MANAGEMENT RECRUITERS
6900 E. Camelback Rd., Suite 935,
Scottsdale, AZ 85251; 602-941-1515
Areas of Specialization: General
Minimum Salary: $25,000

R & K ASSOCIATES, INC.
1296 W. Stacey Lane, Tempe, AZ 85284;
602-961-2983
Areas of Specialization: Technology
Minimum Salary: $45,000

SMITH, ROTH & SQUIRES
6987 N. Oracle Rd., Tucson, AZ 85704; 520-
544-3600
Areas of Specialization: General
Minimum Salary: $60,000

TECHSTAFF, INC.
3900 E. Camelback Rd., Suite 108, Phoenix,
AZ 85018; 602-955-6464
Areas of Specialization: Engineering, Technology
Minimum Salary: $20,000

WARD HOWELL INTERNATIONAL, INC.
2525 E. Arizona Biltmore Circle, Suite 124,
Phoenix, AZ 85016; 602-955-3800
Areas of Specialization: General
Minimum Salary: $90,000

WITT/KIEFFER, FORD, HADELMAN, & LLOYD
432 N. 44th St., Suite 360, Phoenix, AZ
85008; 602-267-1370
Areas of Specialization: General
Minimum Salary: $75,000

ARKANSAS

MANAGEMENT RECRUITERS
1701 Centerview Dr., Suite 314, Little Rock,
AR 72211; 501-224-0801
Areas of Specialization: General
Minimum Salary: $35,000

EXECUTIVE RECRUITERS AGENCY, INC.
14 Office Park Dr., Suite 100, Little Rock, AR
72221; 501-224-7000
Areas of Specialization: General
Minimum Salary: $35,000

CALIFORNIA

ACCORD GROUP, JOHNSON SMITH & KNISELY
44 Montgomery St., Suite 3060, San Francisco, CA 94104; 415- 397-0848

Areas of Specialization: General
Minimum Salary: $150,000

ACCOUNTANTS EXECUTIVE SEARCH
2099 Gateway Pl., Suite 440, San Jose, CA
95110; 408-437-9779
Web: www.aocnet.com
Areas of Specialization: Accounting, Finance
Minimum Salary: $30,000

BOWERSTHOMAS
11150 W. Olympic Blvd., Suite 805, Los
Angeles, CA 90064; 310-477-3244
Areas of Specialization: Law
Minimum Salary: $60,000

DICK BERG & ASSOCIATES, INC.
P.O. Box 927171, San Diego, CA 92192;
619-4546-8680
Areas of Specialization: Technology
Minimum Salary: $25,000

DUNHILL OF SAN FRANCISCO, INC.
268 Bush St., San Francisco, CA 94104; 415-
956-3700
Areas of Specialization: General
Minimum Salary: $30,000

EGON ZEHNDER INTERNATIONAL, INC.
350 S. Grand Ave., Suite3580, Los Angeles,
CA 90071; 213-621-8900
Areas of Specialization: Finance (Mergers
and Acquisitions)
Minimum Salary:$150,000

EASTRIDGE INFOTECH
2355 Northside Dr., Suite 180, San Diego, CA
92108; 619-280-0843
Areas of Specialization: Technology
Minimum Salary: $40,000

HEIDRICK & STRUGGLES, INC.
300 S. Grand Ave., Suite 2400, Los Angeles,
CA 90071; 213-625-8811
Areas of Specialization: General
Minimum Salary: $100,000

KENZER CORP.
6033 W. Century Blvd., Suite 700, Los Angeles, CA 90045; 310-417-3083
Areas of Specialization: General
Minimum Salary: Varies

KORN/FERRY INTERNATIONAL
1800 Century Park E., Suite 900, Los Angeles, CA 90067; 310-552-1834
Areas of Specialization: General
Minimum Salary: $100,000

KORN/FERRY INTERNATIONAL
600 Mongomery St., San Francisco, CA
94111; 415-965-1834
Areas of Specialization: General
Minimum Salary: $100,000

MANAGEMENT RECRUITERS
114 E. Shaw, Suite 207, Fresno, CA 93710;
209-226-5578
Web: www.mri-fresno.com
Areas of Specialization: Engineering, Health
Care
Minimum Salary: $50,000

MACNAUGHTON ASSOCIATES
3600 Lime St., Suite 323, Riverside, CA
92501; 909-788-4951
Areas of Specialization: Education
Minimum Salary: $75,000

POIRIER, HOEVEL & CO.
12400 Wilshire Blvd., Suite 915, Los Angeles, CA 90025; 310-207-3427
Areas of Specialization: General
Minimum Salary:$75,000

WILSON RILES & ASSOCIATES, INC.
400 Capitol Mall, Suite 1540, Sacramento,
CA 95814; 916-448-0600
Web: www.wredu.com
Areas of Specialization: Education
Minimum Salary: Varies

ROMAC AND ASSOCIATES
2101 Webster St., Suite 1500, Oakland, CA
94612; 510- 451-5956
Areas of Specialization: Accounting, Finance
Minimum Salary: $15,000

SEARCH GROUP
1328 Sierra Alta Way, Los Angeles, CA
90069; 310-550-0292
Areas of Specialization: Engineering
Minimum Salary: $35,000

SPENCER STUART
10900 Wilshire Blvd., Suite 800, Los Angeles, CA 90024; 310-209-0610
Areas of Specialization: General
Minimum Salary: $150,000

SPENCER STUART
525 Market St., Suite 3700, San Francisco,
CA 94105; 415-495-4141
Areas of Specialization: General
Minimum Salary: $150,000

YORMAK & ASSOCIATES
3780 Kilroy Airport Way, Suite 200, Long

Beach, CA 90806; 562-988-6555
Areas of Specialization: Accounting
Minimum Salary: Varies

COLORADO

BENAMATI & ASSOCIATES
12247 E. Iowa Dr., Aurora, CO 80012; 303-671-5344
Areas of Specialization: Engineering
Minimum Salary: Varies

EXECUTIVE SEARCH PLACEMENTS, INC.
P.O. Box 17403, Boulder, CO 80308; 303-776-0094
Web: www.concentric.net/-espinc
*Areas of Specialization:*Accounting, Finance
Minimum Salary: $50,000

HUNT PATTON & BRAZEAL, INC.
1200 17th St., Suite 1000, Denver, CO 80202;
303-372-0751
Areas of Specialization: General
Minimum Salary: $25,000

ROCKY MOUNTAIN RECRUITERS, INC.
1801 Broadway, Suite 810, Denver, CO
80202; 303-296-2000
Areas of Specialization: Accounting, Finance
Minimum Salary: $30,000

SPECTRA INTERNATIONAL LLC
4045 S. Nonchalant Circle, Suite 7, Colorado
Springs, CO 80917; 719-572-0225
Areas of Specialization: General
Minimum Salary: $25,000

CONNECTICUT

DUBRUL MANAGEMENT CO.
30 Division St., Greenwich, CT 06830; 203-629-0164
Areas of Specialization: General
Minimum Salary: Varies

**DUNHILL INTERNATIONAL SEARCH OF
NEW HAVEN**
59 Elm St., New Haven, CT 06510; 203-562-0511
Web: www.internationalsearch.com
Areas of Specialization: Accounting, Finance
Minimum Salary: $30,000

FLYNN, HANNOCK, INC.
1001 Farmington Ave., W. Hartford, CT
06107; 860-521-5005
Areas of Specialization: General
Minimum Salary: $80,000

HOWARD W. SMITH ASSOCIATES
Old State House Station, P.O. Box 230877,

Hartford, CT 06123; 860-549-2060
Areas of Specialization: Finance
Minimum Salary: $70,000

MOYER, SHERWOOD ASSOCIATES, INC.
65 High Ridge Rd., Suite 502, Stamford, CT
06905; 203-656-2220
Areas of Specialization: Advertising,
Public Relations
Minimum Salary: $90,000

SOURCE EDP
111 Founders Plaza, East Hartford, CT 06108;
860-528-0300
Areas of Specialization: Computer Professionals
Minimum Salary: $30,000

DELAWARE

ACSYS RESOURCES, INC.
1300 Market St., Suite 501, Wilmington, DE
19801; 302-658-6181
Web: www.@acsysresources.com
Areas of Specialization: Accounting, Finance
Minimum Salary: $40,000

DISCOVERY, THE STAFFING SPECIALISTS, INC.
3519 Silverside Rd., Suite 102, Wilmington,
DE 19810
Areas of Specialization: Finance
Minimum Salary: Varies

F-O-R-T-U-N-E PERSONNEL CONSULTANTS OF WILMINGTON
254 Chapman Rd, Suite 205, Newark, DE
19702; 302-453-0404
Areas of Specialization: Biopharmacy
Minimum Salary: $40,000

DISTRICT OF COLUMBIA

DEVELOPMENT RESOURCE GROUP
1629 K St., NW, Suite 802, Washington, DC
20006; 202-223-6528
Areas of Specialization: Nonprofit
Minimum Salary: Varies

FINN & SCHNEIDER ASSOCIATES, INC.
1730 Rhode Island Ave. NW, Suite 1212,
Washington, DC 20036; 202-822-8400
Areas of Specialization: Law
Minimum Salary: Varies

HEIDRICK & STRUGGLES, INC.
1301 K St. NW, Washington, DC 20005; 202-289-4451
Areas of Specialization: General
Minimum Salary: $100,000

KORN/FERRY INTERNATIONAL
900 19th St., NW, Suite 800, Washington, DC
20006; 202-822-8127
Areas of Specialization: General
Minimum Salary: $100,000

MCPHERSON SQUARE ASSOCIATES, INC.
805 15th St. NW, Suite 701, Washington, DC
20005; 202-737-8777
Areas of Specialization Law
Minimum Salary: $70,000

TRAVAILLE EXECUTIVE SEARCH
1730 Rhode Island Ave. NW, Suite 401,
Washington, DC 20036; 202-463-6342
Areas of Specialization: Communications (Corporate), Marketing
Minimum Salary: $45,000

FLORIDA

AMERICAN MEDICAL CONSULTANTS, INC.
11625 SW 110th Rd, Miami, FL 33176; 305-271-8664
Areas of Specialization: Medical
Minimum Salary: $75,000

DUNHILL PERSONNEL
4350 W. Cypress St., Suite 225, Tampa, FL
33607; 813-872-8118
Areas of Specialization: General
Minimum Salary: $20,000

EXECUTIVE SEARCH CONSULTANTS, INC.
3116 N. Federal Hwy., Lighthouse Point, FL
33064; 954-783-1890
Web: www.insurancerecruiters.com
Areas of Specialization: Insurance
Minimum Salary: $50,000

HEIDRICK & STRUGGLES, INC.
76 S. Laura St., Suite 2110, Jacksonville, FL
32202; 904-355-6674
Areas of Specialization: General
Minimum Salary: $60,000

HUMAN CAPITAL RESOURCES, INC.
424 Central Ave., 5th Fl, St. Petersburg, FL
33701; 813-898-0314
Areas of Specialization: Finance
Minimum Salary: Varies

MANAGEMENT RECRUITERS
815 NW 57th Ave., Suite 110, Miami, FL
33126; 305-264-4521
Areas of Specialization: General

Minimum Salary: $20,000

PARKER PAGE GROUP
12550 Biscayne Blvd., Suite 225, Miami, FL 33181; 305-892-2822
Areas of Specialization: Finance, Health Services, Hospitality, Technology
Minimum Salary: $40,000

RETAIL EXECUTIVE SEARCH
4620 N. State Rd. 7, Suite 212, Ft. Lauderdale, FL 33319; 954-731-2300
Areas of Specialization: Retail
Minimum Salary: Varies

ROMAC AND ASSOCIATES
111 N. Orange Ave., Suite 1150, Orlando, FL 32801; 407-843-0765
Areas of Specialization: General
Minimum Salary: $30,000

STANEWICK, HART & ASSOCIATES, INC.
7829 Briarcreek Rd., Tallahassee, FL 32312; 904-893-7849
Areas of Specialization: Technical
Minimum Salary $30,000

GEORGIA

DUNHILL OF AUGUSTA
801 Broad St., Suite 411, Augusta, GA 30901; 706-722-5741
Areas of Specialization: General
Minimum Salary: $30,000

EGON ZEHNDER INTERNATIONAL, INC.
1201 W. Peachtree St., NW, 3000 IBM Tower, Atlanta, GA 30309; 404-875-3000
Areas of Specialization: Consulting, Finance (Mergers and Acquisitions)
Minimum Salary: $80,000

FORTUNE PERSONNEL CONSULTANTS
7 E. Congress St., Savannah, GA 31401; 912-233-4556
Areas of Specialization: General
Minimum Salary: $25,000

HEIDRICK & STRUGGLES, INC.
303 Peachtree St., NE, Suite 3100, Atlanta, GA 30308; 404-577-2410
Areas of Specialization: General
Minimum Salary: $50,000

KORN/FERRY INTERNATIONAL
303 Peachtree St., NE, Suite 1600, Atlanta, GA 30308; 404-577-7542
Areas of Specialization: Health Services
Minimum Salary: Varies

LAMALIE AMROP INTERNATIONAL
191 Peachtree St., NE, Suite 800, Atlanta, GA 30303; 404-688-0800
Areas of Specialization: General
Minimum Salary: $75,000

MANAGEMENT RECRUITERS
5901-C Peachtree Dunwoody Rd., Suite 370, Atlanta, GA 30328; 770-394-1300
Areas of Specialization: General
Minimum Salary: $20,000

MANAGEMENT RECRUITERS
233 12th St., Suite 818-A, Columbus, GA 31901; 706-571-9611
Areas of Specialization: General
Minimum Salary: $30,000

RAY & BERNDTSON
191 Peachtree St. NE, Suite 3800, Atlanta, GA 30303; 404-215-4600
Areas of Specialization: General
Minimum Salary: $105,000

SPENCER STUART
3424 W. Peachtree St., NW, Suite 3230, Atlanta, GA 30326; 404-504-4400
Areas of Specialization: General
Minimum Salary: $150,000

WARD HOWELL INTERNATIONAL, INC.
3350 Peachtree Rd., NE, Suite 1600, Atlanta, GA 30326; 404-261-6532
Areas of Specialization: General
Minimum Salary: $90,000

HAWAII

HUMAN RESOURCES MANAGEMENT HAWAII, INC.
210 Ward Ave., Suite 126, Honolulu, HI 96814; 808-536-3438
Areas of Specialization: Accounting, Finance
Minimum Salary: $40,000

PHYSICIAN ASSOCIATES
Eaton Sq., P.O. Box 75113, Honolulu, HI 96836; 808-947-9815
Areas of Specialization: Health Services
Minimum Salary: $40,000

BUTTERFIELD & CO. INTERNATIONAL
15 Omaka Place, Kihei, HI 96753; 808-879-1100
Web: www.butterfield-intl.com
Areas of Specialization: Medical
Minimum Salary: $50,000

IDAHO

F-O-R-T-U-N-E PERSONNEL CONSULTANTS OF BOISE

960 Broadway Ave., Suite 540, Boise, ID
83706; 208-343-5190
Areas of Specialization: Pulp and Paper
Minimum Salary: $80,000

WARD–HOFFMAN & ASSOCIATES
2020 Lakewood Dr., Suite 312, Coeur
d'Alene, ID 83814; 208-667-6095
Areas of Specialization: Mining
Minimum Salary: $30,000

ILLINOIS

AMERICAN RESOURCES CORP.
213 W. Institute Pl., Suite 412, Chicago, IL
60610; 312-587-9160
Web: www.american-resources.com
Areas of Specialization: General
Minimum Salary: $35,000

BUSINESS SYSTEMS OF AMERICA, INC.
200 W. Adams St., Suite 2015, Chicago, IL
60606; 312-849-9222
Web: www.bussysam.com
Areas of Specialization: General
Minimum Salary: Varies

CARPENTER ASSOCIATES, INC.
20 S. Clark St., Suite 2210., Chicago, IL
60603; 312-263-4004
Areas of Specialization: Marketing
Minimum Salary: $25,000

CMW & ASSOCIATES
150th St., Peoria, IL 61370; 618-446-3086
Web: www.cmwassoc.com
Areas of Specialization: General
Minimum Salary: $25,000

DHR INTERNATIONAL, INC.
10 S. Riverside Plaza, Suite 2220, Chicago,
IL 60606; 312-782-1581
Areas of Specialization: General
Minimum Salary: $50,000

EGON ZEHNDER INTERNATIONAL, INC.
1 First National Plaza, Suite 3004, Chicago,
IL 60603; 312-782-4500
Areas of Specialization: General
Minimum Salary: $80,000

EVIE KREISLER ASSOCIATES, INC.
333 N. Michigan, Suite 818, Chicago, IL
60601; 312-251-0077
Areas of Specialization: Consumer
Products
Minimum Salary: $50,000

EXECUTIVE SEARCH CONSULTANTS CORP.
8 S. Michigan Ave., Suite 1205, Chicago, IL

60603
Areas of Specialization: Insurance
Minimum Salary: $50,000

HEIDRICK & STRUGGLES, INC.
233 S. Wacker Dr., Suite4200, Chicago, IL
60606; 312- 496-1200
Web: www.h-s.com
Areas of Specialization: General
Minimum Salary: $100,000

KORN/FERRY INTERNATIONAL
233 S. Wacker Dr., Suite 3300, Chicago, IL
60606; 312-466-1834
Areas of Specialization: General
Minimum Salary: $100,000

LAMALIE AMROP INTERNATIONAL
225 W. Wacker Dr., Suite 2100, Chicago, IL
60606; 312-782-3113
Areas of Specialization: General
Minimum Salary: $100,000

MANAGEMENT RECRUITERS
124 E. Laurel St. Suite B, Springfield, IL
62704; 217-544-2051
Web: www.mrinet.com
Areas of Specialization: General
Minimum Salary: $25,000

RAY & BERNDTSON
233 S. Wacker Dr., Suite 4020, Chicago, IL
60606; 312-876-0730
Areas of Specialization: General
Minimum Salary: $105,000

ROMAC INTERNATIONAL
20 N. Wacker Dr., Suite1360, Chicago, IL
60606; 312-263-0902
Web: www.romacintl.com
Areas of Specialization: Accounting, Finance
Minimum Salary: $30,000

SANFORD ROSE ASSOCIATES
416 E. State St., Rockford, IL 61104; 815-
964-4080
Web: www.sanfordrose.com
Areas of Specialization: General
Minimum Salary: $30,000

MANAGEMENT RECRUITERS
600 N. Commons Dr., Suite 101, Aurora, IL
60504; 630-851-4164
Web: www.mrichicago.com
Areas of Specialization: General
Minimum Salary:$30,000

SEARCH DYNAMICS
9420 W. Foster Ave., Suite 200, Chicago, IL

60656; 773-992-3900
Areas of Specialization: Engineering, Technology
Minimum Salary: $30,000

SPENCER STUART
401 N. Michigan Ave., Chicago, IL 60611; 312-822-0080
Areas of Specialization: General
Minimum Salary: $75,000

WARD HOWELL INTERNATIONAL, INC.
300 S. Wacker Dr., Suite 2940, Chicago, IL 60606; 312-236-2211
Areas of Specialization: General
Minimum Salary: $90,000

INDIANA

THE BENNETT GROUP, INC.
5640 Professional Circle, Indianapolis, IN 46241; 317-247-1240
Areas of Specialization: Automotive, Technology
Minimum Salary: $60,000

DUNHILL
9918 Coldwater Rd., Ft. Wayne, IN 46825; 219-489-5966
Areas of Specialization: General
Minimum Salary: $30,000

F-O-R-T-U-N-E PERSONNEL CONSULT-ANTS
52303 Emmons Rd., Suite 27, South Bend, IN 46637; 219-273-3188
Areas of Specialization: General
Minimum Salary: $25,000

MANAGEMENT RECRUITERS
8200 Haverstick Rd., Suite 240, Indianapolis, IN 46240; 317-257-5411
Web: www.MRIindy.com
Areas of Specialization: General
Minimum Salary: $25,000

RESOURCE NETWORK, INC.
6802 Madison Ave., Indianapolis, IN 46227; 317-786-1564
Areas of Specialization: Engineering, Metals, Technology
Minimum Salary: $60,000

IOWA

AGRA PLACEMENTS, LTD.
4949 Pleasant St., Suite 1, West Des Moines, IA 50266; 515-225-6562
Web: www.agraplacements.com
Areas of Specialization: Agriculture, Horticulture
Minimum Salary: $25,000

CORPORATE SUITE, LTD.
507 Merle Hay Tower, Des Moines, IA 50310; 515-278-2744
Areas of Specialization: Insurance
Minimum Salary: $30,000

DUNHILL STAFFING
1233 Gilbert Ct., Suite A, Iowa City, IA 52245; 319-354-1407
Areas of Specialization: General
Minimum Salary: $25,000

MANAGEMENT RECRUITERS
150 1st Ave., NE, Suite 400, Cedar Rapids, IA 52401; 319-366-8441
Areas of Specialization: General
Minimum Salary: $25,000

MANAGEMENT RECRUITERS
7400 University, Suite D, Des Moines, IA 503259; 515-255-1242
Web: www.mrdsm.com
Areas of Specialization: General
Minimum Salary: Varies

KANSAS

HEALTH SEARCH, INC.
151 Whittier St., Suite 2100, Wichita, KS 67207; 316-681-4401
Areas of Specialization: Health Services
Minimum Salary: $25,000

THE WINN GROUP, INC.
501 Lawrence Ave., Lawrence, KS 66049; 913-842-7111
Areas of Specialization: Insurance
Minimum Salary: $50,000

MANAGEMENT RECRUITERS
3400 SW Van Buren, Topeka, KS 66611; 913-267-5430
Areas of Specialization: Healthcare
Minimum Salary: $25,000

MANAGEMENT RECRUITERS
8100 E. 22nd St. N., Bldg 1500, Suite B, Wichita, KS 67226; 316-682-8239
Areas of Specialization: General
Minimum Salary: $20,000

KENTUCKY

MANAGEMENT RECRUITERS
4360 Brownsboro Rd, Suite 240, Louisville, KY 40207; 502-897-0333
Areas of Specialization: General
Minimum Salary: $20,000

MANAGEMENT RECRUITERS
2350 Sterlington Rd., Lexington, KY 40502; 606-273-5665

Areas of Specialization: General
Minimum Salary: $40,000

OVCA ASSOCIATES, INC.
7 Overlook Rd., Louisville, KY 40207; 502-893-6114
Areas of Specialization: General
Minimum Salary: $75,000

PROFESSIONAL SEARCH CONSULTANTS
2500 Meidinger Tower, Louisville, Ky 40202; 502-583-1530
Areas of Specialization: General, Law
Minimum Salary: $50,000

LOUISIANA

ASTRO EXECUTIVE SEARCH FIRM.
11219 Muriel Ave., Suite 418, Baton Rouge, LA 70816; 504-292-7363
Areas of Specialization: General
Minimum Salary: $50,000

MSI INTERNATIONAL.
701 Poydras St., One Shell Square, Suite 3880, New Orleans, LA 70139; 504-522-1998
Areas of Specialization: Healthcare
Minimum Salary: $40,000

ROMAC AND ASSOCIATES
650 Poydras St., Suite 2523, New Orleans, LA 70130; 504-522-6611
Areas of Specialization: Accounting, Data Processing, Finance
Minimum Salary: $25,000

MAINE

EXECUTIVE RESOURCE GROUP
29 Oakhurst Rd., Cape Elizabeth, ME 04107; 207-871-5527
Areas of Specialization: General
Minimum Salary: $50,000

PRO SEARCH
100 Middle St., Portland, ME 04101; 207-775-7600
Areas of Specialization: General
Minimum Salary: $25,000

SALES CONSULTANTS OF BANGOR
12 Acme Rd., Suite 104, Brewer, ME 04412; 207-989-3889
Areas of Specialization: General
Minimum Salary: $30,000

MARYLAND

BOWIE & ASSOCIATES
612 Norhurst Way, Baltimore, MD 21228; 410-747-1919
Areas of Specialization: Transportation
Minimum Salary: $50,000

D. W. BAIRD & ASSOCIATES
10751 Falls Rd., Suite 250, Baltimore, MD 21093; 410-339-7670
Areas of Specialization: Chemicals, Environment, Health Services, Pharmaceuticals
Minimum Salary: $40,000

EXECUTIVE DYNAMICS, INC.
1107 Kenilworth Dr., Suite 208, Baltimore, MD 21204; 410-494-1400
Areas of Specialization: Finance, Health Services, Insurance
Minimum Salary: $50,000

LARSEN & LEE, INC.
4915 St. Elmo Ave., Suite 504., Bethesda, MD 20814; 301-718-4280
Areas of Specialization: Finance (Tax Specialists)
Minimum Salary: $60,000

MANAGEMENT ASSOCIATES
9735 Magledt Rd., Baltimore, MD 21234; 410-665-6033
Areas of Specialization: General
Minimum Salary: $50,000

MANAGEMENT RECRUITERS
1100 Wayne Ave., Suite 1080, Silver Spring, MD 20910; 301-589-5400
Areas of Specialization: General
Minimum Salary: Varies

WITT/KIEFFER, FORD, HADELMAN, & LLOYD
4550 Montgomery Ave., Suite 615N, Bethesda, MD 20814; 301-654-5070
Areas of Specialization: General
Minimum Salary: $75,000

MASSACHUSETTS

ATLANTIC SEARCH GROUP, INC.
1 Liberty Sq., Boston, MA 02109; 617-426-9700
Areas of Specialization: Accounting, Finance
Minimum Salary: $20,000

CHALONER ASSOCIATES
Box 1097, Back Bay Station, Boston, MA 02117; 617-451-5170
Areas of Specialization: Advertising, Public Relations
Minimum Salary: $35,000

DOUGLAS–ALLEN, INC.
1500 Main St., 24th Floor, Springfield, MA 01115; 413-739-0900
Areas of Specialization: Finance

Minimum Salary: $100,000

HEIDRICK & STRUGGLES, INC.
1 Post Office Sq., Boston, MA 02109; 617-423-1140
Areas of Specialization: General
Minimum Salary: $100,000

THE HUMAN RESOURCE CONSULTING GROUP, INC.
800 Turnpike St., Suite 300, N. Andover, MA 01845; 508-686-5338
Areas of Specialization: General
Minimum Salary: $50,000

KORN/FERRY INTERNATIONAL
1 International Place, 11th Floor., Boston, MA 02110; 617-345-0200
Areas of Specialization: General
Minimum Salary: $100,000

ORGANIZATION RESOURCES, INC.
63 Atlantic Ave., Boston, MA 02110; 617-742-8970
Areas of Specialization: General
Minimum Salary: $90,000

ROMAC AND ASSOCIATES
133 Federal St. Suite 300, Boston, MA 02110; 617-350-0945
Areas of Specialization: Accounting, Finance
Minimum Salary: $15,000

THE TOUCHSTONE GROUP
44 Elm St., Suite 500, Worcester, MA 01609; 508-795-0769
Areas of Specialization: Technology
Minimum Salary: $40,000

MICHIGAN

ACTION MANAGEMENT CORP.
600 Renaissance Center, Suite 1400, Detroit, MI 48243; 313-446-6961
Web: www.action-mgmt.com
Areas of Specialization: Women, Minorities
Minimum Salary: $25,000

DUNHILL
4406 Elmhurst, Saginaw, MI 48603; 517-799-9300
Areas of Specialization: General
Minimum Salary: $25,000

EXECUTIVE RECRUITERS INTERNATIONAL
1150 Griswold St., Suite 3000, Detroit, MI 48226; 313-961-6200

Areas of Specialization: Engineering, Environment
Minimum Salary: $30,000

EXECUQUEST , INC.
2050 Breton SE, Suite 103, Grand Rapids, MI 49546; 616-949-1800
Areas of Specialization: General
Minimum Salary: $75,000

L.J. JOHNSON & CO.
815 Newport Rd., Ann Arbor, MI 48103; 313-663-6446
Areas of Specialization: Engineering
Minimum Salary: $40,000

MANAGEMENT RECRUITERS
300 River Pl., Suite 3000, Detroit, MI 48207; 313-568-4200
Areas of Specialization: General
Minimum Salary: $20,000

STONE ASSOCIATES, LLC
25600 N. Woodward Ave., Suite 214, Royal Oak, MI 48067; 248-548-0445
Areas of Specialization: Finance, Technology
Minimum Salary: $30,000

MINNESOTA

AGRA PLACEMENTS, LTD.
710 N. Broadway St., New Ulm, MN 56073; 507-354-4900
Web: www.agraplacements.com
Areas of Specialization: Agriculture, Horticulture
Minimum Salary: $25,000

CORPORATE RESOURCES PROFESSIONAL PLACEMENT
4205 Lancaster Ln. N, Suite 108, Minneapolis, MN 55441; 612-550-9222
Areas of Specialization: Engineering
Minimum Salary: $40,000

HAYDEN & ASSOCIATES, INC.
7825 Washington Ave. S., Suite 120, Minneapolis, MN 55439; 612-941-6300
Areas of Specialization: General
Minimum Salary: $30,000

KORN/FERRY INTERNATIONAL
4816 IDS Ctr., 80 S. 8th St., Minneapolis, MN 55402; 612-333-1834
Areas of Specialization: General
Minimum Salary: $100,000

ROMAC AND ASSOCIATES
333 S. Seventh St., Suite 1470., Minneapolis,

MN 55402; 612- 288-9777
Areas of Specialization: General
Minimum Salary: $15,000

SOURCE EDP
80 S. 8th St., Minneapolis, MN 55402;
612-332-6460
Areas of Specialization: Technology
Minimum Salary: $25,000

WALKER GROUP, INC.
5305 Ximines Ln, Minneapolis, MN 55442;
612-553-1356
Areas of Specialization: Health Services,
Retail
Minimum Salary: $50,000

MISSISSIPPI

JIM WOODSON & ASSOCIATES, INC.
1080 River Oaks Dr., Suite B-102, Jackson,
MS 39208; 601-936-4037
Areas of Specialization: General
Minimum Salary: $25,000

MANAGEMENT RECRUITERS
2506 Lakeland Dr., Suite 408, Jackson,
MS 39208; 601-936-7900
Areas of Specialization: General
Minimum Salary: $50,000

AMERICAN MEDICAL RECRUITING CO. INC.
P.O. Box 12810, Jackson, MS 39236;
601-898-9963
Areas of Specialization: General
Minimum Salary: Varies

MISSOURI

AGRI-ASSOCIATES
500 Nichols Rd., Kansas City, MO
64112; 816-531-7980
Areas of Specialization: Agriculture, Horticulture
Minimum Salary: $30,000

DEBBON RECRUITING GROUP
P.O. Box 510323, St. Louis, MO 63151; 314-
846-9101
Areas of Specialization: Food and Bev-
erages, Manufacturing, Pharmaceuticals
Minimum Salary: $30,000

HITCHENS & FOSTER, INC.
Pines Office Ctr., 1 Pine Court, St. Louis,
MO 63141; 314-453-0800
Areas of Specialization: Health Services
Minimum Salary: $25,000

KENNISON & ASSOCIATES, INC.
3101 Broadway, Suite 280, Kansas City, MO
64111; 816-753-4401
Web: www.kennison.com
Areas of Specialization: General
Minimum Salary: $18,000

MANAGEMENT SCIENCE ASSOCIATES, INC.
4801 Cliff Ave., Suite 300, Independence,
MO 64055; 816-373-9988
Web: www.mgmtscience.com
Areas of Specialization: Health Services
Minimum Salary: Varies

MEDICAL RECRUITERS, INC.
12400 Olive Blved. Suite 555., St. Louis,
MO 63141; 314-275-8131
Areas of Specialization: Health Services
Minimum Salary: $25,000

MICHAEL LATAS & ASSOCIATES, INC.
1311 Lindbergh Plaza Ctr., St. Louis, MO
63132; 314-993-6500
Areas of Specialization: Architecture,
Construction, Engineering
Minimum Salary: $50,000

SANFORD ROSE ASSOCIATES
5407 E. Riverview St., Springfield, MO
65809; 417-887-0484
Areas of Specialization: Finance, Tecn-
nology
Minimum Salary: $60,000

MONTANA

DAVID S. BURT ASSOCIATES
991 Dixon Circle,Billings, MT 59105; 406-
245-9500
Areas of Specialization: Chemical
Minimum Salary: $35,000

FORTUNE PERSONNEL CONSULTANTS
1104 E. Main St., Suite 302, Bozeman, MT
59715; 406-585-1332
Areas of Specialization: General
Minimum Salary: $30,000

PRESLEY CONSULTANTS, INC.
1815 Wyoming Ave., Billings, MT 59102;
406-248-6001
Areas of Specialization: Health Services
Minimum Salary: $50,000

NEBRASKA

HARRISON MOORE, INC.
7638 Pierce, Omaha, NE 68124; 402-
391-5494
Areas of Specialization: Manufacturing,

Metals, Plastics
Minimum Salary: Varies

MANAGEMENT RECRUITERS
210 Gateway, Suite 434, Lincoln, NE 68505;
402-467-5534
Areas of Specialization: General
Minimum Salary: $20,000

THE REGENCY GROUP, LTD.
256 N. 115th St., Suite 1, Omaha, NE
68154; 402-334-7255
Web: www.regencygroup.com
Areas of Specialization: Technology
Minimum Salary: $30,000

VALUE BASED LEADERSHIP
1716 S. 153rd Ave. Circle, Omaha, NE
68144; 402-333-2648
Areas of Specialization: Health Services
Minimum Salary: $25,000

RAYMOND KARSAN ASSOCIATES
5000 Central Park Dr., Suite 204, Lincoln, NE
68504; 402-464-7979
Areas of Specialization: General
Minimum Salary: Varies

N E V A D A

EASTRIDGE INFOTECH
4220 S. Maryland Pkwy., Las Vegas, NV
89119; 702-732-8859
Areas of Specialization: Technology
Minimum Salary: $40,000

MANAGEMENT RECRUITERS
4530 S. Eastern, Suite A-12, Las Vegas, NV
89119; 702-733-1818
Areas of Specialization: General
Minimum Salary: $20,000

MANAGEMENT RECRUITERS
1025 Ridgeview Dr., Suite 100, Reno,
NV 89509; 702-826-5243
Areas of Specialization: Insurance,
Manufacturing
Minimum Salary: $30,000

N E W   H A M P S H I R E

ACCESS DATA PERSONNEL, INC.
649 Second St., Manchester, NH 03102; 603-
641-6300
Web: home.aol.com/accessdata
Areas of Specialization: Data Processing
Minimum Salary: $20,000

EMERALD LEGAL SEARCH
22 Eastman Ave., Bedford, NH 03110; 603-

623-5300
Areas of Specialization: Law
Minimum Salary: $40,000

FORTUNE PERSONNEL CONSULTANTS
505 W. Hollis St., Suite 208, Nashua, NH
03062; 603-880-4900
Areas of Specialization: Health Services
Minimum Salary: $35,000

N E W   J E R S E Y

BRENTWOOD GROUP, INC.
170 Kinnelon Rd., Suite 29B, Kinnelon,
NJ 07405; 201-283-1000
Areas of Specialization: General
Minimum Salary: $50,000

BROOKS EXECUTIVE PERSONNEL
2337 Lemoine Ave., Ft. Lee, NJ 07024; 201-
585-7200
Web: www.brookspersonnel.com
Areas of Specialization: General
Minimum Salary: $50,000

DALTON MANAGEMENT CONSULTANTS, LTD.
327 Grove St., Suite 279, Jersey City, NJ
07302; 201-309-2351
Areas of Specialization: General
Minimum Salary: $50,000

EXCALIBUR HUMAN RESOURCES, INC.
5 Independence Way, Princeton, NJ 08540;
609-452-0952
Areas of Specialization: Health Services
Minimum Salary: $80,000

L.J. GONZER ASSOCIATES
1225 Raymond Blvd., Newark, NJ 07102;
973-624-5600
Areas of Specialization: General
Minimum Salary: $25,000

SANFORD ROSE ASSOCIATES
12 Minneakoning Rd., Suite 4, Flemington,
NJ 08822; 908-788-7847
Areas of Specialization: Manufacturing
Minimum Salary: $25,000

N E W   M E X I C O

ACC CONSULTANTS
P.O. Box 91240, Albuquerque, NM 87199;
505-298-9177
Areas of Specialization: Energy, Envi-
ronment, Health Services
Minimum Salary: Varies

TRAMBLEY THE RECRUITER
5325 Wyoming Blvd. NE, Suite 200, Albuquerque, NM 87109; 505-821-5440
Areas of Specialization: Manufacturing, Mining
Minimum Salary: Varies

NEW YORK

ALEXANDER ROSS & CO..
21 E. 40th St. at Madison Ave., New York, NY 10016; 212-889-9333
Areas of Specialization: Human Resources
Minimum Salary: $80,000

AMERICAN GROUP PRACTICE, INC.
420 Madison Ave., 7th Floor, New York, NY 10017; 212-371-3091
Areas of Specialization: Health Services (Physicians)
Minimum Salary: $60,000

THE AYERS GROUP, INC.
370 Lexington Ave., 25th Floor, New York, NY 10017; 212-599-5656
Areas of Specialization: Technology
Minimum Salary: $50,000

PEREZ–ARTON CONSULTANTS, INC.
350 Lexingtion Ave., Suite 704, New York, NY 10016; 212-986-1630
Areas of Specialization: Education
Minimum Salary: $75,000

BERT DAVIS PUBLISHING PLACEMENT CONSULTANTS
425 Madison Ave., Suite 14A, New York, NY 10017; 212-838-4000
Areas of Specialization: Publishing
Minimum Salary: $50,000

BISHOP PARTNERS, LTD.
708 Third Ave., Suite 2200, New York, NY 10017; 212-986-3419
Areas of Specialization: Communications, Entertainment
Minimum Salary: $100,000

DUNHILL OF BUFFALO
584 Delaware Ave., Buffalo, NY 14202; 716-885-3576
Areas of Specialization: General
Minimum Salary: $25,000

EGON ZEHNDER INTERNATIONAL, INC.
55 E. 59th St., New York, NY 10022; 212-838-9199
Areas of Specialization: General
Minimum Salary: $150,000

FORTUNE PERSONNEL CONSULTANTS OF NYC, INC.
505 Fifth Ave., Suite 1100, New York, NY 10017; 212-557-1000
Areas of Specialization: Manufacturing
Minimum Salary: $40,000

GOSSAGE REGAN ASSOCIATES
25 W. 43rd St., Suite 812, New York, NY 10036; 212-869-3348
Areas of Specialization: Nonprofit
Minimum Salary: $60,000

GOODRICH & SHERWOOD ASSOCIATES, INC..
250 Mill St., Rochester, NY 14614; 716-777-4060
Areas of Specialization: General
Minimum Salary: $80,000

HEIDRICK & STRUGGLES, INC.
245 Park Ave., Suite 4300, New York, NY 10167; 212-867-9876
Areas of Specialization: General
Minimum Salary: $60,000

THE KAY GROUP OF FIFTH AVENUE
350 Fifth Ave., Suite 2205, New York, NY 10118; 212-947-3131
Areas of Specialization: Accounting, Advertising, Metals
Minimum Salary: $40,000

KORN/FERRY INTERNATIONAL
237 Park Ave., New York, NY 10017; 212-687-1834
Areas of Specialization: General
Minimum Salary: $100,000

LAMALIE AMROP INTERNATIONAL
200 Park Ave., Suite 3100, New York, NY10166; 212-953-7900
Areas of Specialization: General
Minimum Salary: $100,000

MANAGEMENT RECRUITERS
370 Lexington Ave., Suite 1412, New York, NY 10017; 212-972-7300
Web: www.mrnyc.com
Areas of Specialization: General
Minimum Salary: $70,000

RAY & BERNDTSON
245 Park Ave., 33rd Floor., New York, NY
10167; 212-370-1316
Areas of Specialization: General
Minimum Salary: $105,000

RANDALL–HEIKEN, INC.
60 E. 42nd St., Suite 2022, New York, NY
10165; 212-490-1313
Areas of Specialization: General
Minimum Salary: $70,000

SAVIAR, INC.
2-212 Center for Science & Technology,
Syracuse, NY 13244; 315-443-4460
Web: www.saviar.com
Areas of Specialization: Technology
Minimum Salary: $50,000

JOHN WALES ASSOCIATES, INC.
240 Washington Ave. Ext., Albany, NY
12203; 800-544-0678
Areas of Specialization: Medical
Minimum Salary: Varies

SPENCER STUART
277 Park Ave., 29th Floor, New York,
NY10172; 212-336-0200
Areas of Specialization: General
Minimum Salary: $150,000

PATHWAY EXECUTIVE SEARCH, INC.
60 E. 42nd St., Suite 405, New York, NY
10165
Web: pesearch.com
Areas of Specialization: General
Minimum Salary: Varies

WARD HOWELL INTERNATIONAL, INC.
99 Park Ave., Suite 2000, New York, NY
10016; 212-697-3730
Areas of Specialization: General
Minimum Salary: $75,000

NORTH CAROLINA

ARIAIL & ASSOCIATES
210 Friendly Ave., Suite 200, Greensboro,
NC 27401; 910-275-2906
Areas of Specialization: Furniture
Minimum Salary: $100,000

ANDREWS AND ASSOCIATES
6100 Fairview Rd., Charlotte, NC 28210;
704-556-0088
Areas of Specialization: Accounting
Minimum Salary: $25,000

A FIRST RESOURCE
P.O. Box 15451, Winston-Salem, NC
27113; 910-784-5898
Areas of Specialization: General
Minimum Salary: $30,000

DLG ASSOCIATES, INC.
1515 Mockingbird Lane, Suite 560,
Charlotte, NC 28209; 704-522-9993
Areas of Specialization: Marketing
Minimum Salary: $50,000

MANAGEMENT RECRUITERS
P.O. Box 17054, Winston-Salem, NC
27116; 910-723-0484
Web: www.mrinet.com
Areas of Specialization: General
Minimum Salary: $30,000

**MSI INTERNATIONAL/MANAGEMENT
SEARCH OF CHARLOTTE**
4801 Independence Blvd., Suite 408,
Charlotte, NC 28212; 704-535-6610
Areas of Specialization: Health Services
Minimum Salary: $40,000

SNELLING PERSONNEL SERVICES
5838 Faringdon Pl., Suite 1, Raleigh, NC
27609; 919-876-0660
Web: www.webpress.net/recruit
Areas of Specialization: General
Minimum Salary: $20,000

NORTH DAKOTA

DUNHILL PERSONNEL SERVICE
118 Broadway, Fargo, ND 58102; 701-235-3719
Web: www.dunhillstaff.com
Areas of Specialization: Engineering,
Health Services
Minimum Salary: $25,000

OHIO

BRYAN & LOUIS RESEARCH
6263 Mayfield, Rd., Suite 226, Cleveland, OH 44124; 216-442-8744
Areas of Specialization: Manufacturing
Minimum Salary: $25,000

DELTA MEDICAL SEARCH ASSOCIATES
615 Rome-Hilliard Rd., Suite 107, Columbus, OH 43228; 614-878-0550
Areas of Specialization: Health Services
Minimum Salary: $50,000

R. GREEN & ASSOCIATES, INC.
One South St. Clair St., Toledo, OH 43602;
419-249-2800
Areas of Specialization: General
Minimum Salary: $50,000

HEIDRICK & STRUGGLES, INC.
600 Superior Ave. E., Cleveland, OH 44114;
216-241-7410
Areas of Specialization: General
Minimum Salary: $100,000

LAMALIE AMROP INTERNATIONAL
Key Tower, Suite 4110, 127 Public Sq.,
Cleveland, OH 44114; 216-694-3000
Areas of Specialization: General
Minimum Salary: $100,000

MANAGEMENT RECRUITERS
4050 Executive Park Dr., Suite 125, Cin-
cinnati, OH 45241-2020; 513-769-4747
Web: www.mrinet.com/cincinnati
Areas of Specialization: General
Minimum Salary: $40,000

R.A.N. ASSOCIATES, INC.
140 Public Sq., Suite 804, Cleveland, OH
44114; 216-696-6699
Areas of Specialization: General
Minimum Salary: $30,000

ROBERT WILLIAM JAMES & ASSOCIATES
3453 Great Western Blvd., Columbus,
OH 43204; 614-787-7707
Areas of Specialization: General
Minimum Salary: Varies

ROBERT WILLIAM JAMES & ASSOCIATES
2717 Miamisburg-Centerville Rd., Dayton, OH 45414; 937-438-4932
Areas of Specialization: General
Minimum Salary: Varies

SANFORD ROSE ASSOCIATES
265 S. Main St., Suite 100, Akron, OH 44308;
330-762-7162
Areas of Specialization: General
Minimum Salary: $40,000

TAYLOR WINFIELD
5875 Mallview Ct., Columbus, OH 43231;
614-895-6757
Areas of Specialization: Technology
Minimum Salary: $120,000

OKLAHOMA

AMERIRESOURCE GROUP INC.
2525 NW Expressway St., Suite 532,
Oklahoma City, OK 73112; 405-842-
5900
Web: www.flash.net
Areas of Specialization: General
Minimum Salary: $35,000

MANAGEMENT SEARCH, INC.
6051 N. Brookline, Suite 125., Oklahoma
City, OK 73112; 405-842-3173
Areas of Specialization: Agriculture
Minimum Salary: $25,000

HUNT PATTON & BRAZEAL, INC.
2250 E. 73rd St., Suite 120, Tulsa, OK 74136;
918-492-6910
Areas of Specialization: General
Minimum Salary: $25,000

OREGON

BECKER PROJECT RESOURCES, INC.
4526 SW Tarlow Ct., Portland OR
97221; 503-246-6500
Web: www.bpr.com
Areas of Specialization: Technology
Minimum Salary: $50,000

CORPORATE BUILDERS, INC.
812 SW Washington St., Suite 660, Portland,
OR 97205; 503-223-4344
Areas of Specialization: Construction
Minimum Salary: Varies

MANAGEMENT RECRUITERS
61419 S. Hwy. 97, Suite V, Bend, OR
97702; 541-383-8550
Areas of Specialization: General
Minimum Salary: $25,000

PACIFIC COAST RECRUITERS
65 W-1 Division #144, Eugene, OR
97404; 541-345-6866
Areas of Specialization: Insurance
Minimum Salary: $30,000

SOURCE ENGINEERING
10220 SW Greenburg Rd., Suite 625, Portland, OR 97223; 503-768-4546
Areas of Specialization: Engineering
Minimum Salary: Varies

WOODWORTH INTERNATIONAL GROUP
620 SW Fifth Ave., Suite 1225, Portland, OR
97204; 503-225-5000
Areas of Specialization: General
Minimum Salary: $60,000

PENNSYLVANIA

ATOMIC PERSONNEL, INC.
P.O. Box 11244/z3, Philadelphia, PA 19027-0244; 215-885-4223
Areas of Specialization: Engineering
Minimum Salary: $35,000

COLEMAN LEGAL SEARCH CONSULTANTS
1535 JFK Blvd., Two Penn Ctr., Suite 1010, Philadelphia, PA 19102; 215-864-2700
Web: www.colemanlegal.com
Areas of Specialization: Law
Minimum Salary: Varies

JEFFERSON–ROSS ASSOCIATES, INC..
2 Penn Ctr. Plaza, Suite 312, Philadelphia, PA 19102; 215-564-5322
Areas of Specialization: Finance
Minimum Salary: $35,000

KORN/FERRY INTERNATIONAL.
2 Logan Sq., Suite 2530, Philadelphia, PA 19103; 215-496-6666
Areas of Specialization: General
Minimum Salary: $100,000

JACK B. LARSEN & ASSOCIATES, INC.
334 W. 8th St., Erie, PA 16502; 814-459-3725
Areas of Specialization: General
Minimum Salary: $25,000

MANAGEMENT RECRUITERS
325 Chestnut St., Suite 1106., Philadelphia, PA 19106; 215-829-1900
Areas of Specialization: General
Minimum Salary: $20,000

MANAGEMENT RECRUITERS
112 Washington Pl., Suite 1570, Pittsburgh, PA 15219-3423; 412 566-2100
Areas of Specialization: General
Minimum Salary: $20,000

ROMACINTERNATIONAL, INC.
2100 Wharton St., Suite 710, Pittsburgh, PA 15203; 412-481-6015
Areas of Specialization: Accounting, Finance
Minimum Salary: $15,000

SPECIALTY CONSULTANTS, INC.
Gateway Towers, Suite 2710, Pittsburgh, PA 15222; 412-355-8200
Areas of Specialization: Construction, Real Estate
Minimum Salary: $40,000

SPENCER STUART
2005 Market St., Suite 2350, Philadelphia, PA 19103; 215-814-1600
Areas of Specialization: General
Minimum Salary: $75,000

STEWART ASSOCIATES
245 Butler Ave., The Executive Offices, Lancaster, PA 17601; 717-299-9242
Areas of Specialization: General
Minimum Salary: $35,000

WELLINGTON MANAGEMENT GROUP
1601 Market St., Suite 2902, Philadelphia, PA 19103; 215-569-8900
Areas of Specialization: Technology
Minimum Salary: $75,000

RHODE ISLAND

MANAGEMENT SEARCH OF R.I., INC.
1 State St., Suite 501, Providence, RI 02908; 401-273-5511
Areas of Specialization: General
Minimum Salary: $50,000

LYBROOK ASSOCIATES, INC..
P.O. Box 572, Newport, RI 02840; 401-683-6990
Areas of Specialization: Technical
Minimum Salary: $30,000

SALES CONSULTANTS OF RHODE ISLAND, INC.
349 Centerville Rd., Warwick, R.I.02886; 401-737-3200
Areas of Specialization: Sales
Minimum Salary: $25,000

SOUTH CAROLINA

DUNHILL
Personnel16 Berry Hill Rd., Suite 120, Columbia, SC 29210; 803-772-6751
Web: www.dunhillSta.com
Areas of Specialization: Automotive
Minimum Salary: $30,000

FORTUNE CONSULTANTS
25 Woods Lake Rd., Suite 410, Greenville, SC 29607; 864-241-7700
Areas of Specialization: General
Minimum Salary: $40,000

STAFF RESOURCES, INC.
130 E. Main St., Rock Hill, SC 29732; 803-366-0500
Areas of Specialization: Manufacturing
Minimum Salary: $25,000

SOUTH DAKOTA

MANAGEMENT RECRUITERS
2600 S. Minnesota Ave., Suite 202, Sioux Falls, SD 57105; 605-334-9291
Areas of Specialization: General
Minimum Salary: $20,000

TENNESSEE

DOUGHERTY & ASSOCIATES
2345 Ashford Dr., Chattanooga, TN 37421; 423-899-1060
Areas of Specialization: Chemicals, Energy, Natural Resources
Minimum Salary: $35,000

FRYE/JOURE & ASSOCIATES, INC.
4515 Poplar Ave., Suite 215, Memphis, TN 38117; 901-683-7792
Areas of Specialization: General
Minimum Salary: $40,000

PROFESSIONALS AND RECRUITING COMPANY
1028 Cresthaven Rd., Suite 202, Memphis, TN 38119; 901-685-2042
Areas of Specialization: General
Minimum Salary: $40,000

RMA SEARCH
301 Gallaher View Rd., Suite 111, Knoxville, TN 37919; 615-691-4733
Areas of Specialization: General
Minimum Salary: $30,000

SOUTHWESTERN PROFESSIONAL SERVICES
2451 Atrium Way, Nashville, TN 37214; 615-391-2617
Areas of Specialization: General
Minimum Salary: Varies

TEXAS

THE ALEXANDER GROUP
1330 Post Oak Blvd., Suite 2800, Houston, TX 77056; 713-993-7900
Areas of Specialization: General
Minimum Salary: $80,000

ANDERSON BRADSHAW ASSOCIATES, INC.
P.O. Box 934045, Houston, TX 77292; 713-869-6789
Areas of Specialization: Engineering
Minimum Salary: $60,000

DUNHILL SEARCH
1301 S. Bowen Rd., Suite 370, Arlington, TX 76013; 817-265-2291
Areas of Specialization: General
Minimum Salary: $35,000

DUNHILL OF CORPUS CHRISTI, INC.
4455 S. Padre Island Dr., #102, Corpus Christi, TX 78411-4417, 512-225-2580
Web: www.talentscouts.com
Areas of Specialization: General
Minimum Salary: $25,000

THE ELSWORTH GROUP
12910 Queens Forest, Suite B, San Antonio, TX 78230; 210-493-6873
Areas of Specialization: Aerospace
Minimum Salary: $35,000

HEIDRICK & STRUGGLES, INC.
1221 McKinney St., Suite 3050, Houston, TX 77010; 713-237-9000
Areas of Specialization: General
Minimum Salary: $100,000

HEIDRICK & STRUGGLES, INC.
2200 Ross Ave., Suite 4700E, Dallas, TX 75201-2787
Areas of Specialization: General
Minimum Salary: $100,000

KELLY SERVICES–NC TECHNICAL
8340 Gateway E., Suite 210, El Paso, TX 79907; 915-595-2288
Areas of Specialization: Technical
Minimum Salary: Varies

KORN/FERRY INTERNATIONAL
500 N. Akard St., 3232 Lincoln Plaza, Dallas, TX 75201; 214-954-1834
Areas of Specialization: General
Minimum Salary: $100,000

KORN/FERRY INTERNATIONAL
1100 Louisiana St., Suite 2850, Houston, TX 77002; 713-651-1834
Areas of Specialization: General
Minimum Salary: $100,000

LAMALIE AMROP INTERNATIONAL
1601 Elm St., Suite 4150, Dallas, TX 75201; 214-754-0019
Areas of Specialization: General
Minimum Salary: $100,000

LAMALIE AMROP INTERNATIONAL
1301 McKinney St., Suite 3130, Houston, TX 77010; 713-739-8602
Areas of Specialization: General
Minimum Salary: $100,000

LEHMAN MCLESKEY
98 San Jacinto Blvd., Suite 440, Austin, TX 78701; 512-478-1131
Areas of Specialization General

Minimum Salary: $80,000

MANAGEMENT RECRUITERS
15400 Knoll Trail, Suite 230, Dallas, TX 75248; 214-960-1291
Areas of Specialization: Insurance, Pharmaceuticals
Minimum Salary: $35,000

RAY & BERNDTSON
2200 Ross Ave., Suite 4500 W, Dallas, TX 75201; 214-969-7620
Areas of Specialization: General
Minimum Salary: $105,000

SEARCH COM, INC.
12860 Hillcrest, Suite 101, Dallas, TX 75230; 214-490-0300
Areas of Specialization: Advertising, Marketing, Public Relations
Minimum Salary: $50,000

SPENCER STUART
1717 Main St., Suite 5300, Dallas, TX 75201; 214-658-1777
Areas of Specialization: General
Minimum Salary: $150,000

SPENCER STUART
1111 Bagby St., Suite 1616, Houston, TX 77002; 713-672-5200
Areas of Specialization: General
Minimum Salary: $150,000

TEKWORX, INC.
2350 N. Sam Houston Pkwy E., Suite 210, Houston, TX 77032; 281-590-8356
Areas of Specialization: Technology
Minimum Salary: $25,000

WARD HOWELL INTERNATIONAL, INC.
1601 Elm St., Suite 900, Dallas, TX 75201; 214-749-0099
Areas of Specialization: General
Minimum Salary: $75,000

WARD HOWELL INTERNATIONAL, INC.
1000 Louisiana St., Suite 3150, Houston, TX 77002; 713-655-7155
Areas of Specialization: General
Minimum Salary: $75,000

WITT/KIEFFER, FORD, HADELMAN, & LLOYD
8117 Preston Rd., Suite 690, Dallas, TX 75225; 214-739-1370
Areas of Specialization: General
Minimum Salary: $75,000

UTAH

ATLANTIC WEST INTERNATIONAL
6337 S. Highland Dr., Suite 300, Salt Lake City, UT 84121; 801-943-9944
Areas of Specialization: Health Services
Minimum Salary: $60,000

MANAGEMENT RECRUITERS
533 26th St., Suite 203B, Ogden, UT 84401; 801-621-1788
Areas of Specialization: General
Minimum Salary: $30,000

STM ASSOCIATES
230 S. 500 E., Suite 500, Salt Lake City, UT 84102; 801-531-6500
Areas of Specialization: Natural Resources
Minimum Salary: $75,000

VERMONT

MANAGEMENT RECRUITERS
187 St. Paul St., Burlington, VT 05401; 802-865-0541
Areas of Specialization: General
Minimum Salary: $45,000

J.R. PETERMAN ASSOCIATES, INC.
1250 Waterboro Rd.; 802-253-6304
Areas of Specialization: Insurance
Minimum Salary: $50,000

VIRGINIA

A LA CARTE INTERNATIONAL, INC.
3330 Pacifica Ave., Suite 500, Virginia Beach, VA 23451; 757-425-6111
Areas of Specialization: General
Minimum Salary: $65,000

BJB ASSOCIATES
1501 Crystal Dr., Suite 1024, Arlington, VA 22202; 703-413-0541
Areas of Specialization: General
Minimum Salary: $30,000

EXECUTIVE RESOURCE ASSOCIATES
1612 Bay Breeze Dr., Virginia Beach, VA 23454; 757-481-6221
Areas of Specialization: General
Minimum Salary: $45,000

FORTUNE PERSONNEL
4490 Holland Office Park, Suite 129, Virginia Beach, VA 23452; 757-497-7767
Areas of Specialization: Engineering, Technology
Minimum Salary: $40,000

MANAGEMENT RECRUITERS
5001-A Lee Hwy., Suite 102, Arlington, VA 22207; 703-276-1135
Web: www.htinfo.com
Areas of Specialization: General
Minimum Salary: $40,000

MANAGEMENT RECRUITERS
6620 W. Broad St., Suite 406, Richmond, VA 23230; 804-285-2071
Areas of Specialization: General
Minimum Salary: $20,000

MANAGEMENT RECRUITERS
1960 Electric Rd., Suite B, Roanoke, VA 24018; 540-989-1676
Areas of Specialization: General
Minimum Salary: $20,000

PROLINKS, INC..
3682 King St., Alexandria, VA 22302; 703-379-5882
Web: www.Career Resources.com
Areas of Specialization: Sports
Minimum Salary: $60,000

WASHINGTON

KORN/FERRY INTERNATIONAL
1 Union Sq., 600 University Ave., Suite 3111, Seattle, WA 98101; 206- 447-1834
Areas of Specialization: General
Minimum Salary: $75,000

MANAGEMENT RECRUITERS
W. 316 Boone Ave., Suite 370, Spokane, WA 99201; 509- 324-3333
Areas of Specialization: General
Minimum Salary: $20,000

MANAGEMENT RECRUITERS
535 Dock St., Suite 111, Tacoma, WA 98402; 206- 572-7542
Areas of Specialization: General
Minimum Salary: $20,000

MCHALE & ASSOICATES
1001 Fourth Ave., Suite 3200, Seattle, WA 98154; 206-230-9062
Areas of Specialization: Technology
Minimum Salary: $40,000

LARRY SIEGEL & ASSOCIATES
1111 Third Ave., Suite 2880, Seattle, WA 98101; 206- 622-4282
Areas of Specialization: General
Minimum Salary: $70,000

SOURCE ENGINEERING.
500 108th Ave NE, Suite 1780, Seattle, WA 98004; 206-454-6400
Areas of Specialization: Engineering
Minimum Salary: Varies

WEST VIRGINIA

DWYER CONSULTING GROUP, INC.
2 Cecil Pl., Wheeling, WV 26003; 304-243-1600
Areas of Specialization: General
Minimum Salary: $100,000

LOCUS INC.
P.O. Box 930, New Haven, WV 25265-0930; 304-882-2483
Areas of Specialization: Technology
Minimum Salary: $20,000

WISCONSIN

ASSOCIATED RECRUITERS
7144 N. Park Manor Dr., Milwaukee, WI 53224; 414-353-1933
Areas of Specialization: Packaging
Minimum Salary: $35,000

CONSULTANT RECRUITERS.
6842 N. Park Manor Dr., Milwaukee, WI 53224; 414-358-3036
Areas of Specialization: Consulting
Minimum Salary: $75,000

H.S. GROUP, INC.
2611 Libal St., Green Bay, WI 54301; 414-432-7444
Areas of Specialization: General
Minimum Salary: $25,000

KORDUS CONSULTING GROUP
1470 E. Standish Pl., Milwaukee, WI 53217; 414-228-7979
Areas of Specialization: Advertising, Marketing, Public Relations
Minimum Salary: $40,000

MANAGEMENT RECRUITERS, INC.
1711 Woolsey St., Suite D, Delavan, WI 53115; 414-728-8886
Areas of Specialization: General, Human Resources
Minimum Salary: Varies

WOJDULA & ASSOCIATES, LTD.
700 Rayovac Dr., Suite 204, Madison, WI 53711; 608-271-2000
Web: www.wojdula.com
Areas of Specialization: General
Minimum Salary: $75,000

WYOMING

MANAGEMENT RECRUITERS
1008 E. 21st St., Cheyenne, WY 82001; 307-635-8731
Areas of Specialization: General
Minimum Salary: $20,000

SERVICES
SALES RECRUITERS

THE CONSTANT DEMAND FOR QUALIFIED SALESPEOPLE is the primary reason that agencies that specialize in sales recruitment exist. Such sales recruiters can help narrow a search by trying to fill the job hunter's expectations in terms of salary, commission, perks, and territories, as well as clientele and future business prospects.

Many employment agencies and executive search firms also fill sales positions. In addition to the sales recruitment agencies listed below, such groups are also potential sources for sales job openings. Therefore, if you wish to seek employment through an agency as opposed to dealing directly with companies, ►See "Employment Agencies," pp. 569-591, and "Executive Recruiters," pp. 592-609.

Be aware that not all sales jobs are listed with agencies. As a result, if you contact companies as well as agencies directly, you will increase your chances of finding the right sales position.

ALABAMA

SALES CONSULTANTS
2 Office Park Circle, Suite 106, Birmingham, AL 35223; 205-871-1128

ALASKA

ALASKA EXECUTIVE SEARCH
821 North St., Suite 204, Anchorage, AK 99501; 907-276-5707

ARIZONA

SALES CONSULTANTS
6200 E. 14th St., Suite B-230, Tucson, AZ 85711; 520-745-2255

SALES RESOURCES, INC.
4350 E. Camelback Rd., Suite 200F, Phoenix, AZ 85018; 602-952-9060

ARKANSAS

SALES CONSULTANTS
1623 S. Dixieland Rd., Rogers, AR 72756; 501-631-4045

CALIFORNIA

BAST & ASSOCIATES, INC.
11726 San Vicente Blvd., Suite 200, Los Angeles, CA 90049; 310-207-2100

CLANTON & CO.
1095 N. Main St., Suite M, Orange, CA 92667; 714-532-5652

CULVER PERSONNEL, INC.
3447 Atlantic Ave., Suite 190, Long Beach, CA 90807; 310-427-0069

GATEWAY, LTD.
5162 Eagle Rock Blvd., Los Angeles, CA 90041; 213-258-7942

SALES CONSULTANTS
4811 Chippendale Dr., Suite 701, Sacramento, CA 95841; 916-344-3737

SALES CONSULTANTS
9455 Ridgehaven Ct., Suite 205, San Diego, CA 92123; 619-565-6600

SALES CONSULTANTS
2055 Gateway Pl., Suite 420, San Jose, CA 95110; 408-453-9999

SALES PROFESSIONALS PERSONNEL SERVICE
595 Market St., Suite 2500, San Francisco, CA 94105; 415-543-2828

COLORADO

THE PINNACLE SOURCE, INC.
9250 E. Costille Ave., Suite 603, Englewood, CO 80111; 303-792-5300

SALES CONSULTANTS
3033 S. Parker Rd., Suite 304, Aurora, CO 80014; 303-752-2550

SALES CONSULTANTS
13111 E. Briarwood Ave., Englewood, CO
80112; 303-706-0123

CONNECTICUT

DUSSICK MANAGEMENT ASSOCIATION
149 Durham Rd., Madison, CT 06443; 203-
245-9311

SALES CONSULTANTS
111 Prospect St., Stamford, CT 06901; 203-
327-3270

DELAWARE

MANAGEMENT RECRUITERS
501 Silverside Rd., Suite 140, Wilmington,
DE 19809; 302-789-7227

DISTRICT OF COLUM-BIA

MEE DERBY & CO.
1522 K St., NW, Suite 704, Washington, DC
20005; 202-842-8442

FLORIDA

THE DUVAL GROUP
9471 Baymeadows Rd., Suite 204, Jacksonville, FL 32216; 904-737-5770

EXECUTIVE SALES REGISTRY
14029 N. Dale Mabry Highway, Tampa, FL
33618; 813-879-1324

INTERNATIONAL RECRUITING SERVICES
P.O. Box Drawer 533976, Orlando, FL 32753;
407-896-9606

MANAGEMENT RECRUITERS
2121 Ponce de Leon Blvd., Suite 220, Miami,
FL 33134; 305-448-1608

SALES WORLD, INC.
899 W. Cypress Creek Rd., Ft. Lauderdale,
FL 33309; 954-492-0088

GEORGIA

HONOUR HUMAN RESOURCES ASSOCIATION
3400 Peachtree Rd., NE, Suite 123, Atlanta,
GA 30326; 404-261-7077

SALES CONSULTANTS
5901-C Peachtree-Dunwoody Rd., Suite 370,
Atlanta, GA 30328; 404-394-1300

SALES CONSULTANTS
2431 Habersham St., Savannah, GA 31401;
912-232-0132

SALESFORCE
3294 Woodrow Way, NE, Atlanta, GA 30319;
404-252-8566

HAWAII

SALES CONSULTANTS
810 Richards St., Suite 160-M, Honolulu, HI
96813; 808-533-3282

IDAHO

SALES CONSULTANTS
290 Bobwhite Ct., Suite 220, Boise, ID
83706; 208-336-6770

ILLINOIS

ACCURATE RECRUITING
180 N. LaSalle, Chicago, IL 60604; 312-357-
2500

SALES CONSULTANTS
20 N. Wabash, Suite 201, Chicago, IL 60611;
312-836-9100

SNELLING PERSONNEL SERVICES
100 N. LaSalle, Chicago, IL 60604; 312-419-
6100

WYLIE GROUP, LTD.
345 N. Canal St., Chicago, IL 60606; 312-
822-0333

INDIANA

C. J. WILLIAMS GROUP, INC.
5444 E. Indiana St., Suite 303, Evansville, IN
47715; 812-429-0100

MALLARD GROUP
3206 Mallard Cove Lane, Ft. Wayne, IN
46804; 219-436-3970

SALES CONSULTANTS
8200 Haverstick Rd., Suite 240, Indianapolis,
IN 46240; 317-257-5411

IOWA

EXECUTIVE RESOURCES
3716 Ingersoll Ave., Des Moines, IA 50312;
515-287-6880

MANAGEMENT RECRUITERS
150 1st Ave., NE, Suite 400, Cedar Rapids,
IA 52401; 319-366-8441

MANAGEMENT RECRUITERS
707 Cycare Plaza, Dubuque, IA 52001; 319-
583-1554

KANSAS

SALES CONSULTANTS
8441 E. 32nd St. N., Suite 100, Wichita, KS 67226; 316-634-1981

STONEBURNER ASSOCIATES, INC.
10000 W. 75th St., Suite 102, Shawnee Mission, KS 66204; 913-432-0055

KENTUCKY

SALES CONSULTANTS
1032 College St., Suite 102, Bowling Green, KY 42101; 502-843-1325

SALES CONSULTANTS
1930 Bishop Lane, Suite 426, Louisville, KY 40218; 502-456-4330

LOUISIANA

SALES CONSULTANTS
5551 Corporate Blvd., Suite 2-H, Baton Rouge, LA 70808; 504-928-2212

SHIELL PERSONNEL
5400 Jefferson Highway, New Orleans, LA 70123; 504-734-7986

MAINE

SALES CONSULTANTS
66 Pearl St., Suite 326, Portland, ME 04101; 207-775-6565

MARYLAND

ANN BOND ASSOCIATES, INC.
275 West St., Suite 304, Annapolis, MD 21401; 410-280-6002

SALES CONSULTANTS
575 S. Charles St., Suite 401, Baltimore, MD 21201; 410-727-5750

MASSACHUSETTS

DANA ASSOCIATES, INC.
131 State St., Suite 10, Boston, MA 02109; 617-248-0079

SALES AND MARKETING SEARCH, INC.
100 Conifer Dr., Suite 1020, Danvers, MA 01923; 508-777-5600

MICHIGAN

DUNHILL OF DETROIT, INC.
29350 Southfield Rd., Suite 115, Southfield, MI 48084; 810-557-1100

SALES CONSULTANTS
2860 Carpenter Rd., Sparrow Wood Office, Suite 300, Ann Arbor, MI 48108; 313-971-4900

SALES CONSULTANTS
900 E. Paris Ave., SE, Suite 301, Grand Rapids, MI 49546; 616-940-3900

MINNESOTA

BRIGHT SEARCH
8120 Penn Ave. S., Suite 167, Minneapolis, MN 55431; 612-884-8111

SALES CONSULTANTS
7550 France Ave. S., Suite 180, Minneapolis, MN 55435; 612-830-1420

MISSISSIPPI

MANAGEMENT RECRUITERS
2506 Lakeland Dr., Suite 408, Jackson, MS 39208; 601-936-7900

MISSOURI

INTERNATIONAL SALES RECRUITERS
708 W. 48th St., Suite 201, Kansas City, MO 64112; 816-561-5488

IRVIN–EDWARDS & ASSOCIATES
12300 Olive Blvd., Suite 302, St. Louis, MO 63141; 314-453-0200

SALES CONSULTANTS
3301 Rider Trail S., Suite 100, St. Louis, MO 63045; 314-344-0900

MONTANA

PATER SEARCH
561 Pinon Dr., Billings, MT 59105; 406-252-6789

NEBRASKA

RECRUITERS INTERNATIONAL, INC.
11330 Q St., Suite 218, Omaha, NE 68137; 402-339-9839

NEVADA

MANAGEMENT RECRUITERS
6875 W. Charleston Blvd., Suite B, Las Vegas, NV 89117; 702-254-4558

MANAGEMENT RECRUITERS
1025 Ridgeview Dr., Suite 100, Reno, NV 89509; 702-826-5243

SALES RECRUITERS

NEW HAMPSHIRE

LLOYD PERSONNEL
7 Medallion Ctr., Merrimack, NH 03054; 603-424-0020

SALES CONSULTANTS
6 Medallion Ctr., Merrimack, NH 03054; 603-424-3282

NEW JERSEY

RIDGEWOOD INTERMEDIARIES
51 S. Broad St., Ridgewood, NJ 07450; 201-444-9277

SALES CONSULTANTS
2 Hudson Pl., Baker Bldg., Hoboken, NJ 07030; 201-659-5205

NEW MEXICO

ROADRUNNER PERSONNEL
4015 Carlisle Blvd., NE, Suite C, Albuquerque, NM 87107; 505-881-1994

NEW YORK

DIVERSIFIED COMMUNICATION PROFESSIONALS
551 Fifth Ave., Suite 222, New York, NY 10176; 212-867-0066

DLB ASSOCIATES
271 Madison Ave., Suite 1406, New York, NY 10016; 212-953-6460

DON WALDRON AND ASSOCIATES
450 Seventh Ave., Suite 501, New York, NY 10123; 212-239-9110

JANOU PARKER ASSOCIATES
99 Park Ave., New York, NY 10003; 212-898-1288

PSP AGENCY
188 Montague St., Brooklyn, NY 11201; 718-596-3786

REDWOOD/CASEY, INC.
189 Broadway, New York, NY 10007; 212-843-8585

SALES CAREERS
1200 Midtown Tower, Rochester, NY 14604; 716-654-7800

SALES CONSULTANTS OF SYRACUSE, INC.
5730 Commons Park, P.O. Box 727; DeWitt, NY 13214; 315-449-0244

NORTH CAROLINA

SALES CONSULTANTS
5815 Westpark Dr., Suite 106, Charlotte, NC 28217; 704-525-9270

SALES CONSULTANTS
P.O. Box 35254, Greensboro, NC 27425; 919-665-9698

SANFORD ROSE ASSOCIATES
2915 Providence Rd., Suite 300, Charlotte, NC 28211; 704-366-0730

NORTH DAKOTA

JOBNET CAREER SERVICE
109½ Broadway, Fargo, ND 58102; 701-237-9262

OHIO

E. CHRISTIAN AND ASSOCIATES
1422 Euclid Ave., Cleveland, OH 44115; 216-656-0480

LAURIE MITCHELL & CO.
25018 Hazelmere Rd., Cleveland, OH 44122; 216-292-6001

MITCHELL MCCREA AND ASSOCIATES
1701 E. 12th St., Cleveland, OH 44122; 216-292-6001

SALES CONSULTANTS
11311 Cornell Park Dr., Suite 404, Cincinnati, OH 45242; 513-247-0707

SALES CONSULTANTS
20600 Chagrin Blvd., Suite 703, Cleveland, OH 44122; 216-561-6676

OKLAHOMA

SALES CAREERS
5929 N. May Ave., Oklahoma City, OK 73112; 405-848-6858

SALES CONSULTANTS
5801 E. 41st St., Suite 440, Tulsa, OK 74135; 918-663-6744

OREGON

SALES CONSULTANTS
5100 SW Macadam Ave., Suite 270, Portland, OR 97201; 503-241-1230

PENNSYLVANIA

CHASE–OWEN ASSOCIATES, INC.

1218 Chestnut St., Suite 603, Philadelphia, PA 19107; 215-923-0256

SALES CONSULTANTS
125 7th St., Pittsburgh, PA 15222; 412-281-6900

RHODE ISLAND

SALES CONSULTANTS
Office Commons 95, 349 Centerville Rd., Warwick, RI 02886; 401-737-3200

SOUTH CAROLINA

GOLD COAST PARTNERS
3 Cardinal Ct., Suite 239, Hilton Head Island, SC 29926; 803-757-5771

SALES CONSULTANTS
1310 Lady St., Suite 1010, Columbia, SC 29201; 803-779-7333

SOUTH DAKOTA

MANAGEMENT RECRUITERS
2600 S. Minnesota Ave., Suite 202, Sioux Falls, SD 57105; 605-334-9291

TENNESSEE

SALES CONSULTANTS
Shallowford Rd., Suite 520, Chattanooga, TN 37421; 423-894-5500

SALES CONSULTANTS
5865 Ridgeway Ctr., Pkwy. #300, Memphis, TN 38120; 901-761-2086

SOUTHWESTERN PROFESSIONAL SERV-ICES
2451 Atrium Way, Nashville, TN 37230; 615-391-2717

TEXAS

ACKERMAN JOHNSON CONSULTANTS, INC.
333 N. Sam Houston Pkwy. E., Suite 1210, Houston, TX 77060; 713-999-8879

THE ALTERNATIVES GROUP
4004 Belt Line Rd., Suite 210, Dallas, TX 75244; 214-788-9393

J. G. CONSULTANTS
8350 N. Central Expressway, Dallas, TX 75206; 214-696-9196

KLARK AND CO.
1616 W. Loop S., Houston, TX 77027; 713-622-2061

SALES CONSULTANTS
106 E. 6th St., Suite 430, Austin, TX 78701; 512-476-3555

SALES CONSULTANTS
3010 LBJ, Suite 1470, Dallas, TX 75234; 214-488-9191

UNLIMITED SOURCES, INC.
1 Riverway, Suite 1626, Houston, TX 77056; 713-621-4629

UTAH

MANAGEMENT RECRUITERS
6600 S. 1100 E., Suite 420, Salt Lake City, UT 84121; 801-264-9800

VERMONT

MARKET SEARCH ASSOCIATES
E. Hill Rd., Richmond, VT 05477; 802-434-2460

VIRGINIA

SALES CONSULTANTS
6620 W. Broad St., Suite 406, Richmond, VA 23230; 804-285-2071

SALES CONSULTANTS
4092 Foxwood Dr., Suite 102, Virginia Beach, VA 23462; 804-474-2752

SALES CONSULTANTS OF FAIRFAX, INC.
9840 Main St., Suite 201, Fairfax, VA 22033; 703-385-6050

WASHINGTON

RUSSELL LAGER AND ASSOCIATES
2200 6th Ave., Suite 1140, Seattle, WA 98121; 206-448-2616

SALES CONSULTANTS
275 118th Ave., SE, Suite 125, Bellevue, WA 98005; 206-455-1805

WEST VIRGINIA

KENT MANAGEMENT GROUP, INC.
836 6th Ave., Huntington, WV 25701; 304-523-8566

SALES RECRUITERS

WISCONSIN

SALES ASSOCIATES OF AMERICA
2525 N. Mayfair Rd., Suite 302, Milwaukee, WI 53226; 414-774-9800

SALES SEARCH, INC.
1011 N. Mayfair Rd., Milwaukee, WI 53217; 414-771-2828

SALES SPECIALISTS, INC.
5215 N. Ironwood Lane, Suite 106, Milwaukee, WI 53217; 414-228-8810

WYOMING

MANAGEMENT RECRUITERS
1008 E. 21st St., Cheyenne, WY 82001; 307-635-8731

SERVICES

TEMP AGENCIES

TEMPORARY AGENCIES ARE RAPIDLY GROWING in the career market. They specialize in placing employees in long- or short-term assignments in order to fill a company's specific need or to substitute for a permanent employee who is on vacation, leave, and so on. "Temp work" is ideal for those individuals who are in between jobs, who are looking for additional income, or who enjoy the numerous and varied professional opportunities temporary work offers.

Jobs offered by temp agencies vary in pay and responsibility, from entry level to professional. Among office workers, those who have computer, clerical, and communications skills are in demand. In the manufacturing and industrial fields, workers who can handle physically taxing jobs such as moving, painting, and cleaning are also in high demand. These types of jobs are classified as "Light Industrial" in the "Areas of Specialization" found at the end of each listing below.

Many temp agencies deal specifically with certain industries or types of jobs. Refer to the "Areas of Specialization" in the entries for these classifications. Note that "Technology" refers to the computer or electronics field, "Finance" to banking as well as the financial area, and "Trade" to plumbing, carpentry, and so on. Agencies that do not specialize in any particular area are classified as "General."

Since the number of temp agencies has skyrocketed in the last several years, no listing can be comprehensive. Many of the entries in this chapter are the branch offices of many of the larger chains specializing in temporary staffing. Also included are the listings for those agencies in major metropolitan areas that focus on general assignments, as well as those that focus on several of the major U.S. industries that generally employ temp workers.

Most of the agencies listed below are compensated by employers looking to fill positions rather than by job seekers. However, be sure to ask about possible exceptions before accepting work from a temp agency.

ALABAMA

LABOR READY
1601 2nd Ave. N., Birmingham, AL 35233; 205-324-5277
Areas of Specialization: General, Light Industrial

ALASKA

ADAMS AND ASSOCIATES
3201 C St., 402 Calais Ctr. 1, Anchorage, AK 99503; 907-561-5161
Areas of Specialization: General

MANPOWER
4300 B Str., Suite 302A, Fairbanks, AK 99503; 907-563-1440
Areas of Specialization: General, Light Industrial

ARIZONA

CAREER PATH TEMPORARY SERVICES, INC.
3200 E. Camelback Rd., Suite 171, Phoenix, AZ 85018; 602-956-5844
Areas of Specialization: Clerical, Construction, Manufacturing, Sales

LABORREADY
2947 W. Indian School Rd., Phoenix, AZ 85017; 602-233-8005
Areas of Specialization: General, Light Industrial

MANPOWER
645 E. Missouri, Suite 260, Phoenix, AZ 85012; 602-264-0871

WESTERN TEMPORARY SERVICES
316 E. Flower St., Phoenix, AZ 85012; 602-279-5301
Areas of Specialization: Accounting,

Administration, Human Resources, Management, Secretarial

ARKANSAS

SELECT TEMPORARY SERVICES OF FORT SMITH
101 N. 6th St., Suite 16, Ft. Smith, AR 72901; 501-785-3700
Areas of Specialization: General

SNELLING PERSONNEL SERVICE
One Financial Ctr., Suite 312, Little Rock, AR 72211; 501-223-2069
Areas of Specialization: General

CALIFORNIA

APPLE ONE SERVICES
1970 Broadway, Suite 110, Oakland, CA 94612; 510-835-0217
Areas of Specialization: Accounting, Clerical, Finance

BEVERLY HILLS BAR ASSOCIATION PERSONNEL SERVICES
300 S. Beverly Dr., Suite 214, Beverly Hills, CA 90212; 310-553-4575
Areas of Specialization: Law

DENT-ASSIST PERSONNEL SERVICE
725 30th St., Suite 206, Sacramento, CA 95816; 916-443-1113
Areas of Specialization: Health Services (Dental)

EDP/TEMPS AND CONTRACT SERVICES
685 Market St., Suite 470, San Francisco, CA 94105; 415-952-5010
Areas of Specialization: Accounting, Engineering, Finance, Insurance, Manufacturing, Publishing, Science, Technology

EDP/TEMPS OF CALIFORNIA
800 S. Figueroa St., Suite 790, Los Angeles, CA 90017; 213-624-9810
Areas of Specialization: Accounting, Engineering, Finance, Insurance, Manufacturing, Publishing, Science, Technology

INTERIM PERSONNEL
24301 Southland Dr., Suite 207, Hayward, CA 94545; 510-785-5300
Areas of Specialization: General

INTERIM PERSONNEL
2050 W. Chapman Ave., Suite 104, Orange, CA 92668; 714-939-1266
Areas of Specialization: General

KELLY SERVICES
1111 Civic Dr., Suite 240, Walnut Creek, CA 94596; 510-746-1460
Areas of Specialization: General

MANPOWER
355 S. Grand Ave., Los Angeles, CA 90071; 213-680-0917
Areas of Specialization: General, Light Industrial

NORRELL TEMPORARY SERVICES, INC., OF CALIFORNIA
790 E. Colorado, Suite 102, Arcadia, CA 91101; 818-446-8574
Areas of Specialization: Bilingual, Clerical, Data Processing, Technology

NORRELL TEMPORARY SERVICES, INC., OF CALIFORNIA
4525 Wilshire Blvd., Suite 120, Los Angeles, CA 90010; 213-964-9566
Areas of Specialization: Bilingual, Clerical, Data Processing, Technology

OLSTEN TEMPORARY SERVICES
1000 Broadway, Suite 248, Oakland, CA 94607; 510-987-7555
Areas of Specialization: Accounting, Clerical, Law, Secretarial

PERSONNEL POOL OF SACRAMENTO
2862 Arden Way, Suite 225, Sacramento, CA 95825; 916-484-1450
Areas of Specialization: Construction, Food and Beverages, Health Services, Law, Manufacturing, Marketing, Sales

ROBERT HALF INTERNATIONAL
1901 Ave. of the Stars, Suite 490, Los Angeles, CA 90067; 310-286-6800
Areas of Specialization: Accounting, Finance, Technology

STAFF BUILDERS OF CALIFORNIA
9520 Padgent, #104, San Diego, CA 92126; 619-536-8773
Areas of Specialization: General

TECH/AID OF CALIFORNIA
15720 Ventura Blvd., Suite 608, Encino, CA 91436; 818-906-1145
Areas of Specialization: Design, Engineering, Manufacturing, Technology

TECH/AID OF CALIFORNIA
1850 E. 17th St., Suite 109, Santa Ana, CA 92701; 714-953-1717
Areas of Specialization: Design, Engineering, Manufacturing, Technology

TANDEM STAFFING
1010 Broadway Blvd., Chula Vista, CA
91911; 619-476-9675
Areas of Specialization: General, Light Industrial

TANDEM STAFFING
7413 S. Garfield Ave., Monterey Park, CA
91754; 818-727-9243
Areas of Specialization: General, Light Industrial

TANDEM STAFFING
14410 Washington Ave., Suite 120, San Leandro, CA 94578; 510-483-0377
Areas of Specialization: General, Light Industrial

COLORADO

MANPOWER
14305 E. Alameda Ave., Suite 310, Aurora,
CO 80012; 303-364-7261
Areas of Specialization: General, Clerical

PERSONNEL PLUS
770 W. Hamden, Suite 310, Englewood, CO
80110; 303-781-1659
Areas of Specialization: Clerical

TEMP FORCE OF DENVER
140 E. 19th Ave., Suite 500, Denver, CO
80203; 303-831-1096
Areas of Specialization: General

CONNECTICUT

EDP/TEMPS OF CONNECTICUT
727 Post Rd. E., Westport, CT 06880; 203-227-2088
Areas of Specialization: Engineering, Finance, Insurance, Manufacturing, Nonprofit, Publishing, Science, Technology

MANPOWER
65 Bank St., Waterbury, CT 06702; 203-756-8303
Areas of Specialization: Accounting, Clerical, Secretarial, Trades

MANPOWER
10 Columbus Blvd., 8th Floor, Hartford, CT
06106; 860-727-1811

STAFF BUILDERS
1234 Summer St., Stamford, CT 06905; 203-853-1411
Areas of Specialization: General

DELAWARE

PLACERS, INC.
111 Continental Dr., #201, Christiana, DE
19713; 302-456-6800
Areas of Specialization: General, Technology

DISTRICT OF COLUMBIA

DON RICHARD ASSOCIATES OF WASHINGTON, DC
1717 K St., Nw, Suite 1000, Washington, DC
20006; 202-463-7210
Areas of Specialization: Accounting, Finance, Technology

MANPOWER
1130 Connecticut Ave., Suite 530, Washington, DC 20036; 202-331-8300
Areas of Specialization: General, Light Industrial

STAFF BUILDERS, INC., OF WASHINGTON, DC
810 1st St., NE, Suite 410, Washington, DC
20002; 202-682-2200
Areas of Specialization: General

FLORIDA

INTERIM PERSONNEL
2551 Drew St., Suite 102, Clearwater, FL
34625; 813-797-2171
Areas of Specialization: General

INTERIM PERSONNEL
10006 N. Dale Mabry, Suite 108, Tampa, FL
33710; 813-963-0066
Areas of Specialization: General

KELLY SERVICES
3300 PGA Blvd., Suite 330, Palm Beach Gardens, FL 33410; 407-694-0116
Areas of Specialization: Clerical, Manufacturing, Science, Technology

KELLY SERVICES
1700 Palm Beach Lakes Blvd., Suite 520,
West Palm Beach, FL 33401; 407-686-2900
Areas of Specialization: Clerical, Manufacturing, Science, Technology

TANDEM STAFFING
3100 NW 27th Ave., Miami, FL 33142; 305-573-1516
Areas of Specialization: General, Light Industrial

STAFF BUILDERS
3075 W. Oakland Park Blvd., Suite 100, Ft.
Lauderdale, FL 33311; 954-486-5506
Areas of Specialization: General

GEORGIA

TANDEM STAFFING
3523 Memorial Dr., Decatur, GA 30032; 404-284-5000
Areas of Specialization: General, Light Industrial

MANPOWER
41 Perimeter Center E., Suite 150, Atlanta, GA 30346; 770-399-6422
Areas of Specialization: General, Light Industrial

MANPOWER
1820 Wynnton Rd., Columbus, GA 31906; 706-596-1313
Areas of Specialization: General, Technical

NORRELL CORPORATION
3535 Piedmont Rd., NE, Bldg. 14, Atlanta, GA 30305; 404-262-2100
Areas of Specialization: Banking, Clerical

STAFF BUILDERS
1835 Savoy Dr., Suite 205, Atlanta, GA 30341; 404-457-1245
Areas of Specialization: General

HAWAII

INTERIM PERSONNEL
1441 Kapiolani Blvd., Honolulu, HI 96814; 808-942-2333
Areas of Specialization: General

IDAHO

INTERIM PERSONNEL
8783 W. Hackamore, Boise, ID 83704; 208-378-1338
Areas of Specialization: General

MANPOWER
8050 Rifleman, Suite 200, Boise, ID 83704; 208-375-8040

ILLINOIS

BECO GROUP
200 S. Prospect Ave., Park Ridge, IL 60068; 847-825-8000
Areas of Specialization: Accounting, Architecture, Clerical, Engineering, Health Services, Technology

KELLY TEMPORARY SERVICES
1101 W. 31st St., Suite 240, Downers Grove, IL 60515; 630-964-8488
Areas of Specialization: Clerical

MANPOWER
500 W. Madison St., Suite 2950, Chicago, IL 60661; 312-648-4555

NORRELL SERVICES
9399 W. Higgins Rd., Suite 640, Rosemont, IL 60018; 847-518-8500
Areas of Specialization: Accounting, Administration, Industrial, Outsourcing Services

OLSTEN OF CHICAGO, INC.
16 W. Ontario, Chicago, IL 60610; 312-944-3880
Areas of Specialization: General

ROBERT HALF INTERNATIONAL
205 N. Michigan Ave., Suite 3301, Chicago, IL 60601; 312-616-8200
Areas of Specialization: Accounting, Administration, Finance, Law, Technology

TANDEM STAFFING
3348 N. Pulaski, Chicago, IL 60041; 773-282-2300
Areas of Specialization: General, Light Industrial

TANDEM STAFFING
1547 N. Western Ave., Chicago, IL 60622; 773-282-2300
Areas of Specialization: General, Light Industrial

INDIANA

TANDEM STAFFING
1238 N. Pennsylvania Ave., Indianapolis, IN 46202; 317-636-6693
Areas of Specialization: General, Light Industrial

IOWA

ALL STAFF INC.
710 E. Kimber Rd., Davenport, IA 52807; 319-388-4751

TANDEM STAFFING
3921 NE 14th St., Des Moines, IA 50313; 515-266-8802
Areas of Specialization: General, Light Industrial

KANSAS

ACE PERSONNEL FRANCHISE CORP.
6400 Glenwood, Suite 309, Overland Park, KS 66202; 913-362-0090

SNELLING PERSONNEL SERVICE
7123 W. 95ᵗʰ St., Overland Park, KS 66212;
913-385-5100
Areas of Specialization: General

K E N T U C K Y

TANDEM STAFFING
3206 Preston Highway, Louisville, KY
40213; 502-636-3444
Areas of Specialization: General, Light Industrial

L O U I S I A N A

INTERIM PERSONNEL
9634 Airline Highway, Suite 1A, Baton
Rouge, LA 70815; 318-445-9000
Areas of Specialization: General

MANPOWER
2835 Hollywood, Suite 170, Shreveport, LA
71108; 318-631-4242
Areas of Specialization: *General*

TANDEM STAFFING
2025 Canal St., #100, New Orleans, LA
70112; 504-522-1814
Areas of Specialization: General, Light Industrial

M A I N E

AMES PERSONNEL SERVICE
34 Hennessey Ave., P.O. Box 651, Brunswick, ME 04011; 207-729-5158
Areas of Specialization: General

MANPOWER
70 Center St., Portland, ME 04101; 207-774-8258

M A R Y L A N D

ADECCO
300 E. Lombard St., Suite 935, Baltimore,
MD 21202; 410-837-2444
Areas of Specialization: Accounting,
Data Processing, Manual Labor, Secretarial

ADMAN PERSONNEL
1112 Wayne Ave., Silver Spring, MD 20910;
301-565-3900
Areas of Specialization: Accounting,
Clerical, Finance, Marketing, Sales,
Technology

DUNHILL OF ROCKVILLE
414 Hungerford Dr., Suite 252, Rockville,
MD 20850; 301-424-0450
Areas of Specialization: Accounting,

Clerical, Finance

ECHO STAFFING SERVICES
10227 Wincopin Circle, Columbia, MD
21044; 410-992-1940
Areas of Specialization: General

MANPOWER
120 E. Baltimore St., Suite 1810, Baltimore,
MD 21202; 410-685-0697
Areas of Specialization: General, Light Industrial

SNELLING PERSONNEL
20 S. Charles St., Sun Life Bldg., Baltimore,
MD 21201; 410-528-9400
Areas of Specialization: General

STAFF BUILDERS, INC., OF MARYLAND
20 Charles St., Baltimore, MD 21201; 410-525-3000
Areas of Specialization: Health Services

TAC/TEMPS, INC., OF MARYLAND
7500 Greenway Ctr. Dr., Suite 330,
Greenville, MD 20770; 301-963-9590
Areas of Specialization: Accounting,
Advertising, Clerical, Education, Finance, Health Services, Marketing, Sales

TECH/AID OF MARYLAND
7000 Security Blvd., Baltimore, MD 21247;
410-597-9550
Areas of Specialization: Architecture,
Broadcasting, Construction, Engineering,
Manufacturing, Science, Technology

VICTOR TEMPORARY SERVICES OF BALTIMORE
102 W. Pennsylvania Ave., Suite 204, Towson, MD 21204; 410-828-8071
Areas of Specialization: General

M A S S A C H U S E T T S

KELLY TEMPORARY SERVICES
1601 Trapelo Rd., Waltham, MA 02154; 617-890-7778
Areas of Specialization: Clerical, Marketing, Sales

MANPOWER
101 Federal St., Boston, MA 02110; 617-443-4100
Areas of Specialization: General, Light Industrial

MANPOWER
One Monarch Pl., Springfield, MA 01144;

413-732-1171
Areas of Specialization: General

NETWORK PERSONNEL, INC.
1661 Worcester Rd., #101, Framingham, MA
01701; 508-879-9251
Areas of Specialization: Accounting,
Clerical, Manufacturing, Secretarial

NEW BOSTON ASSOCIATES
16 Wheeling Ave., Woburn, MA 01801; 617-
938-1910
Areas of Specialization: Accounting,
Engineering, Finance, Technology

ROMAC AND ASSOCIATES
125 Summer St., Boston, MA 02110; 617-
439-4300
Areas of Specialization: Accounting, Finance

STAFF BUILDERS
529 Main St., Suite 101, Boston, MA 02129;
617-241-0224
Areas of Specialization: Health Services,
Secretarial

TAC/TEMPS
400 Franklin St., Suite 302, Braintree, MA
02184; 617-479-0666
Areas of Specialization: Clerical

TAC/TEMPS
265 Winn St., Burlington, MA 01803; 617-
273-2500
Areas of Specialization: Clerical

TAC/TEMPS
124 Mt. Auburn St., Cambridge, MA 02138;
617-354-5202
Areas of Specialization: Clerical

MICHIGAN

CONTRACT PROFESSIONALS
4141 W. Walton Blvd., Waterford, MI 48329;
313-673-3800
Areas of Specialization: Architecture,
Engineering, Science, Technology

INTERIM PERSONNEL
26329 Southfield Rd., Lathrup Village, MI
48076; 248-557-7444
Areas of Specialization: General

INTERIM PERSONNEL
31509 Plymouth Rd., #813, Livonia, MI
48154; 734-261-3830
Areas of Specialization: General

TANDEM STAFFING
3313 Rochester Rd., Royal Oak, MI 48073;
810-616-0100
Areas of Specialization: General, Light Industrial

MANPOWER
25300 Telegraph Rd., Suite 250, Southfield,
MI 48075; 248-351-0416
Areas of Specialization: General, Light Industrial

METRO STAFF
28500 Southfield Rd., Lathrup Village, MI
48076; 810-557-8700
Areas of Specialization: General

TRILLIUM STAFFING
3401 E. Saginaw, Suite 109, Lansing, MI
48912; 517-351-5553
Areas of Specialization: General

MINNESOTA

INTERIM PERSONNEL
222 S. 9th St., Minneapolis, MN 55402; 612-
333-7557
Areas of Specialization: General

TANDEM STAFFING
1304 E. Lake St., Minneapolis, MN 55407;
612-721-9010
Areas of Specialization: General, Light Industrial

MISSISSIPPI

EXPRESS PERSONNEL SERVICES
1425 Lakeland Dr., Suite 110-B, Jackson, MS
39216; 601-366-8585
Areas of Specialization: General

MANPOWER
3452 Pascagoula Place, Suite 1, Pascagoula,
MS 39567; 228-769-8932
Areas of Specialization: General

MISSOURI

CROWN TEMPORARY SERVICE OF MISSOURI
3316 Broadway St., Kansas City, MO 64111;
816-931-3380
Areas of Specialization: Accounting,
Clerical, Engineering, Finance, Insurance, Law, Manufacturing

CROWN TEMPORARY SERVICE OF MIS-
SOURI
9666 Olive St., Suite 100, Olivette, MO
63132; 314-993-5333
Areas of Specialization: Accounting,
Clerical, Engineering, Finance, Human
Resources, Law, Manufacturing

INTERIM PERSONNEL
1 Busch Pl., St. Louis, MO 63146; 314-577-2187
Areas of Specialization: General

TANDEM STAFFING
1525 N. Broadway, St. Louis, MO 63102; 314-421-5005
Areas of Specialization: General, Light Industrial

MANPOWER
200 N. Broadway, St. Louis, MO 63102; 314-241-1356
Areas of Specialization: General, Light Industrial

OLSTEN SERVICES—HEADQUARTERS
2025 Craigshire Dr., P.O. Box 28369, St. Louis, MO 63146; 314-434-2800
Areas of Specialization: Accounting, Health Services, Law, Manufacturing, Secretarial

PERSONNEL POOL OF AMERICA, INC.
9738 Lackland, St. Louis, MO 63114; 314-427-5555
Areas of Specialization: Clerical, Food and Beverages, Law, Manufacturing

MONTANA

EXPRESS PERSONNEL SERVICES
317 16th St. W., Billings, MT 59102; 406-252-5050
Areas of Specialization: General

MANPOWER
1018 Burlington, Suite 100, Missoula, MT 59801; 406-549-5330
Areas of Specialization: General

NEBRASKA

MANPOWER
1001 S. 70th St., Suite 219, Lincoln, NE 68510; 402-484-5533

TANDEM STAFFING
2412 Cumming St., Omaha, NE 68131; 402-341-7200
Areas of Specialization: General, Light Industrial

NEVADA

INTERIM PERSONNEL
2245 Renaissance Dr., Las Vegas, NV 89119; 702-736-1585
Areas of Specialization: General

TANDEM STAFFING
1509 S. Commerce St., Las Vegas, NV 89102; 702-384-4300
Areas of Specialization: General, Light Industrial

NEW HAMPSHIRE

MANPOWER
310 Highlaaander Way, Manchester, NH 03103; 603-625-6994
Areas of Specialization: Technical

TAC/TEMPS, INC., OF NEW HAMPSHIRE
2 Wellman Ave., Stabile Ctr., Nashua, NH 03060; 603-882-4200
Areas of Specialization: Accounting, Advertising, Clerical, Education, Health Services, Insurance, Law, Sales

NEW JERSEY

MANPOWER
212 Carnegie Center, Suite 108, Princeton, NJ 08540; 609-452-8484
Areas of Specialization: General

UNITEMP TEMPORARY PERSONNEL
38 Meadowland Pkwy., Secaucus, NJ 07094; 201-867-2581
Areas of Specialization: Secretarial

NEW MEXICO

TANDEM STAFFING
1600 San Pedro Dr., NE, Albuquerque, NM 87110; 505-268-8352
Areas of Specialization: General, Light Industrial

NEW YORK

CAMEO TEMPORARY SERVICES, INC.
507 Fifth Ave., New York, NY 10017; 212-986-1122
Areas of Specialization: General

ECHO TEMPORARIES
33 Walt Whitman Rd., Huntington, NY 11746; 516-673-6005
Areas of Specialization: Finance, Food and Beverages, Law, Secretarial

MANPOWER
161 Ave. of the Americas, New York, NY 10013; 212-366-6005
Areas of Specialization: General, Light Industrial

MANPOWER
540 Broadway, 5th Floor, Albany, NY 12207;
518-434-8251
Areas of Specialization: General

MANPOWER
135 Delaware Ave., 2nd Floor, Buffalo, NY
14202; 716-854-4000
Areas of Specialization: General

STAFF BUILDERS, INC., BUSINESS SERVICES
122 E. 42nd St., Suite 201, New York, NY
10168; 212-867-2345
Areas of Specialization: General

TEMP FORCE OF LONG ISLAND
425 Broadhollow Rd., Melville, NY 11747;
516-293-7050
Areas of Specialization: General

TEMP FORCE OF NEW YORK
180 Broadway, Suite 1101, New York, NY
10038; 212-267-TEMP
Areas of Specialization: General

TEMPOSITIONS, INC.
420 Lexington Ave., Room 555, New York,
NY 10170; 212-490-7400
Areas of Specialization: Accounting,
Advertising, Finance, Law, Publishing

TEMPS & SERVICES, INC.
2 Penn Plaza, Suite 1190, New York, NY
10121; 212-947-6033
Areas of Specialization: Accounting,
Engineering, Finance, Insurance, Manufacturing, Science, Technology

WALKER BUSINESS SERVICES
23 W. State St., Wellsville, NY 14895; 716-
593-6129
Areas of Specialization: General

NORTH CAROLINA

INTERIM PERSONNEL
4300 Six Forks Rd., Raleigh, NC 27615; 919-
420-0026
Areas of Specialization: Accounting,
Clerical, Finance

OLSTEN STAFFING
2301 W. Meadowview Rd., Suite 100,
Greensboro, NC 27407; 919-852-0500
Areas of Specialization: General

NORTH DAKOTA

INTERIM PERSONNEL
1450 S. 25th St., Fargo, ND 58103; 701-298-
8300
Areas of Specialization: General

OHIO

ADECCO EMPLOYMENT SERVICES
3655 Soldano Blvd., Columbus, OH 43228;
614-279-6614
Areas of Specialization: Clerical, Construction, Food and Beverages, Human
Resources

CROWN TEMPORARY SERVICES OF CIN-CINNATI
230 Northland Blvd., Cincinnati, OH 45246;
513-772-7242
Areas of Specialization: Accounting,
Clerical, Engineering, Finance, Insurance, Law, Manufacturing

CROWN TEMPORARY SERVICES OF CLEVELAND
5010 Mayfield Rd., Lyndhurst, OH 44124;
216-692-0707
Areas of Specialization: Accounting,
Clerical, Engineering, Finance, Insurance, Law, Manufacturing

INTERIM PERSONNEL
832 Terminal Tower, Suite 832, Cleveland,
OH 44113; 216-781-3100
Areas of Specialization: General

INTERIM PERSONNEL
25 Milford Rd., Suites 8 & 9, Hudson, OH
44236; 216-650-4334
Areas of Specialization: General

MANPOWER
1 Cleveland Ct., 1375 E. 9th St., Cleveland,
OH 44114; 216-771-5474
Areas of Specialization: General, Light Industrial

MANPOWER
895 Central Ave., Suite 101, Cincinnati, OH
45202; 513-621-7330
Areas of Specialization: General, Light
Industrial

MANPOWER
2536 Scarborough Blvd., Columbus, OH
43232; 614-863-3400
Areas of Specialization: Technical

MICRO/TEMPS AND EDP/TEMPS OF OHIO
1440 Snow Rd., Parma, OH 44134; 216-749-
0516
Areas of Specialization: Accounting,
Engineering, Finance, Insurance, Manufacturing, Publishing, Science, Technology

NORRELL SERVICES
124 N. Summitt, Suite 200A, Toledo, OH
43604; 419-874-9114
Areas of Specialization: Accounting,
Clerical, Human Resources

TANDEM STAFFING
5287 Northfield Rd., Bedford Heights, OH
44146; 216-662-9960
Areas of Specialization: General, Light Industrial

OKLAHOMA

INTERIM PERSONNEL
6801 S. Western, Suite 201, Oklahoma City,
OK 73139; 405-634-7422
Areas of Specialization: General

OREGON

TANDEM STAFFING
2424 E. Burnside, Portland, OR 97214; 503-233-3649
Areas of Specialization: General, Light Industrial

PENNSYLVANIA

ADECCO
1760 Market St., Philadelphia, PA 19103;
215-567-2390
Areas of Specialization: General

ADVANCE PERSONNEL
P.O. Box 8383, Reading, PA 19603; 610-374-4089
Areas of Specialization: Administration,
Clerical, Customer Service, Data Processing, Law, Secretarial

CAREERS U.S.A.
1825 JFK Blvd., Philadelphia, PA 19103;
215-561-3800
Areas of Specialization: General

INTERIM PERSONNEL
1617 JFK Blvd., Suite 240, Philadelphia, PA
19103; 215-561-3322
Areas of Specialization: Clerical, Secretarial

KEY SERVICES, INC.
1055 Westlakes Dr., Berwin, PA 19312; 215-251-9813
Areas of Specialization: Clerical

MANPOWER
10 Penn Ctr., Suite 615, 801 Market St.,
Philadelphia, PA 19103; 215-568-4050
Areas of Specialization: General, Light Industrial

MANPOWER
881 Marcon Blvd., Allentown, PA 18103;
610-266-2510
Areas of Specialization: General

MANPOWER
100 State St., Suite 101, Erie, PA 16507; 814-453-7901
Areas of Specialization: General

OLSTEN TEMPORARY SERVICES OF PHILADELPHIA
1617 JFK Blvd., Suite 420, Philadelphia, PA
19103; 215-568-7795
Areas of Specialization: General

PROTOCOL
400 Market St., Philadelphia, PA 19106; 215-592-7111
Areas of Specialization: General

STAFF BUILDERS
1 Bala Plaza, Suite 127, Bala Cynwyd, PA
19004; 215-783-0306
Areas of Specialization: General

TAC/TEMPS, INC., OF PENNSYLVANIA
1617 JFK Blvd., Suite 326, Philadelphia, PA
19103; 215-568-4466
Areas of Specialization: Advertising,
Clerical, Education, Finance, Health
Services, Insurance, Law, Sales, Transportation

RHODE ISLAND

KELLY TEMPORARY SERVICES
70 Jefferson Blvd., Warwick, RI 02888; 401-674-4627
Areas of Specialization: Clerical, Marketing, Sales

SOUTH CAROLINA

ADVANTAGE TEMPORARY SERVICES, INC.
P.O. Box 2952, Spartanburg, SC 29304; 864-585-6562
Areas of Specialization: Clerical, Manufacturing, Secretarial

MANPOWER
4975 La Cross Rd., Suite 157, N. Charleston,
SC 29418; 803-554-0285
Areas of Specialization: General

MANPOWER
209 Stoneridge Dr., Suite 101, Columbia, SC
29210; 803-765-2971
Areas of Specialization: General

TALENT TREE
25 Woodslake Rd., Suite 222, Greenville, SC
29607; 864-233-4301
Areas of Specialization: General

SOUTH DAKOTA

INTERIM PERSONNEL
2600 S. Minnesota, Sioux Falls, SD 57105;
605-335-6010
Areas of Specialization: General

TENNESSEE

FEDERAL DATA SERVICES
4013 LaMar Ave., Memphis, TN 38116; 901-360-9088
Areas of Specialization: Engineering, Health Services, Marketing, Sales, Technology

NORRELL SERVICES
3100 Directors Row, Memphis, TN 38131;
901-332-1110
Areas of Specialization: Accounting, Clerical, Finance, Insurance, Secretarial

OLSTEN TEMPORARY SERVICES OF KNOXVILLE
6906 Kingston Pike, Suite 100, Knoxville, TN 37919; 423-694-9449
Areas of Specialization: General

SOUTHERN TEMP, INC.
701 Cherokee Blvd., Suite A, Chattanooga, TN 37405; 423-266-8367
Areas of Specialization: General

STAFF BUILDERS, INC., OF TENNESSEE
6060 Primacy Pkwy., Suite 238, Memphis, TN 38119; 901-767-8233
Areas of Specialization: General

TEXAS

ASHLEY SERVICES
318 W. Main St., Suite 101, Arlington, TX 76010; 817-277-2691
Areas of Specialization: General

ATTORNEY RESOURCE, INC.
2301 Cedar Springs Rd., Suite 350, Dallas, TX 75201; 214-922-8050
Areas of Specialization: Law

CDI CORPORATION
P.O. Box 612225, Dallas, TX 75261; 214-480-8333
Areas of Specialization: Architecture, Engineering, Manufacturing, Science, Technology

FINANCIAL PROFESSIONALS
4100 Spring Valley Rd., Suite 307, Dallas, TX 75244; 214-991-8999
Areas of Specialization: Finance

INTERIM PERSONNEL
5177 Richmond, Suite 245, Houston, TX 77056; 713-629-1080
Areas of Specialization: General

KELLY TEMPORARY SERVICES
1800 Teague Dr., Suite 100, Sherman, TX 75090; 903-893-7777
Areas of Specialization: Accounting, Clerical, Engineering, Food and Beverages, Health Services, Science, Technology

TANDEM STAFFING
9336 Irvington Blvd., Houston, TX 77022; 713-699-8367
Areas of Specialization: General, Light Industrial

MANPOWER
1616 S. Kentucky, Suite 325, Amarillo, TX 79102; 806-358-6221
Areas of Specialization: General, Light Industrial

MANPOWER
440 Louisiana, Suite 470, Houston, TX 77002; 713-228-3131
Areas of Specialization: General, Light Industrial

MANPOWER
5402 S. Staples St., Suite 103, Corpus Christi, TX 78411; 512-991-1196
Areas of Specialization: General, Light Industrial

NORRELL SERVICES OF HOUSTON
2727 Allen Pkwy., Suite 810, Houston, TX 77019; 713-227-6673
Areas of Specialization: Clerical

TEMPORARIES, INC.
1555 Mockingbird Lane, Suite 218, Dallas, TX 75235; 214-630-0365
Areas of Specialization: General

VOLT TEMPORARY SERVICES OF DALLAS
12900 N. Preston Rd., Suite 150, Dallas, TX 75230; 214-386-6968
Areas of Specialization: Clerical, Engineering, Manufacturing, Science, Technology

UTAH

INTERIM PERSONNEL
175 E., 6100 S., Salt Lake City, UT 84107;
801-261-8880
Areas of Specialization: General

MANPOWER
4155 Harrison Blvd., Suite 103, Ogden, UT 84403; 801-621-5228
Areas of Specialization: General

VERMONT

PERSONNEL CONNECTION, INC.
272 S. Main St., Rutland, VT 05701;
802-773-3737
Areas of Specialization: General

MANPOWER
1795 Williston Rd., S. Burlington, VT 05403;
802-862-5747
Areas of Specialization: General

VIRGINIA

CORE PERSONNEL
8201 Greensborough Rd., Suite 1219,
McLean, VA 22102; 703-556-9610
Areas of Specialization: Technology

MANPOWER
11832 Rock Landing Dr., Suite 204, Newport
News, VA 23606; 757-873-2260
Areas of Specialization: General

MANPOWER
1051 E. Cary, Suite 102, Richmond, VA
23219; 804-780-1800
Areas of Specialization: General

ROBERT HALF INTERNATIONAL
1100 Wilson Blvd., Suite 900, Arlington, VA
22209; 703-243-3600
Areas of Specialization: Accounting,
Clerical, Data Processing, Finance

TAC/TEMPS, INC.
1700 N. Moore St., Suite 1225, Arlington, VA
22209; 703-522-4988
Areas of Specialization: General

TAC/TEMPS OF VIRGINIA
2095 Chain Bridge Rd., Suite 100, Vienna,
VA 22182; 703-893-5260
Areas of Specialization: Advertising,
Clerical, Education, Health Services,
Law, Marketing, Sales, Transportation

WASHINGTON

GILMORE TEMPORARY PERSONNEL
2722 Colby Ave., Suite 414, Everett, WA
98201; 360-252-1195
Areas of Specialization: General

TANDEM STAFFING
4069 Rainier Ave. S., Seattle, WA 98118;
206-725-6911
Areas of Specialization: General, Light Industrial

MANPOWER
U.S. Bank Ctr., Suite 1750, 1420 5th Ave.,
Seattle, WA 98101; 206-583-0880
Areas of Specialization: General, Light In-
dustrial

STAFF BUILDERS, INC., OF WASHINGTON
10740 Meridian Ave. N., Suite 102, Seattle,
WA 98133; 206-364-0535
Areas of Specialization: General

WEST VIRGINIA

INTERIM PERSONNEL
1613 Canal Blvd. W., Charleston, WV 25301;
304-345-7665
Areas of Specialization: General

MANPOWER
528 Fifth Ave., Huntington, WV 25708; 304-
529-3031
Areas of Specialization: General

WISCONSIN

TANDEM STAFFING
322 E. Ray St., Milwaukee, WI 53207; 414-
744-7670
Areas of Specialization: General, Light Industrial

MANPOWER
1427 State Road 16, La Crosse, WI 54601;
608-781-8899
Areas of Specialization: General, Light Industrial

WYOMING

EXPRESS PERSONNEL SERVICES
2205 E. Pershing Blvd., Cheyenne, WY
82001; 307-634-1635
Areas of Specialization: General

MANPOWER
907 N. Poplar St., Suite 242, Casper, WY
82601; 307-237-2523

ORGANIZATIONS

Professional organizations abound that can provide valuable information and opportunities for job seekers. At home or abroad, in the trades and in the professions, there are organizations you should know about, which are discussed in the chapters in this section.

ORGANIZATIONS
CHAMBERS OF COMMERCE

CHAMBERS OF COMMERCE AROUND THE WORLD can be useful for those who seek jobs overseas. There are different types of chambers in this chapter. They are divided into three categories:

1. U.S. Chambers of Commerce Abroad
2. Foreign Chambers of Commerce Abroad
3. Foreign Chambers of Commerce in the United States

Before you depart to seek employment in a foreign nation, it is suggested that you contact the chambers within that nation. ➥**See Foreign Chambers of Commerce Abroad," pp. 633-640.** In addition to these offices, most nations have a chamber in the United States, which can and should be contacted prior to your departure. ➥**See "Foreign Chambers of Commerce in the United States," pp. 640-643.** Both can be potentially helpful. A third contact, a U.S. Chamber of Commerce on foreign soil, is also likely to be helpful. ➥**See "U.S. Chambers of Commerce Abroad," pp. 628-589.**

All three categories of chambers of commerce are primarily interested in promoting commerce among nations. As such, they are knowledgeable about companies within their nations. Some of them will provide American job seekers with lists of these companies to prospect. In addition, some will circulate resumes, others will post ads for you, and still others will do even more. Since there is no standard fare offered by chambers of commerce as a whole, a phone call or letter is suggested in order to ascertain what services specific ones can provide.

Chambers can also provide job seekers with information on the import-export activities within a country or between countries. This information can, in turn, serve as an industry overview for a particular country or region, or provide a good place to begin investigating foreign job prospects.

In the listings of "U.S. Chambers of Commerce Abroad" and "Foreign Chambers of Commerce Abroad" that follow, note that many cities—not given here—have chambers of their own. If you are interested in a particular city, consult local telephone directories or the overall chamber for specific information on such offices.

It would be wise before traveling to another country to learn as much as possible about the local political and economic situation, which can change rapidly. Such things as civil unrest, religious turmoil, and political instability can all affect your chances of successful employment—to say nothing of your chances of settling in comfortably and safely. On the other hand, there may be many employment opportunities available in unlikely places, so do not immediately rule out certain nations or regions without researching them first.

U.S. Chambers of Commerce Abroad

ARABIAN PENISULA

Also see: Individual Arabian nations, which are listed alphabetically by country name

AMERICAN BUSINESS COUNCIL OF THE GULF COUNTRIES
Bahrain 11471; **973-722-517**

ARGENTINA

AMERICAN CHAMBER OF COMMERCE IN ARGENTINA
Av. Leandro N. Alem 1110, Piso 8, 1053, Buenos Aires, Argentina; **54-1-371-4500**

ASIA

Also see: Individual Asian nations, which are listed alphabetically by country name

ASIA–PACIFIC COUNCIL OF AMERICAN CHAMBERS OF COMMERCE
c/oAmCham Hong Kong, 1904 Bank of America Tower, 12 Harcourt Rd., Hong Kong; **852--2-526-0165**

AUSTRALIA

AMERICAN CHAMBER OF COMMERCE IN AUSTRALIA
Suite 4, Gloucester Walk, 88 Cumberland St., 2000, Sydney, NSW, Australia; **61-2-9241-1907**

AMERICAN CHAMBER OF COMMERCE IN AUSTRALIA—MELBOURNE BRANCH
Level 21, 500 Collins St., 3000, Melbourne, Victoria, Australia; **61-3-9614-7744**

AUSTRIA

AMERICAN CHAMBER OF COMMERCE IN AUSTRIA
Porzellangasse 35, 1090, Vienna, Austria; **43-1-319-5751**

AZERBAIJAN

AMERICAN CHAMBER OF COMMERCE IN AZERBAIJAN
33 Huseyn Javid St., 4th Floor, Baku, Azerbaijan 370143; **994-1-297-5022**

BELARUS

AMERICAN CHAMBER OF COMMERCE IN BELARUS
Starozhevkaya 7, 74-1, Belarus; **375-172-690376**

BELGIUM

AMERICAN CHAMBER OF COMMERCE IN BELGIUM
Avenue des Arts 50, Boite 5, B-1040, Brussels, Belgium; **32-2-513-67-70**

BOLIVIA

AMERICAN CHAMBER OF COMMERCE OF BOLIVIA
P.O. Box 8268M 140, La Paz, Bolivia; **591-2-432-573**

BRAZIL

AMERICAN CHAMBER OF COMMERCE FOR BRAZIL
C.P. 916, Praca Pio X-15, 5th Floor, 20.040, Rio de Janeiro, Brazil; **55-21-203-2477**

BULGARIA

AMERICAN CHAMBER OF COMMERCE IN BULGARIA
19 Patriarh Evtimii Blvd., Sofia 1000, Bulgaria; **359-2-981-4340**

CHILE

CHILEAN-AMERICAN CHAMBER OF COMMERCE
Av Americo Vespucio sur 80-9 Piso, 82 Correo 34, Santiago, Chile; **56-2-208-4140**

CHINA

AMERICAN CHAMBER OF COMMERCE IN BEIJING
Great Wall Sheraton Hotel, Room444, North Donghuan Ave., 100026, Beijing, China; **86-10-65005566, ext. 2271**

AMERICAN CHAMBER OF COMMERCE IN SHANGHAI
Shanghai Centre, Room 435, 1376 Nanjing Rd. W., 200040 Shanghai, China; **36-21-279-7119**

COLOMBIA

COLOMBIAN-AMERICAN CHAMBER OF COMMERCE
Transversal 19 #122-63, P.O. Box 8008, Santa Fe De Bogota, Bogota, Colombia; **57-1-215-8859**

COSTA RICA

COSTA RICAN-AMERICAN CHAMBER OF COMMERCE
P.O. Box 4946, 1000, San Jose, Costa Rica; **506-220-2200**

CÔTE D'IVOIRE

AMERICAN CHAMBER OF COMMERCE—CÔTE D'IVOIRE
01 B.P. 3394, 01, Abidjan, Côte d'Ivoire; **225-21-46-16**

CZECH REPUBLIC

AMERICAN CHAMBER OF COMMERCE IN THE CZECH REPUBLIC
U Boziho oka, Mala Stupartska 7/634, Prague, Czech Republic; **420-2-2481-4280**

DOMINICAN REPUBLIC

AMERICAN CHAMBER OF COMMERCE OF THE DOMINICAN REPUBLIC
P.O. Box 95-2, Santo Domingo, Dominican Republic; **809-544-2222**

ECUADOR

ECUARDORIAN-AMERICAN CHAMBER OF COMMERCE
Edif Multicentro 4P, La Nina y Avda. 6 de Diciembre, Quito, Ecuador; **593-2-507-450**

EGYPT

AMERICAN CHAMBER OF COMMERCE IN EGYPT
Cairo Marriott Hotel #1541, P.O. Box 33, Zamalek, Cairo, Egypt; **20-2-340-8888**

EL SALVADOR

AMERICAN CHAMBER OF COMMERCE OF EL SALVADOR
87 Av. Norte #720 Apt. A, Col. Escalon, San Salvador, El Salvador; **503-224-6003**

ENGLAND

See: United Kingdom

EUROPE

Also see: Individual European nations, which are listed alphabetically by country name

EUROPEAN COUNCIL OF AMERICAN CHAMBERS OF COMMERCE
5309 Burling Terr., Bethesda, MD 20814; **301-215-9076**

FRANCE

AMERICAN CHAMBER OF COMMERCE IN FRANCE
21, ave. George V, 75008, Paris, France; **33-1-47-20-1862**

GERMANY

AMERICAN CHAMBER OF COMMERCE IN GERMANY—BERLIN OFFICE
Budapesterstrasse 29, 10787, Berlin 30, Germany; **49-30-261-55-86**

AMERICAN CHAMBER OF COMMERCE IN GERMANY—FRANKFURT OFFICE
P.O. Box 100162, 60311, Frankfurt, Germany; **49-69-9291040**

GREECE

AMERICAN–HELLENIC CHAMBER OF COMMERCE
16 Kanari St., 106 74, Athens, Greece; **30-1-36-23231**

GUATEMALA

AMERICAN CHAMBER OF COMMERCE IN GUATEMALA
6a Avenida 14-77, Zona 10, 01010, Guatemala City, Guatemala; **502-2-66-4822/4716**

HONDURAS

HONDURAN–AMERICAN CHAMBER OF COMMERCE
Hotel Honduras Maya, Seccion Commercial, P.O. Box 1838 Tegucigalpa, Honduras; **504-32-70-43**

HONG KONG

AMERICAN CHAMBER OF COMMERCE IN HONG KONG
1904 Bank of America Tower, 12 Harcourt Rd., Central, Hong Kong; **852-2526-0165**

HUNGARY

AMERICAN CHAMBER OF COMMERCE IN HUNGARY
Deak Ferenc Utca 10, 1052, Budapest, Hungary; **36-1-266-9880**

INDIA

AMERICAN BUSINESS COUNCIL—INDIA
214 American Centre, 24 Kasturba Gandhi Marg, 110, New Delhi, India; **91-11-331-6556**

INDONESIA

AMERICAN CHAMBER OF COMMERCE IN INDONESIA
World Trade Center, 11th Floor, Jalan Sudirman Kav. 29-31, 12084, Jakarta, Indonesia; **62-21-526-2860**

IRELAND

UNITED STATES CHAMBER OF COMMERCE IN IRELAND
23 St. Stephens, 2, Dublin, Ireland; **353-1-661-6201**

ISRAEL

ISRAEL–AMERICA CHAMBER OF COMMERCE AND INDUSTRY
P.O. Box 33174, Tel Aviv, Israel; **972-3-6952341**

ITALY

AMERICAN CHAMBER OF COMMERCE IN ITALY
Via Cantu 1, 20123, Milan, Italy; **39-2-86-90-661**

JAMAICA

AMERICAN CHAMBER OF COMMERCE OF JAMAICA
77 Knutsford Blvd., 5, Kingston, Jamaica; **809-929-7866**

JAPAN

AMERICAN CHAMBER OF COMMERCE OF JAPAN
Bridgestone Toranomon Bldg. 5F, 3-25-2 Toranomon, Minato-Ku, 105, Tokyo, Japan; **81-33-433-5381**

AMERICAN CHAMBER OF COMMERCE IN OKINAWA
P.O. Box 235, 904, Okinawa, Japan; **81-98933-5146**

LATIN AMERICA

Also see: Individual Latin nations, which are listed alphabetically by country name

ASSOCIATION OF AMERICAN CHAMBERS IN LATIN AMERICA
1615 H St., NW, Washington, DC 20062; **202-463-5485**

LATVIA

AMERICAN CHAMBER OF COMMERCE IN LATVIA
Jauniela 24, Room 205, Riga, Latvia; **371-721-5205**

MALAYSIA

AMERICAN MALAYSIAN CHAMBER OF COMMERCE
11-03 AMODA, 22 Jalan Imbi, 55100, Kuala Lumpur, Malaysia; **60-3-248-2407**

MEXICO

AMERICAN CHAMBER OF COMMERCE OF MEXICO
Lucerna 78, Col. Juarez, 06600, Mexico, D.F.; **52-5-724-3800**

AMERICAN CHAMBER OF COMMERCE OF MEXICO—GUADALAJARA
#442, Jard. Del Sol, 45050 Guadalajara, Jalisco, Mexico; **52-3-364-6606**

MOROCCO

AMERICAN CHAMBER OF COMMERCE IN MOROCCO
18, Rue Colbert, 01, Casablanca, Morocco; **212-2-31-14-48**

NETHERLANDS

AMERICAN CHAMBER OF COMMERCE IN THE NETHERLANDS
Van Karnebeeklaan 14, 2585 BB, The Hague, Netherlands; **31-70-3659808**

NEW ZEALAND

AMERICAN CHAMBER OF COMMERCE IN NEW ZEALAND
P.O. Box 106-002, Downtown, 1001, Auckland, New Zealand; **64-9-3099140**

NICARAGUA

AMERICAN CHAMBER OF COMMERCE OF NICARAGUA
P.O. Box 2720, Managua, Nicaragua; **505-2-67-30-99/67-36-33**

NORWAY

THE AMERICANCHAMBER OF COMMERCE IN NORWAY
P.O. Box 244, 1322, M280, Hovik, Norway; **47-67-54-6880**

PAKISTAN

AMERICAN BUSINESS COUNCIL OF PAKISTAN
NIC Bldg., 6th Floor, Abbasi Shaheed Rd., GPO Box 1322, 74000, Karachi, Pakistan; **92-21-567-6436**

PANAMA

AMERICAN CHAMBER OF COMMERCE & INDUSTRY OF PANAMA
Apdo. 168, Balboa, Ancon, Panama City, Panama; **507-69-3881**

PARAGUAY

PARAGUAYAN-AMERICAN CHAMBER OF COMMERCE
Gral. Diaz 521, Edif. Faro int. P4, Asuncion, Paraguay; **595-21-442-135/6**

PERU

AMERICAN CHAMBER OF COMMERCE OF PERU
Ave. Ricardo Palama 836, Miraflores, 18, Lima, Peru; **51-12410708**

PHILIPPINES

AMERICAN CHAMBER OF COMMERCE IN THE PHILIPPINES
P.O. Box 1578, MCC, Manila, Philippines; **63-2-818-7911**

POLAND

AMERICAN CHAMBER OF COMMERCE IN POLAND
Swietokrzyska 36 6, Entrance I, 00-116, Warsaw, Poland; **48-2-2622-5525**

PORTUGAL

AMERICAN CHAMBER OF COMMERCE IN PORTUGAL
Rua De D. Estefania, 155, 5 ESQ, 1000, Lisbon, Portugal; **351-1-57-25-61**

ROMANIA

AMERICAN CHAMBER OF COMMERCE IN ROMANIA
Str. M. Eminescu nr. 105-107, Ap. I, Sector 2, Bucharest, Romania; **40-1-210-9399**

RUSSIA

AMERICAN CHAMBER OF COMMERCE IN RUSSIA
.Kosmodamianskaya Emb 52, Bldg. 1, 8th Floor, Moscow, Russia;

7-095-961-2141

SAUDI ARABIA

AMERICAN BUSINESS ASSOCIATION
P.O. Box 88, Dhahran Airport, 31932,
Dhahran, Saudi Arabia; **966-3-857-6464**

SINGAPORE

AMERICAN BUSINESS COUNCIL OF SINGAPORE
1 Scotts Rd. #16-07 Shaw Centre, 0922,
Singapore; **65-235-0077**

SLOVAKIA

AMERICAN CHAMBER OF COMMERCE IN THE SLOVAK REPUBLIC
 Hotel Danube, Rybne nasestie 1, 811 02,
Bratislova, Slovak Republic; **42-1-534-0000**

SOUTH AFRICA

AMERICAN CHAMBER OF COMMERCE IN SOUTH AFRICA
P.O. Box 1132, Houghton, 2041,
Johannesburg, South Africa; **27-11-788-0265**

SOUTH KOREA

AMERICAN CHAMBER OF COMMERCE IN KOREA
2/F Westin Chosun Hotel, 87 Sokong-dong
Chung-Gu, Seoul, South Korea; **82-2-753-6471**

SPAIN

AMERICAN CHAMBER OF COMMERCE IN SPAIN
Avda. Diagonal 477, 08036, Barcelona,
Spain; **34-3-405-12-66**

AMERICAN CHAMBER OF COMMERCE IN SPAIN—MADRID
 Lexington International Business Center,
Paseo de la Castellana, 141 200, 28046, Madrid, Spain; **34-1-359-6559**

SRI LANKA

AMERICAN CHAMBER OF COMMERCE IN SRI LANKA
P.O. Box 1000, Lotus Rd., Colombo Hilton,
3rd Floor, 1, Colombo, Sri Lanka**94-1-336-074**

SWEDEN

AMERICAN CHAMBER OF COMMERCE IN SWEDEN
Box 5512, 114 85, Stockholm, Sweden; **46-8-666-11-00**

SWITZERLAND

SWISS–AMERICAN CHAMBER OF COMMERCE
Talacker 41, 8001, Zurich, Switzerland; **41-1-211-24-54**

TAIWAN

AMERICAN CHAMBER OF COMMERCE
Room 1012, 96 Chung Shan N. Rd., Sec. 2,
Chia Hsin Bldg. Annex, Taipei, Taiwan; **886-2-581-7089**

THAILAND

AMERICAN CHAMBER OF COMMERCE IN THAILAND
P.O. Box 1095, Nana, 10330, Bangkok,
Thailand; **66-2-251-9266**

TRINIDAD & TOBAGO

AMERICAN CHAMBER OF COMMERCE OF TRINIDAD & TOBAGO
Hilton International, Lady Young Rd., Port of
Spain, Trinidad; **809-627-7986**

TURKEY

TURKISH–AMERICAN BUSINESSMEN'S ASSOCIATION
Barbaros Bulvari, Eer. Apt. 48, K.5 D.16,
80700 Balmumcu, Istanbul, Turkey; **90-212-275-9316**

UKRAINE

AMERICAN CHAMBER OF COMMERCE IN UKRAINE
7 Kudriavsky Uzviz #212, 254053, Kiev,
Ukraine; **7044-417-1015**

UNITED ARAB EMIRATES

AMERICAN BUSINESS COUNCIL OF DUBAI/NORTH EMIRATES
P.O. Box 9281, Dubai, United Arab Emirates;
971-431-4735

UNITED KINGDOM

AMERICAN CHAMBER OF COMMERCE OF THE UNITED KINGDOM
75 Brook St., London W1Y 2EB, England;
44-71-493-03-81

URUGUAY

CHAMBER OF COMMERCE URUGUAY—USA
Calle Bartolome Mitre 1337, Casilla de Correo 809, Montevideo, Uruguay; **598-2-95-90-48**

VENEZUELA

VENEZUELAN–AMERICAN CHAMBER OF COMMERCE & INDUSTRY
Torre Credival, Piso 10, 2da. Ave. de Campo Alegre, Apdo. 5181, 1010-A, Caracas, Venezuela; **58-2-2630833**

VIETNAM

AMERICAN CHAMBER OF COMMERCE IN VIETNAM
17 Ngo Quyen, Unite #01, First Floor, Hanoi, Vietnam; **84-4-825-1950**

Foreign Chambers of Commerce Abroad

ALBANIA

ALBANIAN CHAMBER OF COMMERCE
Kavaja St. 6, Tirana, Albania; **355-42-22934**

ALGERIA

NATIONAL CHAMBER OF COMMERCE
6, Blvd. Amilcar Cabral, Palais Consulaire, Place des Martyrs, Algiers, Algeria; **213-2-57-44-44**

AMERICAN SAMOA

CHAMBER OF COMMERCE IN AMERICAN SAMOA
P.O. Box 2446, AS 96799, Pago Pago, American Somoa; **684-633-5583**

ANTIGUA & BARBUDA

ANITGUA & BARBUDA CHAMBER OF COMMERCE & INDUSTRY
Redcliffe St., P.O. Box 774, St. John's, Antigua; **809-462-0743**

ARGENTINA

ARGENTINA CHAMBER OF COMMERCE
Al. L.N. Alem 36, 1003, Buenos Aires, Argentina; **54-1-3318051**

ARUBA

ARUBA CHAMBER OF COMMERCE & INDUSTRY
Zoutmanstraat 21, P.O. Box 140, Oranjestad, Aruba; **297-8-21566**

AUSTRALIA

AUSTRALIAN CHAMBER OF COMMERCE
P.O. Box E14, 2600, Melbourne, Victoria, Australia; **61-6-273-2311**

AUSTRIA

FEDERAL ECONOMIC CHAMBER OF COMMERCE
Wiedner Hauptstrasse 63, A-1045, Vienna, Austria; **43-1-50105-4503**

BAHAMAS

BAHAMAS CHAMBER OF COMMERCE
Shirley St. & Collins Ave., P.O. Box N-665, Nassau, Bahamas; **242-322-3320**

BAHRAIN

BAHRAIN CHAMBER OF COMMERCE & INDUSTRY
P.O. Box 248, Manama, Bahrain; **973- 229555**

BANGLADESH

THE FEDERATION OF BANGLADESH CHAMBER OF COMMERCE & INDUSTRY
Federation Bhaban, 60 Motijhell CA, G.P.O. Box 2079, 1000, Dhaka, Bangladesh; **880-2-240102**

BARBADOS

BARBADOS CHAMBER OF COMMERCE & INDUSTRY
P.O. Box 189, Bridgetown, Barbados; **246-426-2056**

BELGIUM

BRUSSELS CHAMBER OF COMMERCE
Avenue Louise 500, 1050, Brussels, Belgium; **32-02-648-50-02**

BELIZE

BELIZE CHAMBER OF COMMERCE & INDUSTRY
#63 Regent St., P.O. Box 291, Belize City, Belize; **501-2-73148**

BENIN

BENIN CHAMBER OF COMMERCE & INDUSTRY
Avenue du General-de-Gaulle, BP 31, Cotonou, Benin; **229-31-32-99**

BERMUDA

BERMUDA CHAMBER OF COMMERCE
Box HM 655, HM CX, Hamilton, Bermuda; **809-295-4201**

BOLIVIA

CAMARA NACIONAL DE COMERCIO
Mcal. Santa Cruz #1392, P.O. Box 7, La Paz, Bolivia; **591-2-350042**

BOSNIA AND HERZE-GOVINA

BOSNIA AND HERZEGOVINA CHAMBER OF COMMERCE
Mitra Trifunovica-Uce 118, BIH-75000, Tuzla; 387-75-281374

BOTSWANA

BOTSWANA CONFEDERATION OF COMMERCE, INDUSTRY, & MANPOWER
Debswana House, P.O. Box 432, Gaborone, Botswana; 267-353459

BRAZIL

BRAZIL CHAMBER OF COMMERCE
Avenida General Justo 307-4, 20-022, Rio de Janeiro, Brazil; 55-21-533-1295

BULGARIA

BULGARIAN CHAMBER OF COMMERCE & INDUSTRY
11-a Saborna St., 1000, Sofia, Bulgaria; 359-87-26-31

BURKINA FASO

CHAMBER OF COMMERCE & INDUSTRY
P.O. Box 502, Ouagadougou, Burkina Faso; 226-306114

BURUNDI

CHAMBRE DE COMMERCE ET D'INDUSTRIE DU BURUNDI
B.P. 313, Bujumbura, Burundi; 257-22-2280

CAMEROON

CHAMBER OF COMMERCE, INDUSTRY, & MINES OF CAMEROON
B.P. 4011, Douala, Cameroon; 237-42-6787

CAYMAN ISLANDS

CAYMAN ISLANDS CHAMBER OF COMMERCE
P.O. Box 1000 GT, Georgetown, Grand Cayman, Cayman Islands; 809-949-8090

CENTRAL AFRICAN REPUBLIC

BANGUI CHAMBER OF COMMERCE
B.P. 813, Bangui, Central African Republic; 236-20-94

CHILE

CAMARA DE COMERCIO DE SANTIAGO
Santa Lucia 302, P.O. Box 1297, Santiago, Chile; 56-2-3607051

CHINA

CHINA COUNCIL FOR THE PROMOTION OF INTERNATIONAL TRADE
1 Fuxingmenwai St., 100860, Beijing, China; 86-10-685-13344

COLOMBIA

CARTAGENA CHAMBER OF COMMERCE
Centro, calle Santa Teresa No 32-41, P.O. Box A.A. 16, Cartagena, Colombia; 57-56-655520

COSTA RICA

CHAMBER OF COMMERCE OF COSTA RICA
P.O. Box 1114-1000, San Jose, Costa Rica; 506-221-0005

CÔTE D'IVOIRE

CHAMBRE D'INDUSTRIE DE CÔTE D'IVOIRE
11, avenue Lamblin, 01 BP 1758, 01, Abidjan, Côte d'Ivoire; 225-331600

CROATIA

CROATIAN CHAMBER OF COMMERCE
Rooseveltov trg 2, P.O. Box 630, 1000, Zagreb, Croatia; 385-38-456-1555

CUBA

CHAMBER OF COMMERCE OF THE REPUBLIC OF CUBA
Calle 21, No. 661, Vedado, Havana, Cuba; 53-7-30-3356

CYPRUS

CYPRUS CHAMBER OF COMMERCE & INDUSTRY
38 Grivas Dhigenis Ave. & 3 Deligiorgis St., P.O. Box 1455, 1509, Nicosia, Cyprus; 357-2-449500

CZECH REPUBLIC

CZECHOSLOVAK CHAMBER OF COMMERCE
Argentinska 38, 170 OS, 7, Praha, Czech Republic; 422-879-134 (fax only)

DENMARK

DENMARK CHAMBER OF COMMERCE
Borsen, DK-1217, Copenhagen, Denmark; 45-339500500

DJIBOUTI

CHAMBRE INTERNATIONALE DE COMMERCE ET D'INDUSTRIE
P.O. Box 4, Djibouti, Republic of Djibouti; 253-35-10-70

DOMINICAN REPUB-LIC

CHAMBER OF COMMERCE & PRODUCT OF DO-MINICAN REPUBLIC
Arz. Nouel 206, P.O. Box 815, Santo Domingo, Dominican Republic; **809-682-2688**

ECUADOR

INTERNATIONAL CHAMBER OF COMMERCE
P.O. Box 09-01-7515, Guayaquil, Ecuador; **593-4-325967**

EGYPT

FEDERATION OF EGYPTIAN CHAMBERS OF COMMERCE
4, Midan El Falaky, Cairo, Egypt; **20-2-98-71-03**

EL SALVADOR

CAMARA DE COMERCIO E INDUSTRIA DE EL SALVADOR
9 Avenida Norte y 5 Calle Poniente, P.O. Box 1640, San Salvador, El Salvador; **503-81-6622**

ENGLAND

See: United Kingdom

ERITREA

ASMARA CHAMBER OF COMMERCE
P.O. Box 859, Asmara, Eritrea; **291-1-121388**

ESTONIA

ESTONIAN CHAMBER OF COMMERCE
Toom-Kooli 17, EE0001, Tallinn, Estonia; **372-6-460244**

FINLAND

CENTRAL CHAMBER OF COMMERCE OF FIN-LAND
Marja-Liisa Peltola, P.O. Box 1000, 00101, Helsinki, Finland; **358-9-696969**

FRANCE

FRENCH CHAMBER OF COMMERCE
9, boulevard Malesherbes, 75008, Paris, France; **33-1-42-65-1266**

GABON

CHAMBER OF COMMERCE, AGRICULTURE, & INDUSTRY
B.P. 2234, Libreville, Gabon; **241-722064**

GAMBIA

GAMBIA CHAMBER OF COMMERCE & INDUS-TRY
Buckle St., P.O. Box 333, Banjul, Gambia; **220-227765**

GERMANY

DEUTSCHER INDUSTRIE UND HANDELSTAG
Adenauerallee 148, 5300, PF. 1446, Bonn, Germany; **49-228-104-0**

GHANA

GHANA NATIONAL CHAMBER OF COMMERCE
P.O. Box 2325, Accra, Ghana; **233-21-775311**

GREECE

UNION OF CHAMBER OF COMMERCE & INDUS-TRY OF GREECE
27 Kaningos St., 10682, Athens, Greece; **30-1-363-2702**

GRENADA

GRENADA CHAMBER OF INDUSTRY & COM-MERCE
Mt. Gay, P.O. Box 129, Saint George's, Grenada; **809-440-2937**

GUAM

GUAM CHAMBER OF COMMERCE
173 Aspinall Ave., #102, P.O. Box 283, 96910, Agana, Guam; **671-472-6311**

GUATEMALA

CAMARA DE COMERCIO DE GUATEMALA
10a Calle 3-80, zona 1, 01001, Guatemala City, Guatemala; **502-300266**

GUINEA-BISSAU

BISSAU CHAMBER OF COMMERCE
Caixa Postal 88, Bissau, Guinea; **224-2583**

GUYANA

GEORGETOWN CHAMBER OF COMMERCE & INDUSTRY
156 Waterloo St., P.O. Box 10110, Georgetown, Guyana; **592-02-56451**

HAITI

CHAMBRE DE COMMERCE & D'INDUSTRIE D'HAITI
P.O. Box 982, Port-au-Prince, Haiti; **509-23-0786**

HONDURAS

TEGUCIGALPA CHAMBER OF COMMERCE & INDUSTRY
P.O. Box 3444, Blvd. Centroamerica, Tegucigalpa, Honduras; **504-32-8110**

HONG KONG

HONG KONG GENERAL CHAMBER OF COM-MERCE
22/F United Centre, 95 Queensway, P.O. Box 852, Hong Kong; **852-5299229**

HUNGARY

HUNGARIAN CHAMBER OF COMMERCE
P.O. Box 106, 1389, Budapest, Hungary; **36-1-153-3333**

ICELAND

ICELAND CHAMBER OF COMMERCE
House of Commerce, Kringlan 7, IS 103
Reykjavik, Iceland; **354-588-6666**

INDIA

FEDERATION OF INDIAN CHAMBERS OF COMMERCE & INDUSTRY
Federation House, Tansen Marg, 110 001,
New Delhi, India; **91-11-3319251**

INDONESIA

INDONESIAN CHAMBER OF COMMERCE & INDUSTRY
Jalan Merdeka Timur No. 11, Jakarta Pusat,
Indonesia; **62-364247**

IRAN

TEHRAN CHAMBER OF COMMERCE, INDUSTRIES, & MINES
254 Taleghani Ave., 15814, Tehran, Iran; **98-21-8846031**

IRELAND

CHAMBERS OF COMMERCE OF IRELAND
22 Merrion Sq., 2, Dublin, Ireland; **353-1-6612888**

ISRAEL

FEDERATION OF ISRAELI CHAMBERS OF COMMERCE
84 Hahashmonaim St., P.O. Box 20027,
61200, Tel Aviv, Israel; **972-3-5631022**

ITALY

ITALIAN CHAMBER OF COMMERCE
Via XX Settembre N. 5, IT-00187, Rome, Italy; **39-6462-438**

JAMAICA

JAMAICA CHAMBER OF COMMERCE
7-8 E. Parade, P.O. Box 172, Kingston,
Jamaica; **809-922-0150**

JAPAN

JAPAN CHAMBER OF COMMERCE & INDUSTRY
3-2-2 Marunouchi, Chiyoda-ku, 100, Tokyo,
Japan; **81-3-3283-7851**

JORDAN

FEDERATION OF JORDANIAN CHAMBERS OF COMMERCE
P.O. Box 7029, 111 18, Amman, Jordan; **962-6-665492**

KENYA

KENYA NATIONAL CHAMBER OF COMMERCE
Haile Selassie Ave., P.O. Box 47024, Nairobi,
Kenya; **254-220866**

KUWAIT

KUWAIT CHAMBER OF COMMERCE & INDUSTRY
Ali Al-Salem St., P.O. Box 775 (Safat),
13008, Kuwait City, Kuwait; **965-2416391**

KYRGYZSTAN

CHAMBER OF COMMERCE OF THE KYRGYZ REPUBLIC
Kievskaya St. 107, 72001; **7-3312-210565**

LATVIA

LATVIA CHAMBER OF COMMERCE & INDUSTRY
21 Brivibas Blvd., LV 1849, Riga, Latvia;
371-7332269

LEBANON

CHAMBER OF COMMERCE & INDUSTRY OF BEIRUT
Sanayeh 2100, P.O. Box 11-1801, Beirut,
Lebanon; **961-1-353390**

LESOTHO

CHAMBER OF COMMERCE & INDUSTRY
P.O. Box 79, Maseru, Lesotho; **266-323482**

LIBERIA

LIBERIA CHAMBER OF COMMERCE
Capitol Hill, P.O. Box 92, Monrovia, Liberia;
231-223-738

LITHUANIA

ASSOCIATION OF LITHUANIAN CHAMBERS OF COMMERCE & INDUSTRY
V. Kudirkos St. 18, 2022, Vilnius, Lithuania;
370-2-222617

LUXEMBOURG

GRAND DUCHY OF LUXEMBOURG CHAMBER OF COMMERCE
7 Rue Alcide de Gasperi, B.P. 1503, 2981,
Luxembourg City, Luxembourg; **352-43-58-53**

MADAGASCAR

CHAMBER OF COMMERCE, INDUSTRY, & AGRICULTURE OF ANTANANARIVO
rue Paul Dussac, P.O. Box 166, 101,
Antananarivo, Madagascar; **261-202-11**

MALAWI

ASSOCIATED CHAMBERS OF COMMERCE & INDUSTRY OF MALAWI
P.O. Box 258, Blantyre, Malawi; **265-671-988**

MALAYSIA

MALAYSIA INTERNATIONAL CHAMBER OF COMMERCE & INDUSTRY
10th Floor, Wisma Damansara, Jalan Semantan, P.O. Box 12921, 50792, Kuala Lumpur, Malaysia; **60-3-2542677**

MALTA

MALTA CHAMBER OF COMMERCE
Exchange Bldgs., Republic St., VLT05, Valletta, Malta; **356-247233**

MARSHALL ISLANDS

CHAMBER OF COMMERCE
96960, Majuro, Marshall Islands; **692-625-3560**

MAURITIUS

MAURITIUS CHAMBER OF COMMERCE & INDUSTRY
3 Royal St., Port Louis, Mauritius; **230-208-3301**

MEXICO

MEXICAN CHAMBER OF COMMERCE
Donato Guerra 25, Col. Centro, Mexico DF, 06048, Mexico City, Mexico; **52-5-592-35-71**

MONGOLIA

MONGOLIAN CHAMBER OF COMMERCE & INDUSTRY
J. Sambuugiin St., Ulaanbaatar, Mongolia; **976-24620**

MOROCCO

MOROCCO CHAMBER OF COMMERCE
4, rue du Rhone, 01, Casablanca, Morocco; **212-30-97-16**

MOZAMBIQUE

CAMARA DE COMERCIO DE MOZAMBIQUE
452 Mateus Sansao Muthenba St., P.O. Box 1836, 452, Maputo, Mozambique; **258-491970**

MYANMAR

MYANMAR CHAMBERS OF COMMERCE & INDUSTRY
No. 74 Bo Son Pat St., Pabedan Township, Yangon, Myanmar; **95-70749**

NAMIBIA

NAMIBIA NATIONAL CHAMBER OF COMMERCE & INDUSTRY
P.O. Box 9355, Windhoek, Namibia; **264-61-228809**

NEPAL

FEDERATION OF NEPALESE CHAMBERS OF COMMERCE & INDUSTRY
TNT Bldg., Teenkune, P.O. Box 269, Kathmandu, Nepal; **977-1-475032**

NETHERLANDS

KAMER VAN KOOPHANDEL EN FABRIEKEN VOOR AMSTERDAM
De Ruyterkade 5, 1013 AA, Amsterdam, The Netherlands; **31-020-5236600**

NEW ZEALAND

NEW ZEALAND CHAMBERS OF COMMERCE
Enterprise House, Church St., P.O. Box 11-043, Wellington, New Zealand; **64-4-723-376**

NICARAGUA

CAMARA DE COMERCIO DE NICARAGUA
Frente A La Loteria Popular, P.O. Box 135-C-001, Managua, Nicaragua; **505-670718**

NIGERIA

NIGERIAN ASSOCIATION OF CHAMBERS OF COMMERCE, INDUSTRY, MINES, & AGRICULTURE
P.M.B. 12816, Lagos, Nigeria; **234-1-4964727**

NORWAY

NORWEGIAN ASSOCIATION OF CHAMBERS OF COMMERCE
Drammensveien 30, P.O. Box 2483, Solli, Oslo, Norway; **47-22-541700**

OMAN

OMAN CHAMBER OF COMMERCE & INDUSTRY
P.O. Box 1400, 112, Ruwi, Oman; **968-707674**

PAKISTAN

FEDERATION OF PAKISTAN CHAMBERS OF COMMERCE
10th Floor, Adamjee House, I.I. Chundrigar Rd., Karachi, Pakistan; **92-21-222655**

PANAMA

CAMARA DE COMERCIO & INDUSTRIAS DE PANAMA
P.O. Box 74, 1, Panama City, Panama; **507-27-1233**

PERU

LIMA CHAMBER OF COMMERCE

Gregorio Escobedo 398, 100, Lima, Peru; **51-14-63-3434**

PHILIPPINES

PHILIPPINE CHAMBER OF COMMERCE & INDUSTRY
G/F East Wing, PICC Secretariat Bldg., CCP Complex, Roxas Blvd., Pasay City, Philippines; **632-833-8591**

POLAND

TREBACKA CHAMBER OF COMMERCE
ul. Trebacka 4, 00-916, Warsaw, Poland; **48-22-260221**

PORTUGAL

PORTUGAL CHAMBER OF COMMERCE & INDUSTRY
Rua das portas de Santo Antao, 89, 1194, Lisbon, Portugal; **351-1-346-33-04**

QATAR

QATAR CHAMBER OF COMMERCE & INDUSTRY
P.O. Box 402, Doha, Qatar; **974-621131**

ROMANIA

CHAMBER OF COMMERCE & INDUSTRY OF ROMANIA
22 N. Balcescu Blvd., 79302, Bucharest, Romania; **40-1-3121312**

RUSSIAN FEDERATION

UNION OF CHAMBERS OF COMMERCE & INDUSTRY OF THE RUSSIAN FEDERATION
6 Ilyinka Str., 103684, M9, 430, Moscow, Russia; **7-095-9290009**

RWANDA

RWANDA CHAMBER OF COMMERCE & INDUSTRY
P.O. Box 319, Kigali, Rwanda; **250-83541**

SAINT KITTS & NEVIS

SAINT KITTS & NEVIS CHAMBER OF INDUSTRY, & COMMERCE
S. Independence Sq. St., P.O. Box 332, Basseterre, Saint Kitts; **809-465-2980**

SAINT LUCIA

SAINT LUCIA CHAMBER OF COMMERCE, INDUSTRY, & AGRICULTURE
Micoud St., P.O. Box 482, Castries, Saint Lucia; **809-452-3165**

SAUDI ARABIA

COUNCIL OF SAUDI CHAMBERS OF COMMERCE & INDUSTRY
Chamber of Commerce Bldg., P.O. Box 16683, 11474, Riyadh, Saudi Arabia; **966-1-4053200**

SCOTLAND

EDINBURGH CHAMBER OF COMMERCE & MANUFACTURING
3 Randolph Crescent, EH3 7UD, Edinburgh, Scotland; **031-250-5851**

SENEGAL

CHAMBER OF COMMERCE & INDUSTRY
1 Place de L'Independance, P.O. Box 118, Dakar, Senegal; **221-23-71-89**

SIERRA LEONE

SIERRA LEONE CHAMBER OF COMMERCE, INDUSTRY, & AGRICULTURE
5th Floor, Guma Bldg., Lamina Sankoh, P.O. Box 502, Freetown, Sierra Leone; **232-26305**

SINGAPORE

SINGAPORE FEDERATION OF CHAMBERS OF COMMERCE & INDUSTRY
47 Hill St. #03-01, Chincese Chamber of Commerce Bldg., 0617, Singapore; **65-3389761**

SLOVAKIA

SLOVAK CHAMBER OF COMMERCE & INDUSTRY
Gorkeho 9, 816 03, Bratislava, Slovak Republic; **42-7-333272**

SLOVENIA

CHAMBER OF ECONOMY OF SLOVENIA
Slovenska 41, 61000, Ljubljana, Slovenia; **386-61-12-50-122**

SOUTH AFRICA

SOUTH AFRICAN CHAMBER OF BUSINESS
P.O. Box 44164, Linden, 2104, Johannesburg, South Africa; **27-11-4822524**

SOUTH KOREA

THE KOREA CHAMBER OF COMMERCE & INDUSTRY
C.P.O. Box 25, 100-600, Seoul, South Korea; **82-2-316-3114**

SPAIN

SPAIN CHAMBER OF COMMERCE
Avinguda Diagonal 452-454, 08006, Barcelona, Spain; **34-3-219-13-00**

SRI LANKA

CEYLON CHAMBER OF COMMERCE
No. 50 Navam Mawatha, P.O. Box 274, 2,
Colombo, Sri Lanka; **94-1-421745-47**

SUDAN

KHARTOUM CHAMBER OF COMMERCE
P.O. Box 81, Khartoum, Sudan; **249-72959**

SURINAME

CHAMBER OF COMMERCE & INDUSTRY
P.O. Box 149, Paramaribo, Suriname; **597-473527**

SWAZILAND

SWAZILAND CHAMBER OF COMMERCE
Warner St., P.O. Box 72, Mbabane,
Swaziland; **268-44408**

SWEDEN

STOCKHOLM CHAMBER OF COMMERCE
Vastra Tradgardsgatan 9, Box 16050, S-103
22, Stockholm, Sweden; **46-08-23-1200**

SWITZERLAND

SWITZERLAND CHAMBER OF COMMERCE
Mainaustrasse 49, Postfach 690, 8034,
Zurich, Switzerland; **41-1-382-23-23**

SYRIA

FEDERATION OF SYRIAN CHAMBERS OF COMMERCE
Moussa Bin Nousair St., P.O. Box 5909,
Damascus, Syria; **963-11-3337344**

TANZANIA

DAR-ES-SALAAM CHAMBER OF COMMERCE
P.O. Box 41, Kelvin House Bldg.,
Dar-es-Salaam, Tanzania; **255-21893**

THAILAND

THE THAI CHAMBER OF COMMERCE
150 Rajbopit Rd., 10200, Bangkok, Thailand;
66-2-2250086

TOGO

CHAMBER OF COMMERCE, AGRICULTURE, & INDUSTRY OF TOGO
P.O. Box 360, Lomé, Togo; **228-21-20-65**

TONGA

TONGA CHAMBER OF COMMERCE, WORKERS, & INDUSTRY
P.O. Box 838, Nuku'alofa, Tonga; **676-21-316**

TRINIDAD & TOBAGO

TRINIDAD & TOBABO CHAMBER OF INDUSTRY COMMERCE
P.O. Box 499, P 1,200,000, Port of Spain,
Trinidad; **809-637-6966**

TUNISIA

CHAMBRE DE COMMERCE ET D'INDUSTRIE DE TUNIS
1, Rue des Entrepreneurs, 1000, Tunis,
Tunisia; **216-1-242-810**

TURKEY

UNION OF CHAMBERS, INDUSTRY, & COMMODITY EXCHANGES
Ataturk Bulvari No. 149, Bakanliklar, 06582,
Ankara, Turkey; **90-1255614**

UGANDA

UGANDA NATIONAL CHAMBER OF COMMERCE & INDUSTRY
P.O. Box 3809, Kampala, Uganda; **256-41-258791**

UNITED ARAB EMIRATES

FEDERATION OF UAE CHAMBERS OF COMMERCE & INDUSTRY
P.O. Box 8886, Dubai, United Arab Emirates;
971-02-214144

UNITED KINGDOM

ASSOCIATION OF BRITISH CHAMBERS OF COMMERCE
9 Tufton St., SW1P 3QB, London, England;
44-71-222-1555

URUGUAY

URUGUAYAN CHAMBER OF COMMERCE
Misiones 1400, 11000, Montevideo,
Uruguay; **598-2-96-12-77**

VENEZUELA

CAMARA DE INDUSTRIALES DE CARACAS
Edf. camara de Industriales, piso 2 y 3, Esq.
Puente Anauco, Caracas, Venezuela; **58-02-5714202**

YEMEN

ADEN CHAMBER OF COMMERCE
P.O. Box 4345, Craer Aden, Yemen; **967-51104**

YUGOSLAVIA

YUGOSLAV CHAMBER OF COMMERCE
Terazije 23, 11000, Belgrade, Yugoslavia;
381-11-3248123

ZAIRE

ZAIRE NATIONAL ASSOCIATION OF ENTER-PRISES
B.P. 7247, Kinshasa, Zaire; **243-22286**

ZAMBIA

ZAMBIA ASSOCIATION OF CHAMBERS OF COMMERCE & INDUSTRY
P.O. Box 30844, Lusaka, Zambia; **260-252369**

ZIMBABWE

ZIMBABWE NATIONAL CHAMBER OF COMMERCE
Equity House, Rezende St., P.O. Box 1934, Harare, Zimbabwe; **263-4-708611**

Foreign Chambers of Commerce in the United States

AFRICA

Also see: Individual African nations, which are listed alphabetically by country name

AFRICA–USA CHAMBER OF COMMERCE & INDUSTRY
One World Trade Ctr., #800, Long Beach, CA 90831; **310-983-8193**

ARGENTINA

ARGENTINE–AMERICAN CHAMBER OF COMMERCE
10 Rockefeller Plaza, New York, NY 10020; **212-698-2238**

AUSTRALIA

AUSTRALIAN CONSULATE GENERAL
630 5th Ave., New York, NY 10111; **212-408-8400**

AUSTRIA

U.S.–AUSTRIAN CHAMBER OF COMMERCE
165 W. 46th St., New York, NY 10036; **212-819-0117**

BELGIUM

BELGIAN–AMERICAN CHAMBER OF COMMERCE IN THE U.S.
350 Fifth Ave., #1322, New York, NY 10118; **212-967-9898**

BRAZIL

BRAZILIAN–AMERICAN CHAMBER OF COMMERCE
22 W. 48th St., #404, New York, NY 10036; **212-575-9030**

CENTRAL AMERICA

CENTRAL AMERICAN–U.S. CHAMBER OF COMMERCE
2100 Ponce de Leon Blvd., Suite 1180, Miami, FL 33134; **305-569-9113**

CHILE

NORTH AMERICAN–CHILEAN CHAMBER
220 E. 81st St., New York, NY 10028; **212-288-5691**

CHINA

U.S. REP OFFICE—CHINA CHAMBER OF INTERNATIONAL COMMERCE
4301 Connecticut Ave., NW, #136, Washington, DC 20008; **202-244-3244**

COLOMBIA

COLOMBIAN–AMERICAN CHAMBER OF COMMERCE
2355 S. Salzedo, Coral Gables, FL 33134; **305-446-2542**

CYPRUS

CYPRUS TRADE CENTER
13 E. 40th St., New York, NY 10016; **212-213-9100**

DENMARK

DANISH–AMERICAN CHAMBER OF COMMERCE
885 Second Ave., New York, NY 10017; 212-980-6240

ECUADOR

ECUADORIAN–AMERICAN CHAMBER OF COMMERCE OF MIAMI
1390 Brickell Ave., Miami FL 33131; **305-539-0010**

ENGLAND

See: United Kingdom

EUROPE

Also see: Individual European nations, which are listed alphabetically by country name

EUROPEAN–AMERICAN CHAMBER OF COMMERCE IN WASHINGTON, DC
801 Pennsylvania Ave., NW, Washington, DC 20004; **202-347-9292**

FINLAND

FINNISH–AMERICAN CHAMBER OF COMMERCE
380 Madison Ave., New York, NY 10017; **212-808-0978**

FINNISH–AMERICAN CHAMBER OF THE MIDWEST
321 N. Clark St., #2880, Chicago, IL 60610; **312-670-4700**

FRANCE

FRENCH–AMERICAN CHAMBER OF COMMERCE
6380 Wilshire Blvd., #1608, Los Angeles, CA 90048; **213-651-4741**

FRENCH–AMERICAN CHAMBER OF COMMERCE
1350 Avenue of the Americas, 6th Floor, New York, NY 10019; **212-371-4460**

GERMANY

GERMAN–AMERICAN CHAMBER OF COMMERCE
40 W. 57th St., New York, NY 10019; **212-974-8830**

GERMAN–AMERICAN CHAMBER OF COMMERCE OF ATLANTA
3475 Lenox Rd., NW, #620, Atlanta, GA 30326; **404-239-9494**

GERMAN–AMERICAN CHAMBER OF COMMERCE OF CHICAGO
401 N. Michigan Ave., Suite 2525, Chicago, IL 60611; **312-644-2662**

GERMAN–AMERICAN CHAMBER OF THE WESTERN U.S.
465 California St., Suite 506, San Francisco, CA 94104; **415-392-2262**

GREECE

HELLENIC–AMERICAN CHAMBER OF COMMERCE
960 Ave. of the Americas, New York, NY 10001; **212-629-6380**

HUNGARY

HUNGARIAN–AMERICAN CHAMBER OF COMMERCE
250A Twin Dolphin Dr., Redwood City, CA 94065; **415-595-0444**

MIDAMERICA HUNGARIAN CHAMBER OF COMMERCE
707 Forest Ave., Evanston, IL 60202; **847-328-4279**

ICELAND

ICELANDIC–AMERICAN CHAMBER OF COMMERCE
800 3rd Ave., 36th Floor, New York, NY 10022; **212-593-2700**

INDIA

INDIA AMERICAN CHAMBER OF COMMERCE
P.O. Box 873, Grand Central Station, New York, NY 10163; **212-755-7181**

IRELAND

IRELAND CHAMBER OF COMMERCE IN THE U.S.
1305 Post Rd., #205, Fairfield, CT 06430; **203-255-4774**

ISLAMIC NATIONS

Also see: Individual Islamic and Middle Eastern nations, which are listed alphabetically by country name

AMERICAN ISLAMIC CHAMBER OF COMMERCE
P.O. Box30807, Albuquerque, NM 87190; **505-881-3433**

ISRAEL

AMERICAN–ISRAEL CHAMBER OF COMMERCE & INDUSTRY
310 Madison Ave., Suite 1103, New York, NY 10117; **212-661-4106**

AMERICAN–ISRAEL CHAMBER OF COMMERCE & INDUSTRY OF METRO CHICAGO
180 N. Michigan Ave., #911, Chicago, IL 60601; **312-641-2937**

ITALY

ITALIAN–AMERICAN CHAMBER OF COMMERCE OF CHICAGO
30 S. Michigan Ave., #504, Chicago, IL 60603; **312-553-9137**

ITALY–AMERICA CHAMBER OF COMMERCE

11520 San Vincente Blvd., #203, Los Angeles, CA 90272; **310-826-9898**

ITALY–AMERICAN CHAMBER OF COMMERCE
730 Fifth Ave., #600, New York, NY 10019; **212-279-5520**

JAPAN

JAPANESE CHAMBER OF COMMERCE & INDUSTRY OF CHICAGO
401 N. Michigan Ave., Room 602, Chicago, IL 60611; **312-332-6199**

JAPANESE CHAMBER OF COMMERCE & INDUSTRY OF NEW YORK
145 W. 57th St., New York, NY 10019; **212-246-8001**

JAPANESE CHAMBER OF COMMERCE OF SOUTHERN CALIFORNIA
244 S. San Pedro St., #504, Los Angeles, CA 90012; **213-626-3067**

LATIN AMERICA

Also see: Individual Latin American nations, which are listed alphabetically by country name

AMERICAS SOCIETY OF THE U.S.
680 Park Ave., New York, NY 10021; **212-249-8950**

LATIN AMERICAN MANAGEMENT ASSOCIATION
419 New Jersey Ave., SE, Washington, DC 20003; **202-546-3803**

LATIN CHAMBER OF COMMERCE
1417 W. Flagler St., Miami, FL 33135; **305-642-3870**

LUXEMBOURG

LUXEMBOURG AMERICAN CHAMBER OF COMMERCE
825 3rd Ave., 36th Floor, New York, NY 10122; **212-888-6701**

MEXICO

MEXICAN INTERNATIONAL CHAMBER OF COMMERCE & INDUSTRY
P.O. Box 163, San Diego, CA 92153; **619-463-9426**

U.S.–MEXICO CHAMBER OF COMMERCE
1726 M St. NW, Suite 704, Washington, DC 20036; **202-296-5198**

MIDDLE EAST

Also see: Individual Middle Eastern and Islamic nations, which are listed alphabetically by country name

NATIONAL U.S.–ARAB CHAMBER
1100 New York Ave., NW, Washington, DC 20005; **202-289-5920**

NATIONAL U.S.–ARAB CHAMBER OF COMMERCE
208 S. LaSalle St., #706, Chicago, IL 60604; **312-782-0320**

NATIONAL U.S.–ARAB CHAMBER OF COMMERCE
420 Lexington Ave., #2739, New York, NY 10170; **212-986-8024**

SOUTHWEST U.S.–ARAB CHAMBER OF COMMERCE
2915LBJ Freeway, #260, Dallas, TX 75234; **214-241-9992**

U.S.–ARAB CHAMBER OF COMMERCE (PACIFIC)
P.O. Box 422218,
San Francisco, CA 94142; **415-398-9200**

NETHERLANDS

NETHERLANDS CHAMBER OF COMMERCE IN THE U.S.
2015 S. Park Pl., Suite 110, Atlanta, GA30339 **770-993-9040**

NETHERLANDS CHAMBER OF COMMERCE IN THE U.S.
303 E. Wacker Dr., #412, Chicago, IL 60601; **312-938-9050**

NETHERLANDS CHAMBER OF COMMERCE IN THE U.S.
One Rockefeller Plaza, #1420, New York, NY 10020; **212-265-6460**

NORWAY

NORWEGIAN–AMERICAN CHAMBER OF COMMERCE
800 Foshay Tower, 821 Marquette Ave., Minneapolis, MN 55402; **612-332-3338**

NORWEGIAN–AMERICAN CHAMBER OF COMMERCE
800 Third Ave., New York, NY 10022; **212-421-9210**

NORWEGIAN–AMERICAN CHAMBER OF COMMERCE
20 California St., San Francisco, CA 94111;
415-986-0770

PERU

PERUVIAN–U.S. CHAMBER OF COMMERCE
444 Brickell Ave., #M-126, Miami, FL
33131; **305-375-0885**

PHILIPPINES

PHILIPPINE CHAMBER OF COMMERCE
2457 W. Peterson, #3, Chicago, IL 60659;
773-271-8008

RUSSIA

RUSSIAN–AMERICAN CHAMBER OF COMMERCE
P.O. Box 15343, Washington, DC 20003;
202-546-2103

SAUDI ARABIA

ROYAL EMBASSY OF SAUDI ARABIA—COMMERCIAL OFFICE
601 New Hampshire Ave., NW, Washington,
DC 20037; **202-337-4088**

SINGAPORE

SINGAPORE TRADE DEVELOPMENT BOARD
LA World Trade Ctr., 350 S. Figueroa St.,
#909, Los Angeles, CA 90071; **213-617-7358**

SINGAPORE TRADE DEVELOPMENT BOARD
55 E. 59th St., Suite 21B, New York, NY
10022; **212-421-2207**

SPAIN

CHAMBER OF COMMERCE OF SPAIN
350 Fifth Ave., #2029, New York, NY 10118;
212-967-2170

SPAIN–U.S. CHAMBER OF COMMERCE IN FLORIDA
2655 Le Jeune Rd., #1108, Coral Gables, FL
33134; **305-446-1992**

SWEDEN

SWEDISH–AMERICAN CHAMBER OF COMMERCE
5118 S. Broadway, Englewood, CO 80110;
303-761-3285

SWEDISH–AMERICAN CHAMBER OF COMMERCE
599 Lexington Ave., New York, NY 10022;
212-838-5530

SWEDISH–AMERICAN CHAMBER OF COMMERCE OF THE WESTERN U.S.
230 California St., #405, San Francisco, CA
94111; **415-781-4188**

SWITZERLAND

SWISS–AMERICAN CHAMBER OF COMMERCE
347 5th Ave., Suite 1008., New York,
NY10016; **212-213-0482**

THAILAND

THAI TRADE CENTER
5 World Trade Center, Suite 3443, New York,
NY 10048; **212-466-1777**

UNITED KINGDOM

BRITISH–AMERICAN CHAMBER OF COMMERCE
52 Vanderbilt Ave., New York, NY 10017;
212-661-4060

BRITISH–AMERICAN CHAMBER OF COMMERCE
41 Sutter St., #303, San Francisco, CA 94104;
415-296-8645

BRITISH–AMERICAN CHAMBER OF COMMERCE
1640 Fifth St., #203, Santa Monica, CA
90401; **310-394-4977**

VENEZUELA

VENEZUELAN–AMERICAN CHAMBER OF COMMERCE & INDUSTRY
2199 Ponce de Leon Mezzanine, Coral Gables, FL 33134; **305-461-8283**

ORGANIZATIONS
PROFESSIONAL ASSOCIATIONS

ALMOST ALL MAJOR INDUSTRIES, and many minor ones, have associations dedicated to providing information and updates to the professionals working within the field. Professional associations—through their publications, company directories, annual conferences, and placement/referral services—often serve as ideal networking resources for employees already immersed in the industry, as well as for job hunters looking for contacts. In addition, the information provided in their publications can be of great value.

Information about some of the resources made available by different professional associations appears in each entry below. Often, these associations publish numerous materials related to the nuances of the industry in which they are situated.

Numerous occupational fields are represented in this chapter. While the fields themselves are broken down fairly specifically, you may wish to look at other areas as well to find resources pertaining to your interests. For instance, resources aimed at engineers will certainly be found in the "Engineering" section, but there also may be publications of interest to engineers in other fields, such as aerospace and manufacturing.

Other chapters in this book may also be useful. ➤See "Professional Magazines/Journals," pp. 131-147; and "Industry Directories," pp. 148-155.

INDUSTRY LIST

ACCOUNTING (*Also see*: Finance)
ADVERTISING (*Also see*: Consumer Products, Marketing, Public Relations, Retail, Sales)
AEROSPACE (*Also see*: Aviation, Engineering)
AGRICULTURE
APPAREL (*Also see*: Arts, Consumer Products, Design)
ARCHITECTURE (*Also see*: Construction)
ARTS (*Also see*: Apparel, Broadcasting, Cultural Organizations, Dance, Design, Entertainment)
AUTOMOTIVE
AVIATION (*Also see*: Aerospace, Engineering)
BANKING (*Also see:* Finance)
BROADCASTING (*Also see*: Arts, Entertainment)
CONSTRUCTION (*Also see*: Architecture)
CONSUMER PRODUCTS (*Also see*: Advertising, Apparel, Food and Beverages, Hospitality, Retail, Sales)
CULTURAL ORGANIZATIONS (*Also see*: Arts, Government)
DANCE (*Also see:* Arts)

DESIGN (*Also see*: Apparel, Arts)
EDUCATION (*Also see:* Library Science)
ENGINEERING (*Also see*: Aerospace, Aviation, Manufacturing, Science, Technology)
ENTERTAINMENT (*Also see*: Arts, Broadcasting)
FINANCE (*Also see*: Accounting, Banking)
FOOD AND BEVERAGES (*Also see:* Consumer Products, Hospitality)
FOREST/PAPER PRODUCTS
GENERAL BUSINESS
GOVERNMENT (*Also see:* Cultural Organizations)
HEALTH SERVICES
HOSPITALITY (*Also see*: Consumer Products, Food and Beverages, Travel)
HUMAN RESOURCES
HUMAN SERVICES
INSURANCE
LAW
LIBRARY SCIENCE (*Also see*: Education)
MANUFACTURING (*Also see*: Engineering, Technology)
MARKETING (*Also see*: Advertising, Public Relations, Sales)

NATURAL RESOURCES (*Also see*: Petroleum, Utilities)

PETROLEUM (*Also see*: Natural Resources, Utilities)

PUBLIC RELATIONS (*Also see*: Advertising, Marketing, Sales)

PUBLISHING

REAL ESTATE

RETAIL (*Also see*: Advertising, Consumer Products, Sales)

SALES (*Also see*: Advertising, Consumer Products Marketing, Public Relations, Retail),

SCIENCE (*Also see*: Engineering, Technology)

SECRETARIAL

TECHNOLOGY (*Also see*: Engineering, Manufacturing, Science)

TELECOMMUNICATIONS (*Also see*: Technology)

TRANSPORTATION

TRAVEL (*Also see:* Hospitality)

UTILITIES (*Also see:* Natural Resources, Petroleum)

WASTE MANAGEMENT

❶ ACCOUNTING

AMERICAN ACCOUNTING ASSOCIATION
5717 Bessie Dr., Sarasota, FL 34223; 941-921-7747
Resources Available: Publishes *The Accounting Review.*

AMERICAN INSTITUTE OF CERTIFIED PUBLIC ACCOUNTANTS
1211 Avenue of the Americas, New York, NY 10036; 212-596-6200
Resources Available: Publishes the *CPA Letter*, which contains career information.

AMERICAN SOCIETY OF WOMAN ACCOUNTANTS
1255 Lynnfield Rd., Suite 257, Memphis, TN 38119; 901-680-0470
Resources Available: Publishes career information.

NATIONAL SOCIETY OF PUBLIC ACCOUNTANTS
1010 N. Fairfax St., Alexandria, VA 22314; 703-549-6400
Resources Available: Periodical contains job listings, a directory, and other resources.

❶ ADVERTISING

AMERICAN ADVERTISING FEDERATION
1101 Vermont Ave., NW, Suite 500, Washington, DC 20005; 202-898-0089
Resources Available: Annual report lists current and new members; other publications cover the ad industry.

AMERICAN ASSOCIATION OF ADVERTISING AGENCIES
405 Lexington Ave, 18th Floor., New York, NY 10074; 212-682-2500
Resources Available: Publishes several publications including a roster and an association bulletin.

INTERNATIONAL ADVERTISING ASSOCIATION
521 Fifth Ave., Suite 1807, New York, NY 10175; 212-557-1133

Resources Available: Publications include a journal covering the industry, a newsletter for marketing executives, and a membership directory.

❶ AEROSPACE

AEROSPACE INDUSTRIES ASSOCIATION OF AMERICA
1250 I St., NW, Washington, DC 20005; 202-371-8400
Resources Available: Publishes an annual report, a newsletter, and industry facts and figures.

NATIONAL AIR TRANSPORTATION ASSOCIATION
4226 King St., Alexandria, VA 22302; 703-845-9000

Resources Available: Various publications provide many employment resources.

❶ AGRICULTURE

AGRICULTURE COUNCIL OF AMERICA
927 15th St., Suite 800, Washington, DC 20005; 202-682-9200
Resources Available: Publishes ACA information and a semimonthly newsletter.

WOMEN IN AGRIBUSINESS
P.O. Box 414937, Kansas City MO 64141;
Resources Available: Provides employment resources.

❶ APPAREL

AMERICAN APPAREL MANUFACTURERS ASSOCIATION
2500 Wilson Blvd., Suite 301, Arlington, VA 22201; 703-524-1864
Resources Available: Publishes an annual membership directory and numerous materials pertaining to the apparel industry.

AMERICAN FASHION ASSOCIATION
2300 Stemmons Fwy, Suite 1A11, Dallas, TX
75258; 214-631-0821
Resources Available: Publications contain
extensive industry information.

**CLOTHING MANUFACTURERS ASSOCIATON OF
THE USA**
730 Broadway, 9th Floor, New York, NY
10003; 212-529-0823
Resources Available: Publishes a weekly
news bulletin and reports containing industry
data and trend analysis.

**INTERNATIONAL ASSOCIATION OF CLOTHING
DESIGNERS**
475 Park Ave. S., New York, NY 10016; 212-
685-6602
Resources Available: Publishes a quarterly
newsletter, a convention yearbook, and
forecast information.

❶ ARCHITECTURE

AMERICAN INSTITUTE OF ARCHITECTS
1735 New York Ave., NW, Washington, DC
20006; 202-626-7300
Resources Available: Periodical provides
employment leads and a directory.

**AMERICAN SOCIETY OF LANDSCAPE ARCHI-
TECTS**
4401 Connecticut Ave., NW, Washington, DC
20008; 202-686-2752
Resources Available: Publishes industry
information.

❶ ARTS

AMERICANS FOR THE ARTS
1 E. 53rd St., New York, NY 10022; 212-223-
2787
Resources Available: Publishes a career
guide.

NATIONAL ENDOWMENT FOR THE ARTS
1100 Pennsylvania Ave., NW, Washington,
DC 20506; 202-682-5400
Resources Available: Awards grants and
funds to artists.

PROFESSIONAL PHOTOGRAPHERS OF AMERICA
57 Forsyth St., NW, Suite 1600, Atlanta, GA
30303; 404-522-8600
Resources Available: Periodical contains
career resources.

❶ AUTOMOTIVE

**AMERICAN AUTOMOBILE MANUFACTURERS
ASSOCIATION**
1401 H St.NW, Suite 900, Washington, DC
20005; 202-326-5500

Resources Available: Publishes a quarterly
containing analysis of employment and other
industry concerns; also issues various reports
and a data book.

**NATIONAL AUTOMOBILE DEALERS ASSOCIA-
TION**
8400 Westpark Dr., McLean, VA 22102; 703-
821-7000
Resources Available: Publishes various
automotive industry guides.

❶ AVIATION

AIR LINE EMPLOYEES ASSOCIATION
6520 S. Cicero Ave., Bedford Park, IL 60638;
708-563-9999
Resources Available: Publishes job listings.

AIR TRANSPORT ASSOCIATION OF AMERICA
1301 Pennsylvania Ave., NW, Suite1100,
Washington, DC 20004; 202-626-4000
Resources Available: Publishes an annual,
fact sheets, studies, and other industry-related
material.

**AMERICAN ASSOCIATION OF AIRPORT EXECU-
TIVES**
4212 King St., Alexandria, VA 22302; 703-
824-0500
Resources Available: Numerous publications
include job listings.

**AVIATION DISTRIBUTORS AND MANUFACTUR-
ERS ASSOCIATION**
1900 Arch St., Philadelphia, PA 19103; 215-
564-3484
Resources Available: Publishes a bimonthly
newsletter and an annual directory.

**GENERAL AVIATION MANUFACTURERS ASSO-
CIATION**
1400 K St., NW, Washington, DC 20005;
202-393-1500
Resources Available: Publishes an annual
databook and various industry overviews.

❶ BANKING

AMERICAN BANKERS ASSOCIATION
1120 Connecticut Ave., NW, Washington, DC
20036; 202-663-5000
Resources Available: Publications provide
job resources.

NATIONAL BANKERS ASSOCIATION
1513 P St. NW., Washington, DC 20005; 202-
588-5432
Resources Available: Provides job referral
service for members.

❶ BROADCASTING

ACADEMY OF TELEVISION ARTS AND SCIENCES
5220 Lankershim Blvd., North Hollywood, CA 91601; 818-754-2000
Resources Available: Publications contain information on internships, competitions, and awards.

CORPORATION FOR PUBLIC BROADCASTING
901 E St., NW, Washington, DC 20004; 202-874-9600
Resources Available: Provides numerous job resources, including a computerized referral service and an employment outreach program.

NATIONAL ASSOCIATION OF BROADCASTERS
1771 N St., NW, Washington, DC 20036; 202-429-5300
Resources Available: Publications provide career resources.

❶ CONSTRUCTION

AMERICAN SUBCONTRACTORS ASSOCIATION
1004 Duke St., Alexandria, VA 22314; 703-684-3450
Resources Available: Publishes a monthly newsletter containing industry overviews and membership news.

ASSOCIATED GENERAL CONTRACTORS OF AMERICA
1957 E St., NW, Washington, DC 20006; 202-393-2040
Resources Available: Publications include directories that contain company profiles and a biweekly newsletter.

NATIONAL ASSOCIATION OF HOME BUILDERS
1201 15th St., NW, Washington, DC 20005; 202-822-0200
Resources Available: Various publications contain extensive industry overviews and information on trends.

NATIONAL CONSTRUCTORS ASSOCIATION
1730 M St., Suite503, Washington, DC 20036; 202-466-8880
Resources Available: Publishes an annual directory and a quarterly newsletter.

❶ CONSUMER PRODUCTS

ASSOCIATION OF HOME APPLIANCE MANUFACTURERS
20 N. Wacker Dr., Chicago, IL 60606; 312-984-5800
Resources Available: Publishes shipment data.

COSMETIC, TOILETRY, AND FRAGRANCE ASSOCIATION
1101 17th St., NW, Suite 300, Washington, DC 20006; 202-331-1770
Resources Available: Publications include a membership directory and newsletters.

NATIONAL HOUSEWARES MANUFACTURERS ASSOCIATION
6400 Shafer Ct., Suite 650, Rosemont, IL 60018; 847-292-4200
Resources Available: Publications range from financial reports to membership directories.

❶ CULTURAL ORGANIZATIONS

AMERICAN ASSOCIATION OF MUSEUMS
1225 I St., NW, Washington, DC 20005; 202-289-1818
Resources Available: Periodical provides career resources.

❶ DANCE

AMERICAN DANCE GUILD
31 W. 21st St., New York, NY 10018; 212-932-2789
Resources Available: Publishes *ADG Quarterly*, containing award news, conference notices, and scholarship information, as well as a newsletter containing job listings.

❶ DESIGN

AMERICAN SOCIETY OF FURNITURE DESIGNERS
P.O. Box 2688, High Point, NC 27261; 910-884-4074
Resources Available: Magazine lists job openings, directories, and placement services.

AMERICAN SOCIETY OF INTERIOR DESIGNERS
608 Massachusetts Ave., NE, Washington, DC 20002; 202-546-3480
Resources Available: Provides career pamphlets.

GRAPHIC ARTISTS GUILD
90 John St., Suite 403, New York, NY 10038; 212-791-3400
Resources Available: Publishes a quarterly called *Guild News* and *The Graphic Artists Guild Handbook*, an annual regarding ethics and pricing.

NATIONAL COMPUTER GRAPHICS ASSOCIATION
2722 Merrilee Dr., Reston, VA 22031; 703-698-9600
Resources Available: Publishes a variety of materials related to industry trends, as well as a newsletter.

❶ EDUCATION

AMERICAN ASSOCIATION OF HIGHER EDUCATION
1 Dupont Circle, NW, Suite 360, Washington, DC 20036; 202-293-6440
Resources Available: Holds conferences and publishes materials regarding higher education.

AMERICAN ASSOCIATION OF SCHOOL ADMINISTRATORS
1801 N. Moore St., Arlington, VA 22209; 703-528-0700
Resources Available: Publishes *Leadership News*, a monthly that provides job listings.

AMERICAN COUNCIL ON EDUCATION
1 Dupont Circle, NW, Washington, DC 20036; 202-939-9300
Resources Available: Tracks industry trends and publishes a periodical.

ASSOCIATION FOR SCHOOL, COLLEGE, AND UNIVERSITY STAFFING
1600 Dodge Ave., S-330, Evanston, IL 60201; 847-864-1999
Resources Available: Publication contains job resources.

ASSOCIATION OF AMERICAN LAW SCHOOLS
1201 Connecticut Ave., NW, Suite 800, Washington, DC 20036; 202-296-8851
Resources Available: Publishes a bulletin that lists faculty and administrative job openings and publishes an annual membership directory.

MODERN LANGUAGE ASSOCIATION
10 Astor Pl., New York, NY 10003; 212-475-9500
Resources Available: Provides job listings for English and foreign-language college teachers.

NATIONAL ART EDUCATION ASSOCIATION
1916 Association Dr., Reston, VA 22191; 703-860-8000
Resources Available: Works as a placement service.

❶ ENGINEERING

AMERICAN ASSOCIATION OF ENGINEERING SOCIETIES
1111 19th St., NW, Suite403, Washington, DC 20036; 202-296-2237
Resources Available: Provides listings of a multitude of engineering associations and publishes salary information.

AMERICAN INSTITUTE OF CHEMICAL ENGINEERS
3 Park Ave., New York, NY 10016; 212- 591-7338
Resources Available: Periodical provides career information, job listings, and placement referrals.

AMERICAN SOCIETY OF CIVIL ENGINEERS
1015 15th St. NW, Suite 600, Washington, DC 20005; 202-789-2200
Resources Available: Periodical provides job listings, referral services, and other resources.

AMERICAN SOCIETY OF MECHANICAL ENGINEERS
345 E. 47th St., New York, NY 10017; 800-843-2763
Resources Available: Periodical provides job listings.

INSTITUTE OF ELECTRICAL AND ELECTRONICS ENGINEERS
345 E. 47th St., New York, NY 10017; 212-705-7900
Resources Available: Publishes *IEEE Spectrum*, a monthly that provides job listings.

NATIONAL SOCIETY OF PROFESSIONAL ENGINEERS
1420 King St., Alexandria, VA 22314; 703-684-2800
Resources Available: Publishes a directory.

❶ ENTERTAINMENT

ACADEMY OF MOTION PICTURE ARTS AND SCIENCES
8949 Wilshire Blvd., Beverly Hills, CA 90211; 310-247-3000
Resources Available: Publishes a directory and an index of motion picture credits.

ACTORS' EQUITY ASSOCIATION (LOS ANGELES OFFICE)
6430 Sunset Blvd., Hollywood, CA 90028; 213-462-2334
Resources Available: Publishes *Equity*, a newsletter about the entertainment industry.

ACTORS' EQUITY ASSOCIATION (NEW YORK OFFICE)
165 W. 46th St., New York, NY 10036; 212-869-8530
Resources Available: Publishes *Equity*, a newsletter about the entertainment industry.

AMERICAN FILM INSTITUTE
Kennedy Center for the Performing Arts, Washington, DC 20566; 800-774-4234
Resources Available: Awards grants and internships.

AMERICAN SOCIETY OF CINEMATOGRAPHERS
1782 N. Orange Dr., Hollywood, CA 90028;
800-448-0145
Resources Available: Publishes a monthly
magazine and various skills-enhancement
manuals.

ASSOCIATION OF INDEPENDENT VIDEO AND FILMMAKERS
304 Hudson St., 6th Floor, New York, NY
10013; 212- 807-1400
Resources Available: Publishes guides to
festivals, distributors, and production
resources, as well as a monthly.

DIRECTORS GUILD OF AMERICA
7920 Sunset Blvd., Los Angeles, CA 90046;
310-289-2000
Resources Available: Publishes profession-
related information.

MOTION PICTURE ASSOCIATION OF AMERICA
1600 I St. NW, Washington, DC 20006; 202-
293-1966
Resources Available: Publishes profession-
related information.

NATIONAL ACADEMY OF RECORDING ARTS AND SCIENCES
3402 Pico Blvd., Santa Monica, CA 90405;
310-392-3777
Resources Available: Publishes industry
information.

PRODUCERS GUILD OF AMERICA
400 S. Beverly, Suite 211, Beverly Hills, CA
90212; 310-557-0807
Resources Available: Publishes profession-
oriented information.

RECORDING INDUSTRY ASSOCIATION OF AMERICA
1330 Connecticut Ave., Suite 300, Washington, DC 20036; 202-775-0101
Web: www.rica.com
Resources Available: Publishes profession-
oriented information.

SCREEN ACTORS GUILD
5757 Wilshire Blvd., Los Angeles, CA 90036;
213-954-1600
Resources Available: Publishes profession-
related information.

❶ FINANCE

ASSOCIATION FOR INVESTMENT MANAGEMENT AND RESEARCH
P.O. Box 3668, Charlottesville, VA 22903;
804-977-6600
Resources Available: Provides job resources
for members.

CREDIT UNION NATIONAL ASSOCIATION
P.O. Box 431, Madison, WI 53701; 608-231-
4000
Web: www.cuna.org.
Resources Available: Promotes membership,
publishes directory.

FINANCIAL INSTITUTIONS MARKETING ASSOCIATION
401 N. Michigan Ave., Suite 2200, Chicago,
IL 60604; 312-644-6610
Resources Available: Publishes a directory
and trend reports, among other material.

NATIONAL ASSOCIATION OF CREDIT MANAGEMENT
8815 Centre Park Dr., Columbia, MD 21045;
410-740-5560
Resources Available: Publishes a magazine,
an executive handbook, and materials
pertaining to commerical laws.

❶ FOOD AND BEVERAGES

AMERICAN BAKERS ASSOCIATION
1350 I St., NW, Washington, DC 20005; 202-
789-0300
Resources Available: Sends a bulletin to
members.

AMERICAN FROZEN FOOD INSTITUTE
2000 Corporate Ridge, Suite 1000, McLean,
VA 22102; 703-821-0770
Web: www.affi.com
Resources Available: Publishes directory

GROCERY MANUFACTURERS OF AMERICA
1010 Wisconsin Ave., NW, Suite 800,
Washington, DC 20007; 202-337-9400
Resources Available: Publishes an annual
directory.

NATIONAL ASSOCIATION OF SPECIALTY FOOD AND CONFECTION BROKERS
11044 Wood Elves Way, Columbia, MD
21044; 301-596-4859
Resources Available: Publishes training
materials and industry coverage.

NATIONAL FOOD PROCESSORS ASSOCIATION
1401 New York Ave., NW, Suite 400,
Washington, DC 20005; 202-639-5900
Resources Available: Publishes information
letters and various reports and pamphlets.

NATIONAL SOFT DRINK ASSOCIATION
1101 16th St., NW, Washington, DC 20036;
202-463-6732
Resources Available: Publishes a
membership directory and bimonthly
newsletter that covers the industry.

❶ FOREST/PAPER PRODUCTS

AMERICAN FOREST AND PAPER ASSOCIATION
1111 19th St. NW, Suite 700, Washington, DC 20036; 202-463-2700
Resources Available: Publishes industry information.

NATIONAL HARDWOOD LUMBER ASSOCIATION
P.O. Box 34518, Memphis, TN 38184; 901-377-1818
Resources Available: Publishes factbooks, an annual report, and a membership directory, among other materials.

NATIONAL PAPER TRADE ASSOCIATION
111 Great Neck Rd., Great Neck, NY 11021; 516-829-3070
Resources Available: Publishes a monthly devoted to management news.

❷ GENERAL BUSINESS

NATIONAL ASSOCIATION FOR FEMALE EXECUTIVES
135 W. 50th St., 16th Floor, New York, NY 10020; 212-445-6235
Resources Available: Publishes a variety of career-related materials for women.

❸ GOVERNMENT

AMERICAN SOCIETY FOR PUBLIC ADMINISTRATION
1120 G St., NW, Suite 700, Washington, DC 20005; 202-393-7878
Resources Available: Publishes a newsletter with career resources as well as a magazine.

CAPITOL HILL WOMEN'S CAUCUS
P.O. Box 599, Longworth House, Independence and New Jersey Aves., Washington, DC 20515; 202-986-0994
Resources Available: Publishes various informational materials.

INTERNATIONAL CITY/COUNTY MANAGEMENT ASSOCIATION
777 N. Capitol St., NE, Washington, DC 20002; 202-289-4262
Resources Available: Publishes informational materials.

❹ HEALTH SERVICES

AMERICAN ACADEMY OF PHYSICIAN ASSISTANTS
950 N. Washington St., Alexandria, VA 22314; 703-836-2272
Resources Available: Periodicals provide career resources.

AMERICAN ASSOCIATION OF HOMES AND SERVICES FOR THE AGING
901 E. St. NW, Suite 500, Washington, DC 20004; 202-783-2242
Web: www.aahsa.org
Resources Available: Publishes directory.

AMERICAN CHIROPRACTIC ASSOCIATION
1701 Clarendon Blvd., Arlington, VA 22209; 703-276-8800
Resources Available: Periodical provides job listings.

AMERICAN COLLEGE OF SPORTS MEDICINE
P.O. Box 1440, Indianapolis, IN 46206; 317-637-9200
Resources Available: Periodical provides job listings.

AMERICAN DENTAL ASSOCIATION
211 E. Chicago Ave., Chicago, IL 60611; 312-440-2500
Resources Available: Periodical provides job listings and career resources.

AMERICAN HEALTH CARE ASSOCIATION
1201 L St., NW, Washington, DC 20005; 202-842-4444
Resources Available: Publishes many materials pertaining to industry policy and trends.

AMERICAN HOSPITAL ASSOCIATION
1 N. Franklin, Suite 27, Chicago, IL 60606; 312-422-3000
Resources Available: Provides resources primarily for administrators including a periodical with vocational information and a hospital directory.

AMERICAN MEDICAL ASSOCIATION
515 N. State St., Chicago, IL 60610; 312-464-5000
Resources Available: Publishes periodicals and has many affiliations.

AMERICAN PHARMACEUTICAL ASSOCIATION
2215 Constitution Ave., NW, Washington, DC 20037; 202-628-4410
Resources Available: Publishes industry information.

AMERICAN PUBLIC HEALTH ASSOCIATION
1015 15th St., NW, Washington, DC 20005; 202-789-5600
Resources Available: Provides career resources.

AMERICAN SOCIETY OF HOSPITAL PHARMACISTS
7272 Wisconsin Ave., Bethesda, MD 20814; 301-657-3000
Resources Available: Publishes industry information

AMERICAN SOCIETY FOR TRAINING AND DE-VELOPMENT
1640 King St., Alexandria, VA 22313; 703-683-8100
Resources Available: Publishes industry information, directory

HEALTH INDUSTRY MANUFACTURERS ASSO-CIATION
1200 G St., NW, Suite 400, Washington, DC 20005; 202-783-8700
Resources Available: Publishes a directory, manuals, and a monthly.

NATIONAL ASSOCIATION OF EMERGENCY MEDICAL TECHNICIANS
102 W. Leake St., Clinton, MS 39056; 601-924-7744
Resources Available: Provides a placement service.

❶ HOSPITALITY

AMERICAN HOTEL AND MOTEL ASSOCIATION
1201 New York Ave., NW, Suite 600, Washington, DC 20005; 202-289-3100
Resources Available: Publication provides job listings.

HOSPITALITY SALES AND MARKETING ASSO-CIATION
1300 L St., NW, Suite 800, Washington, DC 20005; 202-789-0089
Resources Available: Publishes a quarterly review, a directory, pamphlets, and updates.

NATIONAL RESTAURANT ASSOCIATION
1200 17th St., NW, Suite 800, Washington, DC 20036; 202-331-5900
Resources Available: Publishes a large assortment of industry information.

❶ HUMAN RESOURCES

ASSOCIATION OF EXECUTIVE SEARCH CON-SULTANTS
500 5th Ave., Suite 930, New York, NY10110; 212-949-9556
Resources Available: Publishes industry information.

NATIONAL ASSOCIATION OF EXECUTIVE RE-CRUITERS
222 S. Westmonte Dr., Suite 101, Altamonte Springs, FL 32714; 407-774-7880
Resources Available: Publishes industry information.

NATIONAL ASSOCIATION OF PERSONNEL SERVICES
3133 Mt. Vernon Ave., Alexandria, VA 22305; 703-684-0180

Resources Available: Publishes industry information.

NATIONAL ASSOCIATION OF TEMPORARY SERVICES
119 S. Asaph St., Alexandria, VA 22314; 703-549-6287
Resources Available: Publishes industry information.

❶ HUMAN SERVICES

AMERICAN ASSOCIATION ON MENTAL RETAR-DATION
444 N. Capitol St., NW, Suite 846, Washington, DC 20001; 202-387-1968
Resources Available: Publications provide job information.

AMERICAN COUNSELING ASSOCIATION
5999 Stevenson Ave., Alexandria, VA 22304; 800-545-2223
Resources Available: Provides employment services and publishes job resources.

NATIONAL ASSOCIATION OF SOCIAL WORKERS
750 First St., NW, Washington, DC 20002; 202-408-8600
Resources Available: Periodical contains job listings.

❶ INSURANCE

AMERICAN ACADEMY OF ACTUARIES
1100 17th St., NW, Washington, DC 20036; 202-223-8196
Resources Available: Offers career resources.

AMERICAN COUNCIL OF LIFE INSURANCE
1001 Pennsylvania Ave. NW, Washington, DC 20004; 202-624-2000
Web: www.acli.com
Resources Available: Offers career resources.

AMERICAN INSURANCE ASSOCIATION
1130 Connecticut Ave. NW, Suite 1000, Washington DC 20036; 202-828-7100
Resources Available: Various publications primarily pertain to industry practices and regulations.

HEALTH INSURANCE ASSOCIATION OF AMERICA
555 13th St. NW, Suite 600E, Washington, DC20004; 202-824-1600
Resources Available: Publications provide coverage of the private health insurance business.

INSURANCE INFORMATION INSTITUTE
110 William St., New York, NY 10038; 212-669-9200

Resources Available: Association composed of liability and property insurance companies provides insurance information to the public.

INTERNATIONAL INSURANCE COUNCIL
900 19th St. NW, Suite 250, Washington, DC 20006; 202-682-2345
Resources Available: Advocate for trade policy. Publishes industry information.

NATIONAL ASSOCIATION OF INDEPENDENT INSURERS
2600 River Rd., Des Plaines, IL 60018; 847-297-7800
Resources Available: Publishes directories, surveys, studies, and bulletins, among other materials.

❶ L A W

AMERICAN BAR ASSOCIATION
750 N. Lake Shore Dr., Chicago, IL 60611; 312-988-5000
Resources Available: Publishes directories, information, and industry materials for legal professionals.

❶ L I B R A R Y S C I E N C E

AMERICAN LIBRARY ASSOCIATION
50 E. Huron St., Chicago, IL 60611; 312-944-6780
Resources Available: Publishes *American Libraries*, a monthly that provides job listings.

❶ M A N U F A C T U R I N G

INDUSTRIAL RESEARCH INSTITUTE
1550 M St., NW, Washington, DC 20005; 202-296-8811
Resources Available: Publishes research results pertaining to the manufacturing industry.

NATIONAL ASSOCIATION OF MANUFACTURERS
1331 Pennsylvania Ave., NW, Suite 1500, N. Lobby, Washington, DC 20004; 202-637-3000
Resources Available: Publishes a variety of materials about association activities.

NATIONAL ASSOCIATION OF PHARMACEUTICAL MANUFACTURERS
320 Old County Rd., Suite 205, Garden City, NY 11530; 516-741-3699
Resources Available: Publishes a variety of materials about industry activities.

NONPRESCRIPTION DRUG MANUFACTURERS ASSOCIATION
1150 Connecticut Ave. NW, Washington, DC 20036; 202-429-9260
Resources Available: Publishes directory.

RUBBER MANUFACTURERS ASSOCIATION
1400 K St. NW, Washington, DC 20005; 202-682-4800
Resources Available: Publishes newsletter, directory.

❶ M A R K E T I N G

AMERICAN MARKETING ASSOCIATION
250 S. Wacker Dr., Suite 200, Chicago, IL 60606; 312-648-0536
Resources Available: Periodical provides career resources.

DIRECT MARKETING ASSOCIATION
1120 Avenure of the Americas, New York, NY 10036; 212-768-7277
Resources Available: Provides placement services and job listings and publishes a directory.

❶ N A T U R A L R E S O U R C E S

AMERICAN SOCIETY FOR METALS INTERNATIONAL
9639 Kinsman Rd., Material Park, OH 44073; 216-338-5151
Resources Available: Publications contain help wanted ads.

IRON AND STEEL SOCIETY
410 Commonwealth Dr., Warrendale, PA 15086; 412-776-1535
Resources Available: Publishes a monthly magazine that contains a help wanted section.

NATIONAL MINING ASSOCIATION
1130 17th St., NW, Washington, DC 20036; 202-463-2625
Resources Available: Publishes industry information.

STEEL MANUFACTURERS ASSOCIATION
1730 Rhode Island Ave. NW, Suite 907, Washington, DC20036; 202-342-1160
Resources Available: Publishes industry information.

❶ P E T R O L E U M

AMERICAN GAS ASSOCIATION
1515 Wilson Blvd., Arlington, VA 22209; 703-841-8400
Resources Available: Publishes an abundance of materials pertaining to the petroleum industry.

AMERICAN PETROLEUM INSTITUTE
1220 L St., NW,, Washington, DC 20005;
202-682-8000
Resources Available: Publishes an abundance of materials ranging from product descriptions to employment trends.

❶ PUBLIC RELATIONS

PUBLIC RELATIONS SOCIETY OF AMERICA
33 Irving Pl., New York, NY 10003; 212-995-2230
Resources Available: Publishes studies, a semiannual journal, and a newspaper, among other materials.

❶ PUBLISHING

AMERICAN BOOKSELLERS ASSOCIATION
828 S. Broadway, Tarrytown, NY 10591;
800-637-0037
Resources Available: Publishes newsletter, directory.

ASSOCIATION OF AMERICAN PUBLISHERS
71 Fifth Ave., New York, NY 10003; 212-255-0200
Resources Available: Publishes an annual calendar of international fairs, a directory, a guide to college publishers, and a monthly report.

EDITORIAL FREELANCERS ASSOCIATION
71 W. 23rd St., Suite 1504, New York, NY 10010; 212-929-5400
Resources Available: Provides job listings for members.

INVESTIGATIVE REPORTERS AND EDITORS
138 Neff Hall, School of Journalism, Columbia, MO 65205; 573-882-2042
Web: www.ire.org
Resources Available: Keeps an informal job bank.

MAGAZINE PUBLISHERS OF AMERICA
919 Third Ave., New York, NY 10022; 212-872-3700
Resources Available: Publishes reports on industry trends.

NATIONAL NEWSPAPER ASSOCIATION
1525 Wilson Blvd., Suite 550, Arlington, VA 22209; 703-907-7900
Resources Available: Publishes a directory of newspapers and its own newspaper, which contains industry coverage.

WRITERS GUILD OF AMERICA
7000 W. 3rd St., Los Angeles, CA 90048;
213-951-4000
Resources Available: Publishes profession-related information.

❶ REAL ESTATE

NATIONAL ASSOCIATION OF REAL ESTATE APPRAISERS
8383 E. Evans Rd., Scottsdale, AZ 85260;
602-948-8000
Resources Available: Publishes appraisal guidelines, a newsletter, and a directory.

NATIONAL ASSOCIATION OF REALTORS
430 N. Michigan Ave., Chicago, IL 60611;
800-874-6500
Resources Available: Publishes information on trends and industry overviews.

SOCIETY OF INDUSTRIAL AND OFFICE REALTORS
700 11th St. NW, Suite 510, Washington, DC 20001; 202-737-1150
Resources Available: Publications include brochures, market reports, and industry overviews.

❶ RETAIL

INTERNATIONAL COUNCIL OF SHOPPING CENTERS
665 Fifth Ave., New York, NY 10022; 212-421-8181
Resources Available: Publishes a magazine, a directory, and various industry-related publications.

INTERNATIONAL MASS RETAIL ASSOCIATION
1901 Pennsylvania Ave., Washington, DC 20006; 202-861-0774
Resources Available: Publishes industry information.

NATIONAL RETAIL FEDERATION
325 7th St. NW, Suite 1000, Washington, DC 20004-2802; 202-783-7971
Resources Available: Magazine contains extensive industry coverage.

PHOTO MARKETING ASSOCIATION INTERNATIONAL
300 Picture Pl., Jackson, MI 49209; 517-788-8100
Resources Available: Publishes newsletter, directory.

❶ SCIENCE

AMERICAN ANTHROPOLOGICAL ASSOCIATION
4350 N. Fairfax Dr., Suite 640, Arlington, VA 22203; 703-528-1902
Resources Available: Publications provide job information, employment opportunities, and placement services.

AMERICAN CHEMICAL SOCIETY
1155 16th St. NW, Washington, DC 20036;
800-872-4600
Resources Available: Various publications provide numerous career resources.

PROFESSIONAL ORGANIZATIONS—SCIENCE—TECHNOLOGY

AMERICAN GEOLOGICAL INSTITUTE
4220 King St., Alexandria, VA 22302; 703-379-2480
Web: www.agiweb.org
Resources Available: Magazine contains job listings.

AMERICAN INSTITUTE OF BIOLOGICAL SCIENCES
730 11th St., NW, Washington, DC 20001; 202-628-1500
Resources Available: Provides numerous vocational resources.

AMERICAN INSTITUTE OF CHEMISTS
501 Wythe St., Alexandria, VA 22314-1917; 703-836-2090
Web: www.thealc.org
Resources Available: Publications provide career resources including job listings and a job placement service.

AMERICAN INSTITUTE OF PHYSICS
1 Physics Ellipse, College Park, MD 20740; 301-209-3100
Web: www.aip.org
Resources Available: Has many affiliated associations and publishes job listings.

AMERICAN MATHEMATICAL SOCIETY
P.O. Box 6248, Providence, RI 02940; 401-455-4000
Resources Available: Periodical provides job listings and a directory.

ASSOCIATION OF AMERICAN GEOGRAPHERS
1710 16th St., NW, Washington, DC 20009; 202-234-1450
Resources Available: Provides placement services and job announcements.

CHEMICAL MANUFACTURERS ASSOCIATION
1300 Wilson Blvd, Arlington, VA 22209; 703-741-5000
Resources Available: Provides industry information.

DRUG, CHEMICAL AND ALLIED TRADES ASSOCIATION
2 Roosevelt Ave., Suite 301, Syosset, NY 11791; 516-496-3317
Resources Available: Publishes career information.

INSTRUMENT SOCIETY OF AMERICA (ISA)
67 Alexander Dr., Research Triangle Park, NC 27709; 919-549-8411
Web: www.isa.org
Resources Available: Publishes newsletter.

❶ SECRETARIAL

NATIONAL ASSOCIATION OF EXECUTIVE SECRETARIES & ADMINISTRATIVE ASSISTANTS
900 S. Washington St., Suite G-13, Falls Church, VA 22046; 703-237-8616
Resources Available: Allows members to advertise their availability in the newsletter.

PROFESSIONAL SECRETARIES INTERNATIONAL
10502 NW Ambassador Dr., P.O. Box 20404, Kansas City, MO 64153; 816-891-6600
Resources Available: Publishes *The Secretary Magazine.*

❶ TECHNOLOGY

AMERICAN ELECTRONICS ASSOCIATION
520 Great American Way, Suite 520, Santa Clara, CA 95054; 408-987-4200
Resources Available: Publishes a directory and newsletters.

ASSOCIATION FOR COMPUTING MACHINERY
1515 Broadway, New York, NY 10036; 212-869-7440
Resources Available: Provides a resume databank for members.

COMPUTING TECHNOLOGY INDUSTRY ASSOCIATION
450 E. 22nd St., Suite 230, Lombard, IL 60148; 630-268-1818
Resources Available: Publishes information for computer industry professionals pertaining to industry trends.

ELECTRONIC INDUSTRIES ASSOCIATION
2500 Wilson Blvd., Arlington, VA 22201; 703-907-7500
Web: www.eia.org
Resources Available: Publishes industry information.

INFORMATION INDUSTRY ASSOCIATION
1625 Massachusetts Ave. NW, suite 700, Washington, DC 20036; 202-986-0280
Web: www.infoindustry.org
Resources Available: Publishes numerous materials including a directory listing key executives and company profiles.

INFORMATION TECHNOLOGY ASSOCIATION OF AMERICA
1616 N. Ft. Myer Dr., Suite 1300, Arlington, VA 22209; 703-522-5055
Resources Available: Publications pertain to industry developments and forecasts.

INFORMATION TECHNOLOGY INDUSTRY COUNCIL
1250 I St. NW, Suite 200, Washington, DC 20005; 202-737-8888

Resources Available: Publishes materials relating to industry.

SOFTWARE PUBLISHERS ASSOCIATION
1730 M St. NW, Suite 700, Washington, DC 20036; 202-452-1600
Web: www.spa.org
Resources Available: Publications relating to industry.

❶ TELECOMMUNICATIONS

COMPETITIVE TELECOMMUNICATIONS ASSOCIATION
1900 M St. NW, Suite 800, Washington, DC 20036; 202-296-6650
Web: www.comptel.org
Resources Available: Publishes industry information.

MULTIMEDIA TELECOMMUNICATIONS ASSOCIATION
2500 Wilson Blvd., Suite 300, Arlington, VA 22201; 202-296-9800
Resources Available: Publishes industry trends.

NATIONAL CABLE TELEVISION ASSOCIATION
1724 Massachusetts Ave. NW, Washington, DC 20036; 202-775-3550
Resources Available: Publishes career trends, industry information.

TELECOMMUNICATIONS ASSOCIATION
300 W. Franklin St., 102W, Richmond, VA 23220; 804-780-1776
Resources Available: Publishes a membership roster and a bimonthly newsletter.

UNITED STATES TELEPHONE ASSOCIATION
1401 H St., NW, Suite 600, Washington, DC 20005; 202-326-7300
Resources Available: Publishes extensive industry information.

❶ TRANSPORTATION

AMERICAN BUREAU OF SHIPPING
2 World Trade Ctr.,106th Floor, New York, NY 10048; 212-839-5000
Resources Available: Publishes industry information.

AMERICAN TRUCKING ASSOCIATION
2200 Mill Rd., Alexandria, VA 22314; 703-838-1700
Resources Available: Weekly publication provides an extensive help wanted section.

ASSOCIATION OF AMERICAN RAILROADS
American Railroad Bldg., 50 F St., NW, Washington, DC 20001; 202-639-2100
Web: www.aar.org

Resources Available: Publications include industry updates and information materials.

NATIONAL ASSOCIATION OF MARINE SUPPLIERS
5458 Wagonmaster Dr., Colorado Springs, CO 80917; 719-573-5946
Resources Available: Publishes a news quarterly, a directory of suppliers and members, and a register, among other materials.

❶ TRAVEL

AMERICAN SOCIETY OF TRAVEL AGENTS
1101 King St., Alexandria, VA 22314; 703-739-2782
Web: www.astanet.com
Resources Available: Publishes numerous informational publications including a newsletter and a monthly magazine.

TRAVEL INDUSTRY ASSOCIATION OF AMERICA
1100 New York Ave. NW, Suite 405, Washington, DC 20005; 202-408-8422
Resources Available: Publishes a directory of contacts, a media directory, and an industry calendar, among other materials.

❶ UTILITIES

AMERICAN PUBLIC GAS ASSOCIATION
P.O. Box 11094D, Lee Highway, Suite 102, Fairfax, VA 22030; 703-352-3890
Web: www.apga.org
Resources Available: Publishes a directory and a newsletter.

AMERICAN PUBLIC POWER ASSOCIATION
2301 M St., NW, Washington, DC 20037; 202-467-2900
Web: www.appanet.org
Resources Available: Publishes industry information.

ELECTRIC POWER RESEARCH INSTITUTE
3412 Hillview Ave., Palo Alto, CA 94304; 415-855-2000
Resources Available: Publishes research findings.

NATIONAL UTILITY CONTRACTORS ASSOCIATION
4301 N. Fairfax Dr., Suite 360, Arlington, VA 22203; 703-358-9300
Resources Available: Publishes a variety of materials pertaining to the industry.

❶ WASTE MANAGEMENT

NATIONAL SOLID WASTES MANAGEMENT ASSOCIATION
5 Commonwealth Rd., Natick MA 01760; 508-650-6224
Resources Available: Publishes industry information.

INDEX TO COMPANIES & EMPLOYERS